PSYCHOLOGY

PSYCHOLOGY

FIFTH EDITION

Douglas A. Bernstein
University of South Florida
University of Surrey

Alison Clarke-Stewart
University of California, Irvine

Louis A. Penner
University of South Florida

Edward J. Roy
University of Illinois at Urbana-Champaign

Christopher D. Wickens
University of Illinois at Urbana-Champaign

Houghton Mifflin Company   **Boston**   **New York**

To the researchers, past and present, whose work embodies psychology today, and to the students who will follow in their footsteps to shape the psychology of tomorrow.

Senior Sponsoring Editor: Kerry T. Baruth
Associate Editors: Jane Knetzger, Marianne Stepanian
Senior Project Editor: Janet Young
Editorial Assistant: Nasya Laymon
Senior Production/Design Coordinator: Sarah Ambrose
Senior Cover Design Coordinator: Deborah Azerrad Savona
Senior Manufacturing Coordinator: Priscilla Bailey
Senior Marketing Manager: Pamela Laskey

Cover designed by Rebecca Fagan

Anatomical illustrations by Joel Ito

CREDITS
Chapter-opening photos: Copyright ©99 PhotoDisc, Inc.
Credits continue following Index.

Printed in the U.S.A.

Library of Congress Catalog Card Number: 99-72034

ISBN: 0-395-94503-8

2 3 4 5 6 7 8 9-VH-03 02 01 00

BRIEF CONTENTS

CONTENTS

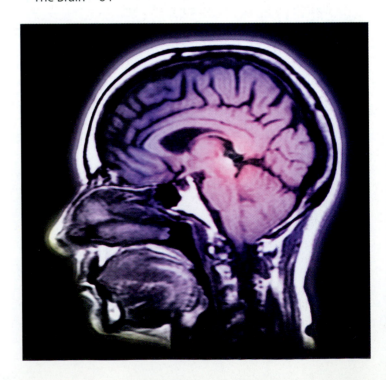

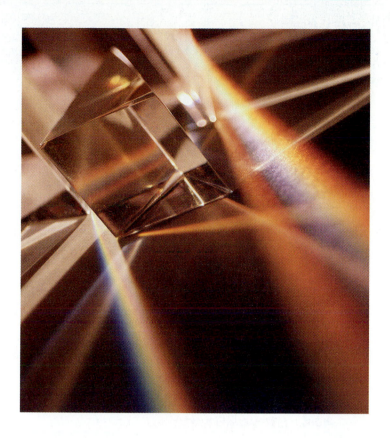

4 SENSATION

5 PERCEPTION

LEARNING

MEMORY

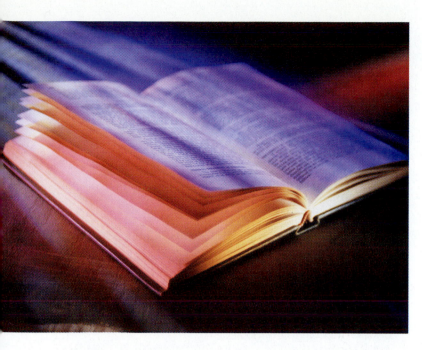

8 COGNITION AND LANGUAGE

9 CONSCIOUSNESS

10   MENTAL ABILITIES

11   MOTIVATION AND EMOTION

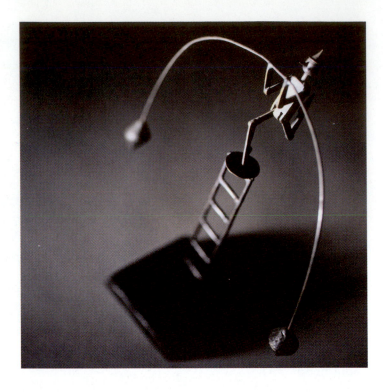

14 PERSONALITY

15 PSYCHOLOGICAL DISORDERS

16 TREATMENT OF PSYCHOLOGICAL DISORDERS

17 SOCIAL COGNITION

18   SOCIAL INFLUENCE

FEATURES

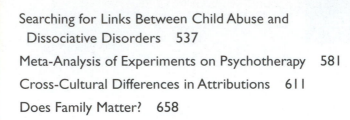

**THINKING
CRITICALLY**

PREFACE

IN REVISING *Psychology* we have rededicated ourselves to the goals we pursued in the first four editions:

- To explore the full range of psychology, from cell to society, in an eclectic manner as free as possible of theoretical bias.
- To balance our need to explain the content of psychology with an emphasis on the doing of psychology, through a blend of conceptual discussion and description of research studies.
- To foster scientific attitudes and to help students learn to think critically by examining the ways that psychologists have solved, or failed to solve, fascinating puzzles of behavior and mental processes.
- To produce a text that, without oversimplifying psychology, is clear, accessible, and enjoyable to read.
- To demonstrate that, in spite of its breadth and diversity, psychology is an integrated discipline in which each subfield is linked to other subfields by common interests and overarching research questions. The productive cross-fertilization among social, clinical, and biological psychologists in researching health and illness is just one example of how different types of psychologists benefit from and build on one another's work.

Preparing the Fifth Edition provided us with new ways to do justice to our goals.

We sought to respond to the needs of instructors who wanted us to reduce or expand coverage of various topics. For example, many instructors asked us to increase the amount of material on applied psychology without losing the book's emphasis on basic research in psychology. As a result, we have added material relating to applied areas such as industrial/organizational psychology throughout the book, wherever appropriate.

We have also added a new coauthor, Louis Penner of the University of South Florida, to help us with our coverage of personality and social psychology. Lou is an active researcher in these areas; he also teaches introductory psychology, as well as graduate and undergraduate courses in personality and social psychology.

As always, we sought to strike an ideal balance between classic and current research. The important historic findings of psychological research are here, but so is coverage of much recent work. Approximately one-third of the research citations are new to the Fifth Edition, and we have added the latest information on such topics as

- Methods for evaluating claims for the effectiveness of eye movement desensitization (Chapter 2)
- Techniques for studying the brain (Chapter 3)
- Pheromones in humans (Chapter 4)
- The impact of subliminal stimuli (Chapter 5)
- The effects of punishment on children (Chapter 6)
- Biological bases of memory (Chapter 7)
- Human-computer interactions (Chapter 8)
- How expectancies about alcohol affect behavior (Chapter 9)
- How anxiety can affect test performance (Chapter 10)
- What motivates people to volunteer (Chapter 11)
- Risk and resiliency in children (Chapter 12)
- Psychological reactions to stress (Chapter 13)
- Temperament, personality, and health-related behaviors (Chapter 14)
- The relationship between child abuse and adult dissociative disorders (Chapter 15)
- Empirically validated psychotherapies (Chapter 16)
- Strategies to change attitudes (Chapter 17)
- Environmental factors and aggression (Chapter 18)

The Fifth Edition also contains substantial material on culture and human diversity. Throughout the text students will encounter recent research on multicultural phenomena occurring in North America and around the world. We introduce this multicultural emphasis in Chapter 1, and we follow up on it in other chapters through such topics as

- Selecting human participants for research (Chapter 2)
- Culture, experience, and perception (Chapter 5)
- Classrooms across cultures (Chapter 6)
- Cultural differences in formal reasoning (Chapter 8)
- Knowledge, language, and culture (Chapter 8)
- Bilingualism (Chapter 8)
- Cross-cultural differences in the meaning of words (Chapter 8)
- The impact of stereotypes on mental-ability testing (Chapter 10)
- Ethnic differences in IQ (Chapter 10)
- Flavor, cultural learning, and food selection (Chapter 11)
- Social and cultural factors in sexuality (Chapter 11)
- Cultural and gender differences in achievement motivation (Chapter 11)
- Cultural aspects of emotional expression (Chapter 11)
- Culture and cognitive development (Chapter 12)
- Cultural background and heart disease (Chapter 13)
- Personality, culture, and human development (Chapter 14)

- Ethnic bias in psychodiagnosis (Chapter 15)
- Sociocultural factors in psychological disorders (Chapter 15)
- Gender and cultural differences in depression and suicide (Chapter 15)
- Cultural factors in psychotherapy (Chapter 16)
- Ethnic differences in responses to drug treatment (Chapter 16)
- Cultural differences in attribution (Chapter 17)
- The roots of ethnic stereotyping and prejudice (Chapter 17)
- Cultural factors in social norms (Chapter 18)
- Culture and social loafing (Chapter 18)
- Cultural factors in aggression (Chapter 18)

We also have increased our coverage of behavioral genetics and evolutionary psychology. These topics are introduced in Chapters 1 and 2 and in a revised behavioral genetics appendix. They are also explored wherever appropriate—for example, when we discuss

- Gene manipulation research on the causes of Alzheimer's disease (Chapter 3)
- Biopreparedness for learning (Chapter 6)
- Genetic components of intelligence (Chapter 10)
- Genetic components of sexual orientation (Chapter 11)
- Evolutionary explanations of mate selection (Chapter 11)
- Innate expressions of emotion (Chapter 11)
- The genetics of prenatal development (Chapter 12)
- The heritability of personality (Chapter 14)
- Genetic factors in psychological disorders (Chapter 15)
- Evolutionary/genetic explanations for aggression, helping, and altruism (Chapter 18)

CHAPTER ORGANIZATION

We have refrained from grouping the book's eighteen chapters into sections. Indeed, we designed each chapter to be a free-standing unit so that you may assign chapters in any order you wish. For example, many instructors prefer to teach the material on human development relatively late in the course, which is why it appears as Chapter 12 in the Fifth Edition. But that chapter can be comfortably assigned earlier in the course as well.

SPECIAL FEATURES

Psychology contains a number of special features designed to promote efficient learning and students' mastery of the material. Most of the features from previous editions have been revised and enhanced in the Fifth; one feature is new to the Fifth Edition.

Linkages

In our experience, most students enter the introductory course thinking that psychology concerns itself mainly with personality, psychological testing, mental disorders, psychotherapy, and other aspects of clinical psychology. They have little or no idea

of how broad and multifaceted psychology is. Many students are surprised, therefore, when we ask them to read about neuroanatomy, neural communication, the endocrine system, sensory and perceptual processes and principles, prenatal risk factors, and many other topics that they tend to associate with disciplines other than psychology.

We have found that students are better able to appreciate the scope of psychology when they see it not as a laundry list of separate topics but as an interrelated set of subfields, each of which contributes to and benefits from the work going on in all of the others. To help students see these relationships, we have built into the book an integrating tool called "Linkages." There are five elements in the Linkages program:

1. Beginning with Chapter 2, a Linkages diagram presents a set of questions that illustrate three of the ways in which material in the chapter is related to other chapters in the book. For example, the Linkages diagram in Chapter 3, Biological Aspects of Psychology, contains questions that show how biological psychology is related to human development ("How do our brains change as we get older?"), consciousness ("Is there a way to drink alcohol without getting drunk?"), and treatment of psychological disorders ("How do drugs help people who suffer from depression or schizophrenia?").

2. The Linkages diagrams now appear at the end of each chapter rather than at the beginning. We moved them so that the students will be more familiar with the material to which each linkage refers when they encounter this feature. To help students notice the Linkages diagrams and appreciate their purpose, we now provide an explanatory caption with each.

3. The page numbers following each question in the Linkages diagram direct the student to pages that carry further discussion of that question. There, the linking question is repeated in the margin alongside the discussion.

4. One of the questions in each chapter's Linkages diagram is treated more fully in a special section in the chapter entitled, appropriately enough, Linkages.

5. Each chapter contains at least one captioned photo illustrating yet another way in which the content of that chapter is related to the content of another chapter.

The Linkages elements combine with the text narrative to highlight the network of relationships among psychology's subfields. This Linkages program is designed to help students see the "big picture" that is psychology—no matter how many chapters their instructor assigns, or in what sequence.

Thinking Critically

We try throughout the book to describe research on psychological phenomena in a way that reveals the logic of the scientific enterprise, that identifies possible flaws in design or interpretation, and that leaves room for more questions and further research. In other words, we try to display critical thinking processes. The "Thinking Critically" sections in each chapter are designed to make these processes more explicit and accessible by providing a framework for analyzing evidence before drawing conclusions. The framework is built around five questions that the reader should find useful in analyzing not only studies in psychology but other forms of communication as well. These questions, first introduced when we discuss the importance of critical thinking in Chapter 2, are

1. What am I being asked to believe or accept?

2. What evidence is available to support the assertion?

3. Are there alternative ways of interpreting the evidence?

4. What additional evidence would help to evaluate the alternatives?

5. What conclusions are most reasonable?

All the Thinking Critically sections retained from the Fourth Edition have been extensively revised and updated. Thinking Critically sections new to the Fifth Edition include

- Recovered memories—true or false? (Chapter 7)
- Is marijuana dangerous? (Chapter 9)
- Are some therapies better than others? (Chapter 16)

Focus on Research Methods

This feature, appearing in Chapters 3 through 18, examines the ways in which the research methods described in Chapter 2, Research in Psychology, have been applied to help advance our understanding of some aspect of behavior and mental processes. To make this feature even more accessible, it is now organized around answers to the following questions:

1. What was the researcher's question?

2. How did the researcher answer the question?

3. What did the researcher find?

4. What do the results mean?

5. What do we still need to know?

Examples of these Focus on Research Methods sections include the use of case-study methods to track the problem-solving methods that led to the invention of the airplane (Chapter 8, Cognition and Language), the use of experiments to study attention (Chapter 5, Perception), learned helplessness (Chapter 6, Learning), the development of physical knowledge (Chapter 12, Human Development), and attribution (Chapter 17, Social Cognition). Other sections illustrate the use of quasi-experimental, survey, longitudinal, and laboratory analogue designs. All of the Focus on Research Methods sections retained from the Fourth Edition were revised and updated and several new ones were added. A full list of topics appears on pp. xv–xvi.

Behavioral Genetics Appendix

This feature is designed to amplify the coverage of behavioral genetics methodology that is introduced in Chapter 2, Research

in Psychology. The appendix includes a section on the basic principles of genetics and heredity, a brief history of genetic research in psychology, a discussion of what it means to say that genes influence behavior, and an analysis of what behavioral genetics research can—and cannot—tell us about the origins of such human attributes as intelligence, personality, and mental disorders.

In Review Charts

In Review charts summarize information in a convenient tabular format. We have placed two or three In Review charts strategically in each chapter to help students synthesize and assimilate large chunks of information—for example, on drug effects, key elements of personality theories, and stress responses and mediators.

Key Terms

A feature new to the Fifth Edition is the presentation of Key Terms at the end of each chapter. This list of all the boldfaced terms in each chapter is designed to help students to review, and to be sure they understand, the most important concepts and terms in each chapter. These terms and their definitions also appear in the glossary at the end of the book.

TEACHING AND LEARNING SUPPORT PACKAGE

Many useful materials have been developed to support *Psychology*. Designed to enhance the teaching and learning experience, they are well integrated with the text and include some of the latest technologies. Several components are new to this edition.

Annotated Instructor's Edition

To help instructors coordinate the many print, software, and video supplements available with the text, an Annotated Instructor's Edition shows which materials apply to the content on every page of the student text. These materials include learning objectives, test questions, discussion and lecture ideas, handouts, active learning and critical thinking activities from the *Study Guide*, videodisc segments and stills, lecture starter videos, overhead transparencies and PowerPoint® images, as well as three psychology readers.

Print Ancillaries

Accompanying this book are, among other ancillaries, a *Test Bank*, an *Instructor's Resource Manual*, and a *Study Guide*. Because these items were prepared by the lead author and a number of colleagues who have worked with him over the years at the University of Illinois psychology department, you will find an especially high level of coordination between the textbook and these supplements. All three are unified by a shared set of learning objectives, and all three have been revised and enhanced for the Fifth Edition.

Test Bank   The *Test Bank,* by David Spurlock, Sandra S. Goss, and Douglas A. Bernstein, contains more than 3,000 multiple-choice items plus three essay questions for each chapter of the text. Half of the multiple-choice questions are new; in all others, the response alternatives have been scrambled. All multiple-choice items are keyed to pages in the textbook and to the learning objectives listed in the *Instructor's Resource Manual* and *Study Guide.* In addition, questions that ask students to apply their knowledge of the concepts are distinguished from those that require factual recall. More than 1,600 questions have already been class-tested with between 500 and 2,500 students and are accompanied by graphs indicating the question's discriminative power and level of difficulty, the percentage of students who chose each response, and the relationship between students' performance on a given item and their overall performance on the test in which the item appeared.

Instructor's Resource Manual   The *Instructor's Resource Manual,* by Joel I. Shenker, Sandra S. Goss, and Douglas A. Bernstein, contains for each chapter a complete set of learning objectives, detailed chapter outlines, suggested readings, and numerous specific teaching aids—many of them new to the Fifth Edition—including ideas for discussion, class activities, research focus sections, and the accompanying handouts. It also contains sections on pedagogical strategies such as how to implement active learning and critical thinking techniques and how to make full use of the Linkages and research focus supplements. In addition, it contains material geared towards teachers of large introductory courses, such as a section on classroom management and the administration of large multi-section courses.

Study Guide   The *Study Guide,* by Linda Lebie, Amanda Allman, and Douglas A. Bernstein, employs numerous techniques that help students to learn. Each chapter contains a detailed outline, a key-terms section that presents fresh examples and aids to remembering, plus a fill-in-the-blank test, learning objectives, a concepts and exercises section that shows students how to apply their knowledge of psychology to everyday issues and concerns, a critical thinking exercise, and personal learning activities. In addition, each chapter concludes with a two-part self-quiz consisting of forty multiple-choice questions. An answer key tells the student not only which response is correct but also why each of the other choices is wrong, and quiz analysis tables enable students to track patterns to their wrong answers, either by topic or by type of question—definition, comprehension, or application.

Succeed in College!   *Succeed in College!* is a skills-building booklet containing selected chapters from Walter Pauk's best-selling study skills text *How to Study in College.* This booklet, which offers time-tested advice on notetaking, test-taking, and other topics, as well as a newly revised section on careers in psychology by John P. Fiore, can be shrink-wrapped free of charge with new copies of the student text.

Internet Guide for Psychology   Houghton Mifflin's *Internet Guide for Psychology,* by David Mahony of St. John's University, is available at no cost to students who purchase *Psychology.* This handy manual introduces students to electronic mail, discussion groups, Usenet newsgroups, the World Wide Web, APA reference style for the Internet, and more, and it provides students with step-by-step exercises and a wealth of addresses and sites relevant to psychology.

Introductory Psychology Readers   *Psychology in Context: Voices and Perspectives,* Second Edition, by David N. Sattler and Virginia Shabatay, contains engaging first-person narratives and essays keyed to major psychological concepts. Coursewise Publishing offers two readers by Laura Freberg. *Perspectives: Introductory Psychology* comprises recent articles relating to key topics in introductory psychology courses, and *Stand! Introductory Psychology* contains articles that explore contending ideas and opinions relating to fundamental issues in introductory psychology courses.

Electronic and Video Ancillaries

In keeping with the technological needs of today's campus, we provide the following electronic and video supplements to *Psychology:*

Power Presentation Manager Software   This powerful program allows instructors to create exciting and well-organized classroom presentations. It provides line art, tables, lecture outlines, preplanned PowerPoint® presentations, and access to *The Psychology Show* videodisc material. Instructors can also add their own PowerPoint® slides and presentations to the overhead transparency images and textbook outlines provided, as well as access their own text and image files.

Computerized Test Bank   The *Computerized Test Bank* allows instructors to generate exams and to integrate their own test items with those on the disk.

PsychAbilities   PsychAbilities is a "hands-on, minds-on" Web site dedicated to facilitating the learning and teaching of introductory psychology. PsychAbilities offers instructors and students access to current events and contemporary issues in psychology, interactive activities, practice tests, teaching materials, and more.

The Psychology Show   Houghton Mifflin's video supplement for introductory psychology is available in both videodisc and videotape formats to qualified adopters. Containing nineteen motion segments plus nearly 100 still images, *The Psychology Show* is designed to expand on text coverage and to stimulate class discussion through the length of the course. An accompanying instructor's guide offers information on each motion segment and still image and provides bar codes for videodisc use.

Lecture Starter Video and Guide   The Lecture Starter Video contains a series of high-interest, concise segments that instructors can use to begin a class meeting or change to a new topic. The accompanying guide briefly describes each segment, indicates concepts that can be addressed using each segment, and offers suggestions on how to use each segment.

Transparencies   The accompanying transparency set contains more than 150 full-color images from both the text and sources outside the text.

Other Multimedia Offerings   A range of videos, CD-ROMs, and other multimedia materials relevant to psychology are available free to qualified adopters. Houghton Mifflin sales representatives have further details.

ACKNOWLEDGMENTS

Many people provided us with the help, criticism, and encouragement we needed to create the Fifth Edition.

Once again we must thank Katie Steele, who got the project off the ground in 1983 by encouraging us to stop talking about this book and start writing it.

We are indebted to a number of our colleagues for their expert help and advice on the revisions of a number of chapters for the Fifth Edition. These colleagues include, for Chapter 5, Melody Carswell, University of Kentucky; for Chapter 6, J. Bruce Overmier, University of Minnesota; for Chapter 7, George Mastroianni, United States Air Force Academy; for Chapter 8, Leslie Whitaker, University of Dayton; for Chapter 10, Deborah Beidel, University of Maryland; for Chapter 13, Shelley Taylor, University of California, Los Angeles; for Chapter 15, Thomas Widiger, University of Kentucky; for Chapter 16, Geoffrey Thorpe, University of Maine; and for the behavioral genetics appendix, Robert Plomin, University of London.

We also owe an enormous debt to the colleagues who provided prerevision evaluations of, or reviewed the manuscript for, the Fifth Edition as it was being developed: James F. Calhoun, University of Georgia; Sheree Dukes Conrad, University of Massachusetts at Boston; Joesph R. Ferrari, DePaul University; Gary Gillund, College of Wooster; Linda A. Jackson, Michigan State University; Kerry Kilborn, University of Glasgow; Rich Robbins, Washburn University; Donna J. Tyler Thompson, Midland College; Teresa A. Treat, Indiana University; and Douglas Wardell, University of Alberta, Edmonton. Their advice and suggestions for improvement were responsible for many of the good qualities you will find in the book. If you have any criticisms, they probably involve areas these people warned us about. We especially want to thank these friends and colleagues: Sandra S. Goss, University of Illinois at Urbana-Champaign; Lawrence Pervin, Rutgers University; and Harry Triandis, University of Illinois at Urbana-Champaign, for their help.

The process of creating the Fifth Edition was greatly facilitated by the work of many dedicated people in the College Division at Houghton Mifflin Company. From the sales representatives and sales managers who told us of faculty members' suggestions for improvement to the marketing staff who developed innovative ways of telling our colleagues about the changes we have made, it seems that everyone in the division had a hand in shaping and improving the Fifth Edition. Several people deserve special thanks, however. Former sponsoring editor David Lee, senior associate editor Jane Knetzger, and editor-in-chief Kathi Prancan gave us invaluable advice about structural, pedagogical, and content changes for the new edition, and Jane, especially, acted as the project's main shepherd. When Jane took maternity leave, Marianne Stepanian ably filled in for her. Joanne Tinsley, our developmental editor, applied her editorial expertise and disciplined approach to helping us create this manuscript. She suggested changes based on reviewers' comments and our own goals, and she kept these suggestions and goals in mind as, chapter by chapter, she worked diligently to find ever better ways to organize the book and clarify its content. Janet Young, the project editor, contributed her considerable organizational skills and a dedication to excellence that was matched by a wonderfully helpful and cooperative demeanor. We also wish to thank Charlotte Miller for her stellar work in the creation and updating of the art program for the Fifth Edition; and Naomi Kornhauser for her creativity in developing new photo ideas and for her diligence in selecting and locating them. And a great big thank-you goes to Christine Arden for once again doing an outstanding job of copyediting the manuscript and to Elaine Kehoe for her copyediting help on the final chapters. Thanks also to Barbara Price and Nasya Laymon, who checked and rechecked each stage of proof to ensure its typographical accuracy. Without these people, and those who worked with them, this revision simply could not have happened. Finally, we want to express our deepest appreciation to our families and friends. Once again, their love saw us through an exhilarating but demanding period of our lives. They endured our hours at the computer, missed meals, postponed vacations, and occasional irritability during the creation of the First Edition of this book, and they had to suffer all over again during the lengthy process of revising it once more. Their faith in us is more important than they realize, and we will cherish it forever.

D. A. B.
A. C.-S.
L. A. P.
E. J. R.
C. D. W.

PSYCHOLOGY

1

Introducing Psychology

chapter

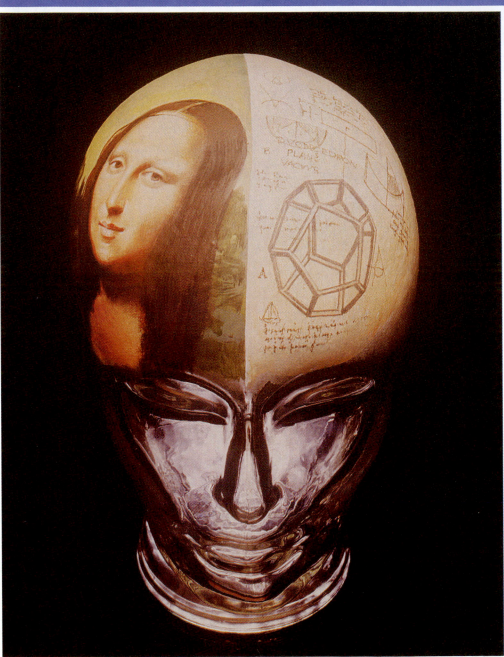

On the afternoon of July 24, 1998, the United States Capitol Building was already crowded with tourists as new arrivals lined up to go through a security checkpoint at the public entrance. Russell Eugene Weston, Jr., was in line, too, but he wasn't there to tour the building. Because he knew that the metal detector at the checkpoint would be set off by the .38 caliber pistol he carried, he tried to walk around it. When Capitol police officer Jacob Chestnut attempted to stop him, Weston drew his weapon and shot the officer in the head, killing him. Though hit by bullets fired by other police officers, Weston managed to run down a hallway and burst into the offices of Congressman Tom DeLay, where another Capitol guard, special agent John Gibson, rose to challenge him. After an exchange of gunfire, Gibson, too, lay dead and Weston was gravely wounded. As investigators tried to find out what prompted Weston's deadly attack, it emerged that he had been diagnosed in 1996 as a paranoid schizophrenic and placed in a mental hospital. This was after years of odd behavior, which included Weston's claims that both the Kennedy family and President Clinton were his close friends and that he was being spied on by the government through his neighbors' TV satellite dishes. Weston was later released from the hospital because his doctors believed that he was not a threat to himself or others if he took his prescribed antipsychotic medication.

How could the hospital staff's judgments and decisions about Weston have been so wrong? Do all mental patients pose a similar threat to society? If not, how can we tell which of them are dangerous and which are not? Are mental disorders such as schizophrenia caused by faulty genes, imbalances in brain chemicals, bad childhood experiences, or all of these factors? Can people like Weston be cured by drugs or psychotherapy? Will those who witnessed Weston's murderous attack be able to accurately recall what they saw and provide useful testimony at a trial? How will the witnesses' own lives be affected? Will they ever recover from their traumatic experience? Finally, why do newspaper and television accounts of this and other similar incidents so strongly affect millions of people who are thousands of miles away from the scene of the tragedy?

Psychologists study questions like these because **psychology** is the science that seeks to understand behavior and mental processes, and to apply that understanding in the service of human welfare. They have not yet provided final answers; but as you will see in later chapters, psychologists' research in areas such as judgment and decision making, psychological disorders, memory, stress and coping, and social cognition has yielded important clues and valuable theories about why people think, feel, and behave as they do. That research tells part of the story of psychology, but there is much more. We wrote this book to give you a better understanding of what psychology is, what psychologists study, where and how they work, what they have—and have not—discovered so far, and how their discoveries are being put to practical use. In this chapter we present an overview of psychology as it exists today, and as it developed. Then we describe the unity and diversity of contemporary psychology, including the differing approaches to understanding psychological phenomena, and the many subfields in which psychologists work.

THE WORLD OF PSYCHOLOGY: AN OVERVIEW

Consider the subject matter of psychology: *behavior and mental processes.* Obvious examples are eating, talking, reading, and thinking, but the realm of behavior and mental processes that psychologists study includes many other phenomena as well. To appreciate just how many, consider how you would answer the question, "Who are you?" Would you describe your personality? Your interests? Your aspirations? Your accomplishments? You could mention these and dozens of other things as well, and every one of them would probably reflect some aspect of what psychologists mean by behavior and mental processes. No wonder, then, that the chapters to come cover such

The Scope of Psychology

Like other living creatures, humans are biological beings, but they are more than just a collection of specialized cells. Throughout our lives, we develop and display remarkable capabilities to experience the world, to remember and think about it, to make decisions, solve problems, and take actions, to have feelings and strive for goals, to form relationships and attachments, and, unfortunately, to suffer distress and disorder. These are just some of the behaviors and mental processes that psychologists seek to understand. Throughout this book you will see how their research has provided knowledge and insights that are being used every day to promote human welfare.

a wide range of topics, including some—such as vision and hearing—that you might not have expected in a book about psychology. The topics have to be diverse in order to capture the full range of behaviors and mental processes that make you who you are and that come together in other ways in people of every culture around the world.

The Scope of Behavior and Mental Processes

So who are you, anyway? For one thing, you are a collection of cells that make up your bones and muscles, your skin and hair, your brain, liver, and other organs. Part of what we mean by behavior and mental processes is the activity of these cells, especially their ability to communicate with one another—as described in the chapter on biological aspects of psychology. To illustrate this point, stop reading for a moment and feel your pulse. You stay alive because your heart beats and your lungs breathe—all thanks to the activity of cells in your brain and elsewhere. Further, as shown in the chapter on human development, it was your cells' ability to divide and carry out specific functions that allowed you to blossom from the single fertilized cell you once were into the complex physical being you are now.

Some of your specialized cells make possible another remarkable aspect of behavior and mental processes: your capacity to sense information coming from the outside world and from inside your body. Again, stop reading for a moment and, this time, look left and right. The images of whatever you saw just then, like those you are seeing on the page right now, are the result of an amazing process through which cells in your eyes convert light into nervous activity that reaches your brain. Barring physical dis-

FIGURE 1.1

Husband and Father-in-Law

This figure is called "Husband and Father-in-Law" (Botwinick, 1961) because it can be seen as two different people, depending upon how you mentally organize the features of the figure. The elderly father-in-law faces to your right and is turned slightly toward you. He has a large nose, and the dark areas represent his coat pulled up to his protruding chin. However, the tip of his nose can also be seen as the tip of a younger man's chin; the younger man is in profile, also looking to your right, but away from you. The old man's mouth is the young man's neck band. Both men are wearing broad-brimmed hats. Your ability to see two different figures in a drawing that does not physically change—and to choose which one to see at any given moment—demonstrates the active nature of your perceptual processes. You manipulate incoming information rather than just passively receiving it.

ability, cells in your sense organs provide your brain with information that allows you not only to see your world but to hear, smell, taste, and feel it as well. Now snap your fingers, or at least try to. It was cells in your brain and motor system that allowed you to move your fingers as you did, just as they allow you to produce the coordinated patterns of behavior we call walking, dancing, talking, and the like. If you have an impairment in your ability to see, hear, or move, the problem lies somewhere in the structure or function of cells in your brain or in your sensory or motor systems. These cells and systems are described in the chapters on biological psychology and sensation.

Are you, then, only a bundle of cells that passively receives information and automatically reacts to it? You know you are much more than that, and we can help you prove it. Look at Figure 1.1. Although the drawing does not change, two different images emerge depending on which of its features you emphasize. Indeed, you don't just take in raw information; you also interpret it and give it meaning. This fascinating aspect of behavior and mental processes is discussed in the chapter on perception.

In addition to interpreting information, you can think about it and decide how to respond. Suppose you see someone standing in front of you with a knife. You recognize the knife as dangerous and you understand the meaning of the words, "Give me your money," so you decide to comply. However, if the person smiles and says, "Happy birthday," you will probably reach for the knife to cut your cake. Your decision about what to do in these two situations is guided not only by immediate circumstances but also by your capacity for learning and memory. If you couldn't understand the words you hear, or couldn't recall the faces of your family or what you have learned about muggers and birthdays, you would be at a loss. You can read more about these aspects of behavior and mental processes in the chapters on learning, memory, and cognition and language.

So far, you seem to be an utterly rational being, capable of coolly processing information under any circumstances. But would you experience only logical thought in the knife situations we described? Probably not. Chances are, you would also experience an emotion, probably fear or happiness. You are capable of feeling many other emotions as well. Where do these emotions come from, and why are they sometimes so difficult to control? You might ask the same questions about your wants and needs. Perhaps you do volunteer work, love to read, compete fiercely, work two jobs, skydive, knit, or eat more than you should. Why you behave as you do, what your behavior makes you feel, and how your feelings influence your behavior add yet other dimensions to your being and reflect yet other aspects of behavior and mental processes. These are discussed in the chapter on motivation and emotion.

Above all, you are an individual, in many ways unlike anyone else on earth. You have your own personality, mental abilities, values, attitudes, beliefs, and probably even a special set of problems of one kind or another. Your individuality arises partly from the unique set of physical characteristics and behavioral tendencies you inherited from your parents, and partly from the experiences you had while growing up in your particular family and culture. The kaleidoscope of individual differences in behavior and mental processes is discussed throughout this book but receives special attention in the chapters on mental abilities; health, stress, and coping; personality; psychological disorders; and treatment.

Finally, because you are an individual in a social world, your answer to the question, "Who are you?" would probably include something about how and where you fit into that world. You might mention the size of your family, your place in the organizations you belong to, or your attitudes about the government. Indeed, as discussed in the chapters on social cognition and social influence, no definition of behavior and mental processes is complete without some reference to how people think about, and relate to, other people. And no wonder. Great human achievements—from the performance of a symphony to the exploration of space—can result when people work together. And great human tragedies—from the Holocaust to terrorism and war—can occur when prejudice and hatred turn people against one another.

Research: The Foundation of Psychology

To help face the challenge of understanding these various aspects of behavior and mental processes, most psychologists rely on a philosophical view known as *empiricism*. Empiricists see knowledge as coming through experience and observation, not through speculation. Accordingly, psychologists use the methods of science to conduct *empirical* research, meaning that they perform experiments and other scientific procedures to systematically gather and analyze information about psychological phenomena.

For example, Michael Morris and Kaiping Peng (1994) were interested in learning more about how people explain other people's actions. Previous research in North America and other Western cultures had shown that people in those cultures tend to see other people's behavior as caused mainly by their personality traits and other individual characteristics. Morris and Peng wondered if this tendency occurred in all cultures. They had reason to believe it did not. North American cultures tend to place great emphasis on self-esteem, personal achievement, and other individual traits and goals. In other cultures, such as those in China and Japan, the individual tends to be seen as less important than the groups to which the individual belongs. These cultural differences affect the way people think about what is important in life, but could they also affect the way people explain other people's behavior? Morris and Peng predicted that whereas Americans would tend to see behavior as caused by *personal* characteristics such as laziness or bravery, people from China would tend to see behavior as caused by social pressure, lack of money, or other *situational* factors.

To test this idea, Morris and Peng gave American students and Chinese students (who were studying in the United States) two newspaper stories about two real murders. In one, the murderer was Chinese; in the other, he was American. After reading the articles, both groups of students were asked to rate the extent to which each murder was due to the personal attributes of the murderer (e.g., personality problems) and the extent to which it was due to the situation in which the murderer found himself (e.g., being provoked by the victim).

The results of this study are presented in Figure 1.2. As Morris and Peng had predicted, American students were more inclined to attribute the murders to the murderer's personality than to the situation he was in. In sharp contrast, the Chinese

FIGURE 1.2

American and Chinese Students' Explanations of a Murder

When American students were asked to explain why someone committed a murder, they tended to attribute the act to the murderer's personal characteristics; but Chinese students tended to attribute it to the circumstances in which the murderer found himself. This experiment illustrates how psychologists conduct empirical research to objectively study psychological phenomena. It also shows how culture can affect mental processes (Morris & Peng, 1994).

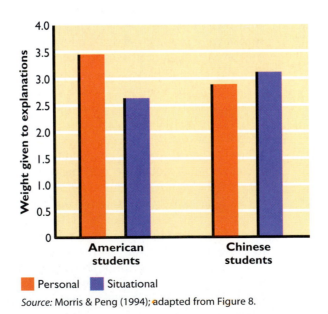

Source: Morris & Peng (1994); adapted from Figure 8.

students gave more weight to the situation as the cause of the murderer's actions. This study, along with many others described in later chapters, provides part of the empirical basis for psychologists' assertion that cultural factors can have a strong influence on people's thoughts, feelings, and actions.

In other words, psychologists do more than speculate about behavior and mental processes; they also use scientific methods to test the validity of their theories. They conduct empirically oriented scientific inquiries and draw informed conclusions from their results. Even psychologists who do not carry out research themselves are constantly applying the results of their colleagues' work to enhance the quality, currency, and effectiveness of their own teaching, writing, or service to clients and organizations.

The rules and methods of science that guide psychologists in their research are summarized in the next chapter. We have placed this material about research early in the book in order to underscore the fact that, without scientific methods and the foundation of empirical data they provide, psychologists' statements and recommendations would be no more credible than those of astrologers, tabloid newspapers, or talk-show guests who offer empirically unsupported opinions. Indeed, throughout this book, the results of scientific research in psychology shape not only our presentation of what is known so far about behavior and mental processes but also our evaluation of psychologists' efforts to apply that knowledge to improve the quality of human life.

A Brief History of Psychology

The birthdate of modern psychology is usually given as 1879, the year that Wilhelm Wundt (pronounced "voont") established the first formal psychology research laboratory at the University of Leipzig, Germany. However, the roots of psychology can be traced back through centuries of history in philosophy and science. Since at least the time of Socrates, Plato, and Aristotle, there has been lively debate about such topics as the source of human knowledge, the nature of mind and soul, the relationship of mind to body, and the possibility of scientifically studying these matters (Wertheimer, 1987).

The philosophy of empiricism was particularly important to the development of scientific psychology. Beginning in the seventeenth century, proponents of empiricism—especially the British philosophers John Locke, George Berkeley, and David Hume—challenged the view held by philosophers from Plato to Descartes that some knowledge is innate. As mentioned earlier, empiricists see everything we know as coming through the experience of our senses. At birth, they said, our minds are like a blank slate (*tabula rasa,* in Latin) upon which experience writes a lifelong story.

Wundt and the Structuralism of Titchener   By the nineteenth century, a number of German physiologists, including Hermann von Helmholtz and Gustav Fechner, were conducting scientific studies of the structure and function of vision, hearing, and the other sensory systems and perceptual processes that empiricism identified as important to human knowledge. Fechner's work was especially valuable because he realized that one could study these mental processes by observing people's reactions to changes in sensory stimuli. By exploring, for example, how much brighter a light must become before a person sees it as twice as bright, Fechner discovered complex but predictable relationships between changes in the *physical* characteristics of stimuli and changes in people's *psychological* experience of them. Fechner's approach, which he called *psychophysics,* paved the way for much of the research on perception described in Chapter 5.

As a physiologist, Wundt, too, analyzed sensory-perceptual systems using the methods of laboratory science, but his explicit goal was to study *consciousness,* the immediate experience arising from these systems. Wundt wanted to describe the basic elements of consciousness, how they are organized, and how they relate to one another (Schultz & Schultz, 2000). He developed numerous ingenious laboratory methods to study these elements, including the speed of mental events. In an attempt to observe conscious experience, Wundt used the technique of *introspection,* which means

Wilhelm Wundt (1832–1920)

In a classic experiment on the speed of mental processes, Wundt (third from left) measured how quickly people could respond to a light by releasing a button they had been holding down. He then determined how much longer the response took when people held down one button with each hand and had to decide, based on the color of the light, which one to release. Wundt reasoned that the additional time revealed how long it took to perceive the color and decide which hand to move. The logic behind this experiment remains a part of research on cognitive processes today.

FIGURE 1.3

A Stimulus for Introspection

Look at this object and try to describe, not what it is, but only how intense and clear are the sensations and images (such as redness, brightness, and roundness) that make up your experience of it. This was the difficult task that Wilhelm Wundt, and especially Edward Titchener, set for carefully trained research participants in a search for the building blocks of consciousness.

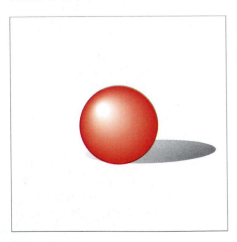

"inward looking." For example, participants specially trained in this method were exposed to a light or sound and, on repeated trials, they tried to describe the sensations and feelings the stimulus created. Wundt concluded that "quality" (e.g., cold or blue) and "intensity" (e.g., brightness or loudness) are the two essential elements of any sensation and that feelings can be described in terms of pleasure-displeasure, tension-relaxation, and excitement-depression (Schultz & Schultz, 2000). In short, with Wundt's work, psychology had evolved from the *philosophy* of mental processes to the *science* of mental processes.

Edward Titchener, an Englishman who had been a student of Wundt, used introspection in his own laboratory at Cornell University to study Wundt's basic elements as well as images and other aspects of conscious experience that are harder to quantify (see Figure 1.3). One result was that Titchener added "clarity" as an element of sensation (Watson, 1963). Though often associated with Wundt, *structuralism* is the name given solely to Titchener's approach because of his efforts to define the structure of consciousness.

Wundt was by no means alone in the scientific study of psychology, nor was his work universally accepted. In psychology laboratories established by German contemporaries such as Hermann Ebbinghaus, the use of introspection to dissect consciousness was seen as less important than conducting experiments on the capacities, limitations, and other characteristics of mental processes such as learning and memory. Indeed, Ebbinghaus's experiments—in which he himself was the subject—formed the basis for much of what we know about memory today. Another group of German colleagues, including Max Wertheimer, Kurt Koffka, and Wolfgang Köhler, criticized Wundt on the grounds that introspection can be misleading. They pointed to visual illusions of the type shown in Figure 1.1 (on page 5) to support their argument that our experience of a whole stimulus pattern is not the same as the sum of its parts. These Gestalt psychologists (*Gestalt* means, roughly, "unified whole" in German) argued that consciousness can be best understood by observing it as a total experience, rather than trying to break it down into a cluster of component elements. Thus, for example, although movies are in fact long strips of film containing thousands of still photographs, describing each of those photographs in turn would not capture a person's *experience* of watching a movie.

Freud and Psychoanalysis   While Wundt and his colleagues in Leipzig were conducting scientific research on consciousness, Sigmund Freud (1856–1939) was in Vienna, beginning to explore the unconscious. As a physician, Freud had presumed that all behavior and mental processes have *physical* causes somewhere in the nervous system. He began to question that assumption in the late 1800s, however, after encountering a series of patients who displayed a variety of physical ailments that had no apparent physical cause. Using hypnosis and other methods, Freud found evidence that convinced him that the roots of these people's "neuroses" lay in shocking experiences from the distant past that the patients had pushed out of consciousness (Breuer & Freud, 1896). He eventually came to believe that all behavior—from everyday slips of the tongue to severe forms of mental disorder—is motivated by *psychological processes*, especially unconscious conflicts within the mind. For the next forty years, Freud revised and expanded his ideas into a body of work known as *psychoanalysis*, which included a theory of personality and mental disorder, as well as a set of treatment methods. Freud's ideas were (and still are) controversial, but they have had an undeniable influence on the thinking of many psychologists around the world.

William James and Functionalism   It was also during the late 1800s that scientific research in psychology took root outside Europe, especially in the United States and Canada. The first U.S. psychology laboratory was founded by William James at Harvard University, at around the same time Wundt established his laboratory in Leipzig. However, most historians believe that James used his laboratory mainly for conducting demonstrations for his students; it was not until 1883 that G. Stanley Hall, at Johns Hopkins University, established the first psychology research laboratory in the United States. Six years later, in 1889, the first Canadian laboratory was established at the University of Toronto by James Mark Baldwin, Canada's first modern psychologist and a pioneer in research on child development.

Like the Gestalt psychologists, William James rejected both Wundt's approach and Titchener's structuralism. Influenced by Darwin's theory of evolution, James was more interested in understanding how consciousness *functions* to help people adapt to their environments (James, 1890, 1892). This idea came to be called *functionalism*, and it

William James's Lab

James (1842–1910) established this psychology demonstration laboratory at Harvard University in the late 1870s. James saw structuralism as a scientific dead end; in one paper, he noted that trying to understand consciousness by studying its components is like trying to understand a house by looking at individual bricks (James, 1884). He preferred to study instead the functions served by consciousness.

focused on the ongoing "stream" of consciousness—the ever-changing pattern of images, sensations, memories, and other mental events. James wanted to know how the whole process works for the individual. Why, for example, do most people remember recent events better than things that happened in the remote past?

The functionalist view encouraged North American psychologists to look not only at how mental processes work in general but also at how they vary from person to person. Accordingly, some psychologists began to measure individual differences in learning, memory, and other mental processes associated with intelligence, made recommendations for improving educational practices in the schools, and even worked with teachers on programs tailored to children in need of special help (Nietzel, Bernstein & Milich, 1998).

John Watson and Behaviorism   Besides fueling James's functionalism, Darwin's theory led psychologists—especially in North America after 1900—to study animals as well as humans. If all species evolved in adaptive ways, perhaps their behavior and mental processes would follow the same or similar laws. Psychologists could not expect cats or rats or chickens to introspect, so they observed animal behavior in mazes and other experimental situations. From these observations, they made inferences about conscious experience, learning, memory, intelligence, and other mental processes.

John B. Watson, a psychology professor at Johns Hopkins University, agreed that overt behavior in animals and humans was the most important source of scientific information for psychology. However, Watson believed it was utterly unscientific to use behavior as the basis for *inferences* about consciousness, as structuralists and functionalists did—let alone about the unconscious, as Freudians did. In 1913, Watson published an article called "Psychology as the Behaviorist Views It." In it, he argued that psychologists should ignore mental events and base psychology only on what they can actually observe about overt behavior and its response to various stimuli (Watson, 1913, 1919). Watson's *behaviorism* recognized the existence of consciousness but considered it useless as a target of research since it would always be private and unobservable by scientific methods. Preoccupation with consciousness, said Watson, would prevent psychology from ever being a true science. Influenced by Ivan Pavlov's research on classical conditioning in dogs (described in Chapter 6), Watson believed that *learn-*

John B. Watson (1878–1958)

The founder of behaviorism, Watson argued that by focusing on observable behavior, such as this baby's grasping reflex, psychologists would not have to rely on people's potentially distorted self-reports.

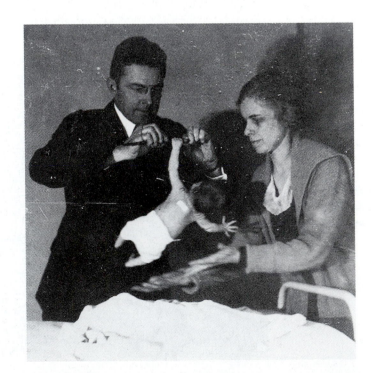

ing is the most important determinant of behavior, and that it is through learning that organisms are able to adapt to their environments. He was famous for claiming that, with enough control over the environment, he could create learning experiences that would turn any infant into a doctor, a lawyer, or even a criminal.

American psychologist B. F. Skinner was another early champion of behaviorism. From the 1930s until his death in 1990, Skinner worked on mapping out the details of how rewards and punishments shape, maintain, and change behavior through what he termed "operant conditioning." His *functional analysis of behavior* helped explain, for example, how children's tantrums are sometimes inadvertently encouraged by the attention they attract from parents and teachers, and how a virtual addiction to gambling can result from the occasional and unpredictable rewards it brings.

Many psychologists were drawn to Watson and Skinner's vision of psychology as the learning-based science of observable behavior. Behaviorism dominated psychological research from the 1920s through the 1960s, while the study of consciousness languished, especially in the United States.

Psychology Today   Psychologists continue to study all kinds of overt behavior in humans and in animals. By the 1960s, however, many had become dissatisfied with the limitations imposed by behaviorism (some, especially in Europe, had never accepted it in the first place). They grew uncomfortable ignoring mental processes that might be important in more fully understanding behavior (e.g., Ericsson & Simon, 1994). The advent of the computer age gave these psychologists just what they needed. Computers provided a new way to think about mental activity—as information processing. They also enabled psychologists to measure mental activity far more accurately than ever before. At the same time, progress in computer-supported biotechnology began to offer psychologists exciting new ways to study the biological bases of mental processes, to literally see what is going on in the brain when, for example, a person thinks or makes decisions (see Figure 1.4).

Armed with ever more sophisticated research tools, psychologists today are striving to do what Watson thought was impossible: to study mental processes with precision and scientific objectivity. In fact, there are probably as many contemporary psychologists studying cognitive and biological processes as those studying observable behaviors. So mainstream psychology has come full circle, once again accepting consciousness—in the form of cognitive processes—as a legitimate topic for scientific research and justifying the definition of psychology as the science of behavior and mental processes (Robins, Gosling, & Craik, 1999).

FIGURE 1.4

Visualizing Brain Activity

Technological advances such as magnetic resonance imaging (MRI) allow psychologists and other scientists to study brain activity accompanying various mental processes. This study, for example, found that males (left) and females (right) show different patterns of brain activity (indicated by the brightly colored areas) while reading (Shaywitz et al., 1995).

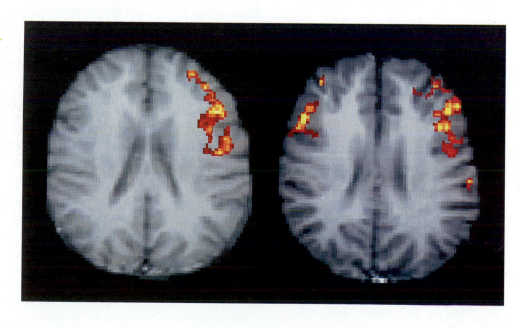

Gilbert Haven Jones (1883–1966)

When Gilbert Haven Jones graduated from the University of Jena, Germany, in 1909, he became one of the first African-Americans to earn a Ph.D. in psychology. Many others were to follow, including J. Henry Alston, who was the first African-American to publish research in a major U.S. psychology journal (Alston, 1920).

Mary Whiton Calkins (1863–1930)

Mary Whiton Calkins studied psychology at Harvard University with William James, and her research on memory helped her to be named, in 1905, the first woman president of the American Psychological Association. Because she was a woman, however, Harvard would only grant her doctoral degree through Radcliffe, an affiliated women's school. She refused that arrangement. When Margaret Washburn (1871–1939) encountered similar sex discrimination at Columbia University, she transferred to Cornell, became the first woman to earn a doctorate in psychology and, in 1921, the second woman president of the APA.

A final point about the history of psychology: If you looked only at the photographs on the preceding pages, you might think that psychology was founded and shaped entirely by male Caucasians. It is true that, as in many other realms of human endeavor in the nineteenth and early twentieth centuries, white males dominated the world of psychology. But there is much more to the story. Women and people of color made important early contributions to psychology (Schultz & Schultz, 2000), and throughout this book you will find the work of their modern counterparts.

Indeed, the contributions of women and ethnic minorities in psychology have increased in tandem with their growing representation in the field. In the United States, women now constitute about 38 percent of all psychologists holding doctoral degrees (National Science Foundation, 1994), and they are earning 60 percent of the new doctorates awarded each year (American Psychological Association, 1995a). Moreover, nearly 10 percent of new doctoral degrees are being earned by members of ethnic minorities (American Psychological Association, 1995b). These numbers reflect continuing efforts by psychological organizations and governmental bodies, especially in the United States and Canada, to promote the recruitment, graduation, and employment of women and ethnic minorities in psychology (DeAngelis, 1995b).

UNITY AND DIVERSITY IN PSYCHOLOGY

Psychologists today are unified by their commitment to empiricism and scientific research, by their linked interests, and by the debt they owe to predecessors whose work has shaped psychology over its 120-year history. However, they approach behavior and mental processes in many different ways. In this section, we review these various approaches and describe the network of linked subfields into which psychology has evolved. We conclude by highlighting psychologists' efforts to ensure that their research is as inclusive of, and as applicable to, as much of humankind as possible.

Approaches to Psychology

Suppose you are a psychologist trying to understand some aspect of the behavior and mental processes we have reviewed. Perhaps, like Morris and Peng, you are interested in cross-cultural differences in thought processes; or maybe you want to identify the

Recording Brain Waves

The biological approach to psychology seeks to understand how behavior and mental processes relate to internal bodily events and activities. Here, researchers record the brain waves of a person who is performing a task similar to that of an air traffic controller (ATC). Psychologists in the Navy and elsewhere are working on systems that could warn ATCs and radar/sonar operators that they are failing to attend to important information.

origins of aggression, pinpoint the causes of schizophrenia, or solve the riddle of drug abuse. Where would you look for answers? In brain cells and hormones? In inherited characteristics? In what people have learned from their parents? The direction of your research efforts will be determined largely by your *approach* to psychology—that is, by the set of assumptions, questions, and methods that you believe will be most helpful for understanding the behavior and mental processes you wish to explore.

Whereas some psychologists adopt one particular approach, many others are *eclectic*, combining features of two or more approaches because they believe that no single perspective can fully account for all aspects of psychological phenomena. Psychologists today no longer refer to themselves as structuralists or functionalists, but the psychodynamic and behavioral approaches remain, along with others known as the biological, evolutionary, cognitive, and humanistic approaches. Some of these approaches are more influential than others, but we will briefly review the essential features of all of them in order to give you a better understanding of why psychologists over the years have conducted their research as they have. In later chapters we will examine the value—and the limitations—of each approach for understanding many psychological phenomena.

The Biological Approach   Investigating the possibility that aggressive behavior or schizophrenia, for example, might be traceable to a hormonal imbalance or a brain disorder reflects the biological approach to psychology. As its name implies, the biological approach assumes that behavior and mental processes are largely shaped by biological processes. Psychologists who take this approach study the psychological effects of hormones, genes, and the activity of the nervous system, especially the brain. Thus, if they are studying memory, they might try to identify the changes taking place in the brain as information is stored there. Or if they are studying thinking, they might look for patterns of brain activity associated with, say, making quick decisions or reading a foreign language.

Research discussed in nearly every chapter of this book reflects the enormous influence of the biological approach on psychology today. To help you better understand the terms and concepts used in that research, the behavioral genetics appendix discusses some basic principles of genetics and Chapter 3 explains other biological aspects of psychology.

The Evolutionary Approach   Biological processes also figure prominently in the evolutionary approach to psychology. The foundation for this approach was English naturalist Charles Darwin's book, *The Origin of Species*. Darwin argued that the forms

Evolution and Behavior

In animals, such as insects, birds, and fish, species-specific behaviors often appear as relatively rigid rituals, called *fixed action patterns,* which are not altered much by learning and which tend to be triggered by specific cues called *sign stimuli.* Here, a herring gull chick pecks for food in a characteristic way, but only after seeing the red spot on the parent's beak that serves as a target.

A Behavioral Prevention Program

The behavioral approach to psychology suggests that most human behaviors are learned and that problematic behaviors can be changed, or even prevented, by the development of alternative responses. In this program, for example, teenagers participate in role-playing exercises that help them to develop the behavioral skills they will need to "say no" to drugs.

of life present in the world today are the result of evolution—of changes in life forms that occur over many generations—and, more specifically, that evolution occurs through *natural selection.* Darwin believed that natural selection operates at the level of individuals, but most contemporary evolutionists maintain that it operates at the level of genes. At either level, the process is the same. Those genes that result in characteristics and behaviors that are adaptive and useful in a certain environment will enable the creatures that possess them to survive, reproduce, and thereby pass these genes on to subsequent generations (Buss & Kenrick, 1998). Genes that result in characteristics that are not adaptive in that environment will not be passed on to subsequent generations because the creatures possessing them will not be able to survive and reproduce. Thus, evolutionary theory says that many (but not all) of the genes we possess today are the result of natural selection.

Scientists who study animal behavior in the natural environment—called **ethologists**—have identified the effects of natural selection not only in inherited physical characteristics, such as the camouflage coloration that helps animals escape predators, but also in instinctive or, more properly, *species-specific* behaviors that aid survival.

In psychology, the evolutionary approach holds that the behavior of animals and humans today is the result of evolution through natural selection. Psychologists who take an evolutionary approach therefore try to understand (1) the adaptive value of behavior, (2) the anatomical and biological mechanisms that make it possible, and (3) the environmental conditions that encourage or discourage it. The evolutionary approach has generated a growing body of research (Buss & Kenrick, 1998). You will read about its influence in later chapters in relation to topics as diverse as helping and altruism, mental disorders, temperament, and interpersonal attraction.

The Psychodynamic Approach　　The **psychodynamic approach** offers a different slant on the role of inherited instincts and other biological forces in human behavior. Rooted in Freud's psychoanalysis, this approach asserts that all behavior and mental processes reflect the constant and mostly unconscious psychological struggles that rage within each person. Usually, these struggles involve conflict between the impulse to satisfy instincts or wishes (for food, sex, or aggression, for example) and the need to abide by the restrictions imposed by society. From this perspective, hostility and aggression reflect the breakdown of civilizing defenses against the expression of primitive urges, whereas anxiety, depression, or other disorders are the overt signs of inner turmoil.

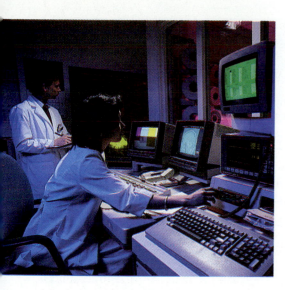

Cognitive Science

Some psychologists are working on a "computational theory of the mind" in which they use computer programs to simulate how humans perceive, remember, reason, and otherwise process information. In Chapter 8, on cognition and language, we discuss their progress in creating "artificial intelligence" in computers that can make medical diagnoses, analyze maps for the presence of mineral deposits, pick stocks, and perform other complex cognitive tasks.

The psychodynamic approach is reflected in a number of the contemporary theories of personality, psychological disorders, and treatment discussed in Chapters 14, 15, and 16. However, the orthodox Freudian perspective is far less influential in psychology now than in the past (Robins, Gosling, & Craik, 1999). Most psychologists today who take a psychodynamic approach prefer one of the many revised versions of Freud's original theories described in Chapter 14. For example, they may focus on how people's relationship with their parents forms a template for intimate relationships later in their lives (e.g., Baldwin, 1992).

The Behavioral Approach   The behavioral approach to psychology stands in stark contrast to the psychodynamic, biological, and evolutionary approaches. As founded by John Watson, the behavioral approach characterizes behavior and mental processes as primarily the result of *learning*. From Watson's point of view, biological, genetic, and evolutionary factors provide the raw material on which rewards, punishments, and other experiences act to shape each individual. Thus, whether the topic is aggression or drug abuse, self-confidence or helping, behaviorists seek to understand it in terms of an individual's learning history, especially the patterns of reward and punishment the individual has experienced. They also believe that people can change problematic behaviors, from overeating to criminality, by unlearning old habits and developing new ones.

Today, many behaviorists have come to endorse a variation on behaviorism. The *cognitive-behavioral* view (also called the social-cognitive view) adds the study of reportable mental processes to the traditional behavioral emphasis on observable actions (Beck & Weishaar, 1995; Ellis, 1995). The cognitive-behavioral approach explores how learning affects the development of thoughts and beliefs and, in turn, how these learned cognitive patterns affect overt behavior.

The Cognitive Approach   Recognition by many behaviorists of the importance of cognitive factors reflects the influence of a broader cognitive approach to psychology. The cognitive approach focuses on how people take in, mentally represent, and store information; how they perceive and process that information; and how cognitive processes are related to the integrated patterns of behavior we can see. In other words, the cognitive approach guides psychologists to study the rapid series of mental events—including those taking place outside of awareness—that accompany overt behavior. Consider, for example, how an incident in which one person shoves another in front of a theater might be analyzed cognitively: The aggressor (1) perceives that someone has cut into the theater line, (2) uses stored memories and concepts to decide that this act is inappropriate, (3) attributes the act to the culprit's obnoxiousness, (4) considers possible responses and their likely consequences, (5) decides that shoving the person is the best response, and (6) executes that response.

Psychologists taking the cognitive approach are interested in discovering how people process information in domains ranging from decision making and interpersonal attraction to intelligence testing and group problem solving, to name but a few. Some of them work with researchers from computer science, the biological sciences, engineering, linguistics, philosophy, and other disciplines in a multidisciplinary field called *cognitive science,* which analyzes intelligent systems. Cognitive scientists attempt to discover the building blocks of cognition and to determine how these components produce complex behaviors such as remembering a fact, naming an object, or writing a word (Azar, 1997a; Medin & Ross, 1997).

The Humanistic Approach   Another view of the role of mental events in psychology is provided by the humanistic approach (also known as the phenomenological approach). From the humanistic perspective, behavior is determined primarily by each person's capacity to choose how to think and act. And humanistic psychologists see these choices as dictated, not by instincts, biological processes, or rewards and punishments, but by each individual's unique perceptions. If you perceive the world as a friendly place, you are likely to feel happy and secure. If you view it as dangerous and

APPROACHES TO PSYCHOLOGY

Approach	Characteristics
Biological	Emphasizes activity of the nervous system, especially of the brain; the action of hormones and other chemicals; and genetics.
Evolutionary	Emphasizes the ways in which behavior and mental processes are adaptive for survival.
Psychodynamic	Emphasizes internal conflicts, mostly unconscious, which usually pit sexual or aggressive instincts against environmental obstacles to their expression.
Behavioral	Emphasizes learning, especially each person's experience with rewards and punishments.
Cognitive	Emphasizes mechanisms through which people receive, store, retrieve, and otherwise process information.
Humanistic	Emphasizes individual potential for growth and the role of unique perceptions in guiding behavior and mental processes.

hostile, you will probably be defensive and anxious. So, like cognitively oriented psychologists, humanists would see aggression in a theater line as stemming from a perception that aggression is justified.

However, unlike those who take a cognitive approach, humanistic psychologists do not search for general laws that govern people's perceptions, judgments, decisions, and actions. Instead, the humanistic approach celebrates immediate, individual experience. Many of its proponents assert that behavior and mental processes can be fully understood only by appreciating the perceptions and feelings experienced by each individual. Humanistic psychologists also believe that people are essentially good, that they are in control of themselves, and that their main innate tendency is to grow toward their highest potential.

The humanistic approach began to attract attention in North America in the 1940s through the writings of Carl Rogers (1902-1987), a psychologist who had been trained in, but later rejected, the psychodynamic tradition. His views on personality and his methods of therapy are discussed in Chapters 14 and 16. The humanistic approach also shaped Abraham Maslow's (1943) influential hierarchy-of-needs theory of motivation, which is described in Chapters 11 and 14. Today, however, the impact of the humanistic approach to psychology is limited, mainly because many psychologists find humanistic concepts and predictions too vague to be expressed and tested scientifically. (For a summary of the approaches we have discussed, see "In Review: Approaches to Psychology.")

Subfields of Psychology

The world's approximately half-million psychologists can be categorized not only in terms of the particular approach to psychology they prefer (such as the biological or the behavioral approach) but also in terms of what they are most interested in study-

Engineering Psychology

Research by cognitive psychologists whose special interest is *engineering psychology*—also known as *human factors*—has guided the development of realistic computer-controlled flight simulators used in pilot training. Their research also guides the placement of controls, instruments, and warning lights so that pilots will react to them quickly and correctly. Cognitive psychologists' findings are also being applied by engineers and designers striving to create computer keyboards, nuclear power plant control panels, and even VCR remote controls that are logical and easy to use without error (Wickens, Gordon, & Liu, 1998).

Mental Processes and the Brain

Biological psychologists study differences in the way each half of the brain processes information. Here, in one of her experiments on this topic, Marie Banich explains to a participant that pictures of faces will be flashed to only the left or the right side of his brain.

ing. In other words, choosing an approach helps shape *how* psychologists think about behavior and mental processes in general, but they still have to decide what to study. One can use the biological approach, for example, to explore the mechanisms behind color vision, or what goes on in the brain when people learn, or how hormones contribute to aggression, or the degree to which genes shape personality and mental disorder. A psychologist taking a behavioral approach might study how rewards and punishments influence child development, alcoholism and drug abuse, the learning of fear or depression, the appearance of healthy—or unhealthy—lifestyles, the morale and productivity of employees, or the success of a community's recycling efforts.

The hundreds of topics available for study tend to cluster into groups that define psychology's specialty areas, or *subfields,* and most psychologists choose to focus their work on just one or two of them. The diversity of these subfields—and the career opportunities they offer—can be quite surprising to anyone who thinks of psychology only as the study and treatment of mental disorders.

Cognitive Psychology   Those whose research focuses on basic mental processes and their relation to behavior tend to be known as **cognitive psychologists.** They study things like sensation, perception, learning, memory, judgment, decision making, and problem solving. (In the tradition of Wundt, some of these researchers prefer to be called **experimental psychologists,** but this label applies much more widely now because psychologists in *all* subfields use experiments and other empirical methods in their work.)

Biological Psychology   Biological psychologists, also called **physiological psychologists,** analyze how biology shapes behavior and mental processes. Their work has helped us understand, for example, how the brain controls physical movements, regulates eating, and receives information from the senses. Biological psychologists address questions such as the role of genetics and brain anatomy in schizophrenia, whether patterns of brain activity can reveal that someone is lying, or how stress-related hormones can suppress the body's immune system.

Social Psychology   Social psychologists study the many ways in which people influence one another. Among the topics on their research agenda is the effectiveness of social influence strategies such as advertising in promoting safe sex and other behaviors that can halt the spread of AIDS. Social psychologists also seek the roots of ethnic prejudice and ways to help eradicate it. And even more than the rest of us, social psychologists are interested in interpersonal attraction—whom we like, and why.

A Persuasive Message

Social psychologists' research on how people's attitudes and behaviors can be influenced by persuasive messages has been applied in public health campaigns designed to promote health and prevent illness, as well as in advertising campaigns for consumer products.

Personality Psychology   Whereas some psychologists seek laws that govern the behavior of people in general, **personality psychologists** focus on characteristics that make each person unique. One relatively new test to come out of this subfield measures five dimensions on which most people can be described and which can be used to make predictions about how they will tend to behave (look for the "Big-Five" model in Chapter 14). Personality psychologists also study personality traits in children that might help predict the occurrence of alcoholism, drug abuse, aggressiveness, or other problems in later life.

Developmental Psychology   Behavior and mental processes change over the life span. **Developmental psychologists** describe these changes and try to understand their causes and effects. They are interested in discovering when children begin to form friendships, whether strict parental discipline leads to conformity or rebellion, and whether a midlife crisis is inevitable. Developmental psychologists also explore the development of thought. In one study, children were asked to draw a picture indicating where they would place a third eye, if they could have one. The youngest children showed they were still in an early stage of cognitive development by drawing the extra eye on their forehead "as a spare." More complex thinking was revealed in slightly older

Planning Environments

Environmental psychologists' research on how floor plans, availability of natural light, and a building's other physical features can affect occupants' mood, energy, interaction, stress level, and productivity helps architects create optimal designs for workplaces, nursing homes, schools, prisons, private homes, and even campus residence halls (Sommer, 1999).

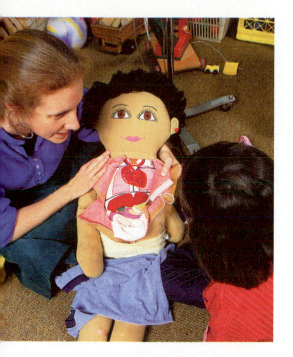

Getting Ready for Surgery

Research by health psychologists has guided the development of specialized programs for helping medical patients prepare for, cope with, and recover from surgery with a minimum of distress. As shown here, hospital pre-surgery programs for children often employ dolls to help young patients understand what their operations will involve and how they can expect to feel afterward.

Keeping Their Cool

Sport psychologists use a variety of methods, including training in relaxation skills, to help athletes combat stress and perform at their peak.

children, one of whom placed the extra eye in his palm—"so I can see what's in the cookie jar better" (Shaffer, 1973).

Industrial/Organizational Psychology Industrial/organizational psychologists try to improve the efficiency, productivity, and satisfaction of workers and the organizations that employ them (Druckman, Singer, & VanCott, 1997). Thus, they conduct research on topics such as improving the selection of new employees, increasing the motivation of current employees, and making organizations more responsive to workers' needs and concerns.

Clinical, Counseling, and Community Psychology Clinical and counseling psychologists conduct research on the causes of behavior disorders and offer services to help troubled people overcome those disorders. Community psychologists create systems to ensure that psychological services reach the homeless and others who need help but tend not to seek it. They also try to *prevent* psychological disorders by working for changes in schools and other social systems in hopes of reducing the poverty and other stresses of life that so often lead to disorder.

Educational and School Psychology Educational psychologists conduct research and develop theories about teaching and learning. The results of their work are applied to improving teacher training and—through refinement of school curricula, for example—to helping students learn more efficiently (Hoy, 1999). School psychologists specialize in IQ testing, diagnosing learning disabilities and other academic problems, and setting up programs to improve students' achievement and satisfaction in school.

Quantitative Psychology To what extent is intelligence inherited, and to what extent can it be influenced by the environment? As you will see in Chapter 10, on mental abilities, this is one of the hottest topics in psychology, and quantitative psychologists are right in the middle of it. They develop ever more sophisticated statistical methods for analyzing the vast amounts of data collected by their colleagues in other subfields (e.g., Russell, 1995), they evaluate the validity of tests (including tests of mental ability), and they seek mathematical methods to tease apart the effects of such closely entwined variables as heredity and environment.

Still other subfields of psychology deal with other aspects of behavior and mental processes. For example, health psychologists study the effects of behavior on health and the impact of illness on behavior and emotion (Taylor, 1998a), sport psychologists

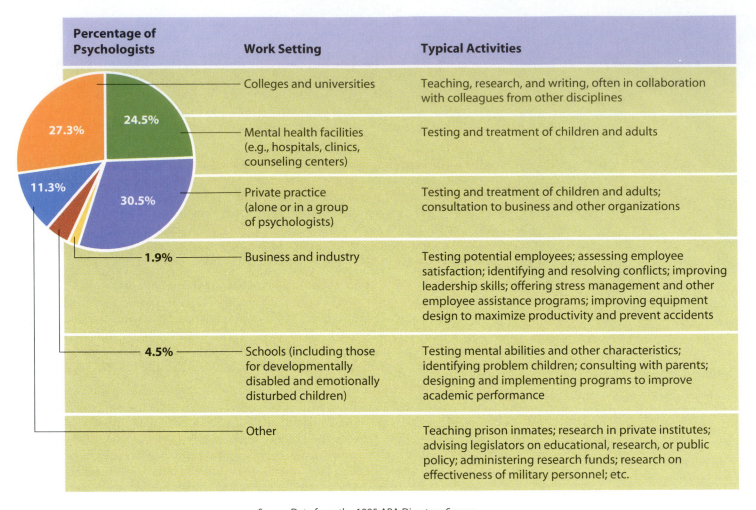

Percentage of Psychologists	Work Setting	Typical Activities
24.5%	Colleges and universities	Teaching, research, and writing, often in collaboration with colleagues from other disciplines
27.3%	Mental health facilities (e.g., hospitals, clinics, counseling centers)	Testing and treatment of children and adults
30.5%	Private practice (alone or in a group of psychologists)	Testing and treatment of children and adults; consultation to business and other organizations
1.9%	Business and industry	Testing potential employees; assessing employee satisfaction; identifying and resolving conflicts; improving leadership skills; offering stress management and other employee assistance programs; improving equipment design to maximize productivity and prevent accidents
4.5%	Schools (including those for developmentally disabled and emotionally disturbed children)	Testing mental abilities and other characteristics; identifying problem children; consulting with parents; designing and implementing programs to improve academic performance
11.3%	Other	Teaching prison inmates; research in private institutes; advising legislators on educational, research, or public policy; administering research funds; research on effectiveness of military personnel; etc.

Source: Data from the 1995 APA Directory Survey.

TABLE 1.1

Typical Activities and Work Settings for Psychologists

The fact that psychologists can work in such a wide variety of settings and perform such a wide range of functions helps account for the popularity of psychology as an undergraduate major (Murray, 1996). Psychology courses also provide excellent background for students planning to enter medicine, law, business, and other fields (Pauk & Fiore, 1989).

search for the keys to maximum athletic performance (Roberts & Treasure, 1999), and environmental psychologists explore the effects of the physical environment on behavior and mental processes (Sommer, 1999). Where do the psychologists in all these subfields work? Table 1.1 summarizes the latest figures on the settings in which they can be found and the kinds of things they typically do there.

Linkages Within Psychology and Beyond

No doubt you noticed that psychology's subfields overlap. For example, we mentioned developmental psychologists who study thought processes, biological psychologists who explore mental disorders, and social psychologists who are concerned with health psychology. The interests of psychologists are linked, in some cases, because they are investigating a common topic, such as violence or language, and in other cases because they are dealing with a common issue, such as how biological and cultural influences interact (Saudino & Plomin, 1997).

Even when psychologists do not themselves conduct research that crosses subfields, they often draw on, and contribute to, the knowledge developed in other subfields. Their theories, methods, findings, and applications to daily life are closely linked (Stec & Bernstein, 1999). Recognizing linkages among subfields is an important part of understanding psychology as a whole. To help you appreciate these linkages, we illustrate just a few of them at the end of each chapter in a Linkages diagram similar to the one shown here. Each question in the diagram illustrates a way in which the topics of two chapters are connected to each other; the page numbers indicate where the questions are discussed. To help you keep these linkages in mind as you read, each linking question will appear in the margin next to the major discussion of that question (see, for example, p. 74). By examining the Linkages diagram in each chapter, you can see how the topic of that chapter is related to other subfields of psychology. One of these relationships is given special attention in a section of each chapter entitled "Linkages." You might find it interesting to identify some of the many other linkages we do not mention.

Much as psychology's subfields are linked to one another, psychology is linked to many other academic disciplines. Sometimes these linkages occur because psychologists and researchers from other disciplines have common interests. Cognitive science, which we described earlier, is one example. Another is *neuroscience,* a multidisciplinary research enterprise that examines the structure and function of the nervous system in animals and humans, at levels ranging from the individual cell to overt behavior. This integrated field includes biological psychologists as well as specialists in neuroanatomy, neurophysiology, neurochemistry, genetics, and computer science. Someday, biological psychologists, like the colleagues with whom they work, may be known simply as "neuroscientists."

Psychology is also linked to other disciplines because research and theory from one discipline is applicable to another. For example, psychologists have applied chaos theory—which was developed in physics and mathematics to understand natural systems such as weather—to detect underlying order in apparently random patterns of violence, drug abuse, depression, or family conflict (e.g., Vallacher & Nowack, 1997). Economists and political scientists apply social psychologists' research on cooperation, conflict, and negotiation to help them understand economic trends and explain international tensions (e.g., Azar, 1997b). And genetic counselors use psychological knowledge about decision making and stress management to help clients decide whether, given a risky gene profile, they should have children (Shiloh, 1996).

The questions in this diagram illustrate some of the relationships between the topics discussed in this chapter and the topics of other chapters. Time and again throughout this book, you will see how psychology's subfields and approaches are linked to one another. Diagrams like this one appear at the end of each chapter to illustrate some of these linkages. The page number following each question indicates where that question is discussed. Of course, there are many more linkages than could be included in the diagrams; we hope that the diagrams will prompt you to look for these additional linkages. This kind of detective work can be enjoyable and useful. You may find it easier to remember material in one chapter by relating it to linked material in other chapters. You might also want to use the questions as a self-testing device when studying for quizzes and exams.

LINKAGES
to
Introducing Psychology

PERCEPTION

Can subliminal messages help you lose weight? *(p. 141)*

TREATMENT OF PSYCHOLOGICAL DISORDERS

Does psychotherapy work? *(p. 582)*

SOCIAL INFLUENCE

What makes some people so aggressive? *(p. 647)*

Or you might want to read the discussions of some questions before reading the chapter to clarify how it relates to the rest of psychology. Most of all, by staying alert to linkages as you read this book, you will come away not only with threads of knowledge about each subfield but with an appreciation of the interwoven fabric of psychology as a whole.

This book is filled with examples of other ways in which psychological theories and research have been applied to fields as diverse as medicine, dentistry, law, business, engineering, architecture, aviation, public health, and sports. Cognitive psychologists' research on memory has influenced the ways in which attorneys question eyewitnesses and judges instruct juries (e.g., Kassin, 1997); developmental psychologists' work on understanding the social and emotional aspects of aging is reshaping nursing-home policies on sexual behavior; and research by industrial/organizational psychologists is helping budding businesses in Russia and other Eastern European countries adjust and survive as they move from a communist economy to a market-driven one.

Human Diversity and Psychology

There was a time when many psychologists implicitly assumed that all people are essentially the same, and that whatever principles emerged from research with local volunteer participants would apply to people everywhere. Since about 90 percent of researchers in psychology work at universities in North America and Europe, they tended to study local college students, mostly white and middle-class, and more often men than women (Graham, 1992). Most of the psychologists, too, tended to be white, middle-class, and male (Walker, 1991).

From one perspective, studying a narrow sample of humankind need not limit the usefulness of psychological research, because, in many ways, people *are* very much alike. They tend to live in groups, develop religious beliefs, and create rules, music, and games. Similarly, the principles governing nerve cell activity or reactions to heat or a sour taste are the same in men and women the world over, as is their recognition of a smile.

But are the forces that motivate people to achieve, or the development of their moral thought, or their patterns of interpersonal communication universal as well? Do the principles derived from research on European-American males living in the Midwestern United States apply to African-American women or to people in Greece, Korea, Argentina, or Egypt? Not always. What people experience and what they learn from that experience are shaped by *sociocultural variables,* which are variations in social identity and background such as gender, ethnicity, social class, and culture. As described earlier in the study about how people from different countries explained a murderer's actions, these variables create many significant differences in behavior and mental processes, especially from one culture to another (Triandis, 1996).

The Impact of Culture

Culture helps shape virtually every aspect of our behavior and mental processes, from how we dress to what we think is important. Because we grow up immersed in our culture, it is easy to forget its influence, until—like these participants at a U.N. World Conference on Women—we encounter people whose culture has shaped them differently.

TABLE 1.2

Some Characteristics of Behavior and Mental Processes Typical of Individualist vs. Collectivist Cultures

Cultural factors do not act as cookie cutters that make everyone in a culture the same, but certain broad tendencies in behavior and mental processes have been associated with particular kinds of cultures. For example, individualist cultures tend to accept people who place personal goals ahead of the goals of the collective (such as the family or work group), whereas collectivist cultures tend to reject such people and to encourage putting the goals of the collective ahead of personal goals (Fiske et al., 1998). Cultures also vary in the degree to which they impose tight or loose rules for social behavior, value achievement or self-awareness, seek dominion over nature or integration with it, and emphasize the importance of time (Triandis, 1996).

Variable	Individualist	Collectivist
Personal identity	Separate from others	Connected to others
Major goals	Self-defined; be unique; realize your personal potential; compete with others	Defined by others; belong; occupy your proper place; meet your obligations to others; be like others
Criteria for self-esteem	Ability to express unique aspects of the self; be self-assured	Ability to restrain the self and be part of a social unit; be self-effacing
Sources of success and failure	Success comes from personal effort, failure from external factors	Success due to help from others; failure due to personal faults
Major frame of reference	Personal attitudes, traits, and goals	Family, work group

Culture has been defined as the accumulation of values, rules of behavior, forms of expression, religious beliefs, occupational choices, and the like for a group of people who share a common language and environment (Fiske et al., 1998). As such, culture is an organizing and stabilizing influence. It encourages or discourages particular behaviors and mental processes; it also allows people to understand and anticipate the behavior of others in that culture. It is a kind of group adaptation, passed by tradition and example rather than by genes from one generation to the next. Culture determines, for example, whether children's education will focus on skill at hunting or reading, how close people stand when they converse, and whether or not they form lines in public places (Munroe & Munroe, 1994).

Psychologists as well as anthropologists have isolated many respects in which cultures differ (Triandis, 1996). Table 1.2 outlines one way of analyzing these differences; it shows that many cultures can be described as either individualist or collectivist. Many people in *individualist* cultures, such as those typical of North America and Western Europe, tend to value personal rather than group goals and achievement. Competitiveness to distinguish oneself from others is common in these cultures, as is a sense of isolation. By contrast, many people in *collectivist* cultures, such as Japan, tend to think of themselves mainly as part of family or work groups. Cooperative effort aimed at advancing the welfare of such groups is highly valued, and whereas loneliness is seldom a problem, fear of rejection by the group is common. Many aspects of U.S. culture—from self-reliant cowboy heroes and bonuses for "top" employees to the invitation to "help yourself" at a buffet table—reflect its tendency toward an individualist orientation.

Culture is often associated with a particular country, but in fact most countries are multicultural; in other words, they host many *subcultures* within their borders (Oyserman, 1993). Often, these subcultures are formed by people of various ethnic origins. The population of the United States, for instance, encompasses African-Americans, Hispanic-Americans, Asian-Americans, and American Indians as well as European-Americans with Italian, German, English, Polish, Irish, and other origins (see Figure 1.5). In each of these groups, the individuals who identify with their cultural heritage tend to share behaviors, values, and beliefs based on their culture of origin and, hence, form a subculture (Phinney, 1996).

Like fish unaware of the water in which they are immersed, people often fail to notice how their culture or subculture has shaped their patterns of thinking and behavior until they come in contact with people whose culture or subculture has shaped different patterns. For example, sending a letter-opener as a birthday gift to a

FIGURE 1.5

Cultural Diversity in the United States

The people of the United States represent a wide array of cultural backgrounds, as illustrated in this figure.

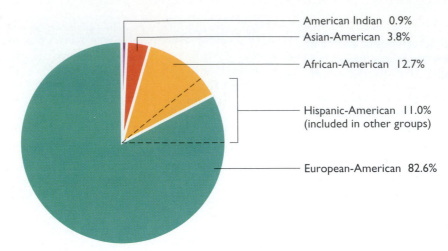

American Indian 0.9%
Asian-American 3.8%
African-American 12.7%
Hispanic-American 11.0%
(included in other groups)
European-American 82.6%

Source: Data from U.S. Bureau of the Census, 1997.

Mexican friend might be a mistake because, to some people in Mexico, the gift of a knife can mean that the sender wishes to sever the relationship. Even some of the misunderstandings that occur between men and women in the same culture are traceable to subtle, culturally influenced differences in their communication patterns (Tannen, 1994). In the United States, for example, women's efforts to connect with others by talking may be perceived by many men as "pointless" unless the discussion is aimed at solving a specific problem; thus women often feel frustrated and misunderstood by men who, in lieu of conversation, tend to offer well-intentioned but unwanted advice.

For decades, psychologists interested in *cross-cultural* research have studied cultural differences (Triandis, 1964), but now the influence of sociocultural variables is of growing interest to psychologists in general (Miller, 1999). As psychology strives to be the science of all behavior and mental processes, researchers need to take into account gender and other sociocultural variables (Hall, 1997). The trend in this direction will be evident in much of the research described in the chapters to come.

SUMMARY

Psychology is the science that seeks to understand behavior and mental processes, and to apply that understanding in the service of human welfare.

THE WORLD OF PSYCHOLOGY: AN OVERVIEW

The concept of "behavior and mental processes" is a broad one, encompassing virtually all aspects of what it means to be a human being.

The Scope of Behavior and Mental Processes

Among the topics studied by psychologists are the activity of individual nerve cells and organ systems; the operation of sensory and perceptual systems; the capacity for thought and decision making; the experience of emotion; the sources and effects of motivation, personality traits and other individual characteristics; and the effects people have upon each other.

Research: The Foundation of Psychology

Psychologists use the methods of science to conduct empirical research. This means that they perform experiments and use other scientific procedures to systematically gather and analyze information about psychological phenomena.

A Brief History of Psychology

The founding of modern psychology is usually marked as 1879, when Wilhelm Wundt established the first psychology research laboratory. Wundt used laboratory methods to study the building blocks of consciousness—an approach later called structuralism. At about the same time, in the United States, William James offered an alternative perspective known as functionalism, suggesting that psychologists should study how consciousness functions to help us adapt to our environments. In 1913, John B. Watson founded behaviorism, arguing that, to be scientific, psychologists should study only the behavior they can see, not private mental events. Behaviorism dominated psychology for decades, but psychologists are once again studying consciousness, now called cognitive processes. Most of the prominent figures in psychology's history were white males, but women and members of ethnic minority groups made important contributions from the start, and continue to do so.

UNITY AND DIVERSITY IN PSYCHOLOGY

Psychologists are unified by their commitment to empirical research and scientific methods, by their linked interests, and by the legacy of psychology's founders.

Approaches to Psychology

Psychologists differ in their approaches to psychology—that is, in the assumptions, questions, and methods they believe will be most helpful in their work. Some adopt one particular approach; many combine features of two or more approaches. Those adopting a *biological approach* examine how physiological processes shape behavior and mental processes. Research by *ethologists* helped stimulate the *evolutionary approach*, which emphasizes the inherited, adaptive aspects of behavior and mental processes. The *psychodynamic approach* sees behavior and mental processes as a struggle to resolve conflicts between impulses and the demands made by society to control those impulses. Psychologists who take the *behavioral approach* see behavior as determined primarily by learning based on experiences with rewards and punishments. The *cognitive approach* assumes that behavior can be understood through analysis of the basic mental processes that underlie it. The *humanistic approach* views behavior as controlled by the decisions that people make about their lives based on their perceptions of the world.

Subfields of Psychology

Because the subject matter of psychology is so diverse, most psychologists work in particular subfields within the discipline. For example, *experimental psychologists*, now usually called *cognitive psychologists*, focus on basic psychological processes such as learning, memory, and perception in both animals and humans; they also study judgment, decision making, and problem solving. *Biological psychologists*, also called *physiological psychologists*, study topics such as communication among nerve cells and the role played by the nervous system in regulating behavior. *Social psychologists* examine questions regarding how people influence one another. *Personality psychologists* focus on characteristics that set people apart from one another. *Developmental psychologists* specialize in trying to understand the development of behavior and mental processes over a lifetime. *Industrial/organizational psychologists* study ways to increase efficiency and productivity in the workplace. *Clinical* and *counseling psychologists* provide direct service to troubled people and conduct research on abnormal behavior. *Community psychologists* work to prevent mental disorders, and to extend mental health services to those who need them. *Educational psychologists* conduct and apply research on teaching and learning, whereas *school psychologists* specialize in assessing and alleviating children's academic problems. Among other things, *quantitative psychologists* develop methods for statistical analysis of research data. *Health psychologists, sport psychologists,* and *environmental psychologists* exemplify some of psychology's many other subfields.

Linkages Within Psychology and Beyond

Psychologists often work in more than one subfield and usually share knowledge with colleagues in many subfields. Psychologists also draw on and contribute to knowledge in other disciplines such as biology, chemistry, physics, anthropology, economics, and political science.

Human Diversity and Psychology

Psychologists are increasingly taking into account the influence of *culture* and other sociocultural variables such as gender and ethnicity in shaping human behavior and mental processes.

KEY TERMS

behavioral approach (14)
biological approach (13)
biological psychologists (17)
clinical psychologists (19)
cognitive approach (15)
cognitive psychologists (17)
community psychologists
 (19)
counseling psychologists
 (19)
culture (23)

developmental psychologists
 (18)
educational psychologists
 (19)
environmental psychologists
 (20)
ethologists (14)
evolutionary approach (13)
experimental psychologists
 (17)

health psychologists (19)
humanistic approach (15)
industrial/organizational
 psychologists (19)
personality psychologists
 (18)
physiological psychologists
 (17)
psychodynamic approach
 (14)

psychology (3)
quantitative psychologists
 (19)
school psychologists (19)
social psychologists (17)
sport psychologists (19)

2

Research in Psychology

Francine Shapiro, a clinical psychologist practicing in northern California, had an odd experience one day in 1987. She was walking in the woods, thinking about some distressing events, when she noticed that her emotional reaction to them was fading away (Shapiro, 1989a). Upon reflection, she realized that she had been unconsciously moving her eyes back and forth. Did the eye movements have anything to do with the change? When she made the eye movements deliberately, the emotion-reducing effect was even stronger. Curious, she examined the effect in others, first among friends and colleagues, then with clients who had suffered traumatic experiences such as childhood sexual abuse, military combat, or rape. She asked these people to think about their unpleasant experiences while following her finger with their eyes as she moved it back and forth in front of them. Like her, they said that their reactions to the memories faded. And her clients reported that emotional flashbacks, nightmares, fears, and other trauma-related problems dropped dramatically, often after only one session (Shapiro, 1989a).

Dr. Shapiro eventually called her new treatment *eye movement desensitization and reprocessing,* or *EMDR* (Shapiro, 1991). Today, Dr. Shapiro and other therapists are using EMDR to treat a wide range of anxiety-related problems, from simple phobias to disorders caused by the trauma of military combat (e.g., Manfield, 1998; Parnell, 1997; Shapiro, 1996). But the question remains: Can severe anxiety be permanently reduced by anything as simple as eye movements?

Psychologists still do not know what to make of EMDR. Is it a breakthrough in the treatment of anxiety disorders or a flash in the pan? When one is examining any aspect of behavior and mental processes, it is vital to determine, first, what specific questions to ask about the phenomenon of interest and, then, how to go about searching for the answers. Deciding on what questions to ask depends on an ability to think critically about the world; making progress toward answers depends on translating critical thinking into scientific research methods. As described in Chapter 1, psychologists use these methods to study a wide range of behavior and mental processes. In the pages that follow, we summarize some of the basic questions that emerge from thinking critically about psychology, describe the methods of science, show how some of these methods have been applied in evaluating the effectiveness of EMDR, and discuss the importance of ethics in scientific research. At the conclusion of the chapter, we present the first "Linkages" section, containing a discussion of how the contents of this chapter are related to another subfield of psychology. As we mentioned in the first chapter, discussions of this sort, and corresponding diagrams, appear throughout the book.

THINKING CRITICALLY ABOUT PSYCHOLOGY (OR ANYTHING ELSE)

Often, people simply accept what they are told because it comes from a believable source or because "everyone knows" it is true (see Table 2.1, page 28). Indeed, some advertisers, politicians, TV evangelists, and social activists hope for this kind of easy acceptance when they seek your money, vote, or allegiance. They want you to believe their promises or claims without careful thought; they don't want you to think critically. Often, they get their wish. In 1997, for example, when a Canadian gold mining company called Bre-X claimed to have found the world's largest vein of gold in a remote area of Indonesia, thousands of people poured millions of dollars into its stock. Their uncritical belief in this claim eventually cost them every last penny because, after the stock skyrocketed—and the company's president and chief geologist made a fortune by selling out—the company was forced to admit that there was no gold (Spaeth, 1997). And this is just the tip of the iceberg. Millions of people waste billions of dollars every year on worthless psychic predictions, on bogus "cures" for cancer, heart disease, and arthritis, on phony degrees offered by nonexistent "universities" on the Internet, and on "miracle defrosting trays" and other consumer products that simply don't work (Beyerstein, 1997; Tuerkheimer & Vyse, 1997; Wolke, 1997).

Critical thinking is the process of assessing claims and making judgments on the basis of well-supported evidence (Wade, 1988). Consider Shapiro's EMDR treatment. Does it reduce anxiety-related problems, as reports by Shapiro and others suggest? One strategy for applying critical thinking to this or any other topic is to ask the following five questions:

1. *What am I being asked to believe or accept?* In this case, the assertion to be examined is that EMDR causes reduction or elimination of anxiety-related problems.

TABLE 2.1

Ten Myths About Human Behavior

Myth	Fact
Many children are injured each year in the United States when razor blades, needles, or poison are put in Halloween candy.	Reported cases are rare, most turn out to be hoaxes, and in the only documented case of a child dying from poisoned candy, the culprit was the child's own parent (Brunvand, 1989).
A drunken person can sober up by taking a shower and drinking coffee.	A drunken person who takes a shower and drinks coffee will be wet, wide awake, and drunk. Neither cold water nor caffeine alters the rate at which the body metabolizes alcohol (see Chapter 9).
If your roommate commits suicide during the school term, you automatically get A's in all your classes for that term.	No college or university anywhere has ever had such a rule.
If you visit the Microsoft Corporation homepage on the Internet, your computer will be infected by a virus that wipes out all your files.	Not true, but word of this virus kept thousands of people from visiting the Microsoft homepage in 1996.
People have been known to burst into flames and die from fire erupting from within their own bodies.	In rare cases, human bodies have been totally consumed by fire that causes relatively little damage to the surrounding area. However, each alleged "spontaneous human combustion" case has been traced to an external source of ignition (Benecke, 1999). The same phenomenon was duplicated in a laboratory demonstration in 1998.
Most big-city police departments rely on the advice of psychics to help them solve murders, kidnappings, and missing-persons cases.	Only about 35 percent of urban police departments ever seek psychics' advice, and that advice is virtually never more helpful than other means of investigation (Nickell, 1997; Wiseman, West, & Stemman, 1996).
As part of their initiation, some urban street gang members in the United States drive with their lights off at night. If you blink your own lights at them, they will follow you home and kill you.	Warnings about this "ritual" were rampant in the summer of 1993, but no police department ever issued them, nor has any such gang rite ever been documented (Brunvand, 1995).
Murders, suicides, and mental disorders are more likely to occur when the moon is full.	Crime statistics and mental hospital admissions data show no evidence to support this common belief (Rotton & Kelly, 1985).
You can't fool a lie detector.	Lie detectors can be helpful in solving crimes, but they are not perfect; their results can free a guilty person or send an innocent person to jail (see Chapter 11).
Viewers never see David Letterman walking to his desk after the opening monologue because his contract prohibits him from showing his backside on TV.	When questioned about this story on the air, Letterman denied it and, to prove his point, lifted his jacket and turned a full circle in front of the cameras and studio audience (Brunvand, 1989).

Uncritically accepting claims for the value of psychic readings, "get-rich-quick" schemes, new therapies, or proposed government policies can be embarrassing, expensive, and sometimes dangerous. Critical thinkers carefully evaluate evidence for *and against* such claims before reaching a conclusion about them.

DOONESBURY

2. *What evidence is available to support the assertion?*   Shapiro began her research on EMDR by gathering information about whether the reduction of her own emotional distress was related to her eye movements or simply a coincidence. When she found the same effect in others, coincidence became a less plausible explanation.

3. *Are there alternative ways of interpreting the evidence?*   The dramatic effects experienced by Shapiro's friends and clients might be due not to EMDR but to factors such as their motivation to change or their desire to please her. Even the most remarkable evidence cannot be accepted as confirming an assertion until all equally plausible alternative assertions have been ruled out, which leads to the next step in critical thinking.

4. *What additional evidence would help to evaluate the alternatives?*   The ideal method would be to identify three groups of people who are identical in every way except for the anxiety treatment they received. If a group receiving EMDR improved to a much greater extent than those given an equally motivating but inherently useless treatment, or no treatment at all, it would become less likely that EMDR effects could be explained on the basis of clients' motivation or the mere passage of time. The ways in which psychologists and other scientists collect evidence to test alternative explanations constitute the methods of scientific research, which we describe in detail later.

5. *What conclusions are most reasonable?*   The evidence available thus far has not yet ruled out alternative explanations for the effects of EMDR (e.g., people's *beliefs* in EMDR rather than the treatment itself may be responsible for its positive effects), so the only reasonable conclusions to be drawn at this point are that (a) EMDR remains a controversial treatment, (b) it seems to have an impact on clients, and (c) further research is needed in order to understand it.

Does that sound wishy-washy? Critical thinking sometimes does seem indecisive because conclusions must be tempered by the evidence available. But critical thinking also opens the way to understanding. To help you hone your critical thinking skills, we include in each subsequent chapter of this book a section called "Thinking Critically" in which we examine an issue by considering the same five questions we asked here about EMDR.

Critical Thinking and Scientific Research

Imagine that you are Dr. Shapiro. You begin, as scientists often do, with curiosity about a phenomenon. Curiosity frequently provokes stimulating questions, but they may be too general to be investigated scientifically. In Dr. Shapiro's place, you might at first have wondered, Can eye movements reduce anxiety? However, critical thinking requires that you make your question more specific, in order to clarify the assertion to be evaluated.

Psychologists and other scientists typically phrase their questions about behavior and mental processes in terms of a **hypothesis**—a specific, testable proposition about something they want to study. Researchers state hypotheses in order to establish in clear, precise terms what they think may be true, and how they will know if it is not. In this case, the hypothesis might be as follows: *EMDR treatment causes significant reduction in anxiety.* To make it easier to understand and objectively evaluate hypotheses, scientists employ **operational definitions,** which are statements describing the exact operations or methods they use to manipulate and/or measure the variables in their research. In the hypothesis just presented, "EMDR treatment" might be operationally defined as inducing a certain number of back-and-forth eye movements per second for a particular period of time, whereas "significant reduction in anxiety" might be operationally defined as a decline of ten points or more on a scale that measures the clients' self-reported anxiety. The kind of treatment a client is given (say, EMDR versus no treatment) and the results of that treatment (how much anxiety reduction occurred) are examples of research **variables,** specific factors or characteristics that are manipulated and measured in research.

To evaluate whether the results of a study support a hypothesis, the researcher usually looks at objective, quantifiable evidence—numbers or scores that represent the variables of interest and provide the basis for conclusions. This kind of evidence is usually called **data** (which is the plural of *datum*), or a *data set.* Even though data themselves are objective, it is all too easy for scientists to look only for those numbers or scores that confirm a hypothesis, especially if they expect the hypothesis to be true or hope that it is. This common human failing is called "confirmation bias," and it is described in Chapter 8. Scientists have a special responsibility to combat confirmation bias by looking for contradictory as well as supporting evidence for even their most cherished hypotheses. They must not only gather evidence but also assess its quality. Usually, the quality of evidence is evaluated in terms of two characteristics: reliability and validity. *Reliability* is the degree to which the data are stable and consistent; the *validity* of data is the degree to which they accurately represent the topic being studied. For example, the initial claims for EMDR stemmed from Dr. Shapiro's use of the treatment with her colleagues and clients. If she had not been able to repeat, or *replicate,* the initial effects—if clients sometimes showed improvement and sometimes did not—she would question the reliability of the data. Alternatively, if the clients' reports of improvement were not supported by, say, corroborating reports from family members, she would doubt the validity of the data.

The Role of Theories

After examining the evidence from research on particular phenomena, scientists often begin to favor certain explanations. Sometimes, they organize these explanations into a **theory,** which is an integrated set of statements designed to account for, predict, and even suggest ways of controlling certain phenomena. For example, Dr. Shapiro's theory about the results of her new treatment suggests that the eye movements of EMDR activate parts of the brain where information about trauma or other unpleasant experiences have been stored but never fully processed. EMDR, she says, allows this information to be processed so that the emotional and behavioral problems it has been causing can be resolved (Shapiro, 1995). In Chapter 1, we reviewed broader and more famous examples of explanatory theories, including Charles Darwin's theory of evolution and Sigmund Freud's theory of psychoanalysis. Throughout this book you will encounter other theories designed to explain phenomena such as color vision, sleep, memory, and aggression.

Theories are tentative explanations that must themselves be subjected to scientific evaluation based on critical thinking. For example, Dr. Shapiro's theory about EMDR has been criticized as being vague, lacking empirical support, and being less plausible than other, simpler explanations (e.g., Dunn et al., 1996; Steketee & Goldstein, 1994). In other words, theories are based on research results, but they also generate hypotheses for further research. Predictions flowing from a theory proposed by one psychologist will be tested by many other psychologists. If research does not support a theory, the theory is revised or, sometimes, abandoned. Without research results, there would be nothing to explain; without explanatory theories, the results might never be organized in a usable way. The continuing interaction of theory and research lies at the heart of the process that has created the knowledge generated in psychology over the past century.

As later chapters illustrate, the constant formulation, evaluation, reformulation, and abandonment of theories have generated many competing explanations of behavior and mental processes. A sometimes frustrating consequence of this continuing search for answers in psychology is that we cannot offer as many definite conclusions as you might want. The conclusions we *do* draw about many of the phenomena described in this book are tentative and almost always accompanied by a call for additional research. Indeed, it is rare for a piece of research not to raise more questions than it answers. Keep this point in mind the next time you hear someone confidently regaling a talk-show audience with easy answers to complex problems or offering simple formulas for ideal parenting or a happy marriage. These self-proclaimed experts—called "pop" (for popular) psychologists by the scientific community—tend to oversimplify issues, cite evidence for their views without concern for its reliability or validity, and ignore good evidence that contradicts their pet theories. Psychological scientists must be more cautious—often suspending final judgments about complex aspects of behavior and mental processes until they have acquired better data.

Nevertheless, current knowledge and tentative conclusions can be put to good use. EMDR and many other forms of treatment, for example, are being applied and studied every day. Indeed, psychologists in all subfields are using today's knowledge as the foundation for the research that will increase tomorrow's understanding. In the rest of this chapter, we describe their research methods and some of the pitfalls that lie in the path of progress toward their goals.

RESEARCH METHODS IN PSYCHOLOGY

Like other scientists, psychologists strive to achieve four main goals in their research: to *describe* a phenomenon, to make *predictions* about it, and to introduce enough *control* over the variables in their research to allow them to *explain* the phenomenon with some degree of confidence. Certain methods are especially useful for gathering the evidence needed to attain each of these goals. Specifically, psychologists tend to use *naturalistic observation, case studies,* and *surveys* to describe and predict behavior and mental processes. They use *experiments* to control variables and thus establish

Scientific Research

In this study, the researcher is trying to determine the age at which babies can begin to tell the difference between colors. In the "classic" scientific research sequence, explanations result when initial observations of sensory abilities or other phenomena suggest a hypothesis about them. As in Francine Shapiro's work with EMDR, these observations lead to predictions, further observations, more precise predictions, and then experiments to eliminate alternative explanations and establish cause-effect relations between variables. This sequence is not set in stone, however. Sometimes, for example, a theory about some phenomenon sparks the curiosity that guides researchers' choices of what topics to explore.

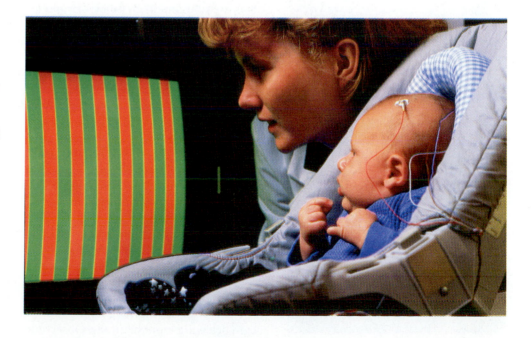

Naturalistic Observation

Observing people in natural settings can provide important clues to understanding social interaction and other aspects of behavior and mental processes.

An Ethologist at Work

Konrad Lorenz used naturalistic observation to describe many examples of the inborn but environmentally triggered behaviors we discussed under the evolutionary approach in Chapter 1. One of the most delightful of these is shown here. Baby geese follow their mother because her movement and honking provide signals that are naturally attractive. After Lorenz squatted and made mother-goose noises in front of orphaned newborn geese, the goslings began following him wherever he went.

unambiguous *cause-effect relationships,* in which one variable can be shown to have actually caused a change in another. Thus, Francine Shapiro initially *described* the EMDR effect on the basis of observations of her own reactions; then she tested the *prediction* that similar results might occur in other cases. Later we discuss an experiment designed to introduce enough *control* over the variables of interest to begin evaluating alternative explanations for the effect, and thus to explore whether EMDR itself is actually the cause of clients' improvement. Let's look at how these goals and methods are blended in psychologists' work.

Naturalistic Observation

Sometimes, the best way to gather descriptive data is through **naturalistic observation,** the process of watching without interfering with a phenomenon as it occurs in the natural environment. This method is especially valuable in cases where other methods are likely to be disruptive or misleading. For example, if you studied animals only by observing them in the laboratory, you might conclude that learning alone determines most of what they do, because you would not see how they normally use cues in their natural environment. In fact, many animals—like the herring gull chicks shown in Chapter 1—display inherited patterns of behavior that are predictable, stereotyped, and triggered automatically by environmental events.

Naturalistic observation of people can also be revealing. For example, much of what we know about gender differences in how children play and communicate with one another has come from psychologists' observations of children in classrooms and playgrounds (e.g., Newcomb & Bagwell, 1995). Observations of adults, too, have helped psychologists see that gender differences already evident in childhood might underlie some of the conflict and miscommunication that occurs in marriages and other intimate relationships (Bradbury, Campbell, & Fincham, 1995). As they work to alleviate relationship problems, therapists are aided by their understanding of gender differences that first came to light through observational research.

Although naturalistic observation can provide large amounts of rich information, it is not problem-free (Nietzel, Bernstein, & Milich, 1998). For one thing, when people know they are being observed (and ethics usually require that they do know), they tend to act differently than they otherwise would. Researchers typically combat this problem by observing long enough for participants to get used to the situation and begin behaving more naturally. Observations can also be distorted if observers expect to see certain behaviors. If, in a study of the effects of EMDR on anxiety, observers know which clients received treatment and which did not, they might tend to rate treated participants as less anxious no matter how they actually behave. To get the most out of naturalistic observation, psychologists must counteract problems such as these. For example, in the EMDR study just mentioned, the researchers might videotape the clients and then ask observers who don't know which clients have received the treatment to view the tapes and rate the clients' anxiety.

Case Studies

Observations are often an important part of a **case study,** which is an intensive examination of a phenomenon in a particular individual, group, or situation. Case studies may also include tests, interviews, and analysis of written records. Case studies are especially useful when a phenomenon is new, complex, or relatively rare. The EMDR method, for example, first attracted psychologists' attention through Dr. Shapiro's reports of cases in which her clients' anxiety was reduced (Shapiro, 1989a).

Case studies have a long tradition in clinical work. Freud's theory of psychoanalysis, for example, was largely developed from case studies of people whose paralysis or other physical symptoms disappeared when they were hypnotized or asleep. Case studies have also played a special role in *neuropsychology,* the study of the relationships among brain activity, thinking, and behavior. Consider the case of Dr. P., a patient described by Oliver Sacks (1985). A distinguished musician with superior intelligence, Dr. P. began to display odd symptoms, such as the inability to recognize familiar people or to distinguish between people and inanimate objects. During a visit to a neurologist, Dr. P. mistook his foot for his shoe. When he rose to leave, he tried to lift off his wife's head—like a hat—and put it on his own. He could not name even the most common objects when he looked at them, although he could describe them. When handed a glove, for example, he said, "A continuous surface, infolded on itself. It appears to have . . . five outpouchings, if this is the word. . . . A container of some sort." Only later, when he put it on his hand, did he exclaim, "My God, it's a glove!" (Sacks, 1985, p. 13).

Using case studies like this one, pioneers in neuropsychology noted the deficits suffered by people with particular kinds of brain damage or disease (Banich, 1997). Eventually, neuropsychologists were able to tie specific disorders to certain types of injuries, tumors, poisons, and other causes. (Dr. P.'s symptoms may have been caused by a large brain tumor.) Case studies do have their limitations, however. They may contain only the evidence that a particular researcher considered important, and, of course, they are unlikely to be representative of people in general. Nonetheless, case studies can provide valuable raw material for further research. They can also be vital sources of information about particular people, and they serve as the testing ground for new treatments, training programs, and other applications of research.

Surveys

Whereas case studies provide close-up views of individuals, surveys give broad portraits of large groups. In a **survey,** researchers use interviews or questionnaires to ask people about their behavior, attitudes, beliefs, opinions, or intentions. Just as politicians and advertisers rely on opinion polls to gauge the popularity of policies or products, psychologists use surveys to gather descriptive data on just about everything related to behavior and mental processes, from parenting practices to sexual behavior. However, the validity of survey data depends partly on how questions are worded (Schwarz, 1999; Schwarz, Groves, & Schuman, 1998). This point was vividly illustrated in a survey conducted by the Gallup polling organization in August of 1998. Specifically, people in the United States were asked their opinion of President Clinton after the speech in which he first admitted his adulterous affair with a young White House intern. Of the people who responded, only 40 percent said their opinion was favorable—a dramatic 20-percentage-point drop from previous polls assessing Mr. Clinton's popularity. However, the wording of the question about Mr. Clinton had changed from previous surveys. In the 1998 poll, respondents were asked, "Now, thinking of Bill Clinton as a

The Survey Method

Avoiding embarrassment and protecting respondent privacy may increase the validity of survey results. For example, not all rape victims are willing to tell a survey researcher about their experience, and one study found that people were more honest about their unsafe-sex practices in a computer-based self-interviewing method than in a live telephone interview (Turner et al., 1996).

person, do you have a favorable or unfavorable opinion *of him?*" In the previous polls, respondents had been presented with the names of several well-known people, including Mr. Clinton. As each name was read, respondents were asked, "Do you have a favorable or unfavorable opinion *of this person?*" When this original wording was reinstated in a survey conducted one day later, 55 percent of respondents said they had a favorable opinion of President Clinton. This figure represented a drop of only 5 percentage points from the pre-speech polls (*New York Times,* August 20, 1998).

A survey's validity also depends on the *representativeness* of the people surveyed; that is, the people in the sample must be representative of the larger group in which you are interested. For example, if only people who had voted for Mr. Clinton were included in the polls taken after his speech, his favorability rating after the speech would probably have been much higher. But that result would reflect only the views of Clinton supporters, not those of the general population of voters in the United States.

Other limitations of the survey method are more difficult to avoid. For example, people may be reluctant to admit undesirable or embarrassing things about themselves, or they may say what they believe they *should* say about an issue. To the extent that such tendencies distort responses, survey results—and the conclusions drawn from them—will be distorted, too (Jouriles et al., 1997; Turner, Miller, & Rogers, 1998). Still, surveys provide a relatively efficient way to gather large amounts of data about people's attitudes, beliefs, or other characteristics.

Experiments

Naturalistic observation, case studies, and surveys are valuable for describing and making predictions about behavior and mental processes, but these methods can only offer clues about the reasons behind their results. For example, surveys have described steady increases in domestic violence in the United States over the last several decades (FBI, 1997), but they do not *explain* the upward trend. Perhaps this trend is due not to changes in behavior but to more accurate reporting of violence, made possible by networked police computers, the advent of rape crisis centers, and greater attention to child abuse. And if there *is* more violence, the increase might be due to crowding, frustration, televised violence, air pollution, or other factors. In order to choose among alternative explanatory hypotheses and establish cause-effect relationships, psychologists must exert some *control* over variables, not just describe them. This kind of research usually takes the form of an experiment. **Experiments** are situations in which the researcher manipulates one variable and then observes the effect of that manipulation on another variable, while holding all other variables constant. The variable manipulated by the experimenter is called the **independent variable.** The variable to be observed is called the **dependent variable** because it is affected by, or *depends on,* the independent variable.

Francine Shapiro performed an experiment in an attempt to better understand the effects of EMDR. As illustrated in Figure 2.1, she first identified twenty-two people suffering the ill effects of traumas such as rape or military combat. These were her research participants. She assigned the participants to two groups. The first group received a single session of EMDR treatment for about fifty minutes; the second

FIGURE 2.1

A Simple Two-Group Experiment

Ideally, the only difference between the experimental and control groups in experiments like this one is whether the participants receive the treatment the experimenter wishes to evaluate. Under such ideal circumstances, at the end of the experiment any difference in the two groups' reported levels of anxiety (the dependent variable) should be attributable to whether or not they received treatment (the independent variable).

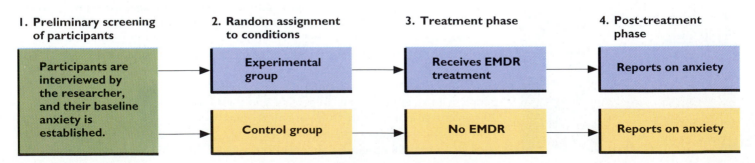

I. Preliminary screening of participants	2. Random assignment to conditions	3. Treatment phase	4. Post-treatment phase
Participants are interviewed by the researcher, and their baseline anxiety is established.	Experimental group	Receives EMDR treatment	Reports on anxiety
	Control group	No EMDR	Reports on anxiety

focused on their unpleasant memories for eight minutes, but without moving their eyes back and forth (Shapiro, 1989b). The experimenter manipulated whether EMDR treatment was administered to each participant, so the presence or absence of treatment was the independent variable. The participants' anxiety level while thinking about their traumatic memories was the dependent variable.

The group that receives the experimental treatment is called, naturally enough, the **experimental group.** The group that receives no treatment, or some other treatment, is called the **control group.** Control groups provide baselines against which to compare the performance of others. In Shapiro's experiment, having a control group allowed her to measure how much change in anxiety could be expected from exposure to bad memories without EMDR treatment. If everything about the two groups is exactly the same *before* the exposure to treatment, then any difference in anxiety between the groups *afterward* should be due to the treatment. At the same time, hypotheses about alternative causes of improvement, such as the passage of time, become less plausible.

The results of Dr. Shapiro's (1989b) experiment showed that participants receiving EMDR treatment experienced a complete and nearly immediate reduction in anxiety related to their traumatic memories, whereas participants in the control group showed no change. At this point, you might be ready to believe that the treatment caused the difference. Before coming to that conclusion, however, look again at the structure, or design, of the experiment. The treatment group's session lasted about fifty minutes, but the control group focused on their memories for only eight minutes. Would the people in the control group have improved, too, if they had spent fifty minutes focusing on their memories? We don't know, because the experiment did not compare methods of equal duration.

Anyone who conducts or relies on research must be on guard for such flaws in experimental design and control. Before drawing any conclusions from research, experimenters need to consider other factors—especially variables that could confound, or confuse, interpretation of the results. Any factor that might have affected the dependent variable, along with or instead of the independent variable, may be such a **confounding variable.** When confounding variables are present, the experimenter cannot know whether the independent variable or the confounding variable produced the results. Here we examine three sources of confounding: random variables, participants' expectations, and experimenter bias.

Random Variables   In an ideal research world, everything about the experimental and control groups would be identical except for their exposure to the independent variable (such as whether or not they received treatment). In reality, however, there are always other differences, especially those introduced by **random variables.** Random variables are uncontrolled, sometimes uncontrollable, factors such as differences among the participants—in terms of their backgrounds, personalities, physical health, or vulnerability to stress, for example—as well as differences in research conditions such as the time of day, temperature, or noise level.

Differences among the participants are so numerous that no experimenter can create groups that are equivalent on all of them. A common solution to this problem is to flip a coin or use some other random process to assign each research participant to experimental or control groups. Such procedures—called **random assignment**—are intended to distribute the impact of these uncontrolled variables randomly (and probably about equally) across groups, thus minimizing the chance that they will distort the results of the experiment (Shadish, Cook, & Campbell, in press).

Participants' Expectations   After eight minutes of focusing on negative memories, participants in the control group in Shapiro's (1989b) experiment were asked to begin moving their eyes. At that point they, too, started to experience a reduction in anxiety. Was this improvement caused by the eye movements themselves, or could it be that the instructions made the participants feel more confident that they were now getting "real" treatment? This question illustrates a second source of confounding: differences in what people think about the experimental situation. If participants who receive an

They Are All the Same

In July of 1998, scientists in Hawaii succeeded in cloning dozens of mice and then creating a second generation of clones from the original group. Having lots of these genetically identical animals is important because researchers can assign them to various experimental and control groups without having to worry about the effects of individual differences on the dependent variable. Ethical concerns rule out creating a pool of cloned people, so random assignment will remain a vital component of psychological research with human beings.

impressive treatment expect that it will help them, they may try harder to improve than those in a control group who receive no treatment or a less impressive one. Improvement created by a participant's knowledge and expectations is called the *placebo effect.* A **placebo** (pronounced "pla-SEE-boe") is a treatment that contains nothing known to be helpful, but that nevertheless produces benefits because a person believes it will be beneficial. People sometimes improve after receiving medical or psychological treatment, not because of the treatment itself but because of their belief that it will help them.

How can researchers determine the extent to which a result is caused by the independent variable or by a placebo effect? Often they include a special control group that receives *only* a placebo treatment. Then they compare results for the experimental group, the placebo group, and those receiving no treatment. In one smoking-cessation study, for example, participants in a placebo group took sugar pills described by the experimenter as "fast-acting tranquilizers" that would help them learn to endure the stress of giving up cigarettes (Bernstein, 1970). These people did as well at quitting as those in the experimental group, who received extensive treatment. This result suggested that the success of the experimental group may have been due largely to the participants' expectations, not to the treatment methods. Research on EMDR treatment similarly suggests that the eye movements themselves may not be responsible for improvement, inasmuch as staring, finger tapping, or listening to rapid clicks while focusing on traumatic memories have also produced benefits (e.g., Devilly, Spence, & Rapee, 1998; Dunn et al., 1996; Feske & Goldstein, 1997). Indeed, although EMDR appears to have positive effects (e.g., Shapiro, 1996; Wilson, Becker, & Tinker, 1997), we cannot draw final conclusions about its inherent value until it has been compared to impressive placebo treatments in controlled experiments (DeBell & Jones, 1997; Herbert et al., in press; Lohr et al., 1999).

Experimenter Bias Another potential confounding variable comes from **experimenter bias,** the unintentional effect that experimenters may exert on results. Robert Rosenthal (1966) was one of the first to demonstrate the power of one kind of experimenter bias, *experimenter expectancies.* His research participants were laboratory assistants who were asked to place rats in a maze. Rosenthal told some of the assistants that their rats were bred to be particularly "maze-bright"; he told the others that their rats were "maze-dull." In fact, both groups of rats were randomly drawn from the same population and had equal maze-learning capabilities. But the "maze-bright" animals learned the maze significantly faster than the "maze-dull" rats. Why? Rosenthal concluded that the result had nothing to do with the rats and everything to do with the experimenters. He suggested that the assistants' expectations about their rats' supposedly superior (or inferior) capabilities caused them to subtly alter their training and handling techniques, which in turn speeded (or slowed) the animals' learning. Similarly, when administering different kinds of anxiety treatments to different groups, experimenters who believe one treatment will be the best may do a slightly better job with that treatment and thus unintentionally improve its effects.

To prevent experimenter bias from confounding results, experimenters often use a **double-blind design.** In this arrangement, both the research participants *and* those giving the treatments are unaware of, or "blind" to, who is receiving a placebo, and do not know what results are expected from various treatments. Only the director of the study—a person who makes no direct contact with participants—has this information, and he or she does not reveal it until the experiment is over. The fact that double-blind studies of EMDR have not yet been conducted is another reason for caution in drawing conclusions about this treatment.

In short, experiments are vital tools for examining cause-effect relationships between variables, but like the other methods we have described, they are vulnerable to error. To maximize the value of their experiments, scientists try to eliminate as many confounding variables as possible, replicate their work to ensure consistent results, then temper their interpretation of the results to take into account the limitations or problems that remain.

A Quasi-Experiment?

Researchers might be able to draw stronger conclusions about the effects of day care on children's development if they could conduct true experiments in which children are randomly assigned to day-care versus no-day-care groups. As described in Chapter 12, however, research ethics require that psychologists address such questions through quasi-experiments in which they compare the characteristics of children whose parents have, or have not, chosen to put them in day care.

Quasi-Experiments

Sometimes a researcher may want to conduct a true experiment, with strict controls and random assignment, but cannot do so because it would be impossible or unethical. Consider the problem of testing the hypothesis that a pregnant woman's use of drugs causes abnormalities in her developing baby. From an experimental design standpoint, it would be ideal to take a large group of newly pregnant women, randomly assign them to either use or not use, say, cocaine, and then observe the condition of the babies they deliver. Such an experiment would be unthinkable, however. In evaluating hypotheses like this one, psychologists must conduct **quasi-experiments.** These are studies whose designs approximate the control of a true experiment (*quasi-* means "resembling") but do not include the random assignment of participants to treatment groups (Campbell & Stanley, 1966; Shadish, Cook, & Campbell, in press). Indeed, even when random assignment of participants to different conditions is impossible, a quasi-experiment can provide useful information about the differences between people who have and have not been exposed to those different conditions. Thus, for example, researchers might be able to measure differences in the mental, physical, and behavioral characteristics of children whose mothers did or did not use drugs during pregnancy.

The conclusions that can be drawn from quasi-experiments are usually not as firm as those from true experiments, but, especially when their results are replicated many times with large numbers of people, they can inspire considerable confidence. They also allow scientific research to be conducted on topics and in settings that would otherwise be impossible.

Selecting Human Participants for Research

As with surveys, the results of naturalistic observation, case studies, and experiments will be limited if they do not include a representative sample of participants. (For a review of all these methods, see "In Review: Methods of Psychological Research", on page 38.) Just as visitors from another galaxy would err wildly if they tried to describe the typical earthling after meeting only Sinbad, Fidel Castro, and the Spice Girls, psychologists can wander astray if they do not study a sample of people that provides a

in review

METHODS OF PSYCHOLOGICAL RESEARCH

Method	Features	Strengths	Pitfalls
Naturalistic observations	Observation of human or animal behavior in the environment where it typically occurs	Provide descriptive data about behavior presumably uncontaminated by outside influences	Observer bias and participant self-consciousness can distort results
Case studies	Intensive examination of the behavior and mental processes associated with a specific person or situation	Provide detailed descriptive analyses of new, complex, or rare phenomena	May not provide representative picture of phenomena
Surveys	Standard sets of questions asked of a large number of participants	Gather large amounts of descriptive data relatively quickly and inexpensively	Sampling errors, poorly phrased questions, and response biases can distort results
Experiments	Manipulation of an independent variable and measurement of its effects on a dependent variable	Can establish a cause-effect relationship between independent and dependent variables	Confounding variables may prevent valid conclusions
Quasi-experiments	Measurement of dependent variables when random assignment to groups is impossible or unethical	Can provide strong evidence suggesting cause-effect relationships	Lack of random assignment may weaken conclusions
All of the above	Choosing among alternative hypotheses; sometimes generating theories	Can expand our understanding of behavior and mental processes	Errors, limitations, and biases in research evidence can lead to incorrect or incomplete explanations

fair representation of the larger group of people about which they want to draw conclusions (the "population").

The process of selecting participants for research is called **sampling.** Sampling is an extremely important component of the research enterprise because it can affect not only what results one gets but also what they mean. If all the participants in a study come from a particular subgroup (say, male Asian-American musicians), the research results might apply, or *generalize,* only to people like them. This outcome would be especially likely if the researcher is studying a behavior or mental process that is affected by age, gender, ethnicity, cultural background, socioeconomic status, sexual orientation, disability, or other characteristics specific to the participants. When, as is often the case, these variables are likely to have an impact on research results, the sample of participants studied must be representative of people in general if the researcher wants results that are applicable to people in general.

If every member of a population to be studied has the same chance of being chosen as a research participant, the individuals selected would constitute a **random sample.** If not everyone has a chance of participating, those selected constitute a **biased sample.** In reality, few researchers try to draw a random sample from the general population. The practical alternative is to identify a specific target population (e.g., female college students or members of Britain's Labour Party) and draw a random sample

Selecting Research Participants

Obtaining a sample of people that fairly represents a population of interest is a major challenge in psychological research.

from that group. This sample would contain people who fairly represent the characteristics of the population from which they were selected.

Note that, although the names are similar, *random sampling* is *not* the same thing as *random assignment*. As mentioned earlier, random assignment is used in experiments to create *equivalence* among various groups, whereas random sampling is used in many kinds of research to ensure that the people studied are *representative* of some larger group.

Sometimes, however, such representative samples are not necessary, or even desirable. If you are studying language development in children, a case study of an unfortunate child raised in solitary confinement by a parent who provided no language instruction might provide more valuable information than observations of a representative sample of average youngsters (Rymer, 1992). Further, if you *want* to learn about male Asian-American musicians, or pregnant teenagers, or Hispanic-American women executives, all your participants should be randomly selected from those groups, not from the general population.

For convenience, researchers often begin their work by studying a particular population, such as local college students or, as in Dr. Shapiro's case, friends and colleagues; then they attempt to replicate their results with broader, more representative samples. If outcomes are consistent across a diverse group of participants, researchers can more confidently draw future samples from whatever willing group is available without worrying too much about finding a diverse sample. However, it is vital to show, rather than merely to assume, that age, gender, ethnicity, or other participant variables do not limit the breadth of conclusions that can be drawn from research data.

Psychologists must also guard against allowing their preconceptions about these participant variables to influence the questions they ask, the research designs they create, and the way they analyze, interpret, and report their data (Denmark et al., 1988; Hall, 1997). When designing a study on gender and job commitment, for example, the researcher must be sure to sample men and women in jobs of equal status. Comparing male executives with female secretaries might create a false impression of greater male commitment, because people in lower-status positions tend to change jobs more often, regardless of gender. Similarly, researchers who use a male-only sample should give this fact the same prominence in their research report as is customarily the case when only females are studied (Ader & Johnson, 1994). To do otherwise would imply that males provide a standard against which females' behavior and mental processes are to be compared. Finally, researchers must report whatever results appear. After all, it is just as valuable to know that men and women, or African-Americans and European-Americans, did *not* differ on a test of leadership ability as to know that they did. Stephanie Riger (1992) suggests that one of psychologists' greatest challenges is to "disengage themselves sufficiently from commonly shared beliefs so that those beliefs do not predetermine research findings" (p. 732).

STATISTICAL ANALYSIS OF RESEARCH RESULTS

Whether psychologists conduct naturalistic observations, case studies, surveys, or experiments, their investigations usually generate a large amount of *data. Statistical analyses* are the methods most often used to summarize and analyze those data. These methods include **descriptive statistics,** which are the numbers that psychologists use to describe and present a data set, and **inferential statistics,** which are mathematical procedures used to draw conclusions from data and to make inferences about what they mean. Here, we describe a few statistical terms that you will encounter in later chapters; you can find more information about these terms in the statistics appendix.

Descriptive Statistics

The three most important descriptive statistics are *measures of central tendency,* which describe the typical score (or value) in a set of data; *measures of variability,* which describe the spread, or dispersion, among the scores in a set of data; and *correlation coefficients,* which describe relationships between variables.

TABLE 2.2

A Set of Pretreatment Anxiety Ratings

Here are scores representing people's ratings, on a 1–100 scale, of their fear of the dark.

Data from II Participants		Data from I2 Participants	
Participant Number	*Anxiety Rating*	*Participant Number*	*Anxiety Rating*
1	20	1	20
2	22	2	22
3	28	3	28
4	35	4	35
5	40	5	40
6	45 (Median)	6	45 (Median = 46*)
7	47	7	47
8	49	8	49
9	50	9	50
10	50	10	50
11	50	11	50
		12	100
Measures of central tendency		**Measures of central tendency**	
Mode = 50		Mode = 50	
Median = 45		Median = 46	
Mean = 436/11 = 39.6		Mean = 536/12 = 44.7	
Measures of variability		**Measures of variability**	
Range = 30		Range = 80	
Standard deviation = 11.064		Standard deviation = 19.763	

*When there is an even number of scores, the exact middle of the list lies between two numbers. The median is the value halfway between those numbers.

The Impact of Variability

Suppose you are a substitute teacher who comes to a new school hoping for an easy day's work. You are offered either of two classes. In each, the students' mean IQ is 100. At first glance, there would appear to be no major difference between the classes, but it turns out that the standard deviation (SD) of IQs in one class is 16; the SD in the other is 32. Since a higher standard deviation means more variability, the class with the SD of 32 is likely to be more difficult to teach because its students vary more in ability. The standard deviation is a particularly important descriptive statistic in any data set.

Measures of Central Tendency   Suppose you want to test the effects of EMDR treatment on fear of the dark. Looking for participants, you collect the eleven anxiety ratings listed on the left side of Table 2.2. What is the typical score, the central tendency, that best represents the group's anxiety level? There are three measures designed to capture this typical score: the mode, the median, and the mean.

The **mode** is the value or score that occurs most frequently in a data set. You can find it by ordering the scores from lowest to highest. On the left side of Table 2.2, the mode is 50, because the score of 50 occurs more often than any other. Notice, however, that in this data set the mode is actually an extreme score. Sometimes, the mode acts like a microphone for a small but vocal minority, which, though it speaks most frequently, does not represent the views of the majority.

Unlike the mode, the median takes all of the scores into account. The **median** is the halfway point in a set of data: Half the scores fall above the median, half fall below it. For the scores on the left side of Table 2.2, the halfway point—the median—is 45.

The third measure of central tendency is the **mean,** which is the *arithmetic average* of the scores. When people talk about the "average" in everyday conversation, they are usually referring to the mean. To find the mean, add the scores and divide by the number of scores. For the scores on the left side of Table 2.2, the mean is 436/11 = 39.6.

Like the median (and unlike the mode), the mean reflects all the data to some degree, not just the most frequent data. Notice, however, that the mean reflects the actual values of all the scores, whereas the median gives each score equal weight, whatever its value. This distinction can have a big effect on how well the mean and median represent the scores in a particular set of data. Suppose, for example, that you add to your sample a twelfth participant whose anxiety rating is 100. When you re-analyze the anxiety data (see the right side of Table 2.2), the median hardly changes, because the new participant counts as just one more score. However, when you compute the new mean, the actual *amount* of the new participant's rating is added to everyone else's ratings; as a result, the mean jumps 5 points. Sometimes, as in this example, the median is a better measure of central tendency than the mean because the median is less sensitive to extreme scores. But because the mean is more representative of the values of all the data, it is often the preferred measure of central tendency.

Measures of Variability   The variability (also known as spread or dispersion) in a set of data can be quantified by the range and the standard deviation. The **range** is simply the difference between the highest and the lowest scores in the data set (it would be 30 for the data on the left side of Table 2.2 and 80 for the data on the right side). In contrast, the **standard deviation,** or **SD,** measures the average difference between each score and the mean of the data set. It provides information on the extent to which scores in a data set vary, or differ, from one another. The more variable the data are, the higher the standard deviation will be. For example, the SD for the eleven participants on the left side of Table 2.2 is 11.064, but it rises to 19.763 once the very divergent twelfth score is added on the right side. In the statistics appendix, we show how to calculate the standard deviation.

Correlation and Correlation Coefficients   Does the number of fears people have tend to decrease with age? In general, yes (Kleinknecht, 1991); but to test hypotheses about questions such as this, psychologists must have a way to measure how, and to what extent, variables such as age and fearfulness are correlated.

Correlation means just what it says—"co-relation." In statistics, it refers both to how strongly one variable is related to another *and* to the direction of the relationship. A *positive correlation* means that two variables increase together or decrease together. A *negative correlation* means that the variables move in opposite directions: When one increases, the other decreases. For example, James Schaefer observed 4,500 customers in 65 bars and found that the tempo of jukebox music was negatively correlated with the rate at which the customers drank alcohol; the slower the tempo, the faster the drinking (Schaefer et al., 1988).

Correlation and Causation

In order to support a claim that the rate of drinking in a bar is caused by, rather than simply correlated with, the tempo of background music, a researcher would have to exert some control over the situation. Usually, this means conducting an experiment.

Three Correlations

The strength and direction of the correlation between two variables can be seen in a graph called a *scatterplot*. In part (A), we have plotted the cost of a gasoline purchase against the number of gallons pumped. Since the number of gallons is *positively* and perfectly correlated with their cost, the scatterplot appears as a straight line, and you can predict the value of either variable from a knowledge of the other. Part (B) shows a perfect *negative* correlation between the number of miles traveled toward a destination and the distance remaining. Again, one variable can be exactly predicted from the other. Part (C) illustrates a correlation of +.81 between the number of high school math courses students had taken and their scores on a college-level final exam in math (Hays, 1981). As correlations decrease, they are represented by ever-greater dispersion in the pattern of dots. A correlation of 0.00 would appear as a shapeless cloud.

Does this mean Schaefer could wear a blindfold and predict exactly how fast people are drinking by timing the music? Or could he plug his ears and determine the musical tempo by watching people's sip rates? No and no, because the accuracy of predictions about one variable from knowledge of another depends on the *strength* of the correlation. Only a perfect correlation between two variables would allow you to predict the exact value of one from a knowledge of the other. The weaker the correlation, the less one variable can tell you about the other.

To describe the strength of a correlation, psychologists calculate a statistic called the **correlation coefficient** (shown in the statistics appendix). The correlation coefficient is given the symbol r, and can vary from $+1.00$ to -1.00. Thus, the coefficient includes (1) an absolute value, such as .20 or .50, and (2) either a plus sign or a minus sign.

The *absolute value* of r indicates the strength of the relationship. An r of $+0.01$ between people's shoe size and the age of their cars, for example, indicates that there is virtually no relationship between the variables, whereas an r of $+1.00$ indicates a perfectly predictable relationship between two variables (see Figure 2.2). Unfortunately,

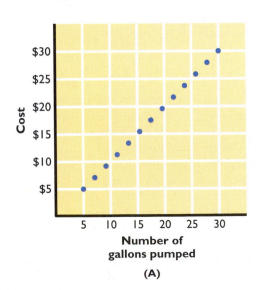

(A)

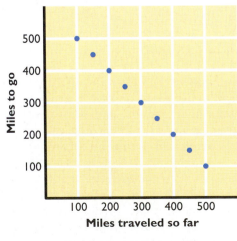

(B)

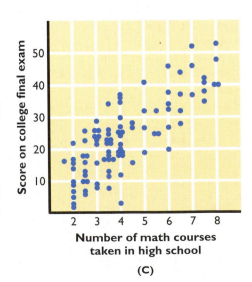

(C)

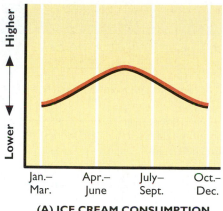

(A) ICE CREAM CONSUMPTION

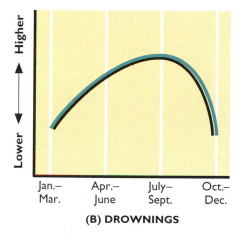

(B) DROWNINGS

FIGURE 2.3

Correlation and Causation

These graphs show that, in the United States, ice cream consumption and drownings tend to rise and fall together. However, this positive correlation does not mean that eating ice cream *causes* drownings. A correlation between variables says nothing about whether one variable actually exerts an impact on the other; it would take experiments to confirm that. In this case, the correlation probably reflects a third variable—time of year—that affects both ice cream sales and the likelihood of swimming and boating.

the variables of interest in psychology are seldom perfectly correlated. Throughout this book, you will find many correlation coefficients whose absolute values range from .20 to .90, reflecting relationships of intermediate strength in which knowing about one variable tells us something, but not everything, about the other.

The *sign* of a correlation coefficient indicates its direction. A plus sign signifies a *positive* correlation between variables; a minus sign indicates a *negative* correlation.

Psychologists use correlation coefficients to help them describe and predict phenomena, to evaluate existing hypotheses, and, often, to generate new hypotheses, but they must be very careful when interpreting correlations. Consider, for example, the positive correlation that has been found between watching violent television programs and behaving violently. Does seeing violence on TV cause viewers to be violent, or does being violent to begin with cause a preference for violent shows? Perhaps neither causes the other; violent behavior *and* TV choices could both be due to a third factor, such as stress. (In Chapter 6, on learning, we discuss how researchers have evaluated these possibilities.) In short, just because two variables are *correlated* doesn't mean that one is *causing* an effect on the other. And even if it is, a correlation coefficient doesn't indicate which variable is influencing which. Correlations can reveal and describe relationships, but correlations alone cannot explain them (see Figure 2.3).

Inferential Statistics

The task of understanding the meaning of research results summarized in correlations or other descriptive statistics is not an easy one. Is a correlation between college grade-point averages and the consumption of certain foods large enough to support the hypothesis that diet is important for mental functioning? Is the anxiety reduction following EMDR sufficiently greater than that following other treatments to justify the recommendation of EMDR? The answers to questions such as these are based largely on the results of analyses that use *inferential statistics*.

Inferential statistics employ certain rules to evaluate the likelihood that a correlation or a difference between groups reflects a real relationship and not just the operation of chance factors on the particular sample that was chosen for study. Suppose, for example, that participants who received EMDR showed a mean decrease of 10 points on a test of fear of the dark, whereas the scores of a no-treatment control group decreased by a mean of 7 points. How important or meaningful is this difference? Traditionally, psychologists have answered questions like this by using tests of statistical significance to estimate how likely it is that an observed difference was due to chance alone (Shrout, 1997). When such tests show that a correlation coefficient or the difference between the means of two groups is larger than would be expected by chance alone, that correlation or difference is said to be **statistically significant.** In the statistics appendix we describe some of these tests and discuss how their results are affected by the size of mean differences or correlations, the number of participants studied, and the amount of variability in the data.

Keep in mind, however, that statistical significance tests alone do not necessarily constitute final "proof" that a particular research result is or is not important. Indeed, some psychologists have begun to suggest that other information (e.g., the typical size of a correlation or a mean difference) should also be used to evaluate research findings (Cohen, 1994; Hunter, 1997; Loftus, 1996). But whatever quantitative methods are used, psychological scientists pay the most attention to correlations or other research findings that statistical analyses suggest are robust and not a fluke. Thus, when one is thinking critically about research, part of the process of evaluating evidence about hypotheses requires asking whether a researcher's results have withstood careful statistical analysis—and whether they can be replicated. (For a review of the statistical measures discussed in this section, see "In Review: Descriptive and Inferential Statistics," on page 44.)

in review

DESCRIPTIVE AND INFERENTIAL STATISTICS

Statistic	Characteristics	Information Provided
Mode	Describes the central tendencies of a set of scores	The score that occurs most frequently in a data set
Median	Describes the central tendencies of a set of scores	The halfway point in a data set; half the scores fall above this score, half below
Mean	Describes the central tendencies of a set of scores	The arithmetic average of the scores in a data set
Range	Describes the variability of a set of scores	The difference between the highest and lowest scores in a data set
Standard deviation	Describes the variability of a set of scores	The average difference between each score and the mean of a data set
Correlation coefficient	Describes the relationship between two variables	How strongly the two variables are related and whether the relationship is positive (variables move in same direction) or negative (variables move in opposite directions)
Tests of significance	Help make inferences about the relationships between descriptive statistics	How likely it is that the difference between measures of central tendencies or the size of a correlation coefficient is due to chance alone

Statistics and Research Methods as Tools in Critical Thinking

It is important to use the critical thinking skills outlined earlier in this chapter when assessing the statistical and methodological aspects of research results, especially when those results are dramatic or unexpected. This point was well illustrated several years ago when Douglas Biklen (1990) claimed that a procedure called "facilitated communication" (FC) could help people with autistic disorder (described in Chapter 15) use language for the first time. These people, said Biklen, have language skills and coherent thoughts, but no way to express themselves. He reported case studies in which autistic people were apparently able to answer questions or convey intelligent messages on a computer keyboard when assisted by a "facilitator" who physically supported their unsteady hands. Controlled experiments showed this claim to be groundless, however (Jacobson, Mulick, & Schwartz, 1995). The alleged communication abilities of these autistic people disappeared under conditions in which the facilitator (1) did not know the question being asked of the participant or (2) could not see the keyboard (Delmolino & Romanczyk, 1995). The discovery that facilitators were—perhaps inadvertently (Spitz, 1997)—guiding their participants' hand movements has allowed those who work with autistic patients to see FC in a different light.

The role of experiments and other scientific research methods in understanding behavior and mental processes is so important that, in each chapter to come, we include a special feature called "Focus on Research Methods." These features describe in detail the specific procedures employed in a particularly interesting research project. Our hope is that, by reading these sections, you will see how the research methods discussed in this chapter are applied in every subfield of psychology.

ETHICAL GUIDELINES FOR PSYCHOLOGISTS

The obligation to analyze and report research fairly and accurately is one of the ethical requirements that guide psychologists. Preserving the welfare and dignity of their participants, animal and human, is another. Although researchers could measure severe anxiety by putting a loaded gun to people's heads, or study marital conflicts by telling one partner that the other has been unfaithful, such methods are potentially harmful and, therefore, unethical.

In each of these examples, the ethical course of action is obvious: The psychologist must find another way to conduct the research. In practice, however, ethical choices are often more complicated, and psychologists must decide how to balance conflicting values. Many experiments reflect a compromise between the need to protect participants from harm and the need to learn about the unknown. In finding ways to help people cope with anxiety, for example, researchers may ask them to try new coping skills while enduring an anxiety-provoking, but not traumatic, situation.

Before almost any psychological study can be conducted, a local human-research committee must review it and decide that the potential benefits of the work, in terms of new knowledge and human welfare, outweigh any potential harm. The researchers themselves must minimize any discomfort and risk involved in the study, and they must act to prevent participants from suffering any long-term negative consequences. They must also inform potential participants about every aspect of the study that might influence their decision to participate and ensure that each person's involvement is voluntary. But what if a researcher must withhold information about a study because full disclosure beforehand would bias participants' behavior? Or what if participants must be given inaccurate information in order to create mild annoyance, a sense of time urgency, or some other temporary condition essential to the study? In such cases, the researcher must "debrief" the participants as soon as the study is over by revealing all relevant information about the research and correcting any misimpressions it created.

The obligation to protect participants' welfare also extends to animals, which are used in a small percentage of psychological research studies (Plous, 1996; Shapiro, 1991). Psychologists study animals partly because their behavior is interesting in and of itself and partly because research with animals can yield information that would be impossible or unethical to collect from humans (Mason, 1997). For example, researchers can use cloned animals to create absolutely identical groups of research participants, but the same thing could not ethically be done with humans.

Contrary to the allegations of some animal-rights activists, animals used in psychological research are not routinely subjected to extreme pain, starvation, or other inhumane conditions (Novak, 1991). Even in the small proportion of studies that require the use of electric shock, the discomfort created is mild, brief, and not harmful. The recently revised Animal Welfare Act, the National Institutes of Health's *Guide for the Care and Use of Laboratory Animals*, the American Psychological Association's *Principles on Animal Use*, and other laws and regulations set high standards for the care and treatment of animal participants. In those relatively rare studies that require animals to undergo short-lived pain or other forms of moderate stress, legal and ethical standards require that funding agencies—as well as local committees charged with monitoring animal research—must first determine that the discomfort is justified by the expected benefits to human welfare.

The responsibility for conducting research in the most humane fashion is just one aspect of the *Ethical Principles of Psychologists and Code of Conduct* developed by the American Psychological Association (APA, 1992b). The main purpose of these standards is to protect and promote the welfare of society and those with whom psychologists work. For example, as teachers, psychologists should strive to give students a complete, accurate, and up-to-date view of each topic, not a narrow, biased point of view. Psychologists should perform only those services and use only those techniques for which they are adequately trained; a biological psychologist untrained in clinical

Caring for Animals in Research

Psychologists are careful to protect the welfare of animal participants. They take no pleasure in animals' suffering, and besides, inflicting undue stress on animals can create reactions that can act as confounding variables. For example, in a study of how learning is affected by the size of food rewards, the researcher could starve animals to make them hungry enough to want the experimental rewards. But this would introduce discomfort that would make it impossible to separate the effects of the reward from the effects of starvation.

methods should not try to offer psychotherapy. Except in the most unusual circumstances (to be discussed in Chapter 16), psychologists should not reveal information obtained from clients or students, and they should avoid situations in which a conflict of interest might impair their judgment or harm someone else. They should not, for example, have sexual relations with their clients, their students, or their employees.

Despite these guidelines, doubt and controversy arise in some cases about whether a proposed experiment or a particular practice, such as deceiving participants, is ethical (e.g., Fisher & Fyrberg, 1994; Rosenthal, 1994a). Indeed, ethical principles for psychologists will continue to evolve as psychologists face new and more complex ethical issues (Biaggio, Paget, & Chenoweth, 1997; Fisher & Younggren, 1997; Prilleltensky, 1997).

LINKAGES

How much of our behavior is due to genetics and how much to our environment? (A Link to Biological Aspects of Psychology)

LINKAGES

Psychological Research and Behavioral Genetics

One of the most fascinating and difficult challenges in psychology is to find research methods that can help us understand the ways in which people's genetic inheritance—their biological *nature*—intertwines with environmental events and conditions before and after birth—often called *nurture*—to shape their behavior and mental processes. Questions about nature and nurture surface in relation to perception, personality, mental ability, mental disorder, and many other topics discussed throughout this book. Psychologists' efforts to explore the influences of nature and nurture in relation to these phenomena have taken them into the field of **behavioral genetics,** the study of how genes and heredity affect behavior. In this section, we describe the logic—and some results—of research methods in behavioral genetics. The basic principles of genetics and heredity that underlie these methods are described as part of a more detailed discussion in the behavioral genetics appendix.

Researchers in behavioral genetics realize that most behavioral tendencies can be influenced by many different genes, but also by the environment. Accordingly, they do not expect to find specific genes that control specific behavioral tendencies—such as aggression or shyness—in particular people. Instead, research in behavioral genetics is designed to explore the *relative roles* of genetic and environmental factors in creating differences in behavioral tendencies in *groups* of people.

Early research in behavioral genetics relied on the selective breeding of animals. For example, Robert Tryon (1940) mated rats who were fast maze learners with other fast learners and mated slower learners with other slow learners. After repeating this procedure for several generations, he found that the offspring of the fast learners were significantly better at maze learning than those of the slow learners.

Selective-breeding studies must be interpreted with caution, however, because it is not specific behaviors that are inherited but, rather, differing sets of physical structures, capacities, and the like, which in turn make certain behaviors more or less likely. These behavioral tendencies are often narrow, and they can be altered by the environment. For example, "maze-dull" rats performed just as well as "maze-bright" rats on many tasks other than maze learning (Searle, 1949). And, when raised in an environment containing tunnels and other stimulating features, "dull" animals did as well at maze learning as "bright" ones; both groups did equally poorly in the maze after being raised in an environment that lacked stimulating features (Cooper & Zubek, 1958).

Research on behavioral genetics in humans must be interpreted with even more caution because environmental influences have an enormous impact on human behavior and because legal, moral, and ethical considerations prohibit manipulations such as selective breeding. Instead, research in human behavioral genetics depends on studies where control is imperfect. Some of the most important designs in behavioral genetics research are family studies, twin studies, and adoption studies (Plomin, DeFries, & McClearn, 1990; Segal, 1993).

FIGURE 2.4

Family Studies of Schizophrenia

Data from family studies show that the risk of developing schizophrenia, a severe mental disorder described in Chapter 15, is highest for the siblings and children of schizophrenics and decreases progressively with genetic distance; the risk is lowest for people with no genetic relationship to a schizophrenic. Does this mean that schizophrenia is inherited? The data are certainly consistent with that interpretation, but the question cannot be answered through family studies alone. Other factors, including environmental stressors that close relatives share, could also play an important role in the development of the disorder.

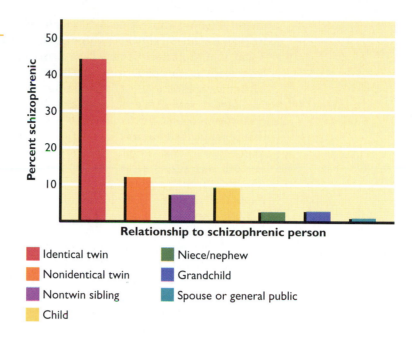

Relationship to schizophrenic person

- Identical twin
- Nonidentical twin
- Nontwin sibling
- Child
- Niece/nephew
- Grandchild
- Spouse or general public

In *family studies,* researchers examine whether similarities in behavior and mental processes are greater among people who are closely related than among more distant relatives or unrelated individuals. If increasing similarity is associated with closer family ties, the similarities might be inherited. For example, data from family studies suggest a genetic basis for schizophrenia because this severe mental disorder appears much more often in the closest relatives of schizophrenics than in other people (see Figure 2.4). But family studies alone cannot establish the role of genetic factors in mental disorders or other characteristics, because close relatives tend to share environments as well as genes. Thus, similarities among close relatives might stem from environmental factors instead of, or in addition to, genetic ones.

Twin studies explore the heredity-environment mix by comparing the similarities seen in identical twins with those of nonidentical pairs. Twins usually share the same environment and may also be treated very much the same by parents and others, so if

Research in Behavioral Genetics

Like other identical twins, each member of this pair has identical genes. Twin studies and adoption studies employ quasi-experimental designs that help illuminate the interaction of genetic and environmental influences on human behavior and mental processes. Cases in which identical twins who had been separated at birth have similar interests, personality traits, and mental abilities suggest that these characteristics have a significant genetic component.

identical twins (whose genes are exactly the same) are more alike on some characteristic than nonidentical twins (whose genes are no more similar than those of other siblings), that characteristic may have a significant genetic component. As we will see in later chapters, this pattern of results holds for a number of characteristics, including some measures of intelligence and some mental disorders.

Adoption studies take advantage of the naturally occurring quasi-experiments that occur when babies are adopted very early in life. The logic underlying these studies is that if adopted children's characteristics are more like those of their biological parents than those of their adoptive parents, genetically inherited ingredients in the nature-nurture mix play a clear role in that characteristic. For example, as described in Chapter 14, the personalities of young adults who were adopted at birth tend to be more like those of their biological parents than those of their adoptive parents. Adoption studies can be especially valuable when they focus on identical twins who were separated at or near birth. If identical twins show similar characteristics after years of living in very different environments, the role of heredity in those characteristics is highlighted. Adoption studies of intelligence, for example, tend to support the role of genetics in variations in mental ability, but they show that environmental influences are important as well.

As you read in later chapters about the role of genetics in human development and in differences in personality and mental abilities, remember that research on human behavioral genetics can help illuminate the relative roles of heredity and environment that underlie *group differences,* but it cannot determine the degree to which a particular person's behavior is due to heredity or environment. The two factors are too closely entwined in an individual to be separated that way.

LINKAGES

As noted in Chapter 1, all of psychology's many subfields are related to one another. Our discussion of behavioral genetics illustrates just one way in which the content of this chapter, research in psychology, is linked to the subfield of biological psychology (Chapter 3). The Linkages diagram shows ties to two other subfields as well, and there are many more ties to be found throughout the book. Looking for linkages among subfields as you read will help you to see how they all fit together and better appreciate the big picture that is psychology.

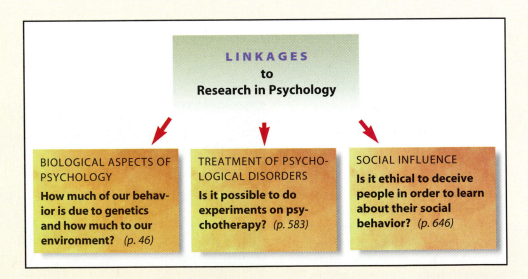

LINKAGES
to
Research in Psychology

BIOLOGICAL ASPECTS OF PSYCHOLOGY

How much of our behavior is due to genetics and how much to our environment? *(p. 46)*

TREATMENT OF PSYCHOLOGICAL DISORDERS

Is it possible to do experiments on psychotherapy? *(p. 583)*

SOCIAL INFLUENCE

Is it ethical to deceive people in order to learn about their social behavior? *(p. 646)*

SUMMARY

THINKING CRITICALLY ABOUT PSYCHOLOGY (OR ANYTHING ELSE)

Critical thinking is the process of assessing claims and making judgments on the basis of well-supported evidence.

Critical Thinking and Scientific Research

Often, questions about psychological phenomena are phrased in terms of *hypotheses* about *operationally defined variables.* Tests of hypotheses are based on objective, quantifiable evidence, or *data,* representing the variables of interest. If data are to be useful, they must be evaluated for reliability and validity.

The Role of Theories

Explanations of phenomena often take the form of *theories,* which are integrated sets of propositions that can be used to account for, predict, and even control certain phenomena. Theories must be subjected to rigorous evaluation.

RESEARCH METHODS IN PSYCHOLOGY

Research in psychology, as in other sciences, focuses on four main goals: description, prediction, control, and explanation.

Naturalistic Observation

Naturalistic observation entails watching without interfering as behavior occurs in the natural environment. This method can be revealing, but care must be taken to ensure that observers are unbiased and do not alter the behavior being observed.

Case Studies

Case studies are intensive examinations of a particular individual, group, or situation. They are useful for studying new or rare phenomena and for evaluating new treatments or training programs.

Surveys

Surveys ask questions, through interviews or questionnaires, about behavior, attitudes, beliefs, opinions, and intentions. They provide an excellent way to gather large amounts of data from a large number of people at relatively low cost, but their results can be distorted if questions are poorly phrased, answers are not given honestly, or respondents do not constitute a representative sample.

Experiments

In *experiments,* researchers manipulate an *independent variable* and observe the effect of that manipulation on a *dependent vari-able.* Participants receiving experimental treatment are called the *experimental group;* those in comparison conditions are called *control groups.* Experiments can reveal cause-effect relationships between variables, but only if researchers use *random assignment, placebo* conditions, *double-blind designs,* and other strategies to avoid being misled by *random variables, participants' expectations, experimenter bias,* and other *confounding variables.*

Quasi-Experiments

When ethics or other concerns prevent random assignment of participants, researchers sometimes conduct *quasi-experiments,* which approximate the control of true experiments. The results of quasi-experiments can be as useful as those obtained with true experiments.

Selecting Human Participants for Research

Psychologists' research can be limited if their *sampling* procedures do not give them a fair cross-section of the population they want to study and about which they want to draw conclusions. Anything less than a *random sample* is said to be a *biased sample* of participants. In most cases, samples consist of people who are representative of specified target populations rather than of the general population.

STATISTICAL ANALYSIS OF RESEARCH RESULTS

Psychologists use descriptive and inferential statistical analyses to summarize and analyze data.

Descriptive Statistics

Descriptive statistics include measures of central tendency (such as the *mode, median,* and *mean*), measures of variability (such as the *range* and *standard deviation*), and *correlation coefficients.* Although they can be valuable, *correlations* alone cannot establish that two variables are causally related; nor can they determine which variable might affect which, or why.

Inferential Statistics

Psychologists employ *inferential statistics* to guide conclusions about data and, especially, to determine if correlations or differences between means are *statistically significant*—that is, larger than would be expected by chance alone.

Statistics and Research Methods as Tools in Critical Thinking

Scientific evaluation of research requires the use of critical thinking to carefully assess the statistical and methodological aspects of even the most dramatic or desirable results.

ETHICAL GUIDELINES FOR PSYCHOLOGISTS

Ethical guidelines promote the protection of humans and animals in psychological research, and set the highest standards for behavior in all other aspects of psychologists' scientific and professional lives.

KEY TERMS

behavioral genetics (46)
biased sample (38)
case study (33)
confounding variable (35)
control group (35)
correlation (41)
correlation coefficient (42)
critical thinking (28)
data (30)

dependent variable (34)
descriptive statistics (40)
double-blind design (36)
experimental group (35)
experimenter bias (36)
experiments (34)
hypothesis (29)
independent variable (34)
inferential statistics (40)

mean (41)
median (41)
mode (41)
naturalistic observation (32)
operational definitions (30)
placebo (36)
quasi-experiments (37)
random assignment (35)
random sample (38)

random variables (35)
range (41)
sampling (38)
standard deviation (SD) (41)
statistically significant (43)
survey (33)
theory (30)
variables (30)

3

Biological Aspects of Psychology

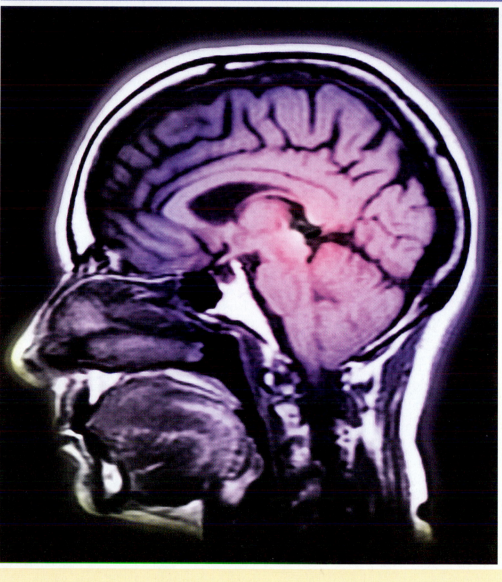

Today millions of people who suffer from depression or anxiety take drugs such as Prozac, because doctors now believe these conditions result from biological imbalances. Diseases of the brain can cause an elderly woman to forget her own children's names and a young man to be unable to pick up a glass of water without shaking. Maybe you yourself worry that your body's metabolism is working against your best efforts to lose or gain weight.

These examples of biological explanations for behavior and mental processes reflect the biological approach to psychology discussed in Chapter 1. The popularity and influence of that approach stems from the fact that brain cells, hormones, genes, and other biological factors are intimately related to all behavior and mental processes, from the fleeting memory you had a minute ago to the movements of your eyes as you read right now. In this chapter, we describe these biological factors in more detail. Reading it will take you into the realm of **biological psychology,** which is the study of the cells and organs of the body and the physical and chemical changes involved in behavior and mental processes. It is here that we begin to consider the relationship between your body and your mind, your brain and your behavior. Throughout the chapter you will see examples of the role of biology in many human behaviors and mental processes.

People often assume that if a behavior or mental process has a strong biological basis, it is beyond control, that "biology is destiny." Accordingly, many smokers don't even try to quit because they assume that a biological addiction to nicotine will doom them to failure. This is not necessarily true, as millions of ex-smokers can attest. Indeed, the fact that all behavior and mental processes are *based* on biological processes does not mean that they can be fully understood through the study of biological processes alone. Those who would reduce all of psychology to the analysis of brain chemicals vastly oversimplify the interactions between our biological selves and our psychological experiences, between our genes and our environments.

For one thing, just as all behaviors and mental processes are influenced by biology, all biological processes are influenced by the environment. Height, for example, is a biologically determined characteristic, but how tall you actually become also depends on nutrition and other environmental factors (Tanner, 1992). As discussed in Chapter 2 and the behavioral genetics appendix, hereditary and environmental influences combine to determine height, intelligence, personality, mental disorders, and many other characteristics.

In short, understanding behavior and mental processes requires that we synthesize information from many levels of analysis, from the activity of cells and organ systems to the activity of individuals and groups in social contexts. This chapter focuses on the biological level, not because it reveals the whole story of psychology but because it tells an important part of that story.

We begin by considering your **nervous system,** a complex combination of cells that allows you to gain information about what is going on inside and outside your body and to respond appropriately. In doing so, the nervous system displays the components of an information-processing system: It has input, processing, and output activities (see Figure 3.1). You receive *input* in the form of sensory signals from the world. During *processing,* you integrate the information with past experiences and decide what to do about it. And *output* occurs as your brain activates your muscles to act on the information. It is a fundamental tenet of scientific psychology that every thought, every feeling, every action, is represented somehow in the nervous system and that none of these events could occur without it.

The nervous system is able to do what it does partly because it is made up of cells that *communicate with each other.* Like all cells in the body—indeed, like cells in all life forms—those in the nervous system can respond to outside influences. Many of the signals that cells respond to come in the form of *chemicals* released by other cells. So even as various cells specialize during prenatal development to become skin, bone, hair, and other tissues, they still "stay in touch" to some extent through chemical signals. Bone cells, for example, add or drop calcium in response to hormones secreted in another part of the body. Cells in the bloodstream respond to viruses and other

FIGURE 3.1

**Three Functions of
the Nervous System**

The nervous system's three main functions involve receiving information (input), integrating that information with past experiences (processing), and guiding actions (output). These functions work in various situations in the service of your motivational state and your goals, helping you do everything from satisfying hunger to getting a job.

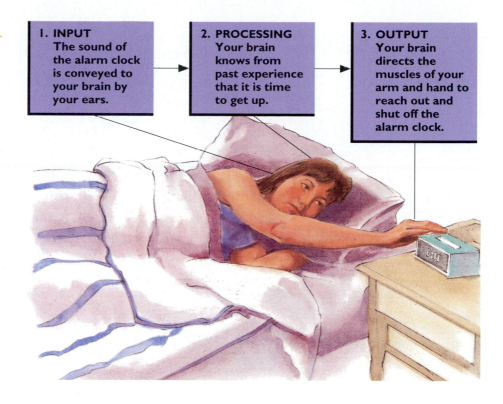

I. INPUT
The sound of the alarm clock is conveyed to your brain by your ears.

2. PROCESSING
Your brain knows from past experience that it is time to get up.

3. OUTPUT
Your brain directs the muscles of your arm and hand to reach out and shut off the alarm clock.

invaders by destroying them. We focus first on the cells of the nervous system because their ability to communicate is the most efficient and complex.

THE NERVOUS SYSTEM

Scientists explore the nervous system at many levels, from the workings of molecules and cells to the wonders of how vast networks of brain cells accomplish such tasks as recognizing visual patterns and learning a language. We begin our exploration of the nervous system at the "bottom," with a description of the individual cells and molecules that compose it. Then we consider how these cells are organized to form the structures of the human nervous system.

Cells of the Nervous System

One of the most striking findings in current research on the cells of the nervous system is how similar they are to other cells in the body, and how similar all cells are in all living organisms, from bacteria to plants to humans. For example, bacteria, plant cells, and brain cells all synthesize similar proteins when they are subjected to reduced oxygen or elevated temperatures. The implications of this similarity are clear: We can learn much about humans by studying animals, and much about brain cells by studying cells in simple organisms. For example, *Alzheimer's disease* is a disease of cells in the brain that usually occurs among older people; it causes a progressive and dramatic deterioration in reasoning and a broad range of other cognitive abilities (see the Focus on Research Methods section in this chapter). Recently, studies of cells in simple worms have provided clues to the causes of this terrible illness (Mattson et al., 1998).

Figure 3.2 illustrates three of the characteristics that cells of the nervous system share with every other kind of cell in the body. First, they have an *outer membrane* that, like a fine screen, lets some substances pass in and out while blocking others. Second, nervous system cells have a *cell body,* which contains a *nucleus.* The nucleus carries the genetic information that determines how a cell will function. Third, nervous system cells contain *mitochondria,* which are structures that turn oxygen and glucose into energy. This

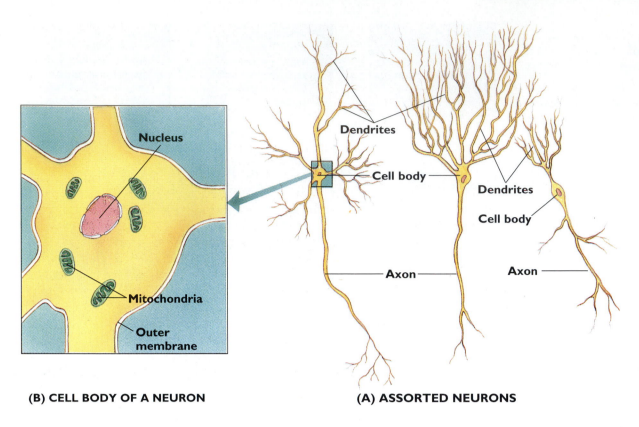

(B) CELL BODY OF A NEURON

(A) ASSORTED NEURONS

FIGURE 3.2

The Neuron

Part (A) shows three examples of *neurons,* which are cells in the nervous system. The fibers extending outward from each cell body—the axons and dendrites—are among the features that make neurons unique. Part (B) is an enlarged drawing of the cell body of a neuron. The cell body of every neuron has typical cell elements, including an outer membrane, a nucleus, and mitochondria.

process is especially vital to brain cells. Although the brain accounts for only 2 percent of the body's weight, it consumes more than 20 percent of the body's oxygen (Sokoloff, 1981). All of this energy is required because brain cells transmit signals among themselves to an even greater extent than do cells in the rest of the body.

Two major types of cells—called neurons and glial cells—allow the nervous system to carry out its complex signaling tasks so efficiently. **Neurons** are cells that are specialized to rapidly respond to signals and quickly send signals of their own. Most of our discussion of brain cells will be about neurons, but glial cells are important as well. Glial means "glue," and scientists had long believed that glial cells did no more than hold neurons together. Recent research shows, however, that **glial cells** also help neurons communicate by directing their growth, keeping their chemical environment stable, secreting chemicals to help restore damage, and even responding to signals from neurons (Cai & Kimelberg, 1997). Without glial cells, neurons could not function.

Neurons have three special features that enable them to communicate signals efficiently. The first is their structure. Although neurons come in many shapes and sizes, they all have long, thin fibers that extend outward from the cell body (see Figure 3.2). When these fibers get close to other neurons, communication between the cells can occur. The intertwining of all these fibers with fibers from other neurons allows each neuron to be in close proximity to thousands or even hundreds of thousands of other neurons.

The fibers extending from a neuron's cell body are called axons and dendrites. **Axons** are the fibers that carry signals away from the cell body, out to where communication occurs with other neurons. Each neuron generally has only one axon leaving the cell body, but that one axon may have many branches. Axons can be very short or several feet long, like the axon that sends signals from the spinal cord all the way down to the big toe. **Dendrites** are the fibers that receive signals from the axons of other neurons and carry those signals to the cell body. A neuron can have many dendrites. Dendrites, too, usually have many branches. Remember that *a*xons carry signals *a*way from the cell body, whereas *d*endrites *d*etect those signals.

The neuron's ability to communicate efficiently also depends on two other features: the "excitable" surface membrane of some of its fibers, and the minute gap between neurons called a **synapse.** In the following sections we examine how these features allow a signal to be sent rapidly from one end of the neuron to the other and from one neuron to another.

Action Potentials

To understand the signals in the nervous system, you first need to know something about cell membranes and the chemical molecules within and outside the cell. The cell membrane is *selectively permeable;* that is, it lets some molecules pass through, but excludes others. Many molecules carry a positive or negative electrochemical charge and are referred to as **ions.** Normally, the membrane maintains an uneven distribution of positively and negatively charged ions inside and outside the cell. The result is that the inside of the cell is slightly more negative than the outside, and the membrane is said to be *polarized.* Because molecules with a positive charge are attracted to those with a negative charge, a force called an *electrochemical potential* drives positively charged molecules toward the inside of the cell; many, however, are kept outside by the membrane.

For communication in the nervous system, the two most important "excluded" molecules are sodium (the same sodium found in table salt) and calcium. Positively charged sodium and calcium ions are highly concentrated on the outside of the cell and are strongly attracted to negatively charged molecules inside the cell. However, sodium and calcium can pass through the membrane only by going through special openings, or channels, in the membrane. These channels are distributed along the axon and dendrites and act as gates that can be opened or closed.

Normally the sodium channels along the axon are closed, but changes in the environment of the cell can *depolarize* the membrane, making the area inside the membrane less negative. If the membrane is depolarized to a point called the *threshold,* then the gates swing open and the sodium ions rush in (see Figure 3.3). When this happens, the adjacent area of the axon becomes more depolarized, thereby causing the neighboring gate to open. This sequence continues, and the change in electrochemical potential spreads rapidly all the way down the axon.

This abrupt change in the potential of an axon is called an action potential, and its "contagious" nature is referred to as its *self-propagating property.* When an action potential shoots down an axon, the neuron is said to have *fired.* This is an *all-or-none* type of communication: The cell either fires at full strength or does not fire at all. For many years, scientists believed that only axons were capable of generating action

FIGURE 3.3

The Beginning of an Action Potential

This diagrammatic view of a polarized nerve cell shows the normally closed sodium gates in the cell membrane. The electrochemical potential across the membrane is generated by an uneven distribution of positive and negative ions. For example, there are more positive ions, such as sodium (Na^+), on the outside than on the inside. There are also more negative ions, such as negatively charged proteins (Pr^-) on the inside than on the outside. If stimulation causes depolarization near a particular sodium gate, that gate may swing open, allowing sodium to rush into the axon, stimulating the next gate to open, and so on down the axon. The cell is repolarized when the sodium gates are closed and gates are opened for potassium (K^+) to flow out. Calcium gates allow action potentials to spread along dendrites in a similar fashion.

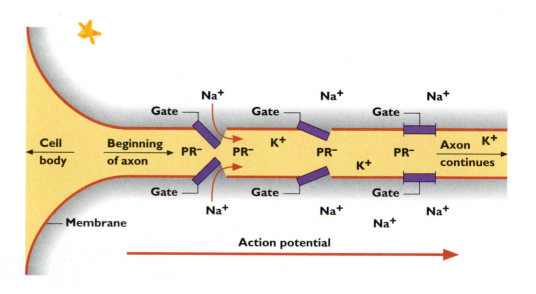

potentials. However, research has recently revealed that action potentials also occur in dendrites (Stuart et al., 1997). So action potentials may go in different directions in different neurons. In some, the action potential begins at the axon and shoots down the axon, as already described. In others, action potentials are generated in the dendrites and send a signal into the cell body and on down the axon. In still others, action potentials beginning in the axon go in both directions—down the axon and also "backward" through the cell body and into the dendrites. Action potentials that spread into the dendrites from the cell body appear to invade some branches and not others, leading scientists to conclude that these messages may be important in strengthening particular connections between neurons (Magee & Johnston, 1997).

The speed of the action potential as it moves down an axon is constant for a particular cell, but in different cells the speed ranges from 0.2 meters per second to 120 meters per second (about 260 miles per hour). The speed depends on the diameter of the axon—larger ones are faster—and on whether myelin is present. **Myelin** (pronounced "MY-a-lin") is a fatty substance that wraps around some axons and speeds action potentials. Larger, myelinated cells are usually found in the parts of the nervous system that carry the most urgently needed information. For example, the sensory neurons that receive information from the environment about onrushing trains, hot irons, and other dangers are fast-acting, myelinated cells. Multiple sclerosis, a severe brain disorder that destroys myelin, occurs because of a virus that is very similar to a component of myelin (Hausmann & Wucherpfennig, 1997). When the victim's immune system attacks this virus, it attacks and destroys vital myelin as well, resulting in disruption of vision, speech, balance, and other important functions.

Although each neuron fires or does not fire in an "all-or-none" fashion, its *rate* of firing varies. It can fire over and over because the sodium gates open only briefly and then close. Between firings there is a very short rest, called a **refractory period.** During this time, gates for positively charged potassium open briefly; because of their high concentration on the inside of the axon, these ions flow out of the axon, and the membrane becomes repolarized. At that point the neuron can fire again. Because the refractory period is so short, a neuron can send action potentials down its axon at rates of up to 1,000 per second. The *pattern* of repeated action potentials amounts to a coded message. We describe some of the codes used by the nervous system in Chapter 4, on sensation.

Synapses and Communication Between Neurons

How does the action potential in one neuron affect the next neuron? For communication to occur *between* cells, the signal must be transferred across the synapse between neurons. Usually, the axon of one cell delivers its signals across a synapse to the dendrites of a second cell; those dendrites, in turn, transmit the signal to their cell body, which may relay the signal down its axon to a third cell, and so on. But other commu-

FIGURE 3.4

A Synapse

This photograph taken through an electron microscope shows part of a neural synapse magnified 50,000 times. Clearly visible are the mitochondria; the neurotransmitter-containing vesicles in the ending of the presynaptic cell's axon; the synapse itself, which is the narrow gap between the cells; and the dendrite of the postsynaptic cell.

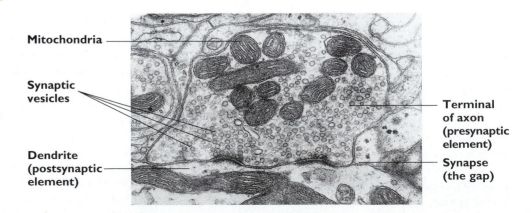

Mitochondria

Synaptic vesicles

Dendrite (postsynaptic element)

Terminal of axon (presynaptic element)

Synapse (the gap)

FIGURE 3.5

Communication Between Neurons

When a neuron fires, a self-propagating action potential shoots to the end of its axon, triggering the release of a neurotransmitter into the synapse. This stimulates neighboring cells. One type of stimulation is *excitatory,* causing depolarization of the neighboring cells. This depolarization, in turn, will cause those neurons to fire an action potential if threshold is reached. New evidence indicates that action potentials can also sometimes occur in dendrites.

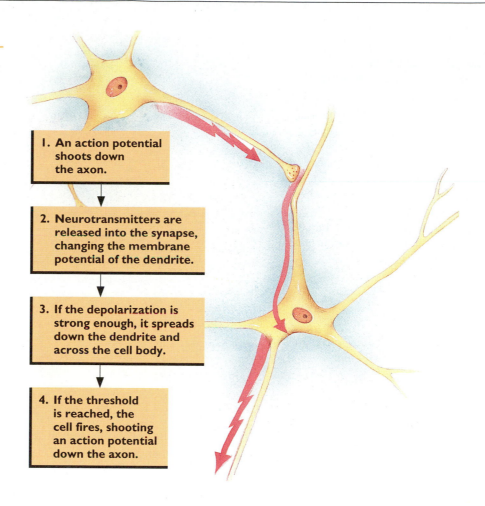

1. An action potential shoots down the axon.

2. Neurotransmitters are released into the synapse, changing the membrane potential of the dendrite.

3. If the depolarization is strong enough, it spreads down the dendrite and across the cell body.

4. If the threshold is reached, the cell fires, shooting an action potential down the axon.

nication patterns also occur. Axons can signal to other axons or even directly to the cell body of another neuron; dendrites of one cell can send signals to the dendrites of other cells (Pinault, Smith, & Deschenes, 1997). These varied communication patterns allow the brain to conduct extremely complex information-processing tasks.

Neurotransmitters   Unlike the communication down the axon, which uses electrochemical signals, communication at the synapse between neurons relies solely on chemicals. The transfer of information across a synapse is accomplished by chemicals called **neurotransmitters.** These chemicals are stored in numerous little "bags," called *vesicles,* at the tips of axons (see Figure 3.4). When an action potential reaches the end of an axon, a neurotransmitter is released into the synapse, where it spreads to reach the next, or *postsynaptic,* cell (see Figure 3.5).

At the membrane of the postsynaptic cell, neurotransmitters attach to proteins called **receptors.** Like a puzzle piece fitting into its proper place, a neurotransmitter snugly fits, or "binds" to, its own receptors but not to receptors for other neurotransmitters (see Figure 3.6 on page 58). Although each receptor "recognizes" only one type of neurotransmitter, each neurotransmitter type can bind to several different receptor types. As a result, the same neurotransmitter can have different effects depending on the type of receptor to which it binds.

The binding of a neurotransmitter to a receptor stimulates channels in the postsynaptic cell to open (much like the sodium channels involved in action potentials), allowing ions to flow in or out. The ion channel may be an integral part of the receptor, allowing a rapid influx of ions, or the receptor may initiate slower chemical changes in the postsynaptic cell that eventually result in a change in ion flow. The flow of ions into and out of the postsynaptic cell produces a change in its membrane

FIGURE 3.6

The Relationship Between Neurotransmitters and Receptors

Neurotransmitters influence postsynaptic cells by stimulating special receptors on the surface of those cells' membranes. Each type of receptor receives only one type of neurotransmitter; the two fit together like puzzle pieces or like a key in a lock. Stimulation of these receptors by their neurotransmitter causes them, in turn, to either help or hinder the generation of a wave of depolarization in their cell's dendrites.

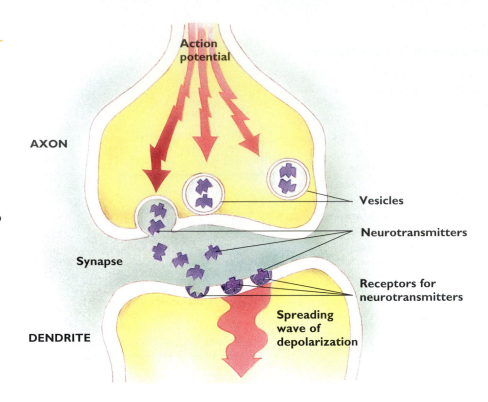

potential; thus, the chemical signal at the synapse creates an electrochemical signal within the postsynaptic cell.

Excitatory and Inhibitory Signals   Scientists can record the extremely small electrochemical changes that occur as ions flow through a single ion channel, as Figure 3.7 illustrates (Sakmann, 1992). The change in the membrane potential of the dendrite or cell body of the postsynaptic cell is called the postsynaptic potential. It can make the cell either more likely or less likely to fire. If positively charged ions (such as sodium or calcium) flow into the neuron, it becomes slightly *less* polarized, or *depolarized*. Because depolarization of the membrane can lead the neuron to fire an action potential, a depolarizing postsynaptic potential is called an excitatory postsynaptic potential, or EPSP. However, if positively charged ions (such as potassium) flow out of the neuron (because the concentration of potassium is higher on the inside), or if negatively charged ions flow in, the neuron becomes slightly more polarized, or *hyperpolarized*. Hyperpolarization makes it less likely that the neuron will fire an action potential. For this reason, a hyperpolarizing postsynaptic potential is called an inhibitory postsynaptic potential, or IPSP.

FIGURE 3.7

Electrical Recording of a Single Sodium Channel

Scientists are now able to record the electrical changes that occur when a single sodium channel opens and closes. Using a tiny glass tube only 1/25,000th the diameter of a human hair, they suck up a small "patch" of cell membrane that contains a channel. When the channel opens, sodium ions flow through and cause the section of membrane to be less polarized. Amazingly, when neurotransmitter-sensitive ion channels are inserted into non-neural cells, those cells begin to behave like neurons when neurotransmitters are applied.

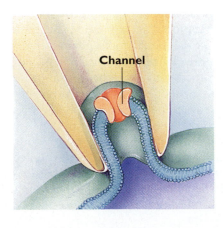

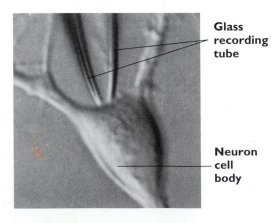

FIGURE 3.8

Integration of Neural Signals

Most of the signals that a neuron receives arrive at its dendrites or at its cell body. These signals, which typically come from many neighboring cells, can be conflicting. Some are excitatory, stimulating the cell to fire; others are inhibitory signals that tell the cell not to fire. Whether the cell actually fires or not at any given moment depends on whether excitatory or inhibitory messages predominate at the junction of the cell body and the axon.

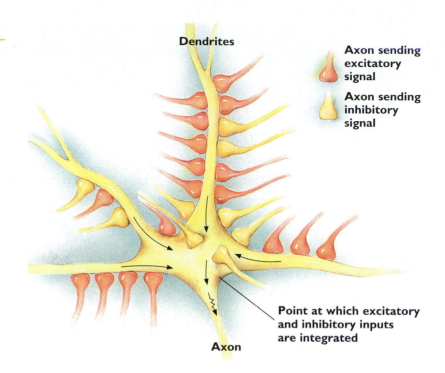

Dendrites

Axon sending excitatory signal

Axon sending inhibitory signal

Point at which excitatory and inhibitory inputs are integrated

Axon

The postsynaptic potential spreads along the membrane of the postsynaptic cell. But unlike the action potential in an axon, which remains at a constant strength, the postsynaptic potential fades as it goes along. Usually, it is not strong enough to pass all the way along the dendrite and through the cell body to the axon, so a single EPSP will not cause a neuron to fire. However, each neuron is constantly receiving EPSPs and IPSPs. The combined effect of rapidly repeated potentials or potentials from many locations can create a signal strong enough to reach the junction of the axon and cell body, a specialized region where new action potentials are generated.

Whether or not the postsynaptic cell fires and how rapidly it fires depend on whether, at a given moment, there are more excitatory ("fire") or more inhibitory ("don't fire") signals from other neurons at this junction (see Figure 3.8). Thus, as neurotransmitters transfer information across many neurons, each neuron constantly integrates or processes this information.

Several of the major neurotransmitters will be discussed later in this chapter, and in other chapters as well, because their effects touch on virtually every aspect of psychology. In the next chapter, for example, we describe some of the neurotransmitters used in pathways that convey pain messages throughout the brain and spinal cord. In Chapter 15, on psychological disorders, we discuss the role that neurotransmitters play in schizophrenia and depression. And in Chapter 16, on treatment, we consider how therapeutic drugs act on neurotransmitters and the cells they affect. Thinking itself requires communication among neurons, and neurotransmitters and their receptors are key links in this vital process.

Organization and Functions of the Nervous System

Impressive as individual neurons are (see "In Review: Neurons, Neurotransmitters, and Receptors"), an understanding of their functions requires that we look at the organization of groups of neurons. In the brain and spinal cord, neurons are organized into groups called neural networks. Many neurons in a network are closely connected, sending axons to the dendrites of many other neurons in the network. Signals from one network also go to other networks, and small networks are organized into bigger collections. By studying these networks, neuroscientists have begun to see that the nervous system conveys information not so much by the activity of single neurons

in review

NEURONS, NEUROTRANSMITTERS, AND RECEPTORS

Part	Function	Type of Signal Carried
Axon	Carries signals away from the cell body	The action potential, an all-or-none electrochemical signal, that shoots down the axon to vesicles at the tip of the axon, releasing neurotransmitters
Dendrite	Carries signals to the cell body	The postsynaptic potential, an electrochemical signal that fades as it moves toward the cell body
Synapse	Provides an area for the transfer of signals, usually between axon and dendrite	Chemicals that cross the synapse and reach receptors on another cell
Neurotransmitter	Chemical released by one cell that binds to the receptors on another cell	A chemical message telling the next cell to fire or not to fire its own action potential
Receptor	Proteins on cell membrane that receive chemical signals	Changes in the flow of ions through the cell membrane

sending single messages with a particular meaning, but by the activity of *groups* of neurons firing together in varying combinations. Thus, the same neurons may be involved in producing different patterns of behavior, depending on which combinations of them are active. Such combinations have been identified in the incredibly complex human brain (Sanes et al., 1995) and in the extremely simple nervous system of the sea slug (Xin, Weiss, & Kupfermann, 1996).

The groups of neurons in the nervous system that provide input about the environment are known as the senses, or sensory systems. These systems—including hear-

Nerve Cells in the Spinal Cord

Neurons in the central nervous system are connected to each other, forming complex communication networks.

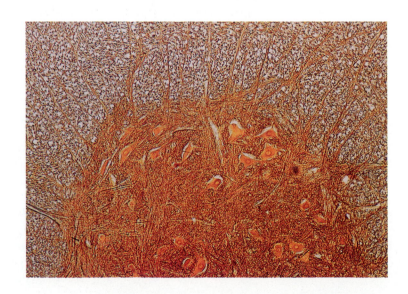

FIGURE 3.9

Organization of the Nervous System

The bone-encased central nervous system (CNS) is made up of the brain and spinal cord and acts as the body's central information processor, decision maker, and director of actions. The peripheral nervous system (PNS) includes all nerves not housed in bone and functions mainly to carry messages. The somatic subsystem of the PNS transmits sensory information to the CNS from the outside world and conveys instructions from the CNS to the muscles. The autonomic subsystem conveys messages from the CNS that alter the activity of organs and glands, and sends information about that activity back to the brain.

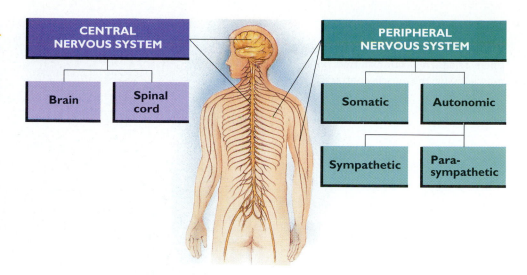

ing, vision, taste, smell, and touch—are described in the next chapter. Integration and processing of information occur mainly in the brain. Output flows through motor systems, which are the parts of the nervous system that influence muscles and other organs to respond to the environment.

The nervous system has two major divisions, which work together: the peripheral nervous system and the central nervous system (see Figure 3.9). The peripheral nervous system (PNS), which includes all of the nervous system that is not housed in bone, carries out sensory and motor functions. The central nervous system (CNS) is the part encased in bone. It includes the brain, which is inside the skull, and the spinal cord, which is inside the spinal column (backbone). The CNS is the "central executive" of the body; in other words, information is usually sent to the CNS to be processed and acted on. Let's take a closer look at these divisions of the nervous system.

THE PERIPHERAL NERVOUS SYSTEM: KEEPING IN TOUCH WITH THE WORLD

As shown in Figure 3.9, the peripheral nervous system has two components, each of which performs both sensory and motor functions.

The Somatic Nervous System

The first component is the somatic nervous system; it transmits information from the senses to the CNS and carries signals from the CNS to the muscles that move the skeleton. For example, when you lie in the sun at the beach, the somatic nervous system is involved in sending signals from the skin to the brain that become sensations of warmth. The somatic nervous system is also involved in every move you make. Neurons extend from the spinal cord to the muscles, where the release of a neurotransmitter onto them causes the muscles to contract. In fact, much of what we know about neurotransmitters was discovered in laboratory studies of this "neuromuscular junction," especially in the frog's hind leg. At the neuromuscular junction, the action of a neurotransmitter allows a quick response that can mean the difference between life and death, for a frog or anyone else.

The Autonomic Nervous System

The second component of the peripheral nervous system, the autonomic nervous system, carries messages back and forth between the CNS and the heart, lungs, and other organs and glands (Janig, 1996). These messages increase or decrease the activity of the organs and glands to meet varying demands placed on the body. As you lie

The Neuromuscular Junction

When nerve cells (shown here as green fibers) release neurotransmitters onto muscle tissue, the muscle contracts.

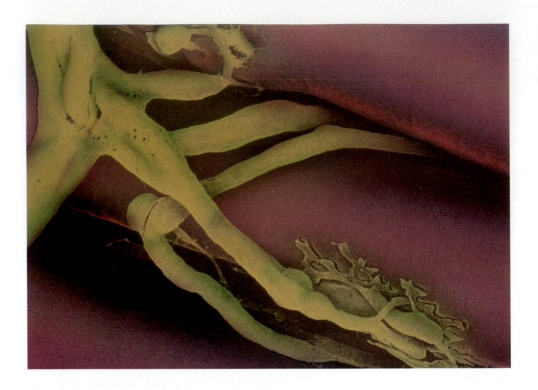

on the beach, it is your autonomic nervous system that makes your heart beat a little faster when an attractive person walks by and smiles.

The name *autonomic* means "autonomous" and suggests independent operation. This term is appropriate because, although the autonomic nervous system is influenced by the brain, it controls activities that are normally outside of conscious control, such as digestion and perspiration. The autonomic nervous system exercises this control through its two divisions: the sympathetic and parasympathetic branches. Generally, the sympathetic system mobilizes the body for action in the face of stress; the responses that result are sometimes collectively referred to as the "fight-or-flight" response. The parasympathetic system regulates the body's functions to conserve energy. Thus, these two branches often create opposite effects. For example, the sympathetic nervous system can make the heart beat faster, whereas the parasympathetic nervous system can slow it down.

The functions of the autonomic nervous system may not get star billing, but you would miss them if they were gone. Just as a race-car driver is nothing without a good pit crew, the somatic nervous system depends on the autonomic nervous system in order to get its job done. For example, when you want to move your muscles, you create a demand for energy; the autonomic nervous system fills the bill by increasing sugar fuels in the bloodstream. If you decide to stand up, you need increased blood pressure so that your blood does not flow out of your brain and settle in your feet. Again, the autonomic nervous system makes the adjustment. Disorders of the autonomic nervous system can make people sweat uncontrollably or faint whenever they stand up; they can also lead to other problems, such as an inability to have sex. We examine the autonomic nervous system in more detail in Chapter 11, on motivation and emotion.

THE CENTRAL NERVOUS SYSTEM: MAKING SENSE OF THE WORLD

The amazing speed and efficiency of the neural networks that make up the central nervous system—the brain and spinal cord—have prompted many people to compare it to the central processor in a computer. In fact, to better understand how human and other brains work and how they relate to sensory and motor systems, *computational neuroscientists* have created neural network models on computers (Koch & Davis, 1994). Figure 3.10 shows an example of how the three components of the nervous system (input, processing, and output) might be represented in a neural network model. Notice that input simultaneously activates several paths in the network, so that information is processed at various places at the same time. Accordingly, the activity of these models is described as *parallel distributed processing.* In the chapters on sensation, perception, learning, and memory, we describe how parallel distributed processing often characterizes the activity of the brain. Although neural network models were initially intended to help scientists better understand the nervous system, the principles of neural networks have been applied to a variety of problems that are not directly related to neurons or the brain. Specifically, neural network models can be programmed into computers, allowing them to perform functions that previously only humans could do. For example, using neural networks, computers are able to determine the quality of pork from scans of pig carcasses (Berg, Engel, & Forrest, 1998) and to predict which cancer patients will relapse after chemotherapy (Burke et al., 1998).

Neural network models are neatly laid out like computer circuits or the carefully planned streets of a new suburb, but the flesh-and-blood central nervous system is more difficult to follow. In fact, the CNS looks more like Boston or Paris, with distinct neighborhoods, winding back streets, and multilaned expressways. Its "neighborhoods" are collections of neuronal cell bodies called **nuclei.** The "highways" of the central nervous system are made up of axons that travel together in bundles called **fiber tracts** or **pathways.** Like a freeway ramp, the axon from a given cell may merge with and leave fiber tracts, and it may send branches into other tracts. The pathways travel from one nucleus to other nuclei, and scientists have learned much about how the brain works by determining the anatomical connections among nuclei. To begin our description of some of these nuclei and anatomical connections, let's consider a practical example of nervous system functioning.

At 6 A.M., your alarm goes off. The day begins innocently enough with what appears to be a simple case of information processing. Input in the form of sound from the alarm clock is received by your ears, which convert the sound into neural signals that reach your brain. Your brain compares these signals with previous experiences stored in memory and correctly associates the sound with "alarm clock." However, your output is somewhat impaired because your brain's activity has not yet reached the waking state. It directs your muscles poorly: Stumbling into the kitchen, you touch a glowing heating element as you reach for the coffeepot. Now things get more lively. Heat energy activates sensory neurons in your fingers, and action potentials flash along fiber tracts going into the spinal cord.

The Spinal Cord

The spinal cord receives signals from peripheral senses, including pain and touch from the fingertips, and relays those signals to the brain through fibers within the cord. Neurons in the spinal cord also carry signals downward, from the brain to the muscles.

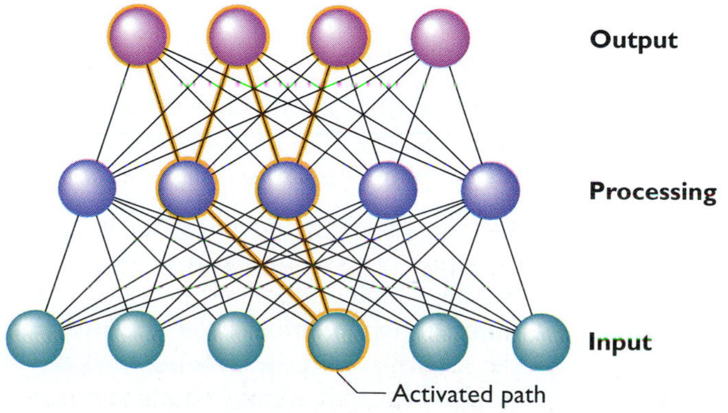

FIGURE 3.10

A Neural Network Model

A simple, computer-based neural network model includes three fundamental components: an input layer, a processing layer, and an output layer. More complex models may have additional processing layers. Each element in each layer is connected to every other element in the other layers. In a typical model, the connections can be either excitatory or inhibitory, and the strengths of connections between the elements can be modified depending on the results of the output; in other words, the network has the capacity to learn. Research on neural network models is part of *cognitive science,* whose linkages with psychology were mentioned in Chapter 1.

Output

Processing

Input

Activated path

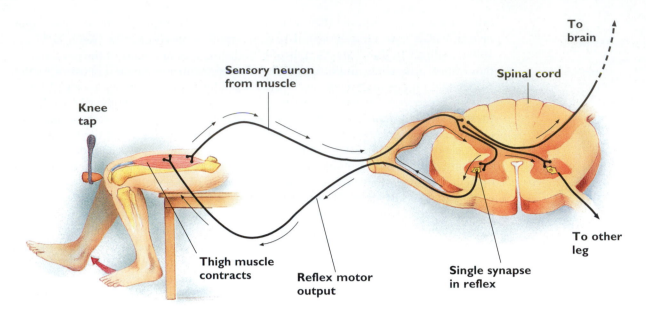

FIGURE 3.11

A Reflex Pathway

A tap on the knee sets off an almost instantaneous sequence of events, beginning with the stimulation of sensory neurons that respond to movement in the muscle. When those neurons fire, their axons, which end in the spinal cord, stimulate the firing of neurons with axons ending in the thigh muscle. The result is a contraction of the thigh muscle and a kicking of the lower leg and foot. Information about the knee tap and about what the leg has done also ascends to the cerebral cortex, but the reflex occurs without any guidance from the brain.

In addition, cells of the spinal cord can direct some simple behaviors without instructions from the brain. These behaviors are called **reflexes** because the response to an incoming signal is directly "reflected" back out (see Figure 3.11).

For example, when you touched that heating element, impulses from sensory neurons in your fingers reflexively activated motor neurons, which caused muscles in your arm to contract and quickly withdraw your hand. Because spinal reflexes like this one include few time-consuming synaptic links, they are very fast. And because spinal reflexes occur without instructions from the brain, they are considered involuntary; but they also send action potentials along fiber tracts going to the brain. Thus, you officially "know" you have been burned a fraction of a second after your reflex got you out of trouble.

The story does not end there, however. When a simple reflex set off by touching something hot causes one set of arm muscles to contract, an opposing set of muscles relaxes. If this did not happen, the arm would go rigid. Furthermore, muscles have receptors that send impulses to the spinal cord to let it know how extended they are, so that a reflex pathway can adjust the muscle contraction to allow smooth movement. Thus, the spinal cord is another example of a *feedback system*, a series of processes in which information about the consequences of an action goes back to the source of the action so that adjustments can be made.

In the spinal cord, sensory neurons are often called *afferent* neurons and motor neurons are termed *efferent* neurons, because *afferent* means "coming toward" and *efferent*, "going away." To remember these terms, notice that *afferent* and *approach* both begin with *a*; *efferent* and *exit* both begin with *e*.

The Brain

The brain has three major subdivisions: the hindbrain, the midbrain, and the forebrain. Figures 3.12 and 3.13 and Table 3.1 (on page 66) describe and illustrate some of the techniques scientists use to learn about these structures and how they function.

The Hindbrain   Incoming signals first reach the hindbrain, which is actually a continuation of the spinal cord. As you can see in Figure 3.14 (on page 67), the hindbrain lies inside the skull. Blood pressure, heart rate, breathing, and many other vital autonomic functions are controlled by nuclei in the hindbrain, particularly in an area called the **medulla.** Threading throughout the hindbrain and into the midbrain is a collection of cells that are not arranged in any well-defined nucleus. Because the collection

FIGURE 3.12

PET Scans of Changes in Brain Activity with Practice

In a study of brain activity, PET scans were conducted while participants performed a simple mental task. Specifically, they were asked to generate a verb after being presented with a noun (e.g., dog–walk). The participants learned to generate verbs more quickly with practice—as reflected in changes in their brain activity. Before practice on this task, the left frontal cortex was activated during verb generation (Section A). After practice, the frontal cortex was no longer activated while the identical task was performed (Section B), but when participants were presented with a list of new nouns, the frontal cortex was again activated (Section C). Similar changes in brain activation can be observed in PET scans of people learning a motor task (Petersen et al., 1998).

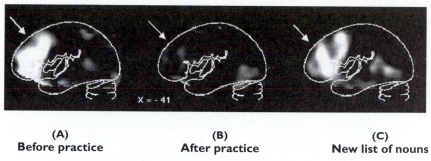

(A)	(B)	(C)
Before practice	**After practice**	**New list of nouns**

BRAIN ACTIVITY IN LEFT PREFRONTAL CORTEX

Source: Petersen et al. (1998), Figure 3.

FIGURE 3.13

The Use of Functional MRI to Bridge Eastern Medicine and Western Neuroscience

Acupuncture is an ancient Asian medical practice in which physical disorders are treated by stimulating specific locations in the skin with needles. Most acupuncture points are distant from the organ being treated. For example, vision problems are treated by the insertion of needles at "acupoints" in the foot (Section A). Recently, scientists have investigated the role of the brain in the effects of acupuncture (Cho et al., 1998). As shown in Section B, a functional MRI (fMRI) reveals that acupuncture stimulation of the acupoints in the foot related to visual problems activates the same area of the brain that responds to light reaching the eyes. However, stimulation of points on the foot only 2 centimeters from the visual acupoint region have no effect on this vision-related brain area.

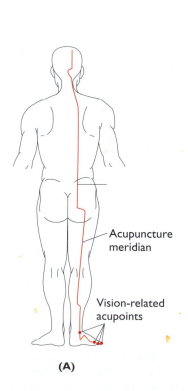

Acupuncture meridian

Vision-related acupoints

(A)

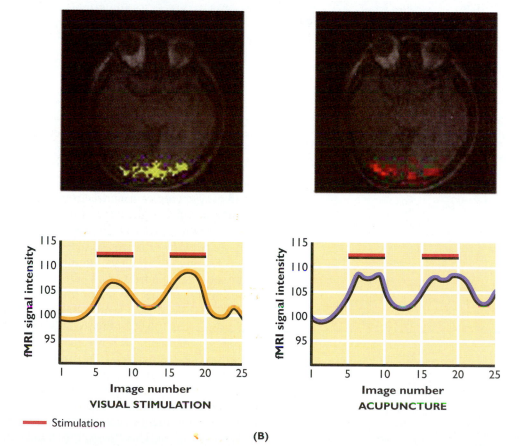

VISUAL STIMULATION

ACUPUNCTURE

— Stimulation

(B)

Source: Cho et al. (1998), Figures 2 and 4.

TABLE 3.1

Noninvasive Techniques for Studying Human Brain Function and Structure

Neuroscientists have developed a number of techniques for studying the structure and functions of the brain.

Technique	What It Shows	Advantages (+) and Disadvantages (−)
EEG (electroencephalogram) Multiple electrodes are pasted to outside of head	A single line that charts the summated electrical fields resulting from the activity of billions of neurons	+Detects very rapid changes in electrical activity, allowing analysis of stages of cognitive processing −Provides poor spatial resolution of source of electrical activity
PET (positron emission tomography) and SPECT (single photon emission computed tomography) Positrons and photons are emissions from radioactive substances	An image of the amount and localization of any molecule that can be injected in radioactive form, such as neurotransmitters, drugs, tracers for blood flow or glucose use (which indicate specific changes in neuronal activity)	+Allows functional and biochemical studies +Provides visual image corresponding to anatomy −Requires exposure to low levels of radioactivity −Provides spatial resolution better than that of EEG but poorer than that of MRI −Cannot follow rapid changes (faster than 30 seconds)
MRI (magnetic resonance imaging) Exposes the brain to magnetic field and measures radiofrequency waves	Traditional MRI provides high-resolution image of brain anatomy, and newer functional MRI (fMRI) provides images of changes in blood flow (which indicate specific changes in neuronal activity)	+Requires no exposure to radioactivity +Provides high spatial resolution of anatomical details (<1 mm) +Provides high temporal resolution (<1/10 of a second)

resembles a net, it is called the **reticular formation** (*reticular* means "netlike"). This network is very important in altering the activity of the rest of the brain. It is involved, for example, in arousal and attention; if the fibers from the reticular system are disconnected from the rest of the brain, a person goes into a permanent coma. Some of the fibers carrying pain signals from the spinal cord make connections in the reticular formation, which immediately arouses the rest of the brain from sleep. Within seconds, the hindbrain causes your heart rate and blood pressure to increase.

Activity of the **reticular formation** also leads to activity in a small nucleus **within** it called the **locus coeruleus,** (pronounced "LO-kus seh-ROO-lee-us"), which means "blue spot" (see Figure 3.14). There are relatively few cells in the locus coeruleus—only about 30,000 of the 100 billion or so in the human brain (Foote, Bloom, & Aston-Jones, 1983)—but each sends out an axon that branches extensively, making contact with as many as 100,000 other cells. Studies of rats, monkeys, and humans suggest that the locus coeruleus is **involved in directing attention** (Aston-Jones, Chiang, & Alexinsky, 1991; Smythies, 1997). In humans, abnormalities in the locus coeruleus have been linked to depression (Leonard, 1997).

The **cerebellum** is also part of the hindbrain. It allows the eyes to track a moving target accurately (Krauzlis & Lisberger, 1991), and it may be the **storehouse for well-rehearsed movements,** such as those associated with ballet, piano playing, and athletics (McCormick & Thompson, 1984). Indeed, for a long time its primary function was thought to be control of finely coordinated movements, such as threading a needle.

FIGURE 3.14

Major Structures of the Brain

This view from the side of a section cut down the middle of the brain reveals the forebrain, midbrain, hindbrain, and spinal cord. Many of these subdivisions do not have clear-cut borders, since they are all interconnected by fiber tracts. Indeed, though beautifully adapted to its functions, the brain was not the work of a city planner. Its anatomy reflects its evolution over millions of years. Newer structures (such as the cerebral cortex, which is the outer surface of the forebrain) that handle higher mental functions were built on older ones (like the medulla) that coordinate heart rate, breathing, and other more basic functions.

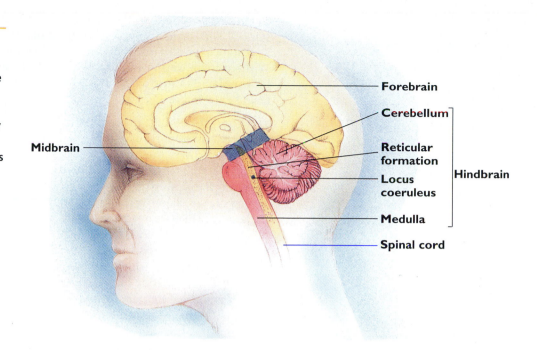

However, because the human cerebellum has grown more in size than any other brain structure, researchers have begun to rethink and reinvestigate the cerebellum's role in more uniquely human tasks such as language and symbolic thought. Recent work on the function of the cerebellum highlights the fact that there are different ways to think about what various parts of the brain do. For instance, you can think of coordinated movements simply as "motor functioning" or as an example of the more general activity of "sequencing and timing" (Gibbon et al., 1997). The importance of sequencing has become increasingly apparent in the study of nonmovement activities, particularly language. To speak fluently, you must put together a sequence of words rapidly and in the correct order and temporal rhythm. It now appears that the cerebellum plays a vital role in normal speech by integrating moment-to-moment feedback about vocal sounds with a sequence of precise movements of the lips and tongue (Leiner, Leiner, & Dow, 1993). When this process of integration and sequencing is disrupted, stuttering can result. Even nonstutterers who hear their own speech with a slight delay begin to stutter. (This is why radio talk-show hosts ask callers to turn off their radios. A momentary gap occurs before the shows are actually broadcast, and listening to the delayed sound of their own voice on the radio can cause callers to stutter.) Recent MRI studies indicate that the cerebellum is one of a number of brain regions that are concurrently involved in stuttering (Fox et al., 1996).

Reflexes and feedback systems are important to the functioning of the hindbrain, just as they are in the spinal cord. For example, if blood pressure drops, heart action increases reflexively to compensate for that drop. If you stand up very quickly, your blood pressure can drop so suddenly that it produces lightheadedness until the hindbrain reflex "catches up." If the hindbrain does not activate autonomic nervous system mechanisms to increase blood pressure, you will faint.

The Midbrain   Above the hindbrain is the midbrain. In humans it is a small structure, but it serves some very important functions. Certain types of automatic behaviors that integrate simple movements with sensory input are controlled there. For example, when you move your head, midbrain circuits allow you to move your eyes smoothly in the opposite direction, so that you can keep your eyes focused on an object despite the movement of your head. And when a loud noise causes you to turn your head reflexively and look in the direction of the sound, your midbrain circuits are at work.

One vital nucleus in the midbrain is the **substantia nigra,** meaning "black substance." This small area and its connections to the **striatum** (named for its "striped" appearance) in the forebrain are necessary for the smooth initiation of movement. Without them, you would find it difficult, if not impossible, to get up out of a chair, lift your hand to swat a fly, move your mouth to form words, or, yes, reach for that coffeepot at 6:00 A.M.

The Forebrain   Like the cerebellum, the human **forebrain** is another region that has grown out of proportion to the rest of the brain, so much so that it folds back over and completely covers the other parts. It is responsible for the most complex aspects of behavior and mental life. As Figure 3.15 shows, the forebrain includes structures known as the *diencephalon* and the *cerebrum;* the latter is covered by the *cerebral cortex.*

The diencephalon includes two structures deep within the brain. The first is the **thalamus,** which relays pain signals from the spinal cord as well as signals from the eyes and most other sense organs to upper levels in the brain. It also plays an important role in processing and making sense out of this information. The other is the **hypothalamus,** which lies under the thalamus (*hypo-* means "under") and is involved in regulating hunger, thirst, and sex drives. It has many connections to and from the autonomic nervous system and the endocrine system, as well as to other parts of the brain. Destruction of one section of the hypothalamus results in an overwhelming urge to eat. Damage to another area of the male's hypothalamus causes the sex organs to degenerate and the sex drive to decrease drastically. There is also a fascinating part of the hypothalamus that contains the brain's own timepiece: the **suprachiasmatic nuclei.** The suprachiasmatic nuclei keep an approximately twenty-four-hour clock that determines your biological rhythms. (You may be familiar with some of the many bodily processes that vary on a twenty-four-hour cycle, such as mental and physical performance, hormone levels, sensitivity to alcohol, and pain tolerance.) We discuss the functions of the hypothalamus in more detail in the chapter on motivation and emotion.

The largest part of the forebrain is the **cerebrum.** Two structures within it, the **amygdala** and **hippocampus,** are important in memory and emotion. For example, the amygdala associates features of stimuli from two different senses, as when we link the shape and feel of objects in memory (Murray & Mishkin, 1985). It is also involved

FIGURE 3.15

Some Structures of the Forebrain

The forebrain is divided into the cerebrum and the diencephalon. The structures of the cerebrum are covered by the outer "bark" of the cerebral cortex. This diagram shows some of the structures that lie deep within the cerebrum, as well as structures of the diencephalon.

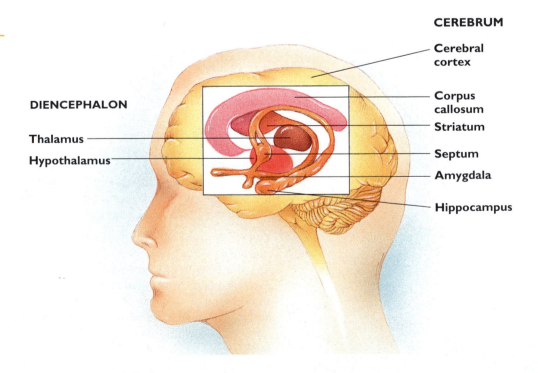

DIENCEPHALON

Thalamus

Hypothalamus

CEREBRUM

Cerebral cortex

Corpus callosum

Striatum

Septum

Amygdala

Hippocampus

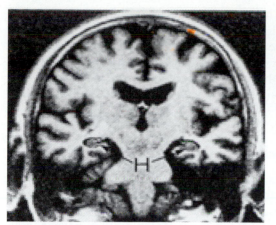
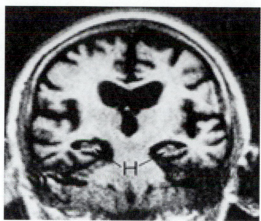
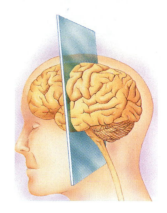

FIGURE 3.16

Source: Seab et al., 1988.

Alzheimer's Disease and the Hippocampus

These magnetic resonance images of living brains show that, compared to the normal person (left), a patient with Alzheimer's disease shows degeneration in the hippocampus (marked H). On average, the hippocampus of Alzheimer's patients has been found to be substantially smaller than in normal people; indeed, a smaller than average hippocampus in the elderly predicts the onset of the disease (Jack et al., 1999). Damage to the hippocampus may be responsible for the severe memory impairments in Alzheimer's patients.

in fear and other emotions (Davis, Rainnie, & Cassell, 1994; LeDoux, 1995); its activity has been found to be altered in people suffering from posttraumatic stress disorder, which is described in Chapter 13. Damage to the hippocampus results in an inability to form new memories of events. In one case, a patient known as R.B. suffered a stroke (an interruption of blood flow to the brain) that damaged only his hippocampus. Although tests indicated that his intelligence was above average and he could recall old memories, he was almost totally unable to build new memories (Squire, 1986). Research using MRI scans and tests of the decline of memory function in normal elderly people suggests that memory ability is correlated with the size of the hippocampus (Golomb et al., 1994); a small hippocampus predicts severe memory problems even before they are evident (Kaye et al., 1997). Animal studies have also shown that damage to the hippocampus within a day of a mildly painful experience erases memories of the experience, but that removal of the hippocampus several days after the experience has no effect on the memory. Thus, memories are not permanently stored in the hippocampus but are transferred elsewhere. As described in Chapter 7, your storehouse of memories depends on the activities of many parts of the brain.

The hippocampus and amygdala, and other interconnected structures such as the hypothalamus and the septum, are part of the limbic system. The limbic system plays an important role in regulating emotion and memory. Studies of the brains of people who died from Alzheimer's disease have found severe degeneration of neurons in the hippocampus and other limbic structures (see Figure 3.16). This may explain why Alzheimer's disease is a major cause of *dementia,* the deterioration of cognitive capabilities often associated with aging. About 10 percent of people over the age of sixty-five, and more than 30 percent of people over eighty-five, suffer from this disorder (Small et al., 1997). The financial cost of Alzheimer's disease is more than $100 billion a year (Small et al., 1997); the cost in human suffering is incalculable. Thus, the search for its causes and cures has a high priority among researchers who study the brain.

FOCUS ON RESEARCH METHODS

Manipulating Genes in Animal Models of Human Disease

About ninety years ago a German neurologist, Alois Alzheimer, conducted a postmortem examination of the brain of a woman who died after years of progressive mental deterioration and dementia. He was trying to find the cause of her disorder. His examination disclosed that cells in her cerebral cortex were bunched up like a rope tied in knots and that cellular debris had collected around the affected nerves. These features came to be known as tangles and plaques. *Tangles* are twisted fibers within neurons; their main protein component is called *tau*. *Plaques* are deposits of protein and parts of dead cells found between neurons. The major component of plaques is a small protein called *beta-amyloid,* which is produced from a larger protein called beta-amyloid precursor protein. Since the discovery of these proteins, researchers have been trying to discover their role in the disease named after this German doctor—Alzheimer's disease.

■ What was the researchers' question?

One specific question that researchers have addressed is whether the biochemicals found in plaques and tangles are the causes of Alzheimer's disease.

As noted in Chapter 2, a causal relationship cannot be inferred from a correlation. Therefore, to discover if beta-amyloid and tau might cause the death of neurons seen in Alzheimer's disease, researchers needed to conduct controlled experiments. As also noted in Chapter 2, experiments involve manipulating an independent variable and measuring its effect on a dependent variable. In this case, the experiment would involve creating plaques and tangles (the independent variable) and looking for their effects on memory (the dependent variable). Because such experiments cannot ethically be conducted on humans, scientists began looking for an "animal model" of Alzheimer's disease. However, progress in finding the causes of Alzheimer's was slowed by the lack of Alzheimer's-like conditions in *any* species of animal.

■ How did the researchers answer the question?

Previous studies of the genes of people with Alzheimer's disease had revealed that a mutation in the beta-amyloid precursor protein was associated with the disease. However, many Alzheimer's patients exhibited mutations not in this protein but in another one, which researchers called "presenilin" because it was associated with senility. (It turns out that presenilin is related to Alzheimer's because it affects the way in which beta-amyloid precursor protein is modified.) At this point, the researchers hoped to determine whether these mutated proteins actually cause the brain damage and memory impairment associated with Alzheimer's disease. Armed with new genetic engineering tools, they were able to create, literally, an animal model of Alzheimer's with mutated human genes.

The first attempts to create this animal model involved the insertion of a mutant form of beta-amyloid precursor protein into the cells of mice. If Alzheimer's disease is caused by faulty beta-amyloid precursor protein, so the logic went, inserting the gene for this faulty protein into mouse cells should cause deposits of beta-amyloid and the loss of neurons in the same parts of the brain as those seen in human Alzheimer's victims. No such changes should be observed in a control group of untreated animals. Of course, finding this result just once is not enough; an experiment's results must be replicable in order to be reliable.

■ What did the researchers find?

Indeed, in 1992, a group of scientists reported success in creating a model of Alzheimer's disease in mice, only to retract their statements when they could not repeat their results. Three years later researchers at a biotechnology company encountered a different problem. Although they succeeded in implanting the faulty protein into mice and found damage characteristic of Alzheimer's disease (Games et al., 1995), they did not observe any memory impairment in the mice.

More recently, however, other scientists have found that a variety of different mutations of beta-amyloid precursor protein inserted into mice produce both brain damage and memory impairment (Hsiao et al., 1996; Nalbantoglu et al., 1997). One group

Gene Manipulation in Mice

In one study, the gene for a particular type of neurotransmitter receptor was "knocked out" in these black mice. As shown here, the animals were much more aggressive than a control group of brown mice (Nelson et al., 1995).

subsequently claimed that the best animal model of Alzheimer's appears to involve mice with mutations in both beta-amyloid precursor protein and presenilin. These mice exhibit both severe brain pathology and memory impairment at a younger age than that seen in other experiments (Holcomb et al., 1998). Another group has claimed that its model better mimics the tau-containing tangles of Alzheimer's disease in humans (Sturchler-Pierrat et al., 1997). Ultimately, comparisons of results from many different experiments will determine which animal model of the disease is best. The scientists will then use that model to evaluate the critical roles of mutations in beta-amyloid precursor protein, presenilin, and tau in causing Alzheimer's disease.

■ What do the results mean?

This research is important not only because it might eventually solve the mystery of Alzheimer's disease, but also because it illustrates the power of experimental modification of animal genes for testing all kinds of hypotheses about biological factors influencing behavior. Besides *inserting* new or modified genes into brain cells, scientists can manipulate an independent variable by "knocking out" specific genes, then looking at the effect on dependent variables. One research team has shown, for example, that knocking out a gene for a particular type of neurotransmitter receptor causes mice to become obese and to overeat even when given appetite-suppressant drugs (Tecott et al., 1995). And genetic elimination of another type of receptor in mice canceled out the stimulating effects of cocaine (Xu et al., 1996). Of course, researchers must be careful not to inadvertently affect other genes while modifying the particular gene they are interested in. And they must be sure that the modified gene has not influenced the mice's behavior in unexpected and important ways. For example, if the gene significantly affects sensory or motor functions, a behavioral change could mistakenly be attributed to a change in brain function. (After all, a mouse with defective legs cannot run through a memory maze.) Careful behavioral analyses of the mouse model of Alzheimer's will also be needed to determine what components of memory processes are impaired.

■ What do we still need to know?

The scarcity of animal models of obesity, drug addiction, Alzheimer's disease, and other problems has impeded progress in finding biological treatments for them. In the case of Alzheimer's, for example, only one type of drug has had any effect on memory impairment, and its effects are quite minor (Small et al., 1997). As animal models for these conditions become more available through gene modification techniques, they will pave the way for new types of animal studies that are directly relevant to human problems. The next challenge will be to use these animal models to develop and test treatments that might effectively be applied to humans.

The Cerebral Cortex

So far, we have described some key structures *within* the forebrain; now we turn to a discussion of other structures on its surface. The outermost part of the cerebrum appears rather round and has right and left halves that are similar in appearance. These halves are called the **cerebral hemispheres.** The outer part of the cerebral hemispheres, the cerebral cortex, has a surface area of one to two square feet—an area that is larger than it looks because of the folds that allow the cortex to fit compactly inside the skull. The **cerebral cortex** is much larger in humans than in most other animals (dolphins are an exception). It is associated with the analysis of information from all the senses, control of voluntary movements, higher-order thought, and other complex aspects of human behavior and mental processes.

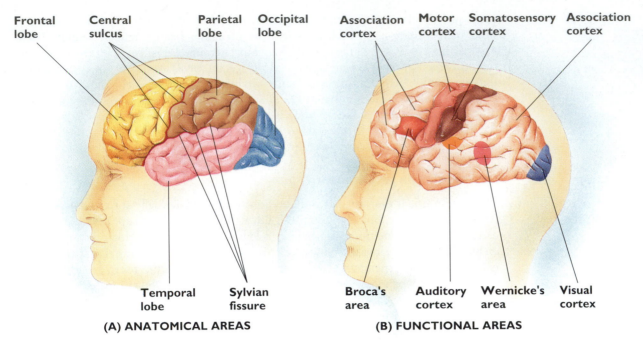

| Frontal lobe | Central sulcus | Parietal lobe | Occipital lobe | | Association cortex | Motor cortex | Somatosensory cortex | Association cortex |

| Temporal lobe | Sylvian fissure | | Broca's area | Auditory cortex | Wernicke's area | Visual cortex |

(A) ANATOMICAL AREAS   (B) FUNCTIONAL AREAS

FIGURE 3.17

The Cerebral Cortex (viewed from the left side)

The ridges (gyri) and valleys (sulci) are landmarks that divide the cortex into four lobes: the frontal, the parietal, the occipital, and the temporal. These terms describe anatomical regions, but the cortex is also divided in terms of function. These functional areas include the motor cortex (which controls movement), sensory cortex (which receives information from the senses), and association cortex (which integrates information). Also illustrated are Wernicke's area, which is involved in the interpretation of speech, and Broca's area, a region vital to the production of speech. (These two areas are found only on the left side of the cortex.)

LINKAGES

A Large Cortex

The dolphin is one of the only mammals whose cerebral cortex is larger than that of humans. As discussed in Chapter 8, this characteristic has led some psychologists to study language abilities in dolphins.

Figure 3.17(A) shows the *anatomical* or physical features of the cerebral cortex. The folds of the cortex give the surface of the human brain its wrinkled appearance, its ridges and valleys. The ridges are called *gyri* and the valleys are called *sulci* or *fissures*. As you can see in the figure, several deep sulci divide the cortex into four areas: the *frontal, parietal, occipital,* and *temporal* lobes. Thus, the gyri and sulci provide landmarks for describing the appearance of the cortex. Figure 3.17(B) depicts the areas of the cerebral cortex in which various *functions* or activities occur. The functional areas do not exactly match the anatomical areas, inasmuch as some functions occur in more than one area. Three of these functional areas—the sensory cortex, the motor cortex, and the association cortex—are discussed below, along with related areas.

Sensory Cortex   The sensory cortex lies in the parietal, occipital, and temporal lobes and is the part of the cerebral cortex that receives information from our senses. Different regions of the sensory cortex receive information from different senses. Visual information is received by the *visual cortex,* made up of cells in the occipital lobe; auditory information is received by the *auditory cortex,* made up of cells in the temporal lobe; and information from the skin about touch, pain, and temperature is received in the *somatosensory cortex,* made up of cells in the parietal lobe.

Information about skin sensations from neighboring parts of the body comes to neighboring parts of the somatosensory cortex, as Figure 3.18 illustrates. It is as if the outline of a tiny person, dangling upside down, determined the location of the infor-

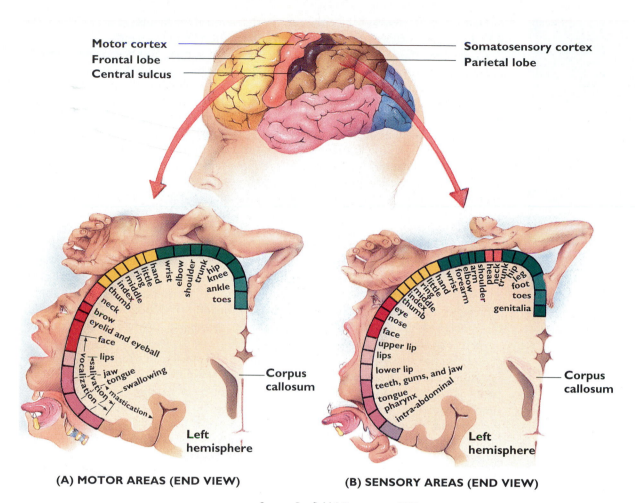

(A) MOTOR AREAS (END VIEW)

(B) SENSORY AREAS (END VIEW)

Source: Penfield & Rasmussen, 1968.

Note: Did you notice the error in this classic drawing? (The figure shows the right side of the body, but the left hand and left side of the face.)

FIGURE 3.18

Motor and Somatosensory Cortex

The areas of cortex that move parts of the body (motor cortex) and receive sensory input from body parts (somatosensory cortex) occupy neighboring regions on each side of the central sulcus. These regions appear in both hemispheres; here we show cross-sections of only those on the left side, looking from the back of the brain toward the front. The cross-sections also show how areas controlling movement of neighboring parts of the body, like the foot and leg, occupy neighboring parts of the motor cortex. Areas receiving input from neighboring body parts, such as the lips and tongue, are near one another in the sensory cortex.

mation. This pattern is called the *homunculus,* Latin for "little man." The organization of the homunculus has long been assumed to be unchanging, but recent work has shown that the amount of sensory cortex that responds to particular sensory inputs can be modified by experience. The experience may be as traumatic as the loss of a limb (whereby sensory areas of the brain formerly stimulated by that limb are now stimulated by other regions of skin) or something as mundane as practicing the violin (which can increase the number of neurons responding to touch). These changes appear to be coordinated partly by brain areas outside the cerebral cortex, which reassign more neurons to process particular sensory inputs. For example, activity in the basal nucleus of the forebrain can generate a massive reorganization of the sensory cortex involved in sound processing (Kilgard & Merzenich, 1998).

Motor Cortex   Neurons in specific areas of the **motor cortex,** which is in the frontal lobe, initiate voluntary movements in specific parts of the body. Some control movement of the hand; others stimulate movement of the foot, the knee, the head, and so on. The specific muscles activated by these regions are linked not to specific neurons but, as mentioned earlier, to the patterned activity of many neurons. Some of the same neurons are active in moving different fingers, for example, but the *combinations* of neurons differ from finger to finger (Schieber & Hibbard, 1993). The motor cortex is arranged in a way that mirrors the somatosensory cortex. For example, as you can see

Movement and the Brain

Smooth movements require the coordination of neural activity in both the brain and the spinal cord. This presents a challenge to researchers developing implants to restore movement for individuals with paralysis. Delivering computer-controlled electrical stimulation to the leg muscles allows walking to be achieved, but the movements are jerkier than normal.

LINKAGES

Where are the brain's language centers? (a link to Cognition and Language)

in Figure 3.18, the parts of the motor cortex that control the hands are near parts of the somatosensory cortex that receive sensory information from the hands.

Controlling the movement of the body may seem simple: You have a map of body parts in the motor cortex, and you activate cells in the hand region if you want to move your hand. But the actual process is much more complex. Recall again your sleepy reach for the coffeepot. The motor cortex must first translate the coffeepot's location in space into coordinates relative to your body; for example, your hand might have to be moved to the right or to the left of your body. Next, the motor cortex must determine which muscles must be contracted to produce those movements. Populations of neurons work together to produce just the right combinations of direction and force in the particular muscle groups necessary to create the desired effects. Many interconnected areas of the motor cortex are involved in making these determinations.

Association Cortex   The parts of the cerebral cortex not directly involved with either receiving specific sensory information or initiating movement are referred to as association cortex. These are the areas that perform such complex cognitive tasks as associating words with images. The term *association* is appropriate because these areas either receive information from more than one sense or combine sensory and motor information. Association cortex occurs in all of the lobes and forms a large part of the cerebral cortex in human beings. For this reason, damage to association areas can create severe deficits in all kinds of mental abilities.

One of the most devastating deficits, called *aphasia,* creates difficulty in understanding or producing speech and can involve all the functions of the cerebral cortex. Language information comes from the auditory cortex (for spoken language) or from the visual cortex (for written language); areas of the motor cortex produce speech (Geschwind, 1979). But the complex function known as language also involves activity in association cortex. In the 1800s, two areas of association cortex involved in different aspects of language were delineated. Paul Broca described the difficulties that result from damage to the association cortex in the frontal lobe near motor areas that control facial muscles, an area now called *Broca's area* (see Figure 3.17 on page 72). When Broca's area is damaged, the mental organization of speech suffers. Victims have great difficulty speaking, and what they say is often grammatically incorrect. Each word comes slowly. Other language problems result from damage to a portion of the association cortex first described by Carl Wernicke (pronounced "VER-nick-ee") and thus called *Wernicke's area.* As Figure 3.17 (on page 72) shows, it is located in the temporal lobe, near an area of the cortex that receives information from the ears and eyes. Wernicke's area is involved in the interpretation of both speech and written words. Damage to this area can leave fluency intact but disrupt the ability to understand the meaning of words or to speak comprehensibly.

One study illustrates the different effects of damage to each area (Lapointe, 1990). In response to the request "Tell me what you do with a cigarette," a person with chronic Broca's aphasia replied, "Uh . . . uh . . . cigarette (pause) smoke it." Though halting and ungrammatical, this speech was meaningful. In response to the same request, a person with chronic Wernicke's aphasia replied, "This is a segment of a pegment. Soap a cigarette." This speech, by contrast, was fluent but without meaning. A fascinating aspect of Broca's aphasia is that when a person with the disorder sings, the words come fluently and correctly. Presumably, words set to music are handled by a different part of the brain than normal spoken words (Besson et al., 1998). Capitalizing on this observation, "melodic intonation" therapy helps Broca's aphasia patients gain fluency in speaking by teaching them to speak in a "singsong" manner (Lapointe, 1990).

It appears that differing areas of association cortex are activated depending on whether language is spoken or written and whether particular grammatical and conceptual categories are involved (see Figure 3.12 on page 65). For example, consider the cases of two women who had strokes that damaged different language-related parts of their association cortex (Caramazza & Hillis, 1991). Neither woman had difficulty speaking or writing nouns, but both had difficulty with verbs. One woman could write

"Whoa! *That* was a good one! Try it, Hobbs — just poke his brain right where my finger is."

FIGURE 3.19

The Brain's Left and Right Hemispheres

The brain's two hemispheres are joined by a core bundle of nerve fibers known as the corpus callosum; in this figure the corpus callosum has been cut and the two hemispheres are separated. The two cerebral hemispheres look nearly the same but perform somewhat different tasks. For one thing, the left hemisphere receives sensory input from and controls movement on the right side of the body. The right hemisphere senses and controls the left side of the body.

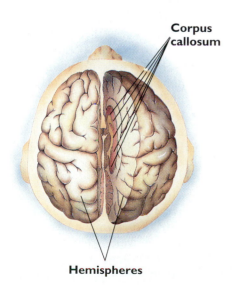

Corpus callosum

Hemispheres

verbs but could not speak them: She had difficulty pronouncing *watch* when it was used as a verb in the sentence "I watch TV" but spoke the same word easily when it appeared as a noun in "My watch is slow." The other woman could speak verbs but had difficulty writing them. Another bizarre language abnormality following brain damage is "foreign accent syndrome," illustrated by a thirty-two-year-old stroke victim whose native language was English. His speech was slurred immediately after the stroke, but as it improved, he began to speak with a Scandinavian accent, adding syllables to some words ("How are you today-ah?") and pronouncing *hill* as "heel." His normal accent did not fully return for four months (Takayama et al., 1993). Case studies of "foreign accent syndrome" suggest that specific regions of the brain are involved in the sound of language, whereas others are involved in various aspects of its meaning.

The Divided Brain in a Unified Self

A striking idea emerged from observations of people with damage to the language areas of the brain. Researchers noticed that damage to limited areas of the *left hemisphere* impaired the ability to use or comprehend language, whereas damage to corresponding parts of the *right hemisphere* usually did not. Perhaps, they reasoned, the right and left halves of the brain serve different functions.

This concept was not entirely new. It had long been understood, for example, that most sensory and motor pathways cross over as they enter or leave the brain. As a result, the *left hemisphere* receives information from and controls movements of the *right* side of the body, whereas the *right hemisphere* receives input from and controls the *left* side of the body. However, both sides of the brain perform these functions. In contrast, the fact that language centers, such as Broca's area and Wernicke's area, are almost exclusively on the left side of the brain suggested that each hemisphere might be specialized to perform some functions almost independently of the other hemisphere.

In the late 1800s there was great interest in the hypothesis that the hemispheres might be specialized, but no techniques were available for testing it. Renewed interest in the issue grew out of studies during the 1960s by Roger Sperry, Michael Gazzaniga, and their colleagues.

Split-Brain Studies Sperry studied *split-brain* patients—people who had undergone a radical surgical procedure in an attempt to control severe epilepsy. Before the surgery, their seizures began in one hemisphere and then spread to engulf the whole brain. As a last resort, surgeons isolated the two hemispheres from each other by severing the **corpus callosum,** a massive bundle of more than a million fibers that connects the two hemispheres (see Figure 3.19).

After the surgery, researchers used a special apparatus to present visual images to only one side of these patients' split brains (see Figure 3.20). They found that severing the tie between the hemispheres had dramatically affected the way these people thought about and dealt with the world. For example, when the image of a spoon was presented to the left, language-oriented side of one patient's split brain, she could say what the spoon was; but when the spoon was presented to the right side of her brain, she could not describe the spoon in words. She still knew what the object was, however. Using her left hand (controlled by the right hemisphere), she could pick out the spoon from a group of other objects by its shape. But when asked what she had just grasped, she replied, "A pencil." The right hemisphere recognized the object, but the patient could not describe it because the left (language) half of her brain did not see or feel it (Sperry, 1968).

Although the right hemisphere has no control over spoken language in split-brain patients, it does have important capabilities, including some related to nonspoken language. For example, a split-brain patient's right hemisphere can guide the left hand in spelling out words with Scrabble tiles (Gazzaniga & LeDoux, 1978). Thanks to this ability, researchers discovered that the right hemisphere of split-brain patients has

FIGURE 3.20

Apparatus for Studying Split-Brain Patients

When the person stares at the dot on the screen, images briefly presented on one side of the dot go to only one side of the brain. For example, a picture of a spoon presented on the left side of the screen goes to the right side of the brain. Thus the right side of the brain could find the spoon and direct the left hand to touch it; but because the language areas on the left side of the brain did not see it, the person would not be able to identify the spoon verbally.

self-awareness and normal learning abilities. In addition, it is superior to the left on tasks dealing with spatial relations (especially drawing three-dimensional shapes) and at recognizing human faces.

Lateralization of Normal Brains   Sperry concluded from his studies that each hemisphere in the split-brain patient has its own "private sensations, perceptions, thoughts, and ideas all of which are cut off from the corresponding experiences in the opposite hemisphere. . . . In many respects each disconnected hemisphere appears to have a separate mind of its own" (Sperry, 1974). But when the hemispheres are connected normally, are certain functions, such as mathematical reasoning or language skills, lateralized? A **lateralized** task is one that is performed more efficiently by one hemisphere than by the other.

To find out, researchers presented images to just one hemisphere of people with normal brains and then measured how fast they could analyze information. If information is presented to one side of the brain and that side is specialized to analyze that type of information, a person's responses will be faster than if the information must first be transferred to the other hemisphere for analysis. These studies have confirmed that the left hemisphere has better logical and language abilities than the right, whereas the right hemisphere has better spatial, artistic, and musical abilities (Springer & Deutsch, 1989). PET scans of normal people receiving varying kinds of auditory stimulation also demonstrate these asymmetries of function (see Figure 3.21). The language abilities of the left hemisphere are not specifically related to auditory information, since deaf people also use the left hemisphere more than the right for sign language (Hickok, Bellugi, & Klima, 1996).

The precise nature and degree of lateralization vary quite a bit among individuals. For example, in about a third of left-handed people, either the right hemisphere or both hemispheres control language functions (Springer & Deutsch, 1989). In contrast, only about 5 percent of right-handed people have language controlled by the right hemisphere. Evidence about sex differences in brain laterality comes from studies on the cognitive abilities of normal men and women, the effects of brain damage on cognitive function, and anatomical differences between the sexes. Among normal individuals there are sex differences in the ability to perform tasks that are known to be lateralized in the brain. For example, women are better than men at perceptual fluency

FIGURE 3.21

Lateralization of the Cerebral Hemispheres: Evidence from PET Scans

These PET scans show overhead views of a section of a person's brain that was receiving different kinds of stimulation. At the upper left, the person was resting, with eyes open and ears plugged. Note that the greatest brain activity (as indicated by the red color) was in the visual cortex, which was receiving input from the eyes. As shown at the lower left, when the person listened to spoken language, the left (more language-oriented) side of the brain, especially the auditory cortex in the temporal lobe, became more active, but the right temporal lobe did not; the visual and frontal areas were also active. However, when the person listened to music (lower right), there was intense activity in the right temporal lobe but little in the left. When the person heard both words and music, the temporal cortex on both sides of the brain became activated. Here is visual evidence of the involvement of each side of the brain in processing different kinds of information (Phelps & Mazziotta, 1985).

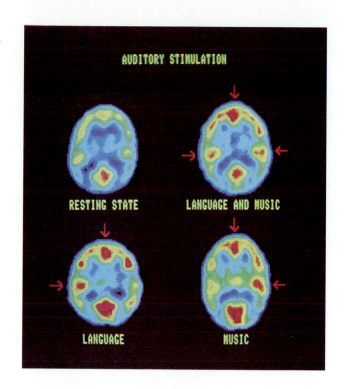

tasks, such as rapidly identifying matching items, and at arithmetic calculations. Men are better at imagining the rotation of an object in space and tasks involving target-directed motor skills, such as guiding projectiles or intercepting them. But as can be seen in any video-game arcade, males tend to practice this type of skill more than females. Perhaps the performance difference would be reduced if practice effects were equated.

Damage to just one side of the brain is more debilitating to men than to women. In particular, men show larger deficits in language ability than women when the left side is damaged (McGlone, 1980). This difference may reflect a wider distribution of language abilities in the brains of women compared with those of men. When participants in one study performed language tasks, such as thinking about whether particular words rhyme, MRI scans showed increased activity on the left side of the brain for men but on both sides for women (Shaywitz et al., 1995; see also Figure 1.4 on page 11). Women reportedly have proportionately more of their association cortex devoted to language tasks (Harasty et al., 1997). Note, however, that although humans and animals show definite sex differences in brain anatomy and metabolism (Allen et al., 1989; Gur et al., 1995), no particular anatomical feature has been identified as underlying sex differences in lateralization. One highly publicized report claimed that the corpus callosum is larger in women than men (de Lacoste–Utamsing & Holloway, 1982), but numerous subsequent investigations have all failed to replicate this finding (Bishop & Wahlsten, 1997). (The original report of a sex difference in the corpus callosum continues to be cited, however, despite overwhelming evidence against it, suggesting that scientists are sometimes not entirely unbiased.)

Having two somewhat specialized hemispheres allows the brain to more efficiently perform some tasks, particularly difficult ones (Hoptman & Davidson, 1994), but the differences between the hemispheres should not be exaggerated. Indeed, the corpus callosum usually integrates the functions of the "two brains." As a result, the hemispheres work so closely together, and each makes up so well for whatever lack of ability the other may have, that people are normally unaware that their brains are made up of two partially independent, somewhat specialized halves (Banich & Heller, 1998).

Plasticity in the Brain

The brain has a remarkable property called synaptic plasticity, which is the ability to strengthen neural connections at synapses as well as to establish new synapses. This property provides the basis for the capacity to learn from experiences and form memories, processes that are described in Chapters 6 and 7. Such plasticity occurs throughout the nervous system; even the simplest reflex in the spinal cord can be modified by experience (Feng-Chen & Wolpaw, 1996). However, the brain's plasticity is severely limited when it comes to repairing damage. So while there are heroic recoveries from brain damage following a stroke, for example, more often the victim is permanently disabled in some way.

Why is it difficult for the brain to repair damage? For one thing, adult animals generally do not produce new neurons. During prenatal development, neurons divide and multiply as other cells do; but as the brain matures, most neurons stop dividing. They grow new axons, but except in very restricted areas they do not produce new cells, even in response to injury (Eriksson et al., 1998). Second, the axons and dendrites of any new neurons would have to reestablish all their former communication links. In the peripheral nervous system, the glial cells form "tunnels" that guide the regrowth of axons. But in the central nervous system, reestablishing communication links is almost impossible, because glial cells actively suppress new connections (Olson, 1997). Nevertheless, the brain does try to heal itself. For example, healthy neurons attempt to take over for damaged ones, partly by changing their own function and partly by sprouting axons whose connections help neighboring regions take on new functions (Cao et al., 1994). Unfortunately, these changes rarely result in total restoration of lost functions. Indeed, it is the brain's inability to replace dead or damaged neurons that underlies the unremitting progression of some diseases of the brain.

Several new methods are being employed to help people recover from brain damage. One approach is to replace lost tissue with tissue from another brain. Scientists have transplanted, or grafted, tissue from a still-developing fetal brain into the brain of an adult animal of the same species. If the receiving animal does not reject it, the graft sends axons out into the brain and makes some functional connections. This treatment has reversed animals' learning difficulties, movement disorders, and other results of brain damage. The technique has also been used to treat a small number of people with *Parkinson's disease*—a disorder characterized by tremors, rigidity of the arms and legs, difficulty in initiating movements, and poor balance (Carlson, 1998). The preliminary results are very encouraging (Kordower et al., 1995). Exciting new work with animals has shown that the effectiveness of brain tissue grafts can be greatly enhanced by adding naturally occurring proteins called growth factors, or *neurotrophic factors,* which promote the survival of neurons (Takayama et al., 1995). One of the most effective of these proteins is Glial-cell Derived Neurotrophic Factor, or GDNF (Henderson et al., 1994). The brain tissue transplant procedure is promising, but because its use with humans requires tissue from aborted fetuses, it has generated considerable controversy. In another twist on this strategy, scientists recently succeeded in transplanting neural cells from a fetal pig into a human with Parkinson's disease (Deacon et al., 1997). Suppression of the patient's immune system was necessary to prevent rejection of the graft, but the graft and the patient survived for seven months—an encouraging result that suggests the feasibility of additional cross-species transplants in the future. Two even more unusual treatments have recently been reported. Russian physicians transplanted neural tissue from fruit flies into the brains of Parkinson's patients, with therapeutic benefits and no reported side effects (Saveliev et al., 1997). And American researchers found that immune-resistant cells taken from testicles have growth-promoting effects on some neurotransmitters, and that cells from the testes transplanted into the brains of rats with Parkinson's disease reduced symptoms of the disease (Sanberg et al., 1997).

In another approach to treating brain diseases and damage, researchers have "engineered" cells from rats to produce *nerve growth factor,* a substance that helps stimulate

A Patient with Parkinson's Disease

Cells from a person's own adrenal gland have been used as an alternative to brain tissue in transplant treatment for Parkinson's disease. Adrenal gland cells act like neurons when placed in the brain, and people can live with just one adrenal gland. In early attempts at this therapy, the benefit was temporary and a significant number of patients died during surgery. More recently, however, adrenal tissue has been mixed with peripheral nerve tissue, and the grafts show more prolonged effectiveness with fewer side effects (Watts et al., 1997).

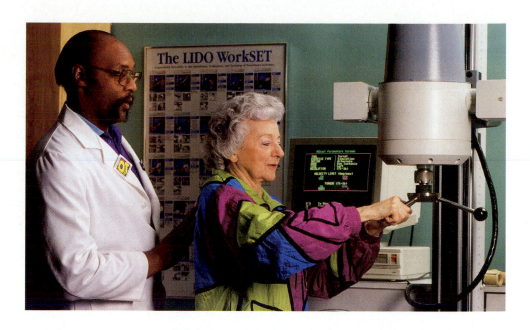

and guide the growth of newly sprouted axons in the central nervous system. When the engineered cells were implanted into the brains of rats with brain damage or disease, the cells secreted nerve growth factor. In many cases, brain damage was reversed, with surviving neurons sprouting axons that grew toward the graft (Rosenberg et al., 1988). Based on these animal studies, nerve growth factor has been infused directly into the brain of a person with Alzheimer's disease (Seiger et al., 1993). The results were encouraging, and trials with other patients are in progress. In addition, studies of nerve growth factor led to the discovery of other growth factors that may provide new avenues for treatment. Interestingly, physical exercise increases concentrations of brain growth factor in rats (Neeper et al., 1995). Although evidence for the same effect in humans has not yet been found, research suggests that older people who exercise regularly are more mentally alert than those who live sedentary lives (Hassmen & Koivula, 1997).

Yet another prospect for reversing brain damage was originally suggested by studies of bird brains (Nottebohm, 1985). Each year, the male canary learns new songs, then forgets many of them at the end of the breeding season. This phenomenon appears to be related to the fact that as the days get shorter, neurons die in a part of his brain related to the learning of songs (Kirn & Schwabl, 1997); then, when spring comes, the same brain region grows by neuronal cell division. If scientists could discover what is different about this part of the bird brain, perhaps the same processes could be generated in the human brain, allowing it to heal itself by producing new neurons. Some progress has already been made in discovering factors that might allow the birth of new neurons in adult mammals. For example, cells were taken from the brains of mice and maintained in a dish with nutrients and oxygen. When the cells were treated with a growth factor known as *epidermal growth factor (EGF)*, some of them divided and produced new neurons and glial cells (Reynolds & Weiss, 1992). In fact, researchers have also stimulated *human* fetal brain cells with EGF and then implanted them into the brains of rats, where the cells developed into both new neurons and glial cells (Svendsen et al., 1997). Additional encouraging evidence comes from research showing that, in rodents and monkeys and even humans, small parts of the hippocampus continue to generate new neurons in adulthood, and that their formation is partly controlled by stress hormones (Eriksson et al., 1998; Gould et al., 1998) and by an enriched environment (Kempermann, Kuhn, & Gage, 1997). The source of these new neurons has recently been identified as "stem cells," which reside in the lining of the ventricles of the brain (Johansson et al., 1999). The discovery of these stem cells, which have the potential to develop into many types of cells, including neurons, creates the exciting possibility that degenerative disorders such as Alzheimer's disease and Parkinson's disease may eventually be cured by actually replacing dying neurons with new neurons.

Immature Movement

The broad, sweeping motion of young babies' limbs is partly related to immaturity in parts of the brain that control movement. As those regions mature over time, this child's movements will become more coordinated.

LINKAGES

Human Development and the Changing Brain

Fortunately, most of the changes that take place in the brain throughout life are not the kind that produce Parkinson's disease and Alzheimer's disease. What are these changes, and what are their effects? How are they related to the developments in sensory and motor capabilities, mental abilities, and other characteristics described in Chapter 12, on human development?

Classical anatomical studies—and, more recently, PET scans and functional MRI scans—are beginning to answer these questions. They have uncovered some interesting correlations between changes in neural activity and the behavior of human newborns and young infants. Among newborns, activity is relatively high in the thalamus but low in the striatum. This pattern may be related to the way newborns move: They make nonpurposeful, sweeping movements of the arms and legs, much like adults who have a hyperactive thalamus and a degenerated striatum (Chugani & Phelps, 1986). During the second and third months of life, activity increases in many regions of the cortex, a change that is correlated with the loss of subcortically controlled reflexes such as the grasping reflex. When infants are around eight or nine months old, activity in the frontal cortex increases, a development that correlates well with the apparent beginnings of cognitive activity in infants (Chugani & Phelps, 1986).

LINKAGES

How do our brains change as we get older? (a link to Human Development)

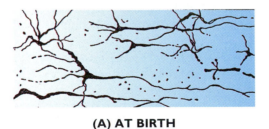

(A) AT BIRTH

(B) SIX YEARS OLD

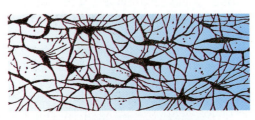

(C) FOURTEEN YEARS OLD

FIGURE 3.22

Changes in Neurons of the Cerebral Cortex During Development

During childhood, the brain overproduces neural connections, establishes the usefulness of certain connections, and then "prunes" the extra connections (Cowan, 1979). Overproduction of synapses, especially in the frontal cortex, may be essential for infants to develop certain intellectual abilities (Goldman-Rakic, 1987). Some scientists believe that the pruning of connections may reflect a process whereby those connections that are used survive, whereas others die.

Source: Reprinted by permission of the publisher from *The Postnatal Development of the Human Cerebral Cortex,* Vol. I–VIII by Jesse LeRoy Conel, Cambridge, Mass.: Harvard University Press, Copyright © 1939–1975 by the President and Fellows of Harvard College.

in review

ORGANIZATION OF THE BRAIN

Major Division	Some Important Structures	Some Major Functions
Hindbrain	Medulla	Regulation of breathing, heart rate, and blood pressure
	Reticular formation (also extends into midbrain)	Regulation of arousal and attention
	Cerebellum	Control of finely coordinated movements
Midbrain	Various nuclei	Relay of sensory signals to forebrain; creation of automatic responses to certain stimuli
	Substantia nigra	Smooth initiation of movement
Forebrain	Hypothalamus	Regulation of hunger, thirst, and sex drives
	Thalamus	Interpretation and relaying of sensory information
	Hippocampus	Formation of new memories
	Amygdala	Connection of sensations and emotions
	Cerebral cortex	Analysis of sensory information; control over voluntary movements, abstract thinking, and other complex cognitive activity
	Corpus callosum	Transfer of information between the two cerebral hemispheres

These changes reflect brain plasticity, not the appearance of new cells. After birth, the number of dendrites and synapses increases. In one area of the cortex, the number of synapses increases tenfold from birth to twelve months of age (Huttenlocher, 1990). Moreover, the number of synapses in cortical regions devoted to hearing peaks earlier than the number of synapses in areas involved in more complex mental processes (Huttenlocher & Dabholkar, 1997). Surprisingly, by the time children are six or seven years old, their brains have more dendrites and use twice as much metabolic fuel as those of adults (Chugani & Phelps, 1986). In early adolescence, the number of dendrites and neural connections actually drops, so that the adult level is reached by about the age of fourteen (see Figure 3.22). MRI scans show an actual loss of gray-matter volume in the cortex throughout the adolescent years (Jernigan et al., 1991).

Even as dendrites are reduced, the brain retains its plasticity and "rewires" itself to form new connections throughout life. Our genes apparently determine the basic pattern of growth and the major lines of connections, the "highways" of the brain and its general architecture. (For a summary of this architecture, see "In Review: Organization of the Brain.") But the details of the connections depend on experience, including such factors as how complex and interesting the environment is. For example, researchers have compared the brains of rats raised alone with only a boring view of the side of their cages to the brains of rats raised with interesting toys and stimulating playmates. The cerebral cortex of those from the enriched environment had more and longer dendrites as well as more synapses than the cortex of animals from barren, individual housing (Turner & Greenough, 1985). Furthermore, the number of cortical synapses increased when isolated animals were moved to an enriched environment (Green, Greenough, & Schlumpf, 1983). To the extent that these ideas and research findings apply to humans, they hold obvious implications for how people raise children and treat the elderly.

In any event, this line of research highlights the interaction of environmental and genetic factors. Some overproduced synapses may reflect genetically directed preparation for certain types of experiences. Generation of these synapses is an "experience expectant" process, and it accounts for sensitive periods during development when certain things can be most easily learned. But overproduction of synapses also occurs in response to totally new experiences; this process is "experience dependent" (Greenough, Black, & Wallace, 1987). Within constraints set by genetics, interactions with the world mold the brain itself.

THE CHEMISTRY OF PSYCHOLOGY

So far, we have described how the cells of the nervous system communicate by releasing neurotransmitters at their synapses, and we have outlined some of the basic structures of the nervous system and their functions. Let's now pull these topics together by considering two questions about neurotransmitters and the nervous system. First, which neurotransmitters occur in which structures? As noted earlier, different sets of neurons use different neurotransmitters; a group of neurons that communicates using the same neurotransmitter is called a **neurotransmitter system.** Second, how do neurotransmitter systems affect behavior? It appears that certain neurotransmitter systems play a dominant role in particular functions, such as emotion or memory, and in particular problems, such as Alzheimer's disease. Our discussion will also reveal that drugs affect behavior and mental processes by altering these systems. Details about how these *psychoactive drugs* work are presented later in the book, when we discuss drugs of abuse—such as cocaine and heroin (see Chapter 9)—and drugs used in treating mental disorders (see Chapter 16).

Chemical neurotransmission was first demonstrated, in frogs, by Otto Loewi in 1921. Since then, about 100 different neurotransmitters have been identified. Some of the chemicals that act on receptors at synapses have been called *neuromodulators,* because they act slowly and often modify or "modulate" a cell's response to other neurotransmitters. The distinction between "neurotransmitter" and "neuromodulator" is not always clear, however. Depending on the type of receptor it acts on at a given synapse, the same substance can function as either a neuromodulator or a neurotransmitter. A more radical modification of the concept of neurotransmitter occurred following the discovery that nitric oxide—a toxic gas and a major constituent of air pollution—is also a neurotransmitter (Dawson & Dawson, 1995). When nitric oxide is released by neurons, it diffuses to other neurons nearby and sends a signal that acts on chemical reactions *inside* those neurons rather than on receptors on the surface of the neurons. Nitric oxide appears to be one of the neurotransmitters responsible for such diverse functions as penile erection and the formation of memories—not at the same site, obviously.

Seven Major Neurotransmitters

The following sections describe seven of the most important neurotransmitters: acetylcholine, norepinephrine, serotonin, dopamine, GABA, glutamate, and endorphins. Usually the suffix *-ergic* is added to the name of a neurotransmitter to make the word an adjective. Thus, a group of neurons using dopamine as a neurotransmitter is called a *dopaminergic system* and a group using acetylcholine is termed *cholinergic.*

Acetylcholine   The first compound to be identified as a neurotransmitter was **acetylcholine** (pronounced "a-see-tull-KO-leen"), which is used by neurons in both the peripheral and the central nervous systems. In the peripheral nervous system, cholinergic neurons control the contraction of muscles by releasing acetylcholine onto muscle tissues. It is also the neurotransmitter used by neurons of the parasympathetic nervous system to slow the heartbeat and activate the gastrointestinal system. In the brain, cholinergic neurons are especially plentiful in the striatum, where they occur in circuits that are important for movement (see Figure 3.23). Axons of cholinergic neurons also make up major pathways in the limbic system, including the hippocampus, and in other areas of the cerebrum that are involved in memory (Jerusalinsky, Kornisiuk, & Izquierdo, 1997). Drugs that interfere with acetylcholine prevent the formation of new memories. In Alzheimer's disease, there is a nearly complete loss of cholinergic neurons in a nucleus in the forebrain that sends fibers to the cerebral cortex and hippocampus—a nucleus that normally enhances plasticity in these regions (Kilgard & Merzenich, 1998).

Norepinephrine   Neurons that use **norepinephrine** (pronounced "nor-eppa-NEF-rin") are called *adrenergic*, because norepinephrine is also called *noradrenaline.* Like acetylcholine, norepinephrine occurs in both the central and the peripheral nervous systems; in both places, it contributes to arousal. Noradrenaline (and its close relative, adrenaline) are the neurotransmitters used by the sympathetic nervous system to activate you and prepare you for action. Approximately half of the norepinephrine in the entire brain is contained in cells of the locus coeruleus, which is near the reticular formation in the hindbrain (see Figure 3.23). Because adrenergic systems cover a lot of territory, it is logical that norepinephrine affects several broad categories of behavior. Indeed, norepinephrine is involved in the appearance of wakefulness and sleep, in learning, and in the regulation of mood.

Serotonin   The neurotransmitter **serotonin** is similar to norepinephrine in several ways. First, most of the cells that use it as a neurotransmitter occur in an area along the midline of the hindbrain; the region for serotonin is the *raphe nuclei* (see Figure 3.23). Second, serotonergic axons send branches throughout the forebrain, including the hypothalamus, the hippocampus, and the cerebral cortex. Third, serotonin affects sleep and mood.

Serotonin differs from norepinephrine, however, in that the brain can get one of the substances from which it is made, *tryptophan,* directly from food. As a result, what you eat can affect the amount of serotonin in your brain. Carbohydrates increase the amount of tryptophan getting into the brain and therefore affect how much serotonin is made; so a meal high in carbohydrates produces increased levels of serotonin. Serotonin, in turn, normally causes a reduction in the desire for carbohydrates. Some researchers suspect that malfunctions in the serotonin feedback system are responsible for the disturbances of mood and appetite seen in certain types of obesity, premenstrual tension, and depression (Wurtman & Wurtman, 1995). Serotonin has also been implicated in aggression and impulse control. One of the most consistently observed relationships between a particular neurotransmitter system and a particular behavior

FIGURE 3.23

Examples of Neurotransmitter Pathways

Neurons that release a certain neurotransmitter may be concentrated in one particular region (indicated by dots) and send fibers into other regions, to which they communicate across synapses (see arrows). Four examples are shown here.

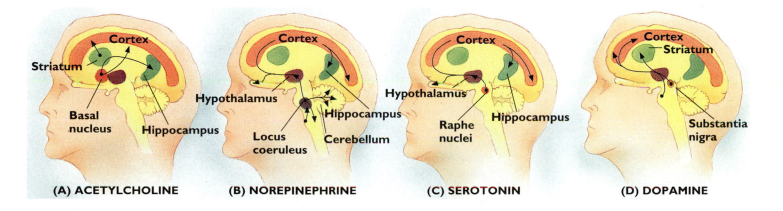

(A) ACETYLCHOLINE   (B) NOREPINEPHRINE   (C) SEROTONIN   (D) DOPAMINE

is the low level of serotonin metabolites in the brains of suicide victims, who tend to show a combination of depressed mood, self-directed aggression, and impulsivity (Mann, 1998).

Dopamine   Figure 3.23 shows that **dopamine** is the neurotransmitter used in the substantia nigra and striatum, which are important for movement. Indeed, malfunctioning of the dopamine system in these regions contributes to movement disorders, including Parkinson's disease. As dopamine cells in the substantia nigra degenerate, Parkinson's disease victims experience severe shakiness and difficulty at initiating movement. Parkinson's is most common in elderly people, and available evidence suggests that it results from sensitivity to an as yet unidentified environmental factor or toxin (Ben-Shlomo, 1997). Parkinson's has been treated, with partial success, using drugs that enable neurons to make more dopamine, or that stimulate dopamine receptors (Chase, 1998).

Other dopaminergic systems send axons from the midbrain to the forebrain, including the cerebral cortex. Some of these neurons are important in the experience of reward, or pleasure, which is vital in shaping and motivating behavior (Wise & Rompre, 1989). Animals will work intensively to receive a direct infusion of dopamine into the forebrain. These dopaminergic systems play a role in the rewarding properties of many drugs, including cocaine (Bardo, 1998). Malfunctioning of other dopaminergic neurons that go to the cortex may be partly responsible for *schizophrenia,* a psychological disorder in which perception, emotional expression, and thought are severely distorted (Egan & Weinberger, 1997).

GABA   Neurons in widespread regions of the brain use **GABA,** which stands for "gamma-amino butyric acid." GABA reduces the likelihood that postsynaptic neurons will fire an action potential; in fact, it is the major inhibitory neurotransmitter in the central nervous system. When you fall asleep, neurons that use GABA deserve part of the credit.

Malfunctioning of GABA systems has been implicated in a variety of disorders, including severe anxiety and *Huntington's disease,* an inherited and incurable disorder in which the victim is plagued by uncontrollable jerky movement of the arms and legs, along with dementia. Huntington's disease results in the loss of many GABA-containing neurons in the striatum. Normally these GABA systems inhibit dopamine systems; so when they are lost through Huntington's disease, the dopamine systems may run wild, impairing many motor and cognitive functions.

Because drugs that block GABA receptors produce intense repetitive electrical discharges, known as *seizures,* researchers suspect that malfunctioning GABA systems probably contribute to *epilepsy,* a brain disorder associated with seizures and convulsive movements. Repeated or sustained seizures can result in permanent brain damage; drug treatments can reduce their frequency and severity, but completely effective drugs are not yet available.

Glutamate   The major excitatory neurotransmitter in the central nervous system is **glutamate.** Glutamate is used by more neurons than any other neurotransmitter; its synapses are especially plentiful in the cerebral cortex and the hippocampus.

Glutamate is particularly important because it plays a major role in the ability of the brain to "strengthen" its synaptic connections—that is, to allow messages to cross the synapse more efficiently. This process is necessary for normal development and may be at the root of learning and memory (Kaczmarek, Kossut, & Skangiel-Kramska, 1997). At the same time, overactivity of glutamate synapses can cause neurons to die. In fact, this overactivity is the main cause of the brain damage that occurs when oxygen is cut off from neurons during a stroke. Glutamate can "excite neurons to death," so blocking glutamate receptors immediately after a brain trauma can prevent permanent brain damage (Bittigau & Ikonomidou, 1997). Glutamate may also contribute to the loss of cells from the hippocampus that occurs in Alzheimer's disease (Olney, Wozniak, & Farber, 1997).

in review

MAJOR NEUROTRANSMITTERS

Neurotransmitter	Normal Function	Disorder Associated with Malfunctioning Neurotransmitter Systems
Acetylcholine	Movement, memory	Alzheimer's disease
Norepinephrine	Sleep, learning, mood	Depression
Serotonin	Mood, appetite, aggression	Depression
Dopamine	Movement, reward	Parkinson's disease, schizophrenia
GABA	Movement	Huntington's disease, epilepsy
Glutamate	Memory	Neuron loss after stroke
Endorphins	Modulation of pain	No established disorder

Endorphins   One family of neurotransmitters was discovered in the 1970s by scientists who were interested in *opiates,* which are substances derived from poppy flowers. Opiates such as morphine and heroin can relieve pain, produce euphoria, and, in high doses, bring on sleep. After marking morphine with a radioactive substance, researchers traced where it became concentrated in the brain. They found that opiates bind to receptors that were not associated with any known neurotransmitter. Since it was unlikely that the brain had developed opiate receptors just in case a person might want to use morphine or heroin, researchers reasoned that the body must contain a substance similar to opiates. This hypothesis led to the search for a naturally occurring, or endogenous, morphine, which was called *endorphin,* a contraction of "endogenous morphine." As it turned out, there are many natural opiate-like compounds. Thus, the term **endorphin** refers to any neurotransmitter that can bind to the same receptors stimulated by opiates. Neurons in several parts of the brain use endorphins, including pathways that modify pain signals to the brain. (For a summary of the main neurotransmitters and the consequences of malfunctioning neurotransmitter systems, see "In Review: Major Neurotransmitters.")

THINKING CRITICALLY

Are There Drugs That Can Make You Smarter?

Neurotransmitter systems provide humans with all sorts of remarkable capabilities. It is hard not to be impressed by how effectively and efficiently these systems work to affect behavior and mental processes. And it is hard not to be concerned by the severe disorders that occur when the major neurotransmitter systems malfunction, as is the case with Alzheimer's disease. A wide variety of drugs have been developed in an effort to correct such malfunctions. Some people believe that drugs like these might also improve the functioning of neurotransmitters in normal individuals. Advertisements and articles in many health magazines and on literally tens of thousands of websites describe an incredible array of "smart drugs" and dietary supplements. (The drugs are called *nootropics*—from *noos,* which is Greek for "mind.") It is claimed that these substances will improve mental sharpness and reduce or slow the effects of degenerative brain diseases. Belief in the value of nootropics is not confined to health-food fanatics; many respected scientists agree with some of the less extreme claims about some of these substances. Although the use of "smart drugs" is still not common in the United States, it is increasing; and in some countries (India, for example), it is already substantial (Geary, 1997). Are "smart drugs" really effective, or are they modern-day snake oil, giving no more than the illusion of a sharpened mind?

■ What am I being asked to believe or accept?

Proponents of "smart drugs" and dietary supplements claim that these substances can enhance memory and reverse the effects of degenerative brain diseases. This notion was popularized in a 1990 book by John Morgenthaler and Ward Dean, *Smart Drugs and Nutrients.* In an interview that year, Morgenthaler said he had been taking "smart drugs" for ten years, about eight pills twice a day. "It's not a scientific study; I may have gotten smarter just from growing up, educating myself and stimulating my brain. But I do stop taking the drugs every now and then, and I know that I have better concentration, attention and memory when I'm on them" (Greenwald, 1991).

■ What evidence is available to support the assertion?

There is certainly an element of truth to the idea that some of these drugs can improve cognitive performance under some circumstances. Animals given the drugs under controlled conditions show statistically significant improvements in performance on tasks requiring attention and memory. The chemicals used in these drugs include piracetam, extracts from the herb known as ginkgo biloba, and vasopressin. The drugs not only affect behavior but also have measurable biochemical effects on the brain. Some have general effects on brain metabolism and also increase blood sugar levels; others affect specific neurotransmitters such as acetylcholine, glutamate, serotonin, and dopamine (Pepeu, 1994).

Do "smart drugs" work with humans? One review of the scientific literature on the effects of nootropics in elderly humans describes improvement in cognitive functioning associated with forty-five different medications (van Reekum et al., 1997). In other words, you can probably find a study supporting the effectiveness of virtually any nootropic drug.

■ Are there alternative ways of interpreting the evidence?

One alternative explanation of the effects of nootropics is that they represent *placebo effects.* As noted in Chapter 2, placebo effects occur when a person's beliefs about a drug rather than the drug itself are responsible for any changes that occur. In their book on "smart drugs," Dean and Morgenthaler (1990) acknowledge the possibility that placebo effects may be responsible for many of the glowing testimonials about smart drugs; but then they themselves present such testimonials to help readers decide which substances to take, and they encourage readers to send in their own accounts of the benefits they have derived from a particular food or dietary supplement. This is hardly the kind of objective, empirical evidence that psychologists seek when evaluating theories and treatments.

Steven Rose (1993) suggests other serious flaws in many of the experiments that apparently show the benefits of nootropic drugs. Specifically, some researchers used only small numbers of participants in their studies, and others failed to test whether positive findings could be reproduced in their own or other researchers' laboratories. Studies that have examined whether the effects of "smart drugs" can be reproduced have yielded mixed results. For example, some experimenters have reported positive effects of ginkgo biloba while others—using exactly the same dosages and memory tasks—have not (Warot et al., 1991).

A third concern is that the effects of "smart drugs" are simply not very substantial. For example, the first drug (*tacrine*) approved by the United States Food and Drug Administration for the treatment of Alzheimer-related memory problems has repeatedly been shown to "significantly" improve memory, but the actual improvement is always minor. (This drug also poses a major risk of potentially fatal liver damage.) Other nootropic drugs that have positive effects on memory primarily affect attentiveness; they are no more effective than a cup of coffee (Service, 1994). Overall, the evidence from properly designed studies shows nootropic drugs to be a major disappointment (Riedel & Jolles, 1996).

■ What additional evidence would help to evaluate the alternatives?

Researchers are evaluating several promising new categories of nootropic drugs in animals (Staubli, Izrael, & Xu, 1996). However, it will take years of study to determine which drugs are truly effective for memory enhancement, and under what circumstances. It will also take time to learn whether the results with animals are applicable to humans. Research with humans will require carefully controlled double-blind studies that eliminate the effects of participants' and investigators' expectancies so that the direct effects of the drugs or other treatments can be separated from placebo effects. One critical question to be addressed in such research is whether drugs that can reduce the memory loss associated with Alzheimer's disease will also improve the memories of normal, healthy people and vice versa. And of course we still need to determine how these drugs work, what their potential side effects are, and whether they affect memory alone or also related processes such as motivation or attention.

■ What conclusions are most reasonable?

The scientific community is somewhat divided regarding the present benefits and the long-term potential of nootropic drugs (Geary, 1997). It is much too soon to hail them as the long-sought cure for all sorts of problems in cognitive functioning, but also too soon to write them off as a pseudoscientific fad. Moreover, although the drugs currently available for improving memory are limited in effectiveness, proponents argue that even if such drugs only delay the institutionalization of Alzheimer's patients for several months, the savings to society are substantial. Accordingly, researchers continue to investigate new drugs such as aricept, which acts on neurotransmitters, does not cause liver damage, and may have positive effects on memory in elderly persons (Barner & Gray, 1998). Overall, however, the scientific jury is still deliberating on the value of nootropic drugs.

The same "wait and see" attitude is *not* justified with respect to the herbs, potions, and drinks that are supposed to make you smarter. You can buy them in health food stores and "smart bars," but be sure they taste good, because their effect on mental powers is minimal. Indeed, the memory strategies described in Chapter 7 are likely to be far more effective in helping you remember information and do well in school. Your cognitive functioning is also more likely to be influenced by your environment and life experiences. For example, educational achievement, and a life of working at a job that engages the mind, has been associated with a lowered risk for Alzheimer's disease (Evans et al., 1997), perhaps because education and other factors that increase cerebral blood flow reduce the risk of this disorder (Crawford, 1998).

THE ENDOCRINE SYSTEM: COORDINATING THE INTERNAL WORLD

As noted earlier, neurons are not the only cells that can use chemicals to communicate with one another in ways that affect behavior and mental processes. Another class of cells with this ability resides in the **endocrine system,** which regulates functions

FIGURE 3.24

Some Major Glands of the Endocrine System

Each of the glands shown releases its hormones into the bloodstream. Even the hypothalamus, a part of the brain, regulates the adjacent pituitary gland by secreting hormones.

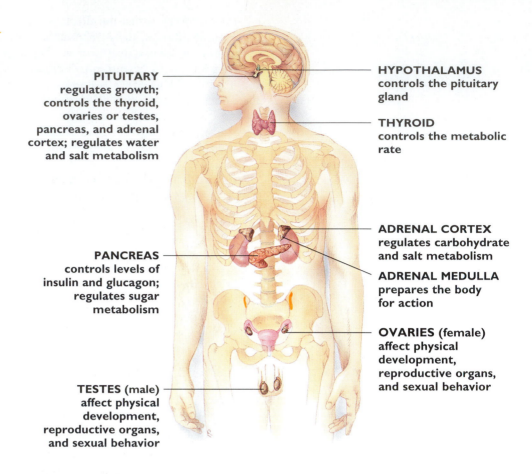

PITUITARY regulates growth; controls the thyroid, ovaries or testes, pancreas, and adrenal cortex; regulates water and salt metabolism

HYPOTHALAMUS controls the pituitary gland

THYROID controls the metabolic rate

ADRENAL CORTEX regulates carbohydrate and salt metabolism

PANCREAS controls levels of insulin and glucagon; regulates sugar metabolism

ADRENAL MEDULLA prepares the body for action

OVARIES (female) affect physical development, reproductive organs, and sexual behavior

TESTES (male) affect physical development, reproductive organs, and sexual behavior

ranging from stress responses to physical growth. The cells of endocrine organs, or **glands,** communicate by secreting chemicals, much as neurons do. In the case of endocrine organs, the chemicals are called **hormones.** Figure 3.24 shows the location and functions of some of the major endocrine glands.

Hormones from the endocrine organs are similar to neurotransmitters. In fact, many such chemicals, including norepinephrine and the endorphins, act both as hormones and as neurotransmitters. However, whereas neurons secrete neurotransmitters into synapses, endocrine organs put their chemicals into the bloodstream, which carries them throughout the body. In this way, endocrine glands can stimulate cells with which they have no direct connection. But not all cells receive the hormonal message. Hormones, like neurotransmitters, can influence only those cells with receptors capable of receiving them (McEwen, 1994). Organs whose cells have receptors for a hormone are called *target organs.*

Each hormone acts on many target organs, producing coordinated effects throughout the body. For example, when the sex hormone *estrogen* is secreted by a woman's ovaries, it activates her reproductive system. It causes the uterus to grow in preparation for nurturing an embryo; it enlarges the breasts to prepare them for nursing; it stimulates the brain to enhance interest in sexual activity; and it stimulates the pituitary gland to release another hormone that causes a mature egg to be released by the ovary for fertilization.

The brain has ultimate control over the secretion of hormones. Through the hypothalamus, it controls the pituitary gland, which in turn controls endocrine organs in the body. The brain is also one of the target organs for most endocrine secretions. Thus, the endocrine system typically involves four elements: the brain, the pituitary gland, the endocrine organ, and the target organs, which include the brain. Each element in the system uses hormones to signal the next element, and the secretion of each hormone is stimulated or suppressed by other hormones.

For example, in stress-hormone systems, the brain controls the pituitary gland by signaling the hypothalamus to release hormones that stimulate receptors of the pituitary gland, which secretes another hormone, which stimulates another endocrine gland to secrete its hormones. Specifically, when the brain interprets a situation as threatening, the pituitary releases the hormone *ACTH,* which causes the adrenal glands to release the hormone *cortisol* into the bloodstream. These hormones, in turn, act on cells throughout the body. The combined effects of the adrenal hormones and the activation of the sympathetic system result in a set of responses called the **fight-or-flight syndrome,** which, as mentioned earlier, prepares the animal or person for action in response to danger or other stress. The heart beats faster, the liver releases glucose into the bloodstream, fuels are mobilized from fat stores, and the organism usually enters a state of high arousal.

However, the hormones also provide feedback to the brain as well as to the pituitary gland. Just as a thermostat and furnace regulate heat, this feedback system regulates hormone secretion so as to keep it within a certain range. If a hormone rises above a certain level, feedback about this situation signals the brain and pituitary to stop stimulating its secretion. Thus, after the immediate threat is over, feedback about cortisol's action in the brain and in the pituitary terminates the secretion of ACTH and, in turn, cortisol. Because the feedback suppresses further action, this arrangement is called a **negative feedback system.**

As an additional example of the effect of hormones, consider another class of sex hormones, the *androgens.* Pituitary hormones cause the male sex organs to secrete androgens such as testosterone, stimulate the maturation of sperm, increase a male's motivation for sexual activity, and increase his aggressiveness (Rubinow & Schmidt, 1996). The relationship between androgens and aggressiveness in humans is complicated and controversial; we discuss it further in Chapter 18.

Can differences between hormones in men and women account for some of the differences between the sexes? During development and in adulthood, sex differences in hormones are relative rather than absolute: Both men and women have androgens and estrogens, but men have relatively higher concentrations of androgens whereas women have relatively higher concentrations of estrogens. There is plenty of evidence from animal studies that the presence of higher concentrations of androgens in males during development creates both structural sex differences in the brain and sex differences in adult behaviors. Humans, too, may be similarly affected by hormones early in development. For example, studies of girls who were exposed to high levels of androgens before birth found that they were later more aggressive than their sisters who had not

Hormones at Work

The appearance of a threat activates a pattern of hormonal secretions and other physiological responses that prepare animals and humans to either confront or flee the danger. This pattern is known as the "fight-or-flight syndrome."

had such exposure (Berenbaum & Resnick, 1997). And, as shown in Figure 1.4 on page 11, MRI studies have revealed specific regions of the brain that function differently in men and women. However, such sex differences may not be simple, inevitable, or due to the actions of hormones alone. For example, just the act of practicing finger-tapping for ten minutes a day over several weeks can create alterations in the activity of the motor cortex that are detectable with functional MRI (Karni et al., 1998). Most likely, the sex differences we see in behavior depend not only on hormones but also on complex interactions of biological and social forces, as described in the chapter on motivation and emotion.

THE IMMUNE SYSTEM: LINKING THE BRAIN AND THE BODY'S DEFENSE SYSTEM

Like the nervous system and endocrine system, the **immune system** serves as both a sensory system and a surveillance system. It monitors the internal state of the body and detects unwanted cells and toxic substances that may invade the body. It recognizes and remembers foreign substances, and engulfs and destroys foreign cells as well as cancer cells. Individuals whose immune system is underresponsive—AIDS patients, for example—face certain death from invading bacteria or malignant tumors. However, if

FIGURE 3.25

Relations Among the Nervous System, Endocrine System, and Immune System

All three systems interact and influence one another. The nervous system affects the endocrine system by controlling secretion of hormones via the pituitary gland. It also affects the immune system via the autonomic nervous system's action on the thymus gland. The thymus, spleen, and bone marrow are sites of generation and development of immune cells. Hormones of the pituitary gland and adrenal gland modulate immune cells. Immune cells secrete cytokines and antibodies to fight foreign invaders; cytokines are blood-borne messengers that regulate development of immune cells and also influence the central nervous system.

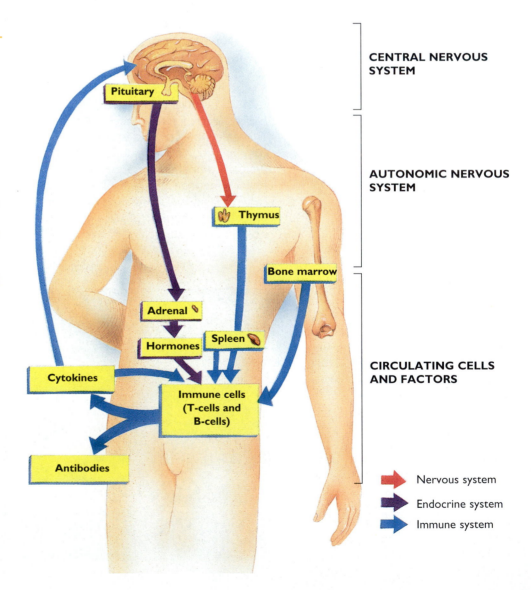

The Common Cold

The interaction of the immune system and the nervous system is exemplified by some of the symptoms associated with routine "sickness." Sleepiness, nausea, and fever are actually a result of chemicals released by immune cells, collectively called *cytokines,* which act directly on the brain through specific receptors (Pousset, 1994).

the system becomes overzealous, the results can be just as devastating: Many diseases, including arthritis and cancer, are now recognized as **autoimmune disorders,** in which cells of the immune system attack normal cells of the body, including brain cells.

The immune system is perhaps as complex as the nervous system, and it contains as many cells as the brain. Some of these cells are in identifiable organs such as the thymus and spleen, whereas others circulate in the bloodstream and enter tissues throughout the body (see Figure 3.25). In Chapter 13, on health, stress, and coping, we describe a few of the immune system's many cell types and how they work.

The nervous system and the immune system were once thought of as completely separate (Ader, Felten, & Cohen, 1990). However, five lines of evidence suggest important interactions between the two.

First, stress can alter the outcome of disease in animals, and, as discussed in Chapter 13, there is growing evidence that psychological stressors also affect disease processes in humans (McEwen, 1998). Second, immune responses can be "taught" using some of the principles of learning outlined in Chapter 6. In one study with humans, for example, exposure to the taste of sherbet was repeatedly associated with an injection of epinephrine, which increases immune system activity. Subsequently, an increase in immune system activity could be prompted by the taste of sherbet alone (Buske-Kirschbaum et al., 1994). Third, animal studies have shown that stimulating or damaging specific parts of the hypothalamus, the cortex, or the brainstem that control the autonomic nervous system can enhance or impair immune functions (Felten et al., 1998). Fourth, activation of the immune system can produce changes in the electrical activity of the brain, in neurotransmitter activity, in hormonal secretion, and in behavior—including "sickness behavior" (Elmquist, Scammell, & Saper, 1997). Finally, immune cells produce some of the same substances as those used by the brain as neurotransmitters and by the endocrine system as hormones (Weigent & Blalock, 1997). These include endorphins, which are the body's natural painkillers, and ACTH, the hormone that stimulates the adrenal gland to produce glucocorticoids during stress.

These converging lines of evidence point to important relationships that illustrate the intertwining of biological and psychological functions, the interaction of body and mind. They highlight the ways in which the immune system, nervous system, and endocrine system—all systems of communication between and among cells—are integrated to form the biological basis for a smoothly functioning self that is filled with interacting thoughts, emotions, and memories and is capable of responding to life's challenges and opportunities with purposeful and adaptive behavior.

LINKAGES

As noted in Chapter 1, all of psychology's many subfields are related to one another. Our discussion of developmental changes in the brain illustrates just one way in which the topic of this chapter, biological aspects of psychology, is linked to the subfield of developmental psychology (Chapter 12). The Linkages diagram shows ties to two other subfields as well, and there are many more ties throughout the book. Looking for linkages among subfields will help you see how they all fit together and better appreciate the big picture that is psychology.

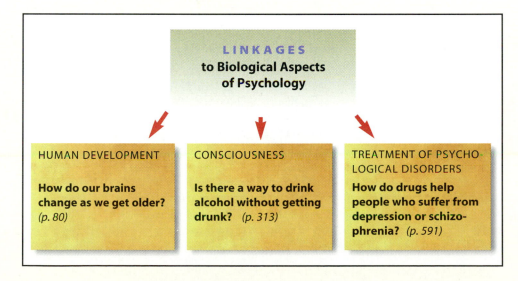

LINKAGES
to Biological Aspects
of Psychology

HUMAN DEVELOPMENT	CONSCIOUSNESS	TREATMENT OF PSYCHOLOGICAL DISORDERS
How do our brains change as we get older? (p. 80)	**Is there a way to drink alcohol without getting drunk?** (p. 313)	**How do drugs help people who suffer from depression or schizophrenia?** (p. 591)

SUMMARY

Biological psychology focuses on the biological aspects of our being, including the nervous system, which provide the physical basis for behavior and mental processes. The *nervous system* is a system of cells that allows an organism to gain information about what is going on inside and outside the body and to respond appropriately.

THE NERVOUS SYSTEM

Much of our understanding of the biological aspects of psychology has stemmed from research on animal and human nervous systems at levels ranging from single cells to complex organizations of cells.

Cells of the Nervous System

The fundamental units of the nervous system are cells called *neurons* and *glial cells.* Neurons are especially good at receiving signals from, and transmitting signals to, other neurons. Neurons have cell bodies and two types of fibers, called *axons* and *dendrites.* Axons usually carry signals away from the cell body, whereas dendrites usually carry signals to the cell body. Neurons can transmit signals because of the structure of these fibers, the excitable surface of some of the fibers, and the *synapses,* or gaps, between cells.

Action Potentials

The selectively permeable membrane of neurons normally keeps the distribution of electrochemically charged molecules, or *ions,* uneven between the inside of cells and the outside, creating an electrochemical force called a potential. The membrane surface of the axon can transmit a disturbance in this potential, called an *action potential,* from one end of the axon to the other. The speed of the action potential is fastest in neurons sheathed in *myelin.* Between firings there is a very brief rest, called a *refractory period.*

Synapses and Communication Between Neurons

When an action potential reaches the end of an axon, the axon releases a chemical called a *neurotransmitter.* It crosses the synapse and interacts with the postsynaptic cell at special sites called *receptors,* creating either an *excitatory* or an *inhibitory postsynaptic potential* that makes the postsynaptic cell more likely or less likely to fire an action potential. Thus, whereas communication within a neuron is electrochemical, communication between neurons is chemical. Because the fibers of neurons have many branches, each neuron can interact with thousands of other neurons. Each neuron constantly integrates signals received at its many synapses; the result of this integration determines how often the neuron fires an action potential.

Organization and Functions of the Nervous System

Neurons are organized in *neural networks* of closely connected cells. *Sensory systems* receive information from the environment, and *motor systems* influence the actions of muscles and other organs. The two major divisions of the nervous system are the *peripheral nervous system (PNS)* and the *central nervous system (CNS),* which includes the brain and spinal cord.

THE PERIPHERAL NERVOUS SYSTEM: KEEPING IN TOUCH WITH THE WORLD

The peripheral nervous system has two components.

The Somatic Nervous System

The first is the *somatic nervous system,* which transmits information from the senses to the CNS and carries signals from the CNS to the muscles that move the skeleton.

The Autonomic Nervous System

The second is the *autonomic nervous system;* it carries messages back and forth between the CNS and the heart, lungs, and other organs and glands.

THE CENTRAL NERVOUS SYSTEM: MAKING SENSE OF THE WORLD

The CNS is laid out in interconnected groups of neuron cell bodies, called *nuclei,* whose collections of axons travel together in *fiber tracts* or *pathways.*

The Spinal Cord

The *spinal cord* receives information from the peripheral senses and sends it to the brain; it also relays messages from the brain to the periphery. In addition, cells of the spinal cord can direct simple behaviors, called *reflexes,* without instructions from the brain.

The Brain

The brain's major subdivisions are the *hindbrain, midbrain,* and *forebrain.* The hindbrain includes the *medulla,* the *cerebellum,* and the *locus coeruleus.* The midbrain includes the *substantia nigra.* The *reticular formation* is found in both the hindbrain and the midbrain. The forebrain is the largest and most highly developed part of the brain; it includes the diencephalon and cerebrum. The diencephalon includes the *hypothalamus* and *thalamus.* A part of the hypothalamus called the *suprachiasmatic nuclei* maintains a clock that determines biological rhythms. Structures within the *cerebrum* include the *striatum, hippocampus,* and *amygdala.* Several of these structures form the *limbic system,* which plays an important role in regulating emotion and memory.

The Cerebral Cortex

The outer surface of the *cerebral hemispheres* is called the *cerebral cortex;* it is responsible for many of the higher functions of the brain, including speech and reasoning. The functional areas of the cortex include the *sensory cortex, motor cortex,* and *association cortex.*

The Divided Brain in a Unified Self

The right and left hemispheres of the cerebral cortex are specialized to some degree in their functions. In most people, the left hemisphere is more active in language and logical tasks; and the right hemisphere, in spatial, musical, and artistic tasks. A task that is performed more efficiently by one hemisphere than the other is said to be *lateralized.* The hemispheres are connected through the *corpus callosum,* allowing them to operate in a coordinated fashion.

Plasticity in the Brain

The brain's *synaptic plasticity,* the ability to strengthen neural connections at its synapses as well as to establish new synapses, forms the basis for learning and memory. Scientists are studying ways to increase plasticity following brain damage.

THE CHEMISTRY OF PSYCHOLOGY

Neurons that use the same neurotransmitter form a *neurotransmitter system.*

Seven Major Neurotransmitters

There are seven particularly important neurotransmitters. *Acetylcholine* systems in the brain influence memory processes and movement. *Norepinephrine* is released by a small number of neurons whose axons spread widely throughout the brain; it is involved in arousal, mood, and learning. *Serotonin,* another pervasive neurotransmitter, is active in systems regulating mood, attention, and appetite. *Dopamine* systems are involved in movement and higher cognitive activities; both Parkinson's disease and schizophrenia involve a disturbance of dopaminergic function. *GABA* is an inhibitory neurotransmitter involved in anxiety and epilepsy. *Glutamate* is the most common excitatory neurotransmitter; it is involved in learning and memory and, in excess, may cause neuronal death. *Endorphins* are neurotransmitters that affect pain pathways.

THE ENDOCRINE SYSTEM: COORDINATING THE INTERNAL WORLD

Like nervous system cells, those of the *endocrine system* communicate by releasing a chemical that signals other cells. However, the chemicals released by endocrine organs, or *glands,* are called *hormones* and are carried by the bloodstream to remote target organs. *Negative feedback systems* are involved in the control of most endocrine functions. The brain is the main controller: Through the hypothalamus, it controls the pituitary gland, which in turn controls endocrine organs in the body. The brain is also a target organ for most endocrine secretions. The target organs often produce a coordinated response to hormonal stimulation. One of these is the *fight-or-flight syndrome,* which is set off by adrenal hormones that prepare for action in times of stress. Hormones also modulate the development of the brain, contributing to sex differences in brain and behavior.

THE IMMUNE SYSTEM: LINKING THE BRAIN AND THE BODY'S DEFENSE SYSTEM

The *immune system* serves as a sensory system that monitors the internal state of the body and as a protective system for detecting, then destroying, unwanted cells and toxic substances that may invade the body. *Autoimmune disorders* result when cells of the immune system attack normal cells of the body. There are important reciprocal relationships among the immune system, nervous system, and endocrine system.

KEY TERMS

acetylcholine (82)
action potential (55)
amygdala (68)
association cortex (74)
autoimmune disorders (91)
autonomic nervous system (61)
axons (54)
biological psychology (52)
central nervous system (CNS) (61)
cerebellum (66)
cerebral cortex (71)
cerebral hemispheres (71)
cerebrum (68)
corpus callosum (75)
dendrites (54)
dopamine (84)
endocrine system (87)
endorphin (85)

excitatory postsynaptic potential (EPSP) (58)
fiber tracts (63)
fight-or-flight syndrome (89)
forebrain (68)
GABA (84)
glands (88)
glial cells (54)
glutamate (84)
hindbrain (64)
hippocampus (68)
hormones (88)
hypothalamus (68)
immune system (90)
inhibitory postsynaptic potential (IPSP) (58)
ions (55)
lateralized (76)
limbic system (69)

locus coeruleus (66)
medulla (64)
midbrain (67)
motor cortex (73)
motor systems (61)
myelin (56)
negative feedback system (89)
nervous system (52)
neural networks (59)
neurons (54)
neurotransmitters (57)
neurotransmitter system (82)
norepinephrine (83)
nuclei (63)
pathways (63)
peripheral nervous system (PNS) (61)
postsynaptic potential (58)

receptors (57)
reflexes (64)
refractory period (56)
reticular formation (66)
sensory cortex (72)
sensory systems (60)
serotonin (83)
somatic nervous system (61)
spinal cord (63)
striatum (68)
substantia nigra (68)
suprachiasmatic nuclei (68)
synapse (55)
synaptic plasticity (78)
thalamus (68)

4

Sensation

chapter

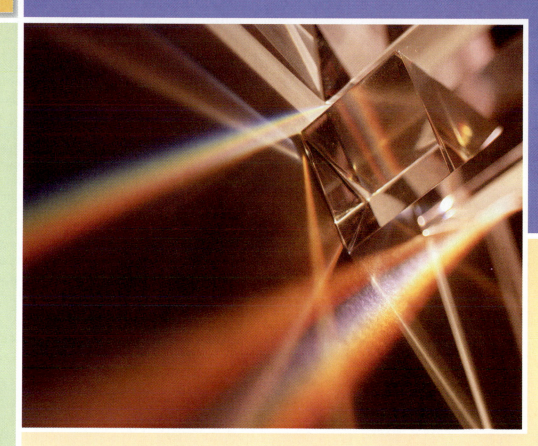

Before you read the next sentence, look at the background on the previous page. What color would you say it is? If you asked the nearest three-year-old this question, the child might call the color "blue," because she is still learning to attach labels to specific sensations of color. But by the time she reaches college age, she will probably label it the same as you do. People in the same culture tend to learn the same names for colors. But does the background color really look exactly the same to others as it does to you? This may seem a foolish question because most people think there is an objective reality that is the same for everyone. The seat you sit on and the book you are reading are solid objects. You can see and feel them with your senses. But sensory psychologists tell us that reality is not so simple, that the senses do not reflect an objective reality. On the contrary, the senses of each individual actively shape information about the outside world to create a *personal* reality. The sensory experiences of different species—and individual humans—vary. You do not see the same world a fly sees, people from California may not hear music quite the same way as do people from Singapore, and different people may experience a color differently, even if they give it the same name.

In order to understand how sensory systems create reality, consider some basic information about the senses. A **sense** is a system that translates information from outside the nervous system into neural activity. For example, vision is the system through which the eyes convert light into neural activity. This neural activity tells the brain something about the source of the light (e.g., that it is bright) or about objects from which the light is reflected (e.g., that there is a round, red object out there). These messages from the senses are called **sensations.** Because they provide the link between the self and the world outside the brain, sensations help shape many of the behaviors and mental processes studied by psychologists.

Traditionally, psychologists have distinguished between sensation—the initial message from the senses—and *perception,* the process through which messages from the senses are given meaning. Thus, you do not actually sense a cat lying on the sofa; you sense shapes and colors—visual sensations. You use your knowledge of the world to interpret, or perceive, these sensations as a cat. However, it is impossible to draw a clear line between sensation and perception. Research shows that the process of interpreting sensations begins in the sense organs themselves. For example, the frog's eye immediately interprets any small black object as "fly!"—thus enabling the frog to attack the fly with its tongue without waiting for its brain to process the sensory information (Lettvin et al., 1959).

This chapter covers the first steps of the sensation-perception process; the next chapter deals with the later phases. Together, these chapters illustrate how we human beings, with our sense organs and brains, create our own realities. In this chapter we explore how sensations are produced, received, and acted upon. First, we consider what sensations are and how they inform us about the surrounding world. Then, we examine the physical and psychological mechanisms involved in the auditory, visual, and chemical senses. And finally we turn to a discussion of the somatic senses, which enable us to feel things, to experience temperature and pain, and to know where the parts of the body are in relation to one another. Collectively, the senses play a critical role in our ability as humans to adapt to and survive in our environment.

SENSORY SYSTEMS

The senses gather information about the world by detecting various forms of energy, such as sound, light, heat, and physical pressure. Specifically, the eyes detect light energy, the ears detect the energy of sound, and the skin detects the energy of heat and pressure. Humans depend primarily on vision, hearing, and the skin senses to gain information about the world; they depend less than other animals on smell and taste. To your brain, "the world" also includes the rest of your body, and there are sensory systems that provide information about the location and position of your body parts.

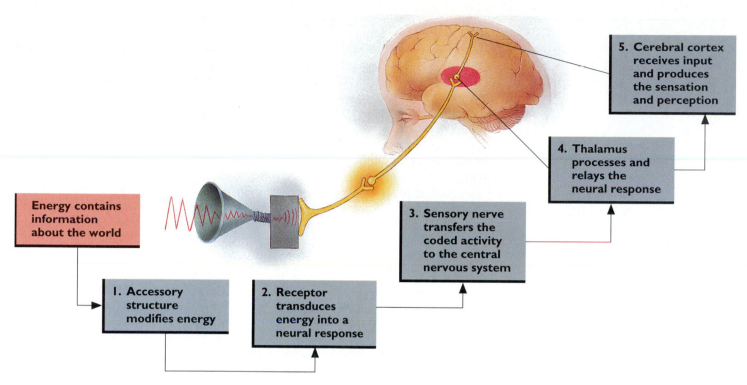

FIGURE 4.1

Elements of a Sensory System

Objects in the world generate energy that is focused by accessory structures and detected by sensory receptors, which convert the energy into neural signals. As the signals are transferred through parts of the brain, information is extracted and analyzed.

All of these senses must detect stimuli, encode them into neural activity, and transfer this coded information to the brain. Figure 4.1 illustrates these basic steps in sensation. At each step, sensory information is "processed" in some way: The information that arrives at one point in the system is not the same as the information that goes to the next step.

In some sensory systems, the first step in sensation involves **accessory structures,** which modify the energy created by something in the person's environment—for example, another person talking or a flashing sign. (See step 1 in Figure 4.1.) The outer part of the ear is an accessory structure that collects sound; the lens of the eye is an accessory structure that changes incoming light by focusing it.

The second step in sensation is **transduction,** which is the process of converting incoming energy into neural activity (step 2 in Figure 4.1). Just as a radio receives energy and transduces it into sounds, the ears receive sound energy and transduce it into neural activity that people recognize as voices, music, and other auditory experiences. Transduction takes place at structures called **sensory receptors,** specialized cells that detect certain forms of energy. Sensory receptors are somewhat like the neurons that we described in Chapter 3; they respond to incoming energy by changing their membrane potential and can release neurotransmitters to send a signal to neighboring cells. (However, some sensory receptors do not have axons and dendrites, as neurons do.) Sensory receptors respond best to changes in energy. A constant level of stimulation usually produces **adaptation,** a process through which responsiveness to an unchanging stimulus decreases over time. This is why the touch sensations you get from your glasses (or even your heavy flannel shirt) disappear shortly after you have put them on.

Next, sensory nerves carry the output from receptors to the central nervous system, including the brain (step 3 in Figure 4.1). For all the senses except smell, the information is taken first to the thalamus (step 4), which relays it to the sensory portion of the cerebral cortex (step 5). It is in the sensory cortex that the most complex processing occurs.

The Problem of Coding

When receptors transduce energy, they must somehow code the physical properties of the stimulus into patterns of neural activity that, when analyzed by the brain, allow you to make sense of the stimulus—to determine, for example, whether you are looking at a cat, a dog, or a person. For each psychological dimension of a sensation, such as the brightness or color of light, there must be a corresponding physical dimension coded by sensory receptors.

As a way of thinking about the problem of coding, imagine that for your birthday you receive a Pet Brain. You are told that your Pet Brain is alive, but it does not respond when you open the box and talk to it. You remove it from the box and show it a hot-fudge sundae; no response. You show it pictures of other attractive brains; still no response. You are about to deposit your Pet Brain in the trash when you suddenly realize that the two of you are probably not talking the same language. Upon rereading Chapter 3 of this book, you recall that the brain usually receives information from sensory neurons and responds via motor neurons, and that these exchanges are carried out through *action potentials*—electrochemical changes in the axons of neurons. Thus, if you want to communicate with your Pet Brain, you have to stimulate its sensory nerves (so that you can send it messages) and record signals from its motor nerves (so that you can read its responses).

After having this brilliant insight and setting up an electric stimulator and recorder, you are faced with an awesome problem. How do you describe a hot-fudge sundae in terms of action potentials? This is the problem of coding. **Coding** is the translation of the physical properties of a stimulus into a pattern of neural activity that specifically identifies those physical properties.

If you want the brain to visualize the sundae, you should stimulate the optic nerve (the nerve from the eye to the brain) rather than the auditory nerve (the nerve from the ear to the brain). This idea is based on the doctrine of **specific nerve energies:** Stimulation of a particular sensory nerve provides codes for that one sense, no matter how the stimulation takes place. For example, if you apply gentle pressure to your eyeball, you will produce activity in the optic nerve and sense little spots of light.

Having chosen the optic nerve to convey visual information, you must next develop a code for the specific attributes of the sundae: the soft white curves of the vanilla ice cream, the dark richness of the chocolate, the bright red roundness of the cherry on top. These dimensions must be coded in the language of neural activity—that is, action potentials.

Some attributes of a stimulus are coded relatively simply. For example, a bright light will cause some neurons in the visual system to fire faster than will a dim light. This is a **temporal code,** because it involves changes in the *timing* of firing. Temporal codes can be more complex as well; for example, a burst of firing followed by a slower firing rate means something different than a steady rate. The other basic type of code is **spatial,** in which the *location* of firing neurons relative to their neighbors provides information about the stimulus. For example, neurons that carry sensations from the fingers travel close to those carrying information from the arms, but far from those carrying information from the feet. Information can be recoded at several relay points as it makes its way through the brain.

Now, if everything goes as planned, your Pet Brain will know what a sundae looks like. Indeed, the problem of coding is solved by means of sensory systems, which allow the brain to receive detailed, accurate, and useful information about stimuli in its environment. Shortly, we discuss how this remarkable feat is accomplished.

LINKAGES

How is information from the senses organized in the brain? (a link to Biological Aspects of Psychology)

LINKAGES

Sensation and Biological Aspects of Psychology

As sensory systems transfer information to the brain, they also organize that information. This organized information is called a *representation*. If you have read Chapter 3, you are already familiar with some characteristics of sensory representations. In humans, representations of vision, hearing, and the skin senses in the cerebral cortex share the following features:

1. The information from each of these senses reaches the cortex via the thalamus. (Figure 3.15, on page 68, shows where these areas of the brain are.)

2. The representation of the sensory world in the cortex is *contralateral* to the part of the world being sensed. For example, the left side of the visual cortex "sees" the right side of the world, while the right side of that cortex "sees" the left side of the world. This happens because nerve fibers from each side of the body cross on their way to the thalamus. Why they cross is still a mystery.

3. The cortex contains maps, or **topographical representations,** of each sense. Accordingly, features that are next to each other in the world stimulate neurons that are next to each other in the brain. For example, two notes that are similar in pitch activate neighboring neurons in the auditory cortex, and the neurons that respond to sensations in the elbow and in the forearm are relatively close to one another in the somatosensory cortex. There are multiple maps representing each sense, but the area that receives input directly from the thalamus is called the **primary cortex** for that sense.

4. The density of nerve fibers in any part of a sense organ determines its representation in the cortex. For example, the skin on a fingertip, which has a higher density of receptors for touch than the skin on the back, has a larger area of cortex representing it than does the back.

5. Each region of primary sensory cortex is divided into columns of cells that have similar properties. For example, some columns of cells in the visual cortex respond most to diagonal lines.

6. For each of the senses, regions of cortex other than the primary areas do additional processing of sensory information. As described in Chapter 3, these areas of *association cortex* may contain representations of more than one sense.

In short, sensory systems convert some form of energy into neural activity, as described in Figure 4.1. Often the energy is first modified by accessory structures; then a sensory receptor converts the energy to neural activity. The pattern of neural activity encodes physical properties of the energy. The codes are modified as the information is transferred to the brain and processed further. In the remainder of this chapter we describe these processes in specific sensory systems.

HEARING

In 1969, when Neil Armstrong became the first human to step onto the moon, millions of people back on earth heard his radio transmission: "That's one small step for a man, one giant leap for mankind." But if Armstrong had taken off his space helmet and shouted, "Whoo-ee! I can moonwalk," another astronaut, a foot away, would not have heard him. Why? Because Armstrong would have been speaking into airless, empty space. **Sound** is a repetitive fluctuation in the pressure of a medium, such as air. Thus, in a place like the moon, which has almost no atmospheric medium, sound cannot exist.

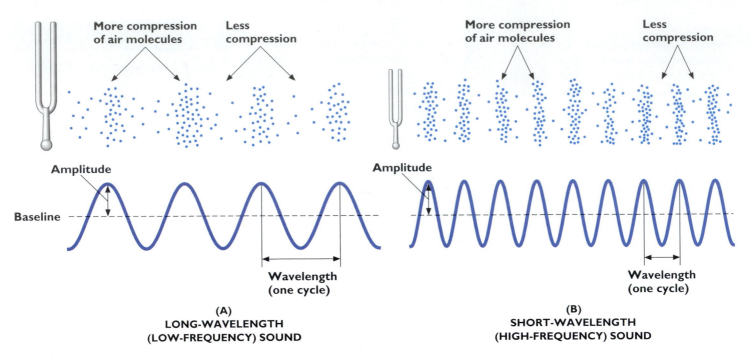

(A)
LONG-WAVELENGTH
(LOW-FREQUENCY) SOUND

(B)
SHORT-WAVELENGTH
(HIGH-FREQUENCY) SOUND

FIGURE 4.2

Sound Waves and Waveforms

Sound is created when objects, such as a tuning fork, vibrate. They create alternating regions of greater and lesser compression of air molecules, which can be represented as a *waveform*. The point of greatest compression is the peak of the graph. The lowest point, or trough, is where compression is lowest.

Sound

The fluctuations in pressure that constitute sound are produced by the vibrations of an object. Each time the object moves outward, it increases the pressure in the medium around it. As the object moves back, the pressure drops. In speech, for example, the vibrating object is the vocal cord, and the medium is air. When you speak, your vocal cords vibrate, producing fluctuations in air pressure that spread as waves. A *wave* is a repetitive variation in pressure that spreads out in three dimensions. The wave can move great distances, but the air itself barely moves. Imagine a jam-packed line of people waiting for a movie. If someone at the rear of the line shoves the next person, a wave of people jostling against people may spread all the way to the front of the line, but the person who shoved first is still no closer to getting into the theater.

Physical Characteristics of Sound   Sound is represented graphically by waveforms like those in Figure 4.2. A *waveform* represents the wave that moves through the air.

Three characteristics of the waveform are important in understanding sounds. First, the difference in air pressure from the baseline to the peak of the wave is the **amplitude** of the sound, or its intensity. Second, the distance from one peak to the next is called the **wavelength.** Third, **frequency** is the number of complete waves, or cycles, that pass by a given point in space every second. Frequency is described in a unit called *hertz,* abbreviated *Hz* (for Heinrich Hertz, a nineteenth-century physicist). One cycle per second is 1 hertz. Because the speed of sound is constant in a given medium, wavelength and frequency are related: The longer the wavelength, the lower the frequency; the shorter the wavelength, the higher the frequency. Most sounds are mixtures of many different frequencies and amplitudes. In contrast, a pure tone is made up of only one frequency and can be represented, as in Figure 4.2, by what is known as a *sine wave.*

Psychological Dimensions of Sound   The amplitude and frequency of sound waves determine the sounds that you hear. These physical characteristics of the waves produce the psychological dimensions of sound known as loudness, pitch, and timbre.

Loudness is determined by the amplitude of the sound wave; waves with greater amplitude produce sensations of louder sounds. Loudness is described in units called *decibels,* abbreviated *dB.* By definition, 0 decibels is the minimal detectable sound for normal hearing. Table 4.1 gives examples of the loudness of some common sounds.

Noise Eliminators

Complex sound, including noise, can be analyzed into its component, simple sine waves by means of a mathematical process called *Fourier analysis.* This technique can be used to eliminate engine, wind, and other repetitive noises in moving vehicles. After the waveforms are analyzed, a sound synthesizer produces the opposite waveforms. The opposing waves cancel each other out, and the amazing result is silence. Several versions of these noise eliminators are now sold as consumer products, and doctors are using related devices to treat *tinnitus,* or "ringing in the ear."

Pitch, or how high or low a tone sounds, depends on the frequency of sound waves. High-frequency waves are sensed as sounds of high pitch. The highest note on a piano has a frequency of about 4,000 hertz; the lowest note has a frequency of about 50 hertz. Humans can hear sounds ranging from about 20 hertz to about 20,000 hertz. Almost everyone experiences pitch as a relative dimension; that is, they can tell whether one note is higher than, lower than, or equal to another note. However, a few people have *perfect pitch,* which means they can identify specific frequencies and the notes they represent—they can say, for example, that a 262 Hz tone is middle C. It was once thought that perfect pitch occurs only in gifted people; but we now know that, if taught before the age of six, children can learn that specific frequencies are particular notes (Takeuchi & Hulse, 1993).

Timbre (pronounced "TAM-ber") is the quality of sound; it is determined by complex wave patterns that are added onto the lowest, or *fundamental,* frequency of a sound. The extra waves allow you to tell, for example, the difference between a note played on a flute and a note played on a clarinet.

The Ear

The human ear converts sound energy into neural activity through a series of accessory structures and transduction mechanisms.

TABLE 4.1

Intensity of Sound Sources

Sound intensity varies across an extremely wide range. A barely audible sound is, by definition, 0 decibels, and every increase of 20 dB represents a tenfold increase in the amplitude of the sound waves. Thus an office that is at 40 db is 10 times as intense as a whisper; and traffic noise that is at 100 dB is 10,000 times as intense as the whisper.

Source	Sound Level (dB)
Spacecraft launch (from 45 m)	180
Loudest rock band on record	160
Pain threshold (approximate)	140
Large jet motor (at 22 m)	120
Loudest human shout on record	111
Heavy auto traffic	100
Conversation (at about 1 m)	60
Quiet office	40
Soft whisper	20
Threshold of hearing	0

An Accessory Structure

Some animals have a large pinna that can be rotated to help localize the source of a sound.

Auditory Accessory Structures　Sound waves are collected in the outer ear, beginning with the *pinna,* the crumpled, oddly shaped part of the ear. The pinna funnels sound down through the ear canal (see Figure 4.3). At the end of the ear canal, the sound waves reach the middle ear, where they strike a tightly stretched membrane known as the eardrum, or **tympanic membrane.** The sound waves set up vibrations in the tympanic membrane.

Next, the vibrations of the tympanic membrane are passed on by a chain of three tiny bones: the *malleus,* or *hammer;* the *incus,* or *anvil;* and the *stapes,* or *stirrup* (see Figure 4.3). These bones amplify the changes in pressure produced by the original sound waves, by focusing the vibrations of the tympanic membrane onto a smaller membrane, the *oval window.*

Auditory Transduction　When sound vibrations pass through the oval window, they enter the inner ear, or **cochlea** (pronounced "COCK-lee-ah"), the structure in which transduction occurs. The cochlea is wrapped into a coiled spiral. (*Cochlea* is derived from the Greek word for "snail.") If you unwrapped it, you would see that a fluid-filled tube runs down its length. The **basilar membrane** forms the floor of this long tube (see Figure 4.4). Whenever a sound wave passes through the fluid in the tube, it moves the basilar membrane, and this movement deforms *hair cells* of the *organ of Corti,* a group of cells that rests on the membrane. These hair cells connect with fibers from the **auditory nerve,** a bundle of axons that go into the brain. Mechanical deformation of the hair cells stimulates the auditory nerve, changing the electrical activity of some of its neurons and thus sending a coded signal to the brain about the amplitude and frequency of sound waves, which you sense as loudness and pitch.

Deafness　Problems with the three tiny bones of the middle ear are one cause of deafness. Sometimes, the bones fuse together, preventing accurate reproduction of vibrations. This condition is called *conduction deafness.* It may be treated by breaking the bones apart or replacing the natural bones with plastic ones; a hearing aid that amplifies the input can also be helpful.

If the auditory nerve or, more commonly, the hair cells are damaged, *nerve deafness* results. Hair cell damage occurs gradually with age, but it can also be caused by loud noise, such as that created by jet engines, noisy equipment, and intense rock music

FIGURE 4.3

Structures of the Ear

The outer ear (pinna and ear canal) channels sounds into the middle ear, where the vibrations of the tympanic membrane are amplified by the delicate bones that stimulate the cochlea. In the cochlea the vibrations are transduced into changes in neural activity, which are sent along the auditory nerve to the brain.

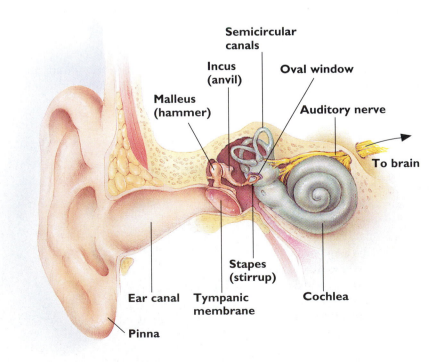

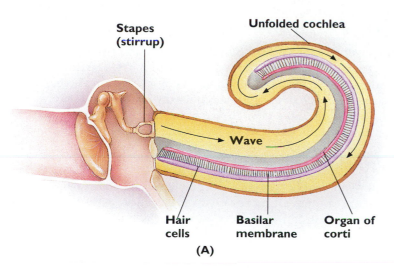

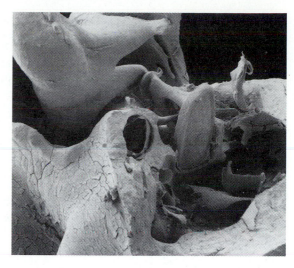

Stapes (stirrup)

Unfolded cochlea

Wave

Hair cells

Basilar membrane

Organ of corti

(A)

FIGURE 4.4

The Cochlea

As shown in part (A), the vibrations of the stirrup set up vibrations in the fluid inside the cochlea. The coils of the cochlea are unfolded in this illustration to show the path of the fluid waves along the basilar membrane. Movements of the basilar membrane stimulate the hair cells of the organ of Corti, which transduce the vibrations into changes in neural firing patterns. In part (B) is an electron micrograph of the stapes and the region around it.

(Goldstein, 1999; see Figure 4.5). For example, two popular rock musicians from the 1970s, Stephen Stills and Pete Townshend, have become partially deaf as a result of their many years of performing extremely loud music (Ackerman, 1995). In the United States and other industrialized countries, people born after World War II are experiencing hearing loss at a younger age than did their forebears, possibly because noise pollution has increased during the past fifty years.

Although hair cells can regenerate in chickens (who seldom listen to rock music), such regeneration was long believed to be impossible in mammals (Salvi et al., 1998). However, evidence that mammals can regenerate a related kind of inner-ear hair cell has fueled optimism about finding a way to stimulate regeneration of human auditory hair cells (Stone, Oesterle, & Rubel, 1998). The feat might be accomplished by treating damaged areas with growth factors similar to those used to repair damaged brain cells (see Chapter 3). Indeed, hair cell regeneration could revolutionize the treatment of nerve deafness because this form of deafness cannot be overcome by conventional hearing aids. Meanwhile, scientists have developed artificial cochleas (called *cochlear implants*) that can stimulate the auditory nerve in cases involving congenital nerve deafness (Clark, 1998). However, the use of these devices for deaf children is controversial. Some members of the deaf community argue that cochlear implants prevent children from fully entering the deaf culture without adequately repairing their hearing deficit (Clay, 1997).

FIGURE 4.5

Effects of Loud Sounds

High–intensity sounds can actually tear off the hair cells of the inner ear. Part (A) shows the organ of Corti of a normal guinea pig. Part (B) shows the damage caused by exposure to twenty-four hours of 2000 Hz sound at 120 decibels. Generally, any sound loud enough to produce ringing in the ears causes some damage. In humans, small amounts of damage can accumulate over time to produce a significant hearing loss by middle age—as many middle-aged rock musicians can attest.

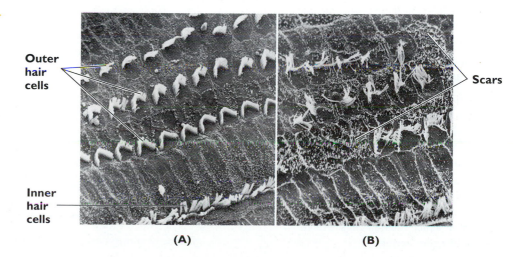

Outer hair cells

Scars

Inner hair cells

(A)

(B)

The Downside of Being a Rock Star

Pete Townshend, a rock musician and one of the composers of the rock opera *Tommy*, has suffered substantial hearing loss as a result of long-term exposure to extremely loud music at his concerts.

Coding Intensity and Frequency

People can hear an incredibly wide range of sound intensities. The faintest sound that can be heard moves the hair cells less than the diameter of a single hydrogen atom (Hudspeth, 1997). Sounds more than a trillion times more intense can also be heard. Between these extremes, the auditory system codes intensity in a straightforward way: The more intense the sound, the more rapid the firing of a given neuron.

Recall that the pitch of a sound depends on its frequency. How do people tell the difference between frequencies? Differences in frequency appear to be coded in two ways, which are described by place theory and frequency-matching theory.

Place Theory   Georg von Bekesy performed some pioneering experiments in the 1930s and 1940s to figure out how frequency is coded (von Bekesy, 1960). Studying human cadavers, he made a hole in the cochlear wall and observed the basilar membrane. He then presented sounds of different frequencies by mechanically vibrating a rubber membrane that was installed in place of the oval window. With sensitive optical instruments, von Bekesy observed ripples of waves moving down the basilar membrane. He noticed that the outline of the waves, called the *envelope*, grows and reaches a peak; then it quickly tapers off to smaller and smaller fluctuations, much like an ocean wave that crests and then dissolves.

As shown in Figure 4.6, the critical feature of this wave is that the place on the basilar membrane where the envelope peaks depends on the frequency of the sound. High-frequency sounds produce a wave that peaks soon after it starts down the basilar membrane. Lower-frequency sounds produce a wave that peaks farther along the basilar membrane, farther from the oval window.

How does the location of the peak affect the coding of frequency? According to **place theory,** also called *traveling wave theory,* the greatest response by hair cells occurs at the peak of the wave. Because the location of the peak varies with the frequency of the sound, it follows that hair cells at a particular place on the basilar membrane respond most to a particular frequency of sound, called a *characteristic frequency*. Thus, place theory describes a spatial code for frequency. One important result of this arrangement is that if extended exposure to a very loud sound of a particular frequency destroys hair cells at one spot on the basilar membrane, the ability to hear sounds of that frequency is lost as well.

Frequency-Matching Theory   Although place theory accounts for a great deal of data on hearing, it cannot explain the coding of very low frequencies, such as that of a deep bass note, because there are no auditory nerve fibers that have very low characteristic frequencies. Since humans can hear frequencies as low as 20 hertz, however, the frequencies must be coded somehow. The answer is **frequency matching,** which refers to the fact that the firing rate of a neuron in the auditory nerve matches the frequency of a sound wave. Frequency matching provides a temporal code for frequency. For example, one neuron might fire at every peak of a wave. Thus, a sound of 20 hertz could be coded by a neuron that fires twenty times per second.

F I G U R E   4 . 6

Movements of the Basilar Membrane

As vibrations of the cochlear fluid spread along the basilar membrane, the membrane is bent and then recovers. As shown in these three examples, the point at which the bending of the basilar membrane reaches a maximum is different for each sound frequency. According to place theory, these are the locations at which the hair cells receive the greatest stimulation.

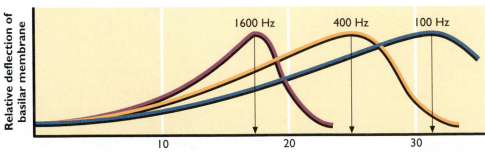

Distance along basilar membrane from oval window in millimeters

in review

HEARING		
Aspect of Sensory System	**Elements**	**Key Characteristics**
Energy	Sound—pressure fluctuations of air produced by vibrations	The amplitude, frequency, and complexity of sound waves determine the loudness, pitch, and timbre of sounds.
Accessory structures	Ear—pinna, tympanic membrane, malleus, incus, stapes, oval window, basilar membrane	Changes in pressure produced by the original wave are amplified.
Transduction mechanism	Hair cells of the organ of Corti	Frequencies are coded by the location of the hair cells receiving the greatest stimulation (place theory) and by the firing rate of neurons (frequency matching).
Pathways and representations	Auditory nerve to thalamus to primary auditory cortex	Neighboring cells in auditory cortex have similar preferred frequencies, thus providing a map of sound frequencies.

In this simple form, however, frequency matching would apply to few sounds, because no neuron can fire faster than 1,000 times per second. A slightly more complicated process accounts for the coding of moderate frequencies above 1,000 hertz. These frequencies can be matched, not by a single neuron, but by the summed activity of a group of neurons firing in concert. Some neurons in the group might fire, for example, at every other wave peak, others at every fifth peak, and so on, producing a *volley* of firing at a combined frequency higher than any could manage alone. Indeed, the frequency-matching theory is sometimes called the **volley theory** of frequency coding.

In summary, the nervous system uses more than one way to code the range of audible frequencies. The lowest sound frequencies are coded by frequency matching, whereby the frequency is matched by the firing rate of auditory nerve fibers. Low to moderate frequencies are coded by both frequency matching and the place on the basilar membrane where the wave peaks. High frequencies are coded exclusively by the place where the wave peaks.

Auditory Pathways and Representations

Before sounds can be heard, the information coded in the activity of auditory nerve fibers must be conveyed to the brain and processed further. (For a review of how changes in air pressure become signals in the brain that are perceived as sounds, see "In Review: Hearing.") The auditory nerve, the bundle of axons that conveys this information, crosses the brain's midline and reaches the thalamus. From the thalamus, the information is relayed to the **primary auditory cortex**. As discussed in Chapter 3, this is an area located in the temporal lobe of the cerebral cortex, close to areas of the brain involved in language perception and production (see Figure 3.17 on page 72).

Various aspects of sound are processed separately as the auditory nerve stimulates the auditory cortex. For example, the location of sounds and their frequency are processed in different regions of the cortex (Rauschecker, 1997). Moreover, neighboring cells in the cortex have similar preferred frequencies; thus the auditory cortex provides a map of sound frequencies. The same is true of the neurons in the auditory nerve; that is, some neurons are more responsive to some frequencies than others. However, although each neuron in the auditory nerve has a characteristic frequency to which it best responds, each also responds to some extent to a range of frequencies. Therefore, the auditory cortex must examine the pattern of activity of a number of neurons in order to determine the frequency of a sound.

Sensing frequency is not always as simple as you might expect, however. Mixtures of frequencies, as in musical chords, can produce sounds of ambiguous pitch. In fact, the same sequence of chords can sound like an ascending scale to one person and a descending scale to another. Cultural factors are partly responsible for the way in which pitch is sensed. For example, people in the United States tend to hear *ambiguous scales* as progressing in directions that are opposite to the way they are heard by people from Canada and England (Dawe, Platt, & Welsh, 1998). Although this cross-cultural difference appears to be a reliable one, researchers do not yet know exactly why it occurs.

The location of sounds is also analyzed by the auditory cortex. This analysis is based partly on the difference in the times at which a sound arrives at your two ears (it reaches the closer ear slightly earlier) and on the difference in sound intensity (sounds that are closer to one ear are slightly louder in that ear). So you can determine where a voice or other sound is coming from even when you can't see its source. Indeed, your brain can detect differences in the arrival time of sounds of as little as a few millionths of a second (Hudspeth, 1997). The brain can determine the location of the sound source by analyzing the activities of groups of neurons that individually signal only a rough approximation of the location (Fitzpatrick, Olsen, & Suga, 1998). Thus, the overall code that allows judgments of sound localization is a *temporal* one; the frequencies of firing by many neurons in the auditory cortex combine to create a kind of "Morse code" that describes where a sound is coming from (Middlebrooks et al., 1994).

Processing Language

As this student and teacher communicate using American Sign Language, the visual information they receive from each other's hand movements is processed by the same areas of their brains that allow hearing people to understand spoken language.

Hearing and Language Language is the auditory stimulation that humans depend upon most, and scientists are learning how the cortex processes sound signals that we recognize as words. We already know, for example, that temporal processing is particularly important in distinguishing some consonants; indeed, recent studies have found that children with language learning problems often have deficits in the temporal processing of sounds in general (Merzenich et al., 1996). Fortunately, these children can be trained to more efficiently process the temporal aspects of sounds. Such training dramatically improves their language acquisition (Tallal et al., 1996). Interestingly, the brain regions involved in processing language are the same whether it comes to hearing individuals in the form of sounds or, to deaf individuals, in the form of sign language (Neville et al., 1998).

VISION

Soaring eagles have the incredible ability to see a mouse move in the grass from a mile away. Cats have special "reflectors" at the back of their eyes that help them to see even in very dim light. Through natural selection, over eons of time, each species has developed a visual system uniquely adapted to its way of life. The human visual system is also adapted to do many things well: It combines great sensitivity and great sharpness, enabling people to see objects near and far, during the day and night. Our night vision is not as acute as that of some animals, but our color vision is excellent. This is not a bad tradeoff, since being able to appreciate a sunset's splendor seems worth an occasional stumble in the dark. In this section, we consider the human visual sense and how it responds to light.

Light

Light is a form of energy known as *electromagnetic radiation.* Most electromagnetic radiation—including x-rays, radio waves, television signals, and radar—passes through space undetected by the human eye. **Visible light** is electromagnetic radiation that has a wavelength from just under 400 nanometers to about 750 nanometers (a *nanometer* is one-billionth of a meter; see Figure 4.7). Unlike sound, light does not need a medium to pass through. So, even on the airless moon, astronauts can see one another even if they can't hear one another without radios. Light waves are like particles that pass through space, but they vibrate with a certain wavelength. Thus light has some properties of waves and some properties of particles, and it is correct to refer to light as either *light waves* or *light rays.*

Sensations of light depend on two physical dimensions of light waves: intensity and wavelength. **Light intensity** refers to how much energy the light contains; it determines

---

FIGURE 4.7

The Spectrum of Electromagnetic Energy

Compared to the overall spectrum of electromagnetic energy, the range of wavelengths that the human eye can see as visible light is very limited— encompassing a band of only about 370 nanometers. To detect energy outside this range, people rely on electronic instruments such as radios, TV sets, radar, and infrared night-vision scopes that can "see" this energy as their own kind of light.

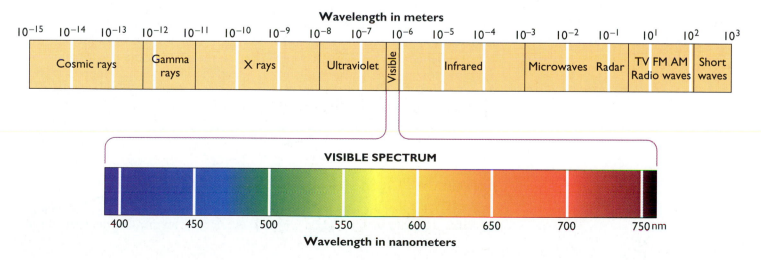

FIGURE 4.8

Major Structures of the Eye

As shown in this top view of the eye, light rays bent by the combined actions of the cornea and the lens are focused on the retina, where the light energy is transduced into neural activity. Nerve fibers known collectively as the optic nerve pass out the back of the eye and continue to the brain.

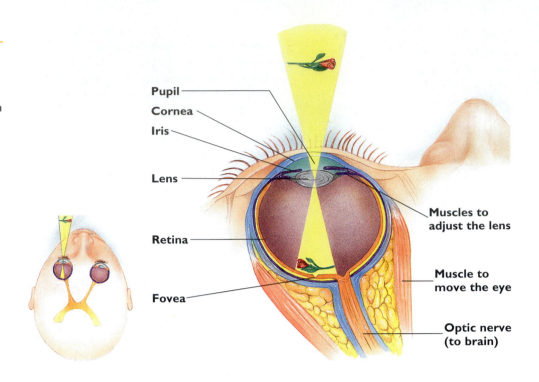

the brightness of light, much as the amplitude of sound waves determines the loudness of sound. What color you sense depends mainly on **light wavelength.** At a given intensity, different wavelengths produce sensations of different colors, much as different sound frequencies produce sensations of different pitch. For instance, 440-nanometer light appears violet-blue, and 600-nanometer light appears orangish-red.

Focusing Light

Just as sound energy is converted to neural activity in the ear, light energy is transduced into neural activity in the eye. First, the accessory structures of the human eye focus light rays into a sharp image. The light rays enter the eye by passing through the curved, transparent protective layer called the **cornea** (see Figure 4.8). Then the light passes through the **pupil,** the opening just behind the cornea. The **iris,** which gives the eye its color, adjusts the amount of light allowed into the eye by constricting to reduce the size of the pupil or relaxing to enlarge it. Directly behind the pupil is the **lens.** The cornea and the lens of the human eye are both curved so that, like the lens of a camera, they bend light rays. The light rays are focused into an image on the surface at the back of the eye; this surface is called the **retina.**

The lens of the human eye bends light rays from a point source so that they meet at a point on the retina (see Figure 4.9). If the rays meet either in front of the retina or behind it, the image will be out of focus. The muscles that hold the lens adjust its shape so that either near or far objects can be focused on the retina. If you peer at something very close, for example, your muscles must tighten the lens, making it more curved, to obtain a focused image. This ability to change the shape of the lens to bend light rays is called **accommodation.** Over time, the lens loses some of its flexibility, and accommodation becomes more difficult. This is why most older people need glasses for reading or close work; the lens no longer flexes enough to properly position the image on the retina.

Converting Light into Images

Visual transduction, the conversion of light energy into neural activity, takes place in the retina. The word *retina* is Latin for "net"; the retina is an intricate network of cells.

Reading and Nearsightedness

Visual experience can modify the eye, as when large amounts of reading leads to nearsightedness (Young et al., 1969). When special goggles blur chicks' vision to mimic slight nearsightedness, their eyeballs become shorter in order to restore focus (Schaeffel & Howland, 1991). When chicks are raised with goggles that allow diffused, unpatterned light through, their eyeballs become elongated and they become nearsighted (Wallman et al., 1987). Humans may be vulnerable to the same elongation because reading presents areas around the fovea with a constant, relatively unpatterned image.

Before transduction can occur, light rays must actually pass through several layers in this network to reach photoreceptor cells.

Photoreceptors   The **photoreceptors** are specialized cells in the retina that convert light energy into neural activity. They contain **photopigments,** chemicals that respond to light. When light strikes a photopigment, the photopigment breaks apart, changing the membrane potential of the photoreceptor cell. This change in membrane potential provides a signal that can be transferred to the brain.

After a photopigment has broken down in response to light, new photopigment molecules are put together. This takes a little time, however. So when you first come from bright sunshine into, say, a dark theater, you cannot see because your photoreceptors do not yet have enough photopigment. In the dark, your photoreceptors synthesize more photopigments, and your ability to see gradually increases. This increasing ability to see in the dark as time passes is called **dark adaptation.** Overall, your sensitivity to light increases about 10,000-fold after about half an hour in a darkened room.

FIGURE 4.9

The Lens and the Retinal Image

Light rays from the top of an object are focused at the bottom of the image on the retinal surface, whereas rays from the right side of the object end up on the left side of the retinal image. The brain rearranges this upside-down and reversed image so that people see the object as it is.

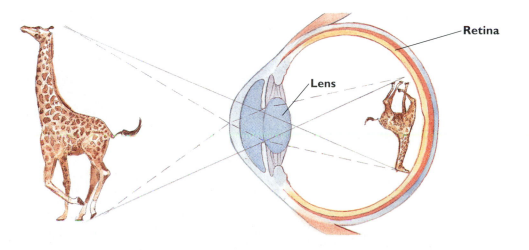

The retina has two basic types of photoreceptors: **rods** and **cones.** As their names imply, these cells differ in shape. They also differ in composition and response to light. The photopigment in rods includes a substance called *rhodopsin,* whereas the photopigment in cones includes one of three varieties of *iodopsin.* The multiple forms of iodopsin provide the basis for color vision, which we explain later. Because rods have only one pigment, they are unable to discriminate colors. However, the rods are more sensitive to light than cones. Thus, rods allow you to see even when there is very little light, as on a moonlit night. In dim light, then, you are seeing with your rods, which cannot discriminate colors; at higher light intensities, the cones, with their ability to detect colors, become most active. As a result, you may put on what you thought was a matched pair of socks in a darkened bedroom, only to go outside and discover that one is dark blue and the other is dark green.

The rods and cones also differ in their distribution in the eye. Cones are concentrated in the center of the retina, a region called the **fovea.** This concentration makes the ability to see details, or **acuity,** greatest in the fovea. Indeed, the fovea is precisely where the eye focuses the light coming from objects you look at. Variations in the density of cones in the fovea probably account for individual differences in visual acuity (Curcio et al., 1987). Interestingly, animals who live where the terrain is very flat (cheetahs on the plains and sea birds near the ocean, for example) do not have a circular fovea. Theirs is a horizontal streak of densely packed photoreceptors corresponding to the unbroken horizon (Land & Fernald, 1992).

Interactions in the Retina   If the eye simply transferred to the brain the stimuli that are focused on the retina, the resulting images would resemble a somewhat blurred TV picture. Instead, the eye actually sharpens visual images. How? The key lies in the interactions among the cells of the retina, which are illustrated in Figure 4.10. The most direct connections from the photoreceptor cells to the brain go first to *bipo-*

FIGURE 4.10

Cells in the Retina

Light rays actually pass through several layers of cells before striking the photoreceptive rods and cones. Signals generated by the rods and cones then go back toward the surface of the retina, passing through bipolar cells, ganglion cells, and on to the brain. Interconnections among interneurons, bipolar cells, and ganglion cells allow the eye to begin analyzing visual information even before that information leaves the retina.

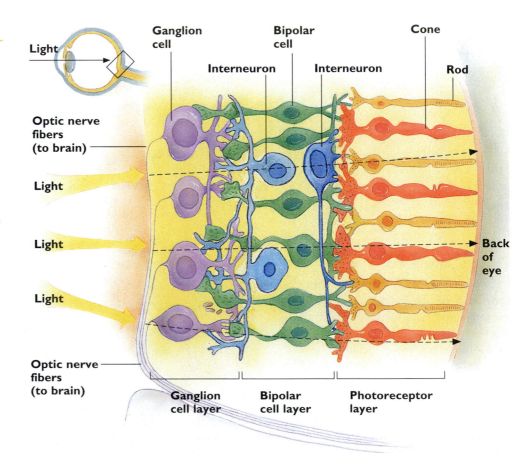

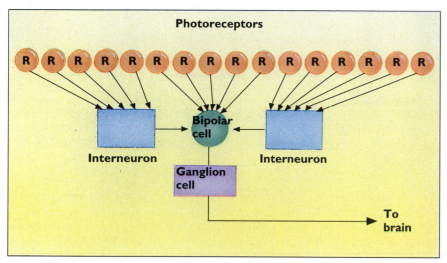

(A) CONVERGENCE

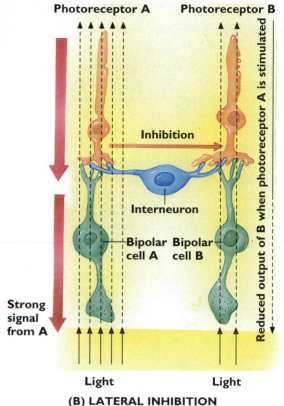

(B) LATERAL INHIBITION

FIGURE 4.11

Convergence and Lateral Inhibition Among Retinal Cells

Part (A) shows that input from many photoreceptors converges onto bipolar cells in the retina, either directly or by influencing interneurons. Part (B) illustrates that this influence is often inhibitory. The bipolar cell of photoreceptor A makes a lateral connection to an interneuron that synapses on the bipolar cell of photoreceptor B. When A is stimulated, it excites the interneuron, which inhibits the bipolar cell of B.

lar cells and then to *ganglion cells;* the axons of the ganglion cells form the optic nerve, which extends out of the eye and into the brain. However, this direct path to the brain is modified by interactions with other cells. Two types of interactions are especially important.

In the first of these, **bipolar cells** receive input from many photoreceptors, as illustrated in Figure 4.11(A). This arrangement is called convergence. **Convergence** increases the sensitivity of each bipolar cell, because light striking any of the photoreceptors to which the cell is connected will stimulate it. However, convergence reduces acuity, because information about exactly *which* photoreceptor was stimulated is lost. Thus, it is not surprising that there is little convergence among the cones of the fovea, an area that is good at detecting fine details but is not very sensitive to light.

Second, photoreceptor cells make connections to other types of cells in the retina, called **interneurons,** which make lateral (sideways) connections between bipolar cells. Through these lateral connections, the response to light by one cell can excite or, more commonly, inhibit the response of a neighboring cell. Figure 4.11(B) illustrates **lateral inhibition.**

These lateral interactions enhance the sensation of *contrast.* Why? Most of the time, the amounts of light reaching two photoreceptors will differ. As Figure 4.11(B) illustrates, through its lateral connections the photoreceptor receiving more light inhibits the output to the brain from the photoreceptor receiving less light, making it seem as if there is less light at that cell than there really is. Therefore, the brain actually receives a *comparison* of the light hitting two neighboring points, and whatever difference that exists between the light reaching the two photoreceptors is exaggerated. This exaggeration is important, because specific features of objects can create differences in amounts of incoming light. For example, the visual image of the edge of a table contains a transition from a lighter region to a darker region. Lateral inhibition in the retina enhances this difference, creating contrast that sharpens the edge and makes it more noticeable.

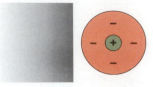 

Medium activity   Higher activity   Low activity
(light on center   (light on center;   (dark on both
and surround)   dark on surround)   center and
                                                  surround)

FIGURE 4.12

Center-Surround Receptive Fields of Ganglion Cells

Center-surround receptive fields allow ganglion cells to act as edge detectors. An edge is a region of light next to a region of relative darkness. If, as shown at the left, an edge is outside the receptive field of a center-on ganglion cell, there will be a uniform amount of light on both the excitatory center and the inhibitory surround, thus creating a moderate amount of activity. If, as shown in the middle drawing, the dark side of an edge covers a large portion of the inhibitory surround but leaves light on the excitatory center, the output of the cell will be high, signaling an edge in its receptive field. When, as shown at right, the dark area covers both the center and the surround of the ganglion cell, its activity will be lower, because neither segment of the cell's receptive field is receiving much stimulation.

Ganglion Cells and Their Receptive Fields   Photoreceptors, bipolar cells, and interneurons communicate by releasing neurotransmitters. But, as discussed in Chapter 3, neurotransmitters cause only small, graded changes in the membrane potential of the next cell, which cannot travel the distance from eye to brain. The cells in the retina that generate action potentials capable of traveling that distance are **ganglion cells.** Ganglion cells are stimulated by bipolar cells and modulated by interneurons, and their axons extend out of the retina to the brain.

What message do ganglion cells send to the brain? The answer depends on each cell's **receptive field,** which is the part of the retina *and* the corresponding part of the visual world to which a cell responds (Sekuler & Blake, 1994). Most ganglion cells have *center-surround receptive fields.* That is, most ganglion cells compare the amount of light stimulating the photoreceptors in the center of their receptive fields with the amount of light stimulating the photoreceptors in the area surrounding the center. This comparison results from the lateral interactions in the retina that enhance contrast. Some center-surround ganglion cells (*center-on cells*) are activated by light in the center of their receptive field; light in the regions surrounding the center inhibits their activity (see Figure 4.12). Other center-surround ganglion cells (*center-off cells*) work in just the opposite way. They are inhibited by light in the center and activated by light in the surrounding area.

The center-surround receptive fields of ganglion cells make it easier for you to see edges and, as illustrated in Figure 4.13, also create a sharper contrast between darker and lighter areas than actually exists. By enhancing the sensation of important features, the retina gives your brain an "improved" version of the visual world.

FIGURE 4.13

Visual Effects of Lateral Inhibition

The larger grid of black boxes and white stripes, called the Hermann grid, demonstrates the effects of lateral inhibition among retinal cells. As you look at the grid, dark spots appear in the intersections of the white stripes. To understand why this happens, look at the four black boxes in the smaller grid. The circles superimposed on this smaller grid represent the receptive fields of two center-on ganglion cells. At the intersection of the white stripes, a center-on ganglion cell has more whiteness shining on its inhibitory surround. Thus, its output is reduced compared to that of the one on the right, and the spot on the left appears darker. When you look directly at the intersection, the dark spot disappears, because ganglion cells in the fovea have smaller receptive fields than elsewhere in the retina, so more excitatory centers are being stimulated.

Seeing Color

Like beauty, color is in the eye of the beholder. Many animals see only shades of gray even when they look at a rainbow, but for humans color is a highly salient feature of vision. An advertising agent might tell you about the impact of color on buying preferences, a poet might tell you about the emotional power of color, but we will tell you about how you see colors—a process that is itself a thing of beauty and elegance.

Wavelengths and Color Sensations   We noted earlier that, at a given intensity, each wavelength of light is sensed as a certain color (look again at Figure 4.7 on page 107). However, the eye is seldom if ever presented with pure light of a single wavelength. Sunlight, for example, is a mixture of all wavelengths of light. When sunlight passes through a droplet of water, the different wavelengths of light are bent to different degrees, separating into a colorful rainbow. The spectrum of color found in the rainbow illustrates an important concept: The sensation produced by a mixture of different wavelengths of light is not the same as the sensations produced by separate wavelengths. Thus, just as most sounds are a mixture of sound waves of different frequencies, so most colors are a mixture of light of different wavelengths.

Characteristics of the mixture of wavelengths striking the eyes determine the color sensation. There are three separate aspects of this sensation: hue, saturation, and brightness. These are *psychological* dimensions that correspond roughly to the physical properties of light. **Hue** is the essential "color," determined by the dominant wavelength in the mixture of the light. For example, the wavelength of yellow is about 570 nanometers, and that of red is about 600 nanometers. Black, white, and gray are not considered hues because no wavelength predominates in them. **Saturation** is related to the purity of a color. A color is more saturated and more pure if just one wavelength is relatively more intense—contains more energy—than other wavelengths. If many wavelengths are added to a pure hue, the color is said to be *desaturated*. For example, pastels are colors that have been desaturated by the addition of whiteness. **Brightness** refers to the overall intensity of all of the wavelengths making up light.

The color circle shown in Figure 4.14 arranges hues according to their perceived similarities. If lights of two different wavelengths but equal intensity are mixed, the color you sense is at the midpoint of a line drawn between the two original colors on

FIGURE 4.14

The Color Circle

Ordering the colors according to their psychological similarities creates a color circle that predicts the result of additive mixing of two colored lights. The resulting color will be on a line between the two starting colors, the exact location on the line depending on the relative proportions of the two colors. For example, mixing equal amounts of pure green and pure red light will produce yellow, the color that lies at the midpoint of the line connecting red and green. (Nm stands for nanometers, the unit in which wavelengths are measured.)

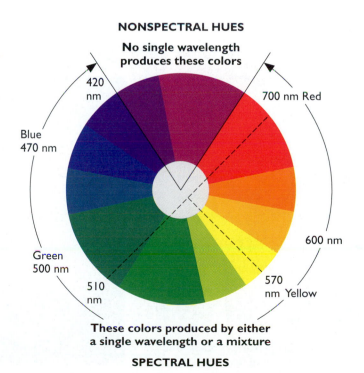

NONSPECTRAL HUES

No single wavelength produces these colors

420 nm

700 nm Red

Blue 470 nm

600 nm

Green 500 nm

570 nm Yellow

510 nm

These colors produced by either a single wavelength or a mixture

SPECTRAL HUES

the color circle. This process is known as *additive color mixing,* because the effects of the wavelengths from each light are added together. If you keep adding different colored lights, you eventually get white (the combination of all wavelengths). You are probably more familiar with a very different form of color mixing called *subtractive color mixing,* which occurs when paints are combined. Like other physical objects, paints reflect certain wavelengths and absorb all others. For example, grass is green because it absorbs all wavelengths except wavelengths that are sensed as green. White objects are white because they reflect all wavelengths. Light reflected from paints or other colored objects is seldom a pure wavelength, so predicting the color resulting from mixing paint is not as straightforward as combining pure wavelengths of light. But if you keep combining different colored paints, all of the wavelengths will eventually be subtracted, resulting in black. (The discussion that follows refers to *additive color mixing,* the mixing of light.)

By mixing lights of just a few wavelengths, we can produce different color sensations. How many wavelengths are needed to create any possible color? Figure 4.15 illustrates an experiment that addresses this question, using a piece of white paper, which reflects all wavelengths and therefore appears to be the color of the light shined upon it. The answer to the question of how many lights are needed to create all colors helped lead scientists to an important theory of how people sense color.

The Trichromatic Theory of Color Vision   Early in the nineteenth century, Thomas Young and, later, Hermann von Helmholtz established that they could match any color by mixing pure lights of only three wavelengths. For example, by mixing blue light (about 440 nanometers), green light (about 510 nanometers), and red light (about 600 nanometers) in different ratios, they could produce *any* other color. Young and Helmholtz interpreted this evidence to mean that there must be three types of visual elements, each of which is most sensitive to different wavelengths, and that information from these three elements combines to produce the sensation of color. This theory of color vision is called the *Young-Helmholtz theory,* or the **trichromatic theory.**

Support for the trichromatic theory has come from recordings of the responses of individual photoreceptors to particular wavelengths of light and from electrical recordings from human cones (Schnapf, Kraft, & Baylor, 1987). This research reveals that there are three types of cones. Although each type responds to a broad range of wavelengths, each is most sensitive to particular wavelengths. *Short-wavelength* cones respond most to light of about 440 nanometers (a shade of blue). *Medium-wavelength* cones are most sensitive to light of about 530 nanometers (a shade of green). Finally,

FIGURE 4.15

Matching a Color by Mixing Lights of Pure Wavelengths

A target color is presented on the left side of this display; the participant's task is to adjust the intensity of different pure-wavelength lights until the resulting mixture looks exactly like the target. A large number of colors can be matched with just two mixing lights, but *any* color can be matched by mixing *three* pure-wavelength lights. Experiments like this generated the information that led to the trichromatic theory of color vision.

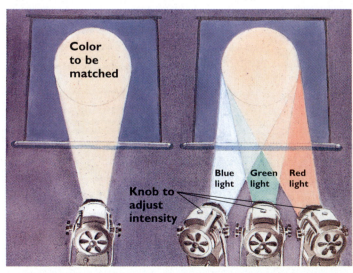

Mixture of many wavelengths   Each projector produces one pure wavelength color

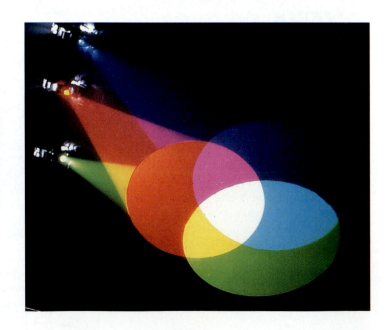

FIGURE 4.16

**Relative Responses of Three
Cone Types to Different
Wavelengths of Light**

Each type of cone responds to a range of wavelengths but responds more to some wavelengths than to others. Thus, it is possible to generate the same pattern of output—and hence the same sensation of color—by more than one combination of wavelengths. For example, a pure light of 570 nanometers (A in the figure) stimulates long-wavelength cones at 1.0 relative units and medium-wavelength cones at about 0.7 relative units. This ratio of cone activity (1/0.7 = 1.4) yields the sensation of yellow. In fact, any combination of wavelengths at the proper intensity that generates the same ratio of activity in these cone types will produce the sensation of yellow.

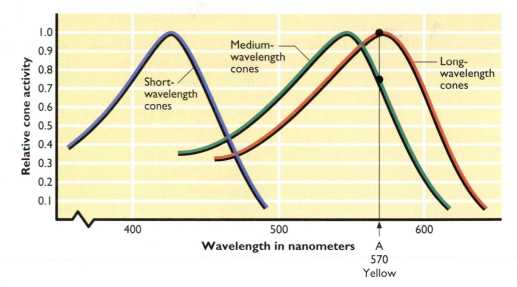

FIGURE 4.17

**Afterimages Produced by
the Opponent-Process Nature
of Color Vision**

Stare at the dot in the flag for at least thirty seconds, then fixate on the dot in the white space below it.

long-wavelength cones respond best to light of about 560 nanometers (a shade of yellow, although these cones have traditionally been called "red cones").

Note that no single cone, by itself, can signal the color of a light. It is the *ratio* of the activities of the three types of cones that indicates what color will be sensed. Color vision is therefore coded by the pattern of activity of the different cones. For example, a light is sensed as yellow if it has a pure wavelength of about 570 nanometers; this light stimulates both medium- and long-wavelength cones, as illustrated by arrow A in Figure 4.16. But yellow is also sensed whenever any mixture of other lights stimulates the same pattern of activity in these two types of cones.

The Opponent-Process Theory of Color Vision   Brilliant as it is, the trichromatic theory in its simplest form cannot explain some aspects of color vision. For example, it cannot account for the phenomenon of color afterimages. If you stare at the flag in Figure 4.17 for thirty seconds and then look at the blank white space below it, you will see an afterimage. What was yellow in the original image will be blue in the afterimage, what was green before will appear red, and what was black will now appear white.

This type of observation led Ewald Hering to offer an alternative to the trichromatic theory of color vision, called the **opponent-process theory.** It holds that the visual elements sensitive to color are grouped into three pairs and that the members of each pair oppose, or inhibit, each other. The three pairs are a *red-green element,* a *blue-yellow element,* and a *black-white element.* Each element signals one color or the other—red or green, for example—but never both. This theory explains color afterimages. When one part of an opponent pair is no longer stimulated, the other is activated. Thus, as in Figure 4.17, if the original image you look at is green, the afterimage will be red.

The opponent-process theory also explains the phenomenon of complementary colors. Two colors are **complementary** if gray results when lights of the two colors are mixed together. Actually, the neutral color of gray can appear as anything from white to gray to black depending on the intensity of the light. On the color circle shown in Figure 4.14 (on page 113), complementary colors are roughly opposite to one another. Red and green lights are complementary, as are yellow and blue. Notice that complementary colors are *opponent* colors in Hering's theory. According to opponent-process theory, complementary colors stimulate the same visual element (e.g., red-green) in opposite directions, canceling each other out. Thus, the theory helps explain why mixing lights of complementary colors produces gray.

A Synthesis and an Update   The trichromatic and opponent-process theories seem quite different, but both are correct to some extent, and together they can explain most of what is now known about color vision. Electrical recordings made from different types of cells in the retina paved the way for a synthesis of the two theories.

At the level of the photoreceptors, a slightly revised version of the trichromatic theory is correct. There *are* three types of cones. However, molecular biologists who isolated the genes for cone pigments have found variations in the genes for the cones sensitive to middle-wavelength and long-wavelength light. These variants have slightly different sensitivities to different wavelengths of light. Thus, we can have two, three, or even four genes for long-wavelength pigments (Neitz & Neitz, 1995). Individual differences in people's long-wavelength pigments become apparent in color-matching tasks. When asked to mix a red light and a green light to match a yellow light, a person with one kind of long-wavelength pigment will choose a different red-to-green ratio than someone with a different long-wavelength pigment. So the answer to the question we asked at the beginning of the chapter—as to whether a certain color looks the same to everyone—is "Not necessarily."

As noted earlier, the output from many photoreceptors feeds into each ganglion cell, and the output from the ganglion cell goes to the brain. Recall that the receptive fields of most ganglion cells are arranged in center-surround patterns. The center and the surround are color coded, as illustrated in Figure 4.18. The center responds best to one color, and the surround responds best to a different color. This color coding arises because varying proportions of the three cone types feed into the center and the surround of the ganglion cell.

When either the center or the surround of a ganglion cell is stimulated, the other area is inhibited. In other words, the colors to which the center and the surround of a given ganglion cell are most responsive are opponent colors. Recordings from many ganglion cells show that three very common pairs of opponent colors are those predicted by Hering's opponent-process theory: red-green, blue-yellow, and black-white. Stimulating both the center and the surround cancels the effects of either light, producing gray. Black-white cells receive input from all types of cones, so it does not matter what color stimulates them. Cells in specific regions of the visual cortex, too, respond in opponent pairs sensitive to the red-green and blue-yellow input coming from ganglion cells in the retina (Engel, Zhang, & Wandell, 1997).

In summary, color vision is possible because the three types of cones have different sensitivities to different wavelengths, as the trichromatic theory suggests. The sensation of different colors results from stimulating the three cone types in different ratios. Because there are three types of cones, any color can be produced by mixing three different wavelengths of light. But the story does not end there. The output from cones is fed into ganglion cells, and the center and surround of the ganglion cells respond to different colors and inhibit each other. This activity provides the basis for afterimages. Therefore, the trichromatic theory describes the properties of the photoreceptors,

FIGURE 4.18

Color Coding and the Ganglion Cells

The center-surround receptive fields of ganglion cells form the anatomical basis for opponent colors. Some ganglion cells, like **G₂**, have a center whose photoreceptors respond best to red wavelengths and a surround whose photoreceptors respond best to green wavelengths. Other ganglion cells pair blue and yellow, whereas still others receive input from all types of photoreceptors.

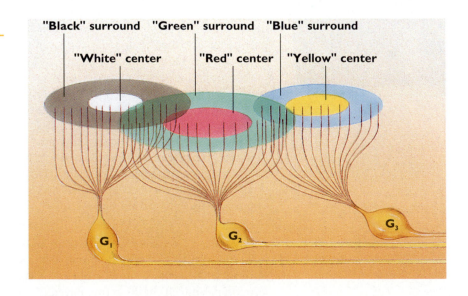

"Black" surround   "Green" surround   "Blue" surround

"White" center   "Red" center   "Yellow" center

FIGURE 4.19

What Do Colorblind People See?

At the upper left is a photo as it appears to people who have all three cone photopigments. The other photos simulate how colors appear to people who are missing photopigments for short wavelengths (lower left), long wavelengths (upper right), or medium wavelengths (lower right). If any of these photos look to you just like the one at the upper left, you may have a form of colorblindness.

whereas the opponent-process theory describes the properties of the ganglion cells. Both theories are needed to account for the complexity of visual sensations of color.

Colorblindness   People who have cones containing only two of the three possible color-sensitive pigments are described as *colorblind* (see Figure 4.19). They are not actually blind to all color; they simply discriminate fewer colors than other people. Two centuries ago, a colorblind chemist named John Dalton carefully described the colors he sensed—to him, a red ribbon appeared the same color as mud—and hypothesized that the fluid in his eyeball must be tinted blue. He instructed his doctor to examine the fluid after he died, but it was clear. However, his preserved retinas were examined recently by molecular biologists. They were not surprised to find that, just as most colorblind people today lack the genes that code one or more of the pigments, Dalton had no gene for medium-length pigment (Hunt et al., 1995).

Visual Pathways

The brain performs even more elaborate processing of visual information than does the retina. The information reaches the brain via the axons of ganglion cells, which leave the eye as a bundle of fibers called the **optic nerve** (see Figures 4.8 and 4.10 on pages 108 and 110). Because there are no photoreceptors at the point where the optic nerve exits the eyeball, a **blind spot** is created, as Figure 4.20 demonstrates.

After leaving the retina, about half the fibers of the optic nerve cross over to the opposite side of the brain at a structure called the **optic chiasm.** (*Chiasm* means "cross" and is pronounced "KI-asm"). Fibers from the inside half of each eye, nearest to the nose, cross over; fibers from the outside half of each eye do not (see Figure 4.21). This arrangement brings all the visual information about the right half of the visual world to the left hemisphere of the brain and information from the left half of the visual world to the right hemisphere of the brain.

The optic chiasm is part of the bottom surface of the brain; beyond the chiasm, the fibers ascend into the brain itself. The axons from most of the ganglion cells in the retina form synapses in the thalamus, in a specific region called the **lateral geniculate nucleus (LGN).** Neurons in the LGN then send the visual input to the **primary visual cortex,** which lies in the occipital lobe at the back of the brain. Visual information is

FIGURE 4.20

FIGURE 4.20

The Blind Spot

There is a blind spot where axons from the ganglion cells leave the eye and become the optic nerve. To "see" your blind spot, cover your left eye and stare at the cross just to the right of the head. Move the page closer and then farther away, and at some point the dot to the right should disappear. However, the vertical lines around the dot will probably look continuous, because the brain tends to fill in visual information at the blind spot. We are normally unaware of this "hole" in our vision because the blind spot of one eye is in the visual field of the other eye.

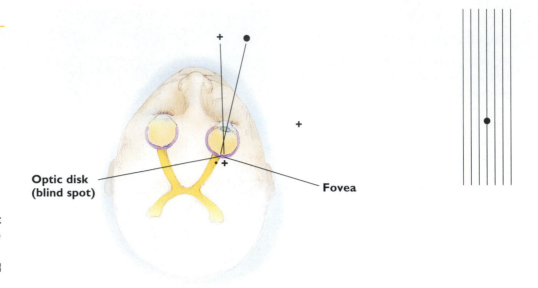

Optic disk (blind spot)   Fovea

also sent from the primary visual cortex for processing in many other areas of cortex. In studies of monkeys, 32 separate visual areas interconnected by more than 300 pathways have been identified so far (Van Essen, Anderson, & Felleman, 1992).

The retina has a topographical map of the visual world, such that neighboring points on the retina receive information from neighboring points in the visual world. This topographical map is also maintained in the brain, in the primary visual cortex, and in each of the many other visual areas of the cortex. That is, neighboring points in the retina are represented in neighboring cells in the brain. (This is a spatial coding system.) The map is a distorted one, however. A larger area of cortex is devoted to the areas of the retina that have many photoreceptors. For example, the fovea, which is densely packed with photoreceptors, is represented in an especially large segment of cortex.

FIGURE 4.21

Pathways from the Ganglion Cells into the Brain

Light rays from the right side of the visual field (the right side of what you are looking at) end up on the left half of each retina (shown in red). Light rays from the left visual field end up on the right half of each retina (shown in blue). From the right eye, axons from the nasal side of the retina (the side nearer the nose, which receives information from the right visual field) cross over the midline and travel to the left side of the brain with those fibers from the left eye that also receive input from the right side of the visual world. A similar arrangement unites left visual-field information from both eyes in the right side of the brain.

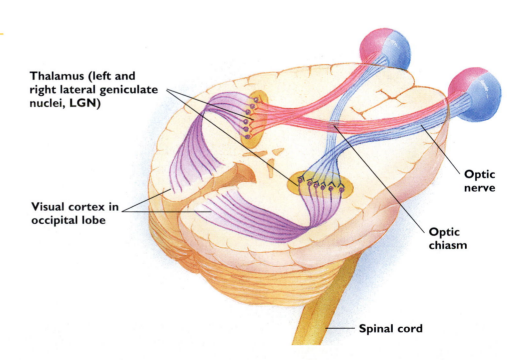

Thalamus (left and right lateral geniculate nuclei, LGN)

Visual cortex in occipital lobe

Optic nerve

Optic chiasm

Spinal cord

Visual Representations

The normally effortless experience of sight is due to a very complex system, in which visual sensations are transmitted from the retina through various cortical regions. We can appreciate some of these complexities by considering the receptive fields of neurons at each point along the way. Two of the processes that characterize these receptive fields are *parallel processing of visual properties* and *hierarchical processing of visual information*.

Parallel Processing of Visual Properties   Like ganglion cells, neurons of the LGN in the thalamus have center-surround receptive fields. However, the LGN is organized in multiple layers of neurons, and each layer contains a complete map of the retina. Neurons of different layers respond to particular aspects of visual stimuli. In fact, four separate aspects of a visual scene are simultaneously handled by *parallel processing*

FIGURE 4.22

Separate Processing of Color and Movement

Different aspects of a visual image are processed in parallel by different parts of the visual system. PET scans show that a brightly colored image causes activation of one area of the brain, whereas black-and-white moving images trigger activity in a completely different area. Both types of images activate the primary visual cortex, but within that region the neurons stimulated by each type of image are segregated.

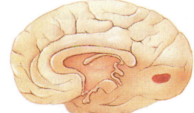

(A) ACTIVATED BY BRIGHTLY COLORED IMAGES

(B) ACTIVATED BY BLACK-AND-WHITE MOVING IMAGES

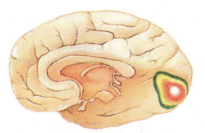

(C) ACTIVATED BY EITHER TYPE OF IMAGE

FIGURE 4.23

Construction of a Feature Detector

The output from several center-on ganglion cells goes to cells in the lateral geniculate nucleus (LGN) and is then fed into one cell in the cortex. This "wiring" makes the cortical cell respond best when all of its LGN cells are excited, and they are most excited when light falls on the center of the receptive fields of their ganglion cells. Because those receptive fields lie in an angled row, it takes a bar-shaped light at that angle to stimulate all their centers. In short, this cortical cell responds best when it detects a bar-shaped feature at a particular angle. Rotating the bar to a different orientation would no longer stimulate this particular cortical cell.

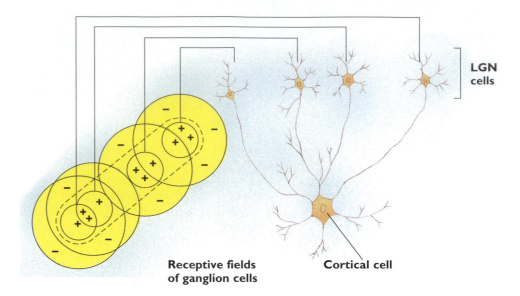

Receptive fields
of ganglion cells

Cortical cell

LGN cells

systems (Livingstone & Hubel, 1988). The form of objects and their color are handled by one system (the "what" system), whereas their movement and cues to distance are handled by another (the "where" system).

These sensations are then sent to the cortex, but the question of where in the cortex they are finally assembled into a unified conscious experience is still being debated. Some researchers argue that there is no one region where all the separate streams of processing converge (Engel et al., 1992). Instead, they say, connections among the regions of cortex that process separate aspects of visual sensation appear to integrate their activity, making possible a distributed but unified experience (Gilbert, 1992). For example, functional MRI scans of monkeys and humans have revealed integration of "what" and "where" information in the prefrontal cortex, an area known to involve short-term memory for vision (Ungerleider, Courtney, & Haxby, 1998).

PET scans, too, have provided evidence of separate processing channels in humans. As shown in Figure 4.22 (on page 119), one area of visual cortex is activated when a person views a colorful painting; a different area is activated by viewing black-and-white moving images (Zeki, 1992). Brain damage may also reveal the separate channels. Damage in one area can leave a person unable to see colors, or even remember them, while still able to see and recognize objects. Damage in another area can leave a person able to see only stationary objects; as soon as the object moves, it disappears. People with brain damage in still other regions can see only moving objects, not stationary ones (Zeki, 1992). Even in visual imagination, the same separate processing channels apparently operate. Thus, some patients with brain damage can recall parts of a visual image, but not their correct spatial relationship. For example, they may be able to "see" a mental image of a bull's horns and ears, but cannot assemble them mentally to form a bull's head (Kosslyn, 1988).

Hierarchical Processing of Visual Information   Multiple inputs from the LGN converge on single cells of the cortex, as Figure 4.23 illustrates. Cells of the cortex that receive input from the LGN in the thalamus have more complex receptive fields than the center-surround fields of LGN cells. For example, a specific cell in the cortex might respond only to vertical edges, but it responds to vertical edges anywhere in its receptive field. Another class of cells responds only to moving objects; a third class responds only to objects with corners. Because cortical cells respond to specific characteristics of objects in the visual field, they have been described as **feature detectors** (Hubel & Wiesel, 1979).

Feature detectors illustrate how cortical processing is partly *hierarchical* in nature. Complex feature detectors may be built up out of more and more complex connections among simpler feature detectors (Hubel & Wiesel, 1979). For example, several

in review

SEEING		
Aspect of Sensory System	**Elements**	**Key Characteristics**
Energy	Light—electromagnetic radiation from about 400 nm to about 750 nm	The intensity, wavelength, and complexity of light waves determine the brightness, hue, and saturation of visual sensations.
Accessory structures	Eye—cornea, pupil, iris, lens	Light rays are bent to focus on the retina.
Transduction mechanism	Photoreceptors (rods and cones) in the retina	Rods are more sensitive to light than cones, but cones discriminate among colors. Sensations of color depend first on the cones, which respond differently to different light wavelengths, and then on processing by ganglion cells. Interactions among cells of the retina exaggerate differences in the light stimuli reaching the photoreceptors, enhancing the sensation of contrast.
Pathways and representations	Optic nerve to optic chiasm to LGN of thalamus to primary visual cortex	Neighboring points in the visual world are represented at neighboring points in the LGN and primary visual cortex. Neurons there respond to particular aspects of the visual stimulus—such as color, movement, distance, or form.

center-surround cells might feed into one cortical cell to make a line detector, and several line detectors might feed into another cortical cell to make a cell that responds to a particular spatial orientation, such as vertical. With further connections, a more complex detector, such as a "box detector," might be built from simpler line and corner detectors.

Cells with similar receptive-field properties are organized into columns in the cortex. The columns are arranged perpendicular (at right angles) to the surface of the cortex. For example, if you locate a cell that responds to diagonal lines in a particular spot in the visual field, most of the cells in a column above and below that cell will also respond to diagonal lines. Other properties are represented by whole columns of cells, so, for example, there are columns in which all of the cells are most sensitive to a particular color. Recent work has also revealed that individual neurons in the cortex perform several different tasks, allowing complex visual processing (Schiller, 1996). ("In Review: Seeing" summarizes how the nervous system gathers the information that allows people to see.)

THE CHEMICAL SENSES: SMELL AND TASTE

There are animals without vision, and there are animals without hearing, but there are no animals without some form of chemical sense, some sense that arises from the interaction of chemicals and receptors. **Olfaction** (smell) detects chemicals that are airborne, or volatile. **Gustation** (taste) detects chemicals in solution that come into contact with receptors inside the mouth.

FIGURE 4.24

The Olfactory System: The Nose and the Rose

Airborne chemicals from the rose reach the olfactory area through the nostrils and through the back of the mouth. Fibers pass directly from the olfactory area to the olfactory bulb in the brain, and from there signals pass to areas such as the hypothalamus and amygdala, which are involved in emotion.

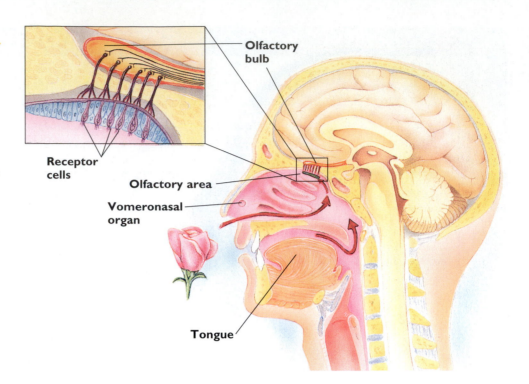

Olfaction

People sense odors in the upper part of the nose (see Figure 4.24). Odor molecules can reach olfactory receptors there either by passing directly through the nostrils or by rising through an opening in the palate at the back of the mouth, allowing us to sample odors from food as we eat it. The olfactory receptors themselves are located on the dendrites of specialized neurons that extend into the moist lining of the nose. Odor molecules bind to these receptors, causing depolarization of the dendrites' membrane, which in turn leads to changes in the firing rates of the neurons. A single molecule of an odorous substance can cause a change in the membrane potential of an olfactory neuron, but detection of the odor by a human normally requires about fifty such molecules (Menini, Picco, & Firestein, 1995); the average hot pizza generates lots more than that.

Olfactory neurons are continuously replaced with new ones, as each lives only about two months. Scientists are very interested in this process because, as noted in Chapter 3, most neurons cannot divide to create new ones. An understanding of how new olfactory neurons are generated—and how they make appropriate connections in the brain—may someday be helpful in treating brain damage.

Substances that have similar chemical structures tend to have similar odors. The precise means by which olfactory receptors in the nose discriminate various smells and send coded messages about them to the brain has only recently been determined (Buck, 1996). In contrast to vision, which makes use of only four basic receptor types (rods, and three kinds of cones), the olfactory system employs about 1,000 different types of receptors. The genes for these olfactory receptors make up about one to two percent of the human genome. A given odor stimulates these receptors to varying degrees, and the combination of receptors stimulated creates codes for a particular odor. The many combinations possible allow humans to discriminate tens of thousands of different odors.

Olfaction is the only sense that does not send its messages through the thalamus. Instead, axons from neurons in the nose extend through a bony plate and directly into the brain, where they have a synapse in a structure called the **olfactory bulb.** Connections from the olfactory bulb spread diffusely through the brain, but

A "Mating Ball"

Among snakes there is intense competition for females—dozens of males will wrap themselves around a single female in a "mating ball." Snakes' forked tongues allow them to sample airborne chemicals at two different points and, hence, to follow an olfactory trail (Schwenk, 1994). Males with the best olfactory tracking abilities are the ones most likely to reach a female first and thus to pass on their genes to the next generation.

they are especially plentiful in the amygdala, a part of the brain involved in emotional experience.

These unusual anatomical features of the olfactory system may account for the strong relationship between olfaction and emotional memory. For example, associations between a certain experience and a particular odor are not weakened much by time or subsequent experiences (Lawless & Engen, 1977). Thus, catching a whiff of the cologne once worn by a lost loved one can reactivate intense feelings of love or sadness associated with that person. Odors can also bring back accurate memories of significant experiences linked with them (Engen, Gilmore, & Mair, 1991).

The mechanisms of olfaction are remarkably similar in species ranging from humans to worms. Different species vary considerably, however, in their sensitivity to smell, and in the degree to which they depend on it for survival. For example, humans have about 9 million olfactory neurons, whereas there are about 225 million such neurons in dogs, which are far more dependent on smell to identify food, territory, and receptive mates. In addition, dogs and many other species have an accessory olfactory system that is able to detect pheromones. **Pheromones** (pronounced "FER-o-mones") are chemicals that are released by one animal and, when detected by another, can shape the second animal's behavior or physiology. For example, when male snakes detect a chemical exuded on the skin of female snakes they are stimulated to "court" the female.

In mammals, pheromones can be nonvolatile chemicals that animals lick and pass into a portion of the olfactory system called the **vomeronasal organ.** In female mice, for example, the vomeronasal organ detects chemicals in the male's urine; by this means a male can cause a female to ovulate and become sexually receptive, and an unfamiliar male can cause a pregnant female to abort her pregnancy (Bruce, 1969).

The role of pheromones in humans is much more controversial. Some perfume companies want potential customers to believe that they have created sexual attractants that act as pheromones, subconsciously influencing the behavior of desirable partners. At the other extreme are those who argue that, in humans, the vomeronasal organ is an utterly nonfunctional vestige, like the appendix. The best current scientific evidence suggests that the human vomeronasal organ is capable of responding to certain hormonal substances and can influence certain hormonal secretions (Berliner et al., 1996). And pheromones themselves are definitely capable of producing physiological changes in humans that are related to reproduction. For example, pheromonal signals secreted in the perspiration of a woman can shorten or prolong the menstrual cycle of other women nearby (Stern & McClintock, 1998). In such cases, pheromones are responsible for *menstrual synchrony,* the tendency of women living together to menstruate at the same time. However, despite some suggestive findings (e.g., Cutler, Friedmann, & McCoy, 1998), there is still no solid evidence for a sexual attractant pheromone in humans, or even in nonhuman primates.

Still, learned associations between certain odors and emotional experiences may enhance a person's readiness for sex. People also use olfactory information in other social situations. For example, after just a few hours of contact, mothers can usually identify their newborn babies by the infants' smell (Porter, Cernich, & McLaughlin, 1983). And if infants are breast-fed, they can discriminate their mothers' odor from that of other breast-feeding women, and appear to be comforted by it (Porter, 1991). Indeed, individual mammals, including humans, have a distinct "odortype," which is determined by their immune cells and other inherited physiological factors (Beauchamp et al., 1995). During pregnancy, a woman's own odortype combines with the odortype of her fetus to form a third odortype. Each of these three odors is distinguishable, suggesting that recognition of odortypes may help establish the mother-infant bonds discussed in Chapter 12.

Gustation

The chemical sense system in the mouth is gustation, or taste. The receptors for taste are in the taste buds, which are grouped together in structures called **papillae**

Taste Receptors

Taste buds are grouped into structures called papillae. Two kinds of papillae are visible in this greatly enlarged photo of the surface of the human tongue.

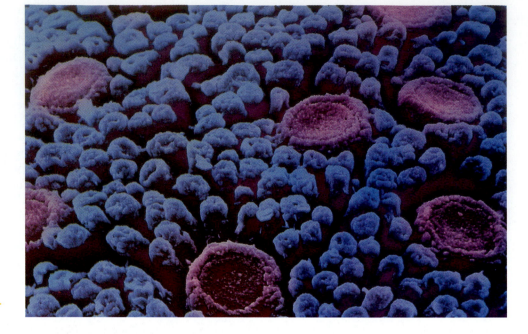

FIGURE 4.25

The Taste Buds of Supertasters

There may be genetically determined differences in the ability to taste things. So-called "supertasters" have thousands of taste buds on their tongues, whereas "nontasters" have only hundreds of buds. Most people fall between these extremes. Having different numbers of taste buds may help account for differences in people's food intake, and weight problems. For example, Linda Bartoshuk has found that, compared with overweight people, thin people have many more taste buds (Duffy et al., 1999). Perhaps they do not have to eat as much to experience the good tastes of food.

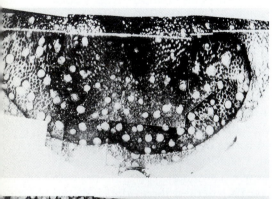

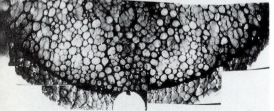

(pronounced "pa-PILL-ee"). Normally, there are about 10,000 taste buds in a person's mouth, mostly on the tongue but also on the roof of the mouth and on the back of the throat.

In contrast to the olfactory system, which can discriminate thousands of different odors, the human taste system detects only a few elementary sensations. The most familiar of these are sweet, sour, bitter, and salty. Each taste bud responds best to one or two of these categories, but it also responds weakly to others. The sensation of a particular substance appears to result from the responses of taste buds that are relatively sensitive to a specific category. Behavioral studies and electrical recordings from taste neurons have also established two additional taste sensations (Rolls, 1997). One, called *umami*, enhances other tastes and is produced by certain proteins as well as by monosodium glutamate (MSG). The other, called *astringent*, is the taste produced by tannins, which are found in teas, for example.

Different tastes are transduced into neural activity by quite different types of taste receptors, and in different ways (Stewart, DeSimone, & Hill, 1997). For example, sweet and bitter are signaled when chemicals fit into specific receptor sites, whereas sour and salty act through more direct effects on the ion channels in membranes of taste cells. Knowledge of the chemistry of sweetness is allowing scientists to design new chemicals that fit into sweetness receptors and taste thousands of times sweeter than sugar. Many of these substances are now being tested for safety and may soon allow people to enjoy low-calorie hot-fudge sundaes.

A taste component in its own right, saltiness also enhances the taste of food by suppressing bitterness (Breslin & Beauchamp, 1997). In animals, taste responses to salt are determined during early development, before and after birth. Research with animals has shown that if mothers are put on a low-salt diet, their offspring are less likely to prefer salt (Hill & Przekop, 1988). In humans, experiences with salty foods over the first four years of life may alter the sensory systems that detect salt and contribute to enduring preferences for salty foods (Hill & Mistretta, 1990).

About 25 percent of the population are "supertasters"—individuals who have an especially large number of papillae on their tongues (Bartoshuk et al., 1996; see Figure 4.25). Supertasters are more sensitive than other people to bitterness, as revealed in their reaction to foods such as broccoli, soy products, and grapefruit (Drewnowski, Henderson, & Shore, 1997).

Smell, Taste, and Flavor

If you have a stuffy nose, everything tastes like cardboard. Why? Because smell and taste act as two components of a single system, known as *flavor* (Rozin, 1982). Most of the properties that make food taste good are actually odors detected by the olfactory system, not activities of the taste system. The olfactory and gustatory pathways converge in the orbitofrontal cortex (Rolls, 1997), where neurons also respond to the sight and texture of food. The responses of neurons in this "flavor cortex" are also influenced by conditions of hunger and satiety ("fullness").

Both tastes and odors prompt strong emotional responses. For tastes, the repugnance of bitter flavors is inborn, but the associations of emotions with odors are all learned (Bartoshuk, 1991). Many animals easily learn taste aversions to particular foods when the taste is associated with nausea, but humans learn aversions to odors more readily than to tastes (Bartoshuk & Wolfe, 1990).

Variations in one's nutritional state affect taste and flavor, as well as the motivation to consume particular foods. For example, food deprivation or salt deficiency makes sweet or salty things taste better. Intake of protein and fat are influenced more indirectly. Molecules of protein and fat have no inherent taste or smell; the tastes and smells of foods that contain these nutrients actually come from small amounts of other volatile substances. So adjustments in intake of these nutrients are based on associations between olfactory cues from the volatile substances and the nutritional consequences of eating the foods (Bartoshuk, 1991). These findings have implications for dieting, which is discussed in Chapter 11.

Flavor includes other characteristics of food as well: its tactile properties (how it feels in your mouth) and especially its temperature. Warm foods are experienced as sweeter, but temperature does not alter saltiness (Frankmann & Green, 1987). Also, warming releases aromas that rise from the mouth into the nose and create more flavor sensations. This is why some people find hot pizza delicious and cold pizza disgusting. Spicy "hot" foods actually stimulate pain fibers in the mouth because they contain a substance called capsaicin (pronounced "cap-SAY-a-sin"), which opens specific ion channels in pain neurons that are also opened by heat. Such foods are thus experienced as physiologically "hot" (Caterina et al., 1997). Why do people eat spicy foods even though they stimulate pain? The practice may have originated because many "hot" spices have antibacterial properties. In fact, researchers have found a strong correlation between frequent use of antibacterial spices and living in climates that promote bacterial contamination (Billing & Sherman, 1998).

SOMATIC SENSES AND THE VESTIBULAR SYSTEM

Some senses are not located in a specific organ, such as the eye or the ear. These are the **somatic senses,** also called **somatosensory systems,** which are spread throughout the body. The somatic senses include the skin senses of touch, temperature, and pain, as well as kinesthesia, the sense that tells the brain where the parts of the body are. Closely related to kinesthesia is the vestibular system, which tells the brain about the position and movements of the head. Though not strictly a somatosensory system, it will also be considered in this section.

Touch and Temperature

Touch is crucial. People can function and prosper without vision, hearing, or smell, but a person without touch would have difficulty surviving. Without a sense of touch, you could not even swallow food.

Stimulus and Receptors for Touch   The energy detected by the sense of touch is a mechanical deformation of tissue, usually of the skin. The skin covers nearly two square yards of surface and weighs more than twenty pounds. The hairs distributed

The Sense of Touch

Touch provides information about the world that is vital to survival. Its importance is revealed in many other aspects of behavior as well. For example, this computer software developer can work without his sight, but not without touch.

virtually everywhere on the skin do not sense anything directly, but when bent, they deform the skin beneath them. The receptors that transduce this deformation into neural activity are in, or just below, the skin.

Many nerve endings in the skin are candidates for the role of touch receptor. Some neurons come from the spinal cord, enter the skin, and simply end; these are called *free nerve endings.* Many other neurons end in a variety of elaborate, specialized structures. However, there is generally little relationship between the type of nerve ending and the type of sensory information carried by the neuron. Many types of nerve endings respond to mechanical stimuli, but the exact process through which they transduce mechanical energy is still unknown. These somatosensory neurons are unusual in that they have no dendrites. Their cell bodies are outside the spinal cord, and their axon splits and extends both to the skin and to the spinal cord. Action potentials travel from the nerve endings in the skin to the spinal cord, where they communicate across a synapse to dendrites of other neurons.

People do more than just passively respond to whatever happens to come in contact with their bodies. For humans, touch is also an active sense that is used to get specific information. In much the same way as you can look as well as just see, you can also touch as well as feel. When people are involved in active sensing, they usually use the part of the sensory apparatus that has the greatest sensitivity. For vision, this is the fovea; for touch, the fingertips. (The area of primary somatosensory cortex devoted to the fingertips is correspondingly large.) Fingertip touch is the principal way people explore the textures of surfaces. It can be extremely sensitive, as evidenced by blind people who can read Braille as rapidly as 200 words per minute (Foulke, 1991).

Adaptation of Touch Receptors   Constant input from all the touch neurons would provide an abundance of unnecessary information. Once you get dressed, for example, you do not need to be constantly reminded that you are wearing clothes. Thanks in part to the process of adaptation mentioned earlier, you do not continue to feel your clothes against your skin.

Changes in touch (for example, if your pants suddenly fall down) constitute the most important sensory information. The touch sense emphasizes these changes and filters out the excess information. How? Typically, a touch neuron responds with a burst of firing when a stimulus is applied, then quickly returns to baseline firing rates, even though the stimulus may still be in contact with the skin. If the touch pressure increases, the neuron again responds with an increase in firing rate, but then it again slows down. A few neurons adapt more slowly, continuing to fire at an elevated rate as long as pressure is applied to the skin. By attending to this input, you can sense a constant stimulus.

Coding and Representation of Touch Information   The sense of touch codes information about two aspects of an object in contact with the skin: its weight and its location. The *intensity* of the stimulus—how heavy it is—is coded by both the firing rate of individual neurons and the number of neurons stimulated. A heavy object produces a higher rate of firing and stimulates more neurons than a light object. *Location* is coded much as it is for vision: by the spatial organization of the information.

Touch information is organized such that signals from neighboring points on the skin stay next to each other, even as they ascend from the skin through the spinal cord to the thalamus and on to the somatosensory cortex. Accordingly, just as there is a topographical map of the visual field in the brain, the area of cortex that receives touch information resembles a map of the surface of the body. (To confirm this, look again at Figure 3.18 on page 73.) As with the other senses, these representations are contralateral; that is, input from the left side of the body goes to the right side of the brain, and vice versa. In nonhuman primates, however, touch information from each hand is sent to both sides of the brain. This arrangement appears to amplify information from manual exploration of objects and to improve feedback from hand movements (Iwamura, Iriki, & Tanaka, 1994).

Temperature   When you dig your toes into a sandy summer beach, the pleasant experience you get comes partly from the sensation of warmth. Touch and temperature seem to be separate senses, and to some extent they are; but the difference between the two senses is not always clear.

Some of the skin's sensory neurons respond to a change in temperature, but not to simple contact. There are "warm fibers" that increase their firing rates when the temperature changes in the range of about 95° to 115°F (35° to 47°C). Temperatures above this range are painful and stimulate different fibers. Other fibers are "cold fibers"; they respond to a broad range of cool temperatures. However, many of the fibers that respond to temperature also respond to touch, so sensations of touch and temperature sometimes interact. For example, warm and cold objects can feel up to 250 percent heavier than body-temperature objects (Stevens & Hooper, 1982). Also, if you touch an object made up of alternating warm and cool bars, you will have the sensation of intense heat (Thunberg, 1896; cited in Craig & Bushnell, 1994).

Stimulation of the touch sense can have some interesting psychological and physiological effects. For example, premature human infants gain weight 47 percent faster when they are given massages; they do not eat more but, rather, process the food more efficiently. In children with asthma, massage therapy increases air flow (Field et al., 1998); in children with arthritis, it reduces pain and lowers stress hormone levels (Field et al., 1997). In adults, massage can reduce anxiety, increase brainwave (EEG) patterns associated with alertness, and improve performance on math tests (Field et al., 1996).

Pain

The skin senses can convey a great deal of pleasure, but a change in the intensity of the same kind of stimulation can create a distinctly different sensation: pain. Pain provides you with information about the impact of the world on your body; it can tell you, "You have just crushed your left thumb with a hammer." Pain also has a distinctly negative emotional component. Researchers have focused on the information-carrying aspects of pain, its emotional components, and the various ways that the brain can adjust the amount of pain that reaches consciousness.

LINKAGES

The Complex Nature of Pain

If pain were based only on the nature of incoming stimuli, this participant in a purification ceremony in Singapore would be hurting. However, as described in Chapter 9, on consciousness, the experience of pain is a complex phenomenon affected by psychological and biological variables that can make it more, or as in this case less, intense.

Pain as an Information Sense   The information-carrying aspect of pain is very similar to that of touch and temperature. The receptors for pain are free nerve endings. For example, capsaicin, the active ingredient in chili peppers, creates pain in the mouth by specifically stimulating these pain nerve endings. Painful stimuli cause the release of chemicals that fit into specialized receptors in pain neurons, causing them to fire. The axons of pain-sensing neurons release neurotransmitters not only near the spinal cord, thus sending information to the brain, but also near the skin, causing local inflammation.

Two types of nerve fibers carry pain signals from the skin to the spinal cord. *A-delta fibers* carry sharp, pricking pain sensations; they are myelinated to carry the sharp pain message quickly. *C fibers* carry chronic, dull aches and burning sensations. Some of these same C fibers also respond to nonpainful touch, but with a different pattern of firing.

Both A-delta and C fibers carry pain impulses into the spinal cord, where they form synapses with neurons that carry the pain signals to the thalamus and other parts of the brain (see Figure 4.26). Different pain neurons are activated by different degrees of painful stimulation. Numerous types of neurotransmitters are used by different pain neurons, a phenomenon that has allowed the development of a variety of new drugs for pain management.

The role of the cerebral cortex in experiencing pain is still being explored. Earlier studies of humans undergoing brain surgery for epilepsy concluded that pain has little, if any, cortical representation (Penfield & Rasmussen, 1968). More recently, functional MRI studies of healthy volunteers have compared cortical activity during a pain experience or an attention-demanding task (Davis et al., 1997). The scans show activation of the somatosensory cortex under both conditions, and additional activity during pain in the anterior cingulate cortex, an evolutionarily primitive region thought to be important in emotions. When hypnosis has been used to manipulate the unpleasantness of pain, there are corresponding changes in cingulate cortex activity but not in

FIGURE 4.26

Pain Pathways

Pain messages are carried to the brain by way of the spinal cord. *A-delta fibers* carry information about sharp pain. Unmyelinated *C fibers* carry several types of pain, including chronic, dull aches. Pain fibers make synapses in the reticular formation, causing arousal. They also project to the thalamus and from there to the cortex.

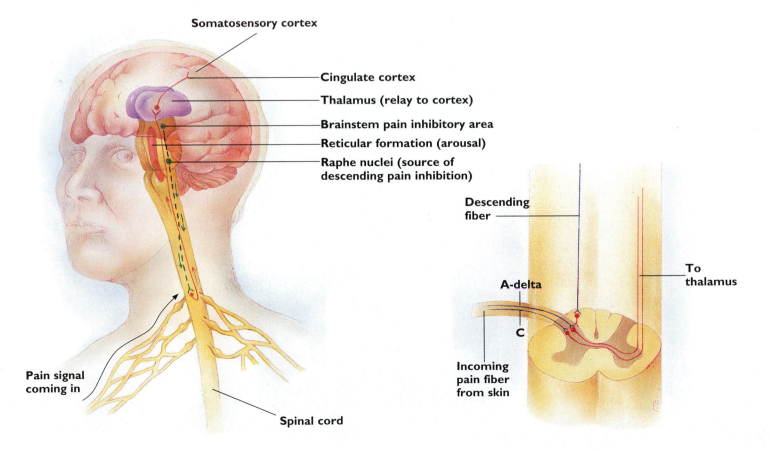

Somatosensory cortex

Cingulate cortex

Thalamus (relay to cortex)

Brainstem pain inhibitory area

Reticular formation (arousal)

Raphe nuclei (source of descending pain inhibition)

Descending fiber

A-delta

C

To thalamus

Incoming pain fiber from skin

Pain signal coming in

Spinal cord

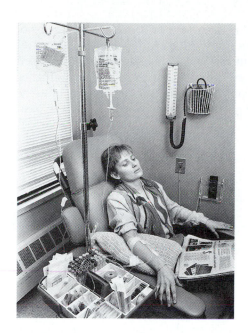

Easing Pain

Candy containing capsaicin is sometimes given for the treatment of painful mouth sores associated with cancer chemotherapy (Berger et al., 1995). Capsaicin is what makes chili peppers "hot," but eating enough of it results in desensitization and a corresponding reduction in pain sensations (Bevan & Geppetti, 1994).

somatosensory cortex activity—yet another finding consistent with the hypothesized role of this brain region in pain perception (Rainville et al., 1997). Research also suggests that pain can be experienced without any external stimulation of pain receptors. In such cases, the pain appears to *originate* in the thalamus and in cortical regions of the brain (Canavero & Bonicalzi, 1998; Gawande, 1998).

Emotional Aspects of Pain   All senses can have emotional components, most of which are learned responses. For example, the smell of baking cookies can make you feel good if it has been associated with happy childhood times. The emotional response to pain is more direct. Specific pathways carry an emotional component of the painful stimulus to areas of the hindbrain and reticular formation (see Figure 4.26), as well as to the cingulate cortex via the thalamus (Craig et al., 1994).

Nevertheless, the overall emotional response to pain depends greatly on cognitive factors. For example, experimenters compared responses to a painful stimulus in people who were informed about the nature of the stimulus and when to expect it, and in people who were not informed. Knowing about pain seemed to make it less objectionable, even though the sensation was reported to be just as noticeable (Mayer & Price, 1982). Another factor affecting emotional responses to pain sensations is the use of pain-reducing strategies, such as focusing on distracting thoughts (Young et al., 1995).

Modulation of Pain: The Gate Control Theory   Pain is extremely useful, because in the long run it protects you from harm. However, there are times when enough is enough. Fortunately, the nervous system has several mechanisms for controlling the experience of pain.

One explanation of how the nervous system controls the amount of pain that reaches the brain is the **gate control theory** (Melzack & Wall, 1965). It holds that there is a "gate" in the spinal cord that either lets pain impulses travel upward to the brain or blocks their progress. The details of the original formulation of this theory turned out to be incorrect, but recent work supports the idea that natural mechanisms can block pain sensations (Stanton-Hicks & Salamon, 1997). For example, input from other skin senses can come into the spinal cord at the same time the pain gets there and "take over" the pathways that the pain impulses would have used. This appears to be why rubbing the skin around a wound temporarily reduces the pain that is felt, why electrical stimulation of the skin around a painful spot relieves the pain, and why scratching relieves itching. (Itching is actually low-level activity in pain fibers.)

The brain can also close the gate to pain impulses by sending signals down the spinal cord. The control of sensation by messages descending from the brain is a common aspect of sensory systems (Willis, 1988). In the case of pain, these messages from the brain block incoming pain signals at spinal cord synapses. The result is **analgesia,** the absence of the sensation of pain in the presence of a normally painful stimulus. For example, if part of a rat's brainstem is electrically stimulated, pain signals generated in the skin never reach the brain (Reynolds, 1969). Permanently implanting stimulating electrodes in the same region of the human brain has reduced severe pain in some patients, but unfortunately it also produces a profound sense of impending doom (Hoffert, 1992).

Natural Analgesics   At least two substances play a role in the brain's ability to block pain signals: (1) the neurotransmitter *serotonin,* which is released by neurons descending from the brain, and (2) natural opiates called *endorphins.* As described in the previous chapter, endorphins are natural painkillers that act as neurotransmitters at many levels of the pain pathway, including the spinal cord, where they block the synapses of the fibers that carry pain signals. Endorphins may also relieve pain when the adrenal and pituitary glands secrete them into the bloodstream as hormones.

Several conditions are known to cause the body to ease its own pain. For example, during the late stages of pregnancy an endorphin system reduces the mother's labor pains (Facchinetti et al., 1982). Further, an endorphin system is activated when people

Natural Analgesia

The stress of athletic exertion causes the release of endorphins, natural painkillers that have been associated with pleasant feelings called "runner's high."

believe they are receiving a painkiller even when they are not (Benedetti & Amanzio, 1997); this may be one reason for the placebo effect, discussed in Chapter 2. Physical or psychological stress can also activate natural analgesic systems. Stress-induced release of endorphins may account for instances in which injured soldiers and athletes continue to perform in the heat of battle or competition with no apparent pain.

There are also mechanisms for reactivating pain sensitivity once a crisis is past. Studies with animals show that they can learn that certain situations signal "safety," and that these safety signals prompt the release of a neurotransmitter that counteracts endorphins' analgesic effects (Wiertelak, Maier, & Watkins, 1992).

THINKING CRITICALLY

Does Acupuncture Relieve Pain?

*A*cupuncture is an ancient and widely used treatment in Asian medicine that is alleged to relieve pain. The method is based on the idea that body energy flows along lines called *channels* (Vincent & Richardson, 1986). There are fourteen main channels, and a person's health supposedly depends on the balance of energy flowing in them. Stimulating the channels by inserting very thin needles into the skin and twirling them is said to restore a balanced flow of energy. The needles produce an aching and tingling sensation called *Teh-ch'i* at the site of stimulation, but they relieve pain at distant, seemingly unrelated parts of the body.

■ What am I being asked to believe or accept?

Acupuncturists assert that twirling a needle in the skin can relieve pain caused by everything from tooth extraction to cancer.

■ What evidence is available to support the assertion?

There is no scientific evidence for the existence of energy channels as described in the theory underlying acupuncture. But what about the more specific assertions that acupuncture relieves pain and that it does so through direct physical mechanisms?

In studies of acupuncture, it is very difficult to control for the placebo effect, especially in double-blind fashion. (How could a therapist not know whether the treatment being given is acupuncture or not? And from the patient's perspective, what placebo treatment could look and feel like having a needle inserted and twirled in the skin?) Nevertheless, researchers have tried to separate the psychological and physical effects of acupuncture by, for example, using mock electrical nerve stimulation, in which electrodes are attached to the skin but no electrical stimulation is given.

Numerous studies show positive results in patients treated by acupuncture for various kinds of pain (Richardson & Vincent, 1986). In one controlled study of headache pain, for example, 33 percent of the patients in a placebo group improved following mock electrical nerve stimulation (which is about the usual proportion of people responding to a placebo), but 53 percent reported reduced pain following real acupuncture (Dowson, Lewith, & Machin, 1985). Another headache study found both acupuncture and drugs to be superior to a placebo. Each reduced the frequency of headaches, but the drugs were more effective than acupuncture at reducing the severity of headache pain (Hesse, Mogelvang, & Simonsen, 1994). Such well-controlled studies are rare, however, and their results are often contradictory (Ter Riet, Kleijnen, & Knipschild, 1990).

There is evidence that acupuncture activates the endorphin system. It is associated with the release of endorphins in the brain, and drugs that slow the breakdown of opiates also prolong the analgesia produced by acupuncture (He, 1987). Furthermore, the pain-reducing effects of acupuncture during electrical stimulation of a tooth can be reversed by *naloxone*, a substance that blocks the painkilling effects of endorphins (and other opiate drugs). This finding suggests that acupuncture somehow activates the body's natural painkilling system. In cases where acupuncture activates endorphins, is this activation brought about only through the placebo effect? Probably not entirely, because acupuncture produces naloxone-reversible analgesia in monkeys and rats, who could not have developed positive expectancies by reading about acupuncture (Ha et al., 1981; Kishioka et al., 1994).

■ Are there alternative ways of interpreting the evidence?

Evidence about acupuncture might be interpreted as simply confirming that the body's painkilling system can be stimulated by external means. Acupuncture may merely provide one activating method; there may be other, even more efficient methods for doing so. We already know, for example, that successful placebo treatments for human pain appear to operate by activating the endorphin system.

■ What additional evidence would help to evaluate the alternatives?

Researchers need to focus not only on the effects of acupuncture but on the general relationship between internal painkilling systems and external methods for stimulating them. Regarding acupuncture itself, scientists do not yet know what factors govern whether it will activate the endorphin system. Other important unknowns include the types of pain for which acupuncture is most effective, the types of patients who respond best, and the precise procedures that are most effective.

■ What conclusions are most reasonable?

There seems little doubt that in some circumstances acupuncture relieves pain. It is not a panacea, however. For example, in the United States the National Institutes of Health (NIH) recently stated that acupuncture can be effective, but the statement focused mainly on the treatment of nausea—and, in any case, new anti-nausea drugs have since proven more effective than acupuncture (Taub, 1998). Because more than $2 million in NIH-funded research has failed to establish its superiority over more conventional pain-relieving procedures, some have argued that further expenditures for research on acupuncture are not warranted (Taub, 1998).

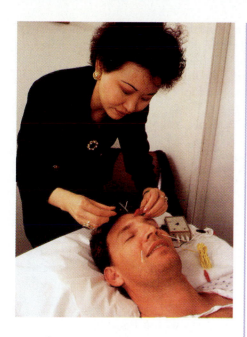

How Does Acupuncture Work?

This acupuncturist is inserting fine needles in her patient's face in hopes of treating poor blood circulation in his hands and feet. Acupuncture treatments appear to alleviate a wide range of problems, including many kinds of pain, but the mechanisms through which it works are not yet determined.

Proprioception

Most sensory systems receive information from the external world, such as the light reflected from a flower or the feeling of cool water. But as far as the brain is concerned, the rest of the body is "out there" too. You know about the position of your body and what each of its parts is doing only because sensory systems provide this information to the brain. These sensory systems are called **proprioceptive** ("received from one's own").

Vestibular Sense   The **vestibular sense** tells the brain about the position of the head (and hence the body) in space and about its general movements. It is often thought of as the sense of balance. People usually become aware of the vestibular sense only when they overstimulate it and become dizzy.

Two vestibular sacs and three semicircular canals that are part of the inner ear are the organs for the vestibular sense. (You can see the semicircular canals in Figure 4.3 on page 102; the vestibular sacs connect these canals and the cochlea.) The **vestibular sacs** are filled with fluid and contain small crystals called **otoliths** ("ear stones") that rest on hair endings. The **semicircular canals** are fluid-filled, arc-shaped tubes; tiny hairs extend into the fluid in the canals. When your head moves, the otoliths shift in the vestibular sacs and the fluid moves in the semicircular canals, stimulating hair endings. This process activates neurons that travel with the auditory nerve, signaling to the brain the amount and direction of head movement.

The vestibular system has neural connections to the cerebellum, to the part of the autonomic nervous system (ANS) that affects the digestive system, and to the muscles of the eyes. The connections to the cerebellum help coordinate bodily movements. The connections to the ANS help create the nausea that sometimes follows overstimulation of the vestibular system—by amusement park rides, for example. Finally, the connections to the eye muscles create *vestibular-ocular reflexes*. For instance, when your head moves in one direction, your eyes reflexively move in the opposite direction. This reflex allows your eyes to fixate on a point in space even when your head is moving around, so you can track a ball in flight as you are running to catch it. You can dramatize this reflex by having a friend spin you around on a stool for a while; when you stop, try to fix your gaze on one point in the room. You will be unable to do so, because the excitation of the vestibular system will cause your eyes to move repeatedly in the direction opposite to that in which you were spinning. Moreover, because vestibular reflexes adapt to the lack of gravity in outer space, astronauts returning to earth have postural and movement difficulties until their vestibular systems readjust to the effects of gravity (Paloski, 1998).

Kinesthesia   The sense that tells you where the parts of your body are with respect to each other is **kinesthesia** (pronounced "kin-es-THEE-zha"). You probably do not think much about kinesthetic information, but you definitely use it—as the following exercise demonstrates. Close your eyes, hold your arms out in front of you, and try to touch your two index fingers together. You probably did this well because your kinesthetic sense told you where each finger was with respect to your body. You also depend on kinesthetic information to guide all your movements. Otherwise, it would be impossible to develop or improve any motor skill, from basic walking to complex athletic movements. These movement patterns become simple and fluid because, with practice, the brain uses kinesthetic information automatically.

Normally, kinesthetic information comes primarily from the joints but also from muscles. Receptors in muscle fibers send information to the brain about the stretching of muscles (McCloskey, 1978). When the position of the bones changes, receptors in the joints transduce this mechanical energy into neural activity, providing information about both the rate of change and the angle of the bones. This coded information goes to the spinal cord and is sent from there to the thalamus along with sensory information from the skin. Eventually it goes to the cerebellum and to the somatosensory cortex (see Figures 3.14, on page 67, and 3.17, on page 72), both of which are involved in the smooth coordination of movements.

Proprioception is thus a critical sense in the context of physical therapy and rehabilitative medicine, especially for people who have to relearn how to move their muscles after strokes or other problems. Recent work in a branch of physics called "nonlinear dynamics" has been applied to problems in proprioception. Utilizing the discovery that the right amount of random, background noise can actually improve the detection of signals, rehabilitation neurologists have found that adding a small amount of vibration (or "noise") to muscle and joint sensations dramatically increases patients' ability to detect joint movements and position (Glanz, 1997).

Balancing Act

The smooth coordination of all physical movement, from scratching your nose to complex feats of balance, depends on kinesthesia, the sense that provides information about where each part of the body is in relation to all the others.

FOCUS ON RESEARCH METHODS

The Case of the Disembodied Woman

Near the beginning of this chapter you read about the problem of coding sensation—of translating the physical properties of some stimulus into neural signals that make sense to the brain. Then, in later sections you learned how this problem is "solved" for the different senses. But what happens when the brain does not receive the sensory information it needs? You are already aware of the most common examples of this problem—deafness and blindness. The case study described next concerns a much less common problem—the loss of a proprioceptive sense.

■ What was the researcher's question?

Oliver Sacks, a well-known clinical neurologist, has spent years treating people with "neurological deficits"—that is, impairments or incapacities of neurological functions. One of his most memorable cases was that of "Christina," who had apparently lost the sense of kinesthesia and, thus, was unable to feel the position of her own body.

In 1977, Christina was a healthy young woman who entered a hospital in preparation for some minor surgery. The night before her operation, she dreamt that she was unsteady on her feet, "could hardly feel anything in her hands . . . and kept dropping whatever she picked up" (Sacks, 1985, p. 43). Her dream soon became a horrible reality. The next day, Christina tried to get out of bed but flopped onto the floor like a rag doll. She was unable to hold onto objects and had trouble moving. She felt "weird—disembodied." A psychiatrist diagnosed Christina's problem as a *conversion disorder*—a psychological problem (described in Chapter 15) involving apparent, but not actual, damage to sensory or motor systems. Sacks, however, wondered if there might be another reason for Christina's strange condition.

■ How did the researcher answer the question?

Sacks conducted electrical tests of Christina's nerve and muscle functions, performed a spinal tap to examine the fibers that carry sensory information to the brain, and studied the portion of her brain that receives proprioceptive information.

Sacks's approach exemplifies the *case study* method of research. As noted in Chapter 2, case studies focus intensively on a particular individual, group, or situation. Sometimes they lead to important insights about clinical problems or other phenomena that occur so rarely that they cannot be studied through surveys or controlled experiments.

■ What did the researcher find?

Sacks's examination of Christina ruled out a psychological disorder. The electrical tests disclosed that the signals from her nerves and muscles that normally told her brain about the location of her body parts were simply not being sent. And the spinal tap indicated that the sensory neurons that carry proprioceptive information had, for unknown reasons, degenerated. As a result, Christina seemed to have become disconnected from her body. On one occasion, for example, she became annoyed at a visitor whom she thought was tapping her fingers on a table top. But it was she, not the visitor, who was doing it. Her hands were acting on their own; her body was doing things she did not know about.

■ What do the results mean?

In his analysis of this case, Sacks noted that the sense we have of our bodies is provided partly through our experience of seeing it, but also partly through proprioception. Christina put it this way: "Proprioception is like the eyes of the body, the way the body sees itself. And if it goes, it's like the body's blind." With great effort and determination, Christina was ultimately able to regain some of her ability to move about. If she looked intently at her arms and legs, she could coordinate their movement to some degree. Eventually, she left the hospital and resumed many of her normal activities. But Christina never recovered her sense of self. She still feels like a stranger in her own body.

■ What do we still need to know?

The story of Christina and the other fascinating case studies in Sacks's popular books, such as *The Man Who Mistook His Wife for a Hat* (1985) and *An Anthropologist on Mars*

(1996) not only contribute substantially to our knowledge of sensory and neurological systems but also illustrate the incredible complexity and fragility of sensory processes. However, the case study methodology, by itself, does not provide a full understanding of how sensory processes work and what happens when they go wrong. As noted in Chapter 2, it is difficult to identify causes using this methodology. The immediate source of Christina's difficulty was selective degeneration of nerve fibers. But what was the cause of that degeneration? Case studies can rarely answer this kind of question.

Although the case study of Christina did not confirm any hypotheses or identify causal relationships as an experiment might have, it *did* focus attention on a rare kinesthetic disorder. This condition was almost unknown when Sacks first reported it, but it has since been diagnosed in several individuals. Specifically, it is found among people taking megadoses of vitamin B6, also known as pyridoxine (Sacks, 1985). These high doses—but also lower doses taken over a long period of time—can damage sensory neurons (Dordain & Deffond, 1994). We still need to learn how vitamin B6 might cause such damage and whether kinesthetic disorders like Christina's can have other causes. Thus, much research remains to be done. Through this work, psychologists and other scientists will continue to unravel the mysteries of our sensory processes.

LINKAGES

As noted in Chapter 1, all of psychology's many subfields are related to one another. Our discussion of the representation of the sensory system in the brain illustrates just one way in which the topic of this chapter, sensation, is linked to the subfield of biological psychology (Chapter 3). The Linkages diagram shows ties to two other subfields as well, and there are many more ties throughout the book. Looking for linkages among subfields will help you see how they all fit together and better appreciate the big picture that is psychology.

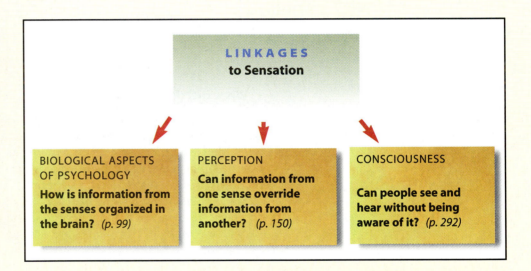

LINKAGES
to Sensation

BIOLOGICAL ASPECTS OF PSYCHOLOGY
How is information from the senses organized in the brain? *(p. 99)*

PERCEPTION
Can information from one sense override information from another? *(p. 150)*

CONSCIOUSNESS
Can people see and hear without being aware of it? *(p. 292)*

SUMMARY

A *sense* is a system that translates information from outside the nervous system into neural activity. Messages from the senses are called *sensations.*

SENSORY SYSTEMS

The first step in sensation involves *accessory structures,* which collect and modify sensory stimuli. The second step is *transduction,* the process of converting incoming energy into neural activity; it is accomplished by *sensory receptors,* cells specialized to detect energy of some type. *Adaptation* takes place when receptors receive unchanging stimulation. Neural activity is transferred through the thalamus (except in the case of olfaction) and on to the cortex.

The Problem of Coding

Coding is the translation of physical properties of a stimulus into a pattern of neural activity that specifically identifies those physical properties. It is the language the brain uses to describe sensations. Coding is characterized by *specific nerve energies:* Stimulation of a particular sensory nerve provides codes for that one sense no matter how the stimulation takes place. There are two basic types of sensory codes: *temporal* and *spatial.*

HEARING

Sound is a repetitive fluctuation in the pressure of a medium such as air; it travels in waves.

Sound

The *frequency* (which is related to *wavelength*) and *amplitude* of sound waves produce the psychological dimensions of *pitch* and *loudness,* respectively. *Timbre,* the quality of sound, depends on complex wave patterns added to the basic frequency of the sound.

The Ear

The energy from sound waves is collected and transmitted to the *cochlea* through a series of accessory structures, including the *tympanic membrane.* Transduction occurs when sound energy stimulates hair cells of the organ of Corti on the *basilar membrane* of the cochlea, which in turn stimulate the *auditory nerve.*

Coding Intensity and Frequency

The intensity of a sound stimulus is coded by the firing rate of auditory neurons. *Place theory* describes the coding of high frequencies: They are coded by the place on the basilar membrane where the wave envelope peaks. Each neuron in the auditory nerve is most sensitive to a specific frequency (its characteristic frequency). Very low frequencies are coded by *frequency matching,* which refers to the fact that the firing rate of a neuron matches the frequency of a sound wave; according to *volley theory,* some frequencies may be matched by the firing rate of a group of neurons. Low to moderate frequencies are coded through a combination of these methods.

Auditory Pathways and Representations

Auditory information is relayed through the thalamus to the *primary auditory cortex* and to other areas of auditory cortex. Sounds of similar frequency activate neighboring cells in the cortex, but loudness is coded temporally.

VISION

Light

Visible light is electromagnetic radiation with a wavelength from about 400 to about 750 nanometers. *Light intensity,* or the amount of energy in light, determines its brightness. Differing *light wavelengths* are sensed as different colors.

Focusing Light

Accessory structures of the eye include the *cornea, pupil, iris,* and *lens.* Through *accommodation* and other means, these structures focus light rays on the *retina,* the netlike structure of cells at the back of the eye.

Converting Light into Images

Photoreceptors in the retina—*rods* and *cones*—have *photopigments* and can transduce light into neural activity. Rods and cones differ in their shape, their sensitivity to light, their ability to discriminate colors, and their distribution across the retina. The *fovea,* the area of highest *acuity,* has only cones, which are color sensitive. Rods are more sensitive to light but do not discriminate colors; they are distributed in areas around the fovea. Both types of photoreceptors contribute to *dark adaptation.* From the photoreceptors, energy transduced from light is transferred to *bipolar cells* and then to *ganglion cells,* with *interneurons* making lateral connections between the bipolar and ganglion cells. As a result of *convergence* and *lateral inhibition,* most ganglion cells in effect compare the amount of light falling on the center of their *receptive fields* with that falling on the surrounding area. The result is that the retina enhances the contrast between dark and light areas.

Seeing Color

The color of an object depends on which of the wavelengths striking it are absorbed and which are reflected. The sensation of color has three psychological dimensions: *hue, saturation,* and *brightness.* According to the *trichromatic* (or Young-Helmholtz) *theory,* color vision results from the fact that the eye includes three types of cones, each of which is most sensitive to short, medium, or long wavelengths; information from the three types combines to produce the sensation of color. Individuals may have slight variations in the number and sensitivity of their cone pigments. According to the *opponent-process* (or Hering) *theory,* there are red-green, blue-yellow, and black-white visual elements; the members of each pair inhibit each other so that only one member of a pair may produce a signal at a time. This theory explains color afterimages as well as the fact that lights of *complementary* colors cancel each other out and produce gray when mixed together.

Visual Pathways

The ganglion cells send action potentials out of the eye, at a point where a *blind spot* is created. Axons of ganglion cells leave the eye as a bundle of fibers called the *optic nerve;* half of these fibers cross over at the *optic chiasm* and terminate in the *lateral geniculate nucleus (LGN)* of the thalamus. Neurons in the LGN send visual information on to the *primary visual cortex,* where cells detect and respond to features such as lines, edges, and orientations.

Visual Representations

Visual form, color, movement, and distance are processed by parallel systems. *Feature detectors* are hierarchically built out of simpler units.

THE CHEMICAL SENSES: SMELL AND TASTE

The chemical senses include olfaction and gustation.

Olfaction

Olfaction detects volatile chemicals that come into contact with olfactory receptors in the nose. Olfactory signals are sent to the *olfactory bulb* in the brain without passing through the thalamus. *Pheromones* are odors from one animal that change the physiology or behavior of another animal, acting through the *vomeronasal organ*.

Gustation

Gustation detects chemicals that come into contact with taste receptors in *papillae* on the tongue. Elementary taste sensations are limited to sweet, sour, bitter, salty, umami, and astringent. The combined responses of many taste buds determines a taste sensation.

Smell, Taste, and Flavor

The senses of smell and taste interact to produce flavor.

SOMATIC SENSES AND THE VESTIBULAR SYSTEM

The *somatic senses*, or *somatosensory systems*, include skin senses and proprioceptive senses. The skin senses include touch, temperature, and pain.

Touch and Temperature

Nerve endings in the skin generate touch sensations when they are mechanically stimulated. Some nerve endings are sensitive to temperature, and some respond to both temperature and touch. Signals from neighboring points on the skin stay next to each other all the way to the cortex.

Pain

Pain provides information about damaging stimuli. Sharp pain and dull, chronic pain are carried by different fibers—A-delta and C fibers, respectively. The emotional response to pain depends on how the painful stimulus is interpreted. According to the *gate control theory*, pain signals can be blocked by messages sent from the brain down the spinal cord, producing *analgesia*. Endorphins act at several levels of the pain systems to reduce sensations of pain.

Proprioception

Proprioceptive senses provide information about the body. The *vestibular sense* provides information about the position of the head in space through the *otoliths* in *vestibular sacs* and the *semicircular canals*, and *kinesthesia* provides information about the positions of body parts with respect to one another.

KEY TERMS

accessory structures (97)
accommodation (*108*)
acuity (110)
adaptation (97)
amplitude (100)
analgesia (129)
auditory nerve (102)
basilar membrane (102)
bipolar cells (111)
blind spot (117)
brightness (113)
cochlea (102)
coding (98)
complementary colors (115)
cones (110)
convergence (111)
cornea (108)
dark adaptation (109)
feature detectors (120)
fovea (110)
frequency (100)

frequency matching (104)
ganglion cells (112)
gate control theory (129)
gustation (121)
hue (113)
interneurons (111)
iris (108)
kinesthesia (132)
lateral geniculate nucleus
   (LGN) (117)
lateral inhibition (111)
lens (108)
light intensity (107)
light wavelength (108)
loudness (100)
olfaction (121)
olfactory bulb (122)
opponent-process theory
   (115)
optic chiasm (117)
optic nerve (117)

otoliths (131)
papillae (123)
pheromones (123)
photopigments (109)
photoreceptors (109)
pitch (101)
place theory (104)
primary auditory cortex
   (106)
primary cortex (99)
primary visual cortex (117)
proprioceptive (131)
pupil (108)
receptive field (112)
retina (108)
rods (110)
saturation (113)
semicircular canals (131)
sensations (96)
sense (96)
sensory receptors (97)

somatic senses (125)
somatosensory systems (125)
sound (99)
spatial code (98)
specific nerve energies (98)
temporal code (98)
timbre (101)
topographical
   representations (99)
transduction (97)
trichromatic theory (114)
tympanic membrane (102)
vestibular sacs (131)
vestibular sense (131)
visible light (107)
volley theory (105)
vomeronasal organ (123)
wavelength (100)

5

Perception

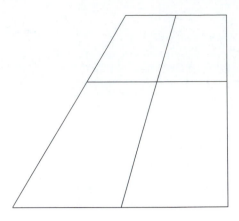

FIGURE 5.1

What Do You See?

A t a traffic circle in Scotland, fourteen fatal accidents occurred in a single year, partly because drivers failed to slow down as they approached the circle. When warning signs failed to solve the problem, Gordon Denton, a British psychologist, proposed an ingenious solution. White lines were painted across the road leading to the circle, in a pattern that looked something like this:

/   /   /   /   /   / / /

Crossing these ever-closer lines at a constant speed gave drivers the illusion that they were accelerating, and their automatic response was to slow down (Denton, 1980). During the fourteen months after Denton's idea was implemented, there were only two fatalities at the traffic circle. Denton's solution to this problem relied heavily on his knowledge of the principles of human perception.

Perception is the process through which sensations are interpreted, using knowledge and understanding of the world, so that they become meaningful experiences. Thus, perception is not a passive process of simply absorbing and decoding incoming sensations. If it were, people's understanding of the environment would be a constantly changing and confusing mosaic of light and color. Instead, our brains take sensations and create a coherent world, often by filling in missing information and using past experience to give meaning to what we see, hear, or touch. For example, the raw sensations coming from the stimuli in Figure 5.1 convey only the information that there is a series of intersecting lines. But your perceptual system automatically interprets this image as a rectangle (or window frame) lying on its side.

We begin this chapter by considering the complexity of such perceptual processes and the various approaches that psychologists have taken in trying to understand them. Then we explore how people detect incoming sensory stimuli, organize these sensations into distinct and stable patterns, and recognize those patterns. We also examine the role of attention in guiding the perceptual system to analyze some parts of the world more closely than others. Finally, we provide some examples of how basic research on perception has been applied to some practical problems.

THE PERCEPTION PARADOX

As the drivers who found themselves slowing at the traffic circle discovered, much of our perceptual work is done automatically, without conscious awareness. Indeed, the

FIGURE 5.2

A Perceptual Task

Which line is longer—A-C on the left or A-B on the right? If you are like most people, you will say A-C, but this judgment is wrong: The lines are exactly the same length. Understanding why our perceptual systems make this kind of error has helped psychologists understand the basic principles of perception.

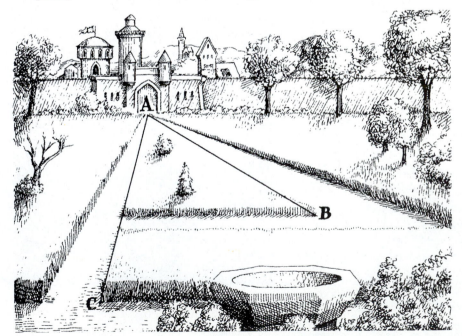

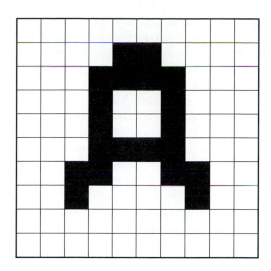

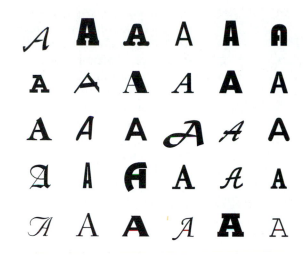

FIGURE 5.3

**Human Versus Computer
Pattern Recognition**

The grid on the left represents a recognition pattern, or template, that might be programmed into a computer to enable it to recognize the letter *A*. On the right are many different versions of the letter *A*, all of which humans have no trouble recognizing. However, because many versions do not match the template, they would not be recognized as *A* by the computer. Recognition skills that are quite easy for humans are difficult to program into a computer.

Source: From Solso, Robert L., *Cognitive Psychology*, 5/e. Copyright © 1998 by Allyn & Bacon. Reprinted by permission.

rapid, often effortless nature of perceptual processing may lead you to conclude that perception is a rather simple affair. But the fundamental paradox of perception is that what seems so easy for the perceiver is exceedingly difficult for psychologists to understand and explain. The difficulty lies in the fact that, to function so effectively and efficiently, our perceptual systems must be exceedingly complex.

To illustrate the workings of these complex systems, psychologists draw attention to *perceptual failures*, instances in which our perceptual experience differs from the actual characteristics of some stimulus. Figure 5.2 provides a clear example. Perceptual errors are clues not only to the problems that perception must solve—such as estimating length—but also to the solutions that it achieves. Ask yourself, for example, *why* you saw the two lines in Figure 5.2 as differing in length even though they are the same. Part of the answer is that your visual system tries to interpret all stimuli as three-dimensional, even when they are not. A three-dimensional interpretation of this drawing would lead you to see the two lines as defining edges of two parallel paths, one of which ends closer to you than the other. Because your eyes tell you that the two paths originate from about the same point (the castle entrance), you solve the perceptual problem by assuming that the closer line must be the longer of the two.

Figure 5.3 provides another example of the complexity of perceptual processing. Perceptual tasks such as recognizing a letter are quite easy for most people; but one of the challenges faced by scientists trying to create *artificial vision* is that it is very difficult to "teach" computers to recognize even simple patterns.

THREE APPROACHES TO PERCEPTION

Psychologists have taken three main approaches in their efforts to understand human perception. Those who take the **computational approach** try to determine the *computations* that a machine would have to perform to solve perceptual problems. Understanding these computations in machines, they believe, will help explain how complex computations within the nervous system of humans and other animals might turn raw sensory stimulation into a representation of the world (Green, 1991).

The computational approach owes much to two earlier, but still influential, views of perception: the constructivist approach and the ecological approach. Psychologists who take the **constructivist approach** argue that our perceptual systems construct a representation of reality from fragments of sensory information. They are particularly interested in situations where the same physical stimulus gives rise to different perceptions in different people. For example, optical illusions that work in one culture may not work in another if the people in the two cultures have not had similar experience with the objects that are represented in the illusions (Leibowitz et al., 1969). In other words, constructivists emphasize that perception is strongly influenced by expectations

Is Anything Missing?

Because you know what animals look like, you perceive a normal, healthy cat in this picture even though its mid-section is hidden from view. The constructivist approach to perception emphasizes our ability to use knowledge and expectations to fill in the gaps in partially obscured objects and to perceive them as unified wholes, not disjointed parts.

and inferences based on past experiences and prior knowledge (Rock, 1983). For example, if a desk prevents you from seeing the lower half of a person seated behind it, you would still "see" the person as a whole human being because your experience tells you that people remain intact even when parts of them are obscured.

Researchers influenced by the ecological approach to perception claim that, rather than depending on interpretations, inferences, and expectations, most of our perceptual experience is due directly to the wealth of information contained in the stimulus array presented by the environment. For example, J. J. Gibson (1979), founder of the ecological approach, argues that the primary goal of perception is to *support actions*, such as walking, grabbing, or flying a plane, by "tuning in" to the part of the environmental stimulus array that is most important for performing those actions. Thus, these researchers would have little interest in our interpretation of the person behind the desk, but great interest in how we might use visual information from that person, from the desk, and from other objects in the room to guide us as we walk toward a chair and sit down.

In summary: To explain perception, the computational approach focuses on the nervous system's manipulations of incoming signals, the constructivist approach emphasizes the inferences that people make about the environment, and the ecological approach emphasizes the information provided by the environment. Evidence in support of each approach is discussed later in this chapter.

PSYCHOPHYSICS

How can psychologists measure people's perceptions when there is no way to get inside their heads to experience what they are experiencing? One solution to this problem is to present people with lights, sounds, and other physically measurable stimuli and ask them to report their perception of the stimuli, using special scales of measurement. This method of studying perception, called **psychophysics,** describes the relationship between *physical energy* in the environment and our *psychological experience* of that energy.

Absolute Thresholds: Is Something Out There?

How much stimulus energy is needed to trigger a conscious perceptual experience? The minimum detectable amount of light, sound, pressure, or other physical energy is called the *absolute threshold* (see Table 5.1). Stimuli that fall below this threshold—that are too weak or too brief to evoke awareness of their presence—are traditionally referred to as **subliminal stimuli.** Stimuli that fall above the threshold are referred to as **supraliminal stimuli.**

TABLE 5.1

Some Absolute Thresholds

Here are examples of stimuli at the absolute threshold for the five primary senses.

Human Sense	Absolute Threshold
Vision	A candle flame seen at 30 miles on a clear night
Hearing	The tick of a watch under quiet conditions at 20 feet
Taste	One teaspoon of sugar in two gallons of water
Smell	One drop of perfume diffused into the entire volume of air in a six-room apartment
Touch	The wing of a fly falling on your cheek from a distance of one centimeter.

Source: Galanter, 1962.

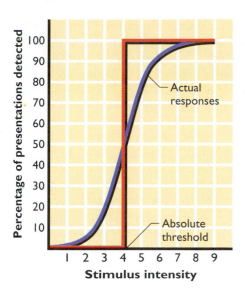

FIGURE 5.4

The Absolute Threshold

The curve shows the relationship between the physical intensity of a signal and the likelihood that it will be detected. If the absolute threshold were indeed absolute, all signals at or above a particular intensity would always be detected, and no signal below that intensity would ever be detected (see red line). Because this response pattern almost never occurs, the "absolute" threshold is defined as the intensity at which the signal is detected with 50 percent accuracy.

LINKAGES

Can subliminal messages help you to lose weight? (a link to Introducing Psychology)

If you were participating in a typical experiment to measure the absolute threshold for vision, you would be seated in a darkened laboratory. After your eyes have adapted to the darkness, brief flashes of light would be presented at varying intensities. Each time, you would be asked if you saw the stimulus. If your absolute threshold was indeed "absolute," your detection accuracy should jump from 0 percent to 100 percent at the exact brightness level that constitutes your threshold—as illustrated by the point at which the red line in Figure 5.4 suddenly rises. In actuality, however, your responses would form a curve much like the green line in that figure. As you can see, your "absolute" threshold is not really an all-or-none phenomenon. Thus, for example, a stimulus at an intensity of 3 will still be perceived 20 percent of the time. So, is that stimulus *subliminal* or *supraliminal?* Psychologists have dealt with questions of this sort by redefining the **absolute threshold** as the minimum amount of energy that can be detected 50 percent of the time. By this definition, your "absolute" threshold would be at intensity level 4; an intensity level of 3 would be subliminal, even though you sometimes perceive it.

It is said that in the late 1950s, while the audience in a New Jersey movie theater watched the movie *Picnic*, messages such as "Drink Coke" and "Buy popcorn" were flashed on the screen. The story goes that, because the messages were on the screen so briefly, the people in the theater did not notice them, but these subliminal stimuli caused a 15 percent increase in Coke sales and a 58 percent increase in popcorn sales. Can such "mind control" really work? Many people seem to think so: They spend millions of dollars each year on audiotapes and videos that promise subliminal help to those who want to lose weight, raise self-esteem, quit smoking, make more money, or achieve other goals.

THINKING CRITICALLY

Can Subliminal Stimuli Influence Your Behavior?

■ What am I being asked to believe or accept?

Two types of claims have been made about subliminal stimuli. The more general, and weaker, of these is that subliminal stimuli can influence our behavior in some way; the nature of this influence, however, is not specified. The second, much stronger assertion is that subliminal stimuli provide an effective means of changing people's buying habits, political opinions, self-confidence, and other complex attitudes and behaviors, with or without their awareness or consent.

■ What evidence is available to support the assertion?

Most evidence for the first claim—that subliminal stimuli can influence behavior—comes from research on visual perception. For example, using a method called *subliminal priming,* participants are presented with clearly visible (supraliminal) stimuli, such as pictures of people, and then asked to make some sort of judgment about these stimuli. Unbeknownst to the participants, however, each of the visible pictures is preceded by other pictures or words flashed so briefly that the participants are unaware of them. The critical question is whether the information in the subliminal stimuli influences—or, more specifically, has a "priming effect" on—participants' responses to the supraliminal stimuli that follow them.

In one subliminal priming study, *supraliminal* pictures of individuals were preceded by *subliminal* pictures that were either "positive" (e.g., happy children) or "negative" (e.g., a monster). The participants in this study judged the people in the visible pictures as more likable, polite, friendly, successful, and reputable when their pictures had been preceded by a positive subliminal picture than by a negative subliminal one (Krosnick, Jussim, & Lynn, 1992). Another study found that people with eating disorders ate more crackers after being exposed to a subliminal presentation of the phrase "Mama is leaving me" than after either a supraliminal presentation of that phrase or after a subliminal presentation of the neutral phrase "Mama is loaning it" (Masling, 1992). More recently, researchers have found that subliminally presented words can influence subsequent decisions about the meaning of similar words. For example, after being exposed to subliminal presentations of a man's name (e.g., "Tom"), participants were able to decide more rapidly whether a supraliminal stimulus (e.g., "John") was a man's or woman's name. It should be noted, however, that the impact of the subliminally presented name lasted for only about one-tenth of a second (Greenwald, Draine, & Abrams, 1996).

Other research shows that subliminal stimuli can lead to a change in people's physiological responses. In one such study, participants were shown slides of written messages at subliminal speed while researchers recorded their *galvanic skin resistance (GSR),* a measure of physiological arousal. Although the slides were flashed too quickly to be consciously perceived, participants exhibited higher GSRs after messages such as "No one loves me" than after equally long, nonemotional messages such as "No one lifts it" (Masling & Bornstein, 1991). In another study, subliminally presented slides of snakes, spiders, flowers, and mushrooms were presented to participants. Even though the slides were impossible to perceive at a conscious level, participants who were afraid of snakes or spiders exhibited increased GSR (and reported fear) in response to slides of snakes and spiders (Öhman & Soares, 1994).

The results of such studies provide some evidence for the weaker claim noted earlier: that subliminal information can have an impact on behavior, in this case judgment and emotion. However, these studies say little or nothing about the effectiveness of subliminal advertising or the value of subliminal self-help tapes for changing one's life. The primary support for claims regarding subliminal tapes, for example, comes from the reports of satisfied customers (e.g., McGarvey, 1989).

■ Are there alternative ways of interpreting the evidence?

One major difficulty in assessing the results of experiments on subliminal perception is knowing whether the participants were really unaware of the supposedly subliminal stimuli. For example, in cases where the researcher's definition of the absolute threshold is based on the 50 percent rule, the participants would have been able to detect *subthreshold* stimuli on some trials. Indeed, as used in most of these experiments, the term *subliminal* really means "marginally perceptible." Critics have also noted that the effects of subliminal stimuli are extremely small and often difficult to replicate in subsequent, independent experiments. In addition, we may never know how many studies failed to produce subliminal perception effects because, whereas studies with significant results for subliminal stimuli stand a good chance of appearing in professional journals, studies with nonsignificant results are rarely published.

As for subliminal advertising or subliminal perception products, such as subliminal self-help tapes, there is no scientific evidence that they have significant effects. Many commercial claims for subliminal perception—including those reported in the New Jersey theater case mentioned above—have turned out to be publicity stunts using fabricated data (Pratkanis, 1992). And the testimonials from people who have purchased subliminal tapes may be biased by what these people would *like* to believe about the product they bought. This interpretation is supported by experiments that manipulate the beliefs of participants regarding the messages they will receive on subliminal tapes. In one study, half the participants were told they would be listening to tapes containing subliminal messages that would improve their memory; the other half were told that subliminal messages would improve their self-esteem. However, half the participants expecting self-esteem tapes actually received memory-improvement tapes and half the participants expecting memory-improvement tapes actually received self-esteem tapes. Regardless of which tapes they *actually* heard, participants who thought they had heard memory-enhancement messages reported improved memory; those who thought that they had heard self-esteem messages said that their self-esteem had improved (Pratkanis, Eskenazi, & Greenwald, 1994). In other words, the effects of the tapes were determined by the listeners' expectations—not by the tapes' subliminal content.

■ What additional evidence would help to evaluate the alternatives?

To address more fully the effectiveness of subliminal products such as self-help tapes, researchers need to conduct further experiments—such as the one just mentioned—that carefully control for the expectations of participants and of the researchers themselves. For example, in a *double-blind, placebo-controlled experiment,* some participants receive subliminal tapes whose content is consistent with the stated purpose of the tapes (e.g., weight control) whereas others receive tapes with inconsistent content or no content at all. Further, neither the participants nor the researchers would know who got which tape until after all the results are in. Ultimately, the effects of the three types of subliminal tapes would be compared to one another *and* to the effects of tapes containing supraliminal (audible) self-help messages.

■ What conclusions are most reasonable?

The available data do provide some support for the claim that subliminal perception does occur. However, there is little or no evidence that subliminal perception can be used as the basis for "mind control" (Greenwald, Klinger, & Schuh, 1995). Subliminal effects are usually small and extremely short-lived, and they mainly affect simple judgments and general measures of overall arousal. Most researchers agree that subliminal messages have no special power to induce major changes in people's needs, goals, skills, or actions (Pratkanis, 1992). Indeed, advertisements, political speeches, and other messages that people can perceive consciously have far stronger persuasive effects.

Signal-Detection Theory

One implication of Figure 5.4 (on page 141) is that participants in a perception experiment can fail to detect stimuli on some occasions even though they had successfully detected them before. Why is there so much variability in what people can detect from trial to trial? And what about the even more puzzling type of error whereby people say they perceive a stimulus on trials when no stimulus was presented? Why would people ever claim to see a stimulus when there is no stimulus for them to see? Some answers to these questions are provided by signal-detection theory.

Signal-detection theory is a mathematical model of the factors that determine how people decide to respond when asked to detect faint stimuli (Green & Swets, 1966). It begins with the premise that even during trials in which the stimulus, or *signal,* is

Detecting Vital Signals

According to signal detection theory, the likelihood that security personnel will detect the outline of a bomb or other weapon in a passenger's luggage depends partly on the sensitivity of their visual systems as they look at x-ray images, and partly on their response criterion, which is affected by their expectations that weapons might appear, and by how motivated they are to look carefully for them. To help keep inspectors' response criteria sufficiently low, those responsible for airport security occasionally attempt to smuggle a simulated weapon through a checkpoint. This procedure serves to assess the quality of security, and also prevents guards from becoming complacent.

absent, people will experience some sort of perceptual stimulation, or noise. **Noise** is any stimulation caused by a source other than the signal. It can come from outside the person, as when lab equipment emits an unintended electrical hum. It can also come from inside the person; *internal* or *neural noise,* caused by the spontaneous, random firing of cells in the person's nervous system, occurs in varying degrees whether or not an external signal is present. Because noise, in one form or another, is always present and its levels are constantly fluctuating, participants in a signal-detection experiment are faced with the task of deciding whether they are experiencing either noise alone or a signal in addition to noise. According to signal-detection theory, two factors determine this decision.

The first is **sensitivity**—a person's ability to correctly discriminate a stimulus from its background. Sensitivity is influenced by internal noise, the intensity of the stimulus, and the capacity of the person's sensory systems. Once again, imagine that you are participating in a threshold experiment. When presented with faint signals, you may find it impossible to distinguish accurately between trials involving noise alone and those involving a signal plus noise. Sometimes, noise levels may be so high that you think something must surely be "out there," in which case you report that the stimulus is present when, in fact, it is not. This type of error is called a *false alarm.* At other times, the signal is so faint that it does not produce enough perceptual stimulation for you to detect it—causing an error known as a *miss.* But a person with a more sensitive sensory system might correctly detect the stimulus—a situation called a *hit.* Thus your response to a signal is determined partly by its strength, the amount of noise surrounding it, and your ability to detect and tell the difference between the two.

The second factor affecting a person's performance when presented with a faint stimulus is called the **response criterion;** it reflects the person's willingness to say that the stimulus is present. This willingness, in turn, is affected by the person's motivation (wants and needs) and expectancies. Consider, for example, the security checkpoints at major airports, where inspectors spend long hours looking at x-rays of people's handbags, briefcases, and other luggage. The "signal" in this situation is a weapon, whereas the "noise" consists of harmless objects in a person's luggage, vague or distorted images on the viewing screen, and anything else that is not a weapon. If a terrorist bombing, or the threat of one, has recently been reported and the airport is on alert, the inspector's response criterion for saying that some ambiguous object on the x-ray might be a weapon will be much lower than if the airport were not on alert.

Thus, detecting a stimulus depends on two independent factors: one's ability to differentiate signal from noise and one's willingness to say that the signal is present. These facts led researchers to conclude that the measurement of absolute thresholds could never be more precise than the 50 percent rule mentioned earlier. As a result, they abandoned the notion of absolute thresholds and focused instead on signal-detection theory.

Because it allows precise measurement of people's sensitivity to stimuli of any kind, signal-detection theory provides a way to understand and predict responses in a wide range of situations (Swets, 1992). Consider weather forecasting. Signal-detection theory can be valuable in understanding why weather forecasters, using the latest radar systems, sometimes fail to warn of a tornado that local residents can see with the naked eye (Stevens, 1995). The forecaster's task is not easy because the high-tech systems they use may respond not only to dangerous shifts in wind direction (wind shear) and a tornado's spinning funnel but also to such trivial stimuli as swirling dust and swarming insects. Thus, the telltale radar "signature" of a tornado appears against a potentially confusing background of visual "noise." Whether or not that signature will be picked out and reported depends both on the forecaster's sensitivity to the signal and on the response criterion being used. In establishing the criterion for making a report, the forecaster must consider certain consequences. Setting the criterion too high might cause evidence of a tornado to go unnoticed. Such a *miss* could cost many lives if it left a populated area with no warning of danger. If the response criterion is set too low, however, the forecaster might deliver a tornado *false alarm* that would unnecessarily disrupt people's lives, activate costly emergency plans, and reduce the credibility of

Perfect!

This chef's ability to taste the difference in his culinary creation before and after he has adjusted the spices depends on psychophysical laws that also apply to judging differences in visual, auditory, and other sensory stimuli.

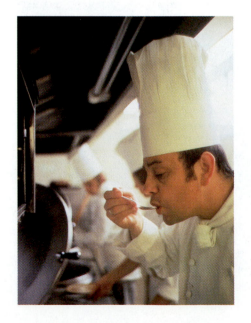

Tornado present?

	Yes	No
Forecaster's decision **Yes**	Hit	False alarm
Forecaster's decision **No**	Miss	Correct rejection

(A) POSSIBLE OUTCOMES

Tornado present?

	Yes	No
Forecaster's decision **Yes**	Hit 70%	False alarm 30%
Forecaster's decision **No**	Miss 30%	Correct rejection 70%

(B) TORNADO PRESENT IN 50% OF THE STORMS

Tornado present?

	Yes	No
Forecaster's decision **Yes**	Hit 90%	False alarm 40%
Forecaster's decision **No**	Miss 10%	Correct rejection 60%

(C) TORNADO PRESENT IN 90% OF THE STORMS

FIGURE 5.5

Signal Detection

Part (A) shows that the possible outcomes of examining a radar display for signs of a tornado include a *hit* (correctly detecting the tornado), a *miss* (failing to detect the tornado), a *correct rejection* (seeing no tornado when there is none), or a *false alarm* (reporting a tornado when none exists). The remainder of the figure illustrates the impact of two different response criteria: Part (B) represents outcomes of a high response criterion, which is set under storm conditions where tornadoes are usually present only 50 percent of the time; Part (C) represents outcomes of a low response criterion, which operates under storm conditions where tornadoes are usually present 90 percent of the time.

future warnings (see Figure 5.5A). In short, there is a tradeoff. To minimize false alarms, the forecaster could set a very high response criterion, but doing so would also make misses more likely.

Let's examine how various kinds of expectations or assumptions can change the response criterion, and how those changes might affect the accuracy of a forecaster's decisions. If a forecaster knows it's a time of year when tornadoes exist in only about 50 percent of the storm systems seen on radar, a rather high response criterion is likely to be used; it will take relatively strong evidence to trigger a tornado warning. The hypothetical data in Figure 5.5B show that, under these conditions, the forecaster correctly detected 70 percent of actual tornadoes but missed 30 percent of them; also, 30 percent of the tornado reports were false alarms. Now suppose the forecaster learns that a different kind of storm system is on the way, and that about 90 percent of such systems spawn tornadoes. This information is likely to increase the forecaster's expectancy for seeing a tornado signature, thus lowering the response criterion. The forecaster will now require less visual evidence of a tornado before reporting one. Under these conditions, the hit rate might rise from 70 percent to, say, 90 percent, but the false-alarm rate might also increase from 30 percent to 40 percent (see Figure 5.5C).

Sensitivity to tornado signals will also affect a forecaster's hit rate and false alarm rate. Forecasters with greater sensitivity to these signals will have a high hit rate and low false-alarm rate. Forecasters with less sensitivity are still likely to have a high hit rate, but their false-alarm rate will also be higher.

As Figure 5.5 suggests, people do sometimes make mistakes at signal detection, whether it involves spotting tornadoes, inspecting aircraft, diagnosing medical conditions, searching for oil, or looking for clues at a crime scene. Research on these and other perceptual abilities has led psychologists to suggest ways of improving people's performance on signal-detection tasks (Wickens, 1992a). For example, they recommend that manufacturers occasionally place flawed items among a batch of objects to be inspected. This strategy increases inspectors' expectations of seeing flaws, thus lowering the response criterion and raising the hit rate.

Judging Differences Between Stimuli

Often people must not only detect a stimulus but also determine whether two stimuli are the same or different. For example, when tuning up, musicians must decide if notes played by two instruments have the same pitch. And when repainting part of a wall, a painter needs to decide if the new paint matches the old. The study of perceptual comparisons focuses on two questions. First, what is the smallest difference between stimuli that people can detect? If you want to make your soup more spicy, what is the minimum amount of spice you have to add to it before you are able to taste a difference? This minimum detectable difference is called the **difference threshold** or **just-noticeable difference** (**JND**). The second question involves how accurate people are at judging the size of a detectable difference. For example, if you had two differently seasoned bowls of soup, could you say exactly how much spicier one is compared with the other? Let's now consider both of these questions.

Just-Noticeable Differences   Our ability to detect a difference in the amount of stimulation we receive is primarily determined by two factors. The first is how much of the stimulus there was to begin with. Specifically, as the magnitude of the stimulus increases, the ability to detect differences in it declines. For example, if you are comparing the weight of two envelopes, you will be able to detect a difference of as little as a fraction of an ounce. But if you are comparing two boxes weighing around fifty pounds, you may not notice a difference unless it is a pound or more. The second factor that affects detection is which sense is being stimulated, because the ability to detect a difference in stimulation varies from one sense to another.

These two factors are represented in one of the oldest laws in psychology. Named after the nineteenth-century German physiologist Ernst Weber (pronounced "VAY-ber"), **Weber's law** states that the smallest detectable difference in stimulus energy is a fixed proportion of the intensity of the stimulus. This proportion, often

Stimulus	K
Pitch	.003
Brightness	.017
Weight	.020
Odor	.05
Loudness	.100
Pressure on skin	.140
Saltiness of taste	.200

TABLE 5.2

The Weber's Fraction (*K*) for Different Sensory Stimuli

The value of Weber's fraction, *K*, differs from one sense to another. Differences in *K* demonstrate the *adaptive* nature of perception. Humans, who depend more heavily on vision than on taste for survival, are more sensitive to vision than to taste.

called *Weber's constant* or *fraction,* is given the symbol *K*. As shown in Table 5.2, *K* is different for each of the senses. The smaller *K* is, the more sensitive a sense is to stimulus differences.

In algebraic terms, Weber's law says that JND = *KI*, where *K* is the Weber's constant for a particular sense, and *I* is the amount, or intensity, of the stimulus. Thus, to compute the JND for a particular stimulus, we must know its intensity and what sense it is stimulating. For example, as shown in Table 5.2, the value of *K* for weight is .02. If an object weighs 25 pounds (*I*), the JND is only half a pound (.02 x 25 pounds). So, for 25 pounds of luggage or groceries, an increase or decrease of half a pound is necessary before you can detect a change in heaviness. But candy thieves beware: It takes a change of only two-thirds of an ounce to determine that someone has been into a two-pound box of chocolates!

Weber's constants vary somewhat among individuals, and as we get older we tend to become less sensitive to stimulus differences. There are exceptions to this rule, however. For example, if you like candy, you will be happy to learn that Weber's fraction for sweetness stays fairly constant throughout life (Gilmore & Murphy, 1989).

Weber's law does not hold when stimuli are very intense or very weak, but it does apply to complex as well as simple stimuli. Accordingly, we all tend to have our own personal Weber's fractions that describe how much prices can increase before we notice the change, or become concerned about it. For example, if your Weber's fraction for cost is .10, then you would surely notice a fifty-cent increase in a one-dollar bus fare. But the same fifty-cent increase in monthly rent would be less than a JND and thus unlikely to cause notice, let alone concern.

Magnitude Estimation   How much must the volume on a stereo system increase before it will seem twice as loud? How many pounds of groceries can you add to a shopping bag before it seems twice as heavy? Weber's law does not address questions like these, but in 1860 Gustav Fechner (pronounced "FECK-ner") used that law to look for an answer. He reasoned that if JNDs become progressively larger as stimulus magnitude increases, then so, too, must the amount of change in the stimulus required to double or triple the perceived intensity, or magnitude, of the stimulus. For example, it would take only a small increase in volume to make a soft sound seem twice as loud, but imagine how much additional volume it would take to make a rock band seem twice as loud. To put it another way, constant increases in physical energy will produce

FIGURE 5.6

Length Illusions

People can usually estimate line lengths very accurately, but, as this figure illustrates, conditions can be created that seriously impair this ability. Although the pairs of lines marked A and B are the same length in each drawing, most observers report that line A appears longer than line B throughout. These optical illusions, like the one in Figure 5.2, may occur because of our tendency to see two-dimensional figures as three-dimensional. With the exception of the top hat, all or part of line A in each illustration can easily be interpreted as being farther away than line B. When two equal-size objects appear to be at different distances, the visual system tends to infer that the more distant object must be the larger one.

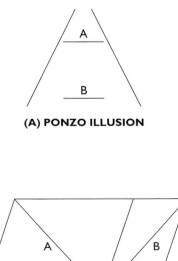

(A) PONZO ILLUSION

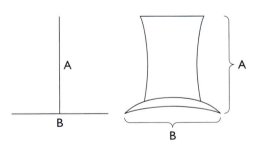

(B) HORIZONTAL-VERTICAL ILLUSION

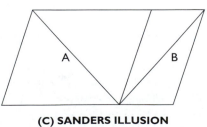

(C) SANDERS ILLUSION

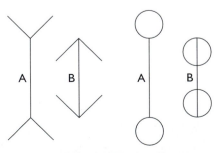

(D) MÜLLER-LYER ILLUSION AND VARIATION

(A)

(B)

FIGURE 5.7

Reversible Images

These are called *reversible* (or multi-stable) images because they can be organized by your perceptual system in two ways. If you perceive Part (A) as the word *figure,* the space around the letters becomes meaningless background. When your perceptual system emphasizes the word *ground,* however, what had stood out as the word *figure* a moment ago now becomes background. Similarly, in Part (B), if you perceive the image as two people facing each other, the space between their faces is the ground—the background behind their faces. But you can also perceive the figure as a vase or candle holder, and when you do, the spaces on each side, which had been meaningful figures, become the ground.

progressively smaller increases in perceived magnitude. This observation, when expressed as a mathematical equation relating actual stimulus intensity to perceived intensity, became known as *Fechner's law.*

Fechner's law applies to most, but not all, stimuli. Whereas light and sound must increase more and more to create the same amount of change in perceived magnitude, the reverse is true for the perceived intensity of electric shock. Thus, it would take a relatively large increase in shock intensity to make a weak shock seem twice as intense, but if the shock is already painful, it would take only a small increase in intensity before you said it was twice as strong. Because of these shortcomings in Fechner's law, S. S. Stevens offered another formula (known as *Stevens's power law*) for magnitude estimation that works for a wider array of stimuli, including electric shock, temperature, and sound and light intensity. Stevens's law is still used today by psychologists who need to determine how much larger, louder, longer, or more intense a stimulus must be for people to perceive a specific difference or amount of change.

Overall, people are reasonably good at estimating differences between stimuli. For example, we are very good at estimating how much longer one line is than another. Yet, as we saw in Figure 5.2 (on page 138), even this perceptual comparison process can be led astray when the lines are embedded in more complex figures. (See Figure 5.6 for some additional examples of lines that appear to be different lengths but in actuality are not.) Thus, the perceptual laws that we have discussed, as well as the exceptions to these laws, emphasize a central principle in perception—that perception is not absolute, but relative. Our experience of one stimulus depends on its relationship to others. The way in which the human perceptual system relates one stimulus to another is the focus of research on our next topic, perceptual organization.

ORGANIZING THE PERCEPTUAL WORLD

Suppose for a moment that you are driving down a busy road while searching for Barney's Diner, an unfamiliar restaurant where you are to meet a friend. The roadside is crammed with signs of all shapes and colors, some flashing, some rotating. If you are ever to recognize the sign that says "Barney's Diner," you must impose some sort of organization on this overwhelming array of visual information.

Principles of Perceptual Organization

Perceptual organization is the task performed by the perceptual system to determine what edges and other stimuli go together to form an object. In this case, the object would be the sign for Barney's Diner. It is perceptual organization, too, that makes it possible for you to separate the sign from its background of lights, colors, letters, and other competing stimuli. Two basic principles—*figure-ground processing* and *grouping*—guide this initial organization.

When you look at a complex scene or listen to a noisy environment, your perceptual apparatus automatically picks out certain features, objects, or sounds to be emphasized and relegates others to be *ground*—the less relevant background. For example, as you drive toward an intersection, a stop sign becomes a figure, standing out clearly against the background of trees, houses, and cars. A *figure* is the part of the visual field that has meaning, stands in front of the rest, and always seems to include the contours or edges that separate it from the less relevant background (Rubin, 1915). As described in Chapter 4, edges are one of the most basic features detected by our visual system; they combine to form figures.

Figure-Ground Processing   To fully appreciate the process of figure-ground processing, look at the drawings in Figure 5.7. These drawings are called *reversible figures* because you can repeatedly reverse your perceptual organization of what is figure and what is ground. Your ability to do this shows that perception is not only an active process, but a categorical one. People usually organize sensory stimulation into one perceptual category or another, but rarely into both or into something in between. In Figure 5.7, for instance, you cannot easily see both faces *and* a vase, or the words *figure* and *ground,* at the same time.

THE FAR SIDE   By GARY LARSON

The deadly couch cobra — coiled and alert in its natural habitat.

The natural camouflage of certain animals works by blurring cues for figure and ground, thus making immobile objects much less noticeable. If the snake depicted here were to move, however, it would stand out more and become much easier to see.

FIGURE 5.8

Gestalt Laws of Perceptual Grouping

We tend to perceive (A) as two groups of two circles plus two single circles, rather than as three groups of two circles or some other arrangement. In (B), we see two columns of X's and two columns of O's, not four rows of XOXO. We see the X in (C) as being made out of two continuous lines—one straight and one curved—not a combination of the odd forms shown. We immediately perceive the disconnected segments of (D) as a triangle and a circle. In (E), the different orientation of the lines in one quadrant of the rectangle makes that quadrant stand out from the others. In (F), we see the same three-dimensional cube from different angles, but the one on the left is normally perceived as a two-dimensional hexagon with lines running through it; the other, as a three-dimensional cube. In (G) we tend to pair up dots in the same oval even though they are far apart.

Grouping   Why is it that certain parts of the world become figure and others become ground, even when nothing in particular stands out in the physical pattern of light falling on the retina? The answer is that certain inherent parts of the stimulus environment lead people to group them together more or less automatically. In the early 1900s, several German psychologists used demonstrations like those in Figure 5.8 to assert the existence of specific laws of perceptual organization. They argued that people perceive sights and sounds as organized wholes. These wholes, they said, are different from, and more than, just the sum of the individual sensations, much as water is something more than just an assortment of hydrogen and oxygen atoms. Because the German word meaning (roughly) "whole figure" is *Gestalt*, these researchers became known as **Gestalt psychologists.** They proposed a number of principles, or "Gestalt laws," that describe how perceptual systems organize a stimulus array of raw sensations into a world of shapes and objects.

The most enduring of these principles include the following:

1. **Proximity.**   The closer objects or events are to one another, the more likely they are to be perceived as belonging together, as Figure 5.8(A) illustrates.

2. **Similarity.**   Similar elements are perceived to be part of a group, as in Figure 5.8(B). For example, people wearing the same school colors at a stadium will be perceived as belonging together even if they are not seated close together.

3. **Continuity.**   Sensations that appear to create a continuous form are perceived as belonging together, as in Figure 5.8(C).

4. **Closure.**   People tend to fill in missing contours to form a complete object, as in Figure 5.8(D).

5. **Texture.**   When basic features of stimuli have the same texture (such as the orientation of certain elements), people tend to group those stimuli together, as in Figure 5.8(E). Thus, you group standing trees together and perceive them as separate from their fallen neighbors.

6. **Simplicity.**   People tend to group features of a stimulus in a way that provides the simplest interpretation of the world. In Figure 5.8(F), for example, perceiving the image on the left as a two-dimensional hexagon with six radii is much simpler than perceiving it as a three-dimensional cube, so the two-dimensional perception usually prevails. For the image on the right, however, it is the two-dimensional perception that is more complex (try describing it in words!), so we tend to see it as a cube at an angle.

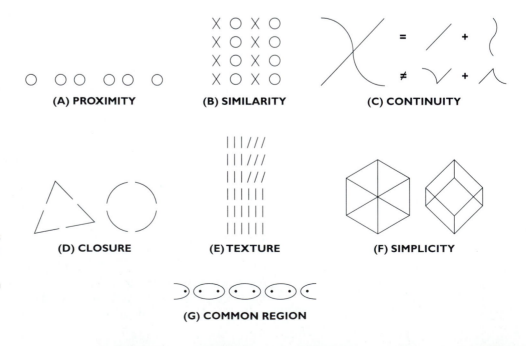

(A) PROXIMITY   (B) SIMILARITY   (C) CONTINUITY

(D) CLOSURE   (E) TEXTURE   (F) SIMPLICITY

(G) COMMON REGION

THE FAR SIDE By GARY LARSON

"Wait! Wait! . . . Cancel that, I guess it says 'helf.'"

The principle of closure allows us to fill in the blanks in what we see and hear. Without it, the world would appear as fragmented images and sounds that would confuse everyone, including would-be rescuers.

Common Fate

When numerous objects move together, they are seen as a group. This perceptual phenomenon is often put to good use by marching bands in half-time shows at college football games.

7. **Common region.** Stephen Palmer (1992) has proposed the principle of common region, which holds that elements located within some boundary tend to be grouped together. The boundary can be created by an enclosing perimeter, as in Figure 5.8(G), a region of color, or other factors.

8. **Common fate.** Sets of objects that are moving in the same direction at the same speed are perceived together. Choreographers and marching-band directors often use the principle of common fate, arranging for groups of dancers or musicians to move identically, creating the illusion of waves of motion or of large moving objects.

These principles are generally consistent with both the ecological and computational approaches to perception. The properties of the stimuli can account quite well for most of these principles of perceptual organization, as ecological psychologists have argued. At the same time, research in neurophysiology is demonstrating how neural pathways detect edges, lines, and texture in a way that can allow these organizational processes to be carried out early in perception, in an essentially automatic way.

However, psychologists who take a constructivist view of perception emphasize the role of experience-based expectations in perceptual organization. For example, they suggest that we see a cube in the righthand side of Figure 5.8(F) not so much because that is the simplest organization, but because of the **likelihood principle,** which says that we tend to perceive objects in the way that experience tells us is the most likely physical arrangement (Pomerantz & Kubovy, 1986). As with most perceptual principles, the likelihood principle operates automatically and accurately most of the time, but as shown in Figure 5.9, when we use it to organize stimuli that violate our expectations it can lead to frustrating misperceptions.

Auditory Scene Analysis Grouping principles such as similarity, proximity, closure, and continuity apply to what we hear as well as to what we see (Bartlett, 1993). For example, sounds that are similar in pitch tend to be grouped together, much like sounds that come close together in time. Through closure, we hear a tone as continuous even if it is repeatedly interrupted by bursts of static. **Auditory scene analysis** (Bregman, 1990) is the perceptual process of mentally representing and interpreting sounds. First, the flow of sound energy is organized into a series of segments based on characteristics such as frequency, intensity, location, and the like. Sounds with similar characteristics are then grouped into separate auditory *streams,* which are sounds perceived as coming from the same source. It is through auditory scene analysis that the potentially overwhelming world of sound is organized into separate, coherent patterns of speech, music, or even noise.

FIGURE 5.9

Impossible Objects

These objects can exist as two-dimensional drawings, but not as the three-dimensional objects that experience tells us to expect them to be. So when we use the likelihood principle to try to organize them in three-dimensional space, we discover that they are "impossible."

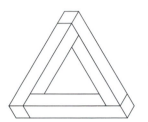

A Case of Depth Misperception

The runner in this photo is actually farther away than the man on the pitcher's mound. But because he is lower, not higher in the visual field—and because his leg seems to be in front of, not behind, the pitcher's leg—the runner appears smaller than normal rather than farther away.

Perception of Location and Distance

One of the most important perceptual tasks we face is to determine where objects and sound sources are located in the world around us. This task involves knowing both their two-dimensional position (left or right, up or down) and their distance from us.

Two-Dimensional Location   Visually determining whether an object is to your right or your left appears to be simple. All the perceptual system has to do, it seems, is determine where the object's image falls on the retina. For example, if the image falls on the center of the retina, then the object must be straight ahead. But when an object is, say, far to your right, and you focus its image on the center of your retina by turning your head and eyes toward it, you do not assume it is straight ahead. A computational approach to this location problem suggests that your brain uses an equation that takes information about where an image strikes the retina and adjusts it based on information about movement of your eyes and head. The result of these computations provides an estimate of the object's true location relative to your body.

As mentioned in Chapter 4, localization of sounds depends on cues about differences in the information received by your two ears. If a sound is continuous, sound waves coming toward the right side of your head will reach the right ear before reaching the left ear. Similarly, a sound coming toward the right side of your head will be a little bit louder to the right ear than to the left ear, because the head blocks some of the sound to the latter. The brain uses these slight differences in both the timing and the intensity of a sound as cues to locate its source. Visual cues are often integrated with auditory cues to determine the exact identity and location of the sound source. Most often, information from the eyes and the ears converge on the same likely sound source. However, there are times when the two senses produce conflicting impressions; in such cases, we tend to believe our eyes rather than our ears. This bias toward using visual information is known as *visual dominance*. The phenomenon is easily illustrated by our impression that the sound of a television program is coming from the screen rather than the speaker. Next time you are watching someone talking on TV, close your eyes. If your television has a single speaker below or to the side of the screen, you will notice that the sound no longer seems to be coming from the screen but from the speaker itself. As soon as you open your eyes, however, the false impression resumes: Words once again seem to come from the obvious visual source of the sound—the person on the screen.

FIGURE 5.10

Stimulus Cues for Depth Perception

See if you can identify how cues of relative size, interposition, linear perspective, and texture gradient combine to create a sense of three-dimensional depth in this drawing.

Depth Perception   One of the oldest puzzles in psychology is the question of how we are able to experience the world in three-dimensional depth even though the visual information we receive from it is projected onto two-dimensional retinas. The answer lies in the many depth cues provided by the environment and by some special properties of the visual system.

To some extent, people perceive depth through the same cues that artists use to create the impression of depth and distance on a two-dimensional canvas. These cues are actually characteristics of visual stimuli and therefore illustrate the ecological approach to perception. Figure 5.10 demonstrates several of these cues.

■ One of the most important depth cues is **interposition,** or *occlusion:* Closer objects block the view of things farther away. This cue is illustrated on the left side of Figure 5.10, where the two people are conversing; since they block part of the building, they are perceived as closer than the building.

■ The two men at the far left side of Figure 5.10 illustrate **relative size:** Given that they are assumed to be about equal in size, the one who casts the larger image on the retina is perceived to be closer.

■ A related cue, known as **texture gradient,** involves a graduated change in the "grain" of the visual field. Texture appears less detailed as distance increases; so, as the texture of a surface changes across the retinal image, people perceive a change in distance. In Figure 5.10, for instance, the center line in the road appears progressively less distinct, as do the birds near the "back" of the photo on page 152.

■ The figure crossing the center line in Figure 5.10 is seen as very far away, partly because she is near the horizon line, which we know is quite distant. She appears far

Texture Gradient

The details of a scene fade gradually as distance increases. This texture gradient helps us to perceive the less detailed animals in this photo as farther away.

away also because she is near a point where the road's edges, like all parallel lines that recede into the distance, appear to converge toward a single point. This apparent convergence provides a cue called **linear perspective.** Objects that are nearer the point of convergence are seen as farther away.

Still other depth cues depend on *clarity, color,* and *shadows.* Distant objects often appear hazier and tend to take on a bluish tone. (Thus, beginning artists are often taught to add a little blue when mixing paint for their background features.) Light and shadow also contribute to the perception of depth (Ramachandran, 1988). The buildings in the background of Figure 5.10 are seen as three-dimensional, not flat, because of the shadows on their right faces. Figure 5.11 gives another example of shadows' effect on depth perception.

An important visual depth cue that cannot be demonstrated in Figure 5.10, or in any other still picture, comes from looking at moving objects. You may have noticed,

FIGURE 5.11

Light, Shadow, and Depth Perception

The shadows cast by these protruding rivets and deep dents make it easy to see them in three dimensions. But if you turn the book upside down, the rivets now look like dents and the dents look like bumps. This reversal in depth perception occurs, in part, because people normally assume that illumination comes from above and interpret the pattern of light and shadow accordingly. With the picture upside down, light coming from the top would produce the observed pattern of shadows only if the circles were dents, not rivets.

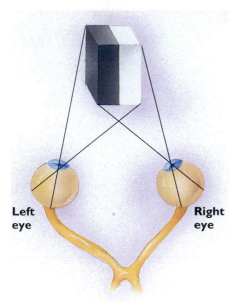

Left eye   **Right eye**

Images go to brain where they are compared

FIGURE 5.12

Binocular Disparity

The difference between each eye's view of the block decreases as distance from it increases. The resulting reduction in binocular disparity helps us perceive the block as farther away. To see how binocular disparity changes with distance, hold a pencil vertically about six inches in front of you, then close one eye and notice where the pencil is in relation to the background. Now open that eye, close the other one, and notice how much the pencil "shifts." These are the two rather different views your eyes have of the pencil. If you repeat this procedure while holding the pencil at arm's length, you will notice less disparity or "shift" because there is less difference in the angles at which the two eyes see the pencil.

for example, that when you look out the window of a moving car, objects nearer to you seem to speed across your visual field whereas objects in the distance seem to move slowly, if at all. This difference in the apparent rate of movement is called **motion parallax,** and it provides cues to differences in the distance of various objects.

Several additional depth cues result from the way human eyes are built and positioned. One of these cues is related to facts discussed in Chapter 4, on sensation. To bring an image into focus on the retina, the lens of the eye changes shape, or *accommodates.* To accomplish this feat, muscles surrounding the lens either tighten, to make the lens more curved for focusing on close objects, or relax, to flatten the lens for focusing on more distant objects. Information about such muscle activity is relayed to the brain, and this **accommodation** cue helps create the perception of distance.

The relative location of our two eyes produces two other depth cues. One is **convergence:** because each eye is located at a slightly different place on the skull, the eyes must converge, or rotate inward, in order to project an image on each retina. The brain receives and processes information from the eye muscles about this activity. The closer the object, the more the eyes must converge, and the greater the proprioceptive information going to the brain.

Second, because of their differing locations, each eye receives a slightly different view of the world, as Figure 5.12 illustrates. The difference between the two retinal images of an object is called **binocular disparity.** For any particular object, this disparity decreases with increasing distance. The brain combines the two images, processes information about the amount of disparity, and generates the impression of a single object having depth as well as height and width. View-Master slide viewers and 3-D movies create the appearance of depth by displaying to each eye a separate photograph of a scene, each taken from a slightly different angle.

The wealth of depth cues available to us is consistent with the ecological approach to perception. However, researchers taking the constructivist and computational approaches argue that, even when temporarily deprived of these depth cues, we can still move about and locate objects in an environment. In one study, for example, participants viewed a target object from a particular vantage point. Then, with their eyes closed, they were guided to a point well to the side of the target object and asked to walk toward it from this new position. The participants were amazingly accurate at this task, leading the researchers to suggest that seeing an object at some point in space creates a spatial model in the minds of perceivers—a model that remains intact even when immediate depth cues are removed.

Perception of Motion

Sometimes the critical property of an object is not its size or shape or distance but its motion—how fast it is going and where it is heading. For example, a car in front of you may change speed or direction, requiring that you change your own speed or direction, often very quickly.

How are you able to perceive such changes in motion? As with the detection of location and depth, the answer seems to be that you can efficiently "tune in" to a host of useful cues. Many of these cues make use of *optical flow,* or the changes in retinal images across the entire visual field. One particularly meaningful pattern of optical flow is known as **looming,** the rapid expansion in the size of an image so that it fills the retina. When an image looms, you tend to interpret it as an approaching stimulus. Your perceptual system quickly assesses whether the expansion on the retina is about equal in all directions or greater to one side than to the other. If it is greater to the right, for example, the approaching stimulus will miss you and pass to your right. However, if the retinal expansion is approximately equal on all sides—then duck!

Two questions, in particular, have interested psychologists who study motion perception. First, how do we know whether the flow of images across the retina is due to the movement of objects in the environment or to our own movements? If changes in retinal images were the only factor contributing to motion perception, then turning your head around or even rotating your eyeballs would create the perception that

Stroboscopic Motion

No movement takes place in any of these still photos, but if the sequence of images of this athlete's handspring were presented to you one at a time and in quick succession, an illusion called stroboscopic motion would cause you to perceive him to be moving.

everything in the visual field is moving. This is not the case because, as noted earlier, the brain also receives and processes information about the motion of the eyes and head. If the brain determines that such bodily movement accounts for all the movement of images on the retina, then the outside world is perceived as stable, not moving. To demonstrate this, close one eye and wiggle your open eyeball by gently pushing your lower eyelid. Because your brain receives no signals that your eye is being moved by its own muscles, the world is perceived as moving.

A second question involves the time lag—about one-twentieth of a second—between the moment when an image is registered on the retina and the moment when messages about that image reach the brain. In theory, each momentary perception of, say, your dog running toward you is actually a perception of where your dog was approximately one-twentieth of a second earlier. How does the perceptual system deal with this time lag so as to accurately interpret information about both motion and location? Psychologists have found that when a stimulus is moving along a relatively constant path, the brain seems to correct for the image delay by predicting where the stimulus should be one-twentieth of a second in the future (Nijhawan, 1997).

Motion perception is of great interest to sport psychologists. They try to understand, for example, why some individuals are so proficient at perceiving motion. One team of British psychologists has discovered a number of cues and computations apparently used by "expert catchers." In order to catch a ball, such individuals seem to be sensitive to the angle between their "straight ahead" gaze (i.e., a position with the chin parallel to the ground) and the gaze they use when looking up at a moving ball. Their task is to move the body—continuously and, often, quickly—to make sure that this "gaze angle" never becomes too small (such that the ball falls in front of them) or too large (such that the ball sails overhead). In other words, these catchers appear to unconsciously use a specific mathematical rule: "Keep the tangent of the angle of gaze elevation to zero" (McLeod & Dienes, 1996).

LINKAGES

How can the senses be fooled? (a link to Sensation)

Humans sometimes perceive motion even when no actual movement has occurred. These illusions of motion can tell us something about how the brain processes the flow of information from images moving across the retina. The most important motion illusion, called **stroboscopic motion,** occurs because of our tendency to interpret as continuous motion a series of still images flashed in rapid succession.

Stroboscopic motion is the basis for our ability to see movement in the still images presented by films and videos. Films consist of sequences of snapshots—presented at a rate of twenty-four per second. Each snapshot is slightly different from the preceding one, and each is separated by a brief blank-out produced by the shutter of the film projector. Videotapes show thirty such snapshots per second. As we watch, the "memory" of each image lasts long enough in the brain to bridge the gap until the next image appears. Thus, we are usually unaware that we are seeing a series of still pictures—and that, about half the time, there is actually no image on the screen!

Perceptual Constancy

Suppose that one sunny day you are watching someone walking toward you along a tree-lined sidewalk. The visual sensations produced by this person are actually rather bizarre. For one thing, the size of the image on your retinas keeps getting larger as the person gets closer. To see this for yourself, hold out a hand at arm's length and look at someone far away. The retinal image of that person will be so small that you can cover it with your hand. If you try to do the same thing when the person is three feet away, the retinal image will now be too large. But you perceive the person as being closer now, not bigger. Similarly, if you watch people pass from bright sunshine through the shadows of trees, your retinas receive images that are darker, then lighter, then darker again. Still, you perceive individuals whose coloring remains the same.

These examples illustrate **perceptual constancy,** the perception of objects as constant in size, shape, color, and other properties despite changes in their retinal image. Without perceptual constancy, the world would be an Alice-in-Wonderland kind of place in which objects continuously change their properties.

Size Constancy   Why does the perceived size of objects remain more or less constant, no matter what changes occur in the size of their retinal image? One view, which emphasizes the computational aspects of perception, suggests that as objects move closer or farther away, the brain perceives the change in distance and automatically adjusts the perception. Thus, the perceived size of an object is equal to the size of the retinal image multiplied by the perceived distance (Holway & Boring, 1941). As an object moves closer, its retinal image increases, but the perceived distance decreases at the same rate, so the perceived size remains constant. If, instead, an unmoving balloon is inflated in front of your eyes, perceived distance remains constant, and the perceived size (correctly) increases as the retinal image size increases.

The computational perspective is reasonably good at explaining most aspects of size constancy, but it cannot fully account for the fact that people are better at judging the true size (and distance) of familiar rather than unfamiliar objects. This phenomenon suggests that there is an additional mechanism for size constancy, one that is consistent with the constructivists' emphasis on the knowledge-based aspects of perception. Indeed, your knowledge and experience tell you that most objects (aside from balloons) do not suddenly change size.

The perceptual system usually produces size constancy correctly and automatically, but it can sometimes fail, resulting in size illusions such as the one illustrated in Figure 5.13. Because this figure contains strong linear perspective cues (lines converging in the "distance"), and because objects nearer the point of convergence are interpreted as farther away, we perceive the monster near the top of the figure as the bigger of the two—even though it is exactly the same size as the other one. The consequences of such illusions can be far more serious when the objects involved are, say, moving automobiles. For example, if there are few other depth cues available, we may perceive objects with smaller retinal images to be farther away than those with larger images. This error may explain why, in countries where cars vary greatly in size, small cars have higher accident rates than large ones (Eberts & MacMillan, 1985). A small car produces a smaller retinal image than a large one at the same distance, easily causing the driver of a following vehicle to overestimate the distance to the small car (especially at night) and therefore fail to brake in time to avoid a collision. Such misjudgments illustrate the *inferential* nature of perception emphasized by constructivists: People make logical inferences or hypotheses about the world based on the available cues. Unfortunately, if the cues are misleading, or the inferences are wrong, perceptual errors may occur.

Shape Constancy   The principles behind shape constancy are closely related to those of size constancy. To see shape constancy at work, remember what page you are on, close this book, and tilt it toward and away from you several times. The book will continue to look rectangular, even though the shape of its retinal image changes

FIGURE 5.13

A Size Illusion

To most people, the monster that is higher in the drawing appears larger than the other one, but in fact they are the same size. Why does this illusion occur? First, the converging lines of the tunnel provide strong depth cues that tell us which monster is farther away. Then, because the monster "farther away" casts an image on our retinas that is just as big as that cast by the "nearer" monster, we assume that the more distant monster must be bigger. (Look again at Figure 5.6(A) on page 146 for another illustration of this illusion.)

Shape Constancy

Trace the outline of this floating object onto a piece of paper. The tracing will be oval-shaped, but shape constancy causes you to perceive it as the circular life ring that it actually is.

in review

PRINCIPLES OF PERCEPTUAL ORGANIZATION AND CONSTANCY

Principle	Description	Example
Figure-ground processing	Certain objects or sounds are automatically identified as figures, whereas others become meaningless background.	You see a person standing against a building, not a building with a person-shaped hole in it.
Grouping (Gestalt laws)	Properties of stimuli lead us to automatically group them together. These include proximity, similarity, continuity, closure, texture, simplicity, common fate, and common region.	People who are sitting together, or are dressed similarly, are perceived as a group.
Perception of location and depth	Knowing an object's two-dimensional position (left and right, up and down) and distance enables us to locate it. The image on the retina and the orientation of the head position provide information about the two-dimensional position of visual stimuli; auditory localization relies on differences in the information received by the ears. Depth or distance perception uses stimulus cues such as occlusion, relative size, texture gradients, linear perspective, clarity, color, and shadow.	Large, clear objects appear closer than small, hazy objects.
Perceptual constancy	Objects are perceived as constant in size, shape, color, and other properties, despite changes in their retinal images.	A train coming toward you is perceived as getting closer, not larger; a restaurant sign is perceived as rotating, not changing shape.

dramatically as you move it. The brain automatically integrates information about retinal images and distance as movement occurs. In this case, the distance information involves the difference in distance between the near and far edges of the book.

As with size constancy, much of the ability to judge shape constancy depends on automatic computational mechanisms in the nervous system, but expectations about the shape of objects also play a role. For example, in Western cultures, most corners are at right angles. Knowledge of this fact helps make "rectangle" the most likely interpretation of the retinal image shown in Figure 5.1 (on page 138).

Brightness Constancy No matter how the amount of light striking an object changes, the object's perceived brightness remains relatively constant. You can demonstrate brightness constancy by placing a charcoal briquette in sunlight and a piece of

FIGURE 5.14

Brightness Constancy

You probably perceive the inner rectangle on the left to be lighter than the inner rectangle on the right. But carefully examine the inner rectangles alone (covering their surroundings). You will see that both are of equal intensity. The brighter surround in the righthand figure leads you to perceive its inner rectangle as relatively darker.

 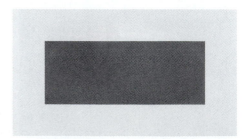

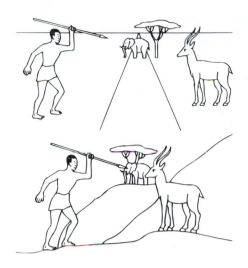

Source: Hudson, 1960.

FIGURE 5.15

The Hudson Test

Viewing these pictures from the Hudson Test, people are asked to judge which animal is closer to the hunter. Those familiar with pictured depth cues choose the antelope, which is at the same distance from the viewer as the hunter. Those less familiar with such cues may choose the elephant, which, though closer on the page, is more distant when depth cues are considered. Some have argued that cultural differences in perception might actually stem from differences in attention, experience with test materials, or the like (Biederman, 1987). Still, reported cultural differences in perception are consistent with what we know about the role of experience in perception.

white paper in nearby shade. The charcoal will look very dark and the paper very bright, even though a light meter would reveal much more light energy reflected from the sun-bathed coal than from the shaded paper. One reason the charcoal continues to look dark, no matter the illumination, is that you know that charcoal is nearly black, illustrating once again the knowledge-based nature of perception. Another reason is that the charcoal is still the darkest object relative to its background in the sunlight, and the paper is the brightest object relative to its background in the shade. The brightness of an object is perceived in relation to its background (see Figure 5.14).

For a summary of this discussion, see "In Review: Principles of Perceptual Organization and Constancy."

Culture, Experience, and Perception

So far, we have talked as if all aspects of perception work or fail in the same way for everyone. Differing experiences, however, do affect people's perceptions. To the extent that people in different cultures are exposed to substantially different visual environments, some of their perceptual experiences may be different as well. For example, researchers have compared responses to pictures containing depth cues by people from cultures that do and do not use pictures and paintings to represent reality (Derogowski, 1989). This research suggests that people in cultures that provide minimal experience with pictorial representations, like the Me'n or the Nupa in Africa, have a more difficult time judging distances shown in pictures (see Figure 5.15). These individuals also tend to have a harder time sorting pictures of three-dimensional objects into categories, even though they can easily sort the objects themselves (Derogowski, 1989).

Other research shows that the perception of optical illusions varies from culture to culture and is related to cultural differences in perceptual experiences. In one study, researchers enhanced the Ponzo illusion shown in Figure 5.6(A), on page 146, by superimposing its horizontal lines on a picture of railroad tracks. This familiar image added depth cues for American subjects but not for people on Guam, where railroad tracks were absent at the time of the research (Leibowitz et al., 1969). In short, although the structure and principles of human perceptual systems tend to create generally similar views of the world for all of us, our perception of reality is also shaped by experience, including the experience of living in a particular culture. Unfortunately, as more and more cultures are "westernized," the visual stimulation they present to their children will become less distinctive; eventually, research on the impact of differential experience on perception may become impossible.

RECOGNIZING THE PERCEPTUAL WORLD

In discussing how people organize the perceptual world, we have set the stage for addressing one of the most vital questions that perception researchers must answer: How do people recognize what objects are? If you are driving in search of Barney's Diner, exactly what happens when your eyes finally locate the pattern of light that spells out "Barney's Diner"? How do you know that you have finally found what you have been looking for?

In essence, the brain must analyze the incoming pattern and compare that pattern to information stored in memory. If it finds a match, recognition takes place and the stimulus is classified into a *perceptual category*. Once recognition occurs, your perception of a stimulus may never be the same again. Look at Figure 5.16 (on page 158). Do you see anything familiar? If not, turn to Figure 5.22 (on page 161), then look at Figure 5.16 again. You should now see it in an entirely new light. The difference between your "before" and "after" experiences of Figure 5.16 is the difference between the sensory world before and after a perceptual match occurs and recognition takes place.

Exactly how does such matching occur? Some aspects of recognition begin at the "top"—that is, at a conceptual level, guided by knowledge, expectations, and other psychological factors. This phenomenon is called **top-down processing** because it involves higher-level, knowledge-based information. Other aspects of recognition

FIGURE 5.16

Perceptual Categorization

For the identity of this figure, turn to page 161.

begin at the "bottom," relying on specific, detailed information elements from the sensory receptors that are integrated and assembled into a whole. This latter phenomenon is called **bottom-up processing** because it begins with basic information units that serve as a foundation for recognition. Let's consider the contributions of bottom-up and top-down processing to recognition, as well as the use of neural network models to understand both.

Bottom-Up Processing

Research on the visual system is providing a detailed picture of how bottom-up processing works. As described in Chapter 4, on sensation, all along the path from the eye to the brain, certain cells respond to selected features of a stimulus, so that the stimulus is actually analyzed into basic features before these features are recombined to create the perceptual experience.

What features are subjected to separate analysis? Again, as discussed in Chapter 4, there is strong evidence that certain cells specialize in responding to stimuli having specific orientations in space (Hubel & Wiesel, 1979). For example, one cell in the cor-

FIGURE 5.17

Feature Analysis

Feature detectors operating at lower levels of the visual system detect such features of incoming stimuli as the corners and angles shown on the left side of this figure. Later in the perceptual sequence, bottom-up processing might recombine these features to aid in pattern recognition, as in the examples on the right.

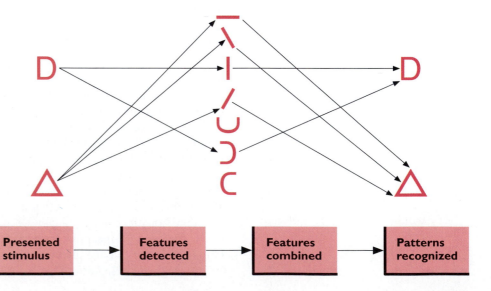

tex might fire only in response to a diagonal line, so it acts as a *feature detector* for diagonal lines. Figure 5.17 illustrates how the analysis by such feature detectors, early in the information-processing sequence, may contribute to recognition of letters or judgments of shape. Color, motion, and even corners are other sensory features that appear to be analyzed separately—in different parts of the brain—prior to full perceptual recognition (Beatty, 1995; Cowey, 1994).

In addition, the brain apparently analyzes *spatial frequencies*—that is, patterns of light and darkness in the visual scene (Graham, 1992). Some cortical cells are especially sensitive to high spatial frequencies, such as the very fine visual "grain" that characterizes the leaves of a tree seen from a distance. Other cells are more sensitive to low spatial frequencies—that is, to large-scale patterns with few light-to-dark shifts, such as a blank white wall. Analysis of the difference between high and low spatial frequencies may allow you to perceive texture gradients that help in making depth judgments and to recognize the general shape of blurry images or an object's fine details.

Features such as color, motion, overall shape, and fine details can all contribute to our ability to recognize objects, but some carry more weight than others in various situations. In the case of face recognition, for example, not all features are equally weighted when we decide who it is that we are seeing (Sinha & Poggio, 1996). Take just a brief look at Figure 5.18 and see if you recognize the person on the *left*. If you are like most people, it will take a second look to realize that your first glance led you to an erroneous conclusion. Such recognition errors are evidence that, at least initially, we tend to rely on large-scale features, such as hair and head shape, to recognize people.

How do psychologists know that feature analysis is actually involved in pattern recognition? Again, as noted in Chapter 4, recordings of brain activity indicate that the sensory features we have listed here cause particular sets of neurons to fire. Further, as described in Chapter 4, people with certain kinds of brain damage show selective impairment in the ability to perceive certain sets of sensory features, such as an object's color or movement (Banks & Krajicek, 1991).

Irving Biederman (1987) has proposed that people recognize three-dimensional objects by detecting and then combining simple forms, which he calls *geons;* Figure 5.19 shows some of these geons. (Notice how these geons can be recombined to form a variety of recognizable objects.) Evidence for Biederman's theory comes from

FIGURE 5.18

The Face Looks Familiar

How long did it take you to identify the two men pictured here? Was your first impression correct? Initially, most people see Bill Clinton and Al Gore, but look more closely. The image on the left is really a mixture of the head shape and hair of Gore with the facial features of Clinton. The tendency to incorrectly identify the composite as Gore suggests that large-scale features, such as overall shape, may be more important than small-scale features for recognition of faces and perhaps other stimuli as well.

FIGURE 5.19

Recognizing Objects from Geons

Research suggests that we use geons—the forms in the top row—to recognize complex objects. Some examples of objects that can be recognized based on the spatial layout and combination of only two or three geons are shown in the bottom row. For example, the coffee cup is made up of geons 2 and 4. Other combinations, such as an elongated cylinder (geon 2) on top of a cone (geon 3), might produce a broom. Can you make a kettle? The solution is on page 160.

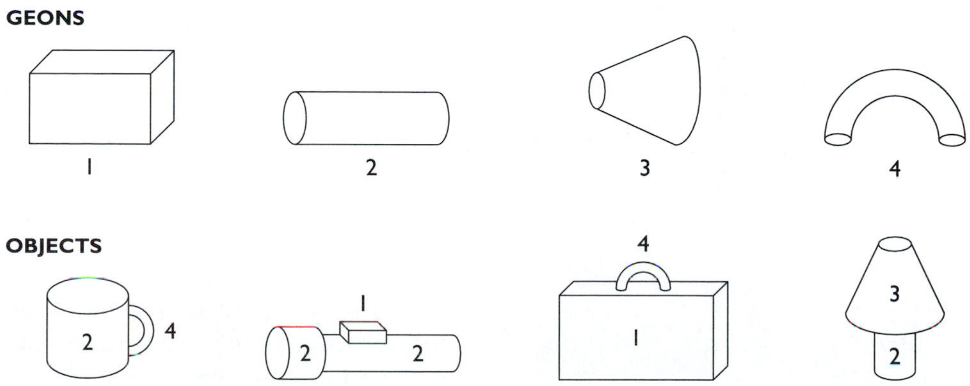

GEONS

l   2   3   4

OBJECTS

FIGURE 5.20

Recognition of Objects With and Without Their Geons Destroyed

The drawings in columns 2 and 3 have had the same amount of ink removed, but in column 3 the deletions have destroyed many of the geons used in object recognition. The drawings in column 2 are far easier to recognize because their geons are intact.

You can create a kettle by adding a cone (geon 3) to a combination of geons 2 and 4 (the coffee cup).

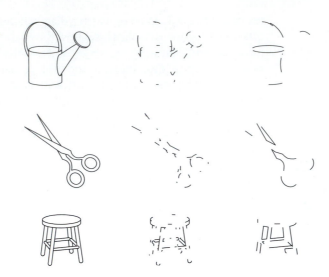

LINKAGES

The Eye of the Beholder

Top-down processing can affect our perception of people as well as objects. As noted in Chapter 17, for example, if you expect everyone in a certain ethnic or social group to behave in a certain way, you may perceive a particular group member's behavior in line with this prejudice. On the other hand, have you ever come to perceive someone as physically more attractive or less attractive as you got to know the person better? This change in perception occurs largely because new information alters, in top-down fashion, your interpretation of the raw sensations you get from the person.

experiments in which people must identify drawings when some of the details have been eliminated. Recognition becomes particularly difficult when the geons are no longer intact, as Figure 5.20 demonstrates.

Top-Down Processing

Bottom-up feature analysis can explain why you recognize the letters in a sign for Barney's Diner. But why is it that you will recognize the sign more easily if it appears where you were told to expect it rather than a block earlier? And why can you recognize it even if a few letters are missing from the sign? Top-down processing seems to be at work in these cases. In top-down processing, people use their knowledge in making inferences or "educated guesses" to recognize objects, words, or melodies, especially when sensory information is vague or ambiguous (DeWitt & Samuel, 1990; Rock, 1983). For example, once you knew that there was a dog in Figure 5.16, it became much easier for you to perceive it.

Many aspects of perception can best be explained by higher-level cognitive influences, especially by expectancy and context. Consider, once again, the two faces in Figure 5.18. Do you think that you'd have been as likely to mistakenly identify the man on the left as Al Gore if the man on the right had been, say, British Prime Minister Tony Blair, or John Travolta, rather than Bill Clinton? Probably not. Through bottom-up processing you correctly identified the combination of features on the right as Bill Clinton; and given your knowledge of Clinton, you reasonably expected to see certain individuals at his side, such as Al Gore. In short, your perceptual system made a quick "educated guess." This example illustrates that whereas top-down processing often aids us by allowing identification to occur before processing of features is complete, or when features are missing or distorted, it can also sometimes lead us to erroneous conclusions.

Top-down processing may also be implicated in many sightings of unusual images or "visions." Figure 5.21 shows a pattern of light reflected from a building in Clearwater, Florida that many people saw as the image of the Virgin Mary. In this case, knowledge of paintings and engravings of the Virgin Mary would have been a necessary precursor to recognition of the pattern as a religious image. The beliefs and motivations of the observers may also have played a role. And expectancy was almost certainly responsible for a substantial number of sightings: Many people who had not learned about the image through the news media probably looked at the building and walked right past without noticing anything unusual.

These examples illustrate that top-down processing can have a strong influence on pattern recognition. Our experiences create **schemas,** which are mental representations of what we know and have come to expect about the world. Schemas can bias our

FIGURE 5.21

A Vision of the Virgin Mary?

What image do you see in the window? Many people in Clearwater, Florida, saw this pattern of light reflected from an office building as an outline of the Virgin Mary. Recognition of such ambiguous images requires a combination of bottom-up and top-down processing. The feature detectors of the visual system automatically register the edges and colors of the image, while knowledge, beliefs, and expectancies impart meaning to these features. Given the importance of context and expectancies, it is not surprising that the image was first noticed a few days before Christmas. A person from a Moslem or Hindu culture might not see the Virgin Mary in the reflection. (Ask a friend to say what this image is, but don't mention what it might be. What was the result?)

perception toward one recognition or another by creating a *perceptual set,* a readiness or predisposition to perceive a stimulus in a certain way. Perceptual sets can save us the time consumed by additional detailed processing of stimulus features, but they can also lead to perceptual errors.

Motivation is another aspect of top-down processing that can affect perception. A hungry person, for example, might misperceive a sign for "Burger's Body Shop" as indicating a place to eat. Similarly, if you have ever watched an athletic contest, you probably remember a time when an obviously demented referee incorrectly called a foul on your favorite team. You knew the call was wrong because you clearly saw the other team's player at fault. But suppose you had been cheering for that other team. The chances are good that you would have seen the referee's call as the right one.

Network Processing

Researchers taking a computational approach to perception have attempted to explain various aspects of object recognition in terms of both top-down *and* bottom-up processing. Consider the following recognition phenomenon, for example. When participants were asked to say whether a particular feature, like the dot and angle at the left side of Figure 5.23 (on page 162), appeared within a pattern that was briefly flashed on a computer screen, the feature was detected faster when it was embedded in a pattern resembling a three-dimensional object than when it appeared within a random pattern of lines (Purcell & Stewart, 1991; Weinstein & Harris, 1974). This result is called the *object superiority effect.* There is also a *word superiority effect:* When strings of letters are briefly flashed on a screen, people's ability to detect target letters is better if the string forms a word than a nonword (Prinzmetal, 1992).

To explain these and related findings, researchers have turned to neural network models. As described in Chapter 3, each element in these networks is connected to every other element, and each connection has a specific strength. Applying network processing models to pattern recognition involves focusing on the interactions among the various feature analyzers we have discussed (Rumelhart & Todd, 1992). More specifically, some researchers explain recognition using **parallel distributed processing (PDP) models** (Rumelhart & McClelland, 1986). According to PDP models, the units in a network operate in parallel—simultaneously. Connections between units either excite or inhibit other units. If the connection is excitatory, activating one unit spreads the activation to connected units. Using a connection may strengthen it.

How does this process apply to recognition? According to PDP models, recognition occurs as a result of the simultaneous operation of connected units. Units are activated

FIGURE 5.22

Another Version of Figure 5.16

Now that you can identify a dog in this figure, it should be much easier to recognize when you look back at the original version.

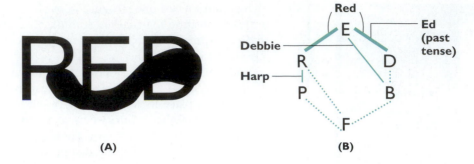

(A)   **(B)**

Source: Rumelhart & McClelland, 1986.

FIGURE 5.24

Recognizing a Word

The first letter of the word shown in (A) could be *R* or *P,* the second *E* or *F,* and the third *D* or *B.* Yet the pattern is quickly recognized as the word *RED.* According to PDP models, recognition occurs because, *together,* the letters excite each other's correct interpretation. This mutual excitation process is illustrated in (B) by a set of letter "nodes" (corresponding to activity sites in the brain), surrounded by some of the words they might activate. These nodes will be activated if the feature they detect appears in the stimulus array. They will also be activated if nodes to which they are linked become active. The stronger the link between nodes, the more activation will occur. Thus, all six letters shown in (B) will initially be excited when the stimulus in (A) is presented, but mutual excitement along the strongest links will guarantee that the word *RED* is perceived (Rumelhart & McClelland, 1986).

FIGURE 5.23

The Object Superiority Effect

When people are asked to say whether the feature on the left appears in patterns briefly flashed on a computer screen, the feature is more likely to be detected when it appears in patterns like those at the top, which most resemble three-dimensional objects. This "object superiority effect" supports the importance of network processing in perception.

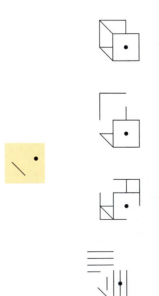

Source: Reprinted with permission from figures by Weisstein & Harris, *Science,* 1974, 186, 752–755. Copyright © 1974 by American Association of the Advancement of Science.

when matched by features in a stimulus. To the extent that features such as the letters in a word or the angles in a box have occurred together in the past, their connective links will be stronger, and detection of any of them will be made more likely by the presence of all the others. This appears to be what happens in the word and object superiority effects; and the same phenomenon is illustrated in Figure 5.24.

PDP models, sometimes called *connectionist* models, clearly represent the computational approach to perception. Indeed, researchers have achieved many advances in theories of pattern recognition by programming computers to carry out the kinds of complex computations that neural networks are assumed to perform in the human perceptual system (Grossberg, 1988). These computers have "learned" to read and recognize speech, and even faces, in a manner that is strikingly similar to the way humans learn and perform the same perceptual tasks (see "In Review: Mechanisms of Pattern Recognition" on page 165).

LINKAGES

Perception and Human Development

We have seen the important role that knowledge and experience play in recognition, but are they also required for more basic aspects of perception? Which perceptual abilities are babies born with, and which do they acquire by seeing, hearing, smelling, touching, and tasting things? How do their perceptions compare to those of adults?

To learn about infants' perception, psychologists have studied two inborn patterns called *habituation* and *dishabituation.* For example, infants stop looking when they repeatedly see stimuli that are perceived to be the same. This is habituation. If a stimulus appears that is perceived to be different, looking resumes. This is dishabituation.

FIGURE 5.25

Infants' Perception of Human Faces

Newborns show significantly greater interest in the facelike pattern at the far left than in any of the other patterns. Evidently, some aspects of face perception are innate.

   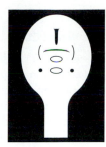

| Face | Configuration | Linear | Scrambled |

Source: Johnson et al., 1991.

LINKAGES

What does the world look like to infants? (a link to Human Development)

Researchers have used the habituation/dishabituation technique, along with measurements of electrical responses in the brain, to study color perception in infants. It seems that newborns can perceive differences between stimuli showing different amounts of black-and-white contrast, but are unable to distinguish between particular hues (Burr, Morrone, & Fiorentini, 1996). Other researchers have used similar methods to show that newborns can perceive differences in the angles of lines (Slater et al., 1991). These and other studies suggest that we are born with some, but not all, of the basic components of feature detection.

Do we also have an innate ability to combine features into perceptions of whole objects? This question generates lively debate among specialists in infant perception. Some research indicates that at one month of age, infants concentrate their gaze on one part of an object, such as the corner of a triangle (Goldstein, 1999). By two months, though, the eyes systematically scan the perimeter of the object, suggesting that only then has the infant begun to perceive the pattern, or shape of the object, not just its component features. However, other researchers have found that newborns, once habituated to specific combinations of features, show dishabituation (that is, pay attention) when those features are combined in a novel way. The implication is that even newborns notice, and keep track of, the way some features are put together (Slater et al., 1991).

There is evidence that infants may be innately tuned to perceive at least one important complex pattern—the human face. In one study of newborns, some less than an hour old, patterns like those in Figure 5.25 were moved slowly past the infants' faces (Johnson et al., 1991). The infants moved their heads and eyes to follow these patterns, but they tracked the face-like pattern shown on the left side of Figure 5.25 significantly farther than any of the nonfaces. The difference in tracking indicates that the infants could discriminate between faces and nonfaces, and are more interested in the former. Why should this be? The investigators suggest that interest in human faces is adaptive, in evolutionary terms, because it helps newborns focus on their only source of food and care.

Other research on perceptual development suggests that our ability to use certain distance cues develops more slowly than recognition of object shapes. For example, infants' ability to use binocular disparity and relative motion cues to judge depth appears to develop some time after about three months of age (Yonas, Arterberry, & Granrud, 1987; see Figure 5.26). And infants do not use texture gradients and linear perspective as cues about depth until they are five to seven months old (Arterberry, Yonas, & Bensen, 1989).

In summary, there is little doubt that many of the basic building blocks of perception are present within the first few days after birth. The basics include organ-based cues to depth such as accommodation and convergence. Maturation of the visual system adds to these basics as time goes by. For example, over the first few months after birth, the eye's fovea gradually develops the number of cone cells necessary for high visual acuity and perception of small differences in hue (Goldstein, 1999). However, visual experience may also be necessary if the infant is to recognize some unified patterns and objects in frequently encountered stimuli, to interpret depth and distance

FIGURE 5.26

FIGURE 5.26

The Visual Cliff

The *visual cliff* is a glass-topped table that creates the impression of a sudden drop-off. Shown here is a ten-month-old who, placed at what looks like the edge, will calmly crawl across the shallow side to reach a parent, but will hesitate and cry rather than crawl over the "cliff" (Gibson & Walk, 1960). Changes in heart rate show that infants too young to crawl also perceive the depth, but are not frightened by it (Campos, Langer, & Krowitz, 1970). Here again, nature and nurture interact adaptively: Depth perception appears shortly after birth, but fear and avoidance of dangerous depth do not develop until an infant is old enough to crawl into trouble.

cues, and to use them in moving safely through the world. Thus, like so many aspects of human psychology, perception is the result of a blending of heredity and environment. From infancy onward, the perceptual system creates a personal reality based in part on the experience that shapes each individual's feature-analysis networks and knowledge-based expectancies.

ATTENTION

Believe it or not, you still haven't found Barney's Diner! By now, you understand *how* you will recognize the right sign when you perceive it, but how can you be sure you *will* perceive it? As you drive, the diner's sign will appear as but one piece in a sensory puzzle that also includes road signs, traffic lights, sirens, talk radio, and dozens of other stimuli. You can't perceive all of them at once, so to find Barney's you are going to have to be sure that the information you select for perceptual processing includes the stimuli that will help you reach your goal. In short, you are going to have to pay attention. **Attention** is the process of directing and focusing certain psychological resources to enhance perception, performance, and mental experience. We use attention to *direct* our sensory and perceptual systems toward certain stimuli, to *select* specific information for further processing, to *allocate* the mental energy required to do that processing, and to *regulate* the flow of resources necessary for performing a task or coordinating several tasks at once.

Psychologists have discovered three important characteristics of attention. First, it *improves mental processing;* you often need to concentrate attention on a task to do your best at it. If your attentional system temporarily malfunctions, you might drive right past Barney's Diner. Second, attention takes *effort*. Prolonged concentration of attention can leave you drained, and when you are fatigued, focusing attention on anything becomes more difficult. Third, attentional resources are *limited*. When your attention is focused on reading this book, for example, you have less attention left over to listen to a conversation in the next room.

To experience attention as a process, try "moving it around" a bit. When you finish reading this sentence, look at something behind you, then face forward and notice the next sound you hear, then visualize your best friend, then focus on how your tongue feels. You just used attention to direct your perceptual systems toward different aspects

in review

MECHANISMS OF PATTERN RECOGNITION

Mechanism	Description	Example
Bottom-up processing	Raw sensations from the eye or the ear are analyzed into basic features, such as color or movement; these features are then recombined at higher brain centers, where they are compared to stored information about objects or sounds.	You recognize a dog as a dog because its physical features—four legs, barking, panting—match your perceptual category for "dog."
Top-down processing	Knowledge of the world and experience in perceiving allow people to make inferences about the identity of stimuli, even when the quality of raw sensory information is low.	On a dark night, a small, vaguely seen blob pulling on the end of a leash is recognized as a dog because the stimulus occurs at a location where we would expect a dog to be.
Network, or PDP, processing	Recognition depends on communication among feature-analysis systems operating simultaneously and enlightened by past experience.	A dog standing behind a picket fence will be recognized even though each disjointed "slice" of the stimulus may not look like a dog.

of your external and internal environments. Sometimes, as when you looked behind you, shifting attention involves *overt orienting*—pointing sensory systems at a particular stimulus. But you were able to shift attention to an image of your friend's face without having to move a muscle; this is called *covert orienting*. There is a rumor that students sometimes use covert orienting to shift their attention from the lecturer they are looking at to thoughts that have nothing to do with the lecture.

An Experiment in "Mind Reading"

Everyone knows what it is like to covertly shift attention, but how can we tell when someone else is doing it? The study of covert attention requires the sort of "mind reading" that has been made possible by innovative experimental research methods. These techniques are helping psychologists to measure where a person's attention is focused.

■ What was the researchers' question?

Michael Posner and his colleagues were interested in finding out what changes in perceptual processing occur when observers covertly shift their attention to a specific location in space (Posner, Nissen, & Ogden, 1978). Specifically, these researchers addressed the question of whether such attentional shifts lead to more sensitive processing of stimuli in the location attended to.

■ How did the researchers answer the question?

Posner and his colleagues took advantage of an important property of mental events: Even though such events do not produce movements that can be observed and

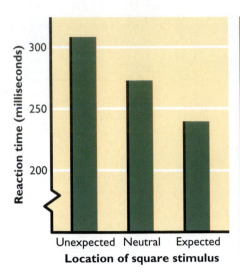

FIGURE 5.27

Measuring Covert Shifts in Attention

It took people less time (measured in thousandths of a second) to detect a square appearing at an expected location than at an unexpected location. This result suggests that, even though their eyes did not move, they covertly shifted attention to the expected location before the stimulus was presented.

recorded, they *do* take time. Moreover, the time taken by mental events may vary considerably, thus providing important clues about internal processes such as covert attention. Accordingly, the researchers designed a study in which participants were asked to focus their eyes on a fixation point that appeared at the center of a computer screen. One second later, a tiny square appeared at either the right or left edge of the screen. The participants were then asked to indicate, by pressing a key as quickly as possible, when they detected the square. However, because their vision was focused on the fixation point, they could detect the square only out of the "corners" of their eyes.

On any given trial, a participant could never be 100 percent sure where the square would be located. However, the researchers provided "hints" on some of the trials. At the start of some trials, participants were given a cue at the fixation point. Sometimes, the cue was an arrow pointing to the right edge of the screen (→). This cue was correct 80 percent of the time. On other trials, participants were presented with an arrow pointing to the left edge of the screen (←); this cue was also correct 80 percent of the time. On still other trials, participants saw a "+" which indicated that the square was equally likely to appear on the left or the right.

The researchers reasoned that when the plus sign appeared, the best strategy for quickly detecting the square would be to maintain visual attention on the center of the screen and to shift it only after the square appeared. However, in cases where one of the arrow cues was presented, the best strategy would involve covertly shifting attention in the direction indicated by the arrow before the square appeared. If the participants were, in fact, using covert attention shifts, so the logic went, they should have been able to detect the square fastest when the cue provided accurate information about the location of the target square—even though they were not actually moving their eyes.

The dependent variable in this study was the speed of target detection, measured in milliseconds. The independent variable was the type of cue given: valid, invalid, or neutral. Valid cues were arrows that correctly predicted the target location; invalid ones were arrows that pointed the wrong way. Neutral cues gave no guidance.

■ **What did the researchers find?**

As shown in Figure 5.27, the square stimulus was detected significantly faster when the cue gave valid information about where the square would appear. Invalid cues, however, resulted in a distinct cost to performance: When participants were led to shift their attention in the wrong direction, they were much slower in detecting the square.

■ **What do the results mean?**

The data provide evidence that the participants used cues to shift their attention to the expected location, thus readying their perceptual systems to detect information there. When a cue led them to shift their attention to the wrong location, they were less ready to detect information at the correct location and their detection was slowed. In short, whereas attention can enhance the processing of information at one retinal location, it does so at the expense of processing information elsewhere.

■ **What do we still need to know?**

Since the publication of this pioneering work by Posner and his colleagues, the costs and benefits associated with perceptual expectancies have been studied by many other researchers interested in attention (e.g., Ball & Sekuler, 1992). For the most part, their results are consistent with the findings of Posner's team. However, psychologists are still trying to answer a variety of questions as to how covert attention actually operates. Some of these questions include the following: How quickly can we shift attention from one location to another? And how quickly can we shift attention between sensory modalities—from watching to listening, for example? These questions, though methodologically difficult to address, are fundamental to our understanding of the efficiency with which we are able to deal with the potential overload of stimuli that reach our sensory receptors.

Experiments designed to answer such questions not only expand our understanding of attention, but illustrate the possibility of measuring hidden mental events through observation of overt behavior.

Allocating Attention

As shown in Posner's experiment on "mind reading," attending to some stimuli makes us less able to attend to others. In other words, attention is *selective;* it is like a spotlight that can illuminate only a part of the external or internal environment at any particular moment. How do you control, or allocate, your attention?

Control over attention can be voluntary or involuntary (Yantis, 1993). *Voluntary,* or goal-directed, attention control occurs when you purposely focus it in order to perform a task, such as reading a book in a noisy room or watching for a friend in a crowd. Voluntary control reflects top-down processing because attention is guided by knowledge-based factors such as intentions, beliefs, expectations, and motivation. As people learn certain skills, they voluntarily direct their attention to information they once ignored. For example, the skilled driver looks farther down the road than the novice does. If you are watching a sports event, learning where to allocate your attention is important if you are to understand what is going on. And if you are a competitor, the proper allocation of attention is absolutely essential for success on the playing field (Moran, 1996).

When, in spite of these top-down factors, some aspect of the environment—such as a loud noise—diverts your attention, attentional control is said to be *involuntary.* In this case, it is a bottom-up or stimulus-driven process. Stimulus characteristics that tend to capture attention include abrupt changes in lighting or color (such as flashing signs), movement, and the appearance of unusual shapes (Folk, Remington, & Wright, 1994). Indeed, some psychologists use the results of attention research to help design advertisements, logos, and product packaging that "grab" potential customers' attention.

Divided Attention

In many situations, people can divide their attention efficiently enough to allow them to perform more than one activity at a time (Damos, 1992). In fact, as Figure 5.28

Capturing Attention

Advertisers use stimulus features such as movement, contrast, color, and intensity to make us involuntarily attend to their products or services. Knowing that attention is selective, magicians use sudden movements or other stimuli to distract our attention from the actions that lie behind their tricks.

BLUE   GREEN
GREEN   ORANGE
PURPLE ORANGE
GREEN   BLUE
RED   RED
GRAY   GRAY
RED   BLUE
BLUE   PURPLE

FIGURE 5.28

The Stroop Task

Look at this list of words and try, as rapidly as possible, to call out the color of the *ink* in which each word is printed. This *Stroop task* (Stroop, 1935) is not easy because the brain automatically processes the *meaning* of these familiar words, which then competes for attention with the response you are supposed to give. To do well, you must focus on the ink color and not allow your attention to be divided between color and meaning. Children just learning to read have far less trouble with this task, because they do not yet process the meaning of words as automatically as experienced readers do.

illustrates, it is sometimes difficult to keep our attention focused rather than divided. We can walk while talking, or drive while listening to music, but we find it virtually impossible to read and talk at the same time. Why is it sometimes so easy and at other times so difficult to do two things at once?

When one task is so *automatic* as to require little or no attention, it is usually easy to do something else at the same time, even if the other task takes some attention (Schneider, 1985). Even when two tasks require attention, it may still be possible to perform them simultaneously, as long as each taps into different kinds of attentional resources (Wickens, 1992a). For example, some attentional resources are devoted to perceiving incoming stimuli, whereas others handle making responses. This specialization of attention allows a skilled pianist to read musical notes and press keys simultaneously even the first time through a piece. Apparently, the human brain has more than one type of attentional resources and more than one spotlight of attention (Navon & Gopher, 1979; Wickens, 1989). This notion of different types of attention also helps explain why a driver can listen to the radio while steering safely and why voice control can be an effective way of performing a second task in an aircraft while the pilot's hands are busy manipulating the controls (Wickens, 1992a).

Attention and Automatic Processing

Your search for Barney's Diner will be aided by your ability to voluntarily allocate attention to a certain part of the environment, but it would be made even easier if you knew that Barney's had the only green sign on that stretch of road (see "In Review: Attention"). Your search would not take much effort in this case because you could simply "set" your attention to filter out all signs except green ones. Psychologists describe this ability to search for targets rapidly and automatically as *parallel processing*; it is as if you can examine all nearby locations at once (in parallel) and rapidly detect the target no matter where it appears.

Thus, if Waldo—the target to be found in Figure 5.29—were bright red and twice as large as any other character, you could conduct a parallel search and he would quickly "pop out." The automatic, parallel processing that allows detection of color or size suggests that such features are analyzed before the point at which attention is

FIGURE 5.29

Where's Waldo?

Find Waldo. (He's the only person wearing a striped shirt and glasses.)

Illustration by Martin Handford.

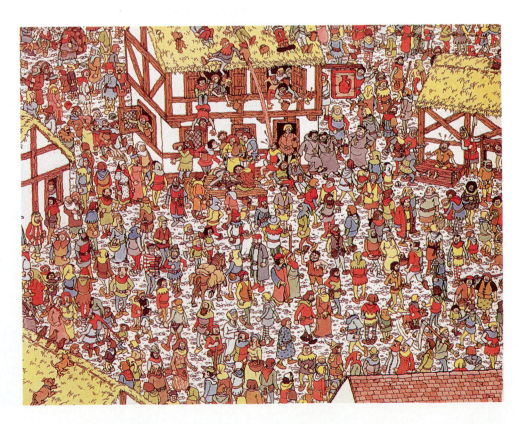

in review

ATTENTION		
Characteristics	**Functions**	**Mechanisms**
Improves mental functioning	Directs sensory and perceptual systems toward stimuli	Overt orienting (e.g., cupping your ear to hear a whisper)
Requires effort	Selects specific information for further processing	Covert orienting (e.g., thinking about spring break while looking at the notes in front of you)
Has limits	Allocates mental energy to process information	Voluntary control (e.g., purposefully looking for cars before crossing a street)
	Regulates the flow of resources necessary for performing a task or coordinating multiple tasks	Involuntary control (e.g., losing your train of thought when you're interrupted by a thunderclap)
		Automatic processing (e.g., no longer thinking about grammar rules as you become fluent in a foreign language)
		Divided attention (e.g., looking for an open teammate while you dribble a soccer ball down the field)

required. However, because Waldo shares many features with the other characters in the figure, you must conduct a slower, serial search, examining each one in turn (Treisman, 1988). The more nontarget elements there are in a display, the longer a serial search will take. The "pop out" test offers a good way to determine which kinds of information are processed in parallel, leaving spare attention for use elsewhere, and which kinds require serial processing and thus more focused attention.

Attention and the Brain

If directing attention to a task causes extra mental work to be done, there should be evidence of that work in brain activity. Such evidence has been provided by positron emission tomography (PET) scans, which reveal increased blood flow to regions of the brain associated with the mental processing necessary for the task. In one study, for example, people were asked either to focus attention on reporting only the color of a stimulus or to divide attention in order to report its color, speed of motion, and shape (Corbetta et al., 1991). When attention was focused on color alone, increased blood flow appeared only in the part of the brain where that stimulus feature was analyzed; when attention was divided, the added supply of blood was shared between two locations. Similarly, particular patterns of blood flow have been observed in different areas of the brain involved in different reading processes, such as attending to the shape, sound, or meaning of words (Peterson et al., 1990). Because attention appears to be a linked set of resources that improve information processing at several levels and locations in the brain, it is not surprising that no single brain region has been identified as an "attention center" (Posner & Peterson, 1990).

APPLICATIONS OF RESEARCH ON PERCEPTION

Throughout this chapter we have mentioned ways in which perceptual systems shape people's ability to handle a variety of tasks, from recognizing restaurant signs to detecting tornadoes. We have also seen how perception research is used in designing advertisements and increasing traffic safety. In this section we examine two areas in which perception is particularly important: aviation and human-computer interaction.

Avoiding Perceptual Overload

The pilot of a commercial jetliner is faced with a potentially overwhelming array of visual and auditory signals that must be correctly perceived and interpreted to ensure a safe flight. Engineering psychologists are helping to design instrument displays that make this task easier.

Aviation Psychology

Much of the impetus for research on perception in aviation has come from accidents caused in part by failures of perception (O'Hare & Roscoe, 1991; Wiener & Nagel, 1988). To land an aircraft safely, for example, pilots must make accurate judgments of how far they are from the ground, and how fast and from what angle they are approaching a runway. Normally, the bottom-up perceptual cues providing this information are rich and redundant, and the pilots' perception is correct (Gibson, 1979). Further, the ground surface they are approaching matches their expectations based on experience, thus adding top-down processing to produce an accurate perception of reality. But suppose there are few depth cues because the landing occurs at night, and suppose the lay of the land is different from the pilot's normal experience. With both bottom-up and top-down processing impaired, the pilot's interpretation of reality may be disastrously incorrect.

If, for example, the runway is much smaller than a pilot expects, it might be perceived as farther away than it actually is—especially at night—and thus may be approached too fast (O'Hare & Roscoe, 1991). (This illusion is similar to the one mentioned earlier in which drivers overestimate their distance from small cars.) Or if a pilot expects the runway to be perfectly flat but it actually slopes upward, the pilot might falsely perceive that the aircraft is too high. Misguided attempts to "correct" a plane's altitude under these circumstances have caused pilots to fly in too low, resulting in a series of major nighttime crashes in the 1960s (Kraft, 1978). Psychologists have helped to prevent similar tragedies by recommending that airline training programs remind pilots about the dangers of visual illusions and the importance of relying on their flight instruments during landings, especially at night.

Unfortunately, the instruments in a typical aircraft cockpit present information that bears little resemblance to the perceptual world. A pilot depending on these instruments must do a lot of time-consuming and effortful serial processing in order to perceive and piece together the information necessary to understand the aircraft's position and movement. To address this problem, engineering psychologists have helped to develop displays that present a realistic three-dimensional image of the flight environment—similar in some ways to a video-game display. This image more accurately captures the many cues for depth perception that the pilot needs (Haskell & Wickens, 1993; Lintern, 1991; Theunisson, 1994).

Research on auditory perception has also contributed to aviation safety, both in the creation of warning signals that are most likely to catch the pilot's attention and in efforts to minimize errors in cockpit communications. Air-traffic control communications use a special vocabulary and standardized phrases in order to avoid ambiguity. But as a result, the communications are also usually short, with little of the built-in redundancy that, in normal conversation, allows people to understand a sentence even if some words are missing. If a pilot eager to depart on time perceives an expected message as "take off" when the actual message is "hold for takeoff," the results can be catastrophic. Problems like these are being addressed, "bottom-up," through "noise canceling" microphones and visual message displays (Kerns, 1991), as well as through the use of slightly longer messages that aid top-down processing by providing more contextual cues.

Human-Computer Interaction

The principles of perception are also being applied by engineering psychologists who serve as key members of design teams at various computer manufacturing and software companies. For example, in line with the ecological approach to perception, they are trying to duplicate in the world of computer displays many of the depth cues that help people navigate in the physical world (Preece et al., 1994). The next time you use a word-processing or spreadsheet program, notice how shading cues make the "buttons" on the application toolbar at the top or bottom of the screen seem to protrude from their background as real buttons would. Similarly, when you open several documents or spreadsheets, interposition cues make them appear to be lying on top of one another.

The results of research on attention have been applied to your cursor. It blinks to attract your attention, making it possible to do a quick parallel search rather than a slow serial search when you are looking for the cursor amid all the other stimuli on the screen (Schneiderman, 1992). Perceptual principles have also guided creation of the pictorial images, or icons, that are used to represent objects, processes, and commands in your computer programs (Preece et al., 1994). These icons speed your use of the computer if their features are easy to detect, recognize, and interpret (Rogers, 1989). This is why a little trash-can icon is used in some software programs to show you where to click when you want to delete a file; a tiny eraser or paper shredder would also work, but its features might be harder to recognize, making the program confusing. In short, psychologists are applying research on perception to make computers easier to use.

LINKAGES

As noted in Chapter 1, all of psychology's many subfields are related to one another. Our discussion of how perceptual processes develop in infants illustrates just one way in which the topic of this chapter, perception, is linked to the subfield of developmental psychology (Chapter 12). The Linkages diagram shows ties to two other subfields as well, and there are many more ties throughout the book. Looking for linkages among subfields will help you see how they all fit together and better appreciate the big picture that is psychology.

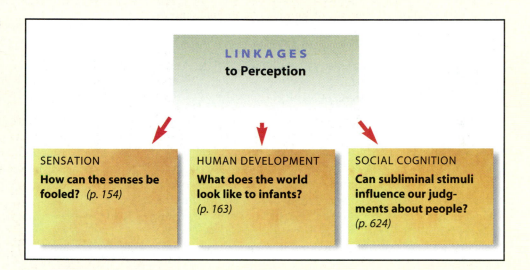

LINKAGES to Perception

SENSATION
How can the senses be fooled? *(p. 154)*

HUMAN DEVELOPMENT
What does the world look like to infants? *(p. 163)*

SOCIAL COGNITION
Can subliminal stimuli influence our judgments about people? *(p. 624)*

SUMMARY

Perception is the process through which people actively use knowledge and understanding of the world to interpret sensations as meaningful experiences.

THE PERCEPTION PARADOX

Because perception often seems so rapid and effortless, one might conclude that it is a rather simple operation; however, this is not the case. An enormous amount of processing is required to transform energy received by receptors into perceptual experience. The complexity of perception is revealed by perceptual errors (e.g., illusions) and the difficulties encountered in creating artificial pattern-recognition systems.

THREE APPROACHES TO PERCEPTION

The *computational approach* to perception emphasizes the computations performed by the nervous system. The *constructivist approach* suggests that the perceptual system constructs the experience of reality, making inferences and applying knowledge in order to interpret sensations. The *ecological approach* holds that the environment itself provides the cues that people use to form perceptions.

PSYCHOPHYSICS

Psychophysics is the study of the relationship between stimulus energy and the psychological experience of that energy.

Absolute Thresholds: Is Something Out There?

Psychophysics has traditionally been concerned with matters such as determining *absolute thresholds* for the detection of stimuli. Research shows that this threshold is not, in fact, absolute. Thus, it has been redefined as the minimum amount of energy that can be detected 50 percent of the time. *Supraliminal stimuli* fall above this threshold; *subliminal stimuli* fall below it.

Signal-Detection Theory

Signal-detection theory describes how people respond to faint or ambiguous stimuli. Detection of a signal is affected by external and internal *noise, sensitivity,* and the *response criterion.* Signal-detection theory has been applied to understanding decision making and performance in areas such as the detection of tornadoes on radar.

Judging Differences Between Stimuli

Weber's law states that the minimum detectable amount of change in a stimulus—the *difference threshold,* or *just-noticeable difference (JND)*—increases in proportion to the initial amount of the stimulus. The less the initial stimulation, the smaller the change must be in order to be detected. Fechner's law and Stevens's power law concern *magnitude estimation* and describe the relation between the magnitude of a stimulus and its perceived intensity.

ORGANIZING THE PERCEPTUAL WORLD

Principles of Perceptual Organization

Perceptual organization is the process whereby order is imposed on the information received by your senses. The perceptual system automatically distinguishes figure from ground, and groups stimuli into patterns. *Gestalt psychologists* proposed laws or principles that guide such grouping: *proximity, similarity, continuity, closure, texture, simplicity, common region,* and *common fate.* The *likelihood principle,* which reflects our expectations about the way the world is, also influences perceptual organization. The process of mentally representing and interpreting sounds is called *auditory scene analysis.*

Perception of Location and Distance

Visual localization requires information about the position of the body and eyes, as well as information about where a stimulus falls on the retinas. Auditory localization depends on detecting differences in the information that reaches the two ears, including differences in timing and intensity.

Perception of distance, or depth perception, depends partly on stimulus cues and partly on the physical structure of the visual system. Some of the stimulus cues for depth perception are *interposition, relative size, texture gradient, linear perspective,* and *motion parallax.* Cues based on the structure of the visual system include *accommodation* (the change in the shape of the lenses as objects are brought into focus), *convergence* (the fact that the eyes must move to focus on the same object), and *binocular disparity* (the fact that the eyes are set slightly apart).

Perception of Motion

The perception of motion results, in part, from the movement of stimuli across the retina. Expanding or *looming* stimulation is perceived as an approaching object. Movement of the retinal image is interpreted along with information about movement of the head, eyes, and other parts of the body, so that one's own movement can be discriminated from the movement of external objects. *Stroboscopic motion* is an illusion that accounts for our ability to see smooth motion in films and videos.

Perceptual Constancy

Because of *perceptual constancy,* the brightness, size, and shape of objects can be seen as constant even though the sensations received from those objects may change. Size constancy and shape constancy depend on the relationship between the retinal image of the object and the knowledge-based perception of its distance. Brightness constancy depends on the perceived relationship between the brightness of an object and its background.

Culture, Experience, and Perception

To the extent that visual environments of people in different cultures differ, their perceptual experiences—as evidenced by their responses to perceptual illusions—may differ as well.

RECOGNIZING THE PERCEPTUAL WORLD

Both *bottom-up processing* and *top-down processing* may contribute to recognition of the world. The ability to recognize objects is based on finding a match between the pattern of sensations organized by the perceptual system and a pattern that is stored in memory.

Bottom-Up Processing

Bottom-up processing seems to be accomplished by the analysis of stimulus features, or combinations of features, such as form, color, motion, depth, and spatial frequencies.

Top-Down Processing

Top-down processing is influenced by expectancy and motivation. *Schemas* based on past experience can create a perceptual set, the readiness or predisposition to perceive stimuli in certain ways. Expectancies can also be created by the context in which a stimulus appears.

Network Processing

Research on pattern recognition has focused attention on network, or *parallel distributed processing (PDP),* models of perception. These emphasize the simultaneous activation and interaction of feature-analysis systems and the role of experience.

ATTENTION

Attention is the process of focusing psychological resources to enhance perception, performance, and mental experience. We can shift attention overtly—by moving the eyes, for example—or covertly, without any movement of sensory systems.

Allocating Attention

Attention is selective; it is like a spotlight that illuminates different parts of the external environment or various mental processes. Control over attention can be voluntary and knowledge-based or involuntary and driven by environmental stimuli.

Divided Attention

Although there are limits to how well people can divide attention, they can sometimes attend to two tasks at once. For example, tasks that are extensively practiced or automatic can often be performed along with more demanding tasks, and tasks that require very different types of processing, such as driving and conversing, can sometimes be performed together because each task depends on a different supply of mental resources.

Attention and Automatic Processing

Some information can be processed automatically, in parallel, whereas other situations demand focused attention and a serial search.

Attention and the Brain

Although the brain plays a critical role in attention, no single brain region has been identified as the attention center.

APPLICATIONS OF RESEARCH ON PERCEPTION

Research on human perception has numerous practical applications.

Aviation Psychology

Accurate size and distance judgments, top-down processing, and attention are all important to safety in aviation.

Human-Computer Interaction

Perceptual principles relating to recognition, depth cues, and attention are being applied by psychologists who work with designers of computers and computer programs.

KEY TERMS

absolute threshold (141)
accommodation (153)
attention (164)
auditory scene analysis (149)
binocular disparity (153)
bottom-up processing (158)
closure (148)
common fate (149)
common region (149)
computational approach (139)
constructivist approach (139)

continuity (148)
convergence (153)
difference threshold (145)
ecological approach (140)
Gestalt psychologists (148)
interposition (151)
just-noticeable difference (JND) (145)
likelihood principle (149)
linear perspective (152)
looming (153)
motion parallax (153)
noise (144)

parallel distributed processing (PDP) models (161)
perception (138)
perceptual constancy (155)
perceptual organization (147)
proximity (148)
psychophysics (140)
relative size (151)
response criterion (144)
schemas (160)
sensitivity (144)

signal-detection theory (143)
similarity (148)
simplicity (148)
stroboscopic motion (154)
subliminal stimuli (140)
supraliminal stimuli (140)
texture (148)
texture gradient (151)
top-down processing (157)
Weber's law (145)

6 Learning

Can you recall how you felt on your first day of kindergarten? Like many preschoolers, you may have been bewildered, even frightened, as the comforting familiarity of home or day care was suddenly replaced by an environment filled with new names and faces, rules and events. But, like most youngsters, you probably adjusted to this new environment within a few days.

This adjustment, or *adaptation,* to a changed environment can take many forms. Some are simple, as when once-startling sounds from a malfunctioning heating system are eventually ignored. Others are more complex. Ringing bells, roll call, and other strange new events become part of children's pattern of expectancies about the world. Youngsters come to expect that certain events, such as the arrival of the music teacher, signal the likely occurrence of other events that are pleasant or unpleasant. They also develop knowledge about which aspects of their school behavior are likely to be rewarded and which are likely to be punished. Some behaviors are appropriate only under certain circumstances, and those circumstances must be identified and differentiated. Talking at will, for example, may not be as acceptable at school as at home, but enthusiastic finger painting—perhaps forbidden at home—may bring praise at school. Children also learn that there are things they can do to prevent unwanted consequences. For example, starting out for school earlier or walking faster can prevent being kept after school for tardiness. Finally, schoolchildren acquire facts about the world and develop skills ranging from kickball to story reading.

Adaptation through learning is not confined to school. The entire process of development, from birth to death, involves adapting to increasingly complex, ever-changing environments, using continuously updated knowledge gained through experience. Though perhaps most highly developed in humans, the ability to adapt to changing environments appears to varying degrees in members of all species. According to the evolutionary approach to psychology, it is individual variability in the capacity to adapt that shapes the evolution of appearance and behavior in animals and humans. As Darwin noted, individuals who don't adapt may not survive to reproduce, and learning enables members of a species to adapt to a wide range of life's challenges.

Many forms of animal and human adaptation follow the principles of learning. **Learning** is the process through which experience modifies pre-existing behavior and understanding. The pre-existing behavior and understanding may have been present at birth, acquired through maturation, or learned earlier. Indeed, learning plays a central role in most aspects of human behavior, from the motor skills we need to walk or tie a shoe to the language skills we use to communicate and the object categories—such as food, vehicle, or animal—that help us organize our perceptions and think logically about the world.

People learn primarily by experiencing events and observing relationships between events and noting the regularity in the world around them. When two events repeatedly take place together, people can predict the occurrence of one from knowledge of the other. They learn that a clear blue sky means dry weather, that too little sleep makes them irritable, that they can reach someone on the telephone by dialing a certain number, that screaming orders motivates some people and angers others.

Psychologists' research on the content, causes, and course of learning have been guided mainly by the following three questions: (1) Which events and relationships do people learn about? (2) What circumstances determine whether and how people learn? (3) How quickly can people learn? In other words, is learning a slow cumulative process requiring lots of practice, or does it involve sudden flashes of insight? In this chapter we provide some of the answers to these questions.

We first consider the simplest forms of learning—learning about individual stimuli. Then we examine the two major kinds of learning that involve associations between stimuli—classical conditioning and operant conditioning. Next we consider some higher forms of learning and cognition, and we conclude by discussing how research on learning might help people learn better. As you read, notice how learning principles operate in such arenas as education, the workplace, medical treatment, psychotherapy, and many other aspects of people's lives.

Learning to Live with It

People who move to a big city may at first be distracted by the din of traffic, low-flying aircraft, and other loud urban sounds, but after a while the process of habituation makes all this noise far less noticeable.

LEARNING ABOUT STIMULI

In a changing world, people are constantly bombarded by stimuli. If we tried to pay attention to every sight and sound, our information-processing systems would be overloaded, and we would be unable to concentrate on anything. People appear to be genetically tuned to attend to and orient toward certain kinds of events, such as loud sounds, special tastes, or pain. *Novel* stimuli also tend to attract our attention. By contrast, our responsiveness to *unchanging* stimuli—as when an event is repeated—decreases over time. In other words, we *adapt* to such stimuli. This adaptation is a form of learning called **habituation**. For example, we eventually cease to notice the loud ticking of a clock; in fact, we may become aware of the clock again only when it stops, because, now, something in our environment has changed. Habituation is not limited to stimuli as neutral as a ticking clock; it can also occur in relation to pleasurable or aversive sights, sounds, smells, or other stimuli. This simple form of learning has been observed in all animals, from humans to simple sea snails (Pinel, 1993).

When an organism habituates, it changes; but the change does not occur because the organism has learned about a relationship or association among stimuli or events. Rather, it is the result of just one stimulus acting on the organism (Barker, 1997). Habituation provides organisms with a useful way to adapt to their environments. For example, they learn not to respond to stimuli that either pose no threat to them or might distract them from other, more important stimuli (Schwartz & Reisberg, 1991).

Habituation has a direct connection to the impact of stimuli that produce affective responses such as emotions. According to Richard Solomon's (1980) *opponent-process theory,* habituation to repeated stimuli is the result of two interacting processes. The first, the *A-Process,* is a fixed, automatic, emotional, and unlearned response of the organism to a stimulus. The second process, the *B-Process,* is an initially slower reaction, triggered by the onset of the A-Process, that counteracts the effects of the A-Process. For example, a painful event produces an increase in heart rate, the A-Process; then the B-Process is triggered to compensate and decreases the heart rate somewhat. If the painful event is repeated over time, the B-Process is triggered more and more quickly and with greater intensity (see Figure 6.1). As the net effect of the opposing A and B processes becomes smaller and smaller with repeated exposure to a stimulus, the change in heart rate becomes less and less noticeable. In other words, habituation results.

The habituation process may explain some of the dangers associated with certain drugs. Consider, for example, what happens when someone first uses a drug such as heroin or crack cocaine. The initial, pleasant reaction (the A-Process) to a fixed dose is eventually countered or neutralized as the opposing unpleasant B-Process becomes quicker and stronger. Thus, progressively larger doses of the drug are required to obtain the same drug "high." According to Solomon, these opponent processes form the basis for the development of drug tolerance and addiction.

FIGURE 6.1

Solomon's Opponent-Process Theory

Richard Solomon explains habituation to repeated stimuli as follows: The automatic, unlearned response to a stimulus—called the A-Process—is followed by a smaller, but opposite, B-Process that reduces the size of the A-Process to produce a somewhat smaller net affective response (shown as the green line). Over time, the B-Process occurs more quickly and with greater intensity, eventually resulting in a minimal net affective response that we call habituation.

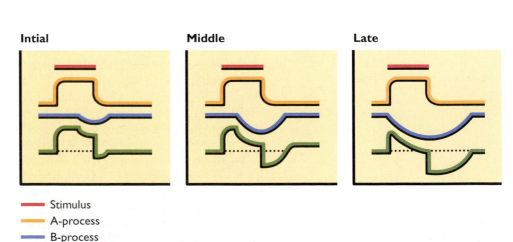

Intial   Middle   Late

■ Stimulus
■ A-process
■ B-process
■ Net response

Solomon's analysis may also explain some accidental drug overdoses. If the B-Process becomes strongly associated with environmental stimuli that are regularly present when the drug is taken, those stimuli may become capable of triggering the B-Process by themselves. Suppose that a person now takes a normal drug dose in a very different environment. The strength of the A-Process (the drug effect) will still be the same; but without the environmental cues that normally help elicit the B-Process, the counteracting process may be diminished. The net effect may be a stronger-than-usual drug reaction, possibly leading to the trauma of an overdose (Siegel et al., 1982; Turkkan, 1989).

Notice that this explanation of drug overdoses is based not just on simple habituation, but also on a *learned association* between certain environmental stimuli and certain responses. Indeed, habituation cannot, by itself, explain many of the behaviors and mental processes that are the focus of psychology. To better understand how learning affects our thoughts and behaviors, we need to consider forms of learning that involve the building of associations between various stimuli, and between stimuli and responses. One major type of associative learning is called classical conditioning.

CLASSICAL CONDITIONING: LEARNING SIGNALS AND ASSOCIATIONS

At the opening bars of the national anthem, a young ballplayer's heart may start pounding; those sounds signal that the game is about to begin. A flashing light on a control panel may make an airplane pilot's adrenaline flow, because it means that something may be wrong. These people were not born with such reactions; they learned them from observed relations or associations between events in the world. The experimental study of this kind of learning was begun, almost by accident, by Ivan Petrovich Pavlov.

Pavlov's Discovery

Pavlov is one of the best-known figures in psychology, but he was not a psychologist. A Russian physiologist, Pavlov won a Nobel Prize in 1904 for his research on the digestive processes of dogs. In the course of this work, Pavlov noticed a strange phenomenon: His dogs sometimes salivated—the first stage of the digestive process—when no food was present. For example, the dogs began to salivate when they saw the assistant who normally brought their food, even if the assistant was empty-handed.

Pavlov devised a simple experiment to determine why salivation occurred in the absence of an obvious physical cause. First he performed a simple operation to divert a dog's saliva into a container, so that the amount secreted could be measured precisely. He then placed the dog in an apparatus similar to the one shown in Figure 6.2 (on page 178). The experiment had three phases.

In the first phase of the experiment, Pavlov and his associates (Anrep, 1920) confirmed that when meat powder was placed on the dog's tongue, the dog salivated, but that it did not salivate in response to a neutral stimulus—a musical tone, for example. Thus, the researchers established the existence of the two basic components for Pavlov's experiment: a natural reflex (the dog's salivation when meat powder was placed on its tongue) and a neutral stimulus (the sound of the tone). A *reflex* is the swift, automatic response to a stimulus, such as shivering in the cold or jumping when you are jabbed with a needle. A *neutral stimulus* is one that initially does not elicit the reflex being studied, although it may elicit other responses. For example, when the tone is first sounded, the dog pricks up its ears, turns toward the sound, and sniffs around; but it does not salivate.

It was the second and third phases of the experiment that showed how one type of learning can occur. In the second phase, the tone sounded and then a few seconds later meat powder was placed in the dog's mouth. The dog salivated. This *pairing*—the tone followed immediately by meat powder—was repeated several times. The tone

FIGURE 6.2

Apparatus for Measuring Conditioned Responses

In this more elaborate version of Pavlov's original apparatus, the amount of saliva flowing from a dog's cheek is measured, then recorded on a slowly revolving drum of paper.

Pen recording on cylinder

predicted the subsequent presentation of the meat powder, but the question remained: Would the animal learn this association? Yes. In the third phase of the experiment the tone was sounded and, even though no meat powder was presented, the dog again salivated. In other words, the tone by itself now elicited salivation.

Pavlov's experiment was the first laboratory demonstration of a basic form of *associative* learning. Today, it is called **classical conditioning**—a procedure in which a neutral stimulus is repeatedly paired with a stimulus that already triggers a reflexive response until the previously neutral stimulus alone evokes a similar response. Figure 6.3 shows the basic elements of classical conditioning. The stimulus that elicits a response without conditioning, like the meat powder in Pavlov's experiment, is called the **unconditioned stimulus (UCS).** The automatic, unlearned reaction to this stimulus is called the **unconditioned response (UCR).** The new stimulus being paired with the unconditioned stimulus is called the **conditioned stimulus (CS),** and the response it comes to elicit is the **conditioned response (CR).**

FIGURE 6.3

Classical Conditioning

Before classical conditioning has occurred, meat powder on a dog's tongue produces salivation, but the sound of a tone—a neutral stimulus—does not. During the process of conditioning, the tone is repeatedly paired with the meat powder. After classical conditioning has taken place, the sound of the tone alone acts as a conditioned stimulus, producing salivation.

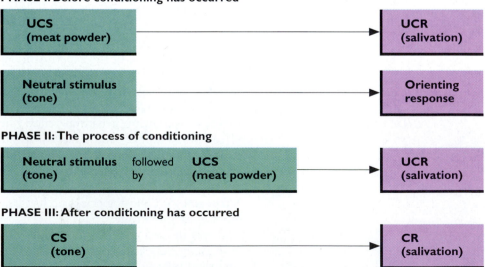

PHASE I: Before conditioning has occurred

| UCS (meat powder) | → | UCR (salivation) |
| Neutral stimulus (tone) | → | Orienting response |

PHASE II: The process of conditioning

| Neutral stimulus (tone)   followed by   UCS (meat powder) | → | UCR (salivation) |

PHASE III: After conditioning has occurred

| CS (tone) | → | CR (salivation) |

FIGURE 6.4

Changes Over Time in the Strength of a Conditioned Response (CR)

As the CS and UCS are repeatedly paired during initial conditioning, the strength of the CR increases. During extinction, CR strength drops as more trials occur in which the CS is presented without the UCS; eventually the CR disappears. However, after a brief period, the CR reappears if the CS is again presented.

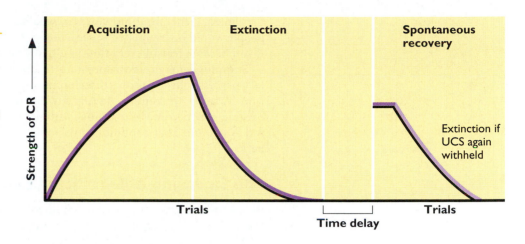

FIGURE 6.5

Stimulus Generalization

The strength of a conditioned response (CR) is greatest when the original conditioned stimulus (CS) occurs, but the CR also appears following stimuli that closely resemble the CS. Here, the CS is the sound of a buzzer at 1,000 hertz, and the CR is salivation. Notice how the CR generalizes well to stimuli at 990 or 1010 hertz, but gets weaker and weaker following stimuli that are less and less similar to the CS.

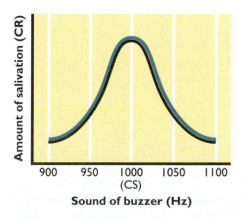

Conditioned Responses Over Time: Extinction and Spontaneous Recovery

Continued pairings of a conditioned stimulus (CS) with an unconditioned stimulus (UCS) strengthen conditioned responses (CR). The curve on the left side of Figure 6.4 shows an example: Repeated associations of a tone (CS) with meat powder (UCS) caused Pavlov's dogs to increase their salivation (CR) to the tone alone.

What if the meat powder is no longer given? In general, unless the unconditioned stimulus continues to be paired at least occasionally with the conditioned stimulus, the conditioned response will gradually disappear through a process known as **extinction** (see the center section of Figure 6.4). If the conditioned stimulus and the unconditioned stimulus are again paired after the conditioned response has been extinguished, the conditioned response returns to its original strength very quickly, often after only one or two trials. This quick relearning of a conditioned response after extinction is called **reconditioning.** Because reconditioning takes much less time than the original conditioning, extinction must not have completely erased the conditioned response.

Additional evidence for this conclusion is illustrated on the right side of Figure 6.4: An extinguished conditioned response will temporarily reappear if, after some time delay, the conditioned stimulus is presented again—even without the unconditioned stimulus. This reappearance of the conditioned response after extinction (and without further CS-UCS pairings) is called **spontaneous recovery.** In general, the longer the time between extinction and the re-presentation of the conditioned stimulus, the stronger the recovered conditioned response. (However, unless the UCS is again paired with the CS, extinction rapidly occurs again.) Thus, when a person hears a song or smells the cologne associated with a long-lost lover, there is a ripple of emotion—a conditioned response. Through its association with that person, the song or fragrance, which originally had no particular significance, became a conditioned stimulus that—even years later—can provoke conditioned emotional reactions.

Stimulus Generalization and Discrimination

After a conditioned response is acquired, stimuli that are similar but not identical to the conditioned stimulus also elicit the response—but to a lesser degree. This phenomenon is called **stimulus generalization.** Usually the greater the similarity between a new stimulus and the conditioned stimulus, the stronger the conditioned response will be. Figure 6.5 shows an example.

Stimulus generalization has obvious adaptive advantages. For example, it is important for survival that a person who becomes sick after drinking sour-smelling milk later avoids dairy products that give off an odor resembling the smell associated with the illness. Generalization, however, would be problematic if it had no limits. Most people would be frightened to see a lion in their home, but imagine the inconvenience if you became fearful every time you saw a cat or a picture of a lion.

Stimulus generalization does not run amok because it is balanced by a complementary process called **stimulus discrimination.** Through stimulus discrimination, organisms learn to differentiate among similar stimuli. Thus, the sound of your own dog barking may become a conditioned stimulus that triggers a conditioned response that wakes you up. That conditioned response might not occur when someone else's dog barks.

The Signaling of Significant Events

Is classical conditioning entirely automatic? Pavlov's research suggested that it is, that classical conditioning allows the substitution of one stimulus (the CS) for another (the UCS) in producing a reflexive response. The animal or person may thus prepare for the arrival of the unconditioned stimulus. It is certainly useful and adaptive for a dog to prepare for the arrival of food; having saliva flowing in advance makes it easier to swallow a meal. For years the study of classical conditioning focused mainly on its role in the control of such automatic, involuntary behavior. However, psychologists now recognize the wider implications of classical conditioning (Hollis, 1997). Some argue that organisms acquire conditioned responses when one event reliably predicts, or *signals,* the appearance of another. In other words, these psychologists believe that, instead of giving rise to simple robot-like reflexes, classical conditioning leads to responses based on the information provided by conditioned stimuli. As a result, animals and people develop *mental representations* of the relationships between important events in their environment and expectancies about when such events will occur (Rescorla, 1988). These representations and expectancies aid adaptation and survival (Williams, Butler, & Overmier, 1990).

What determines whether and how a conditioned response is learned? Important factors include the timing, predictability, and strength of signals; the amount of attention they receive; and how easily the signals can be associated with other stimuli.

Timing   Classical conditioning works best when the conditioned stimulus precedes the unconditioned stimulus, an arrangement known as *forward conditioning.* In essence, the conditioned stimulus is a signal that prepares the organism for the unconditioned stimulus. In an arrangement called *backward conditioning,* the conditioned stimulus signal *follows* the unconditioned stimulus. In such cases, conditioning takes place very slowly, if at all. When the conditioned stimulus and unconditioned stimulus arrive at the same time (an arrangement known as *simultaneous conditioning*), conditioning is much less likely to take place than it is in either forward or backward conditioning, and special techniques are required to detect its occurrence.

Research shows that forward conditioning usually works best when there is only a short delay between the conditioned stimulus and the unconditioned stimulus—no more than a second or so (Ross & Ross, 1971). This "optimum interval" makes adaptive sense. Normally, the presence of food, predators, or other significant events is most reliably predicted by smells or growls or similar stimuli that occur just before their appearance (Einhorn & Hogarth, 1982). Thus, it is logical that organisms are "wired" to form associations most easily between things that occur in a tight time sequence.

Predictability   Is it enough that the conditioned stimulus precedes the unconditioned stimulus—that two events are close together in time—in order for classical conditioning to occur? Think about it. Suppose your dogs, Dashiell and Harley, have very different personalities. When Harley growls, he sometimes bites, but sometimes doesn't. Other times, he bites without growling first. Dashiell, however, growls *only* before biting. Your conditioned fear response to Harley's growl will probably occur slowly, if at all, because his growl is a stimulus that does not reliably signal the danger of a bite. But you are likely to quickly develop a classically conditioned fear response to Dashiell's growl, because classical conditioning proceeds most rapidly when the con-

Conditioning Consumers

Advertisers commonly link their products with images of attractive people or other stimuli which are likely to evoke good feelings. Ideallly, those good feelings will be associated with the products through second-order conditioning.

ditioned stimulus *always* signals the unconditioned stimulus, and *only* the unconditioned stimulus. Thus, even if both dogs provide the same number of pairings of the conditioned stimulus (growl) and unconditioned stimulus (bite), it is only in Dashiell's case that the conditioned stimulus *reliably* predicts the unconditioned stimulus (Rescorla, 1968).

Signal Strength   A conditioned response will be greater if the unconditioned stimulus is strong than if it is weak. Thus a predictive signal associated with a strong shock (a UCS) will come to evoke more fear than one associated with a weak shock. As with timing and predictability, the effect of signal strength on classical conditioning makes adaptive sense: It is more important to be prepared for major events than for those that have little impact.

   How quickly a conditioned response is learned also depends on the strength of the conditioned stimulus. As described in Chapter 5, on perception, louder tones, brighter lights, or other more salient events tend to get attention, so they are most rapidly associated with an unconditioned stimulus—as long as they remain reliable predictive signals.

Attention   In the natural environment, more than one potential conditioned stimulus often precedes an unconditioned stimulus. Attention can influence which conditioned stimulus becomes associated with that unconditioned stimulus. For example, suppose that just before being nearly struck by lightning, a small child was tasting a cookie, listening to a song, and watching a nearby dog. Which of these stimuli is most likely to become a conditioned stimulus for fear? It depends in part on where the child's attention was focused. The stimuli were probably not receiving equal attention just before the lightning hit. Accordingly, the stimulus most closely attended to, and thus most fully perceived at that moment, is the one likely to be more strongly associated with the lightning than any of the others (Hall, 1991).

Second-Order Conditioning   When a child suffers the pain of an injection (an unconditioned stimulus) at a doctor's office, noticeable stimuli—like the doctor's white coat—that precede and predict the unconditioned stimulus can become conditioned stimuli for fear. Once the white coat evokes a conditioned fear response, it may take on some properties of an unconditioned stimulus. Thus, at future visits, the once-neutral sound of a nurse calling the child's name can become a conditioned stimulus for fear because it signals the appearance of the white coat, which in turn signals pain. When a conditioned stimulus acts like an unconditioned stimulus, creating conditioned stimuli out of events associated with it, the phenomenon is called **second-order conditioning.** Conditioned fear, and the second-order conditioning that can be based on it, illustrates one of the most important adaptive characteristics of classical conditioning: the ability to prepare the organism for damaging or life-threatening events—unconditioned stimuli—when these are predictably signaled by a conditioned stimulus.

Taste Aversions

Humans can develop classically conditioned taste aversions, even to preferred foods. Ilene Bernstein (1978) gave one group of cancer patients Mapletoff ice cream an hour before they received nausea-provoking chemotherapy. A second group ate the same kind of ice cream on a day they did not receive chemotherapy. A third group got no ice cream. Five months later, the patients were asked to taste several ice cream flavors. Those who had never tasted Mapletoff and those who had not eaten it in association with chemotherapy chose it as their favorite. Those who had eaten Mapletoff before receiving chemotherapy found it very distasteful.

Biopreparedness   After Pavlov's initial demonstration of classical conditioning, many psychologists believed that associations formed through classical conditioning were like Velcro. Just as Velcro pieces of any size or shape can be attached with equal ease, it was believed that any conditioned stimulus—such as the taste of food or the sight of a dog in our lightning example—have an equal potential for becoming associated with any unconditioned stimulus, as long as the two occur in the right time sequence. This view, called *equipotentiality,* was later challenged by experiments showing that certain signals or events are especially suited to form associations with other events (Logue, 1985; LoLordo, 1979). Indeed, the apparent natural affinity for certain events to become linked suggests that organisms are "biologically prepared" or "genetically tuned" to develop certain conditioned associations.

The most dramatic example of the *biopreparedness* of organisms is conditioned taste aversion. Consider the results of a study in which rats were either shocked or made nauseous in the combined presence of a bright light, a loud buzzer, and saccharin-flavored water. Only certain conditioned associations were formed. Specifically, the animals that had been shocked developed a conditioned fear response to the light and the buzzer, but not to the flavored water. Those who had been made nauseous developed a conditioned aversion to the flavored water, but showed no particular response to the light or buzzer (Garcia & Koelling, 1966). Notice that these associations are useful and adaptive: Nausea is more likely to be produced by something that is eaten or drunk than by a noise or some other external stimulus. Accordingly, nausea is more likely to become a conditioned response to an internal stimulus, such as a saccharine flavor, than to an external stimulus, such as a light or buzzer. In contrast, sudden pain is more likely to have been caused by an external stimulus, so it makes evolutionary sense that organisms should be "tuned" to associate pain with external stimuli like sights or sounds.

Notice, too, that conditioned taste aversion violates the usual timing rules of classical conditioning. In taste aversion, strong conditioning develops despite the long delay between the conditioned stimulus (the taste) and the unconditioned stimulus (the nausea). Poisons do not usually produce their effects until minutes or hours after being ingested, but people who experience food poisoning may never again eat the type of food that made them ill—even though that illness was delayed far longer than the optimal CS-UCS interval of a second or so. In evolutionary terms, organisms that are biologically prepared to link taste signals with illness, even if it occurs after a considerable delay, are more likely to survive than those not so prepared.

Evidence from several sources suggests other ways in which animals and people are innately prepared to learn associations between certain stimuli and certain responses. For example, people are much more likely to develop a conditioned fear of harmless dogs, snakes, and rats than of equally harmless doorknobs or stereos (Kleinknecht, 1991). And experiments with animals suggest that they are prone to learn the type of associations that are most common in or most relevant to their environment (Staddon & Ettinger, 1989). For example, birds of prey, so strongly dependent upon their vision in searching for food, may develop taste aversions on the basis of visual stimuli. Coyotes and rats, who depend more on their sense of smell, tend to develop aversions related to odor.

Some Applications of Classical Conditioning

"In Review: Basic Processes of Classical Conditioning" summarizes the principles of classical conditioning. These principles have proven useful in fighting diseases, overcoming fears, and controlling predators, to name just a few examples.

Learned Immune Responses   After patients receive an organ transplant, they are given drugs that cause suppression of the *immune system;* this is done because the same biological mechanisms that protect the body from infection may also cause the body to reject the transplanted organ. However, these medications have serious side effects, so it would be ideal if the immune system could be suppressed without long-term administration of drugs. Research suggests that, through classical conditioning,

in review

BASIC PROCESSES OF CLASSICAL CONDITIONING

Process	Description	Example
Acquisition	A neutral stimulus and an unconditioned stimulus (UCS) are paired. The neutral stimulus becomes a conditioned stimulus (CS), eliciting a conditioned response (CR).	A child learns to fear (conditioned response) the doctor's office (conditioned stimulus) by associating it with the reflexive emotional reaction (unconditioned response), to a painful injection (unconditioned stimulus).
Stimulus generalization	A conditioned response is elicited not only by the conditioned stimulus but also by stimuli similar to the conditioned stimulus.	A child fears most doctors' offices and places that smell like them.
Stimulus discrimination	Generalization is limited so that some stimuli similar to the conditioned stimulus do not elicit the conditioned response.	A child learns that his mother's doctor's office is not associated with the unconditioned stimulus.
Extinction	The conditioned stimulus is presented alone, without the unconditioned stimulus. Eventually the conditioned stimulus no longer elicits the conditioned response.	A child visits the doctor's office several times for a checkup, but does not receive a shot. Fear may eventually cease.

No Fear

Humans may be biologically prepared to learn certain fears, including the fear of snakes, but this tendency may be counteracted by cultural traditions and personal experiences. These children, who live in a Brazilian jungle, feel the same affection for their harmless pet snakes as children elsewhere feel for the family dog or cat.

decreased activity in the body's immune system can become a conditioned response to certain tastes and odors (CSs) that have been paired with the administration of immune-suppressing drugs (Ader & Cohen, 1993; Markovif, Dimitrijevif & Jankovif, 1993; Olness & Ader, 1992). Such tastes and odors are now being used to elicit classically conditioned suppression of the immune system; when combined with the effects of intermittently administered immune-suppressing drugs, these conditioned stimuli can help prevent rejection of transplanted organs while subjecting patients to minimal drug dosages and side effects (Grochowicz et al., 1991).

These results raise the possibility that beneficial *increases* in the immune response might also be conditioned. In one study, a particular sherbet flavor was paired with an injection of adrenaline, the unconditioned effect of which is to increase the activity of the immune system's natural killer cells. Eventually this sherbet flavor alone elicited the immune response (Buske-Kirschbaum et al., 1994). Another possibility is to associate placebos with active drugs and then administer the placebos alone in the hope that they might trigger beneficial effects as a conditioned response (Turkkan, 1989).

Phobias Classical conditioning can play a role in the development not only of mild fears (such as a child's fear of doctors in white coats) but also of much stronger ones, called phobias. *Phobias* are extreme fears of objects or situations that either are not objectively dangerous—public speaking, for example—or are less dangerous than the phobic person's reaction suggests. In some instances, phobias can seriously disrupt a person's life. A child who is frightened by a large dog may learn a dog phobia that is so intense and generalized that it creates avoidance of all dogs. Dangerous situations, too, can produce classical conditioning of very long-lasting fears. Decades after their war experiences, some military veterans still respond to simulated battle sounds with large changes in heart rate, blood pressure, and other signs of emotional arousal (Edwards & Acker, 1972). These symptoms, combined with others such as distressing dreams about the troubling events, characterize posttraumatic stress disorder (PTSD; see Chapter 13, on health, stress, and coping).

Predator Control Through Conditioning

After learning to associate the taste of mutton with severe nausea created by lithium chloride, wolves and coyotes were placed in a pen with live sheep (mutton on the hoof—the CS). They started to attack, but after biting and smelling the sheep, they withdrew (the CR). When the doors of the pen were opened, the predators were chased away by the sheep! Today ranchers often lace a carcass with enough lithium chloride to make wolves and coyotes ill, thus "teaching" them not to kill sheep.

Classical conditioning procedures can be employed to treat phobias, and even PTSD. Joseph Wolpe (1958; Wolpe & Plaud, 1997) pioneered the development of this methodology. Using techniques first developed with laboratory animals, Wolpe showed that irrational fears could be relieved through systematic desensitization, which involves two conditioning components: (1) extinction of the classically conditioned fear response through harmless exposure to the feared stimulus, and (2) classical conditioning of a new response, such as relaxation, to the feared stimulus. Desensitization is discussed in more detail in Chapter 16, on treatment of psychological disorders.

Predator Control   The power of classically conditioned taste aversion has been put to work to help ranchers who are plagued by wolves and coyotes that kill and eat their sheep. To alleviate this problem without killing the predators, some ranchers have set out lithium-laced mutton for marauding wolves and coyotes to eat. The dizziness and severe nausea caused by the lithium becomes associated with the smell and taste of mutton, thus making sheep an undesirable meal for these predators and protecting the ranchers' livelihood (Garcia, Rusiniak, & Brett, 1977; Gustavson et al., 1974).

OPERANT CONDITIONING: LEARNING THE CONSEQUENCES OF BEHAVIOR

Much of what people learn cannot be described in terms of classical conditioning. In classical conditioning, neutral and unconditioned stimuli are predictably paired, and the result is an association between the two. The association is shown by the conditioned response that occurs when the conditioned stimulus appears. Notice that both stimuli occur *before* or *along with* the conditioned response. But people also learn associations between specific actions or responses and the stimuli that *follow* them—in other words, between behavior and its consequences. A child learns to say "Please" in order to get a piece of candy; a headache sufferer learns to take a pill to escape pain; a dog learns to "shake hands" to get a treat. This form of learning is called *operant conditioning*, and it constitutes the second major type of associative learning.

From the Puzzle Box to the Skinner Box

Much of the groundwork for research on the consequences of behavior was done by Edward L. Thorndike, an American psychologist. While Pavlov was exploring classical conditioning in animals, Thorndike was studying animals' intelligence and ability to

FIGURE 6.6

Thorndike's Puzzle Box

This drawing illustrates the kind of "puzzle box" used in Thorndike's research. His cats learned to open the door and reach food by pushing down on the pedal, but the learning came very gradually. Some cats actually took longer to get out of the box on one trial than on a previous trial.

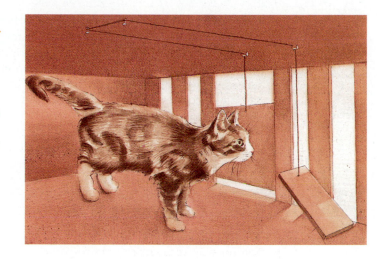

solve problems. He would place an animal, usually a hungry cat, in a *puzzle box*, where it had to learn some response—say, stepping on a pedal—in order to unlock the door and get to some food (see Figure 6.6). The animal would solve the puzzle, but very slowly. It did not appear to understand, or suddenly gain *insight* into, the problem (Thorndike, 1898).

So, what were Thorndike's cats learning? Thorndike argued that any response (such as pressing the pedal) that produces a satisfying effect (escape from the box and access to food) gradually becomes stronger, whereas any response (such as pacing or meowing) that does not produce a satisfying effect gradually becomes weaker. The cats' learning, said Thorndike, is governed by the **law of effect.** According to this law, if a response made in the presence of a particular stimulus is followed by satisfaction (such as a reward), that response is more likely to be made the next time the stimulus is encountered. Conversely, responses that produce discomfort are less likely to be performed again. Thorndike described this kind of learning as **instrumental conditioning** because responses are strengthened when they are instrumental in producing rewards (Thorndike, 1905).

Edward L. Thorndike (1874–1949) and B. F. Skinner (1904–1990)

Thorndike (left) and Skinner studied instrumental and operant conditioning, respectively. Though similar in most respects, these forms of conditioning differ in one way. In instrumental conditioning, the experimenter defines each opportunity for a response, and conditioning is usually measured by how long it takes for the response to appear. In operant conditioning, the response can occur at any time; conditioning is measured by the *rate* of response. In this chapter, the term *operant conditioning* refers to both.

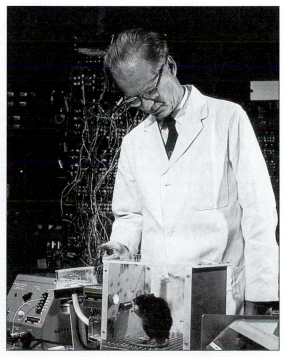

About forty years after Thorndike published his work, B. F. Skinner extended and formalized many of Thorndike's ideas. Skinner (1938) emphasized that during instrumental conditioning an organism learns a response by *operating on* the environment, so he called the process of learning these responses **operant conditioning.** His primary aim was to analyze *how* behavior is changed by its consequences. To study operant conditioning, Skinner devised a chamber known as the *Skinner box,* a version of which is shown in the photo on page 185. There is one primary difference between Thorndike's puzzle box and Skinner's apparatus: In the puzzle box, learning was measured in terms of whether an animal successfully completed a trial (i.e., escaped from the box), whereas in the Skinner box, learning is measured in terms of how often an animal responds during a specified period of time (Barker, 1997).

Basic Components of Operant Conditioning

The tools Skinner devised allowed him and other researchers to precisely arrange relationships between an arbitrary response and its consequences and then to analyze how those consequences affected behavior over time. They found that the basic processes involved in classical conditioning—for example, stimulus generalization, stimulus discrimination, extinction, and spontaneous recovery—also occur in operant conditioning. However, operant conditioning involves additional concepts and processes as well. Let's consider these now.

Operants and Reinforcers   Skinner introduced the term *operant* or *operant response* to distinguish the responses in operant conditioning from those in classical conditioning. Recall that in classical conditioning the conditioned response does not affect whether or when the stimulus occurs. Dogs salivated when a buzzer sounded, but the salivation had no effect on the buzzer or on whether food was presented. In contrast, an **operant** is a response that has some effect on the world; it is a response that *operates on* the environment. For example, when a child says, "Momma, I'm hungry" and is then fed, the child has made an operant response that influences when food will appear.

A **reinforcer** increases the probability that an operant behavior will occur again. There are two main types of reinforcers: positive and negative. **Positive reinforcers** are events that strengthen a response if they are experienced after that response occurs. They are roughly equivalent to rewards. The food given to a hungry pigeon after it pecks a key is a positive reinforcer; its presentation increases the pigeon's key pecking. For people, positive reinforcers can include food, smiles, money, and other desirable outcomes. Presentation of a positive reinforcer after a response is called *positive reinforcement.* **Negative reinforcers** are stimuli such as pain, threats, or a disapproving frown that strengthen a response if they are *removed* after the response occurs. For example, if the response of taking aspirin is followed by the removal of headache pain,

FIGURE 6.7

Positive and Negative Reinforcement

Both positive and negative reinforcement *increase* the chances that a behavior will occur in the future. Behavior is strengthened through *positive reinforcement* when something pleasant or desirable occurs following the behavior. Behavior is strengthened through *negative reinforcement* when the behavior results in the removal or termination of something unpleasant.

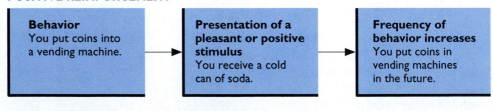

POSITIVE REINFORCEMENT

| **Behavior** You put coins into a vending machine. | → | **Presentation of a pleasant or positive stimulus** You receive a cold can of soda. | → | **Frequency of behavior increases** You put coins in vending machines in the future. |

NEGATIVE REINFORCEMENT

| **Behavior** In the middle of a boring date, you say you have a headache. | → | **Removal of an unpleasant stimulus** The date ends early. | → | **Frequency of behavior increases** You use the same tactic on future boring dates. |

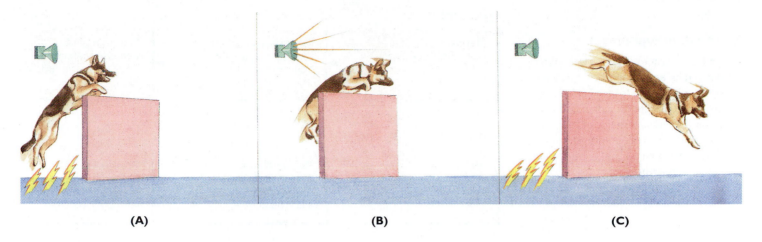

(A) (B) (C)

FIGURE 6.8

A Shuttle Box

A shuttle box has two compartments, usually separated by a barrier, and its floor is an electric grid. Shock can be administered through the grid to each compartment independently. In escape conditioning (A), the animal can get away from shock by jumping over the barrier when the shock occurs. In avoidance conditioning, a buzzer signals the onset of shock (B), and the animal can avoid the shock if it jumps as soon as the buzzer sounds (C).

aspirin taking is likely to occur when similar pain appears again. The process of strengthening behavior by following it with the removal of an aversive stimulus is called negative reinforcement. Note that whether it takes the form of presenting something pleasant or removing something aversive, reinforcement always *increases* the likelihood of the behavior that precedes it (see Figure 6.7).

Escape and Avoidance Conditioning The effects of negative reinforcement can be seen in escape conditioning and in avoidance conditioning. **Escape conditioning** takes place when an organism learns to make a response in order to end an aversive stimulus, or negative reinforcer. Dogs learn to jump over the barrier in a shuttle box to escape shock (see Figure 6.8); parents often learn to give in to children's demands because doing so stops their whining. Now let's consider avoidance conditioning. Imagine that a signal—say, a buzzer or blinking light—occurs just a few seconds before the grid in one side of a shuttle box is electrified. If, at this signal, the animal jumps over the barrier, it can avoid the shock. Children sometimes avoid a scolding by apologizing for misdeeds as soon as they see a parent's frown. When an animal or person responds to a signal in a way that avoids exposure to an aversive stimulus, **avoidance conditioning** has occurred. Remember that in escape conditioning an organism learns to make a response to *terminate* an aversive stimulus, whereas in avoidance conditioning an organism learns to make a response to *prevent* the aversive event from occurring.

Avoidance conditioning is also more complex than escape conditioning, in part because it involves elements of both classical and operant conditioning. The buzzer or blinking light that predicts a shock becomes a *conditioned stimulus,* signaling the aversive event to be avoided. Then, through classical conditioning, the signal comes to elicit a conditioned fear response. Like the shock itself, conditioned fear is an unpleasant internal sensation. The operant response of jumping the barrier is reinforced by its consequences—which include reducing the unpleasant fear stimulus.

In short, avoidance conditioning takes place through a two-step learning process. The first step involves classical conditioning (pairing a signal with a coming shock); the second step involves operant conditioning (learning to make a response to avoid the shock).

Along with positive reinforcement, avoidance conditioning is one of the most important influences on everyday behavior. Most people go to work even when they would rather stay in bed, and they stop at red lights even when they are in a hurry. Each of these behaviors reflects avoidance conditioning, because each behavior allows people to avoid a negative consequence, such as lost pay or a traffic ticket.

Avoidance is a difficult habit to break, partly because avoidance responses continue to be reinforced by fear reduction long after the aversive stimulus has ceased to be a risk (Solomon, Kamin, & Wynne, 1953). Furthermore, avoidance responses prevent the opportunity to learn that the "rules" may have changed and that avoidance is no

FIGURE 6.9

Two Kinds of Punishment

In one form of punishment, a behavior is followed by an aversive or unpleasant stimulus. In a second form of punishment, sometimes called penalty, a pleasant stimulus is *removed* following a behavior. In either case, punishment decreases the chances that the behavior will occur in the future.

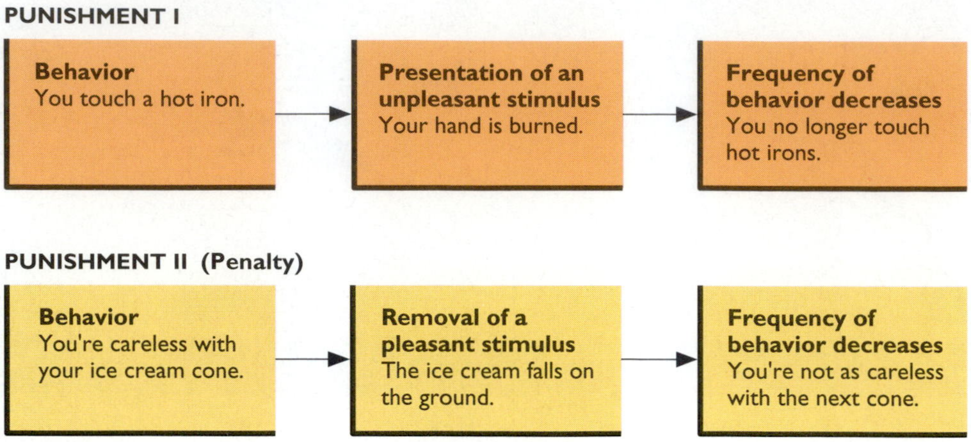

PUNISHMENT I

| **Behavior** You touch a hot iron. | → | **Presentation of an unpleasant stimulus** Your hand is burned. | → | **Frequency of behavior decreases** You no longer touch hot irons. |

PUNISHMENT II (Penalty)

| **Behavior** You're careless with your ice cream cone. | → | **Removal of a pleasant stimulus** The ice cream falls on the ground. | → | **Frequency of behavior decreases** You're not as careless with the next cone. |

longer necessary. If you fear elevators and therefore avoid them, you will never discover that they are safe and comfortable. Avoidance conditioning may also prevent people from learning new, more desirable behaviors. For example, fear of doing something embarrassing may cause people with limited social skills to shy away from social situations.

Punishment   Positive and negative reinforcement both *increase* the frequency of a response. In contrast, **punishment** involves the presentation of an aversive stimulus or the removal of a pleasant one in order to *decrease* the probability that an operant behavior will occur again. Shouting "No!" and swatting your dog when it begins chewing on the rug illustrates punishment that presents a negative stimulus following a response. Taking away a child's TV privileges because of rude behavior is a kind of punishment—sometimes called *penalty*—that removes a positive stimulus (see Figure 6.9).

Punishment and negative reinforcement are often confused, but they are quite different. Reinforcement of any sort always *strengthens* behavior; punishment *weakens* it. If shock is *turned off* when a rat presses a lever, that is negative reinforcement; it increases the probability that the rat will press the lever when shock occurs again. But if shock is *turned on* when the rat presses the lever, that is punishment; the rat will be less likely to press the lever again.

Although punishment can change behavior, it has several potential drawbacks. First, it does not "erase" an undesirable habit; it merely suppresses it. And because this suppression is usually controlled by the stimuli present at the time of punishment, people often repeat previously punished acts when they think they can avoid detection. Second, punishment is often ineffective, especially with animals or young children, unless it is given immediately after the response and each time the response is made. If a child gets into a cookie jar and enjoys a few cookies before being discovered and punished, the effect of the punishment will be greatly reduced. Third, punishment sometimes produces unwanted side effects. For example, if a parent punishes a child for swearing, the child may associate the parent with the punishment and simply end up fearing the parent. Similarly, if a child confesses to wrongdoing and is then punished, the punishment may discourage honesty rather than eliminate undesirable behavior. Fourth, physical punishment when administered by an angry person can become aggression and even abuse. Because children tend to imitate what they see, frequent punishment may lead children to behave aggressively themselves. Finally, although punishment signals that inappropriate behavior occurred, by itself it does not specify correct alternatives. An "F" on a term paper says the assignment was poorly done, but the grade alone tells the student nothing about how to improve.

In the 1970s and 1980s, concerns over these drawbacks led many parents and professionals to discourage spanking and other forms of punishment as a means of controlling children's behavior (Rosellini, 1998). The debate about punishment has been reopened recently by studies suggesting that spanking can be an effective behavior control technique with children three to thirteen years of age. These studies found that occasional spanking is not detrimental to children's development, if used in combination with other disciplinary practices such as requiring that the children pay some penalty for their misdeeds, having them provide some sort of restitution to the victims of their actions, and making them aware of what they had done wrong (Gunnoe & Mariner, 1997; Larzelere, 1996).

When used *properly*, then, punishment can work, and in some instances, it may be the only effective treatment (see Figure 6.10). However, punishment is most useful when several guidelines are followed. First, to prevent development of a general fear of the punisher, he or she should specify why punishment is being given and that the behavior, not the person, is being punished. Second, without being abusive, punishment should be immediate and salient enough to eliminate the undesirable response. A halfhearted "Quit it" may actually reinforce a child's misdeeds because almost any attention is reinforcing to some children. Moreover, if children become habituated to very mild punishment, the parent may end up using substantially more severe punishment to stop inappropriate behavior than would have been necessary if a stern, but moderate, punishment had been used in the first place. (You may have witnessed this *escalation effect* in grocery stores or restaurants, where parents are often not initially firm enough in dealing with their children's misbehavior.) Finally, punishment should not be administered in isolation; more appropriate responses should be identified and positively reinforced. As the frequency of appropriate behavior increases through reinforcement, the frequency of undesirable responses (and the need for further punishment) should decline.

When these guidelines are not followed, the potentially beneficial effects of punishment may be wiped out or only temporary (Hyman, 1995). As illustrated in many criminal justice systems, punishment is typically meted out long after the undesirable behavior occurs, and initial punishments are often relatively mild—as when offenders are repeatedly given probation rather than a jail sentence. And punishment by imprisonment alone does not usually lead to rehabilitation (Brennan & Mednick, 1994). Currently, there are nearly 2 million criminals in prison in the United States alone (Gilliad & Beck, 1998), and about two-thirds of them are likely to be rearrested for serious crimes within three years of completing their sentences (U.S. Department of Justice, 1997).

FIGURE 6.10

Life-Saving Punishment

This child suffered from chronic ruminative disorder, a condition in which he regurgitated all food. At left, the boy was approximately one year old and had been vomiting for four months. At right is the same child thirteen days after punishment with electric shock had eliminated the vomiting response; his weight had increased 26 percent. He was physically and psychologically healthy when tested six months, one year, and two years later (Lang & Melamed, 1969).

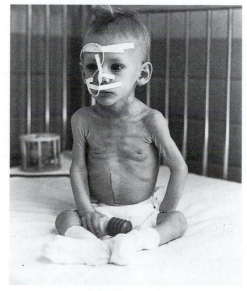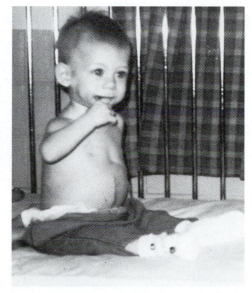

Source: Lang & Melamed, 1969.

FIGURE 6.11

Stimulus Discrimination

In this experiment the rat could jump from a stand through any one of three doors, but it was reinforced only if it jumped through the door that differed from the other two. The rat learned to do so quite well: On this trial, it discriminated vertical from horizontal stripes.

Discriminative Stimuli and Stimulus Control   One of the most important benefits of operant conditioning is that it enables organisms to adapt quickly to changes in their environment—an ability that, in the real world, has survival value. For example, even pigeons are readily able to learn when they should respond and when they should not. If they are reinforced with food for pecking a key when a red light is on but are not reinforced for pecking when a green light is on, they will eventually peck only when they see a red light. Their behavior demonstrates the effect of **discriminative stimuli,** which are stimuli that signal whether reinforcement is available if a certain response is made. When an organism learns to make a particular response in the presence of one stimulus but not another, *stimulus discrimination* has occurred (see Figure 6.11). Another way to say this is that the response is now under *stimulus control.* In general, stimulus discrimination allows people or animals to learn what is appropriate (reinforced) and inappropriate (not reinforced) in particular situations. For both animals and humans, discrimination develops fastest when the discriminative stimulus signals that a behavior is appropriate, and it develops slowest when the stimulus signals that a behavior is inappropriate (Newman, Wolff, & Hearst, 1980).

Stimulus generalization also occurs in operant conditioning; that is, organisms often perform a response in the presence of a stimulus that is similar, but not identical, to the one that previously signaled the availability of reinforcement. As in classical conditioning, the more similar the new stimulus is to the old, the more likely it is that the response will be performed. As an example, consider the student who gets an A after engaging in lively dialogue with a friendly, informal instructor who encouraged discussion. The student will be more likely to repeat the same approach in future classes with other informal instructors than with those who are more aloof.

As in classical conditioning, stimulus discrimination and stimulus generalization often complement each other in operant conditioning. In one study, for example, pigeons received food for pecking a key when they saw only certain works of art (Watanabe, Sakamoto, & Wakita, 1995). As a result, these birds learned to discriminate the works of the impressionist painter Claude Monet from those of the cubist painter Pablo Picasso. Later, when the birds were shown new paintings by other impressionist and cubist artists, they were able to generalize from the original artists to other artists who painted in the same style. We humans learn to place people and objects into even more finely detailed categories, such as "honest" or "dangerous." We discriminate one stimulus from another and then, through generalization, respond similarly to all those we perceive to be in a particular category. This ability to respond in a similar way to all mem-

Although the artist may not have intended it, this cartoon nicely illustrates how discriminative stimuli affect behavior.

"Oh, not bad. The light comes on, I press the bar, they write me a check. How about you?"

bers of a category can save us considerable time and effort, but unfortunately it can also lead to the development of unwarranted prejudice against certain groups of people (see Chapter 17).

Forming and Strengthening Operant Behavior

Daily life is full of examples of operant conditioning. People go to movies, parties, classes, and jobs primarily because doing so brings reinforcement. What is the effect of the type or timing of the reinforcer? How can new responses be established through operant conditioning?

Shaping   Imagine that you want to train your dog, Henry, to sit and to "shake hands." The basic method using positive reinforcement is obvious: Every time Henry sits and shakes hands, you give him a treat. But the problem is also obvious: Smart as Henry is, he may never spontaneously make the desired response, so you will never be able to give the reinforcer. Instead of your teaching and Henry's learning, the two of you will just stare at each other.

The way around this problem is to shape Henry's behavior. **Shaping** is accomplished by reinforcing *successive approximations*—that is, responses that come successively closer to the desired response. For example, you might first give Henry a treat whenever he sits down. Then you might reinforce him only when he sits and partially lifts a paw. Next, you might reinforce more complete paw lifting. Eventually, you would require that Henry perform the entire sit-lift-shake sequence before giving the treat. Shaping is an extremely powerful, widely used tool. Animal trainers have used it to teach chimpanzees to roller-skate, dolphins to jump through hoops, and pigeons to play Ping-Pong (Breland & Breland, 1966; Coren, 1999).

Secondary Reinforcement   Often, operant conditioning begins with the use of **primary reinforcers,** events or stimuli—such as food—that are inherently rewarding. But Henry's training will be somewhat disrupted if he must stop and eat every time he makes a correct response. Furthermore, once he gets full, food will no longer act as an effective reinforcer. To avoid these problems, animal trainers and others in the teaching business capitalize on the principle of secondary reinforcement.

A **secondary reinforcer** is a previously neutral stimulus that, if paired with a stimulus that is already reinforcing, will itself take on reinforcing properties. In other words, secondary reinforcers are rewards that people or animals learn to like. For example, if you say "Good boy!" just before feeding Henry, the words will become

Getting the Hang of It

Learning to eat with a spoon is, as you can see, a hit-and-miss process at first. However, this child will learn to hit the target more and more often as the food reward gradually shapes a more efficient, and far less messy, pattern of behavior.

Secondary Reinforcement

A touch, a smile, and a look of love are among the many social stimuli that can serve as positive reinforcers for humans.

reinforcing after a few such pairings and can then be used alone to reinforce Henry's behavior (especially if the words are paired with food now and then). Does this remind you of classical conditioning? It should, because the primary reinforcer (food) is an unconditioned stimulus; if the sound of "Good boy!" predictably precedes and thus signals food, it becomes a conditioned stimulus. For this reason, secondary reinforcers are sometimes called *conditioned reinforcers.*

Secondary reinforcement greatly expands the power of operant conditioning (Schwartz & Reisberg, 1991). Money is the most obvious secondary reinforcer; some people will do anything for it (even though it tastes terrible!). Its reinforcing power lies in its association with the many rewards it can buy. Smiles and other forms of social approval (like the words "Good job!") are also important secondary reinforcers for human beings. However, what becomes a secondary reinforcer can vary a great deal from person to person and culture to culture. For example, tickets to a rock concert may be an effective secondary reinforcer for some people, but not all. A ceremony honoring outstanding job performance might be highly reinforcing to most employees in individualist cultures, but it might be embarrassing for some from cultures in which group cooperation is valued more than personal distinction (Fiske et al., 1998). Still, when chosen carefully, secondary reinforcers can build or maintain behavior even when primary reinforcement is absent for long periods.

Delay and Size of Reinforcement   Much of human behavior is learned and maintained because it is regularly reinforced. But many people overeat, smoke, drink too much, or procrastinate, even though they know these behaviors are bad for them and even though they want to eliminate them. They just cannot seem to change; they seem to lack "self-control." If behavior is controlled by its consequences, why do people perform acts that are ultimately self-defeating?

Part of the answer lies in the timing of reinforcers. The good feelings (positive reinforcers) that follow, say, drinking too much are immediate; hangovers and other negative consequences are usually delayed. Recall that in classical conditioning, increasing the delay between the conditioned stimulus and the unconditioned stimulus usually weakens the conditioned response. Similarly, operant conditioning is stronger when delivery of the reinforcer is immediate (Kalish, 1981). Thus, under some conditions, delaying a positive reinforcer for even a few seconds can decrease the effectiveness of positive reinforcement. (An advantage of praise or other secondary reinforcers is that they can easily be delivered immediately after a desired response occurs.)

The size of a reinforcer is also important. In general, conditioning generates more vigorous behavior when the reinforcer is large than when it is small. For example, a strong electrical shock will elicit a faster avoidance or escape response than a weak one.

Schedules of Reinforcement   So far, we have described reinforcement as if a reinforcer were delivered every time a particular response occurs. Sometimes it is, and this arrangement is called a **continuous reinforcement schedule.** Very often, however, reinforcement is administered only some of the time; the result is a **partial,** or **intermittent, reinforcement schedule.**

Most intermittent schedules can be classified according to (1) whether the delivery of reinforcers is determined by the number of responses made or by the time that has elapsed since the last reinforcer, and (2) whether the delivery schedule is fixed or variable. This way of classifying schedules produces four basic types of intermittent reinforcement.

1. **Fixed-ratio (FR) schedules** provide reinforcement following a fixed number of responses. Rats might receive food after every tenth bar press (FR 10) or after every twentieth one (FR 20); factory workers might be paid for every five lamps they assemble (FR 5).

2. **Variable-ratio (VR) schedules** also call for reinforcement after a given number of responses, but that number varies from one reinforcement to the next. On a VR 30 schedule, a rat might sometimes be reinforced after ten bar presses, sometimes after fifty bar presses, but an *average* of thirty responses would occur before reinforcement

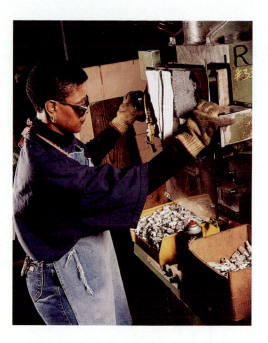

LINKAGES

Reinforcement Schedules on the Job

Workers at the Lincoln Electric Company, in Cleveland, Ohio, are paid for every piece of welding equipment they produce. This fixed ratio reinforcement schedule results in very high production rates and in annual incomes of up to $85,000. While most of the employees like the reward system, they are not necessarily satisfied with their jobs. This may be because, as described in Chapter 11, on motivation and emotion, job satisfaction is usually based on factors other than high pay.

is given. Gambling also offers a variable-ratio schedule; a slot machine, for example, pays off only after a frustratingly unpredictable number of lever pulls, averaging perhaps one in twenty.

3. **Fixed-interval (FI) schedules** provide reinforcement for the first response that occurs after some fixed time has passed since the last reward, regardless of how many responses have been made during that interval. For example, on an FI 60 schedule, the first response after sixty seconds have passed will be rewarded. Some radio stations use fixed-interval schedules to discourage "professional contestants" by stating that listeners cannot win a prize more than once every thirty days.

4. **Variable-interval (VI) schedules** reinforce the first response after some period of time, but the amount of time varies. On a VI 60 schedule, for example, the first response to occur after an *average* of one minute is reinforced, but the actual time between reinforcements might vary from, say, 1 second to 120 seconds. Teachers use VI schedules when they give "points"—at unpredictably varying intervals—to children who are in their seats. A VI schedule has also been successfully used to encourage seatbelt use: During a ten-week test in Illinois, police stopped drivers at random times and awarded prizes to those who were buckled up (Mortimer et al., 1988).

Different schedules of reinforcement produce different patterns of responding, as Figure 6.12 shows (Skinner, 1961a). The figure illustrates two important points. First, both fixed- and variable-ratio schedules produce very high rates of behavior, because in both cases the frequency of the reward depends directly on the rate of responding. Industrial/organizational psychologists have used this principle to help companies increase worker productivity and lower absenteeism. Workers who are paid on the basis of the number of items they produce or the number of days they show up for work usually produce more items and miss fewer workdays (Muchinsky, 1993; Yukl, Latham, & Purcell, 1976). Similarly, gamblers reinforced on a variable-ratio schedule for pulling the slot machine's handle tend to maintain a high rate of responding.

The second important aspect of Figure 6.12 relates to the "scallops" shown in the fixed-interval schedule. Under this schedule, it does not matter how many responses are made during the time between rewards. As a result, the rate of responding typically drops dramatically immediately after reinforcement and then increases as the time for another reward approaches. When teachers schedule quizzes on the same day each week, for example, most students will study just before each quiz

FIGURE 6.12

Schedules of Reinforcement

These curves illustrate the patterns of behavior typically seen under different reinforcement schedules. The steeper the curve, the faster the response rate; the thin diagonal lines crossing the curves show when reinforcement was given. In general, the rate of responding is higher under ratio schedules than under interval schedules.

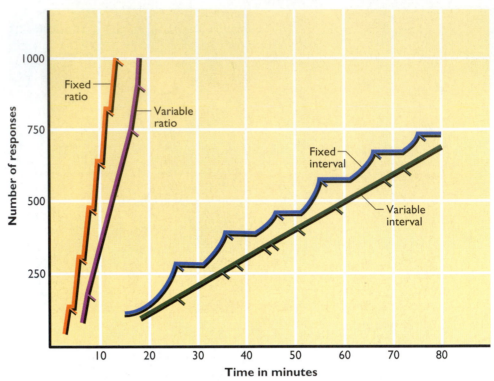

Source: Adapted from Skinner, 1961.

and then almost cease studying immediately afterward. Behavior rewarded on variable-interval schedules looks quite different. The unpredictable timing of rewards typically generates slow but steady responding. Thus, if you know that a "pop quiz" might occur any day, your studying is likely to be relatively steady from day to day.

Schedules and Extinction   Just as breaking the link between a conditioned and unconditioned stimulus weakens a classically conditioned response, ending the causal relationship between an operant response and its consequences weakens that response. In other words, failure to reinforce a response *extinguishes* that response; the response occurs less often and eventually may disappear. If bar-pressing no longer brings food, a rat stops pressing; if repeated e-mail messages to a friend are not answered, you eventually stop sending them. As in classical conditioning, extinction in operant conditioning does not totally erase learned relationships. If a signaling stimulus reappears some time after an operant response has been extinguished, that response may recur (spontaneously recover), and, if again reinforced, it will be relearned even faster.

In general, behaviors learned under a partial reinforcement schedule are far more difficult to extinguish than those learned on a continuous reinforcement schedule. This phenomenon—called the **partial reinforcement extinction effect**—is easy to understand if you imagine yourself in a gambling casino, standing near a broken slot machine and a broken candy machine. If you deposit money in the candy machine, you will probably extinguish (stop putting money in) very quickly. Because the machine is supposed to deliver its goodies on a continuous reinforcement schedule, it is easy to tell that it is not going to provide a reinforcer. But because slot machines are known to offer rewards on an intermittent and unpredictable schedule, you might put in coin after coin, on the assumption that the machine is simply not paying off at the moment.

Partial reinforcement also helps explain why superstitious behavior is so resistant to extinction (Chance, 1988). Suppose you take a shower just before hearing that you passed an important exam. The shower did nothing to cause this outcome; the reward followed it through sheer luck. Still, for some people, this *accidental reinforcement* can

Superstition and Partial Reinforcement

Partial reinforcement can create superstitious athletic rituals such as a fixed sequence of actions prior to shooting a free-throw in a basketball game. If the ritual has preceded success often enough, failure to execute it may upset the player and disrupt performance. Jeff Hornacek always wipes the right side of his face three times before shooting the ball, as a hello to his three children.

function like a partial reinforcement schedule, strengthening actions that precede, and thus appear to cause, reward (Chance, 1988). Thus, someone who wins a lottery while wearing a particular shirt may begin wearing the "lucky shirt" more often. The laws of chance dictate that if you wear a "lucky shirt" often enough, a rewarding event will follow now and then, on a very sparse partial schedule (Vyse, 1997).

Why Reinforcers Work

What makes reinforcers reinforcing? For primary reinforcers, at least, the reason could be that they satisfy hunger, thirst, and other physiological needs basic to survival. This explanation is incomplete, however, because stimuli like saccharin, which have no nutritional value, can wield as much reinforcing power as sugar, which is nutritious. Other activities, like taking addictive drugs, are powerful reinforcers, despite their long-term threat to the health of the individual. Hence psychologists have sought other explanations for the mechanisms of reinforcement.

Some psychologists have argued that reinforcement is based, not on a stimulus itself, but on the opportunity to engage in an activity that involves the stimulus. According to David Premack (1965), for example, at any moment each person has a hierarchy of behavioral preferences, ranked from most to least desirable, like a kind of psychological "Top 10." The higher on the hierarchy an activity is, the greater its power as a reinforcer. And a preferred activity can serve as a reinforcer for any other activity that is less preferred at the moment. Thus, when parents allow their teenager to use the car after she mows the lawn, they are offering activities high on the teenager's preference hierarchy to reinforce performance of activities lower on the hierarchy. This idea is known as the *Premack principle*.

Other psychologists contend that virtually any activity can become a reinforcer if access to that activity has been restricted. Thus, different activities will be reinforcing at different times and in different situations. This *disequilibrium hypothesis* (Timberlake, 1980; Timberlake & Farmer-Dougan, 1991) can be illustrated by imagining a man who prefers eating over all other activities. In accordance with the Premack principle, as long as he is hungry, the opportunity to eat can be used as a reinforcer for almost any behavior. But once his hunger is satisfied, eating will temporarily lose its power as a reinforcer. What activity will now become the strongest reinforcer for this person? The disequilibrium hypothesis says it can be almost anything the man was *prevented* from doing during the time that eating was allowed. For instance, if he had been denied the opportunity to drink water, a disequilibrium would result, the man would be motivated to get water, and drinking would become a powerful reinforcer. A disequilibrium can be created even when the reinforcers do not involve basic survival needs. As an example, suppose a student normally prefers studying over participating in gym class. If she is not allowed to engage in any gym activities for some time, gym activity would be held below its natural "baseline" level, thus increasing its value as a reinforcer enough that it could be used to reinforce studying! Thus, even an activity that is normally less preferred can sometimes become a reinforcer for a normally more preferred activity.

Note that the disequilibrium hypothesis also explains why money is such a powerful secondary reinforcer: It can be exchanged for whatever a person finds reinforcing at the moment. Indeed, recent research suggests that the disequilibrium hypothesis may provide a better overall explanation of why reinforcers work than the Premack principle (Hergenhahn & Olson, 1997).

Psychologists taking a biological approach suggest that the stimuli and activities known as reinforcers may work by exerting particular effects within the brain. This possibility was suggested when James Olds and Peter Milner (1954) discovered that mild electrical stimulation of certain areas of the hypothalamus can be such a powerful reinforcer that a hungry rat will ignore food in a Skinner box, preferring to press for hours a lever that stimulates these "pleasure centers" of its brain (see also Olds, 1973). It is not yet clear whether physiological mechanisms underlie the power of all

REINFORCEMENT AND PUNISHMENT

Concept	Description	Example or Comment
Positive reinforcement	Increasing the frequency of behavior by following it with the presentation of a positive reinforcer—a pleasant, positive stimulus or experience.	Saying "Good job" after someone works hard to perform a task.
Negative reinforcement	Increasing the frequency of behavior by following it with the removal of a negative reinforcer—an unpleasant stimulus or experience.	Pressing the "mute" button on a TV remote control removes the sound of an obnoxious commercial.
Escape conditioning	Learning to make a response that ends a negative reinforcer.	A little boy learns that crying will cut short the time that he must stay in his room.
Avoidance conditioning	Learning to make a response that avoids a negative reinforcer.	You slow your car to the speed limit when you spot a police car, thus avoiding arrest and reducing the fear of arrest. Very resistant to extinction.
Punishment	Decreasing the frequency of behavior by either presenting an unpleasant stimulus or removing a pleasant one.	Swatting the dog after she steals food from the table, or taking a favorite toy away from a child who misbehaves. A number of cautions should be kept in mind before using punishment.

reinforcers, but evidence available thus far certainly suggests that these mechanisms are important components of the process. For example, as mentioned in Chapter 3, activation of dopamine systems is associated with the pleasure of many stimuli, including food, sex, and addictive drugs.

Operant Conditioning of Human Behavior

The principles of operant conditioning were originally developed with animals in the laboratory, but they are valuable for understanding human behavior in an endless variety of everyday situations. ("In Review: Reinforcement and Punishment" summarizes some key principles of operant conditioning.) The unscientific but effective use of rewards and punishments by parents, teachers, and peers is vital to helping children learn what is and is not appropriate behavior at the dinner table, in the classroom, or at a birthday party. Indeed, people learn how to be "civilized" in their own particular culture partly through positive ("Good!") and negative ("Stop that!") responses from others. As described in Chapter 12, on human development, differing patterns of rewards and punishments for boys and girls also underlie the development of behaviors that fit culturally approved *gender roles*.

The scientific study of operant conditioning has led to numerous treatment programs for altering problematic behavior. Behavioral programs that combine the use of rewards for appropriate actions and extinction, or carefully administered punishment for inappropriate behaviors have helped countless mental patients, mentally retarded individuals, autistic children, and hard-to-manage youngsters to develop the behavior patterns they need to live happier and more productive lives.

When people cannot do anything about the consequences of a behavior, discriminative stimuli may hold the key to changing the behavior. For example, people trying to quit smoking often find initial abstinence easier if they stay away from bars and other places that contain discriminative stimuli for smoking. Stimulus control can also help alleviate insomnia. Insomniacs are much more likely than other people to use their beds for nonsleeping activities such as watching television, writing letters, reading magazines, worrying, and so on. Soon the bedroom becomes a discriminative stimulus for so many activities that relaxation and sleep become less and less likely. But if insomniacs begin to use their beds only for sleeping, there is a good chance that they will sleep better (Morin et al., 1993).

COGNITIVE PROCESSES IN LEARNING

During the first half of the twentieth century, psychologists in North America tended to look at classical and operant conditioning through the lens of behaviorism, the theoretical approach that was dominant in psychology at the time. As described in Chapter 1, behaviorism stresses the importance of empirical observation of lawful relationships in animal and human behavior. Behaviorists tried to identify the stimuli responses, and consequences that build and alter overt behavior. In other words, they saw learning as resulting from the automatic, unthinking formation or modification of associations between observable stimuli and observable responses. Behaviorists gave virtually no consideration to the role of conscious mental activity that might accompany the learning process.

This strictly behavioral view of classical and operant conditioning is challenged by the cognitive approach, which has become increasingly influential in recent decades. Cognitive psychologists see a common thread in these apparently different forms of learning. Both classical and operant conditioning, they argue, help animals and people to detect causality, to understand what causes what (Schwartz & Robbins, 1995). By extension, both types of conditioning may result not only from automatic stimulus-response associations but also from the conscious mental processes that organisms use to understand their environments and to interact with them adaptively.

Certainly there is evidence that cognitive processes—how people represent, store, and use information—play an important role in learning. This evidence includes

LINKAGES

Learning Cultural Values

As described in Chapter 18, the prevalence of aggressive behavior varies considerably from culture to culture, in part because some cultures reward it more than others. For example, in some Inuit cultures (like the group shown here), aggressive behavior is actively discouraged and extremely rare (Oatley, 1993); such behavior is much more common among the Yanomamo, a South American Indian group in which a male's status is based on his ability to fight and even kill.

research on learned helplessness, latent learning, cognitive maps, insight, and observational learning.

Learned Helplessness

Babies learn that crying brings parental attention, children learn which button causes the TV to turn on, and adults learn what behaviors bring success in the workplace. Moreover, on the basis of this learning, people come to *expect* that certain actions on their part cause certain consequences. If this learning is disrupted, problems may result. One such problem is **learned helplessness,** a tendency to give up any effort to control the environment (Seligman, 1975).

Learned helplessness was first demonstrated in animals. As described earlier, dogs placed in a shuttle box (see Figure 6.8 on page 187) will normally learn to jump over a partition to escape a shock. However, if the dogs are first placed in a harness so that they cannot escape, they do not even *try* to escape when shocked again after the harness has been removed (Overmier & Seligman, 1967). It is as if the animals had learned that "there is nothing I can do to control events in the world."

FOCUS ON RESEARCH METHODS

A Two-Factor Experiment on Human Helplessness

The results of animal studies on learned helplessness led to speculation that learned helplessness might play a role in human psychological problems, but researchers had to deal with more basic questions first. One of the most important of these questions is whether lack of control over the environment can lead to helplessness in humans.

■ What was the researcher's question?

Donald Hiroto (1974) conducted an experiment to test the hypothesis that people would develop learned helplessness after either experiencing lack of control or simply being *told* that their control was limited.

■ How did the researcher answer the question?

The first independent variable manipulated in Hiroto's experiment was the ability or inability of male and female volunteer participants to control a series of thirty randomly timed bursts of loud, obnoxious noise. Like dogs receiving inescapable shock, one group of participants had no way to stop the noise. A second group did have control; they could press a button to turn off the noise. A third group heard no noise at all.

After this preliminary phase, all participants were exposed to eighteen more bursts of obnoxious noise, each preceded by a red warning light. During this second phase, all participants could stop the noise by moving a lever to the left or right and, if they acted quickly enough, could even prevent it from starting. However, the participants did not know which lever direction would be correct on any given trial.

Before these new trials began, the experimenter manipulated a second independent variable: *expectation* about control. For half the participants, instructions emphasized personal control, noting that avoiding or escaping noise depended on skill. For the other half, control was downplayed; these participants were told that, no matter how hard they tried, success would be a matter of chance. This was a *two-factor* experiment because the dependent variable—the degree to which participants acted to control noise—could be affected by either or both of two independent variables: prior experience with noise (control, lack of control, or no noise) and expectation (skill or chance) about the ability to influence the noise.

■ What did the researcher find?

On the average, participants who had previously experienced lack of control now failed to control noise on almost four times as many trials (50 percent versus 13 percent) as did those who had earlier been in control. Further, regardless of whether participants had experienced control before, those who expected control to depend on their *skill* exerted control on significantly more trials than did those who expected chance to govern the outcome.

■ What do the results mean?

These results support Hiroto's hypothesis that people, like animals, tend to make less effort to control their environment when prior experience leads them to expect their efforts to be in vain. Unlike animals, however, people can develop expectations of helplessness either through personally experiencing lack of control or through being told that they are powerless. Hiroto's (1974) results appear to reflect a general phenomenon: When people's prior experience leads them to believe that nothing they do can change their lives or control their destiny, they generally stop trying to improve their lot (Peterson, Maier, & Seligman, 1993). Instead, they tend to passively endure aversive situations and, at the cognitive level, to attribute negative events to their own enduring and widespread shortcomings rather than to changeable external circumstances (Abramson, Metalsky, & Alloy, 1989; Seligman, Klein, & Miller, 1976).

■ What do we still need to know?

Although it seems clear that helplessness can be learned, not all of its consequences are known or understood. For example, Martin Seligman (1975) originally proposed that learned helplessness was a major cause of depression and other mental disorders in humans, but subsequent research (Abramson, Metalsky, & Alloy, 1989; Metalsky et al., 1993) indicates that the causal picture is more complicated. One study suggests that learned-helplessness experiences give rise to a more general *pessimistic explanatory style* that can produce depression and other mental disorders (Peterson & Seligman, 1984). People with this style see the good things that happen to them as transitory and due to external factors (e.g., luck), and the bad things as permanent and due to internal factors (e.g., lack of ability). A pessimistic explanatory style has, in fact, been associated with negative outcomes, such as poor grades, poor sales performance, and health problems (Peterson & Barrett, 1987; Seligman & Schulman, 1986; Taylor, 1998a). However, the mechanism responsible for this connection remains unknown (Wiebe & Smith, 1997); understanding how pessimistic (or optimistic) explanatory styles can lead to negative (or positive) consequences will be an important new focus of research (Salovey, Rothman, & Rodin, 1998).

Latent Learning and Cognitive Maps

The study of cognitive processes in learning goes back at least to the 1920s and Edward Tolman's research on maze learning in rats (see Figure 6.13 on page 200). The rats' task was to find the goal box, where food awaited them. The rats typically took many wrong turns but over the course of many trials made successively fewer mistakes. The behavioral interpretation was that the rats learned a long chain of turning responses that were reinforced by the food. Tolman disagreed and offered evidence for a cognitive interpretation.

In one of Tolman's studies, three groups of rats were placed in the same maze once a day for several consecutive days (Tolman & Honzik, 1930). For Group A, food was placed in the goal box on each trial. As shown in Figure 6.13, these rats gradually improved their performance so that, by the end of the experiment, they

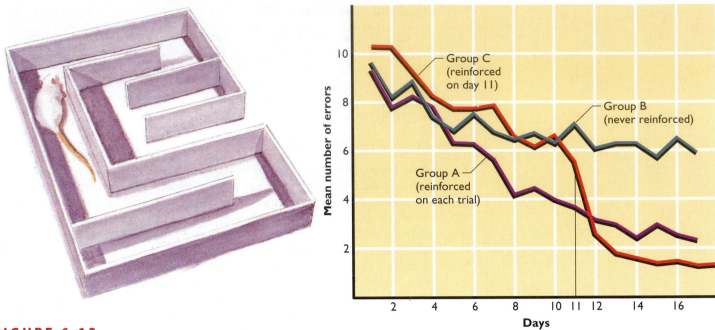

FIGURE 6.13

Latent Learning

Notice that when rats in Group C did not receive food reinforcement, they continued to make many errors in locating the goal box of this maze. The day after first finding food there, however, they took almost no wrong turns! The reinforcement, argued Tolman, affected only the rats' performance; they must have learned the maze earlier, without reinforcement.

made only one or two mistakes as they ran through the maze. Group B also ran the maze once a day, but there was never any food in their goal box. These animals continued to make many errors throughout the experiment. Neither of these results is surprising, and each is consistent with a behavioral view of learning.

The third group of rats, Group C, was the critical one. For the first ten days, they received no reinforcement for running the maze and continued to make many mistakes. But on the eleventh day, food was placed in their goal box for the first time. Then a very surprising thing happened: On the day after receiving reinforcement, these rats made almost no mistakes. In fact, their performance was as good as that of the rats who had been reinforced every day. In other words, for Group C the single reinforcement trial on day 11 produced a dramatic change in performance the next day.

Tolman argued that these results supported two conclusions. First, the reinforcement on day 11 could not have significantly affected the rats' *learning* of the maze itself; it simply changed their subsequent *performance*. They must have learned the maze earlier. Therefore, the rats demonstrated **latent learning**—learning that is not evident when it first occurs. Second, because the rats' performance changed immediately after the first reinforcement trial, the results he obtained could occur only if the rats had earlier developed a **cognitive map**—that is, a mental representation of the particular spatial arrangement of the maze.

Tolman concluded that cognitive maps develop naturally through experience, even in the absence of any overt response or reinforcement. Research on learning in the natural environment has supported these views. For example, we develop mental maps of shopping malls and city streets, even when we receive no direct reward for doing so (Tversky, 1991).

Thus, much as the Gestalt psychologists argued that the whole of a perception is different from the sum of its parts, cognitive views of learning hold that learning is more than the sum of reinforcement effects and stimulus-response associations. Just as perception may depend on the meaning attached to sensations, so, too, some forms of learning require higher mental processes and depend on how the learner attaches meaning to events.

Insight and Learning

Wolfgang Köhler was a Gestalt psychologist whose work on the cognitive aspects of learning happened almost by accident. A German, he was visiting the island of Tenerife when World War I broke out. The British confined Köhler to the island for the duration of the war, and he devoted his time to studying problem solving in chimpanzees housed on the island (Köhler, 1924).

For example, Köhler would put a chimpanzee in a cage and place a piece of fruit so that it was visible but out of the animal's reach. He sometimes hung the fruit from a string too high to reach, or laid it on the ground too far outside the cage to be retrieved. Many of the chimps overcame these obstacles easily. If the fruit was out of reach on the ground outside the cage, some chimps looked around the cage and, finding a long stick, used it to rake in the fruit. Surprised that the chimpanzees could solve these problems, Köhler tried more difficult tasks. Again, the chimps proved very adept, as Figure 6.14 illustrates.

In contrast to Thorndike, who thought that animals learn gradually, through the consequences of their actions, Köhler argued that animals' problem solving does not have to depend on automatic associations developing slowly through trial and error. He buttressed his claim with three observations. First, once a chimpanzee solved a particular problem, it would immediately do the same thing in a similar situation. In other words, it acted as if it understood the problem. Second, Köhler's chimpanzees rarely tried a solution that did not work. Third, they often reached a solution quite suddenly. When confronted with a piece of fruit hanging from a string, for example, a chimp might jump for it several times. Then it would stop jumping, look up, and pace back and forth. Finally it would run over to a wooden crate, place it directly under the fruit, and climb on top of it to reach the fruit. Once, when there were no other objects available, a chimp went over to Köhler, dragged him by the arm until he stood beneath the fruit, and then started climbing up his back!

Köhler believed that the only explanation for these results was that the chimpanzees suddenly had **insight** into the problem as a whole, not just stimulus-response associations between its specific elements. However, conclusively demonstrating that a

FIGURE 6.14

Insight

Here are three impressive examples of problem solving by chimpanzees. In (A) the animal fixed a fifteen-foot pole in the ground, climbed to the top, and dropped to the ground after grabbing the fruit. In (B) the chimp stacked up two boxes from different areas of the compound, climbed to the top, and used a pole to knock down the fruit. The chimp in (C) stacked three boxes and climbed them to reach the fruit.

Source: Kohler, 1976.

(A)

(B)

(C)

particular performance is the product of insight will require experiments more sophisticated than those conducted by Köhler. Indeed, some cognitive psychologists today argue that insight may not occur as suddenly as Köhler assumed. They suggest that insight results only after a "mental trial and error" process in which people (and some animals) envision a course of action, mentally simulate its results, compare it to the imagined outcome of other alternatives, and settle on the course of action most likely to aid complex problem solving and decision making (Klein, 1993).

Observational Learning: Learning by Imitation

Research on the role of cognitive processes in learning has been further stimulated by the finding that learning can occur not only by doing but also by observing what others do. Learning by watching others—called **observational learning,** or *social learning*—is efficient and adaptive. It occurs in both animals and humans. For example, young chimpanzees learn how to use a stone to crack open nuts by watching their mothers perform this action (Inoue-Nakamura & Matsuzawa, 1997). And we don't have to find out for ourselves that a door is locked or an iron is hot if we have just seen someone else try the door or suffer a burn.

Children are particularly influenced by the adults and peers who act as models for appropriate behavior in various situations. In one classic experiment, Albert Bandura showed nursery school children a film featuring an adult and a large, inflatable, bottom-heavy "Bobo" doll (Bandura, 1965). The adult in the film punched the Bobo doll in the nose, kicked it, threw objects at it, and hit its head with a hammer while saying things like "Sockeroo!" There were different endings to the film. Some children saw an ending in which the aggressive adult was called a "champion" by a second adult and rewarded with candy and soft drinks. Some saw the aggressor scolded and called a "bad person." Some saw a neutral ending in which there was neither reward nor punishment. After the film, each child was allowed to play alone with a Bobo doll. How the children played in this and similar studies led to some important conclusions about learning and about the role of cognitive factors in it.

Bandura found that children who saw the adult rewarded for aggression showed the most aggressive acts in play; they had received **vicarious conditioning,** a kind of observational learning in which one is influenced by seeing or hearing about the conse-

Learning by Imitation

Much of our behavior is learned by imitating others, especially those who serve as role models.

FIGURE 6.15

Observational Learning

After children have observed an aggressive model, they often reproduce many of the model's acts precisely, especially if the model's aggression was rewarded.

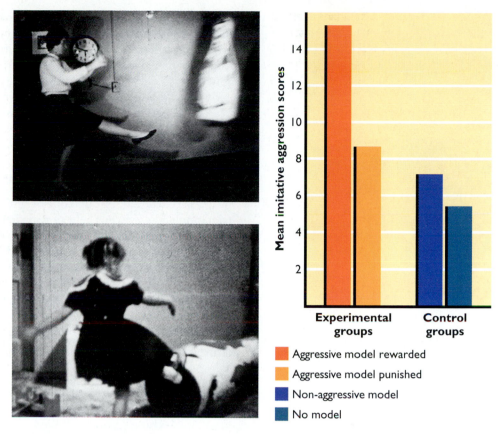

Source: Bandura, Ross & Ross, 1963.

quences of others' behavior. Those who had seen the adult punished for aggressive acts initially showed less aggression, but they still learned something. When later offered rewards for all the aggressive acts they could perform, these children displayed just as many as the children who had watched the rewarded adult. Observational learning can occur even when there are no vicarious consequences; many children in the neutral condition also imitated the model's aggression (see Figure 6.15).

Observational learning seems to be a powerful source of the *socialization process* through which children learn about which behaviors are—and are not—appropriate in their culture. Experiments show, for example, that children are more willing to help and share after seeing a demonstration of helping by a friendly, powerful model—even after some months have elapsed (Schroeder et al., 1995). Still other studies suggest that anxiety disorders such as phobias may be learned through observation of fearful models (Cook & Mineka, 1987).

If observational learning is important, then surely television—and televised violence—must teach children a great deal. For one thing, it is estimated that the average child in the United States spends more time watching television than attending school (Liebert & Sprafkin, 1988; Nielsen Media, 1990). Much of what children see is violent; prime-time programs in the United States present an average of 5 violent acts per hour; some Saturday morning cartoons include more than 20 per hour (Radecki, 1990; Seppa, 1997). As a result, the average

THINKING CRITICALLY

Does Watching Violence on Television Make People More Violent?

child will have witnessed at least 8,000 murders and more than 100,000 other acts of televised violence *before graduating from elementary school* (Kunkel et al., 1996).

Psychologists have speculated that watching so much violence might be emotionally arousing, making viewers more likely to react violently to frustration (Huston & Wright, 1989). Televised violence might also provide models that viewers imitate, particularly if the violence is carried out by attractive, powerful models—the "good guys," for example (Bandura, 1983). And recent research suggests that exposure to media violence can trigger or amplify viewers' aggressive thoughts and feelings, thus increasing the likelihood that they will *act* aggressively (Anderson, 1997; Bushman, 1998).

■ What am I being asked to believe or accept?

Many have argued that, through one or more of these mechanisms, watching violence on television causes violent behavior in viewers (Eron et al., 1996; Huesmann, 1998). Indeed, in 1993 a National Academy of Science report concluded that "overall, the vast majority of studies, whatever their methodology, showed that exposure to television violence resulted in increased aggressive behavior, both contemporaneously and over time" (Reiss & Roth, 1993, p. 371). An American Psychological Association Commission on Violence and Youth reached the same conclusion (American Psychological Association, 1993).

■ What evidence is available to support the assertion?

Three types of evidence back up the claim that watching violent television programs increases violent behavior. Some evidence comes from anecdotes and case studies. Children have poked one another in the eye after watching the Three Stooges appear to do so on television (Associated Press, 1984). And adults have claimed that watching TV shows prompted them to commit murders or other violent acts matching those seen on the shows.

Second, many longitudinal studies have found a correlation between watching violent television programs and later acts of aggression and violence. One such study tracked people from the time they were six or seven (in 1977) until they reached their early twenties (in 1992). Those who watched more violent television as children were significantly more aggressive as adults (Huesmann et al., 1997) and more likely to engage in criminal activity (Huesmann, 1995). They were also more likely to use physical punishment on their own children, who themselves tended to be much more aggressive than average. These latter results were also found in the United States, Israel, Australia, Poland, the Netherlands, and even Finland, where the number of violent TV shows is very small (Huesmann & Eron, 1986).

Finally, the results of numerous laboratory experiments also support the view that TV violence increases aggression among viewers (American Psychological Association, 1993; Paik & Comstock, 1994; Reiss & Roth, 1993). In one study, groups of boys watched violent or nonviolent programs in a controlled setting and then played floor hockey (Josephson, 1987). Boys who had watched the violent shows were more likely than those who had watched nonviolent programs to behave aggressively on the hockey floor. This effect was greatest for those boys who had the most aggressive tendencies to begin with. More extensive experiments in which children are exposed for long periods to carefully controlled types of television programs also suggest that exposure to large amounts of violent activity on television results in aggressive behavior (Huesmann, Laperspetz, & Eron, 1984).

■ Are there alternative ways of interpreting the evidence?

Anecdotal reports and case studies are certainly open to different interpretations. If people face imprisonment or execution for their violent acts, how much credibility can we give to their claims that their actions were triggered by television programs? And how many other people might say that the same programs made them *less* likely to be violent? Anecdotes alone do not provide a good basis for drawing solid scientific conclusions.

What about the correlational evidence from longitudinal studies? Recall from Chapter 2 that a correlation between two variables does not necessarily mean that one caused the other; both might be caused by a third factor. Why, for example, are certain people watching so much television violence in the first place? This question suggests a possible "third factor" that might account for the observed relationship between watching TV violence and acting aggressively: People who tend to be aggressive may prefer to watch more violent TV programs *and* behave aggressively toward others. Thus, personality may account for the observed correlations (e.g., Aluja-Fabregat & Torrubia-Beltri, 1998).

The results of controlled experiments on the effects of televised violence have been criticized as well (Geen, 1998). The major objection is that both the independent and dependent variables in these experiments are artificial and thus may not apply beyond the laboratory (Anderson & Bushman, 1997). For example, the kinds of violent shows viewed by the participants during some of these experiments, as well as the ways in which their aggression has been measured, may not reflect what goes on in the "real-world" situations we most want to know about.

■ What additional evidence would help to evaluate the alternatives?

Given the ambiguities inherent in correlational findings, a useful alternative source of evidence would be controlled experiments in which equivalent groups of people would be given different, long-term "doses" of the violence actually portrayed on TV, and its effects on their subsequent behavior would be observed in real-world situations. Such experiments could also explore the circumstances under which different people (e.g., children versus adults) are affected by various forms of violence. However, studies like these create a potential ethical dilemma. If watching violent television programs does cause violent behavior, are psychologists justified in creating conditions that might lead some people to be more violent? If such violence occurred, would the researchers be partly responsible to the victims and to society? Difficulty in answering questions like these is partly responsible for the prevalence of short-term experiments and correlational research in this area and for some of the remaining uncertainty about the effects of television violence.

■ What conclusions are most reasonable?

The preponderance of evidence collected so far, including recent statistical analyses of correlational findings (e.g., Huesmann et al., 1997), makes it reasonable to conclude that watching TV violence may be one cause of violent behavior (Smith & Donnerstein, 1998). However, a causal relationship between watching TV violence and acting violently is not inevitable, and there are many circumstances in which the effect does not occur (Charleton, Gunter, & Coles, 1998; Freedman, 1992). Parents, peers, and other environmental influences, along with personality factors, may dampen or amplify the effect of watching televised violence. Indeed, the viewers most likely to be affected by TV violence may be those who are most aggressive or violence-prone in the first place, a trait that could well have been acquired by observing the behavior of parents or peers (Huesmann et al., 1997).

Still, the fact that violence on television *can* have a causal impact on violent behavior is reason for serious concern and continues to influence public debate about what should and should not be aired on television.

T aking a cognitive approach to learning does not mean that associations are unimportant in the learning process. Associations between conditioned stimuli and reflexes or between responses and their consequences play an important role even in

LINKAGES

Neural Networks and Learning

FIGURE 6.16

An Associative Network

Here is an example of a network of associations to the concept of "dog." Network theorists suggest that the connections shown here represent patterns of neural connections in the brain.

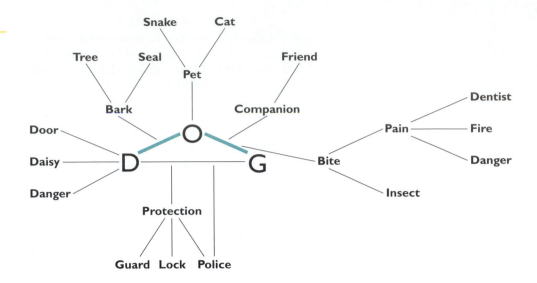

LINKAGES

How can neural network models help us to understand learning? (a link to Perception)

the mental processes that allow us to understand which events predict which other events. As a result of experience, some things remind us of other things, which remind us of still others, and so on.

How are associations actually stored in the brain? No one yet knows for sure, but the neural network models discussed in Chapter 5 provide a good way of thinking about this process. Indeed, networks of neural connections are believed to play a critical role not only in the rapid and accurate recognition of objects (Hintzman, 1991) but also in the learning process itself (Hergenhahn & Olson, 1997). These associative networks can be very complex. Consider the word *dog*. As shown in Figure 6.16, each person's experience builds many associations to this word, and the strength of each association will reflect the frequency with which "dog" has been mentally linked to the other concepts in that person's life.

Using what they know about the laws of learning and about the way neurons communicate and alter their synaptic connections, psychologists have been trying to develop models of how these associations are established. We discussed some of these efforts in Chapter 5 in terms of *neural networks* and *parallel distributed processing models* of how perception takes place. A crucial aspect of such models is the idea of *distributed memory* or *distributed knowledge*. These models suggest, for example, that the knowledge of "dog" does not lie in a single location, or node, within the brain. Instead, knowledge is distributed throughout the network of associations that connect the letters *D, O,* and *G,* along with other "dog-like" experiences. In addition, as shown in Figure 6.16, each of the interconnected nodes that makes up your knowledge of "dog" is connected to many other nodes as well. Thus, the letter *D* will be connected to "Daisy," "Danger," and a host of other things. Networks of connections also appear to be the key to explaining how people come to understand the words and sentences they read (Wolman, van den Broek, & Lorch, 1997).

Neural network models of learning focus on how these connections are laid down as a function of experience (Hanson & Burr, 1990). For example, suppose you are learning a new word in a foreign language. Each time you read the word and associate it with its English equivalent, you strengthen the neural connections between the sight of the letters forming that word and all of the nodes activated when its English equivalent is brought to mind. Neural network or *connectionist* models of learning predict how much the strength of each linkage grows (in terms of the likelihood of neural communication between the two connected nodes) each time the two words are experienced together.

The details of various theories about how these connections grow are very complex (see Hanson & Burr, 1990; Schwartz & Reisberg, 1991), but a theme common to many is that the weaker the connection between two items, the greater the increase in connection strength when they are experienced together. Thus, in a simple classical conditioning experiment, the connections between the nodes characterizing the conditioned stimulus and those characterizing the unconditioned stimulus will show the greatest increase in strength during the first few learning trials. Notice that this prediction nicely matches the typical learning curve shown in Figure 6.4, on page 179 (Rescorla & Wagner, 1972).

Few neural network models today can handle the learning of complex tasks, nor can they easily account for how people adapt when the "rules of the game" are suddenly changed and old habits must be unlearned and replaced (Hintzman, 1991). Nevertheless, a better understanding of what we mean by associations may very well lie in future research on neural network models (Tryon, 1995).

USING RESEARCH ON LEARNING TO HELP PEOPLE LEARN

Teaching and training—explicit efforts to assist learners in mastering a specific skill or body of material—are major aspects of socialization in virtually every culture. Therefore, the study of how people learn has important implications for improved teaching in our schools (Tharinger et al., 1996; Woolfolk-Hoy, 1999) and for helping people develop skills ranging from typing to tennis.

Classrooms Across Cultures

Many people believe that schools in the United States are not doing a very good job (Associated Press, 1997; Carnegie Task Force, 1996; Penner et al., 1994). The average performance of U.S. students on tests of reading, math, and other basic academic skills has tended to fall short of that of youngsters in other countries, especially Asian countries (Stigler, 1992; U.S. Department of Commerce, 1992). In one comparison study, Harold Stevenson (1992) followed a sample of pupils in Taiwan, Japan, and the United States from first grade, in 1980, to eleventh grade in 1991. In the first grade, the Asian students scored no higher than their U.S. peers on tests of mathematical aptitude and skills, nor did they enjoy math more. However, by the fifth grade the U.S. students had fallen far behind. Corresponding differences were seen in reading skills.

Important potential causes of these differences were found in the classroom itself. In a typical U.S. classroom session, teachers talked to students as a group; then students worked at their desks independently. Reinforcement or other feedback about performance on their work was usually delayed until the next day or, often, not provided at all. In contrast, the typical Japanese classroom placed greater emphasis on cooperative work between students (Kristof, 1997). Teachers provided more immediate feedback on a one-to-one basis. And there was an emphasis on creating teams of students with varying abilities, an arrangement in which faster learners help teach slower ones. However, before concluding that the differences in performance are the result of social factors alone, we must consider another important distinction: The Japanese children practiced more. They spent more days in school during the year and on average spent more hours doing homework. Interestingly, they were also given longer recesses than U.S. students and had more opportunities to get away from the classroom during a typical school day.

Although the significance of these cultural differences in learning and teaching is not yet clear, the educational community in the United States is paying attention to them. Indeed, psychologists and educators are considering how principles of learning can be applied to improve education (Woolfolk-Hoy, 1999). For example, one study concluded that the most successful educational techniques apply basic principles of operant conditioning, offering positive reinforcement for correct performance and immediate corrective feedback following mistakes (Walberg, 1987).

Can machines help provide such feedback? For decades, psychologists have been working on *teaching machines* that offer automatic, but individualized, programs of

Reciprocal Teaching

Ann Brown and her colleagues (1992) have demonstrated the success of *reciprocal teaching,* in which children take turns actively teaching each other, a technique that closely parallels the cooperative arrangements characteristic of Japanese education.

instruction and rewards for progress (Holland, 1960). The first such machine did little more than present multiple-choice questions in a window area on a rotating drum device. It was not until after B. F. Skinner's machine appeared in 1954 that automated teaching and programmed instruction gained popularity in North American schools (Skinner, 1958). The window area of his device presented course material, with some words left blank. Students read the material, filled in the blanks, then discovered if their responses were correct. Skinner's idea was to use immediate reinforcement to shape correct responses to gradually more difficult tasks while minimizing frustrating errors. Today, computerized teaching machines use the same principle, but they also feature an interactive capability that allows student and computer to "talk" to one another. Using artificial intelligence systems, these new adaptive teaching systems can constantly adjust the level of instruction to meet the needs of each student (Anderson, 1995).

Active Learning

The importance of cognitive processes in learning is apparent in instructional methods that emphasize *active learning* (Bonwell & Eison, 1991). These methods take many forms, including, for example, small-group problem-solving tasks, discussion of "one-minute essays" written in class, use of "thumbs up" or "thumbs down" to indicate agreement or disagreement with the instructor's assertions, and multiple-choice questions that give students feedback about their understanding of the previous fifteen minutes of lecture. There is little doubt that, for many students, the inclusion of active learning experiences makes classes more interesting and enjoyable (Mehta, 1995). Active learning methods also provide immediate reinforcement and help students to go beyond memorizing isolated facts by encouraging them to think more deeply about new information, consider how it relates to what they already know, and apply it in new situations.

The elaborate mental processing associated with active learning makes new information not only more personally meaningful but also easier to remember because of elaborated associative networks. Indeed, active learning strategies have been found to be superior to passive teaching methods in a number of experiments with children and adults (Meyers & Jones, 1993). Consider this simple study of questioning methods in a fifth-grade science class. On some days, the teacher called on only those students whose hands were raised; the rest listened passively. On other days, all students were required to answer every question by holding up a card on which they had written their response. Scores on next-day quizzes and biweekly tests showed that students remembered more of the material covered on the active learning days than on the "passive" days (Gardner, Heward, & Grossi, 1994). Similarly, in two consecutive medical school classes taught by the same instructor, scores on the final exam were significantly higher when students learned mainly through small-group discussions and case studies than mainly through lectures (Chu, 1994). Finally, high school and college students who passively listened to a physics lecture received significantly lower scores on a test of lecture content than did those who participated in a virtual reality lab that allowed them to "interact" actively with the physical forces covered in the lecture (Brelsford, 1993). Results such as these have fueled the popularity of active learning methods, but rigorous experimental research is still needed to compare their short- and long-term effects with those of more traditional methods in the teaching of different kinds of material.

Skill Learning

The complex action sequences, or *skills*, that people learn to perform in everyday life—tying a shoe, opening a door, operating a computer, shooting a basketball, driving a car—develop through direct and vicarious learning processes involving imitation, instructions, reinforcement, and, of course, lots of practice. Some skills, like those of a

Virtual Surgery

Using a virtual reality system called "Surgery in 3-D," this medical student at the University of North Carolina can actively learn and practice eye surgery skills before working with real patients.

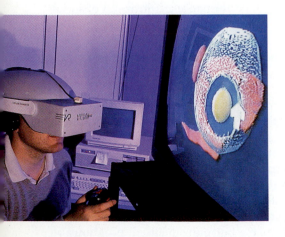

Active Learning

Field trips provide students with firsthand opportunities to see and interact with the things they study in the classroom. These experiences are just one example of the active learning exercises that many teachers offer in addition to lectures and reading assignments as a way of helping students become more deeply involved in the learning process.

basketball player or violinist, demand exceptional perceptual-motor coordination. Others, like those involved in scientific thinking, have a large cognitive component, requiring rapid understanding. In either case, the learning of skills usually involves practice and feedback.

Practice—the repeated performance of a skill—is the most critical component of skill learning (Howe, Davidson, & Sloboda, 1998). For perceptual-motor skills, both physical and mental practice are beneficial (Druckman & Bjork, 1994). To be most effective, practice should continue past the point of correct performance until the skill can be performed automatically, with little or no cognitive attention. For many cognitive skills, what counts most seems to be practice in retrieving relevant information from memory. Trying to recall and write down facts that you have read, for example, is a more effective learning tool than simply reading them a second time—as active learning research would predict.

Large amounts of guidance may produce very good performance during practice, but too much of it may impair later performance (Wickens, 1992). Coaching students about correct responses in math, for example, may impair their ability later to retrieve the correct response from memory on their own. Independent practice at retrieving previously learned responses or information requires more effort, but it is critical for skill development (Ericsson & Charness, 1994; Ericsson, Krampe, & Tesch-Römer, 1993). Indeed, there is little or no evidence to support "sleep learning" or similar schemes designed to make learning effortless (Druckman & Bjork, 1994; Phelps & Exum, 1992). In short, "no pain, no gain."

So the most effective practice is carried out by learners who make independent choices and actions, but what if those choices are wrong? Suppose that a grade schooler starts "flailing" while practicing multiplication tables, coming up with essentially random answers. In this case it is necessary to provide feedback about the correctness of the response. Our discussion of operant conditioning emphasized the importance for learning of prompt feedback in the form of reinforcement or punishment. But certain forms of feedback may not aid skill learning (Schmidt & Bjork, 1992). If given too soon after an action occurs or while it is still taking place, feedback may divert the learner's attention from understanding how that action was achieved and what it felt like to perform it. Similarly, if detailed feedback occurs for virtually everything the learner does, it can have the same negative effects as too much guidance during practice.

Try It This Way

Good coaches provide enough guidance and performance feedback to help budding athletes develop their skills to the fullest, but not so much that the coaching interferes with the learning process. Striking this delicate balance is one of the greatest challenges faced by coaches, and by teachers in general.

LINKAGES

As noted in Chapter 1, all of psychology's many subfields are related to one another. Our discussion of neural networks as possible models of learning illustrates just one way in which the topic of this chapter, learning, is linked to the subfield of perception (Chapter 5). The Linkages diagram shows ties to two other subfields as well, and there are many more ties throughout the book. Looking for linkages among subfields will help you see how they all fit together and better appreciate the big picture that is psychology.

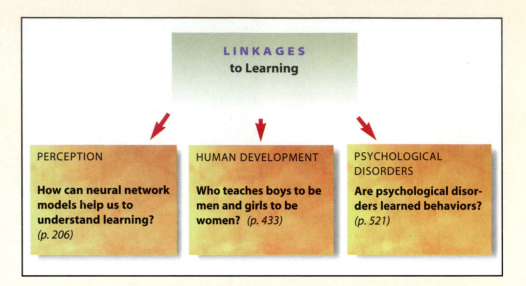

LINKAGES
to Learning

PERCEPTION

How can neural network models help us to understand learning? (p. 206)

HUMAN DEVELOPMENT

Who teaches boys to be men and girls to be women? (p. 433)

PSYCHOLOGICAL DISORDERS

Are psychological disorders learned behaviors? (p. 521)

SUMMARY

Individuals adapt to changes in the environment through the process of *learning,* which is the modification through experience of pre-existing behavior and understanding.

LEARNING ABOUT STIMULI

One kind of learning is *habituation,* which involves adaptation to events that are repeated often. According to Solomon's opponent-process theory, habituation is the result of a relatively automatic, involuntary A-Process and a B-Process that follows and counteracts the A-Process. This theory may help explain drug tolerance and some cases of drug overdose.

CLASSICAL CONDITIONING: LEARNING SIGNALS AND ASSOCIATIONS

Pavlov's Discovery

One form of associative learning is *classical conditioning.* It occurs when a *conditioned stimulus,* or *CS* (such as a tone), is repeatedly paired with an *unconditioned stimulus,* or *UCS* (such as meat powder on a dog's tongue), which naturally brings about an *unconditioned response,* or *UCR* (such as salivation). Eventually the conditioned stimulus will elicit a response, known as the *conditioned response,* or *CR,* even when the unconditioned stimulus is not presented.

Conditioned Responses Over Time: Extinction and Spontaneous Recovery

In general, the strength of a conditioned response grows as CS-UCS pairings continue. If the UCS is no longer paired with the

CS, the conditioned response eventually disappears; this is *extinction.* Following extinction, the conditioned response often reappears if the conditioned stimulus is presented after some time; this is *spontaneous recovery.* In addition, if the conditioned and unconditioned stimuli are paired once or twice after extinction, *reconditioning* occurs; that is, the conditioned response reverts to its original strength.

Stimulus Generalization and Discrimination

Because of *stimulus generalization,* conditioned responses occur to stimuli that are similar but not identical to conditioned stimuli. Generalization is limited by *stimulus discrimination,* which prompts conditioned responses to some stimuli but not to others.

The Signaling of Significant Events

Classical conditioning involves learning that the conditioned stimulus is an event that predicts the occurrence of another event, the unconditioned stimulus. The conditioned response is not just an automatic reflex but a means through which animals and people develop mental models of the relation between events. Classical conditioning works best when the conditioned stimulus precedes the unconditioned stimulus, an arrangement known as forward conditioning. In general, a conditioned response develops best if the interval between the conditioned stimulus and unconditioned stimulus is no more than a second or so. Conditioning is also more likely when the conditioned stimulus reliably signals the unconditioned stimulus. In general, the strength of a conditioned response and the speed of conditioning increase as the intensity of the unconditioned stimulus—and the strength or salience of the conditioned stimulus—increase. The particular conditioned stimulus likely to be linked to a subsequent unconditioned stimulus depends in part on which stimulus was being attended to when the unconditioned stimulus occurred. *Second-order conditioning* occurs when a conditioned stimulus becomes powerful enough to make conditioned stimuli out of stimuli associated with it. Some stimuli are easier to associate than others; organisms seem to be biologically prepared to learn certain associations, as exemplified by taste aversions.

Some Applications of Classical Conditioning

Research suggests that changes in the body's immune response can be classically conditioned. Classical conditioning also plays a role in the development and treatment of phobias and in the humane control of predators in the wild.

OPERANT CONDITIONING: LEARNING THE CONSEQUENCES OF BEHAVIOR

Learning occurs not only through associating stimuli but also through associating behavior with its consequences.

From the Puzzle Box to the Skinner Box

The *law of effect,* postulated by Edward Thorndike, holds that any response that produces satisfaction becomes more likely to occur again and any response that produces discomfort becomes less likely. He called this type of learning *instrumental conditioning.* Skinner called the same basic process *operant conditioning.* In operant conditioning the organism is free to respond at any time, and conditioning is measured by the rate of responding.

Basic Components of Operant Conditioning

An *operant* is a response that has some effect on the world. A *reinforcer* increases the probability that the operant preceding it will occur again; in other words, reinforcers strengthen behavior. There are two types of reinforcers: *positive reinforcers,* which strengthen a response if they are presented after that response occurs, and *negative reinforcers,* which strengthen a response if they are removed after it occurs. *Escape conditioning* results when behavior terminates a negative reinforcer. *Avoidance conditioning* results when behavior prevents or avoids an aversive stimulus; it reflects both classical and operant conditioning. Behaviors learned through avoidance conditioning are highly resistant to extinction. *Punishment* decreases the frequency of a behavior by following it either with an unpleasant stimulus or with the removal of a pleasant one. Punishment modifies behavior but has several drawbacks. It only suppresses behavior; fear of punishment may generalize to the person doing the punishing; it is ineffective when delayed; it can be physically harmful and may teach aggressiveness; and it teaches only what not to do, not what should be done to obtain reinforcement. *Discriminative stimuli* indicate whether reinforcement is available for a particular behavior.

Forming and Strengthening Operant Behavior

Complex responses can be learned through *shaping,* which involves reinforcing successive approximations of the desired response. *Primary reinforcers* are inherently rewarding; *secondary reinforcers* are rewards that people or animals learn to like because of their association with primary reinforcers. In general, operant conditioning proceeds more quickly when the delay in receiving reinforcement is short rather than long, and when the reinforcer is large rather than small. Reinforcement may be delivered on a *continuous reinforcement schedule* or on one of four basic types of *partial,* or *intermittent, reinforcement schedules: fixed ratio (FR), variable ratio (VR), fixed interval (FI),* and *variable interval (VI).* Ratio schedules lead to a rapid rate of responding. Behavior learned through partial reinforcement, particularly through variable schedules, is very resistant to extinction; this phenomenon is called the *partial reinforcement extinction effect.* Partial reinforcement is involved in superstitious behavior, which results when a response is coincidentally followed by a reinforcer.

Why Reinforcers Work

Research suggests that reinforcers are rewarding because they provide an organism with the opportunity to engage in desirable activities, which may change from one situation to the next. Another possibility is that activity in the brain's pleasure centers plays a role in reinforcement.

Operant Conditioning of Human Behavior

The principles of operant conditioning have been used in many spheres of life, including the teaching of everyday social skills, the treatment of sleep disorders, and the improvement of classroom education.

COGNITIVE PROCESSES IN LEARNING

Cognitive processes—how people represent, store, and use information—play an important role in learning.

Learned Helplessness

Learned helplessness appears to result when people believe that their behavior has no effect on the world.

Latent Learning and Cognitive Maps

Both animals and humans display *latent learning.* They also form *cognitive maps* of their environments, even in the absence of any reinforcement for doing so.

Insight and Learning

Experiments on *insight* suggest that cognitive processes and learned strategies also play an important role in learning, perhaps even by animals.

Observational Learning: Learning by Imitation

The process of learning by watching others is called *observational learning,* or social learning. Some observational learning occurs through *vicarious conditioning,* in which one is influenced by seeing or hearing about the consequences of others' behavior. Observational learning is more likely to occur when the person observed is rewarded for the observed behavior. Observational learning is a powerful source of socialization.

USING RESEARCH ON LEARNING TO HELP PEOPLE LEARN

Research on how people learn has implications for improved teaching and for the development of a wide range of skills.

Classrooms Across Cultures

The degree to which learning principles, such as immediate reinforcement and extended practice, are used in teaching varies considerably from culture to culture.

Active Learning

The importance of cognitive processes in learning is seen in active learning methods designed to encourage people to think deeply about and apply new information instead of just memorizing isolated facts.

Skill Learning

Observational learning, practice, and corrective feedback play important roles in the learning of skills.

KEY TERMS

avoidance conditioning (187)
classical conditioning (178)
cognitive map (200)
conditioned response (CR) (178)
conditioned stimulus (CS) (178)
continuous reinforcement schedule (192)
discriminative stimuli (190)
escape conditioning (187)
extinction (179)
fixed-interval (FI) schedules (193)

fixed-ratio (FR) schedules (192)
habituation (176)
insight (201)
instrumental conditioning (185)
intermittent reinforcement schedule (192)
latent learning (200)
law of effect (185)
learned helplessness (198)
learning (175)
negative reinforcers (186)
observational learning (202)
operant (186)

operant conditioning (186)
partial reinforcement extinction effect (194)
partial reinforcement schedule (192)
positive reinforcers (186)
primary reinforcers (191)
punishment (188)
reconditioning (179)
reinforcer (186)
secondary reinforcer (191)
second-order conditioning (181)
shaping (191)
spontaneous recovery (179)

stimulus discrimination (180)
stimulus generalization (179)
unconditioned response (UCR) (178)
unconditioned stimulus (UCS) (178)
variable-interval (VI) schedules (193)
variable-ratio (VR) schedules (192)
vicarious conditioning (202)

7

Memory

Several years ago an air-traffic controller at Los Angeles International Airport cleared a US Airways flight to land on runway 24L. A couple of minutes later, the US Airways pilot radioed the control tower that he was on approach for runway 24L, but the controller did not reply because she was preoccupied by a confusing exchange with another pilot. After finishing that conversation, the controller told a Sky West commuter pilot to taxi onto runway 24L for takeoff, completely forgetting about the US Airways flight that was about to land on the same runway. The US Airways jet hit the commuter plane, killing thirty-four people. The controller's forgetting was so complete that she assumed the fireball from the crash was an exploding bomb. How could the controller's memory have failed her at such a crucial time?

Memory is full of paradoxes. It is common, for example, for people to remember the name of their first-grade teacher but not the name of someone they met just a minute ago. And consider Rajan Mahadevan. He once set a world's record by reciting from memory the first 31,811 places of pi (the ratio of the circumference of a circle to its diameter), but on repeated visits to the psychology building at the University of Minnesota, he had trouble recalling the location of the nearest restroom (Biederman et al., 1992). Like perception, memory is selective. Whereas people retain a great deal of information, they also lose a great deal (Bjork & Vanhuele, 1992).

Memory plays a critical role in your life. Without memory, you would not know how to shut off your alarm clock, take a shower, get dressed, or recognize objects. You would be unable to communicate with other people because you would not remember what words mean, or even what you had just said. You would be unaware of your own likes and dislikes, and you would have no idea of who you are in any meaningful sense (Kihlstrom, 1993). In this chapter we describe what is known about both memory and forgetting. First, we discuss what memory is—the different kinds of memory and the different ways we remember things. Then we examine how new memories are acquired and later recalled, and why they are sometimes forgotten. We continue with a discussion of the biological bases of memory, and we conclude with some practical advice for improving memory and studying skills.

THE NATURE OF MEMORY

Mathematician John Griffith estimated that, in an average lifetime, a person will have stored roughly five hundred times as much information as can be found in all the volumes of the *Encyclopedia Britannica* (Hunt, 1982). The impressive capacity of human memory depends on the operation of a complex mental system (Schacter, 1999).

Basic Memory Processes

We know a psychologist who sometimes drives to work and sometimes walks. On one occasion, he drove, forgot that he had driven, and walked home. When he failed to find his car in its normal spot the next morning, he reported the car stolen. The police soon called to say that "some college kids" had probably stolen the car because it was found on campus (next to the psychology building!). What went wrong? There are several possibilities, because memory depends on three basic processes—encoding, storage, and retrieval (see Figure 7.1).

First, information must be put into memory, a step that requires encoding. Just as incoming sensory information must be coded so that it can be communicated to the brain, information to be remembered must be put in a form that the memory system can accept and use. In the memory system, sensory information is put into various memory codes, which are mental representations of physical stimuli. Imagine that you see a billboard that reads "Huey's Going Out of Business Sale," and you want to remember it so you can take advantage of the sale later. If you encode the sound of the words as if they had been spoken, you are using acoustic encoding, and the information is represented in your memory as a sequence of sounds. If you encode the image of the letters as they were arranged on the sign, you are using visual encoding, and the

Drawing on Memories

The human memory system allows people to encode, store, and retrieve a lifetime of experiences. Without it, you would have no sense of who you are.

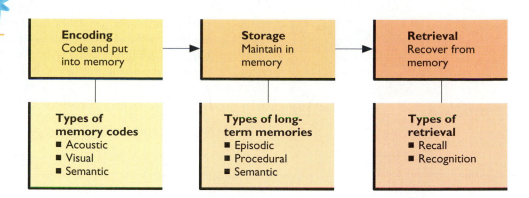

FIGURE 7.1

Basic Memory Processes

Remembering something requires, first, that the item be encoded—put in a form that can be placed in memory. It must then be stored and, finally, retrieved, or recovered. If any of these processes fails, forgetting will occur.

information is represented in your memory as a picture. Finally, if you encode the fact that you saw an ad for Huey's, you are using semantic encoding, and the information is represented in your memory by its general meaning. The type of encoding used can influence what is remembered. For example, semantic encoding might allow you to remember that a car was parked in your neighbors' driveway just before their house was robbed. If there was little or no other encoding, however, you might not be able to remember the make, model, or color of the car.

The second basic memory process is storage, which refers to the maintenance of information over time, often over a very long time. When you find it possible to use a pogo stick or to recall a vacation from many years ago, you are depending on the storage capacity of your memory.

The third process, retrieval, occurs when you locate information stored in memory and bring it into consciousness. Retrieving stored information such as your address or telephone number is usually so fast and effortless that it seems automatic. Only when you try to retrieve other kinds of information—such as the answer to a quiz question that you know but cannot quite recall—do you become aware of the searching process. Retrieval processes include both recall and recognition. To *recall* information, as on an essay test, you have to retrieve it from memory without much help. *Recognition* is retrieval aided by clues, such as the alternatives given in a multiple-choice test item. Accordingly, recognition tends to be easier than recall.

Types of Memory

When was the last time you made a credit card purchase? What part of speech is used to modify a noun? How do you keep your balance when you are skiing? To answer these questions, you must use your memory. However, each may require a different type of memory (Brewer & Pani, 1984). To answer the first question, you must remember a particular event in your life; to answer the second one, you must recall a piece of general knowledge that is unlikely to be tied to a specific event. And the answer to the final question is difficult to put into words but appears in the form of your remembered actions when you get up on skis. How many types of memory are there? No one is sure, but most research suggests that there are at least three basic types. Each is named for the kind of information it handles (Reed, 1992).

Memory of a specific event that happened while you were present—that is, during an "episode" in your life—is called episodic memory. Examples are what you had for dinner yesterday, what you did last summer, or where you were last Friday night. Generalized knowledge of the world that does not involve memory of a specific event is called semantic memory. For instance, you can answer a question like "Are wrenches pets or tools?" without remembering any specific event in which you learned that wrenches are tools. As a general rule, people convey episodic memories by saying, "I remember when . . . ," whereas they convey semantic memories by saying, "I know that . . ." (Tulving, 1982). Finally, memory of how to do things, such as skiing without falling (and riding a bike, reading a map, tying a shoelace), is called procedural memory. Often, procedural memory consists of a complicated sequence of

movements that cannot be described adequately in words. For example, a gymnast might find it impossible to describe the exact motions in a particular routine.

Many activities require all three types of memory. Consider the game of tennis. Knowing the official rules or how many sets are needed to win a match involves semantic memory. Remembering which side served last requires episodic memory. Knowing how to lob or volley involves procedural memory.

Explicit and Implicit Memory

Memory can also be categorized in terms of its effects on thoughts and behaviors. For example, you make use of explicit memory when you deliberately try to remember something and are consciously aware of doing so (Masson & MacLeod, 1992). Let's say that someone asks you about your last vacation; as you attempt to remember where you went, you would be using explicit memory to recall this episode from your past. Similarly, if you have to answer a question on an examination, you would be using explicit memory to retrieve the information needed to give a correct answer. In contrast, implicit memory is the unintentional recollection and influence of prior experiences (Nelson, 1999). For example, while watching a movie about a long car trip, you might begin to feel tense because you subconsciously recall the time you had engine trouble on such a trip. But you are not aware that it is this memory that is making you tense. Implicit memory operates automatically and without conscious effort. As another example, perhaps you've found yourself disliking someone you just met, but didn't know why. One explanation is that implicit memory may have been at work. Specifically, you may have reacted in this way because the person bears a resemblance to someone from your past who treated you badly. In such instances, people are usually unable to recall the person from the past and, indeed, are unaware of any connection between the two individuals (Lewicki, 1985). Episodic, semantic, and procedural memories can be explicit or implicit, but procedural memory usually operates implicitly. This is why, for example, you can skillfully ride a bike even though you cannot explicitly remember all the procedures necessary to do so.

It is not surprising that experience affects how people behave. What is surprising is that they are often unaware that their actions have been influenced by previous events. Because some influential events cannot be recalled even when people try to do so, implicit memory has been said to involve "retention without remembering" (Roediger, 1990).

LINKAGES

Learning By Doing

Procedural memories involve skills that can usually be learned only through repetition. This is why parents not only tell children how to tie a shoe but also show them the steps and then let them practice. Factors that enhance skill learning are described in Chapter 6.

FOCUS ON RESEARCH METHODS

Measuring Explicit Versus Implicit Memory

In Canada, Endel Tulving and his colleagues undertook a series of experiments to map the differences between explicit and implicit memory (Tulving, Schacter, & Stark, 1982).

■ What was the researcher's question?

Tulving knew he could measure explicit memory by giving a recognition test in which participants simply said which words on a list they remembered seeing on a previous list. The question was, How would it be possible to measure implicit memory?

■ How did the researcher answer the question?

First, Tulving asked the participants in his experiment to study a long list of words—the "study list." An hour later, they took a recognition test involving explicit memory—saying which words on a new list had been on the original study list. Then, to test their implicit memory, Tulving asked them to perform a "fragment completion" task (Warrington & Weiskrantz, 1970). In this task, participants were shown a "test list" of word fragments, such as *d–l—iu–*, and asked to complete the word (in this case, *delir-*

Making Implicit Memories

By the time they reach adulthood, these boys may have no explicit memories of the interactions they had in early childhood with friends from differing ethnic groups, but research suggests that their implicit memories of such experiences could have an unconscious effect on their attitudes toward and judgments about members of those groups.

FIGURE 7.2

Measures of Explicit and Implicit Memory

This experiment showed that the passage of time greatly affected people's recognition (explicit memory) of a word list but left fragment completion (implicit memory) essentially intact. Results such as these suggest that explicit and implicit memory may be different memory systems.

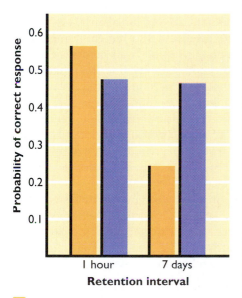

Recognition (explicit)

Fragment completion (implicit)

Source: Tulving, Schacter, & Stark, 1982.

ium). On the basis of *priming* studies such as those described in Chapter 9, Tulving assumed that memory from a previous exposure to the correct word would improve the participants' ability to complete the fragment, even if they were unable to consciously recall having seen the word before. A week later, all participants took a second test of their explicit memory (recognition) and implicit memory (fragment completion) of the study list. Some of the words on this second test list had been on the original study list, but none had been used in the first set of memory tests. The independent variable in this experiment, then, was the amount of time that elapsed since the participants read the study list (one hour versus one week), and the dependent variable was performance on each of the two types of memory tests, explicit and implicit.

■ What did the researcher find?

As shown in Figure 7.2, explicit memory for the study list decreased dramatically over time, but implicit memory was virtually unchanged. Results from several other experiments also show that the passage of time affects one type of memory but not the other (Komatsu & Naito, 1992; Mitchell, 1991). For example, it appears that the aging process has fewer negative effects on implicit memory than on explicit memory (Light, 1991).

■ What do the results mean?

The work of Tulving and others supports the idea of a dissociation, or independence, between explicit and implicit memory, suggesting that the two may operate on different principles (Gabrieli et al., 1995). Indeed, some researchers believe that explicit and implicit memory may involve the activity of distinct neural systems in the brain (Squire, 1987; Tulving & Schacter, 1990).

■ What do we still need to know?

Psychologists are now studying the role of implicit memory (and dissociations between explicit and implicit memory) in such important psychological phenomena as amnesia (Schacter, Church, & Treadwell, 1994; Tulving, 1993), depression (Elliott & Greene, 1992), problem solving (Jacoby, Marriott, & Collins, 1990), prejudice and stereotyping (Fiske, 1998), the development of self-concept in childhood (Nelson, 1993), and even the power of ads to associate brand names with good feelings (Duke & Carlson, 1993). The results of these studies should shed new light on implicit memory and how it operates in the real world.

While some researchers claim that implicit memory and explicit memory involve different structures in the brain (Schacter, 1992; Squire, 1987; Tulving & Schacter, 1990), others argue that the two types of memory entail different cognitive processes (Nelson, McKinney, & Bennett, in press; Roediger, Guynn, & Jones, 1995). Indeed, some social psychologists are trying to determine whether consciously held attitudes are independent of *implicit social cognitions*—past experiences that unconsciously influence a person's judgments about a group of people (Greenwald & Banaji, 1995). A case in point would be a person whose explicit thoughts about members of some ethnic group are positive but whose implicit thoughts are negative. Early work on implicit memory for stereotypes seemed to indicate that explicit and implicit stereotypes are indeed independent (Devine, 1989), but more recent research suggests that they are to some extent related (Lepore & Brown, 1997). Further research is needed to determine what mechanisms are responsible for implicit versus explicit memory and how they are related to one another (Nelson et al., in press).

Models of Memory

People remember some information far better and longer than other information. For example, suppose your friends throw a surprise party for you. Upon entering the room, you might barely notice, and later fail to recall, the flash from a camera. And you might forget in a few seconds the name of a person you met at the party. But if you live to be a hundred, you will never forget where the party took place or how surprised and pleased you were. Why do some stimuli leave no more than a fleeting impression and others remain in memory forever? In the following sections we examine four theoretical models of memory, each of which provides an explanation for this phenomenon.

Levels of Processing   The levels-of-processing model suggests that the most important determinant of memory is how extensively information is encoded or processed when it is first received. Consider situations in which people try to memorize something by mentally rehearsing it. There appear to be two basic types of mental rehearsal: maintenance and elaborative. Maintenance rehearsal involves simply repeating an item over and over. This method can be effective for remembering information for a short time. If you need to look up a phone number, walk across the room, and then dial the number, maintenance rehearsal would work just fine. But what if you need to remember something for hours or months or years? Far more effective in these cases is elaborative rehearsal, which involves thinking about how new material relates to information already stored in memory. For example, instead of trying to remember a new person's name by simply repeating it to yourself, try thinking about how the name is related to something you already know. If you are introduced to a man named Jim Crews, you might think, "He is as tall as my Uncle Jim, who always wears a crew cut."

Study after study has shown that memory is enhanced when people use elaborative rather than maintenance rehearsal (Anderson, 1990b). According to the levels-of-processing model, this enhancement occurs because of the degree or "depth" to which incoming information is mentally processed during elaborative rehearsal. The more you think about new information, organize it, and relate it to existing knowledge, the "deeper" the processing, and the better your memory of it becomes.

Transfer-Appropriate Processing   Level of processing is not the only factor affecting what we remember (Baddeley, 1992). The transfer-appropriate processing model suggests that a critical determinant of memory is how well the encoding process matches up with what is ultimately retrieved. Consider an experiment in which people

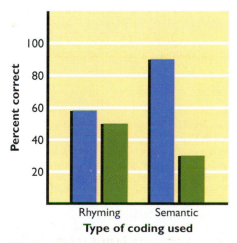

FIGURE 7.3

The Match Between Encoding and Retrieval

People who were asked to recognize words seen earlier did better if they had encoded the words on the basis of their meaning (semantic coding) rather than on the basis of what they rhymed with. But if asked to identify words that *rhymed* with those seen before, they did better on those that had been encoded using a rhyming code. These results support the transfer-appropriate processing model of memory.

were shown a series of sentences with one word missing and were then asked one of two types of questions about the missing word (Morris, Bransford, & Franks, 1977). Some questions were designed so that participants would use a semantic (meaning) code for the target word. For example, one sentence read "A _____ is a building" and participants were asked whether the target word *house* should go in the blank space. Other questions were designed to elicit a rhyming code, as when participants were shown the sentence "_____ rhymes with *legal*" and asked whether the target word *eagle* rhymed with *legal*.

Later, the participants were given two kinds of memory tasks. On one task, they were asked to select from a list the target words they had been shown earlier. As Figure 7.3 shows, the participants did much better at recognizing the words for which they had used a semantic code rather than a rhyming code. But on the other task, in which they were asked to pick out words that *rhymed* with the ones they had seen (e.g., *grouse*, which rhymes with *house*), they did much better at identifying words that rhymed with those for which they had used a rhyming code rather than a semantic code. Results like these inspired the concept of *transfer-appropriate processing*, which suggests that our memory is better when the encoding process matches up with what we are trying to retrieve.

Parallel Distributed Processing   Still another approach to memory is based on parallel distributed processing (PDP) models of memory (Rumelhart & McClelland, 1986). These models suggest that new experiences don't just provide new facts that are

FIGURE 7.4

The Three Stages of Memory

This traditional information-processing model analyzes the memory system into three stages.

later retrieved individually; they also become integrated with people's existing knowledge or memories, changing their overall knowledge base and altering in a more general way their understanding of the world and how it operates. For example, if you compare your knowledge of college life today with what it was when you first arrived, chances are it has changed day by day in a way that is much more general than any single new fact you learned.

PDP memory theorists begin by asking how neural networks might provide a functional memory system (Anderson, 1990b). We describe the essential features of neural networks in Chapters 5 and 6, on perception and learning. In the case of memory, each unit of knowledge is ultimately connected to every other unit, and the connections between units become stronger as they are experienced together more frequently. From this perspective, then, "knowledge" is distributed across a dense network of associations. When this network is activated, *parallel processing* occurs; that is, different portions of the network operate simultaneously, allowing people to quickly and efficiently draw inferences and make generalizations. Just seeing the word *sofa*, for example, allows us immediately to gain access to knowledge about what a sofa looks like, what it is used for, where it tends to be located, who might buy one, and the like.

Information Processing   Historically, the most influential and comprehensive theories of memory have been based on a general information-processing model (Roediger, 1990). The information-processing model originally suggested that in order for information to become firmly embedded in memory, it must pass through three stages of mental processing: sensory memory, short-term memory, and long-term memory (Atkinson & Shiffrin, 1968; see Figure 7.4).

In *sensory memory*, information from the senses—sights or sounds, for example—is held in *sensory registers* for a very brief period of time, often less than one second. Information in the sensory registers may be attended to, analyzed, and encoded as a meaningful pattern; this is the process of *perception*. If the information in sensory memory is perceived, it can enter *short-term memory*. If nothing further is done, the information will disappear in about eighteen seconds. But if the information in short-term memory is further processed, it may be encoded into *long-term memory*, where it may remain indefinitely.

Contemporary versions of the information-processing model emphasize the constant interactions among sensory, short-term, and long-term memory (Massaro & Cowan, 1993). For example, sensory memory can be thought of as that part of one's knowledge base (or long-term memory) that is momentarily activated by information

FIGURE 7.5

The Role of Memory in Comprehension

Read the passage shown here, then turn away and try to recall as much of it as possible. Then read the footnote on page 222 and reread the passage. The second reading probably made a lot more sense and was much easier to remember because knowing the title of the passage allowed you to retrieve from long-term memory your knowledge about the topic (Bransford & Johnson, 1972).

> The procedure is actually quite simple. First, you arrange items into different groups. Of course, one pile may be sufficient, depending on how much there is to do. If you have to go somewhere else due to lack of facilities that is the next step; otherwise, you are pretty well set. It is important not to overdo things. That is, it is better to do too few things at once than too many. In the short run, this may not seem important, but complications can easily arise. A mistake can be expensive as well. At first, the whole procedure will seem complicated. Soon, however, it will become just another facet of life. It is difficult to foresee any end to the necessity for this task in the immediate future, but then, one never can tell. After the procedure is completed, one arranges the materials into different groups again. Then they can be put into their appropriate places. Eventually they will be used once more, and the whole cycle will then have to be repeated. However, that is part of life.

in review

MODELS OF MEMORY	
Model	**Assumptions**
Levels of processing	The more deeply material is processed, the better the memory of it.
Transfer-appropriate processing	Retrieval is improved when we try to recall material in a way that matches how the material was encoded.
Parallel distributed processing (PDP)	New experiences add to and alter our overall knowledge base; they are not separate, unconnected facts. PDP networks allow us to draw inferences and make generalizations about the world.
Information processing	Information is processed in three stages: sensory, short-term, and long-term memory.

sent to the brain via the sensory nerves. And short-term memory can be thought of as that part of one's knowledge base that is the focus of attention at any given moment. Like perception, memory is an active process, and what is already in long-term memory influences how new information is encoded (Cowan, 1988). To understand this interaction better, try the exercise in Figure 7.5.

For a summary of the four models we have discussed, see "In Review: Models of Memory." Each of these models provides an explanation of why we remember some things and forget others, but which one offers the best explanation? The answer is that more than one model may be required to understand memory. Just as it is helpful for physicists to characterize light in terms of both waves and particles, psychologists find it useful to think of memory as both a serial or sequential process, as suggested by the information-processing model, and a parallel process, as suggested by parallel distributed processing models.

ACQUIRING NEW MEMORIES

The information-processing model suggests that sensory, short-term, and long-term memory each provide a different type of storage system.

Sensory Memory

In order to recognize incoming stimuli, the brain must analyze and compare them to what is already stored in long-term memory. Although this process is very quick, it still takes time. The major function of sensory memory is to hold information long enough for it to be processed further. This maintenance is the job of the sensory registers, whose storage capability retains an almost complete representation of a sensory stimulus (Best, 1992). There is a separate register for each of the five senses, and every register is capable of storing a relatively large amount of stimulus information.

Memories held in the sensory registers are fleeting, but they last long enough for stimulus identification to begin (Eysenck & Keane, 1995). As you read a sentence, for example, you identify and interpret the first few words. At the same time, subsequent words are being scanned, and these are maintained in your visual sensory register until you can process them as well.

In many ways, sensory memory brings coherence and continuity to the world. To appreciate this fact, turn your head slowly from left to right. Although your eyes may seem to be moving smoothly, like a movie camera scanning a scene, this is not what happens. Your eyes fixate at one point for about one-fourth of a second and then rapidly jump to a new position. The sensation of smoothness occurs because the scene is held in the visual sensory register until your eyes fixate again. Similarly, when you listen to someone speak, the auditory sensory register allows you to experience a smooth flow of information. Information persists for varying amounts of time in the five sensory registers. For example, information in the auditory sensory register lasts longer than information in the visual sensory register. This difference probably reflects humans' adaptation to a world in which visual images can often be looked at again if necessary, whereas sounds tend to be one-time occurrences that may be lost forever if not stored a bit longer.

The fact that sensory memories quickly fade if they are not processed further is another adaptive characteristic of the memory system (Martindale, 1991). One simply cannot deal with all of the sights, sounds, odors, tastes, and tactile sensations that impinge on the sense organs at any given moment. As mentioned in Chapter 5, selective attention focuses mental resources on only part of the stimulus field, thus controlling what information is processed further. Indeed, it is through perception that the elusive impressions of sensory memory are captured and transferred to short-term memory.

Short-Term, or Working, Memory

The sensory registers allow your memory system to develop a representation of a stimulus, but they do not allow the more thorough representation and analysis needed if the information is going to be used in some way. These functions are accomplished by short-term memory (STM), the part of our memory system that stores limited amounts of information for up to about eighteen seconds. When you check *TV Guide* for the channel number of a show and then switch to that channel, you are using short-term memory.

Once viewed mainly as a temporary storehouse for information, short-term memory is now recognized as a more complex operation that serves a number of purposes. Accordingly, many researchers refer to STM as **working memory** because it enables people to do much of their mental work, from dialing a phone number to solving a complex math problem (Baddeley, 1992). Suppose, for example, you are buying something for 83 cents. You go through your change and pick out two quarters, two dimes, two nickels, and three pennies. To do this you must remember the price, retrieve the rules of addition from long-term memory, and keep a running count of how much change you have so far. Alternatively, try to recall how many windows there are on the front of the house or apartment where you grew up. In attempting to answer this question, you probably formed a mental image of the building, which required one kind of working-memory process, and then, while maintaining that image in your mind, you "worked" on it by counting the windows.

In other words, more is involved in short-term memory than just storing information. In fact, some researchers view STM as one part of a more elaborate working-memory system whose components function together on a semi-independent basis (Baddeley & Hitch, 1974).

Encoding in Short-Term Memory   The encoding of information in short-term memory is much more elaborative and varied than that in the sensory registers (Brandimonte, Hitch, & Bishop, 1992). Often, *acoustic encoding* seems to dominate. Evidence in support of this assertion comes from an analysis of the mistakes people make when encoding information in short-term memory. These mistakes tend to be acoustically related, which means that they involve the substitution of similar sounds. For example, Robert Conrad (1964) showed people strings of letters and asked them to repeat the letters immediately. Their mistakes tended to involve replacing the correct letter—say, *C*—with another that sounded like it, such as *D, P,* or *T*. These mistakes occurred even though the letters were presented visually, without any sound.

Note: The title of the passage on page 220 is "Washing Clothes."

FIGURE 7.6

Capacity of Short-Term Memory

Here is a test of your immediate, or short-term, memory span. Ask someone to read to you the numbers in the top row at the rate of about one per second; then try to repeat them back in the same order. Then try the next row, and the one after that, until you make a mistake. Your immediate memory span is the maximum number of items you can repeat back perfectly. Similar tests can be performed using the rows of letters and words.

```
9 2 5                      G M N
8 6 4 2                    S L R R
3 7 6 5 4                  V O E P G
6 2 7 4 1 8                X W D X Q O
0 4 0 1 4 7 3              E P H H J A E
1 9 2 2 3 5 3 0            Z D O F W D S V
4 8 6 8 5 4 3 3 2          D T Y N R H E H Q
2 5 3 1 9 7 1 7 6 8        K H W D A G R O F Z
8 5 1 2 9 6 1 9 4 5 0      U D F F W H D Q D G E
9 1 8 5 4 6 9 4 2 9 3 7    Q M R H X Z D P R R E H
```

CAT BOAT RUG
RUN BEACH PLANT LIGHT
SUIT WATCH CUT STAIRS CAR
JUNK LONE GAME CALL WOOD HEART
FRAME PATCH CROSS DRUG DESK HORSE LAW
CLOTHES CHOOSE GIFT DRIVE BOOK TREE HAIR THIS
DRESS CLERK FILM BASE SPEND SERVE BOOK LOW TIME
STONE ALL NAIL DOOR HOPE EARL FEEL BUY COPE GRAPE
AGE SOFT FALL STORE PUT TRUE SMALL FREE CHECK MAIL LEAF
LOG DAY TIME CHESS LAKE CUT BIRD SHEET YOUR SEE STREET WHEEL

Visual as well as acoustic codes are used in short-term memory (Zhang & Simon, 1985). However, information that is coded visually tends to fade much more quickly (Cornoldi, DeBeni, & Baldi, 1989).

Storage Capacity of Short-Term Memory You can easily determine the capacity of short-term memory by conducting the simple experiment shown in Figure 7.6 (Howard, 1983). The maximum number of items you are able to recall perfectly after one presentation is called your **immediate memory span**. If your memory span is like most people's, you can repeat about six or seven items from the test in this figure. The interesting thing is that you should come up with about the same number whether you estimate your immediate memory span with digits, letters, words, or virtually any type of unit (Pollack, 1953). When George Miller (1956) noticed that studies of a wide variety of tasks showed the same limit on the ability to process information, he pointed out that the limit seems to be a "magic number" of seven plus or minus two. This is the capacity of short-term memory. In addition, the "magic number" refers not to a certain number of discrete elements but to the number of meaningful *groupings* of information, called **chunks**.

To see the difference between discrete elements and chunks, read the following letters to a friend, pausing at each dash: *MT-VVC-RC-IAU-SAB-MW*. The chances are that your friend will not be able to repeat this string of letters perfectly. Why? There are fifteen letters, a total that exceeds most people's immediate memory span. But if you read the letters so that they are grouped as *MTV-VCR-CIA-USA-BMW*, your friend will probably repeat the string easily (Bower, 1975). Although the same fifteen letters are involved, they will be processed as only five meaningful chunks of information.

The Power of Chunking Chunks of information can become very complex. If someone read to you, "The boy in the red shirt kicked his mother in the shin," you could probably repeat the sentence very easily. Yet it contains twelve words and forty-three letters. How can you repeat the sentence so effortlessly? The answer is that people can build bigger and bigger chunks of information (Ericsson & Staszewski, 1989). In this case, you might represent "the boy in the red shirt" as one chunk of information rather than as six words or nineteen letters. Similarly, "kicked his mother" and "in the shin" represent separate chunks of information.

Chunking in Action

Those who provide instantaneous translation during international negotiations must store long, often complicated segments of speech in short-term memory while searching long-term memory for the equivalent second-language expressions. The task is made easier by chunking the speaker's words into phrases and sentences.

Learning to use bigger and bigger chunks of information can enhance short-term memory. Children's memories improve in part because they gradually become able to hold as many as seven chunks in memory, but also because they become better able to group information into chunks (Servan-Schreiber & Anderson, 1990). Adults, too, can greatly increase the capacity of their short-term memory by more appropriate chunking (Waldrop, 1987); one man increased his immediate memory span to approximately one hundred items (Chase & Ericsson, 1981). In short, although the capacity of short-term memory is more or less constant—five to nine chunks of meaningful information—the size of those chunks can vary tremendously.

Duration of Short-Term Memory   Imagine what life would be like if you kept remembering every phone number you ever dialed or every conversation you ever heard. This does not happen because most people usually forget information in short-term memory quickly unless they continue repeating it to themselves (through maintenance rehearsal). You may have experienced this adaptive, though sometimes inconvenient, phenomenon if you have ever been interrupted while repeating to yourself a new phone number you were about to dial, and then couldn't recall the number.

How long does unrehearsed information remain in short-term memory? To answer this question, John Brown (1958) and Lloyd and Margaret Peterson (1959) devised the **Brown-Peterson procedure**, which is a method for preventing rehearsal. A person is presented with a group of three letters, such as *GRB*, and then counts backward by threes from some number until a signal is given. Counting prevents the person from rehearsing the letters. At the signal, the person stops counting and tries to recall the letters. By varying the number of seconds that the person counts backward, the experimenter can determine how much forgetting takes place over a certain amount of time. As you can see in Figure 7.7, information in short-term memory is forgotten gradually but rapidly: After eighteen seconds, participants can remember almost nothing. Evidence from these and other experiments suggests that *unrehearsed* information can be maintained in short-term memory for no more than about eighteen seconds.

Long-Term Memory

Short-term, or working, memory holds information so briefly that it is not what people usually have in mind when they talk about memory. Usually, they are thinking about **long-term memory** (LTM), which we now consider.

Encoding in Long-Term Memory   Some information is encoded into long-term memory automatically, without any conscious attempt to memorize it (Ellis, 1991). However, encoding information into long-term memory is often the result of a relatively deep level of conscious processing, which usually involves some degree of *seman-*

FIGURE 7.7

Forgetting in Short-Term Memory

This graph shows the percentage of nonsense syllables recalled after various intervals during which rehearsal was prevented. Notice that virtually complete forgetting occurred after a delay of eighteen seconds.

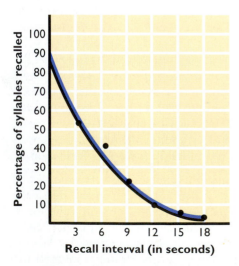

Source: Data from Peterson & Peterson, 1959.

FIGURE 7.8

Encoding into Long-Term Memory

Which is the correct image of a U.S. penny? (See page 226 for the answer.)

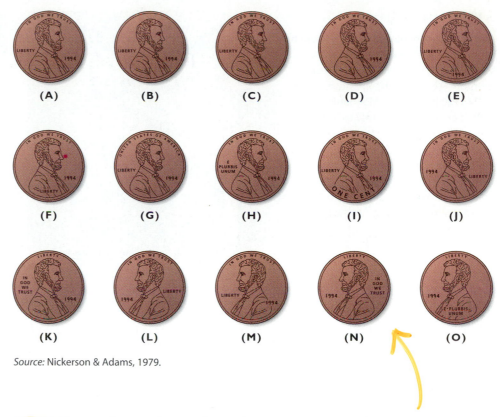

Source: Nickerson & Adams, 1979.

tic encoding. In other words, encoding in long-term memory often ignores details and instead encodes the general, underlying meaning of the information.

The dominance of semantic encoding in long-term memory was demonstrated in a classic study by Jacqueline Sachs (1967). First, people listened to tape-recorded passages. Then Sachs gave them sentences and asked whether each exact sentence had been in the taped passage. People did very well when they were tested immediately (using mainly short-term memory). However, after only twenty-seven seconds, at which point the information had to be retrieved from long-term memory, they could not determine which of two sentences they had heard if both sentences expressed the same meaning. For example, they could not determine whether they had heard "He sent a letter about it to Galileo, the great Italian scientist" or "A letter about it was sent to Galileo, the great Italian scientist." In short, they remembered the general meaning of what they had heard, but not the exact wording.

Counterfeiters depend on the fact that people encode the general meaning of visual stimuli rather than specific details. For example, look at Figure 7.8 and find the correct drawing of the United States penny (Nickerson & Adams, 1979). Most people from the United States are unsuccessful at this task, just as people from Great Britain do poorly at recognizing their country's coins (Jones, 1990). This finding helps explain why the United States Treasury has begun using more distinctive drawings on the paper currencies it distributes.

Long-term memory normally involves semantic encoding, but people can also use visual encoding to process images into long-term memory. In one study, people viewed 2,500 pictures. Although it took sixteen hours just to present the stimuli, the participants later correctly recognized more than 90 percent of the pictures tested (Standing, Conezio, & Haber, 1970). One reason pictures are remembered so well is that these stimuli may be represented in terms of both a visual code and a semantic code. *Dual coding* theory suggests that information is remembered better when it is represented in both codes rather than in only one (Paivio, 1986).

Storage Capacity of Long-Term Memory Whereas the capacity of short-term memory is limited, the capacity of long-term memory is extremely large; most theorists believe it is literally unlimited (Matlin, 1998). It is impossible to prove this, but

A Photographic Memory

Franco Magnani had been away from his hometown in Italy for more than 30 years, but he could still paint it from memory (see comparison photo; Sacks, 1992). People like Mr. Magnani display *eidetic imagery,* commonly called *photographic memory;* they have automatic, detailed, and vivid images of virtually everything they have ever seen. About 5 percent of all school-age children have eidetic imagery, but almost no adults have it (Haber, 1979; Merritt, 1979).

Drawing (A) shows the correct penny image in Figure 7.8.

there are no cases of people being unable to learn something new because they had too much information stored in long-term memory. We know for sure that people store vast quantities of information in long-term memory, and that they often remember it remarkably well for long periods of time. For example, people are amazingly accurate at recognizing the faces of their high school classmates after not having seen them for over twenty-five years (Bruck, Cavanagh, & Ceci, 1991), and they do surprisingly well on tests of a foreign language or high school algebra fifty years after having formally studied these subjects (Bahrick & Hall, 1991; Bahrick et al., 1994). However, long-term memories are sometimes subject to distortion. In one study, college students were asked to recall their high-school grades. Even though the students were motivated to be accurate, they correctly remembered 89 percent of their "A" grades but only 29 percent of their "D" grades. And, perhaps not surprisingly, when they made errors, these usually involved recalling grades as being higher than they actually were (Bahrick, Hall, & Berger, 1996).

Distinguishing Between Short-Term and Long-Term Memory

Some psychologists believe that there is no need to distinguish between short-term and long-term memory: What people call short-term, or working, memory is simply that part of memory that they happen to be thinking about at any particular time, whereas long-term memory is the part of memory that they are not thinking about at any given moment. However, other psychologists argue that short-term and long-term memory are qualitatively different, that they obey different laws (Cowan, 1988). Determining whether short-term and long-term memory are functionally separate has become one of the most important topics in memory research. Evidence that information is transferred from short-term memory to a distinct storage system comes from experiments on recall.

Experiments on Recall   To conduct your own recall experiment, look at the following list of words for thirty seconds, then look away and write down as many of the words as you can, in any order: *bed, rest, quilt, dream, sheet, mattress, pillow, night, snore, pajamas.* Which words you recall depends in part on their *serial position*—that is, on where the words are in the list, as Figure 7.9 shows. This figure is a *serial-position curve,* which shows the chances of recalling words appearing in each position in a list. For the first two or three words in a list, recall tends to be very good, a characteristic

FIGURE 7.9

A Serial-Position Curve

The probability of recalling an item is plotted here as a function of its serial position in a list of items. Generally, the first several items and the last several items are most likely to be recalled.

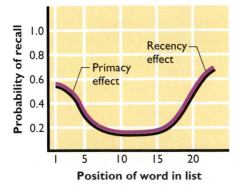

that is called the **primacy effect**. The probability of recall decreases for words in the middle of the list and then rises dramatically for the last few words. The ease of recalling words near the end of a list is called the **recency effect**. It has been suggested that the primacy effect reflects rehearsal that puts early words into *long-term memory*, and that the recency effect occurs because the last few words are still in *short-term memory* when we try to recall the list (Glanzer & Kunitz, 1966; Koppenaal & Glanzer, 1990).

K. Anders Ericsson and Walter Kintsch (1995) have proposed another way of thinking about the relationship between short-term and long-term memory. Studies of people who display unusually good memory abilities—such as waiters or waitresses renowned for their ability to remember dinner orders—suggest the operation of a "long-term working memory." According to these researchers, skilled use of memory appears to be related to an interaction between working memory and long-term memory that enables both the rapid transfer of items into long-term storage and the activation of networks of related information already in long-term storage. The excellent memories exhibited by chess masters, physicians, and, indeed, good restaurant staff, may thus reflect their ability to use chunking and other strategies to manipulate larger amounts of information than is typically associated with working memory by taking advantage of long-term memory stores in a flexible and dynamic way.

RETRIEVING MEMORIES

Have you ever been unable to recall the name of an old television show or movie star, only to think of it the next day? Remembering something requires not only that it be appropriately encoded and stored but also that you have the ability to bring it into consciousness—in other words, to retrieve it.

Retrieval Cues and Encoding Specificity

Stimuli that help people retrieve information from long-term memory are called **retrieval cues**. They allow people to recall things that were once forgotten and help them to recognize information stored in memory. In general, recognition tasks are easier than recall tasks because they contain more retrieval cues. As noted earlier, it is usually easier to recognize the correct alternative on a multiple-choice exam than to recall material for an essay test.

The effectiveness of cues in aiding retrieval depends on the degree to which they tap into information that was encoded at the time of learning (Tulving, 1979; Tulving & Thomson, 1973). This rule, known as the **encoding specificity principle**, is consistent with the transfer-appropriate processing model of memory. Because long-term memories are often encoded semantically, cues that evoke the meaning of the stored information tend to work best. For example, imagine you have learned a long list of sentences, one of which is either (1) "The man lifted the piano" or (2) "The man tuned the piano." Having the cue "something heavy" during a recall test would probably help you remember the first sentence, because you probably encoded something about the weight of a piano, but "something heavy" would probably not help you recall the second sentence. Similarly, the cue "makes nice sounds" would be likely to help you recall the second sentence, but not the first (Barclay et al., 1974).

Context and State Dependence

In general, people remember more when their efforts at recall take place in the same environment in which they learned, because they tend to encode features of the environment where the learning occurred (Richardson-Klavehn & Bjork, 1988). These features may later act as retrieval cues. In one experiment, people studied a series of pictures while in the presence of a particular odor. Later, they reviewed a larger set of photos and tried to identify the ones they had seen earlier. Half of these people were tested in the presence of the original odor and half in the presence of a different odor. Those who smelled the same odor during learning and testing did significantly better

Context-Dependent Memories

Some parents find that being in their child's schoolroom for a teacher conference provides context cues that bring back memories of their own grade school days.

FACTORS AFFECTING RETRIEVAL FROM LONG-TERM MEMORY

Process	Effect on Memory
Encoding specificity	Retrieval cues are effective only to the extent that they tap into information that was originally encoded.
Context dependence	Retrieval is most successful when it occurs in the same environment in which the information was originally learned.
State dependence	Retrieval is most successful when people are in the same psychological state as when they originally learned the information.

on the recognition task than those who were tested in the presence of a different odor. The matching odor served as a powerful retrieval cue (Cann & Ross, 1989).

When memory can be helped or hindered by similarities in environmental context, it is termed context-dependent. One study found that students remember better when tested in the classroom in which they learned the material than when tested in a different classroom (Smith, Glenberg, & Bjork, 1978). This context-dependency effect is not always strong (Saufley, Otaka, & Bavaresco, 1985; Smith, Vela, & Williamson, 1988), but some students do find it helpful to study for a test in the classroom where the test will be given.

Like the external environment, the internal psychological environment can be encoded when people learn and thus can act as a retrieval cue. When a person's internal state can aid or impede retrieval, memory is called state-dependent. For example, if people learn new material while under the influence of marijuana, they tend to recall it better if they are also tested under the influence of marijuana (Eich et al., 1975). Similar effects have been found with alcohol (Overton, 1984), other drugs (Eich, 1989), and mood states. College students remember more positive incidents from their diaries or from their earlier life when they are in a positive mood at the time of recall (Ehrlichman & Halpern, 1988). More negative events tend to be recalled when people are in a negative mood (Lewinsohn & Rosenbaum, 1987). These *mood congruency effects* are strongest when people try to recall personally meaningful episodes, because such events were most likely to be colored by their mood (Eich & Metcalfe, 1989).

Retrieval from Semantic Memory

All of the retrieval situations we have discussed so far are relevant to episodic memory ("In Review: Factors Affecting Retrieval from Long-Term Memory" summarizes this material). However, *semantic memory*, which stores general knowledge about the world, is also important in everyday functioning. Researchers studying semantic memory typically ask participants general-knowledge questions such as (1) Are fish minerals? (2) Is a beagle a dog? (3) Do birds fly? and (4) Does a car have legs? As you might imagine, most people virtually always respond correctly to such questions. By measuring the amount of time people take to answer the questions, however, psychologists gain important clues about how semantic memory is organized and how information is retrieved.

Semantic Networks   One of the most influential theories of semantic memory suggests that concepts are represented in a dense network of associations (Collins & Loftus, 1975). Figure 7.10 presents a graphic representation of what a fragment of a *semantic memory network* might look like. In general, semantic network theories sug-

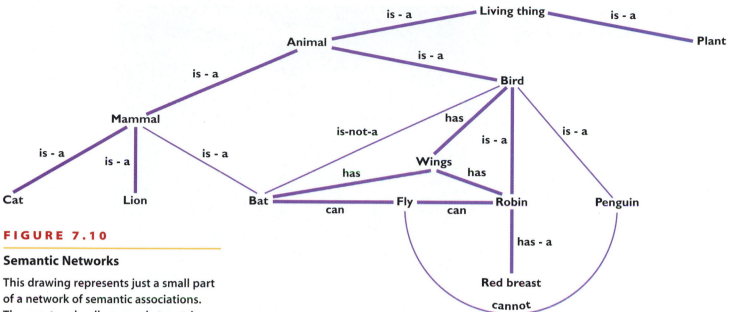

FIGURE 7.10

Semantic Networks

This drawing represents just a small part of a network of semantic associations. These networks allow people to retrieve specific pieces of previously learned information and to make new inferences about concepts.

gest that information is retrieved from memory through spreading activation (Eysenck & Keane, 1995). That is, whenever you think about some concept, it is activated in the network, and spreading activation (in the form of neural energy) begins to travel down all the paths related to it. For example, if a person is asked to say whether "A robin is a bird" is true or false, the concepts of both robin and bird will become activated and the spreading activation from each will intersect in the middle of the path between them.

Some associations within the network are stronger than others. Differing strengths are depicted by the varying thicknesses of the lines in Figure 7.10; spreading activation travels more quickly along thick paths than along thin ones. For example, most people probably have a stronger association between "bat" and "can fly" or "has wings" than "bat" and "is a mammal." Accordingly, most people respond more quickly to "Can a bat fly?" than to "Is a bat a mammal?"

Because of the tight organization of semantic networks and the speed at which activation spreads through them, people gain access to an enormous body of knowledge about the world quickly and effortlessly. They retrieve not only facts that they have learned directly but also knowledge that allows them to infer or to compute other facts about the world (Matlin, 1998). For example, imagine answering the following two questions: (1) Is a robin a bird? and (2) Is a robin a living thing? You can probably answer the first question "directly" because you probably learned this fact at some point in your life. However, you may never have consciously thought about the second question, so answering it requires some inference. Figure 7.10 illustrates the path to that inference. Because you know that a robin is a bird, a bird is an animal, and animals are living things, you infer that a robin must be a living thing. As you might expect, however, it takes slightly longer to answer the second question than the first.

Retrieving Incomplete Knowledge   Figure 7.10 also shows that concepts are represented in semantic memory as unique collections of features or attributes. Often, people can retrieve some features but not enough to identify a whole concept. Thus, you might know that there is an animal that has wings, can fly, but is not a bird, and yet be unable to retrieve its name (Connor, Balota, & Neely, 1992). In such cases you are said to be retrieving incomplete knowledge.

A common example of incomplete knowledge is the tip-of-the-tongue phenomenon. In a typical experiment on this phenomenon, dictionary definitions of words are read to people and they are asked to name each word (Brown & McNeill, 1966). If they cannot recall a defined word, they are asked whether they can recall any feature of it, such

A Constructed Memory

Through constructive memory processes, subjects who waited in this office "remembered" having seen books in it, even though none were present (Brewer & Treyens, 1981). Let a friend examine this photo for a minute or so (cover the caption), then close the book and ask whether each of the following items appeared in the office; chair, wastebasket, bottle, typewriter, coffeepot, and book. If your friend reports having seen a wastebasket or book, you will have demonstrated constructive memory.

PDP Models and Constructive Memory

If you were to hear that "our basketball team won last night," your schema about basketball might prompt you to encode, and later retrieve, the fact that the players were men. Such spontaneous, though often incorrect, generalizations associated with PDP models of memory help account for constructive memory.

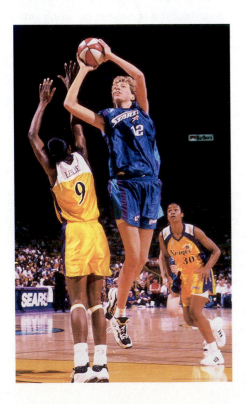

as its first letter or how many syllables it has. People are surprisingly good at this task, indicating that they are able to retrieve at least some knowledge of the word (Brennen et al., 1990).

Another example of retrieving incomplete knowledge is the *feeling-of-knowing experience,* which is often studied by asking people trivia questions (Reder & Ritter, 1992). When they cannot answer a question, they are asked to estimate the probability that they could recognize the correct answer if they were given several options. Again, people are remarkably good at this task; even though they cannot recall the answer, they can retrieve enough knowledge to determine whether the answer is actually stored in memory (Costermans, Lories, & Ansay, 1992).

Constructing Memories

The generalized knowledge about the world that each person has stored constantly affects memory (Harris, Sardarpoor-Bascom, & Meyer, 1989). People use their existing knowledge to organize new information as they receive it and to fill in gaps in the information they encode and retrieve. In this way, memories are constructed.

To study this process, which is sometimes called *constructive memory,* William Brewer and James Treyens (1981) asked undergraduates to wait for several minutes in the office of a graduate student. When later asked to recall everything that was in the office, most of the students mistakenly "remembered" that books were present, even though there were none. Apparently, the general knowledge that graduate students read many books influenced the participants' memory of what was in the room.

Relating Semantic and Episodic Memory: PDP Models   Parallel distributed processing models offer one way of explaining how semantic and episodic information become integrated in constructive memories. As noted earlier, PDP models suggest that newly learned facts alter our general knowledge of what the world is like. Figure 7.11 shows a simple PDP network model of just a tiny part of someone's knowledge of the world (Martindale, 1991). At its center lie the intersections of several learned associations between specific facts about five people, each of whom is represented by a circle. Thus, the network "knows" that Joe is a male European-American professor who likes Brie cheese and drives a Subaru. It also "knows" that Claudia is a female African-

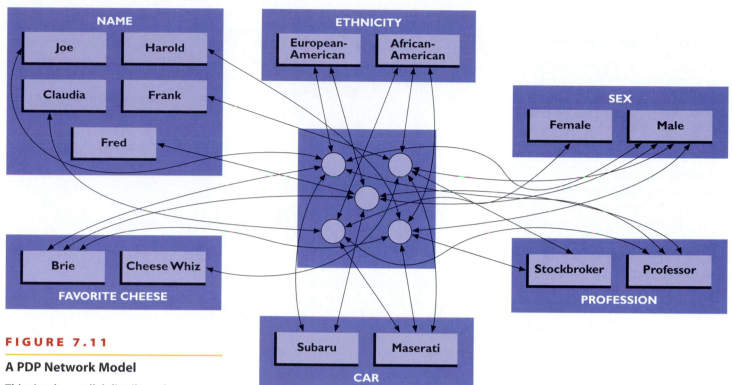

FIGURE 7.11

A PDP Network Model

This simple parallel distributed processing network model represents what someone knows about the characteristics of five people and how they are related to one another. Note that each arrow between a rectangle and a circle connects a characteristic with a person. More complex versions of such network models are capable of accounting not only for what people know but also for the inferences and generalizations they tend to make.

Source: From *Cognitive Psychology,* 1st edition, by C. Martindale, © 1991. Reprinted with permission of Wadsworth Publishing, a division of International Thomson Publishing. Fax 800-730-2215.

American professor who drives a Maserati. Notice that the network has never learned what type of cheese she prefers.

Suppose Figure 7.11 represents your memory and that you now think about Claudia. Because of the connections in the network, the facts that she is a female African-American professor and drives a Maserati would be activated; you would automatically remember these facts about Claudia. However, "likes Brie cheese" would also be activated because it is linked to other professors in the network. If the level of activation for Brie cheese is low, then the proposition that Claudia likes Brie cheese might be considered a hypothesis or an educated guess. But suppose *every other professor* you know likes Brie. In that case, the connection between professors and "likes Brie cheese" would be strong, and the conclusion that Claudia likes Brie cheese would be held so confidently that it would take overwhelming evidence for you to change your mind (Rumelhart & McClelland, 1986).

PDP networks also produce *spontaneous generalizations*. If a friend told you she just bought a new car, you would know without asking that—like all other cars you have experienced—it has four wheels. However, spontaneous generalizations can create significant errors if the network is based on limited or biased experience with a class of objects. For example, if the network in Figure 7.11 were asked what European-American males are like, it would think that all of them drive Japanese cars.

This aspect of PDP networks—generalizing from scanty information—is actually an accurate reflection of human thought and memory. Virtually all people make spontaneous generalizations about males, females, European-Americans, African-Americans, and many other categories (Martindale, 1991).

Schemas   Parallel distributed processing models also help us understand constructive memory by explaining the operation of the schemas that guide it. Schemas are mental representations of categories of objects, events, and people. For example, most Americans have a schema for *baseball game,* so that simply hearing these words is likely to activate whole clusters of information in long-term memory, including the rules of the game, images of players, bats, balls, a green field, summer days, and, perhaps, hot dogs and stadiums. The generalized knowledge contained in schemas provides a basis for making inferences about incoming information during the encoding stage. So if

FIGURE 7.12

The Effect of Schemas on Recall

In one early experiment, participants were shown figures like these, along with labels designed to activate certain schemas (Carmichael, Hogan, & Walter, 1932). For example, when showing the top figure, the experimenter said either "This resembles eyeglasses" or "This resembles a dumbbell." When the participants were asked to reproduce the figures from memory, their drawings tended to resemble the items mentioned by the experimenter. In other words, their memory had been altered by the labels.

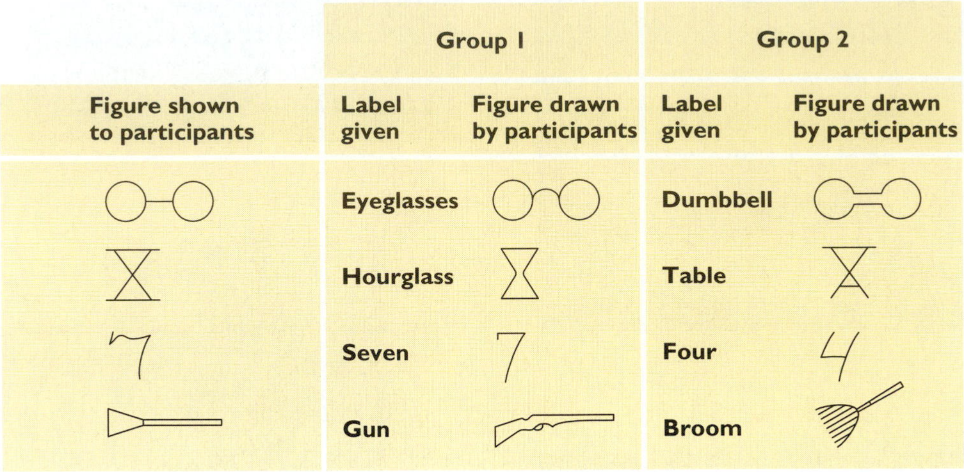

Figure shown to participants	Group 1		Group 2	
	Label given	Figure drawn by participants	Label given	Figure drawn by participants
○—○	Eyeglasses	○○	Dumbbell	○=○
✕	Hourglass	✕	Table	✕
7	Seven	7	Four	4
▷——	Gun	(gun)	Broom	(broom)

you hear that a baseball player was injured, your schema about baseball might prompt you to encode the incident as game related, even though the cause was not mentioned. As a result, you are likely to recall the injury as having occurred during a game (see Figure 7.12 for another example).

LINKAGES

Do forgotten memories remain in the subconscious? (a link to Consciousness)

THINKING CRITICALLY

Recovered Memories— True or False?

In 1989, Eileen Franklin-Lipsker told police in California that, upon looking into her young daughter's eyes one day, she suddenly had a vivid memory of seeing her father kill her childhood friend more than twenty years earlier. Her father, George Franklin, Sr., was sent to prison for murder on the basis of her testimony about that memory (Loftus & Ketcham, 1994). This case sparked a controversy that has continued to grow in intensity, involving not only psychologists but the American legal system as well. The controversy concerns the validity of claims of recovered memory. Some psychologists accept the idea that it is possible for people to repress, or push into unconsciousness, memories of traumatic incidents and then recover these memories many years later. Other psychologists, however, are more skeptical about recovered memory claims.

■ What am I being asked to believe or accept?

The prosecution in the Franklin case successfully argued that Eileen had recovered the memory of a traumatic event. Similar arguments in other cases resulted in the imprisonment of a number of parents whose now-adult children claim to have recovered childhood memories of physical or sexual abuse. The juries in these trials accepted the assertion that people can be unconsciously motivated to forget traumatic events and that, under the right conditions, complete and accurate memories of the events can reappear (Kihlstrom, 1995; Loftus, 1997a). Jurors are not the only believers in this phenomenon. Recently, a news organization in the United States reported that U.S. troops had illegally used nerve gas during the war in Vietnam—a story based, in part, on a Vietnam veteran's recovered memories of a gas attack (*New York Times*, July 3, 1998).

■ What evidence is available to support the assertion?

Proponents of the recovered memory argument point to several lines of evidence to support their claims. First, there is evidence that a substantial amount of mental activity occurs outside conscious awareness (Kihlstrom, 1996; see Chapter 9). Second, research on implicit memory shows that information of which we are unaware can still influence our behavior (Schacter, Chiu, & Ochsner, 1993). Third, research on *motivated*

Exploring Memory Processes

Research by cognitive psychologist Elizabeth Loftus has demonstrated mechanisms through which false memories can be created. Her work has helped to focus scientific scrutiny on reports of recovered memories, especially those arising from contact with therapists who assume that most people have repressed memories of abuse.

forgetting suggests that people may be more likely to forget unpleasant rather than pleasant events (Erdelyi, 1985). In one study, a psychologist kept a detailed record of his daily life over a six-year period. When he later tried to recall these experiences, he remembered more than half of the positive ones, but only one-third of the negative ones. In another study, 38 percent of women who, as children, had been brought to a hospital because of sexual abuse could not recall the incident as adults (Williams, 1994a). Fourth, retrieval cues can help people accurately recall memories that had previously been inaccessible to conscious awareness (Landsdale & Laming, 1995). For example, there are carefully documented cases of soldiers recovering, after many years, vivid and accurate memories of the circumstances in which they were wounded (Karon & Widener, 1997). Finally, there is the confidence with which people report recovered memories; they say they are just too vivid to be anything but real.

■ Are there alternative ways of interpreting the evidence?

Those who are skeptical about recovered memories do not deny the operation of subconscious memory and retrieval processes (Greenwald, 1992). They also recognize that, sadly, child abuse and other traumas are all too common. But these facts do not eliminate the possibility that any given "recovered" memory may actually be a distorted, or constructed, memory (Loftus, 1998; Loftus & Pickrell, 1995). As already noted, our recall of past events is affected by what happened at the time, what we knew beforehand, and everything we experience since. The people who "remembered" nonexistent books in a graduate student's office constructed that memory based on what prior knowledge led them to *assume* was there (see photo on page 230).

Research shows that *false memories*—distortions of actual events and the recall of events that didn't actually happen—can be at least as vivid as accurate ones, and people can be just as confident in them (Brainerd & Reyna, 1998; Brainerd, Reyna, & Brandse, 1995; Roediger & McDermott, 1995). In one case study, for example, a teenager named Chris was given descriptions of four incidents from his childhood and asked to write about each of them every day for five days (Loftus, 1997a). One of these incidents—being lost in a shopping mall at age five—never really happened. Yet Chris not only eventually "remembered" this event but added many details about the mall and the stranger whose hand he was supposedly found holding. He also rated this (false) memory as being more vivid than two of the other three (real) incidents. The same pattern of results has appeared in more formal experiments on the planting of emotion-laden false memories (Hyman & Pentland, 1996). For example, researchers have been able to create vivid and striking, but *completely false*, memories of events that people thought they experienced when they were one day old (DuBreuil, Garry, & Loftus, in press). And the "recovered memory" of the Vietnam veteran mentioned earlier appears to have no basis in fact; the news story about the alleged nerve gas attack was later retracted.

Why would anyone "remember" an event that did not actually occur—especially a traumatic one? Elizabeth Loftus (1997b) suggests that, for one thing, popular books such as *The Courage to Heal* (Bass & Davis, 1988) and *Secret Survivors* (Blume, 1990) have planted in many minds the idea that anyone who experiences guilt, depression, low self-esteem, overemotionality, or any of a long list of other problems is harboring repressed memories of abuse. This message, says Loftus, tends to be reinforced and extended by therapists who specialize in using guided imagination, hypnosis, and other methods to "help" clients recover repressed memories (Polusny & Follette, 1996; Poole et al., 1995). In so doing, these therapists may influence people to construct false memories (Olio, 1994). As one client described her therapy, "I was rapidly losing the ability to differentiate between my imagination and my real memory" (Loftus & Ketcham, 1994, p. 25). To such therapists, a client's failure to recover memories of abuse, or refusal to accept their existence, is evidence of "denial" of the truth.

The possibility that recovered memories might actually be false memories has led to dismissed charges or not-guilty verdicts for defendants in some repressed memory cases, and to the release of previously convicted defendants in others (George Franklin's conviction was overturned.) Concern over the potential damage resulting from false memories has led to the establishment of the False Memory Syndrome Foundation, a support group for families affected by abuse accusations stemming from allegedly repressed memories. More than 100 such families have filed lawsuits against therapists and hospitals (False Memory Syndrome Foundation, 1997). In 1994, California winery executive Gary Ramona received $500,000 in damages from two therapists who had "helped" his daughter recall alleged sexual abuse at his hands. A more recent suit led to a $2 million judgment against a Minnesota therapist whose client realized that her "recovered" memories of childhood abuse were false; a similar case in Illinois resulted in a $10.6 million settlement (Loftus, 1998).

■ What additional evidence would help to evaluate the alternatives?

Evaluating reports of recovered memories would be aided by more information about how common it is for people to forget traumatic events. So far, we know that intense emotional experiences usually produce memories that are vivid and long-lasting (Shobe & Kihlstrom, 1997). Some are called *flashbulb memories* because they preserve particular experiences in great detail (Brown & Kulik, 1977). Indeed, many people who live through trauma are *unable* to forget it. In the sexual abuse study mentioned earlier, for example, 62 percent of the abuse victims did recall their trauma. More studies like this one—which track the fate of memories in known abuse cases—would not only help estimate the prevalence of this kind of forgetting but might also offer clues as to the kinds of people and events most likely to be associated with it.

It would also be valuable to know more about what mechanisms might be responsible for recovered memories and how they relate to empirically established theories and models of human memory. Thus far, cognitive psychologists have not found evidence of such mechanisms (Shobe & Kihlstrom, 1997).

■ What conclusions are most reasonable?

An objective reading of the available research evidence supports the view that recovery of memories of trauma is at least possible, but that the implantation of false memories is also possible—and has been demonstrated experimentally.

The intense conflict between the False Memory Syndrome Foundation and those psychologists who accept as genuine most of the memories recovered in therapy reflects a fundamental disagreement about recovered memories: Client reports constitute "proof" for therapists who deal daily with victims of sexual abuse and other traumas, and who rely more on personal experiences than on scientific research findings. Those reports may not be accepted as valid by empirically oriented psychologists.

In short, whether one believes a claim of recovered memory may be determined by the relative weight one assigns to personal experiences and intuition versus empirical evidence. Still, the apparent ease with which false memories can be created should lead judges, juries, and the general public to exercise great caution before accepting as valid unverified memories of traumatic events. At the same time, we should not automatically and uncritically reject the claims of people who appear to have recovered memories. Perhaps the wisest course is to use all the scientific and circumstantial evidence available to carefully and critically examine such claims, while keeping in mind that constructive memory processes *might* have influenced them. This careful, scientific approach is vital if we are to protect the rights and welfare of those who report recovered memories, as well as of those who face accusations arising from them.

FORGETTING

The frustrations of forgetting—where you left your keys, the answer to a test question, an anniversary—are apparent to most people nearly every day. In this section we look more closely at the nature of forgetting, and at some of the mechanisms that are responsible for it.

*"As I get older, I find I rely more and more
on these sticky notes to remind me."*

Durable Memories

This woman has not used a pogo stick since she was ten. Her memory of how to do it is not entirely gone, however, so she will show some "savings": It will take her less time to relearn the skill than it took to learn it initially.

The Course of Forgetting

About a hundred years ago, Hermann Ebbinghaus, a German psychologist, began the systematic study of memory and forgetting, using only himself as the subject of his research. His aim was to study memory in its "pure" form, uncontaminated by emotional reactions and other pre-existing associations between new material and what was already in memory. To eliminate such associations, Ebbinghaus created the *nonsense syllable*, a meaningless set of two consonants and a vowel, such as *POF*, *XEM*, and *QAL*. He read a list of nonsense syllables aloud, to the beat of a metronome—a mechanical device that emits a sound at constant intervals. Then he tried to recall the syllables.

To measure forgetting, Ebbinghaus devised the **method of savings**, which involves computing the difference between the number of repetitions needed to learn a list of items and the number of repetitions needed to relearn it after some time has elapsed. This difference is called the *savings.* If it took Ebbinghaus ten trials to learn a list and ten more trials to relearn it, there would be no savings, and forgetting would have been complete. If it took him ten trials to learn the list and only five trials to relearn it, there would be a savings of 50 percent.

As you can see in Figure 7.13 (on page 236), Ebbinghaus found that savings decline (and forgetting increases) as time passes. However, the most dramatic drop in what people retain in long-term memory occurs during the first nine hours, especially in the first hour. After this initial decline, the rate of forgetting slows down considerably. In Ebbinghaus's study, some savings existed even thirty-one days after the original learning.

Ebbinghaus's research had some important limitations, but it produced two lasting discoveries. One is the shape of the forgetting curve depicted in Figure 7.13. Psychologists have subsequently substituted words, sentences, and even stories for nonsense syllables. In virtually all cases the forgetting curve shows the same strong initial drop in memory, followed by a much more moderate decrease over time (Slamecka & McElree, 1983). Of course, people remember sensible stories better than nonsense syllables, but the shape of the curve is the same no matter what type of material is involved (Davis & Moore, 1935). Even the forgetting of daily events from one's life tends to follow Ebbinghaus's forgetting function (Thomson, 1982).

The second of Ebbinghaus's important discoveries is just how long-lasting "savings" in long-term memory can be. Psychologists now know from the method of savings

FIGURE 7.13

Ebbinghaus's Curve of Forgetting

Ebbinghaus found that most forgetting takes place during the first nine hours after learning, especially in the first hour

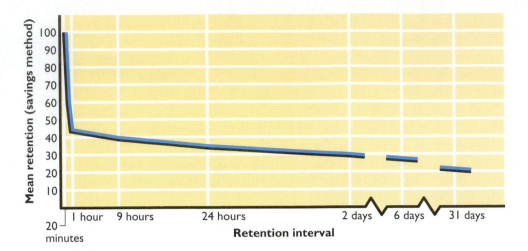

that information about everything from algebra to bike-riding is often retained for decades (Matlin, 1998). Thus, you may forget something you have learned if you do not use the information, but it is easy to relearn the material if the need arises, indicating that the forgetting was not complete (MacLeod, 1988).

The Roles of Decay and Interference

Nothing we have said so far explains why forgetting occurs. In principle, either of two processes can be responsible (Reed, 1992). One process is *decay*, the gradual disappearance of the mental representation of a stimulus, much as letters engraved on a piece of steel are eaten away by rust and become less distinct over time. Forgetting might also occur because of *interference*, a process through which either the storage or retrieval of information is impaired by the presence of other information. Interference might occur either because one piece of information actually *displaces* other information, pushing it out of memory, or because one piece of information makes storing or recalling other information more difficult.

In the case of short-term memory, we noted that if an item is not rehearsed or thought about, memory of it decreases consistently over the course of eighteen seconds or so. Thus decay appears to play a prominent role in forgetting information in short-term memory. But interference through displacement also produces forgetting from short-term memory (Klatzky, 1980). Displacement is one reason why the phone number you just looked up is likely to drop out of short-term memory if you read another

FIGURE 7.14

Procedures for Studying Interference

To recall the two types of interference, remember that the prefixes—*pro* and *retro*—indicate directions in time. In *pro*-active interference, previously learned material interferes with *future* learning; *retro*active interference occurs when new information interferes with the recall of *past* learning.

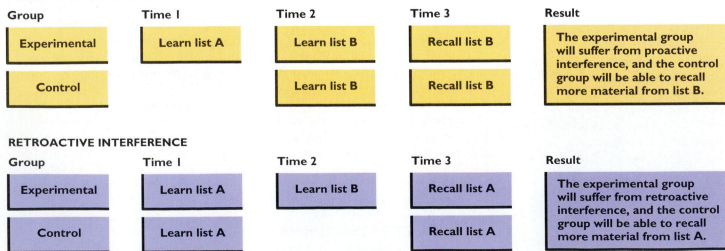

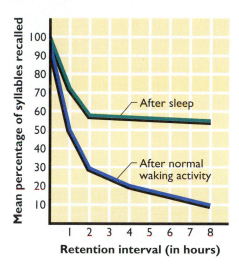

Source: Minimi & Dallenbach, 1946.

FIGURE 7.15

Interference and Forgetting

Forgetting is more rapid if college students engage in normal activity after learning than if they spend the time asleep. These results suggest that interference is more important than decay in forgetting information in long-term memory.

number before dialing. Rehearsal prevents displacement by continually re-entering the same information into short-term memory.

Analyzing the cause of forgetting from long-term memory is more complicated. In long-term memory there can be **retroactive interference**, in which learning of new information interferes with recall of older information, or **proactive interference**, in which old information interferes with learning or remembering new information. For example, retroactive interference would help explain why studying French vocabulary this term might make it more difficult to remember the Spanish words you learned last term. And because of proactive interference, the French words you are learning now might make it harder to learn German next term. Figure 7.14 outlines the types of experiments used to study the influence of each form of interference in long-term memory.

Suppose a person learns something and then, when tested on it after various intervals, remembers less and less as the delay becomes longer. Is this forgetting due to decay or to interference? It is not easy to tell, because longer delays produce both more decay and more retroactive interference as the person is exposed to further information while waiting. To separate the effects of decay from those of interference, Karl Dallenbach sought to create situations in which time passed but there was no accompanying interference. Evidence of forgetting in such a situation would suggest that decay, not interference, was operating.

In one of Dallenbach's studies, college students learned a list of nonsense syllables and then either continued with their waking routine or were sheltered from interference by going to sleep (Jenkins & Dallenbach, 1924). Although the delay (and thus the potential for decay) was held constant for both groups, the greater interference associated with being awake produced much more forgetting, as Figure 7.15 shows.

Results like these suggest that although it is possible that decay sometimes occurs, interference is the major cause of forgetting from long-term memory. But does interference push the forgotten information out of memory, or does it merely hinder the ability to retrieve it? To find out, Endel Tulving and Joseph Psotka (1971) presented people with different numbers of word lists. Each list contained words from one of six semantic categories, such as types of buildings (*hut, cottage, tent, hotel*) or earth formations (*cliff, river, hill, volcano*). Some people learned a list and then recalled as many of the words as possible. Other groups learned the first list and then learned different numbers of other lists before trying to recall the first one.

The results were dramatic. As the number of intervening lists increased, the number of words that people could recall from the original list declined consistently. This finding reflected strong retroactive interference. Then the researchers gave a second test, in which they provided people with a retrieval cue by telling them the category of

FIGURE 7.16

Retrieval Failures and Forgetting

On the initial test in Tulving and Psotka's experiment, people's ability to recall a list of items was strongly affected by the number of other lists they learned before being tested on the first one. When item-category (retrieval) cues were provided on a second test, however, retroactive interference from the intervening lists almost disappeared.

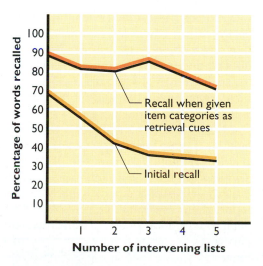

Source: Tulving & Psotka, 1971.

the words (such as types of buildings) to be recalled. Now the number of intervening lists had almost no effect on the number of words recalled from the original list, as Figure 7.16 shows. These results indicate that the words were still represented in long-term memory; they had not been pushed out, but the participants had been unable to recall them without appropriate retrieval cues. In other words, the original forgetting was due to a failure in retrieval. Thus, putting more and more information in long-term memory may be like placing more and more CDs into a storage case. Although none of the CDs disappears, it becomes increasingly difficult to find the specific one you are looking for.

LINKAGES

Memory and Perception in the Courtroom

LINKAGES

How accurate is eyewitness testimony? (a link to Perception)

As described in Chapter 5, in order for incoming information to be encoded into memory, it must first be perceived. Perception, in turn, is influenced by a combination of the stimulus features we find "out there" in the world and what we already know, expect, or want—that is, by both bottom-up and top-down processing. The relationship between memory and perception, especially the impact of top-down processing on memory, is made dramatically evident in the courtroom.

Consider, for example, the accuracy of eyewitness memory and how it can be affected by extraneous information (Loftus, 1993). The most compelling evidence a lawyer can provide is that of an eyewitness, but eyewitnesses make many mistakes (Loftus & Ketcham, 1991). During a federal arson trial in Chicago, for example, a witness was asked if she could identify the man she saw running from a burning building. "That's the guy," she said, looking toward a corner of the courtroom. The judge asked her to single out the man—whereupon she walked over and pointed at an assistant defense attorney (Gottesman, 1992).

Eyewitnesses can remember only what they perceived, and they can have perceived only what they attended to (Backman & Nilsson, 1991). The witnesses' task is to report as accurately as possible what they saw or heard; but no matter how hard they try to be accurate, there are limits to how faithful their reports can be (Kassin, Rigby, & Castillo, 1991). Further, new information, including the form of a lawyer's question, can alter a witness's memory (Loftus, 1979). Experiments show that when witnesses are asked, "How fast was the blue car going when it slammed into the truck?" they are likely to recall a higher speed than when asked, "How fast was the blue car going when it hit the truck?" (Loftus & Palmer, 1974; see Figure 7.17). There is also evidence that an object mentioned after the fact is often mistakenly remembered as having been there in the first place (Dodson & Reisberg, 1991). For example, if a lawyer says that a screwdriver was lying on the ground (when it was not), witnesses often recall with great certainty having seen it (Ryan & Geiselman, 1991). Some theorists have speculated that mentioning an object creates retroactive interference, making the original memory more difficult to retrieve (Tversky & Tuchin, 1989). However, there is now considerable evidence that, when objects are subsequently mentioned, they are integrated into the old memory representation and subsequently are not distinguished from what was originally seen (Loftus, 1992).

For jurors, the credibility of a witness often depends as much (or even more) on *how* the witness presents evidence as on the content or relevance of that evidence (Leippe, Manion, & Romanczyk, 1992). Many jurors are impressed, for example, when a witness can recall a large number of details. Extremely detailed testimony from prosecution witnesses is especially likely to lead to guilty verdicts, even when the details reported are irrelevant (Bell & Loftus, 1989). Apparently, when a witness gives very detailed testimony, jurors infer that the witness paid especially close attention or has a particularly accurate memory. At first glance, these inferences might seem reasonable. However, as discussed in the chapter on perception, the ability to divide attention is limited. As a result, a witness might focus attention on the crime and the criminal or

FIGURE 7.17

The Impact of Leading Questions on Eyewitness Memory

After seeing a filmed traffic accident, people were asked, "About how fast were the cars going when they (smashed, hit, or contacted) each other?" As shown here, the witnesses' responses were influenced by the verb used in the question; "smashed" was associated with the highest average speed estimates. A week later, people who heard the "smashed" question remembered the accident as being more violent than did people in the other two groups (Loftus & Palmer, 1974).

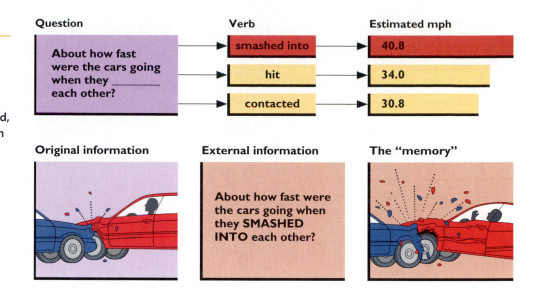

Question	Verb	Estimated mph
About how fast were the cars going when they _____ each other?	smashed into	40.8
	hit	34.0
	contacted	30.8

Original information | External information | The "memory"

About how fast were the cars going when they SMASHED INTO each other?

on the surrounding details, but probably not on both. Hence, witnesses who accurately remember unimportant details of a crime scene may not accurately recall the criminal's facial features or other identifying characteristics (Backman & Nilsson, 1991).

Juries also tend to believe a confident witness (Leippe, Manion, & Romanczyk, 1992), but witnesses' confidence about their testimony is frequently much higher than its accuracy (Shaw, 1996). In fact, repeated exposure to misinformation and the repeated recall of misinformation can increase a witness's confidence in objectively incorrect testimony (Lamb, 1998; Mitchell & Zaragoza, 1996; Roediger, Jacoby, & McDermott, 1996).

▸BIOLOGICAL BASES OF MEMORY

LINKAGES

Where are memories stored? (a link to Biological Aspects of Psychology)

While most psychologists study memory by focusing on conscious and subconscious mental processes, some also consider the physical, electrical, and chemical changes that take place in the brain when people encode, store, and retrieve information. The story of the scientific search for the biological bases of memory begins with the work of Karl Lashley and Donald Hebb, who spent many years studying how memory is related to brain structures and processes. Lashley (1950) taught rats new behaviors and then observed how damage to various parts of the rats' brains changed their ability to perform the tasks they had learned. Lashley hoped that his work would identify the brain area which contained the "engram"—the physical manifestation of memory in the brain. However, after many experiments, he concluded that memories are not localized in one specific region, but, instead, are distributed throughout large areas of brain tissue (Lashley, 1950).

At around the same time, Hebb, who was a student of Lashley's, proposed another biological theory of memory. Hebb believed that a given memory is represented by a group of interconnected neurons in the brain. This set of neurons, which he called a *cell assembly,* formed a network in the cortex. The connections among these neurons were strengthened, he said, when the neurons were simultaneously stimulated through sensory experiences (Hebb, 1949). Though not correct in all its details, Hebb's theory stimulated much research and contributed to an understanding of the physical basis of memory. It is also consistent, in many respects, with contemporary parallel distributed processing models of memory (Hergenhahn & Olson, 1997).

Let's now consider more recent research on the biochemical mechanisms and brain structures that are most directly involved in memory processes.

FIGURE 7.18

Some Brain Structures Involved in Memory

Combined neural activity in many parts of the brain allows us to encode, store, and retrieve memories. The complexity of the biological bases of these processes is underscored by research showing that different aspects of a memory—such as the sights and sounds of some event— are stored in different parts of the cerebral cortex.

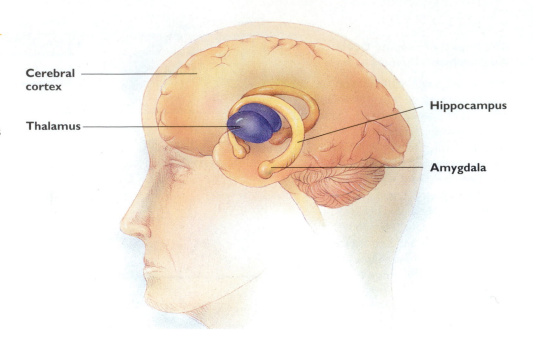

Biochemical Mechanisms

As described in Chapter 3, communication among brain cells takes place at the synapses between axons and dendrites, and it depends on chemicals, called *neurotransmitters*, released at the synapses. There is evidence that new memories are associated with at least two kinds of changes in synapses.

First, environmental stimulation can promote the formation of new synapses, which increases the complexity of the communication networks through which neurons receive information (Black & Greenough, 1991; Rosenzweig & Bennett, 1996). It is likely that these new synapses are involved in the storage of new memories.

Second, functional changes can occur at existing synapses. The enhancement of existing synapses has been most clearly demonstrated in brain tissue studied in a laboratory dish or in living marine snails. By studying individual synapses as a new memory is formed, researchers have discovered that simultaneous activation of two inputs to a synapse later makes it easier for a signal from a single input to cross the synapse (Sejnowski, Chattarji, & Stanton, 1990). Changing the pattern of electrical stimulation can also weaken synaptic connections (Malenka, 1995).

In the hippocampus (see Figure 7.18), these changes appear to occur at synapses that use glutamate as a neurotransmitter. One type of glutamate receptor is initially activated only if the postsynaptic neuron is being stimulated by input from more than one neuron (Cotman, Monaghan, & Ganong, 1988). After these multiple stimulations are repeated a number of times, this type of glutamate receptor appears to become sensitized so that input from just one neuron is sufficient to produce a response. Such a change in sensitivity could account for the development of conditioned responses, for example.

Acetylcholine also plays a prominent role in memory. The memory problems of Alzheimer's patients appear to be related to a deficiency in neurons that use acetylcholine and send fibers to the hippocampus and the cortex (Muir, 1997). Drugs that interfere with acetylcholine neurotransmission impair memory, and drugs or dietary supplements that increase the amount of acetylcholine in the brain sometimes improve memory in aging experimental animals and humans (Parnetti, Senin, & Mecocci, 1997). However, increasing general acetylcholine levels probably won't improve memory. A more appropriate goal might be to selectively enhance acetylcholine activity at the synapses used in memory. One way of doing so in the future might be to implant in the brain some cells that have been genetically modified to produce acetylcholine. When this procedure was performed on brain-damaged animals, it improved their memory (Li & Low, 1997; Winkler et al., 1995).

In short, research has shown that changes in individual synapses help to strengthen networks that are activated repetitively—specifically, by improving transmission through the networks. This finding provides some support for the ideas formulated by Hebb many years ago.

Brain Structures

Where in the brain do memory-related mechanisms occur? Researchers have concluded that memory involves both specialized regions for memory formation and widespread areas for storage (McCarthy, 1995; Zola-Morgan & Squire, 1990). In the formation of new memories, several brain regions are vital (see Figure 7.18), including the hippocampus and nearby parts of the cortex and the thalamus (Brewer et al., 1998; Squire & Zola, 1996).

The Impact of Brain Damage   Studies of how brain injuries affect memory provide evidence about the brain regions involved in various kinds of memory (Martinez, Scalds, & Weinberger, 1991). For example, damage to the hippocampus, which is part of the limbic system, often results in **anterograde amnesia,** a loss of memory for any event occurring after the injury.

A striking example is seen in the case of H.M. (Milner, 1966). Part of H.M.'s hippocampus had been removed in order to end severe epileptic seizures. Afterward, both his long-term and short-term memory appeared normal, but he had a severe problem. The operation had been performed when he was twenty-seven years old. Two years later, he still believed that he was twenty-seven. When his family moved into a new house, H.M. could not remember the new address or even how to get there. When told that his uncle had died, he grieved in a normal way. But soon thereafter, he began to ask why his uncle had not visited him. Each time he was told of his uncle's death, H.M. became just as upset as when he was first told. In short, the surgery had apparently destroyed the mechanism that transfers information from short-term to long-term memory.

Interestingly, although such patients cannot form new episodic memories following hippocampal damage, they can use their *procedural memory*. For example, H.M. was presented with a complicated puzzle on which mistakes are common and performance gradually improves with practice. Over several days his performance steadily improved, just as it does with normal people, and eventually became virtually perfect. But each time he tried the puzzle, he insisted that he had never seen it before (Cohen & Corkin, 1981; see Figure 9.3 on page 296).

Other researchers, too, have found intact procedural memories in patients who have anterograde amnesia for any new episodic material (Squire & McKee, 1992; Tulving, Hayman, & Macdonald, 1991). These patients are also able to keep information temporarily in working memory, which depends on the activity of dopamine neurons in the prefrontal cortex (Williams & Goldman-Rakic, 1995). Thus, while the hippocampus is crucial in the formation of new episodic memories, procedural memory and working memory appear to be governed by other regions of the brain (Squire, 1992).

Retrograde amnesia, which involves a loss of memory for events *prior* to a brain injury, is also consistent with the idea that memory processes are widely distributed. Often, a person with this condition is unable to remember anything that took place in the months, or even years, before the injury. In most cases, the memories return gradually. The most distant events are recalled first, and the person gradually regains memory for events leading up to the injury. Recovery is seldom complete, however, and the person may never remember the last few seconds before the injury. For example, one man received a severe blow to the head after being thrown from his motorcycle. After regaining consciousness, he claimed that he was eleven years old. Over the next three months, he gradually recovered his memory right up until the time he was riding his motorcycle the day of the accident. But he was never able to remember what happened just before

A Case of Retrograde Amnesia

Trevor Rees-Jones (in the brown jacket), a bodyguard for Diana, Princess of Wales, arrives at a Paris courthouse to testify during the investigation of her death in a 1997 car crash. It was hoped that, as the sole survivor, he could shed light on what happened, but the head injury he received left him with retrograde amnesia, and it was months before he could begin to recall anything about the events leading up to the accident. He may never remember the accident itself.

the accident (Baddeley, 1982). Those final events must have been encoded into short-term memory, but apparently they were never transferred into long-term memory.

An additional clue to the role of specific brain areas in memory comes from research on people with *Korsakoff's syndrome*, a disorder that usually occurs in chronic alcoholics. These people's brains become unable to use glucose as fuel, resulting in severe and widespread brain damage. Damage to the mediodorsal nucleus of the thalamus is particularly implicated in the memory problems typical of these patients, which can include both anterograde and retrograde amnesia (Squire, Amara, & Press, 1990). Moreover, like patients with hippocampal damage, Korsakoff's patients show impairments in the ability to form new episodic memories but retain some procedural-memory abilities. Research has demonstrated that damage to the prefrontal cortex (also common in Korsakoff's patients) is related to disruptions in remembering the order in which events occur (Squire, 1992). Other studies have found that the prefrontal cortex is involved in working memory in both animals and humans (D'Esposito et al., 1995; Goldman-Rakic, 1994, 1995).

It seems clear that neither the hippocampus nor the thalamus provides permanent long-term storage for memories. But both structures send nerve fibers to the cerebral cortex, and it is in the cortex that memories are probably stored (Squire & Zola-Morgan, 1991). Memory function is impaired by hippocampal and thalamic damage at least in part because injury to these areas disrupts pathways leading to the cortex. As described in Chapters 3 and 4, messages from different senses are represented in different regions of the cortex; specific aspects of an experience are probably stored near these regions. Support for this contention is provided by a study showing that memory for sounds is disrupted by damage to the auditory association cortex (Colombo et al., 1990). A memory, however, involves more than one sensory system. Even in the simple case of a rat remembering a maze, the experience of the maze entails vision, olfaction, specific movements, and the like. Thus, memories are both localized and distributed; certain brain areas store specific aspects of each remembered event, but many brain systems are involved in experiencing a whole event (Brewer et al., 1998; Gallagher & Chiba, 1996).

How does knowledge about the role of particular brain structures in memory fit with various models of memory? The memory deficits observed in cases of damage to various brain areas are consistent with the view that short-term and long-term memory are distinct systems, and that the deficits themselves result from an inability to transfer information from one system to the other. However, the precise physiological processes involved in this transfer are not yet clear. According to one line of thought, a physiological trace that codes the experience must be gradually transformed and stabilized, or consolidated, if the memory is to endure (Verfaellis & Cermak, 1991). This interpretation calls to mind Hebb's idea of cell assemblies as the basis for the formation of memories.

It seems likely that memory consolidation depends primarily on the movement of electrochemical impulses within clusters of neurons in the brain (Berman, 1991). Events that suppress neural activity in the brain (e.g., physical blows to the head, anesthetics, carbon monoxide and other types of poisoning) can disrupt the transfer of information from short-term to long-term memory—as can strong but random sets of electrical impulses, such as those that occur in the electroshock treatments sometimes used to treat psychological disorders. The information being transferred from short-term to long-term memory seems to be particularly vulnerable to destruction during the first minute or so (Donegan & Thompson, 1991).

The more scientists learn about the physiology of memory, the more they see that no single explanation can account for all types of memory. Further, no single brain structure or neurotransmitter is exclusively involved in memory formation or storage.

APPLICATIONS OF MEMORY RESEARCH

Even though some basic questions about what memory is and how it works resist final answers, psychologists know a great deal about how people can use the findings from memory research to improve their memories and function more effectively.

Improving Your Memory

The most valuable memory-enhancement strategies are based on the elaboration of incoming information, and especially on linking new information to what you already know.

Mnemonics   People with normal memory skills (Harris & Morris, 1984) as well as brain-damaged individuals (Wilson, 1987) can benefit from mnemonics, which are strategies for placing information into an organized context in order to remember it. For example, to remember the names of the Great Lakes, you might use the acronym HOMES (for Huron, Ontario, Michigan, Erie, and Superior). Verbal organization is the basis for many mnemonics. You can link items by weaving them into a story or a sentence or a rhyme. To help customers remember where they have parked their cars, some large garages have replaced section designations such as "A1" or "G8" with labels such as color names or months. Customers can then tie the location of their cars to information already in long-term memory—for example, "I parked in the month of my mother's birthday."

One simple but powerful mnemonic is called the *method of loci* (pronounced "LOW-sigh"), or the method of places. To use this method, first think about a set of familiar locations—your home, for example. You might imagine walking through the front door, around all four corners of the living room, and through each of the other rooms. Next, imagine that each item to be remembered is in one of these locations. Whenever you want to remember a list, use the same locations, in the same order. Vivid images of interactions or relationships seem to be particularly effective (Kline & Groninger, 1991). For example, tomatoes smashed against the front door or bananas hanging from the bedroom ceiling might be helpful in recalling these items on a grocery list.

All mnemonic systems require that you have a well-learned body of knowledge (such as locations) that can be used to provide a context for organizing incoming information (Hilton, 1986). The success of these strategies demonstrates again the importance of relating new information to knowledge already stored in memory.

Guidelines for More Effective Studying   When you want to remember more complex material, such as a textbook chapter, the same principles apply (Palmisano & Herrmann, 1991). Indeed, you can improve your memory for text material by first creating an outline or some other overall context for learning, rather than by just reading

Understand and Remember

Research on memory suggests that students who simply read their textbooks will not remember as much as those who, like this woman, read for understanding using the SQ3R method. Further, memory for the material is likely to be better if you read and study it over a number of weeks rather than in one marathon session on the night before a test.

and rereading (Glover et al., 1990). Repetition may seem effective, because it keeps material in short-term memory; but for retaining information over long periods, repetition alone tends to be ineffective, no matter how much time you spend on it (Bjorklund & Green, 1992). In short, "work smarter, not harder."

In addition, spend your time wisely. *Distributed practice* is much more effective than *massed practice* for learning new information. If you are going to spend ten hours studying for a test, you will be much better off studying for ten one-hour blocks (separated by periods of sleep and other activity) than "cramming" for one ten-hour block. By scheduling more study sessions, you will stay fresh and tend to think about the material from a new perspective each session. This method will help you elaborate the material and remember it.

Reading a Textbook   More specific advice for remembering textbook material comes from a study that examined how successful and unsuccessful college students approach their reading (Whimbey, 1976). Unsuccessful students tend to read the material straight through; they do not slow down when they reach a difficult section; and they keep going even when they do not understand what they are reading. In contrast, successful college students monitor their understanding, reread difficult sections, and periodically stop to review what they have learned. In short, effective learners engage in a deep level of processing. They are active learners, thinking of each new fact in relation to other material, and they develop a context in which many new facts can be organized effectively.

Research on memory suggests two specific guidelines for reading a textbook. First, make sure that you understand what you are reading before moving on (Herrmann & Searleman, 1992). Second, use the SQ3R method (Thomas & Robinson, 1972), which is one of the most successful strategies for remembering textbook material (Anderson, 1990b). SQ3R stands for five activities to engage in when you read a chapter: survey, question, read, recite, review. These activities are designed to increase the depth to which you process the information you read.

1. *Survey*   Take a few minutes to skim the chapter. Look at the section headings and any boldfaced or italicized terms. Obtain a general idea of what material will be discussed, the way it is organized, and how its topics relate to one another and to what you already know. Some people find it useful to survey the entire chapter once and then survey each major section in a little more detail before reading it.

2. *Question*   Before reading each section, ask yourself what content will be covered and what information should be extracted from it.

3. *Read*   Read the text, but think about the material as you read. Are the questions you raised earlier being answered? Do you see the connections between the topics?

4. *Recite*   At the end of each section, recite the major points. Resist the temptation to be passive and say, "Oh, I remember that." Be active. Put the ideas into your own words by reciting them aloud.

5. *Review*   Finally, at the end of the chapter, review all the material. You should see connections not only within a section but also among the sections. The objective is to see how the material is organized. Once you grasp the organization, the individual facts will be far easier to remember. This is because you will be using top-down processing to help you remember.

By following these procedures you will learn and remember the material better and you will also save yourself considerable time.

Lecture Notes   Effective note-taking is an acquired skill. Research on memory suggests some simple strategies for taking and using notes effectively.

Realize first that, in note-taking, more is not necessarily better. Taking detailed notes of everything requires that you pay close attention to unimportant as well as important content, leaving little time for thinking about the material. Note-takers who concentrate on expressing the major ideas in relatively few words remember more than

in review

IMPROVING YOUR MEMORY

Domain	Helpful Techniques
Lists of items	Use mnemonics. Look for meaningful acronyms. Try the method of loci.
Textbook material	Follow the SQ3R system. Allocate your time to allow for distributed practice. Read actively, not passively.
Lectures	Take notes, but record only the main points. Think about the overall organization of the material. Review your notes as soon after the lecture as possible in order to fill in missing points.
Studying for exams	Write a detailed outline of your lecture notes rather than passively reading them.

those who try to catch every detail (Howe, 1970). In short, the best way to take notes is to think about what is being said, draw connections with other material in the lecture, and then summarize the major points clearly and concisely (Kiewra, 1989).

Once you have a set of lecture notes, review them as soon as possible after the lecture so that you can fill in missing details. (As noted earlier, most forgetting from long-term memory occurs within the first few hours after learning.) When the time comes for serious study, use your notes as if they were a chapter in a textbook. Write a detailed outline. Think about how various points are related. Once you have organized the material, the details will make more sense and will be much easier to remember. ("In Review: Improving Your Memory" summarizes tips for studying.)

Design for Memory

The scientific study of memory has influenced the design of the electronic and mechanical devices that play an increasingly important role in our lives. Designers of computers, VCRs, cameras, and even stoves are faced with a choice: Either place the operating instructions on the devices themselves, or assume that the user remembers how to operate them. Understanding the limits of both working memory and long-term memory has helped designers distinguish between information that is likely to be stored in (and easily retrieved from) the user's memory, and information that should be presented in the form of labels, instructions, or other cues that reduce memory demands (Norman, 1988). Placing unfamiliar or hard-to-recall information in plain view makes it easier to use the device as intended, and with less chance of errors (Segal & Suri, 1999).

Psychologists have influenced advertisers and designers to create many other "user-friendly" systems (Wickens, Gordon, & Liu, 1998). For example, in creating toll-free numbers, they take advantage of chunking, which, as we have seen, provides an efficient way to maintain information in working memory. Which do you think would be easier to remember: "1-800-447-4357" or "1-800-GET-HELP"? Similarly, automobile designers ensure that the turn signals on your car emit an audible cue when turned on, a feature that reduces your memory load while driving, thus leaving you with enough working memory capacity to keep in mind that there is a car in your "blind spot."

As more and more complex devices come into the marketplace, it will be increasingly important that instructions about their operation are presented clearly and memorably. With guidance from research on memory it should be possible for almost anyone to operate such devices efficiently. Yes, even the programming of a VCR will no longer be a mystery!

LINKAGES

As noted in Chapter 1, all of psychology's many subfields are related to one another. Our discussion of the accuracy of eyewitnesses' memories illustrates just one way in which the topic of this chapter, memory, is linked to the subfield of perception (Chapter 5). The Linkages diagram shows ties to two other subfields as well, and there are many more ties throughout the book. Looking for linkages among subfields will help you see how they all fit together and better appreciate the big picture that is psychology.

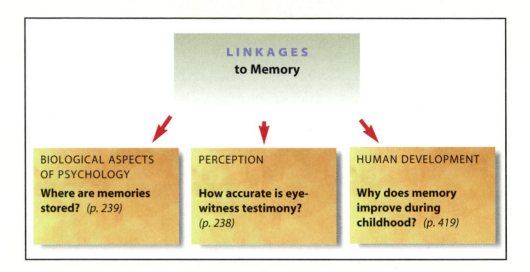

LINKAGES
to Memory

BIOLOGICAL ASPECTS OF PSYCHOLOGY

Where are memories stored? *(p. 239)*

PERCEPTION

How accurate is eyewitness testimony? *(p. 238)*

HUMAN DEVELOPMENT

Why does memory improve during childhood? *(p. 419)*

SUMMARY

THE NATURE OF MEMORY

Human memory depends on a complex mental system.

Basic Memory Processes

There are three basic memory processes. *Encoding* transforms stimulus information into some type of mental representation. Encoding can be *acoustic* (by sound), *visual* (by appearance), or *semantic* (by meaning). *Storage* maintains information in the memory system over time. *Retrieval* is the process of gaining access to previously stored information.

Types of Memory

Most psychologists agree that there are at least three types of memory. *Episodic memory* contains information about specific events in a person's life. *Semantic memory* contains generalized knowledge about the world. *Procedural memory* contains information about how to do various things.

Explicit and Implicit Memory

Most research on memory has concerned *explicit memory*, the processes through which people deliberately try to remember something. Recently, psychologists have also begun to examine *implicit memory*, which refers to the unintentional recollection and influence of prior experiences.

Models of Memory

Four theoretical models of memory have guided most research. According to the *levels-of-processing model*, the most important determinant of memory is how extensively information is encoded or processed when it is first received. In general, *elaborative rehearsal* is more effective than *maintenance rehearsal* in learning new information because it represents a deeper level of processing. According to the *transfer-appropriate processing model*, the critical determinant of memory is not how deeply information is encoded but whether the encoding process produces memory codes that are later accessed at the time of retrieval. *Parallel distributed processing (PDP) models* of memory suggest that new experiences not only provide specific information but also become part of, and alter, a whole network of associations. And the *information-processing model* suggests that in order for information to become firmly embedded in memory, it must pass through three stages of processing: sensory memory, short-term memory, and long-term memory.

ACQUIRING NEW MEMORIES

Sensory Memory

Sensory memory maintains incoming stimulus information in the *sensory registers* for a very brief time. *Selective attention*, which focuses mental resources on only part of the stimulus field, controls what information in the sensory registers is actually perceived and transferred to short-term memory.

Short-Term, or Working, Memory

Short-term memory (STM), which is also known as *working memory*, has two major functions: It constructs and updates an internal model of the environment, and it provides a system in which people can store, organize, and integrate facts and thereby solve problems and make decisions. Various memory codes can be used in short-term memory, but acoustic codes seem to be preferred in most verbal tasks. Studies of the *immediate memory span* indicate that the capacity of short-term memory is approximately seven *chunks*, or meaningful groupings of information. Studies using the *Brown-Peterson procedure* show that information in short-term memory is usually forgotten within about eighteen seconds if it is not rehearsed.

Long-Term Memory

Long-term memory (LTM) normally involves semantic encoding, which means that people tend to encode the general meaning of information, not specific details, in long-term memory. The capacity of long-term memory to store new information is extremely large, perhaps unlimited.

Distinguishing Between Short-Term and Long-Term Memory

According to some psychologists, there is no need to distinguish between short-term and long-term memory. Still, some evidence suggests that these systems are distinct. For example, the *primacy* and *recency effects* that occur when people try to recall a list of words may indicate the presence of two different systems.

RETRIEVING MEMORIES

Retrieval Cues and Encoding Specificity

Retrieval cues help people remember things that they would otherwise not be able to recall. The effectiveness of retrieval cues follows the *encoding specificity principle:* Cues help retrieval only if they match some feature of the information that was originally encoded.

Context and State Dependence

All else being equal, memory may be better when one attempts to retrieve information in the same environment in which it was learned; this is called *context-dependent* memory. When a person's internal state can aid or impede retrieval, memory is said to be *state-dependent*.

Retrieval from Semantic Memory

Researchers usually study retrieval from semantic memory by examining how long it takes people to answer world knowledge questions. It appears that ideas are represented as associations in a dense semantic memory network, and that the retrieval of information occurs by a process of *spreading activation*. Each concept in the network is represented as a unique collection of features or attributes. The tip-of-the-tongue phenomenon and the feeling-of-knowing experience represent the retrieval of incomplete knowledge.

Constructing Memories

In the process of constructive memory, people use their existing knowledge to fill in gaps in the information they encode and retrieve. Parallel distributed processing models provide one explanation of how people make spontaneous generalizations about the world. They also explain the *schemas* that shape the memories people construct.

FORGETTING

The Course of Forgetting

In his research on long-term memory and forgetting, Hermann Ebbinghaus introduced the *method of savings*. He found that most forgetting from long-term memory occurs during the first several hours after learning and that savings can be extremely long lasting.

The Roles of Decay and Interference

Decay and *interference* are two mechanisms of forgetting. Although there is evidence of both decay and interference in short-term memory, it appears that most forgetting from long-term memory is due to either *retroactive interference* or *proactive interference*.

BIOLOGICAL BASES OF MEMORY

Biochemical Mechanisms

Research has shown that memory can result as new synapses are formed in the brain, and as communication at existing synapses is improved. Several neurotransmitters appear to be involved in the strengthening that occurs at synapses.

Brain Structures

Studies of *anterograde amnesia, retrograde amnesia, Korsakoff's syndrome*, and other kinds of brain damage provide information about the brain structures involved in memory. For example, the hippocampus and thalamus are known to play a role in the formation of memories. These structures send nerve fibers to the cerebral cortex, and it is there that memories are probably stored. Memories appear to be both localized and distributed throughout the brain.

APPLICATIONS OF MEMORY RESEARCH

Improving Your Memory

Among the many applications of memory research are *mnemonics*, devices that are used to remember things better. One of the simplest but most powerful mnemonics is the method of loci. It is useful because it provides a context for organizing material more effectively. Guidelines for effective studying have also been derived from memory research. For example, the key to remembering textbook material is to read actively rather than passively. One of the most effective ways to do this is to follow the SQ3R

method: survey, question, read, recite, and review. Similarly, to take lecture notes or to study them effectively, organize the points into a meaningful framework and think about how each main point relates to the others.

Design for Memory

Research on the limits of memory has helped product designers to create electronic and mechanical systems and devices that are "user-friendly."

KEY TERMS

acoustic encoding (214)
anterograde amnesia (241)
Brown-Peterson procedure (224)
chunks (223)
context-dependent (228)
decay (236)
elaborative rehearsal (218)
encoding (214)
encoding specificity principle (227)
episodic memory (215)
explicit memory (216)
immediate memory span (223)
implicit memory (216)

information-processing model (220)
interference (236)
levels-of-processing model (218)
long-term memory (LTM) (224)
maintenance rehearsal (218)
method of savings (235)
mnemonics (243)
parallel distributed processing (PDP) models (219)
primacy effect (227)

proactive interference (237)
procedural memory (215)
recency effect (227)
retrieval (215)
retrieval cues (227)
retroactive interference (237)
retrograde amnesia (241)
schemas (231)
selective attention (222)
semantic encoding (215)
semantic memory (215)
sensory memory (221)
sensory registers (221)

short-term memory (STM) (222)
spreading activation (229)
state-dependent (228)
storage (215)
transfer-appropriate processing model (218)
visual encoding (214)
working memory (222)

8

Cognition and Language

D r. Joyce Wallace, a New York City internist, was having trouble figuring out what was the matter with a forty-three-year-old patient, "Laura McBride." Laura reported pains in her stomach and abdomen, aching muscles, irritability, occasional dizzy spells, and fatigue (Rouéché, 1986). The doctor's initial hypothesis was iron-deficiency anemia, a condition in which the level of oxygen-carrying hemoglobin in the blood is too low. There was some evidence to support that hypothesis. A physical examination revealed that Laura's spleen was somewhat enlarged, and blood tests showed low hemoglobin and high production of red blood cells, suggesting that her body was attempting to compensate for the loss of hemoglobin. However, other tests revealed normal iron levels. Perhaps she was losing blood through internal bleeding, but an additional test ruled that out. Had Laura been vomiting blood? She said no. Blood in the urine? No. Abnormally heavy menstrual flow? No. During the next week, as Dr. Wallace puzzled over the problem, Laura's condition worsened. She reported more intense pain, cramps, shortness of breath, and severe loss of energy. Her blood was becoming less and less capable of sustaining her, but if it was not being lost, what was happening to it? Finally, the doctor looked at a smear of Laura's blood on a microscope slide. What she saw indicated that some poison was destroying the red blood cells. What could it be? Laura spent most of her time at home, but her teenage daughters, who lived with her, were perfectly healthy. Wallace asked herself, "What does Laura do that the girls do not?" She repairs and restores paintings. Paint. Lead! She might be suffering from lead poisoning! When a blood test showed a lead level seven times higher than normal, Dr. Wallace knew she had solved this medical mystery at last.

To do so, Dr. Wallace relied on her ability to think, solve problems, and make judgments and decisions. She used these higher mental processes to weigh the pros and cons of various hypotheses and to reach decisions about what tests to order and how to interpret them. She also consulted with the patient and other physicians using that remarkable human ability known as language.

This story provides just one example of the thinking, problem solving, decision making, and linguistic communication that occur in human beings all the time. How good are human judgments and decisions? What factors influence them? How are thoughts transformed into language? Many of the answers to these questions come from cognitive psychology, the study of the mental processes by which the information humans receive from their environment is modified, made meaningful, stored, retrieved, used, and communicated to others (Neisser, 1967). In this chapter we examine two major aspects of human cognition—thought and language. First we consider what thought is and the functions it serves. Then we examine the basic ingredients of thought and the cognitive processes people use as they interact with their environment. These cognitive processes include reasoning, problem solving, and decision making. Next, we discuss the basic elements of language and how it is acquired and used. We discuss thought and language in the same chapter mainly because thinking and communicating often involve the same cognitive processes. Moreover, without thought, coherent language would be impossible, and language (both spoken and unspoken) is certainly critical to the operation of many thought processes. Indeed, it can be argued that learning about thought helps us to better understand language, and that learning about language helps us to better understand thought.

BASIC FUNCTIONS OF THOUGHT

To begin our exploration of human cognition, we consider the five core functions of thought, which are to *describe, elaborate, decide, plan,* and *guide action*. These functions can be seen as forming a circle of thought (see Figure 8.1).

The Circle of Thought

Consider how the circle of thought operated in Dr. Wallace's case. It began when she received the information about Laura's symptoms that allowed her to *describe* the

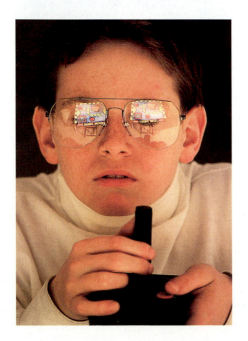

The Circle of Thought

The circle of thought begins as our sensory systems take in information from the world around us. Our perceptual system describes and elaborates this information, which is represented in the brain in ways that allow us to make decisions, formulate plans, and carry out actions. As our actions change our world, we receive new information—and the circle of thought begins again.

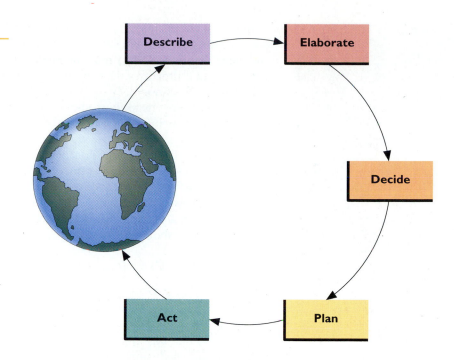

problem. Next, Dr. Wallace *elaborated* on this information by using her knowledge and experience to consider what disorders might cause such symptoms. Then she made a *decision* to investigate a possible cause, such as anemia. To implement this decision, she formulated a *plan*—to order a blood test—and then *acted* on that plan. But the circle of thought did not stop there. Information from the blood test provided new descriptive information, which Dr. Wallace elaborated further to reach another decision, create a new plan, and guide her next action.

Usually, the circle of thought spins so rapidly and its processes are so complex that the task of slowing it down for careful analysis might seem like trying to nail Jell-O to a wall. Some psychologists have approached this task by studying human thought processes as if they were components in a computer-like information-processing system. An **information-processing system** receives information, represents the information with symbols, and then manipulates those representations. According to this information-processing model, then, **thinking** is defined as the manipulation of mental representations. Figure 8.2 shows how an information-processing model might view the sequence of events that form each cycle in the circle of thought. Notice that, according to this model, information from the world is somewhat transformed as it passes through each stage of processing (Wickens, 1992a).

An Information-Processing Model

According to the information-processing model, each stage in the circle of thought takes a certain amount of time. Some stages depend heavily on both short-term and long-term memory and require some attention—that limited supply of mental energy required for information processing to be carried out efficiently.

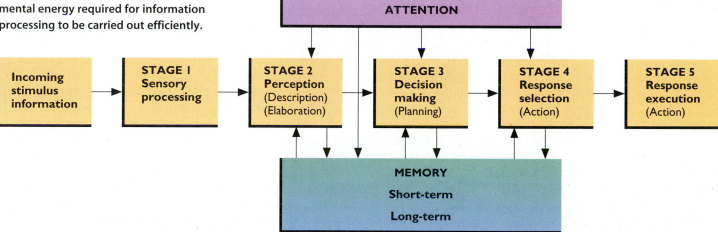

On Your Mark . . .

The runner who reacts most quickly when the starting gun is fired will have an advantage over her competitors, but too much eagerness can cause an athlete to literally jump the gun and lose the race before it starts. At the same time, too much concern over preventing a false start can slow reaction time and cost a precious fraction of a second in getting off the mark. This is the speed-accuracy tradeoff in action.

In the first stage, information about the world reaches the brain by way of the sensory receptors described in Chapter 4. This stage does not require attention. In the second stage, the information must be perceived and recognized, using the attentional and perceptual processes detailed in Chapter 5. It is also during this stage that the information is consciously elaborated, using short-term, or working, memory processes that allow us to think about it in relation to knowledge stored in long-term memory. Once the information has been elaborated in this way, we must decide what to do with it. This third stage—decision making—also demands attention. The decision may simply be to store the information in memory. If, however, a decision is made to take some action, a response must be planned in the third stage, then carried out through a coordinated pattern of responses—the action itself—in the fourth and fifth stages. As suggested in Figure 8.1, this action usually affects the environment, providing new information that, in turn, is "fed back" to the system for processing in the ongoing circle of thought.

Information-Processing Speed: Reaction Time

The information-processing model was developed in part from research on precisely the kind of high-speed thinking that seems so impossible to study. For example, imagine you are driving a little too fast and approach a green traffic light that suddenly turns yellow. You must immediately decide whether to slow down or speed up. Here is a situation in which time is of the essence; in a second or less, the stimulus must be described and elaborated, a decision made, a plan created, and an action executed.

If thinking does involve distinct processes, as the circle of thought implies, then each of these processes must take some time. Indeed, psychologists began the laboratory investigation of thinking by exploring *mental chronometry,* which involves the timing of mental events (Posner, 1978). Specifically, they examined reaction time, the time elapsing between the presentation of a stimulus and the appearance of an overt response. Reaction time, they reasoned, would give us an idea of how long it takes for all the processes shown in Figure 8.2 to occur. A typical reaction-time experiment recreates the traffic light situation mentioned earlier: A person is asked to say a certain word or to push a certain button as rapidly as possible after a stimulus appears. Even in such simple situations, several factors influence reaction times (Wickens, 1992a; Wickens, Gordon, & Liv, 1998).

One important factor in reaction time is the complexity of the decision. The larger the number of possible actions that might be carried out in response to a set of stimuli, the longer the reaction time. The tennis player who knows that her opponent usually serves to the same spot on the court will have a simple decision to make when the serve is completed and will react rapidly. But if she faces an opponent whose serve is less predictable, her reaction will be slower because a more complex decision about which way to move is now required.

Reaction time is also influenced by *stimulus-response compatibility.* If the spatial relationship between a set of stimuli and possible responses is a natural or compatible one, reaction time will be fast. If not, reaction time will be slower. Figure 8.3 illustrates compatible and incompatible relationships. Incompatible stimulus-response relationships are major culprits in causing errors in the use of all kinds of equipment (Proctor & Van Zandt, 1994; Segal & Suri, 1999).

Expectancy, too, affects reaction time. Expected stimuli are perceived more quickly and with greater accuracy than those that are surprising. Expectancy has the same effect on response time: People respond faster to stimuli that they anticipate and more slowly to those that surprise them. Similarly, responses that people expect to make—such as hitting the brakes for a red light—occur more quickly than unexpected ones, such as warding off a purse-snatcher.

Finally, in any reaction-time task there is a *speed-accuracy tradeoff.* If you try to respond quickly, errors increase; if you try for an error-free performance, reaction time increases (Wickens & Carswell, 1997). Sprinters who try too hard to anticipate the starting gun may have especially quick starts but may also have especially frequent false starts that disqualify them.

FIGURE 8.3

Stimulus-Response Compatibility

Imagine standing in front of an unfamiliar stove when a pan starts to boil over. Your reaction time in turning down the heat will depend in part on the stove's design. The response you make will be quicker on stove (A), because each knob is next to the burner it controls; there is compatibility between the source of the stimulus and the location of the response. Stove (B) shows less compatibility; here, which knob you should turn is not as obvious, so your reaction time will be slower.

(A) A COMPATIBLE RELATIONSHIP   **(B) AN INCOMPATIBLE RELATIONSHIP**

Picturing Information Processing: Evoked Brain Potentials

Research on reaction time has helped establish the time required for information processing to occur; it has also revealed how the entire sequence can be made faster or slower. But reaction times alone cannot provide a detailed picture of what goes on between the presentation of a stimulus and the execution of a response. They do not tell us, for example, how long the perception stage lasts, or whether we respond more quickly to an expected stimulus because we perceive it faster or because we make a decision about it faster. Reaction-time measures have been used in many ingenious efforts to make inferences about such things (Coles, 1989); but to analyze mental events more directly, psychologists have turned to other methods, such as the analysis of evoked brain potentials.

The **evoked brain potential** is a small, temporary change in voltage on an *electroencephalogram (EEG)* that occurs in response to specific events (Rugg & Coles, 1995). Figure 8.4 shows an example. Each peak reflects the firing of large groups of neurons, within different regions of the brain, at different times during the information-processing sequence. Thus, the pattern of the peaks provides information that is more precise than overall reaction time. For example, a large positive peak, called P300, occurs 300–500 milliseconds after a stimulus is presented. The exact timing of the P300 is affected by factors that affect the speed of perceptual processes, such as the difficulty of detecting a stimulus. But the timing of the P300 is not affected by factors—such as changes in stimulus-response compatibility—that just alter the speed with which a response is selected and executed (Rugg & Coles, 1995; Siddle et al., 1991). Hence, the length of time before a P300 occurs may reflect the duration of the first two stages of information processing shown in Figure 8.2.

FIGURE 8.4

Evoked Potentials

Shown here is the average EEG, or "brain wave," tracing produced from several trials on which a participant's name was presented. Evoked potentials are averaged in this way so as to eliminate random variations in the tracings. The result is the appearance of a *negative* peak (N100) followed by a large *positive* peak (P300). Traditionally, positive peaks are shown as decreases on such tracings, whereas negative ones are shown as increases.

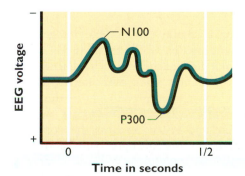

MENTAL REPRESENTATIONS: THE INGREDIENTS OF THOUGHT

Just as measuring, stirring, and baking are only part of the story of cookie-making, describing and timing the processes of thinking tell only part of the story behind the circle of thought. To understand thinking more fully, we also need to know what it is that these processes manipulate. Consistent with the information-processing model, most psychologists usually describe the ingredients of thought as *information*. But this is like saying that you make cookies with "stuff." What specific forms can information take in our minds? In other words, how do we mentally represent information? Researchers in cognitive psychology have found that information can be mentally represented in at least five forms: (1) cognitive maps, (2) mental images, (3) concept schemas and event scripts, (4) propositions, and (5) narratives. In the following sections we consider these ingredients of thought and how people manipulate them as they think.

Cognitive Maps

It is midnight. You are home alone when suddenly the power fails. Even though you can't see a thing, you are still able to find a flashlight or candle, not only because memory tells you where it is but because you carry with you a **cognitive map**—a mental representation of familiar parts of your world (Smythe et al., 1995). In this case, your cognitive map delineates the floor plan, furniture placements, door locations, and other physical features of your home. You would not have this mental map in an unfamiliar house; there, you would have to walk slowly, arms outstretched, to avoid wrong turns and painful collisions. In the chapter on learning we describe how experience shapes cognitive maps that, in turn, help animals navigate mazes and people navigate shopping malls.

What kind of experience do we need in order to create a cognitive map? Looking at our environment is obviously helpful, but research with blind people shows that visual experience is not necessary. For example, Barbara Landau (1986) gave a map with raised features to a young girl who had been blind from birth. The girl had never before touched such a map, but she was immediately able to understand what it was and to use it as effectively as sighted children of her age to plan routes through a room and locate toys. It appears that having the experience of moving through space is enough to allow us to represent information in the form of cognitive maps (Landau, 1986; Millar, 1994).

Useful as they are, cognitive maps are not accurate copies of the environment; they include systematic distortions. One distortion results from *rectangular bias*, a tendency to impose a rectangular north-south-east-west grid on the environment (Wickens, 1992a). For example, when asked to draw a map of Paris, most Parisians straighten out the bends of the Seine River in an effort to make it conform more closely to an east-west flow (Milgram & Jodelet, 1976). The rectangular bias also distorts the sense of relative locations. For example, without looking at a map of the United States, answer the following question: Is Reno, Nevada, east or west of San Diego, California? Most people say it is east (Stevens & Coupe, 1978). After all, most of Nevada is east of California, and Reno is in Nevada. But because southern California "bends" considerably to the east, Reno is, in fact, *west* of San Diego.

Mental Images

Think about how your best friend would look in a clown suit. Did you conjure up a mental picture? Often, thinking is based on the manipulation of **images**—that is, mental representations of visual information. Research suggests that the manipulations performed on mental images of objects are very similar to those that would be performed on the objects themselves (Kosslyn, 1994). For example, Steven Kosslyn (1976) asked people to form a mental image of an object such as a cat and then asked questions about it, such as "Does it have a head?" and "Does it have claws?" The smaller the detail in the question, the longer people took to answer, as if they were mentally zooming in on the detail necessary to respond. The finer the detail required by the question, the greater the zoom and the longer the response time.

Concept Schemas and Event Scripts

As mental representations of our physical world, cognitive maps and images are important ingredients of thought, but understanding that world requires still other ingredients. For one thing, we need ways of thinking about the world that encode the *meaning* of things. Think about anything—dogs, happiness, sex, movies, fame, pizza—and you are manipulating concepts, one of the most basic ingredients of thought. **Concepts** are categories of objects, events, or ideas with common properties (Jahnke & Nowaczyk, 1998). Concepts may be concrete and visual, such as the concepts "round" or "red," but they may also be abstract, such as the concepts "truth" and "justice." To "have a concept" is to recognize the properties, relationships, or *features* that

A Natural Concept

Both a space shuttle and a hot-air balloon are examples of the natural concept "aircraft," but most people would probably think of the space shuttle, with its wings, as the better example. A prototype of the concept is probably an airplane.

are shared by and define members of the category, and to ignore those that are not. For example, the concept "bird" includes such properties as having feathers, laying eggs, and being able to fly.

Concepts are vital to thought because they allow you to relate each object or event you encounter to a category that is already known. Concepts make logical thought possible. If you have the concepts "whale" and "bird," you can decide whether a whale is a bird without having either creature in the room with you.

Types of Concepts   Some concepts—called **artificial concepts**—can be clearly defined by a set of rules or properties such that each member of the concept has all of the defining properties and no nonmember does. For example, the concept "square" can be defined as "a shape with four equal sides and four right-angle corners." Any object that does not have all of these features simply is not a square. To study concept learning in the laboratory, psychologists often use artificial concepts because the members of the concept can be neatly defined (Trabasso & Bower, 1968).

In contrast, try to define the concept "home" or "game." These are examples of **natural concepts**, concepts that have no fixed set of *defining* features but instead share a set of *characteristic* features. Members of a natural concept need not possess all of the characteristic features. One characteristic feature of the natural concept "bird," for example, is the ability to fly; but an ostrich is a bird even though it cannot fly, because it possesses enough other characteristic features of "bird" (feathers, wings, and the like). Having just one bird property is not enough; snakes lay eggs and bats fly, but neither are birds. It is usually a *combination* of properties that defines a concept. Outside the laboratory, most of the concepts people use are natural rather than artificial. These natural concepts include both relatively stable "object" categories, such as "bird" or "house," and temporary goal-related categories, such as "things to put in a suitcase," that help people make plans (Barsalou, 1991, 1993).

The boundaries of a natural concept are fuzzy, and some members of it are better examples of the concept than others because they share more of its characteristic features (Rosch, 1975). A robin, a chicken, an ostrich, and a penguin are all birds. But a robin is a better example than the other three, because a robin can fly and is closer to the size and proportion of what most people, through experience, think of as a typical bird. A member of a natural concept that possesses all or most of its characteristic features is called a **prototype,** or is said to be prototypical (Smith, 1998). Thus, the robin is a prototypical bird. The more prototypical a member of a concept is, the more quickly people can decide if it is an example of the concept. Thus people can decide more rapidly that "a robin is a bird" than that "a penguin is a bird."

Representing Concepts   Concepts tend to be mentally represented as schemas, which, as described in Chapter 7, are generalizations we develop about categories of objects, events, and people. For example, our schema about birds probably includes a robin-like prototype, along with everything else we know about how birds look and act, where they live, and so on. Thus, schemas help us understand what birds are, as well as, say, what cars are, how baseball is played, and how police officers usually dress. Schemas also generate expectations about objects, events, and people—that cars have four wheels, that baseball is played in the summer, that police officers help people, and so on.

Schemas about familiar sequences of events or activities are called **scripts** (Schank & Abelson, 1977). For example, your script of the events that typically occur when you enter a restaurant tells you what you should and should not do in that situation. You also tend to interpret new information and events in line with your scripts. You assume that the person who greets you in a restaurant is an employee, not a mugger. Events that violate scripts may be misinterpreted or even ignored. Thus, you might step over a heart-attack victim on the sidewalk because your script for walking down a city street tells you that someone lying on the sidewalk is drunk, not sick. Indeed, scripts are involved in the top-down processing that prompts people to recognize and react to expected events more quickly and correctly than to unexpected ones. If a bank customer pulls a gun and demands money, the script-violating aspect of the event—though attention getting—may slow observers' perception of the situation and interfere with decisions about a course of action.

Propositions

Often, thinking involves relating one concept to another. Simple ideas about the relationships between and among concepts are called **propositions,** the smallest units of knowledge that can stand as a separate assertion. Propositions may be true or false. Some, such as "dogs chase cats," describe the relationship between concepts; others, such as "birds have wings," describe the relationship between a concept and its properties.

Mental Models   Often, clusters of propositions are represented as **mental models,** which contain our understanding of how things (usually physical things) work. These models then guide our interaction with such things (Norman, 1988). For example, to understand the sequence of commands necessary to edit, save, and retrieve a computer file, you might use a mental model that consists of propositions such as "Each file must have its own name," "Clicking on the 'Save' icon stores the file in a place on the hard drive," and the like. When our mental models are incorrect, we are more likely to make mistakes (see Figure 8.5). Thus, people who hold an incorrect mental model of how physical illness is cured might stop taking an antibiotic when their symptoms begin to disappear, well before the bacteria causing those symptoms have been eliminated (Medin & Ross, 1997).

Narratives

Information can also be mentally represented as a **narrative, or story.** Indeed, story-telling is one of the oldest and most common methods of passing information from one generation to the next. Stylized versions of stories, called *myths* or *parables,* are the basis of many of the world's traditions and religious beliefs and practices.

Accordingly, much of the information we store in, or retrieve from, our memory takes the form of stories. Some stories are told purely for their entertainment value, but many others are used to guide problem solving. Consider the following real example, in which a remembered story was used to solve a problem. During a camping trip in the woods, a family discovered that the gas lantern they had planned to use for light was broken. A gasket had stuck, preventing the gas from fueling the lantern, but no one

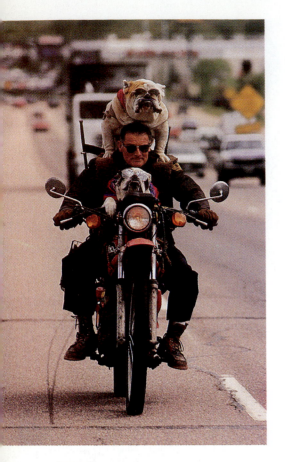

Violating a Schema

Schemas, or learned generalizations about objects, events, and people, result in expectations about the world. People tend to be surprised when schema-based expectations are not met, as in the case of motorcycle-riding dogs or three-wheeled automobiles.

Passing It On

We mentally represent information in many different ways, including as anecdotes, stories, myths, parables, and other narratives that we remember from our own experiences and from what others tell us.

FIGURE 8.5

Applying a Mental Model

Try to imagine the path that the marble will follow when it leaves the curved tube. In one study, most people drew the incorrect (curved) path indicated by the dotted line, rather than the correct (straight) path indicated by the dashed line (McClosky, 1983). Their error was based on a faulty mental model of the behavior of physical objects.

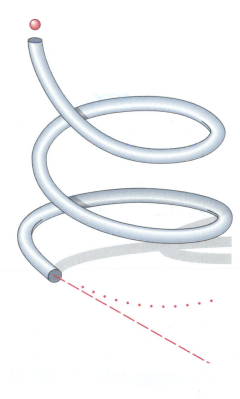

had packed the oil needed to lubricate the gasket. As the hour grew late and the night became stormy, one of the children recalled a time when their father had used motor oil from the car to fix a sticking part on a lawn mower. The whole family could picture that hot summer afternoon and remember how well that solution had worked. After recalling this story it was easy to realize that the car engine's dipstick could be used to get some motor oil and lubricate the lamp gasket. The problem was solved (Whitaker, 1998).

Later in this chapter, we discuss an emerging field of study known as *naturalistic decision making* (Zsambok and Klein, 1997), which emphasizes the importance of remembered stories among expert problem solvers. These experts tend to make extensive use of prior experiences, remembered in the form of narrative descriptions, to make decisions about solutions to current problems.

THINKING STRATEGIES

As already noted, our thinking capacity derives in large measure from our ability to manipulate mental representations—the ingredients of thought—much as a baker manipulates the ingredients of cookies (see "In Review: Ingredients of Thought" for a summary of these representations). But whereas the baker's food processor combines and transforms flour, sugar, milk, and chocolate into a delicious treat, our far more complex information-processing system combines, transforms, and elaborates mental representations in ways that allow us to engage in reasoning, problem solving, and decision making. We begin our discussion of these strategies by considering **reasoning,** the process through which people generate and evaluate arguments, and reach conclusions about them.

Formal Reasoning

Astronomers tell us that the temperature at the core of the sun is about 27 million degrees Fahrenheit. How do they know this? It is not possible to place a temperature probe inside the sun, so the assertion is necessarily based on astronomers' *inferences* from other facts they know about the sun and about physical objects in general. For example, telescopic observations of the sun's volume and mass allowed astronomers to calculate its density, using the formula Density = Mass ÷ Volume. Such observations also enabled them to measure the energy output from a small region of the sun and—

in review

INGREDIENTS OF THOUGHT		
Ingredient	**Description**	**How it is used**
Cognitive maps	Mental representations of familiar locations	Cognitive maps help us describe the world, plan routes, and reach destinations.
Mental images	Visual mental representations of physical objects, events, and scenes	Mental images can be manipulated—rotated, expanded, and examined—to help us think about spatial problems like those involved in navigation.
Concept schemas and event scripts	Generalizations about concepts formed by experience; mental representations of a typical sequence of activity, usually involving people's behavior	Concept schemas represent a large set of specific examples and create expectations; scripts may be used to interpret what will happen or is happening in familiar situations—a component of top-down processing.
Propositions	Smallest unit of knowledge that can stand as a separate assertion	Propositions are usually evaluated as to truth or falsity.
Mental models	Clusters of propositions that represent our understanding of how things work.	Mental models guide our interactions with things; they may be correct or biased.
Narratives	Stories that contain mental representations of important information learned in the past	Narratives are used to retrieve relevant concepts, schemas, and event scripts from memory.

using what geometry told them about the surface area of spheres—to extrapolate that value to the sun as a whole. Further calculations yielded an estimate of how hot a body would have to be to generate that much energy. In short, the astronomers' highly educated guess about the sun's core temperature was based on **formal reasoning** (also called *logical reasoning*), the process of following a set of rigorous procedures for reaching valid, or correct, conclusions. Some of these procedures included the application of specific mathematical formulas to existing data in order to generate new data. Such formulas, in turn, are examples of **algorithms,** systematic methods that always produce a correct solution to a problem, if a solution exists (Jahnke & Nowaczyk, 1998). The astronomers also followed the **rules of logic,** sets of statements that provide a formula for drawing valid conclusions about the world. For example, each step in the astronomers' thinking took the form of "if-then" statements: *If* we know how much energy comes from one part of the sun's surface, and *if* we know how big the whole surface is, *then* we can calculate the total energy output. You use the same formal reasoning processes when you conclude, for example, that *if* your friend José is two years older than you are, *then* his twin brother Juan will be two years older, too.

The rules of logic, which are traceable to the Greek philosopher Aristotle, have evolved into a system for drawing correct conclusions from a set of statements known as *premises.* Consider, for example, what conclusion can be drawn from the following premises:

Premise 1: *People who study hard do well in this course.*

Premise 2: *You have studied hard.*

According to the rules of logic, it would be valid to conclude that you will do well in this course. Logical arguments containing two or more premises and a conclusion are

Using Algorithms

Scientists in many fields use algorithms to perform calculations and draw conclusions about everything from the behavior of subatomic particles and wind-blown skyscrapers to weather systems and solar flares.

Pitfalls in Logical Reasoning

"Elderly people cannot be astronauts; this is an elderly man, therefore, he cannot be an astronaut." The logic of this syllogism is correct, but because the first premise is wrong, so is the conclusion. John Glenn, the astronaut who, in 1962, became the first American to orbit the Earth, returned to space in 1998 at the age of 77 as a full-fledged member of the crew of the space shuttle *Discovery*.

known as **syllogisms**. Notice that the conclusion in a syllogism goes beyond what the premises actually say. The conclusion is an *inference* based on the premises and on the rules of logic. In this case, the logical rule was that if something is true of all members of a category and "A" is in that category, then that something will also be true of "A."

Most of us try to use formal reasoning to reach valid conclusions and avoid erroneous ones (Rips, 1994), but we have to watch out for two pitfalls: incorrect premises and violations of the rules of logic. For example:

Premise 1: *All psychologists are brilliant.*

Premise 2: *The authors of this book are psychologists.*

Conclusion: *The authors of this book are brilliant.*

Do you agree? The conclusion follows logically from the premises, but because the first premise is false, we cannot determine whether or not the conclusion is true. Now consider this syllogism:

Premise 1: *All gun owners are people.*

Premise 2: *All criminals are people.*

Conclusion: *All gun owners are criminals.*

Here, the premises are correct, but the logic is faulty. If "all A's are B" and "all C's are B," it does *not* follow that "all A's are C." In other words, even conclusions based on correct premises can be false if they do not follow the rules of logic.

Psychologists have discovered that both kinds of pitfalls lead people to make errors in formal reasoning, which is one reason why misleading advertisements or speeches can still attract sales and votes (Solso, 1991). Psychologists have identified several specific sources of these errors.

1. **Bias about conclusions.** What do you think of this syllogism? *The United States is a free country. In a free country all people have equal opportunity. Therefore, in the United States all people have equal opportunity.* People who agree with this conclusion often do so not because they have carefully considered the premises but because they hold a prior belief about the conclusion (McGuire, 1968). The same tendency often frustrates district attorneys prosecuting a celebrity, a member of the clergy, or a harmless-looking senior citizen. Jurors may remain unpersuaded by logically sound arguments based on true premises simply because the logical conclusion (that a nice elderly woman poisoned her sister) is at odds with their schemas about such people and with their scripts about how the world operates. In other words, the conclusions that people reach are often based on both logical and wishful thinking (Evans, Barsten, & Pollard, 1983).

2. **The conversion effect.** People often assume that premises are symmetrical—that if A implies B, then B implies A. This is wrong, of course: Being a Democrat implies you are a person, but it does not follow that being a person implies you are a Democrat.

3. **Limits on working memory.** Evaluating syllogisms, particularly long ones, requires you to hold a lot of material in short-term, or working, memory while mentally manipulating it. This task is particularly difficult if elements in a syllogism involve negatives, as in "No dogs are nonanimals." If the amount of material to be manipulated exceeds the capacity of working memory, logical errors can easily result.

Cultural Differences in Formal Reasoning   Most of the time, logic and experience support the same conclusion. If they don't, the ideal option in most Western cultures is to rely on formal reasoning. But this ideal is not universal. In some cultures, direct experience is sometimes considered a surer guide than abstract logic.

For example, Alfred Bloom (1981) found that Chinese residents of Hong Kong showed a culturally based tendency to organize thought around known facts. They had a difficult time responding to questions such as "If the government were to pass a law requiring people to make weekly reports of their activities, how would you react?"

Bloom's research indicated that the Chinese language does not allow easy expression of *counterfactual arguments*, which are arguments that consider hypothetical propositions that are not currently true. Such arguments are rarely found in Chinese newspapers. These results do not mean that the Chinese are incapable of counterfactual thinking (Au, 1992; Liu, 1985); rather, they suggest that people's thinking in certain situations is shaped by both formal reasoning–based schooling and the culture in which that schooling takes place.

Informal Reasoning

The use of algorithms and logic to discover new facts and draw inferences is only one kind of reasoning. A second kind, **informal reasoning,** comes into play in situations where we are trying to assess the *credibility* of a conclusion based on the evidence available to support it. Psychologists use this kind of reasoning when they design experiments and other research methods whose results will provide evidence for (or against) their theories; jurors use informal reasoning when weighing evidence for the guilt or innocence of a defendant.

Formal reasoning is guided by algorithms and the rules of logic, but there are no foolproof methods for informal reasoning. Consider, for example, how many white swans you would have to see before concluding that all swans are white. Fifty? A hundred? A million? A strictly formal, algorithmic approach would require that you observe every swan in existence to be sure they are all white, but such a task would be impossible. A more practical approach is to base your conclusion on the number of observations that some mental rule of thumb leads you to believe is "enough." In other words, you would take a mental "shortcut" to reach a conclusion that is probably, but not necessarily, correct. Such mental shortcuts are called **heuristics.**

Suppose you are about to leave home but cannot find your watch. Applying an algorithm would mean searching in every possible location, room by room, until you find the watch. But you can reach the same outcome more quickly by using a heuristic—that is, by searching only where your experience suggests you might have left the watch. In short, heuristics are often valuable in guiding judgments about which events are probable or which hypotheses are likely to be true. Indeed, they are easy to use and frequently work well.

However, heuristics can also bias cognitive processes and result in errors. For example, if your rule of thumb is to vote for all political candidates in a particular party instead of researching the views of each individual, you might end up voting for someone with whom you strongly disagree on some issues. The degree to which heuristics are responsible for important errors in judgment and decision making is a matter of continuing research and debate by cognitive psychologists (Lopes, 1982; Mellers, Schwartz, & Cooke, 1998). Amos Tversky and Daniel Kahneman (1974, 1993) have described three potentially problematic heuristics that people seem to use intuitively in making judgments.

1. *The anchoring heuristic.* People use the **anchoring heuristic** when they estimate the probability of an event, not by starting from scratch but by adjusting an earlier estimate (Rottenstreich & Tversky, 1997). This strategy sounds reasonable, but the starting value biases the final estimate. Once people have fixed a starting point, their adjustments of the initial judgment tend to be insufficient. It is as if they drop a mental anchor at one hypothesis or estimate and then are reluctant to move very far from that original judgment. Thus, if you thought that the probability of being mugged in New York City is 90 percent and then found evidence that the figure is closer to 1 percent, you might reduce your estimate only to 80 percent. In American courtrooms, the anchoring heuristic presents a challenge for defense attorneys because, once jurors are affected by the prosecution's evidence (which is presented first), their belief in a defendant's guilt or in the amount of money the defendant should have to pay may be difficult to alter (Greene & Loftus, 1998; Hogarth & Einhorn, 1992). Similarly, first impressions of people are not easily shifted by later evidence.

2. *The representativeness heuristic.* Using the **representativeness heuristic,** people decide whether an example belongs in a certain class on the basis of how similar it is to other items in that class. For example, suppose you encounter a man who is tidy, small in stature, wears glasses, speaks quietly, and is somewhat shy. If asked whether this person is likely to be a librarian or a farmer, what would you say? Tversky and Kahneman (1974) found that most of their research participants chose *librarian.* But the chances are that this answer would be wrong. Why? Because of differences in the *base rates,* or commonness, of the two occupations. True, the description is more similar to the prototypical librarian than to the prototypical farmer, but because there are many more farmers in the world than librarians, there are probably more farmers than librarians who match this description. Therefore, a man matching this description is more likely to be a farmer than a librarian. In fact, almost any set of physical features is more likely to belong to a farmer than to a librarian.

Another study found that jurors' decisions to convict or acquit a defendant may depend, in part, on the degree to which the defendant's actions were representative of a crime category. For example, someone who abducts a child and asks for ransom (actions that clearly fit the crime category of kidnapping) is more likely to be convicted than someone who abducts an adult and demands no ransom—even though both crimes constitute kidnapping and the evidence is equally strong in each case (Smith, 1991).

3. *The availability heuristic.* Even when people use probability information to help them judge group membership or to assess a hypothesis, they may employ a third heuristic that can bias their thinking. The **availability heuristic** involves judging the probability that an event may occur or that a hypothesis may be true by how easily the hypothesis or examples of the event can be brought to mind (Eisenman, 1993). Thus, people tend to choose the hypothesis or alternative that is most mentally "available," much as you might choose which sweater to wear on the basis of which is on top in the drawer.

Like other heuristics, this shortcut tends to work well. After all, what people remember most easily are frequent events or likely hypotheses. However, the availability heuristic can lead to biased judgments, especially when mental availability and actual frequency fail to correspond. For example, television news reports showing the grisly aftermath of gang shootings and airline crashes may make these relatively rare events so memorable that people avoid certain cities or refuse to fly because they overestimate the frequency of crime or the probability of a crash (Slovic, 1984).

The three heuristics we have discussed represent only a few of the many strategies that people use intuitively, and they describe only some of the biases and limitations evident in human reasoning (Hogarth & Einhorn, 1992). Other biases and limitations will become clear in the following sections as we consider two important goals of thinking: problem solving and decision making.

PROBLEM SOLVING

If where you are is not where you want to be, and when the path to getting there is not obvious, you have a *problem.* The circle of thought suggests that the most efficient approach to problem solving would be to first diagnose the problem in the elaboration stage, then formulate a plan for solving it, then execute the plan, and finally, evaluate the results to determine whether the problem remains (Bransford & Stein, 1993). But people's problem-solving skills are not always so systematic, which is one reason why medical tests are sometimes given unnecessarily, diseases are sometimes misdiagnosed, and auto parts are sometimes replaced when there is nothing wrong with them.

Strategies for Problem Solving

When you are trying to get from a starting point to some goal, the best path may not necessarily be a straight line. In fact, obstacles may dictate going in the opposite

LINKAGES

Simply knowing about problem-solving strategies, such as decomposition, is not enough. As described in Chapter 11, on motivation and emotion, people must perceive the effort involved to be worth the rewards it is likely to bring.

Calvin and Hobbes   by Bill Watterson

Going for the Top

Whether one is attempting to reach the summit of Mt. Everest or merely organizing a family vacation, working backwards from the final goal through all the steps necessary to reach that goal can provide a helpful approach to solving complex problems.

direction. So it is with problem solving. Sometimes, the best strategy is not to take mental steps aimed straight at your goal. Psychologists have identified several strategies that work better for certain problems.

When a problem is so complicated that all of its elements cannot be held in working memory at once, you can use a strategy called *decomposition* to divide it into smaller, more manageable subproblems. Thus, instead of being overwhelmed by the big problem of writing a major term paper, you can begin by writing just an outline. Next, you can visit a library and search the Internet to find the information most relevant to each successive section of the outline. Then you can write summaries of those materials, then a rough draft of an introduction, and so on.

A second strategy is to *work backward.* Many problems are like a tree. The trunk is the information you are given; the solution is a twig on one of the limbs. If you work forward by taking the "givens" of the problem and trying to find the solution, it will be easy to branch off in the wrong direction. A more efficient approach may be to start at the twig end and work backward (Best, 1995). Consider, for example, the problem of planning a climb to the summit of Mount Everest (Krakauer, 1997). The best strategy is to figure out, first, what equipment and supplies are needed at the highest camp on the night before the summit attempt, then how many people are needed to stock that camp the day before, then how many people are needed to supply those who must stock the camp, and so on until the logistics of the entire expedition are established. Failure to apply this strategy was one reason that six climbers died on Mount Everest in 1996 (Krakauer, 1997).

Third, try finding *analogies.* Many problems are similar to others you have encountered before. A supervisor may find, for example, that a seemingly hopeless impasse between co-workers may be resolved by the same compromise that worked during a recent family squabble. To take advantage of analogies, the problem solver must first recognize the similarities between current and previous problems, and then recall the solution that worked before. Surprisingly, most people are not very good at drawing analogies from one problem to another (Medin & Ross, 1997). They tend to concentrate on the surface features that make problems appear different.

Finally, in the case of an especially difficult problem, a helpful strategy is to allow it to "incubate" by laying it aside for a while. A solution that once seemed out of reach may suddenly appear after a person engages in unrelated mental activity for a period of time (Silviera, 1971). Indeed, the benefits of incubation probably arise from forgetting incorrect ideas that may have been blocking the path to a correct solution (Best, 1995).

The problem-solving strategies just listed were identified mainly by psychologists who conducted laboratory experiments in which they observed volunteers wrestling with, and perhaps "thinking aloud" about, various kinds of problems.

FOCUS ON RESEARCH METHODS

Using Case Studies to Explore Problem-Solving Strategies

◾ What was the researcher's question?

Gary Bradshaw (1993a, 1993b) wondered whether the strategies seen in these laboratory experiments reflect the problem-solving methods that people actually use in the real world.

◾ How did the researcher answer the question?

Bradshaw knew that some psychologists had conducted *case studies* in which they used research notes and other archival evidence to reconstruct the problem-solving strategies associated with major inventions and discoveries (Weber, 1992). However, he also knew that, as a source of evidence, case studies are vulnerable to two important problems: the striking-feature syndrome and causal uncertainty. The *striking-feature syndrome* occurs when an unusual feature in a case chosen for study is given too much weight. Consider the case of a woman who died of a brain tumor not long ago. Her grieving husband focused on a striking feature in her recent life—frequent use of a cellular telephone—and came to the conclusion that the phone's high-frequency magnetic field was responsible for his wife's illness. The phone manufacturer's defense in the resulting lawsuit was based on *causal uncertainty;* the tumor could have been caused by the phone or by something else. As noted in Chapter 2, evidence from a single case study is not sufficient to establish a cause-effect relationship. Indeed, the company presented data showing that cellular telephone users have a *lower* incidence of brain cancer than the general population and, further, that the risk of brain cancer is not positively correlated with the amount of time spent using a cellular phone (Sandler, 1993). On the basis of this more systematic evidence, the judge dismissed the lawsuit.

The limitations of single case studies prompted Bradshaw to use the *comparative case study* method to explore real-world problem-solving strategies. Using this method requires the researcher to collect a large number of cases, then to look for common features that suggest the operation of a particular mental strategy. Bradshaw used comparative case studies to identify the problem-solving strategies that led to the invention of the airplane. His database included turn-of-the-century records from 49 individuals or teams working on what they hoped would be a self-propelled heavier-than-air flying machine. Of the 135 designs developed, only that of the Wright brothers was successful. In fact, the Wrights took only four years to develop the airplane, whereas others labored without success for decades.

◾ What did the researcher find?

When Bradshaw compared the Wright brothers' problem-solving strategies to those of the unsuccessful individuals and teams, he found that it took more than just good luck for the Wrights to solve the problem of heavier-than-air flight. Bradshaw found that several factors might have contributed to their success: (1) As bachelors, they had a lot of spare time to work on their designs; (2) as owners of a bicycle shop, they were familiar with lightweight but sturdy structures; (3) as brothers, they had a rapport that helped them work together; and (4) as mechanics, they were good with their hands. Were any of these striking features causally related to their ultimate success?

Perhaps, but Bradshaw's use of the comparative case study method revealed that everyone else working on the problem of flight shared one or more of these features with the Wright brothers. For example, an engineer named Octave Chanute was good with his hands and familiar with sturdy, lightweight structures. And two other pairs of brothers had worked to invent an airplane. In other words, the comparative case study method showed that the most striking features of the Wrights' case were probably incidental to their success. It also revealed a feature unique to the Wright brothers' approach: They alone devoted large amounts of time and energy to testing more than a dozen aircraft *components* before they field-tested complete machines (see Figure 8.6 on page 264). This feature was important because even the best machines of the day flew for only a few seconds, far too briefly to reveal what was working and what was

FIGURE 8.6

The Wright Brothers' Wind Tunnel

The Wright brothers built this wind tunnel to test the in-flight performance of various wing shapes and propellers. Decomposition of the problem of flight into smaller subproblems was probably the key to the Wrights' success.

not. As a result, other inventors were forced to guess about what to fix, often ending up with an "improved" model that was worse than the previous one. The Wrights' testing program, by contrast, gave them the information they needed to develop an efficient propeller, improve the shape of wings for maximum lift, and refine other vital components of their aircraft.

■ What do the results mean?

Bradshaw's comparative case study method suggests that decomposition of a problem into smaller subproblems, a strategy often seen in laboratory studies of problem solving, may have contributed to some of the world's major inventions and discoveries. His results also highlight the potential value of comparative case studies for helping to establish the applicability of laboratory research results in a wide range of research domains. Lab experiments allow psychologists to identify causal relationships between the independent and dependent variables of interest and can thus be said to have strong *internal validity*. But these experiments are sometimes weak in *external validity*—that is, in how well the results generalize to what goes on outside the laboratory (Shadish, Cook, & Campbell, in press). Comparative case studies tend to have stronger internal validity than the single case study and stronger external validity than some laboratory experiments.

■ What do we still need to know?

The efforts of the Wright brothers and others to develop an airplane represented only one kind of problem, addressed during a particular historical era, using a particular form of technology. In this respect, even the comparative case study methodology employed by Bradshaw lacks external validity: We do not know the extent to which his conclusions generalize to the problem solving methods used by, say, the computer scientists who developed the Internet or the engineers who built the "chunnel" under the English Channel. These well-documented technological achievements provide a rich resource for further research by psychologists interested in real-world problem solving.

Obstacles to Problem Solving

The failure of the Wright brothers' competitors to use decomposition is just one example of the obstacles that face problem solvers every day. Difficulties frequently occur at the start, during the diagnosis stage, when a person forms and then tests hypotheses about a problem.

As a case in point, consider the following true story: In September of 1998, John Gatiss was making a cup of coffee in the kitchen of his rented house in Cheltenham, England, when he heard a faint "meowing" sound. He could not find the source of the sound, but he assumed that a kitten had become trapped in the walls or under the flooring, so he called for the fire brigade to rescue the animal. The sound seemed to be coming from the electric stove, so the rescuers dismantled it, pulling out the power cord in the process. The sound stopped, but everyone assumed that, wherever the kitten was, it had become too frightened to meow. The search was reluctantly abandoned, and the stove was reconnected, but four days later, the meowing began anew. This time, Mr. Gatiss and his landlord called the Royal Society for the Prevention of Cruelty to Animals (RSPCA), whose inspectors heard the kitten in distress and asked the fire brigade rescue squad to return. They spent the next three days searching for the cat. They first dismantled parts of the kitchen walls and ripped up the floorboards, but found nothing. Next, they called in plumbing and drainage specialists who used cables tipped with fiber-optic cameras to search the invisible cavities where a kitten might hide. When the cameras failed to find the little animal, the rescuers enlisted the help of a disaster search team who tried to locate the kitten using acoustic and ultrasonic equipment designed to locate victims trapped in the debris of earthquakes and explosions. Not a sound could be heard. Increasingly concerned about how much longer the kitten could survive, the fire brigade tried to coax it from hiding with the finest quality fish, but to no avail. Suddenly, there was a burst of "purring" that, to everyone's surprise (and the landlord's dismay) the ultrasonic equipment traced to the clock in the electric stove! Later, the landlord commented that everyone assumed that Mr. Gatiss's hypothesis was right—that the "meowing" came from a cat, and that it was trapped in the kitchen. "I just let them carry on. If there is an animal in there, you have to do what it takes. The funniest thing was that it seemed to reply when we called out to it" (London Daily Telegraph, September 19, 1998).

How could fifteen fire-rescue workers, three RSPCA inspectors, four drainage workers, and two acoustics experts waste eight days and cause nearly $2000 in damage to a house in pursuit of a nonexistent kitten? The answer lies in the fact that they, like the rest of us, are prone to four main obstacles to efficient problem solving, described in the following sections.

Multiple Hypotheses Often, people begin to solve a problem with only a vague notion of which hypotheses to test. For example, there may be a dozen reasons why a car will not start. Which of these hypotheses should be tested, and in what order? People seem to have a difficult time entertaining more than two or three hypotheses at a time (Mehle, 1982). The limited capacity of working memory, discussed in Chapter 7, may be part of the reason. As a result, the correct hypothesis is often neglected. Which hypothesis a person considers may depend on the availability heuristic. In other words, the particular hypothesis considered may be the one that most easily comes to mind, not the one most likely to be correct (Tversky & Kahneman, 1974). Thus, Mr. Gatiss diagnosed the sound he heard as a kitten, not a clock, because such sounds usually come from kittens, not clocks.

Mental Sets Sometimes people are so blinded by one hypothesis or strategy that they continue to apply it even when better alternatives should be obvious (a clear case of the anchoring heuristic at work). Once Mr. Gatiss reported hearing a "trapped kitten," his description created an assumption that everyone else accepted and which no one challenged. A laboratory example of this phenomenon devised by Abraham Luchins (1942) is shown in Figure 8.7 on page 266. The object of each problem in the

FIGURE 8.7

The Luchins Jar Problem

The problem is to obtain the quantities of liquid shown in the first column by filling jars with the capacities shown in the next three columns. Each line represents a different problem. See if you can solve the first six without looking at the answer in the text; then try the last one. In dealing with such problems, people often fall prey to mental sets that prevent them from using the most efficient solution.

QUANTITY	JAR A	JAR B	JAR C
1. 21 quarts	8	35	3
2. 10 quarts	6	18	1
3. 19 quarts	5	32	4
4. 21 quarts	20	57	8
5. 18 quarts	8	40	7
6. 6 quarts	7	17	2
7. 15 quarts	12	33	3

Problem: Measure out the above quantities by using jars with the stated capacities (in quarts).

FIGURE 8.8

The Nine-Dot Problem

The problem is to draw no more than four straight lines that run through all nine dots on the page without lifting your pencil from the paper. Figure 8.10 (on page 268) shows two ways of going beyond mental constraints to solve this problem.

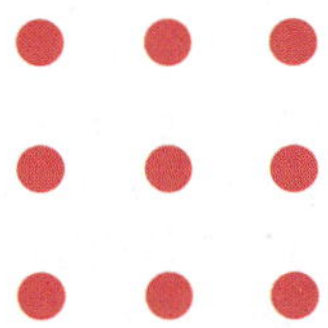

figure is to use three jars with specified capacities to obtain a certain amount of liquid. For example, in the first problem you are to obtain 21 quarts by using three jars that have capacities of 8, 35, and 3 quarts, respectively. The solution is to fill Jar B to its capacity, 35 quarts, and then use its contents to fill Jar A to its capacity of 8 quarts, leaving 27 quarts in Jar B. Then pour liquid from Jar B to fill Jar C to its capacity twice, leaving 21 quarts in Jar B ($27 - (2 \times 3) = 21$). In other words, the general solution is B − A − 2C. Now solve the remaining problems.

If you went through the problems in Figure 8.7, you found that a similar solution worked each time. But what happened with problem 7? If you are like most people, you did not notice that it has a simpler solution (namely, A + C). Instead, you succumbed to a **mental set,** the tendency for old patterns of problem solving to persist (Sweller & Gee, 1978). In the Luchins jar problem, the mental set consists of a tendency to stick with a strategy or solution that worked in the past. Figures 8.8 and 8.10 show that a mental set may also restrict your perception of the problem itself.

Yet another restriction on problem solving may come from experience with objects. Once people become accustomed to using an object for one type of function, they may be blinded to other ways of using it. Thus, experience may produce **functional fixedness**, a tendency to use familiar objects in familiar rather than creative ways. Figure 8.9 illustrates an example. An incubation strategy often helps to break mental sets.

The Confirmation Bias   Anyone who has had a series of medical tests knows that diagnosis is not a one-shot decision. Instead, physicians choose an initial hypothesis on the basis of observed symptoms and then order tests or evaluate additional symptoms to confirm or refute that hypothesis. This process may be distorted by the **confirmation bias:** Humans have a strong bias to confirm rather than to refute the hypothesis they have chosen, even in the face of strong evidence against the hypothesis. In other words, people are quite willing to perceive and accept data that support their hypothesis—that a defendant is guilty, for example—but they tend to ignore information that is inconsistent with it (Aronson, Wilson, & Akert, 1999; Ditto & Lopez, 1992). Thus, the confirmation bias may be seen as a form of the anchoring heuristic, in that it involves reluctance to abandon an initial hypothesis. The would-be rescuers of the "trapped kitten" were so intent on their humanitarian efforts to pinpoint its location that they never stopped to question its existence.

Ignoring Negative Evidence   Often, what does not happen can be as important as what does. For example, when troubleshooting a car problem, you may be led by failed headlights to hypothesize that the battery is low. But if this were the case, other battery-powered equipment should also have failed. The absence of symptoms can provide

FIGURE 8.9

An Example of Functional Fixedness

How would you fasten together two strings that are hanging from the ceiling but are out of reach of each other? Several tools are available, yet most people do not think of attaching, say, the pliers to one string and swinging it like a pendulum until it can be reached while holding the other string. This solution is not obvious because we tend to fixate on the function of pliers as a tool rather than as a weight. People are more likely to solve this problem if the tools are scattered around the room. When the pliers are in a tool box, their function as a tool is emphasized, and functional fixedness becomes nearly impossible to break.

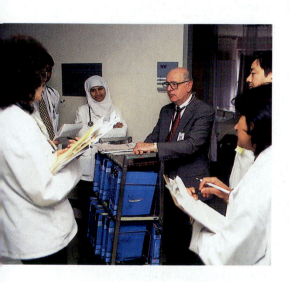

The Voice of Experience

Experts such as this senior physician are usually able to solve problems in their domain of expertise faster than novices can. Their superior performance is due largely to the fact that their long experience allows them to see the similarities between today's problems and those they have solved in the past. However, experience can create mental sets, so the challenge for these experts is to let experience guide them without letting it blind them.

important evidence for or against a hypothesis. Compared with symptoms that are present, however, symptoms or events that do not occur are less likely to be noticed (Hunt & Rouse, 1981). People have a difficult time using the absence of symptoms to help eliminate hypotheses from consideration (Ashcraft, 1989). Thus, in the "trapped kitten" case, when the "meowing" stopped for several days after the stove was unplugged and reconnected, the rescuers assumed that the animal was frightened into silence; they did not pay attention to the possibility that their hypothesis was incorrect in the first place.

Building Problem-Solving Skills

Psychologists have reasoned that it should be possible to train people not to fall prey to the biases that impair problem solving, and attempts to do so have produced some modest benefits. For example, in one study, cautioning people against their tendency to anchor on a hypothesis reduced the magnitude of the confirmation bias and increased their openness to alternative evidence (Lopes, 1982).

How do experts avoid obstacles to problem solving? What do they bring to a situation that a novice does not? Knowledge based on experience is particularly important (Mayer, 1992). Experts frequently proceed by looking for analogies between current and past problems. Compared with novices, they are better able to relate new information and new experiences to past experiences and existing knowledge (Anderson, 1995b; Bedard & Chi, 1992). Accordingly, experts can use existing knowledge to organize new information into chunks, a process described in the chapter on memory. By chunking many elements of a problem into a smaller number of units, experts apparently can visualize problems more clearly and efficiently than novices.

Experts can use their experience as a guide because they tend to perceive the similarity between new and old problems more deeply than novices (Hardimann, Dufresne, & Mestre, 1989). Specifically, experts see the similarity of underlying principles, whereas novices perceive similarity only in superficial features. As a result, experts can more quickly and easily apply these principles to solve the new problem. In one study, expert physicists and novice physics students sorted physics problems into groups (Chi, Feltovitch, & Glaser, 1981). The novices grouped together problems that looked similar (such as those involving blocks lying on an inclined plane), whereas the experts grouped together problems that could be solved by the same principle (such as Newton's second law of motion).

FIGURE 8.10

Two Creative Solutions to the Nine-Dot Problem

Many people find puzzles like this difficult because their mental sets create artificial constraints on the range of solutions. In this case, the mental sets involve the tendency to draw within the frame of the dots and to draw through the middle of each dot. As shown here, however, there are other possibilities.

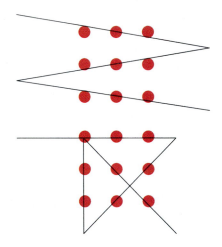

Experience also gives experts a broader perspective on the problem domain, allowing them to perceive the whole problem "tree" so that they can work forward without error, thus avoiding the slower "working backward" strategy more suited to the novice (Medin & Ross, 1997). Finally, successful problem solvers can explain each step in the solution, and can maintain awareness of precisely what is and is not understood along the way (Medin & Ross, 1997).

Although experts are often better problem solvers than novices, expertise also carries a danger: Using past experience can lead to the traps of functional fixedness and mental sets. Top-down, knowledge-driven processes can bias you toward seeing what you expect or want to see and prevent you from seeing a problem in new ways. Indeed, as in the case of the "trapped kitten," confirmation bias sometimes prevents experts from appreciating that a proposed solution is incorrect (Fischoff & Slovic, 1980). Several studies have shown that, although experts may be more confident in their solutions (Payne, Bettman, & Johnson, 1992), they are not always more accurate than novices in such areas as medical diagnosis, accounting, and pilot judgment (Wickens et al., 1992).

In short, there is a fine line between using past experience and being trapped by it. Experience alone does not ensure excellence at problem solving, and practice may not make perfect (see Table 8.1).

Problem Solving by Computer

In view of all the weaknesses of human problem solving, some people hope that computers can take over some aspects of human thinking. (For a summary of our discussion of human problem solving, see "In Review: Solving Problems.") Scientists in the field of **artificial intelligence,** or **AI,** are developing computer systems that imitate the products of human perception and thought. For example, some computers can now beat the best chess masters, and computer programs may be much better at predicting heart attacks from electrocardiograms than even experienced cardiologists (Gawande, 1998).

TABLE 8.1

Some Expert Opinions

Experts typically have a large store of knowledge about their realm of expertise, but even confidently stated opinions based on this knowledge can turn out to be incorrect, as these examples from Christopher Cerf and Victor Navasky's *The Experts Speak* (1998) clearly show.

On the possibility of painless surgery through anesthesia:

"'Knife' and 'pain' are two words in surgery that must forever be associated.... To this compulsory combination we shall have to adjust ourselves." (Dr. Alfred Velpeau, professor of surgery, Paris Faculty of Medicine, 1839)

On the hazards of cigarette smoking:

"If excessive smoking actually plays a role in the production of lung cancer, it seems to be a minor one." (Dr. W. C. Heuper, National Cancer Institute, 1954)

On the stock market (one week before the disastrous 1929 crash that wiped out over $50 billion in investments):

"Stocks have reached what looks like a permanently high plateau." (Irving Fisher, professor of economics, Yale University, 1929)

On the prospects of war with Japan (three years before the December 1941 Japanese attack on Pearl Harbor):

"A Japanese attack on Pearl Harbor is a strategic impossibility." (Major George F. Eliot, military science writer, 1938)

On the value of personal computers:

"There is no reason for any individual to have a computer in their home." (Ken Olson, president, Digital Equipment Corporation, 1977)

On the concept of the airplane:

"Heavier-than-air flying machines are impossible." (Lord Kelvin, mathematician, physicist, and president of the British Royal Society, 1895)

SOLVING PROBLEMS

Steps	Pitfalls	Remedies
Define the problem	Inexperience: the tendency to see each problem as unique.	Gain experience and practice in seeing the similarity between present problems and previous problems.
Form hypotheses about solutions	Availability heuristic: the tendency to recall the hypothesis or solution that is most available to memory.	Force yourself to entertain different hypotheses.
	Anchoring heuristic, or mental set: the tendency to anchor on the first solution or hypothesis and not adjust your beliefs in light of new evidence or failures of the current approach.	Break the mental set, stop, and try a fresh approach.
Test hypotheses	The tendency to ignore negative evidence.	In evaluating a hypothesis, consider the things you should see (but don't) if the hypothesis were true.
	Confirmation bias: the tendency to seek only evidence that confirms your hypothesis.	Look for disconfirming evidence that, if found, would show your hypothesis to be false.

Symbolic Reasoning and Computer Logic   Early efforts at developing artificial intelligence focused on computers' enormous capabilities for formal reasoning and symbol manipulation and on their abilities to follow general problem-solving strategies, such as working backward (Newell & Simon, 1972). This logic-based approach has been reasonably successful at addressing many problems through the development of expert systems. Expert systems are computer programs that solve problems in relatively restricted areas, such as diagnosing infectious diseases, forecasting solar flares, or evaluating bank loan applications (Bradshaw & Shaw, 1992).

Valuable as it is, the logic-based approach to AI has important limitations. Expert systems, for example, are successful only in very narrowly defined fields, and, even within a specific domain, computers show limited ability. There are no ways of putting into computer code all aspects of the reasoning of human experts. Sometimes, the experts can only say, "I know it when I see it, but I can't put it into words" (Dreyfus & Dreyfus, 1988). And making connections among remote knowledge domains is far beyond the grasp of current systems, partly because the builders of the systems seldom know ahead of time which other areas of knowledge might lead to insight. Thus, they can't tell computers where to look for new ideas or how to use them. Yet drawing analogies and noting similarities across domains are important to expert problem solving.

Finally, AI systems based on logical symbolic manipulations depend on "if-then" rules, and it is often difficult to tell a computer how to recognize the "if" condition in the real world (Dreyfus & Dreyfus, 1988). Consider just one example: "If it's a clock, then set it." Humans can recognize all kinds of clocks because they have the natural concept of "clock," but computers are very poor at this task. As discussed earlier, forming natural concepts requires putting into the same category many examples that may have very different physical features—from a bedside digital alarm to Big Ben.

Neural Network Models   Realizing that a large amount of intelligent diagnosis and problem solving depends on recognition and classification of current conditions and ill-defined patterns, many workers in the AI field have moved toward the *connectionist* or *neural network* approach discussed in earlier chapters (Anderson, 1995b). This approach is very effective for modeling many aspects of perceptual recognition. Neural

Artificial Intelligence

Chess master Gary Kasparov had his hands full when he was challenged by "Big Blue," a chess-playing computer that has been programmed so well that it has won games against the world's best competitors, including Kasparov. Still, even the most sophisticated computers cannot perceive and think about the world in general anywhere near as well as humans can. Some observers believe that this situation will eventually change as progress in computer technology—and a deepening understanding of human cognitive processes—leads to dramatic breakthroughs in artificial intelligence.

network approaches to AI have greatly improved computer abilities in areas such as understanding speech and reading print (Churchland & Sejnowski, 1992) and forecasting solar flares (Bradshaw & Shaw, 1992).

Current computer models of neural networks still fall well short of the capacities of the human perceptual system, however (Hofstadter, 1995). For example, they are incredibly slow to learn how to classify visual patterns, and unlike humans, they don't show sudden insights when a key common feature is identified.

Computer-Assisted Problem Solving   For at least the foreseeable future, it may be that computers can best be used to help humans solve problems; indeed, a combined human-computer effort is often more efficient than a computer working alone. For example, today, laboratory technologists who test samples of patients' blood to find the causes of disease are assisted by computer programs that serve three useful functions: (1) to keep track of the findings from previous tests; (2) to provide a systematic listing of the possible tests that remain to be tried; and (3) to indicate either that certain tests have been left undone or that a new sequence of tests should be done (Guerlain, 1993, 1995). Indeed, it has been shown that by using such programs, technologists are able to avoid repeating errors they have made in the past. Note that the computer program does not solve the diagnosis problem for the technologist; instead, it suggests tests that provide information that the technologists know how to interpret.

DECISION MAKING

Dr. Wallace's patient, Laura McBride, faced a simple decision: risk death by doing nothing or protect herself from lead poisoning. Most decisions are not so easy. Patients must decide whether to undergo a dangerous operation; a college senior must choose a career; a corporate executive must decide whether to shut down a factory. Unlike the high-speed decisions discussed earlier, these decisions require considerable time, planning, and mental effort.

Even carefully considered decisions sometimes lead to undesirable outcomes, however, because the world is uncertain. Decisions made when the outcome is uncertain are called *risky decisions* or *decisions under uncertainty*. Psychologists have discovered many reasons why human decisions may lead to unsatisfactory outcomes, and we describe some of them here.

Evaluating Options

Suppose that you must choose between (1) an academic major that fascinates you but is unlikely to lead to a good job, or (2) a major that is uninteresting but virtually guarantees a high-paying career. The fact that each option has positive and negative features, or *attributes,* greatly complicates decision making. Deciding which car to buy, which college to attend, or even how to spend the evening are all examples of *multiattribute decision making* (Edwards, 1987). Often these decisions are further complicated by difficulties in comparing the attributes and in estimating the probabilities of various outcomes.

Comparing Attributes   Multiattribute decisions can be difficult in part because the limited storage capacity of working memory does not permit people to easily keep in mind and compare all of the attributes of all of the options (Bettman, Johnson, & Payne, 1990). Instead, people tend to focus on the one attribute that is most important to them (Kardes, 1999; Tversky, 1972). If, for instance, finishing a degree quickly is most important to you, then you might choose courses based mainly on curricular requirements, without giving much consideration to the reputations of the professors. (Listing the pros and cons of each option offers a helpful way of keeping them all in mind as you contemplate decisions.)

Furthermore, the attributes of the options involved in most important decisions cannot be measured in dollars or other relatively objective terms. Instead, people are forced to compare "apples and oranges." Psychologists use the term utility to describe the subjective, personal value of each attribute. In deciding on a major, for example, you have to think about the positive and negative utilities of each attribute—such as the job prospects and interest level—of each major. Then you must somehow weigh and combine these utilities. Will the positive utility of enjoying your courses be higher than the negative utility of risking unemployment?

Estimating Probabilities   Uncertainty adds other difficulties to the decision-making process: To make a good decision, you should take into account not only the attributes of the options but also the probabilities and risks of their possible outcomes. For example, the economy could change by the time you graduate, closing many of today's job opportunities in one of the majors you are considering and perhaps opening opportunities in the other.

In studying risky decision making, psychologists begin by assuming that the best decision is the one that maximizes expected value, or the total amount of benefit you could expect to receive if the decision were repeated on several occasions. Suppose someone asks you to buy a charity raffle ticket. You know that it costs $2 to enter and that the probability of winning the $100 prize is one in ten (.10). Assuming you are more interested in the prize money than in donating to the charity, the question becomes: Should you enter? The expected value of entering is determined by multiplying the probability of gain (.10) by the size of the gain ($100); this is the average benefit you would receive if you entered the raffle many times. Next, from this product you would subtract the probability of loss, which is 1.0 (the entry fee is a certain loss), multiplied by the amount of the loss ($2). That is, $(.10 \times \$100) - (1.0 \times \$2) = \$8$. Since this eight-dollar expected value is greater than the expected value of not entering (which is zero), you should enter. However, if the odds of winning the raffle were one in a hundred (.01), then the expected value of entering would be $(.01 \times \$100) - (1.0 \times \$2) = -\$1$. In this case, since the expected value is negative, you should not enter the raffle.

Biases and Flaws in Decision Making

In everyday life, people do not always behave so as to maximize expected values (Curim & Sarin, 1992; Gilovich, 1997), and it is important to consider some of the reasons why.

Gains, Losses, and Probabilities   For one thing, positive utilities are not mirror images of negative utilities. Instead, people generally feel worse about losing a certain amount than they feel good about gaining the same amount (Dawes, 1998; Mellers, Schwartz, & Cooke, 1998), a phenomenon known as *loss aversion* (Tversky & Kahneman, 1991). Thus, they may be willing to expend more effort to try collecting a $100 debt than to try winning a $100 prize.

A Highly Unlikely Outcome

By focusing public attention on the very few people who win big lottery prizes, state lottery agencies take advantage of the general human tendency to overestimate the probability of rare events. Lottery ads never show the millions of people whose tickets turn out to be worthless.

It also appears that the utility of a specific gain depends not on the absolute increase in value but on what the starting point was. Suppose you can take some action to receive a coupon for a free dinner worth $10. Does this gain have the same utility as having an extra $10 added to your paycheck? The dollar amount is the same, but people tend to behave as if the difference in utility between $0 and $10 is much greater than the difference between, say, $300 and $310. Thus, they may refuse to drive across town after work to earn a $10 bonus but would gladly make the same trip to pick up a $10 coupon. This tendency calls to mind Weber's law of psychophysics, discussed in Chapter 5, on perception. How much a difference in value means to you depends on how much you already have (Dawes, 1998); the more you have, the less it means.

Biases in the perception of probability are also a source of less than optimal decisions. Two such biases are especially interesting. The first is the tendency to overestimate rare probabilities and to underestimate frequent ones (Kahneman & Tversky, 1984). This bias helps explain not only why people buy insurance but also why they gamble and enter lotteries, even though the odds are against them and the decision to do so has a negative expected value. According to the formula for expected value, buying a $1 lottery ticket when the probability of winning $4,000,000 is one in ten million yields an expected value of −60 cents. But because people overestimate the probability of winning, they believe there is a positive expected value. The tendency to overestimate the likelihood of unlikely events is amplified by the availability heuristic: Vivid memories of rare gambling successes and the publicity given to lottery winners help people recall gains rather than losses when deciding about future gambles (Waagenaar, 1989).

Another bias relating to probability is called the gambler's fallacy: People believe that events in a random process will correct themselves. This belief is false. For example, if you flip a coin and it comes up heads ten times in a row, the chance that it will come up heads on the eleventh try is still 50 percent. Some gamblers, however, will continue feeding a slot machine that hasn't paid off much for hours, assuming it is "due." This assumption may be partly responsible for the resistance to extinction of intermittently reinforced behaviors, as described in Chapter 6.

Yet another factor underlying flaws in human decision making is the tendency for people to be unrealistically confident in the accuracy of their predictions. Baruch Fischoff and Donald MacGregor (1982) used an ingenious approach to study this bias. They asked people whether they believed that a certain event would occur—for example, that a certain sports team would win—and how confident they were about this prediction. After the events took place, the accuracy of the forecasts was computed and compared with the confidence assigned to the predictions. Sure enough, people's confidence in their predictions was consistently greater than their accuracy. This overconfidence operates even when people make predictions concerning the accuracy of their own memory (Plous, 1993).

Overconfidence in one's decisions occurs in many cultures, but it is more common in some than others. For example, Chinese students are more likely to show this bias than Americans. One possible explanation is that students in China are discouraged from challenging what they are told by teachers, so they may be less likely than Americans to question what they tell themselves and thus more likely to be overconfident (Yates, Lee, & Shinotsuka, 1992).

The moral of the story is to be wary when people in any culture express confidence that a forecast or decision is correct. They will be wrong more often than they think.

How Biased Are We?   Although the previous discussion suggests that human decision making is flawed, psychologists are divided on the extent of the biases involved (Cohen, 1993; Payne, Bettman, & Johnson, 1992). Whereas nearly everyone has made decisions they later regret, many human decisions are intended not to maximize expected value but to satisfy some other criterion, such as minimizing expected loss or producing acceptable outcomes with a minimum expenditure of time or mental effort (Zsambok & Klein, 1997). For example, it makes no sense to perform time-consuming mental gymnastics aimed at deciding what to wear each day.

It is also true that the "goodness" or "badness" of many decisions is difficult to assess, because so many of them depend on personal values (utilities), and these vary from person to person and from culture to culture. People in individualist cultures may tend to assign high utilities to attributes that promote personal goals, whereas those in collectivist cultures might place greater value on attributes that bring group harmony and the approval of family and friends (Markus, Kitayama, & Heiman, 1996).

Naturalistic Decision Making

Circumstances in the real world may require a way of making decisions that is entirely different from multiattribute decision making (Klein, 1997). This alternative approach, called *naturalistic decision making,* is utilized when experts—working in organizational teams and facing substantial constraints on time and resources—must find solutions to complex problems. These circumstances make it almost impossible to successfully employ all the steps needed to complete a multiattribute decision process (Zsambok & Klein, 1997).

Naturalistic decision making involves the use of prior experiences to develop mental representations of how organizational systems really work. Suppose that a production team needs some computer graphics to complete a brochure for a sales meeting to be held in three days. The company's stated policy is that all computer graphics work will be completed in two days, but company veterans know that in fact at least a week is required to get the work done. On the basis of prior organizational experience the production team will probably decide to use an outside service to do the graphics task.

Although naturalistic decision making models vary somewhat, most of them predict that experts make decisions based on mental representations that they have developed as a consequence of prior experiences with similar problems. Based on the perceived parallels between current and past experiences, these experts develop what is known as *situation awareness*—the ability to appreciate all elements of a problem as well as all elements of the environment within which it appears, and to make decisions that take them into account simultaneously. Situation awareness is vital to effective decision making and problem solving in the real world.

Groups Working at a Distance

The quality of group problem solving and decision making will become even more important in future years as people increasingly use electronic mail and teleconferencing to work together from a distance. It is not yet clear how "electronic groups" compare to their face-to-face counterparts. Some evidence suggests that group communication via e-mail tends to be more explicit and outspoken (a pattern dubbed "flaming"), and that group solutions tend to be riskier and less conventional (Kiesler & Sproull, 1992).

LINKAGES

Group Processes in Problem Solving and Decision Making

Whether they involve producing a brochure, fighting a fire, balancing a budget, trying a defendant, or choosing a vacation spot, problem solving and decision making are often done in groups. The processes that influence an individual's problem solving and decision making continue to operate when the individual is in a group, but group interactions also shape the outcome.

Typically, group discussions follow a consistent pattern (Hastie, Penrod, & Pennington, 1984). First, various options are proposed and debated until the group sees that no one has strong objections to one option; that option becomes the minimally acceptable solution. From then on, the group criticizes any other proposal and argues more and more strongly for the first minimally acceptable solution, which is likely to become the group's decision. Thus the order in which options are considered can determine the outcome (Wittenbaum & Stasser, 1996).

In many cases, group discussion results in more extreme decisions than people would make if they were alone. For example, if you hold conservative or liberal political opinions, associating with people who share those opinions is likely to result in your becoming more conservative or more liberal (Pascarella & Terenzini, 1991). This tendency toward extreme decisions is called **group polarization** (Kaplan, 1987). Two mechanisms apparently underlie group polarization. First, most arguments presented during group discussion favor the view of the majority, and most criticisms are directed at the minority view. Thus, it seems rational to those favoring the majority view to adopt an even stronger version of it (Stasser, 1991). Second, as a group begins to agree that a particular decision is desirable, members may try to associate themselves with it, perhaps by advocating a more extreme version (Kaplan & Miller, 1987).

Are people better at problem solving and decision making when they work in groups than when on their own? This is one of the questions about human thought studied by social psychologists. In a typical experiment, a group of people is asked to solve a problem like the one in Figure 8.8 (page 266) or to make a decision about the guilt or innocence of a hypothetical defendant. Each person is asked to reach an individual answer and then to join with the others to try to reach a consensus. Such research indicates that on problems whose correct solution can easily be demonstrated to all members, groups will usually outperform individuals (Levine & Moreland, 1998). However, on problems with less clear-cut solutions, groups may not perform any better than their most talented member and may sometimes even perform worse (Hackman, 1998). Moreover, when people work as part of a group, they are often less productive than when working alone (Williams & Sommer, 1997).

Other research (e.g., Stasser, Stewart, & Wittenbaum, 1995) suggests that a critical element in successful group problem solving is the sharing of individual members' unique information and expertise. For example, when asked to diagnose an unknown illness, groups of physicians were much more accurate when they pooled the information possessed by each doctor (Larson et al., in press). However, *brainstorming,* a popular strategy that supposedly encourages group members to generate new and innovative solutions to a problem, may actually produce fewer ideas than those generated by individuals working alone (Levine & Moreland, 1998)—possibly because the input of other group members interferes with the creative process in individuals. Group members who are confident or have high status are most likely to influence a group's deliberations (Levine & Moreland, 1998), but whether these people will help or hurt the group's output depends on whether they express good ideas (Hinsz, 1990). Ironically, there is little evidence that members with the greatest competence (as opposed to status) always contribute more to group deliberations (Hastie, 1986).

As they work to solve a problem, the members of a group experience their own thoughts as words, propositions, images, or other mental representations. How does each member share these private events so as to help the group perform its task? The answer lies in the use of language.

LINKAGES

Do people solve problems better alone or in a group? (a link to Social Influence)

LANGUAGE

Language is the primary means through which we communicate our thoughts to others. We use language not only to share our immediate thoughts and ideas but also to pass on cultural information and traditions from one generation to the next. In this section, we describe the elements that make up a language, the ways that people use language to communicate, and the means by which language is learned.

The Elements of Language

A **language** has two basic elements: **symbols,** such as words, and a set of rules, called **grammar,** for combining those symbols. These two components allow human language to be at once rule-bound and creative. Knowing approximately 50,000 to 100,000 words (the vocabulary of the typical college student), humans can create and understand an infinite number of sentences. All of the sentences ever articulated are created from just a few dozen categories of sounds. The power of language comes from the way these rather unimpressive raw materials are organized according to rules (Miller, 1991). This organization occurs at several levels.

From Sounds to Sentences   Organization occurs first at the level of sounds. A **phoneme** is the smallest unit of sound that affects the meaning of speech. Changing a phoneme changes the meaning of a spoken word, much as changing a letter in a printed word changes its meaning. *Tea* has a meaning different from *sea,* and *sight* is different from *sigh.*

Each spoken language consists of roughly thirty to fifty phonemes. English has twenty-six letters, but it has about forty phonemes. The *a* in *cat* and the *a* in *cake,* for example, are different English phonemes. Many of the letter names are phonemes (including *ell, aitch,* and *em*), but so are the sounds *th* and *sh.* Sounds that are considered one phoneme in English are different phonemes in other languages, and sounds that are different phonemes in English may be just one phoneme in another language. In Spanish, for example, *s* and *z* are considered the same phoneme.

Although changing a phoneme affects meaning, phonemes themselves are not meaningful. They are combined to form a higher level of organization: morphemes. A **morpheme** is the smallest unit of language that has meaning. Word stems like *dog* and *run* are morphemes, but so are prefixes like *un-* and suffixes like *-ed,* because they have meaning even though they cannot stand alone.

Words are made up of one or more morphemes. Words, in turn, are combined to form phrases and sentences according to a set of grammatical rules called **syntax** (Fromkin & Rodman, 1992). For example, according to English syntax, a subject and a verb must be combined in a sentence, adjectives typically appear before the noun that they modify, and so forth. Compare the following sentences:

Fatal accidents deter careful drivers.

Snows sudden floods melting cause.

The first sentence makes sense, but the second sentence violates English syntax. If the words were reordered, however, they would produce the perfectly acceptable sentence "Melting snows cause sudden floods."

Even if you use English phonemes combined in proper ways to form morphemes strung together according to the laws of English syntax, you may not end up with an acceptable English sentence. Consider the sentence "Rapid bouquets deter sudden neighbors." It somehow sounds right, but it is nonsense. Why? It has syntax, but it ignores the set of rules, called **semantics,** that govern the meaning of words and sentences. For example, because of its meaning, the noun *bouquets* cannot be modified by the word *rapid.*

Surface Structure and Deep Structure   So far, we have discussed elements of language that are apparent in the sentences people produce. These elements were the focus of study by linguists for many decades. Then, in 1965, Noam Chomsky started a revolution in the study of language. He argued that if linguists studied only the language that people produce, they would never uncover the principles that account for all the sentences that people create. They could not explain, for example, how the sentence "This is my old friend" has more than one meaning. Nor could they account for the close relationship between the meanings of such sentences as "Don't give up just because things look bad" and "It ain't over 'til it's over."

To take these aspects of language into account, Chomsky proposed a more abstract level of analysis. Behind the word strings that people produce, called **surface structures,** there is, he said, a **deep structure,** an abstract representation of the relationships expressed in a sentence. For example, as Figure 8.11 illustrates, the surface structure "The shooting of the psychologist was terrible" may represent either of two deep structures: (1) that the psychologist had terrible aim, or (2) that it was terrible that someone shot the psychologist.

Chomsky also developed rules for transforming deep structures into surface structures and for relating sentences to one another. Since he proposed his first analysis of deep and surface structures, there have been many revisions of those ideas. For our purposes, what is important about Chomsky's original ideas is that they encouraged psychologists to analyze not just verbal behavior and grammatical rules but also mental representations.

FIGURE 8.11

**Surface Structure
and Deep Structure**

The listener on the right has interpreted
the speaker's message in a way that
differs from the speaker's intended deep
structure. Obviously, identical surface
structures can correspond to distinctly
different deep structures.

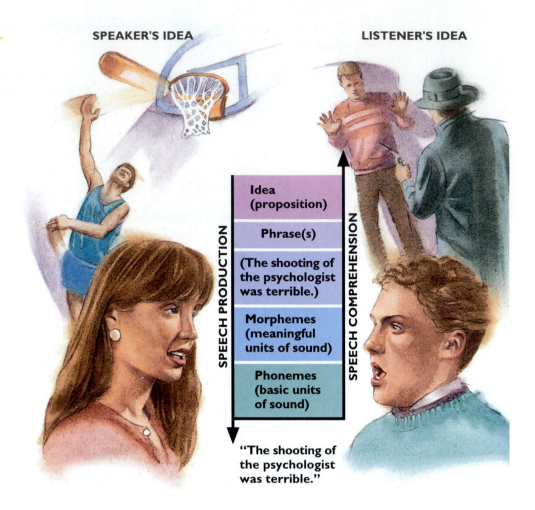

SPEAKER'S IDEA   LISTENER'S IDEA

SPEECH PRODUCTION → SPEECH COMPREHENSION

Idea
(proposition)

Phrase(s)

(The shooting of
the psychologist
was terrible.)

Morphemes
(meaningful
units of sound)

Phonemes
(basic units
of sound)

"The shooting of
the psychologist
was terrible."

Understanding Speech

When you listen to someone speak, your sensory, perceptual, and cognitive systems
reconstruct the sounds into a representation of the speaker's idea: You develop an
internal description of the ideas intended by the speaker. How? Like the perception of
visual images, perception of speech depends not just on bottom-up processing of stimuli but also on top-down processing that uses knowledge, experience, and expectations
to construct a mental representation of what is said (Yule, 1996). This construction
occurs at several levels.

Perceiving Words and Sentences   As someone speaks, you perceive the phonemes
within a word as a continuous string, and you perceive a distinct pause between each
word and the next one. However, as Figure 8.12 demonstrates, the pauses often actually occur *within* the words, not between them. You perceive breaks between the words
because of *top-down processing*. You know what the word should sound like, you recognize the sounds when they occur, and you perceive them as separate units, even if
the physical stimuli are not separated (Miller & Eimas, 1995).
      Similarly, when words are strung together as sentences, knowledge about both sen-
tence structure and the world at large shapes the way they are processed. For example,
people can remember the string "a haky deeb reciled the dison togently um flutests
pav" more easily than the shorter string "Hak deem um flut recile pav togert disen,"
because the first is organized in a sentence-like structure (Altmann, 1997). In other
words, people use their vast store of knowledge about grammatical structure, the
meaning of words, and the world itself in order to process and understand language.

Using Context and Scripts   Suppose you have programmed a computer with all the
rules and knowledge discussed so far—with rules for combining spoken phonemes

Making sure that the surface structures we create accurately convey the deep structures we intend is one of the greatest changes people face when communicating through language.

FIGURE 8.12

A Speech Spectrograph

This *speech spectrograph* indicates what speech looks like as someone says the phrase "Speech we may see." The vertical axis shows the frequencies of the speech sounds; the horizontal axis shows the passage of time. You would hear this phrase as four distinct words. Notice, however, that pauses actually occur not between the words themselves but between the "p" and "ee" in "speech" and again between "ee" and "ch" in the same word.

and written letters into words, rules of syntax, a dictionary of the meanings of words, and an encyclopedia of knowledge of the world. Now you ask your computer to make sense of the following conversation:

A: You goin' to the gym today to work out?

B: Well I *am* flabby, but only if I can hook a ride with Jim. It's a long way.

A: I'm afraid I heard his transmission's conked out, and it's at the shop.

B: Oh [pause], then I guess it won't work out.

The computer would be at a loss. For one thing, certain ambiguous terms have different meanings in different sentences (e.g., *work out* in lines 1 and 4, and *gym* versus *Jim* in lines 1 and 2). Because you understand the gist of the conversation, you understand the meaning of words or phrases like *hook, I'm afraid,* and *conked out,* and you

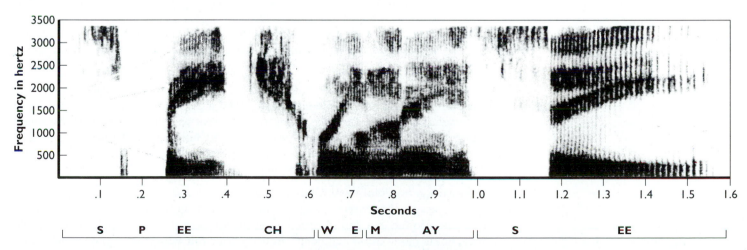

Source: Lachman, Lachman, & Butterfield, 1979.

LINKAGES

Perceiving Spoken Language

Top-down perceptual processes, described in Chapter 5, help explain why speech in a language you do not understand sounds like a continuous stream being spoken faster than speech in your own language. You do not know where each unfamiliar word starts and stops, so, without perceived gaps, the speech sounds run together at what seems to be a faster-than-normal rate.

know that the transmission is part of Jim's car, not a part of Jim. But these are things that the computer could not easily understand.

Difficulties in programming a computer to understand conversations arise first because the use of language relies on the *context* in which words are spoken or written. People use context to interpret and impose meaning on stimuli—including language. A statement like "Wow, are you smart!" can be interpreted as "I think you're an idiot," depending on the context (and perhaps the tone of voice).

Individuals' educational and cultural background also forms part of the context that shapes their understanding of a communication. That background may determine how a listener interprets ambiguous stimuli (Schank & Abelson, 1977). For example, what do you think is going on in this story?

> *Every Saturday night, four good friends get together. When Jerry, Mike, and Pat arrived, Karen was sitting in her living room writing some notes. She quickly gathered the cards and stood up to greet her friends at the door. They followed her into the living room but as usual they couldn't agree on exactly what to play. Jerry eventually took a stand and set things up. Finally, they began to play. Karen's recorder filled the room with soft and pleasant music. Early in the evening, Mike noticed Pat's hand and the many diamonds. As the night progressed the tempo of play increased. Finally, a lull in the activities occurred. Taking advantage of this, Jerry pondered the arrangement in front of him. Mike interrupted Jerry's reverie and said, "Let's hear the score." They listened carefully and commented on their performance. When the comments were all heard, exhausted but happy, Karen's friends went home. (Anderson et al., 1977)*

Researchers found that music majors tended to interpret this passage as describing a musical rehearsal; other students typically read it as the description of a card game (Anderson et al., 1977). The two groups used different scripts as a framework for interpreting ambiguous words like *stand* and *diamonds*. Building scripts into a computer's memory to resolve ambiguities is one of the greatest challenges in developing artificial-intelligence systems for speech recognition.

Conventions and Nonverbal Cues   Social *conventions*, commonly accepted practices and usage, also govern conversation. Although the words alone do not say so, "Will you join me in a cup of coffee?" conveys to most people an invitation to drink coffee, not to climb into a giant cup. Similarly, someone who asks, "Do you know what time it is?" is not expecting a yes or no answer.

People are often also guided to an understanding of conversations by nonverbal cues. The frown, the enthusiastic nod, the bored yawn—all signal differences in understanding or interest that have an important bearing on the exchange of information. Thus it is not surprising that face-to-face conversations are more efficient than those in which speakers cannot see each other—a fact that should be considered when groups or teams must try to solve problems in separate locations, whether by telephone, electronic mail, or other means (Massaro & Stork, 1998).

Learning to Speak: Stages of Language Development

Once people have learned to speak, they use the many rules of language naturally and automatically to generate correct sentences and to reject incorrect ones, even though most people would have a difficult time stating the rules. For example, in an instant you know that the words "Bei mir bist du schön" are not English and that the string of words "Quickly peaches sheep deserve" is not an acceptable sentence. Children the world over learn language with impressive speed and regularity. Developmental psychologists have painstakingly described the steps in this process.

From Babblings to Words Babblings are the first sounds infants make that resemble speech. These alternating consonant and vowel sounds ("bababa," "mamimamima," "dadada") begin at about four months of age. Though meaningless to the baby, they are a delight to parents. During much of the first year, infants of all nationalities make the same babbling sounds. At about nine months, however, babies who hear only English start to lose their German gutturals and French nasals. Their babbling becomes more complex and begins to sound like "sentences" in their native language. Starting around this time, too, infants begin to shorten some of their vocalizations to "da," "duh," and "ma." These sounds seem very much like language. Babies use them in specific contexts and with obvious purpose (Blake & de Boysson–Bardies, 1992). Accompanied by appropriate gestures, they may be used to express joy ("oohwow") or anger ("uh-uh-uh"), to get something that is out of reach ("engh-engh"), or to point out something interesting ("dah!").

Ten- to twelve-month-olds can understand a few words—certainly more words than they can say (Fenson et al., 1994). Proper names and object words are among the earliest words they understand. Often the first word they understand is a pet's name.

Proper names and object words—words like *mama, daddy, cookie, doggy,* and *car*—are also among the first words children are likely to say when, at around twelve to eighteen months of age, they begin to talk. Nouns for simple object categories (*dog, flower*) are acquired before more general nouns (*animal, plant*) or more specific names (*collie, rose*) (Rosch et al., 1976).

Of course, these early words do not sound exactly like adult language. Babies usually reduce them to a shorter, easier form, like "duh" for *duck* or "mih" for *milk.* Children make themselves understood, however, by using gestures, intonations, facial expressions, and interminable repetitions. If they have a word for an object, they may "overextend" it to cover more ground. Thus, they might use *dog* for cats, bears, and horses; they might use *fly* for all insects and perhaps for other small things like raisins and M&M's (Clark, 1983). Children make these "errors" because their vocabularies are limited, not because they fail to notice the difference between dogs and cats or because they want to eat a fly (Fremgen & Fay, 1980; Rescorla, 1981).

Until they can say the conventional words for objects, children overextend the words they have, use all-purpose sounds (like "dat" or "dis"), and coin new words (like *pepping* for "shaking the pepper shaker") (Becker, 1994). During this period, children build up their vocabularies one word at a time. They also use their limited vocabulary one word at a time; they cannot yet put words together into sentences. This one-word stage of speech lasts for about six months.

First Sentences By eighteen to twenty-four months of age, children usually have a vocabulary of some fifty words. Then their language undergoes a rapid acceleration: They may learn several new words a day and begin to put words together (Gleitman &

Getting Ready to Talk

Long before they utter their first words, babies are getting ready to talk. Experiments in Patricia Kuhl's laboratory show that even six-month-olds tend to look longer at faces whose lip movements match the sounds of spoken words. This tendency reflects babies' abilities to focus on, recognize, and discriminate the sounds of speech, especially in their native language. These abilities are crucial to the development of language.

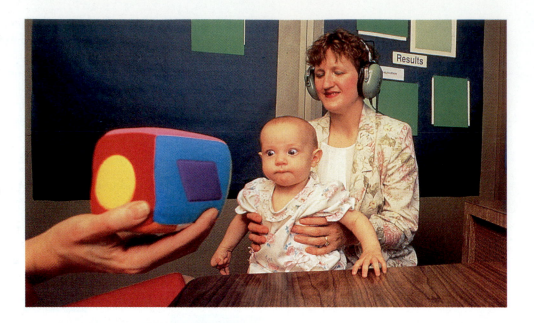

Landau, 1994). At first, children's sentences consist of two-word pairs. These two-word utterances are telegraphic. Brief and to the point, they leave out any word that is not absolutely essential. If she wants her mother to give her a book, the twenty-month-old might first say, "Give book," then, "Mommy give," and, if that does not work, "Mommy book." The child also uses rising intonation to indicate a question ("Go out?") and word stress to indicate location ("Play *park*") or new information ("*Big* car").

Three-word sentences come next in the development of language. They are still telegraphic, but more nearly complete: "Mommy give book." The child can now speak in sentences that have the usual subject-verb-object form of adult sentences. Other words and word endings begin appearing, too, such as the suffix *-ing,* the prepositions *in* and *on,* the plural *-s,* and irregular past tenses ("It broke," "I ate") (Brown, 1973; Dale, 1976). Children learn to use the suffix *-ed* for the past tense ("I walked"), and then they often overapply the rule to irregular verbs that they previously used correctly, saying, for example, "It breaked" or "It broked" or "I eated" (Marcus, 1996).

Children also expand their sentences with adjectives, although, at first, they do not always get the antonyms straight. For example, they are likely to use both *less* and *more* to mean "more" or *tall* and *short* to mean "tall" (Smith & Sera, 1992).

Complex Sentences   By age three or so, children begin to use auxiliary verbs ("Adam is going") and to ask questions using *wh-* words, such as *what, where, who,* and *why.* They begin to put together clauses to form complex sentences ("Here's the ball I was looking for"). Although young children can understand passive sentences that cannot be reversed (e.g., "The ball was thrown by the girl"), they have difficulty with passive sentences that can be interpreted in either direction (e.g., "Charlie was liked by Shannon") (Sudhalter & Braine, 1985). By age five, children have acquired most of the syntax of their native language.

How Is Language Acquired?

LINKAGES

How do we learn to speak? (a link to Human Development)

Despite all that has been discovered about the steps children follow in learning language, mystery and debate still surround the question of just how they learn it. Obviously, children pick up the specific content of language from the speech they hear around them; English children learn English, French children learn French. As parents and children share meals, playtime, and conversations, children learn that words refer to objects and actions and what the labels for them are. One study illustrated the influence of mothers' language input on their toddlers' vocabularies by comparing the language development of U.S. and Japanese children (Tamis-LeMonda et al., 1992). Mothers in the United States were more likely than Japanese mothers to label and describe objects for their toddlers; their children, in turn, were more likely than Japanese children to understand and say these object words. But how do children learn syntax?

Conditioning, Imitation, and Rules   Our discussion of conditioning in Chapter 6 suggests one possibility: Perhaps children learn syntax because their parents reinforce them for using it. In fact, however, parents usually are more concerned about what is said than about its form (Hirsch-Pasek, Treiman, & Schneiderman, 1984). When the little boy with chocolate crumbs on his face says, "I not eat cookie," the mother is more likely to respond, "Yes, you did eat it" than to ask the child to say, "I did not eat the cookie" and then reinforce him for grammatical correctness. Observations suggest, then, that operant conditioning cannot fully explain the learning of syntax.

Learning through modeling, or imitation, appears to be more influential. Children learn syntax most rapidly when adults offer simple revisions of their sentences, implicitly correcting their syntax, and then continue with the topic they are discussing. For example,

Child: Mommy fix.

Mother: Okay, Mommy will fix the truck.

Child: It breaked.

Mother: Yes, it broke.

Child: Truck broke.

Mother: Let's see if we can fix it.

But if children learn syntax by imitation, why would they overgeneralize rules, such as the rule for making the past tense? Why, for example, do children who at one time said "I went" later say "I goed"? Adults never use this form of speech. Its sudden appearance indicates that the child either has mastered the rule of adding *-ed* or has generalized from similar-sounding words (such as "mowed" or "rowed"). In short, neither conditioning nor imitation seems entirely adequate to explain how children learn language. Children must still analyze for themselves the underlying patterns in the welter of language examples they hear around them (Bloom, 1995).

Biological Bases for Language Acquisition   The ease with which children everywhere discover these patterns and learn language encourages some to argue that humans are "prewired," or biologically programmed, to learn language. This biological preparedness is reflected in the unique speech-generating properties of the human mouth and throat (Aitchison, 1983), as well as in brain regions such as Broca's area and Wernicke's area (see Figure 3.17 on page 72).

Chomsky (1965) suggested that human beings are born with a *language acquisition device*—LAD for short—that allows youngsters to gather ideas about the rules of language without being aware of doing so. They then use these ideas to understand and construct their native language. This hypothesis is supported by the observation that children make up words like "goed," which shows that they understand language rules (in this case, the rule for forming past tense). It is also supported by the fact that there is some similarity in the syntax of all languages. Furthermore, children who are born deaf and thus never hear language make up systems of gestures that have several properties of natural spoken language; for example, these systems place subjects before verbs and include agent-action-object sequences, such as "June saw Bob" (Newport & Meier, 1985).

According to Elizabeth Bates (1993), however, one need not assume a special LAD to understand language acquisition. She suggests that the development of children's language is a reflection of their development of other cognitive skills. Thus, for example, children learn short words before long words because limitations in short-term memory and other cognitive abilities lead them to learn easy things before harder ones.

Regardless of whether language learning is guided by a specific language acquisition device or by more general cognitive skills, there appears to be a limited window of

Learning a Second Language

The notion of a critical period for language acquisition is supported by the fact that, after the age of thirteen or fourteen, people learn a second language more slowly (Johnson & Newport, 1989) and virtually never learn to speak it without an accent (Lenneberg, 1967).

opportunity—or *critical period*—for language learning. The idea of such a critical period is supported by cases in which certain unfortunate children spent their early years in isolation from human contact and the sound of adult language. Even after years of therapy and language training, these individuals were not able to combine ideas into sentences (Rymer, 1993). Such cases suggest that, in order to acquire complex features of language, a person must be exposed to speech before a certain age.

Bilingualism   Does trying to learn two languages at once, even before the critical period is over, impair the learning of either? Research suggests just the opposite. Although their early language utterances may be confused or delayed, children who are raised in a bilingual environment before the end of the critical period seem to show enhanced performance in each language (deHouwer, 1995). There is also some evidence that *balanced bilinguals,* those who have roughly equal mastery of two languages, are superior to other children in cognitive flexibility, concept formation, and creativity. It is as if each language offers a slightly different perspective on thinking, and this dual perspective makes the brain more flexible (deHouwer, 1995).

The apparent benefits of bilingualism have important implications for U.S. school systems, where children from non-English-speaking homes often receive instruction in their native language while taking classes in English. Although lack of control over school environments makes it difficult to perform true experiments on the effects of this practice, available evidence suggests that these bilingual programs facilitate educational achievement (Cavaliere, 1996). The evidence also suggests that rapid immersion in an English-only program may do considerable educational harm to children who enter school with no English-language background (Crawford, 1989).

Some psychologists say that it is the ability of humans to acquire and use language that sets them apart from all other creatures. Yet animals use symbols to communicate. Bees dance in a way that indicates the direction and distance of sources of nectar; the grunts and gestures of chimpanzees signify various attitudes and emotions. These forms of communication do not necessarily have the grammatical characteristics of language, however. Are any animals other than humans capable of learning language?

THINKING CRITICALLY

Can Nonhumans Use Language?

■ What am I being asked to believe or accept?

Over the last forty years, several researchers have asserted that nonhumans can master language. Chimpanzees and gorillas have been the most popular targets of study, because at maturity they are estimated to have the intelligence of two- or three-year-old children, who are usually well on their way to learning language. Dolphins, too, have been studied because they have a complex communication system and exceptionally large brains relative to their body size. It would seem that if these animals are unable to learn language, their general intelligence cannot be blamed. Instead, failure would be attributed to the absence of a genetic makeup that permits language learning.

■ What evidence is available to support the assertion?

The question of whether nonhuman mammals can learn to use language is not a simple one, for at least two reasons. First, language is more than just communication, but defining just when animals are exhibiting that "something more" is a source of debate. What seems to set human language apart from the gestures, grunts, chirps, whistles, or cries of other animals is grammar—a formal set of rules for combining words. Using the rules of grammar, people can take a relatively small number of words and create with them an almost infinite number of unique sentences. Also, because of their muscular structures, nonhuman mammals will never be able to "speak" in the same way that humans do (Lieberman, 1991). To test these animals' ability to learn language, investigators therefore must devise novel ways for them to communicate.

David and Ann Premack taught their chimp, Sarah, to communicate by placing different-shaped chips, symbolizing words, on a magnetic board (Premack, 1971). Lana, a chimpanzee studied by Duane Rumbaugh (1977), learned to communicate by pressing keys on a specially designed computer. American Sign Language (ASL), the language of the deaf that is based on hand gestures, has been used by Beatrice and Allen Gardner with the chimp Washoe, and by Herbert Terrace with a chimp named Nim Chimsky (after Noam Chomsky). And Kanzi, a bonobo or pygmy chimp studied by Sue Savage-Rumbaugh (1990; Savage-Rumbaugh et al., 1993), learned to recognize spoken words and communicated through a combination of gesturing and pressing word-symbol keys on a computer that would "speak" them. Kanzi was a special case: He learned to communicate by listening and watching as his mother, Matata, was being taught, then used what he had learned to interact with her trainers.

Studies of all five animals suggested that they could spontaneously use combinations of words to refer to things that were not present. Washoe, Lana, Sarah, Nim, and Kanzi all mastered from 130 to 500 words. Their vocabulary included names for concrete objects, such as *apple* or *me;* verbs, such as *tickle* and *eat;* adjectives, such as *happy* and *big;* and adverbs, such as *again.* The animals combined the words in sentences, expressing wishes like "You tickle me" or "If Sarah good, then apple." Sometimes the sentences referred to things in the past. When an investigator called attention to a wound that Kanzi had received, the animal produced the sentence "Matata hurt," referring to the fact that his mother had recently given him a disciplinary bite (Savage-Rumbaugh, 1990). Finally, all these animals seemed to enjoy their communication tools and used them spontaneously to interact with their caretakers and with other animals.

Most of the investigators mentioned here have argued that their animals mastered a crude grammar (Brakke & Savage-Rumbaugh, 1996; Premack, 1971). For example, if Washoe wanted to be tickled, she would gesture, "You tickle Washoe." But if she wanted to do the tickling, she would gesture, "Washoe tickle you." The correct placement of object and subject in these sentences suggested that Washoe was following a set of rules for word combination—in other words, a grammar (Gardner & Gardner, 1978). Louis Herman and his colleagues documented similar syntactic sensitivity in dolphins, who rarely confused subject-verb order in following instructions given by human hand signals (Herman, Richards, & Wolz, 1984). Furthermore, Savage-Rumbaugh observed several hundred instances in which Kanzi understood sentences he had never heard before. Once, for example, while his back was turned to the speaker, Kanzi heard the

Animal Language?

Koko, a gorilla who is allegedly able to use American Sign Language (ASL), recently spent time answering questions from thousands of people on the Internet. Koko can't read or type, of course, so her trainer relayed the questions to her in ASL and typed her signed responses. This procedure made some questioners wonder whether they were talking to Koko or her trainer.

sentence "Jeanie hid the pine needles in her shirt." He turned around, approached Jeanie, and searched her shirt to find the pine needles. His actions would seem to indicate that he understood this new sentence the first time he heard it.

■ Are there alternative ways of interpreting the evidence?

Many of the early conclusions about primate language learning were challenged by Herbert Terrace and his colleagues in their investigation of Nim (Terrace et al., 1979). Terrace noticed many subtle characteristics of Nim's communications that seemed quite different from a child's use of language, and he argued that animals in other studies demonstrated these same characteristics.

First, he said, their sentences were always very short. Nim could combine two or three gestures but never used strings that conveyed more sophisticated messages. Thus, the ape was never able to say anything equivalent to a three-year-old child's "I want to go to Wendy's for a hamburger, OK?" Second, Terrace questioned whether the animals' use of language demonstrated the spontaneity, creativity, and expanding complexity characteristic of children's language. Many of the animals' sentences were requests for food, tickling, baths, pets, and other pleasurable objects and experiences. Is such behavior qualitatively different from the behavior of the family dog, who learns to sit up and beg for table scraps? Other researchers also concluded that chimps are not naturally predisposed to associate seen objects with heard words, as human infants are (Savage-Rumbaugh et al., 1983). Finally, Terrace questioned whether experimenter bias influenced the reports of the chimps' communications. Consciously or not, experimenters who want to conclude that chimps learn language might tend to ignore strings that violate grammatical order or to reinterpret ambiguous strings so that they make grammatical sense. If Nim sees someone holding a banana and signs, "Nim banana," the experimenter might assume the word order is correct and means "Nim wants the banana" rather than, for example, "That banana belongs to Nim," in which case the word order would be wrong.

■ What additional evidence would help to evaluate the alternatives?

Studies of animals' ability to learn language are expensive and take many years. Accordingly, the amount of evidence in the area is small—just a handful of studies, each based mainly on a single animal. Obviously, more data are needed from more studies that use a common methodology.

It is important, as well, to study the extent to which limits on the length of primates' spontaneous sentences result from limits on working memory (Savage-Rumbaugh & Brakke, 1996). If memory is indeed the main limiting factor, then the failure to produce progressively longer sentences does not necessarily reflect an inability to master language.

Research on how primates might spontaneously acquire language by listening and imitating, as Kanzi did, as well as naturalistic observations of communications among primates in their natural habitat, would also help scientists better understand their capacity to communicate (Sevcik & Savage-Rumbaugh, 1994).

■ What conclusions are most reasonable?

Psychologists are still not in full agreement about whether our sophisticated mammalian cousins can learn language. Two things are clear, however. First, whatever the chimp, gorilla, and dolphin have learned is a much more primitive and limited form of communication than that learned by children. Second, their level of communication does not do justice to their overall intelligence; these animals are smarter than their "language" production suggests. Thus, the evidence to date favors the view that humans have language abilities that are unique, but that under the right circumstances, and with the right tools, other animals can master many language-like skills.

TABLE 8.2

Sometimes a lack of familiarity with the formal and informal aspects of another language can get American advertisers in trouble. Here are some humorous examples.

When the Clairol Company introduced its "Mist Stick" curling iron in Germany, it was unaware that *mist* is a German slang word meaning "manure." Not many people wanted to buy a manure stick.

In Chinese, the Kentucky Fried Chicken slogan "finger lickin' good" came out as "eat your fingers off."

The slogan for Salem cigarettes, "Salem—Feeling Free," when translated into Japanese, read "When smoking Salem, you will feel so refreshed that your mind seems to be free and empty."

In Chinese, the slogan for Pepsi Cola, "Come alive with the Pepsi Generation," became "Pepsi brings your ancestors back from the grave."

Knowledge, Language, and Culture

When ideas from one language are translated into another, the intended meaning can easily be distorted, as shown in Table 8.2. But differences in language and culture may have more serious and important implications as well. The language that people speak forms part of their knowledge of the world, and that knowledge, as noted in Chapter 5, guides perceptions. This relationship raises the question of whether differences among languages create differences in the ways that people perceive and think about the world.

Benjamin Whorf (1956) claimed that language directly influences perception. He noted, for example, that Inuit Eskimos have several different words for *snow* and proposed that this feature of their language should lead to a greater perceptual ability to discriminate among varieties of snow. When the discrimination abilities of Inuits and other people are compared, there are indeed significant differences. But are these differences in perception the *result* of differences in language?

One of the most interesting tests of Whorf's ideas was conducted by Eleanor Rosch (1975). She compared the perception of colors by Americans with that by members of the Dani tribe of New Guinea. In the language of the Dani, there are only two color names, one for dark, "cold" colors and one for lighter, "warm" ones. In contrast, English speakers have names for a vast number of different hues. Of these, it is possible to identify eleven *focal* colors; these are prototypes, the particular wavelengths of light that are the best examples of the eleven major categories (red, yellow, green, blue, black, gray, white, purple, orange, pink, and brown). Thus, fire-engine red is the focal color for red. Rosch reasoned that, if Whorf's views were correct, then English speakers, who have verbal labels for focal colors, should recognize them better than nonfocal colors, but that for the Dani, the focal-nonfocal distinction should make no difference. In fact, however, Rosch found that both the Dani and the English-speaking Americans perceived focal colors more efficiently than nonfocal ones (Heider, 1972).

Thus, the fact that Inuit people have verbal labels for differences among snow textures that, say, Texans or Africans don't even perceive suggests a *correlation* between language and perception in various cultures. But it appears doubtful that language *causes* these differences in perception, as Whorf suggested. It is far more likely that, beneath the differences in both language and perception, there is a third variable: frequency of the use and need for certain objects. Inuits, for example, live in a snowy world. Their lives depend on making fine distinctions about the snow—between the snow bridge that is solid and the one that will collapse, for example. Hence, they learn to discriminate differences that are unimportant to people in warmer climates, and they attach names to these differences.

LINKAGES

As noted in Chapter 1, all of psychology's many subfields are related to one another. Our discussion of group processes in problem solving illustrates just one way in which the topic of this chapter, cognition and language, is linked to the subfield of social influence (Chapter 18). The Linkages diagram shows ties to two other subfields as well, and there are many more ties throughout the book. Looking for linkages among subfields will help you see how they all fit together and better appreciate the big picture that is psychology.

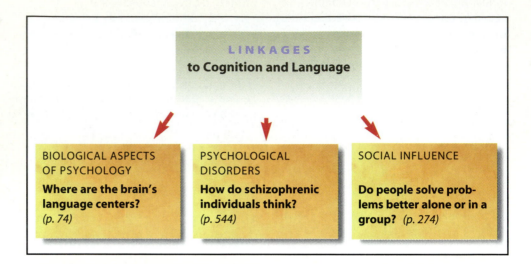

LINKAGES
to Cognition and Language

BIOLOGICAL ASPECTS OF PSYCHOLOGY

Where are the brain's language centers? *(p. 74)*

PSYCHOLOGICAL DISORDERS

How do schizophrenic individuals think? *(p. 544)*

SOCIAL INFLUENCE

Do people solve problems better alone or in a group? *(p. 274)*

SUMMARY

Cognitive psychology is the study of the mental processes by which the information humans receive from their environment is modified, made meaningful, stored, retrieved, used, and communicated to others.

BASIC FUNCTIONS OF THOUGHT

The five core functions of thought are to describe, elaborate, decide, plan, and guide action.

The Circle of Thought

Many psychologists think of the components of the circle of thought as constituting an *information-processing system* that receives, represents, transforms, and acts on incoming stimuli. *Thinking,* then, is defined as the manipulation of mental representations by this system.

Information-Processing Speed: Reaction Time

The time elapsing between the presentation of a stimulus and an overt response is the *reaction time.* Among the factors affecting reaction times are the complexity of the choice of a response, stimulus-response compatibility, expectancy, and the tradeoff between speed and accuracy.

Picturing Information Processing: Evoked Brain Potentials

Using methods such as the EEG, psychologists can also measure mental events as reflected in *evoked brain potentials.*

MENTAL REPRESENTATIONS: THE INGREDIENTS OF THOUGHT

Mental representations take the form of cognitive maps, images, concept schemas and event scripts, propositions, and narratives.

Cognitive Maps

Cognitive maps are mental representations of familiar parts of one's world. In contrast to paper maps, the information in cognitive maps is imprecise and subject to systematic distortion.

Mental Images

Mental images may also be manipulated when people think. Such images can be mentally inspected, expanded, and rotated. They contain details about what objects look like, how their component parts are arranged, and what textures they have.

Concept Schemas and Event Scripts

Concepts are categories of objects, events, or ideas with common properties. They may be natural or artificial. *Artificial concepts* are precisely defined by the presence or absence of certain features. *Natural concepts* are fuzzy; no fixed set of defining properties determines membership in a natural concept. A member of a natural concept that displays all or most of its characteristic features is called a *prototype.* *Schemas* serve as generalized mental representations of concepts and also generate expectations about them. *Scripts* are schemas of familiar patterns or sequences, usually involving human activities; they help people to think about those activities and to interpret new events.

Propositions

The raw material of thought may also take the form of *propositions,* which are assertions that state how different concepts are related or how a concept is related to its properties. Propositions can be true or false. *Mental models* are clusters of propositions describing people's understanding (whether accurate or inaccurate) of physical objects or processes.

Narratives

Information can also be mentally represented as a narrative, or story. Much of the information we store in, or retrieve from, our memory takes the form of stories.

THINKING STRATEGIES

By combining and transforming mental representations, our information-processing system makes it possible for us to reason, solve problems, and make decisions. *Reasoning* is the process through which people generate and evaluate arguments, and reach conclusions about them.

Formal Reasoning

Formal reasoning seeks valid conclusions through the application of rigorous procedures. These procedures include formulas, or *algorithms,* which are guaranteed to produce correct solutions, and the *rules of logic,* which are useful in evaluating sets of premises and conclusions called *syllogisms.* To reach a sound conclusion, people should consider both the empirical truth or falsity of the premises and the logic of the argument itself. People are prone to logical errors; their belief in a conclusion is often affected by the extent to which the conclusion is consistent with their attitudes as well as by other factors, including cultural background.

Informal Reasoning

People use *informal reasoning* to assess the credibility of a conclusion based on the evidence for it. Errors in informal reasoning often stem from the use of *heuristics,* mental shortcuts or rules of thumb. Three important heuristics are the *anchoring heuristic* (estimating the probability of an event by adjusting a starting value), the *representativeness heuristic* (categorizing an event by how representative it is of a category of events), and the *availability heuristic* (estimating probability by how available an event is in memory).

PROBLEM SOLVING

Steps in problem solving include diagnosing the problem, then planning, executing, and evaluating a solution.

Strategies for Problem Solving

Especially when solutions are not obvious, problem solving can be aided by the use of strategies such as decomposition, working backward, finding analogies, and allowing for incubation.

Obstacles to Problem Solving

Many of the difficulties that people experience in solving problems arise when they are dealing with hypotheses. People do not easily entertain multiple hypotheses. Because of *mental sets,* they may persevere in applying one hypothesis even when it is unsuccessful and, through *functional fixedness,* may tend to miss opportunities to use familiar objects in unusual ways. Because of the *confirmation bias,* they may be reluctant to revise or change hypotheses on the basis of new data. And they may fail to use the absence of symptoms as evidence in solving problems.

Building Problem-Solving Skills

Experts are superior to novices in problem solving because of their knowledge and experience. They can draw on knowledge of similar problems, visualize related components of a problem as a single chunk, and perceive relations among problems in terms of underlying principles rather than surface features. Thus, extensive knowledge is the main component of expertise; yet expertise itself can prevent the expert from seeing problems in new ways.

Problem Solving by Computer

Some specific problems can be solved by computer programs known as *expert systems.* These systems are one application of *artificial intelligence (AI).* There are two approaches to AI. One focuses on programming computers to imitate the logical manipulation of symbols that occurs in human thought; the other (involving connectionist, or neural network, models) attempts to imitate the connections among neurons in the human brain. Current problem-solving computer systems deal successfully only with specific domains. They cannot draw insight from different areas.

DECISION MAKING

Evaluating Options

Decisions are sometimes difficult because there are too many alternatives and too many attributes of each alternative to consider at one time. Furthermore, decisions often involve comparisons of *utility,* not of simple objective value. Decision making is also complicated by the fact that the world is unpredictable, which makes decisions risky. People should act in ways that maximize the *expected value* of their decisions.

Biases and Flaws in Decision Making

People often fail to maximize expected value in their decisions because losses are perceived differently from gains of equal size and because they tend to overestimate the probability of rare events, underestimate the probability of frequent events, and feel overconfident in the accuracy of their forecasts. The gambler's fallacy leads people to believe that outcomes in a random process are affected by previous outcomes. People make decisions aimed at goals other than maximizing expected value; these goals may be determined by personal and cultural factors.

Naturalistic Decision Making

Many real-world circumstances require naturalistic decision making, in which prior experiences are used to develop mental representations of how organizational systems really work.

LANGUAGE

The Elements of Language

Language consists of words or word symbols and rules for their combination—a *grammar.* Spoken words are made up of *phonemes,* which are combined to make *morphemes.* Combinations of words must have both *syntax* (grammar) and *semantics* (meaning). Behind the word strings, or *surface structures,* is an underlying representation, or *deep structure,* that expresses the relationship among the ideas in a sentence. Ambiguous sentences occur when one surface structure reflects two or more deep structures.

Understanding Speech

When people listen to speech, the perceptual system allows them to perceive gaps between words, even when these gaps are not physically present. Syntax and semantics also help people understand spoken messages. To understand language generally and conversations in particular, people use their knowledge of the context and of the world. This knowledge is often described through scripts. In addition, communication in conversations is guided by conventions and aided by nonverbal cues.

Learning to Speak: Stages of Language Development

Children develop grammar according to an orderly pattern. *Babblings* and the *one-word stage* of speech come first, then *telegraphic* two-word sentences. Next come three-word sentences and certain grammatical forms that appear in a somewhat predictable order. Once children learn certain regular verb forms and plural endings, they may overgeneralize rules. Children acquire most of the syntax of their native language by the time they are five years old.

How Is Language Acquired?

Conditioning and imitation both play a role in a child's acquisition of language, but neither can provide a complete explanation of how children acquire syntax. Humans may be biologically programmed to learn language. In any event, it appears that language must be learned during a certain critical period if normal language is to occur. The critical-period notion is supported by research on second-language acquisition.

Knowledge, Language, and Culture

Although language has been thought to shape perceptions, it is more likely that environmental conditions and demands shape one's attention to and knowledge of the world and that language evolves to describe in more detail those aspects of the world that are especially important in one's culture.

KEY TERMS

algorithms (258)
anchoring heuristic (260)
artificial concepts (255)
artificial intelligence (AI) (268)
availability heuristic (261)
babblings (279)
cognitive map (254)
cognitive psychology (250)
concepts (254)
confirmation bias (266)
deep structure (275)
evoked brain potential (253)
expected value (271)

expert systems (269)
formal reasoning (258)
functional fixedness (266)
grammar (274)
group polarization (273)
heuristics (260)
images (254)
informal reasoning (260)
information-processing
  system (251)
language (274)
mental models (256)
mental set (266)

morpheme (275)
narrative (256)
natural concepts (255)
one-word stage (279)
phoneme (274)
propositions (256)
prototype (255)
reaction time (252)
reasoning (257)
representativeness
  heuristic (261)
rules of logic (258)
schemas (256)

scripts (256)
semantics (275)
surface structures (275)
syllogisms (259)
syntax (275)
telegraphic (280)
thinking (251)
utility (271)
words (275)

9

Consciousness

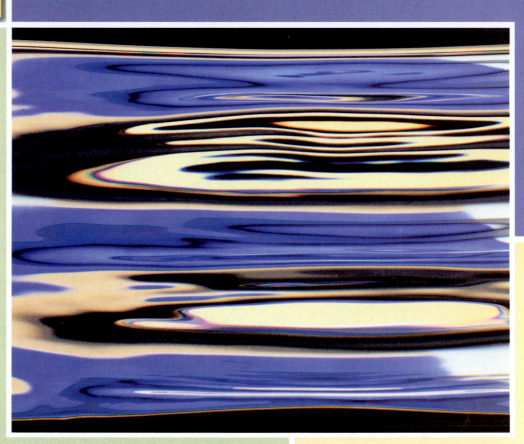

As a teenager, Neil developed a brain tumor. Though successfully treated, it left him with a set of odd symptoms. For example, Neil could remember his childhood and recall other past events, but he now appeared incapable of forming new memories. He was unable to recall what someone had said to him—or what he had read—even a minute earlier. Indeed, within seconds of meeting a new person, Neil would have no memory of having been introduced. Further, although his vision remained normal, Neil was unable to recognize even familiar objects. For example, he could define the word *table* and describe what a table looks like, but when he actually looked at a table, he was unable to say what it was. Once an excellent student, Neil was no longer able to read words, identify numbers, or even match uppercase letters with their lowercase equivalents. Remarkably, however, if he wrote rather than spoke, Neil could accurately describe recent events and correctly name objects. For example, hours after hearing a taped version of a textbook, he could write his reactions to the book and even quote from its contents. But as soon as he finished writing, he would ask, "What does this say?" He appeared to have no memory of having listened to the book on tape, no memory of having written his comments about it, and no idea of what his written words meant (Vargha-Khadem, Issacs, & Mishkin, 1994). Apparently, Neil *could* form memories, recognize objects, and read, but he could not orally report any *conscious* experience of these abilities.

Neil's case illustrates two key aspects of consciousness. First, consciousness is extremely important to us as we go about our daily activities. Imagine, if you can, what it would be like to change places with Neil and spend even one day unable to recall what you had done and what people had said to you, unable to recognize objects in your environment, and unable to understand what you had written. Without some degree of consciousness, it would be extremely difficult, if not impossible, to cope with the demands of the world and interact with other people. Perhaps this is why psychologists have been interested in consciousness ever since Wilhelm Wundt founded the first European psychology laboratory in 1879.

Second, Neil's case illustrates the difficulties that psychologists have when they try to define consciousness. Based on the most common method of inferring consciousness in a person—that person's oral self-reports—Neil appears to have no consciousness. Yet his *written* self-reports suggest that he does. The damage to his brain may have impaired those aspects of consciousness most of us consider to be critical. But in other respects, Neil is capable of conscious experience. The complexities involved in describing exactly what we mean by "consciousness" are also illustrated by the rather disturbing fact that about 1 percent of the people given anesthetics during surgery remain conscious during the entire surgical procedure, even though they appear to be asleep (Ranta, Jussila, & Hynynen, 1990). A few of these people are consciously aware of the pain and remember the trauma to the extent that long after their surgical wounds have healed, they may show signs of posttraumatic stress disorder (Schwender et al., 1995).

Perhaps because of such findings, many researchers believe that consciousness is still not sufficiently well understood to be precisely defined (Crick & Koch, 1998). For our purposes, however, we define **consciousness** as *awareness* of the outside world and of one's own mental processes, thoughts, feelings, and perceptions. This definition suggests that consciousness is a property of many mental processes rather than a unique mental process unto itself. Thus, memories can be conscious, but consciousness is not memory; perceptions can be conscious, but consciousness is not perception. In this chapter we begin by analyzing the nature of consciousness and the ways in which it affects mental activity and behavior. Then we examine what happens when consciousness is altered by sleep, hypnosis, and meditation. Finally, we explore the changes in consciousness that occur when people use certain drugs.

ANALYZING CONSCIOUSNESS

As already noted, psychologists have been fascinated by the study of consciousness for more than a century, but it is only in the last thirty years or so that consciousness has emerged as an active and vital research area in psychology. Why? As you may recall from Chapter 1, because behaviorism dominated psychological research in the United States from the 1920s through the 1960s, little research was conducted on mental processes, including the structure and functions of consciousness. But since the late 1960s, new techniques that allow analysis of brain activity have brought the topic of consciousness back into the mainstream of research in psychology. Scientists who study consciousness sometimes describe their work as *cognitive science* or *cognitive neuroscience* because their research is so closely tied to the subfields of biological psychology, sensation, perception, memory, and human cognition. Indeed, many cognitive psychologists can be said to study consciousness through their work on memory, reasoning, problem solving, and decision making.

Other psychologists study consciousness more directly by addressing three central questions about it. First, like the philosophers who preceded them, psychologists have grappled with the *mind-body problem:* What is the relationship between the conscious mind and the physical brain? One approach, known as *dualism,* sees the mind and brain as different entities. This idea was championed in the seventeenth century by French philosopher René Descartes. Descartes claimed that a person's soul, or consciousness, is separate from the brain but can "view" and interact with brain events through the pineal gland, a brain structure about the size of a grape. Once a popular point of view, dualism has virtually disappeared from psychology.

Another perspective, known as *materialism,* suggests that mind *is* brain. Materialists argue that complex interactions among the brain's nerve cells create consciousness, much as hardware and software interact to create the image that appears on a computer screen. A good deal of support for the materialist view comes from case studies such as Neil's, in which disruptions of consciousness occur following brain damage.

A second question focuses on whether or not consciousness is a unitary entity. According to the *"theater"* view, consciousness is a single phenomenon, a kind of "stage" where all the different events of awareness converge to "play" before the "audience" of your mind. Those adopting this view note that the subjective intensities of lights, sounds, weights, and other stimuli follow similar psychophysical laws (as described in Chapter 5, on perception), as if each sensory system passes its inputs to a single "monitor" that coordinates the experience of magnitude (Teghtsoonian, 1992).

In contrast, *parallel distributed processing (PDP) models* (discussed in Chapter 5) represent the mind as simultaneously processing many parallel streams of information, which are somehow bound together by reciprocal interactions to create a unitary experience of consciousness (Devinsky, 1997). PDP models became influential when research on sensation, perception, memory, cognition, and language suggested that components of these processes are analyzed in separate brain regions. Do these parallel streams eventually unite in common regions? Recent research with animals and humans suggests that they may, thus supporting the theater view of consciousness (Ungerleider, Courtney, & Haxby, 1998).

A third question about consciousness addresses the relationship between nonconscious mental activities and conscious awareness. More than a century ago, Sigmund Freud theorized that some mental processes occur without our awareness and that these processes can affect us in many ways. Most aspects of Freud's theory are not supported by modern laboratory research, but studies have shown that many important mental activities do occur outside of awareness. Let's examine some of these activities and consider the functions they serve.

Some Functions of Consciousness

Francis Crick and Christof Koch have suggested that one function of consciousness is to produce the best current interpretation of sensory information in light of past experience, and to make this interpretation available to those parts of the brain that can act on it (Crick & Koch, 1998). Having a *single* conscious representation, rather than multiple ones, reduces hesitancy in taking action. The conscious brain, then, experiences a representation of the sensory world that is the result of many complex computations;

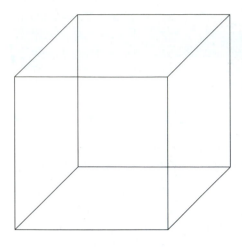

FIGURE 9.1

The Necker Cube

Each of the two squares in the Necker cube can be perceived as either the front or rear surface of the cube. Try to make the cube switch back and forth between these two configurations. Now try to hold only one configuration. You probably cannot maintain the whole cube in consciousness for longer than about 3 seconds before it "flips" from one configuration to the other.

it has access to the *results* of these computational processes but not to the processes themselves. The conscious representation experienced is not necessarily the quickest processing available, however. For example, tennis players may respond to a hard serve before they consciously "see" the ball. However, for complex problems, consciousness allows the most adaptive and efficient interactions among sensory input, motor responses, and a range of knowledge resources in the brain (Baars, 1998).

Even though the contents of consciousness at any given moment are limited by the capacity of working memory, the overall process of consciousness allows access to a vast store of memories and other information. In one study, for example, participants paid brief conscious attention to 10,000 different pictures over several days. A week later they were able to recognize more than 90 percent of the photographs. Evidently, mere consciousness of an event helps to store a recognizable memory that can later be retrieved into consciousness (Kosslyn, 1994).

Almost a hundred years ago William James compared consciousness to a stream, describing it as ever-changing, multilayered, and varying in both quantity and quality. Variations in quantity—in the degree of one's awareness of mental events—result in different *levels of consciousness.* Variations in quality—in the nature of the mental processing available to awareness—lead to different *states of consciousness.* Let's first consider the levels of consciousness.

Levels of Consciousness

At any moment, the mental events that you are aware of are said to exist at the conscious level. For example, look at the Necker cube in Figure 9.1. If you are like most people, you can hold the cube in one configuration for only a few seconds before the other configuration "pops out" at you. The configuration that you experience at any moment is at your conscious level of awareness for that moment.

Some mental events, however, cannot be experienced consciously. For example, you are not directly aware of the fact that your brain constantly regulates your blood pressure. Such mental processing occurs at the **nonconscious level**, totally removed from conscious awareness.

Other mental events are not conscious, but they can either become conscious or influence conscious experience; these mental events make up the *cognitive unconscious* (Reber, 1992), which is further divided into preconscious and unconscious (or subconscious) levels. Mental events at the **preconscious level** are outside of awareness but can easily be brought into awareness. For example, stop reading for a moment and think about last night's dinner. As you do so, you become aware of what and where you ate, and with whom. But moments ago, you were probably not thinking about that information; it was preconscious, ready to be brought to the conscious level. Varying amounts of effort may be required to bring preconscious information into consciousness. In a trivia game you may draw on your large storehouse of preconscious memories to come up with obscure facts, sometimes easily, sometimes only with difficulty.

There are still other mental activities that can alter thoughts, feelings, and actions but are more difficult to bring into awareness (Ratner, 1994). Freud suggested that mental events at the **unconscious level**—especially those involving unacceptable sexual and aggressive urges—are actively kept out of consciousness (see Chapter 14, on personality). Many psychologists do not accept this Freudian view, but still use the term *unconscious* (or *subconscious*) to describe the level of mental activity that influences consciousness but is not conscious (Pervin, 1996).

Mental Processing Without Awareness

LINKAGES

Can people see and hear without being aware of it? (a link to Sensation)

A fascinating demonstration of mental processing without awareness was provided by an experiment with patients who were under anesthesia for surgery. While the still-unconscious patients were in a postoperative recovery room, an audiotape of fifteen word pairs was played over and over. After regaining consciousness, these patients could not say what words had been played in the recovery room—or even whether a

Evidence for the operation of subconscious mental processing includes research showing that surgery patients may be able to hear and later comply with instructions or suggestions given while they are under anesthesia and of which they have no memory (Bennett, Giannini & Davis, 1985). In another study, people showed physiological arousal to emotionally charged words even when they were not paying attention to them (Von Wright, Anderson, & Stenman, 1975).

BLOOM COUNTY   **by Berke Breathed**

Reprinted by permission of International Creative Management, Inc. Copyright ©1999 Berke Breathed.

FIGURE 9.2

Priming Behavior Without Awareness

Participants in this study were primed with rude, polite, or neutral words before being confronted with the problem of interrupting an ongoing conversation. Though not consciously aware of the priming process, participants previously exposed to rude words were most likely to interrupt, whereas those previously exposed to polite words were least likely to do so.

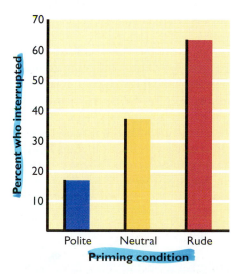

Source: Bargh, Chen, & Burrows, 1996, Figure 1.

tape had been played at all. Yet when given one word from each of the word pairs and asked to say the first word that came to mind, the patients were able to produce the other member of the word pair from the tape (Cork, Kihlstrom, & Hameroff, 1992).

Even when people are conscious and alert, information can sometimes be processed and used without their awareness (Ward, 1997). In one study of this phenomenon, participants watched a computer screen as an *X* flashed in one of four locations. The participants' task was to indicate where the *X* appeared by rapidly pushing one of four buttons. The *X*'s location appeared to vary randomly, but the placement sequence actually followed a set of complex rules, such as "If the *X* moves horizontally twice in a row, then it will move vertically next." The participants' responses became progressively faster and more accurate, but they instantly deteriorated when the rules were dropped and the *X*s began appearing in *truly* random locations. Apparently, the participants in this study had learned a complex rule-bound strategy to improve their performance. However, even when offered $100 to state the rules that had guided the location sequence, they could not do so, nor were they sure that any such rules existed (Lewicki, 1992).

Information processing without awareness has also been demonstrated in research on *priming*. In a typical priming study, people tend to respond faster or more accurately to previously seen stimuli, even when they cannot consciously recall having seen those stimuli (Arndt et al., 1997; Bar & Biederman, 1998; Schacter & Cooper, 1993). In one study, people were asked to look at a set of drawings and decide which of the objects depicted could actually exist in three-dimensional space and which could not. The participants were better at classifying pictures that they had seen before, even when they could not remember having seen them (Cooper et al., 1992b; Schacter et al., 1991).

Other studies show how priming can alter certain behaviors even when participants are not consciously aware of being influenced. In one such study, for example (Bargh, Chen, & Burrows, 1996), participants were asked to unscramble sentences in which the words were out of order (e.g., "*He it finds instantly.*") In one condition of the experiment, the scrambled sentences contained words associated with the attribute of rudeness (e.g., *rude, bother, annoying*); in a second condition, the scrambled words were associated with politeness (e.g., *respect, honor, polite*); and in a third condition, the words were neutral (e.g., *normally, sends, rapidly*). After completing the unscrambling task, the participants were asked to find the experimenter in another room to get further instructions. But by design, the experimenter was always found talking to a research assistant. The dependent variable in this experiment was whether participants in the three conditions to interrupt the experimenter. As shown in Figure 9.2, the participants in the "rude priming" condition were most likely to interrupt, whereas those in the "polite priming" condition were least likely to do so. Those in the "neutral" condition fell in between the other two groups. Interestingly, the three groups of participants did not differ in terms of how polite they thought the experimenter was. Apparently, the priming process affected their behavior without affecting their conscious judgment processes.

Priming studies suggest that unconscious processes can affect people's conscious thoughts and actions. However, the specific mechanisms that produce these effects are difficult to study and still not fully understood.

■ What was the researchers' question?

What is the relationship between conscious and unconscious processes? Anthony Greenwald and Mark Klinger explored one aspect of this question by examining whether stimuli of which people are unaware can improve their performance on a task.

■ How did the researchers answer the question?

Klinger and Greenwald (1995) conducted a two-stage experiment that involved both conscious and unconscious priming. In the first stage, participants looked through a set of viewing tubes that presented each eye with its own computer screen. The same pair of words appeared on each screen, and the participants' task was to press one key if the words were related (as in *eagle-falcon*) and another key if they were unrelated (as in *eagle-polka*). Before the word pairs appeared, a priming word was presented to one eye long enough to be consciously perceived. Sometimes, this priming word was related to one of the words in the pair that followed (for example, *hawk* might appear just before *eagle-falcon* or *eagle-polka*); at other times, the prime was unrelated (*nurse*).

In the second stage of the study, the researchers wanted to present the priming word in such a way that a participant could mentally process it, but without being conscious of doing so. They did this by presenting the priming word to only one eye while showing a meaningless visual pattern, called a "mask," to the other eye. The longer such stimuli are displayed, the easier it is to see the word, but if the visual masking procedure is timed just right, a participant will mentally process the priming word without being aware of seeing it. For each participant, the researchers determined the exposure time at which it became impossible to report whether or not a priming word had appeared on the screen.

■ What did the researchers find?

After analyzing the data from the first stage of the study, Klinger and Greenwald concluded that the expected priming effect had occurred; when the participants were consciously aware of the priming word, they made faster and more accurate decisions about the word pairs when primed by a word that was related to a member of the pair than when primed by an unrelated word.

But what about the effect of the masked priming words in the second stage? As before, the participants' decisions about the word pairs were faster and more accurate when the priming word was related to the word pairs than when it was unrelated. In short, the priming effect occurred even when masking prevented the participants from consciously perceiving the priming word.

In a similar experiment conducted around the same time, Greenwald and his colleagues (1995) found that masked stimuli helped participants on a different kind of task—identifying where a word was located on a computer screen. However, masked primes did not improve their performance when they had to decide whether a word described something pleasant or unpleasant. Thus, priming affected some kinds of performance but not others.

■ What do the results mean?

The results of these experiments provide objective evidence that unconscious processes can affect behavior. Stimuli of which the participants were unaware affected their performance; what's more, the impact was equivalent to that of stimuli that participants could readily recognize. The results of these studies and others like them have another implication as well: They challenge some of the traditional Freudian views about the functions of the unconscious. According to Freud, unconscious processes function mainly to protect us from painful or frightening thoughts, feelings, and memories by keeping such things hidden from consciousness (Pervin, 1996). However, many psychologists studying unconscious processes now believe that, in fact, one of the primary functions of these processes is to help us more effectively carry out mundane, day-to-day mental activities.

■ What do we still need to know?

Numerous questions about the relationship between conscious and unconscious processes remain to be answered. One of the most significant of these is whether conscious and unconscious thoughts occur independently of one another. On the basis of their experiments, Greenwald and his colleagues concluded that the answer is yes. Others question this conclusion, however. For example, one study found a correlation between participants' unconscious indicators of age-prejudice—specifically, implicit memory for negative stereotypes about the elderly—and their consciously held attitudes toward the elderly (Hense, Penner, & Nelson, 1995). Another study (Lepore & Brown, 1997) also found similarity between unconscious and conscious forms of ethnic prejudice. The question remains unresolved because recently it has been shown that some people who consciously disavow ethnic prejudice may unconsciously hold such attitudes (Greenwald, McGhee, & Schwartz, 1998). We consider this issue further in the "Thinking Critically" section of Chapter 17.

The Neuropsychology of Consciousness

The nature of various levels of consciousness and the role of the brain regions that support them can be illuminated by studies of the results of brain damage. Consider the case of Karen Ann Quinlan. After drug-induced heart failure starved her brain of oxygen, Karen entered a coma; she was unconscious, unresponsive, and—in medical terms—"brain-dead." Amid worldwide controversy, her parents obtained a court order that allowed them to shut off Karen's life-support machines; but, to everyone's surprise, she continued to live in a vegetative state for ten more years. A detailed study of her autopsied brain revealed that it had sustained damage mainly in the thalamus, an area described in Chapter 3 as a "relay station" for most sensory signals entering the brain (Kinney et al., 1994). Some researchers have used this finding to argue that the thalamus may be critical for the experience of consciousness (e.g., Bogen, 1995). Indeed, given the recent discovery of reciprocal feedback between the thalamus and the cortex, there is reason to believe that the thalamus plays a role in directing the spotlight of conscious attention to information in particular parts of cortex "where the action is" (Baars, 1998).

The condition known as *prosopagnosia* provides an example of how brain damage can also cause more limited impairments in consciousness. People with prosopagnosia cannot consciously recognize faces—including their own face in the mirror—yet they can still see and recognize many other objects, and can still recognize people by their voices (Young & De Haan, 1992). The problem appears to be relatively specific—one patient who became a farmer could recognize and name his sheep, but never was able to recognize humans! (McNeil & Warrington, 1993). However, when such people see a familiar—but not consciously recognized—face, they show eye movement patterns, changes in brain activity, and autonomic nervous system responses that do not occur when viewing an unfamiliar face (Bruyer, 1991). Thus, some vestige of face recognition is preserved, but it remains unavailable to conscious experience.

Brain damage can also impair conscious access to other mental abilities. Consider *anterograde amnesia,* the inability to form new memories, which often accompanies

FIGURE 9.3

Memory Formation in Anterograde Amnesia

In this experiment, a patient known as H.M., who had anterograde amnesia, was asked to trace the outline of an object while using only a mirror (which reverses left and right) for visual feedback. H.M.'s performance on this difficult task improved from day to day, indicating that he learned and remembered how to do the task. Yet he had no conscious memory of the practice that allowed his skill to develop (Milner, 1965).

(A) MIRROR-TRACING TASK

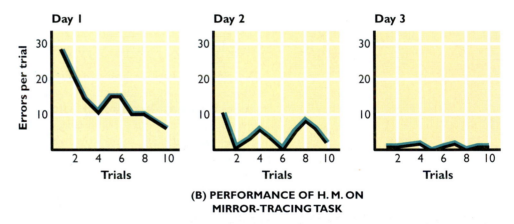

(B) PERFORMANCE OF H. M. ON MIRROR-TRACING TASK

Source: Data from Milner, 1965.

damage to the hippocampus (Eichenbaum, Otto, & Cohen, 1994). Anterograde amnesics seem unable to remember any new information, even about the passage of time. One man who developed this condition in 1957 still needed to be reminded more than thirty years later that it was no longer 1957 (Smith, 1988). Yet as Figure 9.3 shows, anterograde amnesics can learn new skills, even though they cannot consciously recall the practice sessions (Milner, 1965). A 1911 case report offers a dramatic, though cruel, example: A doctor hid a pin in his hand while shaking the hand of a patient with anterograde amnesia. The patient quickly lost conscious memory of the episode but thereafter refused to shake anyone's hand, saying only that "sometimes pins are hidden in people's hands" (Cleparede, 1911; cited in Schacter & Tulving, 1982).

States of Consciousness

Mental activity is always changing. The features of consciousness at any instant—what reaches your awareness, the decisions you are making, and so on—make up your state of consciousness at that moment. Possible states range from deep sleep to alert wakefulness; they can also be affected by drugs and other influences. Consider, for example, the varying states of consciousness that might occur aboard an airplane en route from New York to Los Angeles. In the cockpit, the pilot calmly scans instrument displays while talking to an air-traffic controller. In seat 9B, a lawyer has just finished her second cocktail while planning a courtroom strategy. Nearby, a young father gazes out a window, daydreaming, while his small daughter sleeps in his lap, dreaming dreams of her own.

All these people are experiencing different states of consciousness. Some states are active and some are passive (Hilgard, 1980). The daydreaming father is letting his mind wander, passively noting images, memories, and other mental events that come unbidden to mind. The lawyer is actively directing her mental activity, evaluating various options and considering their likely outcomes.

Most people spend most of their time in a *waking* state of consciousness. Mental processing in this state varies with changes in attention or arousal. Thus, while reading, you may temporarily ignore sounds around you. Similarly, if you are upset or bored, you may miss important environmental cues, making it dangerous to drive a car.

When changes in mental processes are great enough for you or others to notice significant differences in how you function, you have entered an altered state of consciousness (Glicksohn, 1991). In an altered state, mental processing shows distinct changes unique to that state. Cognitive processes or perceptions of yourself or the world may change, and normal inhibitions or self-control may weaken (Martindale, 1981).

The phrase *altered states of consciousness* recognizes waking consciousness as the most common state, a baseline against which "altered" states are compared. However, this is not to say that waking consciousness is universally considered more normal, proper, or valued than other states. In fact, value judgments about different states of consciousness vary considerably across cultures (Ward, 1994).

Consider, for instance, *hallucinations,* which are perceptual experiences—such as hearing voices—that occur in the absence of sensory stimuli. In the United States, hallucinations are viewed as undesirable. Mental patients who hallucinate often feel stress and self-blame; many may opt not to report their hallucinations. Those who do so tend to be considered more disturbed and, thus, may receive more drastic treatments than patients who do not report hallucinations (Wilson et al., 1996). Among the Moche of Peru, however, hallucinations have a culturally approved place. When someone is beset

Altered States and Cultural Values

Different cultures define which altered states of consciousness are approved and which are considered inappropriate. Here we see members of a Brazilian spirit possession cult in various stages of trance, and in Peru, a Moche *curandero,* or curer, attempting to heal an ailing patient by using fumes from a potion—and a drug derived from the San Pedro cactus—to put himself in an altered state of consciousness.

by illness or misfortune, a healer conducts an elaborate ritual to find causes and treatments. During the ceremony, the healer ingests mescaline, a drug that causes hallucinations. These hallucinations are thought to give the healer spiritual insight into the patient's problems (de Rios, 1992). In the context of many other tribal cultures, too, purposeful hallucinations are revered, not demeaned (Grob & Dobkin-de-Rios, 1992).

Thus, states of consciousness differ not only in their basic characteristics but also in their value to members of particular cultures. In the sections to follow, we describe some of the most interesting altered states of consciousness, beginning with the most common one, sleep.

SLEEPING AND DREAMING

According to ancient myths, sleepers lose control of their minds, flirting with death as their souls wander freely. Early researchers thought sleep was a time of mental inactivity. In fact, however, sleep is an active, complex state.

Stages of Sleep

The brain's electrical activity during sleep can be seen on an electroencephalogram (EEG). EEG recordings show "brain waves," which vary in height (amplitude) and speed (cycles per second) as behavior or mental processes change. The brain waves of an awake, alert person have high frequency and low amplitude; they appear as small, closely spaced, irregular EEG spikes, called *beta waves,* occurring at about 13 to 30 cycles per second. A relaxed person with closed eyes shows *alpha waves*—rhythmic brain waves at speeds of 8 to 12 cycles per second (Carlson, 1998).

During a night's sleep, brain waves show distinctive and systematic changes in amplitude and frequency. These EEG changes, along with changes in muscle activity and eye movement, have been used to describe five stages of sleep: four stages of quiet sleep, followed by rapid eye movement (REM) sleep (Dement & Kleitman, 1957).

Stages 1–4: Quiet Sleep   Just before going to sleep you are relaxed, with your eyes closed, but still awake. During this time, EEG activity includes alpha waves; muscle tone and eye movements are normal. Once you fall asleep, you pass through sleep stages 1 through 4, collectively called **quiet sleep** because they are characterized by slowed brain waves, deep breathing, a calm heartbeat, and low blood pressure. Because quiet sleep contrasts with REM sleep (discussed below), it is sometimes called non-REM, or NREM, sleep.

A Sleep Lab

The electroencephalogram (EEG) allows scientists to record brain activity through electrodes attached to the skull. The advent of this technology opened the door to the scientific study of sleep.

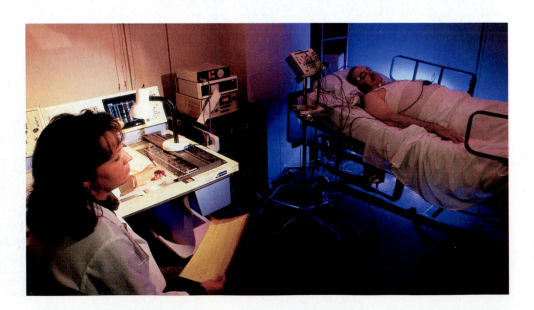

FIGURE 9.4

FIGURE 9.4

EEGs During the Stages of Sleep

EEG recordings of brain wave activity disclose four relatively distinct stages of quiet sleep and one stage of active, or REM, sleep. Notice the regular patterns of alpha waves that occur just before a person goes to sleep, followed by the slowing of brain waves as sleep becomes deeper (stages 1 through 4). When REM sleep begins, brain activity increases dramatically and in some ways resembles the patterns seen in awake and aroused people.

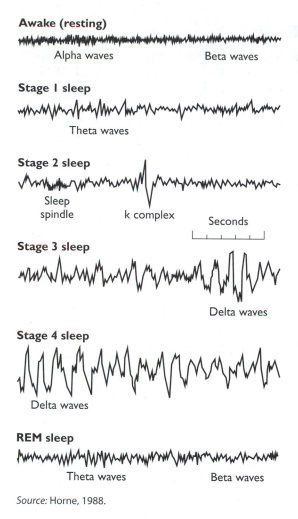

Awake (resting)

Alpha waves   Beta waves

Stage 1 sleep

Theta waves

Stage 2 sleep

Sleep spindle   k complex   Seconds

Stage 3 sleep

Delta waves

Stage 4 sleep

Delta waves

REM sleep

Theta waves   Beta waves

Source: Horne, 1988.

As you enter stage 1 sleep, your eyes start to roll lazily. Rhythmic alpha waves give way to irregular waves known as *theta waves*, which have a speed of between 3.5 and 7.5 cycles per second (see Figure 9.4). Minutes later, stage 2 sleep begins. The EEG shows rapid bursts of waves called *sleep spindles*, along with occasional *K-complexes*, waves with high peaks and deep valleys. Stage 3 sleep shows fewer spindles and K-complexes, but it adds *delta waves,* which are much slower (less than 3.5 cycles per second) and larger in amplitude. When delta waves appear more than half of the time, you are in stage 4 sleep, from which it is quite difficult to be roused. If you are awakened during this stage of deep sleep, you tend to be groggy and confused. The journey from stage 1 to stage 4 has taken about twenty minutes.

REM Sleep After thirty to forty-five minutes in stage 4, you begin a special stage in which delta waves become desynchronized, theta waves reappear, and your eyes move rapidly under closed lids (Jones, 1991). This is called **rapid eye movement (REM) sleep,** or *active sleep.* The EEG now resembles that of an awake, alert person, and physiological arousal—heart rate, breathing, blood pressure—also mimics the waking state. Paradoxically, although the EEG and other measures look like those of an awake person, muscle tone falls to the point of near paralysis. Sudden, twitchy spasms appear, especially in the face and hands, as brainstem and spinal neurons control limb muscle movements (Blumberg & Lucas, 1994). Most of a night's dreams occur during REM sleep (Stickgold, Rittenhouse, & Hobson, 1994) though NREM dreams are common as well (Foulkes, 1985).

A Night's Sleep Most people pass through the cycle of sleep stages four to six times each night. Each cycle lasts about ninety minutes, but with a somewhat different

A Night's Sleep

During a typical night a sleeper goes through this sequence of EEG stages. Notice that sleep is deepest during the first part of the night and more shallow later on, when REM sleep becomes more prominent.

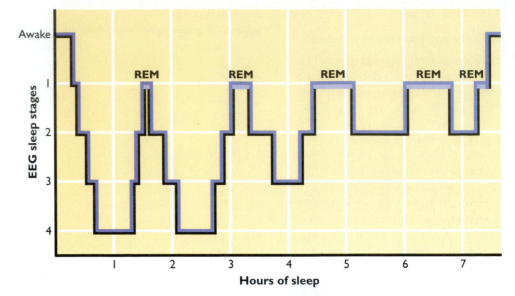

Source: Cartwright, 1978.

itinerary (see Figure 9.5). Early in the night most of the time is spent in stages 3 and 4, with only a few minutes in REM. As sleep continues, though, it is dominated by stage 2 and REM, from which sleepers finally awaken.

Sleep patterns change with age. An average infant sleeps about sixteen hours a day; an average seventy-year-old, only about six hours (Roffwarg, Muzio, & Dement, 1966). The composition of sleep changes with age, too (see Figure 9.6). REM accounts for half of total sleep at birth but less than 25 percent in young adults. People may vary widely from these averages, however; some people feel well-rested after four hours of sleep whereas others of similar age require ten hours to feel satisfied (Clausen, Sersen, & Lidsky, 1974). There are also wide variations among cultural and socioeconomic groups in the tendency to take daytime naps. Interestingly, contrary to the stereotype about the popularity of siestas in Latin and South American countries, urban Mexican college students actually nap *less* than many other college populations (Valencia-Flores et al., 1998).

Sleep Disorders

The most common sleeping problem is **insomnia**, in which one feels daytime fatigue due to trouble falling asleep or staying asleep. Besides being tiring, insomnia is tied to mental distress (Benca et al., 1992). Insomnia is especially associated with depressive and anxiety disorders (Ball, Buchwald, & Waddell, 1995); overall, insomniacs are three times as likely to show a mental disorder as those with no sleep complaints (Ford & Kamerow, 1989). It is unclear from such correlations, however, whether insomnia causes mental disorders, mental disorders cause insomnia, or some other factor causes both.

Sleeping pills can relieve insomnia, but they are dangerous when a person also drinks alcohol and may eventually lead to *increased* sleeplessness (Ashton, 1995). In the long run, methods based on learning principles may be more helpful (Lichstein & Riedel, 1994). For example, stress management techniques such as relaxation training have been shown to help insomniacs reduce unusually strong physiological reactions to stress (Bernstein, Borkovec, & Hazlette-Stevens, 2000; Stepanski et al., 1994). Another option is *sleep restriction therapy,* in which the person goes to bed only when sleepy and gets out of bed if sleep does not come (Spielman, Saskin, & Thorpy, 1987). The goal is for insomniacs to associate their bed with sleeping, not wakefulness.

Narcolepsy is a disturbing daytime sleep disorder that usually begins when a person is between fifteen and twenty-five years old (Choo & Guilleminault, 1998). Its vic-

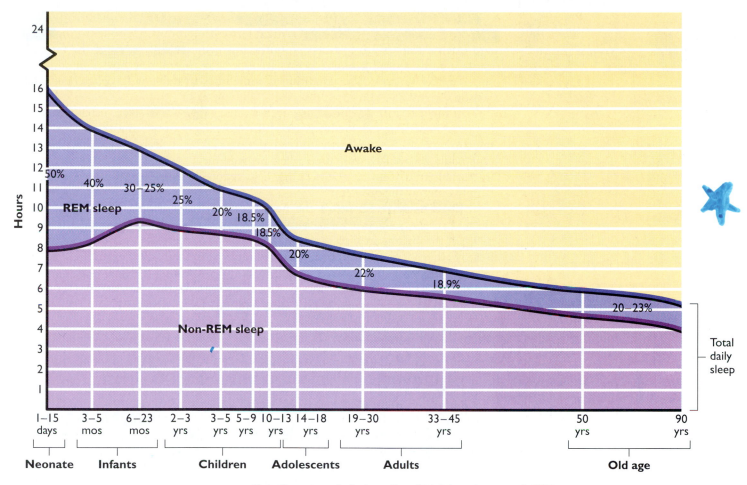

Note: Percentages indicate portion of total sleep time spent in REM.
Source: Roffwarg, Muzio, & Dement, 1966 (revised 1969).

FIGURE 9.6

Sleep and Dreaming over the Life Span

People tend to sleep less as they get older. There is also a sharp reduction in the percentage of REM sleep, from about eight hours per day in infancy to less than an hour per day by age seventy. Non-REM sleep time also decreases but, compared to the drop in REM, remains relatively stable. After age twenty, however, non-REM sleep contains less and less of the deepest, or stage 4, sleep.

tims abruptly switch from active, often emotional waking states, into a few minutes of REM sleep. Because of the loss of muscle tone in REM, the narcoleptic collapses and remains briefly immobile even after awakening. The exact cause of narcolepsy is unknown, but genetic factors do play a role (Mignot, 1998). Stimulants and napping can be helpful treatments, and a promising new drug called Modafinil is currently being tested. It appears to be effective not only for narcolepsy, but for counteracting the effects of sleep deprivation as well (*New York Times,* November 3, 1998).

People suffering from sleep apnea briefly stop breathing hundreds of times every night, waking up each time long enough to resume breathing. In the morning, they do not recall the awakenings, yet they feel tired and tend to show reductions in attention and learning ability (Naëgelé et al., 1995). Apnea has many causes, including obesity and compression of the windpipe. Effective treatments include weight loss and use of a nasal mask that provides a steady stream of air (Wali & Kryger, 1995).

In sudden infant death syndrome (SIDS), a sleeping baby stops breathing and dies. In the United States, SIDS strikes about two of every thousand infants, usually when they are two to four months old (Hirschfeld, 1995). SIDS is less common in cultures where infants and parents sleep in the same bed, suggesting that sleeping position may be important (McKenna et al., 1993). Indeed, about half of apparent SIDS cases may be accidental suffocations caused when infants lie face down on soft surfaces (Guntheroth & Spiers, 1992). Other SIDS cases may stem from exposure to cigarette smoke. Educational campaigns alerting parents to place infants face up in their cribs at bedtime, and to keep them away from cigarette smoke, have dramatically reduced the incidence of SIDS (Henderson-Smart, Ponsonby, & Murphy, 1998).

Disrupted Circadian Rhythms

In 1998, the Brazilian soccer team had to fly all the way to Europe to compete in this World Cup match against Scotland. The disruptive effects of international travel or changes in shift work schedules can be reduced somewhat by exposure to bright light during waking hours. This procedure speeds the process of resetting the body's circadian rhythms, possibly by stimulating cells of the brain's suprachiasmatic nuclei; (Dawson et al., 1995).

Nightmares are frightening REM dreams; **night terrors** are horrific dream images that occur during stage 3 or 4 sleep. A night terror can produce a bloodcurdling scream and intense fear for up to thirty minutes, but people may not recall the terrifying episode in the morning. Night terrors are especially common in boys, but adults can suffer milder versions. The condition is sometimes treatable with drugs (Lillywhite, Wilson, & Nutt, 1994).

Like night terrors, **sleepwalking** occurs during non-REM sleep, usually in childhood (Masand, Popli, & Welburg, 1995). By morning, most sleepwalkers have forgotten their travels. Despite myths to the contrary, waking a sleepwalker is not harmful. One adult sleepwalker was cured when his wife blew a whistle whenever he began a nocturnal stroll (Meyer, 1975). Drugs help reduce sleepwalking, but most children simply outgrow the problem.

In **REM behavior disorder**, the near paralysis that normally accompanies REM sleep is absent, so sleepers move as if acting out their dreams (Watanabe & Sugita, 1998). If the dreams are violent, the disorder can be dangerous to the dreamer or those nearby. Indeed, many sufferers attack sleeping partners. For example, one man grabbed his wife's throat while dreaming he was breaking a deer's neck (or so he claimed). The disorder sometimes occurs along with daytime narcolepsy (Schenck & Mahowald, 1992). Fortunately, drug treatments are usually effective.

Why Do People Sleep?

In trying to understand sleep, psychologists have studied both the functions that sleep serves and the ways in which brain mechanisms shape its characteristics.

Sleep as a Circadian Rhythm   The sleep-wake cycle is one example of the rhythmic nature of life. Almost all animals (including humans) display cycles of behavior and physiology that repeat about every 24 hours in a pattern called a **circadian rhythm** (from the Latin *circa dies,* meaning "about a day") (Kyriacou, 1994). Longer and shorter rhythms also occur, but they are less common. Circadian rhythms are linked, or *entrained,* to signals such as the light and dark of day and night, but most of them continue even without such time cues. Volunteers living for months without external cues maintain daily rhythms in sleeping and waking, hormone release, eating, urination, and other physiological functions. Under such conditions, these cycles repeat about every 25 hours (Hillman et al., 1994).

Disrupting the sleep-wake cycle can create problems. For example, air travel across several time zones often causes **jet lag**, a pattern of fatigue, irritability, inattention, and sleeping problems which can last several days. The traveler's body feels ready to sleep at the wrong time for the new locale. Similar problems affect workers changing between day and night shifts. Because it tends to be easier to stay awake longer than usual than to go to sleep earlier than usual, sleep-wake rhythms readjust to altered

FIGURE 9.7

Westward/Eastward Travel and Jet Lag

Changing time zones causes more intense symptoms of jet lag after eastward travel (when time is lost) than after westward travel (when time is gained). These data show how long it took people flying between London and Detroit (a five-hour time change) to fall asleep once in bed, both on the night before the trip (B1) and on the five nights afterward. Those who flew eastward, from Detroit to London, needed more time to fall asleep than those who flew westward, from London to Detroit (Nicholson et al., 1986).

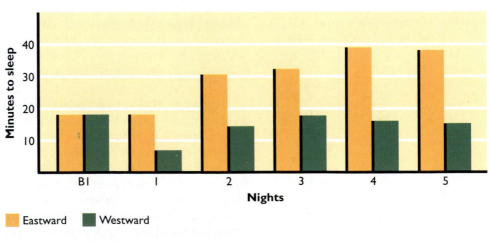

Source: Data from Nicholson et al., 1986.

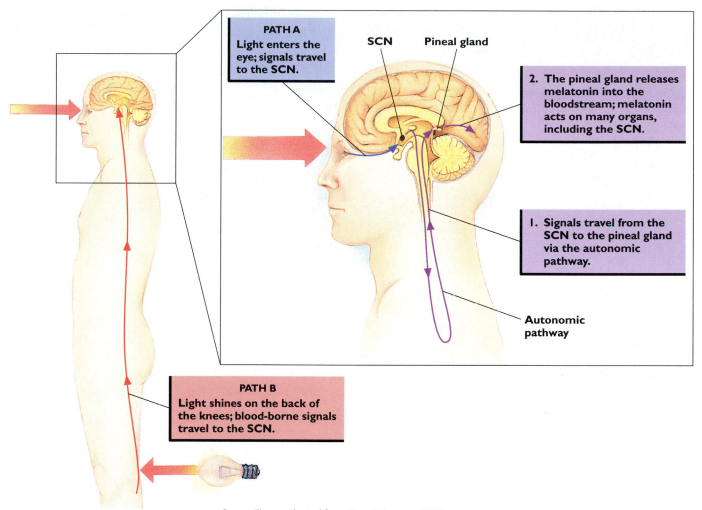

Source: Figure adapted from Oren & Terman, 1998.

FIGURE 9.8

The Suprachiasmatic Nuclei, Light, and Circadian Rhythms

In humans, the body's "biological clock" is in the *suprachiasmatic nuclei* (SCN) of the hypothalamus. The SCN control the release of melatonin from the pineal gland, which affects our circadian rhythms. The amount of light that a person is exposed to can change the setting of this biological clock and shift the timing of these rhythms. The most common pathway by which light reaches the SCN is through the eyes, but recent research suggests that light shining on the back of the knees can also affect SCN neurons and the sleep-wake cycle (Oren & Terman, 1998).

light-dark cycles more easily when sleep is shifted to a later rather than an earlier time (see Figure 9.7).

Since circadian-like rhythms continue without external cues, an internal "biological clock" in the brain must keep track of time. This clock is in the *suprachiasmatic nuclei (SCN)* of the hypothalamus. Signals from the SCN reach areas in the hindbrain that initiate sleep or wakefulness (Moore, 1997). SCN neurons show a 24- to 25-hour rhythm in firing even when removed from the brain and put in a laboratory dish (Gillette, 1986). And when animals with SCN damage receive transplanted SCN cells, the restored circadian rhythms are similar to those of the donor animal (Menaker & Vogelbaum, 1993). SCN neurons also regulate the release of the hormone *melatonin* from the *pineal gland*, via an autonomic pathway. Melatonin, in turn, appears to be important in maintaining circadian rhythms; timely injections of melatonin may reduce fatigue and disorientation stemming from jet lag or other sleep-wake cycle changes by acting on melatonin receptors in the SCN (Liu et al., 1997; Sack et al., 1997).

It was once thought that light coming through the eyes to the SCN provided the only way to shift circadian rhythms in humans. However, researchers have recently discovered that light shining on the back of the knees can have the same effect! (Campbell & Murphy, 1998; see Figure 9.8). A possible explanation for this phenomenom is that light-induced changes in the blood convey a signal to the brain; but regardless of the mechanism, this finding opens the way to new ideas about treatments for rhythm-related psychological problems, including seasonal affective disorder (which we discuss in Chapter 15).

The Functions of Sleep   Examining the effects of sleep deprivation may help explain why people sleep at all. People who go without sleep for as long as a week usually do not suffer serious long-term effects, but sleeplessness does lead to fatigue, irritability, and inattention (Smith & Maben, 1993). Short-term sleep deprivation effects can also take their toll. Most fatal auto accidents in the United States occur during the "fatigue hazard" hours of midnight to 6 A.M. (Coleman, 1992), and fatigue has been implicated as the primary cause of up to 25 percent of all auto accidents (Summala & Mikkola, 1994).

Some researchers believe that sleep, especially non-REM sleep, helps restore the body and the brain for future activity (Adam & Oswald, 1977). The waking brain uses more metabolic fuel than the sleeping brain, and, during wakefulness, the by-products of metabolism accumulate. The accumulation of one such by-product, *adenosine*, inhibits the cholinergic systems in the forebrain and brainstem, inducing sleepiness (Porkka-Heiskanen et al., 1997). During sleep, adenosine levels gradually decline.

Sleep-deprived people do not make up lost sleep hour for hour. Instead, they sleep about 50 percent more than usual, then awake feeling rested. But if people are deprived only of REM sleep, they later compensate more directly. In a classic study, participants were awakened whenever their EEG showed REM sleep. When allowed to sleep uninterrupted the next night, the participants "rebounded," nearly doubling the percentage of time spent in REM (Dement, 1960). Even after *total* sleep deprivation, the next night of uninterrupted sleep includes an unusually high percentage of REM sleep (Feinberg & Campbell, 1993). This apparent need for REM sleep suggests that REM has special functions.

First, REM may improve the functioning of neurons that use norepinephrine (Siegel & Rogawski, 1988). Norepinephrine is a neurotransmitter released by cells in the *locus coeruleus;* during waking hours, it affects alertness and mood. But the brain's neurons lose sensitivity to norepinephrine if it is released continuously for too long. Because the locus coeruleus is almost completely inactive during REM sleep, researchers suggest that REM helps restore sensitivity to norepinephrine, and thus its ability to keep us alert (Steriade & McCarley, 1990). Indeed, animals deprived of REM show unusually high norepinephrine levels and decreased daytime alertness (Brock et al., 1994).

The Effects of Sleep Deprivation

Here, scientists at Loughborough University, England, test the effects of sleep deprivation on motor coordination. Driving while sleep-deprived can be dangerous, but some other functions may not suffer as much. One man reportedly stayed awake for 231 hours and was still lucid and capable of serious intellectual work, including the creation of a lovely poem on his tenth day without sleep (Katz & Landis, 1935).

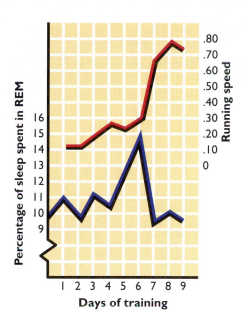

Source: Drucker-Colin & McGaugh, 1977.

FIGURE 9.9

REM Sleep and Learning

The upper curve shows the average running speed of rats as they learned their way around a maze over several days. The lower curve shows the average percentage of REM sleep during the nights between practice sessions. Notice that the rats spent more time in REM on nights during the learning phase than after learning was complete.

REM may also be a time for developing, checking, and expanding the brain's nerve connections (Roffwarg, Muzio, & Dement, 1966). This notion would explain why children and infants, whose brains are still developing, spend so much time in REM (see Figure 9.6 on page 301). In contrast, guinea pigs and other animals born with well-developed brains spend very little sleep time in REM early in their lives (Cartwright, 1978). REM sleep may also help solidify and assimilate the day's experiences. In one study, people who were REM-deprived showed poorer retention of a skill learned the day before than people who were either deprived of non-REM sleep or allowed to sleep normally (Karni et al., 1994b). Further, animals that spend daytime hours engaged in learning tasks display more frequent and longer REM episodes than those that spend the day in their cages (Ambrosini et al., 1992; see also Figure 9.9).

Dreams and Dreaming

We have seen that the brain is active in all sleep stages, but dreams differ from other mental activity in sleep because they are usually story-like, lasting from seconds to minutes. Dreams may be organized or chaotic, realistic or fantastic, calm or exciting (Hobson & Stickgold, 1994). Sometimes, dreams lead to creative insights about waking problems. For example, after trying for days to write a story about good and evil in the same person, author Robert Louis Stevenson dreamed about a man who drank a potion that turned him into a monster (Hill, 1968). This dream inspired *The Strange Case of Dr. Jekyll and Mr. Hyde.* On the whole, however, there are no scientific data indicating that dreams lead to more creative insights than do waking thoughts.

Although they often seem bizarre, dreams often contain a certain amount of logic. In one study, for example, when segments from dream reports were randomly reordered, readers could correctly say which had been rearranged and which were intact (Stickgold, Rittenhouse, & Hobson, 1994).

Daytime activities may influence the content of dreams (Roffwarg, Hermann, & Bowe-Anders, 1978). For example, when people wore red-tinted goggles for a few minutes before going to sleep, they reported more red images in their dreams than people who had not worn the goggles (Roffwarg, Hermann, & Bowe-Anders, 1978). It is also sometimes possible to intentionally direct dream content, especially during lucid dreaming in which the sleeper is aware of dreaming while a dream is happening (LaBerge, 1993).

Research leaves little doubt that everyone dreams during the course of every normal night's sleep. Even blind people dream, although their perceptual experiences are usually not visual. Whether you remember a dream depends on how you sleep and wake up. Recall is better if you awaken abruptly and lie quietly while writing or tape-recording your recollections.

Why do we dream? Theories abound. Some see dreaming as a fundamental process by which all mammals analyze and consolidate information that has personal significance or survival value. Indeed, research clearly indicates that nonhuman animals have REM sleep, although we have no way of knowing whether they are actually dreaming.

According to Freud (1900), dreams are a disguised form of *wish fulfillment,* a way to satisfy unconscious urges or resolve unconscious conflicts that are too upsetting to deal with consciously. Seeing patients' dreams as a "royal road to a knowledge of the unconscious," Freud interpreted their meaning as part of his psychoanalytic treatment of psychological disorders (see Chapters 14 and 16).

In contrast, the *activation-synthesis theory* sees dreams as the meaningless, random by-products of REM sleep (Hobson, 1997). According to this theory, hindbrain arousal during REM creates random messages that *activate* the brain, especially the cerebral cortex. Dreams result as the cortex *synthesizes* these random messages as best it can, using stored memories and current feelings to impose a coherent perceptual organization on confusingly random inputs. From this perspective, dreams represent the brain's attempt to make sense of meaningless stimulation during sleep, much as it does when a person, while awake, tries to find meaningful shapes in cloud formations.

Inducing Hypnosis

In the late 1700s, Austrian physician Franz Anton Mesmer used a forerunner of hypnosis to treat various physical disorders. His procedure, known as mesmerism, began with patients touching afflicted body parts to magnetized metal rods extending from a tub of water. Upon being touched by Mesmer, the patients would fall into a curative "crisis" or trance, sometimes accompanied by convulsions. We now know that hypnosis can be induced without such elaborate rituals, often simply by staring at an object, as this woman did.

If dreams arise from random physiological activity, can their content still have psychological significance? Some psychologists believe that dreams give people a chance to review and address some of the problems they face during waking hours (Cartwright, 1993), whereas others dispute the idea that dreams are particularly helpful in problem solving (Blagrove, 1996). The current concerns of the dreamer *can* affect dream content, however (Fisher & Greenberg, 1996; Hobson, 1988; Stephens, 1996).

HYPNOSIS

The word *hypnosis* comes from the Greek word *hypnos,* meaning "sleep," but hypnotized people are not sleeping. People who have been hypnotized say that their bodies felt "asleep," but their minds were active and alert. **Hypnosis** has traditionally been defined as an altered state of consciousness brought on by special techniques and producing responsiveness to suggestions for changes in experience and behavior (Kirsch, 1994a). Most hypnotized people do not feel forced to follow the hypnotist's instructions; they simply see no reason to refuse (Hilgard, 1965).

Experiencing Hypnosis

Usually, hypnosis begins with suggestions that the participant feels relaxed and sleepy. The hypnotist then gradually focuses the participant's attention on a restricted, often monotonous set of stimuli while suggesting that the participant should ignore everything else and imagine certain feelings.

Not everyone can be hypnotized. Special tests measure *hypnotic susceptibility,* the degree to which people respond to hypnotic suggestions (Gfeller, 1994). Such tests categorize about 10 percent of adults as difficult or impossible to hypnotize (Hilgard, 1982). Hypnotically susceptible people, on the other hand, typically differ from others in several ways. They have a better ability to focus attention and ignore distraction (Crawford, Brown, & Moon, 1993), more active imaginations (Spanos, Burnley, & Cross, 1993), a tendency to fantasize (Lynn & Rhue, 1986), a capacity for processing information quickly and easily (Dixon, Brunet, & Lawrence, 1990), and more positive attitudes toward hypnosis (Gfeller, 1994; Spanos, Burnley, & Cross, 1993). Their *willingness* to be hypnotized is the most important factor of all; contrary to myth, people cannot be hypnotized against their will.

The results of hypnosis can be fascinating. People told that their eyes cannot open may struggle fruitlessly to open them. They may appear deaf or blind or insensitive to pain. They may forget their own names. Some appear to remember forgotten things. Others show *age regression,* apparently recalling or re-enacting their childhood. Hypnotic effects can last for hours or days through *posthypnotic suggestions*—instructions about behavior to take place after hypnosis has ended (such as smiling whenever someone says "England"). Some participants show *posthypnotic amnesia,* an inability to recall what happened while they were hypnotized, even after being told what happened.

Ernest Hilgard (1965, 1992) described the main changes that people display during hypnosis. First, hypnotized people show *reduced planfulness.* They tend not to initiate actions, waiting instead for the hypnotist's instructions. One participant said, "I was trying to decide if my legs were crossed, but I couldn't tell, and didn't quite have the initiative to move to find out" (Hilgard, 1965, p. 6). Second, they tend to ignore all but the hypnotist's voice and whatever it points out; their *attention is redistributed.* Third, hypnosis enhances the ability to *fantasize,* so participants more vividly imagine a scene or relive a memory. Fourth, hypnotized people display increased *role-taking;* they more easily act like a person of a different age or a member of the opposite sex, for example. Fifth, hypnotic participants show *reduced reality testing,* tending not to question if statements are true and more willingly accepting apparent distortions of reality. Thus, a hypnotized person might shiver in a warm room if a hypnotist says it is snowing.

FIGURE 9.10

Can Hypnosis Produce Blindness?

The top row looks like gibberish, but it can be read as the numbers and letters in the lower row if viewed through special glasses *with one eye closed.* Yet when hypnotized subjects who had been given suggestions for blindness in one eye wore the glasses, they were unable to read the display, indicating that both eyes were in fact working normally (Pattie, 1935).

Source: Pattie, 1935.

FIGURE 9.11

Reports of Pain in Hypnosis

This graph shows average reports of pain when peoples' hands were immersed in painfully cold water under three different conditions. The red line represents the reports by nonhypnotized participants. The orange line represents the oral reports by hypnotized participants who were told they would feel no pain. The green line represents the responses by hypnotized participants who were told they would feel no pain but were asked to press a key if "any part of them" felt pain. The key-pressing by this "hidden observer" suggests that under hypnosis the experience of pain was dissociated from conscious awareness (Hilgard, 1977).

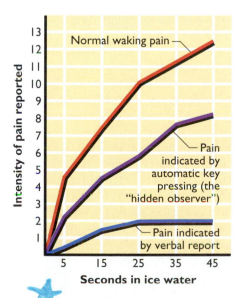

Explaining Hypnosis

Hypnotized people look and act differently from nonhypnotized people (Hilgard, 1965). Do these differences indicate an altered state of consciousness?

Role theory maintains that hypnosis is *not* a special state of consciousness. Proponents of this theory argue that hypnotized participants are merely complying with social demands and acting in accordance with a special social role (Kirsch, 1994b). In other words, they say, hypnosis provides a socially acceptable reason to follow someone's suggestions, much as a doctor's white coat provides a good reason for patients to remove clothing on command.

Support for role theory comes from laboratory experiments indicating that motivated but nonhypnotized volunteers can duplicate many, if not all, aspects of hypnotic behavior, from arm rigidity to age regression (Dasgupta et al., 1995; Orne & Evans, 1965). In other studies, special tests have shown that people rendered blind or deaf by hypnosis can still see or hear, even though their actions and beliefs suggest that they cannot (Bryant & McConkey, 1989; Pattie, 1935; see also Figure 9.10).

Advocates of **state theory** argue that hypnosis does indeed create an altered state of consciousness. They point to the fact that hypnosis can produce dramatic effects—including insensitivity to pain and the disappearance of warts (Noll, 1994)—that are difficult to attribute to social role-taking. They also note that there are subtle differences in the way hypnotized and nonhypnotized people carry out suggestions. In one study, for example, hypnotized people and those who had been asked to simulate hypnosis were told that they would run their hands through their hair whenever they heard the word *experiment* (Orne, Sheehan, & Evans, 1968). Simulators did so only when the hypnotist said the cue word; hypnotized participants complied no matter who said it. Another study found that most hypnotic participants passed a traditional polygraph "lie detector" test when answering questions about their hypnotic experiences, whereas most simulators did not (Kinnunen, Zamansky, & Block, 1994).

Hilgard (1992) has proposed **dissociation theory** to blend role and state theories. He suggests that hypnosis is not one specific state but a general condition in which our normally centralized control of thoughts and actions is temporarily reorganized, or broken up, through a process called *dissociation,* meaning a split in consciousness (Hilgard, 1979). Thus, body movements normally under voluntary control can occur on their own, and normally involuntary processes (such as overt reactions to pain) can be controlled voluntarily. Hilgard argues that this relaxation of central control occurs as part of a *social agreement* to share control with the hypnotist. In other words, people usually decide for themselves how to act or what to attend to, perceive, or remember, but, during hypnosis, the hypnotist is "allowed" to control some of these experiences and actions. To Hilgard, then, hypnosis is a socially agreed-upon display of dissociated mental functions. Compliance with a social role may account for part of the story, he says, but hypnosis also leads to significant changes in mental processes.

Evidence for dissociation theory comes from a study in which hypnotized participants immersed one hand in ice water after being told that they would feel no pain (Hilgard, Morgan, & MacDonald, 1975). With the other hand, participants were to press a key to indicate if "any part of them" felt pain. Participants' oral reports indicated almost no pain, but their key-pressing told a different story (see Figure 9.11).

Hilgard concluded that a "hidden observer" was reporting on pain that was reaching the person but had been separated, or dissociated, from conscious awareness (Hilgard, 1977). Contemporary research continues to test the validity of various explanatory theories of hypnosis (Green & Lynn, 1995). However, traditional distinctions between state and role theories have become less relevant as researchers focus on larger questions, such as the impact of social and cognitive factors in hypnotic phenomena, the nature of the hypnotic experience, and the psychological and physiological basis for hypnotic susceptibility (Kirsch & Lynn, 1995).

Applications of Hypnosis

Whatever hypnosis is, it has proven useful, especially in relation to pain. Hypnosis seems to be the only anesthetic some people need to block the pain of dental work, childbirth, burns, and abdominal surgery (Van Sickel, 1992). For others, hypnosis relieves chronic pain from arthritis, nerve damage, migraine headaches, and cancer (Nolan et al., 1995). Hypnotic suggestion can reduce nausea and vomiting due to chemotherapy (Redd, 1984), and it can help reduce surgical bleeding (Gerschman, Reade, & Burrows, 1980).

Other applications of hypnosis are more controversial, especially the use of hypnosis to aid memory. For example, hypnotic age regression is sometimes attempted in an effort to help people recover lost memories. In actuality, however, the memories of past events reported by age-regressed individuals are *less* accurate than those of nonhypnotized individuals (Lynn et al., 1997). Similarly, it is doubtful that hypnosis can improve the ability of witnesses to recall details of a crime (Lynn, Myers, & Malinoski, in press). Instead, their expectations about and confidence in hypnosis may cause them to unintentionally distort information or reconstruct memories for the events in question (Garry & Loftus, 1994; Weekes et al., 1992).

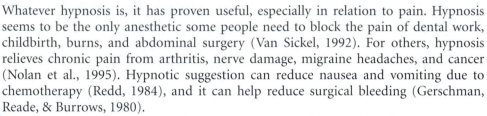

LINKAGES

Does meditation relieve stress? (a link to Health, Stress, and Coping)

LINKAGES

Meditation, Health, and Stress

Meditation provides a set of techniques intended to create an altered state of consciousness characterized by inner peace and tranquillity (Shapiro & Walsh, 1984). Some claim that meditation increases awareness and understanding of themselves and their environment, reduces anxiety, improves health, and aids performance in everything from work to tennis.

In the most common meditation methods, attention is focused on just one thing—a word, sound, or object—until the meditator stops thinking about anything and experiences nothing but "pure awareness" (Benson, 1975).

What a meditator focuses on is far less important than doing so with a passive attitude. To organize attention, meditators may inwardly name every sound or thought that reaches consciousness, focus on the sound of their own breathing, or slowly repeat a *mantra*, which is a soothing word or phrase. During a typical meditation session, breathing, heart rate, muscle tension, blood pressure, and oxygen consumption decrease (Wallace & Benson, 1972). Most forms of meditation induce alpha-wave EEG activity, the brain-wave pattern commonly found in a relaxed, eyes-closed, waking state (see Figure 9.4 on page 299).

Meditators often report significant reductions in stress-related problems such as general anxiety, high blood pressure, and insomnia (Beauchamp-Turner & Levinson, 1992). More generally, meditators' scores on personality tests indicate increases in general mental health, self-esteem, and social openness (Janowiak & Hackman, 1994). Exactly how meditation produces its effects is unclear. Many of its effects can also be achieved by biofeedback, hypnosis, and just relaxing (Holmes, 1984).

PSYCHOACTIVE DRUGS

Every day, most people in the world use drugs that alter brain activity and consciousness (Levinthal, 1996). For example, 80 to 90 percent of people in North America use caffeine, the stimulant found in coffee (Gilbert, 1984). A drug is a chemical not usually needed for physiological activity and that can affect the body upon entering it. (Some people use the word *drug* to mean therapeutic medicines, but refer to nonmedicinal drugs as *substances.*) Drugs that affect the brain, changing consciousness and other psychological processes, are called **psychoactive drugs.** The study of psychoactive drugs is called **psychopharmacology.**

Psychopharmacology

Most psychoactive drugs affect the brain by altering the interactions between neurotransmitters and receptors, as described in Chapter 3, on biological aspects of psychology. To create their effects, these drugs must cross the **blood-brain barrier,** a feature of blood vessels in the brain that prevents some substances from entering brain tissue (Sage & Wilson, 1994). Once past this barrier, a psychoactive drug's effects depend on several factors: With which neurotransmitter systems does the drug interact? How does the drug affect these neurotransmitters or their receptors? What psychological functions are performed by the brain systems that use these neurotransmitters?

Drugs can affect neurotransmitters or their receptors through several mechanisms. As Figure 9.12 shows, neurotransmitters fit into their own receptors; however, some drugs are similar enough to a particular neurotransmitter to fool its receptors. These drugs, called **agonists,** bind to the receptor and mimic the effects of the normal neurotransmitter. Other drugs are similar enough to a neurotransmitter to occupy its receptors but cannot mimic its effects; they bind to a receptor and prevent the normal neurotransmitter from binding. These drugs are called **antagonists.** Still other drugs work by increasing or decreasing the release of a specific neurotransmitter. Finally, some drugs work by speeding or slowing the *removal* of a neurotransmitter from synapses.

Predicting a drug's behavioral effects is complicated by the fact that some drugs interact with many neurotransmitter systems. Also, the nervous system may

FIGURE 9.12

Agonists and Antagonists

In part (A), a molecule of neurotransmitter interacts with a receptor on a neuron's dendrites by fitting into and stimulating it. Part (B) shows a drug moleclue acting as an *agonist,* affecting the receptor in the same way a neurotransmitter would. Part (C) depicts an *antagonist* drug molecule blocking a natural neurotransmitter from reaching and acting upon the receptor.

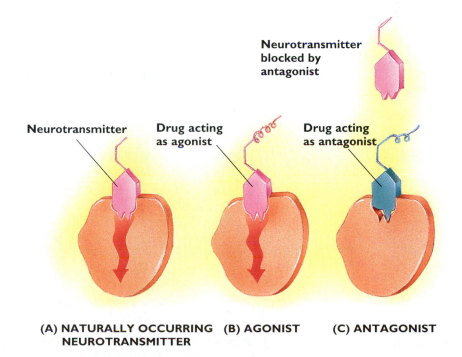

(A) NATURALLY OCCURRING NEUROTRANSMITTER **(B) AGONIST** **(C) ANTAGONIST**

Changing Definitions of Illicit Drugs

The definition of inappropriate drug use can vary across cultures and over time (Weiss & Moore, 1990). For example, in the United States cocaine was once a respectable, commercially available drug; today, it is illegal.

compensate for a disturbance. For example, repeated exposure to a drug that blocks receptors for a certain neurotransmitter often leads to a compensatory increase in the number of receptors available to accept the neurotransmitter.

The Varying Effects of Drugs

Drugs affect biological systems in accordance with their chemical properties. Unfortunately, their medically desirable *main effects,* such as pain relief, are often accompanied by undesirable *side effects,* which may include the potential for abuse. **Substance abuse** is a pattern of use that causes serious social, legal, or interpersonal problems for the user (American Psychiatric Association, 1994).

Substance abuse may lead to psychological or physical dependence. **Psychological dependence** is a condition in which a person continues drug use despite adverse effects, needs the drug for a sense of well-being, and becomes preoccupied with obtaining the drug. Psychological dependence can occur with or without **physical dependence,** or **addiction,** which is a physiological state in which drug use is needed to prevent a **withdrawal syndrome.** Withdrawal symptoms vary across drugs but often include an intense craving for the drug and effects generally opposite to those of the drug itself. Physical dependence can develop gradually, without awareness. Eventually, drug tolerance may appear. **Tolerance** is a condition in which increasingly larger drug doses are needed to produce the same effect (Gilman et al., 1985). With the development of tolerance, many addicts need the drug just to prevent the negative effects of not taking it. However, most researchers believe that a craving for the positive effects of drugs is what keeps addicts coming back to drug use (Wise, 1996).

The potential for "normal" people to develop drug dependence should not be underestimated. All addictive drugs stimulate the brain's "pleasure centers," regions that are sensitive to the neurotransmitter dopamine. Neuronal activity in these areas produces intensely pleasurable feelings; it also helps generate the pleasant feelings of a good meal, a "runner's high," or sex (Grunberg, 1994; Harris & Aston-Jones, 1995).

Neuroscientists long believed that these feelings stem directly from the action of dopamine, but recent research suggests that dopaminergic activity may be more involved in responding to the novelty associated with pleasurable events than in actually creating the experience of pleasure (Garris et al., 1999). In any case, by affecting dopamine regulation and related biochemical processes in "pleasure centers," addictive drugs have the capacity to create tremendously rewarding effects in most people.

Expectations and Drug Effects   Drug effects are determined by more than biochemistry; *learned expectations* also play a role (Goldman, Del Boca, & Darkes, in press). In one experiment, for example, college students reported being drunk after

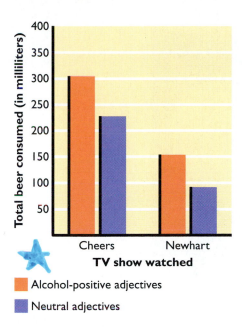

Source: Roehrich & Goldman, 1995, Figure 1.

FIGURE 9.13

Expectancies and Alcohol Consumption

People may drink more when their expectancies about the positive effects of alcohol have been primed. As this study demonstrates, participants who (1) watched a TV show (*Cheers*) in which the characters enjoyed themselves while drinking alcohol and (2) were exposed to adjectives associated with positive expectancies about alcohol subsequently drank more (nonalcoholic) beer than participants who watched a show (*Newhart*) in which alcohol consumption was not portrayed and who were not exposed to the adjectives. None of the participants were consciously aware that their alcohol expectancies had been primed.

consuming drinks that tasted and smelled like alcohol—even though the drinks contained no alcohol (Darkes & Goldman, 1993). Other studies have demonstrated that people's expectancies about the effects of alcohol had a greater influence on their aggressive behavior than did alcohol itself (e.g., Lang et al., 1975). Expectations about drug effects develop, in part, as people watch other people react to drugs. Because what they see can be different from one individual and culture to the next, drug effects vary considerably throughout the world (MacAndrew & Edgerton, 1969). For example, the loss of inhibition and violence commonly associated with alcohol use in the United States is partly attributable to custom, inasmuch as these effects are not universal. Consider the contrasting example of Bolivia's Camba culture, in which people drink, in extended bouts, a brew that is 89 percent alcohol. These people repeatedly pass out, wake up, and start drinking again—all the while maintaining tranquil social relations.

The learned nature of responses to alcohol is also demonstrated by cases in which there are changes in the model for appropriate "drunken comportment." When Europeans brought alcohol to Tahiti in the 1700s, the Tahitians' initial response to drinking it was to become relaxed and befuddled, much as when consuming kava, their traditional—nonalcoholic—tranquilizing drink. But after years of watching European sailors' drunken violence, Tahitian alcohol drinkers became violent themselves. Fortunately, subsequent learning experiences once again made their response to alcohol more peaceful (MacAndrew & Edgerton, 1969).

Expectations about a drug's effects can also influence how much of it people will consume (Goldman, Darkes, & Del Boca, in press). In one study, for example, participants thought they were taking part in a memory experiment, but in fact, their expectations about the positive effects of alcohol were being primed, without their awareness, in one or both of two ways (Roehrich & Goldman, 1995): (1) Participants viewed an episode of a television show (*Cheers*) that portrayed alcohol consumption in a positive light, and (2) they were subtly exposed to positive adjectives associated with alcohol consumption (e.g., *funny, happy, talkative*). Later the participants were given an opportunity to drink what they thought was alcohol (actually nonalcoholic beer) as part of a separate "taste-rating study." Figure 9.13 shows the outcome of this experiment. Although the participants saw no connection between the priming stages of the study and the subsequent taste-test, those who had watched *Cheers* drank more than those who watched a non–alcohol-related TV show (*Newhart*). Moreover, those who were exposed to the positive alcohol-consumption adjectives drank more than those who were exposed to neutral adjectives.

These examples and experiments show that the effects of psychoactive drugs are complex and variable. In Chapter 16 we discuss psychoactive drugs that are used in the treatment of psychological problems. Here, we consider several major categories of psychoactive drugs that are used primarily for the alterations they produce in consciousness, including depressants, stimulants, opiates, and psychedelics.

Depressants

Depressants are drugs that reduce activity of the central nervous system. Examples are alcohol and barbiturates, both of which increase activity of the neurotransmitter GABA. Since GABA inhibits neuron activity, enhancing GABA function reduces the excitability of many neural circuits. Because of their impact on GABA, using depressants creates feelings of relaxation, drowsiness, and sometimes, depression (Hanson & Venturelli, 1995).

Alcohol   In the United States, over 100 million people drink alcohol; it is equally popular worldwide (Alvarez, Delrio, & Prada, 1995). Alcohol affects several neurotransmitters, including dopamine, endorphins, glutamate, serotonin, and, most notably, GABA (Koob et al., 1998). For this reason, drugs that interact with GABA receptors can block some of alcohol's effects, as shown in Figure 9.14 (Suzdak et al., 1986). Alcohol also enhances the effect of endorphins (the body's natural painkillers, described in Chapter 4). This action may underlie the "high" that people feel when

FIGURE 9.14

GABA Receptors and Alcohol

Both of these rats received the same amount of alcohol, enough to incapacitate them with drunkenness. However, the rat on the right then received a drug that reverses alcohol's intoxicating effects by blocking the ability of alcohol to stimulate GABA receptors. Within two minutes, the rat was completely sober. Researchers found a serious problem with the drug, however: It did not reverse the effects of alcohol on hindbrain breathing centers. Thus, if people were drinking to get intoxicated, the drug would frustrate their efforts, and they might consume a lethal overdose of alcohol. Accordingly, the drug's manufacturer ultimately discontinued its development.

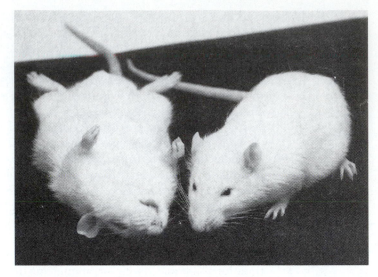

drinking alcohol and may explain why *naltrexone* and *naloxone*, endorphin antagonists, are better than placebos at reducing alcohol craving and relapse rates in recovering alcoholics (Salloum et al., 1998). Alcohol also interacts with dopamine systems, a component of the brain's reward systems. Prolonged alcohol use can have lasting effects on the brain's ability to regulate dopamine levels (Tiihonen et al., 1995), and dopamine agonists reduce alcohol craving and withdrawal effects (Lawford et al., 1995).

Alcohol affects specific brain regions. For example, it depresses activity in the locus coeruleus, an area that helps activate the cerebral cortex (Koob & Bloom, 1988). Reduced cortical activity tends to cause cognitive changes and a release of inhibitions. Some drinkers begin talking loudly, acting silly, or telling others what they think of them. Emotional reactions range from euphoria to despair. Normally shy people may become impulsive or violent. Alcohol's impairment of the hippocampus causes memory problems, making it more difficult to form memories for new information (Givens, 1995). And its suppression of the cerebellum causes poor motor coordination (Rogers et al., 1986). Alcohol's ability to depress hindbrain mechanisms that control breathing and heartbeat can make overdoses fatal.

LINKAGES

Drinking and Driving Don't Mix

Though practice may make it seem easy, driving a car is a complex information-processing task. As described in the chapter on cognition and language, such tasks require constant vigilance, quick decisions, and skillful execution of responses. Alcohol can impair all these processes, as well as the ability to judge the degree of impairment—thus making drinking and driving a deadly combination that kills tens of thousands of people each year in the United States alone.

LINKAGES

Is there a way to drink alcohol without getting drunk? (a link to Biological Aspects of Psychology)

As suggested earlier, some effects of alcohol depend both on biochemical factors and on learned expectations (Goldman, Darkes, & Del Boca, in press). But other effects—especially disruptions in motor coordination, speech, and thought—result from biochemical factors alone (Vuchinich & Sobell, 1978). These biological effects depend on the amount of alcohol the blood carries to the brain. Since the liver breaks down about one ounce of alcohol in an hour, alcohol has milder effects if consumed slowly. Effects increase with faster drinking, or if one drinks on an empty stomach, thereby speeding absorption into the blood. Even after allowing for differences in average male and female body weight, researchers have found metabolic differences that account for the ability of male bodies to tolerate somewhat higher amounts of alcohol. Thus, equal doses of alcohol may create greater effects in women compared to men (York & Welte, 1994).

Genetics also seems to play a role in determining the biochemical effects of alcohol. Evidence suggests that some people have a genetic predisposition toward alcohol dependence (Agarwal, 1997), although the specific genes involved have been difficult to identify (Holden, 1998). Others, such as the Japanese, may have inherited metabolic characteristics that increase the adverse effects of alcohol, thus possibly inhibiting the development of alcohol abuse (Iwahashi et al., 1995).

Barbiturates   Sometimes called "downers" or sleeping pills, *barbiturates* are extremely addictive. Small doses cause relaxation, mild euphoria, loss of muscle coordination, and lowered attention. Higher doses cause deep sleep, but continued use actually distorts sleep patterns (Kales & Kales, 1973). Thus, long-term use of barbiturates as sleeping pills is unwise. Overdoses can be fatal. Withdrawal symptoms are among the most severe for any drug and can include intense agitation, violent outbursts, convulsions, hallucinations, and even sudden death.

Stimulants

Amphetamines, cocaine, caffeine, and nicotine are all examples of **stimulants,** drugs that increase behavioral and mental activity.

Amphetamines   Also called "uppers" or "speed," the *amphetamines* (Benzedrine, for example) increase the release, and decrease the removal, of norepinephrine and dopamine at synapses, causing increased activity at these neurotransmitters' receptors. Dopaminergic activity is probably associated with these drugs' rewarding properties, since taking dopamine antagonists reduces amphetamine use (Holman, 1994).

Amphetamines stimulate both the brain and the sympathetic branch of the autonomic nervous system, raising heart rate and blood pressure, constricting blood vessels, shrinking mucous membranes (thus relieving stuffy noses), and reducing appetite. Amphetamines also increase alertness and response speed, especially in tasks requiring prolonged attention (Koelega, 1993), and may improve memory for verbal material (Soetens et al., 1995).

Amphetamine abuse is usually due to a desire to lose weight, stay awake, or experience a "high." Continued use leads to anxiety, insomnia, heart problems, confusion, paranoia, nonstop talking, and, in some cases, symptoms virtually identical to those of paranoid schizophrenia.

Cocaine   Like amphetamines, cocaine increases norepinephrine and dopamine activity, and thus produces many amphetamine-like effects. Cocaine's particularly powerful effect on dopamine activity and its rapid onset may underlie its remarkably addictive nature (Holman, 1994). Indeed, drugs with rapid onset and short duration are generally more addictive than others (Kato, Wakasa, & Yamagita, 1987), which may explain why crack—a purified, fast-acting, highly potent, smokable form of cocaine— is especially addictive.

Cocaine stimulates self-confidence, a sense of well-being, and optimism. But continued use brings nausea, overactivity, insomnia, paranoia, a sudden depressive "crash," hallucinations, sexual dysfunction, and seizures (Lacayo, 1995). Overdoses, especially of crack, can be deadly, and even small doses can cause a fatal heart attack or

Smoking Crack Cocaine

Cocaine can be smoked, injected, or inhaled nasally (Gossop et al., 1994). It is addictive, very dangerous, and, accordingly, one of the most intensely studied of all psychoactive drugs.

stroke (Marzuk et al., 1995). There is now little doubt that a pregnant woman who uses cocaine harms her fetus (Hurt et al., 1995; Konkol et al., 1994; Snodgrass, 1994). However, many of the severe, long-term behavioral problems seen in "cocaine babies" may have as much to do with poverty and neglect after birth as with the mother's cocaine use beforehand. Indeed, recent research suggests that early intervention can reduce the effects of both cocaine and the hostile environment that confronts most cocaine babies (Wren, 1998).

Ending a cocaine addiction is difficult. One possible treatment involves *buprenorphine*, an opiate antagonist that suppresses cocaine self-administration in addicted monkeys (Mello et al., 1989). The results of other methods have been mixed; success is most likely if addicts remain in treatment for at least a year (Carroll, Rounsaville, & Nich, 1994).

Caffeine   *Caffeine* may be the world's most popular drug (Gilbert, 1984). It is found in coffee, tea, chocolate, and many soft drinks. Caffeine reduces drowsiness by inhibiting receptors for the neuromodulator *adenosine* (Nehlig, Daval, & Debry, 1992), which we discussed earlier in relation to sleep. It improves problem solving, increases the capacity for physical work, and raises urine production (Warburton, 1995). At high doses it induces anxiety and tremors. Caffeine use can result in tolerance as well as physical dependence (Strain et al., 1994). Withdrawal symptoms—including headaches, fatigue, anxiety, shakiness, and craving—appear on the first day of abstinence and last about a week (Silverman et al., 1992). Caffeine may delay conception in women trying to become pregnant (Alderete, Eskenazi, & Sholtz, 1995), but overall, moderate daily caffeine use appears to have few if any negative effects (Kawachi, Colditz, & Stone, 1994; Thompson, 1995).

Nicotine   A powerful stimulant of the autonomic nervous system, *nicotine* is the psychoactive ingredient in tobacco. Nicotine is an acetylcholine agonist, but it also increases neuronal release of glutamate, the brain's primary excitatory neurotransmitter (McGehee et al., 1995). Nicotine has many psychoactive effects, including elevated mood and improved memory and attention (Pomerleau & Pomerleau, 1992). Its ability to create dependence is now well-established (White, 1998). This claim is supported by evidence of a nicotine withdrawal syndrome, which includes craving, anxiety, irritability, lowered heart rate, and weight gain (Hughes, Higgins, & Bickel, 1994). Although nicotine does not create the "rush" characteristic of many drugs of abuse, withdrawal from it reduces activity in the brain's reward pathways (Epping-Jordan et al., 1998). Other research suggests that nicotine creates more psychological than physical dependence (Robinson & Pritchard, 1995), but whatever blend of physical and psychological dependence may be involved, there is no doubt that smoking is a difficult habit for most smokers to break (Shiffman et al., 1997). It is also clearly recognized as a major risk factor for cancer, heart disease, and respiratory disorders (Doll et al., 1994), as discussed in Chapter 13, on health, stress, and coping.

MDMA   "Ecstasy," or *MDMA* (short for 3,4-Methylenedioxymethamphetamine), causes visual hallucinations, a feeling of greater closeness to others, dry mouth, hyperactivity, and jaw muscle spasms resulting in "lockjaw." And since MDMA increases the activity of dopamine-releasing neurons, it leads to some of the same effects as those produced by cocaine and amphetamines (Steele, McCann, & Ricaurte, 1994). At serotonin synapses, MDMA is a receptor agonist and also causes neurotransmitter release, thus possibly accounting for the drug's hallucinatory effects (Green, Cross, & Goodwin, 1995). On the day after using MDMA, people often experience muscle aches, fatigue, depression, and poor concentration (Peroutka, Newman, & Harris, 1988). With continued use, MDMA's positive effects decrease but its negative effects persist.

Although it does not appear to be physically addictive (Peroutka, 1989), MDMA is a dangerous, potentially deadly drug. For one thing, it permanently damages the brain, killing serotonin-containing neurons (Green, Cross, & Goodwin, 1995); the damage increases with higher dosages and continued use (Battaglia, Yeh, & De Souza, 1988). MDMA users may also develop panic disorder, a problem whose symptoms include intense anxiety and a sense of impending death (see Chapter 15).

Giving Up Smoking

The chemical effects of nicotine, combined with strongly learned associations between smoking and relaxation, stimulation, mealtimes, alcohol, and a wide variety of pleasant social interactions, make it extremely difficult for most smokers to give up their unhealthy habit. One of the more promising treatment programs available today combines nicotine replacement (through a patch like the one this woman is wearing) with antidepressant medication and behavioral training in how to cope with smoking-related situations—and with the stress of quitting.

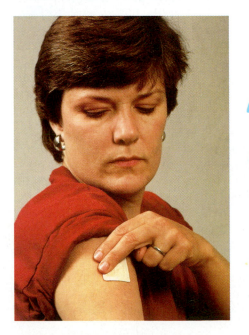

Opiates

The **opiates** (opium, morphine, heroin, codeine) are unique in their capacity for inducing sleep and relieving pain (Julien, 1995). *Opium,* derived from the poppy plant, relieves pain and causes feelings of well-being and dreamy relaxation. One of its most active ingredients, *morphine,* was first isolated in the early 1800s and is used worldwide for pain relief. Percodan and Demerol are two common morphine-like drugs. *Heroin* is derived from morphine but is three times more powerful, causing intensely pleasurable reactions when first taken. In the United States, heroin usage has tripled in the last few years (National Institute on Drug Abuse, 1997).

Opiates have complex effects on consciousness. Drowsy, cloudy feelings occur because opiates depress activity in areas of the cerebral cortex. But they also create excitation in other parts, causing some users to experience euphoria (Bozarth & Wise, 1984). Opiates exert many of their effects through their role as agonists for endorphins. When opiates activate endorphin receptors, they are "tricking" the brain into an exaggerated activation of its pain-killing and mood-altering systems (Julien, 1995).

Opiates are highly addictive, perhaps because they stimulate a particular type of glutamate receptor in the brain that can bring physical changes in a neuron's structure. It may be, then, that opiates alter neurons so that they come to require the drug to function properly. Supporting this idea are data showing that glutamate antagonists appear to prevent morphine dependence yet leave the drug's pain-killing effects intact (Trujillo & Akil, 1991). Beyond the hazards of addiction itself, heroin addicts risk death through overdoses, contaminated drugs, or AIDS contracted by sharing drug-injection needles. In 1995 more than 4,000 people in the United States died of heroin overdoses (National Institute on Drug Abuse, 1997).

Psychedelics

Psychedelics create a loss of contact with reality and alter other aspects of emotion, perception, and thought. They can cause distortions in body image (one may feel gigantic or tiny), loss of identity (confusion about who one actually is), dream-like fantasies, and hallucinations. Since these effects resemble many severe forms of mental disorder, psychedelics are also called *hallucinogens* or *psychotomimetics* (mimicking psychosis).

LSD   One of the most powerful psychedelics is *lysergic acid diethylamide,* or *LSD,* first synthesized from a rye fungus by Swiss chemist Albert Hofmann. In 1938, after Hofmann accidentally ingested a minuscule amount of the substance, he discovered the drug's strange effects in the world's first LSD "trip" (Julien, 1995). LSD's hallucinations can be quite bizarre. Time may seem distorted, sounds may cause visual sensations, and users may feel as if they have left their bodies.

LSD's hallucinatory effects are probably due to its ability to stimulate receptor sites in the forebrain that normally respond to a specific type of serotonin receptor, called 5-HT_{2A} (Carlson, 1998; Leonard, 1992). Indeed, serotonin antagonists greatly reduce LSD's hallucinatory effects (Leonard, 1992).

The precise effects of LSD on a particular individual are unpredictable. Unpleasant hallucinations and delusions can occur during a person's first—or two hundredth—LSD experience. Although LSD is not addictive, tolerance to its effects does develop. Some users suffer lasting side effects, including severe short-term memory loss, paranoia, violent outbursts, nightmares, and panic attacks (Gold, 1994). Distortions in visual sensations can remain years after the end of heavy use (Abraham & Wolf, 1988). Sometimes flashbacks occur, in which a person suddenly returns to an LSD-like state of consciousness weeks or even years after using the drug.

Marijuana   A mixture of the crushed leaves, flowers, and stems from the hemp plant (*Cannabis sativa*) makes up *marijuana.* The active ingredient is *tetrahydrocannabinol,* or *THC.* When inhaled, THC is absorbed in minutes by many organs, including the brain, and it continues to affect consciousness for a few hours. THC tends to collect in fatty deposits of the brain or reproductive organs, where it can be detected for weeks.

MAJOR CLASSES OF PSYCHOACTIVE DRUGS

Drug	Trade/Street Name	Main Effects	Potential for Physical/Psychological Dependence
Depressants			
Alcohol	"booze"	Relaxation, anxiety reduction, sleep	High/High
Barbiturates	Seconal, Tuinal ("downers"), Nembutal		High/High
Stimulants			
Amphetamines	Benzedrine, Dexedrine, Methadrine ("speed," "uppers," "ice") "coke," "crack"	Alertness, euphoria	Moderate/High Moderate to high/High
Cocaine			
Caffeine		Alertness	Moderate/Moderate
Nicotine	"smokes," "coffin nails"	Alertness	High (?)
MDMA	Ecstasy	Hallucinations	Low
Opiates			
Opium		Euphoria	High/High
Morphine	Percodan, Demerol	Euphoria, pain control	High/High
Heroin	"junk," "smack"	Euphoria, pain control	High/High
Psychedelics			
LSD	"acid"	Altered perceptions, hallucinations	Low/Low
Marijuana (cannabis)	"pot," "dope," "reefer"	Euphoria, relaxation	Low/Moderate

The specific receptors for THC include those sensitive to anandamide (from a Sanskrit word meaning "bliss"), a naturally occurring brain substance that research suggests may be a neurotransmitter (Fride & Mechoulam, 1993). Another substance in the brain that binds to THC receptors is called *2-AG*, which may affect the neural substrate for memory in the hippocampus (Stella, Schweitzer, & Piomelli, 1997).

Low doses of marijuana may initially create restlessness and hilarity, followed by a dreamy, carefree relaxation, an expanded sense of space and time, more vivid sensations, food cravings, and subtle changes in thinking (Kelly et al., 1990). For a summary of the effects of marijuana and other psychoactive drugs, see "In Review: Major Classes of Psychoactive Drugs."

Is Marijuana Dangerous?

A recent large-scale study of U.S. teenagers indicated a dramatic rise in their use of marijuana from 1991 to 1996. Usage almost tripled among eighth-graders (from 4 percent to 11 percent) and more than doubled among tenth-graders (from 9 percent to 20 percent). During this same period, the number of students who believed that there is a "great risk" associated with using marijuana declined in about the same proportions (Hall, 1997). In response to such trends, United States government officials have condemned marijuana use as "dangerous, illegal, and wrong." Concern about the drug has also been voiced in countries as diverse as Greece, Britain, France, Japan, Thailand, and Nigeria.

The Cannabis Controversy

Marijuana is illegal in North America and in many other places, too, but the question of whether it should remain so is a matter of hot debate between those who see the drug as a dangerous gateway to more addictive substances and those who view it as a benign source of pleasure that may also have medical benefits.

At the same time, the medical community has been engaged in serious discussion about whether marijuana should be used for medicinal purposes, and in the United States and around the world many individuals and organizations continue to argue for the decriminalization of marijuana use (Hall, 1997).

Proponents of the legalization of marijuana cite its medical benefits; some doctors claim to have successfully used marijuana in the treatment of asthma, glaucoma, epilepsy, chronic pain, and nausea from cancer chemotherapy (Voelker, 1997). But critics insist that medical legalization of marijuana is premature, because its medicinal value has not been established in controlled studies (Bennet, 1994) and because other drugs may be more effective and less dangerous (Schwartz, Voth, & Sheridan, 1997).

■ What am I being asked to believe or accept?

Those who view marijuana as dangerous usually assert four beliefs: (1) that marijuana is addictive; (2) that marijuana leads to the use of "hard drugs" such as heroin; (3) that marijuana intoxication endangers the user and other individuals; and (4) that long-term marijuana use leads to undesirable behavioral changes, disruption of brain functions, and other adverse effects on health.

■ What evidence is available to support the assertion?

Without a doubt, some people do use marijuana to such an extent that it disrupts their lives. According to the criteria normally used to define alcohol abuse, such people are dependent on marijuana—at least psychologically. The issue of *physical* dependence or addiction is less clear, inasmuch as withdrawal from chronic marijuana use does not produce any obvious physical symptoms. However, one recent study conducted with rats found evidence of a subtle withdrawal syndrome—and if the results of this study can be applied to humans, the implication is that withdrawal from marijuana *may* be accompanied by increased anxiety and depression (Rodriguez de Fonseca et al., 1997). Other research (e.g., Tanda, Pontieri, & Di Chiara, 1997) has found that marijuana interacts with the same dopamine and opiate receptors as does heroin, implying that marijuana could be a "gateway drug" to the use of more addictive drugs.

Regardless of whether marijuana is addicting or leads to "harder drugs," it can create a number of problems. It disrupts memory formation, making it difficult to carry out complex tasks (Lichtman, Dimen, & Martin, 1995; Pope & Yurgelun-Todd, 1996). And because marijuana affects muscle coordination, driving while under its influence is quite hazardous. Compounding the danger is the fact that motor impairment continues long after the obvious effects of the drug have worn off. In one study, for example, pilots had difficulty landing a simulated aircraft even a full day after smoking one marijuana cigarette (Yesavage et al., 1985). As for marijuana's effects on intellectual and cognitive performance, one study (Block & Ghoneim, 1993) found that adults who frequently used marijuana scored lower on a twelfth-grade academic achievement test than nonusers with the same IQs.

■ Are there alternative ways of interpreting the evidence?

Those who see marijuana as a benign or even beneficial substance criticize studies like those just mentioned as providing an inaccurate or incomplete picture of marijuana's effects. They argue, for example, that the same dopamine receptors activated by marijuana and heroin are also activated by sex and chocolate—and that few people would call for the criminalization of intimacy and candy bars (Grinspoon et al., 1997). Moreover, the correlation between early marijuana use and later use of "hard drugs" could be due more to the people with whom users become involved than to any property of the drug per se (Fergusson & Horwood, 1997).

The question of marijuana's long-term effects on memory and reasoning is also difficult to resolve, partly because studies of academic achievement scores and marijuana use (e.g., Block & Ghoneim, 1993) tend to be correlational in nature. As noted in

Chapter 2, cause and effect cannot easily be determined in such studies. Does marijuana use lead to poor academic performance, or does poor academic performance lead to increased marijuana use? Both possibilities are credible. Finally, at present, there is no hard evidence of long-term brain damage from marijuana use (Pope, Gruber, & Yurgelun-Todd, 1995).

■ **What additional evidence would help to evaluate the alternatives?**

More definitive evidence on marijuana's short- and long-term effects is obviously needed, but evaluating the meaning of that evidence will be difficult. The issues involved in the marijuana debate involve questions of degree and relative risk. For example, is the risk of marijuana dependence greater than that of alcohol dependence? There are clearly differences among people in the extent to which marijuana use poses a risk for them. Thus far, however, we have not determined what personal characteristics account for such differences. Nor do we know why some people use marijuana only occasionally, whereas others use it so often and in such quantities that it seriously disrupts their ability to function in a normal and adaptive manner. The physical and psychological factors underlying these differences still need to be identified.

■ **What conclusions are most reasonable?**

Those who would decriminalize marijuana use argue that when marijuana was declared illegal in the United States in the 1930s, there was no evidence that it was any more harmful than alcohol or tobacco. Scientific evidence supports that claim, but more by illuminating the dangers of alcohol and tobacco than by exonerating marijuana. Indeed, although marijuana is less dangerous than, say, cocaine or heroin, it is by no means totally benign. Marijuana easily reaches a developing fetus and should not be used by pregnant women (Fried, Watkinson, & Gray, 1992); it suppresses some immune functions in humans (Cabral & Dove Pettit, 1998); and marijuana smoke is as irritating to lungs as tobacco smoke (Roth et al., 1998).

Further, because possession of marijuana is still a crime almost everywhere in the United States as well as in many other countries throughout the world, it would be foolish to flaunt existing laws without regard for the legal consequences of such actions. At the same time, however, scientists must continue to objectively study marijuana's dangers (or lack thereof) as well as its potential value in the treatment of certain diseases. Ultimately, the most reasonable conclusions about marijuana use must await the outcome of further scientific research on its costs and benefits (Joy, Watson, & Benson, 1999).

LINKAGES

As noted in Chapter 1, all of psychology's many subfields are related to one another. Our discussion of meditation, health, and stress illustrates just one way in which the topic of this chapter, consciousness, is linked to the subfield of health psychology (Chapter 13). The Linkages diagram shows ties to two other subfields as well, and there are many more ties throughout the book. Looking for linkages among subfields will help you see how they all fit together and better appreciate the big picture that is psychology.

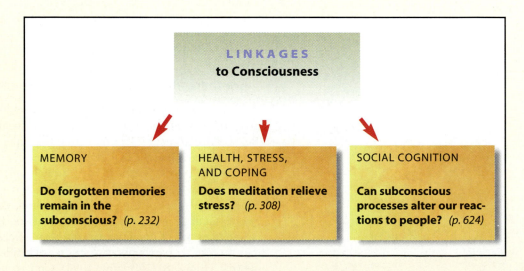

LINKAGES
to Consciousness

MEMORY

Do forgotten memories remain in the subconscious? *(p. 232)*

HEALTH, STRESS, AND COPING

Does meditation relieve stress? *(p. 308)*

SOCIAL COGNITION

Can subconscious processes alter our reactions to people? *(p. 624)*

SUMMARY

Consciousness can be defined as awareness of the outside world and of one's own thoughts, feelings, perceptions, and other mental processes.

ANALYZING CONSCIOUSNESS

Current research on consciousness focuses on three main questions. First, what is the relationship between the mind and the brain? Second, does consciousness occur as a single "point" in the stream of mental processing or as several parallel mental operations that operate independently? Third, what mental processes are outside awareness, and how do they affect conscious processes?

Some Functions of Consciousness

Consciousness produces the best current interpretation of sensory information in light of past experience, and makes this interpretation available to the parts of the brain that plan voluntary actions and speech.

Levels of Consciousness

Variations in how much awareness you have for a mental function are described by different levels of consciousness. The *preconscious level* includes mental activities that are outside of awareness but can easily be brought to the *conscious level.* The *unconscious level* involves thoughts, memories, and processes that are more difficult to bring to awareness. Mental processes that cannot be brought into awareness occur at the *nonconscious level.*

Mental Processing Without Awareness

Awareness is not always required for mental operations. The priming phenomenon shows that people's responses to some stimuli can be speeded, improved, or modified, even when the people are not consciously aware of the priming stimuli.

The Neuropsychology of Consciousness

Brain injuries often reveal ways in which mental processing can occur without conscious awareness. For instance, patients with anterograde amnesia continue to acquire new skills without later awareness of learning them.

States of Consciousness

A person's *state of consciousness* is constantly changing. When the changes are particularly noticeable, they are called *altered states of consciousness.* Examples include sleep, hypnosis, meditation, and some drug-induced states. Different cultures vary considerably in the value placed on different states of consciousness.

SLEEPING AND DREAMING

Sleep is an active and complex state.

Stages of Sleep

Different stages of sleep are defined on the basis of changes in brain activity (as seen on an electroencephalograph, or EEG) and physiological arousal. Sleep normally begins with stage 1 sleep and progresses gradually to stage 4 sleep. Sleep stages 1 through 4 constitute *quiet sleep,* or non-REM sleep. Most dreaming occurs when people enter *rapid eye movement (REM)* sleep, or active sleep. The sleeping person cycles through these stages several times each night, gradually spending more time in stage 2 and REM sleep later in the night.

Sleep Disorders

Sleep disorders can disrupt the natural rhythm of sleep. Among the most common is *insomnia,* in which one feels tired because of trouble falling or staying asleep. *Narcolepsy* produces sudden daytime sleeping episodes. In *sleep apnea,* people briefly but repeatedly stop breathing during sleep. *Sudden infant death syndrome (SIDS)* may be due to brain abnormalities or accidental suffocation. *Nightmares* and *night terrors* are different kinds of frightening dreams. *Sleepwalking* happens most frequently during childhood. *REM behavior disorder* is potentially dangerous because it allows people to act out REM dreams.

Why Do People Sleep?

The cycle of waking and sleeping is a natural *circadian rhythm,* controlled by the suprachiasmatic nuclei in the brain. *Jet lag* can be one result of disrupting the normal sleep-wake cycle. The purpose of sleep is much debated. Non-REM sleep may aid bodily rest and repair. REM sleep may help maintain activity in brain areas that provide daytime alertness, or it may allow the brain to "check circuits," eliminate useless information, and solidify learning from the previous day.

Dreams and Dreaming

Dreams are story-like sequences of images, sensations, and perceptions that occur during sleep. Evidence from research on *lucid dreaming* suggests that people may be able to control their own dreams. Some claim that dreams are the meaningless byproducts of brain activity, but dreams may still have psychological significance.

HYPNOSIS

Hypnosis is a well-known but still poorly understood phenomenon.

Experiencing Hypnosis

Tests of hypnotic susceptibility suggest that some people cannot be hypnotized. Hypnotized people tend to focus attention on the hypnotist and passively follow instructions. They become very good at fantasizing and role-taking. They may exhibit apparent age regression, experience posthypnotic amnesia, and obey posthypnotic suggestions.

Explaining Hypnosis

Role theory suggests that hypnosis creates a special social role that gives people permission to act in unusual ways. *State theory* sees hypnosis as a special state of consciousness. *Dissociation theory* combines aspects of role and state theories, suggesting that hypnotic participants enter into a social contract with the hypnotist to allow normally integrated mental processes to become dissociated and to share control over these processes.

Applications of Hypnosis

Hypnosis is useful in the control of pain and reduction of nausea associated with cancer chemotherapy. Its use as a memory aid is open to serious question.

PSYCHOACTIVE DRUGS

Psychoactive drugs affect the brain, changing consciousness and other psychological processes. *Psychopharmacology* is the field that studies drug effects and their mechanisms.

Psychopharmacology

Psychoactive drugs exert their effects primarily by influencing specific neurotransmitter systems and, hence, certain brain activities. To reach brain tissue, drugs must cross the *blood-brain barrier*. Drugs that mimic the receptor effects of a neurotransmitter are called *agonists*, and drugs that block the receptor effects of a neurotransmitter are called *antagonists*. Some drugs alter the release or inactivation of specific neurotransmitters, thus affecting the amount of neurotransmitter available for receptor effects.

The Varying Effects of Drugs

Adverse effects such as *substance abuse* often accompany the use of psychoactive drugs. *Psychological dependence, physical depen-* dence (addiction), *tolerance,* and a *withdrawal syndrome* may result. Drugs that produce dependence share the property of directly stimulating certain areas of the brain known as pleasure centers. The consequences of using a psychoactive drug depend both on how the drug affects neurotransmitters and on the user's expectations.

Depressants

Alcohol and barbiturates are examples of *depressants.* They reduce activity in the central nervous system, often by enhancing the action of inhibitory neurotransmitters. They have considerable potential for producing both psychological and physical dependence.

Stimulants

Stimulants such as amphetamines and cocaine increase behavioral and mental activity mainly by increasing the action of dopamine and norepinephrine. These drugs can produce both psychological and physical dependence. Caffeine, one of the world's most popular stimulants, may also create dependency. Nicotine is a potent stimulant. MDMA is one of several psychoactive drugs that can permanently damage brain tissue.

Opiates

Opiates such as opium, morphine, and heroin are highly addictive drugs that induce sleep and relieve pain.

Psychedelics

LSD and marijuana are examples of *psychedelics,* or hallucinogens. Psychedelics alter consciousness by producing a temporary loss of contact with reality and changes in emotion, perception, and thought.

KEY TERMS

addiction (310)
agonists (309)
altered state of
  consciousness (297)
antagonists (309)
blood-brain barrier (309)
circadian rhythm (302)
conscious level (292)
consciousness (290)
depressants (311)
dissociation theory (307)
dreams (305)

hypnosis (306)
insomnia (300)
jet lag (302)
lucid dreaming (305)
narcolepsy (300)
nightmares (302)
night terrors (302)
nonconscious level (292)
opiates (315)
physical dependence (310)
preconscious level (292)
psychedelics (315)

psychoactive drugs (309)
psychological dependence
  (310)
psychopharmacology (309)
quiet sleep (298)
rapid eye movement
  (REM) sleep (299)
REM behavior disorder
  (302)
role theory (307)
sleep apnea (301)
sleepwalking (302)

state of consciousness (297)
state theory (307)
stimulants (313)
substance abuse (310)
sudden infant death
  syndrome (SIDS) (301)
tolerance (310)
unconscious level (292)
withdrawal syndrome (310)

10

Mental Abilities

Consider the following sketches of four college seniors and their varying abilities and interests. Do any of these descriptions remind you of anyone you know? Do any of them sound like you?

When Jack got into trouble at his grade school, he was always able to talk his way out of it. His big-city "street smarts" were not reflected in his grades, however. He had great difficulty reading and was a terrible speller. Tests conducted when Jack was thirteen revealed that he had a learning disability, and he was placed in a special reading program. In high school, Jack worked very hard to compensate for his disability, and he graduated with a grade-point average (GPA) of 3.78; but when he took the Scholastic Aptitude Test (SAT) as part of his application for college, his score was only 860 out of a possible 1600. He attended a local college where, because of his learning disability, he was granted extra time to complete exams. He held a half-time job throughout all four years, and his GPA was 2.95. When he completed his undergraduate degree, Jack applied to master's programs in special education.

Deneace grew up in the suburbs and earned straight As in a public grade school. She attended a private high school, where she placed in the top fifth of her class and played the violin as a hobby. Her SAT score was 1340, but because her school did not give letter grades, she had no grade-point average to include in college applications. Instead, she submitted her teachers' written evaluations and a portfolio containing samples of her papers, class projects, and other work. Deneace was accepted at several prestigious small colleges, but not at major research universities. She is enrolled in a pre-med program and has just completed her senior research project. With a GPA of 3.60, Deneace is hoping to be accepted by a medical school.

Ruthie grew up in Chicago, has a wide range of interests, loves physical activities, has many friends, and can talk to anybody about almost anything. Her grades, however, have been only fair, averaging 2.60 in high school. She played four sports, though, and was captain of the state champion volleyball team as well as vice-president of her senior class. She scored rather poorly on a standardized college entrance examination, but received an athletic scholarship at a large university. She majored in sociology, minored in sports therapy, and would now like to become a rehabilitation counselor. Focusing on just one sport has helped her achieve a 3.25 grade-point average. She has applied to graduate schools but has also looked into a job as a city recreation director, for which she had to complete a state employment exam and a full afternoon of interviews.

George comes from a farming region and showed an early interest in computers. As a child, he was quiet and had few friends. In high school, George earned straight A's in math, art, and shop classes, but his overall GPA was only 2.55, placing him in the bottom half of his class. He didn't get along with other students and spent his free time "hacking" on his computer. Everyone was surprised when he scored 1320 on the SAT. George was accepted at a large public university, where he majored in math and computer science. His grades suffered initially as he began to spend time with people who shared his interests, but his GPA is now 3.33. He expresses his artistic talent by writing computer animation software. He has applied to graduate programs in fields relating to artificial intelligence and human factors engineering, and he has also taken a computer programming test for a software company.

Before reading further, take a minute to rank these four people on **mental ability**—the capacity to reason, remember, understand, solve problems, and make decisions. Who came out on top? Now ask a friend to do the same and see if your rankings match. They may not, because each of the students excels in different ways.

Deneace might score highest on general intelligence tests, which emphasize remembering, reasoning, and verbal and mathematical abilities. But would standard tests reflect Ruthie's social skills, Jack's "street smarts," or George's artistic ability? And should they? If you were hiring an employee or evaluating a student, what characteristics would you want a test to measure? Can individuals' test scores be compared without consideration of their social and academic background? The answers to these questions are important from both a theoretical and a practical perspective: Research on mental abilities leads to a better understanding of human cognition and the factors that may help or hinder people's ability to learn from and adapt to their environment; and, as our examples illustrate, measures of mental abilities often determine the kinds of educational and employment opportunities people have or don't have.

There are several kinds of mental abilities, but this chapter focuses primarily on intelligence. Like many other concepts in psychology, intelligence cannot be directly observed. Therefore, we must infer it from what *can* be observed or measured—namely, from scores on tests that are designed to assess this abstract entity. We begin with a brief history of the development of intelligence tests. Then we discuss what attributes make one test good and another one not so good, and we use these criteria to evaluate tests that purport to measure intelligence. Next, we consider some important issues related to intelligence testing, including questions about whether some tests could be biased against certain groups and what test scores actually tell us about a person's innate ability. These questions lead to an examination of different approaches to understanding what intelligence really is. Finally, we look at mental abilities other than intelligence.

TESTING FOR INTELLIGENCE

Usually, it helps to begin the study of a concept by defining it, but defining intelligence has proven to be difficult. Robert Sternberg's (1985) definition of intelligence—which is accepted by many psychologists—is the one we will use as our working definition in this chapter. According to Sternberg, intelligence can be described in terms of three characteristics: the possession of knowledge, the ability to efficiently use knowledge to reason about the world, and the ability to use that reasoning adaptively in different environments. How effectively is intelligence measured by the tests that psychologists use? To begin to answer this question, let's consider the history of intelligence testing.

A Brief History of Intelligence Tests

The story begins in France in 1904, when the French government appointed psychologist Alfred Binet to a commission charged with identifying, studying, and providing special educational programs for children who were not doing well in school. As part of his work on the commission, Binet developed a set, or *battery,* of intellectual test items that provided the model for today's intelligence tests. Binet assumed that intelligence is involved in many reasoning, thinking, and problem-solving activities. Therefore, he looked for tasks that would highlight differences in children's ability to reason, judge, and solve problems (Binet & Simon, 1905). His test included tasks such as unwrapping a piece of candy, repeating numbers or sentences from memory, and identifying familiar objects (Frank, 1976). Binet also assumed that children's abilities increase with age. To select the items for his test, Binet tried them out on children of various ages and then categorized the items according to the age at which the typical child could respond correctly. For example, a "six-year-old item" was one that a substantial majority of six-year-olds could answer. Binet's test was thus a set of *age-graded* items. It measured a child's "mental level"—now called *mental age*—by determining the age level of the most advanced items a child could consistently answer correctly. Children whose mental age equaled their actual or *chronological age* were considered to be of "regular" intelligence (Reisman, 1976).

About a decade after Binet published his test, Lewis Terman at Stanford University developed an English version known as the **Stanford-Binet** (Terman, 1916). Table 10.1 gives examples of the kinds of items included on the test. Terman added items to measure the intelligence of adults and revised the method of scoring. Mental age was divided by chronological age, and the result or "quotient" was multiplied by 100 and called the *intelligence quotient,* or *IQ.* Thus, a child whose mental age and chronological age were equal would have an IQ of 100, which is considered "average" intelligence.

A ten-year-old who scored at the mental age of twelve would have an IQ of 12/10 ×
100 = 120. From this method of scoring came the term **IQ test,** a name that is widely
used for any test designed to measure intelligence on an objective, standardized scale.

The scoring method used with the Stanford-Binet allowed testers to rank people on
IQ. This goal was important to Terman and others who popularized the test in the
United States because, unlike Binet—who suggested that intelligence improves with
practice—they saw intelligence as a fixed and inherited entity. They believed that different individuals possess different amounts of this thing called intelligence and that
IQ tests could pinpoint who did and who did not have a suitable amount of intelligence. In some instances these beliefs led to prejudicial attitudes and acts of discrimination as enthusiasm for testing outpaced understanding of what was being tested.

Even before Terman developed the Stanford-Binet, Henry Goddard had translated
Binet's test for use in studying mentally retarded children. When, in 1910, the U.S. government asked Goddard to help identify mentally defective immigrants, he took his
English-language version of Binet's test and translated it orally into the immigrants'
native languages. Today it is painfully obvious that this test was not a fair measure of
intelligence, but Goddard (1917) used scores on the test to conclude that 83 percent of
Jews, 80 percent of Hungarians, 87 percent of Russians, and 79 percent of Italians

TABLE 10.1

The Stanford-Binet

Here are samples of the type of items
included on the original Stanford-Binet
test. As in Binet's earlier test, an age level
was assigned to each item.

Age	Task
2	Place geometric shapes into corresponding openings; identify body parts; stack blocks; identify common objects.
4	Name objects from memory; complete analogies (e.g., fire is hot; ice is _____); identify objects of similar shape; answer simple questions (e.g., "Why do we have schools?").
6	Define simple words; explain differences (e.g., between a fish and a horse); identify missing parts of a picture; count out objects.
8	Answer questions about a simple story; identify absurdities (e.g., in statements like "John had to walk on crutches because he hurt his arm"); explain similarities and differences among objects; tell how to handle certain situations (e.g., finding a stray puppy).
10	Define more difficult words; give explanations (e.g., about why people should be quiet in a library); list as many words as possible; repeat 6-digit numbers.
12	Identify more difficult verbal and pictured absurdities; repeat 5-digit numbers in reverse order; define abstract words (e.g., *sorrow*); fill in a missing word in a sentence.
14	Solve reasoning problems; identify relationships among points of the compass; find similarities in apparently opposite concepts (e.g., *high* and *low*); predict the number of holes that will appear when folded paper is cut and then opened.
Adult	Supply several missing words for incomplete sentences; repeat 6-digit numbers in reverse order; create a sentence using several unrelated words (e.g., *forest, businesslike,* and *dismayed*); describe similarities between concepts (e.g., *teaching* and *business*).

Source: Nietzel & Bernstein, 1987.

Coming to America

Early in the 20th century, immigrants to the United States, such as these new arrivals being screened at Ellis Island in New York Harbor, were tested for both physical and mental frailties. Especially for those who could not read, speak, or understand English, the intelligence tests they took tended to greatly underestimate their intellectual capacity.

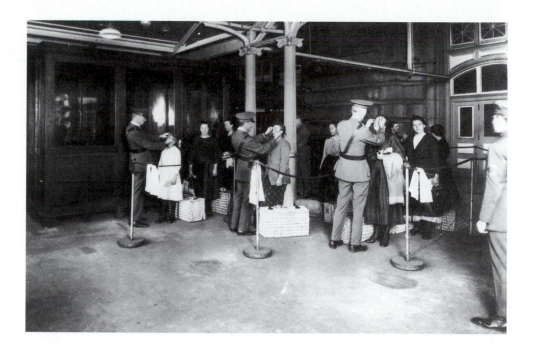

immigrating to America were "feeble-minded"! Ultimately, Goddard came to doubt the accuracy of his own conclusions and retracted them in 1928 (Schultz & Schultz, 2000).

The government also used tests to identify army recruits of low mental ability and to assign appropriate jobs to new soldiers. When the United States entered World War I, a team of psychologists developed the first group-administered tests for these purposes. The Army Alpha test assessed abilities such as arithmetic, analogies, and general knowledge for recruits who could read English. The Army Beta test was for recruits who could not read or did not speak English; it measured ability using non–verbal tasks, such as visualizing three-dimensional objects and solving mazes. Both versions were given in crowded rooms, where instructions were not always audible or, for non-English speakers, understandable. Forty-seven percent of the young men tested scored at a mental age of thirteen years or lower (Yerkes, 1921). On the basis of these results C. C. Brigham (1923) incorrectly concluded that (1) from 1890 to 1915 the mental age of immigrants to America had declined and (2) the main source of this decline was the increase in immigration from Southern and Eastern Europe. Like Goddard, however, Brigham (1930) later retracted his statements and noted that the Army tests were not very good measures of intelligence (Gould, 1983).

New tests developed by David Wechsler (1939, 1949) were designed to correct some of the weaknesses of their predecessors. Like the Army's Alpha and Beta, Wechsler's tests were made up of several subtests, but they significantly improved on those earlier tests in three key ways. First, both the verbal and nonverbal subtests were completed by all test takers. Second, answers depended less on familiarity with a particular culture. And third, each subtest in the Wechsler tests was scored separately, producing a profile that described an individual's performance in terms of several mental abilities.

Intelligence Tests Today

Modern editions of the Wechsler scales and the Stanford-Binet are the most widely used individually administered intelligence tests, but IQ scores are no longer calculated by dividing mental age by chronological age. If you take one of these tests today, the points you earn for each correct answer are summed. Then the summed score is compared with the scores earned by other people. The average score obtained by people at each age level is *assigned* the IQ value of 100. Other scores are assigned IQ values that

FIGURE 10.1

The Normal Distribution of IQ Scores in a Population

This bell-shaped curve represents the normal distribution of IQ scores in the population. Half of those tested score below 100 (the average performance of any given age group) and half above 100; about two-thirds of the IQ scores of an age group fall between 84 and 116; about one-sixth fall below 84 and one-sixth fall above 116.

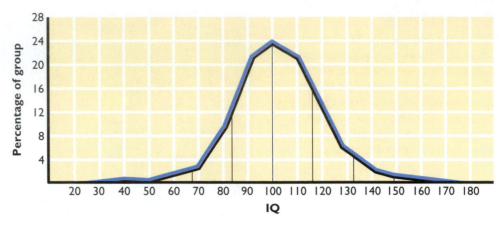

Note: Curve represents distribution of IQ scores in the standardized group for the 1937 version of the Stanford-Binet.

Taking the Wechsler Test

Comparison of verbal and performance scores on the Wechsler test can be useful. For example, a high performance score and a low verbal score could mean that a child has a language deficiency that prevents the verbal scale from accurately measuring the child's mental abilities.

reflect how far each score deviates from that average (see Figure 10.1). If you do better on the test than the average person in your age group, you will receive an IQ score above 100; how far above depends on how much better than average you do. Similarly, a person scoring below the age-group average will have an IQ below 100. This procedure may sound arbitrary, but it is based on a well-documented assumption about many characteristics: Most people's scores fall in the middle of the range of possible scores, creating a bell-shaped curve known as the *normal distribution* shown in Figure 10.1. (The statistics appendix provides a fuller explanation of the normal distribution and how IQ tests are scored.) As a result of this scoring method, your **intelligence quotient,** or **IQ score,** reflects your *relative* standing within a population of your age.

The Wechsler Adult Intelligence Scale–Revised includes eleven subtests. Six require verbal skills and make up the **verbal scale** of the test. These include such items as remembering a series of digits, solving arithmetic problems, defining vocabulary words, and understanding and answering questions (e.g., "What did Shakespeare do?"). The remaining five subtests have little or no verbal content and make up the **performance scale.** They include tasks that require understanding the relations of objects in space and manipulation of materials—tasks such as assembling blocks, solving mazes, and completing pictures. Figure 10.2 gives examples of items from one section of the performance scale of the latest version of the Wechsler test for children. With Wechsler tests, one can compute a verbal IQ, performance IQ, and overall IQ score.

Like the Wechsler scales, the latest edition of the Stanford-Binet also uses subtests. It provides scores on *verbal reasoning* (e.g., "What is similar about an orange, apple, and grape?"), *quantitative reasoning* (e.g., math problems), *abstract/visual reasoning* (e.g., explaining why one should wear a coat in winter), and *working memory* (e.g., repeating a string of numbers in reverse order), along with a composite IQ score (Thorndike, Hagan, & Sattler, 1986).

Both the Wechsler scales and the Stanford-Binet require some degree of verbal fluency on the part of the test taker. But what about people who have difficulty communicating orally with the test giver—those who have speech impediments, for example, or whose native language differs from that of the test giver? One alternative is to administer the test in the language of the test taker. Another is to give a nonverbal test such as the *Raven Progressive Matrices,* in which the test taker has to determine which of eight possible options correctly represents the next in a series of systematically changing geometric designs. There is some controversy regarding the ability of this test to measure overall intelligence, or even the specific aspect of intelligence known as *spatial ability.* Nevertheless, it has proved useful in cases where limited verbal abilities might otherwise influence the accuracy of more traditional intelligence tests.

FIGURE 10.2

Sample Items from the Performance Section of the Wechsler Intelligence Scale for Children (WISC-III)

Items like these tap aspects of intelligence but require little or no verbal ability.

PICTURE COMPLETION
What part is missing from this picture?

PICTURE ARRANGEMENT
These pictures tell a story, but they are in the wrong order. Put them in the right order so that they tell a story.

BLOCK DESIGN

Put the blocks together to make this picture.

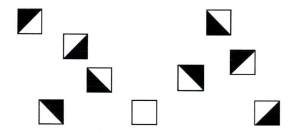

Source: Simulated items similar to those in the Wechsler Intelligence Scales for Adults and Children. Copyright ©: 1949, 1955, 1974, 1981, 1991 by the Psychological Corporation. Reproduced by permission. All rights reserved.

Aptitude and Achievement Tests

Closely related to intelligence tests are aptitude and achievement tests. **Aptitude tests** are designed to measure a person's capability to learn certain things or perform certain tasks. Although such tests may contain questions about what you already know, their ultimate goal is to assess your *potential* to learn (Aiken, 1994). The *SAT* (originally called the Scholastic Aptitude Test) and the *American College Testing Assessment (ACT)* are the aptitude tests most commonly used by many colleges and universities in the United States to help guide decisions about which applicants to admit. Corporations also use aptitude tests as part of the process of selecting new employees; these usually involve brief assessments of mental abilities, such as the *Otis-Lennon Mental Abilities Test* and the *Wonderlic Personnel Test* (Aiken, 1994).

Schools and employers also commonly administer **achievement tests,** which measure what a person has accomplished or learned in a particular area. For example, schoolchildren are tested on what they have learned about language, mathematics, and reading (Rogers, 1995). Their performance on these tests is then compared with that of other students in the same grade to evaluate their educational progress. The achievement tests used by companies in search of new employees typically focus on more specific abilities such as computer or clerical skills.

MEASURING THE QUALITY OF TESTS

Whether a test concerns general intelligence, aptitude, or achievement, it should fairly and accurately measure a person's performance. In fact, schools and companies in the United States are required by law to use fair and accurate tests in situations involving placement of students in particular classes or selection of new employees. Accordingly, many psychologists have devoted themselves to research designed to improve the quality of many kinds of mental abilities tests (American Psychological Association, 1995c; Educational Testing Service, 1995).

Any **test** is a systematic procedure for observing behavior in a standard situation and describing it with the help of a numerical scale or a system of categories (Cronbach, 1990). A test has three major advantages over interviews and other means of evaluating people. First, the administration, scoring, and interpretation of the test are *standardized;* that is, the conditions are as similar as possible for everyone who takes the test. Standardization helps ensure that no matter who gives and scores the test, the results will be the same; incidental factors—such as variations in the way a question is phrased—are less likely to affect test scores. Insofar as the biases of those giving the test do not influence the results, a test is said to be *objective.*

Second, tests summarize the test taker's performance in *quantifiable* terms known as scores. The use of scores allows the calculation of **norms,** which are descriptions of the frequency of particular scores. Norms tell us, for example, what percentage of high school students obtained each possible score on a college entrance exam and whether a particular person's score on that exam is above or below the average. Third, tests are *economical* and *efficient.* Once a test has been developed, it can often be given to many people in less time and for less money than would be expended through other ways of obtaining information.

The two most important characteristics for determining the value of a test are reliability and validity.

LINKAGES

How do you know if a personality test, or any other kind of test, is any good? (a link to Personality)

Reliability

If you stepped on a scale, checked your weight, stepped off, stepped back on, and found that your weight had increased by twenty pounds, you would know it's time to buy a new scale. A good scale, like a good test, must have **reliability;** in other words, the results must be repeatable or stable. A test must measure the same thing in the same way every time it is used. If a person receives a very high score on a reasoning test the first time it is given but gets a very low score when the test is repeated, the test is probably unreliable. The higher the reliability of a test, the less likely it is that its scores will be affected by temperature, hunger, or other irrelevant changes in the environment or the test taker.

To estimate reliability, researchers often obtain two sets of scores on the same test from the same people and compute the *correlation coefficient* between the scores (see Chapter 2 and the statistics appendix). When the correlation is high and positive (usually above +.80 or so), the test is considered reliable. The two sets of scores can be obtained in several ways. The most obvious method is to give the same test to the same people on two occasions. This method is called *test-retest reliability.* Of course, the test-retest method assumes that what is being measured does not change between the two testings. If you practiced typing between tests of typing skill, your second score would be higher than the first, but not because the test is unreliable.

The test-retest method of determining reliability has another limitation: Exposure to the first test can cause some people's second score to improve, thus making the test look unreliable. Other methods of calculating reliability prevent this problem. One method uses an *alternate form* of the test at the second testing, although great care must be taken to ensure that the second test is truly equivalent to the first. And in the *split-half* method, a correlation coefficient is calculated between a person's scores on two comparable halves of the test (Groth-Marnat, 1997). In practice, most researchers employ all these methods to check the reliability of their tests.

Validity

A test may be reliable and still not be valid. The **validity** of a test is the degree to which it measures what it is supposed to measure (Anastasi, 1997). No test has "high" or "low" validity in an absolute sense; *validity depends on how a test is being used.* Thus, measuring how long someone can keep a bare hand immersed in ice water might be a valid test of pain tolerance, but not of intelligence. In other words, the same test can be valid for one purpose but invalid for another.

Most measures of validity are correlation coefficients between test scores and something else. What that "something else" is depends on what the test is supposed to measure. For example, you might want to correlate people's scores on a creativity test with judgments about the quality of their artistic creations; if the correlation is high, the test has high validity as a measure of creativity. Similarly, a correlation between SAT scores and first-year college grades provides a measure of the SAT's validity for predicting success in college.

A test's validity can be studied in three main ways. The first approach is to analyze *content validity,* the degree to which the test's content is related to what the test is supposed to measure. If an instructor spends only five minutes out of twenty lectures discussing the mating behavior of the tree frog and then devotes half of the midterm exam to this topic, that exam would be low on content validity for measuring students' learning in the course. Similarly, a test that measures only math skills would not have acceptable content validity as an intelligence test. A content-valid test includes items relating to the entire area of interest, not just a narrow slice (Lanyon & Goodstein, 1997).

Another way of assessing validity is to look at *construct validity,* the extent to which scores on a test are in accordance with one's theory about what is being tested. For example, if your theory of intelligence says that people get smarter as they get older, then older people should have higher scores on the intelligence test you are evaluating. If they don't—if a positive correlation is not found between test scores and age—then the test has low construct validity with regard to this particular theory of intelligence.

A third approach is to measure *criterion validity,* the extent to which test scores correlate with another direct and independent measure of what the test is supposed to assess. This independent measure is called the *criterion.* Thus a test of eye-hand coordination would have high criterion validity for hiring diamond cutters if its scores are highly correlated with skill at diamond cutting. Why give a test if there is an independent criterion we can measure? The reasons often relate to convenience and cost. It would be silly to hire all job applicants, then fire those who are unskilled, if a ten-minute test can identify the best candidates. When the goal is to predict future behavior, the criterion is some measure of later performance; in such cases, criterion validity is called *predictive validity.*

Again consider the SAT, the test most U.S. universities use to help predict which college applicants will succeed if admitted. As suggested earlier, one can measure the SAT's predictive validity by determining the correlation between SAT scores and a criterion—namely, the grade-point average (GPA) of first-year college students. It turns out that the correlation between total SAT scores and first-year GPA is about + .42 (Donlon, 1984). This figure is reasonably high, but not as high as it might be. The test's predictive validity is limited partly by the fact that many colleges admit only students with high SAT scores. Because these students are then assigned grades from A to F in a more or less normal distribution, some of them will have low GPAs even though they have high SATs. Thus, although SAT scores are generally helpful during the admissions process, it is difficult to predict a particular student's grades on the basis of SAT scores alone.

Criteria for assessing the reliability and validity of tests are incorporated into the testing standards published by the American Psychological Association (1985). These standards are designed to maintain quality in educational and psychological testing by providing guidelines for the administration, interpretation, and application of tests in such areas as therapy, education, employment, certification or licensure, and program evaluation.

EVALUATING IQ TESTS

The meaning of IQ scores must be interpreted with caution, because no particular IQ test can accurately measure all aspects of what various people think of as intelligence. So what does an IQ score say about you? Can it predict your performance in school or on the job? Is it a fair summary of your mental abilities? To scientifically answer questions like these, we must take into account not only the reliability and validity of the tests from which IQ scores come, but also a number of sociocultural factors that might influence those scores.

The Reliability and Validity of IQ Tests

The reliability and validity of IQ tests are generally evaluated on the basis of the stability, or consistency, of IQ scores and the accuracy of these scores in making predictions about people.

How Reliable Are IQ Tests?   IQ scores obtained before the age of seven typically do not correlate very well with scores on IQ tests given later, for two key reasons: (1) Test items used with very young children are different from those used with older children, and (2) as discussed in Chapter 12, cognitive abilities change rapidly in the early years. During the school years, however, IQ scores tend to remain stable (Mayer & Sutton, 1996). The shorter the elapsed time between the two testings and the older the individuals are when first tested, the higher the test-retest correlations tend to be. For teenagers and adults, the reliability of IQ tests is high.

Of course, a person's score may vary from one time to another if testing conditions, degree of motivation or anxiety, or other factors change. But overall, modern IQ tests usually provide exceptionally consistent results—especially compared with most other kinds of mental tests.

How Valid Are IQ Tests?   Scores on various IQ tests correlate well with each other, but this does not necessarily mean they are measuring "intelligence." Because there is no independent criterion of intelligence—recall that psychologists do not fully agree on its definition—it is impossible to determine whether IQ tests are valid measures of intelligence. In short, we can assess their validity only for specific purposes.

IQ tests appear to be most valid for assessing aspects of intelligence that are related to schoolwork, such as abstract reasoning and verbal comprehension. Their predictive

IQ and Job Performance

IQ scores are reasonably good at predicting the ability to learn job-relevant information and to deal with unpredictable, changing aspects of the work environment (Hunter, 1986)—characteristics that are needed for success in complex jobs such as the ones these Navy navigator trainees will undertake.

validity—as measured by correlating IQ scores with high school grades—is reasonably good, about +.50 (Brody & Ehrlichman, 1998).

In addition, there is evidence that employees who score high on tests of verbal and mathematical reasoning tend to perform better on the job (and are paid more) than those who earned lower scores (Arvey, 1986; Barrett & Depinet, 1991; Gottfredson, 1997; Johnson & Neal, 1998). Some industrial/organizational psychologists argue that general mental ability is the best predictor of overall job performance (Borman, Hanson, & Wedge, 1997; Schmidt, 1994). IQ scores also appear to be highly correlated with performance on "real-life" tasks such as reading medicine labels and using the telephone book (Barrett & Depinet, 1991). Later, we describe a study that kept track of people for sixty years and found that children with high IQ scores tended to be well above average in terms of academic and financial success in adulthood (Oden, 1968; Terman & Oden, 1947).

So, by the standard measures for judging psychological tests, IQ tests have good reliability and reasonably good predictive validity for certain criteria, such as success in school. As noted earlier, however, an IQ score is not an infallible measure of how "smart" people are. Because IQ tests do not measure the full array of mental abilities, a particular test score tells only part of the story, and even that part may be distorted. Many factors other than mental ability—including response to the tester—can influence test performance. Children might not do as well if they are suspicious of strangers, for example (Jones & Applebaum, 1989). And older adults who worry about making mistakes in unfamiliar situations may fail to even try to answer some questions, thus artificially lowering their IQ scores (Zelinski, Schaie, & Gribben, 1977).

How Fair Are IQ Tests?   Our review of the history of intelligence testing in the United States suggests that early tests of intelligence were biased against people who were unfamiliar with English or with the vocabulary and experiences associated mainly with middle-class culture at the time. For example, consider the question "Which is most similar to a xylophone? (*violin, tuba, drum, marimba, piano*)." No matter how intelligent children are, if they have never had a chance to see an orchestra or to learn about these instruments, they may miss the question. Test designers today try to avoid obviously biased questions (American Psychological Association, 1985; Educational Testing Service, 1987). Furthermore, because IQ tests now include more than one scale, areas that are most influenced by culture, such as vocabulary, can be assessed separately from dimensions that are less vulnerable to cultural bias.

The solutions to many of the technical problems in IQ tests, however, have not resolved the controversy over the fairness or unfairness of intelligence *testing*. The debate continues partly because results of IQ tests can have important social consequences (Messick, 1982, 1989). Recall that intelligence tests were initially developed to identify and assist children with special educational needs. Yet today, such children may find themselves in special classes that not only isolate them from other students but also carry negative social labels. Obviously, the social consequences of testing can be evaluated separately from the quality of the tests themselves (Maguire, Hattie, & Haig, 1994); but those consequences cannot be ignored, especially if they tend to affect some groups more than others.

Despite attempts to eliminate cultural bias from IQ tests, there are differences in the average scores of various ethnic and cultural groups in the United States (Geary, Fan, & Bow-Thomas, 1992; Herrnstein & Murray, 1994; Humphreys, 1988; Taylor & Richards, 1991). Asian-Americans typically score highest, followed, in order, by European-Americans, Hispanic-Americans, and African-Americans.

THINKING CRITICALLY

Are IQ Tests Unfairly Biased Against Certain Groups?

■ What am I being asked to believe or accept?

Some critics of IQ tests argue that a disproportionately large number of people in some ethnic minority groups score low on IQ tests for reasons that are unrelated to intelligence, job potential, or other criteria that the tests are supposed to predict (Helms, 1992). They say that using IQ tests to make decisions about people may unfairly deprive members of some ethnic minority groups of equal employment or educational opportunities.

■ What evidence is available to support the assertion?

Research reveals several possible sources of bias in tests of mental abilities. First, whatever the content of a test, noncognitive factors such as motivation, trust, and anxiety influence performance on IQ tests and may put certain groups at a disadvantage. Children from some minority groups may be less motivated to perform well on standardized tests and less likely to trust the adult tester (Bradley-Johnson, Graham, & Johnson, 1986; Jones & Appelbaum, 1989). Consequently, differences in test scores may reflect motivational differences among various groups.

Second, many test items are still drawn from the vocabulary and experiences of the dominant middle-class culture in the United States. As a result, these tests often measure achievement in acquiring knowledge valued by that culture. Not all cultures value the same things, however (Serpell, 1994). A study of Cree Indians in northern Canada revealed that words and phrases synonymous with *competent* included *good sense of direction;* at the *incompetent* end of the scale was the phrase *lives like a white person* (Berry & Bennett, 1992). Thus, a European-American might not perform well on a Cree intelligence test based on these criteria. "Culture-fair" tests that reduce, if not eliminate, dependence on knowledge of a specific culture do indeed produce smaller differences between majority and minority groups than more traditional measures. (See Figure 10.3 for an example of an item from a culture-fair test.)

Third, some tests may reward those who interpret questions as expected by the test designer. Conventional IQ tests have clearly defined "right" and "wrong" answers. Yet a person may interpret test questions in a manner that is "intelligent" or "correct" but that produces a "wrong" answer. The fact that you don't give the answer that the test designer was looking for does not mean that you can't. When rice farmers from Liberia were asked to sort objects, they tended to put a knife in the same group as vegetables. This was the clever way to do it, they said, because the knife is used to cut vegetables. When asked to sort the objects as a "stupid" person would, they grouped the cutting tools together, the vegetables together, and so on, much as most North Americans would (Segall et al., 1990).

■ Are there alternative ways of interpreting the evidence?

The evidence might be interpreted as showing that although IQ tests do not provide an unbiased measure of mental ability in general, they do provide a fair test of whether a person is likely to succeed in school or in certain jobs. In short, they may be biased—but not in a way that discriminates *unfairly* among groups. Perhaps familiarity with the

FIGURE 10.3

Culture-Fair Tests

The task on this item from the Learning Potential Assessment Device (LPAD) is to outline the square and two triangles embedded in patterns of dots, using each dot only once.

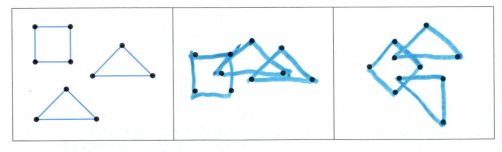

Source: Feuerstein, 1979.

culture reflected in IQ tests is just as important for success at school or work in that culture as it is for success on the tests themselves. After all, the ranking among groups on measures of academic achievement is similar to the ranking for average IQ scores (Sue & Okazaki, 1990). According to this view, it doesn't matter very much if tests that are supposed to measure intellectual aptitude actually measure culture-related achievement as long as they are useful in predicting whatever criterion is of interest. In fact, "culture-fair" tests do not predict academic achievement as well as conventional IQ tests do (Aiken, 1994; Humphreys, 1988).

■ What additional evidence would help to evaluate the alternatives?

Evaluation of whether tests differentiate fairly or unfairly depends on whether the sources of test-score differences are relevant to predicting performance in the environment for which the test is intended. To take an extreme example, perhaps average differences in IQ scores between ethnic groups result entirely from certain test items that have nothing to do with how well the test as a whole predicts academic success. It is important to conduct research on this possibility.

Alternative tests must also be explored, particularly those that include assessment of problem-solving skills and other abilities not measured by most IQ tests (e.g., Sternberg & Kaufman, 1998). If new tests prove to be less biased than traditional tests but have equal or better predictive validity, many of the issues discussed in this section will have been resolved.

■ What conclusions are most reasonable?

The effort to reduce unfair cultural biases in tests is well-founded, but "culture-fair" tests will be of little benefit if they fail to predict success as well as conventional tests do. Whether one considers this circumstance good or bad, fair or unfair, it is important for people to have information and skills that are valued by the culture that establishes criteria for educational and occupational achievement. As long as this is the case, tests designed to predict success in such areas are reasonable insofar as they measure a person's skills and access to the information valued by that culture.

Stopping at that conclusion, however, would mean freezing the status quo, whereby members of certain groups are denied many educational and economic benefits. As discussed later, if attention were to be focused on altering the conditions that result in poverty, poor schools, and inadequate nutrition and health care, many of the reasons for concern about test bias might be eliminated.

IQ Scores as a Measure of Innate Ability

Years of research have led psychologists to conclude that both hereditary and environmental factors interact to influence mental abilities. For example, by asking many questions, bright children help generate an enriching environment for themselves; thus, innate abilities allow people to take better advantage of their environment (Scarr & Carter-Saltzman, 1982). In addition, if their own biologically influenced intelligence allows bright parents to give their children an environment favorable to the development of intelligence, their children are favored by both heredity and environment.

Psychologists have explored the influence of genetics on individual differences in IQ scores by comparing the strength of the correlation between the scores of people who have differing degrees of similarity in their genetic makeup and environment. For example, they have examined the IQ scores of identical twins—pairs with exactly the same genetic makeup—who were separated when very young and reared in different environments. They have also examined the scores of identical twins raised together. (You may want to review the Linkages section of Chapter 2, as well as the behavioral genetics appendix, for more on the designs typically used to analyze hereditary and environmental influences.)

FIGURE 10.4

Correlations of IQ Scores

The correlation between pairs increases as similarity in heredity or environment increases.

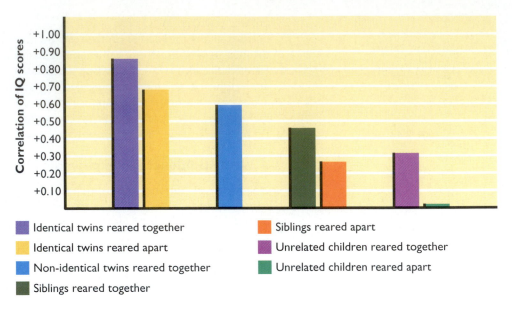

Identical twins reared together
Identical twins reared apart
Non-identical twins reared together
Siblings reared together

Siblings reared apart
Unrelated children reared together
Unrelated children reared apart

Source: Reprinted with permission from "Familial Studies of Intelligence: A Review," T. Bouchard et al., *Science,* Vol. 212, #4498, pp. 1055–9, 29 May 1981. Copyright © 1981 American for the Advancement of Science.

These studies find, first, that hereditary factors are strongly related to IQ scores. When identical twins, separated at birth and adopted by different families, are tested many years later, the correlation between their scores is usually high and positive, at least +.60 (Bouchard et al., 1990). If one twin receives a high IQ score, the other probably will too; if one is low, the other is likely to be low as well. However, studies of IQ correlations also highlight the importance of the environment (Capron & Duyme, 1989). Consider any two people—twins, siblings, or unrelated children—brought together in a foster home. No matter what the degree of genetic similarity in these pairs, the correlation between their IQ scores is higher if they share the same home than if they are raised in different environments, as Figure 10.4 shows (Scarr & Carter-Saltzman, 1982).

The role of environmental influences is also seen in the results of studies that compare children's IQ scores before and after environmental changes such as adoption. Generally, these studies find modest increases in the IQ scores of children from relatively impoverished backgrounds who were adopted into homes with more enriching intellectual environments—environments with interesting materials and experiences, as well as a supportive, responsive adult (Weinberg, Scarr, & Waldman, 1992).

A study of French children who were adopted soon after birth demonstrates the importance of both genetic and environmental influences. When these children were tested after years of living in their adopted homes, those whose biological parents were from upper socioeconomic groups (where higher IQ scores are more common) had higher IQ scores than those whose biological parents came from lower socioeconomic groups, regardless of the socioeconomic status of the adoptive homes (Capron & Duyme, 1989). These findings suggest that a genetic component of the children's mental abilities continued to exert an influence even in the adoptive environment. At the same time, when children from low socioeconomic backgrounds were adopted by parents who provided academically enriched environments, their IQ scores rose by twelve to fifteen points (Capron & Duyme, 1989). Another study found that the IQ scores of adopted children were an average of fourteen points higher than those of siblings who remained with the biological parents in poorer, less enriching environments (Schiff et al., 1978).

Other factors that may have negative effects on mental abilities include poor nutrition, exposure to lead or alcohol, low birth weight, and complications during birth. In contrast, exposure to early interventions that improve academic preparedness and ability tend to improve children's scores on tests of intelligence (Neisser et al., 1996). These intervention programs, some of which are described later, may be responsible

FIGURE 10.5

IQ Test Scores Then and Now

Comparisons of performance on the Stanford-Binet IQ test reveal that today's children are answering more questions correctly than did children in the 1930s. Indeed, the average child today would receive an IQ of 120 on the 1932 test, a very high score! No one is sure why this increase in performance has occurred, but some psychologists suspect that better nutrition and improvements in educational programs are partly responsible.

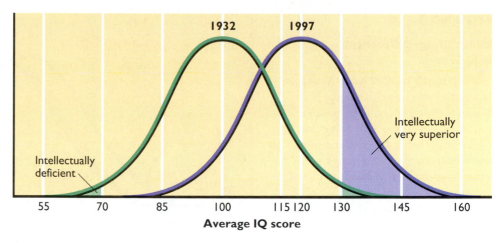

Source: Neisser, 1998.

for the steady increase in average IQ scores throughout the world over the past six decades (Flynn, 1999; Neisser, 1998). Note that this increase cannot be due to the influence of new and "better" genes because genetic changes or mutations simply do not occur this rapidly in humans (see Figure 10.5).

Some researchers have concluded that the influence of heredity and environment on mental abilities appears to be about equal; others see a somewhat larger role for heredity (Herrnstein & Murray, 1994; Loehlin, 1989; Petrill et al., 1998; Plomin, 1994b). For example, one research team has recently reported the discovery of specific genes associated with extremely high IQs (Chorney et al., 1998). Still, it must be emphasized that such estimates of heritability—of the relative contributions of heredity and environment—apply only to groups, not to individuals. Thus, it would be inaccurate to say that 50 percent of *your* IQ score is inherited and 50 percent learned. It is far more accurate to say that about half of the *variability* in the IQ scores of a group of people can be attributed to hereditary influences, and about half can be attributed to environmental influences.

Here is yet another example of nature and nurture working together to shape behavior and mental processes. Further, the relative contributions of nature and nurture can change over time. Environmental influences, for example, seem to be greater at younger ages (Plomin, 1994b) and tend to diminish over the years. Thus, IQ differences in a group of children will probably be affected more by parental help with preschool reading than by, say, the courses available in junior high school ten years later.

Group Differences in IQ Scores

Much of the controversy about differences in IQ scores is not over differences among individuals but over differences in the average scores of groups such as poor people and rich people or Caucasian people and Asian people. This controversy has most recently centered on a book called *The Bell Curve,* in which Richard Herrnstein and Charles Murray (1994) reviewed research on IQ differences across ethnic and socioeconomic groups in North America. The authors concluded that defining intelligence in terms of abilities needed in school—and measuring it with IQ tests—has created a social class system in which members of a "cognitive elite" are likely to succeed while more and more intellectual "have-nots" will drop out of school to face unemployment, poverty, and dependence on welfare to support themselves and their children. Debate about the book focused on what many saw as a negative evaluation of the intelligence and potential of African-Americans and revealed some common misunderstandings about the nature, extent, and meaning of group differences in IQ scores. To correctly interpret these differences and analyze their sources, we must avoid some pitfalls.

FIGURE 10.6

Ethnic Group Differences in IQ Scores

The average IQ score of Asian-Americans is about four to six points higher than that of European-Americans, which in turn averages twelve to fifteen points higher than that of African-Americans and Hispanic-Americans. Notice, however, that the differences among IQ scores within each of these groups is much greater than the differences between the group means.

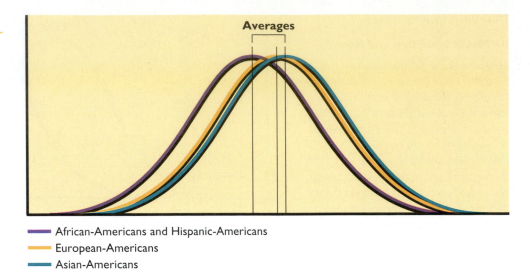

Averages

━━━ African-Americans and Hispanic-Americans
━━━ European-Americans
━━━ Asian-Americans

First, group scores are just that; they do not describe individuals. Although the mean IQ score of Asian-Americans is higher than the mean score of European-Americans, there will still be large numbers of European-Americans who score well above the Asian-American mean and large numbers of Asian-Americans who score below the European-American mean (see Figure 10.6).

Second, increases in IQ scores over the past sixty years (Flynn, 1999; Neisser, 1998) and other similar findings suggest that inherited characteristics are not necessarily fixed. A favorable environment may improve a child's performance somewhat, even if the inherited influences on that child's IQ are negative (Humphreys, 1984).

Socioeconomic Differences   Upper-class communities in the United States have shown average IQ scores seventeen points higher than those of lower-class communities with the same ethnic makeup (Jordan, Huttenlocher, & Levine, 1992; Oakland & Glutting, 1990). IQ score differences associated with socioeconomic status also occur in other countries (Fergusson, Lloyd, & Horwood, 1991; Murthy & Panda, 1987). Why should there be a relationship between IQ scores and family income?

Four factors seem to account for the relationship between IQ and socioeconomic status. First, parents' jobs and status depend on characteristics related to their own intelligence, and this intelligence is partly determined by a genetic component that, in turn, contributes to the child's IQ score. Second, the parents' income affects the child's environment in ways that can increase or decrease the child's IQ score (Cronbach, 1975; MacKenzie, 1984). Third, motivational differences may play a role. Upper- and middle-income families tend to demonstrate greater motivation to succeed and excel in academic endeavors (Atkinson & Raynor, 1974). As a result, children from middle- and upper-class families may exert more effort in testing situations and therefore obtain higher scores (Bradley-Johnson, Graham, & Johnson, 1986; Zigler & Seitz, 1982). Fourth, since colleges, universities, and businesses usually select people with higher scores on IQ tests, those with higher IQs may have greater opportunities to earn more money (Sternberg & Kaufman, 1998).

Ethnic Differences   Some have argued that the mean differences in IQ scores among various ethnic groups in the United States are due mostly to heredity. Note, however, that the existence of hereditary differences *within* groups does not indicate whether differences *between* groups result from similar genetic causes (Lewontin, 1976). As shown in Figure 10.6, variation within ethnic groups is much greater than variation between those groups (Zuckerman, 1990).

There are large differences among the environments in which the average African-American, Hispanic-American, and European-American child grows up. To take only the most blatant evidence, the latest figures available show 26.2 percent of African-American families and 27.8 percent of Hispanic-American families living below the

Helping with Homework

There are differences in the average IQ scores of European-Americans and African-Americans, but those who attribute these differences primarily to hereditary factors are ignoring a number of environmental, social, and other nongenetic factors that are important in creating, and are now narrowing, this IQ gap.

poverty level compared with 8.5 percent of European-American families (*Statistical Abstracts of the United States,* 1997). Among children under age eighteen, the figures show 15.5 percent of European-Americans, 41.5 percent of African-Americans, and 39.3 percent of Hispanic-Americans living below the poverty line. Compared with European-Americans, African-Americans are more likely to have parents with poor educational backgrounds, as well as inferior nutrition, health care, and schools (Wilson, 1997). All of these conditions are likely to pull down scores on IQ tests.

Evidence for the influence of environmental factors on the average black-white difference in IQ scores comes from adoption studies. One such study involved African-American children from disadvantaged homes who were adopted by middle- to upper-class European-American families in the first years of their lives (Scarr & Weinberg, 1976). When measured a few years later, the mean IQ score of these children was 110. A comparison of this mean score with that of nonadopted children from similar backgrounds suggests that the new environment raised the children's IQ scores at least ten points. A ten-year follow-up study of these youngsters showed that their average IQ scores were still higher than the average scores of African-American children raised in disadvantaged homes (Weinberg, Scarr, & Waldman, 1992).

As discussed in the chapter on human development, cultural factors may also contribute to differences between the mean scores of various ethnic groups. For example, those means may partly reflect differences in motivation based on how much value is placed on academic achievement. In one study of 15,000 African-American, Asian-American, Hispanic-American, and European-American high school students, parental and peer influences related to achievement tended to vary with ethnic group (Steinberg, Dornbusch, & Brown, 1992). The Asian-American students received strong support for academic pursuits from both their parents and their peers. European-American students whose parents expected high academic achievement tended to associate with peers who also encouraged achievement, and they tended to do better academically than African-American and Hispanic-American students. The parents of the African-American students in the study supported academic achievement, but because their peers did not, the students may have been less motivated and their performance may have suffered. The performance of the Hispanic-American students may have suffered because, in this study at least, they were more likely than the others to have authoritarian parents, whose emphasis on obedience (see Chapter 12) may have created conflicts with the schools' emphasis on independent learning.

In short, there appear to be important nongenetic factors working to decrease the mean scores of African-American and Hispanic-American children. Indeed, the recently narrowing gap between African-American and European-American children on tests of intelligence and mathematical aptitude may be related to changing environmental conditions for many African-American children (College Board, 1994; Vincent, 1991). Whatever heredity might contribute to children's performance, it may be possible for them to improve greatly, given the right conditions.

Conditions That Can Raise IQ Scores

A number of environmental conditions can help or deter cognitive development (see Chapter 12). For example, lack of caring attention or of normal intellectual stimulation can inhibit a child's mental growth. Low test scores have been linked with poverty, chaos and noise in the home, poor schools, and inadequate nutrition and health care (Humphreys & Davey, 1988; Weinberg, 1989). Can the effects of bad environments be reversed? Not always, but efforts to intervene in the lives of children and enrich their environments have had some success. Conditions for improving children's performance include rewards for progress, encouragement of effort, and creation of expectations for success.

In the United States, the best-known attempt to enrich children's environments is Project Head Start, a set of programs established by the federal government in the 1960s to help preschoolers from lower-income backgrounds. In some of these programs, teachers visit the home and work with the child and parents on cognitive skills. In others, the children attend classes in nursery schools. Some programs emphasize health and nutrition and, in recent years, family mental health and social skills as well (Murray, 1995). Head Start has brought measurable benefits to children's health as well as improvements in their academic and intellectual skills (Lee, Brooks-Gunn, & Schnur, 1988; Zigler & Seitz, 1982). Closely related to Project Head Start are intervention programs for infants at risk because of low birth weight, low socioeconomic status, or low parental IQ scores. Such programs appear to enhance IQ scores by as much as nine points by the age of three; the effects appear especially strong for the infants of mothers with a high school education or less (Brooks-Gunn et al., 1992; Infant Health and Development Program, 1990; Ramey et al., 1992; Wasik et al., 1990).

Project Head Start

This teacher is working in Project Head Start, a program designed to provide children from impoverished backgrounds with the preparation they will need to succeed in grade school.

Do the gains achieved by preschool enrichment programs last? Although program developers sometimes claim long-term benefits (Schweinhart & Weikart, 1991), such claims are disputed (Spitz, 1991). Various findings from more than 1,000 such programs are often contradictory, but the effect on IQ scores typically diminishes after a year or two (Woodhead, 1988). A study evaluating two of the better preschool programs concluded that their effects are at best only temporary (Locurto, 1991a). The fading of effects is probably due to reduced motivation, not loss of mental ability (Zigler & Seitz, 1982). Children may lose motivation when they leave a special preschool program and enter the substandard schools that often serve poor children.

Fading effects were also seen in programs such as the Abecedarian Project (Ramey, 1992), which identified children at risk for mental retardation while they were still in the womb, then offered five years of intense interventions to improve their chances of success once they entered school. At eighteen months of age, children in this enrichment program had IQ scores that were eighteen points higher than those of at-risk children who were not in the program. At age twelve, they still scored higher on IQ tests, but the size of the difference—now just five points—steadily declined over the next several years (Ramey, 1995).

Martin Woodhead (1988) has concluded that the primary benefits of early-enrichment programs probably lie in their effect on children's attitudes toward school. One consistent, though very small, effect is that children who have taken part in enrichment programs are less likely to be held back in school or to need special-education programs (Locurto, 1991b; Palmer & Anderson, 1979). Especially in borderline cases, favorable attitudes toward school may help reduce the chances that children will be held back a grade or placed in special-education classes. Children who avoid these experiences may retain positive attitudes about school and enter a cycle in which gains due to early enrichment are maintained and amplified on a long-term basis (Myerson et al., 1998; Zigler & Styfco, 1994).

IQ Scores in the Classroom

Obviously, IQ scores are neither a crystal ball into some predestined future nor a measure of some fixed quantity, but they can subtly affect how people are treated and how they behave. For example, Robert Rosenthal and Lenore Jacobson (1968) found that labels create *expectancies* that can become self-fulfilling prophecies. Teachers in their study were told that a test could indicate which grade-school students were about to enter a "blooming" period of rapid academic growth, and they were given the names of students who had supposedly scored high on the test. In fact, the experimenters *randomly* selected the "bloomers." But during the next year, the IQ scores of two-thirds of the bloomers dramatically increased, whereas only one-quarter of the children in the control group showed the same increase. Apparently, the teachers' expectancies about the children influenced them in ways that showed up on IQ tests.

Some attempts to replicate Rosenthal and Jacobson's findings have failed (Elashoff, 1979); others have disclosed that the effect of teacher expectancies, though statistically significant, is relatively small (Jussim, 1989; Snow, 1995). Still, there is little doubt that IQ-based teacher expectancies can have an effect on students (Rosenthal, 1994b). To find out how, Alan Chaiken and his colleagues (1974) videotaped teacher-child interactions in a classroom in which teachers had been informed (falsely) that certain pupils were particularly bright. They found that the teachers tended to favor the supposedly "brighter" students—smiling at them more often than at other students, making more eye contact, and reacting more positively to their comments. Children receiving such extra social reinforcement not only get more intense teaching but are also more likely to enjoy school, to have their mistakes corrected, and to continue trying to improve. Later research found that teachers provide a wider range of classroom activities for students for whom they have higher expectations, suggesting another way in which expectancies might influence IQ scores (Blatchford et al., 1989).

These results suggest that the "rich get richer": Those perceived to be blessed with high mental abilities are given better opportunities to improve those abilities. Is there

in review

INFLUENCES ON IQ SCORES		
Source of Effect	Description	Examples of Evidence for Effect
Genetics	Genes appear to play a significant role in differences among people on IQ test performance.	The IQ scores of siblings who share no common environment are positively correlated. There is a greater correlation between scores of identical twins than between those of nonidentical twins.
Environment	Environmental conditions interact with genetic inheritance. Nutrition, medical care, sensory and intellectual stimulation, interpersonal relations, and influences on motivation are all significant features of the environment.	IQ scores have risen among children who are adopted into homes that offer a stimulating, enriching environment. Correlations between IQs of twins reared together are higher than for those reared apart.

also a "poor get poorer" effect? In fact, there is evidence that teachers tend to be less patient, less encouraging, and less likely to try teaching as much material to students whom they do not consider bright (Cooper, 1979; Trujillo, 1986). Further, differential expectations about the academic potential of boys and girls may contribute to gender differences in performance and achievement motivation.

IQ tests have been criticized for being biased and for labeling people on the basis of scores or profiles. ("In Review: Influences on IQ Scores" lists the factors that can shape IQ scores.) However, such tests can also prevent errors by reducing the number of important educational and employment decisions that are made on the basis of inaccurate stereotypes, false preconceptions, and faulty generalizations. For example, boredom or lack of motivation at school can make a child appear mentally slow, even retarded. But a test of mental abilities conducted under the right circumstances is likely to reveal the child's potential. The test can prevent the mistake of moving a child of average intelligence to a class for the mentally handicapped. And, as Alfred Binet had hoped, intelligence tests have been enormously helpful in identifying children who need special educational attention.

LINKAGES

How does excessive emotional arousal affect scores on tests of mental ability? (a link to Motivation and Emotion)

As mentioned earlier, many factors other than mental ability can potentially influence scores on mental ability tests. One of the most important of these factors is emotional arousal. In Chapter 11, we note that people tend to perform best when their arousal level is moderate, whereas too much arousal, or even too little, tends to result in decreased performance. Those whose overarousal compromises their ability to do well in testing situations are said to suffer from *test anxiety*.

Such people fear that they will do poorly on the test and that others will think they are "stupid." In a testing situation, they may experience physical symptoms such as heart palpitations and sweating, as well as negative thoughts such as "I am going to blow this exam" or "The tester will think I am a real idiot." In the most severe cases of test anxiety, individuals may be so distressed that they are unable to successfully complete the test.

LINKAGES

Emotionality and the Measurement of Mental Abilities

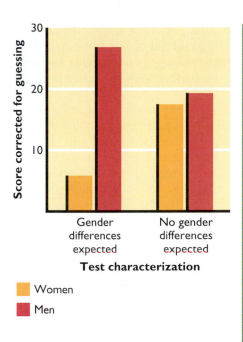

FIGURE 10.7

The Stereotype Threat Effect

In this experiment, male and female college students took a difficult math test. Beforehand, some of the students were told that men usually outscore women on such tests; others were not given this gender-stereotype information. The women who were made aware of this gender stereotype scored lower than those who were not; they also scored lower than the men, even though their mathematical abilities were equal to those of the men. Men's scores were not significantly affected by gender-stereotype information.

Test anxiety may affect up to 40 percent of elementary school students and about the same percentage of college students. General test anxiety afflicts boys and girls equally (Turner et al., 1993). High test anxiety is correlated with lower IQ scores, and even among people with high IQ scores, those who experience severe test anxiety do poorly on achievement tests. Test-anxious grade-school students are likely to receive low grades and to perform poorly on evaluated tasks and those that require new learning (Campbell, 1986). Some children with test anxiety refuse to attend school or they "play sick" on test days, thus becoming caught up in a vicious circle that further harms their performance on standardized achievement tests.

Anxiety and other emotions, such as frustration, may also be at work in a testing phenomenon identified by Claude Steele and his colleagues. In one study, when test instructions were written in such a way as to cause bright African-American students to become more sensitive to negative stereotypes about the intelligence of their ethnic group, these students performed less well on a standardized test than equally bright African-American students whose sensitivity to the stereotypes had not been increased (Steele & Aronson, 1995). In another study, math-proficient women were randomly divided into two groups. The first group was given information that elicited concern over the stereotype that women are less good at math than men; specifically, they were told that men usually do better on the difficult math test they were about to take. The second group was not given such information. As shown in Figure 10.7, those in the second group performed much better on the test than did those in the first. In fact, their performance was equal to that of men who took the same test (Spencer, Steele, & Quinn, 1997). Steele refers to this phenomenon as *stereotype threat:* Concern over negative stereotypes about the mental abilities of the group to which they belong can impair the performance of some women—and some members of ethnic minorities— such that the test scores they earn underestimate their mental abilities.

The good news for people who suffer from test anxiety is that the counseling centers at most colleges and universities have effective programs for dealing with it. Indeed, test anxiety can be remedied through some of the same procedures used to treat other forms of anxiety disorders (see Chapter 16). There is also reason to be cautiously optimistic about reducing the impact of the stereotype threat phenomenon on the academic performance of African-Americans and other minority groups. A program at the University of Michigan that directly addressed this phenomenon produced substantial improvements in the grades of first-year minority students (Steele, 1997).

These and other research findings indicate that the relationship between anxiety and test performance is a complex one, but one generalization seems to hold true: People who are severely test-anxious do not perform to the best of their ability on IQ tests.

UNDERSTANDING INTELLIGENCE

Throughout this chapter we have noted that different researchers and different cultures define intelligence in different ways, and that IQ scores tell only part of the story of intelligence. It is an important part, though, so IQ tests will continue to be used as psychologists work to deepen their understanding of the elusive concept called intelligence. In this section, we consider several of the approaches that these researchers have taken. These approaches should be seen not as competing to be the best explanation of intelligence but, rather, as providing complementary portrayals of a multifaceted concept.

The Psychometric Approach

Standard IQ tests reflect the **psychometric approach,** which is a way of studying intelligence that emphasizes the *products* of intelligence, including IQ scores. Researchers taking this approach ask whether intelligence is one general trait or a bundle of more

LINKAGES

Brainpower and Intelligence

Applying the information-processing model introduced in Chapter 8 to intelligence might suggest that those with the most rapid information-processors (the "fastest" brains) would do best on mental ability tests, including those required for college entrance. Research suggests, however, that this is true only to an extent and that there is more to intelligent behavior than sheer processing speed.

specific abilities. The answer matters, because if intelligence is a single "thing," an employer might assume that someone with a low IQ could not do any tasks well. But if intelligence is composed of many independent abilities, a poor showing in one area—say, spatial abilities—would not rule out good performance in understanding information or solving word problems.

At the turn of the century, statistician Charles Spearman made a suggestion that began the modern debate about the nature of intelligence. Spearman noted that scores on almost all tests of mental abilities were positively correlated (Spearman, 1904, 1927). That is, people who did well on one test also tended to do well on all of the others. Spearman concluded that these correlations were created by general mental ability, which he called **g,** for general intelligence, and a group of special intelligences, which he collectively referred to as **s.** The s-factors, he said, are the specific information and skills needed for particular tasks.

Spearman argued that people's scores on a particular test depend on both g and s. Further examination of test scores, however, revealed correlations that could not be explained by either g or s and were called *group factors.* Although Spearman modified his theory to accommodate these factors, he continued to assert that g represented a measure of mental force, or intellectual power (Gould, 1983).

In 1938, L. L. Thurstone published a paper criticizing Spearman's mathematical methods. Using the statistical technique of factor analysis, he analyzed the correlations among IQ tests to identify the underlying factors, or abilities, being measured by those tests. Thurstone's analyses did not reveal a single, dominating g-factor; instead, he found seven relatively independent *primary mental abilities,* which he labeled as numerical ability, reasoning, verbal fluency, spatial visualization, perceptual ability, memory, and verbal comprehension. Thurstone did not deny that g exists, but he argued that it was not as important as primary mental abilities in describing a particular person. Similarly, Spearman did not deny the existence of special abilities, but he maintained that g tells us most of what we need to know about a person's mental ability.

Raymond B. Cattell (1963) agreed with Spearman, but his own factor analyses suggested that there are two kinds of g, which he labeled fluid and crystallized. **Fluid intelligence,** he said, is the basic power of reasoning and problem solving. It allows us to evaluate the syllogisms described in Chapter 8, to think critically about assertions made in TV commercials, and to understand relationships between concepts (such as "Houses are bigger than people."). **Crystallized intelligence,** in contrast, involves specific knowledge gained as a result of applying fluid intelligence. It produces, for example, a good vocabulary and familiarity with the multiplication tables.

Who is right? After decades of research and debate, most psychologists today agree that there is a positive correlation among various tests of mental ability, a correlation that is due to a factor known as g (Carroll, 1991). However, the brain probably does not "contain" some unified "thing" corresponding to what people call intelligence; g is more likely a collection of subskills and mental abilities—such as reasoning ability, test-taking skill, reading ability, and so forth (Humphreys, 1984)—many of which are needed to succeed on any test of intelligence.

The Information-Processing Approach

The **information-processing approach** analyzes the *process* of intelligent behavior, rather than test answers and other *products* of intelligence (Hunt, 1983; Naglieri et al., 1991; Vernon, 1987). This approach asks, What mental operations are necessary to perform intellectual tasks? What aspects depend on past learning, and what aspects depend on attention, working memory, and processing speed? In other words, the information-processing approach relates the basic mental processes discussed in the chapters on perception, learning, memory, and cognition to the concept of intelligence. Are there individual differences in these processes that correlate with measures of intelligence? More specifically, are measures of intelligence related to differences in the attention available for basic mental processes or in the speed of these processes?

The notion that intelligence may be related to attention builds on the results of research by Earl Hunt and others (Ackerman, 1994; Eysenck, 1987; Hunt, 1980). As discussed in the chapter on perception, attention represents a pool of resources or mental energy. When people perform difficult tasks or perform more than one task at a time, they must call on greater amounts of these resources. Does intelligent behavior depend on the amount of attention that can be mobilized? Early research by Hunt (1980) suggests that it does, that people with greater intellectual ability have more attentional resources available. There is also evidence of a positive correlation between IQ scores and performance on tasks requiring attention, such as mentally tallying the frequency of words in the "animal" category while reading a list of varied terms aloud (Stankov, 1989).

Another possible link between differences in information processing and differences in intelligence relates to processing speed. Perhaps intelligent people have "faster brains" than other people—perhaps they carry out basic mental processes more quickly. When a task is complex, having a "fast brain" might decrease the chance that information will disappear from memory before it can be used (Jensen, 1993; Larson & Saccuzzo, 1989). A "fast brain" might also allow people to do a better job of mastering material in everyday life and therefore to build up a good knowledge base (Miller & Vernon, 1992). Hans Eysenck (1986) even proposed that intelligence can be defined as the error-free transmission of information through the brain. Indeed, some researchers have attempted to measure various aspects of intelligence by looking at electrical activity in particular parts of the brain (Deary & Caryl, 1993; Eysenck, 1994).

These hypotheses sound reasonable, but research suggests that only about 25 percent of the variation seen in people's performance on general mental abilities tests can be accounted for by differences in their information-processing abilities (such as speed of access to long-term memory or the capacity of working memory) (Baker, Vernon, & Ho, 1991; Miller & Vernon, 1992).

The Triarchic Theory of Intelligence

According to Robert Sternberg (1988a), a complete theory of intelligence must deal with three different types of intelligence: analytic, creative, and practical intelligence. *Analytic intelligence,* the kind that is measured by traditional IQ tests, would help you solve a physics problem; *creative* intelligence is what you would use to compose music; and you would draw on *practical* intelligence to figure out what to do if you are stranded on a lonely road during a blizzard. Sternberg's **triarchic theory of intelligence** deals with all three.

Although Sternberg acknowledges the importance of analytic intelligence for success in academics and other areas, he argues strongly that universities and companies should not select people solely on the basis of tests of this kind of intelligence (Sternberg, 1996; Sternberg & Williams, 1997). Why? Because the tasks posed by tests of analytic intelligence are often of little interest to the people taking them, and typically have little relationship to their daily experience; each task is usually clearly defined and comes with all the information needed to find the one right answer (Neisser, 1996). In contrast, the practical problems people face every day are generally of personal interest and related to their actual experiences; they are ill-defined and do not contain all the information necessary to solve them; they typically have more than one correct solution; and there may be several methods by which one can arrive at a solution (Sternberg et al., 1995).

It is no wonder, then, that children who do poorly in school can nevertheless show high degrees of practical intelligence. Some Brazilian street children, for example, are capable of doing the math required for their street business, despite having failed mathematics in school (Carraher, Carraher, & Schliemann, 1985). And a study of avid race-track bettors revealed that even those whose IQ scores were as low as 82 were highly accurate at predicting race odds at post-time by combining many different kinds of complex information about horses, jockeys, and track conditions (Ceci & Liker, 1986). In other words, their practical intelligence was unrelated to measures of

Cognitive Complexity

The outcome of a horse race depends on track conditions, temperature, the horses' training, the skill of the jockeys, and a multitude of other factors. People who can keep in mind and mentally combine numerous interacting factors tend to be especially successful at dealing with complicated situations, whether they involve betting, business decisions, or scientific research.

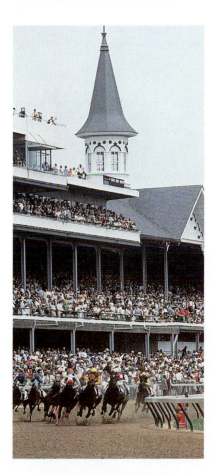

FIGURE 10.8

Testing for Practical and Creative Intelligence

Robert Sternberg believes that traditional IQ tests measure only analytical intelligence. Shown here are sample questions from tests developed by Sternberg to measure practical and creative intelligence. The answers are given below. How did you do?

PRACTICAL

1. Think of a problem that you are currently experiencing in real life. Briefly describe the problem, including how long it has been present and who else is involved (if anyone). Then describe three different practical things you could do to try to solve the problem. *(Students are given up to 15 minutes and up to 2 pages.)*

2. Choose the answer that provides the **best** solution, given the specific situation and desired outcome.

   John's family moved to Iowa from Arizona during his junior year in high school. He enrolled as a new student in the local high school two months ago but still has not made friends and feels bored and lonely. One of his favorite activities is writing stories. What is likely to be the most effective solution to this problem?

   A. Volunteer to work on the school newspaper staff.

   B. Spend more time at home writing columns for the school newsletter.

   C. Try to convince his parents to move back to Arizona.

   D. Invite a friend from Arizona to visit during Christmas break.

3. Each question asks you to use information about everyday things. Read each question carefully and choose the best answer.

   Mike wants to buy two seats together and is told there are pairs of seats available only in Rows 8, 12, 49, and 95–100. Which of the following is not one of his choices for the total price of the two tickets?

   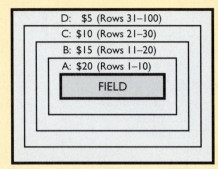

   A. $10.   **B.** $20.   **C.** $30.   **D.** $40.

CREATIVE

1. Suppose you are the student representative to a committee that has the power and the money to reform your school system. Describe your ideal school system, including buildings, teachers, curriculum, and any other aspects you feel are important. *(Students are given up to 15 minutes and up to 2 pages.)*

2. Each question has a "Pretend" statement. You must suppose that this statement is true. Decide which word goes with the third underlined word in the same way that the first two underlined words go together.

   Colors are audible.

   flavor is to *tongue* as *shade* is to

   A. ear.   **B.** light.   **C.** sound.   **D.** hue.

3. First, read how the operation is defined. Then, decide what is the correct answer to the question.

   *There is a new mathematical operation called **flix**.*
   It is defined as follows:
          A flix $B = A + B$, if $A > B$
   but A flix $B = A \times B$, if $A < B$
   and A flix $B = A / B$, if $A = B$
   How much is 4 flix 7?

   A. 28.   **B.** 11.   **C.** 3.   **D.** –11.

ANSWERS. Practical: 2.A, 3.B. Creative: 2.A, 3.A.

Source: Sternberg, 1996.

A Musical Prodigy?

According to Gardner's theory of multiple intelligences, skilled artists, athletes, and musicians—such as the young violinist shown here—display forms of intelligence not assessed by standard intelligence tests.

If only measuring the multifaceted concept of intelligence were this easy!

their IQ. Sternberg and his colleagues (1995) have also found that practical intelligence predicts success on some jobs at least as well as IQ test scores.

Because Sternberg's theory is so broad, however, many parts of it are difficult to test. Determining exactly how to measure practical "street smarts," for example, is a challenge that is now being addressed by researchers (e.g., Sternberg et al., 1995; see Figure 10.8). Nevertheless, Sternberg's theory is important because it extends the concept of intelligence into areas that most psychologists traditionally did not examine and emphasizes what intelligence means in everyday life.

Multiple Intelligences

Many people whose IQ scores are only average have exceptional ability in specific areas. Even some people with below-average IQ scores show incredible ability in narrowly defined areas (Miller, 1999; Treffert, 1988). One child whose IQ score was 50 could correctly state the day of the week for any date between 1880 and 1950 (Scheerer, Rothmann, & Goldstein, 1945). He could also play melodies on the piano by ear and sing Italian operatic pieces he had heard, although he had no understanding of what he was doing. In addition, he could spell—forward or backward—any word spoken to him and could memorize long speeches.

Cases of remarkable ability in specific areas constitute part of the evidence cited by Howard Gardner in support of his theory of multiple intelligences (Gardner, 1993). He suggests that our ideas of intelligence should be based not only on "normal" individuals but also on those who are "gifted" and those who have brain damage. To study intelligence, Gardner focused on how people learn and use symbol systems such as language, mathematics, and music. He asked, Do these systems all require the same abilities and processes, the same "intelligence"? To find out, Gardner looked not just at test scores and information-processing experiments but also at the ways in which children develop, at the exceptional abilities of child prodigies and remarkable adults, at biological research, and at the values and traditions of various cultures.

According to Gardner, all people possess a number of intellectual potentials, or "intelligences," each of which includes skills that allow them to solve problems. Biology provides raw capacities; cultures provide symbolic systems such as language to mobilize those raw capacities. Although the intelligences normally interact, they can function with some independence, and individuals may develop certain intelligences further than others. The specific intelligences that Gardner proposes are (1) linguistic intelligence; (2) logical-mathematical intelligence; (3) spatial intelligence; (4) musical intelligence; (5) body-kinesthetic intelligence (seen in the skills used by dancers, athletes, and surgeons); (6) intrapersonal intelligence (seen in self-understanding); (7) interpersonal intelligence (seen in the ability to understand and interact with others); and (8) naturalistic intelligence, the ability to see patterns in nature (Gardner, 1998). Gardner notes that conventional IQ tests sample only the first three of these intelligences, mainly because these are the forms of intelligence most valued in school. But conventional IQ tests, he claims, fail to do justice to the diversity of intelligences.

Gardner's critics argue that including athletic or musical skill dilutes the validity and usefulness of the intelligence concept, especially as it is applied in school and in many kinds of jobs. Nevertheless, the theory highlights aspects of mental ability that are not measured by traditional IQ tests but that may be important in certain kinds of human activity. ("In Review: Analyzing Mental Abilities" summarizes Gardner's theory, along with the other views of intelligence we have discussed.)

The Ecological Approach

As psychologists become more attuned to the effects of cultural factors on human behavior and mental processes, the ecological approach to intelligence—emphasizing the role of the environment in shaping intelligence—may become more prominent. This approach views intelligence as mental activity that allows people to select, shape, and adapt to those aspects of the environment most relevant to their lives (Krechevsky & Gardner, 1994; Sternberg, 1985). In other words, the ecological approach suggests

in review

ANALYZING MENTAL ABILITIES

Approach	Method	Key Findings or Propositions
Psychometric	Define the structure of intelligence by examining factor analyses of the correlations between scores on tests of mental abilities.	Performance on many tests of mental abilities is highly correlated, but this correlation, represented by g, reflects a bundle of abilities, not just one trait.
Information processing	Understand intelligence by examining the mental operations involved in intelligent behavior.	The speed of basic processes and the amount of attentional resources available make significant contributions to performance on IQ tests.
Sternberg's triarchic theory	Understand intelligence by examining the information processing involved in thinking, changes with experience, and effects in different environments.	There are three distinct kinds of intelligence: analytic, creative, and practical. IQ tests measure only analytic intelligence, but creative intelligence (which involves dealing with new problems) and practical intelligence (which involves adapting to one's environment) may also be important to success in school and at work.
Gardner's theory of multiple intelligences	Understand intelligence by examining test scores, information processing, biological and developmental research, the skills valued by different cultures, and exceptional people.	Biology provides the capacity for eight distinct "intelligences": linguistic, logical-mathematical, spatial, musical, body-kinesthetic, intrapersonal, interpersonal, and naturalistic.

that, as mentioned earlier, intelligence is not the same in all environments. Thus, rather than working on the improvement of tests designed to measure elements of intelligence that are universally shared, the ecological approach would recognize that what is "intelligent" in one situation isn't necessarily the same as what is "intelligent" in another. It will not be easy, however, to construct tests capable of measuring intelligence in a way that takes into account the environment in which a person operates.

LINKAGES

Which research designs are best for studying changes in mental abilities as people age? (a link to Research in Psychology)

The psychometric and information-processing approaches to intelligence have been quite influential in the study of the developmental changes in mental abilities from childhood onward. One major developmental study was focused more specifically on the changes in mental abilities that occur during adulthood.

FOCUS ON RESEARCH METHODS

Tracking Mental Abilities over the Life Span

■ What was the researchers' question?

The researchers began by asking what appears to be a relatively simple question: How do adults' various mental abilities change over time?

■ How did the researchers answer the question?

Answering this question is extremely difficult because findings about age-related changes in mental abilities depend to some extent on the methods that are used to observe them. None of the methods include true experiments because psychologists cannot randomly assign people to be a certain age and then give them mental tests. Thus, changes in mental abilities must be explored through a number of other research designs.

One of these, the *cross-sectional study,* compares data collected simultaneously from people of different ages. However, cross-sectional studies contain a major confounding variable: Because people are born at different times, they may have had very different educational, cultural, nutritional, and medical experiences. This confounding variable is referred to as a *cohort effect.* Suppose two cohorts, or age-groups, are given a test of their ability to imagine the rotation of an object in space. The cohort born around 1940 might not do as well as the one born around 1980, but the difference may be due less to declining spatial ability in the older people than to the younger group's greater experience with video games and other spatial tasks. In short, it may be differences in experience, and not just age, that account for differences in ability among older and younger people in a cross-sectional study.

Changes associated with age can also be examined through *longitudinal studies,* in which a group of people are repeatedly tested as they grow older. But longitudinal designs contain their own inherent problems. For one thing, fewer and fewer members of an age cohort can be tested over time as death, physical disability, relocation, and lack of interest reduce the sample size. Researchers call this problem the *mortality effect.* Further, those remaining are likely to be the healthiest in the group and may also have retained better mental powers than the dropouts (Botwinick, 1977). Hence, longitudinal studies may underestimate the degree to which abilities decline with age. Another confound can come from the *history effect.* In this situation, some event—such as a reduction in health care benefits for senior citizens—may have an effect on mental ability test scores that might be mistakenly attributed to age. Finally, longitudinal studies may be confounded by *testing effects,* meaning that participants may improve over time because of what they learn during repeated testing procedures. People who become "testwise" in this way might even begin to remember answers from one testing session to the next.

As part of the Seattle Longitudinal Study of cognitive aging, K. Warner Schaie (1993) developed a design that measures the impact of the confounds we have discussed and thus allows corrections to be made for them. In 1956, Schaie randomly sampled 5,000 people from the membership of a health maintenance organization, and invited some of them to volunteer for the study. These volunteers, who ranged in age from twenty to eighty, were given a battery of intelligence tests designed to measure Thurstone's primary mental abilities (PMA). The cross-sectional comparisons allowed by this first step were, of course, confounded by cohort effects. To control for those effects, the researchers retested the same participants seven years later, in 1963. Thus, the study's design—called a *cross-sequential with resampling design*—combined cross-sectional and longitudinal methods. By doing so, the size of the *difference* in PMA scores between, say, the twenty-year-olds and twenty-seven-year-olds tested in 1956 could be compared with the size of the *change* in PMA scores for these same people as they aged from twenty to twenty-seven and from twenty-seven to thirty-four. If the size of the longitudinal change were found to be about the same as the size of the cross-sectional difference, the latter could probably be attributed to aging, not to the era in which the participants were born.

What about the effect of confounds on the longitudinal changes themselves? To measure the impact of testing effects, the researchers randomly drew a new set of participants from the pool of 5,000. These people were of the same age range as the original sample, but they had not yet been tested. If the people from that original sample

The Voice of Experience

Even in old age, most people's crystallized intelligence remains intact. Their extensive storehouse of knowledge and experience makes older people a valuable resource for the young.

did better on their second PMA testing than the people of the same age who now took the PMA for the first time, a testing effect would be suggested. (In this case, the size of the difference would indicate the size of the testing effect.) To control for history effects, the researchers examined the scores of people who were the same age in different years. For example, they compared people who were thirty in 1956 with those who were thirty in 1963, people who were forty in 1956 with those who were forty in 1963, and so on. If PMA scores were the same for people of the same age no matter what year they were tested, it is unlikely that events specific to certain years would have influenced test results. The researchers tested participants six times between 1956 and 1991; on each occasion they retested some previous participants and tested others for the first time.

■ What did the researchers find?

The results of the Seattle Longitudinal Study, and other more limited cross-sectional and longitudinal studies, suggest a reasonably consistent conclusion: Unless people are impaired by Alzheimer's disease or other brain disorders, their mental abilities usually remain about the same from early adulthood until about sixty to seventy years of age. Some components of intelligence, but not others, then begin to fail.

Crystallized intelligence, which depends on retrieving information and facts about the world from long-term memory, may continue to grow well into old age. *Fluid intelligence,* which involves rapid and flexible manipulations of ideas and symbols, remains stable during adulthood and then declines in later life (Horn, 1982; Schaie, 1996). Among those over sixty-five or seventy, problems in several areas of information processing may impair problem-solving ability (Sullivan & Stankov, 1990). This decline shows up in the following areas:

1. *Working memory*   The ability to hold and organize material in working memory declines beyond age fifty or sixty, particularly when attention must be redirected (Parkin & Walter, 1991).

2. *Processing speed*   There is a general slowing of all mental processes (Lima, Hale, & Myerson, 1991; Salthouse, Babcock, & Shaw, 1991). Research has not yet isolated whether this slowing is due to reduced storage capacity, impaired processing efficiency, problems in coordinating simultaneous activities, or some combination of these factors (Babcock & Salthouse, 1990; Salthouse, 1990). For many tasks, this slowing does not create obstacles. But if a problem requires manipulating material in working memory, quick processing of information is critical (Rabbitt, 1977). To multiply two two-digit numbers mentally, for example, you must combine the subsums before they are forgotten.

3. *Organization*   Older people seem to be less likely to solve problems by adopting specific strategies, or mental shortcuts (Charness, 1987; Young, 1971). For example, to locate a wiring problem, you might perform a test that narrows down the regions where the problem might be. The tests carried out by older people tend to be more random and haphazard (Young, 1971). This result may occur partly because many older people are out of practice at solving such problems.

4. *Flexibility*   Older people tend to be less flexible in problem solving than their younger counterparts. They are less likely to consider alternative solutions (Salthouse & Prill, 1987), and they require more information before making a tentative decision (Rabbitt, 1977). Laboratory studies suggest that older people are also more likely than younger ones to choose conservative, risk-free options (Botwinick, 1966).

5. *Control of attention*   The ability to direct or control attention declines with age (Kramer, Larish, & Strayer, 1995; Wiegersma & Meertse, 1990). When required to switch their attention from one task to another, older participants typically perform less well than younger ones.

■ What do the results mean?

This study indicates that different kinds of mental abilities change in different ways throughout our lifetime. In general, there is a gradual, continual accumulation of knowledge about the world, some systematic changes in the limits of mental processes, and qualitative changes in the way those processes are carried out. This finding suggests that a general decline in mental abilities during adulthood is neither inevitable nor universal.

■ What do we still need to know?

An important question that the Schaie (1993) study leaves unanswered is why age-related changes in mental abilities occur. Some researchers suggest that these changes are largely due to a decline in the speed with which older people process information (Salthouse, 1993). The implication, if this interpretation is correct, is that older people can perform most of the mental tasks that younger ones can; it just takes them a little longer (Mayer & Sutton, 1996). Finally, it is vital that we learn why some people do not show declines in mental abilities—even when they reach their eighties. By understanding the biological and psychological factors responsible for these exceptions to the general rule, we might be able to reverse or delay some of the intellectual consequences of growing old.

DIVERSITY IN MENTAL ABILITIES

Although psychologists still don't agree on the details of what intelligence is, the study of IQ tests and intelligent behavior has yielded many insights into human mental abilities, and has highlighted the diversity of those abilities. In this section we briefly examine some of that diversity.

Creativity

In every area of human endeavor, there are people who demonstrate **creativity;** in other words, they can produce novel but effective solutions to challenges. Corporate

Creativity and Intelligence

Creative people may share certain personality traits, but being creative says relatively little about one's IQ.

executives and homemakers, scientists and artists, all may be more or less creative. Yet, like intelligence, creativity is difficult to define (Amabile, Goldfarb, & Brackfield, 1990). Does creativity include innovation based on previous ideas, or must it be utterly new? And must it be new to the world—as in Picasso's paintings—or only new to the creator—as when a child "makes up" the word *waterbird* without ever hearing it before? As with intelligence, psychologists have defined creativity not as a "thing" that people have or don't have but, rather, as a process or mental activity that can be inferred from performance on creativity tests.

To measure creativity, some psychologists have generated tests of **divergent thinking**, the ability to think along many paths to generate many solutions to a problem (Guilford & Hoepfner, 1971). The Consequences Test is an example. It contains items such as "Imagine all of the things that might possibly happen if all national and local laws were suddenly abolished" (Guilford, 1959). Divergent-thinking tests are scored by counting the number of *different* but plausible responses that a person can list for each item or by assessing the extent to which a person's answers are different from those given by most test takers.

Of course, the ability to come up with different answers or different ways of looking at a situation does not guarantee that anything creative will be produced. Some believe that creative behavior requires divergent thinking that is *appropriate* for a given situation or problem. To be productive rather than just weird, a creative person must be firmly anchored to reality, understand society's needs, and learn from the experience and knowledge of others (Sternberg & Lubert, 1992). Teresa Amabile has identified three kinds of cognitive and personality characteristics necessary for creativity (Amabile, 1989; Amabile, Hennessey, & Grossman, 1986).

1. Expertise in the field of endeavor, which is directly tied to what a person has learned. For example, a painter or composer must know the paints, techniques, or instruments available.

2. A set of creative skills, including persistence at problem solving, capacity for divergent thinking, ability to break problem-solving habits (mental sets), and willingness to take risks. Amabile believes that training can influence many of these skills (some of which are closely linked to the strategies for problem solving discussed in Chapter 8).

3. The motivation to pursue creative production for internal reasons, such as satisfaction, rather than for external reasons, such as prize money.

In fact, Amabile and her colleagues found that external rewards can deter creativity. They asked groups of children or adults to create artistic products such as collages or stories. Some were simply asked to work on the project. Others were informed that their project would be judged for its creativity and excellence and that rewards would be given or winners announced. Experts, who had no idea which products were created by which group, judged those from the "reward" group to be significantly less creative.

Is creativity inherited? To some extent, perhaps; but there is evidence that the environment influences creative behavior at least as much as it influences intelligence. For example, the correlation between the creativity scores of identical twins reared apart is lower than that between their IQ scores (Nichols, 1978).

Does creativity require a high IQ score? Not necessarily. Correlations between people's scores on IQ tests and on tests of creativity are only modest, between +.10 and +.30 (Barron & Harrington, 1981; Rushton, 1990). This result is not surprising, because creativity as psychologists measure it requires divergent thinking, and traditional IQ tests test **convergent thinking**—the ability to apply logic and knowledge in order to narrow down the number of possible solutions to a problem. Thus, as Sternberg points out, the questions on traditional IQ tests have only one or a small number of acceptable answers. The low correlation between IQ scores and creativity does not mean that the two are completely unrelated, however.

Understanding Mental Retardation

As the limitations and the potential of mentally retarded individuals are better understood, their opportunities and their role in society will continue to expand. The young retarded woman in the center of this picture is a successful, and obviously popular, teacher's assistant.

Unusual Mental Ability

Psychologists' understanding of mental abilities has been advanced by studying people whose mental abilities are unusual—the gifted, the mentally retarded, and those with learning disabilities.

Giftedness   Do all those with unusually high IQs become famous and successful in their chosen fields, or do their remarkable abilities mark them for social maladjustment? One of the best-known studies of the intellectually gifted was conducted by Louis Terman and his colleagues (Oden, 1968; Sears, 1977; Terman & Oden, 1947, 1959). This study began in 1921 with the identification of more than 1,500 children whose IQ scores were very high—most higher than 135 by age ten. Periodic interviews and tests over the next sixty years revealed that few if any became truly creative geniuses—such as world-famous inventors, authors, artists, or composers—but only 11 failed to graduate from high school, and more than two-thirds graduated from college. Ninety-seven earned Ph.Ds; 92, law degrees; and 57, medical degrees. In 1955 their median family income was well above the national average (Terman & Oden, 1959). In general, they were physically and mentally healthier than the nongifted and appear to have led happier, or at least more fortunate, lives (see the Focus on Research Methods section of Chapter 13). Thus, as mentioned earlier, high IQ scores tend to predict success in life, but an extremely high IQ does not guarantee special distinction. Indeed, research by Veronica Dark and Camilla Benbow (1993) suggests that gifted children are not fundamentally different kinds of people; they just have "more" of the same basic mental abilities seen in all children.

Mental Retardation   People whose score on an IQ test is less than about 70 *and* who fail to display the skill at daily living, communication, and other tasks that is expected of those their age have traditionally been described as mentally retarded, although they are now often referred to as "developmentally disabled" or "mentally challenged." People within this very broad category differ greatly in their mental abilities, and in their ability to function independently in daily life. Table 10.2 shows a classification that divides the range of low IQ scores into categories that reflect these differences.

Some cases of mental retardation have a clearly identifiable cause. The best-known example is *Down syndrome*, which is caused by an extra chromosome. Children with

TABLE 10.2

Categories of Mental Retardation

These categories are approximate. Many retarded persons at the upper end of the scale can be taught to handle tasks well beyond what their IQ score might suggest. Furthermore, IQ is not the only diagnostic criterion for retardation. Many people with IQs lower than 70 can function adequately in their everyday environment and hence would not be classified as mentally retarded.

Level of Retardation	IQ Scores	Characteristics
Mild	50–70	A majority of all the mentally retarded. Usually show no physical symptoms of abnormality. Individuals with higher IQs can marry, maintain a family, and work in unskilled jobs. Abstract reasoning is difficult for those with the lower IQs of this category. Capable of some academic learning to a sixth-grade level.
Moderate	35–49	Often lack physical coordination. Can be trained to take care of themselves and to acquire some reading and writing skills. Abilities of a 4- to 7-year-old. Capable of living outside an institution with their families.
Severe	20–34	Only a few can benefit from any schooling. Can communicate vocally after extensive training. Most require constant supervision.
Profound	Below 20	Mental age less than 3. Very limited communication. Require constant supervision. Can learn to walk, utter a few simple phrases, and feed themselves.

LINKAGES

Is mental retardation mainly a matter of poor memory? (a link to Memory)

Down syndrome typically have IQ scores in the 40 to 55 range. Intelligence may also be limited by environmental conditions or traumas such as meningitis or encephalitis contracted during infancy, birth traumas resulting from an oversupply or undersupply of oxygen, and excessive use of drugs or alcohol by the mother during pregnancy.

In most cases, however, no genetic or environmental cause of retardation is directly observed. These are usually cases of mild retardation and are known as **familial retardation** for two reasons: Most people in this group (1) come from families of lower socioeconomic status and (2) are more likely than those suffering from a genetic defect to have a relative who is also retarded (Plomin, 1989). These facts have led psychologists to conclude that familial retardation results from a complex interaction between heredity and environment.

Exactly *how* are the cognitive skills of mentally retarded people deficient? Such people are just as proficient as others at recognizing simple stimuli, and their rate of forgetting information from working memory is no more rapid (Belmont & Butterfield, 1971). But mildly retarded people do differ from other people in three important ways (Campione, Brown, & Ferrara, 1982):

1. They perform certain mental operations more slowly, such as retrieving information from long-term memory. When asked to repeat something they have learned, they are not as quick as a person of normal intelligence.

2. They simply know fewer facts about the world. It is likely that this deficiency is a consequence of a third problem.

3. They are not very good at using particular mental strategies that may be important in learning and problem solving. For example, they do not spontaneously rehearse material that must be held in working memory.

What are the reasons for these deficiencies in using strategies? The differences between normal and retarded children in some ways resemble the differences between older and younger children discussed in Chapter 12. Both younger children and retarded children show deficiencies in ==*metamemory*—the knowledge of how their memory works==. More generally, retarded children are deficient in **metacognition:** the knowledge of what strategies to apply, when to apply them, and how to deploy them in new situations so that new specific knowledge can be gained and different problems mastered (Ferretti & Butterfield, 1989).

It is their deficiencies in metacognition that most limit the intellectual performance of the mildly retarded. If retarded children are simply taught a strategy, they are not likely to use it again on their own or to transfer the strategy to a different task. Because of this characteristic, it is important to teach retarded children to evaluate the appropriateness of strategies (Wong, 1986) and to monitor the success of their strategies. Finally, like other children, retarded children should be shown that effort, combined with effective strategies, pays off (Borkowski, Weyhing, & Turner, 1986).

Despite such difficulties, the intellectual abilities of mentally retarded people can be raised. For example, one program emphasized positive parent-child communications and began when the children were as young as thirty months old. It helped children with Down syndrome to master reading skills at a second-grade level, providing the foundation for further achievement (Rynders & Horrobin, 1980; Turkington, 1987).

Designing effective programs for retarded children is complicated because the way people learn depends not just on cognitive skills but also on social and emotional factors. Much debate has focused on *mainstreaming,* the policy of teaching handicapped children, including those who are retarded, in regular classrooms with those who are not handicapped. Is mainstreaming good for retarded children? A number of studies of the cognitive and social skills of students who have been mainstreamed and those who were separated show few significant differences overall, although it appears that students at higher ability levels may gain more from being mainstreamed than their less mentally able peers (Cole et al., 1991).

Learning Disabilities

People who show a significant discrepancy between their measured intelligence and their academic performance are said to have a *learning disability.* Learning disabilities are often seen in people with average or above-average IQ. For example, the problems with reading, writing, and math that Leonardo da Vinci and Thomas Edison had as children may have been due to such a disability; they certainly did not reflect low IQ!

There are several kinds of learning disabilities (Myers & Hammill, 1990). People with *dyslexia* find it difficult to understand the meaning of what they read because the letters may appear distorted or jumbled; they may also have difficulty in sounding out and identifying written words. *Dysphasia* is difficulty with understanding spoken words or with recalling the words one needs for effective speech. *Dysgraphia*—problems with writing—appears as an inability to form letters, or as the omission or reordering of words and parts of words in one's writing. The least common learning disability, *dyscalculia,* is a difficulty with arithmetic that reflects not poor mathematical ability but, rather, an impairment in the understanding of quantity and/or in the comprehension of basic arithmetic principles and operations, such as addition and subtraction.

The National Joint Committee on Learning Disabilities (1994) suggests that these disorders are caused by dysfunctions in the brain, but specific neurological causes have not yet been found. Accordingly, most researchers describe learning disabilities in terms of dysfunctional information processing (Shaw et al., 1995). Diagnosis of a learning disability includes several steps, the first of which is to look for significant weaknesses in a person's listening, speaking, reading, writing, reasoning, or arithmetic skills (Brinckerhoff, Shaw, & McGuire, 1993). The level of each of these abilities is compared with that predicted by the person's IQ score. Tests for brain damage are also given. To help rule out alternative explanations of poor academic performance, the person's hearing, vision, and other sensory systems are tested and factors such as poverty, family conflicts, and inadequate instruction are reviewed. Finally, alternative diagnoses such as attention deficit disorder (see Chapter 15) are eliminated.

An Inventive Genius

When, as in the case of inventor Thomas Edison, students' academic performance falls short of what intelligence tests say they are capable of, a learning disability may be present. However, poor study skills, lack of motivation, and even the need for eyeglasses are among the many factors other than learning disabilities that can create a discrepancy between IQ scores and academic achievement. Accordingly, accurately diagnosing learning disability is not an easy task.

Edison at Work in Chemical Dept
Orange Lab.

LINKAGES

As noted in Chapter 1, all of psychology's many subfields are related to one another. Our discussion of test anxiety illustrates just one way in which the topic of this chapter, mental abilities, is linked to the subfield of motivation and emotion (Chapter 11). The Linkages diagram shows ties to two other subfields as well, and there are many more ties throughout the book. Looking for linkages among subfields will help you see how they all fit together and better appreciate the big picture that is psychology.

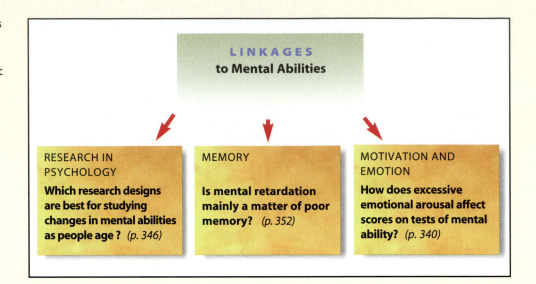

LINKAGES
to Mental Abilities

RESEARCH IN PSYCHOLOGY
Which research designs are best for studying changes in mental abilities as people age ? *(p. 346)*

MEMORY
Is mental retardation mainly a matter of poor memory? *(p. 352)*

MOTIVATION AND EMOTION
How does excessive emotional arousal affect scores on tests of mental ability? *(p. 340)*

SUMMARY

Mental ability refers to the capacity to perform the higher mental processes of reasoning, remembering, understanding, problem solving, and decision making.

TESTING FOR INTELLIGENCE

Psychologists have not reached a consensus on how best to define *intelligence.* Working definitions describe intelligence in terms of reasoning, problem solving, and dealing with the environment.

A Brief History of Intelligence Tests

Binet's pioneering test of intelligence included questions that required reasoning and problem solving of varying levels of difficulty, graded by age. Terman developed a revision of Binet's test that became known as the *Stanford-Binet;* it included items designed to assess the intelligence of adults as well as children and became the model for *IQ tests.* Early IQ tests in the United States required not just mental ability but also knowledge of U.S. culture. Wechsler's tests remedied some of the deficiencies of the earlier IQ tests. Made up of subtests, some of which have little verbal content, these tests allowed testers to generate scores for different aspects of mental ability.

Intelligence Tests Today

The Stanford-Binet and Wechsler tests are the most popular individually administered intelligence tests. Both include subtests and provide scores for parts of the test as well as an overall score. For example, Wechsler subtests that depend heavily on vocabulary are combined into a *verbal scale;* the rest are combined into a *perfor-*

mance scale. Currently, a person's *intelligence quotient,* or *IQ score,* reflects how far that person's performance on the test deviates from the average performance by people in his or her age group. An average performance is assigned an IQ score of 100.

Aptitude and Achievement Tests

Aptitude tests are intended to measure a person's potential to learn new skills; *achievement tests* are intended to measure what a person has already learned. Both kinds of tests are used by schools and companies in situations involving placement or admission of students, or selection of new employees.

MEASURING THE QUALITY OF TESTS

Tests have three key advantages over other techniques of evaluation. They are standardized, so that the performances of different people can be compared; they produce scores that can be compared with *norms;* and they are economical and efficient.

Reliability

A good test must be *reliable,* which means that the results for each person are consistent, or stable. Reliability can be measured by test-retest, alternate-form, and split-half methods.

Validity

A test is said to be *valid* if it measures what it is supposed to measure. A test's validity for a particular purpose can be evaluated by measuring content validity, construct validity, or criterion validity; the last entails measurement of the correlation between the test score and some criterion. If the criterion is a measure of the performance that the test is supposed to predict, criterion validity is called predictive validity.

EVALUATING IQ TESTS

The Reliability and Validity of IQ Tests

IQ tests are reasonably reliable, and they do a good job of predicting academic success. However, IQ tests assess only some of the abilities that might be considered aspects of intelligence, and they may favor those most familiar with middle-class culture. Nonetheless, this familiarity is important for academic and occupational success.

IQ Scores as a Measure of Innate Ability

Both heredity and the environment influence IQ scores, and their effects interact. The influence of heredity is shown by the high correlation between IQ scores of identical twins raised in separate households and by the similarity in the IQ scores of children adopted at birth and their biological parents. The influence of the environment is revealed by the higher correlation of IQ between siblings who share the same environment than by those who do not and by the effects of environmental changes such as adoption.

Group Differences in IQ Scores

Different socioeconomic and ethnic groups have different mean IQ scores. These differences appear to be due to numerous factors, including differences in motivation, family support, educational opportunity, and other environmental conditions.

Conditions That Can Raise IQ Scores

An enriched environment sometimes raises IQ scores. Initial large gains in cognitive performance that result from interventions like Project Head Start may decline over time, but the programs may improve children's attitude toward school.

IQ Scores in the Classroom

Like any label, an IQ score can generate expectations that affect both how other people respond to a person and how that person behaves. Children labeled with low IQ scores may be offered fewer or lower-quality educational opportunities. On the other hand, IQ scores may help educators to identify a student's strengths and weaknesses and to offer the curriculum that will best serve that student.

UNDERSTANDING INTELLIGENCE

The Psychometric Approach

The *psychometric approach* attempts to analyze the structure of intelligence by examining correlations between tests of mental ability. Because scores on almost all tests of mental abilities are

positively correlated, Spearman concluded that such tests measure a general factor of mental ability, called *g*, as well as more specific factors called *s*. As a result of *factor analysis,* other researchers have concluded that intelligence is not a single general ability but a collection of abilities and subskills needed to succeed on any test of intelligence. Cattell distinguished between *fluid intelligence,* the basic power of reasoning and problem solving, and *crystallized intelligence,* the specific knowledge gained as a result of applying fluid intelligence.

The Information-Processing Approach

The *information-processing* approach to intelligence focuses on the process of intelligent behavior. Only small positive correlations have been found between IQ scores and measures of the flexibility and capacity of attention, and between IQ scores and measures of the speed of information processing.

The Triarchic Theory of Intelligence

According to Sternberg's *triarchic theory of intelligence,* there are three different types of intelligence: analytic, creative, and practical. IQ tests typically focus on analytic intelligence, but recent research has suggested ways to assess practical and creative intelligence.

Multiple Intelligences

Gardner's approach to intelligence suggests that biology equips us with the capacities for *multiple intelligences* that can function with some independence—specifically, linguistic, logical-mathematical, spatial, musical, body-kinesthetic, intrapersonal, interpersonal, and naturalistic intelligences.

The Ecological Approach

The ecological approach to intelligence highlights the role of the environment in shaping intellectual abilities that are functional for those in that environment. These abilities may differ somewhat from one culture to another.

DIVERSITY IN MENTAL ABILITIES

Creativity

Tests of *divergent thinking* are used to measure differences in *creativity.* In contrast, IQ tests require *convergent thinking.* Although creativity and IQ scores are not highly correlated, creative behavior requires a certain amount of intelligence, along with expertise in a creative field, skills at problem solving and divergent thinking, and motivation to pursue a creative endeavor for its own sake.

Unusual Mental Ability

Knowledge about mental abilities has been expanded by research on giftedness, mental retardation, and learning disabilities. People with very high IQ scores tend to be successful in life, but are not necessarily geniuses. People are considered retarded if their IQ score is below about 70 and if their communication and daily living skills are less than expected of people their age. In *familial retardation,* no genetic or environmental causes are evident. Compared to those of normal intelligence, retarded people process information more slowly, know fewer facts, and are deficient at *metacognition*—that is, at knowing and using strategies.

Mentally retarded people can be taught strategies, but they must also be taught how and when to use those strategies. People who show a significant discrepancy between their measured intelligence and their academic performance may have a learning disability. Learning disabilities can take several forms and must be carefully diagnosed.

KEY TERMS

achievement tests (327)
aptitude tests (327)
convergent thinking (350)
creativity (349)
crystallized intelligence (342)
divergent thinking (350)
factor analysis (342)

familial retardation (352)
fluid intelligence (342)
g (general intelligence) (342)
information-processing approach (342)
intelligence (323)
intelligence quotient (326)
IQ score (326)

IQ test (325)
mental ability (322)
metacognition (353)
multiple intelligences (345)
norms (328)
performance scale (326)
psychometric approach (341)
reliability (328)

s (special intelligence) (342)
Stanford-Binet (324)
test (328)
triarchic theory of intelligence (343)
validity (329)
verbal scale (326)

11

Motivation and Emotion

I n January 1994, despite temperatures reaching thirty degrees below zero, Brian Carr caught 155 fish, enough to win an annual ice-fishing contest in upstate New York. His first-place finish netted him the grand prize of eight dollars (Shepherd, 1994). Why would Mr. Carr and his competitors go fishing in such harsh conditions for such an apparently small reward? Why, for that matter, do any of us do what we do? Why do we help others or ignore them, overeat or diet, haunt art museums or sleazy bars, attend college or drop out of high school?

These are questions about **motivation,** the factors that influence the initiation, direction, intensity, and persistence of behavior (Evans, 1989). Psychologists who study motivation ask questions such as: What prompts a person to start looking for food, to register for dance lessons, or to act in any other particular way? What determines whether a person chooses to go mountain climbing or to stay home and read? What makes some people go all out to reach a goal while others exert only halfhearted efforts and quit at the first obstacle?

Part of the motivation for behavior is to feel certain emotions, such as the joy of scaling a lofty peak or of becoming a parent. Motivation also affects emotion, as when hunger makes you more likely to become angry if people annoy you. In short, motivation and emotion are closely intertwined.

The first part of this chapter concerns motivation. We begin with some general theories of motivation and then discuss three specific motives—hunger, sexual desire, and the need for achievement. Next, we examine the nature of human emotion as well as some major theories of how and why certain emotions are experienced. The chapter concludes with a discussion of how humans communicate their emotions to one another.

CONCEPTS AND THEORIES OF MOTIVATION

The concept of motivation helps psychologists accomplish what Albert Einstein once called the whole purpose of science: to discover unity in diversity. Suppose that a man works two jobs, refuses party invitations, wears old clothes, drives a beat-up car, eats food others leave behind at lunch, never gives to charity, and keeps his furnace set at sixty degrees all winter. Why does he do these things? One could propose a separate reason for each of these behaviors: Perhaps he likes to work hard, hates parties, fears new clothes and new cars, enjoys other people's leftovers, has no concern for the poor, and likes cold air. Alternatively, one could suggest a **motive,** a reason or purpose that provides a single explanation for this man's diverse and apparently unrelated behaviors. That unifying motive might be the man's desire to save as much money as possible.

This example illustrates the fact that motivation cannot be directly observed; its presence is inferred from what we *can* observe. Psychologists think of motivation, whether it be hunger or thirst or love or greed, as an *intervening variable*—an entity that is used to explain the relationships between environmental stimuli and behavioral responses. The three different responses shown in Figure 11.1, for example, can be understood as guided by a single unifying motive: thirst. Figure 11.1 also shows that motivation can help explain why different stimuli can lead to the same response, and why the same stimulus can evoke different responses.

Motivation also helps explain why behavior varies over time. For example, many people cannot bring themselves to lose weight, quit smoking, or exercise until they experience a heart attack or other serious health problem. Then, in accordance with the health-belief models discussed in Chapter 13, these people may be motivated to eat a low-fat diet, give up tobacco, and exercise regularly. In other words, particular stimuli—including ice cream, cigarettes, and health clubs—elicit different responses at different times.

Sources of Motivation

The number of possible motives for human behavior seems endless. People are motivated to satisfy a need for food and water, of course, but they have many other needs

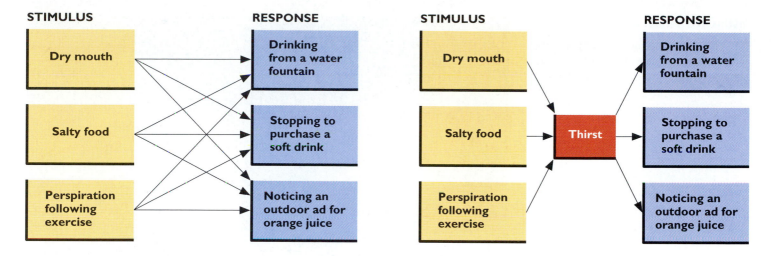

FIGURE 11.1

Motives as Intervening Variables

Motives can act as explanatory links between apparently unrelated stimuli and responses. In this example, seeing thirst as the common motive provides an explanation of why each stimulus elicits the responses shown.

as well. Some people seek the pleasures of creativity, whereas many others are motivated by money or praise or power. And as social creatures, people are also influenced by motives to form emotional attachments to others, to become parents, and to join groups.

These and many other sources of human motivation fall into four general, somewhat overlapping categories. First, human behavior is motivated by basic *biological factors*, particularly the need for food, water, sex, and temperature regulation (Tinbergen, 1989). *Emotional factors* are a second source of motivation (Izard, 1993). Panic, fear, anger, love, and hatred can be crucial to behavior ranging from selfless giving to brutal murder. Third, *cognitive factors* can motivate human behavior (Weiner, 1993). People often behave in a certain way because of their perceptions of the world, their beliefs about what they can do, and their expectations about how others will respond. Fourth, motivation may stem from *social factors*, from reactions to parents, teachers, siblings, friends, television, and other sociocultural forces. The combined influence of such social factors in motivation has a profound effect on almost all human behavior (Baumeister & Leary, 1995).

How do these sources of motivation act on behavior? Does one type dominate? Psychologists have included these factors in various theories of human motivation. No one theory gives a complete explanation of all aspects of motivation, but each of the four most prominent theories—instinct theory, drive reduction theory, arousal theory, and incentive theory—helps tell part of the story.

Instinct Theory and Its Descendants

Early in this century instinct theory was favored by many psychologists as an explanation of motivation. **Instincts** are automatic, involuntary, and unlearned behavior patterns consistently "released" by particular stimuli (Tinbergen, 1989). For example, the male three-spined stickleback fish attacks aggressively when it sees the red underbelly of another male. Such behaviors are often called *fixed-action patterns* because they are unlearned, genetically coded responses to specific "releaser" stimuli.

William McDougall (1908) argued that human behavior, too, is motivated by instincts. He began by listing eighteen human instincts, including self-assertion, reproduction, pugnacity, and gregariousness. Within a few years, McDougall and other theorists had named more than 10,000 instincts, prompting one critic to suggest that his colleagues had "an instinct to produce instincts" (Bernard, 1924). Instincts had become meaningless labels that described behavior without explaining it. Saying that someone gambles because of a gambling instinct, golfs because of a golfing instinct, and works because of a work instinct explains nothing.

Despite the shortcomings of early instinct theories, psychologists have continued to explore the possibility that at least some aspects of human motivation are innate. Their

Instinctive Behavior

The male greater frigate bird displays his red throat as part of a mating ritual. This behavior is instinctive; it does not have to be learned.

interest has been stimulated partly by research showing that a number of human behaviors are present at birth. Among these are sucking and other reflexes, as well as certain facial expressions such as smiling (described later in this chapter). There is also the fact that people do not have to learn to be hungry or thirsty or to want to stay warm, and—as discussed in the chapters on learning and psychological disorders—that they appear to be biologically prepared to fear snakes and other potentially dangerous stimuli. Psychologists who take the evolutionary approach suggest that all such behaviors have evolved because they were adaptive for promoting the survival of the human species. These theorists argue that many other aspects of human behavior, including helping, aggression, and mate selection, are also motivated by inborn factors—specifically, by the desire to pass on our own genes to the next generation.

The evolutionary approach suggests, for example, that our choice of a marriage partner has a biological basis; love and marriage are seen as the result of inborn desires to create and nurture offspring so that our genes will survive in our children. According to this view, biological limits on the number of offspring women can produce make them more psychologically invested than men in the survival and development of their children (Townsend, Kline, & Wasserman, 1995). The evolutionary approach further suggests that, in selecting an opposite-sex mate, females are likely to focus on a male's ability to acquire resources, as signified by maturity, ambition, and earning power (adequate resources increase the chances that an infant will survive), whereas males are likely to place great emphasis on a female's reproductive capacity, as signified by youth, attractiveness, and good health.

These controversial speculations have received some support. For instance, according to a survey of over 10,000 men and women in thirty-three countries on six continents and five isolated islands, males generally preferred youth and good health in prospective female mates, and females generally preferred males who were mature and wealthy (Kenrick, 1994). One example of this sex difference is illustrated in Figure 11.2, which shows the age preferences of men and women who advertised for dates in the "personals" sections of newspapers around the United States. In general, men were interested in women younger than themselves, but women were interested in older men (Kenrick et al., 1995).

Critics argue that such preferences could stem from cultural traditions, not genetic programming. Indeed, among the Zulu of South Africa, where women are expected to build houses, carry water, and perform other physically demanding tasks, men tend to

FIGURE 11.2

Age Preferences Reflected in Personal Advertisements

An analysis of 486 personal advertisements placed in newspapers around the United States showed a sex difference in age preferences: As men got older their preference for younger women increased, whereas women, regardless of age, preferred men who were about their own age or older.

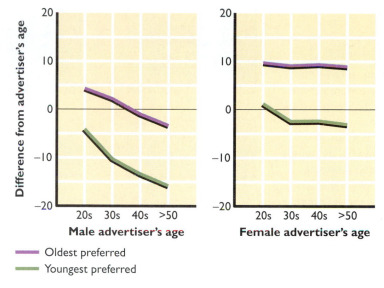

— Oldest preferred
— Youngest preferred

Source: Kenrick et al., 1995, Figure 1.

Evolution at Work?

In this scene from the 1998 film *A Perfect Murder*, Michael Douglas, 55, and Gwyneth Paltrow, 26, portray the worldwide tendency for older men to prefer younger women, and vice versa. This tendency has been interpreted as evidence supporting an evolutionary explanation of mate selection, but skeptics see social and economic forces at work in establishing these preference patterns.

value maturity and ambition in a mate more than women do (Buss, 1989). The fact that women have been systematically denied economic and political power in many cultures may also account for their tendency to rely on the security and economic power provided by men (Silverstein, 1996).

Can the evolutionary approach explain altruistic behavior—the willingness of people to help others in the absence of any observable reward? At first glance, this approach does not seem to work, because people help not only their relatives (who share at least some of their genes) but also total strangers, apparently expecting nothing in return. Evolutionary psychologists have recently hypothesized, however, that people *do* gain something, regardless of whom they help. Specifically, they earn a reputation for being helpful, which may eventually result in their receiving help from others. Mathematical models of such interactions likewise suggest that a person who helps and cooperates ultimately prospers, and is thus more likely to survive to pass on genes to the next generation. The principle at work here is called *indirect reciprocity* (Nowak & Sigmund, 1998).

Drive Reduction Theory

Like instinct theory, drive reduction theory emphasizes biological factors, but it is based on the concept of homeostasis. **Homeostasis** is the tendency for organisms to keep physiological systems at a steady level, or *equilibrium*, by constantly making adjustments in response to change. We described a version of this concept in Chapter 3 when we discussed feedback loops that keep hormones at desirable levels.

According to **drive reduction theory,** an imbalance in homeostasis creates a **need**—a biological requirement for well-being. The brain responds to such needs, in the service of homeostasis, by creating a psychological state called a **drive**—a feeling of arousal that prompts an organism to take action, restore the balance, and, as a result, reduce the drive (Hull, 1943). For example, if you have had no water for some time, the chemical balance of your body fluids is disturbed, creating a biological need for water. One consequence of this need is a drive—thirst—that motivates you to find and drink water. After you drink, the need for water is met, so the drive to drink is reduced. In other words, drives push people to satisfy needs, thus reducing the drives as well as the arousal they create (see Figure 11.3).

Drive reduction theory recognizes the influence of learning on motivation by distinguishing between primary and secondary drives. **Primary drives** stem from biological needs, such as the need for food or water. (Food, water, and other things that satisfy primary drives are called *primary reinforcers;* see Chapter 6, on learning.) As already noted, people do not have to learn either these basic biological needs or the primary

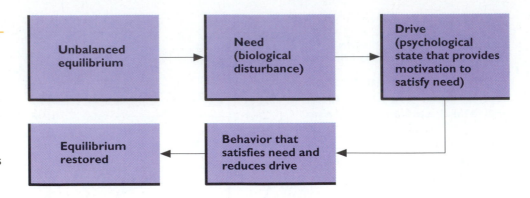

FIGURE 11.3

Drive Reduction Theory and Homeostasis

Homeostatic mechanisms, such as the regulation of body temperature or food and water intake, are often compared to thermostats. If the temperature in a house drops below the thermostat setting, the furnace comes on and brings the temperature up to that pre-set level, achieving homeostasis. When the temperature reaches the pre-set point, the furnace shuts off.

LINKAGES

Optimal Arousal and Personality

People who enjoy high levels of arousal are likely to smoke, drink alcohol, engage in frequent sexual activity, listen to loud music, eat spicy foods, and do things that are novel and risky (Farley, 1986; Zuckerman, 1979). Those with lower optimal arousal tend to behave in ways that bring less intense stimulation and to take fewer risks. Most of the differences in optimal arousal have a strong biological basis and, as discussed in Chapter 14, may help shape broader differences in personality, such as introversion-extraversion.

drives to satisfy them (Hull, 1951). However, we do learn other drives, called **secondary drives.** Once acquired, a secondary drive motivates us to act *as if* we have an unmet basic need. For example, as people learn to associate having money with the satisfaction of primary drives for food, shelter, and so on, having money may become a secondary drive. Having too little money thus motivates many behaviors—from hard work to thievery—to obtain more funds.

By recognizing secondary as well as primary drives, drive reduction theory can account for a wider range of behaviors than instinct theory. But humans and animals often go to extreme lengths to do things that do not obviously reduce *any* drive. Consider curiosity. Animals frequently explore and manipulate their surroundings, even though such activities do not lead to drive reduction. Animals also exert great effort simply to enter a new environment, especially if it is complex and full of novel objects (Bolles, 1975; Loewenstein, 1994). People are no less curious. Most cannot resist checking out anything new or unusual. They go to the new mall, read the newspaper, and travel the world just to see what there is to see.

Arousal Theory

People also go out of their way to ride roller coasters, skydive, eat chili peppers, and do countless other things that, like curiosity-motivated behaviors, do not reduce any known drive (Rozin & Shenker, 1989). In fact, these behaviors *increase* people's levels of activation, or arousal. The realization that people sometimes try to decrease arousal and sometimes try to increase it has led theorists to argue that motivation is tied to the regulation of arousal.

Most of these theorists think of arousal as a general level of activation reflected in the state of several physiological systems (Brehm & Self, 1989). Thus, one's level of arousal can be measured by the brain's electrical activity, by heart action, or by muscle tension (Deschaumes et al., 1991). Normally, arousal is lowest during deep, quiet sleep and highest during panic or great excitement. Many factors increase arousal, including hunger, thirst, intense stimuli, unexpected events, and stimulants (e.g., amphetamines). Interestingly, people who tend to actively seek novelty also tend to be at increased risk for abusing stimulants. This phenomenon may be related to individual differences in the brain's dopamine system, which is activated by novelty and by most drugs of abuse (Bardo, Donohew, & Harrington, 1996). Through an especially creative application of brain imaging techniques, researchers have found that the dopamine system is activated even when a person plays a video game (Koepp et al., 1998).

People perform best, and may feel best, when arousal is moderate (Teigen, 1994). Figure 11.4 illustrates the general relationship between arousal and performance. Overarousal can be harmful to performance; it can also disrupt activities ranging from intellectual tasks to athletic competition (Penner & Craiger, 1992; Wright et al., 1995).

Arousal theories of motivation suggest that people are motivated to behave in ways that keep them at their own *optimal level* of arousal (Hebb, 1955). This optimal level is

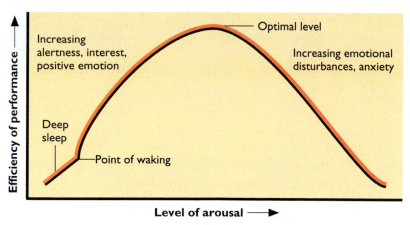

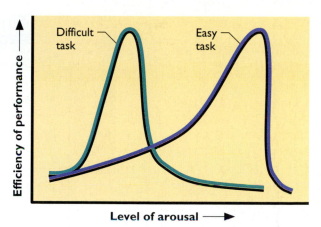

(A) GENERAL RELATIONSHIP BETWEEN PERFORMANCE AND AROUSAL LEVEL

(B) RELATIONSHIP BETWEEN PERFORMANCE AND AROUSAL LEVEL ON DIFFICULT VS. EASY TASKS

FIGURE 11.4

The Arousal-Performance Relationship

Notice in part (A) that performance is poorest when arousal is very low *or* very high and best when arousal is at some intermediate level. When you are either nearly asleep or overly excited, for example, it may be difficult to think clearly or to be physically coordinated. In general, optimal performance comes at a lower level of arousal on difficult or complex tasks and at a higher level of arousal on easy tasks, as shown in part (B). Thus, even a relatively small amount of overarousal can cause students to perform far below their potential on difficult tests (Sarason, 1984). Because animal research early in this century by Robert Yerkes and his colleagues provided supportive evidence, this arousal-performance relationship is sometimes referred to as the Yerkes-Dodson law even though Yerkes never actually discussed performance as a function of arousal (Teigen, 1994).

higher for some people than for others (Zuckerman, 1984). Generally, however, people try to increase arousal when it is too low and decrease it when it is too high. They seek excitement when bored and relaxation when overaroused. After classes and studying, for example, you may want to see an exciting movie. But if your day was spent playing baseball, fiercely debating a political issue, and helping a friend move, an evening of quiet relaxation may seem ideal.

Incentive Theory

Instinct, drive, and arousal theories of motivation all focus on internal processes that prompt people to behave in certain ways. By contrast, **incentive theory** emphasizes the role of environmental stimuli that can motivate behavior by pulling people toward them or pushing people away from them. According to this view, people act to obtain positive incentives and avoid negative incentives. Differences in behavior from one person to another, or from one situation to another, can be traced to the incentives available and the value a person places on them at the time. So if you expect a behavior (such as buying a lottery ticket) to lead to a valued outcome (winning money), you will want to engage in that behavior. The value of an incentive is influenced by biological as well as cognitive factors. For example, food is a more motivating incentive when you are hungry than when you are full (Balleine & Dickinson, 1994).

Contemporary theorists distinguish between two incentive-related systems: wanting and liking. *Wanting* is the process of being attracted to stimuli, whereas *liking* is the immediate evaluation of how pleasurable a stimulus is (Berridge, 1999). Studies with animals have shown that these two systems involve separate parts of the brain, that the wanting system guides behavior to a greater extent than does the liking system, and that the operation of the wanting system varies according to whether an individual has been deprived or not (Nader, Bechara, & Van der Kooy, 1997). For example, different brain regions would affect the motivation to consume a piece of apple pie, depending on whether it is served as an appetizer or as a dessert.

The theoretical approaches we have outlined are complementary (see "In Review: Theories of Motivation" on page 364). Each emphasizes different sources of motivation, and each has helped to guide research into motivated behaviors such as eating, sex, and work-related activities, which we consider in the sections that follow.

HUNGER AND EATING

Hunger is deceptively simple; you get hungry when you do not eat. Much as a car needs gas, you need fuel from food. Is there a bodily mechanism that, like a car's gas gauge, signals the need for fuel? What causes hunger? What determines which foods you eat,

in review

THEORIES OF MOTIVATION	
Theory	**Main Points**
Instinct	Innate biological instincts guide behavior.
Drive reduction	Behavior is guided by biological needs and learned ways of reducing drives arising from those needs.
Arousal	People seek to maintain an optimal level of physiological arousal, which differs from person to person. Maximum performance occurs at optimal arousal levels.
Incentive	Behavior is guided by the lure of rewards and the threat of punishment. Cognitive factors influence expectations of the value of various rewards and the likelihood of attaining them.

and how do you know when to stop? The answers to these questions involve not only interactions between the brain and the rest of the body but also learning, social, and environmental factors (Hill & Peters, 1998).

Biological Signals for Hunger and Satiety

A variety of mechanisms underlie **hunger,** the general state of wanting to eat, and **satiety** (pronounced "se-TY-a-tee"), the general state of no longer wanting to eat. In order to maintain body weight, we must have ways to regulate food intake over the short term (a question of how often we eat, and when we stop eating a given meal) and to regulate the body's stored energy reserves (fat) over the long term.

Signals from the Stomach   The stomach would seem to be a logical source of signals for hunger and satiety. After all, people say they feel "hunger pangs" from an "empty" stomach, and they complain of a "full stomach" after overeating. True, the stomach does contract during hunger pangs, and increased pressure within the stomach can reduce appetite (Cannon & Washburn, 1912; Houpt, 1994). But people who have lost their stomachs due to illness still get hungry when they do not eat and still eat normal amounts of food (Janowitz, 1967). Thus, stomach cues can affect eating, but they do not play a major role in the normal control of eating.

LINKAGES

How does your brain know when you are hungry? (a link to Biological Aspects of Psychology)

Signals from the Blood   The most important signals about the body's fuel level and nutrient needs are sent to the brain from the blood. The brain's ability to "read" blood-borne signals about the body's nutritional needs was shown years ago when researchers deprived rats of food for a long period and then injected them with blood from rats that had just eaten. When offered food, the injected rats ate little or nothing (Davis et al., 1969); something in the injected blood of the well-fed animals apparently signaled the hungry rats' brains that there was no need to eat. What sent that satiety signal? Subsequent research has shown that the brain constantly monitors both the level of food *nutrients* absorbed into the bloodstream from the stomach and the level of *hormones* released into the blood in response to those nutrients and from stored fat.

Some blood-borne signals affect short-term intake—telling us when to start and stop eating a meal—whereas others reflect and regulate the body's long-term supply of fat. The short-term signals are called *satiety factors.* One such signal comes from *cholecystokinin (CCK),* which regulates meal size (Woods et al., 1998). During a meal, cholecystokinin is released as a hormone in the gut and as a neurotransmitter in the brain (Crawley & Corwin, 1994). The activation of CCK in the brain causes animals to stop eating (Parrott, 1994), and even a well-fed animal will start to eat if receptors in the brain for CCK are blocked (Brenner & Ritter, 1995). CCK is also found in humans: Moderate doses cause them to eat less of a given meal, whereas high doses can cause nausea—thus possibly explaining why people sometimes feel sick after overeating. However, research with animals suggests that simply increasing production of CCK would probably not result in weight loss because the animals made up for smaller meals by eating more often. This phenomenon reflects the fact that the brain monitors the long-term storage of fat as well as the short-term status of nutrients.

The nutrients that the brain monitors include *glucose,* the main form of sugar used by body cells. Early on, researchers noted that when the level of blood glucose drops, eating increases sharply (e.g., Mogenson, 1976). More recent work has shown that glucose acts indirectly by affecting certain chemical messengers. For example, when glucose levels rise, the pancreas releases *insulin,* a hormone that most body cells need in order to use the glucose they receive. Insulin may enhance the brain's satiety response to CCK. In one study, animals receiving CCK preceded by insulin infusions into the brain ate less food and gained less weight than animals getting either CCK or insulin alone (Riedy et al., 1995). Insulin itself may also provide a satiety signal; rats injected with insulin eat less than rats injected with a plain saline solution (Vanderweele, 1994).

The long-term regulation of fat stores involves a hormone called *leptin* (from the Greek word *leptos,* meaning "thin"). Leptin is produced by fat cells in response to increased storage of fat; it circulates through the bloodstream and provides information about fat supplies in the body (Carlson, 1998). When leptin levels are high, hunger decreases. Our knowledge of leptin's role in hunger comes from studies of rodents known as *ob* (or *ob/ob) mice,* which exhibit an inherited form of obesity (e.g., Zhang et al., 1994). It turns out that ob mice have a genetic defect that makes them unable to produce leptin, which is the primary reason they are obese. When leptin injections are given to ob mice, or even to animals of normal weight, rapid loss of weight and body fat occurs, with no effect on muscle or other body tissues. Leptin sends its signals directly to the hypothalamus, where special receptors for it are located (Tartaglia et al., 1996). Like ob mice, mice lacking leptin receptors are also obese.

Hunger and the Brain

Many parts of the brain contribute to the control of hunger and eating, but research has focused on three regions of the hypothalamus that may play primary roles in detecting and reacting to the blood's signals about the need to eat (see Figure 11.5 on page 366). These regions include the ventromedial hypothalamus, the lateral hypothalamus, and the paraventricular nucleus. Within these regions several different neurotransmitters and *neuromodulators*—substances that modify the actions of neurotransmitters (Flier & Maratos-Flier, 1998)—play important roles in regulating the overall amount, and specific types, of foods eaten. For example, researchers have recently discovered a new neurotransmitter, *orexin,* that operates in the lateral hypothalamus and stimulates food intake (Sakurai et al., 1998).

When researchers began to study the brain regions that control eating and body weight, the story seemed quite simple. Specifically, they found what appeared to be a "satiety center" and a "feeding center." The *ventromedial hypothalamus* appeared to act as the satiety center. If a rat's ventromedial nucleus is electrically or chemically stimulated, the animal will stop eating (Kent et al., 1994). However, if the ventromedial nucleus is destroyed, the animal will eat ravenously, increasing its weight up to threefold. Then the rat eats enough food to maintain this higher weight (Teitelbaum, 1961). In contrast, the *lateral hypothalamus* acts as a feeding center. When fibers in the lateral hypothalamus are electrically or chemically stimulated, rats begin to eat vast quantities, even if they have just had a large meal (Stanley et al., 1993). When the lateral hypothalamus is destroyed, however, rats stop eating almost entirely. Most eventually resume eating, but they maintain a much-reduced weight (Keesey & Powley, 1975).

One theory suggests that these two hypothalamic regions interact so as to maintain a *set point* of body weight, food intake, or related metabolic signals—much as a home

A Fat Mouse

After surgical destruction of its ventromedial nucleus, this mouse ate enough to triple its body weight. Such animals become picky eaters, choosing only foods that taste good and ignoring all others (Miller, Bailey & Stevenson, 1930; Teitelbaum, 1957).

FIGURE 11.5

The Hypothalamus and Hunger

Studies of the hypothalamus have concentrated on stimulating or destroying fibers that pass through the ventromedial nucleus, the lateral hypothalamus, and the paraventricular nucleus. Here are some of the results of this research.

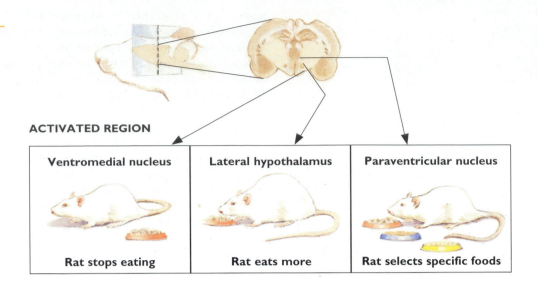

ACTIVATED REGION

Ventromedial nucleus	Lateral hypothalamus	Paraventricular nucleus
Rat stops eating	Rat eats more	Rat selects specific foods

thermostat switches the furnace on and off in order to maintain a chosen temperature setting (Powley & Keesey, 1970). According to this theory, normal animals eat until their set point is reached, then stop eating until desirable intake falls below the set point. Destruction or activation of the lateral or ventromedial hypothalamus may alter the set point.

However, research on neurons in another region of the hypothalamus, the *paraventricular nucleus (PVN),* shows that the brain's control of eating is more complex than just the interaction of "stop-eating" and "start-eating" centers (Winn, 1995). Nearly twenty neurotransmitters have been discovered that together regulate the control of eating and body weight by their actions in the brain (Woods et al., 1998). One function of these neurotransmitters is to influence hungers for specific types of food (Leibowitz, Xuereb, & Kim, 1992). For instance, the neurotransmitter *neuropeptide Y* stimulates carbohydrate eating, reduces energy expenditure, and increases fat deposits (Jhanwar et al., 1993). Neuropeptide Y is normally inhibited by the actions of leptin and insulin, and eliminating it prevents ob mice from becoming obese (Hollopeter, Erickson, & Palmiter, 1998). Conversely, the neurotransmitter serotonin acts to reduce carbohydrate consumption (Blundell & Halford, 1998). Still other neurotransmitters act specifically on fat consumption: *Galanin* motivates the eating of high-fat food (Krykouli et al., 1990), whereas *enterostatin* inhibits it (Lin et al., 1998).

In short, several brain regions and many brain chemicals help to regulate hunger and eating. And although eating is controlled by processes that suggest the existence of a set point, that set point appears variable enough to be overridden by other factors.

Flavor, Cultural Learning, and Food Selection

One factor that can override a set point is the flavor of food. Consider an experiment in which some animals were offered just one type of food while others were offered foods of several different flavors. The group getting the varied menu ate nearly four times more than the one-food group. As each new food appeared, the animals began to eat voraciously, regardless of how much they had already eaten (Peck, 1978). Humans behave similarly. All things being equal, people eat more food during a multicourse meal than when only one food is served. Apparently, the flavor of a food becomes less enjoyable as more of it is eaten (Swithers & Hall, 1994). In one study, for example, people rated how much they liked four kinds of food; then they ate one of the foods and rated all four again. The food they had just eaten now got a lower rating, whereas liking increased for all the rest (Johnson & Vickers, 1993).

Another factor that can override blood-borne signals about satiety is *appetite,* the motivation to seek food's pleasures. For example, the appearance and aroma of certain foods come to elicit conditioned physiological responses—such as secretion of saliva, gastric juices, and insulin—in anticipation of eating those foods. (The process is based on the principles of classical conditioning described in Chapter 6). These responses then augment appetite. Thus, merely seeing a pizza on television may suddenly prompt you to order one, and if you see a delicious-looking cookie, you do not have to be hungry to start eating it. In other words, people eat not only to satisfy nutritional needs but also to experience enjoyment.

A different mechanism appears to be responsible for *specific hungers,* or desires for particular foods at particular times. These hungers appear to reflect the biological need for the nutrients contained in certain foods. In one study, rats were allowed to eat from a bowl of carbohydrate-rich but protein-free food and also from a bowl of protein-rich but carbohydrate-free food. These animals learned to eat from both bowls in amounts that yielded a proper balance of carbohydrates and protein (Miller & Teates, 1985). In another study, rats were given three bowls of tasty, protein-free food and one bowl of bad-tasting food that was rich in protein. Again, the rats learned to eat enough of the unpalatable food to get a proper supply of dietary protein (Galef & Wright, 1995).

These results are remarkable in part because food nutrients such as carbohydrates, fats, and proteins have no inherent taste or odor. How, then, can they guide food choices that maintain nutritional balance? As with appetite, learning principles are probably involved. It may be that *volatile odorants* (odor molecules) in foods come to be associated with the nutritional value of their fat and protein content. Evidence for this kind of learning comes from experiments in which rats received infusions of liquid directly into their stomachs. Some of these infusions consisted of plain water; others included nutritious cornstarch. Each kind of infusion was paired with the presence of a different taste—either sour or bitter—in the animals' normal supply of drinking water. After all the infusions were completed, both sour water and bitter water were made available. When the animals became hungry, they showed a strong preference for the water whose taste had been associated with the cornstarch infusions (Drucker, Ackroff, & Sclafani, 1994). Related research shows that children come to prefer flavors that have been associated with high-fat ingredients (Johnson, McPhee, & Birch, 1991).

The role of learning in food selection is also seen in the social rules and cultural traditions that influence eating. Munching popcorn at movies and hot dogs at baseball games are common examples from North American culture of how certain social situations can stimulate appetite for particular items. Similarly, how much you eat may depend on what others do. Courtesy or custom might prompt you to select foods you might otherwise have avoided. Generally, the mere presence of others, even strangers, tends to increase consumption: Most people consume 60 to 75 percent more food when they are with others than when eating alone (Clendenen, Herman, & Polivy, 1995; Redd & de Castro, 1992).

Eating and food selection are central to the way people function within their cultures. Celebrations, holidays, vacations, and even daily family interactions often revolve around food and what some call a *food culture* (Rozin, 1983). As any world traveler knows, there are wide cultural and subcultural variations in food selection. For example, chewing coca leaves is popular in the Bolivian highlands but illegal in the United States (Burchard, 1992). In China, people in urban areas eat a high-cholesterol diet rich in animal meat whereas those in rural areas eat so little meat as to be cholesterol deficient (Tian et al., 1995). And the insects known as palm weevils, a popular food for people in Papua New Guinea (Paoletti, 1995), are regarded by many Westerners as disgusting (Springer & Belk, 1994). In short, eating serves functions beyond nutrition—functions that help to remind us of who we are and with whom we identify.

Eating Disorders

Problems in the processes regulating hunger and eating may cause an *eating disorder.* The most common and dangerous examples are obesity, anorexia nervosa, and bulimia nervosa.

Bon Appètit!

The definition of "delicacy" differs from culture to culture. At this elegant restaurant in Mexico, diners pay to feast on baby alligators, insects, and other dishes that some people from other cultures would not eat even if the restaurant paid *them.*

Young Couch Potatoes

Inactivity during childhood is thought to contribute to weight gain, and television watching is a major cause of inactivity among overweight children (Dietz, 1991). Studies show that metabolic rates during television watching are even lower than during rest, and that the reduction while watching television may be even greater in obese children compared to those of normal weight (Klesges, Shelton & Klesges, 1993).

Obesity   The World Health Organization defines **obesity** as a condition in which a person's body-mass index (weight in kilograms divided by the square of height in meters) is greater than 30. (In a nonmetric example, a person who is 5'6" and weighs 195 pounds would be considered obese.) Obesity is associated with many health risks, such as diabetes, high blood pressure, and increased risk of heart attack (Pi-Sunyer, 1994). The last two decades have witnessed a significant increase in the number of obese people in many countries around the world. In the United States, for example, the prevalence of obesity increased from 14.5 percent in 1980 to 20 percent in 1999. And obesity appears to be on the rise in regions as diverse as Asia, South America, and Africa (Taubes, 1998). The precise causes of this obesity epidemic are unknown (Hill & Peters, 1998), but possibilities include increased portion sizes at fast-food outlets, greater prevalence of high-fat foods, and decreases in physical activity associated with both work and recreation. (TV remote-control devices are especially implicated in this last category.)

Why do obese people gain so much weight? The body maintains a given weight through a combination of food intake and energy output (Keesey & Powley, 1986). Obese people get more energy from food than their body *metabolizes,* or "burns up"; the excess energy, measured in *calories,* is stored as fat. Metabolism declines during sleep and rises with physical activity. Since women tend to have a lower metabolic rate than men, even when equally active, they tend to gain weight more easily than do men with similar diets (Ferraro et al., 1992).

Most obese people have normal resting metabolic rates and are as active as lean people (Meijer et al., 1992). However, obese people tend to be finicky eaters, eating above-average amounts of high-calorie, tasty foods but below-average amounts of less tasty foods (Kauffman, Herman, & Polivy, 1995; Peck, 1978). And when trying to restrict eating, some obese people greatly underestimate how much they have eaten (Lichtman et al., 1992; Lowe, Kopyt, & Buchwald, 1996).

The fact that most obese people are fat because they eat more of certain foods does not mean that they are "morally lax." For one thing, research on the genetics of the hormone leptin suggests that people may be genetically predisposed to manage fat in different ways. Similarly, both genetic influences and the nature of childhood nutrition can raise a person's set point for body weight and create larger and more numerous fat cells (Grilo & Pogue-Geile, 1991). Such factors may increase obese people's tendency to accumulate fat and also make them feel more hunger than lean people, even when they maintain similar habits of diet and exercise. Leptin deficiency was suggested as a cause of obesity when the hormone was first discovered, and a genetic leptin deficiency does result in obesity in rare cases (Montague et al., 1997); however, most obese humans actually have elevated leptin levels (Sinha & Caro, 1998). It may be that obese individuals are less sensitive to the weight-suppressive effects of leptin—perhaps because of a defect in, or altered regulation of, their leptin receptors. This idea is supported by an animal study involving a strain of mice that maintains normal weight on standard laboratory food but becomes obese when fed a high-fat diet. When obese, the mice have elevated levels of leptin but they are insensitive to it. After losing weight, however, they regain sensitivity to leptin (Campfield, Smith, & Burn, 1998). Drug-company scientists believe that if they can learn how to regulate the leptin receptors in the hypothalamus, they will have found the ideal diet drug for humans.

Genetic variations in the physiology of weight control can interact with environmental factors. For example, members of one tribe of American Indians, the Pima of Arizona, maintained healthy body weight when they actively farmed and ate a diet low in fat. With the introduction of modern lifestyles and foods into their culture, however, prevalence rates of adult obesity in this tribe rose to rank among the highest in the world. In addition, more than 50 percent of Pima adults are diabetic as a consequence of obesity. One study of the tribe's genetic makeup has found a variant of the leptin receptor that predisposes them to obesity (Thompson et al., 1997). Researchers speculate that, in adapting to the rigors of their desert existence, the Pima evolved a very efficient physiology for storing fat—a biological asset that became a dangerous liability when their environment changed.

Psychological explanations for obesity often focus on maladaptive reactions to stress. Many people tend to eat more when under stress, a reaction that may be especially extreme among those who become obese (Friedman & Brownell, 1995). However, obese people are no more likely than normal-weight people to display mental disorders (Stunkard & Wadden, 1992).

Losing weight and keeping it off for at least five years is extremely difficult for many people, especially those who are obese (NIH, 1992). Part of the problem may be due to metabolic changes that accompany weight loss. When food intake is reduced, the process of homeostasis leads to a drop in metabolic rate, thus saving energy and curbing weight loss (Leibel, Rosenbaum, & Hirsch, 1995). This response makes evolutionary sense; conservation of energy during famine, for example, is adaptive for survival. But when obese people try to lose weight, their metabolic rate drops *below* normal. As a result, they can gain weight even while eating amounts that would maintain constant weight in other people.

These facts suggest that attempts to lose a great deal of weight quickly will be met with compensatory changes in one's set point (Brownell & Rodin, 1994). Indeed, animal studies show that losing and then regaining large amounts of weight, so-called cycling, actually leads to a gradual rise in average weight (Archambault et al., 1989). Moreover, people whose body weight "cycles" tend to experience more depression and stress-related symptoms than do people whose average weight is similar but does not fluctuate (Foreyt et al., 1995).

To achieve the kind of gradual weight loss that is more likely to last, obese people are advised to increase regular exercise because it burns calories without slowing metabolism (Tremblay & Bueman, 1995). Indeed, in the long run, regular aerobic exercise raises the metabolic rate (McCarty, 1995). The most effective weight-loss programs include components designed to reduce food intake, change eating habits and attitudes toward food, and increase energy expenditure through exercise (Kirschenbaum & Fitzgibbons, 1995).

Anorexia Nervosa   At the opposite extreme from obesity is **anorexia nervosa,** an eating disorder characterized by self-starvation and severe weight loss. Anorexic individuals often feel strong hunger yet refuse to eat. Some are obsessed with food and its preparation but eat almost nothing. Anorexic self-starvation causes serious, often irreversible, physical damage. Between 4 and 30 percent of anorexics actually starve themselves to death (Bryant & Lask, 1995). About 95 percent of people who suffer from

An Anorexia Fatality

This photo of Christy Henrich, a former member of the U.S. Olympic gymnastics team, was taken in 1993, eleven months before she died of anorexia-related complications. At the time of her death, Christy was twenty-two years old, stood four feet, ten inches tall, and weighed sixty pounds.

in review

MAJOR FACTORS CONTROLLING HUNGER AND EATING

	Stimulate Eating	Inhibit Eating
Biological factors	Levels of glucose and insulin in the blood provide signals that stimulate eating; neurotransmitters that affect neurons in different regions of the hypothalamus also stimulate food intake and influence hungers for specific kinds of foods, such as fats and carbohydrates. Stomach contractions are associated with subjective feelings of hunger, but they do not play a substantial role in the stimulation of eating.	Hormones released into the bloodstream produce signals that inhibit eating; hormones such as leptin, CCK, and insulin act as neurotransmitters or neuromodulators and affect neurons in the hypothalamus and inhibit eating. The ventromedial nucleus of the hypothalamus may be a "satiety center" that monitors these hormones.
Nonbiological factors	Sights and smells of particular foods elicit eating because of prior associations; family customs and social occasions often include norms for eating in particular ways; stress is often associated with eating more.	Values in contemporary U.S. society encourage thinness, and thus can inhibit eating.

anorexia are female. The prevalence of anorexia appears to be on the increase; it now affects about 1 percent of young women in the United States and is a growing problem in many other industrialized nations as well (Feingold & Mazzella, 1998; Thompson, 1996).

The causes of anorexia are not yet clear. Anorexic individuals do have abnormally low levels of certain neurotransmitters; but because these levels return to normal when weight is restored, the deficit may be a response to starvation, not its cause (Kaye et al., 1988). Psychological factors that may contribute to the problem include a self-punishing, perfectionistic personality and a culturally reinforced obsession with thinness and attractiveness (Tiller et al., 1995). The attitudes associated with anorexia begin very early. In the United States, 35 percent of normal-weight girls—and 12 percent of underweight girls!—begin dieting as young as nine to ten years of age. Many of these children are trying to lose weight in response to criticism by their mothers (Schreiber et al., 1996). Anorexics appear to develop a fear of being fat, which they take to dangerous extremes (de Castro & Goldstein, 1995). Many anorexics continue to view themselves as too fat or misshapen even as they are wasting away (Feingold & Mazzella, 1998; Heilbrun & Witt, 1990).

Drugs, hospitalization, and psychotherapy are all used to treat anorexia. In most cases, some combination of treatment and the passage of time brings recovery and maintenance of normal weight (Pike, Loeb, & Vitousek, 1996).

Bulimia Nervosa   Like anorexia, bulimia nervosa involves intense fear of being fat, but the person may be thin, normal in weight, or even overweight (Thompson, 1996). **Bulimia nervosa** involves eating huge amounts of food (say, several boxes of cookies, a half-gallon of ice cream, and a bucket of fried chicken) and then getting rid of the food through self-induced vomiting or strong laxatives (Johnson & Torgrud, 1996). These "binge-purge" episodes may occur as often as twice a day (Weltzin et al., 1995).

Like anorexics, bulimic individuals are usually female; estimates of the frequency of anorexia and bulimia range from 1 to 3 percent of North American women (Thompson, 1996). However, bulimia and anorexia are separate disorders (Pryor, 1995). For one thing, most bulimics see their eating habits as problematic, whereas most anorexics do not. In addition, bulimia nervosa is usually not life-threatening (Thompson, 1996). There are consequences, however, including dehydration, nutritional problems, and intestinal damage. Many bulimics develop dental problems from the acids associated with vomiting. Frequent vomiting, and the insertion of objects to trigger it, can also cause damage to the throat. More generally, preoccupation with eating and avoiding weight gain prevents many bulimics from working productively (Herzog, 1982).

Bulimia nervosa appears to be caused by a combination of factors, including culturally encouraged overconcern with thinness and attractiveness, depression and other emotional problems, and as-yet-undetermined biological problems that might include defective satiety mechanisms (Brewerton et al., 1995). Treatments for bulimia typically include individual or group therapy and, sometimes, antidepressant drugs; these help the vast majority of bulimic people to eat more normally (Crow & Mitchell, 1996).

(For a summary of the processes involved in hunger and eating, see "In Review: Major Factors Controlling Hunger and Eating.")

SEXUAL BEHAVIOR

Unlike food, sex is not necessary for individual survival. A strong desire for reproduction does help ensure the survival of a species, however (Keeling & Roger, 1995). The various factors shaping sexual motivation and behavior differ in strength across species, but they often include a combination of the individual's physiology, learned behavior, and the physical and social environment. For example, one species of desert bird requires adequate sex hormones, a suitable mate, and a particular environment before it begins sexual behavior. As long as the dry season lasts, it shows no interest in sex, but within ten minutes of the first rainfall the birds vigorously copulate.

Rainfall is obviously much less influential as a sexual trigger for humans; indeed, people show a staggering diversity of *sexual scripts,* or patterns of behavior that lead to sex. One survey of college-age men and women identified 122 specific acts and 34 different tactics used for promoting sexual encounters (Greer & Buss, 1994). What happens next? The matter is exceedingly difficult to address scientifically, because most people are reluctant to respond to specific questions about their sexual practices, let alone to allow researchers to observe their sexual behavior.

The most extensive studies of sexual behavior in the United States were done by Alfred Kinsey during the late 1940s and early 1950s (Kinsey, Pomeroy, & Martin, 1948; Kinsey et al., 1953) and in the 1960s by William Masters and Virginia Johnson. Masters and Johnson directly observed sexual relations between volunteers in their laboratory. Although their studies broke new ground in the exploration of human sexuality, critics argued that the people who volunteered for such studies probably did not constitute a representative sample of humankind. Accordingly, the results—and any conclusions drawn from them—may not apply to people in general.

More recently, Edward Laumann and his associates (1994) randomly selected and then interviewed 3,432 Americans, ranging in age from eighteen to fifty-nine. The results challenged some of the popular-culture and mass-media images of sexuality in the United States. For one thing, the survey found that people in the United States have sex less often and with fewer people than many had speculated. For most, sex occurs about once a week in monogamous relationships; about a third of the participants reported having sex only a few times or not at all in the past year. The average male survey participant had only six sexual partners in his entire life; the average female respondent reported a lifetime total of two. Further, the survey data suggested that people in committed, monogamous relationships had the most frequent and the most satisfying sex.

The Biology of Sex

Some aspects of the sexual behavior observed by Masters and Johnson in their laboratory may not have reflected exactly what goes on when people have sex in more familiar surroundings. Still, those observations led to important findings about the **sexual response cycle,** the pattern of physiological arousal during and after sexual activity (see Figure 11.6).

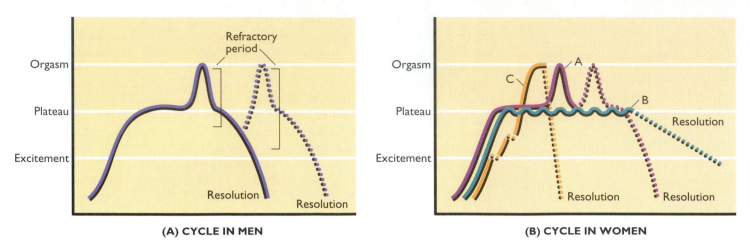

(A) CYCLE IN MEN   (B) CYCLE IN WOMEN

Source: Adapted from Masters & Johnson, 1966.

FIGURE 11.6

The Sexual Response Cycle

Masters and Johnson (1966) found that men show one primary pattern of sexual response, depicted in part (A); and that women display at least three different patterns from time to time (labeled A, B, and C in part (B)). In both men and women, the first, or *excitement*, phase begins with sexually stimulating input from the environment or from one's own thoughts. Continued stimulation leads to intensified excitement in the second, or *plateau*, phase. If stimulation continues, the person reaches the third, or *orgasmic*, stage, which, though it lasts only a few seconds, provides an intensely pleasurable release of physical and psychological tension. The *resolution* phase follows, during which the person returns to a state of relaxation. At this point, men enter a *refractory period* during which they are temporarily insensitive to sexual stimulation. Women are capable of immediately repeating the cycle if stimulation continues.

People's motivation to engage in sexual activity has biological roots in **sex hormones.** The female sex hormones are **estrogens** and **progestins;** the main ones are *estradiol* and *progesterone.* The male hormones are **androgens;** the principal example is *testosterone.* Each sex hormone flows in the blood of *both* sexes, but males have relatively more androgens and women have relatively more estrogens and progestins. Figure 11.7 shows how feedback systems control the secretion of these hormones. Sex hormones have both organizational and activational effects. The *organizational effects* are permanent changes in the brain that alter the way a person thereafter responds to hormones. The *activational effects* are temporary behavioral changes that last only during the time a hormone level remains elevated.

The organizational effects of hormones occur around the time of birth, when certain brain areas are sculpted into a "male-like" or "female-like" pattern. These areas are thus described as *sexually dimorphic.* In rodents, for example, a sexually dimorphic area of the hypothalamus appears to underlie specific sexual behaviors. When these areas are destroyed in male gerbils, the animals can no longer copulate; yet damage to other nearby brain regions does not affect sexual behavior (Yahr & Jacobsen, 1994). Sexually dimorphic areas also exist in the human hypothalamus and other parts of the brain (Breedlove, 1994). For example, a hypothalamic area called *BSTc* is generally smaller in women than in men. Its possible role in some aspects of human sexuality was suggested by a recent study of transsexual men—genetic males who feel like women and who may request sex-change surgery in order to "be" female. The BSTc in these men was smaller than in other men; in fact, it was about the size usually seen in women (Zhou et al., 1995).

Rising levels of sex hormones during puberty have activational effects, resulting in increased sexual desire and interest in sexual behavior. Generally, estrogens stimulate females' sexual interest (Burleson, Gregory, & Trevarthen, 1995). Androgens raise males' sexual interest (Davidson, Camargo, & Smith, 1979), but they may also do so in females (Sherwin & Gelfand, 1987). The activational effects of hormones are evidenced, in part, by the reduced sexual motivation and behavior seen in people whose hormone-secreting ovaries or testes have been removed for medical reasons. Injections of hormones help restore these people's sexual interest and activity (Sherwin, Gelfand, & Brender, 1985).

Generally, hormones affect sexual *desire,* not the physical *ability* to have sex (Wallen & Lovejoy, 1993). This fact may explain why castration does not prevent sex crimes in male offenders. Men with low testosterone levels due to medical problems or castration show less sexual desire, but they still experience physiological responses to erotic stimuli (Kwan et al., 1983). Thus a sex offender treated with androgen antagonists or castration would be less likely to *seek out* sex, but he would still respond as before to his favorite sexual stimuli (Wallen & Lovejoy, 1993).

FIGURE 11.7

The Regulation of Sex Hormones

The secretion of sex hormones is controlled by feedback loops involving the hypothalamus, the pituitary gland, and the ovaries or testes. In males, high levels of testosterone reduce activity in the hypothalamus, which lowers secretion of luteinizing hormone (LH), which causes less testosterone to be secreted. This feedback system tends to keep the secretion of testosterone reasonably constant. In females, the feedback loops are more complex. High levels of estrogen increase hypothalamic activity, causing more LH to be secreted, which causes more estrogen to be secreted. At some point, the secretion of LH increases very rapidly, and a surge of hormone is released. The increased LH not only prompts the release of more estrogen but also causes the ovary to release an egg. Androgens fluctuate across the menstrual cycle just as estrogens and progestins do, and their levels peak around ovulation.

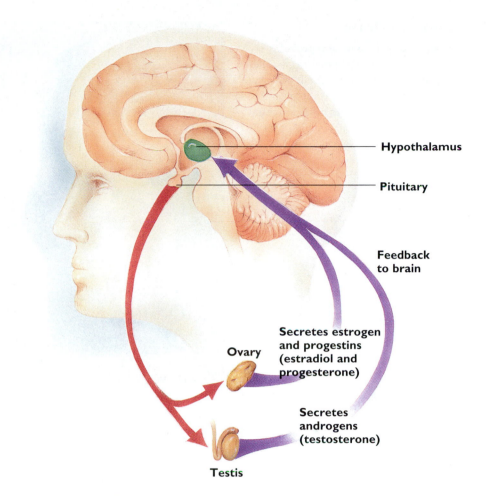

Social and Cultural Factors in Sexuality

In humans, sexuality is profoundly shaped by a lifetime of learning and thinking that modifies the biological "raw materials" provided by hormones. For example, children learn some of their sexual attitudes and behaviors as part of the development of gender roles. The specific attitudes and behaviors learned depend partly on the nature of gender roles in their culture. One survey of the sexual experiences of more than 1,500 college students in the United States, Japan, and Russia found numerous cross-cultural differences in the ways that men and women behave in sexual situations (Sprecher et al., 1994). As just one notable example, consider the finding that more women than men in the United States said they had consented to sex when they did not really want it; in both Russia and Japan, men and women were about equally likely to have had this experience.

Sexual behavior is also shaped by other sociocultural forces. In the United States, for example, concern over transmission of the AIDS virus during sex has prompted mass-media campaigns and school-based educational programs to encourage sexual abstinence prior to marriage or "safe sex" using condoms. These efforts seem to be shaping young people's sexual attitudes and practices. At the beginning of one sex education program, only 36 percent of 1,800 students in grades seven through ten thought premarital sex was a bad idea and only 35 percent saw many benefits in premarital abstinence from sex. By the end of the semester-long program, these figures had risen to 66 percent and 58 percent, respectively (Eisenman, 1994). Another survey of 1,100

Do They Look Ready?

Research on sexual behavior provides psychologists, public health officials, and others who are concerned about poverty and child abuse with important information that helps them to more precisely tailor advertising campaigns and other efforts to prevent these problems.

adolescents and young adults in the United States found that, prior to 1985, first-time intercourse seldom included use of a condom. With growing AIDS awareness since 1985, however, condom use has become common in first-time intercourse (Leigh, Schafer, & Temple, 1995).

Sexual Orientation

Human sexual activity is most often **heterosexual,** involving members of the opposite sex. When sexual behavior is directed toward a member of one's own sex, it is called **homosexual.** People who engage in sexual activities with partners of both sexes are described as **bisexual.** Whether you engage in sexual activities with members of your own sex, the opposite sex, or both is one part of your *sexual orientation.*

In many cultures, heterosexuality has long been regarded as a moral norm, and homosexuality has been seen as a disease, a mental disorder, or even a crime (Hooker, 1993). Attempts to alter the sexual orientation of homosexuals—using psychotherapy, brain surgery, or electric shock—were usually ineffective (Haldeman, 1994). In 1973 the American Psychiatric Association dropped homosexuality from the *Diagnostic and Statistical Manual of Mental Disorders,* thus ending its official status as a form of psychopathology.

Nevertheless, many people still view homosexuality as repugnant and immoral. Because homosexuals and bisexuals are often the victims of discrimination and even hate crimes, many are reluctant to let their sexual orientation be known (Rothblum, 1994). It is difficult, therefore, to obtain an accurate picture of the mix of heterosexual, homosexual, and bisexual orientations in a population. In one national sex survey, 1.4 percent of women and 2.8 percent of men identified themselves as exclusively homosexual (Laumann et al., 1994). However, the survey did not allow respondents to give anonymous answers to questions about sexual orientation. Some researchers suggest that if anonymous responses to those questions had been permitted, the prevalence figures for homosexual and bisexual orientations would have been higher (Bullough, 1995). In fact, studies that have allowed anonymous responding estimate the percentage of homosexual people in the United States and elsewhere at between 6 and 20 percent (Sell, Wells, & Wypij, 1995).

A Committed Relationship

Stable, long-term intimate relationships occur in both heterosexual and homosexual pairs. Behavioral genetics research employing the twin study approach suggests that sexual orientation might be genetically influenced. Richard Pillard, an author of one study of this issue, had personal reasons for suspecting this might be the case. He is gay, as are his brother and sister. He believes that his father was gay, and one of his three daughters is bisexual (Burr, 1993).

THINKING CRITICALLY

Do Genes Determine Sexual Orientation?

The question of where sexual orientation comes from is a topic of intense debate in scientific circles, on talk shows, in everyday conversations, and recently even in the halls of the United States Congress.

■ What am I being asked to believe or accept?

One point of view suggests that genes dictate sexual orientation. According to this view, we do not learn a sexual orientation but rather are born with it.

■ What evidence is available to support the assertion?

Certain variations of a gene called *voila* in male fruit flies alters their brain function and causes them to approach males instead of female flies for sex (Balakireva et al., 1998). A growing body of evidence from research in behavioral genetics (see Chapter 2) suggests that genes might influence sexual orientation in humans as well (Pillard & Bailey, 1998). One study examined pairs of monozygotic male twins (whose genes are identical), nonidentical twin pairs (whose genes are no more alike than those of any brothers), and pairs of adopted brothers (who are genetically unrelated). To participate in this study, at least one brother in each pair had to be homosexual. As it turned out, the other brother was also homosexual or bisexual in 52 percent of the identical-twin pairs, but in only 22 percent of the nonidentical pairs and in just 11 percent of the adoptive pairs (Bailey & Pillard, 1991). Similar findings have been reported for male identical twins raised apart; in such cases, a shared sexual orientation cannot be attributed to the effects of a shared environment (Whitam, Diamond, & Martin, 1993). The few available studies of female sexual orientation have yielded similar results (Bailey & Benishay, 1993).

Other evidence for the role of biological factors in sexual orientation comes from research on the impact of sex hormones. In adults, differences in the level of these hormones are not generally associated with differences in sexual orientation. However, hormonal differences during prenatal development might be involved in the shaping of sexual orientation. Support for this view is provided by research on a congenital disorder that causes the adrenal glands to secrete extremely high levels of androgens prenatally (Carlson, 1998). Women who suffered from this disorder, and who thus had been exposed to high levels of androgens during their fetal development, were much more likely to become lesbians than their sisters who had not been exposed (Meyer et al., 1995). In animals, such hormonal influences alter the structure of the hypothalamus, a brain region known to underlie some aspects of sexual functioning (Swaab & Hofman, 1995). In humans, hormones may likewise be responsible for anatomical differences in the hypothalamus that are seen not only in males versus females but in homosexual versus heterosexual men as well (LeVay, 1991; Swaab & Hofman, 1990). The anterior commissure, an area near the hypothalamus, also appears to differ in people with differing sexual orientations (Allen & Gorski, 1992).

Further support for the influence of hormones on sexual orientation comes from a study of *otoacoustic emissions*, which are faint sounds that come from the human ear (McFadden & Pasanen, 1998). These sounds, known to be affected by hormones during prenatal development, are louder in heterosexual women than in men. In lesbian women, however, the sounds are more similar to men's than to heterosexual women's, suggesting a biological process of sexual differentiation. This study did *not* find a difference between homosexual and heterosexual men, which is contrary to what would be expected if homosexuality were invariably associated with otoacoustic emissions.

Finally, a biological basis for sexual orientation is suggested by the relatively weak effects of the environment on sexual orientation. For example, the sexual orientation of children's caregivers has little or no effect on those children's own orientation. Several studies have shown that children adopted by homosexual parents are no more or less likely to display a homosexual orientation than are children raised by heterosexual parents (Bailey et al., 1995; Tasker & Golombok, 1995).

■ Are there alternative ways of interpreting the evidence?

Correlations between genetics and sexual orientation are, like all correlational data, open to alternative interpretations. As discussed in Chapter 2, a correlation describes the strength and direction of the relationship between two variables, but it does not guarantee that one variable is actually influencing the other. Consider again the data showing that brothers who shared the most genes were also most likely to share a homosexual orientation. It is possible that what they shared was not a gene for homosexuality but, rather, a set of genes that influenced their activity level, emotionality, aggressiveness, or other general aspects of temperament or personality. It could have been these characteristics, and other people's reactions to them, that increased the likelihood of a particular sexual orientation. In other words, sexual orientation could arise as a *reaction* to the way people respond to a genetically determined, but nonsexual, aspect of personality. Prenatal hormone levels, too, could influence sexual orientation by shaping aggressiveness or other nonsexual aspects of behavior.

It is also important to look at behavioral genetics evidence for what it can tell us about the role of *environmental* factors in sexual orientation. When we read that both members of identical twin pairs have a homosexual or bisexual orientation 52 percent of the time, it is easy to ignore the fact that the orientation of the twin pair members was *different* in nearly half the cases. Viewed in this way, the results suggest that genes do not tell the entire story of sexual orientation.

In other words, even if sexual orientation has a biological base, it is probably not determined by unlearned, genetic forces alone. As described in Chapter 3, the bodies we inherit are quite responsive to environmental input; the behaviors we engage in and the environmental experiences we have often result in physical changes in the brain and elsewhere (Wang et al., 1995). For example, physical changes occur in the brain's synapses as we form new memories. Thus, differences in the brains of people with differing sexual orientations could be the effect, not the cause, of their behavior or experiences.

■ What additional evidence would help to evaluate the alternatives?

Much more evidence is needed regarding the extent to which genetic characteristics directly determine sexual orientation, as well as the extent to which genetics shape physical and psychological characteristics that lead to the social construction of various sexual orientations. For example, the few available reports of sexual dimorphism in human brains have yet to be replicated. In studying this issue, researchers need to learn more not only about the genetic characteristics of people with different sexual orientations but also about their mental and behavioral styles. Are there personality characteristics associated with different sexual orientations? If so, do those characteristics have a strong genetic component? To what extent are heterosexuals, bisexuals, and homosexuals similar—and to what extent are they different—in terms of cognitive styles, biases, coping skills, developmental histories, and the like?

The more we learn about sexual orientation generally, the easier it will be to interpret data relating to its origins; but even defining sexual orientation is not simple. Alfred Kinsey and his colleagues (1948) viewed sexual orientation as occurring along a continuum rather than falling into a few discrete categories. Should a man who identifies himself as gay be considered bisexual because he occasionally has heterosexual daydreams? What sexual orientation label would be appropriate for a forty-year-old woman who experienced a few lesbian encounters in her teens but has engaged in exclusively heterosexual sex since then? Progress in understanding the origins of sexual orientation would be enhanced by a generally accepted system for describing and defining what is meant by sexual orientation.

■ What conclusions are most reasonable?

Given the antagonism and physical danger often faced by people with nonheterosexual orientations (Van de Ven, 1994), it seems unlikely that a homosexual or bisexual identity is entirely a matter of choice. Indeed, much of the evidence reviewed suggests that our sexual orientation chooses us, rather than the other way around. In light of this evidence, a reasonable hypothesis is that genetic factors, probably operating via prenatal hormones, create differences in the brains of people with different sexual orientations. Even if this hypothesis is correct, however, the manner in which a person expresses a genetically influenced sexual orientation will be profoundly shaped by what that person learns through social and cultural experiences (Bancroft, 1994). In short, sexual orientation most likely results from the complex interplay of both genetic and nongenetic mechanisms—both nature and nurture. Those who characterize sexual orientation as all "in the genes" are probably no more correct than those who see it as entirely a matter of choice.

Sexual Dysfunctions

The same biological, social, and psychological factors that shape human sexual behavior can also result in **sexual dysfunctions,** problems in a person's desire for or ability to have satisfying sexual activity. Fortunately, most of these problems—which affect 30 to 40 percent of U.S. adults (Laumann et al., 1994)—respond to psychotherapy, drugs, or both (de Silva, 1994). For men, a common problem is *erectile disorder* (once called impotence), a persistent inability to have or maintain an erection adequate for sex. Physical causes—such as fatigue, diabetes, hypertension, aging, and alcohol or other drugs—account for some cases, but psychological causes such as anxiety are also common (Everaerd & Laan, 1994). The recently introduced drug known as *Viagra,* which affects blood flow in the penis, is effectively treating many cases of erectile disorder (Goldstein et al., 1998). *Premature ejaculation,* another common dysfunction, involves a recurring tendency to ejaculate during sex sooner than the man or his partner desires. Most men experience episodes of at least one of these problems at some point in their lives, but such episodes are considered dysfunctions only if they become a distressing obstacle to sexual functioning (American Psychiatric Association, 1994).

For women, the most common sexual dysfunction is *arousal disorder* (once called frigidity), which is characterized by a recurring inability to become physiologically aroused during sexual activity (Wilson et al., 1996). The causes of arousal disorder are not yet fully understood. However, some researchers believe that it may result from the reduction of oxygen-rich blood to the clitoris (Wilson et al., 1996). Arousal disorder also appears to be tied to psychological factors such as guilt or concern about one's sexual performance, which can affect men as well as women (Laan et al., 1993; Palace & Gorzalka, 1990).

ACHIEVEMENT MOTIVATION

This sentence was written at 6 A.M. on a beautiful Sunday in June. Why would someone get up that early to work on a weekend? Why do people take their work seriously and try to do the best that they can? People work hard partly due to *extrinsic motivation*, a desire for external rewards such as money. But work and other human behaviors also reflect *intrinsic motivation*, a desire to attain internal satisfaction.

The next time you visit someone's home or office, look at the mementos displayed there. You may see framed diplomas and awards, trophies and ribbons, pictures of memorable personal events, and photos of children and grandchildren. These badges of achievement affirm that a person has accomplished tasks that merit approval or establish worth. Much of human behavior is motivated by a desire for approval, admiration, and achievement—in short, for *esteem*—from others and from themselves. In this section, we examine two of the most common avenues to esteem: achievement in general and a job in particular.

Need for Achievement

Many athletes who hold world records still train intensely; many people who have built multimillion-dollar businesses still work fourteen-hour days. What motivates such people?

One possible answer is a motive called **need achievement** (Murray, 1938). People with a high need for achievement seek to master tasks—be they sports, business ventures, intellectual puzzles, or artistic creations—and feel intense satisfaction from doing so. They exert strenuous efforts in striving for excellence, enjoy themselves in the process, and take great pride in achieving at a high level (McClelland, 1985).

Individual Differences   How do people with strong achievement motivation differ from others? To find out, researchers gave children a test to measure their need for achievement (Figure 11.8 shows a test for adults) and then asked them to play a ring-toss game. Children scoring low on the need-achievement test usually stood so close to or so far away from the ring-toss target that they either could not fail or could not succeed. In contrast, children scoring high on the need-achievement test stood at a moderate distance from the target, making the game challenging but not impossible (McClelland, 1958).

These and other experiments suggest that people with high achievement needs tend to set challenging—but realistic—goals. They actively seek success, take risks when necessary, and are intensely satisfied with success. But if they feel they have tried their best, people with high achievement motivation are not too upset by failure. Those with low achievement motivation also like to succeed, but instead of joy, success tends to bring them relief at having avoided failure (Winter, 1996).

People with strong achievement motivation tend to be preoccupied with their performance and level of ability (Harackiewicz & Elliot, 1993). They select tasks with clear outcomes, and they prefer feedback from a harsh but competent critic rather than from one who is friendlier but less competent (Klich & Feldman, 1992). They like to struggle with a problem rather than get help, they can wait for delayed rewards, and

FIGURE 11.8

Assessment of Need Achievement

This picture is similar to those included in the Thematic Apperception Test, or TAT (Morgan & Murray, 1935). The strength of people's achievement motivation is inferred from the stories they tell about TAT pictures. A response like "The young woman is hoping that she will be able to make her grandmother proud of her" would clearly reflect achievement motivation.

Source: Murray, 1971.

"Maybe they didn't try hard enough."

they make careful plans for the future (Mayer & Sutton, 1996). In contrast, people who are less motivated to achieve are less likely to seek or enjoy feedback, and they tend to quit in response to failure (Weiner, 1980).

Development of Achievement Motivation   Achievement motivation tends to be learned in early childhood, especially from parents. For example, in one study young boys were given a very hard task at which they were sure to fail. Fathers whose sons scored low on achievement motivation tests often became annoyed as they watched their boys, discouraged them from continuing, and interfered or even completed the task themselves (Rosen & D'Andrade, 1959). A different pattern of behavior emerged among parents of children who scored high on tests of achievement motivation. Such parents tended to (1) encourage the child to try difficult tasks, especially new ones; (2) give praise and other rewards for success; (3) encourage the child to find ways to succeed rather than merely complaining about failure; and (4) prompt the child to go on to the next, more difficult challenge (McClelland, 1985).

Cultural influences also affect achievement motivation. For example, subtle messages about a culture's view of the importance of achievement often appear in the books children read and the stories they hear. Does the story's main character work hard and overcome obstacles (creating expectations of a payoff for persistence) or loaf and then win the lottery (suggesting that rewards come randomly regardless of effort)? If the main character succeeds, is this outcome the result of personal initiative (typical of an individualist culture) or of ties to a cooperative and supportive group (typical of a collectivist culture)? Such themes appear to act as blueprints for reaching culturally approved goals. Not surprisingly, then, ideas about achievement motivation differ from culture to culture. In one study, for example, individuals from Saudi Arabia and from the United States were asked to comment on short stories describing people succeeding at various tasks. Saudis tended to see the people in the stories as having succeeded because of the help they got from others, whereas Americans tended to attribute success to the internal characteristics of each story's main character (Zahrani & Kaplowitz, 1993).

Achievement motivation can be increased even among people whose cultural training had not fostered it in childhood (Mayer & Sutton, 1996). In one study, high school and college students with low achievement motivation were helped to develop fantasies about their own success. They imagined setting goals that were difficult but not impossible. Then they imagined themselves concentrating on breaking a complex problem into small, manageable steps. They fantasized about working hard, failing but not being discouraged, continuing to work, and finally feeling elated at success. Afterward, the students' grades and academic success improved, suggesting an increase in their achievement motivation (McClelland, 1985).

A Model of Achievement Motivation

U.S. Secretary of State Madeleine Albright is but one of the many high-achieving female role models who are influencing girls and young women to set their sights high, no matter what they choose to do in life.

Gender Differences in Achievement Motivation

The behavior of women with high achievement motivation varies more than that of men with equally high achievement motivation. In particular, these women do not always set challenging goals, and they do not always persist when faced with failure (Dweck, 1986). In fact, some withdraw from and even avoid situations in which their achievement could be evaluated.

Gender differences in achievement motivation emerge early in life, perhaps because of differences in the ways that boys and girls learn to think of themselves and their performance (Burns & Seligman, 1989). Females are more likely than males to attribute failure on school-related tasks to lack of ability, and they tend to begin doing so at an early age (Dweck & Gilliard, 1975). Many persist in seeing themselves as incompetent even when grades and other objective evidence show that they excel (Licht & Dweck, 1984).

Girls' readiness to deprecate their own abilities in school may stem in part from the performance feedback they receive from their grade-school teachers. Observational studies show that both boys and girls are often told what they did wrong and what they should do instead. But boys are more likely than girls to also be told that they are not concentrating or are being careless. Thus, boys learn to see failure as due to lack of effort or some other situational factor. In contrast, the feedback that girls hear leads them to attribute failure to lack of ability (Dweck et al., 1978). Support for this view comes from a study in which researchers arranged for girls with high achievement motivation to receive the type of criticism normally directed toward boys. The girls' behavior became more like that of boys with high achievement motivation: They adopted challenging goals, worked hard, and persisted in the face of failure (Dweck, 1986).

In some cultures, gender-role stereotypes discourage achievement motivation in women. These stereotypes may portray the pursuit of excellence and mastery as "unfeminine" and threatening to men. Teachers and parents may communicate gender-role stereotypes about achievement, including ideas about "appropriate" areas of achievement for boys and girls. For example, if boys are expected to be better at math and girls to be better at reading, boys may receive more help and encouragement in math than girls do (Leinhardt, Seewald, & Engel, 1979). Such differential assistance may be one reason that, by the time they enter high school, girls don't do as well as boys in math (Hyde, Fennema, & Lamon, 1990). Sadly, some of the same gender-based treatment appears even among university professors in their dealings with students—and with other professors (Wiley & Crittenden, 1992).

Achievement and Success in the Workplace

In the workplace, there is usually less concern with employees' general level of need achievement than with their motivation to work hard during business hours. Indeed, employers tend to set up jobs in accordance with their ideas about how intrinsic and extrinsic motivation combine to shape employees' performance (Riggio, 1989). Those who see workers as lazy, untrustworthy, ambitionless creatures tend to offer highly structured, heavily supervised jobs that give employees little say in deciding what to do or how to do it. Such employers assume that workers are motivated mainly by extrinsic rewards—money, in particular. They are thus often surprised when, in spite of good pay and benefits, employees sometimes express dissatisfaction with their jobs and show little motivation to work hard (Amabile et al., 1994).

If good pay and benefits alone do not bring job satisfaction and the desire to excel on the job, what does? Research suggests that low worker motivation in Western cultures comes largely from the feeling of having little or no control over the work environment (Rosen, 1991). Compared with those in rigidly structured jobs, workers tend to be more satisfied and productive if they are (1) encouraged to participate in decisions about how work should be done; (2) given problems to solve, without being told how to solve them; (3) taught more than one skill; (4) given individual responsibility; and (5) given public recognition, not just money, for good performance.

Allowing people to set and achieve clear goals is one way to increase both job performance and job satisfaction (Abramis, 1994). Goals that most effectively maintain work motivation have three features (Katzell & Thompson, 1990). First, they are personally meaningful. When a memo from a faceless administrator tells employees that their goal should be to increase production, they tend to feel put upon and not particularly motivated to meet the goal. Second, effective goals are specific and concrete. The goal of "doing better" is usually not a strong motivator. A specific target, such as increasing sales by 10 percent, is a far more motivating goal. It is there for all to see, and whether the goal has been reached is easily determined. Finally, goals are most effective if management supports the workers' own goal-setting, offers special rewards for reaching goals, and gives encouragement after failure (Kluger & DeNisi, 1998).

In short, motivating jobs offer personal challenges, independence, and both intrinsic and extrinsic rewards. They provide enough satisfaction for people to feel excitement and pleasure in working hard. For employers, meanwhile, the rewards are more productivity, less absenteeism, and lower turnover (Ilgen & Klein, 1989).

Promoting Teamwork

Companies in the United States have followed Japanese examples in redesigning jobs to enhance responsibility and flexibility. The goal is to increase both employee productivity and job satisfaction by having employees work in teams that are responsible for solving production problems and making decisions about how best to do the job. Team members are publicly recognized for outstanding work and part of their pay depends on the quality (not just the number) of their products and on the profitability of the whole company.

Thus far we have discussed the motives that underlie relatively self-serving behaviors, such as achievement of personal and occupational success. But what about the motives for altruistic, or "other-oriented" behaviors? In the United States alone, between 45 and 55 percent of adults spend at least some of their time in volunteer work for churches, charities, or other service organizations. The annual value of such efforts is estimated at $180 billion. Cross-cultural studies of volunteerism show similar rates of participation in countries around the world (Curtis, Grabb, & Baer, 1992).

■ What was the researchers' question?

What motivates people to work as volunteers? Allen Omoto and Mark Snyder (1995) addressed a specific form of this question by focusing on the motivation of people who volunteer to help individuals infected with HIV or suffering from AIDS.

■ How did the researchers answer the question?

Studying real-world behaviors such as volunteerism often requires that researchers collect data from people in their homes or at work. In this instance, Omoto and Snyder conducted a telephone survey of volunteers at an AIDS service organization. Working from a list provided by the organization, they contacted 225 active volunteers and offered them each $5 to participate in the survey. A total of 116 of the volunteers agreed to do so. They answered questions about their demographic characteristics (i.e., age, sex, ethnicity), their personality characteristics, their satisfaction with and commitment to the AIDS organization, and, most important, the reasons they had volunteered. To measure this last variable, Omoto and Snyder administered a questionnaire that assessed six motives for volunteering. These motives ranged from altruistic (e.g., concern for others or for the community) to self-centered (e.g., desire to improve one's self-esteem or personal development). Two-and-a-half years later, the researchers obtained information regarding the length of time their respondents had actually served as volunteers. This information was then analyzed in relation to the volunteers' scores on the six motives assessed in the telephone survey.

■ What did the researchers find?

Contrary to what might have been expected, Omoto and Snyder found that the best predictors of time served as volunteers were not the altruistic motives, but the self-centered motives—namely, self-understanding, personal development, and esteem enhancement. Moreover, the more motivated the participants were by self-centered reasons for volunteering, the longer they served as volunteers.

■ What do the results mean?

At the most general level, these findings provide support for the notion that people volunteer to help others for the same basic reason that they do anything else, namely because doing so serves some function or purpose, whether it be perpetuating their genes, reducing a drive, optimizing arousal, or acquiring a positive incentive.

■ What do we still need to know?

While the Omoto and Snyder study provides valuable information about motives for volunteering, at least one question remains unresolved: Are helpful behaviors invariably motivated by self-centered concerns? Probably not, as suggested by the findings of other research on volunteers. For example, Louis Penner and Marcia Finkelstein (1998) found a positive correlation between altruistic motives and the amount of time male volunteers spent working for an AIDS organization and providing direct help to AIDS

Lending a Hand

Members of Habitat for Humanity, including former U.S. President Jimmy Carter, volunteer their services to build houses for poor people in many parts of the world. Are their motives altruistic, self-centered, or both?

sufferers. The same relationship was found in a study of crisis counseling volunteers (Clary & Orenstein, 1991).

Another challenge is to identify the full range of motives that underlie volunteering, inasmuch as the six motives specified by Omoto and Snyder may not represent a complete list. In a recent study, E. Gil Clary and his colleagues (1998) attempted to meet this challenge. The new scale they have developed appears to provide a more comprehensive measure of what motivates people to volunteer.

Recent research has also focused on the motives for prosocial actions that arise in business situations. For example, Sheila Rioux (1998) has identified various motives associated with *organizational citizenship behavior,* which is defined as going beyond the formal requirements of a job in order to help the company or one's co-workers. Further research in this domain may ultimately help industrial/organizational psychologists to better understand why some workers do more than their share and others do less.

RELATIONS AND CONFLICTS AMONG MOTIVES

Suppose you need to study for a test, want to return a friend's phone call, and are also very hungry. Any of these motives might guide your behavior in the next five minutes. What determines which one will?

Maslow's Hierarchy

Abraham Maslow (1970) suggested that human behavior is influenced by a hierarchy of five classes of needs, or motives (see Figure 11.9). Needs at the lowest level of the hierarchy, he said, must be at least partially satisfied before people can be motivated by higher-level goals. From the bottom to the top of Maslow's hierarchy these five motives are as follows:

1. *Biological,* such as food, water, oxygen, activity, and sleep.

2. *Safety,* such as being cared for as a child and having a secure income as an adult.

3. *Belongingness* and *love,* such as being part of various social groups and participating in affectionate sexual and nonsexual relationships.

FIGURE 11.9

Maslow's Hierarchy of Motives

Abraham Maslow saw motives as organized in a hierarchy in which motives at lower levels take precedence over those at higher levels. Although he considered self-actualization to be the essence of mental health, he believed that only rare individuals, such as Mother Teresa or Dr. Martin Luther King, Jr., approach full self-actualization.

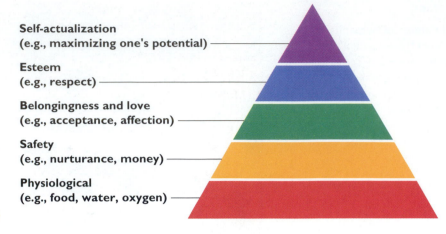

Self-actualization
(e.g., maximizing one's potential)

Esteem
(e.g., respect)

Belongingness and love
(e.g., acceptance, affection)

Safety
(e.g., nurturance, money)

Physiological
(e.g., food, water, oxygen)

Source: Adapted from Maslow, 1943.

4. *Esteem*, being respected as a useful, honorable individual.

5. *Self-actualization*, which means becoming all that one is capable of. People motivated by this need explore and enhance relationships with others, follow interests for intrinsic pleasure rather than status or esteem, and are concerned with issues affecting all people, not just themselves.

In general, research suggests that motives lower in Maslow's hierarchy do take precedence over those higher in the hierarchy (Baumeister & Leary, 1995). But Maslow's system has been criticized as too simplistic. Moreover, people do not always act according to this hierarchy: Even when lower-level needs are unmet, some people continue to be motivated by higher-level needs (Hall et al., 1998). Nevertheless, Maslow's classification is useful for thinking about the relationships among human motives.

LINKAGES

Can motivational conflicts cause stress? (a link to Health, Stress, and Coping)

LINKAGES

Conflicting Motives and Stress

Maslow's hierarchy suggests that differing motives can sometimes conflict. What is the result? Imagine that, while alone and bored on a Saturday night, you think about going to a convenience store for a snack. What are your motives? Hunger might prompt you to go out, as might the prospect of the increased arousal and decreased boredom that a shopping trip will provide. Even sexual motivation might be involved, as you consider the chances of meeting someone exciting in the snack-food aisle. But safety-related motives may give you pause—what if you get mugged? Even an esteem motive might come into play, leading you to avoid being seen alone on a Saturday night.

These are just a few motives that may shape a trivial decision. When the decision is important, the number and strength of motivational pushes and pulls is often greater, creating more internal conflict and acting as a source of stress. Four basic types of motivational conflict have been identified (Miller, 1959):

1. *Approach-approach conflicts* When a person must choose only one of two desirable activities—say, going to a movie or to a play—an *approach-approach conflict* exists. As the importance of the choice increases, so does the difficulty of making it.

2. *Avoidance-avoidance conflicts* An avoidance-avoidance conflict arises when a person must select one of two undesirable alternatives. Someone forced either to sell the family farm or to declare bankruptcy faces an *avoidance-avoidance conflict.* Such conflicts are very difficult to resolve and often create intense emotions.

3. *Approach-avoidance conflicts* If someone you can't stand has tickets to your favorite group's sold-out concert and invites you to come along, what would you do? When a single event or activity has both attractive and unattractive features, an *approach-avoidance conflict* is created. Conflicts of this type are also difficult to resolve and often result in long periods of indecision.

4. *Multiple approach-avoidance conflicts* Suppose you must choose between two jobs. One offers a high salary with a well-known company, but requires long hours and relocation to a miserable climate. The other boasts good advancement opportunities, fringe benefits, and a better climate, but offers low pay and an unpredictable work schedule. This is an example of a *multiple approach-avoidance conflict,* in which two or more alternatives each have both positive and negative features. Such conflicts are difficult to resolve partly because the attributes of each option are often difficult to compare. For example, how many dollars a year does it take to compensate you for living in a bad climate?

Each of these conflicts may create stress, a topic described at length in Chapter 13. Most people in the midst of motivational conflicts are tense, irritable, and particularly vulnerable to physical and psychological problems. These reactions are especially likely when the correct choices are not obvious, when conflicting motives have approximately equal strength, and when a choice can have serious consequences (as in decisions to marry, to divorce, or to approve disconnection of a relative's life-support system). Resolution of such conflicts may take time or may be made impulsively and thoughtlessly, if only to end the discomfort of uncertainty. And even after a conflict is resolved, stress responses may continue in the form of anxiety about the wisdom of the decision or guilt over bad choices. These and other consequences of conflicting motives can even lead to depression or other serious disorders.

Opponent Processes, Motivation, and Emotion

Sometimes people are motivated to engage in behaviors that produce effects that may be in opposition to one another. People who ride roller coasters, for example, often say that the experience gives rise to fear, but also to thrilling excitement. How do they decide whether or not to ride the coaster again? One answer lies in the changing value of incentives and the regulation of arousal described in Richard Solomon's *opponent-process theory,* which is discussed in Chapter 6, on learning (Solomon & Corbit, 1974). As noted there, opponent-process theory is based on two assumptions. The first is that any reaction to a stimulus is followed by an opposite reaction, called the opponent process. For example, being startled by a sudden sound is typically followed by relaxation and relief. Second, after repeated exposure to the same stimulus, the initial reaction weakens, and the opponent process becomes quicker and stronger.

Research on opponent-process theory has revealed a predictable pattern of emotional changes that helps explain some people's motivation to repeatedly engage in arousing but fearsome activities, such as skydiving, bungee-jumping, or roller-coaster riding. Prior to the first several episodes, people usually experience stark terror, followed by intense relief. With more experience, however, the terror becomes mild anxiety, and what had been relief grows to a euphoria that can appear *during* the activity (Solomon, 1980). As a result, says Solomon, some people's motivation to pursue such activities can become a virtual addiction.

The emotions associated with motivational conflicts and with the operation of opponent processes provide just two examples of the intimate links between human motivation and emotion. Motivation can intensify emotion, as when a normally timid person's hunger results in an angry protest over a late pizza delivery. But emotions can also create motivation. Happiness, for example, is an emotion that people want to feel, so they engage in whatever behaviors—studying, artwork, beachcombing—they think

Winners and Losers

Emotional experiences depend in part on our interpretation of situations and how those situations relate to our goals. The stimulus for these drastically different emotional reactions was the same—namely, the announcement of the winners of a cheerleading contest. Each woman's emotional experience following this stimulus depended on whether she perceived the situation as making her a winner or a loser.

will achieve it. Similarly, as an emotion that most people want to avoid, anxiety prompts many behaviors, from leaving the scene of an accident to avoiding poisonous snakes. In the next section of this chapter, we take a closer look at emotions.

THE NATURE OF EMOTION

Everyone seems to agree that joy, sorrow, anger, fear, love, and hate are emotions, but it is hard to identify the shared features that make these experiences emotions rather than, say, thoughts or impulses. In fact, some cultures see emotion and thought as the same thing. The Chewong of Malaysia, for example, consider the liver the seat of both what we call thoughts and feelings (Russell, 1991).

Defining Characteristics

Most psychologists in Western cultures tend to see emotions as organized psychological and physiological reactions to changes in our relationship to the world. These reactions are partly subjective experiences and partly objectively measurable patterns of behavior and physiological arousal. The subjective experience of emotion has several characteristics:

1. Emotion is usually *transitory;* it tends to have a relatively clear beginning and end, and a relatively short duration. Moods, by contrast, tend to last longer.

2. Emotional experience has *valence,* which means it is either positive or negative.

3. Emotional experience is elicited partly by a *cognitive appraisal* of how a situation relates to your goals. The same event can elicit very different emotions depending on the way you interpret what the event means. An exam score of 75 percent may excite you if your previous score had been 50 percent, but it may upset you if you had never before scored below 90 percent.

4. Emotional experience *alters thought processes,* often by directing attention toward some things and away from others. The anguish of parents whose child is killed by a drunken driver, for example, may prompt them to alter their perception of the importance of drunk-driving laws.

5. Emotional experience elicits an *action tendency,* a motivation to behave in certain ways. The grieving parents' anger, for example, may motivate them to harm the driver or to work for stronger penalties for drunk driving.

6. Emotional experiences are *passions* that happen to you, usually without willful intent. You exert some control over emotions inasmuch as they depend partly on how you interpret situations. If you interpret an emotion as fear, for example, your experience of fear may be amplified as a result. Still, you cannot *decide* to experience joy or sorrow; instead, you "fall in love" or are "overcome by grief." Emotional experiences, much like personality traits, have a different relation to the self than conscious cognitions.

The subjective aspects of emotions are, therefore, experiences both *triggered by* the thinking self and felt as *happening to* the self. They reveal an individual as both agent and object, both I and me, both the controller of thoughts and the recipient of passions. The extent to which we are "victims" of our passions versus rational designers of our emotions is a central dilemma of human existence, as much a subject of literature as of psychology.

Objective aspects of emotion include learned and innate *expressive displays* and *physiological responses*. Expressive displays—a smile, a frown—communicate feelings to others. Physiological responses—changes in heart rate, for example—provide biological adjustments needed to perform the action tendencies generated by emotional experience. If you throw a temper tantrum at the object of your anger, for example, your heart must deliver additional oxygen and fuel to your muscles.

In summary, an **emotion** is a transitory, positive or negative experience that is felt with some intensity as happening to the self, generated in part by a cognitive appraisal of situations, and accompanied by both learned and innate physical responses. Through emotion, people communicate their internal states and intentions to others, but emotion also functions to direct and energize a person's own thoughts and actions. Emotion often disrupts thought and behavior, but it also triggers and guides cognitions and organizes, motivates, and sustains behavior and social relations.

The Biology of Emotion

The role of biology in emotion is seen in mechanisms of the central nervous system and the autonomic nervous system. In the *central nervous system,* specific brain areas are involved in the generation of emotions as well as in our experience of those emotions. The *autonomic nervous system* gives rise to many of the physiological changes associated with emotional arousal.

Brain Mechanisms Although many questions remain, researchers have described three basic features of the brain's control of emotion. First, it appears that activity in the *limbic system,* especially in the *amygdala,* is central to various aspects of emotion (see Figure 11.10). Animal research initially demonstrated that disruption of the amygdala's functioning prevented animals from being able to associate fear with a negative stimulus (Davis et al., 1993), and research with humans has highlighted the amygdala's critical role in the learning of emotional associations and the recognizing of emotional expressions in other individuals. In a recent functional magnetic resonance imaging study, when researchers paired an aversively loud noise with pictures of neutral faces, the participants' brains revealed activation of the amygdala while the noise-picture association was being learned (LaBar et al., 1998). In another study, victims of a disease that destroys only the amygdala were found to be unable to judge other people's emotional state by looking at their facial expressions (Adolphs et al., 1994). For example, faces that normal people rated as expressing strong negative emotions were rated by the amygdala-damaged individuals as approachable and trustworthy (Adolphs, Tranel, & Damasio, 1998).

A second aspect of the brain's involvement in emotion is seen in its control over emotional and nonemotional facial expressions (Rinn, 1984). Take a moment to look in a mirror and put on your best fake smile. The voluntary facial movements you just

FIGURE 11.10

Brain Regions Involved in Emotion

Incoming sensory information alerts the brain to an emotion-evoking situation. Most of the information goes through the thalamus; the cingulate cortex and hippocampus are involved in the interpretation of this sensory input. Output from these areas goes to the amygdala and hypothalamus, which control the autonomic nervous system via brainstem connections. There are also connections from the thalamus directly to the amygdala. The locus coeruleus is an area of the brainstem that causes both widespread arousal of cortical areas and changes in autonomic activity.

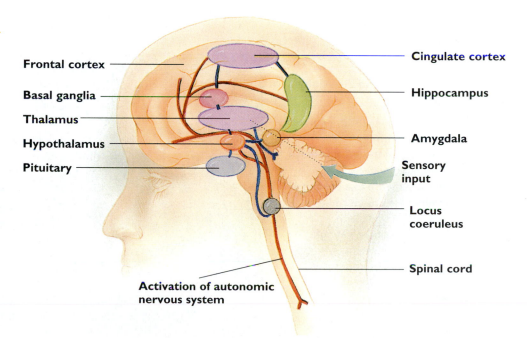

made, like all voluntary movements, are controlled by the *pyramidal motor system*, a brain system that includes the motor cortex (see Figure 3.18 on page 73). However, a smile that expresses genuine happiness is involuntary. That kind of smile, like the other facial movements associated with emotions, is governed by the *extrapyramidal motor system*, which depends on subcortical areas. Brain damage can disrupt either system (see Figure 11.11). Thus, people with pyramidal motor system damage show normal facial expressions during genuine emotion, but cannot fake a smile. In contrast, people with damage to the extrapyramidal system can pose facial expressions at will, but remain straight-faced even when feeling genuine joy or profound sadness (Hopf, Muller, & Hopf, 1992).

A third aspect of the brain's role in emotion is revealed by research on the differing contributions of its two cerebral hemispheres to the perception, experience, and expression of emotion. For example, after suffering damage to the right, but not the left, hemisphere, people no longer laugh at jokes—even though they can still understand the jokes' words, the logic (or illogic) underlying them, and the punch lines (Critchley, 1991). Further, when people are asked to name the emotions shown in slides of facial expressions, blood flow increases in the right hemisphere more than in the left hemisphere (Gur, Skolnic, & Gur, 1994). People are also faster and more accurate at this emotion-naming task when the facial expressions are presented to the right hemisphere than when they are presented to the left (Hahdahl, Iversen, & Jonsen, 1993). Finally, compared with normal people, depressed people display greater electrical activity in the right frontal cortex (Schaffer, Davidson, & Saron, 1983) and perform more poorly on tasks that depend especially on the right hemisphere (Banich et al., 1992; Heller, Etienne, & Miller, 1995).

Yet there is some debate about the relationship between hemispheric differences and emotion. Research has demonstrated that the right hemisphere is activated during many displays of emotion (Heller, 1993), including negative emotion. But some investigators argue that the *experiencing* of positive emotion depends on the left frontal cortex. For example, EEG recordings show that smiling during an experience of genuine positive emotion correlates with greater left frontal activity (Davidson et al., 1990). Corroborating evidence is provided in a recent case study of a sixteen-year-old girl suffering from epilepsy. When an area of her left frontal cortex was given mild electrical stimulation, smiling was elicited, whereas stimulation at a higher intensity elicited robust laughter (Fried et al., 1998). The patient attributed the laughter to whatever external stimulus was present ("You guys are just so funny . . . standing around"). Generally, however, most other aspects of emotion—the *experiencing* of negative emo-

FIGURE 11.11

Control of Voluntary and Emotional Facial Movements

This man has a tumor in his motor cortex that prevents him from voluntarily moving the muscles on the left side of his face. In the photograph at left he is trying to smile in response to a command from the examiner. He cannot smile on command, but he *can* smile with happiness, as the photograph at right shows, because the movements associated with genuine emotion are controlled by the extrapyramidal motor system.

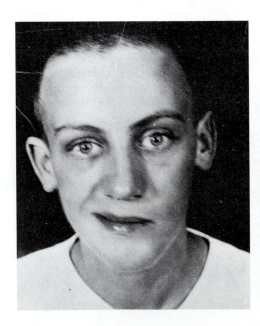
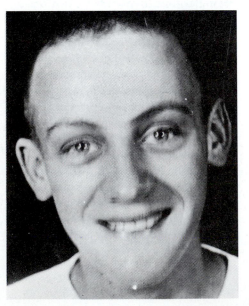

tion, the *perception* of any emotion exhibited in faces or other stimuli, and the facial *expression* of any emotion—depend on the right hemisphere more than on the left (Heller, Nitschke, & Miller, 1998).

If the right hemisphere is relatively dominant in emotion, which side of the face would you expect to be somewhat more involved in expressing emotion? If you said the left side, you are correct because, as described in Chapter 3, movements of each side of the body are controlled by the opposite side of the brain.

Mechanisms of the Autonomic Nervous System   The autonomic nervous system (ANS) is involved in many of the physiological changes that accompany emotions (Vernet, Robin, & Dittmar, 1995). If your hands get cold and clammy when you are nervous, it is because the ANS has increased perspiration and decreased the blood flow in your hands.

As described in Chapter 3, the ANS carries information between the brain and most organs of the body—the heart and blood vessels, the digestive system, and so on. Each of these organs has its own ongoing activity, but ANS input modulates this activity, increasing or decreasing it. By modulating the activity of organs, the ANS coordinates their functioning to meet the body's general needs and to prepare it for change (Porges, Doussard, & Maita, 1995). If you are aroused to take action—to run to catch a bus, say—you need more glucose to fuel your muscles. The ANS frees needed energy by stimulating secretion of glucose-generating hormones and promoting blood flow to the muscles.

Figure 11.12 shows that the autonomic nervous system is organized into two divisions: the sympathetic nervous system and the parasympathetic nervous system.

FIGURE 11.12

The Autonomic Nervous System

Emotional responses involve activation of the autonomic nervous system, which includes sympathetic and parasympathetic subsystems. Which of the bodily responses depicted do you associate with emotional experiences?

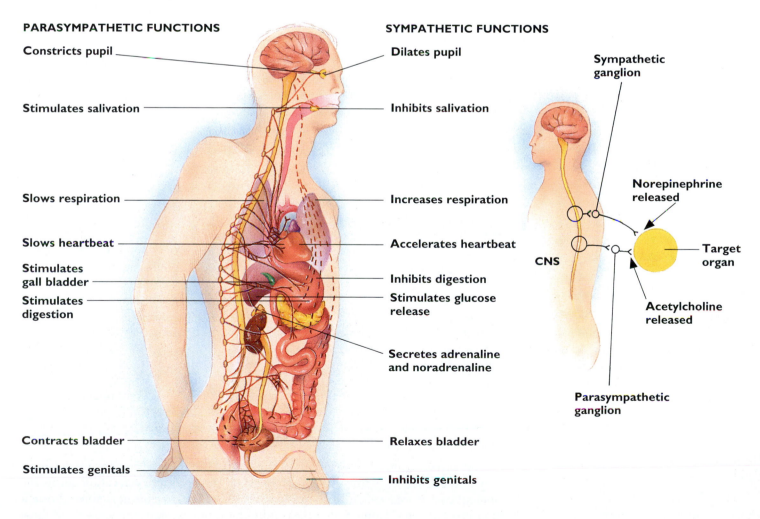

PARASYMPATHETIC FUNCTIONS

Constricts pupil

Stimulates salivation

Slows respiration

Slows heartbeat

Stimulates gall bladder

Stimulates digestion

Contracts bladder

Stimulates genitals

SYMPATHETIC FUNCTIONS

Dilates pupil

Inhibits salivation

Increases respiration

Accelerates heartbeat

Inhibits digestion

Stimulates glucose release

Secretes adrenaline and noradrenaline

Relaxes bladder

Inhibits genitals

Sympathetic ganglion

Norepinephrine released

Target organ

Acetylcholine released

Parasympathetic ganglion

CNS

Emotions can activate either of these divisions, both of which send axon fibers to each organ in the body. Generally, the sympathetic and parasympathetic fibers have opposite effects on these so-called target organs. Axons from the **parasympathetic system** release acetylcholine onto target organs, leading to activity related to the protection, nourishment, and growth of the body. For example, parasympathetic activity increases digestion by stimulating movement of the intestinal system, so that more nutrients are taken from food. Axons from the **sympathetic system** release norepinephrine onto target organs, helping to prepare the body for vigorous activity. When one part of the sympathetic system is stimulated, other parts are activated "in sympathy" with it (Gellhorn & Loofbourrow, 1963). For example, as described in Chapter 13, input from sympathetic neurons to the *adrenal medulla* causes that gland to dump norepinephrine and epinephrine into the bloodstream, thereby activating all sympathetic target organs (see Figure 13.3 on page 457). The result is the **fight-or-flight syndrome,** a pattern of increased heart rate and blood pressure, rapid or irregular breathing, dilated pupils, perspiration, dry mouth, increased blood sugar, piloerection ("goose bumps"), and other changes that help prepare the body to combat or run from a threat.

The ANS is not directly connected to brain areas involved in consciousness, so sensory input about organ activity reaches the brain at a nonconscious level. Thus, you may hear your stomach grumble, but you can't actually feel it secrete acids. Similarly, you cannot consciously experience the brain mechanisms that alter the activity of your autonomic nervous system. This is why most people cannot exert direct, conscious control over blood pressure or other aspects of ANS activity. However, you can do things that have indirect effects on the ANS. For example, to arouse autonomic innervation of your sex organs, you might imagine an erotic situation. And to raise your blood pressure, you might hold your breath or strain your muscles.

THEORIES OF EMOTION

Are the physiological responses associated with emotion sufficient to produce an emotional experience, or are these responses simply by-products of an emotional experience that is created when we cognitively interpret events? In other words, is emotion in the heart, in the head, or both? Questions about the roles played by physiological and cognitive activity in the experience of emotion have been the focus of research for over a century; in this section we highlight two major theories about these questions.

James's Theory

Suppose while walking in the woods you come upon a ferocious bear. Scared to death, you run for dear life. Do you run because you are afraid, or are you afraid because you run? The example and the question come from William James, who offered one of the first formal accounts of how physiological responses relate to emotional experience. James argued that you are afraid *because* you run. Your running and other physiological responses, he said, follow directly from your perception of the bear. Without some form of these responses, you would feel no fear because, said James, recognition of physiological responses *is* fear.

Presented in this simplified way, James's theory of emotion may sound preposterous. It defies common sense, which says that it would be silly to run from something unless you already fear it. James concluded otherwise after examining his own mental processes. He decided that once all physiological responses are stripped away, nothing remains of the experience of an emotion (James, 1890); hence emotion, he reasoned, is simply the result of experiencing a particular set of physiological responses. Because a similar view was offered by Carle Lange, a Danish physician, James's view is sometimes called the *James-Lange theory* of emotion.

Observing Peripheral Responses   Figure 11.13 outlines the components of emotional experience, including those emphasized by James. First, a perception affects the cerebral cortex, said James; "then quick as a flash, reflex currents pass down through their pre-ordained channels, alter the condition of muscle, skin, and viscus; and these

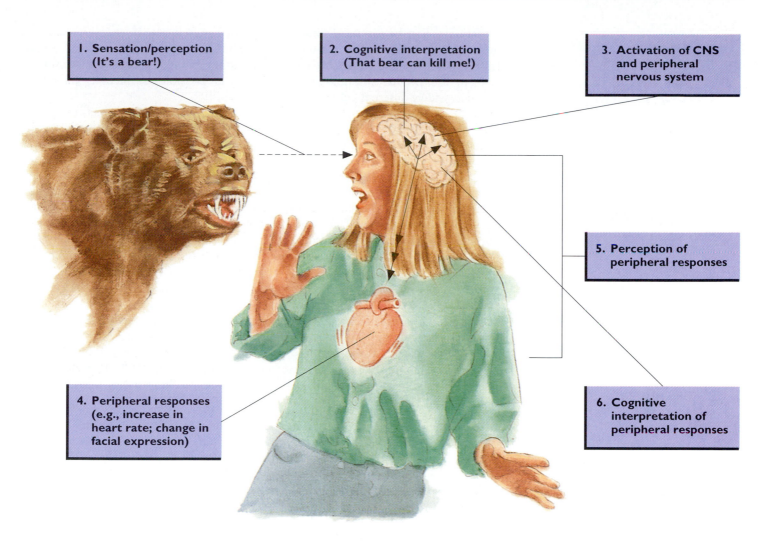

FIGURE 11.13

Components of Emotion

Emotion is associated with activity in the brain and spinal cord as well as with peripheral responses. Emotion theorists have argued about which of these components are essential for emotion. William James emphasized #5, the perception of peripheral responses, such as changes in heart rate. Stanley Schachter, in his modification of James's theory, emphasized #6, the cognitive interpretation and labeling of those peripheral responses. Walter Cannon believed that #3 was sufficient, that emotion could occur wholly in the central nervous system.

alterations, perceived, like the original object, in as many portions of the cortex, combine with it in consciousness and transform it from an object-simply-apprehended into an object-emotionally-felt" (James, 1890, p. 759). In other words, the brain interprets a situation and automatically directs a particular set of peripheral physiological changes—a palpitating heart, sinking stomach, facial grimace, perspiration, and certain patterns of blood flow. We are not conscious of the process, said James, until we become aware of these bodily changes; at that point, we experience an emotion. Thus, James's theory holds that reflexive peripheral responses precede the subjective experience of emotion, and that each particular emotion is created by a particular pattern of physiological responses.

Notice that, according to James's view, there is no emotional experience generated by activity in the brain alone, no special "emotion center" in the brain where the firing of neurons creates a direct experience of emotion. If this theory is accurate, it might account for the difficulty we sometimes have in knowing our true feelings: We must figure out what emotions we feel by perceiving subtle differences in specific physiological response patterns.

Evaluating James's Theory In the English language there are more than 500 labels for emotions (Averill, 1980). Does a distinctly different pattern of physiological activity precede each of these emotions? According to James's theory, for example, fear would follow from one pattern of bodily responses, and anger would follow from a different pattern.

Research shows that certain emotional states are indeed associated with different patterns of autonomic changes. For example, blood flow to the hands and feet increases in association with anger and declines in association with fear (Levenson, Ekman, & Friesen, 1990). Thus, fear involves "cold feet"; anger does not. A pattern of activity associated with disgust includes increased muscle activity, but no change in heart rate. Even when people mentally "relive" different kinds of emotional experiences, they show different patterns of autonomic activity (Ekman, Levenson, & Friesen, 1983). Such emotion-specific patterns of physiological activity have been found in widely different cultures (Levenson et al., 1992).

Furthermore, different patterns of autonomic activity are closely tied to specific emotional facial expressions, and vice versa (Ekman, 1993). When research participants were told to make certain facial movements, various facial configurations led to autonomic changes resembling those normally accompanying emotion (Ekman, Levenson, & Friesen, 1983; see also Figures 11.14 and 11.15). The patterns of autonomic activity produced by expressions of fear, anger, disgust, sadness, and happiness could be distinguished from each other. Also, almost all participants reported feeling the emotion associated with the expression they had created, even though they could not see their own expressions and did not realize that a specific emotion was being portrayed. The emotion created by posed facial expressions can be significant enough to affect social judgments. In one study, participants who were asked to smile tended to form more positive impressions of other people than did those who received no special instructions (Ohira & Kurono, 1993).

Mimicking the face of another person may elicit in you the same feelings that person is having, including autonomic responses, and may thus create empathy. Indeed, people do best at describing another person's emotions when their own physiological responses match those of the other person (Levenson & Ruef, 1992). Edgar Allan Poe noted this relationship between facial expressions and feelings more than a hundred years ago:

> When I wish to find out how wise or how stupid or how good or how wicked is anyone, or what are his thoughts at the moment, I fashion the expression of my face, as accurately as possible, in accordance with the expression of his, and then wait to see what thoughts or sentiments arise in my mind or heart, as if to match or correspond with the expression. (Quoted in Levenson, Ekman, & Friesen, 1990)

FIGURE 11.14

Patterns of Physiological Change Associated with Different Emotions

In this experiment, movements of the face characteristic of different emotions produced different patterns of change in (A) heart rate; (B) peripheral blood flow, as measured by finger temperature; (C) skin conductance; and (D) muscle activity (Levenson, Ekman, & Friesen, 1990). For example, making an angry face caused heart rate and finger temperature to rise, whereas making a fearful face raised heart rate but lowered finger temperature.

Source: Levenson, Ekman, & Friesen, 1990.

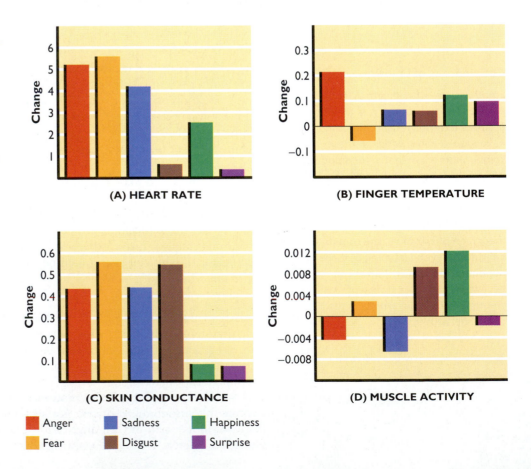

FIGURE 11.15

Voluntary Facial Movements and Emotional Autonomic Responses

This man was instructed to (A) "raise your brows and pull them together"; (B) "raise your upper eyelids"; and (C) "also stretch your lips horizontally, back toward your ears." Carrying out these instructions produced changes in heart rate characteristic of fear *and* the experience of fear.

James's theory implies that the experience of emotion would be blocked if a person were unable to detect physiological changes occurring in the body's periphery. For example, spinal cord injuries that reduce feedback from peripheral responses should reduce the intensity of emotional experiences. This was the result reported in a study performed during the 1960s (Hohmann, 1966). However, more recent studies have shown that when people with spinal injuries actively pursue their life goals, they experience a full range of emotions, including as much happiness as noninjured people (Bermond et al., 1991; Chwalisz, Diener, & Gallagher, 1988). These people reported that their emotional experiences are just as intense as before their injuries, even though they notice less intense physiological changes associated with their emotions.

Such reports seem to contradict James's theory. But spinal cord injuries do not usually affect facial expressions, which James included among the bodily responses that are experienced as emotions. Thus, some researchers have proposed a variant of James's theory, the *facial feedback hypothesis,* which maintains that involuntary facial movements provide sufficient peripheral information to drive emotional experience (Ekman & Davidson, 1993). This hypothesis predicts that feeling yourself smile should make you feel happy. It also helps explain the results mentioned earlier suggesting that voluntarily posed facial expressions create the emotions normally associated with them.

Lie Detection   James's view that different patterns of physiological activity are associated with different emotions forms the basis for the lie detection industry. If people experience anxiety or guilt when they lie, specific patterns of physiological activity accompanying these emotions should be detectable on instruments, called *polygraphs,* that record heart rate, breathing rate, skin conductance (which is affected by slight changes in perspiration), and other autonomic responses.

To identify the perpetrator of a crime, a polygraph tester may ask questions specific to the crime, such as "Did you stab anyone on July 3, 1999?" Responses to such relevant questions are then compared with responses to *control questions,* such as "Have you ever tried to hurt someone?" Innocent people might have tried to hurt someone at some time and might feel guilty when asked, but they should have no reason to feel guilty about what they did on July 3, 1999. Thus, an innocent person should have a stronger emotional response to control questions than to relevant questions (Rosenfeld, 1995).

Most people do have emotional responses when they lie, but statistics about the accuracy of polygraphs are difficult to obtain. Estimates vary widely, from those suggesting that polygraphs detect 90 percent of guilty, lying individuals (Raskin, 1986) to those suggesting that polygraphs mislabel as many as 40 percent of truthful, innocent persons as guilty liars (Ben-Shakhar & Furedy, 1990). Obviously, the results of a polygraph test are not determined entirely by whether a person is telling the truth. What people think about the act of lying, and about the value of the test, can also influence the accuracy of its results. For example, people who consider lying to be acceptable—and who do not believe in the power of polygraphs—are unlikely to display emotion-linked physiological responses while lying during the test. However, an innocent

Searching for Truth

Polygraph tests are not infallible, but they tend to be most effective when the person being tested believes in them. In a small town where the police could not afford a polygraph, one suspect confessed his crime when a "lie detector" consisting of a kitchen colander was placed over his head and attached by wires to a copy machine (Shepard, Kohut, & Sweet, 1989).

person who believes in such tests and who thinks that "everything always goes wrong" might show a large fear response when asked about a crime, thus wrongly suggesting guilt.

Polygraphs can catch some liars, but most researchers agree that a guilty person can "fool" a polygraph lie detector. Thus, the American Psychological Association has expressed "great reservations about the use of polygraph tests to detect deception" (Abeles, 1985). Other lie-detecting devices are now under development. One of these measures the brain waves emitted during certain cognitive operations (Bashore & Rapp, 1992). Such devices may someday prove more accurate than polygraph tests because they do not depend on a link between deception and emotional responses.

Schachter's Modification of James's Theory   In the early 1960s, when many psychologists were raising questions about the validity of James's theory of emotion, Stanley Schachter argued that the theory was essentially correct—but required a few modifications (Cornelius, 1996). In Schachter's view, feedback about physiological changes may not vary enough to create all the subtle shadings of human emotional experiences. Instead, said Schachter, emotions emerge from a *combination* of feedback from peripheral responses and our cognitive interpretation of what caused those responses (Schachter & Singer, 1962). According to Schachter, cognitive interpretation comes into play twice: once when you perceive the situation that leads to bodily responses and again when you identify feedback from those responses as a particular emotion (see Figure 11.13 on page 391). The same physiological responses, therefore, might be given many different labels, depending on your interpretation of those responses.

The labeling of arousal depends on an **attribution,** the process of identifying the cause of some event. People may attribute their physiological arousal to different emotions, depending on the information available about the situation. For example, if you are watching the final seconds of a close ball game, you might attribute your racing heart, rapid breathing, and perspiration to excitement; but you might attribute the same physiological reactions to anxiety if you are waiting for a big exam to begin. Thus, the emotion you experience upon seeing a bear in the woods might be fear, excitement, astonishment, or surprise, depending on how you label your bodily reactions.

Schachter's refinement of James's theory predicts that emotional experience will be less intense if arousal is attributed to a nonemotional cause. So if you notice your heart pounding before an exam but say to yourself, "Sure my heart's pounding—I just drank five cups of coffee!" then you should feel "wired" from caffeine rather than afraid or worried. This prediction has received some support (Schachter & Singer, 1962; Sinclair et al., 1994).

Schachter's theory also predicts that if arousal is artificially induced—by drugs, for example—the emotion that results will depend to a certain extent on external circumstances; that is, people will attribute their arousal to the emotions suggested by cues in the situation they are in. Evidence related to this idea is, at best, mixed. In their original study, Schachter and his colleague, Jerome Singer (1962) did find that situational factors influenced how people labeled drug-induced arousal, and later research has shown that people can be led to misattribute their arousal on the basis of false information from an experimenter (e.g., Storms & Nisbett, 1970). However, other investigators have been unable to replicate these results (Leventhal & Tomarken, 1986; Maslach, 1979). Today, few researchers fully accept Schachter's theory, but it stimulated an enormous amount of valuable research on emotions (Cornelius, 1996). It also directly influenced research on a phenomenon called *transfer of excitation.*

Transfer of Excitation   There is evidence that physiological arousal from nonemotional sources can *intensify* emotional experience (Zillman, 1984). For example, people who have been aroused by physical exercise become more angry when provoked, or experience more intense sexual feelings when in the company of an attractive person, than do people who have been less physically active (Allen et al., 1989).

When arousal from one experience carries over to an independent situation, it is called **transferred excitation** (Reisenzein, 1983). This transfer is most likely to occur when the overt signs of physiological arousal have subsided but the sympathetic nervous system is still active. In one study, people were emotionally "primed" by reading words that were cheerful, neutral, or depressing. Next, they either engaged in physical exercise or sat quietly and then rated their mood, either immediately or after a short delay. Those who had not exercised, or who rated themselves *immediately* after exercise, reported being in no particular mood. However, the mood of those whose reports came several minutes after exercising tended to be positive, neutral, or negative, depending on which priming words they had read earlier. Apparently, the people in this latter group were still somewhat aroused; but because the delay had been long enough to keep them from attributing their lingering arousal to exercise, they instead used the emotional tone of the word list as a guide to labeling their mood (Sinclair et al., 1994).

Arousal created by one emotion can also transfer to intensify another. For example, arousal from fear, like arousal from exercise, can enhance sexual feelings. One study of this transfer took place in British Columbia over a deep river gorge. The gorge could be crossed either by a precarious swinging bridge or by a safe wooden structure. A female researcher asked men who had just crossed each bridge to fill out a questionnaire that included a measure of sexual imagery. The men who met the woman after crossing the dangerous bridge had much higher sexual imagery scores than the men who had crossed the safe bridge. Furthermore, they were more likely to rate her as attractive (Dutton & Aron, 1974). When the person giving out the questionnaire was a male, however, the type of bridge crossed had no impact on sexual imagery. To test the possibility that the men who crossed the dangerous bridge were simply more adventurous in both bridge crossing and sexual encounters, the researchers repeated the study, but with one change. This time, the woman approached the men farther down the trail, long after arousal from the bridge crossing had subsided. Now, the apparently adventurous men were no more likely than others to rate the woman as attractive. Apparently, it was indeed transfer of excitation, not just adventurousness, that produced the original result.

Cannon's Theory

The theories we have considered so far assume that the experience of emotion depends on facial movements and other bodily responses outside the brain. However, Walter Cannon believed that emotion can result from brain activity alone (Cannon, 1927/1987). He argued that you feel fear at the sight of a wild bear even before you take a step because emotional experience starts in the brain—specifically, in the thalamus, the brain structure that relays information from most sense organs to the cortex.

According to Cannon's theory of emotion (also known as the *Cannon-Bard theory*, in recognition of Philip Bard's contribution), sensory information about emotional situations first reaches the thalamus, which sends signals *simultaneously* to the autonomic nervous system and to the cerebral cortex, where the emotion becomes conscious. So when you see a bear, the brain receives sensory information about it, interprets that information as a bear, and directly creates the experience of fear while at the same time sending messages to the heart, lungs, and legs to initiate a rapid departure. In Cannon's theory, then, there is a direct, central nervous system experience of emotion, with or without feedback about peripheral responses (see Figure 11.13 on page 391).

Updating Cannon's Theory   Subsequent research indicates that the thalamus is not the "seat" of emotion, as Cannon had suggested. Still, through its connections to the amygdala (see Figure 11.10 on page 387), the thalamus does participate in some aspects of emotional processing (Lang, 1995; LeDoux, 1995). For example, animal studies show that the emotion of fear is generated by thalamic connections to the amygdala (LeDoux, 1995). The implication is that strong emotions can sometimes bypass the cortex without requiring conscious thought to activate them—thus possibly explaining why people find it so difficult to overcome an intense fear, or phobia, even though they may consciously know the fear is irrational. Consistent with this

THEORIES OF EMOTION		
Theory	**Source of Emotions**	**Evidence for Theory**
James	The CNS generates specific physical responses; observation of the physical responses constitutes emotion.	Different emotions are associated with different physical responses.
Schachter's modification of James's theory	The CNS generates nonspecific physical responses; interpretation of the physical responses in light of the situation constitutes emotions.	Excitation generated by physical activity can transfer to increase emotional intensity.
Cannon	Parts of the CNS directly generate emotions; peripheral physiological responses are not necessary.	People with spinal cord damage experience a full range of emotions without feedback from peripheral responses.

interpretation is the fact that some stimuli, such as angry faces, can elicit physiological signs of arousal without any conscious perception (Morris et al., 1998).

An updated version of Cannon's theory suggests that specific brain areas produce the feelings of pleasure or pain associated with emotion. This idea arose from studies showing that electrical stimulation of certain parts of the brain is rewarding. The researchers found that rats kept returning to the place in their cage where they received stimulation through electrodes in their brains. When these animals were allowed to control delivery of the stimulation by pressing a bar, they pressed it until they were physically exhausted, ignoring even food and water (Olds & Milner, 1954). The brain areas in which stimulation is experienced as especially pleasurable include the dopamine systems, which are activated by drugs of abuse (Bardo, 1998). In contrast, stimulation of other brain regions is so unpleasant that animals work hard to avoid it.

Presumably, part of the direct central experience of emotions involves areas of the brain whose activity is experienced as either pleasurable or aversive. The areas of the brain activated by the kind of events that elicit emotion in humans have widespread connections throughout the brain. Thus, the central nervous system experience of emotion is probably widely distributed, not narrowly localized in any one "emotion center" (Derryberry & Tucker, 1992).

Certain brain areas appear to form a kind of "autonomic nervous system" within the brain (Hartman et al., 1986). Just as the ANS modulates the activity of organs that can function without its input, some neurotransmitter systems modulate the activity of other brain cells. Cells in the locus coeruleus play this "autonomic" role, releasing norepinephrine and modulating the activity of other brain cells, as well as sending signals to the autonomic nervous system in the periphery (Olpe, Steinmann, & Jones, 1985). An "autonomic nervous system" in the brain could be the equivalent of what Walter Cannon envisioned: a central mechanism that arouses the brain *and* activates emotional facial expressions and autonomic visceral responses (Levenson, Ekman, & Friesen, 1990).

Indeed, there is increasing evidence for the main thrust of Cannon's theory: that emotion occurs through the activation of specific parts of the central nervous system. However, different parts of the central nervous system may be activated for different emotions and for different aspects of the total emotional experience.

Conclusions   "In Review: Theories of Emotion" summarizes key elements of the theories we have discussed. It appears that both peripheral autonomic responses (including facial responses) and the cognitive interpretation of those responses add to emotional experience. In addition, the brain itself can apparently generate emotional experience, independent of physiological arousal. So emotion is probably both in the heart and in the head (including the face). The most basic emotions probably occur directly within the brain, whereas the many shades of discernible emotions probably arise from attributions, including evaluations of physiological responses. No theory has completely resolved the issue of which, if any, component of emotion is primary. However, the theories we have discussed have helped psychologists better understand how these components interact to produce emotional experience.

COMMUNICATING EMOTION

Imagine a woman watching television. You can see her face, but not what she sees on the screen. She might be engaged in complex thought, perhaps comparing her investments with those of the experts interviewed in a financial news report. Or she might be thinking of nothing at all as she loses herself in a soap opera. In other words, your observation is not likely to tell you much about what she is thinking. If the television program creates an emotional experience, however, you will be able to make a reasonably accurate guess about which emotion she feels (Patrick, Craig, & Prkachin, 1986). So far, we have described emotion from the inside, as people experience their own emotions. In this section, we examine the social organization of emotion—how people communicate emotions to each other.

Humans communicate emotions partly through tone of voice and body posture or movement, but mainly through facial movements and expressions. The human face can create thousands of different expressions (Zajonc, 1998), and people are good at detecting them. Observers can discern very small facial movements—a twitch of the mouth can carry a lot of information. Are emotional facial expressions innate, or are they learned? And how are they used in communicating emotion?

Innate Expressions of Emotion

Charles Darwin observed that some facial expressions seem to be universal (Darwin 1872/1965). He proposed that these expressions are genetically determined, passed on biologically from one generation to the next. The facial expressions seen today, said Darwin, are those that have been most effective at telling others something about how a person is feeling. If someone is scowling with teeth clenched, for example, you will probably assume that he or she is angry, and you will be unlikely to choose that particular moment to ask for a loan.

Infants provide one source of evidence for the innateness of some facial expressions. Newborns do not need to be taught to grimace in pain or to smile in pleasure or to

The Universal Smile

The innate origin of some emotional expressions is supported by the fact that the facial movement pattern we call a smile is related to happiness, pleasure, and other positive emotions in human cultures throughout the world.

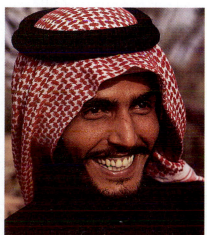

blink when startled (Balaban, 1995). Even blind infants, who cannot imitate adults' expressions, show the same emotional expressions as do sighted infants (Goodenough, 1932).

A second line of evidence for innate facial expressions comes from studies showing that, for the most basic emotions, people in all cultures show similar facial responses to similar emotional stimuli (Zajonc, 1998). Participants in these studies look at photographs of people's faces and then try to name the emotion each person is feeling. The pattern of facial movements we call a smile, for example, is universally related to positive emotions. Sadness is almost always accompanied by slackened muscle tone and a "long" face. Likewise, in almost all cultures, people contort their faces in a similar way when shown something they find disgusting. And a furrowed brow is frequently associated with frustration (Ekman, 1994).

Anger is also linked with a facial expression recognized by almost all cultures. One study examined artwork—including ceremonial masks—of various Western and non-Western cultures (Aronoff, Barclay, & Stevenson, 1988). The angry, threatening masks of all eighteen cultures contained similar elements, such as triangular eyes and diagonal lines on the cheeks. In particular, angular and diagonal elements carry the impression of threat (see Figure 11.16).

Social and Cultural Influences on Emotional Expression

Whereas some basic emotional expressions are innate, many others are neither innate nor universal (Ekman, 1993). Even innate expressions are flexible and modifiable, changing as necessary in the social contexts within which they occur (Fernández-Dols & Ruiz-Belda, 1995; Fridlund, 1994). For example, facial expressions become more intense and change more frequently while people are imagining social scenes as opposed to solitary scenes (Fridlund et al., 1990). Similarly, facial expressions in response to odors tend to be more intense when others are watching than when people are alone (Jancke & Kaufmann, 1994).

Further, although a core of emotional responses is recognized by all cultures, there is a certain degree of cultural variation in recognizing some emotions (Russell, 1995). In one study, for example, Japanese and North American people agreed about which facial expressions signaled happiness, surprise, and sadness, but they frequently disagreed about which faces showed anger, disgust, and fear (Matsumoto & Ekman, 1989). Members of preliterate cultures such as the Fore of New Guinea agree even less with people in Western cultures on the labeling of facial expressions (Russell, 1994). In addition, there are variations in the ways that cultures interpret emotions expressed by tone of voice (Mesquita & Frijda, 1992). An example is provided by a study showing that Taiwanese participants were best at recognizing a sad tone of voice whereas Dutch participants were best at recognizing happy tones (Van Bezooijen, Otto, & Heenan, 1983).

People learn how to express certain emotions in particular ways, as specified by cultural rules. Suppose you say, "I just bought a new car," and all your friends stick their tongues out at you. In North America, this may mean that they are envious or resentful. But in some regions of China, such a display expresses surprise.

Even smiles can vary as people learn to use them to communicate certain feelings. Paul Ekman and his colleagues categorized seventeen types of smiles, including "false smiles," which fake enjoyment, and "masking smiles," which hide unhappiness. They called the smile that occurs with real happiness the *Duchenne smile,* after the French researcher who first noticed a difference between spontaneous, happy smiles and posed smiles. A genuine Duchenne smile includes contractions of the muscles around the eyes (creating a distinctive wrinkling of the skin in these areas) as well as of the muscles that raise the lips and cheeks. Few people can successfully contract the muscles around the eyes during a posed smile, so this feature can be used to distinguish "lying smiles" from genuine ones (Ekman, Friesen, & O'Sullivan, 1988; Frank, Ekman, & Friesen, 1993). In one study, the Duchenne smile was highly correlated with reports of positive emotions experienced while people watched a movie, as well as with a pattern

FIGURE 11.16

Elements of Ceremonial Facial Masks That Convey Threat

Certain geometrical elements are common to threatening masks in many cultures. When people in various cultures were asked which member of each of these pairs was more threatening, they consistently chose those, shown here on the left, containing triangular and diagonal elements. "Scary" Halloween pumpkins tend to have such elements as well.

of brain waves known to be associated with positive emotions. These relationships did not appear for other types of smiles (Ekman, Davidson, & Friesen, 1990).

Learning About Emotions   The effects of learning are seen in a child's growing repertoire of emotional expressions. Although infants begin with an innate set of emotional responses, they soon learn to imitate facial expressions and use them for more and more emotions. In time, these expressions become more precise and personalized, so that a particular expression conveys a clear emotional message to anyone who knows that person well.

If facial expressions become too idiosyncratic, however, no one will know what the expressions mean, and they will fail to elicit responses from others. Operant shaping probably helps keep emotional expressions within certain limits. If you could not see other people's facial expressions or observe their responses to yours, you might show fewer, or less intense, facial signs of emotion. Indeed, as congenitally blind people grow older, their facial expressions tend to become less animated (Izard, 1977).

As children grow, they learn an *emotion culture*—rules that govern what emotions are appropriate in what circumstances and what emotional expressions are allowed. These rules can vary from culture to culture. For example, the people of Ifaluk, a tiny Pacific island, condemn expressions of happiness as disruptive to carrying out one's duties (Lutz, 1987). Similarly, when viewing a distressing movie with a group of peers, Japanese students exhibited much more control over their facial expressions than North American students. When they watched the film while alone, however, the Japanese students' faces showed the same emotional expressions as those of the North American students (Ekman, Friesen, & Ellsworth, 1972).

Emotion cultures shape how people describe and categorize feelings, resulting in both similarities and differences across cultures (Russell, 1991). At least five of the seven basic emotions listed in an ancient Chinese book called the *Li Chi*—joy, anger, sadness, fear, love, disliking, and liking—are considered primary emotions by most Western theorists. Yet whereas English has over 500 emotion-related words, some emotion words in other languages have no English meaning. The Czech word *litost* apparently has no English word equivalent: "It designates a feeling as infinite as an open accordion, a feeling that is the synthesis of many others: grief, sympathy, remorse, and an indefinable longing. . . . *Litost* is a state of torment caused by a sudden insight into one's own miserable self" (quoted in Russell, 1991). The Japanese word *ijirashii* also has no English equivalent; it describes the feeling of seeing a praiseworthy person overcoming an obstacle (Russell, 1991).

Similarly, other cultures have no equivalent for some English emotion words. Many cultures do not see anger and sadness as different, for example. The Ilongot, a Philippine head-hunting group, have only one word, *liget,* for both anger and grief (Russell, 1991). Tahitians have different words for forty-six types of anger, but no word for sadness and, apparently, no concept of it. One Westerner described a Tahitian man as sad over separation from his wife and child, but the man himself felt *pe'a pe'a*—a generic word for feeling ill, troubled, or fatigued—and did not attribute it to the separation.

Social Referencing   Facial expressions, tone of voice, body postures, and gestures not only communicate information about the emotion someone is experiencing; they can also influence others' behavior, especially the behavior of people who are not sure what to do. A novice chess player, for instance, might reach out to move the queen, catch sight of a spectator's grimace, and infer that another move would be better. The process of letting another person's emotional state guide our own behavior is called social referencing (Campos, 1980).

The visual-cliff studies described in the chapter on perception have been used to create an uncertain situation for infants. To reach its mother, an infant in these experiments must cross the visual cliff (see Figure 5.26 on page 164). If the apparent dropoff is very small or very large, there is no ambiguity, and a one-year-old knows to crawl across in the first case and to stay put in the second case. However, if the apparent dropoff is shallow enough to create uncertainty (say, two feet), the infant relies on its mother's facial expressions to decide what to do. In one study, mothers were asked to make either a fearful or a joyful face. When the mothers made a fearful face, no infant crossed the glass floor. But when they posed a joyful face, most infants crossed (Sorce et al., 1981). Here is yet another example of the adaptive value of sending, and receiving, emotional communications.

LINKAGES

As noted in Chapter 1, all of psychology's many subfields are related to one another. Our discussion of conflicting motives and stress illustrates just one way in which the topic of this chapter, motivation and emotion, is linked to the subfield of health psychology (Chapter 13). The Linkages diagram shows ties to two other subfields as well, and there are many more ties throughout the book. Looking for linkages among subfields will help you see how they fit together and better appreciate the big picture that is psychology.

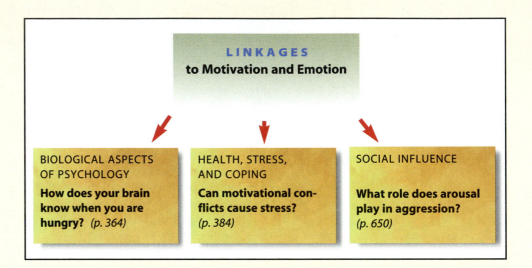

LINKAGES to Motivation and Emotion

BIOLOGICAL ASPECTS OF PSYCHOLOGY

How does your brain know when you are hungry? (p. 364)

HEALTH, STRESS, AND COPING

Can motivational conflicts cause stress? (p. 384)

SOCIAL INFLUENCE

What role does arousal play in aggression? (p. 650)

SUMMARY

Motivation refers to factors that influence the initiation, direction, intensity, and persistence of behavior. Emotion and motivation are often linked: Motivation can influence emotion, and people are often motivated to seek certain emotions.

CONCEPTS AND THEORIES OF MOTIVATION

Focusing on a *motive* often reveals a single theme within apparently diverse behaviors. Motivation is said to be an intervening variable, a way of linking various stimuli to the behaviors that follow them.

Sources of Motivation

The many sources of motivation fall into four categories: biological factors, emotional factors, cognitive factors, and social factors.

Instinct Theory and Its Descendants

An early argument held that motivation follows from *instincts*, automatic, involuntary, and unlearned behavior patterns consistently "released" by particular stimuli. Modern versions of *instinct theory* are seen in evolutionary accounts of helping, aggression, mate selection, and other aspects of social behavior.

Drive Reduction Theory

Drive reduction theory is based on *homeostasis*, a tendency to maintain equilibrium in a physical or behavioral process. When disruption of equilibrium creates a *need* of some kind, people are motivated to reduce the resulting *drive* by behaving in some way that satisfies the need and restores balance. *Primary drives* are unlearned; *secondary drives* are learned.

Arousal Theory

According to *arousal theories* of motivation, people are motivated to behave in ways that maintain a level of *arousal* that is optimal for their functioning.

Incentive Theory

Incentive theory highlights behaviors that are motivated by attaining desired stimuli (positive incentives) and avoiding undesirable ones (negative incentives).

HUNGER AND EATING

Hunger and eating are controlled by a complex mix of learning, culture, and biology.

Biological Signals for Hunger and Satiety

The desire to eat (*hunger*) or to stop eating (*satiety*) depends primarily on signals from blood-borne substances such as cholecystokinin (CCK), insulin, and leptin.

Hunger and the Brain

Activity in the ventromedial nucleus of the hypothalamus results in satiety, whereas activity in the lateral hypothalamus results in hunger. Neurons in the paraventricular nucleus appear to influence hungers for specific types of foods. Multiple neurotransmitters act in these brain areas to maintain a set point of body weight.

Flavor, Cultural Learning, and Food Selection

Eating may also be influenced by the flavor of food and by appetite for the pleasure of food. Food selection is influenced by biological needs (specific hungers) for certain nutrients, as well as by food cravings, social contexts, and cultural traditions.

Eating Disorders

Obesity has been linked to overconsumption of certain kinds of foods, to low energy metabolism, and to genetic factors. People suffering from *anorexia nervosa* starve themselves to avoid becoming fat. Those who suffer from *bulimia nervosa* engage in binge eating, followed by purging through self-induced vomiting or laxatives.

SEXUAL BEHAVIOR

Sexual motivation and behavior result from a rich interplay of biology and culture.

The Biology of Sex

Sexual stimulation generally produces a stereotyped *sexual response cycle*, a pattern of physiological arousal during and after sexual activity. *Sex hormones,* which include male hormones (*androgens*) and female hormones (*estrogens* and *progestins*), occur in different relative amounts in both sexes. They can have organizational effects, such as physical differences in the brain, and activational effects, such as increased desire for sex.

Social and Cultural Factors in Sexuality

Gender-role learning, educational experiences, media influences, and family dynamics are examples of cultural factors that can bring about variations in sexual attitudes and behaviors.

Sexual Orientation

Sexual orientation—*heterosexual, homosexual,* or *bisexual*—is increasingly viewed as a sociocultural variable that affects many other aspects of behavior and mental processes. Though undoubtedly shaped by a lifetime of learning, sexual orientation appears to have strong biological roots.

Sexual Dysfunctions

Common male sexual *dysfunctions* include erectile disorder and premature ejaculation. Females may experience such problems as arousal disorder.

ACHIEVEMENT MOTIVATION

People gain esteem from achievement in many areas, including the workplace.

Need for Achievement

The motive to succeed is called *need achievement.* Individuals with high achievement motivation strive for excellence, persist despite failures, and set challenging but realistic goals.

Gender Differences in Achievement Motivation

Gender differences in achievement motivation often appear at a young age, apparently due to early learning experiences.

Achievement and Success in the Workplace

Workers are most satisfied when they are working toward their own goals and get concrete feedback. Jobs that offer clear and specific goals, a variety of tasks, individual responsibility, and other intrinsic rewards are the most motivating.

RELATIONS AND CONFLICTS AMONG MOTIVES

People's behavior reflects many motives, some of which may be in conflict.

Maslow's Hierarchy

Maslow proposed a hierarchy of five classes of human motives, from meeting basic biological needs to attaining a state of self-actualization. Motives at the lowest levels, according to Maslow, must be at least partially satisfied before people can be motivated by higher-level goals.

Opponent Processes, Motivation, and Emotion

Motivated behavior sometimes gives rise to opponent emotional processes, such as the fear and excitement associated with a rollercoaster ride. Opponent-process theory illustrates the close link between motivation and emotion.

THE NATURE OF EMOTION

Defining Characteristics

An *emotion* is a transitory, valenced experience that is felt with some intensity as happening to the self, is generated in part by a cognitive appraisal of a situation, and is accompanied by both learned and reflexive physical responses.

The Biology of Emotion

Several brain mechanisms are involved in emotion. The amygdala, in the limbic system, is deeply involved in emotional arousal. The expression of emotion through involuntary facial movement is controlled by the extrapyramidal motor system. Voluntary facial movements are controlled by the pyramidal motor system. The brain's right and left hemispheres play somewhat different roles in emotional expression. In addition to specific brain mechanisms, both the *sympathetic* and the *parasympathetic* divisions of the autonomic nervous system are involved in physiological changes that accompany emotional activation. The *fight-or-flight* syndrome, for example, follows from activation of the sympathetic system.

THEORIES OF EMOTION

James's Theory

William James's theory of emotion holds that physiological responses are the primary source of emotion and that self-observation of these responses constitutes emotional experience. James's theory is supported by evidence that, at least for several basic emotions, physiological responses are distinguishable enough for emotions to be generated in this way. Distinct facial expressions are linked to particular patterns of physiological change. Studies of people with spinal cord damage do not support an important role in emotion for autonomic activity in parts of the body beyond the face. Schachter's modification of James's theory proposes that physiological responses are primary sources of emotion but that labeling of emotion—a process that depends on *attribution*—is greatly influenced by the situation in which the arousal occurs. Attributing arousal from one situation to stimuli in another situation can produce *transferred excitation,* intensifying the emotion experienced in the second situation.

Cannon's Theory

Cannon's theory of emotion proposes that emotional experience occurs independent of peripheral physiological responses and that there is a direct experience of emotion based on activity of the central nervous system. Updated versions of this theory suggest that various parts of the central nervous system may be involved in different emotions and different aspects of emotional experience. Some pathways in the brain, such as that from the thalamus to the amygdala, allow strong emotions to occur before conscious thought can take place. And specific parts of the brain appear to be responsible for the feelings of pleasure or pain in emotion. One updated version of Cannon's theory suggests that emotion depends on pathways in the brain, including those from the locus coeruleus, that constitute a kind of "autonomic nervous system" within the brain, modulating the activity of other areas of the brain.

COMMUNICATING EMOTION

In humans, voice tones, bodily movements, and, mainly, facial movement and expressions are involved in communicating emotions.

Innate Expressions of Emotion

Darwin suggested that certain facial expressions of emotion are innate and universal and that these expressions evolved because they effectively communicate one creature's emotional condition to other creatures. Some facial expressions of basic emotions do appear to be innate. Even blind infants smile when happy and frown when experiencing discomfort. And certain facial movements are universally associated with certain emotions.

Social and Cultural Influences on Emotional Expression

Many emotional expressions are learned, and even innate expressions are modified by learning and social contexts. As children grow, they learn an emotion culture, the rules of emotional expression appropriate to their culture. Accordingly, the same emotion may be communicated by different facial expressions in different cultures. Especially in ambiguous situations, other people's emotional expressions may serve as a guide about what to do or what not to do, a phenomenon called *social referencing.*

KEY TERMS

androgens (372)
anorexia nervosa (369)
arousal (362)
arousal theories (362)
attribution (394)
bisexual (374)
bulimia nervosa (370)
drive (361)
drive reduction theory (361)

emotion (387)
estrogens (372)
fight-or-flight syndrome (390)
heterosexual (374)
homeostasis (361)
homosexual (374)
hunger (364)
incentive theory (363)

instincts (359)
instinct theory (359)
motivation (358)
motive (358)
need (361)
need achievement (378)
obesity (368)
parasympathetic system (390)
primary drives (361)

progestins (372)
satiety (364)
secondary drives (362)
sex hormones (372)
sexual dysfunctions (377)
sexual response cycle (370)
social referencing (399)
sympathetic system (390)
transferred excitation (394)

12

Human Development

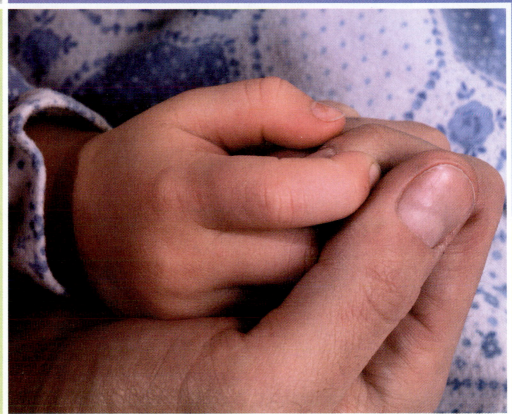

In 1997 through 1999, the towns of Springfield, Oregon; Jonesboro, Arkansas; West Paducah, Kentucky; Edinboro, Pennsylvania; Bethel, Alaska; Pearl, Mississippi; and Littleton, Colorado, shared a common tragedy with the Canadian town of Taber, Alberta—the shooting deaths of students and teachers at local schools. Overall, the number of school homicides was lower during these years than in previous years, but that fact was of little solace to the friends and families of the forty-nine people who were killed and the fifty-five others who were injured in these school shooting sprees. With each new tragedy the cry became louder: *Why did it happen?* The killers were boys ranging in age from 11 to 18. Had they watched too many violent movies and television programs? Were their actions the fault of a "gun culture" that allows children access to firearms? Had they been victims of abuse and neglect? Were their parents too strict—or not strict enough? Did they come from "broken homes" or witness physical violence within their own families? Did they behave violently because they were going through a difficult "stage," because they had not been taught right from wrong, because they wanted to impress their peers, because males are more aggressive in general, or because their brains were "defective"? Were they just "bad kids"?

These are the kinds of questions for which developmental psychologists try to find answers. They investigate when certain behaviors first appear and how they change with age. They explore how development in one area, such as moral reasoning, relates to development in another area, such as aggressive behavior. They attempt to discover whether most people develop at the same rate and, if not, whether slow starters ever catch up to early bloomers. They ask why some children become well-adjusted, socially competent, nurturant, and empathic individuals whereas others become murderers, and why some adolescents go on to win honors in college whereas others drop out of high school. They seek to explain how development throughout the life span is affected by both genetics and the environment, analyzing the extent to which development is a product of what we arrive with at birth—our inherited, biological *nature*—and the extent to which it is a product of what the world provides—the *nurture* of the environment. And they pursue development into adulthood, examining the changes that occur over the years and determining how these changes are related to earlier abilities and later events. In short, **developmental psychology** is concerned with the course and causes of developmental changes over a person's lifetime.

In this chapter we examine many such changes. We begin by describing the physical and biological changes that occur from the moment of conception to the time a child is born. Then we discuss cognitive, social, and emotional development during infancy and childhood. Next, we examine the changes and challenges that confront humans during their adolescence. And we conclude by considering the significant physical, intellectual, and social changes that occur as people move through early, middle, and late adulthood.

EXPLORING HUMAN DEVELOPMENT

Arguments about whether development is the result of nature or nurture can be traced back to philosophers of centuries ago. In essays published in the 1690s, the British philosopher John Locke argued for nurture. He believed that experiences provided by the environment during childhood have a profound and permanent effect. As mentioned in Chapter 1, Locke thought of the newborn as a blank slate, or *tabula rasa*. Adults write on that slate, he said, as they teach children about the world and how to behave in it. Some seventy years later, French philosopher Jean-Jacques Rousseau made the opposite argument. He claimed that children are capable of discovering how the world operates and how they should behave without instruction from adults, and he advocated letting children grow as their natures dictate, with little guidance or pressure from parents.

The first psychologist to systematically investigate the role of nature in behavior was Arnold Gesell. In the early 1900s, Gesell observed many children of all ages. He found that their motor skills, such as standing and walking, picking up a cube, and throwing a ball, developed in a fixed sequence of stages, as Figure 12.1 illustrates. The order of

A Deadly Child

Andrew Golden was barely out of diapers when he was given camouflage clothing and taught to fire a hunting rifle. In March of 1998, at the age of 11, he and his 13-year-old friend Mitchell Johnson used their shooting skills to kill four classmates and a teacher at their elementary school in Jonesboro, Arkansas. Many youngsters learn to hunt; what led these two to commit murder? Researchers in developmental psychology are studying the genetic and environmental factors that underlie the emergence of violent aggression and many other patterns of behavior and mental processes.

FIGURE 12.1

Motor Development

The left end of each bar indicates the age at which 25 percent of the infants tested were able to perform the behavior; 50 percent of the babies were performing the behavior at the age indicated by the vertical line in the bars; the right end indicates the age at which 90 percent could do so (Frankenberg & Dodds, 1967). Although different infants, especially in different cultures, achieve milestones of motor development at slightly different ages, all infants—regardless of their ethnicity, social class, or temperament—achieve them in the same order.

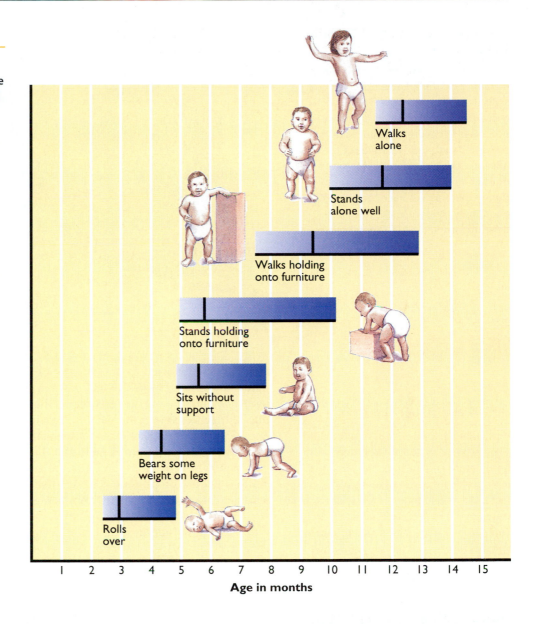

Walks alone

Stands alone well

Walks holding onto furniture

Stands holding onto furniture

Sits without support

Bears some weight on legs

Rolls over

1 2 3 4 5 6 7 8 9 10 11 12 13 14 15

Age in months

the stages and the age at which they develop, he suggested, are determined by nature and relatively unaffected by nurture. Only under extreme conditions such as famine, war, or poverty, he claimed, are children thrown off their biologically programmed timetable. Gesell referred to this type of natural growth or change, which unfolds in a fixed sequence relatively independent of the environment, as **maturation**.

John B. Watson, founder of the behaviorist approach to psychology, disagreed with Gesell. He claimed that the environment, not nature, molds and shapes development. Early in the twentieth century Watson began conducting experiments with children. From these experiments he inferred that children learn everything, from skills to fears.

It was Jean Piaget, a native of Switzerland, who first suggested that nature and nurture work together. The first European psychologist to receive a Distinguished Scientific Contribution Award from the American Psychological Association (Shaffer, 1999), Piaget had a lifelong interest in human intellectual and cognitive development. His ideas, presented in numerous books and articles published from the 1920s until his death in 1980, influenced the field of developmental psychology more than those of any other person before or since (Flavell, 1996).

Most developmental psychologists now accept the idea that nature and nurture contribute jointly to development—in two ways. First, they operate together to make all people *alike* as human beings. For example, we all achieve milestones of physical development in the same order and at roughly the same rate as a result of biological

A Pioneer in the Study of Cognitive Development

Using a variety of research procedures, including his remarkable observational skills, Jean Piaget (1896–1980) investigated the development of cognitive processes in children, including his own son and daughters. He wove his observations and inferences into the most comprehensive and influential theory that had yet been formulated about how thought and knowledge develop from infancy to adolescence.

A Tiger in Training

Human behavior develops as a function of both heredity and environment—of both nature and nurture. The joint and inseparable influence of these two factors in development is nicely illustrated in the case of professional golfer Tiger Woods, shown here as a youngster with his father, who not only provided some of Tiger's genes but also served as his golf teacher.

maturation supported by the nurture of basic care, nutrition, and exercise. Second, nature and nurture also both operate to make each person *unique.* The nature of inherited genes and the nurture of widely different family and cultural environments produce differences among individuals in such dimensions as athletic abilities, intelligence, and personality. Michael Jordan, Stephen Hawking, and Prince William are different from each other and from the rest of us because of their genes *and* their experiences.

Just how much nature and nurture contribute varies from one characteristic to another. Nature shapes some characteristics, such as physical size and appearance, so strongly that only extreme environmental conditions can affect them. It takes a substantial difference in diet, for instance, to make a significant difference in a person's ultimate height. Indeed, variation in height has been estimated to be 80 to 95 percent genetic. Nature affects other characteristics, such as motor skills, slightly less strongly. During infancy and early childhood, motor skills—such as those employed when a baby begins to walk—are only modestly affected by experience. Later, nurture plays a larger role in children's motor abilities, as when they start playing soccer, practicing for the swim team, or taking piano lessons. Other characteristics, such as intelligence, may be more easily affected by the environment during infancy than in subsequent years when heredity seems to play a greater role (Plomin et al., 1997).

Although the relative contributions of nature and nurture are different for specific aspects of development at different times, their influences on *all* human characteristics are inextricably intertwined. One reason they cannot be separated is that heredity and environment are *correlated.* For example, highly intelligent biological parents give their children genes for intelligence *and* typically provide a stimulating environment.

Heredity and environment also affect each other. Just as the environment promotes or hampers an individual's abilities, those inherited abilities to some extent determine the individual's environment. For example, a stimulating environment full of toys, books, and lessons encourages children's mental development and increases the chances that their full inherited intelligence will emerge. At the same time, more intelligent children seek out more stimulating environments, ask more questions, evoke more attention from adults, and, ultimately, learn more from these experiences.

BEGINNINGS

Let's now consider how nature and nurture interact to affect human development. Nowhere is this interaction clearer than in the womb, as a single fertilized egg becomes a functioning infant.

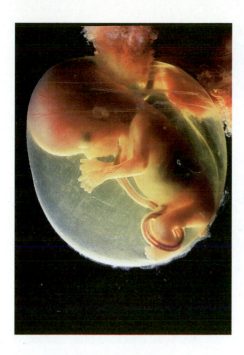

A Fetus at Twelve Weeks

At this point in prenatal development, the fetus can kick its legs, curl its toes, make a fist, turn its head, squint, open its mouth, swallow, and take a few "breaths" of amniotic fluid.

Prenatal Development

The process of development begins when a sperm from the father-to-be penetrates, or fertilizes, the ovum of the mother-to-be and a brand-new cell, called a **zygote**, is formed. This new cell carries a genetic heritage from both mother and father. (See the behavioral genetics appendix.)

Stages of Development   In the first stage of prenatal development, the zygote divides into many more cells, which by the end of the second week have formed an **embryo.** What follows is the *embryonic stage* of development, during which the embryo quickly develops a heart, nervous system, stomach, esophagus, and ovaries or testes. By two months after conception, the inch-long embryo has developed eyes, ears, a nose, a jaw, a mouth, and lips. The tiny arms have elbows, hands, and stubby fingers; the legs have knees, ankles, and toes.

During the remaining seven-month period until birth, called the *fetal stage* of pre-natal development, the organs grow and start to function. By the end of the third month, the **fetus** can kick, make a fist, turn its head, open its mouth, swallow, and frown. In the sixth month, the eyelids, which have been sealed, open. The fetus now has a well-developed grasp and taste buds, and, if born prematurely, can breathe regularly for as long as twenty-four hours at a time. By the end of the seventh month, the organ systems, though immature, are all functional. In the eighth and ninth months, fetuses respond to light and touch, and can hear what is going on outside. They can also learn. For example, they will ignore a stimulus, such as a vibration or a sound, after it has been repeated a number of times (Azar, 1997). In such cases, they have *habituated* to the stimulus—a form of learning that predicts later cognitive abilities.

Prenatal Risks   During prenatal development, a spongy organ called the *placenta*, formed from the outside layer of the zygote, sends nutrients from the mother to the fetus and carries away wastes. It also screens out many potentially harmful substances, including most bacteria. This screening is imperfect, however; severe damage can occur if the baby's mother takes certain drugs, is exposed to toxic substances, or has certain illnesses. A baby whose mother has rubella (German measles) during the third or fourth week after conception, for example, has a 50 percent chance of being blind, deaf, mentally retarded, or of suffering a malformed heart. If the mother has rubella later in the pregnancy, after the infant's eyes, ears, brain, and heart have formed, the likelihood that the baby will have one of these defects drops substantially.

Harmful external substances that invade the womb and result in birth defects are called **teratogens** (pronounced "ta-RAT-a-jens"). Teratogens are especially damaging during the embryonic stage because it is a **critical period** in prenatal development, a time when certain kinds of growth must occur if the infant's development is to pro-ceed normally. If the heart, eyes, ears, hands, and feet do not appear during this period, they cannot form later on, and if they form incorrectly, the defects are permanent. Thus, even before a mother knows she is pregnant, she may accidentally damage her infant by exposing it to teratogens. Later, during the fetal stage, teratogens affect the baby's size, behavior, intelligence, and health, rather than the formation of organs and limbs.

Of special concern today are the effects of drugs on infants' development. Pregnant women who use substances such as cocaine create a substantial risk for their fetuses, which do not yet have the enzymes necessary to break down the drug. "Cocaine babies" or "crack babies" may be born premature, underweight, tense, and fussy (Inciardi, Surratt, & Saum, 1997); they may also suffer delayed physical growth and motor devel-opment (Tarr & Pyfer, 1996). Their kidneys, genitals, or other organs may be mal-formed because the mother's cocaine use leads to a loss of blood to the developing organs. Current research suggests, however, that although "cocaine babies" are more likely to have behavioral and learning problems, their mental abilities are not substan-tially different from those of any baby born into an impoverished environment (Johnson et al., 1997). How well they ultimately do in school depends on how sup-portive that environment turns out to be (Begley, 1997).

A Cocaine Baby

One in ten babies in the United States is exposed to illegal drugs while still in the womb. "Cocaine babies," sometimes called "crack babies," are born with numerous physical defects as the result of their mothers' drug use during pregnancy. To make matters worse, these mothers are likely to respond negatively to their infants because, for example, these babies often turn their heads away when the mother tries to play. This unfortunate reaction can impair the mother–child relationship and lead to a vicious cycle of child abuse in already fragile families.

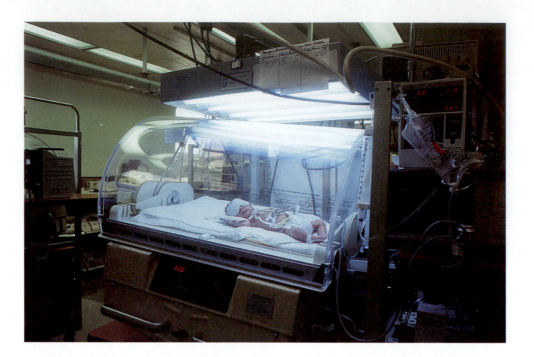

Alcohol is another dangerous teratogen. Pregnant women who drink as little as a glass or two of wine a day can harm their infants' intellectual functioning (Kaufman, 1997; Kraft, 1996). About half the children born to expectant mothers who abuse alcohol will develop fetal alcohol syndrome, a pattern of defects that includes mental retardation and malformations of the face, such as a flattened nose and an underdeveloped upper lip (Jenkins & Culbertson, 1996; Shaffer, 1999). Smoking, too, can affect the developing fetus. Smokers' babies are usually born underweight and often suffer from respiratory problems. They may also have attention problems later on (Milberger et al., 1997).

Interestingly, it may not be only the mothers' health habits that put their babies at risk. There is evidence that fathers who drink heavily in the month prior to conception also have children of lower birth weight (Zigler & Stevenson, 1993). And newborns whose fathers smoke heavily are smaller than those whose fathers are nonsmokers (Friedman & Polifka, 1996). The mechanisms responsible for these outcomes are not yet fully understood.

What we *do* know is that defects due to teratogens are most likely when the negative effects of nature and nurture combine—when a genetically susceptible infant receives a strong dose of a damaging substance during a critical period of prenatal development. Yet despite these vulnerabilities, mental or physical problems resulting from all harmful factors affect fewer than 10 percent of the babies born in Western nations. Mechanisms built into the human organism maintain normal development under all but the most adverse conditions. The vast majority of fetuses arrive at the end of their nine-month gestation averaging a healthy seven pounds and ready to continue a normal course of development in the world.

The Newborn

Determining what newborns are able to see, hear, and do is one of the most fascinating—and frustrating—research challenges in developmental psychology. Young infants are very difficult to study. About 70 percent of the time, they are asleep; and when they are not sleeping, they may be drowsy, crying, or restlessly moving about. It is only when they are in a state of quiet alertness, which occurs infrequently and only for a few minutes at a time, that researchers can assess infants' abilities.

During these brief periods, psychologists show infants objects or pictures, or present sounds to them, and watch where they look and for how long. They film the infants' eye movements and record changes in their heart rates, sucking rates, brain waves, movements, and skin conductance (a measure of perspiration associated with emotion) to learn what infants can see and hear (Aslin, Jusczyk, & Pisoni, 1998; Kellman & Banks, 1998).

Vision and Other Senses Infants can see at birth, but their vision is blurry. Researchers estimate that newborns have 20/300 eyesight; that is, an object 20 feet away looks as clear as it would if viewed from 300 feet away by an adult with normal vision. The reason infants' vision is so limited is that their eyes and brains still need time to grow and develop. Indeed, newborns' eyes are smaller than those of adults. The cells in their fovea—the area of retina on which images are focused—are fewer and far less sensitive. Their eye movements are slow and jerky. And pathways connecting the eyes to the brain are still inefficient, as is the processing of visual information within the brain.

Although infants cannot see small objects on the other side of the room, they are able to see large objects close up. They stare longest at objects that exhibit large visible elements, movement, clear contours, and a great amount of contrast—all qualities that exist in the human face. In fact, from the time they are born, infants will redirect their eyes to follow a moving drawing of a face and they stare at a human face longer than at other figures (Johnson et al., 1991; Valenza et al., 1996). They also exhibit a degree of *size constancy*—the ability to perceive the correct physical size of an object despite changes in the size of its image on the retina. Newborns do not experience *depth perception* until some time later, however; it takes about seven months before they develop the ability to use the pictorial cues to depth described in Chapter 5.

The course of development for hearing is similar to that of vision. Infants at birth are not deaf, but they hear poorly. At two or three days of age, they can hear soft voices and notice the difference between tones about one note apart on the musical scale; they also turn their heads toward sounds (Clifton, 1992). But their hearing is not as acute as that of adults until well into childhood.

Nevertheless, infants' hearing is particularly attuned to the sounds of speech. When they hear voices, babies open their eyes wider and look for the speaker. By four months of age, they can discriminate differences among almost all of the more than fifty phonetic contrasts in adult languages. Infants also prefer certain kinds of speech. They like rising tones spoken by women or children, and they like speech that is high-pitched, exaggerated, and expressive. In other words, they like to hear the *baby talk* used by most adults when they talk to babies.

Newborns' sense of smell is similar to that of adults but, again, less acute. Certain smells and tastes appeal to them more than others. For instance, they like the smell of flowers and the taste of sweet drinks (Ganchrow, Steiner, & Daher, 1983). Contrary to popular myth, however, they dislike the smell of ammonia (in wet diapers). Research indicates that within a few days after birth, breast-fed babies prefer the odor of their own mother to that of another mother (Cernoch & Porter, 1985).

Though limited, these inborn sensory abilities—smell, taste, hearing, and vision—are important for survival and development because they focus the infant's attention

LINKAGES

A Baby's-Eye View of the World

The photograph at left simulates what mother looks like to her infant at three months of age. Although their vision is blurry, infants particularly seem to enjoy looking at faces. As mentioned in Chapter 5, their eyes will follow a moving face-like drawing (Johnson et al., 1991), and by one month of age they will stare at a human face longer than at other figures (Olson & Sherman, 1983).

on the caregiver. For example, the attraction of newborns to the sweet smell and taste of mother's milk helps them locate appropriate food and thus identify their caregiver. Their sensitivity to speech allows them to focus on language and encourages the caregiver to talk to them. And because their vision is limited to the distance at which most interaction with a caregiver takes place and is tuned to the special qualities of faces, the caregiver's face is especially noticeable to them. Accordingly, infants are exposed to emotional expressions and come to recognize the caregiver by sight, further encouraging the caregiver to interact. As infants physically mature and learn from their environment, their sensory capacities become more complex and adult-like.

Reflexes and Motor Skills   In the first few weeks and months after birth, babies demonstrate involuntary, unlearned motor behaviors called **reflexes**. These are swift, automatic movements that occur in response to external stimuli. Figure 12.2 illustrates the *grasping reflex;* more than twenty other reflexes have been observed in newborn infants. For example, the *rooting reflex* causes the infant to turn its mouth toward a nipple (or anything else) that touches its cheek, and the *sucking reflex* causes the newborn to suck on anything that touches its lips. Many of these reflexes evolved because, like seeing and hearing, they were important for infants' survival.

But infants' behavior does not remain under the control of these reflexes for long. Most reflexes disappear after the first three or four months, when infants' brain development allows them to control their muscles voluntarily. At that point, infants can develop motor skills, so they are soon able to roll over, sit up, crawl, stand, and, by the end of the year, walk (see Figure 12.1 on page 405).

Until a few years ago, most developmental psychologists accepted Gesell's view that, barring extreme environmental conditions, these motor abilities occur spontaneously as the central nervous system and muscles mature. Recent research clearly demonstrates, however, that maturation does not tell the whole story (Thelen, 1995). Psychologists have discovered, for example, that infants' motor development also depends on active experimentation. In one study, researchers observed six infants as they learned to crawl on their hands and knees (Freedland & Bertenthal, 1994). Once they had developed sufficient muscle strength to support their abdomens, the infants tried various crawling techniques—moving backward, moving one limb at a time, using the arms only, and so on. It was only after a week or two of trial and error that all six infants arrived at the same method: moving diagonal limbs (right arm and left leg, left arm and right leg) together. This pattern turned out to be the most efficient way of getting around quickly without tipping over. Such observations suggest that as maturation increases infants' strength, they try out motor patterns and select the ones that work best.

In short, motor development results from a combination of maturation and experience. It is not the result of an inexorably unfolding plan that is genetically inscribed in the brain. Yet again, we see that nature and nurture influence one another.

INFANCY AND CHILDHOOD: COGNITIVE DEVELOPMENT

Over the first ten years of life, the crawling infant becomes a competent child who can read a book, write a poem, and argue persistently. Several changes lead to the dramatic shifts in thinking, knowing, and remembering that occur between early infancy and later childhood.

Changes in the Brain

One factor that underlies the cognitive leaps of infancy and childhood is continued growth and development of the brain. When infants are born they already have their full quota of brain cells, but the neural networks connecting the cells are immature. With time, the connections grow increasingly complex and then, with pruning, more

FIGURE 12.2

Reflexes in the Newborn

When a finger is pressed into a newborn's palm, the *grasping reflex* causes the infant to hold on tightly enough to suspend its entire weight. The *Moro reflex* is a response to the sudden sensation of falling: The arms and legs are flung to the sides, hands open and fingers spread, then the arms are brought in toward the body in a hugging motion, hands now fisted, back arched, and legs fully extended. And when a newborn is held upright over a flat surface, the *stepping reflex* leads to walking movements.

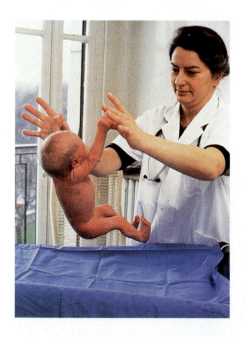

efficient. Studies reveal how, as different regions of the brain develop more complex and efficient neural networks, new cognitive abilities appear (Nelson, 1997).

In the first few months of infancy, the area of the brain that is most mature is the cerebellum. Its early maturation allows infants to achieve simple cognitive abilities such as sucking more when they see their mother's face or hear her voice. Between six and twelve months of age, neurological development in the medial temporal lobe of the cortex makes it possible for infants to remember and imitate an action they have seen earlier, or to recognize a picture of an object they have never seen before but have held in their hands. And neurological development in the frontal cortex, which occurs later in childhood, allows the individual to develop higher cognitive functions such as reasoning. Underlying structures of the brain thus provide the "hardware" for children's *cognitive development*. How their "software" develops is a question pursued by many developmental psychologists, beginning with Jean Piaget.

The Development of Knowledge: Piaget's Theory

Piaget dedicated his life to a search for the origins of intelligence in infancy and the factors that lead to changes in knowledge over the life span. He was the first to chart the fascinating journey from the simple reflexes of the newborn to the complex understandings of the adolescent. Piaget's theory was not correct in every respect—later we discuss some of its weaknesses and shortcomings—but the fact remains that his ideas about cognitive development still guide much research on cognitive development (Fischer & Hencke, 1996).

Piaget proposed that cognitive development proceeds through a series of distinct *periods* or *stages* (outlined in Table 12.1 on page 412). He believed that all children's thinking goes through the same stages, in the same order, without skipping—building on previous stages, then moving progressively to higher ones. Thus, according to Piaget, the thinking of infants is different from the thinking of children, and the thinking of children is different from that of adolescents. Children are not just miniature adults, he inferred, and they are not dumber than adults; they just think in completely different ways. Entering each stage involves a *qualitative* change from the previous stage. What drives children to higher stages is their unceasing struggle to make sense of their experiences. They are active thinkers, constantly trying to construct more advanced understandings of the world.

Building Blocks of Development To explain how infants and children move to ever-higher stages of understanding and knowledge, Piaget used the concept of schemas. As noted in previous chapters, **schemas** are the mental images or generalizations that form as people experience the world; they organize past experiences and provide a framework for understanding future experiences. According to Piaget, schemas are the basic units of knowledge, the building blocks of intellectual development.

At first, infants form simple schemas. For example, a sucking schema consolidates their experiences of sucking into images of what objects can be sucked on—bottles, fingers, pacifiers—and what kinds of sucking can be done—soft and slow, speedy and vigorous. Later, children form more complex schemas, such as a schema for tying a knot or making a bed. Still later, adolescents form schemas about what it is to be in love.

Two complementary processes guide the development of schemas: assimilation and accommodation. In the process of **assimilation,** infants and children take in information about new objects by using existing schemas that will fit the new objects. A baby boy is given a new squeaker toy. What he does with the toy—examine it, suck on it, wave it, and then, perhaps, throw it—will depend largely on the schemas he has developed through his experiences with other toys in the past. He discovers that this new toy, like his familiar rattle, is suckable, wavable, and throwable. So he assimilates the squeaker into his existing schemas of sucking, waving, throwing. A toddler encounters a large dog. How she assimilates this new object depends on her existing schema of

TABLE 12.1

Piaget's Periods of Cognitive Development

According to Piaget, a predictable set of features characterizes each period of children's cognitive development. Note that the ages associated with the stages are approximate; Piaget realized that some children move through the stages slightly faster or slower than others.

Period	Activities and Achievements
Sensorimotor Birth–2 years	Infants discover aspects of the world through their sensory impressions, motor activities, and coordination of the two. They learn to differentiate themselves from the external world. They learn that objects exist even when they are not visible and that they are independent of the infant's own actions. They gain some appreciation of cause and effect.
Preoperational 2–4 years 4–7 years	Children cannot yet manipulate and transform information in logical ways, but they now can think in images and symbols. They become able to represent something with something else, acquire language, and play games of pretend. Intelligence at this stage is said to be intuitive, because children cannot make general, logical statements.
Concrete operational 7–11 years	Children can understand logical principles that apply to concrete external objects. They can appreciate that certain properties of an object remain the same, despite changes in appearance, and sort objects into categories. They can appreciate the perspective of another viewer. They can think about two concepts, such as longer and wider, at the same time.
Formal operational Over 11 years	Only adolescents and adults can think logically about abstractions, can speculate, and can consider what might or what ought to be. They can work in probabilities and possibilities. They can imagine other worlds, especially ideal ones. They can reason about purely verbal or logical statements. They can relate any element or statement to any other, manipulate variables in a scientific experiment, and deal with proportions and analogies. They reflect on their own activity of thinking.

dogs. If she has had positive experiences with a family pet she will have a positive schema and, expecting the dog to behave like her pet, she will greet it enthusiastically. But if she has been frightened by dogs in the past, she may have a negative schema and react with fear to the dog she has just met. Thus, past experiences affect what and how children think about new ones.

Sometimes, like Cinderella's sisters squeezing their oversized feet into the glass slipper, people distort information about a new object to make it fit their existing schema. When squeezing won't work, though, they are forced to change, or accommodate, their schema to the new object. In **accommodation,** the person tries out a familiar schema on a new object, finds that the schema cannot be made to fit the object, and changes the schema so that it will fit (see Figure 12.3). The baby boy is given a cup. He examines it, sucks on it, waves it, and throws it. However, he discovers that to suck on it, he can put only the edge in his mouth; to wave it, he must hold on to the handle; and throwing it will not work at all, because mother removes the cup from his playpen. So, now the schema for playing with a cup is different from the schemas for playing with other objects the baby finds in his playpen, such as stuffed animals, rattles, and squeakers. Similarly, if the toddler with a positive "doggie" schema meets a snarling stray and

FIGURE 12.3

Accommodation

Because the bars of the playpen are in the way, this child discovers that her schema for grasping and pulling objects toward her will not work. Thus she adjusts, or accommodates, her schema in order to achieve her goal.

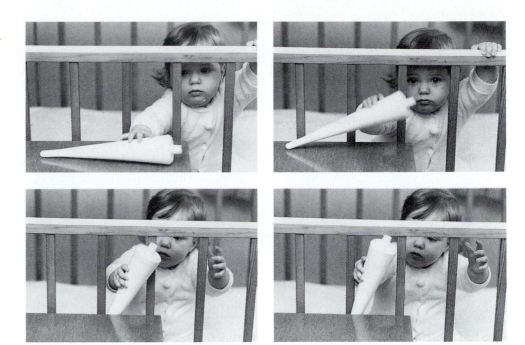

discovers that her original schema does not extend to all dogs, she will need to refine her schema about dogs.

Sensorimotor Development   Piaget (1952) called the first stage of cognitive development the **sensorimotor period** because, he claimed, the infant's mental activity and schemas are confined to sensory functions, like seeing and hearing, and motor skills, like grasping and sucking. According to Piaget, during this stage, infants can form schemas only of objects and actions that are present, things they can see or hear or touch. They cannot think about absent objects because they cannot act on them; thinking, for infants, is doing. They do not lie in the crib thinking about Mother or teddy, because they are not yet able to form schemas that are *mental representations* of objects and actions.

The sensorimotor period ends when infants *can* form mental representations and thus can think about objects and actions even while the objects are not visible or the actions are not occurring. This is a remarkable milestone, according to Piaget; it frees the child from the here-and-now of the sensory environment and allows for the development of thought. One sign that children have reached this milestone is their ability to find a hidden object. Such behavior was of particular interest to Piaget because, for him, it reflected infants' knowledge that they do not have to look at, touch, or suck an object to know that it exists; it exists even when out of sight. Piaget called this knowledge **object permanence.**

Before they acquire a knowledge of object permanence, infants do not search for objects that are placed out of their sight. They act as if out of sight is literally out of mind. The first evidence of developing object permanence appears when infants are four to eight months old. At this age, for the first time, they recognize a familiar object even if part of it is hidden. They know it's their bottle even if they can see only the nipple peeking out from under the blanket. In Piaget's view, infants now have some primitive mental representation of objects. If an object is completely hidden, however, they will not search for it.

Several months later, infants will search briefly for a hidden object, but their search is haphazard and ineffective. Not until they are eighteen to twenty-four months old, said Piaget, do infants appear able to picture and follow events in their minds. They look for the object in places other than where they saw it last, sometimes in completely new places. According to Piaget, their concept of the object as permanent is now fully developed; they have a mental representation of the object that is completely separate from their immediate perception of it.

New Views of Infants   In the years since Piaget's death, psychologists have found new ways to measure what is going on in infants' minds—infrared photography to record infants' eye movements, time-lapse photography to detect subtle hand movements, special equipment to measure infants' sucking rates, and computer technology to track and analyze it all. Their research shows that infants know a lot more, and know it sooner, than Piaget ever thought they did.

Infants are not just sensing and moving in the sensorimotor period; they are already thinking as well. For example, they are able to integrate sights with sounds. In one study, infants were shown two different videotapes at the same time, while the soundtrack for one of them was played through a speaker placed between the two screens. The infants tended to look at the video that went with the soundtrack—at a toy bouncing in time with a tapping sound or at a pair of cymbals accompanied by clanging (Walker-Andrews et al., 1991). Infants can remember, too. As young as two to three months of age, they can recall a particular mobile that was hung over their crib a few days before (Rovee-Collier, 1993; see Figure 12.4).

Other studies suggest that infants as young as five months of age can perform simple addition and subtraction. If you show them two dolls one at a time, hide the dolls behind a screen, and then remove the screen to reveal three dolls, they will stare, presumably in amazement. Findings such as these indicate that infants have some basic knowledge of "numerosity"; they can recognize changes in a group of up to three or four objects or events (Wynn, 1995, 1996).

Young babies also seem to have a sense of object permanence. Piaget had required infants to demonstrate object permanence through rather grand movements, such as removing a cover that had been placed over a hidden object. However, when experimenters simply turn off the lights, infants as young as five months of age have been shown to reach for now-unseen objects in the dark (Clifton et al., 1991). Researchers now recognize that finding a hidden object under a cover requires several abilities: mentally representing the hidden object, figuring out where it might be, and pulling off the cover. Piaget's tests did not allow for the possibility that infants *know* a hidden object still exists but do not have adequate strategies for finding it or memory skills for remembering it while they search. In research situations where infants merely have to stare to indicate that they know where an object is hidden, they demonstrate this cognitive ability even before the age of one (Ahmed & Ruffman, 1998).

In short, developmental psychologists now generally agree that infants develop some mental representations earlier than Piaget had suggested. They disagree, however, about whether this knowledge is "programmed" in infants (Spelke et al., 1992), quickly develops through interactions with the outside world (Baillargeon, 1995), or is constructed through the recombination of old schemas into new ones (Fischer & Bidell, 1991).

What Do Babies Know?

A baby in Karen Wynn's laboratory stares intently at the unexpected disappearance of one of three dolls. By observing how long infants of various ages look at events like this, researchers can make inferences about what babies know about numbers and other aspects of their world.

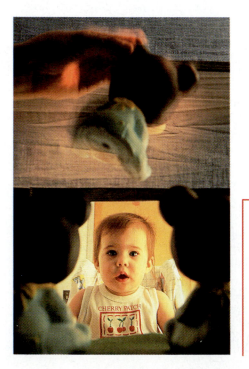

FOCUS ON RESEARCH METHODS

Experiments on Developing Minds

One attempt to settle this disagreement was made by Renee Baillargeon (pronounced "by-ar-ZHAN"), who investigated infants' early understanding of the principles of physics. Whether you realize it or not, you know a lot about physics. You know about gravity and balance, for example. But when did you first understand that "what goes up must come down" and that an unbalanced tray will tip over? Are these things you have always known, or did you figure them out through trial and error?

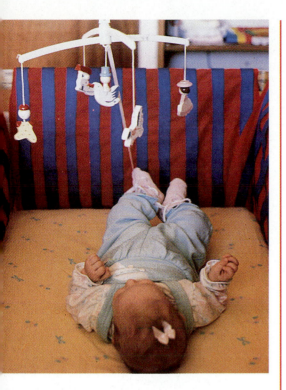

FIGURE 12.4

Infant Memory

Infants as young as two or three months of age can remember a mobile that they had previously learned to move by kicking a foot, which was tied to the mobile by a ribbon. Even a month later, the babies indicate their recognition by kicking vigorously when they see above them this particular mobile as opposed to another one.

■ What was the researcher's question?

Baillargeon wanted to know when and how babies first develop knowledge about balance and gravity—specifically, about the tendency of unsupported objects to fall.

■ How did the researcher answer the question?

Baillargeon (1994a, 1994b) devised a creative experimental method to probe infants' knowledge. She showed infants pairs of events, one of which was physically possible and the other, physically impossible. She then determined the infants' interest in each kind of event by measuring the amount of time they spent looking at it. Their tendency to look longer at new things provided an indication of which events violated what the babies knew about the world. Using this method, Baillargeon explored infants' knowledge of balance and gravity.

The independent variable in these studies was the amount of physical support applied to objects; the dependent variable was the length of time the infants looked at the objects. Specifically, the infants viewed a bright-red gloved hand pushing a box from left to right along the top of a platform. On some trials, they saw physically possible events. For example, the hand pushed the box until its edge reached the end of the platform (see event A in Figure 12.5 on page 416). On other trials, they saw impossible events, as when the hand pushed the box until only the end of its bottom surface rested on the platform or the box was beyond the platform altogether (see events B and C in the figure). On still other trials, the gloved hand held on to the box while pushing it beyond the edge of the platform (as shown in event D). Trials continued until the infants had seen at least four pairs of possible and impossible events in alternating order.

■ What did the researcher find?

Baillargeon found that three-month-old infants looked longest at impossible event C, when the box was entirely off the platform, whereas they were not particularly interested in either event D, when the box was held by the gloved hand, or event A, when the box was still on the platform. At six-and-a-half months old, however, infants stared intently at event B, when only the end of the box was resting on the platform.

■ What do the results mean?

According to Baillargeon (1998), these results suggest that three-month-olds know something about physical support: They expect the box to fall if it is entirely off the platform and act surprised when it does not. But they do not yet know that a box should fall if its center of gravity is unsupported, as in event B. By six-and-a-half months old, however, infants apparently know about centers of gravity—that most of the box must be on the platform or it will fall.

Recently, however, researchers have questioned whether infants' tendency to stare longer at a particular display necessarily indicates "surprise" (Bogartz, Shinskey, & Speaker, 1997). Perhaps they simply recognize that the image is different from what they remember it to be or find the impossible image more noticeable.

■ What do we still need to know?

The question remains as to which of these interpretations is correct. Do infants possess fundamental knowledge about the world that implies an understanding of complex physical principles, or are they just staring at something because it is novel or vivid? The answer to this question will require further research using varied visual stimuli that allow researchers to determine whether infants stare longer at physically possible events that are just as novel and vivid as physically impossible events.

Whether or not such research confirms Baillargeon's view, psychologists are still faced with the task of discovering *how* babies know about physics (Wynn & Chiang, 1998). Does their increasing understanding of physical principles result from their experience with objects, or is the knowledge innate?

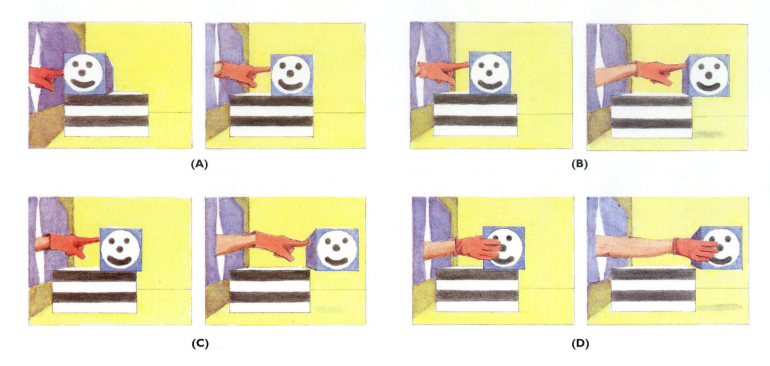

(A)   (B)

(C)   (D)

FIGURE 12.5

Events Demonstrating Infants' Knowledge of Physics

Infants look longer at things that interest them—that is, at new things rather than things they have seen before and find boring. In her research on the development of knowledge, Renee Baillargeon (1995) has found that physically impossible events (B) and (C)—made possible by an experimenter reaching through a hidden door to support a moving box—attract the most attention from infants. These results suggest that humans understand some basic laws of physics quite early in life.

Source: Baillargeon, 1992.

In an attempt to answer this question, Baillargeon conducted another experiment in which she manipulated object-experience. She randomly assigned infants, ranging in age from three to six-and-a-half months, to receive either normal or extra experience with objects (the independent variable) and observed the effect on the infants' understanding of gravity (the dependent variable). After only a few demonstrations in which unsupported objects fell off platforms, infants in the extra object-experience group stared longer at a display of an unsupported object that did not fall. It is still too early to say for sure whether Baillargeon's hypothesis about the importance of experience in developing knowledge is correct, but her results seem to support it.

Preoperational Development   According to Piaget, the sensorimotor stage of development is followed by the **preoperational period.** During the first half of this period, he observed, children begin to understand, create, and use *symbols* to represent things that are not present. They can even appreciate the symbolic function of a miniature model. In one study, for example, three-year-olds shown a scale-model room in which a miniature dog was hidden behind a miniature sofa could then find an actual stuffed dog in a real room (DeLoache, 1987). At two years, for the first time, children begin to play "pretend." They make their fingers "walk" or "shoot" and use a spoon to make a bridge. By the age of three or four, children can symbolize roles and play "house" or "doctor." And as described in the chapter on cognition and language, they also use words as symbols to stand for objects ("This squiggle is a picture of Mommy and Daddy and me going for a walk.") Indeed, the ability to use and understand symbols opens up vast domains for two- to four-year-olds.

During the second half of the preoperational stage, according to Piaget, four- to seven-year-olds begin to make intuitive guesses about the world as they try to figure out how things work. They claim that dreams are real. ("Last night I had a circus in my room.") And they believe that inanimate objects are alive and have intentions, feelings, and consciousness—a belief called *animism.* ("Clouds go slowly because they have no legs." "Empty cars feel lonely.") In short, argued Piaget, preoperational children cannot distinguish between the seen and the unseen, between the physical and the mental world. They are also highly *egocentric,* he said, inasmuch as they appear to believe that the way things

THE FAMILY CIRCUS®   **By Bil Keane**

©1993 Bil Keane, Inc.
Dist. by Cowles Synd., Inc.

Reprinted with special permission of King Features Syndicate.

"I think the moon likes us. It keeps on followin' us."

look to them is also how they look to everyone else. (This helps to explain why they may stand so as to block your view when both of you are trying to watch TV or ask "What's this?" as they look at pictures in a book in the back seat of the car while you're driving.)

Children's thinking is so dominated by what they can see and touch for themselves, Piaget said, that they do not realize that something is the same if its appearance is changed. In one study, for example, preoperational children thought that a cat wearing a dog mask was actually a dog—because that's what it looked like (DeVries, 1969). These children do not yet have what Piaget called **conservation,** the ability to recognize that important properties of a substance or object—including its volume, weight, and species—remain constant despite changes in its shape.

In a test of conservation, Piaget first showed children equal amounts of water in two identical containers. He then poured one of them into a tall, thin glass and the other into a short, wide glass and asked whether one glass contained more water than the other. Children at the preoperational stage of development said that one glass (usually the taller one) contained more. They were dominated by the evidence of their eyes. If the glass looked bigger, they thought it contained more. In short, they did not understand the logical concepts of *reversibility* (you just poured the water from one container to another, so you can pour it back and it will still be the same amount) or *complementarity* (one glass is taller but also narrower; the other is shorter but also wider). Indeed, Piaget named this stage "*pre*operational" because children at this stage do not yet understand logical mental *operations* such as these.

Concrete Operational Thought   Sometime around the age of six or seven, Piaget observed, children do develop the ability to conserve number and amount. When they do so, they enter what Piaget called the stage of **concrete operations.** Now, he said, they can count, measure, add, and subtract; their thinking is no longer dominated by the appearance of things. They can use simple logic and perform simple mental manipulations and mental operations on things. They can also sort objects into classes (such as tools, fruit, and vehicles) or series (such as largest to smallest).

Still, concrete operational children can perform their logical operations only on real, concrete objects—sticks and glasses, tools and fruit—not on abstract concepts like justice and freedom. They can reason only about what is, not about what is possible.

The ability to think logically about abstract ideas comes in the next stage of cognitive development, the *formal operational period,* which we discuss later in the chapter.

Modifying Piaget's Theory

Piaget was right in pointing out that there are significant shifts with age in children's thinking, and that thinking becomes more systematic, consistent, and integrated as children get older. His idea that children are active explorers and constructors of knowledge has been absorbed into contemporary ways of thinking about childhood. And he inspired many other psychologists to test his findings and theory with experiments of their own. The results of these experiments have suggested that Piaget's theory needs some modification.

What needs to be modified most is Piaget's notion of developmental stages. Researchers have shown that changes from one stage to the next are less consistent and global than Piaget thought. For example, three-year-olds *can* sometimes make the distinction between physical and mental phenomena; they know the characteristics of real dogs versus pretend dogs (Woolley, 1997). Moreover, they are not invariably egocentric; as one study demonstrated, children of this age knew that a white card, which looked pink to them because they were wearing rose-colored glasses, still looked white to someone who was not wearing the glasses (Liben, 1978). Preoperational children can even do conservation tasks if they are allowed to count the number of objects or have been trained to focus on relevant dimensions such as number, height, and width (Gelman & Baillargeon, 1983).

Taken together, these studies suggest that children's knowledge and mental strategies develop at different ages in different areas, and in "pockets" rather than at global levels of understanding (Sternberg, 1989). Knowledge in particular areas is demonstrated sooner in children who are given specific experience in those areas or who are presented with very simple questions and tasks. Thus, children's reasoning depends not only on their general level of development but also on (1) how easy the task is, (2) how familiar they are with the objects involved, (3) how well they understand the language being used, and (4) what experiences they have had in similar situations (Siegal, 1997). Research has also shown that the level of a child's thinking varies from day to day and may even shift when the child solves the same problem twice in the same day (Siegler, 1994).

In summary, psychologists today tend to think of cognitive development in terms of rising and falling "waves," not fixed stages—in terms of changing frequencies in children's use of different ways of thinking, not sudden, permanent shifts from one way of thinking to another (Siegler, 1995). They suggest that children systematically try out many different solutions to problems and gradually come to select the best of them.

Information Processing During Childhood

An alternative to Piaget's theory of cognitive development is based on the *information-processing approach* discussed in Chapters 7 and 8. This approach describes cognitive activities in terms of how people take in information, use it, and remember it. Developmental psychologists taking this approach focus on gradual quantitative changes in children's mental capacities, rather than on dramatic qualitative changes in their stages of development. Their research demonstrates that, as children get older, information-processing skills gradually get better. Older children have longer attention spans. They take in information and shift their attention from one task to another more rapidly. And they are faster at processing information after it is received (Miller & Vernon, 1997). They are also more efficient; for instance, they code information into fewer dimensions and divide tasks into steps that can be processed one after another (Halford et al., 1994).

Children's memory also markedly improves with age (Schneider & Bjorklund, 1998). Preschoolers can keep only two or three pieces of information in mind at the same time; older children can remember more. Their short-term memory capacities get larger every year, though only up to a point. (Even most adults can hold only about seven pieces of information in mind at any one time.) Older children retain more information in their long-term memory storage as well. They forget less than younger children, and their ability to remember things longer increases throughout childhood. After about age seven, children are also better at remembering more complex and abstract information, such as the gist of what several people have said during a conversation. Their memories are more accurate, extensive, and well organized. The knowledge they have accumulated allows them to draw more inferences and to integrate new information into a more complete network of facts. (See "In Review: Milestones of Cognitive Development in Infancy and Childhood" on page 420.)

What accounts for these increases in children's attention, information processing, and memory capacities? As we have already suggested, one cause is maturation of the brain. Another is experience. Indeed, researchers have observed that the cognitive abilities of children improve dramatically when they are dealing with familiar rather than unfamiliar material. One study found, for example, that Mayan children in Mexico lagged behind their age-mates in the United States on standard memory tests of pictures and nouns, but they did a lot better when researchers gave them a more familiar task, such as recalling miniature objects in a model of a Mayan village (Rogoff & Waddell, 1982). The amount of experience children have had affects their memory span, presumably by allowing them to process new information more easily and quickly.

Better memorization strategies may also help account for the improvement in children's memories. To a great extent, children acquire these strategies in school. They learn to repeat information over and over to help fix it in memory, to place information into categories, and to use memory aids like "*i* before *e* except after *c*" to help them remember. They also learn what situations call for deliberate memorization and what factors, such as the length of a list, affect memory.

LINKAGES

Why does memory improve during childhood? (a link to Memory)

LINKAGES

What happens to our memories of infancy? (a link to Memory)

LINKAGES

Development and Memory

The ability to remember facts and figures, pictures and objects, improves as we get older and more expert at processing information. But take a minute right now and try to recall anything that happened to you when you were, say, one year old. Most people can accurately recall a few autobiographical memories from age five or six but remember virtually nothing from before the age of three (Schneider & Bjorklund, 1998).

Psychologists have not yet found a fully satisfactory explanation for this "infantile amnesia." Some have suggested that young children lack the memory encoding and storage processes described in Chapter 7. Yet children of two or three can clearly recall experiences that happened weeks or even months earlier (Bauer, 1996). Other psychologists suggest that infantile amnesia occurs because very young children lack a sense of self. They don't recognize themselves in the mirror, so they may not have a framework for organizing memories about what happens to them (Howe, 1995). However, this explanation cannot apply to the entire period up to three years of age, inasmuch as children do recognize themselves in the mirror by the time they are two. Indeed, recent research suggests that infants even younger than two can recognize their own faces, and their voices on tape (Legerstee, Anderson, & Schaffer, 1998).

Another possibility is that early memories, though "present," are implicit rather than explicit. As described in Chapter 7, *implicit memories* form automatically and can affect our emotions and behavior even when we do not consciously recall them. Toddlers' implicit memories were demonstrated in a study in which two-and-a-half-year-olds apparently remembered a strange, pitch-dark room where they had participated in an experiment two years earlier (Perris, Myers, & Clifton, 1990). Unlike children who had never been in the room, these children were unafraid and reached for noisy objects in the dark, just as they had learned to do at the previous session. However, children's implicit memories of their early years, like their explicit memories,

in review

MILESTONES OF COGNITIVE DEVELOPMENT IN INFANCY AND CHILDHOOD

Age*	Achievement	Description
3–4 months	Maturation of senses	Immaturities that limit the newborn's vision and hearing are overcome.
	Voluntary movement	Reflexes disappear, and infants begin to gain voluntary control over their movements.
12–18 months	Mental representation	Infants can form images of objects and actions in their minds.
	Object permanence	Infants understand that objects exist even when out of sight.
18–24 months	Symbolic thought	Young children use symbols to represent things that are not present in their pretend play, drawing, and talk.
4 years	Intuitive thought	Children reason about events, real and imagined, by guessing rather than by engaging in logical analysis.
6–7 years	Concrete operations Conservation	Children can apply simple logical operations to real objects. For example, they recognize that important properties of a substance, such as number or amount, remain constant despite changes in shape or position.
7–8 years	Information processing	Children can remember about seven pieces of information; they begin to learn strategies for memorization.

*These ages are approximate; they indicate the order in which children first reach these milestones of cognitive development rather than the exact ages.

are quite limited. In one study, researchers showed photographs of young children to a group of ten-year-olds (Newcombe & Fox, 1994). Some of the photos were of preschool classmates whom the children had not seen since they were five years old. They explicitly recalled 21 percent of their former classmates, and their skin conductance (an index of emotion) indicated that they had implicit memories of an additional 5 percent. Yet these children had *no* memory of 74 percent of their preschool pals, as compared with adults in another study who correctly identified 90 percent of the photographs of high-school classmates they had not seen for thirty years (Bahrick, Bahrick, & Wittlinger, 1975).

Other psychologists have proposed that our early memories are lost because in those years we did not yet have the language skills to talk about, and thus solidify, our memories. Nor could we be reminded of past events when others talked about them (Fivush, Haden, & Adam, 1995; Hudson & Sheffield, 1998). Still others say that early memories were stored, but, because the schemas we used in early childhood to mentally represent them changed in later years, we no longer possess the retrieval cues necessary to recall them. Another possibility is that early experiences tend to be fused into *generalized event representations,* such as "going to Grandma's" or "playing at the beach," so that it becomes difficult to remember any specific event. Research on hypotheses such as these may someday unravel the mystery of infantile amnesia.

Culture and Cognitive Development

Whereas Piaget focused on the physical world of objects in explaining development, the Russian psychologist Lev Vygotsky (pronounced "vah-GOT-ski") focused on the social world of people. He viewed the human mind as a product of cultural history. The child's mind, said Vygotsky, grows through interaction with other minds. Dramatic support for this idea comes from cases such as the "Wild Boy of Aveyron," a French child who, in the late 1700s, was apparently lost or abandoned by his parents at a very early age and had grown up with animals. At about eleven years of age, he was captured by hunters and sent to Paris, where scientists observed him. What the scientists saw was a dirty, frightened creature who trotted like a wild animal and spent most of his time silently rocking. Although the scientists worked with the boy for more than ten years, he was never able to live unguarded among other people, and he never learned to speak.

Consistent with Vygotsky's ideas, this tragic case suggests that, without society, children's minds would not develop much beyond those of animals—that children acquire their ideas through interaction with parents, teachers, and other representatives of their culture. Followers of Vygotsky have studied the effects of the social world on children's cognitive development—how participation in social routines affects children's developing knowledge of the world. In Western societies, such routines include shopping, eating at McDonald's, going to birthday parties, and attending religious services. In other cultures they might include helping to make pottery, going hunting, and weaving baskets. Quite early, children develop mental representations, called *scripts,* for these activities. By the time they are three, children can accurately describe the scripts for their routine activities (Nelson, 1986). Scripts, in turn, affect children's knowledge and understanding of cognitive tasks. Thus, suburban children can understand conservation problems earlier than inner-city children if the problems are presented, as Piaget's were, like miniature science experiments; but the performance of

Encouraging Academic Achievement

Asian-American children tend to do better in school than European-American children partly because Asian-American children's families tend to provide especially strong support for academic achievement.

inner-city children is improved when the task is presented via a script that is more familiar to them, such as one involving what a "slick trickster" would do to fool someone (White & Glick, 1978).

From a remarkably young age, children's cognitive abilities are influenced by the language of their culture. Consider, for instance, the way people think about relations between objects in space. Those who, as children, learn a language that has no words for spatial concepts—such as *in, on, in front of, behind, to the left,* and *to the right*—acquire cognitive categories that are different from those of people in North America. Indeed, research indicates that such individuals have difficulty distinguishing between the left and right sides of objects, and tend not to invoke the symbolic associations with left and right hands that North Americans do (Bowerman, 1996; Levinson, 1996).

Language influences cognition in the area of academic achievement as well. For example, Korean and Chinese children show exceptional ability at adding and subtracting large numbers (Fuson & Kwon, 1992; Miller et al., 1995). As third-graders, they can do in their heads three-digit problems (such as 702 minus 125) that would stump most North American children. The difference seems traceable in part to the clear and explicit way that Asian languages label numbers from eleven to nineteen. In English, the meaning of the words *eleven* and *twelve,* for instance, is not as clear as the Asian *ten-one* and *ten-two.* A related cultural difference supports this mathematical expertise: Asians use the metric system of measurement and the abacus, both of which are structured around the number ten. And Korean math textbooks emphasize this tens structure by presenting the ones digits in red, the tens in blue, and the hundreds in green. Above all, in Asian cultures, educational achievement, especially in mathematics, is encouraged at home and conscientiously taught in school (Crystal et al., 1994; Stevenson, Azuma, & Hakuta, 1986).

Promoting Cognitive Development

Even within a single culture, some children are mentally advanced whereas others lag behind their peers. Why? As already suggested, heredity is an important factor, but experience also plays a role. To explore the significance of that role, psychologists have studied the cognitive development of children who are exposed to differing environments.

Cognitive development is profoundly delayed if children are raised in environments where they are deprived of the everyday sights, sounds, and feelings provided by conversation and loving interaction with family members, by pictures and books, even by toys and television. Children subjected to such severe deprivation show marked impairment in intellectual development by the time they are two or three years old, and may never fully recover even if they are given special attention later on (Rymer, 1993). Cognitive development is also impaired by less extreme conditions of deprivation, including the neglect, malnourishment, noise, and chaos that occur in many poor households. One study found that children raised in poverty scored nine points lower on IQ tests by the time they were five years old than did children in families whose incomes were twice the poverty level (Duncan, Brooks-Gunn, & Klebanov, 1994). Such differences continue as poor children enter school (Stipek & Ryan, 1997). Children who remain in poverty have lower IQs and poorer school achievement, the result of a build-up of problems which often begin with prenatal complications and continue through childhood with exposure to lead, lack of cognitive stimulation, and harsh and inconsistent parenting (McLoyd, 1998).

In families above the poverty line, too, children's cognitive development is related to their surroundings, their experiences, and, most notably, their parents' behavior. One longitudinal study, for instance, revealed that the parents of gifted children started stimulating their children's cognitive activity very early on (Gottfried, 1997). When they were infants, the parents read to them. When they were toddlers, the parents provided them with reference books, computerized teaching aids, and trips to the museum. And when they were preschoolers and older, the parents drew out their children's natural curiosity about the world and encouraged their tendency to seek out new learning opportunities themselves. In another study, researchers examined how interactions between parents and children are related to IQ scores (Fagot & Gauvain, 1997). When the children were eighteen to thirty months old, they were asked to solve a problem—specifically, to use a hook to remove a stuffed animal from a box. The researchers recorded how the mothers interacted with their children during this task. Later, at the age of five, the children were given IQ tests, at which point the earlier behaviors of the mothers were compared. It turned out that the mothers of children with the highest IQ scores had been the ones who provided cognitive guidance by offering numerous hints and suggestions. In contrast, the mothers of children with the lowest IQ scores had forcefully told them what they needed to do to complete the task.

To improve the cognitive skills of children who do not get the optimum stimulation and guidance at home, developmental psychologists have provided extra lessons, materials, and educational contact with sensitive adults. In a variety of such programs, ranging from weekly home visits to daily preschools, children's cognitive abilities have been enhanced (Ramey & Ramey, 1998). Music lessons have also been shown to promote children's cognitive development (Rauscher et al., 1997). Even electronic games, though no substitute for adult attention, can provide opportunities for school-age children to hone spatial skills that help improve their performance in math and science (Subrahmanyam & Greenfield, 1994). It appears that the earlier the stimulation begins, the better; and for some cognitive abilities, stimulation affects both the brain and behavior throughout much of the life span (Greenough, 1997).

INFANCY AND CHILDHOOD: SOCIAL AND EMOTIONAL DEVELOPMENT

Life for the child is more than learning about objects, doing math problems, and getting good grades. It is also about social relationships and emotional reactions. From the first months onward, infants are both attracted by and attractive to other people.

During the first hour or so after birth, mothers gaze into their infants' eyes and give them gentle touches (Klaus & Kennell, 1976). This is the first opportunity for the mother to display her *bond* to her infant—an emotional tie that begins even before the baby is born. Psychologists once believed that this immediate postbirth contact was critical—that the mother-infant bond would never be strong if the opportunity for early interaction was missed. Research has revealed, however, that such interaction in the first few hours is not a requirement for a close relationship (Myers, 1987). With or without early contact, mothers (and nowadays many fathers as well), whether biological or adoptive, gradually form close attachments to their infants by interacting with them day after day.

At the same time as the mother is gazing at the baby, the baby is gazing back at her (Klaus & Kennell, 1976). By the time infants are two days old, they recognize—and like—their mother's face; they will suck more vigorously to see a videotaped image of her face than to see that of a stranger (Walton, Bower, & Bower, 1992). Soon, they begin to respond to the mother's facial expressions as well. By the time they are a year old, children use their mothers' emotional expressions to guide their own behavior in ambiguous situations (Saarni, Mummer, & Campos, 1998; Thompson, 1998). If the mother looks frightened when a stranger approaches, for example, the child is more likely to avoid the stranger. As discussed in Chapter 11, this phenomenon is called *social referencing*.

Infants also communicate their feelings to their parents. They do so by crying and screaming, but also by more subtle behavior. When they want to interact, they look and smile; when they do not want to interact, they turn away and suck their thumbs (Tronick, 1989).

Individual Temperament

From the moment infants are born, they differ from one another in the emotions they express most often. Some infants are happy, active, and vigorous; they splash, thrash, and wriggle. Others are usually quiet. Some infants approach new objects with

Forming a Bond

Mutual eye contact, exaggerated facial expressions, and shared baby talk are an important part of the early social interactions that promote an enduring bond of attachment between parent and child.

enthusiasm; others turn away or fuss. Some infants whimper; others kick, scream, and wail. Characteristics like these make up the infant's disposition or **temperament**—the individual style of expressing needs and emotions. Temperament has long been known as a reflection of heredity's influence on the beginning of an individual's personality. But recent research suggests that temperament may itself be affected by the prenatal environment—for example, by the mother's level of stress, her intrauterine hormones, and her health habits, such as smoking (Azar, 1997).

Early research on infant temperament indicated that most babies fall into one of three temperament patterns (Thomas & Chess, 1977). *Easy babies*, the most common kind, get hungry and sleepy at predictable times, react to new situations cheerfully, and seldom fuss. *Difficult babies* are irregular and irritable. And *slow-to-warm-up babies* react warily to new situations but eventually come to enjoy them.

Traces of these early temperament patterns weave their way throughout childhood: Easy infants usually stay easy; difficult infants often remain difficult, sometimes developing attention and aggression problems in childhood (Guerin, Gottfried, & Thomas, 1997); timid, or slow-to-warm-up, toddlers tend to become shy preschoolers, restrained and inhibited eight-year-olds, and somewhat anxious teenagers (Schwartz, Kagan, & Snidman, 1995). However, in temperament, as in cognitive development, nature interacts with nurture. Many events take place between infancy and adulthood to shift the individual's development in one direction or another.

If parent and infant are in tune, chances increase that temperamental qualities will be stable. Consider, for example, the temperament patterns of Chinese-American and European-American children. At birth, Chinese-American infants are calmer, less changeable, less perturbable, and more easily consoled when upset than European-American infants, suggesting that there may be an inherited predisposition toward self-control among the Chinese (Kagan et al., 1994). This tendency is then powerfully reinforced by the Chinese culture. Compared with European-American parents, Chinese parents are less likely to reward and stimulate babbling and smiling, and more likely to maintain close control of their young children. The children, in turn, are more dependent on their mothers and less likely to play by themselves; they are less vocal, noisy, and active than European-American children (Smith & Freedman, 1983).

These temperamental differences between children in different ethnic groups illustrate the combined contributions of nature and nurture. There are many other illustrations, as well. Mayan infants, for example, are relatively inactive from birth. The Zinacantecos, a Mayan group in southern Mexico, reinforce this innate predisposition toward restrained motor activity by swaddling their infants and by nursing at the slightest sign of movement (Greenfield & Childs, 1991). This combination of genetic predisposition and cultural reinforcement is culturally adaptive: Quiet Mayan infants do not kick off their covers at night, which is important in the cold highlands where they live; inactive infants are able to spend long periods on their mother's back as she works at the loom; infants who do not begin to walk until they can understand some language do not wander into the open fire at the center of the house. This adaptive interplay of innate and cultural factors in the development of temperament operates in all cultures.

The Infant Grows Attached

During the first year of life, as infants and caregivers watch and respond to one another, the infant begins to form an **attachment**—a deep, affectionate, close, and enduring relationship—to these important figures. John Bowlby, a British psychoanalyst, drew attention to the importance of attachment after he observed children who had been orphaned in World War II. These children's depression and other emotional scars led Bowlby to develop a theory about the importance of developing a strong attachment to one's primary caregivers, a tie that normally keeps infants close to their caregivers and, therefore, safe (Bowlby, 1973). Soon after Bowlby first described his theory, researchers began to investigate how such attachments are formed and what happens when they are not formed, or when they are broken by loss or separation. Some of the most dramatic of these studies were conducted by Harry Harlow.

Motherless Monkeys—and Children Harlow (1959) separated newborn monkeys from their mothers and reared them in cages containing two artificial mothers. One "mother" was made of wire with a rubber nipple from which the infant could get milk (see Figure 12.6); it provided food but no physical comfort. The other artificial mother had no nipple but was made of soft, comfortable terrycloth. Harlow found that the infants preferred the terrycloth mother; they spent most of their time with it, especially when frightened. The terrycloth mother provided feelings of softness and cuddling, which were things the infants needed when they sensed danger.

FIGURE 12.6

Wire and Terrycloth "Mothers"

Here are the two types of artificial mothers used in Harlow's research. Although baby monkeys received milk from the wire mother, they spent most of their time with the terrycloth version and would cling to it when frightened.

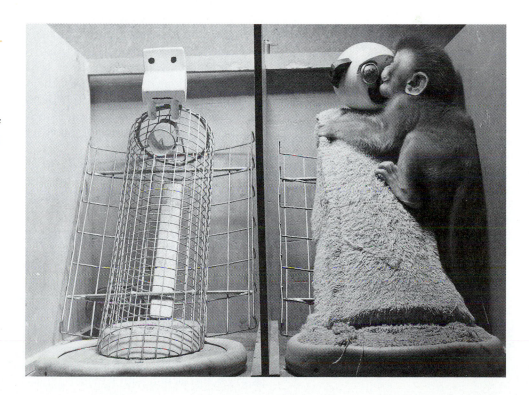

Breaking a Bond

On April 30, 1995, after a four-year battle over his custody, "Baby Richard" was taken from the adoptive parents to whom he formed a strong emotional attachment, and turned over to his biological father. The tearful separation shown here, as Richard is carried away by his biological father, touched many hearts, and raised serious questions about the U.S. legal system, adoption laws, and apparent disregard for psychological research on attachment.

Harlow also investigated what happens when attachments do not form. He isolated some newborn monkeys from all social contact. After a year of this isolation, the monkeys showed dramatic disturbances. When visited by normally active, playful monkeys, they withdrew to a corner, huddling or rocking for hours. As adults, they were unable to have normal sexual relations; but when some of the females did have babies (through artificial insemination), they tended to ignore them. When their infants became distressed, the mothers physically abused and sometimes even killed them.

Tragically, humans who spend their first few years without a consistent caregiver react in a similar manner. At Romanian and Russian orphanages, where many children were abandoned by their mothers and neglected by institutional caregivers, visitors have discovered that the children, like Harlow's deprived monkeys, were withdrawn and engaged in constant rocking (Holden, 1996). These effects continued even after the children were adopted. In one study, researchers observed the behaviors of four-year-old children who had been in a Romanian orphanage for at least eight months before being adopted and compared them to the behaviors of children in two other groups matched for age and gender: those who had been adopted before the age of four months, and those who had remained with their biological parents (Chisholm, 1997). The late-adopted children were found to have many more serious problems. Depressed or withdrawn, they stared blankly, demanded attention, and could not control their tempers (Holden, 1996). They also interacted poorly with their adopted mothers but were indiscriminately friendly with strangers, trying to cuddle and kiss them. Neurologists suggest that the dramatic problems observed in isolated monkeys and humans are the result of developmental brain dysfunction and damage brought on by a lack of touch and body movement in infancy (Prescott, 1996).

Forming an Attachment   Fortunately, most infants do have a consistent caregiver, usually the mother, to whom they can form an attachment. By the age of six or seven months, infants show signs of preferring their mother to anyone else—watching her closely, crawling after her, clambering up into her lap, protesting when she leaves, and brightening when she returns (Ainsworth, 1973). After an attachment has been formed, separation from the mother for even thirty minutes can be a stressful experience (Larson, Gunnar, & Hertsgaard, 1991).

Later on, infants develop attachments to their fathers as well (Lamb, 1976). However, interaction with fathers is typically less frequent, and of a somewhat different nature, than with mothers (Parke, 1996). Mothers tend to feed, bathe, dress, cuddle, and talk to their infants, whereas fathers are more likely to play, jiggle, and toss them, especially sons. In addition, fathers may not do as well as mothers when the baby becomes bored or distressed.

Variations in Attachment   The amount of closeness and contact the infant seeks with either mother or father depends to some extent on the infant. Those who are ill or tired or slow to warm up may require more closeness. Closeness also depends to some extent on the parent. An infant whose parent has been absent, aloof, or unresponsive is likely to need more closeness than one whose parent is accessible and responsive.

Researchers have studied the differences in infants' attachments in a special situation that simulates the natural comings and goings of parents and infants—the so-called *Strange Situation* (Ainsworth et al., 1978). Mother and infant come to an unfamiliar room where they can be videotaped through a one-way window. Here the infant interacts with the mother and an unfamiliar woman in brief episodes. The infant plays with the mother and the stranger, the mother leaves the baby with the stranger for a few minutes, the mother and the stranger leave the baby alone in the room briefly, and the mother returns to the room.

Researchers have found that most infants in the Strange Situation display a *secure attachment* to the mother (Thompson, 1998). In the unfamiliar room, they use the mother as a home base, leaving her side to explore and play but returning to her periodically for comfort or contact. And when the mother returns after the brief separation, these infants are invariably happy to see her and receptive when she initiates contact. These mother-child pairs also tend to have harmonious interactions at home. The mothers themselves are generally sensitive and responsive to their babies' needs and signals (DeWolff & van IJzendoorn, 1997).

Some infants, however, display an *anxious insecure attachment*. Their relationship with the mother may be (1) *avoidant*—they avoid or ignore the mother when she approaches or when she returns after the brief separation; (2) *ambivalent*—they are upset when the mother leaves, but when she returns they act angry and reject her efforts at contact and when picked up they squirm to get down; or (3) *disorganized*—their behavior is inconsistent, disturbed, and disturbing; they may begin to cry again after the mother has returned and comforted them, or they may reach out for the mother while looking away from her.

Cultural Differences in Parent-Child Relations

Variations in the intimacy of family interactions, including whether infants sleep in their parents' bed, may contribute to cross-cultural differences in attachment patterns.

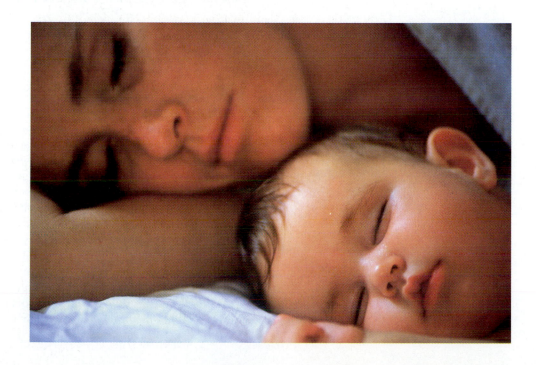

The security of a child's attachment to parents has a number of implications that extend past infancy. Compared with insecurely attached children, those who are securely attached tend to be more socially and emotionally competent, more cooperative, enthusiastic, and persistent, better at solving problems, more compliant and controlled, and more popular and playful (Thompson, 1998). They receive more positive reactions from their peers (Fagot, 1997), report being less lonely (Berlin, Cassidy, & Belsky, 1995), and are less egocentric (Meins et al., 1998). Attachment to the mother also affects the way children process emotional information. Securely attached children tend to remember positive events more accurately than negative events, whereas insecurely attached children tend to do the opposite (Belsky, Spritz, & Crnic, 1996).

Patterns of attachment vary widely in different parts of the world. In northern Germany, for example, the proportion of infants who display avoidant behavior in the Strange Situation is much higher than in the United States (Spangler et al., 1996). In Japan, where mothers are completely devoted to their young children and are seldom apart from them (White, 1987), it is impossible for many mothers to leave their infants in the Strange Situation because the infants are so distressed by separation (Miyake, Chen, & Campos, 1985). And in Israel, kibbutz babies who sleep in infant houses away from their parents are relatively likely to show insecure attachments to them, as well as other attachment difficulties later in life (Sagi et al., 1994). For this reason, "collective sleeping" has been discontinued at most, if not all, kibbutzim (Aviezer et al., 1994). Questions remain, however, about the consequences of other aspects of collective child care practiced at kibbutzim and around the world.

With the mothers of many infants now working outside the home, concern has been expressed about how daily separations from their mothers might affect these infants. Some have argued that leaving infants with a babysitter, or putting them in a day-care center, damages the quality of the mother-infant relationship and increases the babies' risk for psychological problems later on (Gallagher, 1998).

THINKING CRITICALLY

Does Day Care Harm the Emotional Development of Infants?

■ What am I being asked to believe or accept?

The claim to be evaluated is that daily separations brought about by the need for day care undermine the infant's ability to form a secure attachment and inflict emotional harm.

■ What evidence is available to support the assertion?

There is clear evidence that separation from the mother is painful for young children. Furthermore, if separation lasts a week or more, young children may become apathetic and mournful and eventually lose interest in the missing mother (Robertson & Robertson, 1971). But day care does not involve such lasting separations, and research has shown that infants in day care do form attachments to their mothers. In fact, they prefer their mothers to their daytime caregivers (Clarke-Stewart & Fein, 1983).

But are their attachments as *secure* as the attachments formed by infants whose mothers do not work? Researchers first examined this question by comparing infants' behavior in the Strange Situation. A review of the data disclosed that, on average, infants in full-time day care were somewhat more likely to be classified as insecurely attached. Specifically, 36 percent of the infants in full-time care received this classification, compared with 29 percent of the infants not in full-time day care (Clarke-Stewart, 1989). These results appear to support the suggestion that day care hinders the development of infants' attachments to their mothers.

■ **Are there alternative ways of interpreting the evidence?**

Perhaps factors other than day care could explain this difference between infants in day care and those at home with their mothers. One such factor could be the method used to assess attachment—the Strange Situation. Infants in these studies were judged insecure if they did not run to their mothers after a brief separation. But maybe infants who experience daily separations from their mothers are less perturbed by the Strange Situation separations and therefore seek out less closeness with their mothers. A second factor could be differences between the infants' mothers: Working mothers may value independence in themselves and their children, whereas mothers who value closeness may choose to stay home.

■ **What additional evidence would help to evaluate the alternatives?**

Finding a heightened rate of insecure attachment among the infants of working mothers does not, by itself, prove that day care is harmful. To judge the effects of day care, we must use other measures of emotional adjustment. If infants in day care show consistent signs of impaired emotional relations in other situations (at home, say) and with other caregivers (such as the father), this evidence would support the argument that day care harms children's emotional development. Another useful method would be to statistically control for differences in the attitudes and behaviors of parents who do and do not use day care and then examine the differences in their children.

In fact, this research design has already been employed. In 1990 the U.S. government funded a study of infant day care in ten sites around the country. The psychological and physical development of more than 1,300 randomly selected infants was tracked from birth through age three. The results available so far show that when factors such as parents' education, income, and attitudes are statistically controlled for, infants in day care are no more likely to have emotional problems or to be insecurely attached to their mothers than infants not in day care. However, in cases where infants were placed in poor-quality day care, where the caregivers were insensitive and unresponsive, and where mothers were insensitive to their babies' needs at home, the infants were less likely to develop a secure attachment to their mothers.

■ **What conclusions are most reasonable?**

Based on available evidence, the most reasonable conclusion appears to be that day care by itself does not lead to insecure attachment or cause emotional harm to infants. But if the care is of poor quality, it can worsen a risky situation at home and increase the likelihood that infants will have problems forming a secure attachment to their mothers. The U.S. government study is still under way, and the children's progress is being followed into elementary school. Time will tell if other problems develop in the future.

Relationships with Parents and Peers

Erik Erikson (1968) saw the first year of life as the time when infants develop a feeling of basic trust (or mistrust) about the world. According to his psychodynamically oriented theory, an infant's first year represents the first of eight stages of lifelong psychosocial development (see Table 12.2 on page 430). Each stage focuses on an issue or crisis that is especially important at that time of life. Erikson believed that the ways in which people resolve these issues shape their personalities and social relationships. Positive resolution of an issue provides the foundation for characteristics such as trust, autonomy, initiative, and industry. But if the crisis is not resolved positively, according to Erikson, the person will be psychologically troubled and cope less effectively with

TABLE 12.2

Erikson's Stages of Psychosocial Development

In each of Erikson's stages of development, a different psychological issue presents a new crisis for the person to resolve. The person focuses attention on the issue and by the end of the period has worked through the crisis and resolved it either positively, in the direction of healthy development, or negatively, hindering further psychological development.

Age	Central Psychological Issue or Crisis
First year	**Trust versus mistrust** Infants learn to trust that their needs will be met by the world, especially by the mother—or they learn to mistrust the world.
Second year	**Autonomy versus shame and doubt** Children learn to exercise will, to make choices, and to control themselves—or they become uncertain and doubt that they can do things by themselves.
Third to fifth year	**Initiative versus guilt** Children learn to initiate activities and enjoy their accomplishments, acquiring direction and purpose. Or, if they are not allowed initiative, they feel guilty for their attempts at independence.
Sixth year through puberty	**Industry versus inferiority** Children develop a sense of industry and curiosity and are eager to learn—or they feel inferior and lose interest in the tasks before them.
Adolescence	**Identity versus role confusion** Adolescents come to see themselves as unique and integrated persons with an ideology—or they become confused about what they want out of life.
Early adulthood	**Intimacy versus isolation** Young people become able to commit themselves to another person—or they develop a sense of isolation and feel they have no one in the world but themselves.
Middle age	**Generativity versus stagnation** Adults are willing to have and care for children and to devote themselves to their work and the common good—or they become self-centered and inactive.
Old age	**Integrity versus despair** Older people enter a period of reflection, becoming assured that their lives have been meaningful and ready to face death with acceptance and dignity. Or they are in despair for their unaccomplished goals, failures, and ill-spent lives.

later crises. Thus, in Erikson's theory, forming basic feelings of trust during infancy is the bedrock for all future emotional development.

After children have formed strong emotional attachments to their parents, their next psychological task is to begin to develop a more autonomous relationship with them. This task is part of Erikson's second stage, when children begin to exercise their wills, develop some independence from their all-powerful parents, and initiate activities on their own. According to Erikson, children who are not allowed to exercise their wills or initiate their own activities will feel uncertain about doing things for themselves and guilty about seeking independence. The extent to which parents allow or encourage their children's autonomy depends largely on their parenting style.

Parenting Styles   Parents try to channel children's impulses into socially accepted outlets and teach them the skills and rules needed to function in their society. This process, called *socialization,* is shaped by cultural values. Parents in Hispanic cultures of Mexico, Puerto Rico, and Central America, for example, tend to be influenced by the collectivist tradition, in which family and community interests are emphasized over individual goals. Children in these cultures are expected to respect and obey their elders and to do less of the questioning, negotiating, and arguing that is encouraged or allowed in many middle-class European and European-American families (Greenfield, 1995). When parents from Hispanic cultures immigrate to the United States, their values may often conflict with those of their children's European-American teachers (Raeff, Greenfield, & Quiroz, 1995), and their own parenting efforts may become inconsistent (Harwood, Schulze, & Wilson, 1995).

European and European-American parents tend to employ one of three distinct parenting styles, as described by Diana Baumrind (1971). **Authoritarian parents** are relatively strict, punitive, and unsympathetic. They value obedience and try to shape their children's behavior to meet a set standard and to curb the children's wills. They do not encourage independence. They are detached and seldom praise their youngsters. In contrast, **permissive parents** give their children complete freedom and lax discipline. **Authoritative parents** fall between these two extremes. They reason with their children, encouraging give and take. They allow children increasing responsibility as they get older and better at making decisions. They are firm but understanding. They set limits but also encourage independence. Their demands are reasonable, rational, and consistent.

In her research with middle-class parents, Baumrind found that these three parenting styles were related to young children's social and emotional development. Authoritarian parents had children who were unfriendly, distrustful, and withdrawn. The children of permissive parents were immature, dependent, and unhappy; they were likely to have tantrums or to ask for help when they encountered even slight difficulties. Children raised by authoritative parents were friendly, cooperative, self-reliant, and socially responsible (Baumrind, 1986).

Other researchers have found authoritative parenting styles to be associated with additional positive outcomes, including better school achievement (Steinberg et al., 1994), higher sociometric status (Hinshaw et al., 1997), and better psychological adjustment to parental divorce (Hetherington & Clingempeel, 1992). In contrast, children of authoritarian parents are more likely to cheat and to be aggressive, and less likely to be empathic or to experience guilt or accept blame after doing something wrong (Eisenberg & Fabes, 1998).

The results of these studies of parenting styles are interesting, but their limitations must be noted. First, they involve *correlations,* which, as discussed in Chapter 2, do not prove causation. Finding consistent correlations between parents' and children's behavior does not establish that parents are creating the differences seen in their children. In fact, parents' behavior is often shaped to some extent by their children. For example, parents may react differently to children of different ages. Inherited characteristics, such as children's temperament, size, and appearance, may also influence the way parents treat them (Bugental & Goodnow, 1998). Second, some psychologists have suggested that it is not the parents' behavior *per se* that influences children but, rather, how the children perceive the discipline they receive—as stricter or more lenient than what an older sibling received, for example (Dunn & Plomin, 1990).

A third limitation of these studies is that the correlations between parenting styles and children's behavior, though statistically significant, are usually not terribly strong. Expected relationships between parenting styles and children's behavior do not always appear. For example, Baumrind (1971) found a small group of "harmonious" families in which she never observed the parents disciplining the children, yet the children were thriving.

Findings such as these have led some people to suggest that parents play only a minor role in the development of children's personality (e.g., Harris, 1995, 1998). A much greater influence, they propose, is the children's experience outside the home—

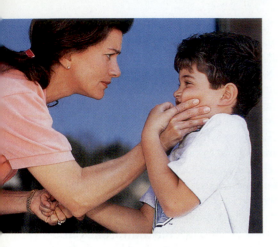

LINKAGES

Parent-Training Programs

Research in developmental psychology on the relationship between parents' socialization styles and children's behavior patterns has helped shape parent-training programs based on both the social-cognitive and the phenomenological approaches to personality described in Chapter 14. These programs are designed to teach parents authoritative methods that can avoid scenes like this.

LINKAGES

Do children perceive others as adults do? (a link to Social Cognition)

especially their interaction with peers. Although this argument has recently gained considerable attention in the media, it is much too early to dismiss parenting styles as irrelevant to the development of children's personality.

In all likelihood, it is the "fit" between parenting style and children's characteristics that affect children the most. Thus, there is no universally "best" style of parenting (Parke & Buriel, 1998). For example, authoritative parenting, so consistently linked with positive outcomes in European-American families, is not related to better school performance in African-American or Asian-American youngsters (Steinberg, Dornbusch, & Brown, 1992). One possible explanation is that different disciplinary styles have different meanings in different cultures. Chinese-American parents use authoritarian discipline more than European-American parents, but their goal is usually to "train" (*chiao shun*) and "govern" (*guan*) children so that they will know what is expected of them (Chao, 1994). By contrast, European-American parents who use authoritarian discipline are more likely to do so to "break the child's will." In other words, each parenting style must be evaluated in its cultural context.

Relationships with Peers   Social development over the years of childhood occurs in a social world that broadens to include brothers and sisters, playmates and classmates. Relationships with other children start very early (Rubin, Bukowski, & Parker, 1998). By two months of age, infants engage in mutual gaze. By six months, they vocalize and smile at each other. By eight months, they prefer to look at another child rather than at an adult (Bigelow et al., 1990). Thus, even infants are interested in each other, but it's a long journey from interest to intimacy.

Observations of two-year-olds show that the most they can do with their peers is to look at them, imitate them, and exchange—or grab—toys. By the time they are three, they can use toys to get a response from another child, but they still don't really play together. Four-year-olds spend most of their time together engaged in parallel play— doing the same thing but not interacting. By this age, though, they can also begin to play "pretend" together, agreeing about roles and themes. This "sociodramatic" play is important because it provides a context for communicating meaning and offers an opportunity to form first "friendships" (Rubin, Bukowski, & Parker, 1998).

In the school years, peer interaction becomes more frequent, complex, and structured. Instead of engaging in pretend play, children play games with rules, play on teams, tutor each other, and cooperate—or compete—in achieving goals. Friends become more important and friendships longer-lasting (Hartup & Stevens, 1997). Schoolchildren understand that feelings, not things, keep friends together (Selman, 1981). In Western cultures, children's friendships are almost always with children of the same sex—presumably because children of the same sex share the same play interests, are attracted to others who are like themselves, and want to avoid those who are different. Children who do not have friends usually experience problems in later life (Bagwell, Newcomb, & Bukowski, 1998).

Social Skills

The changes in peer interactions and relationships over the years of childhood can be traced in part to children's increasing social competencies and skills. Social skills, like cognitive skills, must be learned (Rubin, Bukowski, & Parker, 1998).

One social skill is the ability to engage in sustained, responsive interactions with peers. Such interactions require cooperation, sharing, and taking turns—behaviors that first appear in the preschool years. Parents can aid their children's development of these skills by initiating lots of pretend play and other prosocial activities (Ladd & LeSieur, 1995; Parke & O'Neil, 1997) and by helping the children express their emotions constructively (Eisenberg, 1998). Older siblings, too, can help by acting out social roles during play and by talking about their feelings (Ruffman et al., 1998). Children who have been abused by their parents tend to lack these important interactional skills and are thus more likely to be victimized by their peers (Crick, 1997).

A second social skill learned by children is the ability to detect and interpret other people's emotional signals. Indeed, effective social performance depends on this abil-

Children's Friendships

Though relationships with peers may not always be cordial, they are often among the closest and most positive in a child's life. Friends are more interactive than nonfriends; they smile and laugh together more, pay closer attention to equality in their conversation, and talk about mutual rather than their own idiosyncratic ends.

LINKAGES

Who teaches boys to be men and girls to be women? (a link to Learning)

ity to process information about other people (Slomkowski & Dunn, 1996). Research indicates that girls are able to read emotional signals at younger ages than boys (Dunn et al., 1991). Children who understand another person's perspective, who appreciate how that person might be feeling, and who behave accordingly, tend to be the most popular members of a peer group (Rubin, Bukowski, & Parker, 1998). Children who do not have these skills are rejected or neglected; they may become bullies or the victims of bullies.

A related social skill is the ability to feel what another person is feeling, or something akin to it, and to respond with comfort or help if the person is in distress. This skill allows children to develop both *empathy* and *sympathy*. Affectionate mothers who discuss emotions openly, and who provide clear messages about the consequences of their child's hurtful behavior, effectively encourage the child to be empathic and sympathetic (Eisenberg, 1997).

Yet another social skill that develops in childhood is the ability to control one's emotions and behavior—an ability known as **self-regulation** (Rothbart & Bates, 1998). In the first few years of life, children learn to calm or console themselves by sucking their thumbs or cuddling their favorite blanket. Later, they learn more sophisticated strategies of self-regulation such as planning ahead to avoid a problem (e.g., getting on the first bus when the school bully usually takes the second one) and recruiting social support (casually joining a group of big kids to walk past the bully on the playground). Children who cannot regulate their emotions tend to experience anxiety and distress and have trouble recovering from stressful events. They become overaroused when they see someone in distress and are often unsympathetic and unhelpful (Eisenberg & Fabes, 1998).

Self-regulation is most effectively learned by children who experience harmonious interactions at home under the guidance of supportive and competent parents (Saarni, Mummer, & Campos, 1998). One study revealed that children skilled at regulating their emotions had parents who, when the children were infants, soothed their distress by holding them, talking to them, and providing distractions. Moreover, as the children grew older, the parents gradually began to introduce them to new and potentially uncomfortable events (such as their first haircut), all the while remaining close by as a safe base (Fox, 1997). Another study, specifically involving North American children, found that self-regulation and empathy are fostered by parents who talk about their own feelings and encourage their children to express emotions (Eisenberg, 1997). This phenomenon is not universal, however. For example, Japanese children are better emotion regulators than North American children, even though their parents do not encourage the expression of strong emotion. (Zahn-Waxler et al., 1996).

In recent years, psychologists in the United States have been encouraging schools to teach children the social skills of self-regulation as well as understanding, empathy, and cooperation (Goleman, 1995; Salovey & Sluyter, 1997). It is their hope this "emotional literacy" will reduce the prevalence of childhood depression and aggression.

Gender Roles

An important aspect of understanding other people and being socially skilled is knowing about social roles, including **gender roles**—the general patterns of work, appearance, and behavior associated with being a man or a woman. One survey of gender roles in twenty-five countries found that children learn such roles earliest in Muslim countries (where the roles are perhaps most extreme), but children in all twenty-five countries eventually developed them (Williams & Best, 1990).

Gender roles persist because they are deeply rooted in both nature and nurture. Small physical and behavioral differences between the sexes are evident early on and tend to increase over the years (Eagly, 1996). For example, girls tend to speak and write earlier and to be better at grammar and spelling (Halpern, 1997), whereas boys tend to be more skilled than girls at manipulating objects, constructing three-dimensional forms, and mentally manipulating complex figures and pictures. Girls are likely to be more kind, considerate, and empathic. Their play tends to be more orderly. Boys are

Learning Gender Roles

Socialization by parents and others typically encourages interests and activities traditionally associated with a child's own gender.

more physically active and aggressive; they play in larger groups and spaces, enjoying noisier, more strenuous physical games (Eisenberg & Fabes, 1998). The biological contribution to these male-female differences is supported by studies of differences in anatomy, hormones, and brain organization and functioning (Ruble & Martin, 1998), as well as by cross-cultural research that finds consistent gender patterns even in the face of differing socialization practices. Consider the phenomenon of violence. In one survey, there was not a single culture in which the number of women who killed women was even one-tenth as great as the number of men who killed men; on average, men's homicides outnumbered women's by more than 30 to 1 (Daly & Wilson, 1988).

At the same time, there is strong evidence that socialization influences gender roles. From the moment they are born, boys and girls are treated differently. Adults usually play more gently and talk more to infants they believe to be girls than to infants they believe to be boys. They often shower their daughters with dolls and doll clothes, their sons with trucks and tools. They tend to encourage boys to achieve, compete, and explore; to control their feelings, act independent, and assume personal responsibility. They more often encourage girls to be reflective, dependent, domestic, obedient, and unselfish (Ruble & Martin, 1998). They talk more, and use more supportive speech, with daughters than with sons (Leaper, Anderson, & Sanders, 1998). In these and many other ways, parents, teachers, and television role models consciously or inadvertently pass on their ideas about "appropriate" behaviors for boys and girls (Witt, 1997).

Children also pick up notions of what is gender-appropriate behavior from their peers. Peer pressure exaggerates whatever differences may already exist. For example, boys tend to be better than girls at computer and video games (Greenfield, 1994), but this difference stems in part from the fact that boys encourage and reward each other for skilled performance at these games more than girls do (Law, Pellegrino, & Hunt, 1993). Children are also more likely to play with other children of the same sex, and to act in gender-typical ways, when they are on the playground than when they are at home or in the classroom (Luria, 1992). On the playground, boys are the overtly aggressive ones; they push and they punch (Hyde, 1986). Among girls, the aggression is less obvious; though unlikely to hit other children, they hurt with nasty words and threats to withdraw friendship (Crick, Casas, & Mosher, 1997; Zuger, 1998).

Children are also influenced by **gender schemas**, the generalizations they develop about what toys and activities are "appropriate" for boys versus girls and what jobs are "meant" for men versus women (Fagot, 1995). For example, by the time they are three years old, children tend to believe that dolls are for girls and trucks are for boys. Once they have developed these gender schemas, and know that they themselves are male or female, children tend to choose activities, toys, and behaviors that are "appropriate" for their own gender and to remember actions that are gender-stereotyped better than those that are not (Ruble & Martin, 1998).

In short, social training by both adults and peers tends to bolster and amplify any biological predispositions that distinguish boys and girls, thus creating gender roles that are the joint—and inextricably linked—products of nature and nurture. This and other elements of early development are summarized in "In Review: Social and Emotional Development During Infancy and Childhood."

The efforts of some parents to de-emphasize gender roles in their children's upbringing may be helping to reduce the magnitude of gender differences in areas such as verbal and quantitative skills (Hyde, 1994). However, some observers believe that other gender differences—such as males' greater ability to visualize the rotation of objects in space and females' greater ability to read facial expressions—are unlikely to change much. Evolutionary psychologists see such differences as deeply rooted in our evolutionary past, when males' major activity was hunting and females' was child-rearing (Buss & Kenrick, 1998).

Risk and Resilience

Family instability, child abuse, homelessness, poverty, substance abuse, and domestic violence put many children at risk for various problems in social and emotional devel-

in review

SOCIAL AND EMOTIONAL DEVELOPMENT DURING INFANCY AND CHILDHOOD

Age	Relationships with Parents	Relationships with Other Children	Social Understanding
Birth–2 years	Infants form an attachment to the primary caregiver.	Play focuses on toys, not on other children.	Infants respond to emotional expressions of others.
2–4 years	Children become more autonomous and no longer need their parents' constant attention.	Toys are a way of eliciting responses from other children.	Young children can recognize emotions of others.
4–10 years	Parents actively socialize their children.	Children begin to cooperate, compete, play games, and form friendships with peers.	Children learn social rules, like politeness, and roles, like being a male or female; they learn to control their emotions.

opment. When parents divorce, for example, their children often develop serious interpersonal problems (Hetherington, Bridges, & Insabella, 1998). By two or three years after the divorce, the intense psychological stress is over, and most children are functioning competently (Furstenberg & Cherlin, 1991), but there can be long-lasting effects. Adults whose parents had divorced when they were children may not live as long as those from intact families (Friedman et al., 1995b), and a high proportion of people who were young adolescents when their parents divorced are unable to form committed relationships ten years later (Wallerstein & Blakeslee, 1989). Children are also at risk if their parents have violent fights. Nearly half the children exposed to marital violence exhibit various forms of mental disorder—a rate six times higher than that in the general population (Garber, 1992). How well children ultimately adjust to their parents' fighting or divorce, and whether they lead happy and successful lives, is influenced by numerous factors, including the intensity and duration of the parents' marital conflict, and how well divorcing parents work out a harmonious arrangement that allows both to have regular contact with their children (Hetherington, Bridges, & Insabella, 1998). Even when the odds are against them, though, some children are left virtually unscathed by even the most dangerous risk factors. These children are said to be resilient.

Resilience is a phenomenon that permits successful development in the face of significant challenge. It has been studied in a wide variety of adverse situations throughout the world, including war, natural disaster, family violence, and poverty. This research has consistently identified certain qualities in children and their environments that are associated with resilience (Masten & Coatsworth, 1998). Specifically, resilient children tend to be intelligent and to have easy dispositions, high self-esteem, talent, and faith. They also typically have significant relationships with a warm and authoritative parent, with someone in their extended family, or with other caring adults outside the family, in clubs or religious organizations, or at school.

ADOLESCENCE

The years of middle childhood usually pass smoothly, but adolescence changes things drastically. All adolescents undergo significant changes in size, shape, and physical capacities. Many also experience substantial changes in their social life, reasoning abilities, and views of themselves.

The Challenges of Change

A sudden spurt in physical growth is the most visible sign that adolescence has begun. This growth spurt peaks at about twelve for girls and fourteen for boys (Tanner, 1978; see Figure 12.7). Suddenly, adolescents find themselves in new bodies. At the end of the growth spurt, females begin to menstruate and males produce live sperm. This state of being able for the first time to reproduce is called **puberty.**

In Western cultures, *early adolescence,* the period from age eleven to fifteen or so, is filled with challenges. Sexual interest stirs, and there are opportunities to smoke, drink alcohol, and take other drugs. All of this can be disorienting. Indeed, adolescents may experience bouts of depression and other psychological problems as well. Eating disorders increase in frequency with the onset of adolescence (Wilson et al., 1996), as does the incidence of attempted and completed suicide. In the United States suicide is the third leading cause of death among teenagers, exceeded only by homicides and accidents (U.S. Bureau of the Census, 1996). Between 15 and 30 percent of adolescents drop out of school; their arrest rate is the highest of any age group (Zigler & Stevenson, 1993). For some adolescents, then, early adolescence marks the beginning of a downward spiral that ends up in academic failure, dropping out of school, delinquency, and substance abuse.

Many of the problems of adolescence are associated with challenges to young people's *self-esteem,* their sense of being worthy, capable, and deserving of respect (Harter, 1998). Adolescents are especially vulnerable if many stressors occur at the same time (DuBois et al., 1992). The switch from elementary school to middle school is particularly challenging. Grades tend to drop, especially for students who were already having trouble in school or who don't have confidence in their own abilities (Azar, 1996b). But grades do not affect self-esteem in all teens. For example, some may base their self-esteem on athletic success, and on their peers' opinions of them, rather than on their academic achievement (Osborne, 1997).

Still, making the transition from elementary school to junior high or middle school can be a rude awakening for an eleven-year-old (Eccles, Lord, & Buchanan, 1996). At the new school, teachers may be less friendly and less likely to have time for nurturing relationships with students. They may also exert more control, impose higher standards, and set up more public evaluation of students' work. In addition, junior high school teachers may not be aware of their students' anxieties or insecurities, and may assume that students are adjusting well as long as they are doing well academically (Eccles, Lord, & Roeser, 1996).

The changes and pressures of adolescence are often played out at home, as adolescents try to have a greater say in a parent-child relationship once ruled mainly by their

FIGURE 12.7

Physical Changes in Adolescence

At about ten-and-a-half years of age, girls begin their growth spurt and by age twelve are taller than their male peers. When boys, at about twelve-and-a-half years of age, begin their growth spurt, they usually grow faster and for a longer period of time than girls. Adolescents may grow as much as 5 inches a year. The development of sexual characteristics accompanies these changes in height. The ages at which these changes occur vary considerably across individuals, but their sequence is the same.

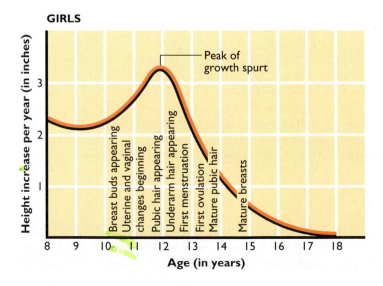

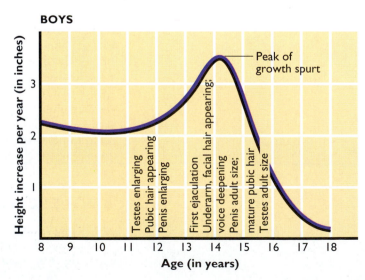

parents. A recent survey of more than 90,000 adolescents from eighty high schools and middle schools in the United States found that teens who do not feel close to their parents are more likely to engage in risky behaviors such as smoking, taking drugs, attempting suicide, and having sex (Resnick, 1997). Fortunately, such closeness is not uncommon; there are also programs that can teach parents what is "normal" behavior for adolescents and how to respond to it. In one study, for example, low-income parents of young adolescents participated in a parenting program in which they learned how to listen and communicate, to invite their children to participate in family decision making, and to reduce nonsupportive behaviors such as scolding, criticizing, and interrogating. The children of these parents adjusted well to the transition to middle school and showed more positive functioning than children in a control group. In addition, their grades stayed stable (whereas the control kids' grades declined), and they exhibited fewer problem behaviors (Bronstein et al., 1998).

Despite the dangers and problems of adolescence, most teens in Western cultures do not experience major personal turmoil or family conflicts (Peterson, 1987; Steinberg, 1990). But when troubles do arise, sex is often involved. Surveys conducted in North America suggest that about 50 percent of teens have had sexual intercourse by age sixteen; fifty years ago, the comparable figure was less than 10 percent (Resnick, 1997). The most dramatic increase has occurred among fifteen-year-old girls, of whom nearly one-third are sexually active (U.S. Department of Health and Human Services, 1992). Sexual activity in adolescence is also related to ethnicity. For instance, teens from Asian-American families are less likely to be sexually active than those from European-American families (McLaughlin et al., 1997).

Teenagers have the highest rates of sexually transmitted diseases (such as gonorrhea, chlamydia, and pelvic inflammatory disease) of any age group (Grady, 1998). One-fifth of all AIDS cases start in adolescence (Brody, 1998). Often, sexual activity also leads to declining school achievement and interest, and, of course, unplanned and unwanted pregnancies. A teenage pregnancy can wreak havoc for the baby as well as the mother. Teenage parents tend to be less positive and stimulating with their children, and more likely to abuse them, than older parents (Coley & Chase-Lansdale, 1998). Their children, in turn, are likely to develop behavior problems and to perform poorly in school. They do better if they have strong attachments to their fathers *and* if their mothers are prepared for their new responsibilities and know about children and parenting even before the baby is born (Miller et al., 1996).

Identity and Development of the Self

A hundred years ago, the end of early adolescence, around the age of fifteen, often marked the beginning of adulthood: of work, parenting, and grown-up responsibilities. Today, in Western societies, the transition from childhood to adulthood often lasts well into the twenties. This lengthened adolescence has created special problems—among them, the matter of finding or forming an identity.

Forming a Personal and Ethnic Identity   Most adolescents have not previously thought deeply about who they are. When preschool children are asked to describe themselves, they often mention a favorite or habitual activity: "I watch TV" or "I do the dishes" (Keller, Ford, & Meacham, 1978). At eight or nine, children identify themselves by giving facts such as their sex, age, name, physical appearance, likes, and dislikes. They may still describe themselves in terms of what they do, but they now include how well they do it compared with other children (Secord & Peevers, 1974). Then, at about age eleven, children begin to describe themselves in terms of social relationships, personality traits, and general, stable psychological characteristics (Damon & Hart, 1982). By the end of early adolescence, they are ready to develop a personal identity as a unique individual.

Their personal identity may be affected by their **ethnic identity**—the part of a person's identity that reflects the racial, religious, or cultural group to which he or she belongs. In melting-pot nations such as the United States, members of ethnic minorities may identify with their ethnic group even more than with their national citizenship. Children are aware of ethnic cues such as skin color before they reach the age of three and prefer to play with children from their own group. Minority-group children reach this awareness earlier than other children (Milner, 1983). In high school, most students hang out with members of their own ethnic group. They tend not to know classmates in other ethnic groups well, seeing them more as members of those groups than as individuals (Steinberg, Dornbusch, & Brown, 1992). These social processes solidify ethnic identity. A positive ethnic identity contributes to self-esteem; seeing their own group as superior makes people feel good about themselves (Fiske, 1998). However, as described in Chapter 17, the same processes that foster ethnic identity can also sow the seeds of ethnic prejudice.

Facing the Identity Crisis   According to Erikson (1968), identity formation is the central task of adolescence. Events of late adolescence, such as graduating from high school, going to college, and forging new relationships, challenge the adolescent's self-concept and precipitate an **identity crisis** (see Table 12.2 on page 430). In this crisis, the adolescent must develop an integrated self-image as a unique person by pulling together self-knowledge acquired during childhood. If infancy and childhood brought trust, autonomy, and initiative, according to Erikson, the adolescent will resolve the identity crisis positively, feeling self-confident and competent. If infancy and childhood resulted in feelings of mistrust, shame, guilt, and inferiority, the adolescent will be confused about his or her identity and goals.

In Western cultures there is some limited empirical support for Erikson's ideas about the identity crisis. In late adolescence, young people do consider alternative identities (Waterman, 1982). They "try out" being rebellious, studious, or detached, as they attempt to resolve questions about sexuality, self-worth, industriousness, and independence. Adolescents who explore identity issues more extensively tend to come from backgrounds that give them opportunities to express and develop their own points of view in a supportive environment at home, at school, and in the community (Grotevant, 1998). By the time they are twenty-one, about half of the adolescents studied resolve the identity crisis in a way that is consistent with their self-image and the historical era in which they are living. They are ready to enter adulthood with self-confidence. Basically the same people who entered adolescence, they now have more mature attitudes and behavior, more consistent goals and values, and a clearer idea of who they are (Savin-Williams & Demo, 1984). Some adolescents fail to resolve identity issues. They either avoid the identity crisis by accepting whatever identity their parents set for them or they postpone dealing with the crisis and remain uncommitted and lacking in direction. For these young people, there are often problems ahead (Hart & Yates, 1997).

Abstract Thought and Moral Reasoning

One reason that adolescents can develop a conscious identity is that they are able to think and reason about abstract concepts. In terms of Piaget's theory, they have reached the **formal operational period.** This stage is marked by the ability to engage in hypothetical thinking, including the imagining of logical consequences. For example, adolescents who have reached this level can consider various strategies for finding a part-time job and recognize that some methods are more likely to succeed than others. They can form general concepts and understand the impact of the past on the present and the present on the future. They can question social institutions, think about the world as it might be and ought to be, and consider the ramifications of love, work, politics, and religion. They can think logically and systematically about symbols and propositions.

Piaget explored adolescents' formal operational abilities by asking them to perform science experiments that involved formulating and systematically investigating hypotheses. Research indicates that only about half the people in Western cultures ever reach the formal operational level necessary to succeed in Piaget's experiments; those who have not had high school science and math are less likely to succeed (Keating, 1990). In other cultures, too, people who have not gone to school are less likely to exhibit formal operations. Consider the following exchange in which a researcher explores the formal operations of an illiterate Kpelle farmer in a Liberian village by giving him a test of logic (Scribner, 1977):

> *Researcher:* All Kpelle men are rice farmers. Mr. Smith is not a rice farmer. Is he a Kpelle man?
>
> *Kpelle farmer:* I don't know the man. I have not laid eyes on the man myself.

Kpelle villagers who had completed some formal schooling answered the question logically: "No, Mr. Smith is not a Kpelle man."

Even people who have been to school do not use a single mode of thinking in all situations. In adulthood, people are more likely to use formal operations for problems based on their own occupations; this is one reason that people whose logic is impeccable at work may still become victims of a home-repair or investment scam (Carraher, Schliemann, & Carraher, 1988).

Kohlberg's Stages of Moral Reasoning   Adolescents are capable of applying their advanced cognitive skills not only to science and logic but also to questions of morality. To examine how people think about morality, psychologists have asked them how they would resolve hypothetical moral dilemmas. Perhaps the most famous of these is the "Heinz dilemma." It requires people to decide whether a man named Heinz should steal a rare and unaffordable drug in order to save his wife from cancer. Using moral dilemmas like this one, Lawrence Kohlberg found that the reasons people give for their moral choices change systematically and consistently with age (Kohlberg & Gilligan, 1971). Kohlberg proposed that moral reasoning develops in six stages, which are summarized in Table 12.3 (on page 440). These stages, he said, are not tightly linked to a person's chronological age; there is a range of ages for reaching each stage, and not everyone reaches the highest level.

Stage 1 and Stage 2 moral judgments, which are most typical of children under the age of nine, tend to be selfish in nature. Kohlberg called this level **preconventional** because reasoning at this level is not based on the conventions or rules that guide social interactions in society. People at this level of moral development are concerned with avoiding punishment or following rules when it is to their own advantage. At the **conventional** level of moral reasoning, Stages 3 and 4, people are concerned about other people; they think that morality consists of following rules and conventions such as duty to the family, to marriage vows, to the country. A conventional thinker would never think it was proper to burn the flag, for example. The moral reasoning of children and adolescents from nine to nineteen is most often at this level. Stages 5 and 6 represent the highest level of moral reasoning, which Kohlberg called **postconventional** because it occurs after conventional reasoning. Moral judgments at this level are based on personal standards or universal principles of justice, equality, and respect for human life rather than on the dictates of authority figures or society. People who have reached this level view rules and laws as arbitrary but respect them because they protect human welfare. They believe that individual rights can sometimes supersede these laws if the laws become destructive. People do not usually reach this level until sometime after the end of adolescence. Stage 6 is seen only rarely in extraordinary individuals. Studies of Kohlberg's stages generally support the sequence he proposed (Colby et al., 1983; Walker, 1989).

Limitations of Kohlberg's Stages   Kohlberg's first four stages appear to be universal; evidence of them has been found in twenty-seven cultures from Alaska to Zambia. Stages 5 and 6, however, do not always appear (Snarey, 1987). Further, some people in collectivist cultures like Papua New Guinea, Taiwan, and in Israeli kibbutzim, for example, explained their answers to moral dilemmas by pointing to the importance of the community rather than to personal standards. People in India included in their moral reasoning the importance of acting in accordance with one's gender and caste

TABLE 12.3

Kohlberg's Stages of Moral Development

Kohlberg's stages of moral reasoning describe differences in how people think about moral issues. Here are some examples of answers that people at different stages of development might give to the "Heinz dilemma" described in the text. Lest you think this dilemma unrealistic, a man was arrested in 1994 for robbing a bank after being turned down for a loan to pay for his wife's cancer treatments.

Stage	What Is Right?	Should Heinz Steal the Drug?
Preconventional		
1	Obeying and avoiding punishment from a superior authority	Heinz should not steal the drug because he will be jailed.
2	Making a fair exchange, a good deal	Heinz should steal the drug because his wife will repay him later.
Conventional		
3	Pleasing others and getting their approval	Heinz should steal the drug because he loves his wife and because she and the rest of the family will approve.
4	Doing your duty, following rules and social order	Heinz should steal the drug for his wife because he has a duty to care for her, or he should not steal the drug because stealing is illegal.
Post-conventional		
5	Respecting rules and laws, but recognizing that they may have limits	Heinz should steal the drug because life is more important than property.
6	Following universal ethical principles, such as justice, reciprocity, equality, and respect for human life and rights	Heinz should steal the drug because of the principle of preserving and respecting life.

and with maintaining personal purity (Shweder et al., 1994). As in other areas of cognitive development, culture plays a significant role in shaping moral judgments.

Gender may also play a role. Carol Gilligan (1982, 1993) has suggested that for females, the moral ideal is not the abstract, impersonal concept of justice that Kohlberg documented in males but, rather, the need to protect enduring relationships and fulfill human needs. Gilligan questioned Kohlberg's assumption that the highest level of morality is based on justice. When she asked her research participants about moral conflicts, the majority of men focused on justice, but only half of the women did. The other half focused on caring. Although this difference between men and women has not been found in many studies, there does seem to be an overall tendency for females to focus on caring more than males and for males to focus on justice more than females (Turiel, 1998).

Taken together, the results of research in many countries and with both genders suggest that moral ideals are not absolute and universal. Moral development is apparently an adaptation to the moral world in which one lives, a world that differs from place to place. Formal operational reasoning may be necessary for people to reach the highest level of moral reasoning, but this alone is not sufficient. To some extent, at the highest levels, moral reasoning is a product of culture and history.

Moral Reasoning and Moral Action   There is some evidence that moral reasoning is related to moral behavior. In one study, adolescents who committed crimes ranging from burglary to murder tended to see obedience to laws mainly as a way of avoiding jail—a Stage 2 belief—whereas their nondelinquent peers, who showed Stage 3 reasoning, believed that one should obey laws because they prevent chaos in society (Gregg, Gibbs, & Basinger, 1994). But having high moral reasoning ability is no guarantee that a person will always act morally; other factors, such as the likelihood of being caught, also affect behavior (Krebs, 1967).

Children and adolescents can be encouraged to move to higher levels of moral reasoning through exposure to arguments at a higher stage, perhaps as they argue about issues with each other. Hearing about moral reasoning that is one stage higher than their own or encountering a situation that requires more advanced reasoning seems to push people into moral reasoning at a higher level (Enright, Lapsley, & Levy, 1983). The development of moral behavior takes more than abstract knowledge, however. Consider a study of inner-city adolescents who were required to take a high school class that involved community service—working at a soup kitchen for the needy (Youniss & Yates, 1997). As part of the course they also had to write essays on their experience. Over time, the students' essays became more sophisticated, going beyond discussion of, say, homelessness to observations about the distribution of wealth in society and other ideological matters. By the end of the course, the behavior of the students had also changed; they were going to the soup kitchen more often than the course required.

For children and adolescents, learning to behave in moral ways requires (1) consistent models of moral reasoning and behavior in the actions of their parents and peers, (2) parents and teachers who promote moral behavior, (3) real-life experience with moral issues, and (4) situational factors that support moral actions. Indeed, both moral reasoning and moral behavior tend to be lower when situational factors—such as excessive use of alcohol—do not support them (Denton & Krebs, 1990). Not only do we sometimes fail to act at the highest level of which we are capable, we sometimes fail even to reason at this level.

ADULTHOOD

Development does not end with adolescence. Adults, too, go through transitions and experience physical, cognitive, and social changes.

Physical Changes

In *early adulthood* (ages twenty to forty), physical growth continues. Shoulder width, height, and chest size increase. People continue to develop their athletic abilities. For most people, the years of early adulthood are the prime of life.

In *middle adulthood* (ages forty to sixty-five), one of the most common physical changes is the loss of sensory acuity (Fozard et al., 1977). By this time, nearly everyone shows some hearing impairment. People in their early forties become less sensitive to light, and their vision deteriorates somewhat. Increased farsightedness is an inevitable change that usually results in a need for reading glasses. Inside the body, bone mass is dwindling, the risk of heart disease is increasing, and fertility declines. In their late forties or early fifties, women generally experience the shutdown of reproductive capability, a process known as **menopause.** Estrogen and progesterone levels drop, and the menstrual cycle eventually ceases.

In *late adulthood* (past age sixty-five), men shrink about an inch, and women about two inches, as their posture changes and cartilage disks between the spinal vertebra become thinner. Hardening of the arteries and a buildup of fat deposits on the artery walls may lead to heart disease. The digestive system slows down and becomes less efficient. In addition, the brain shrinks and the flow of blood to the brain slows. The few reflexes that remained after infancy (such as the knee-jerk reflex) weaken or disappear.

But, as in earlier years, many of these changes can be delayed or diminished by a healthy diet and exercise.

Cognitive Changes

Despite the aging of the brain, cognitive abilities do not normally decline until late adulthood. Indeed, except in cases where limitations are imposed by brain disorders such as Alzheimer's disease, the adult nervous system appears considerably more open to positive change throughout the life span than was previously thought (Nelson & Bloom, 1997). Alert older people can think just as quickly as alert younger people. In fact, older adults may function as well as or better than younger adults in situations that tap their long-term memories and learning skills. The experienced teacher may deal with an unruly child more skillfully than the novice, and the senior lawyer may understand the implications of a new law more quickly than the recent graduate. Their years of accumulating and organizing information can make older adults practiced, skillful, and wise.

Early and Middle Adulthood   In early and middle adulthood, until age sixty at least, important cognitive abilities improve. During this period, adults do better on tests of vocabulary, comprehension, and general knowledge, especially if they use these abilities in their daily lives (Eichorn et al., 1981). Young and middle-aged adults learn new information and new skills; they remember old information and hone old skills.

The nature of thought may also change during adulthood. Adult thought is often more complex, adaptive, and relativistic than adolescent thought (Labouvie-Vief, 1992). Adults can understand, as adolescents cannot, the contradictions inherent in thinking. They see both the possibilities and the problems in every course of action (Riegel, 1975)—in deciding whether to start a new business or to move to a new house, for example. Middle-aged adults are more adept than adolescents or young adults at making rational decisions and at relating logic and abstractions to actions, emotions, social issues, and personal relationships (Tversky & Kahneman, 1981). As they appreciate these relationships, their thought becomes more global, more concerned with broad moral and practical concerns (Labouvie-Vief, 1982).

Late Adulthood   It is not until late adulthood—after sixty-five or so—that some intellectual abilities decline in some people. Generally, these are abilities that require rapid and flexible manipulation of ideas and symbols, active thinking and reasoning, and sheer mental effort (Baltes, 1993, 1994; see Figure 12.8). Older adults do just as well as younger ones at tasks they know well, like naming familiar objects. It is when they are asked to perform an unfamiliar task or to solve a complex problem they have not seen before that older adults are generally slower and less effective than younger ones (Craik & Rabinowitz, 1984). When facing complex problems, older people apparently suffer from having too much information to sift through. They have trouble considering, choosing, and executing solutions (Arenberg, 1982). As people age, they grow less efficient at organizing the elements of a problem and at holding and manipulating more than one idea at a time. They have difficulty doing tasks that require them to divide their attention between two activities (McDowd, Vercruyssen, & Birren, 1991) and are slower at shifting their attention back and forth between two activities (Korteling, 1991). If older adults have enough time, though, and can separate the two activities, they can perform just as well as younger adults (Hawkins, Kramer, & Capaldi, 1993).

Older people also have the ability to think deeply and wisely about life. Psychologists define *wisdom* as expert knowledge in the fundamental pragmatics of life, permitting exceptional insight and judgment involving complex and uncertain matters of the human condition (Smith & Baltes, 1990). Old age does not in itself guarantee wisdom, but if it is combined with experiences conducive to the accumulation and refinement of wisdom-related knowledge, growing old can be associated with high levels of wisdom (Baltes et al., 1995). In a recent study, researchers found that one component of wisdom—the ability to infer what other people are thinking—remained

FIGURE 12.8

Mental Abilities over the Life Span

Mental abilities collectively known as "fluid" intelligence—speed and accuracy of information processing, for example—begin to decline quite early in adult life. Changes in these biologically based aspects of thinking are usually not marked until late adulthood, however. "Crystallized" abilities learned over a lifetime—such as reading, writing, comprehension of language, and professional skills—do not diminish even in old age (see Chapter 10, page 346).

Source: Adapted from Baltes, 1994.

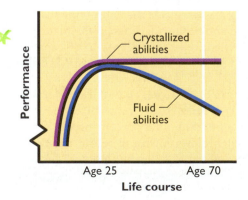

Staying Active

A lifetime of fitness through skiing or other forms of aerobic exercise has been associated with better maintenance of skills on a variety of mental tasks, including reaction time, reasoning, and divided attention (Offenbach, Chodzko-Zajko & Ringel, 1990; Clarkson-Smith & Hartley, 1989; Dustman et al., 1990; Hawkins, Kramer & Capaldi, 1993).

intact and sometimes even improved over the later adult years. When asked to explain why a burglary suspect in a story surrendered to the police, seventy-year-olds gave better answers than younger adults. Their answers included inferences about the suspect's motives, such as "the burglar surrendered because he thought the policeman knew he had robbed the shop" (Happe, Winner, & Brownell, 1998).

Usually the loss of intellectual abilities in older adults is slow and need not cause severe problems. A study of Swedish adults (Nilsson, 1996) found that memory problems among older adults are largely confined to *episodic memory* (e.g., what they ate for lunch yesterday, or what was on a list of words they read half an hour ago) rather than to *semantic memory* (general knowledge, such as the name of the capital of France). People who are healthy and psychologically flexible, who have a high level of education, income, and occupation, and who live in an intellectually stimulating environment with mentally able spouses or companions have a significantly lower risk of cognitive decline (Azar, 1996c). Continued mental exercise—such as doing puzzles, painting, and talking to intelligent friends—can help older adults think and remember effectively and creatively.

Perhaps the greatest threat to cognitive abilities in late adulthood is *Alzheimer's disease*, which strikes 3 percent of the world's population by age seventy-five. As the disease runs its course, its victims become emotionally flat, then disoriented, then incontinent, then mentally vacant, and finally die prematurely. The average duration of the disease, from onset to death, is seven years. But the rate of deterioration depends on a number of factors, such as sex (Molsa, Marttila, & Rinne, 1995), education (Stern et al., 1995), and age of onset (Jagger, Clarke, & Stone, 1995). Women, well-educated people, and those who develop Alzheimer's at an older age deteriorate more slowly.

Social Changes

In adulthood, people develop new relationships, assume new positions, and take on new roles. These changes do not come in neat, predictable stages but, instead, follow various paths, depending on the individual's experiences (Lieberman, 1996). Transitions—such as initiating a divorce, getting fired from a job, going back to school, remarrying, losing a spouse to death, being hospitalized, or getting arrested—are turning points that can redirect a person's life path and lead to changes in personality (Caspi, 1998). Sometimes these events create radical turnarounds. More often they involve gradual and incremental change.

Early Adulthood Men and women in Western cultures typically enter the adult world in their twenties. They decide on an occupation, or at least take a job, and often become preoccupied with their careers. They also become more concerned with issues of love (Whitbourne et al., 1992). They reach the sixth of Erikson's stages of psychosocial development noted in Table 12.2 on page 430: "intimacy versus isolation." This intimacy may include sexual intimacy, friendship, or mutual intellectual stimulation. It may lead to marriage or some other form of committed relationship. Today, intimacy occurs at earlier ages than it did when Erikson formulated his theory three decades ago. Specifically, intimate and sexual peer relationships now become important in late adolescence as well as in early adulthood. Adolescents whose parents are accepting and supportive of their children's growing autonomy tend to develop more mature and comfortable relationships (Dresner & Grolnick, 1996).

Intimate commitments are also related to the young adult's earlier attachment relationships. Although the kind of attachment infants form may not necessarily color all their subsequent intimate relationships, researchers have discovered that young adults' views of intimate relationships parallel the patterns of infant attachment that we described earlier (Horowitz, Rosenberg, & Bartholomew, 1993). For example, individuals whose attachment was avoidant were found to engage in more "one-night stands" and less cuddling than did those whose attachment was secure (Tidwell, Reis, & Shaver, 1996). (This phenomenon is discussed in more detail in Chapter 14, on personality.)

For the many young adults who become parents, the experience represents entry into a major new developmental phase that is accompanied by personal, social, and, often, occupational changes. For many couples, marital satisfaction declines (Belsky & Kelly, 1994). Young mothers may experience particular dissatisfaction, especially if they resent the constraints an infant brings, if they see their career as important, if the infant is temperamentally difficult, and if their partner is not supportive. Researchers have found that when the father does not do his share of caring for the baby, both mothers and fathers are dissatisfied (e.g., Levy-Shiff, 1994).

The ability of young parents to provide adequate care for their babies is related to their own attachment histories. New mothers whose attachment to their own mother was secure are more responsive to their infants, and the infants, in turn, are more likely to develop secure attachments to them (van IJzendoorn, 1995). It appears that inter-generational continuities in emotional well-being and social relations are as strong as continuities across an individual's lifetime.

Another major change that many young adults experience is the end of an intimate relationship. About half of all marriages in the United States end in divorce. Divorce may free people from a bad relationship, but it is also likely to make them feel anxious, guilty, incompetent, depressed, and lonely. It is correlated with health problems and, ultimately, to earlier mortality (Friedman et al., 1995b).

Middle Adulthood   By their forties, many people become concerned with producing something that will outlast them—usually through parenthood or job achievements. Erikson called this concern the crisis of **generativity,** because people are focused on producing or generating something. If people do not resolve this crisis, he suggested, they stagnate.

For many women today the greatest tension occurs between two types of generativity—parenthood versus achievement. The demands of children and career often pull in opposite directions. Devotion to a job may lead to guilt about depriving children of attention; too much emphasis on home life may impair productivity at work. This stressful balancing act can lead to anxiety, frustration, and conflicts at home and on the job. Moreover, women are often frustrated by gender-related limitations on their career paths. For example, one study of financial services companies found that although female executives received the same pay as men at the same level, they managed fewer people, received fewer benefits, and were less likely to receive desirable assignments (Lyness & Thompson, 1997). In addition, they felt they could not go

Building Monuments

Middle adulthood tends to be a time during which people become deeply committed to building personal monuments, either by raising children or through achievements outside the home. This parent seems to have accomplished both goals.

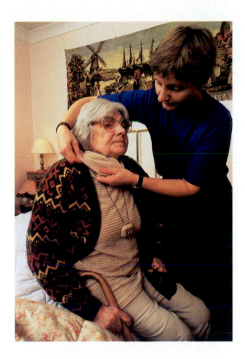

The "Sandwich" Generation

People in the midlife transition may feel caught between the generations, pressured by the expenses of college on one side and retired parents on the other.

much further in their careers. Among nonexecutives, the average female worker earns only 71 percent of what her male counterpart does (Hanges, 1997).

At around age forty, women as well as men go through a midlife transition, during which they may reappraise and modify their lives and relationships. Many feel invigorated and liberated; some may feel upset and have a "midlife crisis" (Beck, 1992; Levinson et al., 1978). The contrast between youth and middle age may be especially upsetting for men who matured early in adolescence and were sociable and athletic rather than intellectual (Block, 1971). Women who chose a career over a family now hear the biological clock ticking out their last childbearing years. Women who have had children, however, become more independent and confident, oriented toward achievement and events outside the family (Helson & Moane, 1987). For both men and women, the emerging sexuality of teenage children, the emptiness of the nest as children leave home, or the declining health of a parent may precipitate a crisis. Preliminary results from a study of over 7,000 adults suggest that the degree of happiness and healthiness people experience during middle adulthood depends on how much control they feel they have over their work, finances, marriage, children, and sex life, as well as how many years of education they completed and what kind of job they have (Azar, 1996a).

Following the midlife transition, the middle years of adulthood are often a time of satisfaction and happiness (MacArthur Foundation, 1999). In a study of professionals in their fifties, both women and men reported that they could not quite believe they were no longer young (Karp, 1991). Most described themselves as healthy but acknowledged that their bodies were slowing down.

Late Adulthood From sixty-five to seventy-five, most people think of themselves as middle-aged, not old (Neugarten, 1977). They are active and influential politically and socially; they often are physically vigorous. Ratings of life satisfaction and self-esteem are on average as high in old age as during any other period of adulthood (Myers & Diener, 1995).

This is the time when men and women usually retire from their jobs, but research shows that many people underestimate older people's ability and willingness to work (Clay, 1996). Such misperceptions were once codified in laws that forced workers to retire at age sixty-five regardless of their abilities. Thanks to changes in those laws,

The Golden Years

Even after the age of seventy-five, many seniors continue living active and satisfying lives.

most workers can now continue working as long as they wish. Being *forced* to retire can result in psychological and physical problems. In one twenty-seven-year study of cardiovascular disease, men who retired involuntarily were found to be more depressed, more unhealthy, and more poorly adjusted than those who retired voluntarily (Swan, 1996). Such problems may also occur when husbands retire before their wives (Rubin, 1998). Men tend to view retirement as a time to wind down; women, as a time to try new things, to reinvent themselves (Helgesen, 1998). In a longitudinal study that followed people from childhood through adulthood, researchers found that when previously employed women reached their seventies, they were more active and more concerned about maintaining their independence and continuing their achievements than women who had been homemakers. They were also happier, and less depressed and anxious (Holahan, 1994).

More people than ever are reaching old age. Indeed, the fastest-growing segment of the population is made up of people past the age of seventy-five. This group is twenty-five times larger today than it was a hundred years ago; among its members, women greatly outnumber men. Old age is not necessarily a time of loneliness and desolation, but it is a time when people generally become more inward looking, cautious, and conforming (Reedy, 1983). It is a time when people develop coping strategies that increasingly take into account the limits of their control—accepting chronic health problems and other things they cannot change (Brandtstadter & Renner, 1990).

In old age, people interact with others less frequently, but they enjoy their interactions more (Carstensen, 1997). They find relationships more satisfying, supportive, and fulfilling than they did earlier in life. As they sense that time is running out, they value positive interactions and become selective about their social partners. During the last twenty years of their lives, people gradually restrict their social network to loved ones. As long as there are at least three close friends or relatives in their network, they tend to be content.

The many changes associated with adolescence and adulthood are summarized in "In Review: Milestones of Adolescence and Adulthood."

Death and Dying

With the onset of old age, people become aware that death is approaching. They watch as their friends disappear. They feel their health deteriorating, their strength waning, and their intellectual capabilities declining. A few years or a few months before death, people may experience a sharp decline in mental functioning known as **terminal drop** (Berkowitz, 1965).

The awareness of impending death brings about the last psychological crisis, according to Erikson's theory, in which people evaluate their lives and accomplishments and affirm them as meaningful (leading to a feeling of *integrity*) or meaningless (leading to a feeling of *despair*). People at this stage tend to become more philosophical and reflective. They attempt to put their lives into perspective. They reminisce, resolve past conflicts, and integrate past events. They may also become more interested in the religious and spiritual side of life. This "life review" may trigger anxiety, regret, guilt, and despair, or it may allow people to face their own death and the deaths of friends and relatives with a feeling of peace and acceptance (Lieberman & Tobin, 1983).

Even the actual confrontation with death does not have to bring despair and depression. People generally want to be told if they are dying (Hinton, 1967). When death finally is imminent, old people strive for a death with dignity, love, affection, physical contact, and no pain (Schulz, 1978). As they think about death, they are comforted by their religious faith, their achievements, and the love of their friends and family (Kastenbaum, Kastenbaum, & Morris, 1989).

Longevity

Facing death with dignity and openness helps people complete the life cycle with a sense of life's meaningfulness and unity, but most of us want to live as long as possible.

in review

MILESTONES OF ADOLESCENCE AND ADULTHOOD

Age	Physical Changes	Cognitive Changes	Social Events and Psychological Changes
Early adolescence (11–15 years)	Puberty brings reproductive capacity and marked bodily changes.	Formal operations and principled moral reasoning become possible for the first time (this occurs only for some people).	Social and emotional changes result from growing sexual awareness, mood swings, physical changes, conflicts with parents.
Late adolescence (16–20 years)	Physical growth continues.	Formal operations and principled moral reasoning become more likely.	An identity crisis accompanies graduation from high school.
Early adulthood (20–39 years)	Physical growth continues.	Increases continue in knowledge, problem-solving ability, and moral reasoning.	People choose a job and often a mate; they may become parents.
Middle adulthood (40–65 years)	Size and muscle mass decrease, fat increases, eyesight declines, reproductive capacity in women ends.	Thought becomes more complex, adaptive, and global.	Midlife transition may lead to change; for most, the middle years are satisfying.
Late adulthood (over 65 years)	Size decreases; organs become less efficient.	Reasoning, mathematical ability, comprehension, novel problem solving, and memory may decline.	Retirement requires adjustments; people look inward; awareness of death precipitates life review.

How can we do so? Researchers studying the factors associated with longer life have discovered that *longevity* is greater among women, people without histories of heavy drinking or heart problems, and people who live independently. Longevity is also related to personality characteristics such as conscientiousness as a child (Friedman et al., 1995a) and curiosity as an adult. Indeed, a study of over 2,000 adults revealed that those who, at age seventy, expressed more curiosity were more likely to still be alive five years later (Swan & Carmelli, 1996). This finding suggests that curiosity makes older people more willing to try new approaches to health care, to live independently for as long as possible, and to stay intellectually flexible.

Older adults can be helped to feel better physically and psychologically if they continue to be socially active and useful. For example, old people who are given parties, plants, or pets are happier and more alert than those who receive less attention, and they do not die as soon (Rodin & Langer, 1977). People who restrict their caloric intake, engage in regular physical and mental exercise, and have a sense of control over their lives are also likely to live longer (Hayflick, 1994; Langer et al., 1984). Engaging in a variety of mental activities also appears to extend the life of nursing-home residents (Alexander et al., 1989).

So eat your veggies, stay physically fit, and continue to think actively—not just to live longer later, but to live better now.

LINKAGES

As noted in Chapter 1, all of psychology's many subfields are related to one another. Our discussion of infantile amnesia illustrates just one way in which the topic of this chapter, human development, is linked to the subfield of memory (Chapter 7). The Linkages diagram shows ties to two other subfields as well, and there are many more ties throughout the book. Looking for linkages among subfields will help you see how they all fit together and better appreciate the big picture that is psychology.

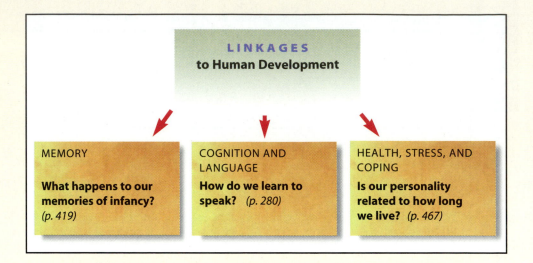

LINKAGES
to Human Development

MEMORY

What happens to our memories of infancy? *(p. 419)*

COGNITION AND LANGUAGE

How do we learn to speak? *(p. 280)*

HEALTH, STRESS, AND COPING

Is our personality related to how long we live? *(p. 467)*

SUMMARY

Developmental psychology is the study of the course and causes of age-related changes in mental abilities, social relationships, emotions, and moral understanding over the life span.

EXPLORING HUMAN DEVELOPMENT

A central question in developmental psychology concerns the relative influences of nature and nurture, a theme that had its origins in the philosophies of Locke and Rousseau. In the twentieth century, Arnold Gesell stressed nature in his theory of development, proposing that development is *maturation*—the natural unfolding of abilities with age. John Watson took the opposite view, claiming that development is learning—shaped by the external environment. In his theory of cognitive development, Jean Piaget described how nature and nurture work together. According to Piaget, knowledge develops as children explore the environment while being guided by internal mental images. Today we accept as given the notion that both nature and nurture affect development and ask how and to what extent each contributes.

BEGINNINGS
Prenatal Development

Development begins with the union of an ovum and a sperm to form a *zygote,* which develops into an *embryo.* The *embryonic stage* is a *critical period* for development, a time when certain organs must develop properly or they never will. Development of organs at this stage is irrevocably affected by harmful *teratogens,* such as drugs and alcohol. After the embryo develops into a fetus, adverse conditions during the *fetal stage* may harm the infant's

size, behavior, intelligence, or health. Babies born to women who drink heavily have a strong chance of suffering from *fetal alcohol syndrome.*

The Newborn

Newborns have limited but effective senses of vision, hearing, taste, and smell. They exhibit many *reflexes:* swift, automatic responses to external stimuli. Motor development proceeds as the nervous system matures, muscles grow, and the infant experiments with and selects the most efficient movement patterns.

INFANCY AND CHILDHOOD: COGNITIVE DEVELOPMENT

Cognitive development refers to the development of thinking, knowing, and remembering.

Changes in the Brain

The development of increasingly complex and efficient neural networks in various regions of the brain provides the "hardware" for the increasingly complex cognitive abilities that arise during infancy and childhood.

The Development of Knowledge: Piaget's Theory

According to Piaget, cognitive development occurs in a fixed sequence of stages, as *schemas* are modified through the complementary processes of *assimilation* (fitting new objects or events into existing schemas) and *accommodation* (changing schemas when new objects will not fit existing ones). During the *sensori-*

motor period, infants progress from using only simple senses and reflexes to forming mental representations of objects and actions. Thus, the child becomes capable of thinking about objects that are not immediately present. The ability to recognize that objects continue to exist even when they are hidden from view is what Piaget called *object permanence.* During the *preoperational period,* children can use symbols, but they do not have the ability to think logically and rationally. Their understanding of the world is intuitive and egocentric. They do not understand the logical operations of reversibility or complementarity. When children develop the ability to think logically about concrete objects, they enter the period of *concrete operations.* At this time they can solve simple problems and have an understanding of *conservation,* recognizing that, for example, the amount of a substance is not altered even when its shape changes.

Modifying Piaget's Theory

Recent research reveals that Piaget underestimated infants' mental abilities. Developmental psychologists now also believe that new levels of cognition are reached not in sharply marked stages of global understanding but more gradually, and in specific areas. Children's reasoning is affected by factors such as task difficulty and degree of familiarity with the objects and language involved.

Information Processing During Childhood

Psychologists who explain cognitive development in terms of information processing have documented age-related improvements in children's attention, their abilities to explore and focus on features of the environment, and their memories.

Culture and Cognitive Development

The specific content of cognitive development, including the development of scripts, depends on the cultural context in which children live.

Promoting Cognitive Development

How fast children develop cognitive abilities depends to a certain extent on how stimulating and supportive their environments are. Children growing up in poverty are likely to have delayed or impaired cognitive abilities.

INFANCY AND CHILDHOOD: SOCIAL AND EMOTIONAL DEVELOPMENT

Infants and their caregivers, from the early months, respond to each other's emotional expressions. When an infant's behavior in an ambiguous situation is affected by the caregiver's emotional expression, social referencing is said to have occurred.

Individual Temperament

Most infants can be classified as having easy, difficult, or slow-to-warm-up *temperaments.* Whether they retain these temperamental styles depends to some extent on their parents' expectations and demands.

The Infant Grows Attached

Over the first six or seven months of life, infants form a deep and abiding emotional *attachment* to their mother or other primary caregiver. This attachment may be secure or anxious insecure, depending largely on whether the caregiver is responsive and loving, or rejecting.

Relationships with Parents and Peers

Parents teach their children the skills and rules needed in their culture using parenting styles described as *authoritarian, permissive,* or *authoritative.* Among European and European-American parents, those with an authoritative style tend to have more competent and cooperative children. Parenting styles depend upon the culture and conditions in which parents find themselves. Over the childhood years, interactions with peers evolve from parallel play to cooperative and competitive encounters. Children come to base their friendships on feelings, not things.

Social Skills

Changes in children's relationships are in part related to their growing social skills and competence. Children become increasingly able to interpret and understand social situations and emotional signals. They begin to express empathy and sympathy, and to *self-regulate* their emotions and behavior. They also learn social rules and roles, including those related to gender.

Gender Roles

Children develop *gender roles* that are based both on biological differences between the sexes and on implicit and explicit socialization by parents, teachers, and peers. Children are also influenced by *gender schemas,* which affect their choices of activities and toys.

Risk and Resilience

Children who lead successful lives despite such adversities as family instability, child abuse, homelessness, poverty, or war are described as having *resilience.* Factors associated with this characteristic include good intellectual functioning and strong relationships with caring adults.

ADOLESCENCE

Adolescents undergo significant changes not only in size, shape, and physical capacity but also, typically, in their social lives, reasoning abilities, and views of themselves.

The Challenges of Change

Puberty brings about physical changes that lead to psychological changes. Early adolescence is a period of shaky self-esteem. It is also a time when conflict with parents as well as closeness and conformity to friends are likely to rise. A particularly difficult challenge for adolescents is the transition from elementary school to junior high or middle school.

Identity and Development of the Self

Late adolescence focuses on finding an answer to the question, Who am I? Events such as graduating from high school and going to college challenge the adolescent's self-concept, precipitating an *identity crisis*. To resolve this crisis the adolescent must develop an integrated self-image as a unique person, an image that often includes *ethnic identity*.

Abstract Thought and Moral Reasoning

For many people, adolescence begins a stage of cognitive development that Piaget called the *formal operational period*. Formal abstract reasoning now becomes more sophisticated, and moral reasoning may begin its progress through *preconventional, conventional,* and *postconventional* stages. Principled moral judgment—shaped by gender and culture—becomes possible for the first time. Such advanced understanding may be reflected in moral action.

ADULTHOOD

Physical, cognitive, and social changes occur throughout adulthood.

Physical Changes

Middle adulthood sees changes that include decreased acuity of the senses, increased risk of heart disease, and declining fertility (*menopause*). Nevertheless, most people do not experience major health problems until late adulthood.

Cognitive Changes

The cognitive changes that occur in early and middle adulthood are generally positive, including improvements in reasoning and problem-solving ability. In late adulthood, some intellectual abilities decline—especially those involved in tasks that are unfamiliar, complex, or difficult. Other abilities, such as recalling facts or making wise decisions, tend not to decline.

Social Changes

In their twenties, young adults make occupational choices and form intimate commitments. In middle adulthood they become concerned with *generativity*, with producing something that will outlast them. Sometime around age forty, adults experience a *midlife transition*, which may or may not be a crisis. The forties and fifties are often a time of satisfaction. In their sixties, people contend with retirement. They generally become more inward looking, cautious, and conforming. Adults' progress through these ages is influenced by the unique personal events that befall them.

Death and Dying

In their seventies and eighties, people confront their own mortality. They may become more philosophical and reflective as they review their lives. They interact with fewer people but enjoy their interactions more. A few years or months before death, they may experience a sharp decline in mental functioning known as *terminal drop*. Older adults feel better and live longer if they receive attention from other people, maintain an open attitude toward new experiences, and keep their minds active. They strive for a death with dignity, love, and no pain.

Longevity

Death is inevitable, but certain factors—including healthy diets, exercise, personality qualities such as conscientiousness and curiosity, and a sense of control over one's life—are associated with living longer and happier lives.

KEY TERMS

accommodation (412)
assimilation (411)
attachment (425)
authoritarian parents (431)
authoritative parents (431)
concrete operations (417)
conservation (417)
conventional moral
  reasoning (439)
critical period (407)
developmental psychology
  (404)

embryo (407)
ethnic identity (437)
fetal alcohol syndrome
  (408)
fetus (407)
formal operational period
  (438)
gender roles (433)
gender schemas (434)
generativity (444)
identity crisis (438)
maturation (405)

menopause (441)
midlife transition (413)
object permanence (413)
permissive parents (431)
postconventional moral
  reasoning (439)
preconventional moral
  reasoning (439)
preoperational period (416)
puberty (436)
reflexes (410)
resilience (435)

schemas (411)
self-regulation (433)
sensorimotor period (413)
temperament (424)
teratogens (407)
terminal drop (446)
zygote (407)

13

Health, Stress, and Coping

Two decades ago, acquired immune deficiency syndrome (AIDS) was a rare and puzzling medical condition. Today, it threatens everyone and is one of the major causes of death in the United States (Centers for Disease Control, 1996). In some African countries, the HIV infection rate among adults is as high as 20 percent. As medical researchers race against time to find a cure for AIDS and a vaccine against HIV, the virus that causes it, others work to find ways to prolong the lives of people infected with HIV or suffering with AIDS.

One important factor that may affect how long AIDS patients live is their expectations about survival. Geoffrey Reed and his associates asked seventy-four male AIDS patients about the extent to which they had accepted their situation and prepared themselves for the worst (Reed et al., 1994). Acknowledging the reality of a terminal illness has been considered by some to be a psychologically healthy adaptation (e.g., Kübler-Ross, 1975); however, Reed and his associates found that the men who had accepted their situation and prepared themselves for death died an average of nine months earlier than those who had neither accepted nor resigned themselves to their situation. This statistically significant difference is all the more impressive because it cannot be accounted for by differences in the patients' general health status, immune system functioning, psychological distress, or other factors that might have affected the time of death. Here is evidence that, compared with those who are "fighters," terminally ill patients who resign themselves to debilitation and death might actually hasten both.

Research like this has made psychologists and the medical community more aware than ever of psychological factors that can affect health and illness. It also reflects the growth of **health psychology,** "a field within psychology devoted to understanding psychological influences on how people stay healthy, why they become ill, and how they respond when they do get ill" (Taylor, 1998a, p. 4). Health psychologists use knowledge from many subfields of psychology to enhance understanding of the psychological and behavioral processes associated with health and illness (Taylor, 1998a). In this chapter we describe some of the ways in which health is related to psychological, social, and behavioral factors as well as what health psychologists are doing to understand these relationships and to apply their research to prevent illness and promote better health. We begin by examining the nature of stressors and people's physical, psychological, and behavioral responses to stress. Then we consider factors that might mediate the impact of stressful life events on a person. Next, we examine the psychological factors responsible for specific physical disorders and some behaviors that endanger people's health. We conclude with a discussion of what health psychologists can tell us about coping with stress and promoting healthy behaviors.

HEALTH PSYCHOLOGY

Although health psychology is relatively new, its underlying themes are ancient. For thousands of years, in many cultures around the world, people have believed that their mental state, their behavior, and their health are linked. Today, there is scientific evidence to support this belief (Taylor, 1998a). We know, for example, that through their impact on psychological and physical processes, the stresses of life can influence physical health. Researchers have also associated anger, hostility, pessimism, depression, and hopelessness with the appearance of physical illnesses. Similarly, poor health has been linked to lack of exercise, inadequate diet, smoking, alcohol and drug abuse, and other behavioral factors.

Health psychology has become increasingly prominent in North America in part because of changing patterns of illness. Until the middle of the twentieth century, the major causes of illness and death in the United States and Canada were acute infectious diseases such as influenza, tuberculosis, and pneumonia. With these afflictions now less threatening, chronic illnesses—such as coronary heart disease, cancer, and diabetes—have joined accidents and injuries as the leading causes of disability and death. Further, psychological, lifestyle, and environmental factors play substantial roles in determining whether a person will fall victim to these modern-day killers (Taylor,

Running for Your Life

Health psychologists have developed programs to help people increase exercise, stop smoking, eat healthier diets, and make other lifestyle changes that lower their risk of illness and death.

1998a). For example, lifestyle choices, such as whether a person smokes, affect the risk for the five leading causes of death in the United States (see Table 13.1). Further, the psychological and behavioral factors that contribute to these illnesses can be altered by psychological interventions, including programs that promote nonsmoking and low-fat diets. Indeed, as many as 50 percent of deaths in the United States are due to potentially preventable lifestyle behaviors (National Cancer Institute, 1994). One major activity of health psychologists is to help people understand the role they can play in controlling their own health and longevity. However, health psychologists have also been instrumental in studying, and helping people understand, the role played by stress in physical health and illness.

STRESS AND STRESSORS

You have probably heard that death and taxes are the only two things you can be sure of in life. If there is a third, it must surely be stress. Stress is basic to life—no matter how wealthy, powerful, attractive, or happy you might be. It comes in many forms—a difficult exam, an automobile accident, waiting in a long line, a day on which everything goes wrong. Mild stress can be stimulating, motivating, and sometimes desirable. But as it becomes more severe, stress can bring on physical, psychological, and behavioral problems.

Stress is the negative emotional and physiological process that occurs as individuals try to adjust to or deal with stressors, which are environmental circumstances that disrupt, or threaten to disrupt, individuals' daily functioning and cause people to make adjustments (Taylor, 1998a). Thus stress involves a transaction between people and their environment. Figure 13.1 on page 454 lists the main types of stressors, and illustrates that, when confronted by stressors, people respond physically (e.g., with nervousness, nausea, and fatigue) as well as psychologically.

As also shown in Figure 13.1, the transaction between people and their environment can be influenced by *stress mediators,* which include such variables as the extent to which people can predict and control their stressors, how they interpret the threat involved, the social support they get, and their stress-coping skills. (We discuss these mediators in greater detail later.) Thus, stress is not a specific event but a *process* in which the nature and intensity of stress responses depend to a large degree on factors such as the way people think about them and the skills and resources they have to cope with them.

For humans, most stressors have both physical and psychological components. Students, for example, are challenged by psychological demands to do well in their courses, as well as by the physical fatigue that can result from a heavy load of classes, combined perhaps with a job and family responsibilities. Here, we focus on psycho-

TABLE 13.1

Lifestyle Behaviors That Affect the Leading Causes of Death in the United States

This table shows five of the leading causes of death in the United States today, along with behaviors that contribute to their development.

	Alcohol	Smoking	Poor diet	Lack of exercise	Stress
Heart disease	x	x	x	x	x
Cancer	x	x	x		?
Accidents and injury	x	x			
Stroke	x	x	x	?	?
Lung disease		x			

Source: National Cancer Institute, 1994.

STRESSORS

- **Life changes and strains**
- **Catastrophic events**
- **Daily hassles**
- **Chronic stressors**

STRESS MEDIATORS

- **Cognitive appraisal**
- **Predictability**
- **Control**
- **Coping resources and methods**
- **Social support**

STRESS RESPONSES

- **Physical**
- **Psychological**
  - **Emotional**
  - **Cognitive**
  - **Behavioral**

FIGURE 13.1

The Process of Stress

Stressful events, a person's responses to those events, and interactions between people and the situations they face are all important components of stress. Note the two-way relationships in the stress process. For example, as effective coping skills minimize stress responses, the experience of having milder stress responses will solidify those skills. And as coping skills (such as refusing unreasonable demands) improve, some stressors (such as a boss's unreasonable demands) may decrease.

logical stressors, which can stimulate some of the same physiological responses as physical stressors (Cacioppo et al., 1995).

Psychological Stressors

Any event that forces people to accommodate or change can be a psychological stressor. Accordingly, even pleasant events can be stressful (Brown & McGill, 1989). For example, the increased salary and status associated with a promotion may be desirable, but the upgrade usually brings new pressures as well. Similarly, people often feel exhausted after a vacation. Still, it is typically negative events that have the most adverse psychological and physical effects (Kessler, 1997). These circumstances include catastrophic events, life changes and strains, chronic stressors, and daily hassles (Sarason, Johnson, & Siegel, 1978).

Catastrophic events are sudden, unexpected, potentially life-threatening experiences or traumas, such as physical or sexual assault, military combat, natural disasters, and accidents. *Life changes* and *strains* include divorce, illness in the family, difficulties at work, moving to a new place, and other circumstances that create demands to which people must adjust (Cohen & Williamson, 1991; see Table 13.2). *Chronic stress*—stressors that continue over a long period of time—can involve anything from living near a noisy airport to being unable to earn a decent living because of adverse economic

U.S. Embassy Bombing in Nairobi, Kenya, 1998

Catastrophic events such as explosions, hurricanes, plane crashes, and other traumas can be psychologically devastating for victims, their families, and rescue workers. Health psychologists and other professionals provide on-the-spot counseling as well as follow-up sessions to help these people deal with the consequences of trauma.

TABLE 13.2

The Undergraduate Stress Questionnaire

Here are some items from the Undergraduate Stress Questionnaire, which asks respondents to indicate whether various stressors have occurred during the past week (Crandall, Preisler, & Aussprung, 1992).

Has this stressful event happened to you at any time during the last week? If it has, please check the space next to it. If it has not, please leave it blank.

——— 1. Assignments in all classes due the same day

——— 2. Having roommate conflicts

——— 3. Lack of money

——— 4. Trying to decide on a major

——— 5. Can't understand your professor

——— 6. Stayed up late writing a paper

——— 7. Sat through a boring class

——— 8. Went into a test unprepared

——— 9. Parents getting divorced

——— 10. Incompetence at the registrar's office

conditions or job discrimination (Evans, Hygge, & Bullinger, 1995). *Daily hassles* include traffic jams, deadlines, and other irritations, pressures, and annoyances that might not be significant stressors by themselves but whose cumulative effects can be significant (Levy et al., 1997).

Measuring Stressors

Which stressors are most harmful? In order to study stress more precisely, psychologists have tried to measure the impact of particular stressors. In 1967, Thomas Holmes and Richard Rahe made a pioneering effort to find a standard way of measuring the stress in a person's life. Working on the assumption that all change, positive or negative, is stressful, they asked a large number of people to rate—in terms of life change events, or LCUs—the amount of change and demand for adjustment represented by events such as divorcing, being fired, retiring, losing a loved one, or becoming pregnant. (Getting married, the event against which raters were told to compare all other

A Daily Hassle

Though not as severe as the death of a loved one or other major stressors, daily hassles—such as traffic jams, noisy neighbors, and computer malfunctions—can accumulate to create significant physical and psychological stress responses.

stressors, was rated as slightly more stressful than losing one's job.) On the basis of these ratings, Holmes and Rahe created the *Social Readjustment Rating Scale*, or *SRRS*. People taking the SRRS receive a stress score equal to the sum of the LCUs for the events they have recently experienced.

Numerous studies show that people scoring high on the SRRS and other life-change scales are more likely to suffer physical illness, mental disorder, or other problems than those with lower scores (e.g., Monroe, Thase, & Simons, 1992). Still, questions were raised about whether life changes themselves—either positive or negative—lead to mental health problems. Accordingly, investigators developed scales such as the *Life Experiences Survey*, or *LES* (Sarason, Johnson, & Siegel, 1978), that go beyond the SRRS to measure not just what life events have occurred but also the respondents' cognitive appraisal of how intensely positive or negative the events were. As you might expect, scales like the LES generally show that negative events have a stronger negative impact on health than positive events do (De Benedittis, Lornenzetti, & Pieri, 1990).

The LES also gives respondents the opportunity to write in and rate any stressors they have experienced that are not on the printed list. This personalized approach is particularly valuable for capturing the differing impact and meaning that experiences may have for men compared to women and for individuals from various cultural or subcultural groups. Divorce, for example, may have very different meanings to people of different religious or cultural backgrounds. Similarly, members of certain ethnic groups are likely to experience stressors—such as prejudice and discrimination—that are not felt by other groups (Lopez & Takemoto-Chock, 1992).

Other researchers have developed questionnaires to assess daily hassles and uplifts (Kanner et al., 1981). Some studies suggest that daily hassles may also predict illness, perhaps even better than major negative life events (e.g., Levy et al., 1997). However, research on this point is not yet clear, and much more information will be needed about the mediating influences shown in Figure 13.1 before accurate predictions about individuals can be made (Pillow, Zautra, & Sandler, 1996).

STRESS RESPONSES

Physical and psychological responses to stress often occur together, especially as stressors become more intense. Furthermore, one type of stress response can set off a stress response in another dimension. For example, a physical stress response—such as mild chest pain—may lead to the psychological stress response of worrying about a heart attack. Still, it is useful to analyze separately each category of stress responses.

Physical Responses

Anyone who has experienced a near accident or some other sudden, frightening event knows that the physical responses to stressors include rapid breathing, increased heartbeat, sweating, and, a little later, shakiness. These reactions are part of a general pattern, or *syndrome*, known as the fight-or-flight syndrome. As described in Chapters 3 and 11, this vital syndrome prepares the body to face or to flee an immediate threat. When the danger is past, fight-or-flight responses subside. However, when stressors are long-lasting, these responses are only the beginning of a sequence of reactions.

The General Adaptation Syndrome   Careful observation of animals and humans led Hans Selye (pronounced "SELL-yay") to suggest that the sequence of physical responses to stress occurs in a consistent pattern and is triggered by the effort to adapt to any stressor. Selye called this sequence the **general adaptation syndrome,** or **GAS** (Selye, 1956, 1976). The GAS has three stages, as Figure 13.2 shows.

The first stage is the *alarm reaction*, which involves some version of the fight-or-flight syndrome. In the face of a mild stressor such as a hot room, the reaction may simply involve changes in heart rate, respiration, and perspiration that help the body regulate its temperature. More severe stressors prompt more dramatic alarm reactions, rapidly mobilizing the body's adaptive energy, much as a burglar alarm alerts the police to take action (Selye, 1956).

FIGURE 13.2

The General Adaptation Syndrome

Hans Selye's research showed that physical reactions to stressors include an initial alarm reaction, followed by resistance and then exhaustion. During the alarm reaction, the body's resistance temporarily drops below normal as it absorbs a stressor's initial impact. Resistance increases, then levels off in the resistance stage, but ultimately declines if the exhaustion stage is reached.

Source: Adapted from Selye, 1974.

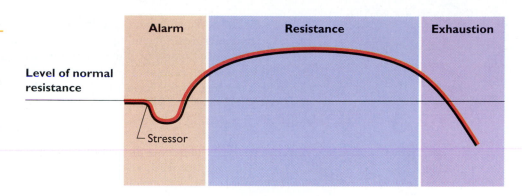

How do alarm reactions occur? They are controlled by the sympathetic branch of the autonomic nervous system (ANS) through organs and glands that make up the *sympatho-adreno-medullary (SAM)* system. As shown on the right side of Figure 13.3, environmental demands (stressors) trigger a process in the brain in which the hypothalamus activates the sympathetic branch of the ANS, which stimulates the medulla (inner part) of the adrenal gland. The adrenal gland, in turn, secretes *catecholamines—*

FIGURE 13.3

Organ Systems Involved in Physical Stress Responses

Stressors produce a variety of physiological consequences that begin in the brain and spread to organs throughout the body. The most important of these are (1) the sympatho-adreno-medullary (SAM) system, represented by blue arrows; and (2) the hypothalamic-pituitary-adrenocortical (HPA) system, represented by purple arrows. The SAM system stimulates the release of catecholamines, which mobilize the body for action; and the HPA system stimulates the release of corticosteroids, which affect higher brain regions.

Source: Taylor, 1998a.

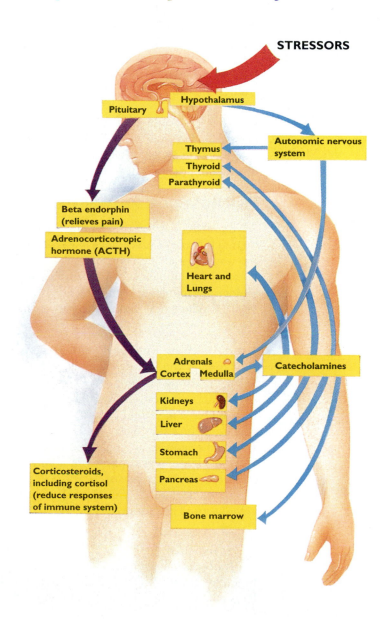

especially adrenaline and noradrenaline—which circulate in the bloodstream, activating various organs including the liver, the kidneys, the heart, and the lungs. The results are increased blood pressure, enhanced muscle tension, increased blood sugar, and other physical changes needed to cope with stressors. Even brief exposure to a stressor can produce major changes in these coordinated regulatory physiological mechanisms (Cacioppo et al., 1995).

If the stressor persists, the *resistance* stage of the GAS begins. Here, obvious signs of the initial alarm reaction diminish as the body settles in to resist the stressor on a long-term basis. The drain on adaptive energy is slower during the resistance stage than it was during the alarm reaction, but the body is working very hard as a second stress response pattern—involving the *hypothalamic-pituitary-adrenocortical (HPA)* system—comes into play. As shown on the left side of Figure 13.3, the hypothalamus activates the HPA system by stimulating the pituitary gland in the brain. The pituitary, in turn, secretes hormones such as adrenocorticotropic hormone (ACTH), which stimulates the adrenal gland's cortex (outer surface) to secrete *corticosteroids* such as cortisol. These hormones help fight inflammation, and also affect higher brain regions.

The overall effect of these stress responses is to generate emergency energy. The more stressors there are and the longer they last, the more resources the body must expend in an effort to resist them. This continued campaign of biochemical resistance is costly. It slowly but surely uses up the body's reserves of adaptive energy. The body then enters the third GAS stage, known as *exhaustion*. In extreme cases, such as prolonged exposure to freezing temperatures, the result is death. More commonly, the exhaustion stage brings signs of physical wear and tear, especially in organ systems that were weak in the first place or heavily involved in the resistance process. For example, if adrenaline and cortisol, which help fight stressors during the resistance stage, remain at high levels for an extended time, they can damage the heart and blood vessels, suppress the functioning of the body's disease-fighting immune system, and promote illnesses ranging from heart disease, high blood pressure, and arthritis to colds and flu (McEwen, 1998). Selye referred to illnesses that are caused or worsened by stressors as **diseases of adaptation.**

Psychological Responses

Selye's model has been very influential, but it has also been criticized for underestimating the role of psychological factors in stress, such as a person's emotional state or the way a person thinks about stressors. These criticisms led to the development of *psychobiological models,* which emphasize the importance of psychological as well as biological variables in regulating and producing stress responses (Lazarus & Folkman, 1984). Psychological responses to stress can involve emotions, thoughts, and behaviors.

Emotional Responses   The physical stress responses we have described are usually accompanied by emotional stress responses. If someone shows a gun and demands your money, you will no doubt experience the GAS alarm reaction, but you will also feel some strong emotion, probably fear, maybe anger. In fact, when people describe stress, they are more likely to say, "I was angry and frustrated!" than "My heart rate increased and my blood pressure went up." In other words, they are likely to mention changes in how they feel.

In most cases, emotional stress responses subside soon after the stressors are gone. However, if stressors continue for a long time or occur in a tight sequence, emotional stress reactions may persist. When people do not have a chance to recover their emotional equilibrium, they commonly report feeling tense, irritable, short-tempered, or anxious more and more of the time.

Cognitive Responses   Reductions in the ability to concentrate, to think clearly, or to remember accurately are typical cognitive stress responses. These problems appear partly because of *ruminative thinking,* the recurring intrusion of thoughts about stressful events (Lyubomirsky & Nolen-Hoeksma, 1995). Ruminative thoughts about problems in a romantic relationship, for example, can seriously interfere with studying for

Children Killed by Terrorists in Northern Ireland

Even severe emotional stress responses usually ease eventually, but people plagued by numerous stressful events in quick succession may experience increasingly intense feelings of fatigue, depression, and helplessness. These reactions can become severe enough to be diagnosed as major depressive disorder, generalized anxiety disorder, or other stress-related mental disorders discussed in Chapter 15.

a test. A related phenomenon is *catastrophizing,* which means dwelling on and overemphasizing the potential consequences of negative events (Sarason et al., 1986). Thus, during examinations, test-anxious college students are likely to say to themselves, "I'm falling behind" or "Everyone else is doing better than I am." As catastrophizing or ruminative thinking impairs cognitive functioning, a person may experience anxiety and other emotional arousal that adds to the total stress response and further hampers performance.

Arousal created by stressors also tends to narrow the scope of attention, making it harder to scan the full range of possible solutions to complex problems (Keinan, Friedland, & Ben-Porath, 1987). In addition, stress-narrowed attention may increase the problem-solving errors described in Chapter 8, on cognition and language. Thus, people under stress are more likely to cling to *mental sets,* which are well learned but not always efficient approaches to problems. Stress can also intensify *functional fixedness,* the tendency to use objects for only one purpose. Victims of hotel fires, for example, sometimes die trapped in their rooms because, in the stress of the moment, it did not occur to them to use the telephone or a piece of furniture to break a window.

Stressors may also impair decision making. People who normally consider all aspects of a situation before making a decision may, under stress, act impulsively and sometimes foolishly (Keinan, Friedland, & Ben-Porath, 1987). High-pressure salespeople try to take advantage of this phenomenon by creating artificially time-limited offers or by telling customers that others are waiting to buy the item they are considering (Cialdini, 1993).

Stress for $500, Alex

The effects of stress on memory and thought are often displayed by participants on "Jeopardy!" and other game shows. Under the intense pressure of time, competition, and the scrutiny of millions of viewers, contestants sometimes miss questions that seem ridiculously easy to those calmly recalling the answers at home.

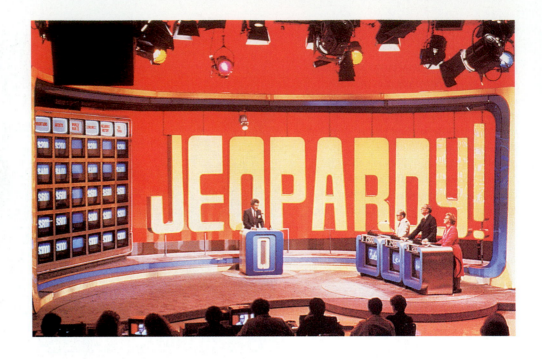

Behavioral Responses   Clues about people's physical and emotional stress responses come from changes in how they look, act, or talk. Strained facial expressions, a shaky voice, tremors or spasms, and jumpiness are common behavioral stress responses. Posture can also convey information about stress, a fact observed by skilled interviewers.

Even more obvious behavioral stress responses appear as people attempt to escape or avoid stressors. Some people quit their jobs, drop out of school, turn to alcohol, or even attempt suicide. Unfortunately, as discussed in the chapter on learning, escape and avoidance tactics deprive people of the opportunity to learn more adaptive ways of coping with stressful environments, including college (Cooper et al., 1992). Aggression is another common behavioral response to stressors. All too often, this response is directed at members of one's own family (Polusny & Follette, 1995). In the months after Hurricane Andrew hit south Florida in 1992, for example, the rate of domestic-violence reports in the devastated area doubled.

LINKAGES

When do stress responses become mental disorders? (a link to Psychological Disorders)

LINKAGES

Stress and Psychological Disorders

Physical, psychological, and behavioral stress responses sometimes appear together in patterns known as burnout and posttraumatic stress disorder. **Burnout** (also called gradual mental stress) is an increasingly intense pattern of physical and psychological dysfunction in response to a continuous flow of stressors or to chronic stress (Maslach & Goldberg, 1998; McKnight & Glass, 1995). As burnout approaches, previously reliable workers or once-attentive spouses may become indifferent, disengaged, impulsive, or accident prone. They may miss work frequently, oversleep, perform their jobs poorly, abuse alcohol or other drugs, and become irritable, suspicious, withdrawn, depressed, and unwilling to talk about stress or anything else (Taylor, 1998a). Burnout is particularly common among individuals who do "people-work," such as teachers and nurses (Schultz & Schultz, 1998). It accounts for some 11 percent of occupational disease claims by U.S. workers (Sauter, Murphy, & Hurrell, 1990).

A different pattern of severe stress reactions is illustrated by the case of Mary, a thirty-three-year-old nurse who was raped at knife-point by an intruder in her apartment (Spitzer et al., 1983). In the weeks following the attack, she became afraid of

Life Hanging in the Balance

Symptoms of burnout and posttraumatic stress disorder often plague fire-fighters, police, emergency medical personnel, air traffic controllers, and others continuously exposed to time pressure, trauma, and other stressors (DeAngelis, 1995; Weiss, et al., 1995). When such symptoms affect those so vital to the safety of the community, burnout and PTSD become a serious problem for us all.

being alone and was preoccupied with the attack and with the fear that it might happen again. She had additional locks installed on her doors and windows but experienced difficulty concentrating and could not immediately return to work. She was repelled by the thought of sex.

Mary suffered from **posttraumatic stress disorder (PTSD),** a pattern of adverse reactions following a traumatic event. Among the characteristic reactions are anxiety, irritability, jumpiness, inability to concentrate or work productively, sexual dysfunction, and difficulty in getting along with others. People suffering from posttraumatic stress disorder may also experience sleep disturbances, guilt, and intense startle responses to noise or other sudden stimuli. Posttraumatic stress disorder is most commonly associated with events such as war, assault, or rape, but researchers now believe that some PTSD symptoms can be triggered by any major stressor (Ironson et al., 1997). The most common feature of posttraumatic stress disorder is re-experiencing the trauma through nightmares or vivid memories. In rare cases, *flashbacks* occur in which the person behaves for minutes, hours, or days as if the trauma were occurring again.

Posttraumatic stress disorder may appear immediately following a trauma, or it may not occur until weeks, months, or even years later. The majority of those affected require professional help, although some seem to recover without it. For most, improvement takes time; for nearly all, the support of family and friends is vital to recovery (Shalev, Bonne, & Eth, 1996).

Stress has also been implicated in the development of a number of other psychological disorders, including depression and schizophrenia (see Chapter 15). The *diathesis-stress model* suggests that certain people are predisposed to these disorders, but that whether or not individuals actual display them depends on the frequency, nature, and intensity of the stressors they encounter.

STRESS MEDIATORS: INTERACTIONS BETWEEN PEOPLE AND STRESSORS

As noted earlier, important aspects of the stress process include the way that people evaluate stressors, and the resources they are willing or able to marshal when stressors occur (see Figure 13.1 on page 454). These stress mediators can substantially affect the impact that stressors have on people's lives.

Consider, for example, that during the 1991 Persian Gulf War, a number of United Nations soldiers were killed by "friendly fire" when pilots flying in close support of ground forces mistakenly identified them as the enemy. Many such tragic errors in decision making are probably a result of the stress of combat (Adler, 1993). But why does stress disrupt the performance of some individuals and not others? More generally, why is it that one individual survives, even thrives, under the same circumstances that lead another to break down, give up, and burn out? Stress mediators provide a partial answer to this question.

How Stressors Are Appraised

As discussed in Chapter 5, our perceptions of the world depend on which stimuli we attend to and how we interpret, or appraise, them. Any potential stressor, be it a hot elevator or a deskful of work, usually has more negative impact on those who perceive it as a threat than on those who see it as a challenge (Goode et al., 1998).

Evidence for the effects of cognition on stress responses comes from both laboratory experiments and surveys. Figure 13.4 shows the results of a classic experiment that demonstrated these effects. In this case, the intensity of physiological arousal during a film depended on how the viewers were instructed to think about the film (Lazarus et al., 1965). Similarly, noise-related distress among people living near airports appears to have more to do with how they evaluate the airport (e.g., as a nuisance or as a source of employment) than with how much noise they must endure (Tracor, Inc., 1971).

The influence of cognitive factors weakens somewhat as stressors become more extreme. For example, if chronic-pain patients feel a sense of control over their pain, they tend to show higher levels of physical activity; but this effect does not hold for patients whose pain is severe (Jensen & Karoly, 1991). Still, even the impact of natural disasters or major stressors such as divorce may be less severe for those who think of them as challenges to be overcome. In short, many stressful events are not inherently stressful; their impact depends partly on how people perceive them (Wiedenfeld et al., 1990). An important aspect of this appraisal is the degree to which the stressors are perceived to be predictable or controllable.

Predictability and Control

Knowing that a particular stressor *might* occur but being uncertain whether it will tends to increase the stressor's impact (Boss, 1999). Thus, predictable stressors tend to have less impact than those that are unpredictable (Lazarus & Folkman, 1984), especially when the stressors are intense and occur for relatively brief periods (Abbott, Schoen, & Badia, 1984). Rats given a reliable warning signal every time they are to receive a shock show less severe physiological responses and more normal eating and drinking habits than animals given no warnings (Weinberg & Levine, 1980). Among humans, men and women whose spouses had died suddenly displayed more immediate disbelief, anxiety, and depression than did those who had weeks or months to prepare for the loss (Parkes & Weiss, 1983). This is not to say that predictability provides total protection against stressors. Laboratory research with animals has shown that predictable stressors, even if relatively mild, can be more damaging than unpredictable ones if they occur over long periods of time (Abbott, Schoen, & Badia, 1984).

Perceptions of control can also mediate the effects of stressors. If people believe they can exert some control over them, stressors usually have less impact (e.g., Christensen, Stephens, & Townsend, 1998). For example, a study of several thousand Swedish employees found that those who held jobs in which they had little or no control over their work environment were twice as likely to die of heart disease as were workers with a high degree of control over their work environment (Hancock, 1996). Can this outcome be attributed solely to the fact that people in low-control jobs experience more stress? Probably not, as suggested by another study that found very similar results after controlling for job stressors (Fox, Dwyer, & Ganster, 1993). Here, the stress responses

FIGURE 13.4

Cognition and Stress

Richard Lazarus gave differing instructions to three groups of students who were about to watch a stressful film showing bloody industrial accidents. There were clear differences in physiological arousal during the film, as measured by sweat-gland activity. The students who were instructed to remain detached from the bloody scenes (the intellectualizers) or to think of them as unreal (the denial group) were less upset than those in an unprepared control group. These results illustrate that people's cognitive appraisal of stressors can affect their responses to those stressors.

Source: Adapted from Lazarus et al., 1965.

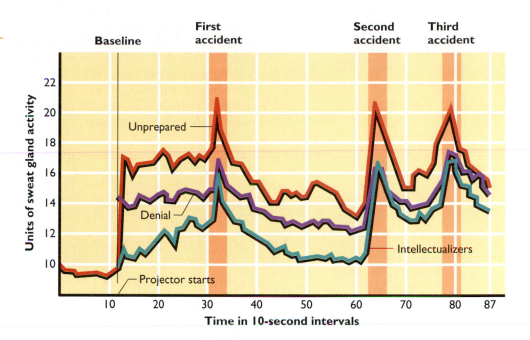

of nurses in high-demand, *low*-control jobs were compared with the stress responses of nurses in high-demand, *high*-control jobs. Even though the jobs were equally demanding, the nurses in low-control jobs exhibited higher blood pressure and more adrenal gland activity than did the nurses in high-control jobs.

In another study, researchers randomly selected a group of patients awaiting surgery and gave them a full explanation of the procedures that they could expect to undergo, along with information that would help them manage post-surgical pain (Egbert et al., 1964). After the surgery was over, patients who had been given this information and who felt they had at least some control over the pain they experienced were not only better adjusted than patients in a control group who received no special preparation, but were discharged from the hospital sooner. So impressive are findings like these that, at many hospitals, it is now standard practice to teach presurgery patients how to manage or control the side effects of surgery (Kiecolt-Glaser et al., 1998).

Simply believing that a stressor is controllable, even if it isn't, can also reduce its impact (Thompson et al., 1993). In one study that examined the cause of panic disorder (discussed in Chapter 15), clients inhaled a mixture of carbon dioxide and oxygen that typically causes such clients to experience intense fear and other symptoms of a panic attack (Sanderson, Rapee, & Barlow, 1989). Half the clients were led to believe (falsely) that they could control the concentration of the mixture. Compared with those who believed they had no control, significantly fewer of the "in control" clients experienced full-blown panic attacks during the session, and their panic symptoms were fewer and less severe.

People who feel they have no control over negative events appear especially prone to physical and psychological problems. They often experience feelings of helplessness and hopelessness that, in turn, may promote depression or other mental disorders (Taylor & Aspinwall, 1996).

Coping Resources and Coping Methods

People usually suffer fewer ill effects from a stressor if they have adequate coping resources and effective coping methods. Coping resources include, for example, the money and time to deal with stressful events. Thus, the physical and psychological responses to your car breaking down are likely to be more negative if you are low on cash and pressed for time than if you have money for repairs and the freedom to take a day off from work.

The impact of stressors can also be reduced by the use of effective coping methods (Sutker et al., 1995). Most of these methods can be categorized as either *problem-focused*, involving efforts to alter or eliminate a source of stress, or *emotion-focused*, involving attempts to regulate the negative emotional consequences of the stressor (Folkman et al., 1986b). These two forms of coping sometimes work together. For example, you might deal with the problem of noise from a nearby airport by forming a community action group to push for tougher noise abatement regulations and, at the same time, calm your anger when noise occurs by mentally focusing on the group's efforts to improve the situation. Susan Folkman and Richard Lazarus (1988) have devised a widely used scale to assess the specific ways that people cope with stressors; Table 13.3 shows some examples from their scale.

Particularly when a stressor is difficult to control, it is sometimes helpful to fully express and think about the emotions one is experiencing in relation to the stressful event (Pennebaker, 1993). For example, although people may not be able to do very much about stressors such as the death of a family member, attempting to see the meaning of the death in relation to their own lives may help them cope more successfully (Bower et al., 1999). The benefits of this cognitive stance can be observed among many devout individuals whose religious beliefs allow them to bring meaning to events that might otherwise be deemed senseless tragedies (McIntosh, Silver, & Wortman, 1993; Paloutzian & Kirkpatrick, 1995).

Humor may also play a role. At least some individuals who use humor to help them cope show better adjustment and lower physiological reactivity to stressful events (Lefcourt et al., 1997).

Social Support

If you have ever benefited from the comforting presence of a good friend during troubled times, you know about another factor that mediates the impact of stressful events—*social support*. Social support consists of resources provided by other persons; the friends and social contacts on whom you can depend for support constitute your **social support network.** The support may take many forms, from eliminating the stressor (as when a friend helps you fix your car) to buffering its impact with companionship, ideas for coping, or reassurance that one is cared about and valued and that everything will be all right (Sarason, Sarason, & Gurung, 1997).

TABLE 13.3

Ways of Coping

Coping is defined as one's cognitive and behavioral efforts to manage specific demands that are appraised as taxing one's resources (Folkman et al., 1986a). This table illustrates two of the most common approaches to coping.

Coping Skills	Example
Problem-focused coping	
Confronting	"I stood my ground and fought for what I wanted."
Seeking social support	"I talked to someone to find out more about the situation."
Planful problem solving	"I made a plan of action and I followed it."
Emotion-focused coping	
Self-controlling	"I tried to keep my feelings to myself."
Distancing	"I didn't let it get to me; I tried not to think about it too much."
Positive reappraisal	"I changed my mind about myself."
Accepting responsibility	"I realized I brought the problem on myself."
Escape/avoidance (wishful thinking)	"I wished that the situation would go away or somehow be over with."

Source: Adapted from Folkman et al., 1986a; Taylor, 1995.

You've Got a Friend

Even when social support cannot eliminate stressors, it can help people, such as these breast cancer survivors, to feel less anxious, more optimistic, more capable of control, and more willing to try new ways of dealing with stressors.

The stress-reducing effects of social support have been documented for a wide range of stressors (Haines, Hurlbert, & Beggs, 1996), including heart disease (Holahan et al., 1997), crowding (Lepore, Evans, & Schneider, 1991), military combat (Bartone et al., 1992), natural disasters (Kaniasty & Norris, 1993), and AIDS (Hays, Turner, & Coates, 1992). Students clearly benefit from social support. Compared with those who are part of a supportive network, students with the least adequate social support suffer more emotional distress and are more vulnerable to upper respiratory infections during times of high academic stress (Lepore, 1995a). One team of researchers concluded that having inadequate social support is as dangerous as smoking cigarettes, in that it nearly doubles a person's risk of dying from disease, suicide, or other causes (House, Landis, & Umberson, 1988). Conversely, having strong social support can reduce the likelihood of illness, improve recovery from existing illness, and promote healthier behaviors (Wickrama, Conger, & Lorenz, 1995).

The Impact of Stress Mediators

Of the nearly 3 percent of U.S. soldiers who developed posttraumatic stress disorder during and after the 1991 Persian Gulf War, most were individuals who had the greatest exposure to combat, the least stress-resistant personalities, and the lowest levels of social support from other soldiers (Bartone et al., 1992).

However, the relationship between social support and the impact of stressors is not a simple one. First, just as the quality of social support may influence people's ability to cope with stress, the reverse may also be true: People's ability to cope may determine the quality of social support they receive (McLeod, Kessler, & Landis, 1992). For example, people who complain endlessly about stressors but never try to do anything about them may discourage social support, whereas those with an optimistic, action-oriented approach may attract reliable support.

Second, social support refers not only to relationships with others but also to the cognitive recognition that others care and will help (Pierce, Sarason, & Sarason, 1991). Some relationships in a social support network may be stormy and fragile, resulting in interpersonal conflicts that can have an adverse effect on health (Malarkey et al., 1994).

Finally, having too much support or the wrong kind of support can be as bad as not having enough. People whose friends and family are overprotective may actually put *less* energy into coping efforts. In one study of physically disabled people, for example, nearly 40 percent were found to have experienced emotional distress in response to the well-intentioned help they received from their spouses. This distress, in turn, was a predictor of depression nearly a year later (Newsom & Schulz, 1998). Similarly, people living in crowded conditions might initially perceive the situation as providing lots of social support, but these conditions may eventually become an added source of stress (Lepore, Evans, & Schneider, 1991). Thus, the efforts of a social support network can sometimes become annoying, disruptive, or interfering, thereby increasing stress and intensifying psychological problems (Broman, 1993).

Stress and Personality

Several of the stress-mediating factors we have discussed reflect individual differences in cognitive styles—how people think about stressors and the world in general. Some cognitive styles, such as those characteristic of "disease-resistant" personalities, help insulate people from the ill effects of stress. One component of the disease-resistant personality seems to be *dispositional optimism,* the belief or expectation that things will work out positively (Scheier & Carver, 1987; Scheier, Carver, & Bridges, 1994). Optimistic students, for example, experience fewer physical symptoms at the end of the academic term (Aspinwall & Taylor, 1992). Optimistic coronary bypass surgery patients have been shown to heal faster than pessimists (Scheier et al., 1989) and to experience a higher quality of life following coronary surgery than those with less opti-

Coping with a Tragedy

In the wake of the brutal murder of University of Wyoming student Matthew Shepard in 1998, people in Laramie and elsewhere employed both emotion-focused coping, such as this candlelight memorial, and problem-focused coping, which included social and political activism aimed at preventing hate crimes against homosexuals and members of other minorities.

mistic outlooks (Fitzgerald et al., 1993). And among HIV-positive men, dispositional optimism has been associated with less psychological distress, fewer worries, and lower perceived risk of acquiring full-blown AIDS (Taylor et al., 1992). These effects appear to be due in part to optimists' tendency to use challenge-oriented, problem-focused coping strategies that attack stressors directly, in contrast to pessimists' tendency to use emotion-focused coping such as denial and avoidance (Taylor, 1998a). Indeed, another study of HIV-positive men showed that active coping strategies are associated with improved functioning of the immune system (Goodkin et al., 1992).

Other cognitive styles, such as those associated with "disease-prone" personalities, may leave people especially vulnerable to the effects of stress (Sutker et al., 1995; Werner, 1995). For example, stress-related health problems tend to be more common among people who persist at mentally evading perceived stressors; who perceive them as long-term, catastrophic threats that they brought on themselves; and who are pessimistic about their ability to overcome negative situations (e.g., Jorgensen et al., 1996; Peterson et al., 1998; Segerstrom et al., in press).

LINKAGES

Is our personality related to how long we live? (a link to Human Development)

FOCUS ON RESEARCH METHODS

Does Personality Affect Health?

Research on stress and personality suggests that dispositional optimism may help people cope with stressors in ways that are beneficial to their physical and psychological health.

■ What was the researchers' question?

Are there other personality characteristics that protect or threaten people's health? This was the research question asked by Howard Friedman and his associates (1995a, 1995b). In particular, they attempted to identify aspects of personality that increase the likelihood that people will develop heart disease or hypertension and die prematurely from these disorders.

■ How did the researchers answer the question?

Friedman suspected that an answer might lie in earlier research—specifically, in the Terman Life Cycle Study of Intelligence, named after Louis Terman, author of the Stanford-Binet Intelligence Test. As described in Chapter 10, the study was originally designed to document the long-term development of 1,528 gifted California children (856 boys and 672 girls)—nicknamed the "Termites" (Terman & Oden, 1947). Friedman and his colleagues found ways of using data from this study to explore the relationship between personality and health (Friedman et al., 1995a, 1995b).

Starting in 1921, and every five to ten years thereafter, Terman's research team had gathered information about the Termites' personality traits, social relationships, stressors, health habits, and many other variables. The data were collected through questionnaires and interviews with the Termites themselves, as well as with their teachers, parents, and other family members. When, by the early 1990s, about half of the Termites had died, Friedman realized that the Terman Life Cycle Study was really a longitudinal study in health psychology. As in most such studies, the independent variable—in this case, personality characteristics—was not actually manipulated (the Termites had obviously not been randomly assigned different personalities by the researchers), but the various personality traits identified in these people could still be related to a dependent variable—namely, how long they lived. Accordingly, Friedman and his colleagues gathered the death certificates of the Termites, noted the dates and causes of death, and then looked for associations between personality and longevity.

■ What did the researchers find?

As it turns out, among the background variables that predicted long life, one of the most important was conscientiousness, or social dependability. Termites who, in childhood, had been seen as truthful, prudent, reliable, hard-working, and free from vanity tended to live longer than those whose parents and teachers had identified them as impulsive and lacking in self-control.

Friedman also used the Terman Life Cycle Study to investigate the relationship between social support and health. He compared the life spans of Termites who came from broken homes or who had been in unstable marriages with those who grew up in stable homes and who had stable marriages. He found that people who had experienced parental divorce during childhood or who themselves had unstable marriages died an average of four years earlier than those whose close social relationships had been less stressful.

■ What do the results mean?

Since Friedman's research was based mainly on correlational analyses, it is difficult to draw conclusions about whether differences in personality traits and social support actually *caused* some Termites to live longer than others. Nevertheless, Friedman and his colleagues searched the Terman data for clues to mechanisms through which personality and other factors might have exerted a causal influence on longevity (Peterson et al., 1998). For example, they evaluated the hypothesis that conscientious, dependable Termites who lived socially stable lives might have followed healthier lifestyles than their impulsive and socially stressed age-mates. Indeed, people in the latter group did tend to eat less healthy diets and were more likely to smoke, drink to excess, or use drugs; but health behaviors alone did not fully account for their shorter average life spans. Another possible explanation is that conscientiousness and stability in social relationships instill a general attitude of caution that goes beyond eating right and avoiding substance abuse. Friedman found some support for this idea in the Terman data—Termites who were impulsive or low on conscientiousness were somewhat more likely to die from accidents or violence than those who were less impulsive. (A similar finding is reported in the Focus on Research Methods section of Chapter 14.)

■ What do we still need to know?

Although the Terman Life Cycle Study cannot provide definitive answers about the relationship between personality and health, it has generated some important clues and a number of intriguing hypotheses to be evaluated in future research with more representative samples of people. Further, Friedman's decision to reanalyze a set of data on psychosocial development as a way of exploring issues in health psychology stands as a fine example of how creative a researcher can be in pursuing answers to complex questions that are difficult or impossible to study via controlled experiments.

Our review of personality and other factors that can alter the impact of stressors should make it obvious that what is stressful for a given individual is not determined simply by predispositions, coping styles, or situations. (See "In Review: Stress Responses and Stress Mediators.") Even more important are interactions between the person and the situation, the mixture of each individual's coping resources and the specific characteristics of the situations encountered (Smith, 1993).

THE PHYSIOLOGY AND PSYCHOLOGY OF HEALTH AND ILLNESS

Several studies mentioned so far have suggested that stress shapes the development of physical illness by affecting cognitive, physiological, and behavioral processes. Those studies are part of a much larger body of research in health psychology that sheds light on the relationship between stress and illness as well as on the issue of how people can behave in ways that preserve their health. In this section, we focus more specifically on the ways in which stress can, directly or indirectly, lead to physical illnesses by affect-

in review

STRESS RESPONSES AND STRESS MEDIATORS

Category	Examples
Responses	
Physical	Fight-or-flight syndrome (increased heart rate, respiration, and muscle tension, sweating, pupillary dilation; SAM and HPA activation (involving release of catecholamines and corticosteroids); eventual breakdown of organ systems involved in prolonged resistance to stressors.
Psychological	*Emotional:* anger, anxiety, depression, and other emotional states. *Cognitive:* inability to concentrate or think logically, ruminative thinking, catastrophizing. *Behavioral:* aggression and escape/avoidance tactics (including suicide attempts).
Mediators	
Appraisal	Thinking of a difficult new job as a challenge will create less discomfort than focusing on the threat of failure.
Predictability	A tornado that strikes without warning may have a more devastating emotional impact than a long-predicted hurricane.
Control	Repairing a disabled spacecraft may be less stressful for the astronauts doing the work than for their loved ones on Earth, who can do nothing to help.
Coping resources and methods	Having no effective way to relax after a hard day may prolong tension and other stress responses.
Social support	Having no one to talk to about a rape or other trauma may amplify the negative impact of the experience.

ing systems of the body involved in the development of disease. One of the most important of these systems is the *immune system*. As noted in Chapter 3, on biological aspects of psychology, components of the immune system act as the body's first line of defense by killing or inactivating foreign or harmful substances in the body such as viruses, bacteria, and cancer cells. Hence this system plays a critical role in fighting infectious diseases, autoimmune diseases (in which the body falsely identifies its own tissue to be that of an invader), and chronic diseases such as AIDS, some cancers, and arthritis.

LINKAGES

Can stress give you the flu? (a link to Biological Aspects of Psychology)

Stress, the Immune System, and Illness

The role of physiological stress responses in the body's ability to fight disease was demonstrated more than a century ago. On March 19, 1878, at a seminar before the Académie de Médecine de Paris, Louis Pasteur showed his distinguished audience three chickens. One healthy bird, the control chicken, had been raised normally. A second bird had been intentionally infected with bacteria but given no other treatment; it was also healthy. The third chicken Pasteur presented was dead. It had been infected with the same bacteria as the second bird, but it had also been physically stressed by being exposed to cold temperatures; as a result, the bacteria killed it (Kelley, 1985).

The First Line of Defense

A patrolling immune system cell sends out an extension known as a *pseudopod* to engulf and destroy a bacterial cell before alerting more defenders. Psychological stressors can alter immune system functions through a number of mechanisms. For example, they can activate neural connections between the sympathetic nervous system and organs of the immune system through response systems that have direct suppressant effects on immune function. These suppressant effects are due largely to the release of cortisol and other corticosteroid hormones from the adrenal cortex (see Figure 13.3 on page 457).

Research conducted since Pasteur's time has greatly expanded knowledge about how stressors affect the body's reaction to disease. **Psychoneuroimmunology** is the field that examines the interaction of psychological and physiological processes that affect the body's ability to defend itself against disease.

The Immune System and Illness   If the immune system is impaired—by stressors, for example—a person is left more vulnerable to colds, mononucleosis, and many other infectious diseases (Cohen & Herbert, 1996). Disabling of the immune system is the process by which the human immunodeficiency virus (HIV) leads to AIDS and leaves the HIV-infected person defenseless against other infections or cancers.

There are many facets to the human immune system. One important component is the action of immune system cells, especially white blood cells, called *leukocytes,* which are formed in the bone marrow and serve as the body's mobile defense units. Leukocytes are called into action when foreign substances are detected. Among the varied types of leukocytes are *B-cells,* which mature in the bone marrow, and *T-cells,* which mature in the thymus. Generally, T-cells kill other cells, and B-cells produce *antibodies,* which are circulating proteins that bind to specific foreign toxins and initiate their inactivation. *Natural killer cells,* another type of leukocyte, destroy a wide variety of foreign organisms, but they have particularly important antiviral and antitumor functions. Yet another type of immune system cell is the *macrophage.* Macrophages engulf foreign cells and digest them in a process called *phagocytosis* ("eating cells"). These scavengers are able to squeeze out of the bloodstream and enter organs where they destroy foreign cells.

The activity of immune system cells can be either strengthened or inhibited by a number of systems, including the endocrine system and the central and autonomic nervous systems. It is through these connections that stress-related psychological and emotional factors can affect the functioning of the immune system (see Figure 3.25 on page 90). The precise mechanisms by which the nervous system affects the immune system are not yet fully understood. There is evidence, however, that the brain can influence the immune system indirectly by altering the secretion of hormones that modify circulating T-cells and B-cells and directly by making connections with the immune organs, such as the thymus, where T-cells and B-cells are stored (Felten et al., 1991).

The Immune System and Stress   Researchers have convincingly shown that people under stress are more likely than their less stressed counterparts to develop infectious diseases and to experience reactivation of latent viruses responsible for oral herpes (cold sores) or genital herpes (Cohen & Herbert, 1996). For example, Sheldon Cohen and his colleagues in the United Kingdom (Cohen et al., 1995) exposed 394 healthy adult volunteers either to one of five respiratory viruses or to a placebo. After being quarantined, the participants were asked about the number and severity of life stresses they had experienced in the previous year. After controlling for factors such as prior history of colds, exposure to other viruses, and health practices, the researchers found that the more stress the participants had experienced, the greater was the likelihood that their exposure to a virus would result in colds and respiratory infections.

These findings are supported by other research showing more directly that a variety of stressors lead to suppression of the immune system. For example, a study of first-year law students found that, as these students participated in class, took exams, and experienced other stressful aspects of law school, they showed a decline in several measures of immune functioning (Segerstrom et al., in press). Similarly, decrements in natural killer cell activity have been observed in both men and women following the death of their spouses (Cohen & Herbert, 1996), and a variety of immune system impairments have been found in people suffering the effects of separation, divorce, lack of social support, and loneliness (Kiecolt-Glaser & Glaser, 1992). Providing care for an elderly relative who is mentally or physically incapacitated is a particularly stressful circumstance that has been reliably shown to diminish immune function (Cacioppo et al., 1998; Shewchuk, Richards, & Elliott, 1998). Many of these stressors have also been associated with depression, which is itself associated with compromised immune system activity (Petitto et al., 1992).

The relationship between stress and the immune system is especially important in persons who are HIV-positive but do not yet have AIDS. Because their immune systems are already seriously compromised, further stress-related decrements could be life threatening. Research indicates that psychological stressors are associated with the progression of HIV-related illnesses (e.g., Kemeny & Dean, 1995). Unfortunately, people with HIV (and AIDS) face a particularly heavy load of immune-suppressing psychological stressors, including bereavement, unemployment, uncertainty about the future, and daily reminders of serious illness. A lack of perceived control and resulting depression can further amplify their stress responses.

Moderators of Immune Function   The effects of social support and other stress-moderating factors can be seen in the activity of the immune system. For example, immune system functioning among students who are able to get emotional assistance from friends during stressful periods appears better than among those with less adequate social support (Cohen & Herbert, 1996).

James Pennebaker (1993) has suggested that social support may help prevent illness by providing the person under stress with an opportunity to express pent-up thoughts and emotions. Keeping important things to oneself, says Pennebaker, is itself a stressor (Pennebaker, Colder, & Sharp, 1990). For example, the spouses of suicide or accidental-death victims who do not or cannot confide their feelings to others are most likely to develop physical illnesses during the year following the death (Pennebaker & O'Heeron, 1984). Disclosing, even anonymously, the stresses and traumas one has experienced is associated with enhanced immune functioning and decreased use of health services among students (Pennebaker, Kiecolt-Glaser, & Glaser, 1988; Petrie et al., 1995). Future research in psychoneuroimmunology promises to reveal vital links in the complex chain of mental and physical events that determine whether people become ill or stay healthy.

Heart Disease and Behavior Patterns

Earlier we discussed the critical role played by the sympatho-adreno-medullary (SAM) system in mobilizing the body during times of threat. This system and its repeated activation in response to stressors are linked in important ways to the development of heart problems, as are certain psychological states and behavior patterns.

For example, a number of stress responses—including anger and hostility—have been related to *coronary heart disease (CHD),* especially in men (Friedman & Rosenman, 1959, 1974). Current research explores a response pattern called *cynical hostility,* which is characterized by suspiciousness, resentment, frequent anger, antagonism, and distrust of others (Helmers & Krantz, 1996; Williams & Barefoot, 1988).

The identification of cynical hostility as a risk factor for coronary heart disease and *myocardial infarction,* or MI (commonly known as heart attack), may be an important breakthrough in understanding an illness that remains the chief cause of death in the United States and most other Western nations. Further, the fact that cynical hostility often develops in childhood (Woodall & Matthews, 1993) raises the possibility that intervention programs might be capable of altering this interpersonal style in time to prevent its negative consequences for health. But is cynical hostility as dangerous as health psychologists suspect?

THINKING CRITICALLY

Does Cynical Hostility Increase the Risk of Heart Disease?

■ **What am I being asked to believe or accept?**

Many researchers contend that individuals displaying cynical hostility are at increased risk for coronary heart disease and heart attack. This risk, they say, is independent of other risk factors such as heredity, diet, smoking, and drinking.

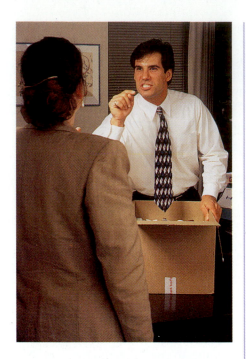

You Can't Fire Me—I Quit!

For a time, researchers believed that anyone who displayed the pattern of aggressiveness, competitiveness, and nonstop work known as "Type A" behavior was at elevated risk for heart disease. More recent research shows, however, that the danger lies not in these characteristics alone, but in cynical hostility, a pattern seen in some, but not all, Type A people.

■ What evidence is available to support the assertion?

The precise mechanism underlying the relationship between hostility and heart disease is not clear, but there are several possibilities (Helmers et al., 1995). The risk of CHD and MI may be elevated in cynically hostile people because these people tend to be unusually reactive to stressors, especially when challenged (Suls & Wan, 1993). Under interpersonally challenging circumstances, for example, people predisposed to hostile behavior display not only overt hostility but also unusually large increases in blood pressure, heart rate, and other aspects of sympatho-adreno-medullary (SAM) reactivity (Suls & Wan, 1993). In addition, it takes hostile individuals longer than normal to get back to their resting levels of SAM functioning. Like a driver who damages a car by simultaneously stepping on the accelerator and applying the brakes, these "hot reactors" may create excessive wear and tear on the arteries and the heart, as their increased heart rate pushes blood through constricted vessels. Increased sympathetic nervous system activation not only puts stress on the coronary arteries but also leads to surges of stress-related hormones from the adrenal glands: the catecholamines (adrenaline and noradrenaline). High levels of these hormones, in turn, are associated with increases in fatty substances, such as blood cholesterol, that are deposited in arteries and contribute to atherosclerosis (hardening of the arteries) and CHD. Plasma lipids, such as cholesterol and triglycerides, do appear to be elevated in hostile people (Dujovne & Houston, 1991).

■ Are there alternative ways of interpreting the evidence?

The studies purporting to show that hostility causes CHD are not true experiments. Researchers cannot manipulate the independent variable, hostility, by creating it in some people but not others; nor can they create experimental conditions in which individuals who differ *only* in terms of hostility are compared on heart disease, the dependent variable. Thus, other explanations of the hostility–CHD/MI relationship must be considered.

Some researchers suggest that higher CHD/MI rates among those high in hostility are due not to the impact of hostility on autonomic reactivity and hormone surges but, rather, to a third variable that accounts for the other two. Specifically, it may be that genetically determined autonomic reactivity increases the likelihood of *both* hostility and heart disease (Krantz et al., 1988). Supporting this alternative interpretation is evidence that people with an inherited predisposition toward strong physiological stress responses to the hassles, challenges, and frustrations of everyday life not only have a higher risk for CHD susceptibility but also tend to experience greater hostility (Cacioppo et al., in press).

Even if hostility is not a direct cause of coronary heart disease or myocardial infarction, it might indirectly increase the incidence of these diseases through its impact on social support. We know, for example, that hostile people may derive fewer benefits from their social support network (Lepore, 1995b). Failure to make use of such support—as well as possible alienation of potential supporters in the process—may intensify the impact of stressful events on hostile people, resulting in increased anger, antagonism, and, ultimately, additional stress on the cardiovascular system (e.g., Hall & Davidson, 1996).

■ What additional evidence would help to evaluate the alternatives?

One way of testing whether hostile people's higher rates of CHD and MI are related to their hostility or to a more general tendency toward intense physiological arousal is to examine how hostile individuals react to stress when they are not angry. Researchers have done exactly this by observing the physiological reactions of hostile people as they undergo surgery. What they have found is that, during surgical stress under general anesthesia, such people show unusually strong autonomic reactivity (Krantz & Durel, 1983). Since these individuals are not conscious, it is more likely that oversensitivity to stressors, not hostile thinking, is causing this exaggerated response.

Obviously, to more fully illuminate hostility's role in the development of CHD and MI, future research will have to take into account a number of important psychobiological possibilities: (1) Some individuals may be biologically predisposed to react to stress and challenge with hostility and increased cardiovascular activity, which in turn may contribute to heart disease; (2) hostile people may amplify and perpetuate their stress through aggressive thoughts and actions, which in turn may provoke others and elicit additional stressors; and (3) those high in hostility may harm their health to a greater extent than less hostile people by smoking, drinking, overeating, failing to exercise, and engaging in other high-risk behaviors (Houston & Vavac, 1991).

■ What conclusions are most reasonable?

Although there is some inconsistency among the relevant studies, most researchers continue to find that hostile individuals have a higher risk of heart disease and heart attacks than nonhostile individuals. However, the causal relationship is probably more complex than researchers first thought; it appears that many interacting factors affect the relationship between hostility and CHD. We must also keep in mind that the relationship between hostility and CHD/MI may not be universal. For example, some studies suggest that this relationship does not hold for women (Davidson, Hall, & MacGregor, 1996) or for individuals in certain ethnic and cultural groups (Delehanty, Dimsdale, & Mills, 1991; Powch & Houston, 1996). Final conclusions must await further research that examines the impact of gender, culture, and ethnicity on the link between hostility and CHD/MI.

Risking Your Life: Health-Endangering Behaviors

As we have seen, many of today's major health problems are caused or amplified by preventable behaviors such as those listed in Table 13.1, on page 453 (USDHHS, 1990).

Smoking　　Smoking is the single most preventable risk factor for fatal illnesses in the United States (Kaplan et al., 1995). Indeed, cigarette smoking accounts for more deaths than all other drugs, car accidents, suicides, homicides, and fires combined. Further, nonsmokers who inhale "secondhand" smoke face an elevated risk for lung cancer and other respiratory diseases (Collins, 1997), a fact that has fueled a militant nonsmokers' rights movement in North America.

Although smoking is on the decline in the United States overall—only about 26 percent of adults now smoke—the habit is actually increasing in some groups, especially Latino men and women and young African-American men (National Center for Health Statistics, 1996). Poorer, less educated people are particularly likely to smoke. Conversely, some American Indian tribes in the Southwest and most Asian groups are less likely than other groups to smoke (Gritz & St. Jeor, 1992; USDHHS, 1990). In many Third World countries, smoking is still the rule rather than the exception. Smoking is a difficult habit to break; long-term success following most smoking cessation programs available today is still only about 35 percent (Killen et al., 1997). Improving this success rate and preventing adolescents from taking up smoking remain among health psychology's greatest challenges.

Alcohol　　Like tobacco, alcohol is a potentially addicting substance that can lead to major health problems. In addition to its association with most leading causes of death, including heart disease, stroke, cancer, and liver disease, alcohol abuse contributes to irreversible damage to brain tissue and to gastrointestinal illnesses, among many others. Both male and female alcohol abusers may experience disruption of their reproductive functions, such as early menopause in women and erectile disorder in men. Alcohol consumption by pregnant women is the most preventable cause of birth defects. The economic costs of alcohol abuse total $70 billion a year (USDHHS, 1990); about 15 percent of U.S. health care costs relate to this problem.

A Deadly Habit

It has been estimated that, if people did not smoke cigarettes, 400,000 fewer U.S. citizens would die in the next twelve months and 25 percent of all cancer deaths and thousands of heart attacks would never occur (USDHHS, 1990).

Preventing AIDS

Adolescent-oriented AIDS prevention efforts focus on safe-sex media campaigns and studies of the cognitive and emotional factors that can enhance their effectiveness. Their impact is still being evaluated.

Unsafe Sex   In just the past decade, almost half a million Americans have been diagnosed as having AIDS and as many as 2 million more have been infected with HIV (Holmberg, 1996). An estimated 75,000 of these people are adolescents (St. Lawrence, 1993). With growing public awareness of how to prevent HIV infection, the rate of new AIDS cases is now falling in the U.S., but not everyone is getting the message.

Unsafe sex—especially sexual relations without the use of a condom—greatly increases the risk of contracting HIV; yet many adolescents and adults continue this dangerous practice (DeAngelis, 1995b). Like smoking and many other health-threatening behaviors, unprotected sex is disproportionately common among low-income individuals, many of whom are members of ethnic minority groups. Among African-American men the risk of contracting AIDS is three times greater than for European-American men; the risk for African-American women is fifteen times higher than for European-American women (Holmberg, 1996).

PROMOTING HEALTHY BEHAVIOR

As noted earlier, health psychologists are concerned with lessening the impact of certain diseases and reducing the incidence of others. In particular, they have facilitated early detection of disease by educating people about the warning signs of cancer, heart disease, and other serious illnesses and prompting them to seek medical attention while life-saving treatment is still possible. Encouraging women to perform breast self-examinations and men to do testicular self-examinations are just two examples of health psychology programs that can save thousands of lives each year (Taylor, 1998a). Health psychologists have also explored the reasons behind some people's failure to follow treatment regimes that are vital to the control of diseases such as diabetes, heart disease, and high blood pressure. Understanding these reasons and devising procedures that encourage greater compliance could speed recovery, prevent unnecessary suffering, and save many lives.

The process of preventing, reducing, or eliminating behaviors that pose risks to health and of increasing healthy behavior patterns is called **health promotion** (Taylor, 1998a). Toward this end, many health psychologists have developed programs which help youngsters as young as nine or ten to develop healthy behaviors and avoid health-compromising behaviors. School systems now offer a variety of these programs, including those that teach children and adolescents the skills necessary to help them avoid cigarettes, drugs, and unprotected sex (e.g., Amaro, 1995; Evans, in press; Kelly et al., 1995). To meet the more difficult challenge of modifying existing health-threatening behaviors, health psychologists have moved into the workplace with the goal of altering diet, smoking, and exercise patterns and teaching stress management techniques to help workers develop healthier lifestyles (Fielding, 1991; Taylor, 1998a). These programs may have the added advantage of creating savings in future medical treatment costs (Kaplan, 1991).

In their health promotion efforts, many health psychologists also conduct and apply research on the cognitive factors associated with the development and alteration of health-related behaviors. The aim is to better understand the thought processes that lead people to engage in health-endangering behaviors and to tailor intervention programs that alter those thought processes, or at least take them into account (Klepp, Kelder, & Perry, 1995).

Health Beliefs and Health Behaviors

The cognitive approach to health psychology is embodied in various *health-belief models.* One of the most influential of these models was developed by Irwin Rosenstock (1974). This model has been extensively tested and is based on the assumption that people's decisions about health-related behaviors (such as smoking) are guided by four main factors:

1. A perception of *personal* threat of, or susceptibility to, developing a specific health problem. (Do you believe that *you* will get lung cancer from smoking?)

2. A perception of the seriousness of the illness and the severity of the consequences of having it. (How serious do *you* think lung cancer is, and what will happen to *you* if you get it?)

3. The belief that a particular practice will reduce the threat. (Will *your* stopping smoking prevent *you* from getting lung cancer?)

4. The decisional balance between the perceived costs of enacting a health practice and the benefits expected from this practice. (Will the reduced chance of getting cancer in the future be worth the discomfort and loss of pleasure associated with not smoking?)

On the basis of this health-belief model, one would expect that the people most likely to quit smoking would be those who believe that they are susceptible to getting cancer from smoking, that cancer is serious and life-threatening, and that the benefits of preventing cancer clearly outweigh the difficulties associated with quitting.

Other belief factors not included in Rosenstock's model may be important as well. For example, people are unlikely to try to quit smoking unless they believe they can succeed. Thus, *self-efficacy,* the belief that one is able to perform some behavior (see Chapter 14, on personality), is an additional determinant of decisions about health behaviors (Bandura, 1986; Taylor, 1998a). A related factor is the *intention* to engage in a behavior designed to improve health (Maddux & DuCharme, 1997).

© Steve Kelley/Copley News Service

Health-belief models have been useful in predicting a variety of health behaviors, including exercise (McAuley, 1992), safe-sex practices among gay men at risk for AIDS (Fisher, Fisher, & Rye, 1995), adherence to medical regimes among diabetic adolescents (Bond, Aiken, & Somerville, 1992), and the decision to undergo mammogram screening for breast cancer (Champion & Huster, 1995). Such models have also guided researchers in the development of interventions to reduce certain health-compromising behaviors. For example, interventions aimed at individuals at high risk for AIDS, particularly adolescents and African-American women, include programs to improve knowledge about the disease and skill in demanding safe sex (e.g., DiClemente & Wingood, 1995).

Changing Health Behaviors: Stages of Readiness

Changing health behaviors depends not only on one's health beliefs but also on one's readiness to change. According to James Prochaska and his colleagues, successful change involves five stages (Prochaska, DiClemente, & Norcross, 1992):

1. *Precontemplation*   The person does not perceive a health-related problem and has no intention of changing in the foreseeable future.

2. *Contemplation*   The person is aware of a problem behavior that should be changed and is seriously thinking about changing it. People often get stuck here. Cigarette smokers, for example, have been known to spend years contemplating quitting.

3. *Preparation*   The person has a strong intention to change, has specific plans to do so, and may already have taken preliminary steps, such as cutting down on smoking.

4. *Action*   The person at this stage is engaging successfully in behavior change. Because relapse is so prevalent in health-related behaviors, people in this stage must remain successful for up to six months before they reach the next stage.

5. *Maintenance*   The person uses skills learned along the way to continue the healthy behavior and to prevent relapse.

The path from precontemplation through maintenance is not a smooth one (Prochaska, 1994). Usually, people relapse and go through the stages again until they finally achieve stability in the healthy behavior they desire (see Figure 13.5). For example, smokers typically require three to four cycles through the stages and up to seven years before they finally reach the maintenance stage.

What factors contribute to movement from one stage to the next? Prochaska and his colleagues found that the factors facilitating progress at one stage may be different from those most important at another. However, decisional balance, the outcome of weighing the pros and cons of changing, is important for predicting progress at any stage (Prochaska et al., 1994). This finding applies to many health-related behaviors, including getting mammograms (Rakowski et al., 1996), participating in exercise programs (Courneya, 1995), consuming a diet high in fruit and vegetables (Laforge, Greene, & Prochaska, 1994), and quitting smoking, among others (Prochaska & DiClemente, 1992).

LINKAGES

How can people manage stress? (a link to Treatment of Psychological Disorders)

Programs for Coping with Stress and Promoting Health

Helping people to tip the decisional balance in favor of healthy change is but one strategy that health psychologists apply in an effort to improve people's coping skills and promote healthier lifestyles. Let's consider a few specific procedures and programs used in this wide-ranging effort.

Planning to Cope   Just as people with extra money in the bank have a better chance of weathering a financial crisis, those with effective coping skills may escape some of the more harmful effects of intense stress (Aspinwall & Taylor, 1997). Like family

FIGURE 13.5

Stages of Readiness to Change Health Behaviors

Many health psychologists are guided by Prochaska's theory that readiness to change health behaviors progresses through predictable stages. To help people quit smoking, for example, they use persuasive communications during the *contemplation* stage and relapse prevention techniques during the *action* stage. Tailoring an intervention to each individual's history of progress through the stages of readiness may increase the likelihood of successful long-term behavior change.

Source: Prochaska, DiClemente, & Norcross, 1992.

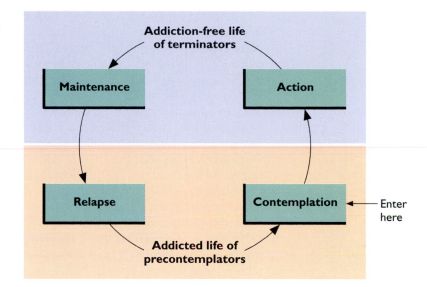

money, the ability to handle stress appears to come naturally to some people, but coping can also be learned.

The first step in learning to cope with stress is to make a systematic assessment of the degree to which stress is disrupting one's life. This assessment involves (1) identifying the specific events and situations, such as conflicts or life changes, that are operating as stressors; and (2) noting the effects of these stressors, such as headaches, lack of concentration, or excessive smoking or drinking.

Table 13.4 lists the other steps in a program to cope with stress. Notice that the second step is to select an appropriate goal. Should you try to eliminate stressors or to alter your response to them? Knowing the difference between changeable and unchangeable stressors is important. Stress-related problems appear especially prevalent among people who either exhaust themselves trying to change stressors that cannot be changed or miss opportunities to change stressors that can be changed (Folkman, 1984).

No single method of coping with stressors is universally successful. For example, denying the existence of an uncontrollable stressor may be fine in the short run but may lead to problems if no other coping method is used (Suls & Fletcher, 1985). Similarly, people who rely exclusively on an active problem-solving approach may handle controllable stressors well but find themselves nearly helpless in the face of uncontrollable ones (Rodin & Salovey, 1989). Individuals most successful at stress management may be those who are best able to adjust their coping methods to the demands of changing situations and differing stressors (Carver, Scheier, & Weintraub, 1989).

TABLE 13.4

Stages in Coping with Stress

Many successful programs for coping with stress systematically guide people through several stages and are aimed at removing stressors that can be changed and at tempering responses to stressors that cannot be changed (Silver & Wortman, 1980).

Stage	Task
1. Assessment	Identify the sources and effects of stress.
2. Goal setting	List the stressors and stress responses to be addressed. Designate which stressors are and are not changeable.
3. Planning	List the specific steps to be taken to cope with stress.
4. Action	Implement coping plans.
5. Evaluation	Determine the changes in stressors and stress responses that have occurred as a result of coping methods.
6. Adjustment	Alter coping methods to improve results, if necessary.

Developing Coping Strategies   Like stress responses, strategies for coping with stress can be cognitive, emotional, behavioral, or physical. *Cognitive coping strategies* change how people interpret stimuli and events. They help people to think more calmly, rationally, and constructively in the face of stress and may generate a more hopeful emotional state. For example, students with heavy course loads may experience anxiety, confusion, discouragement, lack of motivation, and the desire to run away from it all. Frightening, catastrophic thoughts about their tasks (for example, "What if I fail?") can amplify stress responses. Cognitive coping strategies replace catastrophic thinking with thoughts in which stressors are viewed as challenges rather than threats (Ellis & Bernard, 1985). This substitution process is often called **cognitive restructuring** (Lazarus, 1971; Meichenbaum, 1977; see Chapter 16). It can be done by practicing constructive thoughts such as "All I can do is the best I can." Cognitive coping does not eliminate stressors, but it can help people perceive them as less threatening and thus make them less disruptive.

Seeking and obtaining social support from others are effective *emotional coping strategies.* The perception that one has such support, and is cared for and valued by others, tends to be an effective buffer against the ill effects of many stressors (Taylor, 1998a). With social support comes feedback from others, along with advice on how to approach stressors. Having enhanced social support is associated with increased survival time in cancer patients (Anderson, 1992), improved immune function (Kiecolt-Glaser & Glaser, 1992), and more rapid recovery from illness (Taylor, 1998a).

Behavioral coping strategies involve changing behavior in ways that minimize the impact of stressors. Time management is one example. You might keep track of your time for a week and start a time-management plan. The first step is to set out a schedule that shows how your time is now typically spent; then decide how to allocate your time in the future. A time-management plan can help control catastrophizing thoughts by providing reassurance that there is enough time for everything and a plan for handling it all.

Behavioral, emotional, and cognitive coping skills often interact closely. Discussing stressors and seeking feedback from others help people think more rationally and calmly, and make it easier to develop and use sensible plans for behavioral coping. When behavioral coping eliminates or minimizes stressors, people find it easier to think and feel better about themselves.

Physical coping strategies are aimed at directly altering one's physical responses before, during, or after stressors occur. The most common physical coping strategy is some form of drug use. Prescription medications are sometimes an appropriate coping aid, especially when stressors are severe and acute, such as the sudden death of one's child. But if people depend on prescriptions or other drugs, including alcohol, to help them face stressors, they often attribute any success to the drug, not to their own skill. Furthermore, the same drug effects that blunt stress responses may interfere with the ability to apply coping strategies. If the drug is abused, it can become a stressor itself. The resulting loss of perceived control over stressors may make those stressors even more threatening and disruptive.

Nonchemical methods of reducing physical stress reactions include relaxation, physical exercise, and meditation, among others (Taylor, 1998a). Meditation is described in Chapter 9; here, we consider progressive relaxation training.

Progressive relaxation training is one of the most popular physical methods for coping with stress. Edmund Jacobson developed the technique during the 1930s (Jacobson, 1938). Today, progressive relaxation is learned by tensing a group of muscles (such as the hand and arm) for a few seconds, then releasing the tension and focusing on the resulting feelings of relaxation. This procedure is repeated for each of sixteen muscle groups throughout the body (Bernstein, Borkovec, & Hazlette-Stevens, 2000). Once some skill at relaxation is developed, it can be used to calm down anywhere and anytime, often without lying down (Blanchard & Andrasik, 1985; Wolpe, 1982). ("In Review: Methods for Coping with Stress" summarizes our discussion of stress-coping methods.)

Dealing with Chemotherapy

Progressive relaxation training can be used to ease a variety of health-related problems. For example, one study found that this training resulted in significant reductions in anxiety, physiological arousal, and nausea following cancer chemotherapy (Burish & Jenkins, 1992).

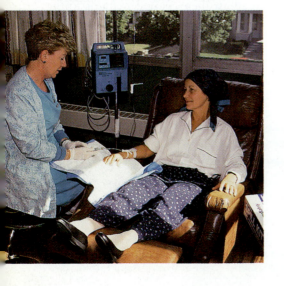

in review

METHODS FOR COPING WITH STRESS	
Type of Coping Method	**Examples**
Cognitive	Thinking of stressors as challenges rather than as threats; avoiding perfectionism.
Emotional	Talking about one's problems to a friend.
Behavioral	Implementing a time-management plan; where possible, making life changes to eliminate stressors.
Physical	Progressive relaxation training, exercise, meditation.

LINKAGES

As noted in Chapter 1, all of psychology's many subfields are related to one another. Our discussion of posttraumatic stress disorder illustrates just one way in which the topic of this chapter, health, stress, and coping, is linked to the subfield of psychological disorders (Chapter 15). The Linkages diagram shows ties to two other subfields as well, and there are many more ties throughout the book. Looking for linkages among subfields will help you see how they all fit together and better appreciate the big picture that is psychology.

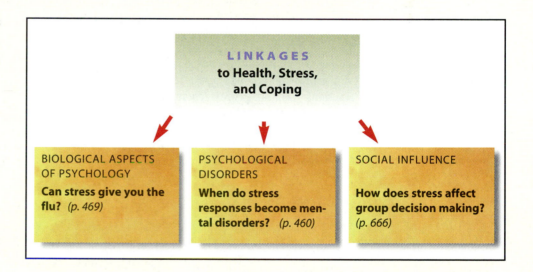

SUMMARY

HEALTH PSYCHOLOGY

The development of *health psychology* was prompted by recognition of the link between stress and illness, as well as the role of behaviors such as smoking, in elevating the risk of illness. Researchers in this field explore how psychological factors are related to physical disease and help people behave in ways that prevent or minimize disease and promote health.

STRESS AND STRESSORS

The term *stress* refers in part to *stressors*, which are events and situations to which people must adjust. More generally, stress is viewed as an ongoing, interactive process that takes place as people adjust to and cope with their environment.

Psychological Stressors

Stressors may be physical or psychological. Psychological stressors include catastrophic events, life changes and strains, and daily hassles.

Measuring Stressors

Stressors can be measured by tests such as the Social Readjustment Rating Scale (SRRS) and the Life Experiences Survey (LES), as well as by surveys of daily hassles, but scores on such tests provide only a partial picture of the stress in a given individual's life.

STRESS RESPONSES

Responses to stressors can be physical or psychological. These stress responses can occur alone or in combination, and the appearance of one can often stimulate others.

Physical Responses

Physical stress responses include changes in SAM activation, such as increases in heart rate, respiration, and many other processes and in HPA activation, including the release of corticosteroids. These responses may be viewed as part of a pattern known as the *general adaptation syndrome,* or *GAS*. The GAS has three stages: the alarm reaction, resistance, and exhaustion. The GAS helps people resist stress but, if present too long, can lead to depletion of physiological resources as well as to physical illnesses, which Selye called *diseases of adaptation.*

Psychological Responses

Psychological stress responses can be emotional, cognitive, and behavioral. Anxiety, anger, and depression are among the most common emotional stress reactions. Cognitive stress reactions include ruminative thinking, catastrophizing, and disruptions in the ability to think clearly, remember accurately, and solve problems efficiently. Behavioral stress responses include irritability, aggression, absenteeism, and even suicide attempts.

STRESS MEDIATORS: INTERACTIONS BETWEEN PEOPLE AND STRESSORS

The fact that different individuals react to the same stressors in different ways can be explained in part by stress mediators, such as the extent to which individuals can predict and control their stressors, how they interpret the threat involved, the social support they get, and their stress-coping skills.

How Stressors Are Appraised

Many stressors are not inherently stressful; their impact depends partly on how people perceive them. In particular, stressors appraised as threats are likely to have greater impact than those appraised as challenges.

Predictability and Control

Knowing that a particular stressor might occur but being uncertain whether it will tends to increase the stressor's impact, as does lack of control over stressors.

Coping Resources and Coping Methods

The people most likely to react strongly to a stressor are those whose coping resources and coping methods are inadequate.

Social Support

Social support, which consists of resources provided by other persons, can lessen the impact of stress. The friends and social contacts on whom a person can depend for support constitute that person's *social support network.*

Stress and Personality

Certain personality characteristics help insulate people from the ill effects of stress. One such characteristic appears to be dispositional optimism, the belief or expectation that things will work out positively.

THE PHYSIOLOGY AND PSYCHOLOGY OF HEALTH AND ILLNESS

Stress, the Immune System, and Illness

When a person is under stress, some of the hormones released from the adrenal gland, such as cortisol, reduce the effectiveness of the cells of the immune system (T-cells, B-cells, natural killer cells, macrophages) in combating foreign invaders such as viruses and cancer cells. *Psychoneuroimmunology* is the field that examines the interaction of psychological and physiological processes that affect the body's ability to defend itself against disease.

Heart Disease and Behavior Patterns

Heart disease is a major cause of death in most developed countries, including the United States. People who are cynically hostile appear to be at greater risk for heart disease than other people. The heightened reactivity to stressors that these people experience may damage their cardiovascular system.

Risking Your Life: Health-Endangering Behaviors

Most of the major health problems in Western cultures are related to preventable behaviors such as smoking and drinking alcohol. Having unsafe sex is a major risk factor for contracting HIV.

PROMOTING HEALTHY BEHAVIOR

The process of altering or eliminating health-risky behaviors and fostering healthy behavior patterns is called *health promotion.*

Health Beliefs and Health Behaviors

People's health-related behaviors are partly guided by their beliefs about health risks and what they can do about them.

Changing Health Behaviors: Stages of Readiness

The process of changing health-related behaviors appears to involve several stages, including precontemplation, contemplation, preparation, action, and maintenance. Understanding which stage people are in, and helping them move through these stages, is an important task in health psychology.

Programs for Coping with Stress and Promoting Health

In order to cope with stress, people must recognize the stressors affecting them and develop ways of coping with those stressors.

Important coping skills include *cognitive restructuring,* acting to minimize the number or intensity of stressors, and using *progressive relaxation training* and other techniques for reducing physical stress reactions. These coping procedures are often part of health psychologists' disease-prevention and health-promotion efforts.

KEY TERMS

burnout (460)
cognitive restructuring (478)
diseases of adaptation (458)
general adaptation syndrome (GAS) (456)

health promotion (474)
health psychology (452)
posttraumatic stress disorder (PTSD) (461)

progressive relaxation training (478)
psychoneuroimmunology (470)

social support network (464)
stress (453)
stressors (453)

14

Personality

It has been estimated that U.S. businesses lose more than $60 billion each year as a result of employee theft (Gatewood & Feild, 1998). Millions more are spent on security and surveillance designed to curb these losses, but it would be far better if companies could simply avoid hiring dishonest employees in the first place. Some firms have tried to screen out potential thieves by requiring prospective employees to take "lie detector" polygraph tests. As described in Chapter 11, however, these tests may not be reliable or valid; the federal government has banned their use in most kinds of employee selection.

Many employers have turned instead to paper-and-pencil "integrity" tests designed to identify job applicants who are likely to steal or behave in other dishonest or irresponsible ways (Hogan & Ones, 1997). Some of these tests simply ask applicants if they have stolen from previous employers and if they might steal in the future. Such questions can screen out people who are honest about their stealing, but most people who steal would probably also lie to conceal previous crimes or criminal intentions. Accordingly, some companies now use tests to assess applicants' general psychological characteristics and compare their scores to those of current or past employees. Applicants whose characteristics are most like the company's honest employees are hired; those who appear similar to dishonest employees are not.

Can employee honesty be predicted on the basis of such tests? To some extent, it can (Murphy, 1993). For example, scores on the *Reliability Scale*—which includes questions about impulse control and disruptive behavior during school years—are significantly correlated with a broad range of undesirable employee behaviors (Hogan & Ones, 1997). But the ability of psychological tests to predict such behaviors is far from perfect; though better than polygraph tests, they still fail to detect dishonesty in some people or, worse, falsely identify some honest people as potential thieves. The best that companies can hope for is to find tests that will help reduce the overall likelihood of hiring dishonest people.

The use of personality tests to help select honest employees is a relatively recent application of theory and research in personality psychology, but it is really only a more formal version of the process that most of us use when we meet someone new. We observe the person's behavior, form impressions, and draw conclusions about how that person will act at other times or under other circumstances. Like the employer, we are looking for clues to personality. Although there is no universally accepted definition, psychologists generally view **personality** as the unique pattern of enduring thoughts, feelings, and actions that characterize a person. Personality research, in turn, focuses on understanding the origins or causes of the similarities and differences among people in their patterns of cognition, emotion, and behavior. With such a large agenda, personality researchers must incorporate information from many other areas of psychology.

Indeed, personality psychology appears to lie at the crossroads of all psychological research (McAdams, 1996); it is the coalescence in a particular individual of all the psychological, behavioral, and biological processes discussed elsewhere in this book. To gain a comprehensive understanding of just one individual's personality, for example, one must know about developmental experiences (including cultural influences), genetic and other biological characteristics, perceptual and other information-processing habits and biases, typical patterns of emotional expression, and social skills. Psychologists also want to know about personality in general, such as how personality develops and changes across the life span, why some people are usually optimistic whereas others are usually pessimistic, and how consistent or inconsistent people's behavior tends to be from one situation to the next.

In this chapter we describe four theoretical approaches to the study of personality and some of the ways in which personality theory and research are being applied. We begin by presenting the psychodynamic approach, which was developed in the late nineteenth century by Sigmund Freud and subsequently modified by a number of people he influenced. Next, we describe the trait approach, which focuses on patterns of characteristic thoughts, feelings, and actions that form individual personalities. Then we present the social-cognitive approach, which explores the roles of learning and cognition in shaping human behavior and personality. Finally, we consider the

Founder of the Psychodynamic Approach

Here is Sigmund Freud with his daughter, Anna, who developed a revised version of her father's psychodynamic theories of personality.

FIGURE 14.1

Freud's Conception of the Personality Structure

According to Freud, some parts of the personality are conscious, whereas others are unconscious. In the preconscious he said, lie memories and other material not usually in awareness but that can be easily brought into consciousness.

Source: Adapted from Liebert & Spiegler, 1990.

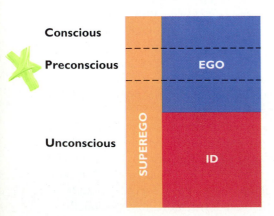

phenomenological approach, with its emphasis on how each person's unique view of the world shapes personality. Our overview of these varying approaches is followed by a description of how psychologists measure and compare people's personalities, along with some examples of how psychological tests are being used in personality research and in other ways as well.

THE PSYCHODYNAMIC APPROACH

Some people think they can understand personality by simply watching people. Someone with an "obnoxious personality," for example, shows it by acting obnoxiously. But is that all there is to personality? Not according to Sigmund Freud, who likened personality to an iceberg whose tip is clearly visible but whose bulk remains hidden underwater.

As a physician during the 1890s, Freud specialized in treating "neurotic" disorders, such as blindness or paralysis for which there was no physical cause and which hypnosis could often remove. These cases led Freud to believe in *psychic determinism,* the idea that personality and behavior are determined more by psychological factors than by biological conditions or current events. He proposed, further, that people may not know why they feel, think, or act the way they do, because these activities are partly controlled by the unconscious portion of the personality—the part of which people are not normally aware. From these ideas Freud created the **psychodynamic approach** to personality, which holds that the interplay of various unconscious psychological processes determines thoughts, feelings, and behavior.

The Structure and Development of Personality

Freud believed that people are born with basic instincts or needs—not only for food, water, and air but also for sex and aggression. He believed that needs for love, knowledge, security, and the like are derived from these more fundamental desires. Each person faces the task of figuring out how to meet his or her needs in a world that often frustrates these efforts. According to Freud, personality develops out of each person's struggle with this task and is reflected in the ways he or she goes about satisfying a range of needs.

Id, Ego, and Superego   As Figure 14.1 illustrates, Freud described the personality as having three major components: the id, the ego, and the superego.

Freud saw the **id** as the inborn, unconscious portion of the personality where instincts reside. The life instincts, which he called *Eros,* promote positive, constructive behavior and reflect a source of energy (sometimes called psychic energy) known as libido. Alternatively, he considered the death instincts, or *Thanatos,* to be responsible for human aggression and destructiveness (Hall, Lindzey, & Campbell, 1998). The id operates on the **pleasure principle,** seeking immediate satisfaction of both kinds of instincts, regardless of society's rules or the rights or feelings of others. The thirsty person who snatches your water bottle at the gym would be satisfying an Eros-driven id impulse.

As parents, teachers, and others place greater restrictions on the expression of id impulses, a second part of the personality—the **ego** (or "self")—evolves from the id. The ego is responsible for organizing ways to get what a person wants in the real world, as opposed to the fantasy world of the id. Operating on the **reality principle,** the ego makes compromises between the id's unreasoning demands for immediate satisfaction and the practical constraints of the real world.

As people gain experience with the rules and values of society, they tend to adopt them. This process of *internalizing* parental and societal values produces the third component of personality: the **superego,** which tells us what we should and should not do. The superego is just as relentless and unreasonable as the id in its demand to be obeyed.

Conflicts and Defenses   Freud called the inner turmoil among personality components *intrapsychic* or *psychodynamic conflicts*, and he believed that the number, nature, and outcome of these conflicts shape each individual's personality.

The ego's primary function is to prevent the anxiety or guilt that would arise if we became conscious of socially unacceptable id impulses or if we thought about violating the superego's rules (Hall, Lindzey, & Campbell, 1998). Sometimes, the ego motivates realistic actions, as when a person seeks help after experiencing impulses to abuse a child. However, it may also resort to **defense mechanisms**, which are unconscious tactics that either prevent threatening material from surfacing or disguise it when it does (see Table 14.1).

Stages in Personality Development   Freud proposed that personality develops during childhood in a series of **psychosexual stages**. Failure to resolve the problems and conflicts that arise at a given stage can leave a person *fixated*—that is, overly attached to or unconsciously preoccupied with the area of pleasure associated with that stage. Freud believed that the stage at which a person has fixated is revealed in adult personality characteristics.

In Freud's theory, a child's first year or so is called the **oral stage**, because the mouth—used by the infant to eat and explore—is the center of pleasure associated

TABLE 14.1

Psychodynamic Defense Mechanisms

Defense mechanisms deflect anxiety or guilt in the short run, but they sap energy. Further, the use of such defenses to avoid dealing with the source of one's problems can be maladaptive in the long run.

Repression	Unconsciously pushing threatening memories, urges, or ideas from conscious awareness: A person may experience loss of memory for unpleasant events.
Rationalization	Attempts to make actions or mistakes seem reasonable: The reasons or excuses given (e.g., "I spank my children because it is good for them") have a rational ring to them, but they are not the real reasons for the behavior.
Projection	Unconsciously attributing one's own unacceptable thoughts or impulses to another person: Instead of recognizing that "I hate him," a person may feel that "He hates me."
Reaction formation	Defending against unacceptable impulses by acting opposite to them: Sexual interest in a married friend might appear as strong dislike instead.
Sublimation	Converting unacceptable impulses into socially acceptable actions, and perhaps symbolically expressing them: Sexual or aggressive desires may appear as artistic creativity or devotion to athletic excellence.
Displacement	Deflecting an impulse from its original target to a less threatening one: Anger at one's boss may be expressed through hostility toward a clerk, a family member, or even the family dog.
Denial	Simply discounting the existence of threatening impulses: A person may vehemently deny ever having had even the slightest degree of physical attraction to a person of the same sex.
Compensation	Striving to make up for unconscious impulses or fears: A business executive's extreme competitiveness might be aimed at compensating for unconscious feelings of inferiority.

with this period. Freud said fixation at the oral stage can stem from early or late weaning and may produce adult characteristics ranging from overeating or alcoholism to child-like dependence or the use of "biting" sarcasm.

The **anal stage** occurs during the second year as the demand for toilet training shifts the focus of pleasure and conflict to the anal area. According to Freud, toilet training that is too harsh, or begins too early or too late, can lead to anal fixation. Adult characteristics associated with fixation at this stage range from being stingy and overly concerned with neatness (thus symbolically withholding feces) to being disorganized or impulsive (symbolically expelling feces at will).

Between the ages of three and five, according to Freud, the child's focus of pleasure shifts to the genital area. Because Freud emphasized male psychosexual development, he called this period the **phallic stage**. It is then, said Freud, that the boy experiences sexual desire for the mother and a desire to eliminate, even kill, the father, with whom the boy competes for the mother's affection. Freud named this constellation of impulses the **Oedipus complex**, because it echoes the plot of the Greek tragedy *Oedipus Rex*. The boy's fantasies create so much fear, however, that the ego represses the incestuous desires, and the boy seeks to identify with and be like his father. It is during this stage that the male's superego begins to develop.

According to Freud, the female child begins the phallic stage with a strong attachment to her mother; but upon realizing that boys have penises and girls don't, she supposedly develops *penis envy* and transfers her love to her father—a phenomenon known as the **Electra complex**. To avoid her mother's disapproval, the girl identifies with and imitates her, thus forming the basis for her own superego.

Freud believed that unresolved conflicts from the phallic stage can lead to problems in adulthood, such as difficulties in dealing with authority figures or the inability to maintain a stable love relationship.

As the phallic stage draws to a close and its conflicts are dealt with by the ego, an interval of peace known as the **latency period** ensues. During adolescence, when sexual impulses reappear, the genitals again become the focus of pleasure. Thus begins the **genital stage**, which, according to Freud, lasts until death.

Variations on Freud's Personality Theory

Freud's ideas—especially those concerning the Oedipus and Electra complexes and the role of infantile sexuality—created instant controversy in public and professional circles. Even many of Freud's followers disagreed with him. Some of these dissenters have been called *neo-Freudian theorists* because, though they differed from Freud on certain points and developed new theories of personality, their theories still contained many of the basic features of Freud's theory. Others are known as *ego psychologists* because their ideas focused more on the ego than on the id (Hall, Lindzey, & Campbell, 1998).

Jung's Analytic Psychology   Many psychologists would identify Carl Jung (pronounced "yoong") as the most prominent dissenter among Freud's early followers. Jung (1916) argued that libido was not just sexual instinct but a more general life force that includes an innate drive for creativity, for growth-oriented resolution of conflicts, and for the productive blending of basic impulses with real-world demands. Jung did not identify specific stages in personality development. He suggested instead that people develop, over time, differing degrees of *introversion* (a tendency to reflect on one's own experiences) or *extraversion* (a tendency to focus on the social world), along with differing tendencies to rely on specific psychological functions such as thinking versus feeling. The combination of these tendencies, said Jung (1933), creates personalities that display distinctive and predictable patterns of behavior.

Jung also argued for the existence of a *collective unconscious,* which he defined as the memories that all of us inherit from our human and nonhuman ancestors (Hall, Lindzey, & Campbell, 1998). According to Jung, we are not consciously aware of these memories, yet they are responsible for our innate tendencies to react in particular ways

An Early Feminist

After completing medical school at the University of Berlin in 1913, Karen Horney (1885–1952) trained as a Freudian psychoanalyst. She accepted some aspects of Freud's psychoanalytic views, including the idea of unconscious motivation, but the neo-Freudian theory she favored differed from his in several respects. For example, she saw the need for security as more important than biological instincts in motivating infants' behavior, and she rejected his male-oriented notion that the psychological development of females is influenced by penis envy.

to certain objects in our environment. For example, Jung believed that our collective memory of mothers influences how each of us perceives our own mother. Although the notion of a collective unconscious is widely accepted by followers of Jung, there is no empirical evidence that it exists. In fact, Jung himself acknowledged that it would be impossible to objectively demonstrate the existence of a collective unconscious (Feist & Feist, 1998).

Other Neo-Freudian Theorists   Jung was neither the first nor the only theorist to challenge Freud. Alfred Adler, originally a loyal disciple of psychoanalysis, came to believe that the impetus for the development of personality is provided not by the id but, rather, by an innate desire to overcome infantile feelings of helplessness. Adler (1927) referred to this process as *striving for superiority*, by which he meant a drive for fulfillment as a person, not just a desire to best others. Other prominent neo-Freudians, including Erik Erikson, Erich Fromm, and Henry Stack Sullivan, focused on how people's personalities are shaped by the people around them. They argued that once biological needs are met, the attempt to meet social needs (to feel protected, secure, and accepted, for example) is the primary influence on personality. The strategies people use to meet social needs, such as dominating other people or being dependent on them, thus become central aspects of the personality.

Another challenge to Freud came from the first feminist personality theorist, Karen Horney (pronounced "HORN-eye"), who disputed Freud's view that women's lack of a penis causes them to envy men and feel inferior to them. In fact, Horney (1937) argued that it is men who envy women: Realizing that they cannot bear children and may play only a small role in raising them, males see their lives as having less meaning or substance than women's. Horney called this condition "womb envy." She argued further that, when women feel inferior, it is because of the personal and political restrictions that men have placed upon them, not because of penis envy. Horney's position on this issue reflected her strong belief that cultural factors, rather than instincts, play a major role in personality development (Feist & Feist, 1998). This greater emphasis on cultural influences is one of the major theoretical differences between Freud and the neo-Freudians generally.

Contemporary Psychodynamic Theories

Today, some of the most influential psychodynamic approaches to personality focus on *object relations*—that is, on how people's perceptions of themselves and others influence their view of and reactions to the world (Feist & Feist, 1998). According to object relations theorists such as Melanie Klein (1991), Otto Kernberg (1976), Heinz Kohut (1984), and Margaret Mahler (1968), early relationships between infants and their love objects, usually the mother and other primary caregivers, are vitally important in the development of personality. These relationships, they say, shape a person's thoughts and feelings about social relationships later in life.

As described in Chapter 12, children ideally form a secure early bond to the mother or other caregiver, tolerate gradual separation from the object of attachment, and finally develop the ability to relate to others as an independent, secure individual (Ainsworth, 1989; Bowlby, 1973). Object relations theory is at least partly responsible for psychologists' current interest in how the nature of early child-parent attachments affects self-image, identity, security, social relationships, and other aspects of personality later in life (Mikelson, Kessler, & Shaver, 1997; Rholes et al., 1997). According to one study, for example, people with a history of secure and stable attachments to others are less likely to abuse alcohol and other drugs (Mikelson, Kessler, & Shaver, 1997). Another study found a correlation between college students' early attachment styles and the quality of their current romantic relationships: Students whose attachments had been anxious or ambivalent tended to have shorter and less satisfying romances (Shaver & Clark, 1996). Similarly, some object relations theorists believe that certain instances of child abuse may be related to abusive parents' perceptions of how their own parents treated them (e.g., van IJzendoorn, 1995).

Early Attachment

While Freud believed that personality problems involved conflicts among the structures of personality, object relations theorists believe that such problems arise from arrested personality development due to difficulties in early relationships and attachments.

Evaluation of the Psychodynamic Approach

Any overall evaluation of Freud and his theories will inevitably be mixed. There is no doubt that his views have influenced modern Western thinking about medicine, literature, religion, sociology, and anthropology, and his contributions to the field of psychology have been considerable. Indeed, Freud's personality theory is probably the most comprehensive and influential psychological theory ever proposed. His ideas have also shaped a wide range of psychotherapeutic techniques and stimulated the development of several personality assessments, including the projective tests described later in this chapter. Further, contemporary theories and research have provided some limited support for certain aspects of Freud's theory. For example, personality psychologists who take an evolutionary approach to human behavior (e.g., A. Buss, 1997) argue that personality can be traced in part to innate human tendencies, which are similar to instincts. Other psychologists have found that people do employ several of the defense mechanisms proposed by Freud (Paulhus, Fridhandler, & Hayes, 1997), although they question whether defense mechanisms operate at an unconscious level. Finally, there is substantial evidence that events and experiences that people are unable to recall can influence their thoughts and actions (Smith, 1998; Westen, 1998).

However, there are several weaknesses in Freud's psychodynamic theories. For one thing, they are based almost entirely on case studies of a few individuals. As discussed in Chapter 2, conclusions drawn from case studies may not apply to people in general. Nor was Freud's sample representative of people in general. Most of his patients were upper-class Viennese women who not only had psychological problems but were raised in a society in which discussion of sex was considered to be uncivilized. Moreover, Freud's thinking about personality and its development reflected Western European and North American values, which may or may not be helpful in understanding people in other cultures (Feist & Feist, 1998). For example, the concepts of ego and self that are so central to Freud's personality theory (and the theories of his followers) are based on the self-oriented values of individualist cultures and thus may be less illustrative of personality development in the more collectivist cultures of, say, Asia and Africa (Triandis, 1997).

Freud's conclusions may have been distorted by other biases as well. Jeffrey Masson (1984) argued that Freud was afraid to accept his patients' accounts of sexual abuse by their parents because doing so would have brought him into conflict with those parents, many of whom had power and influence in Vienna. Instead, claimed Masson, Freud characterized the patients' reports as fantasies and wish fulfillment, not as memories of real events. Freudian scholars have largely rejected Masson's charges (Esterson, 1998), but they do acknowledge other possible problems. They note, for example, that Freud might have (unconsciously?) modified reports of what happened during therapy to better fit his theory (Esterson, 1993). He may also have asked leading questions that influenced patients to "recall" events from their childhood that never really happened (Hall, Lindzey, & Campbell, 1998). Today, there are similar concerns that some patients who recover allegedly repressed memories about childhood sexual abuse by parents may actually be reporting false memories implanted by their therapists (Ofshe & Watters, 1994).

Freud's focus on male psychosexual development and his notion that females envy male anatomy have also caused both female and male feminists to reject some or all of his ideas. In the tradition of Karen Horney, some contemporary female neo-Freudians have proposed theories that focus specifically on the psychosexual development of women (Sayers, 1991).

Finally, as judged by contemporary standards, Freud's theory is not very scientific. His definitions of id, ego, unconscious conflict, and other concepts lack the precision required for scientific measurement and testing (Feist & Feist, 1998). His belief that human beings are driven mainly by unconscious instinctual desires ignores evidence that much human behavior goes beyond instinct gratification. The conscious drive to attain personal, social, and spiritual goals is also an important determinant of behavior, as is learning from others.

Some of the weaknesses in Freudian theory have been addressed by those who have altered some of Freud's concepts and devoted more attention to social influences on personality. Attempts have also been made to increase precision and objectivity in the measurement of psychodynamic concepts (e.g., Barber, Crits-Christoph, & Paul, 1993). Research on psychodynamic theory is indeed becoming more sophisticated and increasingly reflects interest in subjecting psychodynamic principles to experimental tests (e.g., Hardaway, 1990). Still, the psychodynamic approach is better known for generating hypotheses about personality than for scientifically testing them. Accordingly, this approach to personality is less popular today than it was in past decades (Hall, Lindzey, & Campbell, 1998; Robins, Gosling, & Craik, 1999).

THE TRAIT APPROACH

If you were to describe the personality of someone you know, you would probably make a small number of descriptive statements. For example:

She is a truly caring person, a real extravert. She is generous with her time, and she works very hard at everything she does. Yet, sometimes I think she also lacks self-confidence. She is submissive to other people's demands because she wants to be accepted by them.

In other words, most people describe others by referring to the kind of people they are ("extravert") and to the thoughts, feelings, and actions that are most typical of them ("caring," "lacks self-confidence," "works very hard"), or to their needs ("wants to be accepted"). Together, these statements describe personality *traits*—the inclinations or tendencies that help to direct how a person usually thinks and behaves (Johnson, 1997).

The trait approach to personality makes three basic assumptions:

1. Personality traits are relatively stable and therefore predictable over time. Thus, a gentle person tends to stay that way day after day, year after year (Costa & McCrae, 1997).

2. Personality traits are relatively stable across situations, and they can explain why people act in predictable ways in many different settings. A person who is fiercely competitive at work will probably be competitive on the tennis court or at a party.

3. People differ with regard to how much of a particular personality trait they possess; no two people are exactly alike on all traits. The result is an endless variety of unique human personalities.

In short, the **trait approach** views personality as the combination of stable internal characteristics that people display consistently over time and across situations (Carver & Scheier, 1996).

Traits Versus Types   Theories about differences in personality characteristics among people go back at least as far as Hippocrates, a physician of ancient Greece. He suggested that a certain temperament, or basic behavioral tendency, is associated with each of four bodily fluids, or humors: blood, phlegm, black bile, and yellow bile. Personality, said Hippocrates, depends on how much of each humor a person has. His terms for the four humor-driven personalities—sanguine (optimistic), phlegmatic (slow, lethargic), melancholic (sad, depressive), and choleric (angry, irritable)—still survive today.

Notice that Hippocrates described personality *types*, not traits. A *type* is a discrete category; when people are "typed," they belong to one class or another—such as male or female. Type theories of personality thus try to place people in one category or another. There have been other type theories since Hippocrates. For example, an American physician and psychologist named William Sheldon promoted *physiognomy*—the study of the link between personality and physique. To test his theory,

Sheldon obtained nude and seminude photographs of thousands of college students and correlated body measurements taken from the pictures with personality-related data such as career choice and success in life. Among the students who participated in his studies were George Bush, Hillary Rodham Clinton, and Meryl Streep (Rosenbaum, 1995).

Physiognomy was abandoned by almost all psychologists when they discovered that the dazzling range of human personalities cannot be compressed into a few types based on facial or bodily characteristics. Echoes of type theories can still be found, however. One example is the Myers-Briggs personality test, which is based on Jung's (1933) system of sixteen personality types. Although this test is quite popular among nonpsychologists, its validity has been questioned by many personality researchers (Aiken, 1996).

Prominent Trait Theories

Rather than looking for discrete personality types, trait theorists measure the relative strength of the many personality characteristics appearing in each individual (see Figure 14.2).

Allport's Trait Theory   Gordon Allport (1961) spent thirty years searching for the traits that combine to form the normal personality. He found nearly 18,000 dictionary terms that can be used to describe human behavior (Allport & Odbert, 1936; Block, 1995), but he noticed that many of these terms referred to the same thing (for instance, "hostile," "nasty," and "mean" all convey a similar meaning). Accordingly, if you were

FIGURE 14.2

Two Personality Profiles

From the trait perspective, personality is like a fabric of many different-colored threads, some bright, some dull, some thick, some thin, which are never woven together in exactly the same combination twice. Here are trait profiles for Rodney, an inner-city social worker, and James, a sales clerk in a department store. Compared with James, Rodney is about equally industrious, more generous, and less nervous, extraverted, and aggressive.

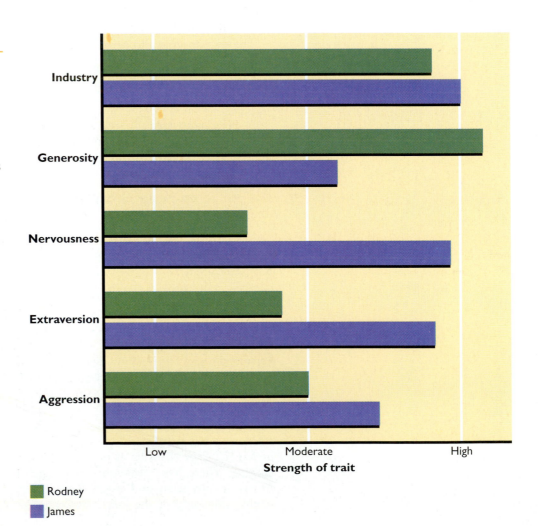

to think of a close relative and quickly jot down the personality traits that describe him or her, you would probably be able to capture your relative's personality using only about seven trait labels. Allport believed that the set of labels chosen to describe a particular person reflects that person's *central traits*, those that are usually apparent to others and comprise characteristics that organize and control behavior in many different situations. Central traits are roughly equivalent to the descriptive terms used in letters of recommendation ("reliable" or "distractible," for example) that are meant to convey what can be expected from a person most of the time (Schultz & Schultz, 2000). Allport also believed that people possess *secondary traits,* those that are more specific to certain situations and control far less behavior. "Dislikes crowds" is an example of a secondary trait.

Allport's research helped to lay the foundation for modern research on personality traits. However, his strong emphasis on the uniqueness of each individual personality made it difficult to draw conclusions about the structure of human personality in general (McAdams, 1997).

Eysenck's Biological Trait Theory   British psychologist Hans Eysenck (pronounced "EYE-sink") used a statistical technique called *factor analysis* to study the structure of both normal and disordered personalities. Factor analysis can reveal, for example, whether someone who is moody is also likely to be anxious, rigid, and unsociable. From his research, Eysenck (1990a, 1990b) concluded that personality can be described in terms of three basic factors or dimensions:

1. *Introversion-extraversion*   Extraverts are sociable and outgoing, enjoy parties and other social activities, take risks, and love excitement and change. Introverts tend to be quiet, thoughtful, and reserved, enjoying solitary pursuits and avoiding excitement and social involvement.

2. *Emotionality-stability*   At one extreme of emotionality-stability are people who exhibit such characteristics as moodiness, restlessness, worry, anxiety, and other negative emotions. People at the opposite end of this dimension are calm, even-tempered, relaxed, and emotionally stable. (This dimension is also often called *neuroticism.*)

3. *Psychoticism*   People high on psychoticism show such attributes as cruelty, hostility, coldness, oddness, and rejection of social customs. Those low on psychoticism do not show these attributes.

Extraversion in Action

This street entertainer enjoys showing off his skills while bantering with the audience. He would probably score high on extraversion if he were to take the Eysenck Personality Inventory.

Eysenck believed that personality traits are determined mainly in terms of where a person falls along these three dimensions, especially introversion-extraversion and emotionality-stability. He presented data to show that scores on tests measuring these dimensions—such as the Eysenck Personality Inventory—can predict people's key characteristics, including specific behavior disorders (see Figure 14.3). Criminals, for example, are likely to be in the "choleric" quadrant and tend to display restless, aggressive, and impulsive behavior. People with anxiety disorders tend to be in the "melancholic" quadrant.

Eysenck argued that variation in personality characteristics can be traced to inherited differences in the brain. These biological differences, he said, explain why some people are more physiologically aroused than others. For example, people who inherit a nervous system with a chronically low level of arousal will be relatively insensitive to the effects of rewards and punishments, and therefore will not readily develop conditioned responses, including conditioned fears. Without such fears, said Eysenck, they will not easily learn to play by society's rules. Further, having a low arousal level may lead such people to look constantly for excitement and change in order to increase their arousal; in short, they will be extraverted. In contrast, Eysenck's theory predicts that people with sensitive, "overaroused" nervous systems are likely to be strongly affected by rewards and punishments, to readily develop conditioned responses such as fears and oversensitivities, and to avoid excessive stimulation—in other words, to be introverted.

The "Big-Five" Model of Personality

In recent years, trait approaches have continued to focus on identifying and describing the core structure of personality. This work owes much to Allport and Eysenck, as well as to Raymond Cattell, another British psychologist. Cattell asked people to rate themselves and other people on many of the trait-descriptive terms identified by Allport. He believed that certain traits would tend to cluster together because they reflect a basic dimension, or *factor*, of personality on which all people can be compared. Using factor

FIGURE 14.3

Eysenck's Major Personality Dimensions

According to Eysenck, varying degrees of emotionality-stability and introversion-extraversion combine to produce predictable trait patterns. For example, an introverted but stable person is likely to be controlled and reliable, whereas an introverted but emotional person is likely to be rigid and anxious. Note that the traits appearing in the quadrants created by crossing these two personality dimensions correspond roughly to Hippocrates' four temperaments.

Source: Eysenck & Rachman, 1965.

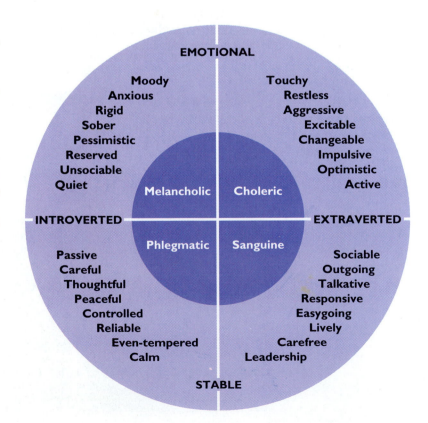

"Personality" Traits in Animals

The notion that personality can be described along five main dimensions is supported not only by research on the "big-five" traits seen in humans, but also by research that has revealed five related, though not identical, traits in some nonhuman species. One observational study of spotted hyenas found, for example, that they differ from one another in terms of dominance, excitability, agreeableness (toward humans), sociability (toward each other), and curiosity. Some of these same traits have also been observed in chimpanzees and other primates (Gosling, 1998).

analysis, Cattell eventually identified sixteen such factors, including shy versus bold, trusting versus suspicious, and relaxed versus tense. Cattell believed that these *common traits* are found in everyone, and he measured their strength through a test called the *Sixteen Personality Factor Questionnaire*, or *16PF* (Cattell, Eber, & Tatsuoka, 1970).

Subsequent factor analyses by researchers such as Paul Costa and Robert McCrae (1992) have led many trait theorists to believe that personality is organized around only five basic factors (Wiggins & Trapnell, 1997). The components of this so-called **big-five** or **five-factor model** of personality are Openness, Conscientiousness, Extraversion, Agreeableness, and Neuroticism (see Table 14.2). The importance of the "big-five" is underscored by the fact that different investigators find these factors (or a set very similar to them) when they factor-analyze data from numerous sources, including personality inventories, peer ratings of personality characteristics, and checklists of descriptive adjectives (Costa & McCrae, 1995; Goldberg & Saucier, 1995). These factors emerge even from participants' ratings of how well drawings of people in social and solitary situations described the participants' own personalities (Paunonen et al., 1992). The fact that some version of the "big-five" factors reliably

TABLE 14.2

Descriptors of the Big-Five Personality Dimensions

Here is a list of the adjectives that define the big-five personality factors. You can more easily remember the names of these factors by noting that their first letters spell the word *ocean*.

Dimension	Defining Descriptors
Openness to experience	Artistic, curious, imaginative, insightful, original, wide interests, unusual thought processes, intellectual interests
Conscientiousness	Efficient, organized, planful, reliable, thorough, dependable, ethical, productive
Extraversion	Active, assertive, energetic, outgoing, talkative, gesturally expressive, gregarious
Agreeableness	Appreciative, forgiving, generous, kind, trusting, noncritical, warm, compassionate, considerate, straightforward
Neuroticism	Anxious, self-pitying, tense, emotionally unstable, impulsive, vulnerable, touchy, worrying

Source: Adapted from McCrae & John, 1992.

appears in many countries and cultures—including Canada, China, Germany, Finland, India, Japan, Korea, the Philippines, and Poland (Benet-Martinez & John, in press; McCrae & Costa, 1997; Narayanan, Menon, & Levine, 1995; Paunonen et al., 1992; Yang & Bond, 1990)—provides further evidence that these few dimensions may represent the basic components of human personality.

Many trait theorists believe that the big-five model represents a major breakthrough in examining the personalities of people who come from different backgrounds, are of different ages, and live in different parts of the world (Goldberg, 1995). It has certainly enabled psychologists to provide a comprehensive description of the basic similarities and differences in people's personalities.

Family Resemblance

Do children inherit personality traits from their parents in the same direct way as they may inherit facial features, coloration, and other physical characteristics? Research in behavioral genetics suggests that personality is the joint product of genetically influenced behavioral tendencies and the environmental conditions each child encounters.

THINKING CRITICALLY

Are Personality Traits Inherited?

Where do the "big-five" factors or other personality traits come from? Do they arise, as some personality psychologists suggest, from our genes? Consider the case of a pair of twins who were separated at five weeks of age and did not meet again for thirty-nine years. Both men drove Chevrolets, chain-smoked the same brand of cigarettes, had divorced a woman named Linda, were remarried to a woman named Betty, had sons named James Allan, had dogs named Toy, enjoyed similar hobbies, and had served as sheriff's deputies (Tellegen et al., 1988).

■ What am I being asked to believe or accept?

Cases like this have helped focus the attention of behavioral geneticists on the possibility that some core aspects of personality might be partly, or even largely, inherited (Rowe, 1997).

■ What evidence is available to support the assertion?

The evidence and the arguments regarding this assertion are much like those presented in Chapter 10, where we discuss the origins of differences in mental abilities. Anecdotes about children who seem to "have" their parents' or grandparents' bad temper, generosity, or shyness are often presented in support of the heritability of personality. Indeed, resemblances in personality among family members do provide one important source of evidence. Several studies have found moderate but significant correlations between children's personality test scores and those of their parents and siblings (Davis, Luce, & Kraus, 1994; Loehlin, 1992).

Stronger evidence comes from studies conducted around the world comparing identical twins raised together, identical twins raised apart, nonidentical twins raised together, and nonidentical twins raised apart (e.g., Saudino, 1998; Waller & Shaver, 1994). Irrespective of whether they are raised apart or together, identical twins (who have exactly the same genes) tend to be more alike in personality than nonidentical twins (whose genes are no more similar than those of other siblings). Further, research consistently shows that identical twins are more alike than nonidentical twins in general temperament, such as how active, sociable, anxious, and emotional they are (Buss, 1995; Rowe, 1997). On the basis of such twin studies, behavioral geneticists have concluded that at least 30 percent and perhaps as much as 60 percent of the variability in adult personality traits is due to genetic factors (Brody & Ehrlichman, 1998).

■ Are there alternative ways of interpreting the evidence?

Family resemblances in personality could reflect genetic or social influence. An obvious alternative interpretation of this evidence, then, might be that family similarities come not from common genes but from a common environment, especially from the modeling that parents and siblings provide. Children learn many rules, skills, and behaviors by watching those around them; perhaps they learn their personalities as well. The fact that nontwin siblings are less alike than twins may well result from what are called *nonshared environments* (Plomin, 1994). A child's place in the family birth order, differences in the way parents treat each of their children, and accidents and illnesses that alter a particular child's life or health are examples of nonshared factors that can have a differential impact on each individual. Nontwins are more likely than twins, especially identical twins, to be affected by nonshared environmental factors.

■ What additional evidence would help to evaluate the alternatives?

One way to evaluate the degree to which personality is inherited would be to study people in infancy, before the environment has had a chance to exert its influence. If the environment were entirely responsible for personality, newborn infants should be essentially alike. However, as discussed in Chapter 12, newborns do show differences in temperament—varying markedly in amount of activity, sensitivity to the environment, tendency to cry, and interest in new stimuli (Buss, 1995). These differences suggest biological and perhaps genetic influences.

To evaluate the relative contributions of nature and nurture beyond infancy, psychologists have examined characteristics of adopted children. An argument for genetic influences on personality is more plausible if adopted children are more like their biological than their adoptive parents. If they are more like their adoptive family, a strong role for environmental factors in personality would be suggested. In actuality, adopted children's personalities tend to resemble the personalities of their biological parents and siblings more than those of the families in which they are raised (Carey & DiLalla, 1994; Loehlin, 1992).

Despite this finding, further research is needed to determine more clearly what aspects of the environment are most important in shaping personality. Thus far, most investigators conclude that elements of the shared environment—factors such as socioeconomic status that affect all children in the same family to varying degrees—do not appear to be responsible for the strong personality similarities that have been observed among identical twins. As noted above, however, nonshared environmental influences appear to be very important in personality development (Halverson & Wampler, 1997; Plomin, 1994). Indeed, some researchers believe that such influences must be considered even in the context of explaining the greater similarities between identical twins reared apart than among nontwin siblings reared together. As of yet, however, the exact impact on personality development of nonshared environmental factors that may be different for twins and nontwin siblings has not been fully or systematically examined. Additional research on the role of nonshared factors in personality development and the ways in which these factors might differentially affect twin and nontwin siblings' development is obviously vital. It will also be important to investigate the ways in which the personalities of individual children may affect the nature of the environment in which they are raised (Halverson & Wampler, 1997; see also the behavioral genetics appendix).

■ What conclusions are most reasonable?

Even those researchers, such as Robert Plomin, who support genetic theories of personality caution that we should not replace "simple-minded environmentalism" with the equally incorrect view that personality is almost completely biologically determined (Plomin, Chipuer, & Loehlin, 1990). As with mental abilities, it is pointless to talk about heredity *versus* environment as causes of personality because nature and nurture always intertwine to exert joint and simultaneous influences. With this caution in mind, we would be well advised to draw rather tentative conclusions about the sources of personality.

The evidence available so far suggests that genetic influences do appear to contribute significantly to the differences among people in many personality traits. However, understanding the implications of such a statement is important. First, the genetic contribution to personality most likely comes in the form of physical

The Trait Approach in the Courtroom

The trait approach to personality is highlighted in the courtroom, where defense attorneys try to show that their clients are not the type of people who would commit certain acts and where lawyers on both sides seek to disqualify jurors who display traits suggesting that they might be unsympathetic to their case. This was certainly the approach taken in a 1997 trial in Boston when attorney Andrew Good, shown here with his client, defended British au pair Louise Woodward against charges that she killed Matthew Eappen, an 8-month-old baby in her care. The jury found her guilty of second-degree murder, but the judge reduced the charge to manslaughter and sentenced her to time already served while awaiting trial.

characteristics and general predispositions toward certain temperaments, as measured by levels of activity, emotionality, and sociability (Buss, 1995). These physical characteristics and temperaments then interact with environmental factors such as family experiences to produce specific features of personality. Thus, children who inherit a frail body and/or high emotionality might play less with other children, withdraw from social interactions, and thereby fail to learn important social skills (Eisenberg, Fabes, & Murphy, 1995). These experiences and tendencies, in turn, might foster the self-consciousness and shyness seen in introverted personalities.

Note, however, that genetic predispositions toward particular personality characteristics may or may not appear in behavior, depending on whether the environment supports or suppresses them. Changes in genetically predisposed traits are not only possible, they may actually be quite common as children develop (Kagan & Snidman, 1991). For example, there is a strong genetic basis for shyness, but many children learn to overcome this tendency and become rather outgoing (Rowe, 1997). Even the personalities of identical twins become less similar over time as they are exposed to differing environmental experiences (McCartney, Harris, & Bernieri, 1990). It appears that rather than inheriting specific traits, people inherit raw materials out of which personality is shaped by the world.

Evaluation of the Trait Approach

The trait approach, especially the big-five model, has gained such wide acceptance that it tends to dominate contemporary research in personality. Yet there are several problems and weaknesses associated with this approach.

For one thing, trait theories seem better at describing people than at understanding them. It is easy to say, for example, that Michelle is nasty to others because she has a strong hostility trait; but other factors, such as the way people treat her, could also be responsible. In short, trait theories say a lot about *how* people behave, but they don't always explain *why* (Funder, 1993; Pervin, 1996). Trait theories also don't say much about how traits are related to the thoughts and feelings that precede, accompany, and follow behavior. Do introverts and extraverts *decide* to act as they do, can they behave otherwise, and how do they feel about their actions and experiences? (Mischel & Shoda, 1995). Some personality psychologists are currently trying to link their research with that of cognitive psychologists in an effort to better understand how thoughts and emotions influence, and are influenced by, personality traits (Snyder & Cantor, 1998).

The trait approach has also been faulted for offering a short list of traits of varying strengths providing, at best, a static and superficial description of personality that fails to capture how traits combine to form a complex and dynamic individual (Block, 1995; McAdams, 1997). Even if the big-five model of personality is correct and universal, its factors are not all-powerful; situations also affect behavior. Thus, people high in extraversion are not always gregarious; whether they behave sociably depends, in part, on where they are and who else may be present.

In fairness, the earliest trait theorists, such as Gordon Allport, did implicitly acknowledge the importance of situations in influencing behavior, but it is only recently that consideration of person-situation interactions have become an explicit part of trait-based approaches to personality. This change is largely the result of research conducted by psychologists who have taken a social-cognitive approach to personality.

THE SOCIAL-COGNITIVE APPROACH

According to the psychodynamic and trait approaches, personality consists of inner dynamics or traits that guide thoughts, feelings, and behavior. In contrast, those taking a **social-cognitive approach** view personality mainly as the array of behaviors that people acquire through learning and display in particular situations. Some aspects of this approach reflect a traditional behavioral assumption—namely, that all behaviors are learned through classical and operant conditioning. However, we shall see that the social-cognitive approach expands that original scope by emphasizing (1) the role of *learned patterns of thought* in guiding our actions and (2) the fact that much of personality is learned in *social situations* through interaction with and observation of other people, including family members (Mischel & Shoda, 1998; Rotter, 1990). Accordingly, this approach is sometimes called the *social-learning* approach; it views personality as the sum total of the behaviors and cognitive habits that develop as people learn through experience in the social world.

Roots of the Social-Cognitive Approach

Elements of the social-cognitive approach can be traced back to John B. Watson. As noted in Chapter 1, Watson (1924) used research on classical conditioning to support his claim that all human behavior, from mental disorder to scientific skill, is determined by learning. B. F. Skinner widened the behavioral approach by emphasizing the importance of operant conditioning in learning. Through what he called **functional analysis,** Skinner sought to understand behavior in terms of the function it serves in obtaining rewards or avoiding punishment. For example, if observation of a schoolboy's aggressive behavior reveals that it occurs mainly when a teacher is present to break up fights, it may be that the aggression is being rewarded by the teacher's attention. Rather than describing personality traits, then, functional analysis summarizes what people find rewarding or punishing, what they are capable of, and what skills they lack.

Once the hallmark of the behavioral approach to personality, classical and operant conditioning principles are still considered vitally important in the development of behavior. However, much as Freud's followers challenged some of his original ideas, many proponents of the behavioral approach became dissatisfied with what they saw as its overly narrow focus on observable behaviors and its lack of attention to the role of thoughts in guiding behavior. The social-cognitive approach to personality resulted from their efforts over the last two decades to address these perceived deficiencies.

Proponents of this very popular approach to personality seek to assess and understand how learned patterns of thought contribute to behavior and how behavior and its consequences alter cognitive activity as well as future actions. In dealing with the aggressive schoolboy, for example, these theorists would want to know not only what he has learned to do under particular circumstances (and how he learned it) but also what he thinks about himself, his teachers, his behavior—and his expectations about each (Mischel & Shoda, 1998).

Prominent Social-Cognitive Theories

Among the most influential social-cognitive or social-learning theories are those of Julian Rotter, Albert Bandura, and Walter Mischel.

Rotter's Expectancy Theory   Rotter (1982) argued that learning creates cognitive expectancies that guide behavior. Specifically, he suggested that a person's decision to engage in a behavior is determined by (1) what the person expects to happen following the behavior and (2) the value the person places on the outcome. For example, people spend a lot of money on clothes to be worn at a job interview because (1) past learning leads them to expect that doing so will help get them the job, and (2) they place a high value on having the job. To Rotter, then, behavior is determined not only by the rewarding consequences Skinner emphasized but also by a cognitive *expectation* that a particular behavior will obtain that reward (Mayer & Sutton, 1996).

Rotter also suggested that people learn general ways of thinking about the world, especially about how life's rewards and punishments are controlled. Some people (*internals*) are more inclined to expect events to be controlled by their own efforts. That is, what they achieve and the reinforcements they obtain are seen as due to efforts they make themselves. Others (*externals*) are more inclined to expect events to be determined by external forces over which they have no control. When "externals" succeed, they are likely to believe that the success was due to chance or luck.

Differences in these generalized expectancies can produce differences in behavior (Rotter, 1990). For example, internally oriented individuals tend to get better grades and to score higher on standardized academic tests than externals (Mayer & Sutton, 1996). Internals are also somewhat more likely than externals to work at staying healthy. They are less likely to smoke and drink, and more likely to exercise and to wear seat belts (Maddux, 1993; Phares, 1991). One study has even shown that alcoholics with an internal orientation toward their drinking are more likely to abstain than are those with an external orientation (Clements, York, & Rohrer, 1995).

Bandura and Reciprocal Determinism   In his social-learning theory, Albert Bandura (1997) has emphasized the complex and constant interaction among patterns

LINKAGES

Expecting Incentives

As noted in Chapter 11, incentive theories of motivation emphasize the role of paychecks and external goals in explaining a wide range of behavior, from physical labor to diligent studying. Incentives also lie at the heart of Rotter's expectancy theory of personality.

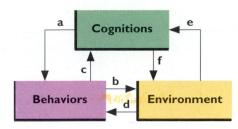

FIGURE 14.4

Reciprocal Determinism

Bandura's model of reciprocal determinism suggests that hostile thinking can lead to hostile behavior (line a), which in turn can intensify hostile thoughts (line c). At the same time, hostile behavior is likely to offend others and create an environment of anger (line b), which calls forth even more negative thoughts and actions (lines d and e). These negative thoughts then alter perceptions, making the environment seem more threatening (line f).

of thought, the environment, and behavior. He points out that whether people learn through direct experience with rewards and punishments or through the observational learning processes described in Chapter 6, their behavior tends to affect their environment, which in turn may affect cognitions, which then may affect behavior, and so on. In short, personality is shaped by what he calls *reciprocal determinism* (see Figure 14.4).

One cognitive element in this web of influence is especially important in Bandura's view: **self-efficacy**, which is the learned expectation of success, the belief that you can successfully perform a certain behavior regardless of past failures or current obstacles. Bandura says that overt behavior is largely controlled by individuals' expectations of their ability to perform. The higher a person's self-efficacy regarding a particular situation or task, the greater will be the actual accomplishments in that situation (Maddux, in press). Thus, going to a job interview with the belief that you have the skills necessary to be hired may help you get the job or, at least, help blunt the impact of rejection.

Self-efficacy about a specific action may interact with expectancies about the outcome of behavior in general, leading to a result that helps shape a person's psychological well-being (Bandura, 1986; Cozzarelli, 1993). Figure 14.5 shows how different interactions among these kinds of cognitions produce different emotions and outcomes. For example, if a person has little self-efficacy and also expects that nothing anyone does has much effect on the world, apathy may result. But if a person with low self-efficacy believes that other people are enjoying the benefits of their efforts, the result may be self-disparagement and depression.

Mischel and Cognitive Processes   Social-cognitive theorists maintain that learned beliefs or expectancies characterize each individual and make that individual different from other people. Walter Mischel calls these characteristics *cognitive person variables*; he believes that they outline the dimensions along which individuals differ (Mischel & Shoda, 1998).

The most important cognitive person variables, according to Mischel, are (1) competencies (the thoughts and actions the person can perform); (2) perceptions (how the person perceives the environment); (3) expectations (what the person expects to follow from various behaviors and what the person believes he or she is capable of doing—again, a matter of self-efficacy); (4) subjective values (the person's ideals and goals); and (5) self-regulation and plans (the person's standards for self-reward and plans for reaching goals) (Mischel & Shoda, 1995).

To best predict how a person might behave, says Mischel, we need to know about these cognitive person variables as well as about the features of the situation the person will face. In short, the person and the situation interact to produce behavior. Mischel does not see his theory as inconsistent with the trait approach, but he does distinguish between cognitive person variables and traditional personality traits. Indeed, his early pessimism about the value of traits as explanations of behavior sparked an intense debate between social-cognitive and trait theorists about whether personality traits or situational factors were more influential in guiding behavior. This debate

FIGURE 14.5

Self-Efficacy and Psychological Well-Being

According to Bandura, if people with high self-efficacy perceive the environment as unresponsive to their best efforts, they may become resentful and socially active. If they perceive the environment as responsive to their efforts, they are more likely to be both active and self-assured.

Source: Bandura, 1982.

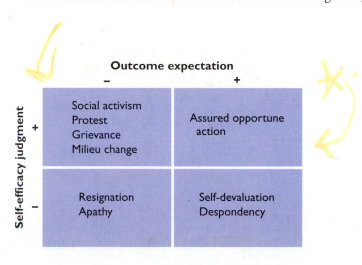

The Impact of Situations

Like the rest of us, professional wrestler Jesse Ventura tends to behave differently in different situations, such as in the ring and in the office where he serves as governor of Minnesota. Mischel's theory of personality underscores the importance of such person-situation interactions in determining behavior.

produced no clear winners, and advocates of both approaches have recently begun to focus on the similarities between the theories rather than on the differences (Mischel & Shoda, 1998; Wiggins, 1997). This trend toward reconciliation has helped to clarify the relationship between personal and situational variables and how they affect behavior under various conditions. Many of the conclusions that have emerged are consistent with Bandura's concept of reciprocal determinism:

1. Personal dispositions (which include traits and cognitive person variables) influence behavior only in relevant situations. The trait of anxiousness, for example, may be predictive of anxiety, but only in situations where the person feels threatened.

2. Personal dispositions can lead to behaviors that alter situations that, in turn, promote other behaviors. Thus, a hostile child can elicit aggression in others and, in turn, precipitate a fight.

3. People choose to be in situations that are in accord with their personal dispositions. Introverts, for instance, are more likely to choose quiet environments, whereas extraverts tend to seek out livelier, more social circumstances.

4. Personal dispositions are more important in some situations than in others. In ambiguous or unconstrained situations—a picnic, for example—people's behavior may be predicted from their dispositions (extraverts will probably play games and socialize while introverts watch). However, in socially constrained situations such as a funeral, personal dispositions will not differentiate one person from another; all are likely to be quiet and somber.

Today, social-cognitive theorists devote much of their research to examining how cognitive person variables develop, how they are related to stress and health, and how they interact with situational variables to affect behavior.

Evaluation of the Social-Cognitive Approach

The traditional behavioral perspective on personality appealed to many people. It offered an objective, experimentally oriented approach that operationally defined its concepts, relied on empirical data for its basic principles, and based its applications on the results of empirical research (Pervin, 1996). However, its successor, the social-cognitive approach, has gained even wider acceptance because it expands the applications of learning principles and the concept of reciprocal determinism to such socially important areas as aggression, the effects of mass media on children, and the development of self-regulatory processes that enhance personal control over behavior. The popularity of this approach also stems from the ease with which its principles can be translated into treatment procedures for many types of psychological disorders (Goldfried & Davison, 1994).

Still, the social-cognitive approach has not escaped criticism. Theories that primarily emphasize learning processes are accused of reducing human beings to a set of learned responses derived solely from relationships with the environment. This view, critics say, is too narrow, minimizes the importance of subjective experience, fails to consider unconscious processes, neglects the contribution of emotion to personality, and tends to exclude genetic, physiological, and other influences not based on learning. Social-cognitive theories have addressed some of these objections through their emphasis on expectancies, self-efficacy, and cognitive person variables, but they are still criticized by some for failing to capture the complexities and richness of human personalities (Hall, Lindzey, & Campbell, 1998). According to such critics, a far more palatable alternative is provided by the phenomenological approach to personality.

THE PHENOMENOLOGICAL APPROACH

Suppose you and a friend meet someone new at a party. Comparing notes later, you discover a major discrepancy in your reactions. You thought the new person was entertaining and warm and showed a genuine interest in others. Your friend saw the same person as a "phony" who merely pretended to be interested. How can two people draw such opposite conclusions from the same conversation? Perhaps it was not the same conversation. Just as each person sees something different in a cloud formation, each of you perceived a different reality, a different conversation, and a different person.

This interpretation reflects the **phenomenological approach** to personality, which maintains that the way people perceive and interpret the world forms their personalities and guides their behavior. Proponents of this view emphasize the fact that, as noted in the chapter on perception, each individual perceives reality somewhat differently, and these differences—rather than instincts, traits, or learning experiences—are central to understanding human personality (Kelly, 1980). From this perspective, no one can understand another person without somehow perceiving the world through that

LINKAGES

What Is Reality?

Everyone present probably has somewhat differing perceptions about what actually happened during the play that precipitated this argument. The disagreement illustrates the phenomenological notion that each person's perceptions of the world shape personality and guide behavior. As described in Chapter 5, those perceptions are often influenced by top-down processing; in this case, expectations and motivation stemming from differing team loyalties are likely to influence reality—and reactions—for each side's players, coaches, and fans.

person's eyes. All behavior, even if it looks bizarre, is meaningful to the person displaying it. Unlike theories that emphasize the instincts and learning processes that humans and lower animals seem to have in common, the phenomenological approach focuses on mental qualities that set humans apart: self-awareness, creativity, planning, decision making, and responsibility. For this reason, the phenomenological approach is also called the *humanistic* view of personality.

This approach to personality has many roots. The idea that each person perceives a different reality reflects the views of existential philosophers such as Kierkegaard and Sartre. That people actively shape their own reality stems in part from the Gestalt psychologists whose work is described in Chapter 5. We can also hear echoes of Adler and other psychodynamic theorists who emphasized the positive aspects of human nature and the importance of the ego in personality development.

According to the phenomenological approach, the primary human motivator is an innate drive toward growth that prompts people to fulfill their unique and natural potential. Like the planted seed that naturally becomes a flower, people are inclined toward goodness, creativity, love, and joy.

Prominent Phenomenological Theories

By far, the most prominent phenomenological theories of personality are those of Carl Rogers and Abraham Maslow.

Rogers' Self Theory   The name of Carl Rogers is almost synonymous with the phenomenological approach (Rogers, 1961, 1970, 1980). Rogers assumed that each person responds as an organized whole to reality as he or she perceives it. He emphasized the **actualizing tendency,** which he described as an innate inclination toward growth and fulfillment that motivates all human behavior. To Rogers, personality is the expression of each individual's actualizing tendency as it unfolds in that individual's uniquely perceived reality (Hall, Lindzey, & Campbell, 1998).

Central to Rogers' theory is the *self,* the part of experience that a person identifies as "I" or "me." According to Rogers, those who accurately experience the self—with all its preferences, abilities, fantasies, shortcomings, and desires—are on the road to *self-actualization.* The progress of those whose experiences of the self become distorted, however, is likely to be slowed or stopped.

Seeking Self-Actualization

According to Rogers, conditions of worth can make it harder for children to become aware of and accept aspects of themselves that conflict with their parents' values. Progress toward self-actualization may be enhanced by associating with those whose positive regard is not conditional on displaying any particular pattern of behavior.

The Joys of a Growth Orientation

Maslow's humanistic theory of personality says the key to personal growth and fulfillment lies in focusing on the skills and experiences that we have, not on the material possessions we do not have.

Very early in life, children learn to need other people's approval or, as Rogers called it, *positive regard.* As a result, evaluations by parents, teachers, and others begin to affect children's self-evaluations. When evaluations by others concur with a child's own evaluation, the child's genuine reaction matches, or is *congruent* with, self-experience. The child not only feels the others' positive regard but also evaluates the self as "good" for having earned approval. The result is a clearly identified and positively evaluated experience of the self. This self-experience becomes part of the self-concept, which is the way one thinks of oneself. Unfortunately, things may not always go so smoothly. If a pleasurable self-experience is evaluated negatively by others, a child must either do without their positive regard or reevaluate the experience. Thus, a little boy who is teased by his parents because he enjoys playing with dolls might adopt a distorted self-experience ("I don't like dolls" or "Feeling good is bad").

In other words, personality is shaped partly by the actualizing tendency and partly by others' evaluations. In this way, people come to like what they are "supposed" to like and to behave as they are "supposed" to behave. Although this process is adaptive, allowing people to get along in society, it often requires that they stifle their actualizing tendency and distort experience. Rogers argued that psychological discomfort, anxiety, or mental disorder can result when the feelings people experience or express are *incongruent* with their true feelings.

Incongruence is likely, said Rogers, when parents and teachers lead a child to believe that his or her worth as a person depends on displaying the "right" attitudes, behaviors, and values. These **conditions of worth** are created whenever *people* are evaluated instead of their behavior. For example, parents who find their toddler smearing Jell-O on the kitchen floor are unlikely to say, "I love you, but I do not approve of this particular behavior." They are more likely to shout, "Bad boy!" or "Bad girl!" thus suggesting that the child is lovable and worthwhile only when well behaved. As a result, the child's self-experience is not "I like smearing Jell-O but Mom and Dad don't approve" but, instead, "Playing with Jell-O is bad, and I am bad if I like it, so I don't like it," or "I like it, so I must be bad." The child may eventually display neat and tidy behaviors that do not reflect the real self but, rather, are part of the ideal self dictated by the parents.

Like Freud's concept of superego, conditions of worth are first set up by external pressure but eventually become part of the person's belief system. Thus, to Rogers, rewards and punishments are important in personality development not just because they shape behavior but also because they can so easily create distorted self-perceptions and incongruence.

Maslow's Humanistic Psychology   Like Rogers, Abraham Maslow (1954, 1971) saw personality as the expression of a basic human tendency toward growth and self-actualization. Maslow believed that self-actualization is not just a human capacity but a human need; as shown in Figure 11.9 on page 384, he described it as the highest in a hierarchy of motives, or needs. Yet, said Maslow, people are often distracted from seeking self-actualization because of needs that are lower on the hierarchy.

Maslow saw most people as controlled by a **deficiency orientation**, a preoccupation with perceived needs for material things. Ultimately, he said, deficiency-oriented people come to perceive life as a meaningless exercise in disappointment and boredom, and they may begin to behave in problematic ways. For example, in an attempt to satisfy the need for love and belongingness, people may focus on what love can give them (security), not on what they can give to another. This deficiency orientation may lead a person to be jealous and to focus on what is missing in relationships; as a result, the person will never truly experience either love or security.

In contrast, people with a **growth orientation** do not focus on what is missing but draw satisfaction from what they have, what they are, and what they can do. This orientation opens the door to what Maslow called *peak experiences,* in which people feel joy, even ecstasy, in the mere fact of being alive, being human, and knowing that they are utilizing their fullest potential.

Evaluation of the Phenomenological Approach

The phenomenological approach to personality coincides with the way many people view themselves. It gives a central role to each person's immediate experience and emphasizes the uniqueness of each individual. The best-known application of the phenomenological approach is the client-centered therapy of Carl Rogers, which is discussed in Chapter 16. The phenomenological approach has also inspired short-term group experiences, such as sensitivity training and encounter groups, designed to help people become more aware of themselves and the way they relate to others, and techniques to teach parents how to avoid creating conditions of worth while maximizing their children's potential (Gordon, 1970).

Yet to its critics, the phenomenological view is naive, romantic, and unrealistic. Are people all as inherently good and growth-oriented as this approach suggests? Phenomenologists have also been faulted for underplaying the importance of inherited characteristics, learning, situational influences, and unconscious motivation in shaping personality. The idea that everyone is directed only by an innate growth potential is viewed by critics as an oversimplification. So, too, is the assumption that all human problems stem from blocked actualization. Like the trait approach, phenomenological theories seem to do a better job of describing personality than explaining it. And like many of the concepts in psychodynamic theories, phenomenological concepts seem too vague to be tested empirically. Thus, among psychologists who rely on empirical research to learn about personality, the phenomenological approach is not favored.

Finally, the phenomenologists' tendency to define healthy people as independent and autonomous individuals may reflect culture-specific ideas about mental health that may not apply outside of North America and other Western cultures (Triandis, 1997). As described in the next section, the foundations of phenomenological self theories may be in direct conflict with the values of non-Western, collectivist cultures. ("In Review: Major Approaches to Personality" (page 506) summarizes key features of the phenomenological approach, along with those of the other approaches we have described.)

LINKAGES

Does culture determine personality?
(a link to Human Development)

LINKAGES

Personality, Culture, and Human Development

In many Western cultures, it is common to hear people encourage others to "stand up for yourself" or to "blow your own horn" in order to "get what you have coming to you." In middle-class North America, for example, the values of achievement and personal distinction are taught to children, particularly male children, very early in life (Markus & Kitayama, 1997). North American children are encouraged to feel special, to want self-esteem, and to feel good about themselves. Those who learn and display these values tend to receive praise and encouragement for doing so.

As a result of such cultural training, many people in North America and Europe develop personalities that are largely based on a sense of high self-worth. In a study by Hazel Markus and Shinobu Kitayama (1991), for example, 70 percent of a sample of U.S. students believed they were superior to their peers and 60 percent believed they were in the top 10 percent on a wide variety of personal attributes! This tendency toward self-enhancement is evident as early as age four.

Indeed, a sense of independence, uniqueness, and self-esteem is seen by many Western personality theorists as fundamental to mental health. As noted in Chapter 12, for example, Erik Erikson included the appearance of personal identity and self-esteem as part of normal psychosocial development. Middle-class Americans who fail to value and strive for independence, self-promotion, and unique personal achievement may be seen as displaying a personality disorder, some form of depression, or other psychological problems.

Working for Group Goals

In Asian cultures where collectivist values prevail, a strong sense of personal self-worth tends to be seen as a less important characteristic of personality than it is in more individualist cultures. In other words, the features of "normal" personality development vary from culture to culture.

Do these ideas reflect universal truths about personality development or, rather, the influence of the cultures that generated them? It is certainly clear that people in many non-Western cultures develop personal orientations very different from those of North Americans and Europeans (Fiske et al., 1998). In China and Japan, for example, an independent, unique self is not emphasized (Ho & Chiu, 1998). In fact, children there are encouraged to develop and maintain harmonious relations with others and *not* to stand out from the crowd, lest they diminish someone else. In the United States, people say that "the squeaky wheel gets the grease"; in Japan, they warn that "the nail that stands out gets pounded down" (Markus & Kitayama, 1997).

In contrast to the *independent* self-system prevalent in individualist cultures (e.g., the United States, Great Britain, Switzerland), countries characterized by a more collectivist orientation (e.g., Japan, China, Brazil, Nigeria) promote an *interdependent* self-system through which people see themselves as a fraction of a whole, as an entity that has little or no meaningful definition without reference to the group. These differences in self-systems may produce differences in the way people experience well-being. In the United States a sense of personal well-being is typically associated with the feeling that one *possesses positive attributes*, whereas in Japan it is more likely to be associated with the feeling that one *lacks negative attributes* (Fiske et al., 1998; Kitayama et al, 1997). Similarly, results from studies of life satisfaction involving thousands of people from around the world indicate that in collectivist cultures, life satisfaction is associated with social approval and harmonious relations with others, whereas in individualist cultures, life satisfaction is associated with high self-esteem and feeling good about one's own life (Kwan, Bond, & Singelis, 1997; Suh et al., 1998).

Given that cultural factors shape notions about ideal personality development, it is important to evaluate various approaches to personality in terms of how well they apply to cultures other than the one in which they were developed (Enns, 1994). Their applicability to males and females must be considered as well. Even within North American cultures, for example, there are gender differences in the development of self-esteem. Females tend to display an interdependent self-system, achieving their sense of self and self-esteem from attachments to others. By contrast, males' self-esteem tends to develop in relation to personal achievement, in a manner more in keeping with an independent self-system (Cross & Madson, 1997). Cross-gender and cross-cultural differences in the nature and determinants of a sense of self underscore the pervasive effects of gender and culture on the development of many aspects of human personality.

MAJOR APPROACHES TO PERSONALITY

Approach	Basic Assumptions About Behavior	Typical Research Methods
Psychodynamic	Determined by largely unconscious intrapsychic conflicts	Case studies
Trait	Determined by traits or needs	Analysis of tests for basic personality dimensions
Social-cognitive	Determined by learning, cognitive factors, and specific situations	Analysis of interactions between people and situations
Phenomenological	Determined by unique perception of reality	Studies of relationships between perceptions and behavior

FOCUS ON RESEARCH METHODS

Longitudinal Studies of Temperament and Personality

Studying the development of personality over the life span requires longitudinal research in which the same people are followed from infancy to adulthood so that their characteristics can be analyzed at different points in their lives. A number of studies have used this longitudinal methodology to explore a variety of questions about changes in personality over time.

■ What was the researchers' question?

The specific question addressed by Avashalom Caspi and his colleagues was whether young children's temperament could predict their personality and behavior as adults (Caspi & Silva, 1995; Caspi et al., 1997; Caspi et al., 1995). As discussed in Chapter 12, *temperament* refers to a general pattern of emotions and behavior exhibited by humans from birth (Buss, 1997). It is generally agreed that differences in temperament are influenced more by heredity than by the environment (Rowe, 1997).

■ How did the researchers answer the question?

Caspi's research team studied all the children born in Dunedin, New Zealand, between April 1972 and March 1973—a total of about 1,000 individuals. When the children were three, an examiner gave each of them a test of their cognitive abilities and motor skills and, using a three-point scale, rated their reactions to the testing situation. Some of the children exhibited explosive or uncontrolled behaviors; some interacted easily; some were withdrawn and unresponsive. (To avoid bias while making their ratings, the examiners were told nothing about the children's typical behavior outside of the testing room.) Based on these ratings, each child was placed into one of five temperament categories: *undercontrolled* (irritable, impatient, emotional), *inhibited* (shy, fearful, easily distracted), *confident* (eager to perform, responsive to questions), *reserved* (withdrawn, uncomfortable), and *well-adjusted* (comfortable, friendly, well-controlled). The children were reexamined at age five, seven, and nine; but each time, a different person did the ratings, thus eliminating the possibility that an examiner's earlier impressions might bias later ratings. Almost all correlations among the independent ratings made at various ages were positive and statistically significant, indicating that the temperament classifications were stable across time.

When the participants were eighteen years old, they completed a standard personality test. Finally, at the age of twenty-one, they were interviewed about the degree to which they engaged in risky and unhealthy behaviors—excessive drinking, violent criminal activities, unprotected sexual activity, and unsafe driving habits. To avoid the possibility that prior knowledge of temperament or personality might bias the interviews, the interviewers were given no information about the participants' previous scores on these measures.

■ What did the researchers find?

Several significant differences were found among the average personality scores for the five temperament categories. For example, participants classified as *inhibited* at the age of three were more likely to avoid dangerous activities at the age of twenty-one than were participants initially classified as *undercontrolled*. In addition to being inclined toward dangerous and exciting activities, *undercontrolled* individuals were more aggressive, alienated, negative, and hostile than any other temperament group. Further, people originally classified as *confident* or *well-adjusted* were more forceful and decisive than were the people classified as *inhibited* or *reserved*. And young adults who, as children, had been classified as *confident* or *well-adjusted* tended to be effective individuals who were likely to assume leadership roles. These findings held true for males and females alike.

Caspi and his colleagues also found small but significant correlations between temperament and health-risk behaviors (Caspi et al., 1997). Participants originally classified as *undercontrolled* were about twice as likely to engage in such behaviors as were people in the general population. The relationship between temperament in childhood and health-risk behaviors in young adulthood was not, however, a direct one. Statistical analyses disclosed that temperament at age three affected personality at age eighteen, which, in turn, affected behavior patterns at age twenty-one.

■ What do the results mean?

The results of Caspi's studies provide persuasive empirical support for a hypothesis long endorsed by personality psychologists: that relatively accurate predictions can be made about individuals' personality and behavior as adults on the basis of information about their temperament as children. However, the strength of these results should not be overstated: The relationships between temperament and personality, and between temperament and health-risk behaviors, though statistically significant, were also relatively modest. For example, not all the participants classified as *undercontrolled* at age three turned out to be aggressive or violent at age twenty-one. The implication is that personality is influenced and shaped by temperament, but not completely determined by it.

The results of these studies also corroborate a point made in Chapter 13: that personality plays a significant role in health. Specifically, personality characteristics predispose people to engage in behaviors that can affect their mental and physical health.

■ What do we still need to know?

Caspi's research has revealed some continuity between temperament in childhood and personality in adulthood. But what factors underlie this continuity? The individual differences in adult behavior within temperament groups shows that a child is not simply biologically programmed to exhibit certain personality traits later. One explanation offered by Caspi and his colleagues draws heavily on social-cognitive theories, particularly on Bandura's notion of *reciprocal determinism*. These researchers believe that long-term consistencies in behavior result from the mutual influence that temperament and environmental events have on one another. They propose, for example, that people tend to put themselves in situations that reinforce their temperament. Thus, *undercontrolled* people might choose to spend time with people who accept and even encourage rude or impolite behavior. When such behavior brings negative reactions, the world seems that much more hostile and they become even more aggressive and negative. Caspi and his colleagues see the results of their studies as evidence that this process of mutual influence between personality and situations can continue over a lifetime.

ASSESSING PERSONALITY

Suppose you are an industrial/organizational psychologist whose job it is to ensure that honest, cooperative, and hard-working employees are hired by your company. How would you know which candidates have these characteristics? There are three basic methods of assessing and describing personality: observations, interviews, and personality tests. The data gathered through these methods are used not only in personnel selection but also in the diagnosis of psychological disorders, in making predictions about a convict's or mental patient's dangerousness, and in other risky decision situations (Borum & Grisso, 1995; Groth-Marnat, 1997).

As noted in Chapter 2, *observational methods* allow direct assessment of many aspects of behavior, including how often, how effectively, and how consistently various actions occur. *Interviews* provide a way to gather information about personality from the person's own point of view. They can be open-ended and tailored to the intellectual level, emotional state, and special needs of the person being assessed. Interviews can also be *structured,* that is, aimed at gathering information about specific topics without spending much time on other issues (Campion, Palmer, & Campion, 1998). Structured interviews are routinely used in personality research because they elicit the same information from each person.

Personality tests offer a way of gathering information that is more standardized and economical than either observations or interviews. To be useful, however, a personality test must be reliable and valid. As described in Chapter 10, reliability refers to how stable or consistent the results of a test are; validity reflects the degree to which a test measures what it is intended to measure. The many personality tests available today are traditionally classified as either objective or projective.

Objective Tests

Objective tests ask direct, unambiguous questions about a person's thoughts, feelings, or behavior; the answers are used to draw inferences about the individual's personality. The questions can be addressed to friends and relatives of the person (e.g., "Does he/she worry a great deal?") or to someone who has known the person for only a short time (e.g., "Did he/she seem at ease in the conversation you just observed?"). However, the most common kind of objective personality test is the *self-report test,* which is usually similar in format to the multiple-choice examinations used in many classrooms. Like multiple-choice exams, self-report personality tests can be administered to many people at the same time; they can also be machine-scored. However, unlike multiple-choice exams, self-reports include questions concerning the characteristics of the respondent (e.g., "Are you nervous when you first meet people?"). And whereas there is only one correct answer for each question in a classroom exam, the "correct" answers on self-report tests depend on who takes them. Each respondent picks out the statement or alternative that best describes him or her.

Ultimately, the respondent's answers to individual questions are combined into a score or set of scores. When compared with the scores of numerous other people who have taken the same test, that score can be used to draw certain conclusions about the respondent's personality. For example, before interpreting your score of "77" on a self-report test of extraversion, a psychologist would compare the score with *norms*, or average scores from others of your age and gender. Only if you were well above these averages would you be considered unusually extraverted.

Some self-report tests focus on one personality trait, such as optimism (Scheier et al., 1989), whereas others measure a set of related traits, such as empathy and social responsibility (Penner et al., 1995). Still others measure the strength of a wider variety of traits to reveal general psychological functioning or signs of psychological disorders.

The most commonly used objective test for diagnosing psychological disorders is the *Minnesota Multiphasic Personality Inventory,* better known as the *MMPI* (Dahlstrom, 1992). This 566-item true-false test was originally developed during the 1930s at the University of Minnesota by Starke Hathaway and J. C. McKinley. It has subsequently been revised and updated in the MMPI-2 (National Computer Systems, 1992).

The MMPI is organized into ten *clinical scales*. These are groups of items that, in earlier research, had elicited a characteristic pattern of responses only from people who displayed particular psychological disorders or personality characteristics (see Figure 14.6). The MMPI and MMPI-2 also contain four *validity scales,* which are item groups designed to detect whether respondents distorted their answers, misunderstood the items, or were uncooperative. For example, someone who responds "true" to items such as "I never get angry" may not be giving honest answers to the test as a whole.

FIGURE 14.6

The MMPI-2: Clinical Scales and Sample Profiles

A score of 50 on the clinical scales is average. Scores at or above 65 mean that the person's responses on that scale are more extreme than at least 95 percent of the normal population. The red line represents the profile of Kenneth Bianchi, the infamous "Hillside Strangler" who murdered thirteen women in the late 1970s. His profile would be interpreted as characteristic of a shallow person with poor self-control and little personal insight who is sexually preoccupied and unable to reveal himself to others. The profile in green comes from a more normal man, but it is characteristic of someone who is self-centered, passive, unwilling to accept personal responsibility for his behavior, and, when under stress, complains of numerous vague physical symptoms.

The clinical scales abbreviated in the figure are as follows:

1. Hypochondriasis (Hs) (Concern with bodily functions and symptoms)

2. Depression (D) (Pessimism, hopelessness, slowed thinking)

3. Hysteria (Hy) (Use of physical or mental symptoms to avoid problems)

4. Psychopathic deviate (Pd) (Disregard for social customs, emotional shallowness)

5. Masculinity/femininity (Mf) (Interests associated with a particular gender)

6. Paranoia (Pa) (Delusions, suspiciousness)

7. Psychasthenia (Pt) (Worry, guilt, anxiety)

8. Schizophrenia (Sc) (Bizarre thoughts and perceptions)

9. Hypomania (Ma) (Overactivity, excitement, impulsiveness)

10. Social introversion (Si) (Shy, insecure)

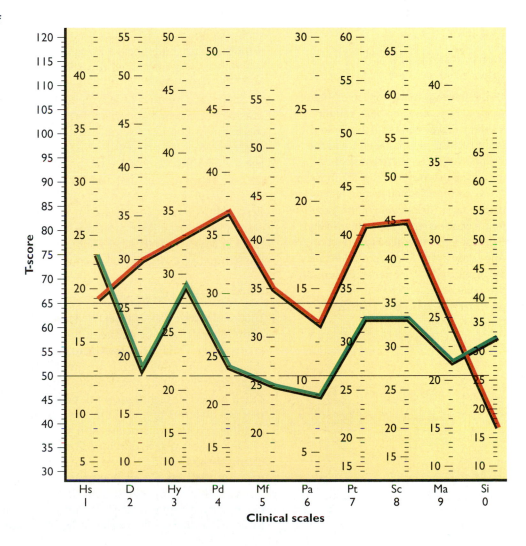

Interpreting the MMPI is largely a matter of comparing respondents' profiles—such as those shown in Figure 14.6—to the profiles of persons already known to display certain personality characteristics. Respondents are generally presumed to share characteristics with the group whose profile theirs most closely resembles. So whereas a very high score on one scale, such as depression, might indicate a problem in the dimension measured by that scale, MMPI interpretation usually focuses on the overall *pattern* in the clinical scales—particularly on the combination of two or three scales on which a person has unusually high scores. Recent years have seen the development of computer programs that "read" such profiles (Lanyon & Goodstein, 1997).

There is considerable evidence for the reliability and validity of MMPI clinical scales, but even the latest editions of the test are far from perfect measurement tools—even when the resulting profiles are interpreted by computers (Groth-Marnat, 1997; Humphrey & Dahlstrom, 1995). The validity of MMPI interpretations may be particularly suspect when—because of cultural factors—the perceptions, values, and experiences of the respondent are notably different from those of the test developers and the people to whom the respondent's results will be compared. Thus, a profile that looks typical of people with a certain disorder might reflect the culture-specific way the respondent interpreted the test items, not a mental problem (Groth-Marnat, 1997).

Even though the MMPI-2 uses comparison norms that represent a more culturally diverse population than did those of the original MMPI, psychologists must remain cautious when interpreting profiles of people who are members of minority subcultures. One reason is that the responses people give on objective personality tests can be influenced by general cultural differences as well as by individual personality traits. For example, Chuansheng Chen and his colleagues (1995) found that when respondents were asked to rate their personal attributes, those from individualist countries such as Canada and the United States tended to select extreme alternatives ("very important" or "much below average"), whereas those from collectivist countries such as China and Japan tended to select more moderate alternatives ("somewhat important" or "average").

There are a number of self-report tests designed to measure personality variables in normal populations, especially the "big-five" personality traits described earlier. One increasingly popular example is the *Neuroticism Extraversion Openness Personality Inventory, Revised* or *NEO-PI-R* (Costa & McCrae, 1992). Table 14.3 shows how the test's results are presented. One innovative feature of the NEO-PI-R is its "private" and "public" versions. The first asks for the respondent's self-assessment; the second asks a person who knows the respondent to rate her or him on various dimensions. Personality descriptions derived from the two versions are often quite similar, but discrepancies may indicate problems. For example, if a person's self-ratings are substantially different from those of a spouse, marital problems may be indicated; in addition, the nature of the discrepancies could suggest a focus for marital therapy.

Projective Tests

Unlike objective tests, **projective tests** contain relatively unstructured stimuli, such as inkblots, which can be perceived in many ways. Proponents of projective tests tend to take a psychodynamic approach to personality. They believe that people's responses to the tests' ambiguous stimuli are guided by unconscious needs, motives, fantasies, conflicts, thoughts, and other hidden aspects of personality. Some projective tests (also called projective techniques) ask people to draw items such as a house, a person, or a tree (see Figure 14.7), to fill in the missing parts of incomplete pictures or sentences, or to say what they associate with a particular word.

One projective test, developed by Henry Murray and Christina Morgan, is called the *Thematic Apperception Test*, or *TAT*. As described in Chapter 11, the TAT is used to measure need for achievement (see Figure 11.8 on page 378). It is also used to assess other needs (e.g., for power or affiliation) that Murray and Morgan saw as the basis for personality. Another widely used projective test, the *Rorschach Inkblot Test*, asks people to say what they see in a series of inkblots (see Figure 14.8 on page 512).

FIGURE 14.7

Interpretations of a Draw-a-Person Test

These drawings came from an eighteen-year-old male who had been caught stealing a television set. A psychologist interpreted the muscular figure as the young man's attempt to boast of masculine prowess, but saw the muscles' "puffy softness" as suggesting feelings of inadequacy. The drawing of the baby-like figure was seen to reveal vulnerability, dependency, and a need for affection. Appealing as these interpretations may be, research does not generally support the value of projective tests in personality assessment (Smith & Dumont, 1995).

Source: Hammer, 1968.

TABLE 14.3

Sample Summary of Results from the NEO-PI-R

The NEO-PI-R assesses the big-five personality dimensions. In this example of the results that a respondent might receive, the five factors scored are, from the top row to the bottom row, neuroticism, extraversion, openness, agreeableness, and conscientiousness. Because people with different NEO profiles tend to have different disorders, this test has also been used to aid in the diagnosis of personality disorders (Trull & Sher, 1994).

Compared with the responses of other people, your responses suggest that you can be described as:

☐ Sensitive, emotional, and prone to experience feelings that are upsetting.	☒ Generally calm and able to deal with stress, but you sometimes experience feelings of guilt, anger, or sadness.	☐ Secure, hardy, and generally relaxed even under stressful conditions.
☐ Extraverted, outgoing, active, and high-spirited. You refer to be around people most of the time.	☐ Moderate in activity and enthusiasm. You enjoy the company of others, but you also value privacy.	☒ Introverted, reserved, and serious. You prefer to be alone or with a few close friends.
☐ Open to new experiences. You have broad interests and are very imaginative.	☐ Practical but willing to consider new ways of doing things. You seek a balance between the old and the new.	☒ Down-to-earth, practical, traditional, and pretty much set in your ways.
☐ Compassionate, good-natured, and eager to cooperate and avoid conflict.	☒ Generally warm, trusting, and agreeable, but you can sometimes be stubborn and competitive.	☐ Hardheaded, skeptical, proud, and competitive. You tend to express your anger directly.
☒ Conscientious and well-organized. You have high standards and always strive to achieve your goals.	☐ Dependable and moderately well-organized. You generally have clear goals but are able to set your work aside.	☐ Easygoing, not very well-organized, and sometimes careless. You prefer not to make plans.

In comparison to objective-test results, responses to projective tests are much more difficult to translate into numerical scores. In an effort to reduce the subjectivity involved in projective-test interpretation, some psychologists have developed more structured—and thus potentially more reliable—scoring systems for instruments such as the Rorschach (Erdberg, 1990; Exner & Ona, 1995). Proponents claim that projective tests make it difficult for respondents to detect what is being measured and what the "best" answers would be. They argue, therefore, that these tests can measure aggressive and sexual impulses and other personality features that people might otherwise be able to hide. The ambiguous stimuli in projective tests may also capture how people respond to the uncertainty that they confront in daily life. In addition, proponents point to specific instances—as in studies assessing achievement motivation via the TAT—where projectives show acceptable reliability and validity (Spangler, 1992). Accordingly, projective tests continue to be used by many clinical psychologists (Chan & Lee, 1995; Watkins et al., 1995).

Overall, however, projective personality tests are less reliable and valid than objective tests (Garb, Florio, & Grove, 1998; Rogers, 1995). Indeed, because of their generally low predictive validity, they often add little beyond what might be inferred from other information. One study showed, for example, that even untrained observers are able to make relatively accurate judgments about an individual's personality characteristics simply by watching a sample of his or her behavior on videotape (Funder & Colvin, 1997).

FIGURE 14.8

The Rorschach Inkblot Test

The Rorschach test consists of ten patterns, some in color, others in black and white. The participant is asked to tell what the blot might be and then to explain why. This pattern is similar to those in the Rorschach test. What do you see? Most scoring methods pay attention to (1) what part of the blot the person responds to; (2) what features (such as details or color) appear to determine each response; (3) the content of responses (for example, animals, maps, body parts); and (4) the popularity or commonness of the participant's responses.

("In Review: Personality Tests" summarizes the characteristics of objective and projective tests, along with some of their advantages and disadvantages.)

Personality Tests and Employee Selection

How good are personality tests at selecting people for jobs? Most industrial/organizational psychologists believe they are valuable tools in the selection of good employees. The MMPI (and even some projective tests) are occasionally employed for such purposes (e.g., Bartol, 1991), but the majority of personality tests used by large organizations are those that measure the big-five personality dimensions or similar characteristics (Borman, Hanson, & Wedge, 1997). Several researchers have found significant relationships between scores on tests of these characteristics and overall job performance (Barrick & Mount, 1991; Ones & Viswesvaran, 1996). And, more generally, a review of studies involving over 300,000 people has shown that objective personality tests are of value in helping businesses reduce thefts and other disruptive employee behaviors (Ones, Viswesvaran, & Schmidt, 1993).

Still, personality tests are far from perfect predictors of behavior—and, as noted earlier, they can lead to incorrect predictions. Many tests measure traits that may be too general to predict specific aspects of job performance (Schneider, Hough, & Dunnette, 1996); and, in any case, personality characteristics may influence performance in some job situations but not in others (Motowidlo, Borman, & Schmit, 1997). Further, some employees see personality tests as an invasion of their privacy. They worry also that test results in their personnel files might later be misinterpreted and hurt their chances for promotion or for employment by other companies. Lawsuits have resulted in a ban on the use of personality tests in the selection of U.S. federal employees. Concerns about privacy and other issues surrounding personality testing have also led the American Psychological Association to publish ethical standards relating to procedures for the development, dissemination, and use of all psychological tests (American Psychological Association, 1974, 1981, 1992b). The goal is not only to improve the reliability and validity of tests but also to ensure that their results are properly used and do not infringe on individuals' rights.

in review

PERSONALITY TESTS			
Type of Test	**Characteristics**	**Advantages**	**Disadvantages**
Objective	Asks direct questions about a person; quantitatively scored	Efficiency, standardization	Subject to deliberate distortion
Projective	Unstructured stimuli create maximum freedom of response; scoring is subjective, though some objective methods exist	"Correct" answers not obvious; designed to tap unconscious impulses; flexible use	Reliability and validity lower than those of objective tests

LINKAGES

As noted in Chapter 1, all of psychology's many subfields are related to one another. Our discussion of personality development illustrates just one way in which the topic of this chapter, personality, is linked to the subfield of developmental psychology (Chapter 12). The Linkages diagram shows ties to two other subfields as well, and there are many more ties throughout the book. Looking for linkages among subfields will help you to see how they all fit together and better appreciate the big picture that is psychology.

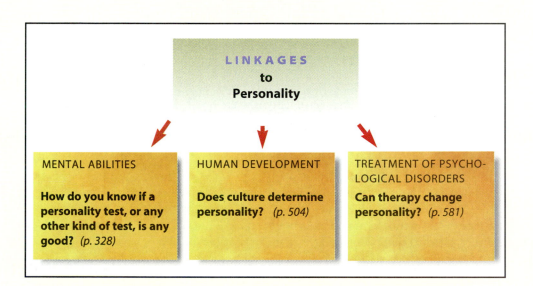

LINKAGES to Personality

MENTAL ABILITIES

How do you know if a personality test, or any other kind of test, is any good? *(p. 328)*

HUMAN DEVELOPMENT

Does culture determine personality? *(p. 504)*

TREATMENT OF PSYCHOLOGICAL DISORDERS

Can therapy change personality? *(p. 581)*

SUMMARY

Personality refers to the unique pattern of psychological and behavioral characteristics by which each person can be compared and contrasted with other people. The four main theoretical approaches to personality are the psychodynamic, trait, social-cognitive, and phenomenological approaches.

THE PSYCHODYNAMIC APPROACH

The *psychodynamic approach*, first proposed by Freud, assumes that personality arises out of conflicts between basic needs and the demands of the real world. Most of these conflicts occur at an unconscious level.

The Structure and Development of Personality

Freud believed that personality has three components—the *id*, which has a reservoir of *libido* and operates according to the *pleasure principle;* the *ego*, which operates according to the *reality principle;* and the *superego*, which internalizes society's rules and values. The ego uses *defense mechanisms* to prevent unconscious conflicts among these components from becoming conscious and causing anxiety. Freud proposed that the focus of conflict changes as the child passes through *psychosexual stages* of development called the *oral stage*, the *anal stage*, the *phallic stage* (during which the *Oedipus* or *Electra complex* occurs), the *latency period*, and the *genital stage*.

Variations on Freud's Personality Theory

Many of Freud's early followers developed new theories that differed from his. Among these theorists were Jung, Adler, and Horney. These and other theorists tended to downplay the role of instincts and the unconscious, emphasizing instead the importance of conscious processes, ego functions, and social and cultural factors. Horney also challenged the male-oriented nature of Freud's original theory.

Contemporary Psychodynamic Theories

Current psychodynamic theories derive from neo-Freudians' emphasis on family and social relationships. According to object relations theorists, personality development depends mainly on the nature of early interactions between an individual and his or her caregivers (objects).

Evaluation of the Psychodynamic Approach

The psychodynamic approach is reflected in many forms of psychotherapy. Despite evidence in support of some psychodynamic concepts and recent attempts to test psychodynamic theories more precisely and objectively, critics still fault the approach for its lack of a scientific base and for its view of human behavior as driven by unmeasurable forces.

THE TRAIT APPROACH

The *trait approach* assumes that personality is made up of stable internal characteristics that appear at varying strengths in different people and guide their thoughts, feelings, and behavior.

Prominent Trait Theories

Gordon Allport believed that personality is created by a small set of central traits in each individual. Hans Eysenck, who used factor analysis to identify common traits or core dimensions of personality, believed that biological factors are responsible for these core dimensions.

The "Big-Five" Model of Personality

Building on the work of Allport and Eysenck, as well as that of Raymond Cattell, contemporary researchers have used factor analysis to identify five basic dimensions of personality, collectively referred to as the *big-five* or *five-factor model*. These dimensions, which have been found in many different cultures, may arise partly from inherited differences in temperament that provide the raw materials out of which experience molds each personality.

Evaluation of the Trait Approach

The trait approach has been criticized for being better at describing personality than at explaining it, for failing to consider mechanisms that motivate behavior, and for underemphasizing the role of situational factors. Nevertheless, the trait approach—particularly the big-five model—currently dominates the field of personality.

THE SOCIAL-COGNITIVE APPROACH

The *social-cognitive approach* assumes that personality is a label that summarizes the unique patterns of thinking and behavior that a person learns in the social world.

Roots of the Social-Cognitive Approach

With roots in research on classical and instrumental conditioning (including Skinner's *functional analysis* of behavior), the social-cognitive approach has expanded on traditional behavioral approaches by emphasizing the role of cognitive factors, such as observational learning, in personality development.

Prominent Social-Cognitive Theories

Julian Rotter's theory focuses on cognitive expectancies that guide behavior, especially general beliefs about whether rewards occur because of personal efforts (internal control) or chance (external control). Albert Bandura believes that personality develops largely through cognitively mediated learning, including observational learning. He sees personality as reciprocally determined by interactions among cognition, environmental stimuli, and behavior. *Self-efficacy*—the belief in one's ability to accomplish a specific task—is an important determinant of behavior. Walter Mischel emphasizes the importance of cognitive processes—and their interactions with the characteristics of particular situations—in determining behavior. According to Mischel, we must look at both cognitive person variables and situational variables in order to understand human consistencies and inconsistencies.

Evaluation of the Social-Cognitive Approach

The social-cognitive approach has led to new forms of psychological treatment and many other applications. However, critics of the approach consider even its latest versions to be too mechanistic and incapable of capturing what most psychologists mean by personality, including beliefs, intentions, and values.

THE PHENOMENOLOGICAL APPROACH

The *phenomenological approach*, also called the humanistic approach, is based on the assumption that personality is determined by the unique ways in which each individual views the world. These perceptions form a personal version of reality and guide behavior as the individual strives to reach his or her fullest human potential.

Prominent Phenomenological Theories

Carl Rogers believed that personality development is driven by an innate *actualizing tendency,* but also that one's *self-concept* is shaped by social evaluations. He proposed that when people are free from the effects of *conditions of worth,* they will be psychologically healthy. Abraham Maslow saw self-actualization as the highest in a hierarchy of needs. Personality development is healthiest, he said, when people have a *growth orientation* rather than a *deficiency orientation.*

Evaluation of the Phenomenological Approach

Applications of the phenomenological approach include certain forms of psychotherapy and group experiences designed to enhance personal growth. Although it has a large following, the phenomenological approach is faulted for being too idealistic, for failing to explain personality development, for being vague and unscientific, and for underplaying cultural differences in "ideal" personalities.

ASSESSING PERSONALITY

Personality is usually assessed through some combination of observations, interviews, and tests. To be useful, personality assessments must be both reliable and valid.

Objective Tests

Objective tests ask direct questions about the individual being assessed; their scores can be compared to group norms. The MMPI and the NEO-PI-R are examples of objective tests.

Projective Tests

Based on psychodynamic theories, *projective tests* present ambiguous stimuli in an attempt to tap unconscious personality characteristics. Two popular projective tests are the TAT and the Rorschach Inkblot Test. In general, projective tests are less reliable and valid than objective personality tests.

Personality Tests and Employee Selection

Objective personality tests are often used to identify the people best suited for certain occupations. Although such tests can be helpful in this regard, those who use them must be aware of the tests' limitations and take care not to violate the rights of test respondents.

KEY TERMS

actualizing tendency (502)
anal stage (486)
big-five model (493)
conditions of worth (503)
defense mechanisms (485)
deficiency orientation (503)
ego (484)
Electra complex (486)
five-factor model (493)

functional analysis (497)
genital stage (486)
growth orientation (503)
id (484)
latency period (486)
libido (484)
objective tests (508)
Oedipus complex (486)
oral stage (485)

personality (483)
phallic stage (486)
phenomenological approach (501)
pleasure principle (484)
projective tests (510)
psychodynamic approach (484)
psychosexual stages (485)

reality principle (484)
self-concept (503)
self-efficacy (499)
social-cognitive approach (497)
superego (484)
trait approach (489)

15

Psychological Disorders

During his freshman year at college, Mark began to worry about news stories describing the deadly diseases resulting from hanta virus, "flesh-eating" strep bacteria, and HIV. He took a blood test for HIV, the virus that causes AIDS, and was relieved when it showed no infection. But then he wondered if he might have contracted HIV after the test. Library research and a call to an AIDS hotline revealed that HIV antibodies may not appear until six months after infection. He took another blood test, also negative, but he still worried when he learned that the AIDS virus can live outside of the human body for anywhere from ten minutes to several hours or even days; no one knows for sure. He also read that no one can explain why hanta virus appears in new places or why some rare forms of bacteria cause deadly lesions.

Given all this uncertainty, Mark concluded that HIV, hanta virus, and "flesh-eating" strep bacteria can live indefinitely outside of the body and could therefore be anywhere and everywhere. He decided that the only safe course was not just sexual abstinence but absolute cleanliness. Mark began to scrub himself whenever he touched door knobs, money, walls, floors—anything. People with HIV or other deadly viruses or bacteria, he thought, could have touched these things, or they might have bled on the street and he might have tracked their infected blood into his car and house and bathroom. Eventually he felt the need to scrub everything around him up to forty times in each direction; it took him several exhausting hours simply to shower and dress. He washed himself and the shower knobs before touching them and, once in the shower, felt that he had to wash his body in cycles of thirteen strokes. If his feet touched the bare floor, he had to wash them again before putting on his underwear to ensure that his feet would not contaminate the fabric. He was sure his hands, rubbed raw from constant washing, were especially susceptible to infection, so he wore gloves at all times except in the summer, when he wrapped his fingers in flesh-colored bandages. The process of protecting himself from infection was wearing him out and severely restricting his activities; he could not go anywhere without first considering the risk of infection.

Mark's case provides an example of someone who suffers from a psychological disorder, also called a mental disorder, or psychopathology. **Psychopathology** involves patterns of thought, emotion, and behavior that result in personal distress or a significant impairment in a person's social or occupational functioning. Psychopathology is thus a social as well as a personal matter, and its presence in an individual is assessed in terms of what a particular society defines as "normal" versus "abnormal."

In Western societies, the definitions of these terms are such that a large number of people can be said to display some form of psychological disorder. Surveys reveal that, in the United States alone, as many as 29.5 percent of the adult population have displayed mild to severe mental disorder within a given year, and that as many as 48 percent have experienced a disorder at some point in their lives (Kessler et al., 1994; Robins & Regier, 1991). Further, more than 22 percent of children in the United States display significant mental disorder in any given year (Costello et al., 1988). These rates of mental disorder are found, with only minor variations, throughout the U.S. (see Figure 15.1 on page 518), among males and females in all ethnic groups (Robins & Regier, 1991). Bear in mind that the actual rates may be higher than the percentages just cited, given that major survey studies have examined fewer than half of all known psychological disorders.

Psychological disorders are enormously costly in terms of human suffering and wasted potential, economic burden and lost resources. They can also cost lives. In this chapter we describe major categories of psychological disorders, discuss some of their possible causes, and examine issues surrounding the nature of psychopathology.

UNDERSTANDING PSYCHOLOGICAL DISORDERS: SOME BASIC ISSUES

A woman's husband dies, and in her grief she stays in bed all day, weeping, refusing to eat, at times holding "conversations" with him. In India, a Hindu holy man on a

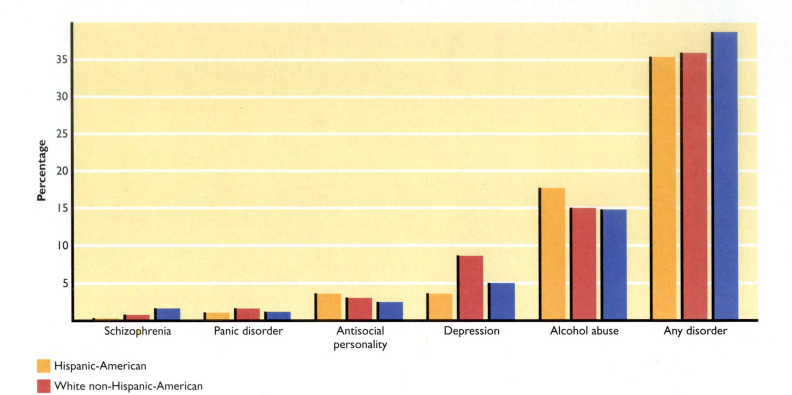

Hispanic-American

White non-Hispanic-American

African-American

FIGURE 15.1

Lifetime Prevalence of Mental Disorders

Surveys of 18,000 adults in five U.S. cities revealed that nearly one-third experienced some form of mental disorder at some time in their lives. Here are the prevalence data for several mental disorders among Hispanics, non-Hispanic whites, and African-Americans. Note that the size of the differences between these groups varies across disorders, but that all such differences are small and none is statistically significant.

Source: Robins & Regier, 1991.

pilgrimage rolls along the ground across 1,000 miles of deserts and mountains, pelted by monsoon rains, until he reaches the sacred place he seeks. Seven percent of adults in the United States say they have seen a UFO (Roper Organization, 1992), and hundreds of people around the world claim to have been abducted by space aliens (e.g., Mack, 1994; Spanos et al., 1993). These and countless other examples raise the question of where to draw the line between normality and abnormality, between eccentricity and mental disorder (Kanner, 1995). We begin our exploration of psychopathology by considering some factors that determine what is considered normal and abnormal in various cultures today.

What Is Abnormal?

There are several criteria for judging whether people's thinking, emotions, or behavior are abnormal. Each criterion has value, but also some flaws.

Infrequency   If we define normality as what most people do, an obvious criterion for abnormality is *statistical infrequency*, that which is atypical or rare. By this criterion, the few people who believe that space aliens are stealing their thoughts would be judged abnormal; the many people who worry about becoming victims of crime would not. Statistical infrequency alone is a poor criterion for abnormality, however, because some characteristics that appear only rarely—creative genius, extraordinary language skills, or world-class athletic ability, for example—may be highly valued. Further, equating rarity with abnormality can result in the oppression of nonconformists who express minority views in a society. Finally, just how rare must a behavior be to warrant the designation of "abnormal"? The dividing line is not easy to locate.

Personal Suffering   Another criterion for abnormality is *personal suffering*. Indeed, the experience of distress is the criterion that people often use in deciding that their psychological problems are severe enough to require treatment. But personal suffering alone is an inadequate criterion for abnormality because it does not take into account the fact that some people may be excessively distressed over behaviors that are not pathological (e.g., homosexuality) or, conversely, that some people with serious psychological disorders may show little distress because the disorders have impaired their ability to recognize how maladaptive their behavior is.

Norm Violation   Abnormality can also be defined in terms of whether someone violates social norms—the cultural rules that tell us how we should and should not behave in various situations, especially in relation to others (see Chapter 18). According to this *norm violation* criterion, when people behave in ways that are bizarre, unusual, or disturbing enough to violate social norms, they are described as abnormal. Like the other criteria, however, norm violation alone is an inadequate measure of abnormality. For one thing, some norm violations are better characterized as eccentric or illegal than as abnormal (Weeks & Weeks, 1995). People who bathe infrequently or who stand too close during conversation violate social norms, but are they abnormal or merely annoying? Further, whose norms are we talking about? Social norms vary across cultures, subcultures, and historical eras, so the behaviors that qualify as abnormal in one part of the world might be perfectly acceptable elsewhere.

Behavior in Context: A Practical Approach   Because no single criterion is entirely adequate for identifying abnormality, mental health practitioners and researchers tend to adopt a *practical approach* that combines aspects of all the criteria we've discussed. They consider the *content* of behavior—that is, what the person does; the *sociocultural context* in which the person's behavior occurs; and the *consequences* of the behavior for that person, and for others. This practical approach pays special attention to whether a person's thoughts, behavior, or emotions cause *impaired functioning*—that is, difficulty in fulfilling appropriate and expected social and work-related roles.

What is "appropriate" and "expected" depends on age, gender, and culture, as well as on the particular situation and historical era in which people find themselves. Thus, for example, the same short attention span that is considered normal in a two-year-old would be described as inappropriate and problematic in an adult. There are gender-specific norms as well. In some countries, for example, it is considered more appropriate for women than for men to display emotion. Kisses, tears of happiness, and long embraces are common when women greet each other after a long absence; men tend to simply shake hands or, at most, hug briefly. Because of cultural differences, hearing a dead relative's voice calling from the afterlife would be considered more acceptable in certain North American Indian tribes than among, say, the families of suburban Toronto. Situational factors are important, too. Falling to the floor and "speaking in tongues" is considered appropriate, even desirable, during the worship services of certain religious groups, but the same behavior would be considered inappropriate, and a sign of disorder, in a college classroom. Finally, judgments about behavior are shaped by changes in social trends and cultural values. For example, the American Psychiatric Association once listed homosexuality as a mental disorder but dropped this category from its *Diagnostic and Statistical Manual of Mental Disorders* in 1973. In taking this step, it was responding to changing views of homosexuality that were prompted in part by the political and educational efforts of gay and lesbian rights groups (Bayer, 1981).

In summary, it is difficult, and probably impossible, to define a specific set of behaviors that everyone, everywhere, will agree constitutes abnormality. Instead, the practical approach sees abnormality as including those patterns of thought, behavior, and emotional reaction that significantly impair people's functioning within their culture (Wakefield, 1992). In keeping with this approach, mental health professionals assign diagnostic labels for the purpose of describing specific cases of impaired functioning (Kutchins & Kirk, 1997; Szasz, 1987).

Explaining Psychological Disorders

Since the dawn of civilization, people throughout the world have tried to understand the causes of psychological disorder. Early on, explanations of abnormal behavior focused on possession by gods or demons. Disordered people were seen either as innocent victims of evil spirits or as social deviants suffering supernatural punishment. In Europe during the late Middle Ages, for example, disbelief in established religious doctrine and other unusual behaviors were viewed as the work of the devil and his witches.

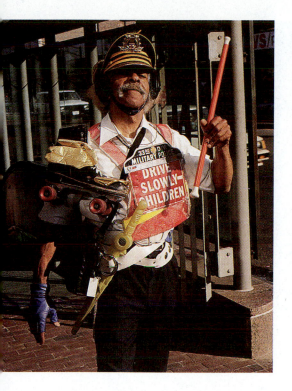

Is This Man Abnormal?

The answer depends on a number of factors, including how abnormality is defined by the culture in which he lives and by those who are most directly affected by his behavior.

Situational Factors and "Abnormality"

Although being nude in designated public places is not considered abnormal, when this California student attended class nude to protest "social repression," complaints from other students led to his dismissal.

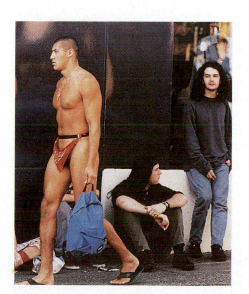

An Exorcism

Though no longer dominant in Western cultures, supernatural explanations of mental disorder, and supernaturally oriented cures, such as the exorcism being performed by this Buddhist monk in Thailand, remain influential in many other cultures and subcultures.

Hundreds of "witches"—mostly women—were burned at the stake, and exorcisms were performed to rid people of controlling demons. Supernatural explanations of psychological disorders are still invoked today in many cultures around the world—including certain ethnic and religious subcultures in North America (Tagliabue, 1999). More generally, however, mainstream authorities in Western cultures attribute the appearance of psychopathology to three other causes: biological factors, psychological processes, and sociocultural context.

Biological Factors   According to the *medical model* of psychopathology, mental disorder is caused by *biological factors*, usually some kind of physical illness or imbalance in bodily processes. One of the earliest proponents of this view was the ancient Greek physician Hippocrates. Psychological disorders, he said, resulted from imbalances among four *humors,* or bodily fluids (blood, phlegm, black bile, and yellow bile). Depression, according to Hippocrates, resulted from an excess of black bile (melancholia). Similarly, in ancient Chinese cultures, psychological disorders were seen as resulting from an imbalance of *yin* and *yang,* the dual forces of the universe flowing in the physical body.

The medical model gave rise to the concept of abnormality as *mental illness*—and, indeed, even though the specifics of the presumed illness are often vague, most people in Western cultures today still tend to seek medical doctors and hospitals for the diagnosis and treatment of psychological disorders. The medical model is now more properly called the **neurobiological model** because it explains psychological disorders in terms of particular disturbances in the anatomy and chemistry of the brain and in other biological processes. The neurobiological model dominates modern research on the causes—and treatments—of psychological disorders. Neuroscientists and others who investigate these disorders approach them as they would approach any physical illness, seeing problematic symptoms stemming from an underlying illness that can be diagnosed, treated, and cured.

The enduring influence of the medical model is based largely on the fact that some forms of abnormality have, in fact, been traced to biological causes (Spitzer et al., 1992). *Dementia,* for example, is characterized by a loss of intellectual functions, including disturbances in memory, personality, and cognitive abilities. The most frequent causes of dementia are progressive deterioration of the brain as a result of aging or long-term alcohol abuse; acute diseases and disorders such as encephalitis, brain

Visiting Bedlam

As the medical model gained prominence in Western cultures after the Middle Ages, specialized hospitals for the insane were established throughout Europe. As shown in Hogarth's portrayal of "Bedlam" (the local name for London's St. Mary's of Bethleham hospital), most of these eighteenth-century *asylums* were little more than prisons where the public could buy tickets to gawk at the patients.

tumors, or head injury; and drug intoxication. Alzheimer's disease is a severe form of dementia seen mostly in the elderly. Research in neuroscience and behavioral genetics has also implicated biological factors in a number of other psychological disorders to be described later, including schizophrenia, bipolar disorders, some forms of anxiety disorder, and autism and attention deficit disorder in children.

Psychological Processes   Another approach to understanding mental disorders views them as arising from psychological processes. If biological factors can be thought of as the "hardware" of mental disorders, then psychological factors are the "software." The roots of this **psychological model** can be seen in ancient Greek literature and drama dealing with *psyche,* or mind—especially with the struggles of the mind to resolve inner conflicts, or with the effects of childhood experiences on adult behavior. These ideas gained far greater prominence in the late 1800s, when Sigmund Freud challenged the assumption that psychological disorders had only physical causes. Freud's explanations of these disorders came as part of a more general *psychodynamic* approach to personality, described in Chapter 14. Freud viewed psychological disorders as the result of unresolved, mostly unconscious clashes between the instinctual desires of the id and the demands of the environment and society. These conflicts, he said, begin early in childhood. Contemporary versions of the psychodynamic model— such as *object relations* theory—focus less on instinctual urges and more on the role of attachment and other early interpersonal relationships (Schultz & Schultz, 2000).

Psychological explanations for mental disorders have also come from other theories of personality. For example, *cognitive-behavioral* theorists, who draw heavily on the social-cognitive approach described in Chapter 14, see most psychological disorders as the result of past learning and current situations. Just as people learn to avoid hot grills after being burned, say these theorists, bad experiences in school or a dental office can "teach" people to fear such places. Cognitive-behavioral theorists also emphasize some of the cognitive processes discussed in Chapter 8. Specifically, they focus on the expectations, schemas, and other ways of thinking (about oneself and others) that people develop as they grow up. Depression, for example, is seen as stemming not only from

LINKAGES

Are psychological disorders learned behaviors? (a link to Learning)

negative events, such as losing a job, but also from irrational or maladaptive thoughts that people have learned to experience in relation to such events—such as "I never do anything right."

According to the humanistic, or *phenomenological,* approach to personality, behavior disorders appear when actualizing tendencies are blocked, usually by a failure to be aware of and to express true feelings. When this happens, one's perceptions of reality become distorted. The greater the distortion, the more serious the psychological disorder. Phenomenologists assume that abnormal behavior, no matter how unusual or seemingly irrational, is a reasonable reaction to the world, as the person perceives it.

LINKAGES

How do societies define what is abnormal? (a link to Social Influence)

Sociocultural Context   Neither biological nor psychological explanations alone can account for all forms of abnormality because, for one thing, many disorders have both biological *and* psychological causes. And even together, these explanations focus on processes *within* the individual. An alternative approach looks *outside* the person for possible causes of psychopathology. As the name implies, **sociocultural explanations** of mental disorder draw attention to social and cultural factors that constitute the *context* in which abnormal behavior has been shaped and within which it must be viewed (Mezzich et al., 1996). As noted earlier, this context includes such factors as gender and age, physical and social situations, cultural values and expectations, and historical eras. These factors influence not only what is and isn't labeled abnormal but also who displays what kind of disorder.

Consider gender, for instance. The greater tolerance in many cultures for open expression of emotional distress among women, but not men, may contribute to the higher rates of depression seen in women compared to men (Nolen-Hoeksema, 1990). And the view held in many cultures that excessive alcohol consumption is less appropriate for women than for men is a sociocultural factor that may help explain higher rates of alcohol abuse among men in those cultures (Helzer et al., 1990).

Sociocultural factors also influence the form that abnormality takes. For example, schizophrenia and depression are *culture-general* disorders—appearing virtually everywhere in the world—but their specific symptoms tend to differ depending on the disordered person's cultural background. In Western cultures, where emotional and physical components of disorder are generally viewed separately, symptoms of depression tend to revolve around despair and other signs of emotional distress (Kleinman, 1991). But in China and certain other Asian cultures where emotional and physical experiences tend to be viewed as one, a depressed person is as likely to report stomach or back pain as to complain of sadness (Brislin, 1993).

There are also *culture-specific* forms of disorder. For instance, Puerto Rican and Dominican Hispanic women sometimes experience *ataques de nervios,* a unique way of reacting to stress that includes heart palpitations, shaking, shouting, nervousness, depression, and, on occasion, fainting or seizure-like episodes (Spiegel, 1994). Another example can be found in Southeast Asia, Southern China, and Malaysia, where a disorder called *koro* is occasionally observed. Victims of this condition, who are usually male, fear that their penis will shrivel, retract into the body, and cause death (in females, the fear relates to shriveling of the breasts). *Koro* appears only in cultures holding the specific supernatural beliefs that explain it. In such cultures, epidemics of *koro* are often triggered by economic hard times (Tseng et al., 1992).

In short, as sociocultural factors create differing social roles, stressors, opportunities, and experiences for people who differ in age, gender, and cultural traditions, they help shape the disorders and symptoms to which certain categories of people are prone. Any attempt to fully explain psychological disorders must take these sociocultural factors into account.

Diathesis-Stress as an Integrative Approach   More generally, research suggests that most psychological disorders arise from a varying combination of sources, including biological imbalances, genetically inherited characteristics, brain damage, enduring psychological traits, socioculturally mediated learning experiences, and stressful life events. All of these *biopsychosocial* causes of disorder are taken into account by the **diathesis-stress model,** which suggests that a person's inherited characteristics, biological processes, and early learning experiences may create a predisposition (or *diathesis*) for a psychological disorder, but that whether or not the disorder appears depends on the stressors the person encounters (National Advisory Mental Health Council, 1996; Zuckerman, 1999).

For example, a person may have inherited a tendency toward neural problems in the brain that are associated with depression or may have learned depressing patterns of thinking, but these predispositions may be expressed as a depressive disorder only during a financial crisis or some other particularly stressful situation. If such circumstances do not often occur, or if the person has skills adequate for coping with them, depressive symptoms may never appear, or may be quite mild. You will encounter the diathesis-stress model in discussions of the causes of a number of psychological disorders described in this chapter. Table 15.1 shows how this approach compares with the neurobiological and psychological approaches in explaining and treating a particular case of psychopathology.

CLASSIFYING PSYCHOLOGICAL DISORDERS

Despite differences of opinion within and across cultures about what constitutes psychological disorder, there is a set of culture-general and culture-specific behavior patterns that most mental health professionals, and other people as well, consider worthy

TABLE 15.1

Five Ways of Explaining Psychopathology

Here are examples of how various approaches to disorder might account for and treat the problems experienced by José, a fifty-five-year-old electronics technician. A healthy and vigorous father of two adult children, he was forced to take medical leave because of a series of sudden, uncontrollable panic attacks in which he experienced dizziness, heart palpitations, sweating, and fear of impending death. The attacks also kept him from his favorite pastime, scuba diving, but he has been able to operate a part-time computer business out of his home. (Panic disorder is discussed in more detail later in this chapter; the outcome of the case is described in the next chapter.)

Explanatory Approach	Possible Cause	Possible Treatment
Medical/neurobiological	Organic disorder (brain tumor?); endocrine (e.g., thyroid) disorder.	Drugs, surgery
Psychodynamic	Unconscious conflicts and desires; instinctual impulses breaking through ego defenses into consciousness, causing panic.	Psychotherapy to gain insight into unconscious
Cognitive-behavioral	Bodily stress symptoms interpreted as signs of serious illness or impending death. Receives reward in the form of relief from work stress and opportunity to work at home.	Develop cognitive coping techniques such as relaxation and noncatastrophic thinking
Phenomenological	Failure to recognize genuine feelings about work and his place in life. Fear of expressing himself.	Therapy to put him in touch with feelings about life and work
Diathesis-stress	Biologically predisposed to be overly responsive to stressors. Stress of work and extra activity exceeds capacity to cope and triggers panic as stress response.	Learn to monitor stress level, learn new stress-coping techniques, and change lifestyle as needed

of being labeled as psychopathology. These behavior patterns correspond roughly to those that the practical approach, with its emphasis on impaired functioning, would define as abnormal. It has long been the goal of those who study abnormal behavior to establish a system of classifying such patterns in order to understand and deal with them.

In 1952 the American Psychiatric Association published the first edition of what has become the "official" North American diagnostic classification system, the *Diagnostic and Statistical Manual of Mental Disorders (DSM)*. Each subsequent edition of the DSM has included more categories of disorders. The latest edition, DSM-IV, contains more than three hundred specific diagnostic labels—a fact that critics say makes it possible for almost anyone to be labeled as having some kind of psychological problem (Kutchins & Kirk, 1997).

Mental health professionals outside North America diagnose mental disorders using the classification system that appears as Chapter V ("Mental and Behavioural Disorders") of the World Health Organization's *International Classification of Diseases,* now in its tenth edition (ICD-10). To facilitate international communication about—and cross-cultural research on—psychopathology, DSM-IV was designed to be compatible with ICD-10. Some inconsistencies still exist between the two systems, however (Frances, Pincus, & Widiger, 1996).

A Classification System: DSM-IV

DSM-IV describes the abnormal patterns of thinking, emotion, and behavior that define various mental disorders. For each disorder, DSM-IV provides specific criteria outlining the conditions that must be met before a person can be diagnosed as having that disorder. A diagnostician using DSM-IV can evaluate a person on five dimensions, or *axes,* which together provide a broad picture of the person's problems and their context. As shown in Table 15.2, major mental disorders, such as schizophrenia or major depressive disorder, are recorded on Axis I, whereas evidence of personality disorders or mental retardation are noted on Axis II. Any medical conditions that might be important in understanding the person's mental or behavioral problems are listed on Axis III. On Axis IV the diagnostician notes any psychosocial and environmental problems (such as loss of a loved one, physical or sexual abuse, discrimination, unemployment, poverty, homelessness, or inadequate health care) that are important for understanding the person's psychological problems. Finally, a rating (from 100 down to 1) of the person's current level of psychological, social, and occupational functioning appears on Axis V. Here is a sample DSM-IV diagnosis for a person who received labels on all five axes.

Axis I   Major depressive disorder, single episode; alcohol abuse.

Axis II   Dependent personality disorder.

Axis III   Alcoholic cirrhosis of the liver.

Axis IV Problems with primary support group (death of spouse).

Axis V   Global assessment of functioning = 50.

It is surprising to many people that *neurosis* and *psychosis* are no longer major categories in the DSM. In earlier editions of the manual, neurosis referred to conditions in which some form of anxiety is the major characteristic, whereas psychosis referred to conditions involving more extreme problems that leave patients "out of touch with reality" or unable to function on a daily basis. However, these categories were eventually deemed too vague for accurate and useful diagnosis. The disorders once grouped under them now appear in various Axis I categories in DSM-IV.

Purposes and Problems of Diagnosis

A major goal in diagnosing psychological disorders is to determine the nature of people's problems so that the characteristics of these problems can be described and understood, and the most appropriate treatment methods can be chosen. Diagnoses

Axis I (Clinical Syndromes)

1. *Disorders usually first diagnosed in infancy, childhood, or adolescence.* Problems such as hyperactivity, childhood fears, abnormal aggressiveness or other notable misconduct, frequent bedwetting or soiling, and other problems in normal social and behavioral development. Autistic disorder (severe impairment in social and behavioral development), as well as other problems in the development of skill in reading, speaking, mathematics, or English.

2. *Delirium, dementia, amnestic, and other cognitive disorders* Problems caused by physical deterioration of the brain due to aging, disease, drugs or other chemicals, or other possible unknown causes. These problems can appear as an inability to "think straight" (delirium) or as loss of memory and other intellectual functions (dementia).

3. *Substance-related disorders* Psychological, behavioral, physical, social, or legal problems caused by dependence on or abuse of a variety of chemical substances, including alcohol, heroin, cocaine, amphetamines, hallucinogens, marijuana, and tobacco.

4. *Schizophrenia and other psychotic disorders* Severe conditions characterized by abnormalities in thinking, perception, emotion, movement, and motivation that greatly interfere with daily functioning. Problems involving false beliefs (delusions) about such things as being loved by some high-status person, having inflated worth or power, or being persecuted, spied on, cheated on, followed, harassed, or kept from reaching important goals.

5. *Mood disorders* (also called *affective disorders*) Severe disturbances of mood, especially depression, over-excitement (mania), or alternating episodes of each extreme (as in bipolar disorders).

6. *Anxiety disorders* Specific fears (phobias), panic attacks, generalized feelings of dread, rituals of thought and action (obsessive-compulsive behavior) aimed at controlling anxiety, and problems caused by traumatic events, such as rape or military combat (see Chapter 13 for more on posttraumatic stress disorder).

7. *Somatoform disorders* Physical symptoms, such as paralysis and blindness, that have no physical cause. Unusual preoccupation with physical health or with nonexistent or elusive physical problems (hypochondriasis, somatization disorder, pain disorder).

8. *Factitious disorders* False physical disorders, which are intentionally produced to satisfy some psychological need.

9. *Dissociative disorders* Psychologically caused problems of consciousness and self-identification, e.g., loss of memory (amnesia) or the development of more than one identity (dissociative identity disorder).

10. *Sexual and gender identity disorders* Problems of (a) finding sexual arousal through unusual objects or situations (like shoes or exposing oneself), (b) unsatisfactory sexual activity (sexual dysfunction; see Chapter 11), or (c) identifying with the opposite gender.

11. *Eating disorders* Problems associated with eating too little (anorexia nervosa) or binge eating followed by self-induced vomiting (bulimia nervosa). (See Chapter 11)

12. *Sleep disorders* Severe problems involving the sleep-wake cycle, especially an inability to sleep well at night or to stay awake during the day. (See Chapter 9)

13. *Impulse control disorders* Compulsive gambling, stealing, or fire setting.

14. *Adjustment disorders* Failure to adjust to or deal well with such stressors as divorce, financial problems, family discord, or other unhappy life events.

Axis II (Personality Disorders and Mental Retardation)

1. *Personality disorders* Diagnostic labels given to individuals who may or may not receive an Axis I diagnosis but who show lifelong behavior patterns that are unsatisfactory to them or that disturb other people. The problematic features of their personality may involve unusual suspiciousness, unusual ways of thinking, self-centeredness, shyness, overdependency, excessive concern with neatness and detail, or overemotionality, among others.

2. *Mental retardation* As described in Chapter 10, the label of mental retardation is applied to individuals whose measured IQ is less than about 70 *and* who fail to display the skill at daily living, communication, and other tasks expected of those their age.

TABLE 15.2

The *Diagnostic and Statistical Manual* (DSM) of the American Psychiatric Association

Axis I of the fourth edition (DSM-IV) lists the major categories of mental disorders. Personality disorders and mental retardation are listed on Axis II.

are also important for research on the causes of mental disorders. If researchers can accurately and reliably classify people into groups with similar disorders, they will have a better chance of spotting commonalities in genetic features, biological abnormalities, cognitive processes, and environmental experiences that might differentiate people in one disorder group from those in other groups, thereby providing clues to the origins of various problems.

How good is the diagnostic system? *Interrater reliability*, the degree to which different diagnosticians give the same person the same diagnostic label, has improved considerably for many diagnoses since about 1980. It was then that, in DSM-III, broad, vague symptom descriptions were replaced with specific criteria for assigning each diagnosis. Nevertheless, mental health professionals still often disagree about diagnoses, particularly for personality disorders and other complex conditions (Kirk & Kutchins, 1992). Overall, agreement appears to be facilitated when diagnosis is based on semistructured interviews that systematically address various areas of functioning and provide uniform guidelines for interpretation of the answers that people give (Rogers, 1995; Widiger & Sanderson, 1995).

Do diagnostic labels give accurate information about people? This *validity* question is difficult to answer because it is hard to find a fully acceptable standard for accuracy: Should a clinician's diagnosis be evaluated by comparing it with the judgments of experts? Or should the value of a diagnosis be tested by checking its predictions about a person's behavior against what the person actually does? Still, there is evidence to support the validity of most DSM criteria (Clark, Watson, & Reynolds, 1995). And validity is likely to improve further as diagnostic labels are refined in future editions of the DSM to reflect what researchers are learning about the characteristics, causes, courses, and treatments of various disorders.

The diagnostic system is far from perfect, however. First, people's problems often do not fit neatly into a single category. Second, the same symptoms may appear as part of more than one disorder. Third, diagnostic judgments are to some extent subjective, raising the possibility that personal bias might creep into the labeling system. All of these factors can lead to misdiagnosis in some cases. Psychiatrist Thomas Szasz (pronounced "zaws") and other critics of the medical model (e.g., Caplan, 1995; Kutchins & Kirk, 1997) also argue that labeling *people* instead of describing problems is dehumanizing because it ignores features that make each person's case unique. Calling people schizophrenics or alcoholics, Szasz says, may actually encourage the behaviors associated with these labels and undermine the confidence of clients (and therapists) about the chances of improvement (Szasz, 1987).

Indeed, no shorthand label can fully describe a person's problems or predict exactly how that person will behave in the future. All that can be reasonably expected of a diagnostic system is that it allows informative, general descriptions of the types of problems displayed by people who have been placed in various categories.

THINKING CRITICALLY

Is Psychological Diagnosis Biased?

Some researchers and clinicians worry that problems with the reliability and validity of the diagnostic system are due partly to bias in its construction and use. They point out, for example, that if the research underlying the diagnostic criteria for a certain disorder focuses mainly on one gender, one ethnic group, or one age group, those criteria might not apply widely enough. Moreover, since diagnosticians, like other people, hold expectations and make assumptions about males versus females, and about individuals from differing cultures or ethnic groups, such cognitive biases could color their judgments, leading them to apply diagnostic criteria in ways that are subtly but significantly different from one case to the next (Garb, 1997; Hartung & Widiger, 1998).

■ What am I being asked to believe or accept?

Here, we focus on ethnicity as a possible source of bias in diagnosing psychopathology. It is of special interest because there is evidence that, like social class and gender, ethnicity is an important sociocultural factor in the development of mental disorder. Thus the assertion to be considered is that clinicians in the United States base their diagnoses partly on the ethnic group to which their clients belong and, more specifically, that there is bias in diagnosing African-Americans.

■ What evidence is available to support the assertion?

Several facts suggest the possibility of ethnic bias in psychological diagnosis. For example, African-Americans receive the diagnosis of schizophrenia more frequently than European-Americans do (Manderscheid & Barrett, 1987). Further, relative to their presence in the general population, African-Americans are overrepresented in public mental hospitals, where the most serious forms of disorder are seen, and underrepresented in private hospitals and outpatient clinics, where less severe problems are treated (Lindsey & Paul, 1989; Snowden & Cheung, 1990).

■ Are there alternative ways of interpreting the evidence?

Differences between ethnic groups in diagnosis or treatment do not automatically indicate bias based on ethnicity. Perhaps real differences in psychological functioning are associated with different ethnic groups. For example, if, relative to other groups, African-Americans are exposed to more poverty, violence, or other major stressors, they could be more vulnerable to more serious forms of mental disorder. And poverty, not diagnostic bias, could be responsible for the fact that African-Americans more often seek help at less expensive public hospitals than at more expensive private ones.

■ What additional evidence would help to evaluate the alternatives?

Do African-Americans actually display more signs of mental disorder, or do diagnosticians just perceive them as more disordered? One way of approaching this question would be to conduct experiments in which diagnosticians assign labels to clients on the basis of case histories, test scores, and the like. Unknown to the diagnosticians, the cases would be selected so that pairs of clients show about the same objective amount of disorder, but one member of the pair is identified as European-American, the other as African-American. Bias among the clinicians would be suggested if the African-American member of each pair more often received a diagnosis—or a more severe diagnosis. Unfortunately, studies like this are difficult to conduct in clinical settings.

A strategy that has been used with real clinical populations is to perform statistical analyses to identify the factors that influence clinicians' diagnostic judgments following extensive interviews with patients. If, after controlling for the type and severity of symptoms, a researcher discovers that African-Americans are still diagnosed with a certain disorder more often than European-Americans, evidence for bias would be rather strong. Studies conducted in hospital settings with African-American and European-American patients show that African-Americans are indeed more frequently diagnosed as schizophrenic (Pavkov, Lewis, & Lyons, 1989). In contrast, a large-scale study of mental disorder found that when people were interviewed and diagnosed in their own homes, the diagnosis of schizophrenia was given only slightly more often to African-Americans than to European-Americans (Robins & Regier, 1991; Snowden & Cheung, 1990). In other words, there is little evidence that schizophrenia is more common among African-Americans in the community, but they appear more likely to receive this diagnosis when entering a hospital. Thus the presence of ethnic bias is suggested, at least in some diagnoses.

■ What conclusions are most reasonable?

Just as DSM-IV is imperfect, so are those who use it. Bias does not necessarily reflect deliberate discrimination, however; it may be unintentional. Cognitive biases and stereotypes shape human thought in matters large and small (see Chapters 8 and 17). No matter how precisely researchers specify the ideal criteria for assigning diagnostic labels, those biases and stereotypes still threaten the objectivity of the diagnostic process.

Minimizing diagnostic bias requires a better understanding of it. Toward this end, Hope Landrine (1991) suggests that diagnosticians need to focus more intently than ever on the fact that their concepts of "normality" and "abnormality" are affected by sociocultural values that they may or may not share with a given client. And Steven Lopez (1989) argues that diagnosticians must become more aware that the same cognitive heuristics and biases (see Chapter 8) that affect everyone else's thinking and decision making can impair their own clinical judgments. Indeed, studies of memory, problem solving, decision making, social attributions, and other aspects of culture and cognition may turn out to be key ingredients in reducing bias in the diagnosis of psychological disorders. Meanwhile, perhaps the best way to counteract clinicians' cognitive shortcomings is to teach them to base their diagnoses solely on published diagnostic criteria and statistically validated decision rules rather than relying on their (potentially biased) clinical impressions (Garb, 1997).

We do not have the space to cover all the DSM-IV categories, so we will sample several of the most prevalent, socially significant, or unusual ones. As you read, try not to catch "medical student's disease." Just as medical students often think they have the symptoms of every illness they read about, some psychology students worry that their behavior (or that of a relative or friend) signals a mental disorder. Remember that everyone has problems sometimes. Before deciding that you or someone you know needs psychological help, see if the nature and frequency of the behavior qualify it as abnormal according to the criteria of the practical approach.

ANXIETY DISORDERS

If you have ever been tense before an exam, a date, or a job interview, you have a good idea of what anxiety feels like. Increased heart rate, sweating, rapid breathing, a dry mouth, and a sense of dread are common components of anxiety. Brief episodes of moderate anxiety are a normal part of life for most people. For others, anxiety is so intense, long-standing, or disruptive that it is called an **anxiety disorder.**

Types of Anxiety Disorders

We discuss four types of anxiety disorders: phobia, generalized anxiety disorder, panic disorder, and obsessive-compulsive disorder. Another type, called posttraumatic stress disorder, is described in Chapter 13, on health, stress, and coping. Together, these are the most common psychological disorders in North America.

Phobia   An intense, irrational fear of an object or situation that is not likely to be dangerous is called a **phobia.** People who experience phobias usually realize that their fears make no sense, but the discomfort and consequent avoidance of the object or event may greatly interfere with daily life. Thousands of phobias have been described (see Table 15.3).

DSM-IV classifies phobias into specific, social, and agoraphobia subtypes. **Specific phobias** involve fear and avoidance of heights, blood, animals, automobile or air travel, and other specific stimuli and situations. In the United States, they are the most prevalent of the anxiety disorders, affecting 7 to 10 percent of adults and children (Kessler et al., 1994; Robins & Regier, 1991). Here is an example.

Mr. L. was a fifty-year-old office worker who became terrified whenever he had to drive over a bridge. For years, he avoided bridges by taking roundabout ways to and from

TABLE 15.3

Common Phobias

Phobia is the Greek word for morbid fear, after the lesser Greek god, Phobos. Phobias are usually named using the Greek word for the feared object or situation, followed by the suffix -*phobia*.

Name	Feared Stimulus	Name	Feared Stimulus
Acrophobia	Heights	Aerophobia	Flying
Claustrophobia	Enclosed places	Entomophobia	Insects
Hematophobia	Blood	Gamophobia	Marriage
Gephyrophobia	Crossing a bridge	Ophdophobia	Snakes
Kenophobia	Empty rooms	Xenophobia	Strangers
Cynophobia	Dogs	Melissophobia	Bees

work, and he refused to be a passenger in anyone else's car, lest they use a bridge. Even this very inconvenient adjustment failed when Mr. L. was transferred to a position requiring frequent automobile trips, many of which were over bridges. He refused the transfer and lost his job.

Social phobias involve anxiety about being negatively evaluated by others or acting in a way that is embarrassing or humiliating. The anxiety is so intense and persistent that the person's normal functioning is impaired. Common social phobias are fear of public speaking, "stage fright," fear of eating in front of others, and fear of using public restrooms. *Generalized social phobia* is a more severe form in which fear occurs in virtually all social situations (Mannuzza et al., 1995).

Agoraphobia is a strong fear of being away from a safe place like home or from a familiar person, such as a spouse or close friend, or of being trapped in a place from which escape might be difficult or where help may be unavailable. Attempts to leave home lead to intense anxiety, so people who suffer severe agoraphobia seldom even try to go out alone. Theaters, shopping malls, public transportation, and other potentially crowded places are particularly avoided. Most individuals who suffer from

It's a Long Way Down

Almost everyone is afraid of something, but as many as 10 percent of U.S. adults suffer from a specific phobia, in which fear interferes significantly with daily functioning. For example, people with acrophobia (fear of heights) would not do well in a job that requires being in this high position.

agoraphobia have a history of panic attacks (which we describe below), and their intense fear of public places is partly attributable to the fact that they don't want to risk triggering an attack by going where they have had one before or where having another one would be harmful or embarrassing.

Like other phobias in Western cultures, agoraphobia is more often reported by women, many of whom have become prisoners in their own homes by the time they seek help. Note, however, that in India, where homebound women are considered less unusual than in the United States, the people labeled as agoraphobic tend to be male (Raguram & Bhide, 1985). Although agoraphobia occurs less frequently than specific phobias (affecting about 2.5 percent of the population in the United States), it is the phobia that most often leads people to seek treatment, mainly because it so severely disrupts everyday life (Barlow, 1988).

Generalized Anxiety Disorder Excessive and long-lasting anxiety that is not focused on any particular object or situation marks **generalized anxiety disorder.** Because the problem occurs in virtually all situations and because the person cannot pinpoint its source, this type of anxiety is sometimes called *free-floating anxiety.* For weeks at a time, the person feels anxious and worried, sure that some disaster is imminent. The person becomes jumpy and irritable; sound sleep is impossible. Fatigue, inability to concentrate, and physiological signs of anxiety are also common. Generalized anxiety disorder affects about 5 percent of the U.S. population at some point in their lives (Kessler et al., 1994). It is more common in women, often accompanying other problems such as depression or substance abuse (Wittchen et al., 1994).

Panic Disorder For some people, anxiety takes the form of **panic disorder.** Like the man described in Table 15.1 (page 523), people suffering from panic disorder experience recurrent, terrifying *panic attacks* that often come without warning or obvious cause. These attacks are marked by intense heart palpitations, pressure or pain in the chest, dizziness or unsteadiness, sweating, and a feeling of faintness; often, victims believe they are having a heart attack. They may worry constantly about suffering future panic episodes and thus curtail activities to avoid possible embarrassment. In fact, as noted earlier, it is often the fear of experiencing panic attacks while alone or away from home that leads to agoraphobia (Barlow, 1988). Panic disorder may become chronic, with periods of improvement followed by recurrence (Ehlers, 1995). As many as 30 percent of adults in the United States have experienced at least one panic attack within the past year, though in most cases this does not lead to full-blown panic disorder (Ehlers, 1995). Here is a case that did.

> Geri, a thirty-two-year-old nurse, had her first panic attack while driving on a freeway. Afterward, she would not drive on freeways. Her next attack occurred while with a patient and a doctor in a small examining room. A sense of impending doom flooded over her and she burst out of the office and into the parking lot, where she felt immediate relief. From then on, fear of another attack made it impossible for her to tolerate any close quarters, including crowded shopping malls. She eventually quit her job because of terror of the examining rooms.

Obsessive-Compulsive Disorder Anxiety is also at the root of **obsessive-compulsive disorder.** As with Mark, whose case opened this chapter, people displaying obsessive-compulsive disorder are plagued by persistent, upsetting, and unwanted thoughts—called *obsessions*—that often center on the possibility of infection, contamination, or doing harm to oneself or others. These obsessive thoughts may motivate ritualistic, repetitive behaviors—called *compulsions*—that the person performs in an effort to avoid some dreaded outcome or to reduce feelings of anxiety associated with the obsessions (Foa & Kozak, 1995). For example, Mark engaged in incessant, ritualized cleaning to protect himself from infection; other common compulsions include rituals such as checking locks, repeating words, images, or numbers, counting things, or arranging objects "just so." Obsessions and compulsions are much more intense than the familiar experience of having a repetitive thought or tune "in the back of your mind" or rechecking that a door is locked. In obsessive-compulsive disorder, the obses-

sions and compulsions are intense, disturbing, and often bizarre intrusions that can severely impair daily activities. Many of those who display this disorder recognize that their thoughts and actions are irrational, but still experience severe agitation and anxiety if they try to interrupt their obsessions or give up their compulsive behaviors.

Causes of Anxiety Disorders

As with all the forms of psychopathology we will consider, the exact causes of anxiety disorders are a matter of debate. All theoretical approaches offer explanations. Research suggests that biological factors, distortions in thinking, and learning are particularly important.

Biological Factors   Genes may play a role in anxiety disorders. Research indicates, for example, that if one identical twin displays generalized anxiety disorder, the other identical twin is likely to do so as well. This co-occurrence is much less probable among nonidentical twins (Kendler et al., 1992). In fact, most anxiety disorders, such as panic disorder, obsessive-compulsive disorder, and generalized social phobia, appear to run in families (Kendler et al., 1995; Pauls et al., 1995; Wittchen et al., 1994). Perhaps, then, anxiety disorders develop out of a physiological predisposition to react with anxiety to a wide range of situations, a predisposition that results, in part, from inheriting an autonomic nervous system that is oversensitive to stress (Zinbarg & Barlow, 1996).

The predisposition to anxiety disorders may stem from abnormalities in the brain's neurotransmitter systems, discussed in Chapter 3. Excessive activity of norepinephrine in certain parts of the brain has been linked with panic disorder, and excessive serotonin has been associated with obsessive-compulsive disorder (Gorman et al., 1989). In addition, there is evidence that anxiety-generating neural impulses may run unchecked when the neurotransmitter GABA is prevented from exerting its normal inhibitory influence in certain neural pathways (Friedman, Clark, & Gershon, 1992; Zorumski & Isenberg, 1991).

Something may also be physically wrong in people with panic disorder. Unlike other people, many of these individuals have a panic episode after receiving an injection of lactate or caffeine, inhaling carbon dioxide, or taking yohimbine (a drug that blocks one type of norepinephrine receptor) (Papp et al., 1993). Because these substances all stimulate brainstem areas that control the autonomic nervous system, one hypothesis is that panic-disorder patients have hypersensitive brainstem mechanisms and are therefore especially prone to fear responses (Gorman et al., 1989).

Although biological predispositions may set the stage for anxiety disorders, most researchers agree that environmental stressors and psychological factors, including cognitive processes and learning, bring about most anxiety disorders (Ley, 1994; Schmidt, Lerew, & Jackson, 1997).

Cognitive Factors   Persons suffering from an anxiety disorder may exaggerate the dangers in their environment, thereby creating an unrealistic expectation that bad events are going to happen (Foa et al., 1996). In addition, they tend to underestimate their own capacity for dealing with threatening events, resulting in anxiety and desperation when feared events do occur (Beck & Emery, 1985).

As an example, consider the development of a panic attack. Whereas the appearance of unexplained symptoms of physical arousal may make a panic attack more likely, the person's cognitive interpretation of those symptoms can determine whether or not the attack actually develops (Clark et al., 1997). One study, for instance, found that panic attacks were much less likely if panic disorder patients believed they could control the source of their discomfort (Rapee et al., 1992). In another study, panic-disorder patients were asked to inhale carbon dioxide, which typically causes panic attacks in such patients. Those who inhaled this substance in the presence of a person they associated with safety were significantly less fearful than patients whose "safe person" was not present (Carter et al., 1995). Results like these suggest the existence of a role for cognitive factors in panic disorder.

LINKAGES

Can we learn to become "abnormal"?
(a link to Learning)

LINKAGES

Psychological Disorders and Learning

Upsetting thoughts—about money or illness, for example—are often difficult to dismiss, especially when people are under stress or feel incapable of dealing effectively with the problems they are worried about. As the thoughts become more persistent, they engender increased anxiety. If an action such as cleaning temporarily relieves the anxiety, that action may be strengthened through the process of negative reinforcement discussed in Chapter 6. But such actions do nothing to eliminate the obsessive thoughts, so the actions become compulsive, endlessly repeated rituals that keep the person trapped in a vicious circle of anxiety (Barlow, 1988). Thus, according to cognitive-behavioral theorists, obsessive-compulsive disorder might be a pattern that is sparked by distressing thoughts and maintained by operant conditioning.

Phobias may also be explained in part by the principles of classical conditioning described in Chapter 6. The object of the phobia becomes an aversive conditioned stimulus through association with a traumatic event that acts as an unconditioned stimulus (Öst, 1992). Fear of dogs, for example, may result from a dog attack. Observing or hearing about other people's bad experiences can produce the same result; most people who fear flying have never been in a plane crash. Once the fear is learned, avoidance of the feared object prevents the person from finding out that there is no need to be afraid. This cycle of avoidance helps explain why many fears do not simply extinguish, or disappear, on their own.

Why are phobias about snakes and spiders so common, even though people are seldom harmed by them? And why are there so few cases of electrical-outlet phobia when people are frequently shocked by them? As discussed in the chapter on learning, the answer may be that people are *biologically prepared* to learn associations between certain stimuli and certain responses. These stimuli and responses, then, would be especially easy to link through conditioning (Hamm, Vaitl, & Lang, 1989). Specifically, people may be biologically prepared to learn to fear and to avoid stimuli that had the potential to harm their evolutionary ancestors (Staddon & Ettinger, 1989).

Learning by Watching

Many phobias, including those of needles, blood, and medical-related situations, are acquired vicariously. Fear developed through observational learning can be as strong as through direct experience (Kleinknecht, 1991), though direct conditioning is the more common pathway to phobia (Öst, 1992). Fearlessness can also be learned vicariously. By simply watching the boy in the dental chair as he learns to relax with his dentist, the other youngster is less likely to be distressed when it is his turn.

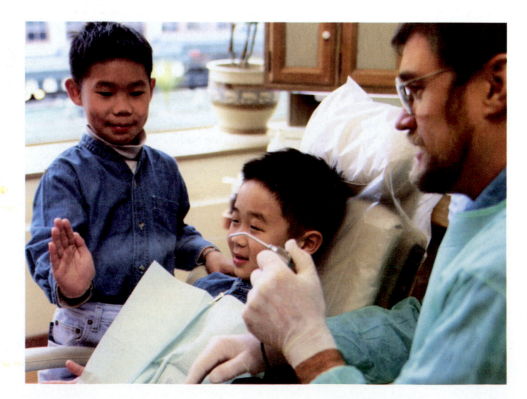

Biological Preparedness

Having a predisposition to learn fear of snakes and other potentially dangerous stimuli makes evolutionary sense. Animals (and humans) who rapidly learn a fear response to objects or situations that they see frightening their parents or peers are more likely to survive to pass on their genes to the next generation.

Some laboratory evidence supports the notion that people are biologically prepared to learn certain phobias. A group of Swedish psychologists attempted to classically condition people to fear certain stimuli by associating the stimuli with electric shocks (Öhman, Dimberg, & Öst, 1985). The participants developed approximately equal conditioned anxiety reactions to slides of houses, human faces, and snakes. Later, however, when they were tested without shock, the reaction to snakes remained long after the houses and faces had failed to elicit a fear response. A series of investigations with animals has also supported preparedness theory (Cook & Mineka, 1990). If a monkey sees another monkey behaving fearfully in the presence of a snake, it quickly develops a strong and persistent fear of snakes. However, if the snake is entwined in flowers, the observer monkeys come to fear only the snake, not the flowers. Thus the fear conditioning was selective, focusing only on potentially dangerous creatures such as snakes or crocodiles (Zinbarg & Mineka, 1991), not on harmless stimuli. Data like these suggest that anxiety disorders probably arise through the combined effects of genetic predispositions and learning.

SOMATOFORM DISORDERS

Sometimes people show symptoms of a *somatic*, or physical, disorder, even though there is no physical cause for the symptoms. Because these conditions reflect psychological problems that take somatic form, they are called **somatoform disorders.** The classic example is **conversion disorder,** a condition in which a person appears to be, but is not, blind, deaf, paralyzed, or insensitive to pain in various parts of the body. (An earlier term for this disorder was *hysteria.*) Conversion disorders are rare, accounting for only about 2 percent of diagnoses. Although they can occur at any point in life, they usually appear in adolescence or early adulthood.

Conversion disorders differ from true physical disabilities in several ways. First, they tend to appear when a person is under severe stress. Second, they often help reduce that stress by enabling the person to avoid unpleasant situations. Third, the person may show remarkably little concern about what is apparently a rather serious problem. Finally, the symptoms may be physiologically impossible or improbable, as Figure 15.2 illustrates. One university student, for example, experienced visual impairment that began each Sunday evening and became total blindness by Monday morning. Her vision would begin to return on Friday evenings and was fully restored in time for

FIGURE 15.2

Glove Anesthesia

In this conversion disorder, lack of feeling stops abruptly at the wrist (B). But as shown in (A) the nerves of the hand and arm blend, so if they were actually impaired, part of the arm would also lose sensitivity. Other neurologically impossible symptoms of conversion disorder include sleepwalking at night on legs that are "paralyzed" during the day.

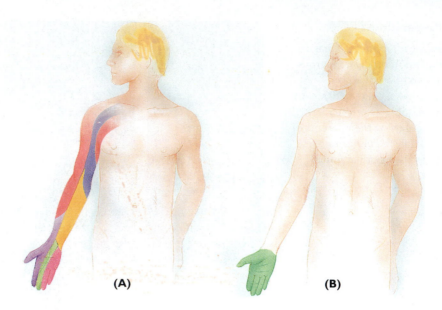

(A)   (B)

weekend football games and other social activities. She expressed no undue concern over her condition (Holmes, 1991).

Can people who display a conversion disorder see and hear, even though they act as if they cannot? Experiments show that they can (Grosz & Zimmerman, 1970), but this does not necessarily mean that they are malingering, or lying. Research on consciousness suggests that people can use sensory input even when they are not consciously aware of doing so (e.g., Blake, 1998). Rather than destroying visual or auditory ability, the conversion process may prevent the person from being aware of information that the brain is still processing.

Another somatoform disorder is **hypochondriasis,** a strong, unjustified fear that one has cancer, heart disease, AIDS, or other serious physical problems. The fear prompts frequent visits to physicians and reports of numerous symptoms. Their preoccupation with illness often leads hypochondriacs to become "experts" on their most feared diseases. In some ways, hypochondriasis resembles a phobic anxiety disorder, but whereas a phobic person might suffer irrational fear of *contracting* a serious illness, the hypochondriac is excessively concerned about already *having* such an illness. A related condition called **somatization disorder** is characterized by dramatic but often vague reports about a multitude of physical problems rather than any specific illness. Finally, **pain disorder** is marked by complaints of severe, often constant pain (typically in the neck, chest, or back) with no physical cause.

Some cases of somatoform disorder may be related to childhood experiences in which a person learns that symptoms of physical illness bring special attention, care, and nurturance (Barsky et al., 1994). Others, including conversion disorder, may be triggered by severe stressors (Spiegel, 1994). Based on such findings, many researchers have adopted a diathesis-stress approach rather than seeking a common cause for all somatoform disorders (e.g., Nietzel et al., 1998). The results of their work suggest that certain people may have biological and psychological traits that make them especially vulnerable to somatoform disorders, particularly when combined with a history of physical illness. Among these traits are oversensitivity to physical sensations and self-consciousness. If such people experience a number of long-lasting stressors, intense emotional conflicts, or severe traumas, they are more likely than others to display physical symptoms in association with emotional arousal (Nietzel et al., 1998). Sociocultural factors may also shape some somatoform disorders. For example, in many Asian, Latin American, and African cultures, it is not unusual for people to experience severe physical symptoms in association with psychological or interpersonal conflicts, whereas in North America such conflicts are more likely to result in anxiety or depression (Brislin, 1993).

A Famous Case of Dissociative Identity Disorder

In this scene from the film *Sybil,* Sally Field portrays a woman diagnosed with dissociative identity disorder, previously known as multiple personality disorder, whose behavior created the appearance of as many as seventeen distinct personalities. The causes of such dramatic cases, and the reasons behind their increasing prevalence in recent years, is a matter of intense debate.

DISSOCIATIVE DISORDERS

Disruptions in a person's memory, consciousness, or identity characterize **dissociative disorders.** Although such disruptions may come on gradually, they are usually sudden and last from a few days to many years. Temporary dissociative states are familiar to most of us. For example, after many hours of highway driving we may suddenly realize that we have little or no recollection of what happened during the last half-hour. Dissociative disorders, however, are much more intense and long-lasting, as in the case of John, a thirty-year-old computer manufacturing executive. John was a meek person who was dependent on his wife for companionship and emotional support. It came as a jolt when she announced that she was leaving him to live with his younger brother. John did not go to work the next day. In fact, nothing was heard from him for two weeks. Then he was arrested for public drunkenness and assault in a city more than three hundred miles from his home. The police discovered that during those two weeks John lived under another name at a cheap hotel and worked selling tickets at a pornographic movie theater. When he was interviewed, John did not know his real name or his home address, could not explain how he reached his present location, and could not remember much about the previous two weeks.

John's case illustrates the dissociative disorder known as **dissociative fugue,** which is characterized by a sudden loss of personal memory and the adoption of a new identity in a new locale. Another dissociative disorder, **dissociative amnesia,** also involves sudden memory loss. As in fugue, all personal identifying information may be forgotten, but the person does not leave home or create a new identity. These rare conditions tend to attract intense publicity because they are so perplexing.

The most famous dissociative disorder is **dissociative identity disorder,** formerly known as—and still commonly called—*multiple personality disorder.* Dissociative identity disorder is a condition in which a person appears to have more than one identity, each of which speaks, acts, and writes in a different way. Each personality seems to have its own memories, wishes, and (often conflicting) impulses. Here is a case example:

> A 42-year-old woman was brought to a psychiatrist by her husband, who complained that during arguments about money or other matters, she would suddenly either change into uncharacteristically flamboyant clothes and go to a nearby bar to flirt with strangers, or curl up on the floor and talk as if she were a young child. An interview conducted under hypnosis revealed that during these times she experienced being "Frieda," the girlfriend of a Russian soldier who had been sexually molested in her native Poland after World War II. Once hypnosis was terminated, she had no memory of "Frieda." (Spitzer et al., 1989)

How do dissociative disorders develop? Psychodynamic theorists see massive repression of unwanted impulses or memories as the basis for creating a "new person" who acts out otherwise unacceptable impulses or recalls otherwise unbearable memories. Behavioral theorists focus on the fact that everyone is capable of behaving in different ways, depending on circumstances (e.g., boisterous in a bar, quiet in a museum); but in rare cases, they say, this variation can become so extreme that an individual feels—and is perceived by others—as a "different person." Further, dissociative symptoms may be strengthened by reward as people find that a sudden memory loss or shift in behavior allows them to escape stressful situations, responsibilities, or punishment for misdeeds.

Evaluating these causal hypotheses has been difficult in part because of the rarity of dissociative disorders. Recently, however, dissociative identity disorder has been diagnosed more frequently, either because clinicians are looking for it more carefully or because the conditions leading to it are more prevalent. The results of one study in Canada suggests that between 5 and 10 percent of the adult population may suffer from some form of dissociative disorder (Ross, Joshi, & Currie, 1990). Research available so far supports three conclusions. First, many people displaying multiple personality disorder have experienced events they would like to forget or avoid. The majority (some clinicians believe all) have suffered severe, unavoidable, persistent abuse in

in review

ANXIETY, SOMATOFORM, AND DISSOCIATIVE DISORDERS

Disorder	Subtypes	Major Symptoms
Anxiety disorders	Phobias	Intense, irrational fear of objectively nondangerous situations or things, leading to disruptions of behavior.
	Generalized anxiety disorder	Excessive anxiety not focused on a specific situation or object; free-floating anxiety.
	Panic disorder	Repeated attacks of intense fear involving physical symptoms such as faintness, dizziness, and nausea.
	Obsessive-compulsive disorder	Persistent ideas or worries accompanied by ritualistic behaviors performed to neutralize the anxiety-driven thoughts.
Somatoform disorders	Conversion disorder	A loss of physical ability (e.g., sight, hearing) that is related to psychological factors.
	Hypochondriasis	Preoccupation with or belief that one has serious illness in the absence of any physical evidence.
	Somatization disorder	Wide variety of somatic complaints that occur over several years and are not the result of a known physical disorder.
	Pain disorder	Preoccupation with pain in the absence of physical reasons for the pain.
Dissociative disorders	Amnesia/fugue	Sudden, unexpected loss of memory, which may result in relocation and the assumption of a new identity.
	Dissociative identity disorder (multiple personality disorder)	Appearance within same person of two or more distinct identities, each with a unique way of thinking and behaving.

childhood (Ross et al., 1991). Second, most of these people appear to be skilled at self-hypnosis, through which they can induce a trance-like state. Third, most found that they could escape the trauma of abuse at least temporarily by creating "new personalities" to deal with stress (Spiegel, 1994). However, as noted below, not all abused children display dissociative identity disorder, and there is evidence that some cases of dissociative identity disorder may have been triggered by media stories or by suggestions made to clients by their therapists (Spanos, 1996).

This evidence has led some skeptics to question the existence of multiple personalities (Acocella, 1998); others suggest that the increased incidence of dissociative identity disorder may simply reflect its status as a socioculturally approved method of expressing distress (Hacking, 1995; Spanos, 1994). Observations such as these prompted the change in its official designation from "multiple personality disorder" to "dissociative identity disorder." The authors of DSM-IV made this change partly to avoid perpetuating the notion that people harbor multiple personalities that can easily be "contacted" through hypnosis or related techniques. The new name was chosen to suggest, instead, that dissociation, or separation, between one's memories and other aspects of identity can be so dramatic that people experiencing it may come to *believe* that they have more than one personality (Spiegel, 1994). Research on the existence and alleged effects of repressed memories—discussed in Chapter 7—is sure to have an impact on our understanding of, and the controversy over, the causes of dissociative identity disorder. ("In Review: Anxiety, Somatoform, and Dissociative Disorders" presents a summary of our discussion of these disorders.)

Searching for Links Between Childhood Abuse and Dissociative Disorders

Professionals who study and treat psychological disorders have become intensely interested in the role of physical and sexual abuse in the development of psychopathology. One hotly debated question in this area is whether abuse in childhood can cause amnesia or other dissociative disorders later on (Acocella, 1998).

LINKAGES

Can people forget traumatic childhood memories? (a link to Memory)

▪ What was the researcher's question?

Linda Meyer Williams (1994a) has addressed one aspect of this important question by asking if is it possible for adults to have no memory of a sexual abuse incident that took place during their childhood.

▪ How did the researcher answer the question?

Williams began by noting that many studies showing a link between abuse in childhood and dissociative disorders or other psychopathology in adulthood had used a retrospective design in which people already diagnosed with some mental disorder were asked if they had been child victims of abuse. Many of the participants in these studies who at first denied, but later remembered, abuse experiences were diagnosed as having dissociative amnesia. Unfortunately, however, the use of retrospective research designs makes it difficult or impossible to confirm whether the reported abuse actually occurred. Given all the media (and therapist) attention currently being devoted to the subject of childhood abuse—and "recovered" memories of it—some people may tend to exaggerate or even falsely recall abuse experiences, especially if they believe that a history of abuse helps to explain or excuse their current behavior problems (Acocella, 1998).

Williams found a way around the problems inherent in retrospective reports by using data from a study on sexual assault published fifteen years earlier (McCahill, Meyer, & Fischman, 1979). The participants in this study, 790 in all, were victims of sexual assaults that had been reported to the police over a two-year period. Each had been brought to a hospital emergency room for treatment and collection of forensic evidence; 206 were girls ranging in age from ten months to twelve years. After obtaining permission to use the hospital's records, Williams (1994a) was able to contact 129 of these female victims, who by then were between eighteen and thirty-one years old. Williams asked them to participate in what she described as a follow-up study of children who had received medical care at the hospital. (As required by research ethics, the women were later informed of the true purpose of the study.)

Each woman was interviewed for approximately three hours by a well-trained and experienced investigator using established procedures for obtaining retrospective reports of childhood sexual experiences. Participants who did not recount the incident that had led to their emergency-room visit were asked questions that explored the possibility that the incident had involved a false report of abuse. They were also asked if any members of their family had ever been accused of sexual misconduct.

▪ What did the researcher find?

Williams (1994a) found that, whereas most of the 129 women recalled the incident of abuse that had put them in the emergency room in childhood, 49 (38 percent) did not. Were the latter participants too embarrassed to be honest? Possibly, but not in every case, given that 68 percent of those who failed to recall the emergency-room visit *did* report other incidents of abuse or assault. In some cases, the failure to recall was quite striking. One woman, for example, denied that she had ever even met the uncle who, according to the emergency-room report, had abused her when she was four, along with a nine-year-old male cousin and a four-year-old male playmate. Her failure to remember this event was all the more remarkable given that she had reported the abuse to her mother, who told the playmate's mother, who then killed the uncle!

In general, the younger the victims had been when the abuse occurred, the less likely they were to report it during the follow-up interview; however, this relationship was not very strong. Those who had been abused when they were four to six years old were almost as likely to fail to remember it as those who were three or younger. Further, recall failure was exhibited by almost 30 percent of those who had been victimized at age seven or older.

Victims who were molested by a stranger were more likely to recall the abuse than those who were molested by a family member, but recall was not related to the severity of the assault.

■ What do the results mean?

Williams' (1994a) study demonstrates that it is possible for women to forget childhood experiences of sexual abuse, but does this finding mean that such women are suffering from a dissociative disorder? Not according to Elizabeth Loftus and her colleagues (Loftus, Garry, & Feldman, 1994), who argued that failure to recall an incident of childhood sexual abuse does not imply the presence of dissociative amnesia or even repression of a traumatic event. Such cases, they said, may involve normal forgetting; indeed, the fact that some of the women forgot one episode of abuse but recalled others suggests that the forgetting may have been due to processes other than pathological dissociation or repression.

In response, Williams (1994b) argued that ordinary forgetting seems an unlikely explanation of her results, especially in cases involving extensive abuse. For example, one girl was abused by her father at least six times, and another was raped and abused by three male cousins from the age of five to the age of seven. As adults, neither victim reported any recollection of these events.

Bear in mind, however, that failure to recall even the most horrendous trauma does not, in and of itself, justify a diagnosis of dissociative amnesia. In order to receive that diagnosis, abuse victims must also be experiencing significant personal distress or substantial problems in important areas of functioning. Williams (1994a, 1994b) did not claim that her research participants satisfied this criterion.

What do we still need to know?

■ Williams' (1994a) study represents an important contribution to research on memory for childhood traumas, but it does not support the notion that sexual abuse in childhood results in dissociative disorder. Indeed, a review of forty-five other studies indicates that, although sexually abused children show more symptoms of disorder (including posttraumatic stress disorder) than nonabused children, such victimization is not consistently followed by a particular set of symptoms, nor does it inevitably condemn the victims to psychopathology in adulthood. In fact, about one-third of the abused children who participated in those studies displayed no symptoms at all (Kendall-Tackett, Williams, & Finkelhor, 1993).

Thus, although at least some cases of virtually every type of adolescent and adult disorder—including dissociative disorders—have been associated with physical or sexual abuse in childhood (e.g., Nietzel et al., 1998; Widom, 1989a), we still do not understand precisely how abuse experiences are related to such diverse symptoms or what factors determine which victims will be scarred for life and which ones will emerge unscathed.

MOOD DISORDERS

Everyone's mood, or *affect,* tends to rise and fall from time to time. However, when people experience extremes of mood—wild elation or deep depression—for long periods, when they shift from one extreme to another, and especially when their moods are not consistent with the events around them, they are said to show a **mood disorder** (also known as *affective disorder*). We will describe two main types: depressive disorders and bipolar disorders.

Depressive Disorders

Depression can range from occasional, normal "down" periods to episodes severe enough to require hospitalization. A person suffering **major depressive disorder** feels sad and overwhelmed for weeks or months, typically losing interest in activities and relationships and taking pleasure in nothing (Coryell et al., 1993). Exaggerated feelings of inadequacy, worthlessness, hopelessness, or guilt are common. Despite one's best efforts, everything, from conversation to bathing, is an unbearable, exhausting effort (Solomon, 1998). Changes in eating habits resulting in weight loss or, sometimes, weight gain often accompany major depressive disorder, as does sleep disturbance or, less often, excessive sleeping. Problems in working, concentrating, making decisions, and thinking clearly are also common. In extreme cases, depressed people may express false beliefs, or **delusions**—worrying, for example, that the government is planning to punish them. Major depressive disorder may come on suddenly or gradually. It may consist of a single episode or, more commonly, repeated depressive periods. Here is one case example:

> Mr. J. was a fifty-one-year-old industrial engineer . . . . Since the death of his wife five years earlier, he had been suffering from continuing episodes of depression marked by extreme social withdrawal and occasional thoughts of suicide . . . . He drank, and when thoroughly intoxicated would plead to his deceased wife for forgiveness. He lost all capacity for joy. . . . Once a gourmet, he now had no interest in food and good wine . . . and could barely manage to engage in small talk. As might be expected, his work record deteriorated markedly. Appointments were missed and projects haphazardly started and left unfinished. (From Davison & Neale, 1990, p. 221)

Many cases of depression do not become this extreme. A less severe pattern of depression is called **dysthymic disorder,** in which the person shows the sad mood, lack of interest, and loss of pleasure associated with major depression, but less intensely and for a longer period. (The duration must be at least two years to qualify as dysthymic disorder.) Mental and behavioral disruption are also less severe; most people exhibiting dysthymic disorder do not require hospitalization.

Major depressive disorder occurs sometime in the lives of up to 17 percent of the North American or European population; at any given time, about 5 percent of these people are affected (Blazer et al., 1994; Kessler et al., 1994; Smith & Weissman, 1992). Anyone can become depressed, but major depressive disorder is most likely to appear during the late teenage and early adult years (Burke et al., 1990); there is also evidence that rates of depression have increased among young people (Cross-National Collaborative Group, 1992). In the United States and other industrialized Western countries, women are two to three times more likely than men to experience major depressive disorder. Worldwide, however, the gender ratio varies greatly across cultures. For example, there are no reported gender differences in depression in many less economically developed countries in the Middle East, Africa, and Asia, including Iran, Korea, Nigeria, and Uganda (Culbertson, 1997).

Suicide and Depression   Suicide is associated with a variety of psychological disorders, but it is most closely tied to depression; some form of depression has been implicated in 40 to 60 percent of suicides (Clark & Fawcett, 1992). Indeed, suicidal thoughts are a symptom of depressive disorders. Hopelessness about the future—another depressive symptom—and a desire to seek instant escape from problems are also related to suicide attempts (Beck et al., 1990).

Suicide rates differ considerably depending on sociocultural variables such as age, gender, and ethnicity. The rate is as high as 25 per 100,000 individuals in some northern European countries and Japan, for example, and as low as 6 per 100,000 in countries with stronger religious prohibitions against suicide, such as Greece, Italy, Ireland, and the Middle East. In the United States, where the overall suicide rate is about 11 per

A Suicide Attempt

About 32,000 people in the United States and about 4,000 people in Canada commit suicide each year (Centers for Disease Control, 1998; Statistics Canada, 1998). Worldwide, the annual death toll from suicide is about 120,000. Suicide is the second leading cause of death among college students; about 10,000 try to kill themselves each year, and about 1,000 succeed. This rate is much higher than for 18- to 24-year-olds in general, but much lower than for the elderly (Centers for Disease Control, 1998).

100,000, suicide is most common—68 per 100,000—among people sixty-five and older (Centers for Disease Control, 1998). However, since 1950 suicide among adolescents—especially fifteen- to nineteen-year-olds—has quadrupled; it is now the third leading cause of death among adolescents (Centers for Disease Control, 1998). Men are about four times as likely as women to commit suicide (Centers for Disease Control, 1998).

Suicide rates also differ across ethnic groups in the United States. For example, although there is wide variation from tribe to tribe, the overall rate for American Indians is 13.6 per 100,000, compared with 12.9 for European-Americans, 9.1 for Asian-Americans, 7.5 for Hispanic-Americans, and 5.7 for African-Americans (Garland & Zigler, 1993; Howard-Pitney et al., 1992; McIntosh, 1992). The suicide rate among adolescent European-American males has stabilized since 1986. Among African-American teens, however, it has increased dramatically: Since 1980 suicides committed by African-Americans between the ages of ten and nineteen have risen by 114 percent (Centers for Disease Control, 1998).

Predicting exactly who will commit suicide is difficult. For one thing, suicidal thoughts are quite common—54 percent of one sample of college students reported having such thoughts (Meehan et al., 1992). Still, the results of hundreds of research studies provide some predictive guidelines. In the United States, at least, suicide is most likely among European-American males, especially those over forty-five, single or divorced, and living alone. The risk of suicide is also heightened among people who have made a specific plan and given away possessions (Clark et al., 1989). A previous suicide attempt may not always be a good predictor of eventual suicide, because such attempts may have been help-seeking gestures, not failed efforts to die. In fact, although about 10 percent of unsuccessful attempters try again and succeed, most people who commit suicide had made no prior attempts (Clark & Fawcett, 1992).

One myth about suicide is that people who talk about it will never try it. On the contrary, those who say they are thinking of suicide are much *more* likely to attempt suicide than people from the general population. In fact, according to Edwin Schneidman (1987), 80 percent of suicides are preceded by some kind of warning, whether direct ("I think I'm going to kill myself") or vague ("Sometimes I wonder if life is worth living"). Although not everyone who threatens suicide follows through, if you suspect that someone you know is thinking about suicide, encourage the person to contact a mental health professional or a crisis hotline. If the danger is imminent, make the contact yourself and ask for advice about how to respond.

Bipolar Disorders

The alternating appearance of two emotional extremes, or poles, characterizes **bipolar I disorder.** We have already described one emotional pole: depression. The other is **mania,** which is a very agitated, usually elated, emotional state. People in a manic state tend to be utterly optimistic, boundlessly energetic, certain of having extraordinary powers and abilities, and bursting with all sorts of ideas. They become irritated with anyone who tries to reason with them or "slow them down." During manic episodes the person may make impulsive and unwise decisions, including spending their life savings on foolish schemes.

In bipolar I disorder, manic episodes may alternate with periods of deep depression (sometimes, periods of relatively normal mood separate these extremes). This pattern has also been called *manic depression.* Bipolar I disorder is rare; it occurs in only about 1 percent of adults, and it affects men and women about equally. However, it can severely disrupt a person's ability to work or maintain social relationships (Goldberg, Harrow, & Grossman, 1995). Even less common is *bipolar II disorder,* which features major depressive episodes alternating with episodes known as *hypomania,* which are less severe than the manic phases seen in bipolar I disorder.

A somewhat more common mood disorder is **cyclothymic disorder,** the bipolar equivalent of dysthymia. Cyclothymic disorder involves episodes of depression and mania, but the intensity of *both* moods is less severe than in cases of bipolar I disorder.

Causes of Mood Disorders

Research on the causes of mood disorders has focused on biological as well as psychological factors.

LINKAGES

> **Are some mental disorders inherited?** (a link to Biological Aspects of Psychology)

Biological Factors The role of genetics in mood disorders, especially bipolar disorders, is suggested by twin studies and family studies. For example, the co-occurrence of a bipolar disorder is much greater among genetically identical twins than among fraternal, or genetically nonidentical, twins (Egeland et al., 1987). Family studies also show that those who are closely related to people with a bipolar disorder are more likely than others to develop that disorder themselves (Winokur et al., 1995). Major depressive disorder is also more likely to co-occur among identical twins than among nonidentical twins, but the difference is smaller than in bipolar disorders (Kendler et al., 1995; Nurnberger, 1993). Researchers continue to look for the specific genes that might be involved in the transmission of elevated risk for mood disorders (Suinn, 1995).

Other potential biological causes of mood disorders include imbalances in the brain's neurotransmitter systems, malfunctioning of the endocrine system, and disruption of biological rhythms. Neurotransmitters such as norepinephrine, serotonin, and dopamine were implicated decades ago when scientists discovered that drugs capable of altering these substances also relieved mood disorders. Early research suggested that depression was triggered by too little of these neurotransmitters whereas unusually high levels caused mania, but the neurochemical causes now appear more complex than that. Recent research suggests, for example, that mood disorders may result in part from changes in the sensitivity of the neuronal receptors at which these chemicals have their effects in the brain. The precise nature of these neurotransmitter-receptor mechanisms, and just how they affect mood, is not yet fully understood (Delgado et al., 1994; Rush, 1993; Schloss & Williams, 1998).

Mood disorders have also been related to malfunctions of the endocrine system, especially the hypothalamic-pituitary-adrenocortical system (HPA) mentioned in Chapter 13 as being involved in the body's responses to stress. For example, research shows that as many as 70 percent of depressed people secrete abnormally high levels of the stress hormone *cortisol* (Lickey & Gordon, 1991).

The cyclical pattern seen in bipolar disorders and in recurring episodes of major depressive disorder suggests that mood disorders may be related to disturbances in the body's biological clock, which is described in Chapter 9 (Goodwin & Jamison, 1990).

Treating SAD

Seasonal affective disorder (SAD) can often be relieved by exposure to full-spectrum light for as little as a couple of hours a day (Campbell & Murphy, 1998; Sato, 1997).

This possibility seems especially likely to apply to the 15 percent of depressed people who consistently experience a calendar-linked pattern of depressive episodes known as *seasonal affective disorder*. During months of shorter daylight, these people slip into severe depression, accompanied by irritability and excessive sleeping (Blehar & Rosenthal, 1989). Their depression tends to lift as daylight hours increase (Faedda et al., 1993). Disruption of biological rhythms is also suggested by the fact that many depressed people tend to have trouble sleeping—perhaps partly because, during the day, their biological clocks are telling them it is the middle of the night. Resetting the biological clock through methods such as sleep deprivation or light stimulation has relieved depression in some cases (Kuhs & Tolle, 1991).

Psychological Factors   Traditional psychodynamic theory proposes that depression stems from unconscious processes associated with the loss of a loved one. According to Freud, in addition to experiencing grief we feel anger over being abandoned, and some of that anger is directed inward, resulting in self-hatred and other symptoms of depression. More recently, psychodynamic theorists have suggested that depression may result when people base too much of their self-esteem on a particular achievement or relationship (Blatt & Ford, 1994; Main, 1996).

A variety of cognitive-behavioral theories also address the causes of depression. One of the earliest stemmed from the research on *learned helplessness* described in Chapter 6. Just as animals become inactive and appear depressed when they have no control over negative events, humans may experience depression as a result of feeling incapable of controlling their lives, especially the stressors besetting them (Klein & Seligman, 1976). But most of us have limited control; why aren't we all depressed? The ways in which people learn to *think* about events in their lives may hold the key. For example, Aaron Beck's (1967, 1976) cognitive theory of depression suggests that depressed people develop mental habits of (1) blaming themselves when things go wrong, (2) focusing on and exaggerating the negative side of events, and (3) jumping to overly generalized, pessimistic conclusions. Such cognitive habits, says Beck, are errors that lead to depressing thoughts and other symptoms of depression. There is ample evidence that depressed people do think about significant negative events in ways that are likely to increase or prolong their depression (Gotlib & Hammen, 1992).

Cognitive-behavioral theories of depression are somewhat consistent with the psychodynamically oriented *object relations* approach discussed in Chapter 14 (Blatt & Maroudas, 1992). Both views suggest that negative patterns of thinking can be acquired through maladaptive experiences in childhood. For example, research indicates that children whose early relationships with parents or other primary caregivers were characterized by deprivation or abuse are especially likely to develop depression in later life (Gotlib & Hammen, 1992). Further, close, protective, predictable, and responsive early relationships may be necessary in order for children to form healthy views of themselves, positive expectations about others, and a sense of control over the environment (Bowlby, 1980; Main, 1996).

Severe, long-lasting depression is especially common among people who attribute the lack of control or other problems they experience to a permanent, generalized lack of personal competence rather than to a temporary lapse or external cause (Abramson, Seligman, & Teasdale, 1978; Seligman et al., 1988). Thus, *attributional style* may be another important cognitive factor in depression. People may be prone to depression when they blame negative events on themselves and believe they will always be incapable of doing better. One version of attributional theory even postulates *hopelessness* as a subtype of depression (Abramson, Metalsky, & Alloy, 1989; Metalsky et al., 1993; Rose et al., 1994).

Depressed people do hold more negative beliefs about themselves and their lives than other people, but the exact significance of these beliefs is not yet clear (Gara et al., 1993). For one thing, pessimistic beliefs may be a symptom of depression rather than its cause. Also, research indicates that the negative beliefs held by depressed persons are often an accurate reflection of these people's unfortunate life situations (Coyne & Whiffen, 1995). In any case, the cognitive-behavioral perspective suggests that whether depression continues, or worsens, depends in part on how people respond once they start to feel depressed. Those who ruminate about negative events, about why they occur, and even about feeling depressed are likely to feel more and more depressed. According to Susan Nolen-Hoeksema (1990), this *ruminative style* is especially characteristic of women and may help explain gender differences in the frequency of depression. When men start to feel sad, she says, they tend to use a *distracting style,* engaging in activity that helps bring them out of their depressed mood (Just & Alloy, 1997; Nolen-Hoeksema, Morrow, & Fredrickson, 1993).

Notice that cognitive-behavioral explanations of depression are consistent with the diathesis-stress model of disorder. These explanations suggest that certain cognitive styles constitute a predisposition (or diathesis) that makes a person vulnerable to depression, the occurrence of which is made more likely by stressors. Indeed, most episodes of major depressive disorder are preceded by the onset of major stressors, such as the loss of a loved one. As suggested in Chapter 13, the depressing effects of these stressors are likely to be magnified by lack of social support, inadequate coping skills, and the presence of other stressful conditions such as poverty.

Given the number and complexity of biological, psychological, and situational factors potentially involved in causing mood disorders, the diathesis-stress model appears to be an especially appropriate guide to future research. One study based on this model looked at the role of genetics and stressful events in shaping mood disorders in a large group of female twin pairs. Both factors were associated with major depression; the women at highest genetic risk were the most likely to become depressed following a significant stressor (Kendler et al., 1995). In the final analysis, it may turn out that each subtype of mood disorder is caused by a unique combination of factors. The challenge for researchers is to identify these subtypes and map out their causal ingredients.

SCHIZOPHRENIA

Here is part of a letter that arrived in the mail a while ago:

Dear Sirs:

Pertaining to our continuing failure to prosecute violations of minor's rights to sovereign equality which are occurring in gestations being compromised by the ingestion of controlled substances, . . . the skewing of androgyny which continues in female

juveniles even after separation from their mother's has occurred, and as a means of pro-
mulflagitating my paying Governor Hickel of Alaska for my employees to have personal
services endorsements and controlled substance endorsements, . . . the Iraqi oil being
released by the United Nations being identified as Kurdistanian oil, and the July, 1991
issue of the Siberian Review spells President Eltsin's name without a letter y.

The disorganization and bizarre content of this letter suggest that its writer suffers from **schizophrenia,** a pattern of severely disturbed thinking, emotion, perception, and behavior that seriously impairs the ability to communicate and relate to others and disrupts most other aspects of daily functioning. Schizophrenia is one of the most severe and disabling of all mental disorders. Its core symptoms are seen virtually everywhere in the world, occurring in about 1 percent of the population (American Psychiatric Association, 1994). In the United States, it appears about equally in various ethnic groups, but, like most disorders, it tends to be diagnosed more frequently in economically disadvantaged populations. Schizophrenia is seen about equally in men and women, although some studies have suggested that, in women, it may appear later in life, be less severe, and respond better to treatment (Seeman, 1995; Syzmanski et al., 1995).

Schizophrenia tends to develop in adolescence or early adulthood. The onset is gradual in some cases and more rapid in others. About 40 percent of people with schizophrenia improve with treatment and are able to function reasonably well; the rest show continuous or intermittent symptoms that permanently impair their functioning (Hegarty et al., 1994). It has been estimated that 10 to 13 percent of homeless individuals suffer from schizophrenia (Fischer & Breakey, 1991).

One of the best predictors of the course of schizophrenia is *premorbid adjustment,* the level of functioning a person had achieved before schizophrenic symptoms first appeared. Improvement is more likely in those who had attained higher levels of education and occupation, and who had established supportive relationships with family and friends (Watt & Saiz, 1991).

Symptoms of Schizophrenia

People displaying schizophrenia have problems in how they think, and what they think. The nineteenth-century psychiatrist Eugen Bleuler coined the word *schizophrenia,* or "split mind," to refer to the peculiarities of schizophrenic thinking. Contrary to popular belief, *schizophrenia* does not mean "split personality," as in dissociative identity disorder (multiple personality), but refers instead to a splitting of normally integrated mental processes, such as thoughts and feelings. Thus, for instance, some schizophrenics may giggle while claiming to feel sad.

LINKAGES

How do schizophrenic individuals think? (a link to Cognition and Language)

Schizophrenic thought and language are often disorganized. *Neologisms* ("new words" that have meaning only to the person speaking them) are common; the appearance of "promulflagitating" in the letter above is one example. That letter also illustrates *loose associations,* the tendency for one thought to be logically unconnected, or only superficially related, to the next. Sometimes the associations are based on double meanings or on the way words sound (*clang associations*). For example, "My true family name is Abel or A Bell. We descended from the clan of Abel, who originated the bell of rights, which we now call the bill of rights." In the most severe cases, a jumble of words known as *word salad* reflects utterly chaotic thoughts. For example, "Upon the advisability of held keeping, environment of the seabeach gathering, to the forest stream, reinstatement to be placed, poling the paddleboat, of the swamp morass, to the forest compensation of the dunce" (Lehman, 1967, p. 627).

The *content* of schizophrenic thinking is also disturbed. Often it includes a bewildering assortment of delusions, especially delusions of persecution. Some patients say that space aliens are trying to steal their thoughts; they may interpret everything from TV commercials to casual hand gestures as part of the plot. Delusions that common events are somehow related to oneself are called *ideas of reference.* Delusions of grandeur may also be present; one young man was convinced that the president of the

United States was trying to contact him for advice. Other types of delusions include *thought broadcasting,* in which patients believe that their thoughts can be heard by others; *thought blocking* or *withdrawal,* the belief that someone is either preventing thoughts or "stealing" them as they appear; and *thought insertion,* the belief that other people's thoughts are appearing in one's own mind. Some patients may believe that, as with puppets, their behavior is controlled by others.

People with schizophrenia often report that they cannot focus their attention. They may feel overwhelmed as they try to attend to everything at once. Various perceptual disorders may also appear. The person may feel detached from the real world and see other people as flat cutouts. The body may feel like a machine, or parts of it may seem to be dead or rotting. **Hallucinations,** or false perceptions, are common, often emerging as voices. These voices may sound like an overheard conversation, or they may urge the person to do or not to do things; sometimes they comment on or narrate the person's actions. Hallucinations can also involve nonexistent sights, smells, tastes, and touches. (As shown in Figure 15.3, the brain areas activated during hallucinations are related to those that respond to real sights and sounds.) The emotional expression of patients with schizophrenia is often muted, but when they do display emotion, it is frequently exaggerated or inappropriate. They may cry for no apparent reason or fly into a rage in response to a simple question.

Some schizophrenia patients are extremely agitated, ceaselessly moving their limbs, making facial grimaces, or pacing the floor in highly ritualistic sequences. Others become so withdrawn that they move very little. Lack of motivation and poor social skills, deteriorating personal hygiene, and an inability to function day to day are other common characteristics of schizophrenia.

FIGURE 15.3

PET Scan Showing Areas of the Brain Activated During Hallucinations

This 23-year-old schizophrenic patient said he saw rolling, disembodied heads that spoke to him and gave him instructions. PET scans revealed heightened activity in visual and auditory (language) association cortex, rather than in the primary cortex regions for these senses. Posterior cingulate cortex (part of the limbic system), which was also activated, is known to be affected by drugs that produce hallucinations (Silbersweig et al., 1995).

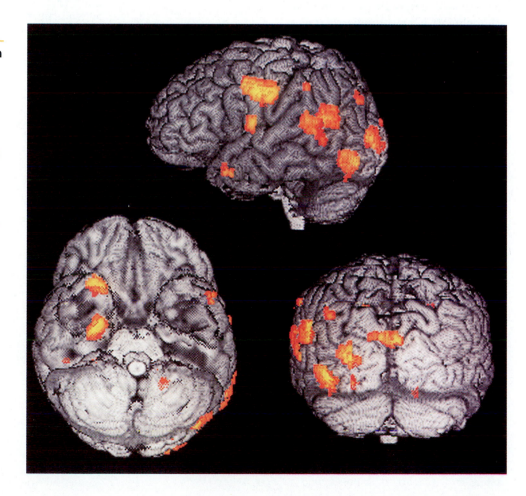

Categorizing Schizophrenia

DSM-IV lists five major subtypes of schizophrenia: paranoid, disorganized, catatonic, undifferentiated, and residual (see Table 15.4). These subtype labels convey a certain amount of useful information. We know, for example, that the prognosis for paranoid schizophrenia is somewhat better than for the other subtypes (Benton & McGlashan, 1991). However, subtype labels do not always provide accurate information about patients' behavior, because some symptoms appear in more than one subtype. Further, people originally diagnosed as suffering from disorganized schizophrenia might later display characteristics of the paranoid subtype. Finally, the DSM-IV subtypes may not be linked very closely to the various biological conditions thought to underlie schizophrenia (Benton & McGlashan, 1991). With these concerns in mind, many researchers are now using methods of categorizing schizophrenia that focus more precisely on the kinds of symptoms that patients display.

One such method highlights the distinction between positive and negative symptoms of schizophrenia. **Positive symptoms** involve distortions or exaggerations of cognitive, perceptual, or behavioral functioning—including disorganized thoughts, hallucinations, and delusions, for example. They are called positive symptoms because they appear as undesirable *additions* to a person's mental life (Andreasen et al., 1995). By contrast, **negative symptoms** appear to *subtract* elements from normal mental life,

TABLE 15.4

Subtypes of Schizophrenia

Mental health professionals still use these DSM-IV subtypes when diagnosing schizophrenia, but many researchers now tend to categorize patients in terms of whether positive or negative symptoms of schizophrenia predominate.

Type	Frequency	Prominent Features
Paranoid schizophrenia	40 percent of schizophrenics; appears late in life (after age 25–30)	Delusions of grandeur or persecution; anger; anxiety; argumentativeness; extreme jealousy; onset often sudden; signs of impairment may be subtle
Disorganized schizophrenia	5 percent of all schizophrenics; high prevalence in homeless population	Delusions; hallucinations; incoherent speech; facial grimaces; inappropriate laughter/giggling; neglected personal hygiene; loss of bladder/bowel control
Catatonic schizophrenia	8 percent of all schizophrenics	Disordered movement, alternating between immobility (stupor) and excitement. In stupor, the person does not speak or attend to communication; the body is rigid or can be posed in virtually any posture (a condition called "waxy flexibility").
Undifferentiated schizophrenia	40 percent of all schizophrenics	Patterns of disordered behavior, thought, and emotion that do not fall easily into any other subtype
Residual schizophrenia	Varies	Applies to people who have had episodes of schizophrenia but are not currently displaying symptoms

Catatonic Stupor

This woman's lack of motivation and other negative symptoms of schizophrenia are severe enough that she appears to be in a stupor. Such patients may become rigid or, as in this case, show a waxy flexibility that allows them to be posed in virtually any position.

inasmuch as they involve a decrease in or loss of normal functioning. These symptoms include *anhedonia* (the absence of feelings of pleasure), *alogia* (lack of speech), *avolition* (loss of motivation), *flat affect* (restricted emotional expression), and other deficits (Andreasen et al., 1995; Nicholson & Neufeld, 1993).

Describing patients in terms of positive and negative symptoms does not require that they be placed in one category or the other. Indeed, many patients exhibit both positive and negative symptoms. However, it is important to know whether negative or positive symptoms predominate, because when symptoms are mainly negative, schizophrenia is generally more severe and less responsive to treatment. In such cases, patients typically experience long-term disability (e.g., Benton & McGlashan, 1994).

Another method involves categorizing schizophrenic symptoms in terms of whether they are *psychotic* (hallucinations or delusions), *disorganized* (incoherent speech, chaotic behavior, inappropriate affect), or *negative* (e.g., alogia or avolition). Some researchers believe that these categories of symptoms represent three separate dimensions of schizophrenia (Buchanan & Carpenter, 1994; Johnstone & Frith, 1996). In support of this interpretation is research suggesting that patients' negative symptoms do not improve, and may even worsen, at the same time that their psychotic symptoms are being reduced through drug treatment (Andreasen et al., 1995). The fact that the three dimensions of schizophrenia are to some extent independent from one another has led to speculation that each may ultimately be traceable to different causes and, further, that each may require different treatments.

Causes of Schizophrenia

The search for the causes of schizophrenia has been more intense than for any other psychological disorder. The findings so far confirm one thing for certain: No single cause can adequately account for all forms of schizophrenia.

Biological Factors   Research in behavioral genetics shows that schizophrenia runs in families (Gottesman, 1991). One longitudinal family study found, for instance, that 16 percent of the children of schizophrenic mothers—compared with 2 percent of those of nonschizophrenic mothers—developed schizophrenia themselves over a twenty-five-year period (Parnas et al., 1993). Even if they are adopted by nonschizophrenic families, the children of schizophrenic parents are ten times more likely to develop schizophrenia than adopted children whose biological parents are not schizophrenic (Kety et al., 1994). Still, it is unlikely that a single gene transmits schizophrenia (Kendler & Diehl, 1993). Among identical-twin pairs in which one member displays schizophrenia, 40 percent of the other members will, too; but 60 percent will not (McGue, 1992). It is more likely that some people inherit a genetic *predisposition,* or diathesis, for schizophrenia (Moldin & Gottesman, 1997).

The search for more specific causes of schizophrenia focuses on a number of abnormalities in the structure, functioning, and chemistry of the brain that tend to appear in schizophrenics. For example, numerous MRI and other brain imaging studies have shown that, compared with other mental patients, many schizophrenia patients have less tissue in thalamic regions, prefrontal cortex, and some subcortical areas (Andreasen, 1997; Breier et al., 1992; Buchsbaum et al., 1992). As shown in Figure 15.4 on page 548, shrinkage of tissue in these regions leads to corresponding enlargement in the brain's fluid-filled spaces, called *ventricles.* The brain areas in which anatomical abnormalities have been found are active in emotional expression, thinking, and information processing—functions that are disordered in schizophrenia. Enlarged ventricles and reduced prefrontal cortex are more often found in patients whose schizophrenic symptoms are predominantly negative; those with mainly positive symptoms tend to have essentially normal-looking brains (Andreasen, 1997).

Hundreds of studies of brain functioning in people diagnosed with schizophrenia provide general support for the idea that their impairments in information-processing and other cognitive abilities are consistent with structural damage (Clementz, McDowell, & Zisook, 1994; Niznikiewicz et al., 1997). For example, patients whose schizophrenic symptoms are predominantly negative are especially likely to display

FIGURE 15.4

Brain Abnormalities in Schizophrenia

Here is a magnetic resonance imaging (MRI) comparison of the brains of identical twins. The schizophrenic twin (on the right) has greatly enlarged ventricles (see arrows) and correspondingly less brain tissue, including that in the hippocampal area, a region involved in memory and emotion. The same results appeared in fourteen other identical-twin pairs; by contrast, no significant differences appeared between members of a seven-pair control group of normal identical twins (Suddath et al., 1990). These results support the idea that brain abnormalities are associated with schizophrenia and, because identical twins have the same genes, that such abnormalities may stem from nongenetic factors.

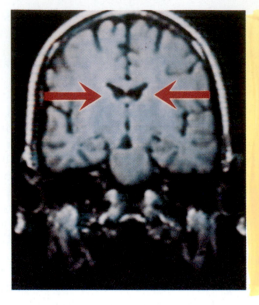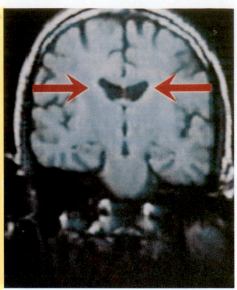

cognitive deficits associated with the frontal-cortex problems often seen in these patients (Buchanan et al., 1994). This research provides important clues, but we still do not know the extent to which, or exactly how, specific structural abnormalities are related to specific forms of schizophrenia. For one thing, not all schizophrenia patients show brain abnormalities, and some normal people do.

Researchers are also investigating the possibility that abnormalities in brain chemistry—especially in neurotransmitter systems that use dopamine—play a role in causing or intensifying schizophrenic symptoms. Because drugs that block the brain's dopamine receptors often reduce hallucinations, disordered thinking, and other positive symptoms of schizophrenia, some investigators speculate that schizophrenia results from excess dopamine. However, as we have seen in connection with neurochemical theories of mood disorders, the relationship between dopamine and schizophrenia appears to be quite complex, in several respects. First, excess dopamine is not always associated with schizophrenia. Second, schizophrenia may involve over- or undersensitivity of dopamine receptors as well as an abnormal amount of dopamine itself. And, third, schizophrenia might be related to *dysregulation* of dopamine mechanisms in several interconnected regions of the brain (e.g., Healy et al., 1998). Some research suggests, for example, that excessive activity in dopamine systems may be related to the appearance of hallucinations, delusions, and other positive symptoms of schizophrenia that are treatable with dopamine-blocking drugs. Abnormally low dopamine system activity, especially in prefrontal brain areas, has been associated with negative symptoms such as withdrawal (Cohen & Servan-Schreiber, 1992; Davis et al., 1991).

Some researchers are integrating genetic and environmental explanations of schizophrenia by looking for *neurodevelopmental abnormalities* (Cannon, 1998). Perhaps, they say, some forms of schizophrenia arise from disruptions in brain development during the period from gestation through childhood, when the brain is growing and its various functions are maturing. Studies have shown, for instance, that prenatal exposure to viral infections or other physical traumas are associated with increased risk for developing schizophrenia (Takei et al., 1994). Similarly, children whose birth weight was low or who experienced oxygen deprivation during birth are more likely to have the brain abnormalities described earlier; these abnormalities are especially likely in children of schizophrenic parents (Cannon et al., 1993). Thus, it may be that the expression of a genetically transmitted predisposition for brain abnormality is enhanced by environmental stressors such as maternal drug use during pregnancy, complications during birth, and childhood malnutrition. Neurodevelopmental factors may help explain why children of schizophrenic parents tend to show the kinds of

SCHIZOPHRENIA	
Aspect	**Key Features**
Common Symptoms	
Disorders of thought	Disturbed content, including delusions; and disorganization, including loose associations, neologisms, and word salad.
Disorders of perception	Hallucinations, or false perceptions; poorly focused attention.
Disorders of emotion	Flat affect; or inappropriate tears, laughter, or anger.
Possible Causes	
Biological	Genetics; abnormalities in brain structure; abnormalities in dopamine systems; neurodevelopmental problems.
Psychological	Learned maladaptive behavior; disturbed patterns of family communication.

in review

subtle cognitive and intellectual problems associated with brain abnormalities (Cannon et al., 1994; Neumann et al., 1995).

Psychological Factors   Early psychodynamic theorists suggested that schizophrenic symptoms represent regression to early childhood—an extreme reaction to anxiety about expressing or becoming aware of unacceptable unconscious impulses (Freud, 1924). Other theorists have attributed schizophrenia to unclear or contradictory communication in the family or to learned, maladaptive efforts at coping with anxiety (Bateson et al., 1956; Mednick, 1958; Ullmann & Krasner, 1975).

None of these hypotheses has received strong research support. Indeed, psychological factors alone are no longer considered to be primary causes of schizophrenia. Contemporary research does suggest, however, that psychological processes, including unfortunate learning experiences and maladaptive family communication patterns, can contribute to the appearance of schizophrenia and influence its course. For example, schizophrenia patients living with relatives who are critical, unsupportive, or emotionally overinvolved are especially likely to relapse following improvement (Kavanagh, 1992). Family members' negative attitudes may be a source of stress that actually increases the chances that disruptive or odd behaviors will persist or worsen (Rosenfarb et al., 1995; Weisman et al., 1993).

The Vulnerability Model: An Integrative View   The causal theories we have discussed are all consistent with the diathesis-stress model, which assumes that stress may activate a person's predisposition for disorder (Fowles, 1992). ("In Review: Schizophrenia" summarizes these causal theories as well as the symptoms of schizophrenia.) The diathesis-stress perspective is embodied in the *vulnerability model* of schizophrenia (Cornblatt & Erlenmeyer-Kimling, 1985). This model suggests that (1) vulnerability to schizophrenia is mainly biological; (2) different people have differing degrees of vulnerability; (3) vulnerability is influenced partly by genetics and partly by neurodevelopmental abnormalities associated with prenatal risk factors, birth complications, and other problems; and (4) psychological components, such as exposure to poor parenting or inadequate coping skills, may play a role in determining whether schizophrenia actually appears, but also may influence the course of the disorder (Susser & Lin, 1992; Walker & Diforio, 1998). Many different blendings of

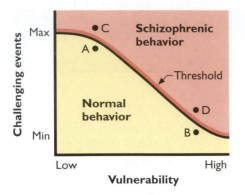

FIGURE 15.5

The Vulnerability Model of Schizophrenia

According to this model, a person can cross the threshold into schizophrenia through many combinations of predisposition and stress. A strong predisposition for schizophrenia and little environmental stress (point D), a weak predisposition and a lot of stress (point C), or any other sufficiently potent combination can lead to disorder.

Source: Zubin & Spring, 1977.

vulnerability and stress can lead to schizophrenia, as Figure 15.5 illustrates. Persons whose genetic characteristics or prenatal experiences leave them vulnerable to develop schizophrenia may be especially likely to do so if they are later exposed to learning experiences or family conflicts and other stressors that elicit and maintain schizophrenic patterns of thought and action. Those same experiences and stressors would not be expected to lead to schizophrenia in people who are less vulnerable to developing the disorder. In other words, schizophrenia is a highly complex disorder (probably more than one disorder) whose origins appear to lie in numerous biological and psychological domains, some of which are yet to be discovered (Durand & Barlow, 1997).

PERSONALITY DISORDERS

Personality disorders are long-standing, inflexible ways of behaving that are not so much severe mental disorders as styles of life. These disorders affect all areas of functioning and, from childhood or adolescence, create problems for those who display them and for others (Millon & Davis, 1996). Some psychologists view personality disorders as interpersonal strategies (Kiesler, 1996) or as the extreme and maladaptive expressions of personality traits that are evident in everyone to varying degrees (Widiger & Costa, 1994).

The ten personality disorders found on Axis II of DSM-IV are grouped into three clusters that share certain features (see Table 15.5). Here, we describe just a few of these disorders. The *odd-eccentric* cluster includes paranoid, schizoid, and schizotypal per-

A Dangerous Case of Antisocial Personality Disorder

Andrew Phillip Cunanan, pictured here on an FBI poster, murdered fashion designer Gianni Versace and several other men across the United States in 1997. His violent crime spree, which ended with his suicide in July of that year, represents the antisocial personality at its worst.

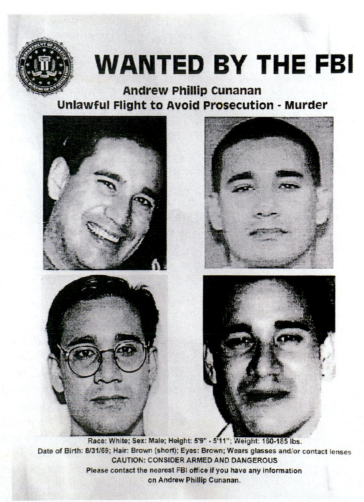

TABLE 15.5

Personality Disorders

Here are brief descriptions of each of the ten personality disorders listed on Axis II of DSM-IV

Type	Typical Features
Paranoid	Suspiciousness and distrust of others, all of whom are assumed to be hostile.
Schizoid	Detachment from social relationships; restricted range of emotion.
Schizotypal	Detachment from, and great discomfort in, social relationships; odd perceptions, thoughts, beliefs, and behaviors.
Dependent	Helplessness; excessive need to be taken care of; submissive and clinging behavior; difficulty in making decisions.
Obsessive-compulsive	Preoccupation with orderliness, perfection, and control.
Avoidant	Inhibition in social situations; feelings of inadequacy; oversensitivity to criticism.
Histrionic	Excessive emotionality and preoccupation with being the center of attention; emotional shallowness; overly dramatic behavior.
Narcissistic	Exaggerated ideas of self-importance and achievements; preoccupation with fantasies of success; arrogance.
Borderline	Lack of stability in interpersonal relationships, self-image, and emotion; impulsivity; angry outbursts; intense fear of abandonment; recurring suicidal gestures.
Antisocial	Shameless disregard for, and violation of, other people's rights.

sonality disorders. People diagnosed as having schizotypal personality disorder, for example, display some of the peculiarities seen in schizophrenia but are not disturbed enough to be labeled as schizophrenic. Rather than hallucinating, these people may report "illusions" of sights or sounds. They may also exhibit "magical thinking," including odd superstitions or beliefs (such as that they have extrasensory perception or that salt under the mattress will prevent insomnia). The *anxious-fearful* cluster includes dependent, obsessive-compulsive, and avoidant personality disorders. The avoidant personality disorder, for example, is akin to social phobia in the sense that persons labeled with this disorder tend to be "loners" with a long-standing pattern of avoiding social situations and of being particularly sensitive to criticism or rejection. They want to be with others but are too inhibited. Finally, the *dramatic-erratic* cluster includes the histrionic, narcissistic, borderline, and antisocial personality disorders. The main characteristics of narcissistic personality disorder, for example, are an exaggerated sense of self-importance, extreme sensitivity to criticism, a constant need for attention, and a tendency to arrogantly overestimate personal abilities and achievements. Persons displaying this disorder feel entitled to special treatment *by* others but are markedly lacking in empathy *for* others.

From the perspective of public welfare and safety, the most serious and most intensively studied personality disorder is **antisocial personality disorder.** It is marked by a long-term pattern of irresponsible, impulsive, unscrupulous, even criminal behavior, beginning in childhood or early adolescence. In the nineteenth century, this pattern was called *moral insanity,* because such persons appear to have no morals or common decency; later, people in this category were called *psychopaths* or *sociopaths*. The current "antisocial personality" label more accurately portrays them as troublesome, but not "insane" by the legal standards we will discuss shortly. About 3 percent of men and about 1 percent of women in the United States fall into this diagnostic category.

At their least troublesome, people exhibiting antisocial personality are a nuisance. They are often charming, intelligent, glib talkers who borrow money and fail to return it; they are arrogant and self-centered manipulators who "con" people into doing things for them, usually by lying and taking advantage of the decency and trust of others. A hallmark of antisocial personality disorder is a lack of anxiety, remorse, or guilt, whether they have wrecked a borrowed car or killed an innocent person (Hare, 1993). Fortunately, these individuals tend to become less active and dangerous after the age of forty (Stoff, Breiling, & Maser, 1997). No method has yet been found for permanently altering their behavior (Rice, 1997), but research suggests that identification of antisocial personalities prior to the development of their more treatment-resistant traits may offer the best hope for dealing with this disorder (Lynam, 1996; Stoff, Breiling, & Maser, 1997).

As for the causes of antisocial personality disorder, theories abound. Some studies suggest a genetic predisposition for the disorder, possibly in the form of chronic underarousal of both the autonomic and central nervous systems (Patrick, Cuthbert, & Lang, 1994; Raine, Venables, & Williams, 1990). This underarousal leads to abnormally low anxiousness, which may make people less sensitive to punishment than is normally the case (Stoff, Breiling, & Maser, 1997). From psychological and social perspectives, broken homes, rejection by parents, poor discipline, lack of good parental models, lack of attachment to early caregivers, impulsivity, conflict-filled childhoods, and poverty have all been suggested as environmental factors contributing to failure to acquire adaptive patterns of conformity to social standards (Lahey et al., 1995; Raine, Brennan, & Mednick, 1994; Tremblay et al., 1994). The diathesis-stress model suggests that antisocial personality disorder results when these environmental conditions interact with genetic predispositions to low arousal and the sensation-seeking and impulsivity associated with it (Rutter, 1997).

A SAMPLING OF OTHER PSYCHOLOGICAL DISORDERS

The disorders described so far represent some of the most prevalent and socially disruptive psychological problems encountered in cultures around the world. Several others are mentioned in other chapters. In Chapter 9, for example, we discuss insomnia, night terrors, and other sleep disorders; mental retardation is covered in Chapter 10; sexual dysfunctions are mentioned in Chapter 11; and posttraumatic stress disorder is described in Chapter 13. Here, we consider two other significant psychological problems: substance-related disorders and some disorders of childhood.

Substance-Related Disorders

When people are consistently unable to control their use of psychoactive drugs and this behavior has harmful consequences for them, they exhibit what the DSM-IV calls **substance-related disorders.** These disorders create major political, economic, social, and health problems worldwide. The substances involved most often are alcohol and other depressants, such as barbiturates; opiates, such as heroin; stimulants, such as cocaine or amphetamines; and psychedelics, such as LSD.

As mentioned in Chapter 9, one effect of using some substances (including alcohol, heroin, and amphetamines) is *addiction,* a physical need for the substance. DSM-IV calls addiction *physiological dependence.* Usually, addiction is evident when the person begins to need more and more of a substance to achieve the desired state; this is called *building a tolerance.* When addicted people stop using the substance, they experience painful, often terrifying and potentially dangerous *withdrawal symptoms* as the body tries to readjust to a substance-free state. However, not all dependence is physiological in nature (Widiger & Smith, 1994). People can also display *psychological dependence,* sometimes called *behavioral dependence;* in such cases, a drug has become their primary source of reward and their lives essentially revolve around getting and using it (Edwards, 1986). People who are behaviorally dependent on a drug often display problems that are at least as serious as, and sometimes more difficult to treat than, those exhibited by people who are physiologically addicted.

Even when use of a drug does not create behavioral or physiological dependence, some people may use it in a way that is harmful to themselves or others. For example, they may rely on the drug to bolster self-confidence, or to avoid depressive, angry, anxious, or other painful feelings, but the drug's effects may create other problems that cause these people to lose their job, neglect their children, or have an auto accident. DSM-IV defines such behavior as *substance abuse,* a pattern of drug use that creates significant social, legal, or interpersonal problems. In short, substance-related disorders can be extremely serious even when they do not involve addiction.

In Chapter 9, we described the impact on consciousness of the psychoactive drugs typically associated with substance dependence and abuse; here we focus on the causes and broader consequences of their use.

Alcohol Use Disorders   More than 7 percent of American adults—nearly 14 million people—display *alcohol dependence or abuse,* a pattern of continuous or intermittent drinking that may lead to addiction and almost always causes severe social, physical, and other problems (NIAAA, 1994). Males outnumber females in this category by a ratio of about 3 to 1, although the problem is on the rise among women and among teenagers of both genders (Blum, Nielsen, & Riggs, 1998; USDHHS, 1997). Prolonged overuse of alcohol can result in life-threatening liver damage, reduced cognitive abilities, vitamin deficiencies that can lead to an irreversible brain disorder called *Korsakoff's psychosis* (severe memory loss), and a host of other physical ailments. Alcohol dependence or abuse, commonly referred to as **alcoholism,** has been implicated in half of all the traffic fatalities, homicides, and suicides that occur each year (NIAAA, 1998); alcoholism also figures prominently in rape and child abuse, as well as in elevated rates of hospitalization and absenteeism from work (USDHHS, 1990; U.S. Department of Justice, 1998).

Several explanations for alcohol abuse have been proposed. Some theorists see it as stemming from impulsivity, neuroticism, and other personality traits (Sher et al., 1991). Those taking a more behavioral approach maintain that people learn to use alcohol because it helps them cope with stressors. But use can become abuse, often

LINKAGES

Alcohol Abuse

It has been estimated that 43 percent of U.S. adults have an alcoholic in their families (NIDA, 1991). Children who grow up in families in which one or both parents abuse alcohol are at increased risk for developing a host of mental disorders, including substance-related disorders (Nietzel et al., 1998). And as described in Chapter 12, children of mothers who abused alcohol during pregnancy may be born with fetal alcohol syndrome.

TABLE 15.6

Social Drinking Versus Alcoholism

Social drinking differs markedly from alcoholism, but it is all too easy for people to drift from social to alcoholic drinking patterns. Alcoholism can include heavy drinking on a daily basis, on weekends only, or in isolated binges lasting weeks or months.

Social Drinkers	Alcoholics
Sip drinks.	Gulp drinks.
Usually drink in moderation and can control the amount consumed.	Drink increasing quantities (develop tolerance). Sometimes drink until blacking out. May not recall events that occur while drinking.
Usually drink to enhance the pleasure of social situations.	Drink for the chemical effect, often to relieve tension or face problems; often drink alone, including in the morning to reduce hangover or to face the day.
Do not usually think about or talk about drinking in nondrinking situations.	Become preoccupied with getting next drink, often sneaking drinks during working hours or at home.
Do not experience physical, social, or occupational problems caused by drinking.	Suffer physical disorders, damaged social relationships, and impaired capacity to work because of drinking.

addiction, if drinking is a person's main coping strategy (Walters, 1992; see also Table 15.6). The stress-reduction theory of alcoholism has been supported by studies indicating that alcohol can reduce animals' learned fear of a particular location and that animals in a stressful conflict situation will choose to drink alcohol if it is available (Freed, 1971). The stress-reducing effects of alcohol have also been shown in humans, but not consistently (Cooper et al., 1992a).

The importance of learning is further suggested by evidence that alcoholism is more common among ethnic and cultural groups (such as the Irish and English) in which frequent drinking tends to be socially reinforced than among groups (such as Jews, Italians, and Chinese) in which all but moderate drinking tends to be discouraged (Wilson et al., 1996). Moreover, differing expressions of social support for drinking can result in differing consumption patterns within a cultural group. For example, one study found significantly more drinking among Japanese men living in Japan (where social norms for males' drinking are quite permissive) compared with those living in Hawaii or California, where excessive drinking is less strongly supported (Kitano et al., 1992). Learning would also help explain why the prevalence of alcoholism is higher than average among people working as bartenders and cocktail servers, and in other jobs where alcohol is available and drinking is socially reinforced, even expected (Fillmore & Caetano, 1980). (Of course, it is also possible that attraction to alcohol led some of these people into such jobs in the first place.)

Learning, then, appears to be implicated in excessive drinking, but heredity may also play a role, especially among males (Azar, 1995b). For example, the sons of alcoholics are more likely than others to become alcoholic themselves; and if the sons are identical twins, both are at increased risk for alcoholism, even when raised apart (Cloninger, 1987; McGue, Pickens, & Svikis, 1992). The role of genetics appears to be greatest among males who begin their alcoholic drinking pattern at an early age and display other conduct problems as teenagers (McGue, Pickens, & Svikis, 1992). For females, and for males whose problem drinking appears later in life, the evidence for genetic causes is much less compelling. In such cases, it may be that any genetic predisposition is too weak to result in alcoholism except when amplified by social and cultural influences that promote drinking (McGue, Pickens, & Svikis, 1992). Indeed, reanalysis of the evidence suggests that the genetic component of alcoholism may not be as strong overall as once believed (Gelernter, Goldman, & Risch, 1993); just what might be inherited, or which genes are involved, is certainly not clear. One possibility involves abnormalities in the brain's neurotransmitter systems or in the body's metabolism of alcohol (Devor, 1994; Kranzler & Anton, 1994). Sons of alcoholics do tend to be less sensitive than other males to the effects of alcohol—a factor that may contribute to greater consumption (Pollack, 1992)—but it is unclear whether this reduced sensitivity reflects a biological predisposition.

Heroin and Cocaine Dependence   Like alcoholics, heroin and cocaine addicts suffer many serious physical problems, both as a result of the drug itself and of the poor eating and other unhealthy habits it engenders. The risk of death from an overdose, contaminated drugs, or AIDS (contracted through blood in shared needles), as well as from suicide, is also always present. Drug dependence tends to be more prevalent among males, especially young males (Warner et al., 1995).

Continued use or overdoses of cocaine can cause problems ranging from nausea and hyperactivity to paranoid thinking, sudden depressive "crashes," and even death. An estimated 1 million Americans have become physiologically dependent on cocaine, and millions more use it on occasion (National Institute on Drug Abuse, 1996). The widespread availability of crack, a powerful and relatively cheap form of cocaine, has made it one of the most dangerous and addicting drugs in existence. Pregnant women who use cocaine are much more likely than nonusers to lose their babies through spontaneous abortions, placental detachments, early fetal death, or stillbirths. The more than 50,000 "crack babies" born each year to cocaine-using mothers are at risk for numerous physical and mental birth defects (Julien, 1992) and—unless preventive measures are taken early—are prone to emotional and academic problems in later life (Wren, 1998).

Although addiction to substances like heroin is largely understood to be a biological process brought about by the physiological effects of the drugs, explaining why people first use them is more complicated. Beyond the obvious and immediate pleasure that these drugs provide, the causes of initial drug abuse are less well established than the reasons for alcohol abuse. One line of theorizing suggests that there might be a genetic tendency toward behavioral dysregulation or compulsion that predisposes some people to abuse many kinds of drugs, including alcohol (Holden, 1991; Smith et al., 1992). A behavioral genetics study supported this idea when it found a link between alcoholism in biological parents and drug abuse in adopted-away sons (Cadoret et al., 1995). The same study also found a link between antisocial personality traits in biological parents and antisocial acts—including drug abuse—in the sons they had put up for adoption.

Psychological factors, such as the need to reduce stress, emulation of drug-using peers, thrill seeking, and social maladjustment, have all been proposed as initial causes of substance abuse. Research has still not established why drugs become a problem for some people and not for others, but, as with so many other disorders, it is likely that some biological predisposition sets the stage on which specific psychological processes and stressors play out their roles.

Psychological Disorders of Childhood

The physical, cognitive, emotional, and social changes seen in childhood—and the stress associated with them—can create or worsen psychological disorders in children. Stress can do the same in adults, but childhood disorders are not just miniature versions of adult psychopathology. Because children's development is still incomplete and because their capacity to cope with stress is limited in important ways, children are often vulnerable to special types of disorders. Two broad categories encompass the majority of childhood behavior problems: externalizing disorders and internalizing disorders (Achenbach, 1997).

The *externalizing,* or *undercontrolled,* category includes behaviors that are particularly aversive to people in the child's environment. Lack of control shows up as *conduct disorders* in 4 to 10 percent of children, mostly boys (Martin & Hoffman, 1990). Conduct disorders are characterized by a relatively stable pattern of aggression, disobedience, destructiveness, and other problematic behaviors (Lahey et al., 1995). Often these behaviors involve criminal activity. A genetic predisposition toward conduct disorders is suggested by the fact that many such children have parents who display antisocial personality disorder. However, environmental and parenting factors undoubtedly help to shape these children's antisocial behavior (Lahey et al., 1995; Patterson, DeBaryshe, & Ramsey, 1989).

Another kind of externalizing problem, also seen primarily in boys, is *attention deficit hyperactivity disorder (ADHD)*. This diagnosis is given to children who are impulsive and unable to concentrate on an activity as well as other children their age can (Schachar & Logan, 1990). Many of these children are *hyperactive;* they have great difficulty sitting still or otherwise controlling their physical activity. Their impulsiveness and lack of self-control contribute to significant impairments in learning, and to an astonishing ability to annoy and exhaust those around them (Henker & Whalen, 1989). Genetic predisposition, the occurrence of brain damage, dietary problems, poisoning from lead or other household substances, and ineffective parenting have all been proposed as possible causes of hyperactivity, but the role played by each of these factors is still uncertain (Daly et al., 1999; Hauser et al., 1993). Also uncertain is exactly what constitutes hyperactivity (Panksepp, 1998). Cultural standards about acceptable activity levels in children vary, so a "hyperactive" child in one culture might be considered merely "active" in another. Indeed, when mental health professionals from four cultures used the same rating scales to judge the presence and severity of hyperactivity in a videotaped sample of children's behavior, the Chinese and Indonesians rated the children as significantly more hyperactive than did their American and Japanese colleagues (Mann et al., 1992). Such findings remind us again that sociocultural factors can be important determinants of what is acceptable, and hence what is abnormal, in various parts of the world.

The second broad category of child behavior problems involves *internalizing,* or *overcontrol.* Children in this category experience distress, especially depression and anxiety, and may be socially withdrawn. Those displaying *separation anxiety disorder,* for example, constantly worry that they will be lost, kidnapped, or injured or that some harm may come to a parent (usually the mother). The child clings desperately to the parent and becomes upset or sick at the prospect of any separation. Refusal to go to school (sometimes called "school phobia") is often the result.

A few childhood disorders do not fall into either the externalizing or internalizing category. An example is *autistic disorder,* a severe and puzzling condition usually identified within the first thirty months of life, in which babies show no sign of attachment to their caregivers, or anyone else. Autistic babies do not smile, laugh, or make eye contact. They will not tolerate being held and cuddled; they seem unable to enter the social realm. As years go by, they ignore others and instead rock themselves repetitively or play endlessly, it seems, with ashtrays, keys, or other inanimate objects. Language development is seriously disrupted in these children. Half never learn to speak at all. Autistic disorder occurs in fewer than five children per ten thousand births; but, with few exceptions, it leads to a life of marginal adjustment, often within an institution.

Possible biological roots of autistic disorder include genetic factors (Bailey, 1993; Cook, Courchesne, & Cox, 1998) or neurodevelopmental abnormalities affecting language and communication (Minshew, Payton, & Sclabassi, 1986; Ornitz, 1989). The specific causes of autistic disorder remain unknown, but researchers today have rejected the once-popular hypothesis that its profound problems are caused by cold and unresponsive parents.

Disorders of childhood differ from adult disorders not only because the patterns of behavior are distinct but also because their early onset renders childhood disorders especially capable of disrupting development. To take one example, children whose separation anxiety causes spotty attendance at school may not only fall behind academically but also fail to form the relationships with other children that promote normal social development. Some children never make up for this deficit. They may drop out of school and risk a life of poverty, crime, and violence. Moreover, children are dependent on others to obtain help for their psychological problems, and all too often those problems may go unrecognized or untreated. For some, the long-term result may be adult forms of mental disorder.

MENTAL ILLNESS AND THE LAW

Cheryl was barely twenty when she married Glen, a graduate student in biology. They moved into a large apartment complex near the university and within three years had two sons. Cheryl's friends had always been impressed by the attention and affection she showered on her boys; she seemed to be the ideal mother. She and Glen had serious marital problems, however, and she felt trapped and unhappy. One day Glen came home to find that Cheryl had stabbed both children to death. At her murder trial, she was found not guilty by reason of insanity and was placed in a state mental institution.

This verdict reflected U.S. laws and rules that protect people with severe psychological disorders when they are accused of crimes. Similar laws and rules are in effect in many other countries as well. The protection takes two forms.

First, under certain conditions, people designated as mentally ill may be protected from prosecution. If, at the time of their trial, individuals accused of a crime are unable to understand the proceedings and charges against them or to assist in their own defense, they are declared to be *mentally incompetent to stand trial*. In such cases, the defendant is sent to a mental institution until he or she becomes mentally competent. If still not competent after a court-specified period, two years in most cases, the defendant may be ruled permanently ineligible for trial and either committed in civil court to a mental institution or released. This is a rare outcome, however, because competency to stand trial requires only minimal mental abilities. If drugs can produce even temporary mental competence, the defendant will usually go to trial (Nietzel, 1999).

Second, the mentally ill may be protected from punishment. In most U.S. states, defendants may be judged *not guilty by reason of insanity* if, at the time of the crime, mental illness prevented them from (1) understanding what they were doing, (2) knowing that what they were doing was wrong, or (3) resisting the impulse to do wrong. The first two of these criteria—understanding the nature or wrongfulness of an act—are "cognitive" criteria known as the *M'Naughton rule*. This rule stems from an 1843 case in England in which a man named Daniel M'Naughton, upon hearing "instructions from God," tried to kill British Prime Minister Robert Peel; he was found not guilty by reason of insanity and put into a mental institution for life. The third criterion is known as the *irresistible-impulse test*. All three criteria are combined in a rule proposed by the American Law Institute (ALI) in 1962 and now followed in about half of the U.S. states:

> *A person is not responsible for criminal conduct if at the time of such conduct as a result of mental disease or defect he lacks substantial capacity either to appreciate the criminality (wrongfulness) of his conduct or to conform his conduct to the requirements of law. (ALI, 1962, p. 66)*

In 1984, after John Hinckley was found not guilty by reason of insanity under the ALI rule for his attempted assassination of President Ronald Reagan, the U.S. Congress passed the Insanity Defense Reform Act that eliminated the lack-of-control criterion from the definition of insanity in federal cases. Such laws highlight the fact that insanity is a legal term, not a psychiatric diagnosis—it does not appear in DSM-IV. Thus, the responsibility falls on judges and juries to weigh evidence and testimony and decide whether or not a defendant should be held responsible for criminal acts. Defendants who are judged not guilty by reason of insanity and who still display a psychological disorder are usually required to receive treatment, typically through commitment to a hospital, until judged to be cured or no longer dangerous.

Insanity rules have been faulted on several grounds. Some critics argue that everyone, even those who meet legal criteria for insanity, should be held responsible for their actions and punished for their crimes. Others point out significant problems in the implementation of insanity rules. For one thing, different experts often give conflicting, highly technical testimony about a defendant's sanity at the time of a crime. (One expert said Cheryl was sane; another concluded she was insane.) Jurors are then left in the difficult position of deciding which expert to believe and what to make of the experts' diagnostic judgments. Their task is complicated by the fact that people suffering from mental disorders—even those as severe as schizophrenia—are still capable of

Incompetent to Stand Trial

As described in Chapter 1, Russell Eugene Weston, Jr.—shown here after his arrest on a drug possession charge in 1991—killed two police officers during an armed rampage at the U.S. Capitol Building in July of 1998. After being examined by a U.S. government psychiatrist, Weston, who had been diagnosed two years earlier as suffering from paranoid schizophrenia, was declared mentally incompetent to stand trial for the killings. He remains confined in a mental hospital. Protection from trial on criminal charges is one of several legal rights accorded to persons who display severe symptoms of mental disorder either during or after their alleged crime.

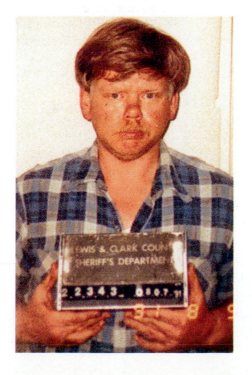

some rational decision making and controlling some aspects of their behavior (Grisso & Applebaum, 1995). Finally, in rare cases, defendants found not guilty by reason of insanity may spend more time in a mental hospital than they would have spent in prison had they simply been convicted (Silver, 1995). These cases leave critics worried that well-intentioned laws can produce a miscarriage of justice.

Can anything be done about such problems? Three U.S. states have taken the radical step of simply abolishing the insanity defense. Three other, less extreme reforms have also been attempted. First, several states now permit a verdict of *guilty but mentally ill.* Defendants found guilty but mentally ill still serve a sentence but are supposed to receive treatment while in a prison or special institution. Critics object that this verdict is a compromise that ensures neither proper treatment nor proper verdicts, because mentally ill prisoners should receive treatment anyway. Second, as already noted, federal courts no longer use the irresistible-impulse criterion in defining insanity. Third, federal courts, and some state courts, now require defendants to prove that they were insane at the time of their crime, rather than requiring the prosecution to prove that the defendants were sane.

Clearly, communities are still seeking the proper balance between protecting the rights of defendants and protecting society from dangerous criminals. Although certain high-profile cases might suggest otherwise, the insanity plea is raised in fewer than 1 percent of criminal cases in the United States—usually when the defendant displays severe psychological disorder—and this plea is successful only a tiny fraction of the time (Applebaum, 1994). Evidently, some of the same sociocultural values that shape people's views about what constitutes abnormality also influence their judgments about the extent to which abnormality relieves people of criminal responsibility for their actions.

LINKAGES

As noted in Chapter 1, all of psychology's many subfields are related to one another. Our discussion of how classical conditioning can lead to phobias illustrates just one way in which the topic of this chapter, psychological disorders, is linked to the subfield of learning (Chapter 6). The Linkages diagram shows ties to two other subfields as well, and there are many more ties throughout the book. Looking for linkages among subfields will help you see how they all fit together and better appreciate the big picture that is psychology.

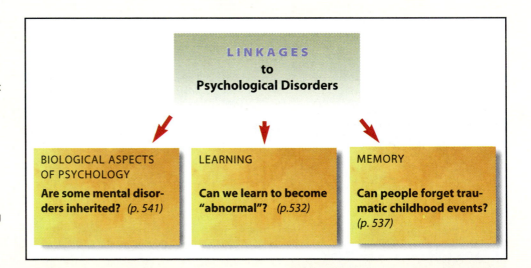

SUMMARY

Psychopathology involves patterns of thinking, feeling, and behaving that cause personal distress or significantly impair a person's social or occupational functioning.

UNDERSTANDING PSYCHOLOGICAL DISORDERS: SOME BASIC ISSUES

The definition of abnormality is largely determined by social and cultural factors.

What Is Abnormal?

The criteria for judging abnormality include statistical infrequency (a comparison to what most people do), personal suffering, and norm violations. Each of these criteria is flawed to some extent. The practical approach, which considers the content, context, and consequences of behavior, emphasizes the question of whether people show impaired functioning in fulfilling the roles appropriate for particular people in particular settings, cultures, and historical eras.

Explaining Psychological Disorders

Abnormal behavior has been attributed, at one time or another, to the action of supernatural forces, to physical disorders (the medical or *neurobiological model*), or to various psychological processes (the *psychological model*) such as unconscious conflicts, maladaptive cognitive schemas, learning, or blocked actualizing tendencies. The neurobiological model of abnormality predominates in most Western cultures, but supernatural interpretations of disorders are still employed in some Western subcultures and in many non-Western cultures. *Sociocultural explanations* focus on factors that help define abnormality and influence the form that disorders take in different parts of the world. No single model can adequately explain all psychological disorders. However, the *diathesis-stress model* takes all of them into account by highlighting inherited biological predispositions or psychological characteristics that interact with stressors to produce disorder.

CLASSIFYING PSYCHOLOGICAL DISORDERS

There seems to be a set of behavior patterns that roughly defines abnormality in most cultures.

A Classification System: DSM-IV

The dominant system for classifying abnormal behavior in North America is the *Diagnostic and Statistical Manual* (DSM-IV) of the American Psychiatric Association. It includes more than three hundred specific categories of mental disorders.

Purposes and Problems of Diagnosis

Diagnosis helps to identify the features, causes, and most effective methods of treating various psychological disorders. Research on the reliability and validity of DSM-IV shows that it is a useful, but imperfect, classification system.

ANXIETY DISORDERS

Long-standing and disruptive patterns of anxiety characterize *anxiety disorders.*

Types of Anxiety Disorders

The most prevalent type of anxiety disorder is phobia, which includes *specific phobias, social phobias,* and *agoraphobia.* Other anxiety disorders are *generalized anxiety disorder,* which involves nonspecific anxiety; *panic disorder,* which brings unpredictable attacks of intense anxiety; and *obsessive-compulsive disorder,* in which uncontrollable repetitive thoughts and ritualistic actions occur.

Causes of Anxiety Disorders

The most influential explanations of anxiety disorders suggest that they may develop as a result of a combination of biological predisposition for strong anxiety reactions and the impact of fear-enhancing thought patterns and learned anxiety responses.

SOMATOFORM DISORDERS

Somatoform disorders include *conversion disorder,* which involves physical problems that have no apparent physical cause; *hypochondriasis,* an unjustified concern over becoming ill; *somatization disorder,* in which the person complains of numerous, unconfirmed physical complaints; and *pain disorder,* in which pain is felt in the absence of a physical cause.

DISSOCIATIVE DISORDERS

Dissociative disorders involve such rare conditions as *dissociative fugue, dissociative amnesia,* and *dissociative identity disorder* (multiple personality disorder), in which a person suffers memory loss or develops two or more identities.

MOOD DISORDERS

Mood disorders, also known as affective disorders, involve extreme moods that may be inconsistent with events.

Depressive Disorders

Major depressive disorder is marked by feelings of inadequacy, worthlessness, and guilt; in extreme cases, *delusions* may also occur. Also seen is *dysthymic disorder,* which includes similar but less severe symptoms persisting for a long period. Suicide is often related to these disorders.

Bipolar Disorders

Alternating periods of depression and *mania* characterize *bipolar I disorder,* which is also known as manic depression. *Cyclothymic disorder,* an alternating pattern of less extreme mood swings, is more common.

Causes of Mood Disorders

Mood disorders have been attributed to biological causes such as genetic inheritance, disruptions in neurotransmitter and endocrine systems, and irregularities in biological rhythms. Self-directed anger, loss of significant sources of reward, and maladaptive patterns of thinking are among the psychological causes proposed. A predisposition toward some of these disorders may be inherited, although their appearance may be determined by a diathesis-stress process.

SCHIZOPHRENIA

Symptoms of Schizophrenia

Schizophrenia is perhaps the most severe and puzzling disorder of all. Among its symptoms are problems in thinking, perception (often including *hallucinations*), attention, emotion, movement, motivation, and daily functioning.

Categorizing Schizophrenia

Although DSM-IV lists five major subtypes of schizophrenia (paranoid, disorganized, catatonic, undifferentiated, and residual), many researchers today favor a descriptive system that focuses on whether patients display mainly *positive symptoms* (such as hallucinations and disorganized thoughts) or *negative symptoms* (such as lack of speech and restricted emotional expression). Each category of symptoms may be traceable to different causes; predominantly negative symptoms tend to be associated with more severe disorder and less successful treatment.

Causes of Schizophrenia

Genetic factors, neurotransmitter problems, abnormalities in brain structure and functioning, and neurodevelopmental abnormalities are biological factors implicated in schizophrenia. Psychological explanations have pointed to regression, unfortunate learning experiences, and disturbed family interactions. The diathesis-stress approach, often described in terms of the vulnerability model, remains a promising framework for research into the multiple causes of schizophrenia.

PERSONALITY DISORDERS

Personality disorders are long-term patterns of maladaptive behavior that, while not always associated with personal discomfort, may be disturbing to others. Examples include schizotypal, avoidant, narcissistic, and *antisocial personality disorders.*

A SAMPLING OF OTHER PSYCHOLOGICAL DISORDERS

Substance-Related Disorders

Substance-related disorders involving alcohol and other drugs affect millions of people. Dependence on, or abuse of, these substances contributes to disastrous personal and social problems, including physical illnesses, accidents, and crime. Genetic factors may create a predisposition for *alcoholism,* but learning, cultural traditions, and other nonbiological processes are also important. In the case of dependence on heroin and cocaine, stress reduction, imitation, thrill seeking, and social maladjustment have been proposed as important factors, along with genetics; but the exact causes of initial use of these drugs are unknown.

Psychological Disorders of Childhood

Childhood disorders can be categorized as externalizing conditions, such as conduct disorders or attention deficit hyperactivity disorder, and as internalizing disorders, in which children show overcontrol, experiencing distress as in separation anxiety disorder. The most severe childhood disorder is autistic disorder, in which the child shows no concern for or attachment to others.

MENTAL ILLNESS AND THE LAW

Current rules protect people accused of crimes from prosecution or punishment if they are mentally incompetent at the time of their trial or if they were legally insane at the time of their crime. Difficulty in establishing the mental state of defendants and other knotty problems have created dissatisfaction with those rules and prompted a number of reforms, including the "guilty but mentally ill" verdict.

KEY TERMS

agoraphobia (529)
alcoholism (553)
antisocial personality disorder (551)
anxiety disorder (528)
bipolar I disorder (541)
conversion disorder (533)
cyclothymic disorder (541)
delusions (539)
diathesis-stress model (522)
dissociative amnesia (535)
dissociative disorders (535)

dissociative fugue (535)
dissociative identity disorder (535)
dysthymic disorder (539)
generalized anxiety disorder (530)
hallucinations (545)
hypochondriasis (534)
major depressive disorder (539)
mania (541)
mood disorder (539)

negative symptoms (546)
neurobiological model (520)
obsessive-compulsive disorder (530)
pain disorder (534)
panic disorder (530)
personality disorders (550)
phobia (528)
positive symptoms (546)
psychological model (521)
psychopathology (517)

schizophrenia (544)
social phobias (529)
sociocultural explanations (522)
somatization disorder (534)
somatoform disorders (533)
specific phobias (528)
substance-related disorders (552)

16 Treatment of Psychological Disorders

In the previous chapter, we described José, a fifty-five-year-old electronics technician who had to take medical leave from his job after experiencing panic attacks (see Table 15.1 on page 523). After four months of diagnostic testing turned up no physical problems, José's physician suggested that he see a psychologist. José resisted at first, insisting that his condition was not "just in his head," but he eventually began psychological treatment. Within a few months, his panic attacks had ceased, and José had returned to all his old activities. After the psychologist helped him to reconsider his workload, José decided to retire from his job in order to pursue more satisfying work at his home-based computer business.

José's case is by no means unique. During any given year in the United States alone, nearly 15 percent of the population is receiving some form of treatment for a psychological disorder (Regier et al., 1993). Although the economic impact of mental disorders—in treatment costs, disability payments, and lost productivity—is staggering, reaching $150 billion per year in the United States, the treatments that are available today for severe disorders can pay for themselves. Indeed, the savings realized from treatment are actually greater than its costs (National Institute of Mental Health, 1998). In this chapter, we describe a variety of treatment methods, most of which are based on the theories of stress and coping, personality, and psychological disorders reviewed in Chapters 13, 14, and 15. By spelling out proposed explanations for what can go wrong in the development of personality and behavior and the role of stress in both, those theories provide important guidelines for treatment.

First we examine the basic features common to all forms of treatment. Then we discuss approaches that rely on **psychotherapy,** the treatment of psychological disorders through psychological methods, such as talking about problems and exploring new ways of thinking and acting; these approaches use methods derived from the psychodynamic, phenomenological, and behavioral approaches to treatment. We then consider biological approaches to treatment, which depend mainly on drugs and other physical therapies.

Although we discuss different approaches in separate sections, keep in mind that the majority of mental health professionals see themselves as *eclectic therapists;* in other words, they might lean toward one treatment approach, but, when working with particular clients or particular problems, they borrow methods from other types of therapy as well (Jensen, Bergin, & Greaves, 1990). Further, many clients receive psychoactive drugs in addition to therapy during the course of psychological treatment (Lickey & Gordon, 1991).

BASIC FEATURES OF TREATMENT

All treatments for psychological, as well as physical, disorders share certain basic features. These common features include a *client* or patient, a *therapist* who is accepted as capable of helping the client, and the establishment of a special relationship between the client and therapist. In addition, all forms of treatment are based on some *theory* about the causes of the client's problems. The theory may presume causes ranging from magic spells to infections and everything in between (Frank, 1973). The theory, in turn, leads to *procedures* for dealing with the client's problems. Thus, traditional healers combat supernatural forces with ceremonies and prayers, medical doctors treat chemical imbalances with drugs, and psychologists focus on altering psychological processes through psychotherapy.

People receiving psychotherapy can be classified into two general categories: inpatients and outpatients. *Inpatients* are treated in a hospital or other residential institution. They are hospitalized because their impairments are severe enough to constitute a threat to their own well-being or the safety of others. Depending on their level of functioning, inpatients may stay in the hospital for a few days or up to several years. Their treatment almost always includes psychoactive drugs. *Outpatients* receive psychotherapy while living in the community. Compared with inpatients, outpatients tend to be younger, are more likely to be female, and typically come from the middle or upper classes.

Medieval Treatment Methods

The methods used to treat psychological disorders are related to the presumed cause of those disorders. In medieval times, when demons were widely blamed for abnormal behavior, magical-religious practitioners tried to make the victim's body inhospitable to evil spirits. Here, many such spirits are shown departing when an afflicted person's head is placed in an oven.

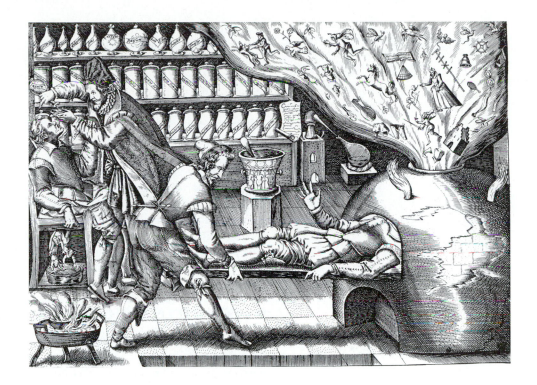

Those who provide psychological treatment are also a diverse group. **Psychiatrists** are medical doctors who complete specialty training in the treatment of mental disorders. Like other physicians, they are authorized to prescribe drugs for the relief of psychological problems. **Psychologists** who offer psychotherapy have usually completed a doctoral degree in clinical or counseling psychology, often followed by additional specialized training. Psychologists are not currently authorized to prescribe drugs, although there is continuing debate over a proposal to extend prescription privileges to clinical psychologists who have been specially trained for this function (Ax, Forbes, & Thompson, 1997; McGuire, 1998; Nietzel, Bernstein, & Milich, 1998; Tatman et al., 1997). Other therapy providers include *clinical social workers, marriage and family therapists,* and *licensed professional counselors,* all of whom typically hold a master's

Group Therapy for Vietnam Veterans

Some psychotherapy consists of one-to-one sessions in an office setting, but no single image can capture all its many formats. Therapy is also conducted with couples, families, and groups in hospitals, community health centers, and facilities for former mental hospital residents. Treatment is also provided in prisons, military bases, drug and alcoholism treatment centers, and other places.

degree in their respective professions and provide treatment in a variety of settings, such as hospitals, clinics, and private practice. *Psychiatric nurses, substance abuse counselors,* and members of the clergy working as *pastoral counselors* also provide various forms of therapy, often as part of a hospital or outpatient treatment team that may include other paraprofessional providers.

The general goal of treatment providers is to help troubled people change their thinking, feelings, and behavior in ways that relieve discomfort, promote happiness, and improve their overall functioning. To reach this goal, some therapists try to help clients gain insight into the hidden causes of problems, others seek to promote growth through more genuine self-expression, and still others help clients learn and practice new ways of thinking and acting. The particular methods employed in each case depend on the problems, preferences, and financial circumstances of the client, the time available for treatment, and the therapist's theoretical and methodological preferences. There are hundreds of specific methods of psychotherapy (Bongar & Beutler, 1995; Eells, 1997), most of which fall into one of three general categories: psychodynamic, phenomenological, and behavioral.

PSYCHODYNAMIC PSYCHOTHERAPY

The field of formal psychotherapy began in the late nineteenth century when, as described in Chapter 14, Sigmund Freud established the psychodynamic approach to personality and mental disorders. Central to his approach, and to modern revisions of it, is the assumption that personality and behavior reflect the efforts of the ego to referee conflicts, usually unconscious, among various components of the personality.

Freud's method of treatment, **psychoanalysis,** is aimed at understanding these unconscious conflicts and how they affect the client. His one-to-one method of studying and treating people, his systematic search for relationships between an individual's life history and current problems, his emphasis on thoughts and emotions in treatment, and his focus on the client-therapist relationship are reflected in almost all forms of psychotherapy. We describe Freud's original methods first, and then consider some more recently developed treatments that are rooted in his psychodynamic approach.

Classical Psychoanalysis

Classical psychoanalysis developed mainly out of Freud's medical practice. He was puzzled by patients who suffered from "hysterical" ailments—blindness, paralysis, or other symptoms that had no physical cause. (As mentioned in Chapter 15, in DSM-IV these ailments are considered to be symptoms of somatoform disorders.) Inspired by his colleague Josef Breuer's dramatic success in using hypnosis to treat hysterical symptoms in a patient known as "Anna O." (Breuer & Freud, 1895/1974), Freud tried similar methods with other hysteria patients but found them to be only partially and temporarily successful. Eventually, Freud stopped using hypnosis and merely asked his patients to lie on a couch and report whatever thoughts, memories, or images came to mind (a process Freud called *free association*).

The results of this "talking cure" were surprising. Freud and Breuer were struck by how many patients reported childhood memories of sexual abuse, usually by a parent or other close relative. Either child abuse was rampant in Vienna at the time or patients' reports were distorted by psychological factors. Freud ultimately concluded that his patients' memories of childhood seduction probably reflected childhood fantasies. (As discussed in Chapter 14, this conclusion has been attacked in recent years.) Freud's reasoning focused classical psychoanalysis on the exploration of unconscious impulses and fantasies. Hysterical symptoms, he concluded, developed out of conflicts about those impulses and fantasies.

Classical psychoanalytic treatment aims to help clients gain insight into their problems by recognizing unconscious thoughts and emotions and then discover, or *work through,* the many ways in which those unconscious elements affect everyday life. The treatment may require as many as three to five sessions per week, usually over several years. Generally, the psychoanalyst tries to maintain a compassionate neutrality during

Freud's Consulting Room

During psychoanalytic sessions, Freud's patients lay on this couch while he sat in the chair behind them. According to Freud, human actions are determined by a combination of conscious intentions and unconscious influences. Even apparently trivial or accidental behavior may hold important messages from the unconscious. Thus, forgetting a dream or the time of a therapy appointment might reflect a client's unconscious resistance to treatment. Even accidents may be meaningful. The waiter who spills hot soup on an elderly male customer might be seen as acting out unconscious aggressive impulses against a father figure.

treatment as the client slowly develops insight into how past conflicts determine current problems (Auld & Hyman, 1991).

To gain glimpses into the unconscious, Freud considered not only his patients' free associations but also their dreams, their everyday behaviors, and their relationship with him. He believed that, hidden beneath the obvious or *manifest content* of dreams, there is *latent content* that reflects the wishes, impulses, and fantasies that the dreamer's defense mechanisms keep out of consciousness during waking hours. Accordingly, Freud devoted considerable time to interpreting the unconscious meanings of dreams. He also looked for meaning in "Freudian slips" of the tongue (such as saying "beast" instead of "best") and other seemingly insignificant behaviors. Similarly, tenderness, fear, dependency, hostility, and other aspects of the client's behavior in therapy sessions were viewed by Freud as part of an unconscious transference to the therapist of feelings and conflicts experienced in childhood in relation to parents and other significant people. Analysis of this *transference,* this "new edition" of the client's childhood conflicts and current problems, became another important psychoanalytic method; Freud believed that focusing on the transference allows clients to see how old conflicts haunt their lives and to resolve these problems from the past (Arlow, 1995).

Contemporary Variations on Psychoanalysis

Though classical psychoanalysis is still practiced, it is not as prevalent as it was several decades ago (Horgan, 1996). The decline is due to such factors as disenchantment with Freud's instinct-based personality theory, the high costs of classical psychoanalysis, its limited usefulness with children, and the availability of many alternative forms of treatment, including variations on classical psychoanalysis.

Many of the variations were developed by the neo-Freudian theorists discussed in Chapter 14. As noted there, these theorists tended to put less emphasis than Freud did on the past and on biologically based drives stemming from the id and unconscious. They also tended to stress the client's current problems and how the power of the ego could be harnessed to solve them. Treatment variations based on these neo-Freudian theories include *ego analysis* (Hartmann, 1958; Klein, 1960), *interpersonal therapy* (Sullivan, 1954), and *individual analysis* (Adler, 1927/1963). Some versions have been designed for use with children (Klein, 1960; A. Freud, 1946). A particularly popular contemporary psychodynamic approach is known as *object relations therapy* (Hamilton, 1994).

Object relations analysts believe that personality, as well as the conflicts among its components, derives from the need for supportive human relationships. The

A Play Therapy Session

Contemporary variants of psychoanalytic treatment include fantasy play and other techniques that make the approach more useful with children. A child's behavior and comments while playing with puppets representing family members, for example, allows a form of free association that the therapist hopes will reveal important unconscious material (such as fear of abandonment).

mother-child relationship and the attachment patterns that arise from it (see Chapter 12, on development) form the prototype for these relationships (Kohut, 1971). (The term *object* refers to anything, from symbols to people, that can have emotional significance for a person.) The powerful need for human contact takes center stage in object relations therapy, since most of the difficulties that bring clients to treatment involve their relationships with others.

Psychotherapists who adopt an object relations perspective take a much more active role in therapy sessions than classical analysts do. The object relations therapist works to develop a nurturing relationship with the client, providing a "second chance" for the client to receive the support that might have been absent in infancy and to counteract some of the consequences of maladaptive early attachment patterns (Lieberman & Pawl, 1988). For example, the therapist takes pains to demonstrate that he or she will not abandon the client.

Other variations on psychoanalysis retain more of Freud's ideas but alter the format of treatment so that it is less intense, less expensive, and more appropriate for a broader range of clients (Hoyt, 1995). For example, *psychoanalytically oriented psychotherapy* and *time-limited dynamic psychotherapy* employ basic psychoanalytic methods but use them more flexibly (Levenson & Strupp, 1997). In these variants, the therapist may be more active than a classical psychoanalyst in directing the client's attention to evidence of particular conflicts. The goal of treatment may range from giving psychological support to achieving basic changes in personality, and therapy may be completed in fewer than thirty sessions. A therapist using these briefer psychodynamic methods encourages clients to focus on concrete, specific goals. For example, the therapist might ask a client to describe how she or he would feel and act if a specific problem were suddenly solved (*Harvard Mental Health Letter,* 1994).

Some version of transference analysis is seen in virtually all variations on classical psychoanalysis. In a short-term psychodynamic treatment called *supportive-expressive therapy,* for example, the therapist looks for a "core conflict"—the *core conflictual relationship theme*—that appears repeatedly across a variety of relationships, including the therapeutic one (Luborsky, 1997). Research shows that core-conflict themes that emerge in therapy sessions are often quite similar to those that also occur in the client's dreams (Popp et al., 1996). The way in which a client might express a core conflict is illustrated in the following excerpt from the treatment of a depressed twenty-two-year-old college student who had been physically abused by his father in childhood.

Client: I feel mad at myself for not standing up to my roommate.

Therapist: What happened?

Client: I was talking to a friend and my roommate interrupted me. He wanted to use my car. I said, "Excuse me, but I am having a conversation." Instead of backing off he continued to interrupt me in a rude manner. I just couldn't stand up to him and when he left, my friend asked me why I just didn't "tell him to go to hell." But I just gave in, and later I started to have all these fantasies.

Therapist: Fantasies?

Client: Yes, things like, I imagined things like punching him in the mouth. Telling him to drop dead. Then I just kind of felt stupid, like I was overreacting and making a big deal out of nothing. I felt really stupid. I started getting down on myself again.

The supportive-expressive therapist might see in this client a core conflict between the desire to stand up for himself and the tendency to criticize himself for having that desire. The therapist would watch for this core conflict to appear in the therapy relationship—perhaps in the form of tentative assertiveness tempered by fear of having done wrong—and then help the client see the links among his fear of asserting himself, his fantasies of getting even, and his childhood abuse experiences. This interpretation is part of the transference analysis (Luborsky, 1997). At the same time, the therapist would support the client's attempts to be more assertive with authority figures without having violent fantasies.

Variants on classical psychoanalysis focus not only on the client's feelings toward the therapist but also on the therapist's feelings toward the client—that is, on *countertransference*. For example, if transference leads a client to treat the therapist as a mother, the therapist might, because of countertransference, unintentionally begin treating the client as her child. Therapists must be alert to countertransference and its effects on their clinical objectivity. Ideally, the development and analysis of this emotionally intimate two-way relationship serves as a stepping stone for the client to develop healthier, more satisfying relationships with others.

An analysis of the transference and countertransference in this therapy relationship would be quite a challenge!

"What do you think I think about what you think I think you've been thinking about?"

With their focus on interpersonal relationships rather than instincts, their emphasis on clients' potential for self-directed problem solving, and the reassurance and emotional support they provide, contemporary variants on classical psychoanalysis have helped the psychodynamic approach retain its influence among mental health professionals (Messer & Wolitzky, 1997).

PHENOMENOLOGICAL PSYCHOTHERAPY

As discussed in Chapters 14 and 15, *phenomenologists*—some of whom are known as *humanistic psychologists*—emphasize the subjective interpretations that people place on events. Phenomenologists view people as capable of consciously controlling their own actions and taking responsibility for their own decisions. Many phenomenological therapists believe that human behavior is not motivated by sexual or aggressive instincts but by an innate drive toward growth that is guided from moment to moment by the way people interpret the world. Disordered behavior, they say, reflects a blockage of natural growth brought on by distorted perceptions or lack of awareness of feelings. Thus, phenomenological therapists operate on the following assumptions:

1. Treatment is an encounter between equals, not a cure provided by an expert. It is a way to help clients restart their natural growth and to feel and behave as they really are.

2. Clients will improve on their own, given the right conditions. These ideal conditions promote clients' awareness, acceptance, and expression of their feelings and perceptions. Thus, as in psychodynamic approaches, therapy promotes insight. Phenomenological therapy, however, seeks insight into current feelings and perceptions, not into unconscious childhood conflicts.

3. Ideal conditions in therapy can best be established through a relationship in which clients feel fully accepted and supported, no matter how problematic or undesirable their *behavior* may be. It is the client's experience of this relationship that brings beneficial changes. (As noted earlier, this assumption is also important in object relations therapy.)

4. Clients must remain responsible for choosing how they will think and behave.

Of the many phenomenological treatments in use today, the most influential are client-centered therapy, developed by Carl Rogers, and Gestalt therapy, developed by Frederick and Laura Perls.

Client-Centered Therapy

Carl Rogers was trained in psychodynamic methods during the 1930s, but he soon began to question their value. He especially disliked being a detached expert observer whose task is to "figure out" the client. He became convinced that a less formal approach would be more effective for the client and more comfortable for the therapist. Accordingly, Rogers developed *nondirective therapy*, which depends on the client's own drive toward growth or actualization. Rogers allowed his clients to decide what to talk about and when, without direction, judgment, or interpretation by the therapist (Raskin & Rogers, 1995). This approach, now called **client-centered** or **person-centered therapy,** relies on the creation of a relationship that reflects three intertwined attitudes of the therapist: unconditional positive regard, empathy, and congruence.

Unconditional Positive Regard   The attitude Rogers called **unconditional positive regard** consists of nothing more nor less than treating the client as a valued person, no matter what. This attitude is communicated through the therapist's willingness to listen without interrupting and to accept what is said without evaluating it. The therapist need not *approve* of everything the client says, but he or she must *accept* each statement as reflecting a part of the person. Because they trust clients to solve their own

A Client-Centered Therapy Group

Carl Rogers (shown here in shirt-sleeves) believed that, as successful treatment progresses, clients become more self-confident, more aware of their feelings, more accepting of themselves, more comfortable and genuine with other people, more reliant on self-evaluation than on the judgments of others, and more effective and relaxed.

problems, Rogerian therapists rarely give advice. Doing so, said Rogers, would carry the subtle message that clients are incompetent, making them less confident and more dependent on help.

Empathy   Client-centered therapists try to appreciate how the world looks from the client's point of view. This involves far more than saying "I know what you mean." The therapist tries to replace an *external frame of reference*—looking at the client from the outside—with an *internal frame of reference* characterized by **empathy,** the emotional understanding of what the client might be thinking and feeling. Client-centered therapists convey empathy by showing that they are *actively listening* to the client. Like other skillful interviewers, they make eye contact with the client, nod in recognition as the client speaks, and give other signs of careful attention. They also use **reflection,** a paraphrased summary of the client's words and especially the feelings and meanings that appear to accompany them; reflection confirms the communication, shows the therapist's interest, and helps the client to perceive and focus on the thoughts and feelings being expressed.

Most clients respond to empathic reflection by elaborating on their feelings. By communicating the desire to listen and understand, the therapist can help the client bring important material into the open without asking disruptive questions. Empathic listening tends to be so effective in promoting self-understanding and awareness that it is used across a wide range of therapies (Greenberg, Rice, & Elliot, 1993). Even outside the realm of therapy, people who are thought of as easy to talk to are usually "good listeners" who reflect back the important messages they hear from others.

Congruence   Sometimes called *genuineness,* **congruence** refers to a consistency between the therapist's feelings and actions. When the therapist's unconditional positive regard and empathy are genuine, the client is able to see that relationships can be built on openness and honesty. Ideally, this experience will help the client become more congruent in other relationships.

Here is an excerpt that illustrates the three therapist attitudes just described.

Client: . . . I cannot be the kind of person I want to be. I guess maybe I haven't the guts or the strength to kill myself and if someone else would relieve me of the responsibility or I would be in an accident I, I . . . just don't want to live.

Therapist: At the present time things look so bad that you can't see much point in living. [Note the use of empathic reflection and the absence of any criticism.]

Nonverbal Cues in Gestalt Therapy

Gestalt therapists pay particular attention to clients' "body language," especially when it conflicts with what they are saying. If this client had just said that she is looking forward to starting her new job, the therapist would probably challenge that statement in an effort to make the client more aware of her ambivalence.

Client: Yes. I wish I'd never started this therapy. I was happy when I was living in my dream world. There I could be the kind of person I wanted to be. But now there is such a wide, wide gap between my ideal and what I am. . . . [Notice how the client responds to reflection by giving more information.]

Therapist: It's really a tough struggle digging into this like you are and at times the shelter of your dream world looks more attractive and comfortable. [Reflection]

Client: My dream world or suicide. . . . So I don't see why I should waste your time—coming in twice a week—I'm not worth it—What do you think?

Therapist: It's up to you. . . . It isn't wasting my time. I'd be glad to see you whenever you come but it's how you feel about it. . . . [Note the congruence in stating an honest desire to see the client and the unconditional positive regard in trusting her capacity and responsibility for choice.]

Client: You're not going to suggest that I come in oftener? You're not alarmed and think I ought to come in every day until I get out of this?

Therapist: I believe you are able to make your own decision. I'll see you whenever you want to come. [Positive regard]

Client: (Note of awe in her voice) I don't believe you are alarmed about—I see—I may be afraid of myself but you aren't afraid for me. [Here the client experiences the therapist's confidence in her. She did not kill herself, by the way.] (Rogers, 1951, p. 49)

Gestalt Therapy

Another form of phenomenological treatment was developed by Frederick S. (Fritz) Perls, along with his wife, Laura. A European psychoanalyst, Perls was greatly influenced by Gestalt psychology. (As noted in Chapter 5, on perception, Gestalt psychologists emphasized the idea that people actively organize their view of the world.) Perls believed that (1) people create their own versions of reality and (2) people's natural psychological growth continues only as long as they perceive, remain aware of, and act on their true feelings. Growth stops and symptoms appear, said Perls, when people are not aware of all aspects of themselves (Perls, Hefferline, & Goodman, 1951).

Like client-centered therapy, **Gestalt therapy** seeks to create conditions in which clients can become more unified, self-aware, and self-accepting and thus ready to grow again. However, Gestalt therapists use more direct and dramatic methods than do Rogerians. Often working in group settings, Gestalt therapists prod clients to become aware of feelings and impulses that they have disowned and to discard feelings, ideas, and values that are not really their own. For example, the therapist or other group members might point out incongruities between what clients say and how they behave. Gestalt therapists may also ask clients to engage in imaginary dialogues with other people, with parts of their own personalities, and even with objects. Like a shy person who can be socially outgoing only while in a Halloween costume, clients often find that these dialogues help to get them in touch with and express their feelings (Paivio & Greenberg, 1995).

BEHAVIOR THERAPY

The psychodynamic and phenomenological approaches assume that if clients gain insight or self-awareness about underlying problems, the symptoms created by those problems will disappear. Behavior therapists emphasize a different kind of insight or self-awareness: They try to help clients view psychological problems as *learned behaviors* that can be changed without first searching for hidden meanings or underlying processes.

For example, suppose you have a panic attack every time you leave home and find relief only when you return. Making excuses when friends invite you out eases your anxiety temporarily but does nothing to solve the problem. Could you reduce your fear without looking for its "meaning"? Behavior therapy would offer just such an alternative by helping you first to understand the learning principles that maintain your fear and then to learn new responses in feared situations.

These goals are based on the behavioral approach, described in Chapters 1, 14, and 15, which sees learning as the basis of normal personality, as well as of most behavior disorders. Indeed, according to this perspective, disordered behavior and thinking are examples of the maladaptive thoughts and actions that the client has learned. For example, behavior therapists believe that agoraphobia, the fear of leaving home and entering crowded public places, develops through associations the client makes (via classical conditioning) between being away from home and having panic attacks. The problem is maintained in part through operant conditioning: Staying home and making excuses for doing so are rewarded by reduced anxiety. Therapists who adopt a behavioral approach argue that if learning experiences can create problems, they can also help to alleviate those problems. So even if the learning that led to phobias and other problems began in the client's childhood, behavior therapists focus on solving those problems by using the principles of learning discussed in Chapter 6 to promote beneficial new experiences.

Inspired by the writings of John B. Watson, I. P. Pavlov, B. F. Skinner, and others who studied learning during the 1920s and 1930s, researchers in the late 1950s and early 1960s began to systematically apply the principles of classical conditioning, operant conditioning, and observational learning to alter disordered human behavior (Thorpe & Olson, 1997). By 1970, behavioral treatment had become a popular alternative to psychodynamic and phenomenological methods.

Some of the most notable features of behavioral treatment include:

1. Developing a good therapist-client relationship. As in other therapies, this relationship enhances clients' confidence that change is possible and makes it easier for them to speak freely and to cooperate in the treatment. In fact, behavior therapists see the therapeutic relationship as central to the success of treatment because it provides the context in which adaptive new learning takes place (Cahill, Carrigan, & Evans, 1998; Wilson, 1995).

2. Careful listing of the behaviors and thoughts to be changed. This assessment—and the establishment of specific goals—sometimes replace the formal diagnosis used in certain other therapy approaches. Thus, instead of treating "depression" or "schizophrenia," behavior therapists work to change the specific thoughts, behaviors, and emotional reactions that cause people to receive these labels.

3. A therapist who acts as a kind of teacher/assistant by providing learning-based treatments, giving "homework" assignments, and helping the client make specific plans for dealing with problems.

4. Continuous monitoring and evaluation of treatment, along with constant adjustments to any procedures that do not seem to be effective.

Behavioral treatment can take many forms. By tradition, those that rely mainly on *classical conditioning* principles are usually referred to as **behavior therapy.** Those that focus on *operant conditioning* methods are usually called **behavior modification.** And behavioral treatment that focuses on changing thinking patterns as well as overt behaviors is called **cognitive-behavior therapy.**

LINKAGES

> **Can people learn their way out of a disorder?** (a link to Learning)

Techniques for Modifying Behavior

Some of the most important and commonly used behavioral treatment techniques are systematic desensitization, modeling, positive reinforcement, extinction, aversive conditioning, and punishment.

Systematic Desensitization   A behavioral treatment often used to help clients deal with phobias and other forms of irrational anxiety was developed by Joseph Wolpe (1958). Called **systematic desensitization,** it is a method in which the client visualizes

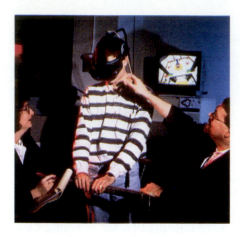

Virtual Desensitization

Here, a client who fears heights wears virtual reality equipment that allows him to gradually experience images of what he would see as a glass elevator rises higher and higher. The images are quite realistic, but the client never leaves the ground.

Source: Hodges et al., 1995.

a series of anxiety-provoking stimuli while maintaining a state of relaxation. Wolpe believed that this process so weakens the learned association between anxiety and the feared object that the fear disappears.

Wolpe first arranged for clients to do something that is incompatible with being afraid. He often used *progressive relaxation training* (described in Chapter 13) to prevent anxiety. Then, while relaxing, the client would be asked to imagine an item from a *desensitization hierarchy,* a sequence of increasingly fear-provoking situations (see Table 16.1). The client would work through the hierarchy gradually, imagining a more difficult scene only after tolerating the previous one without distress. Wolpe found that, once clients can calmly imagine being in feared situations, they are better able to deal with them later. Desensitization may be especially effective if clients actually confront—rather than simply imagine—the fear-provoking stimuli in their hierarchies (Chambless, 1990), but this *in vivo,* or "real life," exposure is not always easy to arrange or control, especially when the fear involves commercial air travel or highway driving, for example. Recently, however, a technique known as *virtual reality graded exposure* has made it possible for clients to "experience" extremely vivid and gradually more intense versions of feared situations without actually being exposed to them. In one study, clients with acrophobia (fear of heights) stood on a platform surrounded by a railing while wearing a head-mounted visual display. The images presented on the virtual reality display gave the impression of standing on bridges that were seven to eighty meters above water, on outdoor balconies at increasing heights, or in a glass elevator as it rose forty-nine floors (Rothbaum, et al., 1995). The same technology has been used successfully in the treatment of a spider phobia (Carlin, Hoffman, & Weghorst, 1997).

Exactly why systematic desensitization works is not clear. Traditionally, clinicians believed that change occurs because of basic learning processes—either through classical conditioning of a new and calmer response to the fear-provoking stimulus or through extinction, as the object or situation that had been a conditioned fear stimulus repeatedly occurs without being paired with pain or any other unconditioned stimulus (Rachman, 1990). More recent accounts supplement these conditioning explanations by emphasizing that desensitization also modifies clients' cognitive processes, including their expectation that they can deal calmly and successfully with previously feared situations (Kehoe & Macrae, 1998).

Modeling   Therapists often teach clients desirable behaviors by demonstrating those behaviors. In **modeling,** the client watches other people perform desired behaviors, thus vicariously learning skills without going through a lengthy shaping process. In fear treatment, modeling can teach the client how to respond fearlessly while vicariously extinguishing conditioned fear responses. For example, one therapist showed a twenty-four-year-old student with a severe spider phobia how to kill spiders with a fly

TABLE 16.1

A Sample Desensitization Hierarchy

Desensitization hierarchies are lists of increasingly fear-provoking stimuli that the client visualizes while using relaxation to remain calm. Here are some items from a hierarchy that was used to reduce a client's fear of flying.

1. You are reading a newspaper and notice an ad for an airline.
2. You are watching a television program that shows a group of people boarding a plane.
3. Your boss tells you that you need to take a business trip by air.
4. You are in your bedroom packing your suitcase for your trip.

        .
        .
        .

12. Your plane begins to move as you hear the flight attendant say, "Be sure your seat belt is securely fastened."
13. You look at the runway as the plane is readied for takeoff.
14. You look out the window as the plane rolls down the runway.
15. You look out the window as the plane leaves the ground.

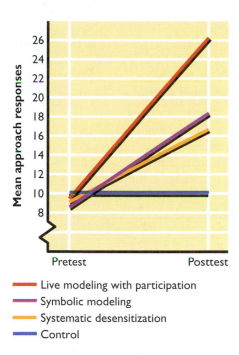

Live modeling with participation
Symbolic modeling
Systematic desensitization
Control

FIGURE 16.1

Participant Modeling

In this study, participant modeling was compared to systematic desensitization, symbolic modeling (watching filmed models), and no treatment (control). Notice that, compared with no treatment, all three methods helped snake-phobic clients approach live snakes, but participant modeling was clearly the best; 92 percent of the participants in that group were virtually free of any fear. The value of participant modeling has been repeatedly confirmed (e.g., Öst, Salkovskis, & Hellström, 1991).

Source: Data from Bandura, Blanchard, & Ritter, 1969.

swatter and had her practice this skill at home with rubber spiders (MacDonald & Bernstein, 1974). The combination of live modeling with gradual practice is called *participant modeling;* it is one of the most powerful treatments for fear (see Figure 16.1).

Modeling is also a major part of **assertiveness training** and **social skills training,** which teach clients how to interact with people more comfortably and effectively. The goals of social skills training range from helping college students with social phobias make conversation on dates to rebuilding mental patients' ability to interact normally with people outside the hospital (Fairweather & Fergus, 1993; Trower, 1995; Wong et al., 1993). In assertiveness training, the therapist helps clients learn to be more direct and expressive in social situations. Note that *assertiveness* does not mean aggressiveness; it means clearly and directly expressing both positive and negative feelings and standing up for one's rights while respecting the rights of others (Alberti & Emmons, 1986). Assertiveness training is often done in groups and involves both modeling and role playing of specific situations. In one program, group assertiveness training helped wheelchair-bound adults more comfortably handle the socially awkward situations in which they sometimes find themselves (Gleuckauf & Quittner, 1992).

Positive Reinforcement Behavior therapists also use systematic **positive reinforcement** to alter problematic behaviors and to teach new skills in cases ranging from childhood tantrums and juvenile delinquency to schizophrenia and self-starvation. Employing operant conditioning principles, they set up contingencies, or rules, that specify the behaviors to be strengthened through reinforcement. In one study, autistic children, who typically have very little language, were given grapes, popcorn, or other items they liked in return for saying "please," "thank you," and "you're welcome" while exchanging crayons and blocks with a therapist. The therapist initially modeled the behavior by saying the appropriate words. The children almost immediately began to utter the phrases spontaneously. The effects generalized to situations involving other toys, and, as indicated in Figure 16.2, the new skills were still evident six months later (Matson et al., 1990).

FIGURE 16.2

A Positive Reinforcement Program for an Autistic Child

During each pretreatment baseline period, the child rarely said "please," "thank you," or "you're welcome," but these statements began to occur spontaneously once they were reinforced. The causal role of reinforcement in producing these changes is supported by the fact that each response remained low until it was specifically reinforced.

Source: Matson et al., 1990.

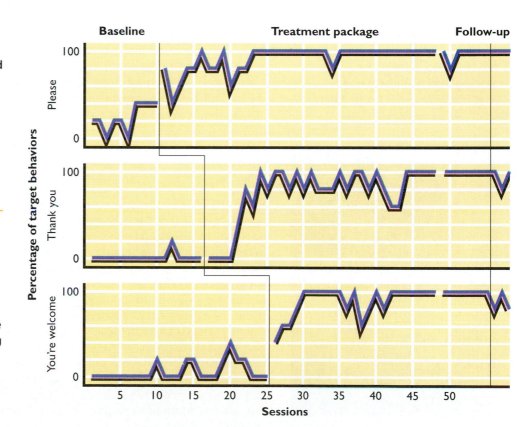

For severely retarded or disturbed clients in institutions, behavior therapists sometimes establish a **token economy,** a system for reinforcing desirable behaviors with poker chips or other tokens that can be exchanged later for snacks, access to television, or other desired rewards (Ayllon & Azrin, 1968; Paul & Lentz, 1977). The goal is to shape behavior patterns that will persist outside the institution (Paul, 2000; Paul, Stuve, & Cross, 1997).

Extinction   Just as reinforcement can be used to make desirable behaviors more likely, other behavioral techniques can make undesirable behaviors less likely. In operant conditioning, **extinction** is the process of removing the reinforcers that normally follow a particular response. If you have ever given up telephoning someone whose line has been busy for hours, you know how extinction works: When a behavior does not "pay off," people usually stop it. Extinction changes behavior rather slowly, but it has been a popular way of treating children and retarded or seriously disturbed adults because it provides a gentle way to eliminate undesirable behaviors.

Another application of extinction is **flooding,** a procedure that keeps people in a feared but harmless situation, depriving them of their normally rewarding escape pattern (Barlow, 1988). (Flooding and related methods based on the extinction of classically conditioned fear responses are also called *exposure techniques.*) When someone is kept in contact with a fear-eliciting conditioned stimulus (a frog, say) without experiencing pain, injury, or any other severe unconditioned stimulus, the fear-eliciting power of the conditioned stimulus eventually diminishes, and the conditioned fear response extinguishes. In one study, clients who feared needles were given extended exposure to the sight and feel of needles, including mild finger pricks, harmless injections, and blood samplings (Öst, Hellström, & Kåver, 1992). After a single two-hour session, nineteen of twenty clients had a blood sample drawn without experiencing significant anxiety. These effects were maintained at a one-year follow-up assessment.

Though often highly effective, flooding is equivalent to immediately exposing a fearful client to the most distressing item on a desensitization hierarchy. Therefore, some therapists and clients prefer more gradual exposure methods, especially in cases of agoraphobia and other problems in which a client's fear is not focused on a specific stimulus (Hecker & Thorpe, 1992). In dealing with agoraphobia, for instance, the therapist might provide gradual exposure by escorting the client away from home for increasing periods and eventually venturing into shopping malls and other previously avoided places (Kleinknecht, 1991; Zuercher-White, 1997). Clients can also practice gradual exposure methods on their own. They might be instructed, for example, to spend a little more time each day looking through photos of some feared animal or to spend some time sitting alone in a dental waiting room or operatory. In one study, clients suffering from various phobias made as much progress after six hours of instruction in gradual self-exposure methods and daily "homework" exercises as did those who received an additional nine hours of therapist-aided gradual exposure (Al-Kubaisy et al., 1992). Effective self-treatment using gradual exposure has also been reported in cases of panic disorder (Hecker et al., 1996) and obsessive-compulsive disorder (Fritzler, Hecker, & Losee, 1997).

Aversive Conditioning   Many unwanted behaviors are so habitual and temporarily rewarding that they must be made less attractive if the client is to have any chance of learning alternatives. Methods for lessening the appeal of certain stimuli are known as **aversive conditioning** because they employ classical conditioning principles to associate physical or psychological discomfort with behaviors, thoughts, or situations the client wishes to stop or avoid.

One form of aversive conditioning, called *covert sensitization,* operates in a way that is the reverse of systematic desensitization. The client first visualizes the stimulus or situation that is to be made less attractive and is then exposed to frightening or disgusting stimuli. For example, covert sensitization was used to treat a man who had been repeatedly arrested for making obscene phone calls. While imagining making an obscene call, the client heard vivid descriptions of his greatest fears: snakes, vomiting, and choking. Finally, he was told to imagine his mother walking in on him during a call. After a month of treatment he was no longer sexually aroused by thoughts of mak-

LINKAGES

Treating Fear Through Flooding

Flooding is designed to extinguish severe anxiety by allowing it to occur without reinforcement. Like other behavioral treatments, flooding stems from the social-learning approach to personality described in Chapter 14, which suggests that disordered behavior, like normal behavior, is learned and can thus be "unlearned."

ing obscene calls, and even two years later he still had not made any (Moergen, Merkel, & Brown, 1990).

Because aversive conditioning is unpleasant and uncomfortable and its effects are often temporary, many therapists avoid this method or use it only long enough to allow the client to learn alternative behaviors.

Punishment   Sometimes the only way to eliminate a dangerous or disruptive behavior is to punish it with an unpleasant but harmless stimulus, such as a shouted "No!" or a mild electric shock. Unlike aversive conditioning, in which the unpleasant stimulus occurs along with the behavior that is to be eliminated (a classical conditioning approach), **punishment** is an operant conditioning technique; it presents the unpleasant stimulus *after* the undesirable response occurs. (Though technically distinct, the two methods may overlap.) Before behavior therapists use punishment (e.g., contingent electric shock) with institutionalized clients, other impaired adults, or children, they must consider certain guidelines based on legal and professional considerations. Among these are the following: Would the client's life be in danger without treatment? Have all other methods failed? Has an ethics committee reviewed and approved the procedures? And has the client or a close relative formally agreed to the treatment? (Kazdin, 1994). Such considerations led to the use of punishment in the case illustrated in Figure 6.10 on page 189.

Cognitive-Behavior Therapy

Psychodynamic and phenomenological therapists have long recognized that problematic thought patterns may lead to depression, anger, or anxiety. Behavior therapists have also addressed these patterns, using methods known collectively as *cognitive-behavior therapy*. In simplest terms, cognitive-behavior therapy helps clients change the way they think, as well as the way they behave. For example, some clients already know *how* to be assertive in social situations but need to identify the habitual thoughts (such as "I shouldn't draw attention to myself") that get in the way of self-expression. Once these cognitive obstacles are brought to light, the therapist encourages the client to try new ways of thinking. The therapist may also help clients learn to say things to themselves that promote desirable behavior and prevent a relapse into undesirable behavior (Meichenbaum, 1995).

Rational-Emotive Behavior Therapy and Cognitive Restructuring   One prominent form of cognitive behavior therapy is **rational-emotive behavior therapy.** Developed by Albert Ellis (1962, 1993, 1995), and originally called *rational-emotive therapy,* rational-emotive behavior therapy is based on the principle that anxiety, guilt, depression, and other psychological problems are caused by how people think about events. Ellis's therapy aims first at identifying self-defeating thoughts such as "I must be loved or approved by everyone" or "I must be perfectly competent, adequate, and achieving to be worthwhile." After the client learns to recognize thoughts like these and to see how they cause problems, the therapist uses modeling, encouragement, and logic to help the client replace these thoughts with more realistic and beneficial ones. Here is part of a rational-emotive behavior therapy session with a thirty-nine-year-old woman who suffered from panic attacks. She has just said that it would be "terrible" if she had an attack in a restaurant and that people "should be able to handle themselves!"

> *Therapist:* . . . The reality is that . . . "shoulds" and "musts" are the rules that other people hand down to us, and we grow up accepting them as if they are the absolute truth, which they most assuredly aren't.
>
> *Client:* You mean it is perfectly okay to, you know, pass out in a restaurant?
>
> *Therapist:* Sure!
>
> *Client:* But . . . I know I wouldn't like it to happen.
>
> *Therapist:* I can certainly understand that. It would be unpleasant, awkward, inconvenient. But it is illogical to think that it would be terrible, or . . . that it somehow bears on your worth as a person.
>
> *Client:* What do you mean?

Albert Ellis

When Albert Ellis reached his 80s and was disabled by chronic diabetes and other health problems, he used the principles of rational-emotive behavior therapy on himself (Ellis, 1997). Instead of complaining about his physical limitations or lamenting life's unfairness, he worked hard at telling himself that his situation, though frustrating, was acceptable—and definitely not awful!

Therapist: Well, suppose one of your friends calls you up and invites you back to that restaurant. If you start telling yourself, "I might panic and pass out and people might make fun of me and that would be terrible," . . . you might find you are dreading going to the restaurant, and you probably won't enjoy the meal very much.

Client: Well, that is what usually happens.

Therapist: But it doesn't have to be that way . . . The way you feel, your reaction . . . depends on what you choose to believe or think, or say to yourself. . . . (Masters et al., 1987).

Cognitive-behavior therapists use many techniques related to rational-emotive behavior therapy to help clients learn to think and act in more adaptive ways. Behavioral techniques aimed at replacing upsetting thoughts with alternative thinking patterns were originally called *cognitive restructuring* (Lazarus, 1971). Using these techniques, clients plan calming thoughts that they can employ during exams, tense discussions, and other anxiety-provoking situations. The calming thoughts might take a form such as "OK, stay calm, you can handle this if you just focus on the task and don't worry about being perfect" (Meichenbaum, 1977). Sometimes, the methods are expanded into *stress inoculation training,* in which clients imagine being in a stressful situation, then practice newly learned cognitive skills to remain calm (Meichenbaum, 1995).

Beck's Cognitive Therapy   In cases involving depression or anxiety disorders, behavior therapists often use Aaron Beck's **cognitive therapy,** which entails another type of cognitive restructuring (Beck, 1976, 1995; Beck & Weishaar, 1995). As described in Chapter 15, Beck bases his approach on the idea that negative cognitive patterns are maintained by errors in logic and erroneous beliefs, such as "I can't do anything right," or by thoughts that minimize the value of one's accomplishments, such as "Anyone could do that." Thoughts and beliefs such as these lead to low self-esteem, depression, and anxiety.

Cognitive therapy is an organized problem-solving approach in which the therapist helps clients notice how certain negative thoughts precede anxiety and depression. Then, much as in the five-step critical thinking system illustrated throughout this book, these thoughts and beliefs are considered as hypotheses to be tested rather than as assertions to be uncritically accepted. Accordingly, therapist and client take the role of "investigators" and develop ways to test beliefs such as "I can never do anything right." For example, they might agree on tasks that the client will attempt as "homework"—such as completing an overdue household project or meeting a new neighbor. Success at accomplishing these tasks provides concrete evidence that allows the client to challenge the erroneous beliefs that cause anxiety and depression, thus helping to alleviate these problems (Beck et al., 1979, 1992).

As mentioned in Chapter 15, however, depressed people's specific thoughts may not be in error; depression may be associated with an overall cognitive style in which people attribute negative events to their own general and enduring incompetence rather than, say, to bad luck or a temporary lack of effort (Peterson, 1994, 1995). Accordingly, cognitive-behavior therapists also help depressed clients to develop more optimistic ways of thinking and to reduce their tendency to blame themselves for negative outcomes (Jacobson & Hollon, 1996).

GROUP, FAMILY, AND COUPLES THERAPY

Although psychotherapy is often conducted with individuals, it can also be done with groups of clients or with family units. **Group therapy** refers to the simultaneous treatment of several clients under the guidance of a therapist who tries to facilitate helpful interactions among group members. Psychodynamic, phenomenological, and behavioral treatments can all be adapted for use in groups. Many groups are organized around one type of problem (such as alcoholism) or one type of client (such as ado-

Aaron T. Beck

The cognitive therapy that Beck pioneered seeks first to identify the negative thoughts that precede a client's anxiety or depression and then to challenge the validity of these thoughts so that they can be overcome.

Source: Wilson et al., 1996.

A Meeting of Overeaters Anonymous

The self-help movement is part of a rapidly growing network of inexpensive mental health and anti-addiction services offered by volunteer helpers, including friends and relatives of troubled people. The services provided by these non-professional groups have come to constitute a significant proportion of the psychological services offered in North America (Kurtz, 1997). Some mental health professionals welcome this trend, but others remain skeptical because of the relatively small amount of empirical evidence available to support the effectiveness of self-help organizations.

lescents). In most cases, six to twelve clients meet with their therapist at least once a week for about two hours. All group members agree to hold confidential everything that occurs during group sessions.

Group therapy offers several features not found in individual treatment (Fuhriman & Burlingame, 1995; Yalom, 1995). First, group therapy allows the therapist to observe clients interacting with one another. Second, clients often feel less alone as they listen to others and recognize that many people struggle with difficulties at least as severe as their own. This recognition tends to raise each client's expectations for improvement, a factor important in all forms of treatment. Third, group members can bolster one another's self-confidence and self-acceptance as they come to trust and value one another and develop group cohesiveness. Fourth, clients learn from one another. They share ideas for solving problems and give one another honest feedback about how each member "comes across." Fifth, perhaps through mutual modeling, the group experience makes clients more willing to share their feelings and more sensitive to other people's needs, motives, and messages. Finally, group therapy allows clients to try out new skills in a supportive environment.

Some of the advantages of group therapy are also put to use in *self-help*, or *mutual-help, organizations.* Self-help groups, such as Alcoholics Anonymous (AA), are made up of people who share some problematic experience and meet to help one another (Zimmerman et al., 1991). There are self-help groups for a wide range of problems, including alcohol and drug addiction, childhood sexual abuse, cancer, overeating, compulsive gambling, and schizophrenia, among many others. The worldwide self-help movement has grown dramatically during the last two decades (Gidron, Chesler, & Chesney, 1991; Kurtz, 1997), partly because many troubled people would rather seek help from friends, teachers, or other "unofficial" helpers before turning to mental health practitioners and partly because some people have been dissatisfied with professional treatment. Dozens of self-help organizations operate through hundreds of thousands of local chapters, enrolling 10 to 15 million participants in the United States and about half a million in Canada (Gottlieb & Peters, 1991; Jacobs & Goodman, 1989). Lack of reliable data makes it difficult to assess the value of many self-help groups, but available information suggests that active members may obtain some moderate improvement in their lives (Morganstern et al., 1997; Noordsy et al., 1996; Ouimette, Finney, & Moos, 1997). Some therapists view these groups as compatible with the therapies they offer and urge clients to participate in self-help groups as part of their treatment (Zweben, 1996). This is especially true for clients with problems such as eating disorders, alcoholism, and other substance-abuse disorders.

As its name implies, **family therapy** involves treatment of two or more individuals from the same "family system," one of whom—often a troubled adolescent or child—is the initially identified client. The term *family system* highlights the idea that the problems displayed by one family member often reflect problems in the entire family's functioning (Clarkin & Carpenter, 1995). This interdependence in family systems can be seen, for example, when one family member's recovery from a mental disorder has an adverse effect on the mental health of another family member. In one case, a woman's recovery from severe depression was followed shortly after by her husband's suicide. The family's therapist concluded that this man's mental stability—and his role in the family—had depended on having a "sick" wife. Cases such as this remind therapists that treating an individual in isolation from the family system can be problematic, and sometimes disastrous (Nichols & Schwartz, 1991).

Ultimately, the family becomes the client, and treatment involves as many members as possible. Indeed, the goal of family therapy is not just to alleviate the identified client's problems but to create harmony and balance within the family by helping each member understand family interaction patterns and the problems they create (Goldenberg & Goldenberg, 1995). As with group therapy, the family format gives the therapist an excellent view of how the initially identified client interacts with others, thus providing a forum for discussion of important issues.

Family therapy has been adapted to fit many theoretical approaches (Goldenberg & Goldenberg, 1995). For example, therapists who emphasize object relations theory point out that if parents have not worked out conflicts with their own parents, these conflicts will surface in relation to their spouses and children. Accordingly, family therapy sessions might focus on the parents' problems with their own parents and, when possible, include members of the older generation (Nugent, 1994). A related approach, called *structural family therapy,* concentrates on family communication patterns (Minuchin & Fishman, 1981). It focuses on changing the rigid patterns and rituals that create alliances (such as mother and child against father) that perpetuate conflict and prevent the communication of love, support, or even anger. Structural family therapists argue that when dysfunctional communication patterns are eliminated, problematic behaviors decrease because they are no longer necessary for survival in the family system.

Working Things Out

Discussions in couples therapy sessions typically focus on identifying and improving the miscommunication, or lack of communication, that is interfering with the couple's happiness and intimacy.

TABLE 16.2

Some "Rules for Talking" in Couples Therapy

Many forms of couples therapy help partners improve communication through rules such as these.

1. Always begin with something positive when stating a problem.
2. Use specific behaviors rather than derogatory labels or overgeneralizations to describe what is bothersome about the other person.
3. Make connections between those specific behaviors and feelings that arise in response to them (e.g., "It makes me sad when you . . . ").
4. Admit your own role in the development of the problem.
5. Be brief; don't lecture or harangue.
6. Maintain a focus on the present or the future; don't review all previous examples of the problem or ask "why" questions such as "Why do you always . . . ?"
7. Talk about observable events; don't make inferences about them (e.g., say "I get angry when you interrupt me" rather than "Stop trying to make me feel stupid").
8. Paraphrase what your partner has said, and check out your own perceptions of what was said before responding. (Note that this suggestion is based on the same principle as Rogers' empathic listening.)

Behavior therapists use family therapy sessions as meetings at which family members can discuss and agree on behavioral "contracts." Often based on operant conditioning principles, these contracts establish rules and reinforcement contingencies that help parents encourage their children's desirable behaviors (and discourage undesirable ones) and help spouses become more supportive of one another (O'Farrell, 1995; Sanders & Dadds, 1993).

Therapists of many theoretical persuasions also offer **couples therapy,** in which communication between partners is the most important focus of treatment (Cordova & Jacobson, 1993). Often, the sessions revolve around learning to abide by certain "rules for talking," such as those listed in Table 16.2. Behavior therapists have even developed a program, called *behavioral premarital intervention,* that is designed to help engaged couples prevent marital problems before they begin and to prepare them to deal effectively with problems that do arise (Hahlweg & Markman, 1988; Sullivan & Bradbury, 1996).

EVALUATING PSYCHOTHERAPY

Psychotherapy has been available for a hundred years, yet people are still asking if it works. ("In Review: Approaches to Psychological Treatment," on page 580) summarizes key features of the main approaches to treatment.) Most psychotherapists and their clients believe in psychotherapy's effectiveness (*Consumer Reports,* 1995); however, confirming this belief with experimental research has proved to be challenging and controversial (Brock, Green, & Reich, 1998; Dawes, 1994; Seligman, 1995, 1996).

The value of psychotherapy was first widely questioned in 1952, when British psychologist Hans Eysenck reviewed studies in which thousands of clients had received either traditional psychodynamic therapy, various other therapies, or no treatment. To the surprise and dismay of many therapists, Eysenck (1952) found that the percentage of clients who improved following any kind of psychotherapy was actually lower than that of people who received no treatment. Eysenck (1961, 1966) later supported his conclusions with additional evidence.

Critics argued that Eysenck was wrong (Bergin, 1971; de Charms, Levy, & Wertheimer, 1954; Luborsky, 1972). They claimed that he ignored studies that supported the value of psychotherapy and misinterpreted his data. They pointed out, for example, that untreated clients may have been less disturbed than those in treatment; that untreated clients may have received informal treatment from their medical doctors; and that physicians who judged untreated clients' progress might have used more lenient criteria than the psychotherapists who rated their own clients. Indeed, other reviewers' subsequent "box score" counts of successes and failures suggested that psychotherapy tends to be *more* helpful than no treatment (Bergin, 1971).

in review

APPROACHES TO PSYCHOLOGICAL TREATMENT

Dimension	Classical Psychoanalytic	Contemporary Psychodynamic	Phenomenological	Behavioral
Nature of the human being	Driven by sexual and aggressive urges	Driven by the need for human relationships	Has free will, choice, and capacity for self-actualization	A product of social learning and conditioning; behaves on the basis of past experience
Therapist's role	Neutral; helps client explore meaning of free associations and other material from the unconscious	Active; develops relationship with client as a model for other relationships	Facilitates client's growth; some therapists are active, some nondirective	Teacher/trainer who helps client replace undesirable thoughts and behaviors; active, action-oriented
Time frame	Emphasizes unresolved unconscious conflicts from the distant past	Understanding the past, but focusing on current relationships	Here and now; focus on immediate experience	Current behavior and thoughts; may not need to know original causes in order to create change
Goals	Psychosexual maturity through insight; strengthening of ego functions	Correction of effects of failures of early attachment; development of satisfying intimate relationships	Expanded awareness, fulfillment of potential; self-acceptance	Changes in thinking and behaving in particular classes of situations; better self-management
Typical methods	Free association; dream analysis, analysis of transference	Analysis of transference and countertransference	Reflection-oriented interviews designed to convey unconditional positive regard, empathy, congruence; exercises to promote self-awareness	Systematic desensitization, modeling, assertiveness and social skills training, positive reinforcement, aversive conditioning, punishment, extinction, cognitive restructuring

Debate over Eysenck's findings—and the contradictory reports that followed them—highlighted several reasons why it is so difficult to definitively answer the apparently simple question, "Does psychotherapy work?" Above all, there is the problem of how to measure improvement in psychotherapy. Should such assessment depend on psychological tests, behavioral observations, interviews, or a combination of all three? For that matter, what *kinds* of tests should be used, where should clients be observed (and by whom), and should equal weight be given to interviews with clients, friends, relatives, therapists, and teachers? The fact that all these measures tend to correlate only moderately with one another makes it that much harder for researchers to compare or combine the results of different studies and, hence, to draw conclusions about the overall effectiveness of treatment (Lambert & Hill, 1994).

The question of effectiveness is further complicated by the broad range of clients, therapists, and treatments involved in the psychotherapy enterprise. Clients differ not only in terms of their problems but also in terms of their motivation to solve them. Therapists differ in skill, experience, and personality—and, as we have seen, their treatment procedures can vary widely. To the extent that a client's improvement is influenced by all these factors, results from an evaluative study of one treatment may not apply to other clients and therapists (Kazdin, 1994). Consider the example of a study in which "kindly college professors" were found to be as effective as experienced psychotherapists in helping people solve their problems (Strupp & Hadley, 1979). This result would appear relevant to the question of psychotherapy's effectiveness, but a careful reading of the study shows that the clients were college students with minor problems, not people with chronic mental disorders. Further, the fact that these students already had a relationship with their professors might have given the professors an edge over unfamiliar therapists (Chambless & Hollon, 1998). Accordingly, the outcome of this study probably does not apply to the outcome of professional psychotherapy in general.

LINKAGES

Can therapy change personality? (a link to Personality)

FOCUS ON RESEARCH METHODS

Meta-Analysis of Experiments on Psychotherapy

While some researchers continue to study the outcome of psychotherapy in independent experiments, others work on summarizing and comparing the results of those experiments.

■ What was the researchers' question?

Mary Smith, Gene Glass, and Thomas Miller (1980) wanted to find a way to look at the "big picture," to answer the question, What objective conclusions can be drawn about the general effectiveness of all kinds of psychotherapy with all kinds of clients and all kinds of disorders?

■ How did the researchers answer the question?

Smith and her colleagues applied a statistical technique known as *meta-analysis* to combine the outcomes of 475 controlled experiments that included almost 25,000 clients and a wide assortment of psychotherapy methods. This meta-analysis involved computing the average difference in improvement between treated and untreated participants in each experiment. These average differences, called *effect sizes,* were obtained for a variety of dependent variables, including clients' reports of improvement, therapists' ratings of client improvement, and the degree of improvement observed by clients' friends and families. Some effect sizes reflected improvement measured immediately after treatment, whereas others were based on measures taken several months later. The researchers averaged all the effect sizes from a given experiment in order to determine how much the average treated client in that experiment improved in comparison to the average untreated person. Then, by averaging the effect sizes for all 475 experiments, they were able to make an overall comparison of the amount of improvement seen in people who did and did not receive treatment.

■ What did the researchers find?

This meta-analytic procedure showed that the average person who received treatment was better off than 80 percent of untreated individuals (see Figure 16.3). Other more recent meta-analyses have reached similar conclusions about the benefits of psychotherapy in general (e.g., Anderson & Lambert, 1995; Weisz et al., 1995) and about specific kinds of cognitive-behavioral interventions for problems such as generalized anxiety disorder (Gould et al., 1997), obsessive-compulsive disorder (Abramowitz, 1996, 1997), and social phobia (Taylor, 1996). In other words, meta-analyses have yielded results that are much more favorable toward psychotherapy than Eysenck's findings.

FIGURE 16.3

A Meta-Analysis of Experiments on Psychotherapy

These curves show the results of one large-scale meta-analysis of the effects of psychotherapy. Notice that, on average, people who received therapy were better off than 80 percent of those who did not.

Source: Data from Smith, Glass, & Miller, 1980.

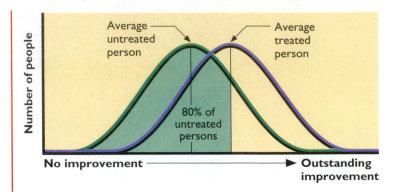

LINKAGES

Does psychotherapy work? (a link to Introducing Psychology)

■ What do the results mean?

Meta-analytic research by Smith and her colleagues (1980) and by others shows that psychotherapy is often more helpful than placebos or no treatment at all (Lambert & Bergin, 1994). Other data suggest that the benefits of therapy tend to be long lasting (Nicholson & Berman, 1983) and statistically significant—that is, greater than would be expected by chance—but that they are not necessarily clinically significant.

To be *clinically significant,* therapeutic changes must be not only measurable but also substantial enough to make important differences in a client's life, as Figure 16.4 illustrates. For example, a reduction in treated clients' anxiety test scores might be *statistically* significant, but if those clients do not feel and act noticeably less anxious in daily life, the change is probably not *clinically* significant. In recent years, the need to demonstrate the clinical significance of treatment effects has become clearer than ever as increasingly cost-conscious clients—and their health insurance companies—decide whether, and how much, to pay for psychotherapy services (Dawes, 1994; Farberman, 1999; Lambert & Hill, 1994; Seligman, 1995).

■ What do we still need to know?

Can therapy ever make people worse? A number of studies conducted since the 1950s suggest that "deterioration effects" sometimes do occur (Lambert & Bergin, 1994; Mays & Franks, 1985; Mohr, 1995). About 5 to 10 percent of all clients in all forms of therapy may experience a worsening of their original problems or the development of new ones, including a sense of failure, low self-esteem, or hopelessness over the inability to profit from therapy (Lambert, Shapiro, & Bergin, 1986; Ogles, Lambert, & Sawyer, 1995). As researchers continue to test the effectiveness of new treatments and as practitioners continue to offer established ones, it will be important to focus on measuring

FIGURE 16.4

Clinical Significance

Evaluation of psychological treatment must consider the clinical, as well as statistical, significance of observed changes. Here, the shaded area shows the range of deviant behaviors per minute displayed at home by normal boys. The solid line shows the average rate of deviant behavior for a group of boys in an operant conditioning treatment for severe behavior problems. The improvement following reinforcement of appropriate behavior was not only statistically significant (compared to the pretreatment baseline) but also clinically significant, inasmuch as the once-deviant behavior came to resemble that of normal boys.

Source: Patterson, 1974.

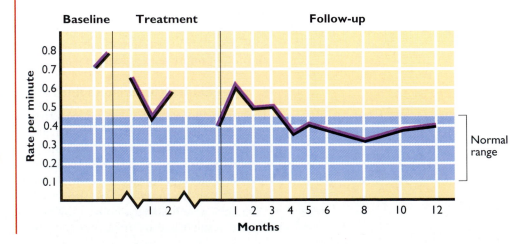

the magnitude of any negative effects, as well as on the dimensions of therapeutic success. As discussed later, ethical standards in research and clinical service require that clients be informed of all foreseeable risks and benefits associated with their involvement in psychotherapy (American Psychological Association, 1992b; Koocher, 1995).

LINKAGES

Is it possible to do experiments on psychotherapy? (a link to Research in Psychology)

THINKING CRITICALLY

Are Some Therapies Better Than Others?

It is reassuring to know that therapy is usually better than no therapy and that therapy-related deterioration is rare, but most people considering treatment also want to know which form of psychotherapy is most likely to bring about clinically significant improvements in their problems. Many clinical psychologists, too, want more empirical data about differences in the effectiveness of the various therapies being used with various clients and disorders. These empirically oriented clinicians are concerned that, all too often, practicing therapists select a particular kind of therapy more on the basis of speculation and hunches about its effectiveness than on the basis of scientific evidence (Davison, 1998). They believe that advocates of any treatment—whether it is object-relations therapy or systematic desensitization—must demonstrate that its benefits are the result of proper administration of the treatment itself rather than of the passage of time, the effects of repeated assessment, the client's motivation and personal characteristics, or other confounding factors (Chambless & Hollon, 1998). They suggest further that the ideal way to evaluate treatment effects is through experiments in which clients are randomly assigned to various treatments or control conditions and their progress is objectively measured. This empirical scientific approach also demands that even the most positive findings be replicated in further experiments by other scientists who have no particular allegiance to the therapy under study.

To help clinicians select treatment methods on the basis of empirical evidence, the American Psychological Association's Division of Clinical Psychology created a task force on effective psychotherapies (Task Force on Promotion and Dissemination of Psychological Procedures, 1995). Working with other scientifically minded clinical psychologists, members of this task force have now published a list of treatments—known as **empirically supported therapies** or **ESTs**—whose effectiveness has been validated by controlled experimental research (DeRubeis & Crits-Christoph, 1998; Kendall, 1998; see Table 16.3, page 584, for a partial listing of ESTs for adult disorders).

■ What am I being asked to believe or accept?

The authors of the empirically supported therapies report claim that experimental research has enabled them to scientifically evaluate various therapies and thus provide a list of methods from which clinicians and consumers can choose with confidence for dealing with specific disorders.

■ What evidence is available to support the assertion?

Support for these claims comes from thousands of empirical studies of psychotherapy for mental disorders in adults, children, and adolescents (DeRubeis & Crits-Christoph, 1998; Kazdin & Weisz, 1998), as well as for marital distress (Baucom et al., 1998) and health-related behavior problems (Compas, et al., 1998). As shown in Table 16.3, the therapies identified as effective for particular problems in adult clients involve behavioral, cognitive, and cognitive-behavioral methods, along with interpersonal therapy, a contemporary psychodynamic approach initially developed to treat depression (Klerman & Weissman, 1993; Markowitz & Swartz, 1997).

Problem	Efficacious and Specific	Efficacious	Possibly Efficacious
Major depressive disorder	Cognitive therapy	Behavior therapy; Interpersonal therapy	Problem-solving therapy for depression
Generalized anxiety disorder	Cognitive therapy	Applied relaxation	
Social phobia	Exposure therapy; Exposure plus cognitive restructuring		
Obsessive-compulsive disorder	Exposure and response prevention		Cognitive therapy
Agoraphobia	Exposure therapy		
Panic disorder	Panic control therapy; Cognitive therapy	Exposure therapy; Applied relaxation	
Posttraumatic stress disorder	Exposure therapy		Stress inoculation training; Eye movement desensitization and reprocessing
Schizophrenia			Social skills training
Alcohol abuse and dependence			Social skills training; Cue exposure; Cue exposure plus coping skills training
Substance dependence (Opiates)			Supportive-expressive therapy; Cognitive therapy; Behavior therapy (reinforcement)
(Cocaine)			Relapse prevention therapy

Source: DeRubeis & Crits-Christoph, 1998.

TABLE 16.3

Empirically Supported Therapies for Adult Mental Health Problems

Treatments listed by the APA task force as "efficacious," or capable of bringing about a desired effect, have been shown to produce greater benefits than no treatment in at least two experiments by independent research teams. Therapies labeled "efficacious and specific" have been shown to produce *clinically significant* benefits that are superior to a placebo treatment or to another treatment of proven value. Treatments listed as "possibly efficacious" have been found effective in only one study or by only one group of researchers.

■ Are there alternative ways of interpreting the evidence?

Those who disagree with the claims embodied in the list of empirically supported therapies argue that it ignores the results of the large meta-analytic studies of psychotherapy described earlier. Those studies did not reveal significant differences in overall effectiveness among psychodynamic, phenomenological, and behavioral approaches to psychotherapy, so these critics suggest that all three approaches are equally effective (Lambert & Bergin, 1994; Smith et al., 1980). This conclusion has been called the "Dodo Bird Verdict," after the *Alice in Wonderland* creature who, when called upon to judge who had won a race, answered, "Everybody has won and all must have prizes" (Luborsky, Singer, & Luborsky, 1975).

Advocates of empirically supported therapies reply that meta-analyses are incapable of detecting genuine differences among treatments. They argue, for example, that the averaging methods used in meta-analyses might obscure important differences in the effectiveness of particular treatments for particular problems (Eysenck, 1978; Wilson, 1985). So even if some specific techniques are more successful than others, meta-analyses are unlikely to reveal the difference because they usually group treatments by theoretical approach (psychodynamic, phenomenological, behavioral) rather than by specific procedures (Giles, 1990; Mahrer & Nadler, 1986; Marmar, 1990).

For their part, critics of the APA task force say that its empirically validated therapies list is based on research that may not be relevant to clinicians practicing in the "real world." They note, for example, that experimental studies of psychotherapy have focused almost exclusively on the therapeutic procedures used rather than on the characteristics and interactions of therapists and clients (Garfield, 1998). This emphasis on procedure is a problem, they say, because the outcome of therapy in these studies might have been affected by whether random assignment of clients to therapists resulted in a match or a mismatch on certain personal characteristics. These critics argue further that although random assignment is a hallmark of experimental research, it does not reflect the way in which clients choose therapists in everyday life (Persons & Silberschatz, 1998; Seligman, 1995). Finally, they point out that therapists participating in experimental research are required to rigidly follow the standardized procedures contained in structured treatment manuals. As a result, those therapists are not free to adapt treatment methods, as they normally would, to the needs of particular clients (Garfield, 1998). So perhaps the experimental procedures that are designed to reveal therapy effects might actually obscure what may be one of the most important components of successful treatment—the skill of the therapist. It may be that therapists who are good at motivating clients to change for the better might be successful even when using mediocre treatment methods (Hubble, Duncan, & Miller, 1999; Lambert, 1989).

In short, rather than considering the empirically supported therapies list a useful guide, some people see it as an incomplete, irrelevant, and ultimately misleading document based on research designed to evaluate the effects of therapy without adequately taking into account either the personal qualities and theoretical biases of those who offer it, or how these factors might interact with the characteristics of the clients who receive it.

■ What additional evidence would help to evaluate the alternatives?

Progress in evaluating psychotherapy will obviously require resolution of the ongoing disagreements among clinicians over how best to do so. However, even if most forms of therapy were to prove about equally effective overall, the Dodo Bird Verdict may actually be the right answer to the wrong question about psychotherapy. Instead of looking only for one "best" approach, researchers also need to explore what Gordon Paul called the "ultimate question" about psychotherapy: "What treatment, by whom, is most effective for this individual with that specific problem, under what set of circumstances?" (Paul, 1969, p. 44).

■ **What conclusions are most reasonable?**

This analysis suggests caution in drawing conclusions about the relative value of various approaches to psychotherapy. Whether we accept particular experimental findings depends on our view of which aspects of psychotherapy are most important in determining outcomes—therapeutic procedures, the personality and skill of the therapist, or the qualities of the client. It would appear, then, that the question "Are some therapies better than others?" has no simple answer. As described in the next section, troubled people or their relatives must carefully consider several factors highlighted by Paul's "ultimate question" when choosing a treatment approach and therapist most likely to be best for them.

Addressing the "Ultimate Question"

The combinations of treatment methods and therapist and client characteristics that are best suited to remedying particular psychological problems have not yet been mapped out, but there are a few trends. For example, when differences do show up in meta-analyses or comparative studies of adult psychotherapy, they tend to reveal a small to moderate advantage for behavioral and cognitive-behavioral methods, especially in the treatment of phobias and certain other anxiety disorders (DeRubeis & Crits-Cristoph, 1998; Lambert & Bergin, 1994; Weisz et al., 1995), as well as bulimia nervosa, an eating disorder (Wilson, 1997). The same tends to be true for child and adolescent clients (Epstein et al., 1994; Weiss & Weisz, 1995; Weisz et al., 1995).

Further, the client-therapist relationship seems to play a major role in the success of all forms of treatment. Certain people seem to be particularly effective in forming productive human relationships. Even without formal training, these people can sometimes be as helpful as professional therapists because of personal qualities that are inspiring, healing, and soothing to others (Stein & Lambert, 1995). Their presence in self-help groups may well underlie some of the success of those groups and, among professionals, may help account for the success of many kinds of formal therapy. (It would be ideal if we could learn their secrets and, if possible, train others to do what they do.)

The choice of therapist and treatment approach, then, should be made with Paul's "ultimate question" in mind. Careful consideration should be given to (1) what treatment approach, methods, and goals the client finds comfortable and appealing, (2) information about the potential therapist's "track record" of clinically significant success with a particular method for treating problems similar to those the client faces, and (3) the likelihood of the client's forming a productive relationship with the therapist. This last consideration assumes special importance when client and therapist do not share similar cultural backgrounds.

Cultural Factors in Psychotherapy

Imagine that after moving to an unfamiliar country to pursue your education or occupation, you become severely depressed. A friend there refers you to a therapist who specializes in such problems. During your first session the therapist stares at you intently, touches your head for a moment, and says, "You have taken in a spirit from the river and it is trying to get out. I will help." The therapist then begins chanting softly and appears to go into a trance. What would you think? Would you return for a second visit? If you are like most people raised in a Western culture you probably wouldn't continue treatment, because this therapist probably does not share your beliefs and expectations about what is wrong with you and what should be done about it.

Similar sociocultural clashes can also occur within a country if clients bring to therapy a cultural or subcultural background or world view that is not shared by their therapist. For example, if a therapist assumes that a client's unexplained abdominal pain is

Preparing for Therapy

When cultural or subcultural differences suggest that clients are unfamiliar with the general rules and procedures of psychotherapy, special pre-treatment orientation programs may be offered. These programs provide a preview of what psychotherapy is, how it can help, and what the client is expected to do to make it work better (Prochaska & Norcross, 1994; Sue, Zane, & Young, 1994).

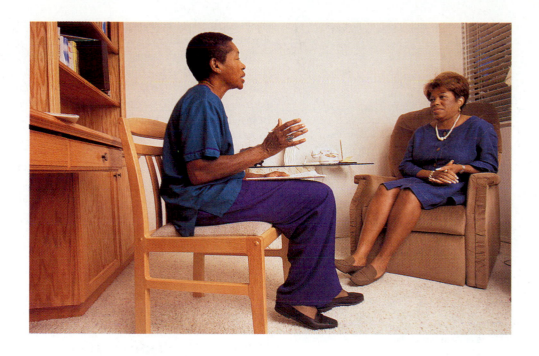

a learned reaction to stress but the client is sure that it comes as punishment for having offended a long-dead ancestor, the client may not easily accept a treatment based on the principles of stress management (Wohl, 1995). In the United States, cultural clashes may be partly to blame for the underuse of or withdrawal from mental health services by recent immigrants, as well as by African-Americans, Asian-Americans, Hispanic-Americans, American Indians, and members of other minority populations (Aponte, Rivers, & Wohl, 1995; Canino & Spurlock, 1994; Casas, 1995; Sue, 1998). Often the problem lies in mismatched goals. A therapist who believes that one should confront and overcome life's problems may encounter a client who believes that one should work at calmly accepting such problems (Sundberg & Sue, 1989). The result may be much like two people singing a duet using the same music but different lyrics (Johnson & Thorpe, 1994).

Major efforts are under way to ensure that cultural differences between clients and therapists do not impede the delivery of treatment to anyone who wants or needs it (Pederson, 1994; Sue, 1998). Virtually every mental health training program in North America is seeking to recruit more students from traditionally underserved minority groups in order to make it easier to match clients with therapists from similar cultural backgrounds (e.g., Hammond & Yung, 1993; Sleek, 1999).

Still, in most cases, minority group clients are likely to encounter a therapist from a differing background, so researchers are also examining the value of matching therapeutic *techniques* with clients' culturally based expectations and preferences (Hays, 1995; Preciado, 1994; Tanaka-Matsumi & Higginbotham, 1994). For example, many clients from collectivist cultures—in which the emphasis is on subjugating personal wishes to the expectations of family and friends—might expect to receive specific instructions from a therapist about how to overcome problems. How would such clients respond to a therapist whose client-centered treatment emphasizes such individualist goals as being independent and taking responsibility for the direction of change? David Sue and his students have investigated the hypothesis that the collectivist values of Asian cultures would lead Asians and Asian-Americans to prefer a directive, problem-solving approach over nondirective, client-centered methods. Sue (1992) found that a preference for directive treatment was highest among foreign-born Asians compared with American-born Asians and European-Americans. However, there are always individual differences; two clients from the same culture may react quite differently to a treatment that group research suggests should be ideal for both of them. In Sue's (1992) study, for example, more than a third of the foreign-born Asians preferred

Making a Connection

The formation of a productive therapeutic relationship can be easier for clients and therapists who share similar sociocultural backgrounds (Sue, 1998).

the nondirective approach and 28 percent of the European-Americans preferred the directive approach.

Today, psychotherapists are more sensitive than ever to the cultural values of particular groups and to the nuances of intercultural communication (LaFromboise, Foster, & James, 1996; Sue, 1998). Indeed, some U.S. states now require psychologists to complete courses on the role of cultural factors in therapy before being licensed. This training helps clinicians appreciate, for example, that it is considered impolite in some cultures to make eye contact with a stranger and, hence, that clients from those cultures are not necessarily depressed, lacking in self-esteem, or inappropriately deferent just because they fix their eyes on the floor during an interview (e.g., Ibrahim, 1991). Graduate students are getting similar training and practical experience as part of their coursework in clinical or counseling psychology (Neville et al., 1996). Research with these students suggests that the training increases their sensitivity to cultural factors in treatment but does not necessarily increase their competence in actually working with members of ethnic minorities (Pope-Davis et al., 1995; Ramirez et al., 1996). Nevertheless, cultural sensitivity training helps therapists to appreciate the client's view of the world and thus to set goals that are in harmony with that view (Sue, 1998; Yutrzenka, 1995). Minimizing the chances of cultural misunderstanding and miscommunication is one of the many obligations that therapists assume whenever they work with a client (Tomes, 1999).

Rules and Rights in the Therapeutic Relationship

Treatment can be an intensely emotional experience, and the relationship established with a therapist can profoundly affect a client's life. Professional ethics and common sense require the therapist to ensure that this relationship does not harm the client. For example, the American Psychological Association's *Ethical Principles of Psychologists and Code of Conduct* forbids a sexual relationship between therapist and client because of the severe harm it can cause the client (American Psychological Association, 1992b; Williams, 1992). To help combat violations of this rule (Wincze et al., 1996), virtually all accredited professional psychology internship programs require their students to receive training in this vital ethical issue (Samuel & Gorton, 1998).

Ethical standards also require therapists, with a few exceptions, to keep strictly confidential everything a client says in therapy. Confidentiality is one of the most important features of a successful therapeutic relationship because it allows the client to discuss unpleasant or embarrassing feelings, behaviors, or events without fear that the therapist might disclose this information to others. Professionals are required not to reveal information to outsiders, even to other treatment providers or members of the client's family, without formal authorization from the client. Since the advent of e-mail, new ethical standards have been proposed to protect the confidentiality and anonymity of clients who seek psychological services via the Internet (American Psychological Association, 1996; Kulynych & Stromberg, 1998). These standards would require therapists to clearly inform clients that others might be able to gain access to their e-mail messages, that no formal client-therapist relationship exists in e-mail exchanges, and that they should seek traditional therapy (Shapiro & Schulman, 1996).

Professional rules about confidentiality are backed up in most U.S. states by laws recognizing that information revealed in therapy—like information given to a priest, a lawyer, or a physician—is privileged communication. In 1996, a U.S. Supreme Court ruling also established psychotherapist-client privilege in the federal courts (DeBell & Jones, 1997; Knapp & VandeCreek, 1997). This means that a therapist can refuse, even in court, to answer questions about a client or to provide personal notes or tape recordings from therapy sessions. The law may require a therapist to violate confidentiality only under special circumstances, including those in which (1) the client is so severely disturbed or suicidal that hospitalization is needed, (2) the client uses his or her mental condition and history of therapy as part of a defense strategy in a civil or criminal trial, (3) the therapist must defend against the client's charge of malpractice, (4) the client reveals information about sexual or physical abuse of a child or an incapacitated adult, and (5) the therapist believes the client may commit a violent act against a specific person.

Rights of the Mentally Ill

Larry Hogue, a homeless crack cocaine addict, had been arrested or sent to mental hospitals more than thirty times in ten years for threatening people on the streets of New York City. However, laws protecting the rights of the mentally ill—and the fact that he had not committed any serious crimes—prevented him from being committed to a hospital against his will. Local authorities' frustration over his case highlights the difficulties inherent in balancing the rights of mental patients and those of the public.

This last condition poses a dilemma. Suppose a client says, "Someday I'm going to kill that brother of mine!" Should the therapist consider this a serious threat and warn the brother? In most cases, the danger is not real, but there have been tragic exceptions. A famous example occurred in 1969. Prosenjit Poddar, a graduate student receiving therapy at the University of California at Berkeley, revealed his intention to kill Tatiana Tarasoff, a young woman whom he had dated the previous year but who later rejected him. The therapist took the threat seriously and consulted his supervisor and the campus police. It was decided that there was no real danger, so neither Tatiana nor her parents were warned. After terminating therapy, the client killed Ms. Tarasoff. Her parents sued the university, the campus police, and the therapist. The parents won their case, thus setting an important precedent. Several states now have laws that make a therapist liable for failing to take steps to protect those who are threatened with violence by the therapist's clients (Bersoff, 1995). Other states allow therapists discretion in warning or protecting potential victims (Stromberg, Schneider, & Joondeph, 1993).

In the United States, clients are protected from being casually committed to mental hospitals. Federal court decisions have given people threatened with commitment the right to have written notice; an opportunity to prepare a defense with the help of an attorney; a court hearing, with a jury if desired; and the right to take the Fifth Amendment to avoid self-incrimination. Furthermore, before people can be forcibly committed, the state must provide "clear and convincing" evidence that they are not only mentally ill but also gravely disabled or an "imminent danger" to themselves or others. Most states now require a periodic review of every committed person's records to determine whether he or she should be released.

Clients have the right to receive treatment while hospitalized, but they also have the right to refuse certain forms of treatment and to be subjected to as little restriction of their freedom as possible (Stromberg et al., 1988). These rules, which are designed to protect hospitalized mental patients from abuse, neglect, coercion, and exploitation, can also create some difficulties. For example, staff members at mental health facilities worry that they might be sued if they keep patients unnecessarily confined *or* if they release a patient who then harms someone. Thus the dilemma: to find a way to balance the legal rights of the patient against those of the public.

BIOLOGICAL TREATMENTS

Hippocrates, a physician of ancient Greece, was among the first to propose that psychological problems have physical causes. He prescribed rest, special diets, laxatives, and abstinence from alcohol or sex as treatments for psychological disorders. In the mental hospitals of Europe and North America during the sixteenth through eighteenth centuries, treatment of psychological disorders was based in part on Hippocrates' formulations and consisted mainly of physical restraints, laxative purges, draining of "excess" blood, and induced vomiting. Cold baths, hunger, and other

The "Crib"

This device, used in the nineteenth century to restrain unmanageable mental patients, was gentle compared with some of the methods endorsed in the late 1700s by Benjamin Rush. Known as the "father" of American psychiatry, Rush advocated curing patients by frightening or disorienting them—for example, by placing them in a coffinlike box which was then briefly immersed in water.

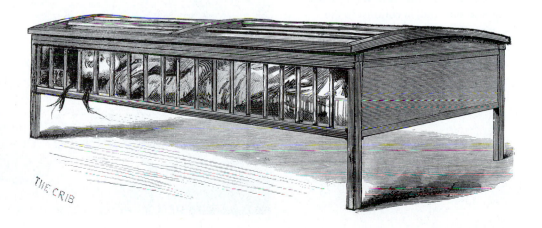

THE CRIB

physical discomforts were also used in efforts to shock patients back to normality (Jones, 1923). Biological treatments for psychological problems have advanced considerably since then and, today, mainly involve the prescription of psychoactive drugs. Earlier in this century, however, the most common biological treatment methods were electroconvulsive therapy and psychosurgery.

Electroconvulsive Therapy

In the 1930s, a Hungarian physician named Von Meduna used a drug to induce convulsions in schizophrenics. He believed—incorrectly—that, since schizophrenia and epilepsy rarely occur in the same person, epileptic-like seizures might combat schizophrenia. In 1938, Italian physicians Ugo Cerletti and Lucio Bini created seizures more easily by passing an electric current through the brains of people diagnosed with schizophrenia. During the next twenty years or so, this procedure, called **electroconvulsive therapy (ECT),** became a routine treatment for schizophrenia, depression, and, sometimes, mania. Upon awakening after an ECT session, the patient typically remembered nothing about the events just preceding the shock and experienced confusion. Although many patients improved, they often relapsed. The benefits of ECT also had to be weighed against such side effects as varying degrees of memory loss, speech disorders, and, in some cases, death due to cardiac arrest (Lickey & Gordon, 1991).

Recent modifications in ECT procedures—such as applying shock to only one side of the brain, ensuring that patients have sufficient oxygen, and inducing profound muscle relaxation—have made modern ECT less hazardous (Abrams, 1993). The most common side effect, memory loss, is temporary and not disabling (*Harvard Mental Health Letter,* 1995a). About 100,000 people a year in the United States and about twice that number in the United Kingdom receive ECT(Fink, 1993; Julien, 1995). Today, ECT is used primarily for patients whose depression is severe, who cannot tolerate or do not respond to antidepressant drugs, or who are at high risk for suicide (American Psychiatric Association, 1993). When ECT is used in combination with other forms of treatment, the reoccurrence of depression is significantly decreased (Lickey & Gordon, 1991; Janicak et al., 1991; NIMH, 1985). ECT is also occasionally used with manic patients (Fink, 1997; Mukherjee, Sackheim, & Schnur, 1994). Contrary to Von Meduna's claim, however, ECT is not an effective treatment for schizophrenia unless the patient is also severely depressed (American Psychiatric Association, 1993).

Electroconvulsive Therapy

To make electroconvulsive therapy (ECT) safer, patients are now given an anesthetic to make them unconscious before the shock is delivered and a muscle relaxant to prevent bone fractures during convulsions. Also, the duration of the shock is now only about a half a second and, in contrast to the dozens of treatments administered decades ago, patients now receive only about six to twelve shocks, one approximately every two days (Abrams, 1993).

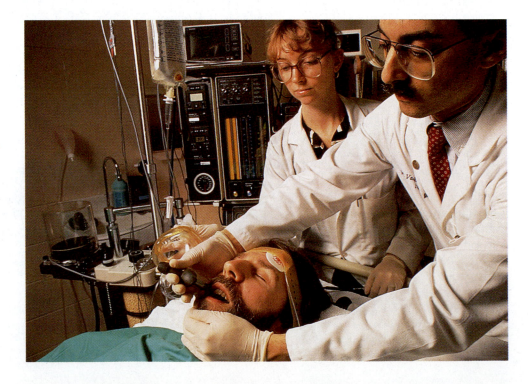

No one knows for sure how ECT works. It may be that it somehow improves neurotransmitter functions and thereby alters mood (Julien, 1995; Kapur & Mann, 1993). Another view is that the neurotransmitters that help the brain recover from convulsions also reduce activity in areas of the brain associated with depression, thus relieving it (Sackeim, 1985). Because shock affects many aspects of brain function, identifying the specific mechanisms underlying ECT's effects on depression is exceedingly difficult (Abrams, 1992; Julien, 1995).

Because of its dramatic and potentially dangerous nature, ECT remains a controversial method of treatment for serious depression. Critics want it outlawed; proponents perceive its benefits as outweighing its potential costs in most cases (Breggin, 1991; Small, Small, & Milstein, 1986).

Psychosurgery

Procedures known as **psychosurgery** involve the destruction of brain tissue for the purpose of treating mental disorder. Among the first to try these procedures was a Portuguese neurosurgeon named António Egas Moniz. In 1935 he developed a technique, called *prefrontal lobotomy,* in which small holes are drilled in the skull and a sharp instrument is inserted and moved from side to side (Egas Moniz, 1948; Freeman & Watts, 1942). The theory was that emotional reactions in disturbed people become exaggerated due to neural processes in the frontal lobes and that the lobotomy disrupts these processes. During the 1940s and 1950s, psychosurgery became almost routine in the treatment of schizophrenia, depression, anxiety, aggressiveness, and obsessive-compulsive disorder (Valenstein, 1980). Unfortunately, brain surgery is risky, sometimes fatal; its benefits are uncertain; and its side effects and complications, including epilepsy, are irreversible. Today, psychosurgery is performed only in rare cases in which all else has failed, and it focuses on much smaller brain areas than those involved in lobotomies (Jenike et al., 1991; Sachdev, Hay, & Cumming, 1992).

LINKAGES

> **How do drugs help people who suffer from depression or schizophrenia?** (a link to Biological Aspects of Psychology)

Psychoactive Drugs

The use of psychosurgery and ECT declined after the 1950s, not only because of their complications and general distastefulness but also because psychoactive drugs had begun to offer more effective treatment alternatives. In Chapters 3 and 9 we discussed how psychoactive drugs affect neurotransmitter systems and consciousness. Here, we describe how drugs are used to combat schizophrenia, depression, mania, and anxiety. Table 16.4 on page 592 lists a few of these drugs, their uses, effects, and side effects.

Neuroleptics The early 1950s saw the introduction of a new group of drugs that revolutionized the treatment of severe mental disorder. Called **neuroleptics** (or *antipsychotics*), these drugs dramatically reduced the intensity of such symptoms as hallucinations, delusions, paranoid suspiciousness, disordered thinking, and incoherence in many mental patients, especially those diagnosed with schizophrenia. As a result of taking these drugs, many mental patients became better able to care for themselves and more responsive to their environments. Thousands were able to leave their hospitals. For those who remained, straightjackets, padded cells, and other once-common restraints were rarely needed.

The most widely used neuroleptics are the *phenothiazines,* of which the first, chlorpromazine (marketed as Thorazine in the United States and as Largactil in Canada and the United Kingdom), has been especially popular. Another neuroleptic called haloperidol (Haldol) is comparable to the phenothiazines in overall effectiveness, but is less sedating (Julien, 1995). Patients who do not respond to one of these neuroleptics may respond to the other. Between 60 and 70 percent of patients receiving these drugs show improvement, though fewer than 30 percent respond well enough to live entirely on their own.

Unfortunately, neuroleptics have problematic side effects, the mildest of which include dry mouth, blurred vision, urinary retention, dizziness, and skin pigmentation problems. More serious side effects include symptoms similar to those of Parkinson's disease, such as muscle rigidity, restlessness, tremors, and slowed movement. Some of

TABLE 16.4

A Sampling of Psychoactive Drugs Used for Treating Psychological Disorders

For Schizophrenia: Neuroleptics (Antipsychotics)		
Chemical Name	Trade Name	Effects and Side Effects
Chlorpromazine Haloperidol	Thorazine Haldol	Reduce hallucinations, delusions, incoherence, jumbled thought processes; cause movement-disorder side effects, including tardive dyskinesia
Clozapine	Clozaril	Reduces psychotic symptoms; causes no movement disorders, but raises risk of serious blood disease
For Mood Disorders: Antidepressants and Mood Elevators		
Tricyclics		
Imipramine Amitriptyline	Tofranil Elavil, Amitid	Act as antidepressants, but also have antipanic action; cause sleepiness and other moderate side effects; potentially dangerous if taken with alcohol
Other Antidepressants		
Fluoxetine Clomipramine Fluvoxamine	Prozac Anafranil Luvox	Have antidepressant, antipanic, and anti-obsessive action
Other Drugs		
Lithium carbonate		Calms mania; reduces mood swings of bipolar disorder; overdose harmful, potentially deadly
For Anxiety Disorders: Anxiolytics		
Benzodiazepines		
Chlordiazepoxide Diazepam	Librium Valium	Act as potent anxiolytics for generalized anxiety, panic, stress; extended use may cause physical dependence and withdrawal syndrome if abruptly discontinued
Alprazolam	Xanax	Also has antidepressant effects; often used in agoraphobia (has high dependence potential)
Other Anti-anxiety Agents		
Buspirone	BuSpar	Has slow-acting anti-anxiety action; no known dependence problems

these side effects can be treated with medication, but the most serious, *tardive dyskinesia,* is an irreversible disorder of the motor system that appears only after years of neuroleptic use. Affecting at least 25 percent of patients who take these drugs, tardive dyskinesia involves grotesque, uncontrollable, repetitive movements of the body, often including tic-like movements of the face and thrusting of the tongue. Sometimes the person's arms or legs flail unpredictably. Indeed, tardive dyskinesia can be far worse than the mental disorder that led to treatment (*Harvard Mental Health Letter,* 1995b).

Clozapine (Clozaril) has effects similar to those of the phenothiazines, but it does not cause movement disorders. Overall, clozapine is no more effective than the phenothiazines, but it has helped many patients who did not respond to the phenothiazines or haloperidol, and it may reduce suicide risk in schizophrenia (Green & Patel, 1996). Unfortunately, for about 2 percent of those who take it, clozapine greatly increases the risk of developing a fatal blood disease called *agranulocytosis,* which is marked by the loss of white blood cells and consequent susceptibility to infectious disease. Weekly blood tests are required to detect early signs of this disease, thus greatly increasing the cost of using clozapine (Lickey & Gordon, 1991).

Several "post-clozapine" drugs are now under intensive study, including *risperidone* (Risperdal), a drug that many physicians see as safer than clozapine. *Olanzapine* (Zyprexa) and *sertindole* (Serlect), currently under review by the United States Food and Drug Administration, may bring improvement in the "negative" symptoms of schizophrenia, such as lack of emotion, social withdrawal, and reduced speech (see Chapter 15).

Antidepressants   Soon after antipsychotic drugs appeared, they were joined by **antidepressants,** which, as their name suggests, were originally designed to relieve symptoms of depression. About 60 to 70 percent of patients who take these drugs show improved mood, greater physical activity, increased appetite, and more deep (stage 4) sleep. Curiously, although these drugs have almost immediate effects on neurotransmitters (usually increasing serotonin or norepinephrine availability), their effects on depressive symptoms do not occur until a week or two after dosage begins; maximum effects take even longer. The mechanism underlying the effects of these drugs is consistent with some theories about the biology of depression discussed in Chapter 15, but the time lag suggests that the effects occur through some sort of long-term compensatory process in the nervous system.

There are several classes of antidepressant drugs. The *monoamine oxidase inhibitors (MAO-I)* are effective in many cases of depression and in some cases of panic disorder, but they can produce severe hypertension if mixed with foods containing tyramine, a substance found in aged cheeses, red wine, and chicken livers (Julien, 1995). Fortunately, a new class of monoamine oxidase inhibitors is now available that does not carry this side-effect risk (Julien, 1995).

Another popular class of antidepressant is the *tricyclics.* Tricyclic antidepressants have been prescribed more frequently than MAO-I drugs because they seem to work somewhat better. They also have fewer side effects, though some patients stop taking tricyclics because of the sleepiness, dry mouth, dizziness, blurred vision, hypotension, constipation, and urinary retention they can cause. Further, the combination of tricyclics and alcohol can increase the effects of both, with potentially fatal results. Still, if side effects are controlled, tricyclics can help many depressed patients and can also reduce the severity and frequency of panic attacks in some patients.

Today, the most popular medications for depressed patients are those that affect serotonin rather than norepinephrine ("Harvard Mental Health Letter," 1998a; Julien, 1995). The most prominent drug in this group is *fluoxetine* (Prozac). Introduced in 1986, fluoxetine has been prescribed for more than 10 million people (Barondes, 1994), making it the most widely prescribed antidepressant in the United States. Its popularity is due to the fact that it is as effective as the tricyclics (about 60 to 80 percent of depressed people who take it find significant relief) and in most cases has milder side effects. An improved version of Prozac, containing a purer active ingredient called R-fluoxetine, is currently being developed. Two other new antidepressants, *venlafaxine* (Effexor) and *nefazodone* (Serzone), show similar promise (Feighner, 1997). Fluoxetine and other serotonin-related drugs, such as *clomipramine* (Anafranil) and *fluvoxamine* (Luvox), are also effective in treating panic disorder and obsessive-compulsive disorder (Julien, 1995; Lickey & Gordon, 1991).

The most recent development in the pharmacological treatment of depression is the use of an herbal remedy from a plant called St. John's wort (*Hypericum*). In Germany, where this treatment is covered by health insurance, it is more popular than Prozac. The active ingredient in St. John's wort may be *hypericin,* a substance thought to enhance serotonin activity and possibly act as a monoamine oxidase inhibitor. However, no firm conclusions can be drawn about the effectiveness of St. John's wort until we have the results of double-blind experiments that control for the placebo effects that may be associated with it (*Harvard Mental Health Letter,* 1998a).

Lithium and Anticonvulsants   Around 1970 a mineral salt of the element *lithium* was found to calm manic patients and, if taken regularly, to prevent both the depression and the mania associated with bipolar disorders (Coppen, Metcalf, & Wood, 1982). Administered as lithium carbonate—often in combination with two or three mood stabilizers or anticonvulsive agents—lithium is effective for about 80 percent of manic patients (Kahn, 1995). Without lithium, the typical bipolar patient has a manic episode about every fourteen months and a depressive episode about every seventeen months (Lickey & Gordon, 1991). With lithium, attacks of mania occur as rarely as every nine years. The lithium dosage, however, must be exact and carefully controlled; taking too much can cause vomiting, nausea, tremor, fatigue, slurred speech, and, with severe overdoses, coma or death. Further, lithium is not useful for treating a manic episode in progress because, as in the case of antidepressants, it takes a week or two of regular use before its effects are seen. So, as with the antidepressants, lithium's effects probably occur through some form of long-term adaptation as the nervous system adjusts to the presence of the drug.

Anticonvulsants are becoming a popular alternative to lithium in treating mania. For example, the anticonvulsant drug *sodium valproate* (Depakote) has fewer side effects than lithium, is less dangerous at higher doses, and is easier to regulate (*Harvard Mental Health Letter*, 1998b).

Anxiolytics   During the 1950s, a new class of drugs called *tranquilizers* was shown to reduce mental and physical tension and the symptoms of anxiety. The first of these drugs, called meprobamate (Miltown or Equanil), act in a manner somewhat similar to barbiturates, meaning that overdoses can cause sleep and even death. Because they do not pose this danger, the *benzodiazepines,* particularly chlordiazepoxide (Librium) and diazepam (Valium), became the worldwide drug treatment of choice for anxiety (Blackwell, 1973). Today, these and other anti-anxiety drugs, now called **anxiolytics,** continue to be the most widely prescribed and used of all legal drugs. They have an immediate calming effect on anxiety and are quite useful in treating the symptoms of generalized anxiety disorder and posttraumatic stress disorder. One of the newest of the benzodiazepines, alprazolam (Xanax), has also become especially popular for the treatment of panic disorder and agoraphobia (Greenblatt, Harmatz, & Shader, 1993).

Benzodiazepines can have bothersome side effects such as sedation, lightheadedness, and impaired psychomotor and mental functioning. Combining these drugs with alcohol can have fatal consequences, and continued use of anxiolytics can lead to tolerance and physical dependence. After heavy or long-term use, attempts to stop taking these drugs, particularly if the change is abrupt, can result in severe withdrawal symptoms, including seizures and a return of anxiety more intense than the patient had initially experienced (Rickels et al., 1993).

An anxiolytic called buspirone (BuSpar) provides an alternative anxiety treatment that eliminates some of these problems, but it acts more slowly. As with the antidepressants, buspirone's effects do not occur for days or weeks after treatment begins; in fact, many patients stop taking it because they think it has no effect other than dizziness, headache, and nervousness (Lickey & Gordon, 1991). Yet buspirone can ultimately equal diazepam in reducing generalized anxiety (Feighner, Merideth, & Hendrickson, 1982; Schnabel, 1987). Further, it does not seem to promote dependence, has fewer side effects than the benzodiazepines, and does not interact negatively with alcohol.

Human Diversity and Drug Treatment   So far, we have talked about drug treatment effects in general ("In Review: Biological Treatments for Psychological Disorders," page 596, summarizes our discussion of drugs and other biological treatments), but there can be significant differences among members of various ethnic groups and between men and women in terms of the psychoactive drug dose necessary to produce clinical effects. For example, Keh-Ming Lin, director of the Center on the Psychobiology of Ethnicity at the University of California at Los Angeles has demonstrated that compared with Asians, Caucasians need to take significantly higher doses of the benzodiazepines, haloperidol, lithium, and possibly the tricyclic antidepressants in order to obtain equally beneficial effects (Lin, Poland, & Nakasaki, 1993; Silver, Poland, & Lin, 1993). In addition, African-Americans may show a faster response to tricyclic antidepressants than European-Americans and respond to lower doses of lithium (Strickland et al., 1991). Whether Hispanics differ from other ethnic groups is not yet clear (Mendoza et al., 1991). Some of these ethnic differences are thought to be a function of genetically regulated differences in drug metabolism, whereas others may be due to dietary practices.

Sex differences in drug response are also being investigated. In the past, much of our knowledge about drug effects in women—and about women's health in general—was based on studies of men, but because these responses can differ in women and men,

BIOLOGICAL TREATMENTS FOR PSYCHOLOGICAL DISORDERS

in review

Method	Typical Disorders Treated	Possible Side Effects	Mechanism of Action
Electroconvulsive therapy (ECT)	Severe depression	Temporary confusion, memory loss	Uncertain
Psychosurgery	Schizophrenia, severe depression, obsessive-compulsive disorder	Listlessness, overemotionality, epilepsy	Uncertain
Psychoactive drugs	Anxiety disorders, depression, obsessive-compulsive disorder, mania, schizophrenia	Variable, depending on drug used: movement disorders, physical dependence	Alteration of neurotransmitter systems in the brain

the male-oriented approach can be potentially dangerous for women. Fortunately, we are now seeing rapid growth in research focused specifically on matters relating to women's health, including their response to drugs (Vogeltanz, Sigmon, & Vickers, 1998). Some of this research suggests that women may maintain higher levels of therapeutic psychoactive drugs in their blood and show better response to neuroleptics, but may also be more vulnerable to adverse effects such as tardive dyskinesia (Yonkers et al., 1992). It may be that hormonal and body-composition differences (such as the ratio of body fat to muscle) are among the factors responsible for sex differences in drug response (Dawkins & Potter, 1991; Yonkers et al., 1992). Continued research on these and other dimensions of human diversity will undoubtedly lead to more effective and safer drug treatments for psychological disorders.

Evaluating Psychoactive Drug Treatments

Despite the widespread success of psychoactive drugs in the treatment of psychological disorders, critics point out several problems with them.

First, even if a disorder has physical components, drugs may mask the problem without curing it. This masking effect is desirable in treating otherwise incurable physical conditions such as diabetes, but it may divert attention from potentially effective nondrug approaches to psychological problems. For example, anti-anxiety drugs may facilitate psychotherapy (Koenigsberg, 1994), but these drugs alone cannot teach people to cope with the source of their anxiety. Critics are concerned that psychiatrists, and especially general practitioners, rely too heavily on anxiolytics and other drugs to solve patients' psychological problems (Beardsley et al., 1988). The antidepressant Prozac, for instance, is being widely prescribed—overprescribed, critics say—for problems ranging from hypersensitivity to criticism and fear of rejection to low self-esteem and premenstrual syndrome (Barondes, 1994). Second, abuse of some drugs (such as the anti-anxiety benzodiazepines) can result in physical or psychological dependence. Third, side effects present a problem. Some are merely annoying, such as the thirst and dry mouth produced by some antidepressants. Other side effects, such as tardive dyskinesia, are far more serious. Although these side effects occur in a minority of patients, some are irreversible, and it is impossible to predict in advance who will develop them.

Still, research on psychoactive drugs holds the promise of creating better drugs, a fuller understanding of the origin and nature of some psychological disorders, and more informed prescription practices (Peuskens, 1995). For example, advances in research on individual variations in the structure of the genes that create different types of dopamine receptors may explain why some people with schizophrenia respond to phenothiazines that bind primarily to one type of dopamine receptor, whereas others respond only to clozapine, which has a preference for another type of dopamine receptor (Van Tol et al., 1992). This research may guide the development of new drugs that are matched to specific receptors, so that the symptoms of schizophrenia can be alleviated without the risk of movement disorders posed by the phenothiazines or the potentially lethal side effects of clozapine. Similarly, research on anxiolytics promises to reveal information about the chemical aspects of anxiety.

Drugs and Psychotherapy

We have seen that both drugs and psychotherapy can be effective in treating psychological disorders. Is one better than the other? Can they be effectively combined? Considerable research is being conducted to address these questions.

Although occasionally a study does show that one approach or the other is more effective, there is no clear consensus; overall, neither form of therapy is clearly superior for treating problems such as anxiety disorders and major depressive disorder (Antonuccio, Danton, & DeNelsky, 1995). One large-scale study on the treatment of depression found that, in general, two forms of psychotherapy (cognitive-behavior therapy and interpersonal therapy) were as effective as treatment with an antidepressant drug (Elkins et al., 1989). There was some indication that the drug was more effective than psychotherapy in the most severe cases of depression, however. Similar results have been reported for panic disorder (Klosko et al., 1990), for generalized anxiety disorder (Gould et al., 1997), and for obsessive-compulsive disorder (Abramowitz, 1997). Further, when a team of Spanish researchers compared the effects of gradual exposure and the anti-anxiety drug alprazolam (Xanax) in the treatment of agoraphobia, they found that clients receiving gradual exposure alone showed better short- and long-term benefits than those getting either the drug alone or a combination of the drug and gradual exposure (Echeburua et al., 1993).

Indeed, most studies that have examined the joint use of drugs and psychotherapy have found that combining them produces surprisingly little overall advantage (Elkins, 1994; Hollon, Shelton, & Loosen, 1991). At the same time, some evidence suggests that a combination of drugs and psychotherapy can be more effective than either method alone in treating certain disorders, including attention deficit hyperactivity disorder, obsessive-compulsive disorder, alcoholism, stammering, compulsive sexual behavior, and panic (e.g., Coleman, 1992; deBeurs et al., 1995; Engeland, 1993). This combined approach is especially valuable to clients who are initially too depressed or anxious to cooperate in psychotherapy (Kahn, 1995). Thus, it has been suggested that the most conservative strategy for treating anxiety and depression is to begin with some form of psychotherapy (which has no major negative side effects) and then to add or switch to drug treatment only if the psychotherapeutic approach is ineffective. Often, clients who do not respond to one method will be helped by the other.

LINKAGES

How do psychoactive drugs work?
(a link to Biological Aspects of Psychology)

LINKAGES

Biological Aspects of Psychology and the Treatment of Psychological Disorders

As noted in Chapter 3, all sensing, perceiving, thinking, feeling, and behaving, whether normal or abnormal, is ultimately the result of biological processes, especially those in the brain, and most especially those involving neurotransmitters and their receptors. Alterations in the availability of these neurotransmitters, in the sensitivity of their receptors, and thus in the activity of the neural circuits they influence, affect the ebb and flow of neural communication, the integration of information in the brain, and ultimately behavior and mental processes.

Because different neurotransmitters are especially prominent in particular brain regions or circuits (see Figure 3.23 on p. 83), altering the functioning of particular neurotransmitter systems will have relatively specific psychological and behavioral effects.

Some of the drugs that we have described for the treatment of psychological disorders were developed specifically to alter a neurotransmitter system that biological theories suggest might be involved in those disorders; in other cases, causal theories evolved from (often accidental) findings that drugs known to affect certain neurotransmitter systems help patients who display some disorder.

Let's consider in a little more detail some of the ways in which therapeutic psychoactive drugs affect neurotransmitters and their receptors. Recall from Chapter 3 that a given neuron can receive excitatory ("fire") or inhibitory ("don't fire") signals via neurotransmitters that facilitate or inhibit firing. Some therapeutic drugs amplify excitatory signals, whereas others increase inhibition. For example, the benzodiazepines (Valium, Xanax) exert their anti-anxiety effects by helping the inhibitory neurotransmitter GABA to bind to postsynaptic receptors and, thus, suppress neuronal firing. This enhanced inhibitory effect acts as a sort of braking system that slows the activity of GABA-sensitive neurons involved in the experience of anxiety. However, benzodiazepines also slow the action of all neural systems that use GABA, including those associated with motor activity and mental processing, which are spread throughout the brain. The result is the decreased psychomotor coordination and reduced clarity of thinking that appear as benzodiazepine side effects.

Other therapeutic drugs reduce postsynaptic activity by serving as receptor antagonists (see Figure 9.12 on page 309), acting to block the receptor site normally used by a particular neurotransmitter. Some neuroleptics, the phenothiazines and haloperidol, for example, exert their antipsychotic effects by blocking receptors for dopamine, a neurotransmitter that, as described in Chapter 3, is important for movement. Thus, these drugs compete with dopamine, blocking the firing of neurons that normally use it. The fact that dopamine blockage seems to normalize the jumbled thinking processes of many schizophrenics suggests that, as discussed in Chapter 15, schizophrenia may be partly due to excess dopamine activity. Unfortunately, reducing this activity can create severe disorders—such as tardive dyskinesia—in the movement systems that are also controlled by dopamine.

Psychoactive drugs can also exert their therapeutic influence by increasing the amount of a neurotransmitter available at receptors, thereby maximizing the effects of the neurotransmitter. This enhanced availability can be accomplished either by stimulating production of the neurotransmitter or, as is more common in therapeutic drugs, by keeping it in circulation in the synapse. Normally, after a neurotransmitter has been released, it flows back to the presynaptic terminal, where it is stored for later use. If this reuptake process is blocked, the neurotransmitter remains in the synapse, ready to work. The tricyclic antidepressants, for example, operate by blocking the reuptake of norepinephrine. Fluoxetine, clomipramine, and other "second generation" antidepressants are called selective serotonin reuptake inhibitors (or SSRIs) because they block the reuptake of serotonin. These effects are consistent with biological theories suggesting that some cases of depression are traceable to faulty norepinephrine or serotonin systems.

COMMUNITY PSYCHOLOGY: FROM TREATMENT TO PREVENTION

It has long been argued that even if psychologists knew exactly how to treat every psychological problem, there would never be enough mental health professionals to help everyone who needs it (Albee, 1968). This view fostered the rise of **community psy-**

Community Mental Health Efforts

Professional and nonprofessional staff of community mental health centers provide traditional therapy and mental health education, along with walk-in facilities or "hotlines" for people who are suicidal or in crises related to rape or domestic violence. They also offer day treatment to former mental patients, many of whom are homeless.

chology, a movement that aims both to treat troubled people in their home communities and to promote social and environmental changes that would minimize or prevent psychological disorders.

One aspect of community psychology, the *community mental health movement*, arose during the 1960s as an attempt to make treatment available to people in their own communities. Thanks to the availability of antipsychotic drugs, as well as to the concern that mental hospitals were little more than warehouses for patients, thousands of people were released from mental institutions. It was expected that they would receive low-cost mental health services in newly funded community mental health centers. This *deinstitutionalization* process did spare patients the oppressive tedium of the hospital environment, but the mental health services available in the community never matched the need for them. As a result, former mental patients have swelled the ranks of the homeless who find themselves in city jails or risking the dangers of life on city streets (Breakey & Thompson, 1997; McBride et al., 1998).

Community psychology also attempts to prevent psychological disorders by addressing unemployment, poverty, overcrowded substandard housing, and other stressful social problems that may underlie some disorders (Albee, 1985; Hawkins et al., 1999). Less ambitious, but perhaps even more significant, are efforts to detect psychological problems in their earliest stages and keep them from becoming worse, as well as to minimize the long-term effects of psychological disorders and prevent their recurrence (e.g., Dadds et al., 1997). Examples of these efforts include suicide prevention programs (Garland & Zigler, 1993), programs that train teachers to identify early signs of child abuse, programs that help emotionally disturbed or mentally retarded individuals develop the skills necessary for semi-independent living (Wallace et al., 1992), and programs, including Project Head Start, that help preschoolers whose backgrounds hurt their chances of doing well in school and put them at risk for delinquency (Tremblay et al., 1995; Zigler, Taussig, & Black, 1992).

LINKAGES

As noted in Chapter 1, all of psychology's many subfields are related to one another. Our discussion of treating psychological disorders through the use of psycho-active drugs illustrates just one way in which the topic of this chapter, the treatment of psychological disorders, is linked to the subfield of biological psychology (Chapter 3). The linkage diagram shows ties to two other subfields as well, and there are many more ties throughout the book. Looking for linkages among subfields will help you see how they fit together and better appreciate the big picture that is psychology.

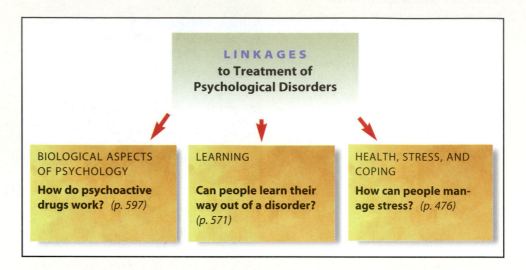

LINKAGES
to Treatment of Psychological Disorders

BIOLOGICAL ASPECTS OF PSYCHOLOGY
How do psychoactive drugs work? *(p. 597)*

LEARNING
Can people learn their way out of a disorder? *(p. 571)*

HEALTH, STRESS, AND COPING
How can people manage stress? *(p. 476)*

SUMMARY

Psychotherapy for psychological disorders is usually based on psychodynamic, phenomenological, or behavioral theories of personality and behavior disorder. Most therapists combine features of these theories in an eclectic approach. The biological approach is reflected in the use of drugs and other physical treatment methods.

BASIC FEATURES OF TREATMENT

All forms of treatment include a client, a therapist, an underlying theory of behavior disorder, a set of treatment procedures suggested by the underlying theory, and the development of a special relationship between the client and therapist, which may make it easier for improvement to occur. Therapy may be offered to inpatients and outpatients in many different settings by *psychologists, psychiatrists,* and other mental health professionals. The goal of treatment is to help people change their thinking, feelings, and behavior so that they will be happier and function better. This goal may be pursued by promoting insight into hidden causes of behavior problems, by fostering personal growth through genuine self-expression, or by helping clients learn new ways of thinking and acting.

PSYCHODYNAMIC PSYCHOTHERAPY

Psychodynamic psychotherapy began with Freud's method of *psychoanalysis* and seeks to help clients gain insight into unconscious conflicts and impulses and then to explore how those factors have created disorders.

Classical Psychoanalysis

Exploration of the unconscious is aided by the use of free association, dream interpretation, and analysis of transference.

Contemporary Variations on Psychoanalysis

Some variations on psychoanalysis focus less on the id, the unconscious, and the past, and more on helping clients to harness the ego to solve problems in the present. Other forms retain most of Freud's principles but use a more flexible format. Object relations therapy, for example, examines the effects of early family relationships on current ones and seeks to improve the latter.

PHENOMENOLOGICAL PSYCHOTHERAPY

Phenomenological psychotherapy helps clients to become more aware of discrepancies between their feelings and their behavior. According to the phenomenological approach, these discrepancies are at the root of behavior disorders and can be resolved by the client once they are brought to light in the context of a genuine, trusting relationship with the therapist.

Client-Centered Therapy

Therapists using Carl Rogers's *client-centered therapy,* also known as *person-centered therapy,* help mainly by adopting attitudes toward the client that express *unconditional positive regard, empathy,* and *congruence.* These attitudes create a nonjudgmental atmosphere that facilitates the client's honesty with the therapist, with himself or herself, and with others. One way of creating this atmosphere is through *reflection.*

Gestalt Therapy

Therapists employing the *Gestalt therapy* of Fritz and Laura Perls use more active techniques than Rogerian therapists, often confronting and challenging clients with evidence of defensiveness, game playing, and other efforts to escape self-exploration.

BEHAVIOR THERAPY

Behavior therapy, behavior modification, and *cognitive-behavior therapy* use learning principles to eliminate clients' undesirable patterns of thought and behavior and to strengthen more desirable alternatives.

Techniques for Modifying Behavior

Common behavioral treatments include *systematic desensitization, modeling, assertiveness training,* and *social skills training.* More generally, behavior therapists use *positive reinforcement* (sometimes in a *token economy*), techniques based on *extinction* (such as *flooding*), *aversive conditioning,* and *punishment* to make desirable behaviors more likely or problematic behaviors less likely.

Cognitive-Behavior Therapy

Many behavior therapists also employ cognitive-behavior therapy to help clients alter the way they think, as well as the way they behave. Among the specific cognitive-behavioral methods are *rational-emotive behavior therapy,* cognitive restructuring, stress inoculation training, and *cognitive therapy.*

GROUP, FAMILY, AND COUPLES THERAPY

Therapists of all theoretical persuasions offer *group therapy, family therapy,* and *couples therapy.* These forms of treatment take advantage of relationships in the group, family, or couple to enhance the effects of treatment. The group format is also adopted in many self-help or mutual-help organizations.

EVALUATING PSYCHOTHERAPY

There is little agreement about exactly how to measure improvement following psychotherapy and how best to ensure that observed improvement was actually due to the treatment itself and not to some other factor. One prominent method for evaluating outcome research is meta-analysis. Recent meta-analyses have found that clients who receive psychotherapy are better off than most people who receive no treatment but that no single approach is uniformly better than all others for all clients and problems. Still, some treatment methods appear effective enough for certain disorders to have been listed as *empirically supported therapies (ESTs).*

Addressing the "Ultimate Question"

Research is needed to discover which combinations of therapists, clients, and treatments are ideally suited to treating particular psychological problems. Several factors, including personal preferences, must be considered when choosing a treatment approach and a therapist.

Cultural Factors in Psychotherapy

The effects of cultural differences in values and goals between therapist and client have attracted increasing attention. Efforts are under way to minimize the problems that these differences can create.

Rules and Rights in the Therapeutic Relationship

Whatever the specific form of treatment, the client's rights include the right to confidentiality and protection from unjustified confinement in a mental hospital.

BIOLOGICAL TREATMENTS

Biological treatment methods seek to relieve psychological disorders by physical rather than psychological means.

Electroconvulsive Therapy

In *electroconvulsive therapy (ECT),* an electric current is passed through the patient's brain, usually in an effort to relieve severe depression.

Psychosurgery

Psychosurgery procedures once involved mainly prefrontal lobotomy; when used today, usually as a last resort, they focus on more limited areas of the brain.

Psychoactive Drugs

Today the most prominent form of biological treatment is the prescription of psychoactive drugs, including those that are used to treat schizophrenia (the *neuroleptics*), mood disorders (*antidepressants,* lithium, and anticonvulsants), and anxiety disorders (*anxiolytics.*). There appear to be significant differences among members of various ethnic groups and between men and women in the dosages of psychoactive drugs necessary to produce clinical effects.

Evaluating Psychoactive Drug Treatments

Psychoactive drugs have proven impressively effective in many cases, but critics point out a number of undesirable side effects associated with these drugs, the risks of abuse, and the dangers of overreliance on chemical approaches to human problems that might have other solutions.

Drugs and Psychotherapy

So far, neither psychotherapy nor drug treatment has been found clearly superior overall for treating problems such as anxiety or depression; however, a combination of the two may be more effective in treating certain disorders than either one alone.

COMMUNITY PSYCHOLOGY: FROM TREATMENT TO PREVENTION

Concern about the effectiveness of individual treatment and the realization that there will never be enough therapists to treat all who need help prompted the development of *community psychology*. Community mental health programs and efforts to prevent mental disorders are the two main elements of community psychology.

KEY TERMS

antidepressants (594)

anxiolytics (595)

assertiveness training (573)

aversive conditioning (574)

behavior modification (571)

behavior therapy (571)

client-centered therapy (568)

cognitive-behavior therapy (571)

cognitive therapy (576)

community psychology (598)

congruence (569)

couples therapy (579)

electroconvulsive therapy (ECT) (590)

empathy (569)

empirically supported therapies (ESTs) (583)

extinction (574)

family therapy (578)

flooding (574)

Gestalt therapy (570)

group therapy (576)

modeling (572)

neuroleptics (591)

person-centered therapy (568)

positive reinforcement (573)

psychiatrists (563)

psychoanalysis (564)

psychologists (563)

psychosurgery (591)

psychotherapy (562)

punishment (575)

rational-emotive behavior therapy (575)

reflection (569)

social skills training (573)

systematic desensitization (571)

token economy (574)

unconditional positive regard (568)

17

Social Cognition

In 1998, at about the same time that Paula Corbin Jones's sexual harassment suit against United States President Bill Clinton was making headlines around the world, another sexual harassment case involving a high-level government employee was in progress—the court-martial of Sergeant Major Gene McKinney. McKinney, the highest ranking noncommissioned officer in the United States Army, had an outstanding record of military service, but six women, who had never met one another, independently accused him of making unwelcome advances toward them and threatening their careers if they refused his requests for sex. If convicted of all the charges against him, McKinney could have served fifty-five years in a military prison. At his trial, jurors heard about two very different Gene McKinneys. According to the prosecution, he was an immoral individual who used his position to exploit, threaten, and degrade women. But according to his defense attorney, Sergeant Major McKinney was a model soldier, a highly moral individual who was the victim of a horrible conspiracy. The evidence against McKinney seemed overwhelming—virtually identical stories from six witnesses—and most people who followed the case assumed he would (and should) be found guilty. After sixteen hours of deliberation, however, the jury found the sergeant major innocent of eighteen of the nineteen charges against him and gave him a relatively minor punishment for the one on which he was convicted.

Why had the jury acquitted Sergeant Major McKinney? Observers offered three possible explanations for the unexpected verdict. First, the jurors simply might not have believed McKinney's accusers. Second, they might have believed parts of the women's stories but not enough to conclude that he was guilty beyond a reasonable doubt. The third and most widely accepted explanation was that the jurors believed the women, but because they themselves were members of the military, and because of their admiration for Sergeant Major McKinney and his distinguished record of military service, they were unwilling to send him to prison (Gross, 1998).

Whatever the case, the outcome of this trial serves to illustrate an important psychological fact: People's *perceptions* of the world have an enormous influence on how they think, feel, and act. The verdict in the McKinney trial, like the verdicts in many other trials, did not depend solely on the facts of the case, or even solely on the "truth." It depended as well on the jurors' thoughts and feelings about the defendant. To paraphrase the famous lawyer Clarence Darrow, juries seldom convict people they like or acquit people they hate. Attorneys know this and try to influence jurors to see their clients in the most favorable light possible. They know that our perceptions of people and their behavior can be influenced by motivation, expectations, contexts, and emotions. The mental processes associated with the ways in which people perceive and react to other individuals and groups is called **social cognition.** Through social cognition, each of us constructs a somewhat different version of the world, including our view of what is true and what is false and what is right and what is wrong (Fiske, 1995; Taylor, 1998).

Understanding the ways in which social cognition affects our behavior is just one aspect of **social psychology,** the study of how people influence, and are influenced by, other people. In the next chapter, we describe how social influences produce various group and interpersonal behaviors, such as conformity, aggression, and altruism. In this chapter, we focus on social cognition, particularly on how our perceptions, thoughts, and feelings affect our relations with people. We examine how people think about themselves and others, why they may like one person but dislike another, how they form and change attitudes, and why and how they use stereotypes to judge other people, sometimes in unfair and biased ways.

SOCIAL INFLUENCES ON THE SELF

Each of us lives in both a private and a public world. You experience your thoughts and feelings privately, but they are products of the social and cultural environment, influenced by others in important ways, and they affect your public behaviors.

In the chapters on human development and personality, we described how each individual develops within a cultural context. We explored the ways in which collectivist and individualist cultures emphasize different core values and encourage contrasting definitions of the self. In this section we look at the processes whereby other people in the culture in which we live affect two important components of the self: **self-concept,** the beliefs we hold about who we are and what characteristics we have, and **self-esteem,** the evaluations we make about how worthy we are as human beings.

Social Comparison

People spend a lot of time thinking about themselves, trying to evaluate their own perceptions, opinions, values, abilities, and so on. Decades ago, Leon Festinger (1954) noted that self-evaluation involves two distinct types of questions: those that can be answered by taking objective measurements and those that cannot. You can determine your height or weight by measuring it, but for other types of questions—about mental ability or athletic prowess, for example—there are no objective criteria. In these cases, according to Festinger's theory of **social comparison,** people evaluate themselves in relation to others. When you wonder how intelligent, interesting, or attractive you are, you use *social* rather than objective criteria (Lyubomirsky & Ross, 1997; Wills, 1991).

Who serves as your basis of comparison? Festinger said that people usually look to others who are similar to themselves. For example, if you are curious about how good a swimmer you are, you are likely to compare yourself with the people against whom you compete, not with Olympic champions. That is, you tend to choose swimmers at your own level of experience and ability (Major, Sciacchtinano, & Crocker, 1993). The categories of people to which you see yourself belonging and to which you habitually compare yourself are called **reference groups.**

The performance of people in a reference group can influence your self-esteem (Baumeister, 1998). For example, if being a good swimmer is very important to you, knowing that someone in your reference group swims much faster than you do can lower your self-esteem. People use a wide variety of strategies to protect their self-esteem (Tesser, 1988). Sometimes they choose to compare themselves with those who are not as good, a strategy called *downward social comparison* (Wills, 1991). Alternatively, they might tell themselves that the superior performer is not really similar enough to them to be in their reference group; they may even *exaggerate* the ability of the other person so that their own performance doesn't look so bad in light of such an able competitor (Alicke et al., 1997). In other words, if you can convince yourself that the opponent who far outscored you in a one-on-one basketball game plays like Michael Jordan or Rebecca Lobo, then you can believe that being badly beaten wasn't so bad and that you would do fine against someone with normal athletic skills.

An unfavorable comparison of your own status with that of others can produce a phenomenon known as **relative deprivation**—the belief that, no matter how much you are getting in terms of recognition, status, money, and so forth, it is less than you deserve (Brewer & Brown, 1998). The concept of relative deprivation explains why an actor who receives $5 million to star in a film feels abused if a co-star is receiving $10 million. If an average person constantly identifies very wealthy people as a reference group, the resultant relative deprivation can make the person depressed and anxious (Taylor & Lobel, 1989). And if a large group experiences relative deprivation, political unrest may follow. The turmoil that leads to great political upheavals, from the American Revolution to the overthrow of European communism, usually starts after the members of an oppressed group experience some improvement in their lives and begin to compare their circumstances with those in other groups (Brewer & Brown, 1998). With this improvement comes elevated expectations about what they deserve.

Social Identity Theory

Stop reading for a moment and fill in the blank in the following sentence: "I am a(n) _____."

Some people complete the sentence by using characteristics such as "hard worker," "good sport," or some other aspect of their *personal* identity. However, many others

The Muhammad Ali Effect

When former heavyweight boxing champion of the world Muhammad Ali was once asked why he did so poorly on an intelligence test, Ali replied, "I only said I was the greatest, not the smartest." Recent research in the United States and in Holland suggests that most people, like Ali, consider it more important to be moral and honest than to be smart. They also believe that they are more honest than other people. This helps to maintain self-esteem (Van Lange & Sedikides, 1998).

All in the Family

For many people, their place in their family is a central aspect of their social identity. For others, it might be their role as part of a political, religious, cultural, or business organization that is most vital to that identity. Whatever the specifics, social identity is an important part of people's self-concept, or view of themselves.

identify themselves by using a word or phrase that reflects their nationality, gender, or religion. These responses reflect **social identity,** our beliefs about the groups to which we belong. Our social identity is thus part of our self-concept (Walsh & Banaji, 1997).

Our social, or group, identity permits us to feel part of a larger whole (Deaux, 1996). Its importance is seen in the pride that people feel when a member of their family graduates from college or when a local team wins a big game (Burris, Branscombe, & Klar, 1997). In wars between national, ethnic, or religious groups, individuals sacrifice and sometimes die for the sake of their group identity. A group identity is also one reason people donate money to people who are in need, support friends in a crisis, and display other helping behaviors toward those with whom they can identify. As we shall see later, however, defining ourselves in terms of a group identity can foster an "us versus them" mentality that sets the stage for prejudice, discrimination, and intergroup conflict (Brewer & Brown, 1998).

LINKAGES

Can negative self-image lead to mental disorders? (a link to Psychological Disorders)

LINKAGES

Social Cognition and Psychological Disorders

Through social comparison and the formation of social identity, people develop mental representations of themselves. These mental representations, called **self-schemas,** not only shape how people think about themselves but also can alter their vulnerability to various forms of psychological disorder. Patricia Linville has found that people vary with respect to the complexity of their self-schemas (Linville & Carlston, 1994). Some individuals have a *unified self-schema;* they think of themselves as having more or less the same characteristics or attributes in every situation (at home, at a party, and so on) and in every role (as student, friend, or romantic partner). In contrast, other individuals have *differentiated self-schemas;* they think of themselves as having different attributes in different roles or situations.

Variations in the way people think about themselves have a strong impact on their emotional experiences (Clark, 1994). For example, students with a unified self-schema are likely to have an especially strong emotional reaction to failing an exam because they would tend to interpret failure in this one area as implying incompetence in all areas (Niedenthal, Setterlund, & Wherry, 1992). After failing, they are likely to lower their opinions of themselves not only as students but also in a variety of other roles—

as sons or daughters, for example. In contrast, people with a differentiated self-schema may think less of themselves as students, but failing an exam will have fewer implications for the way they think of themselves in their other social roles (Kihlstrom & Klein, 1994).

As described in Chapter 15, a tendency to see oneself as generally and permanently inadequate rather than as merely prone to specific or temporary weaknesses may form the cognitive basis for depression and other psychological disorders. In contrast, people with differentiated self-schemas seem better able to separate failure in one part of their life from their total worth as individuals. This ability may be part of the reason they typically become less depressed following the breakup of a romance than do people with unified self-schemas, and they may be less prone to stress-related illness (Smith & Cohen, 1993).

Self-schemas contain information not only about what people are like (the *actual self*) but also about how they want to be (the *ideal self*) and what their moral training says they should be (the *ought self*). For most people, thinking about the discrepancy between the actual self and the ideal self produces emotions such as sadness, disappointment, and dissatisfaction (Higgins, Vookles, & Tykocinski, 1992). In more extreme cases, people may become so focused on such thoughts that they show symptoms of depression (Weary & Edwards, 1994). Discrepancies between the actual self and the ought self usually produce emotions such as guilt and fear of rejection; in some cases these emotions result in anxiety-related disorders (Higgins, 1989; Pittman, 1998).

SOCIAL PERCEPTION

There is a story about a company president who was having lunch with a man being considered for an executive position. When the man salted his food without first tasting it, the president decided not to hire him. The reason, she explained, was that the company had no room for a person who acted before collecting all relevant information. The candidate lost his chance because of social perception, the process through which people interpret information about others, form impressions of them, and draw conclusions about the reasons for their behavior. In this section we examine how and why social perception influences our thoughts, feelings, and actions.

The Role of Schemas

The perception of people follows many of the same laws that govern the perception of objects, including the Gestalt principles of perception discussed in Chapter 5. Consider Figure 17.1. Consistent with Gestalt principles, most people would describe it as "a square with a notch in one side," not as eight straight lines (Woodworth & Schlosberg, 1954). The reason is that they interpret new information using the mental representations, or *schemas*, they already have about squares; in short, they interpret this diagram as a square with a slight modification.

Schemas about people, too, can have a significant influence on our perception of them because, first, schemas influence what we pay attention to and what we ignore. Characteristics or events that are consistent with our schema about another person usually get more attention than those that are inconsistent with that schema. Thus, we tend to process information about the other person more quickly if it confirms our beliefs about that person's gender or ethnic group than if it violates those beliefs (Fiske, 1998). Second, schemas influence what we remember about others. One study demonstrated that if people thought a woman they saw in a videotape was a waitress, they recalled that she had a beer with dinner and owned a TV set; if they thought she was a librarian, they remembered that she was wearing glasses and liked classical music (Cohen, 1981). Finally, schemas affect our judgment about the behavior of others (Fiske, 1995). Thomas Hill and his colleagues (1989) found that participants' ratings of male and female friends' sadness were influenced not only by the friends' actual

FIGURE 17.1

A Schema-Plus-Correction

People who see an object like this tend to use a pre-existing mental representation (their schema of a square) and then correct or modify it in some way (here, with a notch).

Violating a Schema

This particular grandmother probably does not fulfill your schema—your mental representation—of how grandmothers are supposed to look and act. Schemas help us to categorize quickly and respond appropriately to the people we meet, but they can also create narrowmindedness and, as we shall see later, prejudice.

"You are fair, compassionate, and intelligent, but you are perceived as biased, callous, and dumb."

behavior but also by the participants' general schemas about how much sadness men as opposed to women tend to experience.

In other words, through "top-down" processing, schemas can influence—and sometimes bias—person perception in the same manner in which schemas about objects can affect object perception (see Chapter 5). And just as they help us read sentences in which words have missing letters, schemas also allow us to efficiently "fill in the blanks" about people. Accordingly, medical patients and airline passengers do not usually ask their doctors or pilots for credentials. Their schemas about these professionals lead to perceptions that the person who examines them or flies their plane is competent, confident, skilled, experienced, and serious. And usually these perceptions are correct. It is only when our expectations are violated that we realize that schemas can create errors in judgment about other people.

First Impressions

The schemas we have about people act as lenses that shape our first impression of them. That impression, in turn, influences both our subsequent perceptions of their behavior and our reactions to it. First impressions are formed quickly, usually change slowly, and typically have a long-lasting influence. No wonder first impressions are so important in the development of social relations (Gilbert, 1998). How do people form impressions of other people? And why are they so resistant to change?

Forming Impressions   Think about your first impression of a close friend. It probably formed rapidly, because, as mentioned earlier, existing schemas create a tendency to automatically infer a great deal about a person on the basis of limited information (Fiske, 1995). An ethnic name, for example, might have caused you to draw inferences about your friend's religion, food preferences, or temperament. Clothing or hairstyle might have led you to make assumptions about her political views or taste in music. These inferences and assumptions may or may not be accurate; how many turned out to be true in your friend's case?

One schema has a particularly strong influence on our first impressions: the assumption that most people we meet hold attitudes and values similar to our own (Hoyle, 1993). So, all else being equal, we are initially inclined to like other people. However, it does not take much negative information to change our minds. Why? There are numerous reasons why people may behave positively around us—they are nice, they like us, they want to sell us insurance, our best friend likes them, and so on. Negative acts, however, suggest only that they are unfriendly or have other undesirable personality traits (Coovert & Reeder, 1990). Accordingly, negative information attracts more attention and carries more weight in shaping first impressions than positive information (Klein, 1991).

Lasting Impressions   Does your friend seem the same today as when you met? First impressions can change, but the process is usually very slow. One reason is that humans tend to be "cognitive misers" (Fiske, 1995). We maintain our existing beliefs about the world, often using our schemas to preserve a reality that fits our expectations. Holding on to existing impressions appears to be part of this effort. Thus, if your friend has recently said or done something that violates your expectations, your view of her probably did not change much, if at all. In fact, you may have acted to preserve your impression by thinking something like "She is not herself today." In short, impressions are slow to change because the meaning we give to new information about people is shaped by what we already know or believe about them (Sherman & Klein, 1994).

Self-Fulfilling Prophecies   Another reason first impressions tend to be stable is that we often do things that cause others to confirm our impressions (Lord, 1997). If teachers expect particular students to do poorly in mathematics, the students may sense this expectation, exert less effort, and perform below their ability level. Similarly, judges often unintentionally convey their own feelings about a case to jurors (Hart, 1995), and counselors can draw extraverted behavior from clients whom they believe to be extraverted, whether or not they actually are (Copeland & Snyder, 1995). When,

LINKAGES

Self-Fulfilling Prophesies in the Classroom

As discussed in the chapter on mental abilities, first impressions of a student's potential can alter a teacher's behavior. If teachers inadvertently spend less time helping children who impressed them as "dull," those children may in fact not learn as much, thus fulfilling the teachers' expectations. If the girl in the back row has not impressed this teacher as being bright, how likely do you think it is that she will be called on?

without our awareness, schemas cause us to subtly lead people to behave in line with our expectations, a **self-fulfilling prophecy** is at work.

In one experiment on self-fulfilling prophecies, men and women participated in "get acquainted" conversations over an intercom system. Before the conversations took place, the men were shown photographs and told that they were pictures of their partners. Some saw a photograph of an obese woman, whereas others saw a picture of a woman of normal weight. In fact, the photographs bore no relationship to the women's actual appearance. Independent judges who had not seen any of the participants listened to tapes of the ensuing conversations and rated the women's behavior and personalities. The women whom the men thought were of normal weight were judged as more articulate, lively, interesting, exciting, and fun to be with. Apparently, when the men thought their partners were of normal weight, they were more friendly and engaging themselves, and this behavior, in turn, elicited more positive reactions from the women. In contrast, men who thought their partners were overweight behaved in ways that drew comparatively dull responses (Snyder & Haugen, 1994, 1995).

Self-fulfilling prophecies also help maintain judgments about groups. If you assume that members of a certain ethnic group are pushy or aggressive, for example, you might display defensiveness or even hostility toward them. Faced with this behavior, members of the group might become frustrated and angry. Their reactions fulfill your prophecy and perpetuate the impressions that created it (Ross & Jackson, 1991).

Explaining Behavior: Attribution

So far, we have examined how people form impressions about the characteristics of other people. But perceptions of others include another key element: explanations of behavior. People tend to form *implicit theories* about why people (including themselves) behave as they do and about what behavior to expect in the future. Psychologists use the term **attribution** to describe the process people go through to explain the causes of behavior (including their own).

As an example, suppose a classmate fails to return borrowed notes on time. You could attribute the behavior to many causes, from an unanticipated emergency to simple selfishness. Which of these alternatives you choose is important because it will help you to *understand* your classmate's behavior, *predict* what will happen if this person asks to borrow something in the future, and decide how to *control* the situation should it arise again. Similarly, whether a person attributes a spouse's nagging to stress-induced irritability or to lack of love can influence whether that person will work on the marriage or work to dissolve it.

People tend to attribute behavior in a particular situation to either primarily internal causes (characteristics of the person) or primarily external (situational) causes (Bell-Dolan & Anderson, in press). For example, if you thought your classmate's failure to return notes was due to lack of consideration or laziness, you would be making an *internal attribution*. If you thought that the oversight was due to time pressure caused by an upcoming exam or a family crisis, you would be making an *external attribution*. Similarly, if you failed an exam, you could explain it by concluding either that you're not very smart (internal attribution) or that your work schedule left you too little time to study (external attribution). The attribution that you make, in turn, might determine how much you study for the next exam or even whether you decide to stay in school.

Sources of Attributions   Harold Kelley (1973) proposed an influential theory of how people (whom Kelley called *observers*) make attributions about the actions of other people (whom Kelley called *actors*). To illustrate this theory, let's imagine that your father refuses to allow your friend Ralph to eat dinner at your house tonight. According to Kelley, understanding the reasons for your father's behavior requires information about three key variables: consensus, consistency, and distinctiveness (Kelley, 1973).

1. *Consensus* is the degree to which other people's behavior is similar to that of the actor—in this case, your father. If everyone you know avoids Ralph, your father's behavior has a high degree of consensus, and you would attribute his reaction to an external cause (probably something about Ralph). However, if everyone else treats Ralph well, your father's negative response would have low consensus. Accordingly, you would probably attribute it to something about your father, such as his being a grouch or his personal dislike for Ralph.

2. *Consistency* is the degree to which the behavior is the same across time and/or situations. If your father has warmly invited Ralph to dinner several times in the past but rejects him this time, the consistency of his behavior is low. Low consistency suggests that your father's behavior is attributable to external causes, such as the fact that Ralph has just played three hours of basketball and did not shower afterward. Conversely, if his behavior toward Ralph is always hostile, it has high consistency. But is your father's consistent behavior attributable to an internal cause (his consistent grouchiness) or to an external cause (Ralph's consistent offensiveness)? This question is difficult to answer without information about distinctiveness.

3. *Distinctiveness* concerns the extent to which similar stimuli elicit the same behaviors from the actor. If your father is nasty to all your friends, his behavior toward Ralph has low distinctiveness. Behavior that is low in distinctiveness is usually attributable to internal causes, such as a grouchy personality. However, if your dad gets along with everyone except Ralph, his behavior has high distinctiveness, and your attribution about the cause of his behavior is likely to shift toward a cause other than your father's personality, such as how Ralph acts.

In summary, Kelley's theory suggests that people are most likely to make internal attributions about an actor's behavior when there is low consensus, high consistency, and low distinctiveness. If you observe your boss insulting customers (a situation of low consensus, inasmuch as most people in business are polite to customers) every day (high consistency) no matter who the customers are (low distinctiveness), you would probably attribute this behavior to the boss's personality rather than to some external cause such as the weather or the customers' rudeness. On the other hand, if you saw the boss on just one day (low consistency) being rude (low consensus) to one particular customer (high distinctiveness), you would be more likely to attribute the incident to the customer's behavior or some other external factor. External attributions are often made in response to other information patterns as well, as Figure 17.2 illustrates.

FIGURE 17.2

Causal Attribution

Here are the most common patterns of consensus, consistency, and distinctiveness that lead people to attribute other people's behavior to internal or external causes.

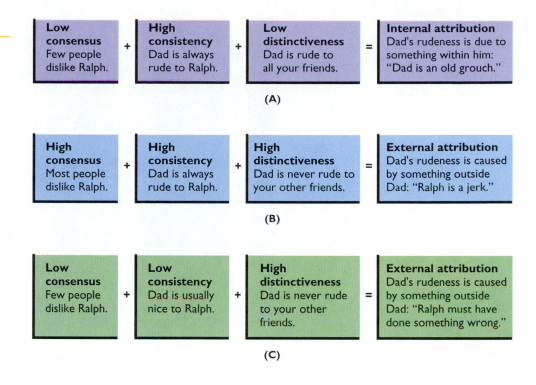

(A)

| Low consensus Few people dislike Ralph. | + | High consistency Dad is always rude to Ralph. | + | Low distinctiveness Dad is rude to all your friends. | = | Internal attribution Dad's rudeness is due to something within him: "Dad is an old grouch." |

(B)

| High consensus Most people dislike Ralph. | + | High consistency Dad is always rude to Ralph. | + | High distinctiveness Dad is never rude to your other friends. | = | External attribution Dad's rudeness is caused by something outside Dad: "Ralph is a jerk." |

(C)

| Low consensus Few people dislike Ralph. | + | Low consistency Dad is usually nice to Ralph. | + | High distinctiveness Dad is never rude to your other friends. | = | External attribution Dad's rudeness is caused by something outside Dad: "Ralph must have done something wrong." |

FOCUS ON RESEARCH METHODS

Cross-Cultural Differences in Attributions

Most theories of causal attribution were developed by North American psychologists who implicitly assumed that the factors leading to internal or external attributions are the same all over the world. These theories predict, for example, that anyone anywhere who sees a woman helping someone who had once helped her would attribute her actions to an obligation to return a favor (an external cause), not to her general helpfulness (an internal cause).

■ What was the researchers' question?

Joan Miller and David Bersoff (1994) asked whether such attributional patterns are, in fact, universal. Using their knowledge of the values and beliefs of Americans from a Judeo-Christian culture and of Indians from a Hindu culture, the researchers hypothesized that the Americans would attribute repayment of a favor to external factors, whereas the Indians would attribute it to internal factors (Miller, 1994; Miller & Bersoff, 1995).

■ How did the researchers answer the question?

Miller and Bersoff conducted a cross-cultural experiment in India and the United States. They asked sixty U.S.-born students at Yale University and sixty Hindu students from the University of Mysore in India to read a brief story about helping. Half the participants were male and half were female, and they each read the story in their own language. The independent variable in the study was the kind of helping that occurred in the stories (reciprocal vs. spontaneous). The dependent variable was the students' explanations for the helping that was portrayed.

Here is a modified version of one of the stories about reciprocal helping:

One day John noticed that a neighbor, Bill, was planting a new garden. John had plenty of free time so he helped Bill plant his garden. Several weeks later, Bill, the man whom

Why Are They Helping?

Helping occurs all around the world, but research shows that people's explanations about why it happens can differ from culture to culture.

John had helped previously, noticed that John was painting a fence in his yard. Bill had plenty of free time, so he offered to help John paint his fence.

In a similar story about spontaneous helping, a man offers to help his friend paint a fence, but in this story the friend had not previously helped him. Half the stories were about males, half about females. Each participant was asked to rate how well each of several reasons explained the helper's actions. Giving a high rating to a reason such as "because he likes to help" would suggest an internal attribution; a high rating for "she owed her a favor" would suggest an external attribution. The students were also asked to say whether they thought the helper felt a general moral responsibility to be helpful (an internal attribution).

■ What did the researchers find?

The results from both male and female students supported the researchers' hypothesis. The American students tended to rate "repaying a favor" (an external cause) as a much better explanation of reciprocal helping than "liking to help" (an internal cause). Less than 2 percent thought that reciprocal helpers felt a moral responsibility to help. In contrast, the Indian students tended to believe that reciprocal helping occurred mainly because the helper liked to help; almost 80 percent also said that helpers who returned a favor felt a moral responsibility to do so. The American students thought that a spontaneous helper enjoyed helping much more than did a reciprocal helper. However, the Indian students thought that a spontaneous helper liked to help slightly *less* than a reciprocal helper.

■ What do the results mean?

Miller (1994) suggested that the differences in the two groups' responses reflected differences in their cultural experiences. She noted that Hindus in India have a "duty-based" moral system in which helping because of social obligation is just as moral as helping in the absence of prior favors. Further, they tend not to distinguish between helping that is motivated by personal traits and helping that is motivated by social duty; they believe that one should help whether or not one likes the person who is helped. In contrast, people from Euro-American cultures tend to believe that while social obligations may force a person to help even if that person does not have a "helpful" personality, they should not have to help someone who doesn't deserve help or whom they don't like (Miller & Bersoff, 1998). In short, helping is seen very differently in India and the United States.

The results of Miller and Bersoff's experiment highlight once again the danger of assuming that phenomena seen in Euro-American cultures generalize to all cultures. Cross-cultural differences in attribution and other aspects of social cognition may help to explain why people in different cultures sometimes have so much difficulty in understanding one another.

■ What do we still need to know?

Many questions remain about cultural differences in social cognition and social perception. For example, are there differences in perceptions of helping *within India?* Hinduism is the dominant religion and culture in India, but it is not the only one; diverse cultures within a given country are likely to shape differing patterns of social perception. It would also be useful to know how the differences found by Miller and Bersoff relate to other cross-cultural differences in social cognition, such as the fact that people from individualist cultures are more likely than those from collectivist cultures to attribute people's behavior to personality traits (Moghaddam, 1998). Finally, we need to know more about the mechanisms through which different cultures teach different patterns of social cognition and how easy or difficult it is to change these learned patterns if they contribute to strained intercultural relations.

Attributional Bias

Men whose thinking is colored by the ultimate attribution error might assume that women who succeed at tasks associated with traditional male gender roles are just lucky, but that men succeed at those tasks because of their skill. When this attributional bias is in operation, people who are perceived as belonging to an out-group, whether on the basis of their gender, age, sexual orientation, religion, ethnicity, or other characteristics, may be denied fair evaluations and equal opportunities.

The Fundamental Attribution Error   Whatever their background, most people are usually logical in their attempts to explain behavior (Trope, Cohen, & Alfieri, 1991). However, they are also prone to *attributional biases* that can distort their view of behavior (Gilbert, 1998).

North American psychologists have paid special attention to the **fundamental attribution error,** a tendency to overattribute the behavior of others to internal factors, such as personality traits (Gilbert & Malone, 1995). Imagine that you hear a student give an incorrect answer in class. You are liable to attribute this behavior to an internal cause and infer that the person is not very smart. In doing so, however, you would fail to take into account possible external factors (such as lack of study time).

The fundamental attribution error has some significant consequences. For one thing, it may lead to unjustified confidence in our ability to predict people's behavior from what we think we know about their personality traits. The fundamental attribution error would explain why, for example, despite the fact that situations often strongly influence behavior, most people believe that behavior is caused mainly by personality traits (Robins & John, 1998).

A related form of cognitive bias is called the *ultimate attribution error,* in which positive actions by members of an *out-group* (people perceived as different) and negative actions by members of an *in-group* (people with whom we identify) are both attributed to external situational factors rather than internal personal ones (Pettigrew, 1979). Because of the ultimate attribution error, members of the out-group receive little credit for their positive actions, and members of the in-group get little blame for their negative actions. Biases such as the ultimate attribution error help maintain stereotypic views of certain groups (Fiske, 1998). For example, when women perform well on traditionally male tasks (e.g., repairing a car), their success is often attributed to luck, but when men succeed at the same task, it is attributed to skill (Deaux & LaFrance, 1998).

In recent years some psychologists, especially those who adopt the trait approach to personality described in Chapter 14, have questioned whether the fundamental attribution error is as serious or widespread as earlier research suggested. Specifically, David Funder has shown that under many circumstances we are capable of making quite accurate judgments of what people are like and what motivates them (Funder & Colvin, 1997). Further, as already mentioned, the attributional tendencies shown by people in Europe and North America are not universal. Cross-cultural studies show that people in collectivist cultures such as India, China, Japan, and Korea are less likely than those in the individualist cultures of North America and Europe to commit the fundamental attribution error or the ultimate attribution error (Fiske et al., 1998; Morris & Peng, 1994). And even within Euro-American cultures themselves, there are individual differences in people's vulnerability to these errors. According to one study, for example, people raised in the southern United States are more inclined than northerners to make external attributions (Sims & Baumann, 1972).

Other Attributional Biases   The inclination toward internal attributions is much less pronounced when people explain their own behavior. Here, in fact, another bias tends to come into play: the **actor-observer bias.** Whereas people often attribute *other* people's behavior to internal causes, they tend to attribute their *own* behavior to external factors, especially when the behavior is inappropriate or inadequate (Baumeister, 1998). For example, when you drive slowly, it is because you are looking for an address, not because you are a dimwitted loser like that jerk who crawled along in front of you yesterday.

The actor-observer bias occurs mainly because people have different kinds of information about their own and others' behavior. When *you* are acting in a situation—giving a speech, perhaps—the stimuli that are most noticeable to you are likely to be external and situational, such as the temperature of the room and the size of the audience. You also have a lot of information about other external factors, such as the amount of time you had to prepare your talk or the upsetting conversation that occurred this morning. If your speech is disorganized and boring, you can easily attribute it to one or all of these external causes. But when you observe someone else, the most noticeable stimulus in the situation is *that person.* You do not know what happened to the person last night or this morning, so you are likely to attribute whatever he or she does to enduring internal characteristics (Gilbert, 1998).

Of course, people do not always attribute their own behavior to external forces. In fact, the degree to which they do so depends on whether the outcome is positive or negative. In one study, researchers asked each of several students to work with a partner on a task and then, regardless of their actual performance, told half of the pairs that they had succeeded and half that they had failed. Students who were told that their team was successful took personal credit for the success; those who had supposedly failed blamed their partner (Sedikides et al., 1998). These students showed a **self-serving bias,** the tendency to take personal credit for success but to blame external causes for failure.

The Self-Protective Functions of Social Cognition

The self-serving bias occurs partly because, as noted earlier, people are motivated to maintain their self-esteem—and ignoring negative information is one way to do so. If you just failed an exam, it is painful to admit that your grade was fair, so you might blame your performance on a picky instructor. Other forms of social cognition, too, help people think about their failures and shortcomings in ways that protect their self-esteem (Lord, 1997).

For some people, even unrealistic optimism is better than no optimism at all.

DILBERT® by Scott Adams

DILBERT © United Feature Syndicate. Reprinted by Permission.

SOME BIASES IN SOCIAL PERCEPTION	
Bias	**Description**
Importance of first impression	Ambiguous information is interpreted in line with a first impression, and the initial schema is recalled better and more vividly than any later correction to it. Actions based on this impression may elicit behavior that confirms it.
Fundamental attribution error	The tendency to attribute the behavior of others to internal factors.
Actor-observer bias	The tendency for actors to attribute their own behavior to external causes and for observers to attribute the behavior of others to internal factors.
Self-serving bias	The tendency to attribute one's successes to internal factors and one's failures to external factors.
Unrealistic optimism	The tendency to assume that positive events are more likely, and negative events are less likely, to occur to oneself than to others.

in review

Unrealistic optimism is one example. Unrealistic optimism is the tendency to believe that positive events (such as financial success or having a gifted child) are more likely to happen to oneself than to others, and that negative events (such as being in an accident or having cancer) are more likely to happen to others than to oneself (Krueger, 1998).

Unrealistic optimism is fueled, in part, by another self-protective form of social cognition called *unique invulnerability.* For example, college students believe that their own chances of contracting a serious illness are substantially less than those of their classmates (Snyder, 1997). Unrealistic optimism tends to persist even in the face of evidence that contradicts it, and it can lead to potentially harmful behaviors. For example, Karina Davidson and Kenneth Prkachin (1997) found that people who were unrealistically optimistic about their health exercised infrequently and knew relatively little about how to prevent heart disease.

Note that *unrealistic* optimism differs from the generally optimistic (but realistic) perspective about life that, as noted in Chapter 13, is positively correlated with good physical and mental health. Unrealistic optimism can have the opposite effects. For example, one reason that people may engage in risky sexual behaviors (e.g., multiple partners, unprotected sex) is that they estimate the risks of unsafe sex to be much lower for themselves than for other people (Taylor et al., 1992).

Self-protective cognitive biases can help us temporarily escape from something painful, but they also set the stage for a somewhat unrealistic view of reality and, in the long run, can create problems. ("In Review: Some Biases in Social Perception" summarizes the common cognitive biases discussed here.) Like the defense mechanisms described in Chapter 14, cognitive strategies such as unrealistic optimism may temporarily decrease anxiety and blunt the impact of stress, but these strategies may also keep people from taking the rational steps necessary for long-term protection of their health, well-being, and safety (Ayanian & Cleary, 1999).

ATTITUDES

People's views about health or safety reflect their attitudes, an aspect of social cognition that social psychologists have studied longer and more intensely than any other. An **attitude** is the tendency to think, feel, or act positively or negatively toward objects in our environment (Eagly & Chaiken, 1998; Petty & Wegener, 1998). Attitudes play an important role in guiding how we react to other people, what political causes we support, which products we buy, and countless other daily decisions.

The Structure of Attitudes

Social psychologists have long viewed attitudes as having three components (Haddock & Zanna, in press; see Figure 17.3). The *cognitive* component is a set of beliefs about the attributes of the attitude object. The emotional, or *affective,* component includes feelings about the object, and the *behavioral* component pertains to the way people act toward the object. Ideally, these components would be in harmony, allowing us to predict people's behavior toward the homeless, for example, on the basis of the thoughts or feelings they express and vice versa. This is often not the case, however (Kraus, 1995). Many people's charitable thoughts and sympathetic emotions regarding the homeless are never translated into actions aimed at helping them.

What determines whether people's behavior will be consistent with the cognitive and affective components of their attitudes? Several factors are important. For one thing, consistency is more likely when the cognitive and affective components are, themselves, in agreement (Lord, 1997). Second, consistency is also more likely when the behavioral component of the attitude is in line with a *subjective norm,* our view of how important people in our lives want us to act. Conflict between attitudes and subjective norms may cause people to behave in ways that are inconsistent with their attitudes (Eagly & Chaiken, 1998). Thus, for example, someone who believes that the rights of gays and lesbians should be protected might not campaign for this cause because doing so would upset family members or co-workers who are strongly against it. Third, attitude-consistent behavior is more likely when people have *perceived control,* the belief that they can actually perform such behavior (Madden, Ellen, & Ajzen, 1992). The cognitive and affective components of your attitude about eliminating homelessness may be positive, but if you don't believe it is possible, you are not likely to even try. Fourth, *direct experience* with the attitude object increases the likelihood of attitude-consistent behavior (Lord, 1997). If your positive attitude toward caviar, say, is based on having actually tasted it, you are more likely to buy it than if your attitude stems solely from caviar's image.

Another explanation of the consistency or discrepancy among the components of attitudes is derived from the cognitive theories of learning and memory described in Chapters 6 and 7. According to this view, attitudes reside in networks of cognitions—interconnected evaluations and beliefs about attitude objects—that are stored in long-

FIGURE 17.3

Three Components of an Attitude

Different attitude components may or may not be consistent with one another. For example, people may deplore drunken driving (cognitive component) *and* be upset by its tragic consequences (affective component), yet not do anything to solve the problem. They may even get behind the wheel after having had one too many (behavioral component).

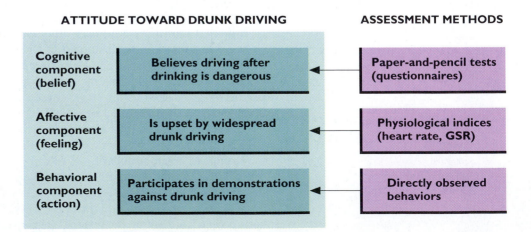

ATTITUDE TOWARD DRUNK DRIVING   ASSESSMENT METHODS

Cognitive component (belief)	Believes driving after drinking is dangerous	Paper-and-pencil tests (questionnaires)
Affective component (feeling)	Is upset by widespread drunk driving	Physiological indices (heart rate, GSR)
Behavioral component (action)	Participates in demonstrations against drunk driving	Directly observed behaviors

A Reminder About Poverty

Photographs like this one are among the cues used by fund-raising organizations to make positive attitudes toward needy people and other social causes more salient and accessible to viewers. As a result, people may be more likely to behave in accordance with their attitudes and make a donation.

FIGURE 17.4

The Elaboration Likelihood Model of Attitude Change

The central route to attitude change involves carefully processing and evaluating a message's content. The peripheral route involves reliance on persuasion cues, such as the attractiveness of the person making the argument, rather than on careful processing of the message (Cacioppo, Petty, & Crites, 1993).

term memory (Ostrom, Skowronski, & Nowack, 1994; see also Figure 7.11 on page 231). When you encounter an attitude object, the cognitions associated with it are activated. If these thoughts and feelings are well defined and come easily to mind, then your behavior is likely to be consistent with them; if not, there may be less consistency (Smith, 1998).

Forming Attitudes

People are not born with specific attitudes toward specific objects, but their attitudes about new objects begin to appear in early childhood and continue to emerge throughout life. How do attitudes form?

The inherited predispositions of temperament described in Chapters 12 and 14 may have some indirect effects (Oskamp, 1991; Tesser, 1993), but the formation of new attitudes is influenced mainly by the learning principles discussed in Chapter 6. In childhood, modeling and other forms of social learning are especially important. Children learn not only the names of objects but also what they should believe and feel about them and how they should act toward them. For example, a parent's words may teach a child not only that snakes are reptiles but also that they should be feared and avoided. So as children learn concepts such as "reptile" or "work," they learn attitudes about those concepts, too (Olson & Zanna, 1993).

Classical and operant conditioning can also shape positive or negative attitudes (Krosnick et al., 1992). Advertisers associate enjoyable music or soothing colors with the products they are trying to sell (Aronson, Wilson, & Akert, 1999; Pratkanis & Aronson, 1991), and parents, teachers, and peers reward children for stating particular views. The *mere-exposure effect* is influential as well: All else being equal, attitudes toward an object will become more positive the more frequently people are exposed to it (Seamon et al., 1997). One study found that even newborns showed a preference for the passages their mother had repeatedly read aloud while they were still in the womb (Cacioppo, Bernston, & Petty, 1997).

Changing Attitudes

The nearly $100 billion a year spent on advertising in the United States alone provides but one example of how people are constantly trying to change our attitudes. Stop for a moment and make a list of other examples, starting, perhaps, with the messages of groups concerned with abortion or recycling—and don't forget your friends who want you to do something that you think is a waste of time.

Two Routes to Attitude Change   Whether a persuasive message succeeds in changing attitudes depends primarily on three factors: (1) the characteristics of the person communicating the message, (2) the content of the message, and (3) the audience who receives it (Cacioppo, Bernston, & Petty, 1997). The **elaboration likelihood model** of attitude change (illustrated in Figure 17.4) provides a framework for understanding when and how these factors affect attitude change. The model is based on the premise that persuasive messages can change people's attitudes through one of two main routes. The first is called the *peripheral route* because, when it is activated, we devote little attention to the actual content of the persuasive message and tend to be affected

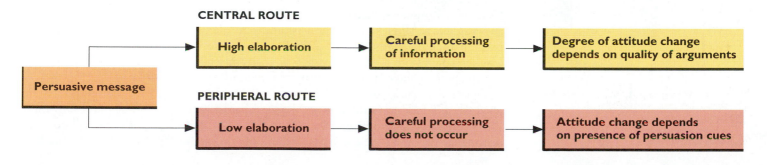

FIGURE 17.5

Personal Involvement and Routes to Attitude Change

In the study represented here, students' reactions to messages advocating exit exams for seniors depended on whether they thought the policy would begin immediately (high involvement) or only after they had graduated (low involvement). In the low-involvement condition, students followed a peripheral route to attitude change, agreeing with messages from highly credible communicators regardless of how logical they were. More involved students followed a central route, changing their minds only if the message contained a strong, logical argument.

Source: Data from Petty, Cacioppo, & Goldman, 1981, and Petty, Cacioppo, & Schumann, 1983.

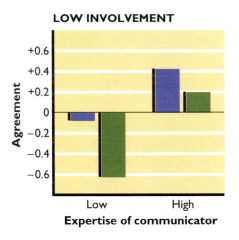

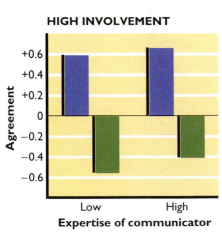

■ Strong arguments
■ Weak arguments

instead by peripheral *persuasion cues,* such as the confidence, attractiveness, or other characteristics of the person delivering the message. Persuasion cues influence attitude change even though they say nothing about the logic or validity of the message content. Commercials in which movie stars or other attractive nonexperts endorse pain relievers are designed to operate via the peripheral route to attitude change. By contrast, when the *central route* to attitude change is activated, the content of the message becomes more important than the characteristics of the communicator in determining attitude change. A person following the central route uses logical steps—like those outlined in the Thinking Critically sections of this book—to rationally analyze the content of the persuasive message, including the validity of its claims, whether it leaves out pertinent information, alternative interpretations of evidence, and so on.

What determines which route people will follow? Personal involvement with message content is one important factor. The elaboration likelihood model proposes that the more personally involving a topic is, the more likely the central route will be activated (Petty, 1995; Petty & Wegener, 1998). Suppose, for example, that you hear someone advocating the abolition of student loans in Chile. This message might persuade you via the peripheral route if it comes from someone who looks attractive and sounds intelligent. However, you are more likely to follow the central route if the message proposes terminating student loans at *your* school. You might be persuaded, but only if the logic of the message is irrefutable (see Figure 17.5). This is why celebrity endorsements tend to be most effective when the products being advertised are relatively unimportant to the audience.

"Cognitive busyness" is another factor affecting which attitude-change route is activated. If you are busy thinking about other things while a message is being delivered, you will be unable to pay much attention to its content—in which case activation of the peripheral route becomes more likely.

Personality characteristics are also related to attitude-change processes. For example, people with a strong *need for cognition* like to engage in thoughtful mental activities and are therefore more likely to use the central route to attitude change (Cacioppo et al., 1996). In contrast, people whose discomfort with uncertainty creates a *need for closure* are more likely to use the peripheral route (Cacioppo et al., 1996).

Persuasive messages are not the only means of changing attitudes. Another approach is to get people to act in ways that are inconsistent with their current attitudes, in the hope that they will adjust those attitudes to match their behavior. Often, such adjustments do occur. Cognitive dissonance theory and self-perception theory each attempt to explain why.

Cognitive Dissonance Theory   Leon Festinger's (1957) classic **cognitive dissonance theory** holds that people want their thoughts, beliefs, and attitudes to be consistent with one another and with their behavior. When people become aware of inconsistency, or *dissonance,* among these elements, they become anxious and are motivated to make them more consistent (Eliot & Devine, 1994; Harmon-Jones et al., 1996). For example, someone who believes that "smoking is bad" but must also acknowledge that "I smoke" would be motivated to reduce the resulting dissonance. Because it is often difficult to change behavior, people usually reduce cognitive dissonance by changing inconsistent attitudes: Rather than quit smoking, the smoker might decide that smoking is not so bad.

In one of the first studies of cognitive dissonance, Festinger and his colleague Merrill Carlsmith (Festinger & Carlsmith, 1959) asked people to turn pegs in a board, a very dull task. Later, some of these people were asked to persuade a person waiting to participate in the study that the task was "exciting and fun." Some were told that they would be paid $1 to tell this lie; others were promised $20. After they had talked to the waiting person, their attitudes toward the dull task were measured.

Figure 17.6 shows the surprising results. The people who were paid just $1 to lie liked the dull task more than those who were paid $20. Why? Festinger and Carlsmith (1959) argued that telling another person that a boring task is enjoyable will produce dissonance (between the thoughts "I think the task is boring" and "I am saying it is

LINKAGES

Unselfish Persuasion

Companies often pay celebrities large sums of money to endorse their products—and for good reason. Celebrity endorsements are effective when the peripheral route to attitude change is activated, because the characteristics of the person delivering the message, rather than the content of the message, become the major influence on consumer attitudes toward the products. As owner of a food company, Paul Newman uses his own status as a movie star to persuade people to buy the company's products, but he donates all the profits to charity. In Chapter 18, on social influence, we discuss several theories that explain why some people are so willing to help others.

FIGURE 17.6

Cognitive Dissonance and Attitude Change

According to cognitive dissonance theory, people who were paid $20 to say a boring task was enjoyable had clear justification for lying and should experience little dissonance between what they said and what they felt about the task. Indeed, their attitude toward the task did not change much. However, participants who received just $1 had little justification to lie and reduced their dissonance mainly by displaying a more positive attitude toward the task.

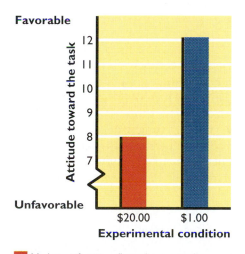

- ■ High justification (low dissonance)
- ■ Low justification (high dissonance)

fun"). To reduce this dissonance, the people who were paid just $1 adopted more favorable attitudes toward the task, making their cognitions consistent: "I think the task is fun" and "I am saying it is fun." But if a person has adequate justification for the behavior, any dissonance that exists will be reduced simply by thinking about the justification. The participants who were paid $20 thought they had adequate justification for lying and so did not need to change their attitudes toward the task.

Hundreds of other experiments have also found that when people publicly engage in behaviors that are inconsistent with their privately held attitudes, they are likely to change their attitudes to be consistent with the public behavior (McGregor, Newby-Clark, & Zanna, in press). More precisely, these experiments have found that behavior-attitude inconsistency will produce attitude change when (1) the inconsistency causes some distress or discomfort in a person and (2) changing attitudes serves to reduce the person's discomfort or distress. But what causes the discomfort? There is considerable debate among attitude researchers about this question (Petty & Wegener, 1998).

Currently, the most popular of several possible answers is that the discomfort is caused by an inconsistency between people's desire to maintain a positive self-concept and the fact that they have, for example, encouraged another person to do something that they themselves didn't believe in or that they themselves wouldn't do. This inconsistency makes most people feel dishonest or hypocritical, and they change their attitudes to reduce or eliminate such feelings (Stone et al., 1997). If people can persuade *themselves* that they really believed in what they did, the perceived inconsistency disappears and their positive self-concept is restored. Changing one's private attitude to match one's public action is one way to accomplish this self-persuasion. Claude Steele's (1988) work on *self-affirmation* supports this explanation of why dissonance causes discomfort. He has found that people will *not* change their attitudes after recognizing their own attitude-behavior inconsistency if they can do something else that makes them look good and feel good about themselves (e.g., showing how smart or competent they are). In other words, when people do not need to change their attitudes to reestablish a positive view of themselves, they don't.

The impact of attitude-behavior inconsistencies on attitude change may be greater in individualist cultures of Europe and North America than in collectivist cultures such as Japan and China. Where group rather than individual identities are emphasized, behaving at odds with one's personal beliefs may create less self-concept discomfort and, thus, less motivation for attitude change. For example, one study found that Canadian students were much more likely to show dissonance-related attitude change than were Japanese students (Heine & Lehman, 1997).

Self-Perception Theory   Over the years cognitive dissonance theory has been challenged by other explanations of why attitudes change when they are inconsistent with behavior (McGregor, Newby-Clark, & Zanna, in press). The first and strongest of these challenges came from Daryl Bem's (1967) **self-perception theory,** which unlike dissonance theory, does not presuppose internal tension when attitudes are inconsistent with behaviors. According to Bem, situations often arise in which people are not quite sure about their attitudes. When this happens, Bem says, people look at their own behavior under particular circumstances and then infer what their attitude must be. That is, a person says, "If I did that under those circumstances, my attitude must be this." This process requires no tension.

Consider, for example, an experiment in which European-American students wrote essays in support of larger scholarships for African-American students—an idea that most of the essay-writers initially opposed. Some students were told by the experimenters that writing the essay was a requirement, whereas others were told they could refuse to write it if they wished. Only students in the second, or free-choice condition, developed more positive attitudes toward African-Americans (Lieppe & Eisenstadt, 1994). Cognitive dissonance theory would say that this difference occurred because the students who were required to write the essay could easily justify the attitude-behavior inconsistency—it was forced on them. However, students who chose to write the essay could not use this rationalization and so they changed their attitudes to resolve the inconsistency.

Self-perception theory would provide a different explanation of the students' responses. Specifically, it would suggest that the students who voluntarily wrote the essay changed their attitudes because they thought to themselves, "I wouldn't have written this if I did not believe African-Americans deserve special help." Conversely, those forced to write the essay could say, "I would never have written this on my own, so I still don't support the idea of special help for African-Americans."

Self-perception theory and cognitive dissonance theory often make the same predictions, and both may be correct to some extent. Self-perception theory seems to apply best when people either have no prior attitude or have an attitude that is weak and ill-defined—for instance, toward a food they have never tasted (Olson, 1992). But when attitudes are strong and clearly defined, and especially when internal consistency is important to one's self-esteem, dissonance theory appears to hold (Thibodeau & Aronson, 1992). ("In Review: Forming and Changing Attitudes" summarizes some of the major processes through which attitudes are formed and changed.)

PREJUDICE AND STEREOTYPES

All of the principles that underlie impression formation, attribution, and attitudes come together to create prejudice and stereotypes. **Stereotypes** are the perceptions, beliefs, and expectations a person has about members of some group; they are schemas about entire groups of people (Fiske, 1998). Usually, they involve the false assumption that all members of a group share the same characteristics. Although the characteristics that make up the stereotype may be positive, they are usually negative. The most prevalent and powerful stereotypes focus on observable personal attributes, particularly ethnicity, gender, and age (Devine, 1995; Eberhardt & Fiske, 1998). As discussed later, people may not be consciously aware of many of the stereotypes they hold (Wegener & Bargh, 1998).

Stereotyping often leads to **prejudice,** which is a positive or negative attitude toward an individual based simply on his or her membership in some group (Lord, 1997). The word *prejudice* means literally "prejudgment." Many theorists believe that prejudice, like other attitudes, has cognitive, affective, and behavioral components. Stereotyped thinking is the cognitive component of prejudicial attitudes. The hatred, admiration, anger, and other feelings people have about stereotyped groups constitute the affective

in review

FORMING AND CHANGING ATTITUDES	
Type of Influence	**Description**
Modeling and conditioning	Attitudes are usually formed through observation of how others behave and speak about an attitude object, as well as through classical and operant conditioning.
Elaboration likelihood model	People change attitudes through either a central or peripheral route, depending on factors such as personal involvement, "cognitive busyness," and personality characteristics.
Cognitive dissonance and self-perception	Inconsistencies between attitudes and behaviors can produce attitude change, as can reviewing one's behavior in light of circumstances.

component. The behavioral component of prejudice involves **discrimination,** which is differential treatment of individuals who belong to different groups.

Theories of Prejudice and Stereotyping

Prejudice and stereotyping may occur for several reasons (Duckitt, 1994). We describe three explanatory theories, each of which has empirical support and accounts for some, but not all, instances of stereotyping and prejudice.

Motivational Theories   For some people, prejudice against certain groups might enhance their sense of security and help them meet certain personal needs. This idea was first proposed by T. W. Adorno and his associates fifty years ago (Adorno et al., 1950) and highlighted more recently by Bob Altemeyer (1988, 1994). Specifically, these researchers suggest that prejudice may be especially likely among people who have a personality trait called *authoritarianism*. According to Altemeyer, authoritarianism is composed of three elements: an acceptance of conventional or traditional values, a willingness to unquestioningly follow the orders of authority figures, and an inclination to act aggressively toward individuals or groups identified by these authority figures as threatening the values held by one's in-group. People with an authoritarian orientation tend to view the world as a threatening place (Winter, 1996), and one way to protect themselves from perceived threat is to identify strongly with their in-group and to reject, dislike, and perhaps even punish anyone who is a member of other groups. Derogating out-group members may help people with authoritarian tendencies to feel safer and better about themselves (Haddock & Zanna, 1998). Some psychodynamic theorists have even suggested that prejudice serves to displace the hostility that authoritarian personalities feel toward their parents onto convenient target groups such as gays and lesbians, African-Americans, and other minorities (Adorno et al., 1950).

A more recent motivational explanation of prejudice invokes the concept of social identity discussed earlier. Recall that whether they are authoritarian or not, most people are motivated to identify with their in-group and tend to see it as better than other groups (Billig & Tajfel, 1973; Brewer & Brown, 1998). As a result, members of an in-group often see all members of out-groups as less attractive and less socially acceptable than in-group members and may thus treat them badly (Dovidio, Gaertner, & Validzic, 1998). In other words, prejudice may result when people's motivation to enhance their own self-esteem causes them to derogate other people.

Cognitive Theories   Stereotyping and prejudice may also result from the social-cognitive processes people use in dealing with the world. There are so many other people, so many situations in which one meets them, and so many possible behaviors they might perform that one cannot possibly attend to and remember them all. Therefore, people must use schemas and other cognitive shortcuts to organize and make sense out of their social world (Fiske, 1998). Often these cognitive processes allow people to draw accurate and useful conclusions about other people, but sometimes they lead to inaccurate stereotypes. For example, one effective way to deal with social complexity is to group people into *social categories*. Rather than remembering every detail about everyone we have ever encountered, we tend to put other people into categories, such as doctor, senior citizen, Republican, student, Italian, and the like (Rothbart & Lewis, 1994). To further simplify perception of these categories, we tend to see their members as being quite similar to one another. Thus, members of one ethnic group may find it harder to distinguish among specific faces within other ethnic groups than within their own (Anthony, Cooper, & Mullen, 1992). People also tend to assume that all members of a different group hold the same beliefs and values and that those beliefs and values differ from their own (Dovidio, Gaertner, & Validzic, 1998). Finally, as noted in the chapter on perception, people's attention tends to be drawn to distinctive stimuli. Thus, noticeably rude behavior by even a few members of an easily identified ethnic group may lead other people to see an *illusory correlation* between rudeness and ethnicity (Hamilton & Sherman, 1994). As a result, they may incorrectly believe that most members of that group are rude. People may be especially likely to recall negative stereotypes when they are in a negative mood (Forgas & Fiedler, 1996).

Learning Theories   Some prejudice results from conflicts between members of different groups, but people also develop negative attitudes toward groups with whom they have had little or no contact. Like other attitudes, prejudice can be learned. Learning theories suggest that children acquire prejudices just by watching and listening to the words and deeds of parents, peers, and others (Rohan & Zanna, 1996). Movies and television may also portray ethnic or other groups in ways that teach stereotypes and prejudice (Liebert & Sprafkin, 1988). And, as mentioned earlier, children may be directly reinforced for expressing prejudice. In fact, small children often know about the supposed negative characteristics of many groups long before they ever meet members of those groups (Mackie et al., 1996; Quintana, 1998).

Reducing Prejudice

One clear implication of the cognitive and learning theories of prejudice and stereotyping is that members of one group are often ignorant or misinformed about the characteristics of people in other groups (Miller & Davidson-Podgorny, 1987). Before 1954, for example, most black and white children in the United States knew very little about one another because they went to separate schools. Then the Supreme Court declared that segregated public schools should be prohibited. By ruling segregation to be unconstitutional, the court created a real-life test of the **contact hypothesis,** which states that stereotypes and prejudice toward a group will diminish as contact with the group increases (Pettigrew, 1997).

Did the desegregation of U.S. schools in the 1960s and 1970s confirm the contact hypothesis? In a few schools, integration was followed by a decrease in prejudice, but in most places either no change occurred or prejudice actually increased (Oskamp & Schultz, 1998). However, these results did not necessarily disprove the contact hypothesis. In-depth studies of schools in which desegregation was successful suggested that contact alone was not enough; integration reduced prejudice only when certain social conditions were created (Brewer & Brown, 1998; Cook, 1985). First, members of the two groups had to be of roughly equal social and economic status. Second, school authorities had to promote cooperation and interdependence among the members of ethnic groups by having them work together on projects that required reliance on one another to reach success. Third, the contact between group members had to occur on

Fighting Ethnic Prejudice

Negative attitudes about members of ethnic groups are often based on negative personal experiences or the negative experiences and attitudes people hear from others. Cooperative contact between equals can help promote mutual respect and reduce ethnic prejudice.

a one-on-one basis; it was only when *individuals* got to know each other that the errors contained in stereotypes became apparent. Finally, the members of each group had to be seen as typical and not unusual in any significant way. When these four conditions were met, the children's attitudes toward one another became more positive. These effects are not restricted to school children in the United States. In Italy, for example, people who had equal-status contact with black immigrants from North Africa displayed less prejudice against them than did Italians who had no contact with the immigrants (Kirchler & Zani, 1995).

Elliot Aronson (1995) describes a teaching strategy, called the *jigsaw technique,* that helps create the conditions that reduce prejudice. The strategy calls for children from several ethnic groups to work as a team to complete a task, such as writing a report about a famous figure in history. Each child learns, and provides the team with, a separate piece of information about this person, such as place of birth (Aronson, 1990). Studies show that children from various ethnic groups who take part in the jigsaw technique and other cooperative learning experiences show substantial reductions in prejudice toward other groups (e.g., Aronson, Wilson, & Akert, 1999). The success reported in these studies has greatly increased the popularity of cooperative learning exercises in classrooms in the United States. Such exercises may not eliminate all aspects of ethnic prejudice in children, but they seem to be a step in the right direction.

Can friendly, cooperative, interdependent contact between adults reduce the more entrenched forms of prejudice? It may. When equal-status adults work jointly toward a common goal, bias and distrust can be reduced. This is especially true if they come to see themselves as members of the same group rather than belonging to opposing groups (Gaertner, Dovidio, & Bachman, 1997). The challenge to be met in creating such cooperative experiences in the real world is that the participants must be of equal status—a challenge made more difficult in many countries by the sizable status differences that still exist between ethnic groups (Dovidio, Gaertner, & Validzic, 1998).

In the final analysis, contact provides only part of the solution to the problems of stereotyping, prejudice, and discrimination. To reduce ethnic prejudice, we must develop additional educational techniques that address the social cognitions and perceptions that lie at the core of bigotry and hatred toward people who are different from us (Monteith, Zuwerink, & Devine, 1994).

LINKAGES

Can subconscious processes alter our reaction to people? (a link to Consciousness)

THINKING CRITICALLY

Is Ethnic Prejudice Too Ingrained Ever to Be Eliminated?

There is little doubt that overt forms of ethnic prejudice have decreased dramatically in the United States over the past thirty to forty years. For example, in the 1950s less than half of European-American college students surveyed said they were willing to live in integrated neighborhoods; today, about 95 percent say they would be willing to do so. And three decades ago, fewer than 40 percent of European-Americans said they would vote for an African-American presidential candidate; over 95 percent now say they might do so (Dovidio & Gaertner, 1998). Nevertheless, polls suggest that most African-Americans in the United States think that prejudice against them is still a very serious problem (Anderson, 1996).

■ What am I being asked to believe or accept?

Even people who see themselves as nonprejudiced and who disavow ethnic stereotypes and discrimination still hold negative stereotypes about ethnic out-groups and, in certain situations, will display prejudice and discrimination toward them (Chen & Bargh, 1997; Devine, 1995). Some people claim, therefore, that negative attitudes toward ethnic out-groups are so deeply ingrained in all of us that ethnic prejudice can never be eliminated.

■ What evidence is available to support the assertion?

Evidence for this assertion focuses primarily on prejudice against African-Americans by European-Americans and comes, first, from studies testing the theory of *aversive racism* (Dovidio & Gaertner, 1998). This theory holds that even though many European-Americans consider ethnic prejudice to be aversive, they will still sometimes display it—especially when they can do so without admitting, even to themselves, that they are prejudiced. In one study of aversive racism, a male experimenter telephoned male and female European-Americans who were known to believe in ethnic equality. The man claimed to be a stranded motorist who had misdialed while trying to call a service station for help. When told he had dialed the wrong number, the man replied that he was out of coins and asked the person he'd reached to call a service station for him. *If* people listened long enough to learn of the man's problem, they were just as likely to contact the service station whether the caller "sounded" European-American or African-American. However, if the caller "sounded" African-American, these supposedly unprejudiced people were almost five times as likely to hang up even before the caller could ask for help (Gaertner & Dovidio, 1986). In other studies, female European-American college students were asked to help another female student who was doing poorly on some task. When the student's poor performance was described as being due to the task's difficulty, the students agreed to help, regardless of the other student's ethnicity. But if the problem was said to be due to lack of effort, help was offered much more often to European-Americans than to African-Americans (Frey & Gaertner, 1986; McPhail & Penner, 1995). These findings suggest that even people who do not display prejudice in most situations may do so in others.

A second line of evidence for the entrenchment of prejudice comes from research showing that many people hold negative stereotypes about ethnic minorities (and women) of which they are unaware. These negative stereotypes can also be activated without conscious awareness, even among people who believe they are free of prejudice. To demonstrate these phenomena, researchers have used the priming procedures described in Chapter 9 to activate unconscious thoughts and feelings that can alter people's reactions to stimuli without their awareness. In one study, for example, white participants were exposed to subliminal presentations of pictures of black individuals (Chen & Bargh, 1997). The participants were not consciously aware that they had seen these pictures, but when they interacted with a black man soon thereafter, those who

LINKAGES

Can subliminal stimuli influence our judgments about people? (a link to Perception)

had been primed with the African-American pictures acted more negatively toward him and saw him as more hostile than did people who had not been primed. Priming apparently activated these participants' negative ethnic stereotypes. It is also possible to prime unconscious negative stereotypes about other groups, including women and the elderly (Blair & Banaji, 1996; Hense, Penner, & Nelson, 1996). All of these findings suggest that stereotypes are so overlearned and ingrained in people that they may be activated automatically and without their conscious awareness (Eberhardt & Fiske, 1998).

■ Are there alternative ways of interpreting the evidence?

The evidence presented so far suggests that it may be impossible to eliminate ethnic prejudice because everyone harbors unconscious negative stereotypes about various groups. But this evidence does not necessarily mean that unconscious stereotypes affect everyone in the same way. Perhaps they have a greater impact on people who are more overtly prejudiced.

■ What additional evidence would help to evaluate the alternatives?

One way to evaluate this possibility is to compare the responses of prejudiced and non-prejudiced people in various experimental situations. In one mock-trial study, for example, overtly prejudiced white jurors recommended the death penalty more often for black defendants than for white defendants guilty of the same crime, but low-prejudice white jurors showed this bias only when they believed that a black juror also favored giving the death penalty (Dovidio et al., 1997). Priming studies, too, show that although negative stereotypes can be primed in both prejudiced and nonprejudiced people, it is easier to do so with people who openly display their ethnic bias. Furthermore, activation of these stereotypes may be less likely to affect the conscious attitudes and behavior of nonprejudiced whites. Thus, when unconscious stereotypes are activated in nonprejudiced people, the effects tend to appear in subtle ways, such as in facial expressions or other nonverbal behaviors (Devine, 1989; Kawakami, Dion, & Dovidio,1998; Lepore & Brown, 1997).

LINKAGES

Can we ever be unbiased about anyone? (a link to Consciousness)

■ What conclusions are most reasonable?

Taken together, research evidence presents a mixed picture regarding the possibility of eliminating ethnic prejudice. Clearly, people in the United States are not nearly as "color-blind" as we might hope, and ethnic prejudice may be so ingrained in some people as to be subconscious. Nonetheless, it makes sense to do everything possible to reduce prejudice in everyone; indeed, even if subconscious thoughts and feelings toward out-groups cannot be altered, the evidence suggests that people can, to a certain extent, control their conscious thoughts and behaviors toward members of minority groups. In the United States, as in any multicultural country, survival as a society demands that people continue fighting against overt forms of stereotyping, prejudice, and discrimination.

INTERPERSONAL ATTRACTION

Research on prejudice helps illuminate some of the reasons for which people, from childhood on, may come to dislike or even hate other people. An equally fascinating aspect of social cognition is why people like or love other people. Folklore tells us that "opposites attract," but it also maintains that "birds of a feather flock together." Though valid to some degree, each of these statements needs to be qualified in important ways. We begin our coverage of interpersonal attraction by discussing the factors that lead to initial attraction; we then examine how liking sometimes develops into more intimate relationships.

Proximity and Liking

In general, the more often people make contact with someone, the more they tend to like that person. This is one reason why next-door neighbors are much more likely to become friends than people who live farther from one another. Chances are, most of your friends are people whom you met as neighbors, co-workers, or classmates.

FIGURE 17.7

Attitude Similarity and Attraction

This graph shows the results of a study in which participants learned about another person's attitudes. Their liking for that person was strongly related to the proportion of his or her attitudes that were similar to the participants' own.

Source: Adapted from Byrne & Nelson, 1965.

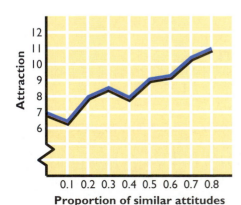

Keys to Attraction

Whether you like someone or not depends partly on situational factors and partly on personal characteristics.

The Environment One of the most important determinants of attraction is simple physical proximity (Berscheid & Reis, 1998). As long as you do not initially dislike a person, your liking for him or her will increase with additional contact (Bornstein, 1992). This phenomenon is another example of the *mere-exposure effect* mentioned earlier. For example, Richard Moreland and Scott Beach (1992) varied the number of times that several experimental assistants (posing as students) attended a class. Even though none of the assistants spoke to anyone in the class, they were rated by the other students as more likable the more often they attended.

The circumstances under which people first meet also influence attraction. Thus, in accordance with the principles of learning discussed in Chapter 6, you are much more likely to be attracted to a stranger you meet in comfortable as opposed to uncomfortable physical conditions. Similarly, if you receive a reward in the presence of a stranger, the chances that you will like that stranger are increased, even if the stranger is not the one giving the reward (Clark & Pataki, 1995). In one study, for example, an experimenter judged one person's creativity while another person watched. Compared with those who received a negative evaluation, participants who were evaluated positively tended to like the observer more (Griffitt & Guay, 1969). At least among strangers, then, liking can occur through associating someone with something pleasant.

Similarity People also tend to like those whom they perceive as similar to themselves on variables such as age, religion, smoking or drinking habits, or being a "morning" or "evening" person. As shown in Figure 17.7, similarity in attitudes is an especially important influence on attraction. This relationship has been found among children, college students, adult workers, and senior citizens (Duck & Barnes, 1992).

Similarity in attitudes toward mutual acquaintances is a particularly good predictor of liking because, in general, people prefer relationships that are *balanced*. Thus, as illustrated in Figure 17.8, if Zoe likes Abigail, the relationship is balanced as long as they agree on their evaluation of a third person, Samantha, regardless of whether they like or dislike that third person. However, the relationship will be imbalanced if Zoe and Abigail disagree on their evaluation of the third person.

One reason why we like people with similar views of the world is that we expect such people to think highly of us (Condon & Crano, 1988). Like many important rela-

FIGURE 17.8

Balanced and Imbalanced Relationships

Shown here are some common examples of balanced and imbalanced patterns of relationships among three people. The plus and minus signs refer to liking and disliking, respectively. Balanced relationships are comfortable and harmonious; imbalanced ones often bring conflict.

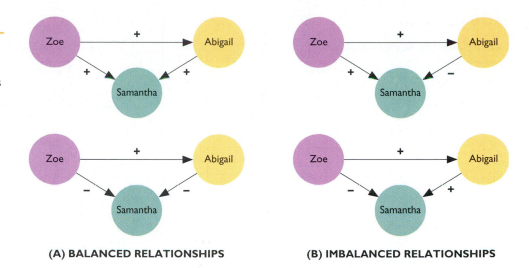

(A) BALANCED RELATIONSHIPS   **(B) IMBALANCED RELATIONSHIPS**

tionships, it's hard to say whether attraction is a cause or an effect of similarity (Berscheid & Reis, 1998). Thus, for example, you might like someone because his attitudes are similar to yours, but it is also possible that, as a result of liking him, your attitudes will become more similar to his. Some people even change their perceptions of a liked person's attitudes so that they seem more similar to their own (Brehm, 1992).

Physical Attractiveness   Physical characteristics are another important factor in attraction, particularly during the initial stages of a relationship (Berscheid & Reis, 1998). From preschool through adulthood, physical attractiveness is a key to popularity with members of both sexes (Aronson, Wilson, & Akert, 1999; Chapdelaine, Levesque, & Cuardo, in press; Dion, 1992). Consistent with the **matching hypothesis** of interpersonal attraction, however, people tend to date, marry, or form other committed relationships with those who are similar in physical attractiveness (Berscheid & Reis, 1998). One possible reason for this outcome: Although people tend to be most attracted to those with the greatest physical appeal, they also want to avoid rejection by such individuals. In short, it may be compromise, not preference, that leads people to pair off with those who are roughly equivalent to themselves in physical attractiveness (Carli, Ganley, & Pierce-Otay, 1991).

Intimate Relationships and Love

There is much about intimate relationships that psychologists do not—and may never—understand, but they are learning all the time. As mentioned in Chapter 11, proponents of evolutionary psychology suggest that men and women employ different strategies to ensure the survival of their genes, and that each gender looks for different attributes in a potential mate (Buss & Kenrick, 1998; Kenrick & Trost, 1997; Sprecher, Sullivan, & Hatfield, 1994). For example, women may be much more concerned than men about the intelligence level of their dating partners (Kenrick & Trost, 1997; see Figure 17. 9 on page 628.)

Intimate Relationships   Eventually, people who are attracted to each other usually become *interdependent*, which means that the thoughts, emotions, and behaviors of one person affect the thoughts, emotions, and behaviors of the other (Clark & Pataki, 1995). Interdependence occurs in large measure as the thoughts and values of one person become part of the self-concept of the other (Agnew et al., 1998). It is thus one of the defining characteristics of intimate relationships.

Another key component of successful intimate relationships is *commitment* to the relationship, which is the extent to which each party is psychologically attached to and wants to remain in the relationship (Rusbult & Van Lange, 1996). People feel committed to a relationship when they are satisfied with the rewards they receive from it, when they have invested considerable resources (both tangible and intangible) in it and

FIGURE 17.9

Sex Differences in Date and Mate Preferences

As discussed in the chapter on motivation and emotion, evolutionary psychologists believe that as humans evolved, men and women developed different strategies for selecting sexual partners. Women became much more selective about mating choices because they could have relatively few children. Men, being able to father large numbers of children, could afford to be somewhat less selective. The data shown here are consistent with this idea. When asked about the intelligence of the partners they would choose for one-night stands, dating, and sexual relationships, women preferred much smarter partners than men did. Only when the choices concerned steady dating and marriage did the men's preference for bright partners equal that of the women. Critics of the evolutionary approach believe that social norms and people's expectations of the way men and women should behave explain this sex difference.

Source: Kenrick et al., 1993.

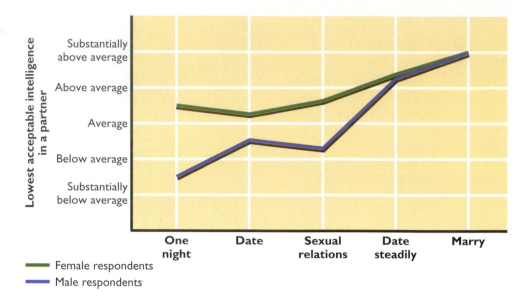

when there are few attractive alternative relationships available to them (Bui, Peplau, & Hill, 1996).

Analyzing Love Affection, emotional expressiveness, social support, cohesiveness, sexuality—these characteristics of intimate relationships are likely to bring something else to mind: love. Yet intimacy and love are not synonymous. Most theorists agree that there are several different types of love (Brehm, 1992). One widely accepted view distinguishes between *passionate love* and *companionate love* (Hatfield & Rapson, 1996). Passionate love is intense, arousing, and marked by both strong physical attraction and deep emotional attachment. Sexual feelings are very strong, and thoughts of the other intrude on a person's awareness frequently. Companionate love is less arousing but psychologically more intimate. It is marked by mutual concern for the welfare of the other (Hendrick & Hendrick, 1986).

Robert Sternberg (1988b) has offered a more comprehensive analysis of love. According to his *triangular theory,* the three basic components of love are *passion, intimacy,* and *commitment.* Various combinations of these components result in quite different types of love, as illustrated in Figure 17.10. For example, Sternberg suggests that

A Wedding in India

In Western cultures, most people tend to marry a person whom they choose on the basis of love, sometimes without regard for discrepancies in religion, ethnicity, and financial or social status. In other cultures, however, it is not uncommon for these sociocultural considerations—and even arrangements made by parents—to largely determine the choice of a marital partner. What factors do you think might have brought this couple together?

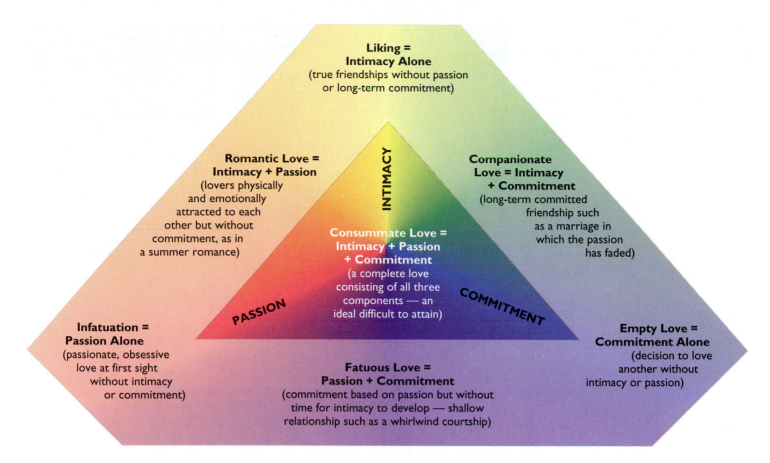

Liking =
Intimacy Alone
(true friendships without passion
or long-term commitment)

Romantic Love =
Intimacy + Passion
(lovers physically
and emotionally
attracted to each
other but without
commitment, as in
a summer romance)

INTIMACY

Companionate
Love = Intimacy
+ Commitment
(long-term committed
friendship such
as a marriage in
which the passion
has faded)

Consummate Love =
Intimacy + Passion
+ Commitment
(a complete love
consisting of all three
components — an
ideal difficult to attain)

PASSION

COMMITMENT

Infatuation =
Passion Alone
(passionate, obsessive
love at first sight
without intimacy
or commitment)

Fatuous Love =
Passion + Commitment
(commitment based on passion but without
time for intimacy to develop — shallow
relationship such as a whirlwind courtship)

Empty Love =
Commitment Alone
(decision to love
another without
intimacy or passion)

FIGURE 17.10

A Triangular Theory of Love

According to Sternberg, different types of love result when the three basic components proposed in his triangular theory occur in different combinations.

Source: "Triangulating Love." In R. J. Sternberg & M. L. Barnes, *The Psychology of Love* New Haven: Yale University Press. (pp. 500, 520).

romantic love involves a high degree of passion and intimacy, yet lacks substantial commitment to the other person. *Companionate love* is marked by a great deal of intimacy and commitment but little passion. And *consummate love* is the most complete and satisfying. It is the most complete because it includes a high level of all three components, and it is the most satisfying because the relationship is likely to fulfill many of the needs of each partner.

Cultural factors have a strong influence on the value that people place on love. In North America and the United Kingdom, for example, the vast majority of people believe that they must love the person they marry. By contrast, in India and Pakistan, about half the people interviewed in a survey said they would marry someone they did not love if that person had other qualities that they desired (Levine et al., 1995). In the former Soviet Union, only 40 percent of the people say that they married for love; rather, most married because of loneliness, shared interests, or an unplanned pregnancy (Baron & Byrne, 1994).

Strong and Weak Marriages Long-term studies of successful and unsuccessful marriages suggest that premarital attitudes and feelings are predictive of marital success. For example, one study found that couples who had a close, intimate relationship and similar attitudes when they were dating were more likely to still be married fifteen years later (Hill & Peplau, 1998). Also, still-married couples were more likely to have had a premarital relationship that was rewarding and balanced.

Among married couples, women—but not men—generally tend to be more satisfied with their marriage when the partners talk a lot about the relationship (Acitelli, 1992). Partners in successful marriages also tend to share one another's view of themselves and each other, even if that view is a negative one (Swann, De La Ronde, & Hixon, 1994). The perception that the relationship is fair or equitable also enhances marital satisfaction (Clark, 1994). After the birth of a first child, for example, many wives find that they have much more work than they had anticipated. If their husbands

Happy and Healthy

People in satisfying marriages and other long-term relationships tend to enjoy better physical and psychological health than those in unsatisfying relationships (Burman & Margolin, 1992).

do not share this work to the degree they expected, wives' marital satisfaction tends to decrease (Hackel & Ruble, 1992). A related determinant of long-term marital satisfaction is how the couple deals with the conflict and anger that occur in virtually all marriages. In unhappy marriages and marriages that end in divorce, both the husband and wife trade increasingly nasty and hurtful remarks until communication breaks down (Gottman et al., 1998). But in happy marriages, the cycle of hostile reactions is ultimately broken, allowing the couple to deal with the problem at hand during moments of calm (Rusbult et al., 1991). Perhaps not surprisingly, long-term research on the causes of divorce suggests that in marriages that last and are happy, husbands and wives are able to generally agree on how they should deal with important marital issues (Gottman et al., 1998).

LINKAGES

As noted in Chapter 1, all of psychology's many subfields are related to one another. Our discussion of self-schemas and psychological disorders illustrates just one way in which the topic of this chapter, social cognition, is linked to the subfield of psychological disorders (Chapter 15). The Linkages diagram shows ties to two other subfields as well, and there are many more ties throughout the book. Looking for linkages among subfields will help you see how they all fit together and better appreciate the big picture that is psychology.

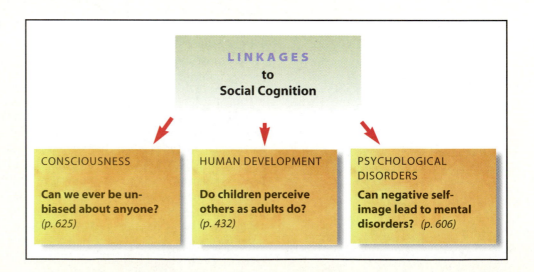

LINKAGES
to
Social Cognition

CONSCIOUSNESS

Can we ever be un-biased about anyone? (p. 625)

HUMAN DEVELOPMENT

Do children perceive others as adults do? (p. 432)

PSYCHOLOGICAL DISORDERS

Can negative self-image lead to mental disorders? (p. 606)

SUMMARY

Social cognition, the mental processes through which people perceive and react to others, is one aspect of *social psychology,* the study of how people influence, and are influenced by, other people. Through social cognition, each person creates a unique perception of reality.

SOCIAL INFLUENCES ON THE SELF

People's social and cultural environments affect their thoughts and feelings about themselves, including their *self-esteem* and their *self-concept.*

Social Comparison

When people have no objective criteria by which to judge themselves, they look to others as the basis for *social comparison.* Such comparison can affect self-evaluation, or self-esteem. Categories of people that are habitually used for social comparison are known as *reference groups.* Comparison to reference groups sometimes produces *relative deprivation,* which, in turn, can cause personal and social turmoil.

Social Identity Theory

A person's *social identity* is formed from beliefs about the groups to which the person belongs. Social identity affects the beliefs we hold about ourselves, our self-concept. Social identity permits people to feel part of a larger group, engendering loyalty and sacrifice from group members but also potentially creating bias and discrimination toward people who are not members of the group.

SOCIAL PERCEPTION

Social perception concerns the processes by which people interpret information about others, form impressions of them, and draw conclusions about the reasons for their behavior.

The Role of Schemas

Schemas, the mental representations about people and social situations that we carry into social interactions, affect what we pay attention to, what we remember, and how we judge people and events.

First Impressions

First impressions are formed easily and quickly, in part because people apply existing schemas to their perceptions of others. First impressions change slowly because people are "cognitive misers"; once we form an impression about another person, we try to maintain it, because doing so simplifies the world. Schemas, however, can create *self-fulfilling prophecies,* leading people to act in ways that bring out in others behavior that is consistent with first impressions.

Explaining Behavior: Attribution

Attribution is the process of explaining the causes of people's behavior, including one's own. Observers tend to attribute behavior to causes that are either internal or external to the actor. In general, they do this by looking at three aspects of the behavior: consensus, consistency, and distinctiveness. People from different cultures may sometimes reach different conclusions about the causes of an actor's behavior. Attributions are also affected by biases that systematically distort one's view of behavior. The most common attributional biases are the *fundamental attribution error* (and its cousin, the ultimate attribution error), the *actor-observer bias,* and the *self-serving bias.* Personal and cultural factors can affect the extent to which people exhibit attributional biases.

The Self-Protective Functions of Social Cognition

People often protect themselves from admitting something threatening about themselves through unrealistic optimism and a feeling of unique invulnerability.

ATTITUDES

An *attitude* is the tendency to respond positively or negatively to a particular object. Attitudes affect a wide range of behaviors.

The Structure of Attitudes

Some theorists believe that attitudes have three components: the cognitive (beliefs), affective (feelings), and behavioral (actions). However, it is often difficult to predict a specific behavior from a person's beliefs or feelings about an object. Cognitive theories propose that attitudes consist of evaluations of an object that are stored in memory. This approach suggests that the likelihood of attitude-behavior consistency depends on the accessibility of evaluations in memory, on subjective norms, on perceived control over the behavior, and on prior direct experience with the attitude object.

Forming Attitudes

Attitudes can be learned through modeling as well as through classical or operant conditioning. They are also subject to the mere-exposure effect: All else being equal, people develop greater liking for a new object the more often they are exposed to it.

Changing Attitudes

The effectiveness of persuasive messages in changing attitudes is influenced by the characteristics of the person who communicates it, by its content, and by the audience receiving it. The *elaboration likelihood model* suggests that attitude change can occur via either the peripheral or the central route, depending on a person's ability and motivation to carefully consider an argument. Another approach to attitude change is to change a person's behavior in the hope that his or her attitude will be adjusted to match the behavior. *Cognitive dissonance theory* holds that inconsistencies between attitudes and behavior can create discomfort about one's self-image; attitude change is one way to reduce this discomfort. *Self-perception theory* holds that people sometimes look to their behavior for clues to what their attitudes are.

PREJUDICE AND STEREOTYPES

Stereotypes often lead to *prejudice* and *discrimination*.

Theories of Prejudice and Stereotyping

Motivational theories of prejudice suggest that some people have a need to derogate and dislike others. This need may stem from the trait of *authoritarianism*, as well as from a strong social identity. In either case, feeling superior to members of out-groups helps these people to feel better about themselves. As a result, in-group members tend to discriminate against out-groups. Cognitive theories suggest that people categorize others into groups in order to reduce social complexity. And learning theories maintain that stereotypes, prejudice, and discriminatory behaviors can be learned from parents, peers, and the media.

Reducing Prejudice

The *contact hypothesis* proposes that intergroup contact can reduce prejudice and lead to more favorable attitudes toward the stereotyped group—but only if it occurs under specific conditions, such as equal status between groups.

INTERPERSONAL ATTRACTION

Keys to Attraction

Interpersonal attraction is a function of many variables. Physical proximity is important because it allows people to meet. And the situation in which they meet is important because positive or negative aspects of the situation tend to be associated with the other person. Characteristics of the other person are also important. Attraction tends to be greater when two people share similar attitudes and personal characteristics. Physical appearance plays a role in attraction; initially, attraction is strongest to those who are most physically attractive. But for long-term relationships, the *matching hypothesis* applies: People tend to choose others whose physical attractiveness is about the same as theirs.

Intimate Relationships and Love

A defining characteristic of intimate relationships is interdependence, and a key component of successful relationships is commitment. Commitment, in turn, is affected by the receipt of satisfactory rewards from the relationship, by the resources invested in it, and by the possible alternatives open to the parties in the relationship. Sternberg's triangular theory suggests that love is a function of three components: passion, intimacy, and commitment. Varying combinations of these three components create different types of love. Couples who have long and successful marriages are likely to have had a close, intimate relationship and similar attitudes when they were dating. Marital satisfaction also depends on communication, having similar views, the perception that the relationship is equitable, the ability to deal effectively with conflict and anger, and agreement about important issues in the marriage.

KEY TERMS

actor-observer bias (614)
attitude (616)
attribution (609)
cognitive dissonance theory (618)
contact hypothesis (622)
discrimination (621)

elaboration likelihood model (617)
fundamental attribution error (613)
matching hypothesis (627)
prejudice (620)
reference groups (605)

relative deprivation (605)
self-concept (605)
self-esteem (605)
self-fulfilling prophecy (609)
self-perception theory (620)
self-schemas (606)

self-serving bias (614)
social cognition (604)
social comparison (605)
social identity (606)
social perception (607)
social psychology (604)
stereotypes (620)

18

Social Influence

Well-publicized suicides are often followed by a rash of other suicides, and the murder rate tends to increase after well-publicized homicides (Garland & Zigler, 1993; Phillips, 1983; Phillips & Cartensen, 1986). Murders even increase following telecasts of major professional boxing matches! Do these correlations mean that media coverage of violence triggers similar violence? As described in Chapter 6, televised violence can play a causal role in aggressive behavior; but there are additional reasons to believe that when suicides and murders become media events, they stimulate people to imitate them. For one thing, many of the people who are murdered soon after a celebrated homicide bear some notable similarity to the victim (Cialdini, 1993). Further, in the days after a professional championship fight in which the loser is white, murders of young white men increase; if the loser is black, a rise in murders of young black men is seen (Miller et al., 1991).

Imitative or "copycat" violence illustrates the effects of *social influence,* the process whereby the words or actions of other people directly or indirectly influence a person's behavior. This chapter begins with a discussion of social influence itself, after which we consider several related aspects of how we are influenced by others, including the processes of conformity, compliance, and obedience. Then we explore the causes and consequences of aggression and altruism. Finally, we examine several different circumstances in which people jointly influence one another's behavior, especially circumstances in which people compete with one another for some scarce resource or work together in groups to solve some problem.

SOCIAL INFLUENCE

As illustrated by copycat violence, people can influence the way other people think, feel, and act, even without specifically trying to do so (Goodwin, 1992). The most pervasive yet subtle form of social influence is communicated through social norms.

Norms are learned, socially based rules that prescribe what people should or should not do in various situations (Cialdini & Trost, 1998). They are transmitted by parents, teachers, clergy, peers, and other agents of culture. Although many cannot be verbalized, norms are so powerful that people often follow them automatically. At movie theaters in North America, for example, norms tell us that we should get in line to buy a ticket rather than crowd around the ticket window; they also lead us to expect that others will do the same. By informing people of what is expected of them and others, norms make social situations less ambiguous and more comfortable.

Robert Cialdini and his associates (1990) have described social norms as being either descriptive or injunctive. *Descriptive norms* indicate how most other people actually behave in a given situation. They tell a person what actions are common in the situation and thereby implicitly give the person permission to act in the same way. The fact that most people do not cross a street until the green light appears is an example of a descriptive norm. *Injunctive norms* give more specific information about the actions that others find acceptable and those that they find unacceptable. Thus, subtle pressure exists to behave in accordance with these norms. A sign that reads, "Do not cross on red" or hearing the person next to you saying the same thing is an example of an injunctive norm.

A study by Raymond Reno and his colleagues (Reno, Cialdini, & Kallgren, 1993) illustrates the differing effects of these two types of norms. The participants were people walking through a parking lot who had just been handed an advertising leaflet. The experimenters arranged for the participants to see another person (who was working with the experimenters) either toss a paper bag on the ground or pick one up. Half the time this event occurred in a littered parking lot and half the time in a clean one. As shown in Figure 18.1, the descriptive norm—seeing another person litter a dirty environment—appeared to communicate that "many people do this," and the percentage of the people who dropped the leaflet in the dirty parking lot themselves

LINKAGES

Clothing and Culture

The social norms that guide how people dress and behave in various situations are part of the culturally determined socialization process described in Chapter 12, on human development. The process is the same worldwide—parents, teachers, peers, religious leaders, and others communicate their culture's social norms to children—but differences in those norms result in quite different behaviors from culture to culture.

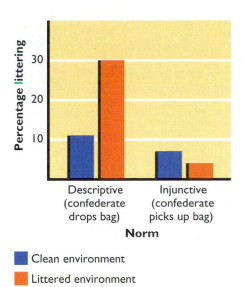

Clean environment
Littered environment

FIGURE 18.1

Descriptive and Injunctive Norms

A descriptive norm communicated by the littering of a messy parking lot led many observers to litter, too. A clean lot changed the descriptive norm, leading fewer observers to imitate a litterer; but an injunctive norm (communicated by the picking up of litter) was not altered significantly by the condition of the lot (Reno, Cialdini, & Kallgren, 1993).

Source: Adapted from Reno, Cialdini, & Kallgren, 1993.

was relatively high. By contrast, the injunctive norm—seeing the confederate pick up litter—appeared to communicate that, even though many people litter, one should not do so. When this norm was evident, fewer than 5 percent of the people dropped the leaflet in the dirty parking lot.

One very powerful injunctive norm is *reciprocity,* the tendency to respond to others as they have acted toward you (Cialdini & Trost, 1998). When an investigator sent Christmas cards to strangers, most responded with a card of their own; some even added a personal note of good cheer (Kunz & Woolcott, 1976). But norms are neither universal nor unchanging (Triandis, 1997). For example, people around the world differ greatly in terms of the physical distance they maintain between themselves and others while interacting. Indeed, people from South America usually stand much closer to one another than do people from North America. Thus, as suggested in Chapter 15 on psychological disorders, behavior considered normal and friendly in one culture may be seen as abnormal, even offensive, in another.

The social influence exerted by norms creates orderly social behavior. But social influence can also lead to a breakdown in order. For example, **deindividuation** is a psychological state in which a person becomes "submerged in the group" and loses the sense of individuality (Prentice-Dunn & Rogers, 1989). When people experience deindividuation, they undergo heightened emotional arousal and an intense feeling of cohesiveness with the group; they appear to become part of the "herd," and they may perform acts that they would not do otherwise. Deindividuation appears to be caused by two factors. The first is the belief that one cannot be held personally accountable for one's actions. The second is a shifting of attention away from internal thoughts and standards and toward the external environment (Lord, 1997). This shift of attention can be intensified when members of the group act in unison, such as by singing together or wearing uniforms (Ku Klux Klan robes, for example).

Deindividuation often results in antisocial acts, and the emotional arousal that is generated makes such behavior difficult to stop (Aronson, Wilson, & Akert, 1999). The greater the sense of anonymity, the more extreme the behavior. An analysis of newspaper accounts of lynchings in the United States over a fifty-year period showed that larger lynch mobs were more savage and vicious than smaller ones (Mullen, 1986). Deindividuation provides an example of how, given the right circumstances, quite normal people can engage in destructive, even violent, behavior.

Deindividuation

Robes, hoods, and group rituals help create deindividuation in these Ku Klux Klansmen by focusing their attention on membership in their organization and on its values. The hoods also hide their identities, thus reducing their sense of personal responsibility and accountability and making it easier for them to engage in hate crimes and other cowardly acts of bigotry. Deindividuation operates in other groups, too, ranging from lynch mobs and paramilitary death squads to political protesters and urban rioters. In short, people who feel themselves to be anonymous members of a group may engage in antisocial acts that they might not perform individually.

LINKAGES

Do people perform better or worse when others are watching? (a link to Motivation and Emotion)

LINKAGES

Motivation and the Presence of Others

In Chapter 11 we noted that social factors such as parental attitudes toward achievement often affect motivation. But a person's current motivational state is also affected by the mere presence of other people. As an illustration, consider what was probably the first experiment in social psychology, conducted by Norman Triplett in 1897.

Triplett noticed that bicyclists tended to race faster when a competitor was near than when all competitors were out of sight. Did seeing one another remind the riders of the need to go faster to win? To test this possibility, Triplett arranged for bicyclists to complete a twenty-five-mile course under three conditions: riding alone, in a race against the clock; riding with another cyclist, but not in competition; or competing directly with another rider. The cyclists went much faster when another rider was present than when they were simply racing against time. This was true even when they were not competing against the other person. Something about the presence of the other person, not just competition, produced increased speed.

The term **social facilitation** describes circumstances in which the mere presence of other people can improve performance. This improvement does not always occur, however. The presence of other people sometimes hurts performance, a process known as **social impairment.** For decades these results seemed contradictory; then Robert Zajonc (pronounced "ZYE-onze") suggested that both effects could be explained by one process: arousal.

The presence of other people, said Zajonc, increases a person's general level of arousal or motivation (Zajonc, 1965). Arousal increases the tendency to perform those behaviors that are most *dominant*—the ones you know best—and this tendency may either help or hinder performance. When you are performing an easy, familiar task such as riding a bike, increased arousal due to the presence of others should allow you to ride even faster than normal. But when a task is hard or unfamiliar, the most dominant responses may be incorrect and cause performance to suffer. Thus, the impact of other people on performance depends on whether the task is easy or difficult. This is true even when the "other person" is a machine that records one's errors at a task (Aiello & Kolb, 1995).

Why does the presence of others increase arousal? One reason is that being watched increases our sense of being evaluated, producing apprehension that in turn increases emotional arousal (Penner & Craiger, 1992). The presence of others may also distract us from the task at hand or cause us to focus on only one part of it, thus impairing performance (Baron, Kerr, & Miller, 1992).

What if a person is not merely in the presence of others but is working on a task with them? Research indicates that the impact of their presence changes slightly under these conditions (Sanna, 1992). When a group performs a task, it is not always possible to identify each individual's contributions. In these situations, people often exert less effort than they do when performing alone, a phenomenon termed **social loafing** (Karau & Williams, 1997). Whether the task is pulling on a rope, clapping as loudly as possible, or trying to solve intellectual puzzles, people tend to work harder when performing alone than with others (Baron, Kerr, & Miller, 1992; Geen, 1991). Steven Karau and Kipling Williams (1993) have proposed that there are two reasons for social loafing: The first is that rewards may come whether or not one exerts maximum effort, and the second is that rewards will be divided among the members of the group. Social loafing is more common in Western cultures (e.g., North America) than Eastern cultures (e.g., China and Japan) and more common among men than women (Smith & Bond, 1999; Williams & Sommer, 1997). These differences probably reflect the collectivist orientation that tends to be associated not only with women but also with people from Eastern cultures. This orientation emphasizes the importance of group performance and discourages social loafing.

Social Facilitation

In their battle for a new home run record during the 1998 baseball season, both Mark McGwire and Sammy Sosa, shown here adding to his total, were able to perform at their best even though large crowds were present. Indeed, the crowds probably helped them hit well because the presence of others tends to increase arousal, which enhances the performance of familiar and well-learned skills, such as their batting swing. However, arousal created by an audience tends to interfere with the performance of unfamiliar and poorly developed skills. Thus, the same professional athletes who show flawless grace in front of thousands of fans are likely to freeze up or blow their lines in front of a small production crew when trying for the first time to tape a TV ad or a public service announcement.

In Western countries social loafing can be seen in groups of all sorts, from volunteer committees to search parties. Because social loafing can reduce productivity in business situations, it is important for managers to develop ways of evaluating the efforts of every individual in a work group, not just the overall output of a team (Shepperd, 1993). Social loafing can also be reduced by strategies that cause people to like the group and identify with it (Karau & Williams, 1997).

CONFORMITY AND COMPLIANCE

Suppose you are with three friends. One says that Franklin Roosevelt was the greatest president in the history of the United States. You think that the greatest president was Abraham Lincoln, but before you can say anything, another friend agrees that it was Roosevelt, and then the other one does as well. What would you do? Disagree with all three? Maintain your opinion but keep quiet? Change your mind?

When people change their behavior or beliefs to match those of other members of a group, they are said to conform. **Conformity** occurs as a result of group pressure, real or imagined (Cialdini & Trost, 1998). You probably have experienced such group pressure when everyone around you stands to applaud a performance you thought was mediocre. You may conform by standing as well, though no one told you to do so; the group's behavior creates a silent but influential pressure to follow suit. **Compliance,** in contrast, occurs when people adjust their behavior because of a request. The request can be either *explicit,* such as your brother saying, "Please pass the salt," or *implicit,* as when your mother looks at you in a certain way to let you know she wants you to take out the trash (Cialdini & Trost, 1998).

The Role of Norms

Conformity and compliance are usually generated by spoken or unspoken norms. In a classic experiment, Muzafer Sherif (1937) managed to chart the formation of a group norm by taking advantage of a perceptual illusion, called the *autokinetic phenomenon,* whereby a stationary point of light in a pitch dark room appears to move. Estimates of this movement tend to stay the same over time—if the observer is alone in the room.

Mass Conformity

The faithful who gather at Mecca, at the Vatican, and at other holy places around the world exemplify the power of religion and other social forces to produce conformity to group norms.

But when Sherif tested several people at once, asking each person to say aloud how far the light moved on repeated trials, their estimates tended to converge; they had established a group norm. Even more important, when the individuals from the group were later tested alone, they continued to be influenced by this norm.

In another classic experiment, Solomon Asch (1956) examined how people would respond when they faced a norm that already existed but was obviously wrong. The participants in this experiment saw a standard line like the one in Figure 18.2(A); then they saw a display like that in Figure 18.2(B). Their task was to pick out the line in the display that was the same length as the one they had initially been shown.

Each participant performed this task in a small group of people who posed as fellow participants, but who were actually the experimenter's assistants. There were two conditions. In the control condition, the real participant responded first. In the experimental condition, the participant did not respond until after the assistants did. The assistants chose the correct response on six trials, but on the other twelve trials they all gave the same obviously incorrect response. Thus, on twelve trials, each participant was confronted with a "social reality" created by a group norm that conflicted with the physical reality created by what the person could clearly see. Only 5 percent of the participants in the control condition ever made a mistake on this easy perceptual task. However, among participants who heard the assistants' responses before giving their own, about 70 percent made at least one error by conforming to the group norm. A meta-analysis of 133 studies conducted in 17 countries reveals that conformity in Asch-type situations has declined somewhat in the United States since the 1950s, but that it still occurs; it is especially likely in collectivist cultures, in which conformity to group norms is emphasized (Bond & Smith, 1996).

Why Do People Conform?

Why did so many people in Asch's experiment give incorrect responses when they were capable of near-perfect performance? One possibility, called *public conformity*, is that they gave an answer they did not believe simply because it was the socially desirable thing to do. Another possibility is called *private acceptance:* Perhaps the participants used the confederates' responses as legitimate evidence about reality, were convinced that their own perceptions were wrong, and actually changed their minds. Morton Deutsch and Harold Gerard (1955) reasoned that if conformity disappeared when people gave their responses without identifying themselves, then Asch's findings must

(A) STANDARD LINE

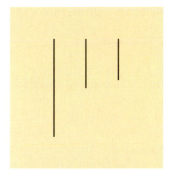

(B) TEST LINES

FIGURE 18.2

Types of Stimulus Lines Used in Experiments by Asch

Participants in Asch's experiments saw a new set of lines like these on each trial. Which line in (B) matches the one in (A)?

Source: Asch, 1955.

reflect public conformity, not private acceptance. In fact, conformity does decrease when people respond anonymously instead of publicly, but it is not eliminated (Deutsch & Gerard, 1955). People sometimes publicly produce responses that they do not believe, but hearing other people's responses also influences their private beliefs (Moscovici, 1985).

Why do group norms wield such power? Research suggests three influential factors (Cialdini & Trost, 1998). First, people are motivated to be correct, and norms provide information about what is right and wrong. This factor may help explain why some extremely disturbed or distressed people consider stories about suicide to be "social proof" that self-destruction is a reasonable way out of their problems (Cialdini, 1993). Second, people are motivated to be liked by other group members, and we generally like those who agree with us. Finally, norms influence the distribution of social rewards and punishments (Cialdini, 1995). From childhood on, people in many cultures learn that going along with group norms is good and earns rewards. (These positive outcomes presumably help compensate for not always being able to say or do exactly what we please.) People also learn that breaking a norm may bring punishments ranging from scoldings for small transgressions to imprisonment for violation of norms that have been translated into laws.

When Do People Conform?

People do not always conform to group influence. In the Asch studies, for example, nearly 30 percent of the participants did not go along with the assistants' obviously erroneous judgments. Countless experiments have probed the question of what combinations of people and circumstances do and do not lead to conformity.

Ambiguity of the Situation   Ambiguity is very important in determining how much conformity will occur. As the physical reality of a situation becomes less certain, people rely more and more on others' opinions, and conformity to a group norm becomes increasingly likely (Aronson, Wilson, & Akert, 1999).

You can demonstrate this aspect of conformity on any street corner. First, create an ambiguous situation by having several people look at the sky or the top of a building. When passers-by ask what is going on, be sure everyone excitedly reports seeing something interesting but fleeting—perhaps a faint light or a tiny, shiny object. If you are especially successful, conforming newcomers will begin persuading other passers-by that there is something fascinating to be seen.

Unanimity and Size of the Majority   If ambiguity contributes so much to conformity, why did so many of Asch's participants conform to a judgment that was unambiguously wrong? The answer has to do with the unanimity of the group's judgment and the number of people expressing it. Specifically, people experience great pressure to conform as long as the majority is unanimous. If even one other person in the group disagrees with the majority view, conformity drops greatly. For example, when Asch (1951) arranged for just one assistant to disagree with the others, fewer than 10 percent of the real participants conformed. Once unanimity is broken, it becomes much easier to disagree with the majority, even if the other nonconformist does not agree with the person's own view (Turner, 1991).

Conformity also depends on the size of the group. Asch (1955) demonstrated this phenomenon by varying the number of assistants in the group from one to fifteen. Conformity to incorrect norms grew as the number of people in the group increased. But most of the growth in conformity occurred as the size of the majority rose from one to about three or four members; further additions had little effect. Several years after Asch's research, Bibb Latané (pronounced "lat-a-NAY") sought to explain this phenomenon via his *social impact theory*. This theory holds that a group's impact on an individual depends not only on group size but also on how important and close the group is to the person. According to Latané (1981), the impact of increasing the size of a majority depends on how big it was originally. Thus, increasing a majority from, say, two to three will have much more impact than increasing it from, say, sixty to sixty-one. The reason is that the increase from sixty to sixty-one is psychologically much smaller than that from two to three; it attracts far less notice in relative terms. Does this explanation sound familiar? The principles underlying it are similar to those of Weber's law, which, as described in Chapter 5, governs our perception of changes in brightness, weight, and other physical stimuli.

Minority Influence   Conformity can also result from **minority influence,** by which a numerical minority in a group influences the behavior or beliefs of a majority (Aronson, Wilson, & Akert, 1999). This phenomenon is less common than majority influence, but minorities can be influential, especially when they persist in their views and show agreement with one another (Moscovici, 1994). William Crano and his associates have found that whereas majority influence tends to affect people immediately and directly, minority influence is *indirect;* that is, minority-influenced change often takes a while to occur and may involve only a moderate adjustment of the majority view in the direction favored by the minority (Alvaro & Crano, 1997; Crano & Chen, 1998).

Gender   Early research on conformity suggested that women conform more than men, but this gender difference stemmed mainly from the fact that the tasks used in those experiments were often more familiar to men than to women. And, indeed, people are especially likely to conform when they are faced with an unfamiliar situation (Cialdini & Trost, 1998). No male-female differences in conformity have been found in subsequent research using materials that are equally familiar to both genders (Maupin & Fisher, 1989). Why then do some people still perceive women as more conforming than men despite evidence to the contrary? Part of the answer may lie in their perception of the relative social status of men and women. Those who think of women as having lower social status than men in most social situations are likely to see women as easier to influence, even though men and women conform equally often (Eagly, 1987).

Inducing Compliance

In the experiments just described, the participants experienced psychological pressure to conform to the views or actions of others, even though no one specifically asked them to do so. In contrast, *compliance* involves changing what you say or do because of a request.

How is compliance brought about? Many people believe that the direct approach is always best: If you want something, ask for it. But salespeople, political strategists, social psychologists, and other experts have learned that often the best way to get something is to ask for something else. Three examples of this strategy are the foot-in-the-door technique, the door-in-the-face procedure, and the low-ball approach.

The *foot-in-the-door technique* works by getting a person to agree to small requests and then gradually presenting larger ones. In the original experiment on this strategy, homeowners were asked to do one of two things. Some were asked to allow a large, unattractive "Drive Carefully" sign to be placed on their front lawn. Approximately 17 percent of the people approached in this way complied with the request. In the foot-in-the-door condition, however, homeowners were first asked only to sign a petition supporting legislation aimed at reducing traffic accidents. Several weeks later, when a different person asked these same people to put the "Drive Carefully" sign on their lawn, 55 percent of them complied (Freedman & Fraser, 1966).

Why should the granting of small favors lead to larger ones? First, people are usually far more likely to comply with a request that costs little in time, money, effort, or inconvenience. Second, complying with a small request makes people think of themselves as being committed to the cause or issue (Cialdini & Trost, 1998). This occurs through the processes of self-perception and cognitive dissonance discussed in Chapter 17. In the study just described, participants who signed the petition might have thought, "I must care enough about traffic safety to do something about it." Compliance with the higher-cost request (displaying the sign) was thus increased

Reaching a Compromise

The door-in-the-face strategy plays a vital role in the bargaining that takes place between labor and management, and between political leaders such as the late Yitzhak Rabin and Yasser Arafat, shown here in 1993 with President Bill Clinton after signing an agreement outlining a plan for Palestinian self-rule in territories occupied by Israel. Each side usually starts out by asking for more than they expect to get so that, by comparison, their later proposals will appear to be a compromise.

because it was consistent with these people's self-perceptions and past actions (Eisenberg et al., 1987).

The foot-in-the-door technique can be quite effective. Steven Sherman (1980) created a 700 percent increase in the rate at which people actually volunteered to work for a charity simply by first getting them to say that, in a hypothetical situation, they would volunteer if asked. For some companies, the foot-in-the-door is a request that potential customers merely answer a few questions; the request to buy something comes later. Others offer a small gift, or "door-opener," as salespeople call it. Acceptance of the gift not only allows a foot in the door but may also invoke the reciprocity norm: Many people who get something free feel obligated to reciprocate by buying something (Cialdini, 1993). Recent research suggests, however, that small favors don't always lead to bigger ones. Specifically, if the request for the larger favor comes immediately after the initial request, people may be unlikely to comply with it (Chartrand, Pinckert, & Burger, in press).

The second approach, known as the *door-in-the-face procedure,* can also be effective in obtaining compliance (Cialdini, 1995; Reeves et al., 1991). This strategy begins with a request for a favor that is likely to be denied. The person making the request then concedes that asking for the initial favor was excessive and substitutes a lesser alternative—which was what he or she really wanted in the first place. Because the person appears willing to compromise and because the new request seems modest in comparison to the first one, it is more likely to be granted than if it had been made at the outset. In this case, compliance appears to be due to activation of the reciprocity norm.

The third technique, called the *low-ball approach,* is commonly used by car dealers and other businesses (Cialdini & Trost, 1998). The first step in this strategy is to obtain a person's oral commitment to do something, such as to purchase a car at a certain price. Once this commitment is made, the cost of fulfilling it is increased, often because of an "error" in computing the car's price. Why do buyers end up paying much more than originally planned for "low-balled" items? Apparently, once people commit themselves to do something, they feel obligated to follow through, especially when the person who obtains the initial commitment also makes the higher-cost request (Burger & Petty, 1981). In other words, as described in relation to cognitive dissonance theory in Chapter 17, people like to be consistent in their words and deeds. In this instance, it appears that people try to maintain a positive self-image by behaving in accordance with their initial oral commitment, even though it may cost them a great deal to do so.

OBEDIENCE

Compliance involves a change in behavior in response to a request. In the case of **obedience,** the behavior change comes in response to a *demand* from an authority figure (Lutsky, 1995). In the 1960s, Stanley Milgram developed a laboratory procedure to study obedience. In his first experiment, he used newspaper ads to recruit forty male volunteers between the ages of twenty and fifty. Among the participants were professionals, white-collar businessmen, and unskilled workers (Milgram, 1963).

Imagine you are one of the people who answered the ad. When you arrive for the experiment, you join a fifty-year-old gentleman who has also volunteered and has been scheduled for the same session. The experimenter explains that the purpose of the experiment is to examine the effects of punishment on learning. One of you—the "teacher"—will help the learner remember a list of words by administering an electric shock whenever he makes a mistake. Then the experimenter turns to you and asks you to draw one of two cards out of a hat. Your card says "TEACHER." You think to yourself that this must be your lucky day.

Now the learner is taken into another room and strapped into a chair, as shown in Figure 18.3. Electrodes are attached to his arms. You are shown a shock generator with thirty switches. The experimenter explains that the switch on the far left administers a mild, 15-volt shock and that each succeeding switch increases the shock by 15 volts; the one on the far right delivers 450 volts. The far left section of the shock generator is labeled "Slight shock." Looking across the panel, you see "Moderate shock," "Very strong shock," and, at the far right, "Danger—severe shock." The last two switches are ominously labeled "XXX." The experimenter explains that you, the teacher, will begin by reading a list of word pairs to the learner. Then you will go through the list again, presenting just one word of each pair; the learner should indicate which word went with it. After the first mistake, you are to throw the switch to deliver 15 volts of shock. Each time the learner makes another mistake, you are to increase the shock by 15 volts.

You begin, following the experimenter's instructions. But after the learner makes his fifth mistake and you throw the switch to give him 75 volts, you hear a loud moan. At 90 volts, the learner cries out in pain. At 150 volts, he screams and asks to be let out of the experiment. You look to the experimenter, who says, "Proceed with the next word."

In fact, no shock was delivered in Milgram's experiments. The "learner" was always an accomplice of the experimenter, and the moans and other signs of pain came from

Proximity and Obedience

Milgram's research suggested that the close proximity of an authority figure enhances obedience to authority (Rada & Rogers, 1973). This principle is employed in the military, where no one is ever far away from the authority of a higher-ranking person.

a prerecorded tape. But you do not know that. What would you do in this situation? Suppose you continue and eventually deliver 180 volts. The learner screams that he cannot stand the pain any longer and starts banging on the wall. The experimenter says, "You have no other choice; you must go on." Would you continue? Would you keep going even when the learner begs to be let out of the experiment and then falls silent? Would you administer 450 volts of potentially deadly shock to a perfect stranger just because an experimenter demands that you do so?

Figure 18.4 shows that only 5 participants in Milgram's experiment stopped before 300 volts, and 26 out of 40 (or 65 percent) went all the way to the 450-volt level. The decision to continue was difficult and stressful for the participants. Many protested repeatedly; but each time the experimenter told them to continue, they did so. Here is a partial transcript of what a typical participant said.

[After throwing the 180-volt switch]: *He can't stand it. I'm not going to kill that man in there. Do you hear him hollering? He's hollering. He can't stand it. What if something happens to him? I'm not going to get that man sick in there. He's hollering in there. Do you know what I mean? I mean, I refuse to take responsibility. He's getting hurt in there. . . . Too many left here. Geez, if he gets them wrong. There are too many of them left. I mean, who is going to take responsibility if anything happens to that gentleman?*

[After the experimenter accepts responsibility]: *All right. . . .*

[After administering 240 volts]: *Oh, no, you mean I've got to keep going up the scale? No sir, I'm not going to kill that man. I'm not going to give him 450 volts.*

[After the experimenter says, "The experiment requires that you go on"]: *I know it does, but that man is hollering in there, sir.*

This participant administered shock up to 450 volts (Milgram, 1974, p. 74).

Factors Affecting Obedience

Milgram had not expected so many people to deliver such apparently intense shocks. Was there something about his procedure that produced this high level of obedience? To find out, Milgram and other researchers varied the original procedure in numerous ways. The overall level of obedience to an authority figure was usually quite high, but the degree of obedience was affected by several characteristics of the situation and procedure.

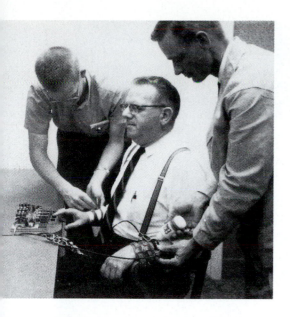

FIGURE 18.3

Studying Obedience in the Laboratory

In this photograph from Milgram's original experiment, a man is being strapped into a chair with electrodes on his arm. Although participants in the experiment do not know it, the man is actually one of the experimenter's research assistants and receives no shock.

FIGURE 18.4

Results of Milgram's Obedience Experiment

When Milgram asked a group of undergraduates and a group of psychiatrists how participants in his experiment would respond, they estimated that fewer than 2 percent would go all the way to 450 volts. In fact, 65 percent of the participants did so.

Source: Milgram, 1963.

Civil Disobedience

In 1955, Rosa Parks was arrested and fingerprinted in Montgomery, Alabama, after refusing an order to move to the "colored" section in the back of a segregated bus. Ms. Parks' courageous act of disobedience sparked the civil rights movement in the United States.

Prestige   One possibility was that the experimenter's status as a Yale University professor helped produce high levels of obedience in Milgram's original experiment. To test the effects of status and prestige, Milgram rented an office in a rundown building in Bridgeport, Connecticut. He then placed a newspaper ad for people to participate in research sponsored by a private firm; there was no mention of Yale. In all other ways, the experimental procedure was identical to the original.

Under these less prestigious circumstances, the level of obedience dropped, but not as much as Milgram expected; 48 percent of the participants continued to the maximum level of shock, compared with 65 percent in the original study. Milgram concluded that people would obey instructions that could cause great harm to another even if the authority figure was not particularly reputable or distinguished.

Presence of Others Who Disobey   To assess how the presence of other people might affect obedience, Milgram (1965) created a situation in which there were apparently three teachers. Teacher 1 (in reality an assistant to the experimenter) read the words to the learner. Teacher 2 (also a research assistant) indicated whether or not the learner's response was correct. And Teacher 3 (the actual participant) was to deliver shock when mistakes were made. At 150 volts, when the learner began to complain that the shock was too painful, Teacher 1 refused to participate any longer and left the room. The experimenter asked him to come back, but he refused. The experimenter then instructed Teachers 2 and 3 to continue by themselves. The experiment continued for several more trials. However, at 210 volts, Teacher 2 said that the learner was suffering too much and also refused to participate further. The experimenter then told Teacher 3 (the actual participant) to continue the procedure. In this case, only 10 percent of the participants (compared with 65 percent in the original study) continued to deliver shock all the way up to 450 volts. Thus, as research on conformity would suggest, the presence of others who disobey appears to be the most powerful factor in reducing obedience.

Personality Characteristics   Were the participants in Milgram's original experiment heartless creatures who would have given strong shocks even if there had been no pressure on them to do so? Quite the opposite; most of them were nice people who were influenced by experimental situations to behave in apparently antisocial ways. In a later demonstration of the same phenomenon, college students playing the role of prison guards behaved with aggressive heartlessness toward other students who were playing the role of prisoners (Zimbardo, 1973).

Still, not everyone is equally obedient to authority. For example, people high in *authoritarianism* (discussed in Chapter 17) are more likely than others to comply with an experimenter's request to shock the learner. The same tends to be true of people who have an external *locus of control* (Blass, 1991). As described in Chapter 14, such people believe that what happens to them is controlled by factors outside of themselves.

Evaluating Milgram's Studies

How relevant are Milgram's thirty-five-year-old studies in today's world? Consider this fact: The U.S. Federal Aviation Administration attributes many commercial airline accidents to a phenomenon it calls "captainitis." This phenomenon occurs when the captain of an aircraft makes an obvious error but none of the other crew members is willing to challenge the captain's authority by pointing out the mistake. As a result, planes have crashed and people have died (Kanki & Foushee, 1990). Obedience to authority may also explain why, a few years ago, when a fire broke out at the airport in Frankfurt, Germany, many travelers followed an airport official's incorrect instructions to move in a direction that took them *toward* the fire rather than away from it. Several of these obedient people died as a result. Obedience to authority appeared to be at work, too, in the case of train crew members in the United States who were ordered to deliver a shipment of weapons despite the fact that a protester was lying on the tracks in front of them; the crew did not even slow down as the train wheels severed the man's legs (Cialdini, 1993). The occurrence of all these phenomena suggest that Milgram's findings are still relevant and important (Saks, 1992). They have been replicated in countries in Europe and the Middle East, with female as well as male participants (Smith and Bond, 1999). However, many aspects of Milgram's work still provoke debates. (For a summary of Milgram's results, plus those of studies on conformity and compliance, see "In Review: Types of Social Influence," page 646.)

Ethical Questions   Although the "learners" in Milgram's experiment suffered no discomfort, the participants did. Milgram (1963) observed participants "sweat, stutter, tremble, groan, bite their lips, and dig their fingernails into their flesh" (p. 375). Against

Following Ghastly Orders

When authority figures issue orders, they tend to be obeyed, sometimes with tragic consequences. Recently, for example, Serbian Army troops and members of Serbian paramilitary groups engaged in the rape and murder of ethnic Albanian civilians in the province of Kosovo in response to orders from their superiors.

in review

TYPES OF SOCIAL INFLUENCE

Type	Definition	Key Findings
Conformity	A change in behavior or beliefs to match those of others	In cases of ambiguity, people develop a group norm and then adhere to it.
		Conformity occurs because people want to be right, because they want to be liked by others, and because conformity to group norms is usually reinforced.
		Conformity usually increases with the ambiguity of the situation, as well as with the unanimity and psychological size of the majority.
Compliance	A change in what is said or done because of a request	Compliance increases with the foot-in-the-door technique, which begins with a small request and works up to a larger one.
		The door-in-the-face procedure can also be used. After making a large request that is denied, the person substitutes a less extreme alternative that was desired all along.
		The low-ball approach also elicits compliance. A person first obtains an oral commitment for something, then claims that only a higher-cost version of the original request will suffice.
Obedience	A change in behavior in response to an explicit demand, typically from an authority figure	People may inflict great harm on others when an authority demands that they do so.
		Even though people obey orders to harm another person, they often agonize over the decision.
		People are most likely to disobey orders to harm someone else when they see another person disobey.

the potential harm inflicted by Milgram's experiments stand the potential gains. For example, people who learn about Milgram's work often take his findings into account when deciding how to react in social situations (Sherman, 1980). But even if social value has come from Milgram's studies, the question remains: Was it ethical for Milgram to treat his participants as he did?

LINKAGES

Is it ethical to deceive people in order to learn about their social behavior? (a link to Research in Psychology)

In the years before his death in 1984, Milgram defended his experiments (e.g., Milgram, 1977). He argued that his debriefing of the participants after the experiment prevented any lasting harm. For example, to demonstrate that their behavior was not unusual, Milgram told them that most people went all the way to the 450-volt level. He also explained that the learner did not experience any shock; indeed, the learner came in and chatted with each participant. On a later questionnaire, 84 percent of the participants said that they had learned something important about themselves and that the experience had been worthwhile. Thus, Milgram argued, the experience was actually a positive one. Still, today's committees charged with protecting human participants in research would be unlikely to approve Milgram's experiments, and less controversial ways to study obedience have now been developed (Sackoff & Weinstein, 1988).

Questions of Meaning   Do Milgram's dramatic results mean that most people are putty in the hands of authority figures and that most of us would blindly follow inhumane orders from our leaders? Some critics have argued that other factors besides obedience to authority were responsible for Milgram's participants' behavior and that the social influence processes identified in his studies might not explain obedience in the real world (Lutsky, 1995). Most psychologists believe, however, that Milgram demonstrated a basic truth about human behavior—namely that under certain circumstances, human beings are capable of unspeakable acts of brutality toward other humans. Sadly, examples abound. One of the most horrifying aspects of Nazi atrocities against the Jews—and of more recent campaigns of genocide against ethnic groups in Eastern Europe and Africa—is that the perpetrators were not necessarily demented, sadistic fiends. Most of them were normal people who, because of the situation they faced, were influenced to behave in a demented and fiendish manner.

Worse, inhumanity can occur even without pressure for obedience. For example, a good deal of people's aggressiveness toward other people appears to come from within. In the next section, we consider human aggressiveness and some of the circumstances that influence its expression.

AGGRESSION

Aggression is an action intended to harm another person. It is all too common. In the United States in 1995, a murder occurred every twenty-four minutes, a rape every five minutes, and an aggravated assault every twenty-nine seconds (Anderson, in press). In many urban areas, murder is the leading cause of death among men under the age of twenty-five (Huesmann & Miller, 1994). Aggression is even likely to occur among friends and lovers. For example, almost half of the dating couples interviewed in one study said that one of them had been physically aggressive toward the other (O'Leary, Malone, & Tyree, 1994). There is less aggression among married couples, but not much less. About one-third of married people in the United States display aggression toward each other that ranges from pushing, shoving, and slapping to beatings and the threatened or actual use of weapons (Pan, Neidig, & O'Leary, 1994).

Why Are People Aggressive?

LINKAGES

What makes some people so aggressive? (a link to Introducing Psychology)

An early theory of human aggression was offered by Freud, who suggested it was partly due to *Thanatos,* the death instincts described in Chapter 14. He proposed that aggression is an instinctive biological urge that gradually builds up in everyone and must at some point be released. Sometimes, he said, release takes the form of physical or verbal abuse against others; at other times, the aggressive impulse is turned inward and leads to suicide or other self-damaging acts.

A slightly more complicated view is offered by evolutionary psychologists. As discussed in Chapters 1 and 11, these psychologists believe that human social behavior is related to our evolutionary heritage. From this perspective, aggression is thought to have helped prehistoric people compete for mates, thus ensuring survival of their genes in the next generation. Through the principles of natural selection, then, aggressive tendencies were passed on through successive generations. Some evolutionary psychologists believe that, even now, aggression sometimes occurs because it promotes the survival of the aggressor's genes (e.g., Buss & Shackelford, 1997).

Freudian and evolutionary theories seem too simplistic to fully account for human aggressiveness, however. For one thing, there are large differences in aggression from culture to culture. In the Philippines, for example, the murder rate is forty-six times higher than in China or Finland, and it is almost nine times higher in the United States than in those latter two countries (Triandis, 1994). Indeed, the homicide rate is higher in the United States than in any other industrialized nation (Geen, 1998b). These data suggest that, even if aggressive *impulses* are universal, the emergence of aggressive *behavior* reflects an interplay of nature and nurture (Geen, 1998b). No equation can predict when people will be aggressive, but years of research have revealed a number of important biological, learning, and environmental factors that combine in various ways to produce aggression in various situations.

Genetic and Biological Mechanisms   The evidence for hereditary influences on aggression is strong, especially in animals (Cairns, Gariepy, & Hood, 1990). In one study, the most aggressive members of a large group of mice were interbred; then the most aggressive of their offspring were also interbred. After this procedure was followed for twenty-five generations, the resulting animals would immediately attack any mouse put in their cage. Continuous inbreeding of the least aggressive members of the original group produced animals that were so nonaggressive that they would refuse to fight even when attacked (Lagerspetz & Lagerspetz, 1983). Research on human twins reared together or apart suggests that there is a genetic component to aggression in people as well (Rushton et al., 1986; Tellegen et al., 1988). However, other research suggests that people do not necessarily inherit the tendency to be aggressive; instead, they may inherit certain temperaments, such as impulsiveness, that in turn make aggression more likely (Baron & Richardson, 1994).

Several parts of the brain influence aggression (Anderson & Anderson, 1998). One is the limbic system, which includes the amygdala, the hypothalamus, and related areas (see Figure 3.15, page 68). Damage to these structures may produce *defensive aggression,* which includes heightened aggressiveness to stimuli that are not usually threatening or a decrease in the responses that normally inhibit aggression (Coccaro, 1989; Eichelman, 1983). The cerebral cortex may also be involved in aggression (see Figure 3.17, page 72). One study found that the prefrontal area of the cortex metabolized glucose significantly more slowly in murderers than in nonmurderers (Raine et al., 1994).

Hormones also play an important role in aggression. One possibility is that aggression is related to one's level of *testosterone,* the masculine hormone that is present in both sexes (Dabbs et al., 1995). Experiments have shown that aggressive behavior increases or decreases dramatically with the amount of testosterone in an animal's body (Frank, Glickman, & Licht, 1991), and violent criminals have been found to have higher levels of testosterone than nonviolent ones (Dabbs et al., 1995). Among normal men, variations in testosterone show a small but statistically significant correlation with aggressiveness (Dabbs & Morris, 1990; Gray, Jackson, & McKinley, 1991).

Testosterone may have its most significant and durable influence not so much through its day-to-day variations as through its impact on early brain development. One natural test of this hypothesis occurred when pregnant women were given testosterone in an attempt to prevent miscarriages. Accordingly, their children were exposed to high doses of testosterone during prenatal development. Figure 18.5 shows that these children grew up to be more aggressive than their same-sex siblings who were not exposed to testosterone during prenatal development (Reinisch, Ziemba-Davis, & Sanders, 1991).

Drugs that affect the central nervous system can also affect the likelihood that a person will act aggressively. Even relatively small amounts of alcohol, for example, can substantially increase some people's aggressiveness (Taylor & Hulsizer, 1998). One study demonstrated that when male alcoholics stopped drinking, the amount of violence directed toward their spouses decreased significantly (O'Farrell & Murphy, 1995). No one knows exactly why alcohol increases aggression, but research suggests that the drug may affect areas of the brain that normally inhibit aggressive responses (Lau, Pihl, & Peterson, 1995).

Research on the effects of other drugs on aggression have produced some surprising findings. One might expect, for example, that using stimulants would increase aggressiveness and that taking tranquilizers would reduce it, but the opposite appears to be true. Whereas amphetamines do not usually make people more aggressive, opiates (e.g., heroin, morphine) and some tranquilizers may do so (Taylor & Hulsizer, 1998). No one knows why heroin users are more likely than amphetamine users to be aggressive. Some have suggested that heroin addicts' aggression reflects their desperate need to get money, by any means, to buy more drugs. But if this were so, we should also see increased aggression among people who are addicted to amphetamines and cocaine—because these addictions, too, are very expensive. Further, ingesting opiates increases people's aggressiveness even in controlled laboratory settings (Taylor & Hulsizer, 1998), suggesting that these drugs have biochemical effects that lead directly to aggression. The nature of these effects is presently unknown.

Learning and Cultural Mechanisms

Although biological factors may increase or decrease the likelihood of aggression, cross-cultural research makes it clear that learn-

---

FIGURE 18.5

Testosterone and Aggression

In the study illustrated here, the children of women who had taken testosterone during pregnancy to prevent miscarriage became more aggressive than the mothers' other children of the same sex who had not been exposed to testosterone during prenatal development. This effect held for both males and females.

Source: Data from Reinisch, Ziemba-Davis, & Sanders, 1991.

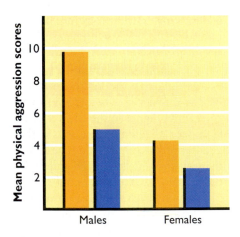

Participants exposed to high doses of testosterone during prenatal development

Unexposed participants

Following Adult Examples

Learning to express aggression is especially easy for children who, like these youngsters at a Hizbollah parade in Beirut, Lebanon, see aggressive acts modeled for them all too often.

ing also plays a role. Aggressive behavior is much more common in individualist than in collectivist cultures, for example (Oatley, 1993). Cultural differences in the expression of aggression appear to stem in part from differing cultural values. Thus, in contrast to many so-called advanced peoples, the Utku, an Inuit culture, view aggression in any form as a sign of social incompetence. In fact, the Utku word for "aggressive" also means "childish" (Oatley, 1993). The effects of culture on aggression can also be seen in the fact that the incidence of aggression in a given culture changes over time as cultural values change (Baron & Richardson, 1994).

In addition, people learn many aggressive responses by watching others (Smith & Donnerstein, 1998). Children, in particular, learn and perform many novel aggressive responses that they see modeled by others (Bandura, 1983). Albert Bandura's "Bobo doll" experiments, which are described in Chapter 6, provide impressive demonstrations of the power of observational learning. The significance of observational learning is highlighted by studies of the effects of televised violence, also discussed in Chapter 6. For example, the amount of violent content watched on television by eight-year-olds predicts aggressiveness in these children even fifteen years later (Huesmann et al., 1997). Fortunately, not everyone who sees aggression becomes aggressive; individual differences in temperament, the modeling of nonaggressive behaviors by parents, and other factors can temper the effects of violent television. Nevertheless, observational learning does play a significant role in the development and display of aggressive behavior (Anderson, 1997).

Immediate reward or punishment can also alter the frequency of aggressive acts; people become more aggressive when rewarded for aggressiveness and less aggressive when punished for aggression (Geen, 1998b). In short, a person's accumulated experiences—including culturally transmitted teachings—combine with daily rewards and punishments to influence whether, when, and how aggressive acts occur (Baron & Richardson, 1994).

When Are People Aggressive?

In general, people are more likely to be aggressive when they are both physiologically aroused and experiencing strong emotions such as anger (Geen, 1998a). People tend either to lash out at those who make them angry or to displace their anger onto defenseless targets such as children or pets. However, aggression can also be made more likely by other forms of emotional arousal. One emotion that has long been considered to be a major cause of aggression is *frustration*.

Frustration and Aggression   Suppose that a friend interrupts your studying for an exam by coming over to borrow a book. If things have been going well that day and you are feeling confident about the exam, you are likely to be friendly and accommodating. But what if you are feeling frustrated because your friend's visit represents the fifth interruption in the last hour? Under these emotional circumstances, you may react aggressively, perhaps berating your startled visitor for not calling ahead (Eron, 1994).

Your aggressiveness in this situation conforms to the predictions of the **frustration-aggression hypothesis,** which was originally developed by John Dollard and his colleagues (Dollard et al., 1939). They proposed that frustration always results in aggression and, conversely, that aggression will not occur unless a person is frustrated. Research on this hypothesis has shown that it is too simple and too general, however. For one thing, frustration sometimes produces depression and withdrawal, not aggression (Berkowitz, 1998). In addition, not all aggression is preceded by frustration (Berkowitz, 1994). In many of the experiments described earlier, for example, participants were not frustrated, but they still made aggressive responses.

After many years of research, Leonard Berkowitz (1998) has suggested some substantial modifications to the frustration-aggression hypothesis. First, he proposed that it may be *stress* rather than frustration *per se* that can produce a readiness to act aggressively. Once this readiness exists, cues in the environment that are associated with aggression will often lead a person to behave aggressively. The cues might be guns or knives, televised scenes of people arguing, and the like. Neither stress alone nor the cues alone are sufficient to set off aggression. When combined, however, they often do. Support for this aspect of Berkowitz's theory has been quite strong (Carlson, Marcus-Newhall, & Miller, 1990).

Second, Berkowitz argues that the direct cause of most kinds of aggression is *negative affect,* or unpleasant emotion, and that whether it is caused by frustration or other sources, the greater the negative affect, the stronger is the readiness to respond aggressively (Berkowitz, 1998). For example, negative affect can stem from pain, and research suggests that people in pain do tend to become aggressive, no matter what caused their pain. In one study, female students whose hands were placed in painfully cold water became more aggressive toward other students than women whose hands were in water of room temperature (Berkowitz, 1998).

LINKAGES

What role does arousal play in aggression? (a link to Motivation and Emotion)

Generalized Arousal   Imagine you have just jogged three miles. You are hot, sweaty, and out of breath, but you are not angry. Still, the physiological arousal caused by jogging may increase the probability that you will become aggressive if, say, a passer-by shouts an insult (Zillmann, 1988). Why? The answer lies in a phenomenon described in Chapter 11, on motivation and emotion: Arousal from one experience may carry over to an independent situation, producing what is called *transferred excitation.* Thus, the physiological arousal caused by jogging may intensify your reaction to an insult (Geen, 1998a).

By itself, however, generalized arousal does not lead to aggression. It is most likely to produce aggression when the situation contains some reason, opportunity, or target for aggression (Zillmann, 1988). In one study, for example, people engaged in two minutes of vigorous exercise. Then they had the opportunity to deliver electric shock to another person. The participants chose high levels of shock only if they were first insulted (Zillmann, Katcher, & Milavsky, 1972). Apparently, the arousal resulting from the exercise made aggression more likely; the insult "released" it. These findings are in keeping with the notion that aggression is not caused solely by either a person's characteristics *or* the particular situation a person is in; rather, the incidence and intensity of aggression are determined by the joint influence of individual characteristics *and* environmental circumstances.

THINKING CRITICALLY

Does Pornography Cause Aggression?

In both men and women, sexual stimulation produces strong, generalized physiological arousal, especially in the sympathetic nervous system. If arousal in general can make a person more likely to be aggressive (given a reason, opportunity, or target), could stimuli that create sexual excitement be dangerous? In particular, does viewing pornographic material make people more likely to be aggressive? Over the years, numerous scholars had concluded that there is no evidence for an overall relationship between any type of antisocial behavior and mere exposure to pornographic material (Donnerstein, 1984b). However, in 1986 the U.S. Attorney General's Commission on Pornography reexamined the question and concluded that pornography is dangerous.

■ **What am I being asked to believe or accept?**

Specifically, the commission proposed that there is a causal link between viewing erotic material and several forms of antisocial behavior, including sexually related violent crimes.

■ **What evidence is available to support the assertion?**

The commission cited several types of evidence in support of its conclusion. First, there was the testimony of men convicted of sexually related crimes. Rapists, for example, are unusually heavy consumers of pornography, and they often say that they were aroused by erotic material immediately before committing a rape (Silbert & Pines, 1984). Similarly, child molesters often view child pornography immediately before committing their crimes (Marshall, 1989).

In addition, the commission cited experimental evidence that men who are most aroused by aggressive themes in pornography are also the most potentially sexually aggressive. One study, for example, showed that men who said they could commit a rape became sexually aroused by scenes of rape and less aroused by scenes of mutually consenting sex; this was not true for men who said they could never commit a rape (Malamuth & Check, 1983).

Perhaps the most compelling evidence cited by the commission, however, came from transferred excitation studies. In a typical study of this type, men are told that a person in a separate room (actually a research assistant) will be performing a learning task and that they are to administer an electric shock every time the person makes a mistake. The intensity of shock can be varied (no shock actually reaches the assistant), but participants are told that changing the intensity will not affect the speed of learning. So the shock intensity (and presumed pain) that the participants choose to administer is taken as an index of aggressive behavior. Some participants watch a sexually explicit film before beginning the learning trials, some do not. The arousal created by the film appears to transfer into aggression, especially when the arousal is experienced in a negative way. For example, after watching a film in which several men have sex with the same woman, the participants became aroused but tended to label the experience as somewhat unpleasant. Their aggressiveness during the learning experiment was greater than that demonstrated by men who did not watch the film (Donnerstein, 1984b).

■ Are there alternative ways of interpreting the evidence?

The commission's interpretation of evidence was criticized on several counts. First, critics argued that some of the evidence should be given little weight. In particular, how credible is the testimony of convicted sex offenders? It may reflect self-serving attempts to lay the blame for their crimes on pornography. These reports cannot establish that exposure to pornography causes aggression. Indeed, it may be that pornography partially *satisfies* sex offenders' aggressive impulses rather than creating them (Aronson, Wilson, & Akert, 1999). Similarly, the fact that potential rapists are most aroused by rape-oriented material may show only that they prefer violence-oriented pornography, not that such materials created their impulse to rape.

What about the evidence from transferred excitation studies? To interpret these studies, you need to know that the pornography that led to increased aggression contained violence as well as sex; the sexual activity depicted was painful for or unwanted by the woman. Thus, the subsequent increase in aggression could have been due to the transfer of sexual arousal, the effects of observing violent behavior, or the effects of seeing sex combined with violence (Donnerstein, Slaby, & Eron, 1995).

In fact, several careful experiments have found that highly arousing sexual themes, in and of themselves, do not produce aggression. When men in transferred excitation studies experience pleasant arousal by viewing a film depicting nudity or mutually consenting sexual activity, their subsequent aggression is actually less than when they viewed no film or a neutral film (Lord, 1997). In short, the transferred excitation studies might be interpreted as demonstrating not that sexually arousing material causes aggression but that portrayals of sexual violence influence aggressiveness.

■ What additional evidence would help to evaluate the alternatives?

Two types of evidence are needed to understand more clearly the effects of pornography on aggression. First, since pornography can include sexual acts, aggressive acts, or both, the effects of each of these components must be more carefully examined (Hall & Hirschman, 1991). Second, factors affecting men's reactions to pornography, particularly pornography that involves violence, must be more clearly understood (Malamuth et al., 1991). Work is in progress on each of these fronts.

Aggressive themes—whether specifically paired with sexual activity or not—do appear to increase subsequent aggression (Malamuth, Heavy, & Linz, 1993). Research has focused on *aggressive pornography,* which contains sexual themes but also scenes of violence against women (Linz, Wilson, & Donnerstein, 1992). In laboratory experiments, men often administer higher levels of shock to women after viewing aggressive pornographic films as opposed to neutral films. Yet there is no parallel increase in aggression against other men, indicating that the films create not a generalized increase in aggression but an increase in aggressiveness directed toward women (Aronson, Wilson, & Akert, 1999). Similarly, viewing aggressive pornography that depicts the *rape myth*—in which the victim of sexual violence appears to be aroused by the aggression—usually leads men to become less sympathetic toward the rape victim and more tolerant of aggressive acts toward women (Donnerstein & Linz, 1995). In general, sexually explicit films that do not contain violence have no effects on attitudes toward rape (Linz, Donnerstein, & Penrod, 1987).

In one study, 35 percent of all college men reported having been exposed to aggressive pornography within the past twelve months (Demare, Briere, & Lips, 1988), and the figure may be even higher in the general population. Are all these men equally likely to become rapists? The evidence available so far suggests that the answer is no. Whether aggressive pornography alters men's behavior and attitudes toward women depends to some extent on the men. For example, a recent national study of over 2,700 American men examined how three factors—a history of sexual promiscuity, feelings of hostility toward women, and the consumption of pornography—were related to sexual aggression against women (Malamuth, 1998). Among men *low* in promiscuity and hostility, viewing pornography was not associated with sexual aggression, but among men who were *high* in promiscuity and hostility, there was such an association. Specifically, 72 percent of the men who were high on all three factors had actually engaged in sexually aggressive acts (see Figure 18.6).

■ What conclusions are most reasonable?

The attorney general's commission appeared to ignore numerous studies showing that the relationship between sexual arousal and aggression is neither consistent nor simple (Lord, 1997). Analysis of this relationship reveals the importance of distinguishing between pornography in general and aggressive pornography in particular. Overall, there is no reason to assume that sexual arousal created by nonaggressive pornography is associated with aggressive behavior. Indeed, for most people, sexual arousal and aggression remain quite separate. However, aggressive pornography is associated with violence against women. Thus, there is reason for concern over the impact of sexual violence commonly seen on television and in films—especially "slasher" movies. Remarkably, in the United States, such films are sometimes given less restrictive ratings ("R" or even "PG-13") than films that are nonviolent but erotic.

So although pornography has little impact on most people, certain segments of the population do seem to be affected by it. Men who are inclined to abuse and exploit women are also inclined to watch a lot of pornography. And watching a lot of pornography can increase the likelihood of their sexually abusing a woman. In short, pornography *per se* is probably not a cause of violence against women, but in combination with other factors it can play a role in sexual aggression.

Environmental Influences on Aggression The link between stress and aggressive behavior points to the possibility that stressful environmental conditions can make aggressive behavior more likely (Anderson & Anderson, 1998). This possibility is one of the research topics in **environmental psychology,** the study of the relationship between people's physical environment and their behavior (Sommer, 1999). One aspect of the environment that clearly affects social behavior is the weather, especially temperature. High temperature is a source of stress and arousal and, thus, might be

FIGURE 18.6

Pornography and Sexual Aggression

Extensive exposure to pornography does not by itself make most men more likely to engage in sexual aggression. However, among men who are hostile toward women and have a history of sexual promiscuity, those who watch a lot of pornography are much more likely to engage in sexual aggression.

Source: Adapted from Malamuth (1998).

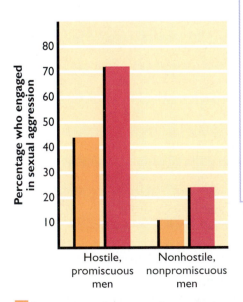

Low amount of pornography watched

High amount of pornography watched

Crowding and Aggression

Studies of prisons suggest that as crowding increases, so does aggression (Paulus, 1988). Accordingly, environmental psychologists are working with architects on the design of prisons that minimize the sense of crowding and may, ideally, help prevent some of the violence that endangers staff and prisoners.

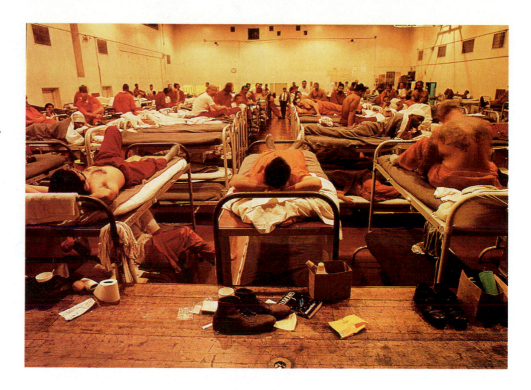

Effects of Temperature on Aggression

Studies from around the world indicate that aggressive behaviors are most likely to occur during hot summer months. These studies support the idea that environmental factors can affect aggression.

Source: Anderson & Anderson (1998).

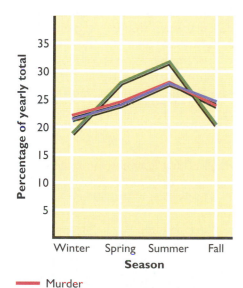

expected to correlate with aggressiveness. The results of many studies conducted in several different countries show that many kinds of aggressive behavior are indeed more likely to occur during hot summer months than at any other time of the year (Anderson & Anderson, 1998; see Figure 18.7).

Air pollution and noise—usually defined as any unwanted sound (Bell et al., 1990)—are also sources of stress, and they can influence whether a person displays aggression (Holahan, 1986). For example, people tend to become more aggressive when breathing air that contains ethyl mercapton, a mildly unpleasant-smelling pollutant common in urban areas (Rotton et al., 1979). A study conducted in Dayton, Ohio, found that the frequency of aggressive family disturbances increased along with the ozone level in the air (Rotton & Frey, 1985). And in laboratory studies, nonsmokers are more likely to become aggressive when breathing smoke-filled rather than clean air (Zillmann, Baron, & Tamborini, 1981). Long-term exposure to toxins such as lead has also been associated with increased aggression (Needleman, 1996). Noise, too, tends to make people more likely to display aggression, especially if the noise is unpredictable and irregular (Geen & McCown, 1984).

Living arrangements also influence aggressiveness. Compared with the tenants of crowded apartment buildings, those in buildings with relatively few residents are less likely to behave aggressively (Bell et al., 1990). This difference appears to be due in part to how people feel when they are crowded. Crowding tends to create physiological arousal and to make people tense, uncomfortable, and more likely to report negative feelings (Epstein, Woolfolk, & Lehrer, 1981). This arousal and tension can influence people to like one another less and to be more aggressive. One study of juvenile delinquents found that the number of behavior problems they displayed (including aggressiveness) was directly related to how crowded their living conditions had become (Ray et al., 1982).

ALTRUISM AND HELPING BEHAVIOR

The first chapter of this book opens with the story of Russell Eugene Weston, Jr., a gunman who killed two people in the U.S. Capitol Building in 1998. One of the schoolyard shootings described at the beginning of Chapter 12 involved Mitchell Johnson and Andrew Golden, two Jonesboro, Arkansas, schoolboys who shot to death four of their

Four Heroes

During urban violence in Los Angeles, California, in 1992, these four people saw live television pictures of rioters near their homes beating Reginald Denny, a truck driver. In a remarkable display of altruism toward a total stranger, they ran to the scene, rescued Denny from his attackers, and got him to a hospital in time to save his life.

A Young Helper

Even before their second birthday, some children offer help to those who are hurt or crying by snuggling, patting, or offering food or even their own teddy bears.

classmates and a teacher. These incidents vividly exemplify human aggression, but they also illustrate its opposite—namely, acts of selflessness and heroism. Jacob Chestnut and John Gibson, the two U.S. Capitol police officers who were killed by Weston, died while trying to protect legislators and the public. And Shannon Wright, the teacher killed at Jonesboro, had placed herself between the shooters and her students, probably saving several of their lives while sacrificing her own. Nor are such remarkable acts confined to people whose job it is to help others. Consider, for example, the people who saved Reginald Denny. Denny had the misfortune to be driving his truck through the center of the riots that broke out in Los Angeles in 1992. As his path was blocked by crowds, four men pulled Denny out of the truck and began to beat him mercilessly. A local TV station's helicopter hovered over the scene and broadcast live pictures of the beating. Among the viewers were two men and two women living in the riot area, who then left the safety of their homes to try to help Denny. Though threatened by Denny's attackers and the crowd, these four people got the severely injured trucker back into his vehicle and drove him to the hospital. Doctors there said that, had he arrived five minutes later, Reginald Denny would have died (Schroeder et al., 1995).

The actions of all of these individuals provide dramatic examples of **helping behavior,** which is defined as any act that is intended to benefit another person. Helping can range from picking up dropped packages to donating a kidney. Closely related to helping is **altruism,** an unselfish concern for another's welfare (Dovidio & Penner, in press). In the following sections we examine some of the reasons for helping and altruism, along with some of the conditions under which people are most likely to help others.

Why Do People Help?

The tendency to help others begins early, although at first it is not spontaneous. In most cultures, very young children generally help others only when they are asked to do so or are offered a reward (Grusec, 1991). Still, Carolyn Zahn-Waxler and her associates (1992) found that almost half of the two-year-olds they observed acted helpfully toward a friend or family member. As they grow older, children use helping behavior to gain social approval, and their efforts at helping become more elaborate. The role of social influence in the development of helping is seen as children follow examples set by people around them; their helping behaviors are shaped by the norms established by their families and the broader culture (Grusec & Goodnow, 1994). In addition, children are praised and given other rewards for helpfulness but scolded for selfishness.

Eventually children come to believe that being helpful is good and that they are good when they are helpful. By the late teens, people often help others even when no one is watching and no one will know that they did so (Cialdini, Baumann, & Kenrick, 1981). There are three major theories about why people help even when they cannot expect any external rewards for doing so.

Arousal: Cost-Reward Theory   One psychological model that attempts to explain why people help is called the **arousal: cost-reward theory** (Piliavin et al., 1981). This theory proposes that people find the sight of a victim distressing and anxiety-provoking and that this experience motivates them to do something to reduce the unpleasant arousal. Indeed, several studies have shown that all else being equal, the more physiologically aroused bystanders are, the more likely they are to help someone in an emergency (Dovidio et al., 1991; Schroeder et al., 1995). Before rushing to a victim's aid, however, the bystander will first evaluate two aspects of the situation: the costs associated with helping and the costs (to the bystander and the other person) of not helping. Whether or not the bystander actually helps depends on the outcome of this evaluation (Dovidio et al., 1991). If the costs of helping are low (as when helping someone pick up a dropped grocery bag) and the costs of not helping are high (as when the other person is physically unable to do this alone), the bystander will almost certainly help. However, if the costs of helping are high (as when helping to load a heavy air conditioner into a car) and the costs of not helping are low (as when the person is extremely strong and could probably manage the task alone), the bystander is unlikely to offer help. One of the strengths of this theory is that it is comprehensive enough to provide a conceptual framework for explaining a number of different research findings on the factors that affect helping. Let's consider some of these factors.

One factor is the *clarity of the need for help*, which has a major impact on whether people provide help (Dovidio et al., 1991). In one study, undergraduate students waiting alone in a campus building observed what appeared to be an accident involving a window washer. The man screamed as he and his ladder fell to the ground, then he began to clutch his ankle and groan in pain. All of the students looked out the window to see what had happened, but only 29 percent of them did anything to help. Other students experienced the same situation with one important difference: The man said he was hurt and needed help. In this case, more than 80 percent of the participants came to his aid (Yakimovich & Saltz, 1971). Why? Apparently, this one additional cue eliminated any ambiguity about whether the person needed help. This cue also raised the

Diffusion of Responsibility

Does the man on the sidewalk need help? The people nearby were probably not sure and might have assumed that, if so, someone else will assist him. Research on factors affecting helping and altruism suggests that if you need help, especially if a number of others are present, it is important not only to clearly ask for help, but to tell a specific onlooker to take specific action (for example, "You, in the yellow shirt, please call an ambulance!").

perceived costs to the victim of not offering help; as these costs become higher, helping becomes more likely.

The *presence of others* also has a strong influence on the tendency to help. Somewhat surprisingly, however, their presence tends to *inhibit* helping behavior. One of the most highly publicized examples of this phenomenon was the Kitty Genovese incident, which occurred on a New York City street in 1964. During a thirty-minute struggle, a man stabbed Ms. Genovese repeatedly, but none of the dozens of neighbors who witnessed the attack intervened or even called the police until it was too late to save her life. Journalists and social commentators expressed dismay about the apathy and callousness that seemed to exist among people who lived in New York and other big cities. But psychologists wondered whether something about the situation that night had deterred people from helping.

The numerous studies of helping behavior stimulated by this tragedy revealed a phenomenon that may explain the inaction of Ms. Genovese's neighbors. This phenomenon is known as the *bystander effect:* usually, as the number of people who witness an emergency increases, the likelihood that one of them will help decreases (Dovidio & Penner, in press). One explanation for why the presence of others often reduces helping is that each person thinks someone else will help the victim. That is, the presence of other bystanders allows each individual to experience a *diffusion of responsibility* for not taking action, which lowers the costs of not helping (Schroeder et al., 1995).

The degree to which the presence of other people will inhibit helping may depend on who those other people are. When they are strangers, perhaps poor communication inhibits helping. People often have difficulty speaking to strangers, particularly in an emergency, and without speaking, they have difficulty knowing what the others intend to do. According to this logic, if people are with friends rather than strangers, they should be less uncomfortable, more willing to discuss the problem, and thus more likely to help.

In one experiment designed to test this idea, a female experimenter left a research participant in a waiting room, either alone, with a friend, with a stranger, or with a stranger who was an assistant to the experimenter (Latané & Rodin, 1969). The experimenter then stepped behind a curtain into an office. For a few minutes, she could be heard opening and closing the drawers of her desk, shuffling papers, and so on. Then there was a loud crash, and she screamed, "Oh, my god . . . My foot, I . . . I can't move it. Oh, my ankle . . . I can't get this . . . thing off me." Then the participant heard her groan and cry.

Would the participant go behind the curtain to help? Once again, people were most likely to help if they were alone. When one other person was present, participants were more likely both to communicate with one another and to offer help if they were friends than if they were strangers. When the stranger was the experimenter's assistant (who had been instructed not to help), very few participants offered to help. Other studies have confirmed that bystanders' tendency to help increases when they know each other (Rutkowski, Gruder, & Romer, 1983).

Research suggests that the *personality of the helper* also plays a role in helping. Some people are just more likely to help than others. Consider, for example, the Christians who risked their lives to save Jews from the Nazi Holocaust. Samuel and Pearl Oliner (1988) interviewed more than 200 of these rescuers and compared their personalities with those of people who had a chance to save Jews but did not do so. The rescuers were found to have more empathy (the ability to understand or experience another's emotional state) (Davis, 1994), more concern about others, a greater sense of responsibility for their own actions, and a greater sense of self-efficacy (confidence in the success of their efforts, as discussed in Chapter 14). Louis Penner and his associates (Penner & Finkelstein, 1998; Penner et al., 1995) have found that these kinds of personality traits predict a broad spectrum of helping behaviors, ranging from the speed with which bystanders intervene in an emergency to the amount of time volunteers spend helping someone with AIDS. Consistent with the arousal: cost-reward theory, these personality characteristics are also correlated with people's estimates of the costs of helping and not helping. For example, empathic individuals usually estimate the costs of not helping as high, and people with a sense of self-efficacy usually rate the costs of helping as low (Penner et al., 1995). These patterns of cost estimation may partially explain why such people tend to be especially helpful.

Other helping-related phenomena cannot be easily explained by the arousal: cost-reward theory. One of these is the impact of *environmental factors* on helping. Research conducted in several countries has revealed, for example, that people in urban areas are generally less helpful than those in rural areas (Aronson, Wilson, & Akert, 1999). Why? It is probably not the simple fact of living in a city but rather the stressors one finds there that tend to make some urban people less helpful. For example, a study conducted in thirty-six North American cities found that people's tendency to help was related more strongly to *population density* (the number of people per square mile) in a community than to the overall size of the city in which people lived (Levine et al., 1994). The higher the density, the less likely people were to help others. Similar results have been found in countries such as the United Kingdom, Saudi Arabia, and Sudan (Hedge & Yousif, 1992; Yousif & Korte, 1995). Two explanations have been suggested for this association between environmental stress and reduced likelihood of helping. The first is that stressful environments create bad moods—and, generally speaking, people in bad moods are less likely to help (Salovey, Mayer, & Rosenhan, 1991). A second possibility is that noise, crowding, and other urban stressors create too much stimulation. To reduce this excessive stimulation, people may pay less attention to their surroundings, including to individuals who need help.

It is also difficult for the arousal: cost-reward theory to predict what bystanders will do when the cost of helping and the cost of not helping are *both* high. In these instances helping (or not helping) may depend on several situational factors and, sometimes, on the personality of the potential helper. There may also be circumstances in which cost considerations may not be the major cause of a decision to help or not help. A second approach to helping considers some of these circumstances.

Empathy-Altruism Theory This second approach is embodied in **empathy-altruism theory,** which maintains that people are more likely to engage in altruistic, or unselfish, helping—even when the cost of helping is high—if they feel empathy toward the person in need (Batson, 1998). In one experiment illustrating this phenomenon, students listened to a recording of an interview with a female student; the interview was not real, but the participants believed that it was. The student told the interviewer that her parents had been killed in an automobile accident, that they had no life insurance, and that she was now faced with the task of finishing college while taking care of a younger brother and sister. She said that these financial burdens might force her to quit school or give up her siblings for adoption. Before listening to the woman's story, half the participants were given other information about her that was designed to promote strong empathy. Later, all the participants were asked to help the woman raise money for herself and her siblings (Batson et al., 1997). The critical question was whether the participants who heard the empathy-promoting information would help more than those who did not. Consistent with empathy-altruism theory, participants in the empathy condition did help more than those in the nonempathy condition (see Figure 18.8).

Were those who offered help in this experiment being utterly altruistic, or could there be a different reason for their actions? This is a hotly debated question. Some researchers dispute Batson's claim that his study illustrated truly altruistic helping and suggest instead that people help in such situations for more selfish reasons, such as relieving the distress they experienced after hearing of the woman's problems (Cialdini et al., 1997). Although the final verdict on this question is not yet in, the evidence appears to support Batson's contention that empathizing with another person can sometimes lead to unselfish helping (Dovidio, Allen, & Schroeder, 1990).

Evolutionary Theory A third approach to explaining helping is based on an evolutionary approach to social psychology, which views many human social behaviors as echoes of actions that contributed to the survival of our prehistoric ancestors (Buss &

FIGURE 18.8

The Effect of Empathy on Helping

After hearing a staged interview with a woman who supposedly needed to raise money for her family, participants in this experiment were asked to help her. Those who empathized with the woman were much more likely to offer to help her than those who did not empathize. These results are consistent with the empathy-altruism theory of helping.

Source: Adapted from Batson et al. (1997).

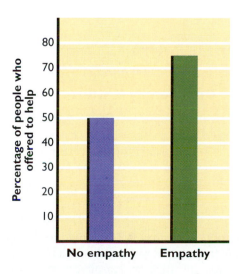

Family Ties

Research indicates that people are more likely to donate organs to family members than to strangers. This pattern may reflect greater attachment or a stronger sense of social obligation to relatives than to others, but psychologists who take an evolutionary approach to helping suggest that when, as in the case of these sisters, one family member donates a kidney to save the life of another, the donor is helping to ensure the survival of the genes he or she shares with the recipient.

Kenrick, 1998). At first glance, it might not seem reasonable to apply evolutionary theory to helping and altruism, because helping others at the risk of one's own well-being does not appear adaptive. If we die while trying to save others, it will be their genes, not ours, that will survive. Indeed, according to Darwin's concept of the "survival of the fittest," helpers—and their genes—should have disappeared long ago. Contemporary evolutionary theorists suggest, however, that Darwin's thinking about natural selection focused too much on the survival of the fittest *individuals* and not enough on the survival of their genes *in others.* Thus, survival of the fittest has been replaced by the concept of *inclusive fitness,* the survival of one's genes in future generations (Hamilton, 1964). Because we share genes with our relatives, helping or even dying for a cousin, a sibling, or, above all, our own child potentially increases the likelihood that at least some of our genetic characteristics will be passed on to the next generation through the beneficiary's future reproduction (Batson, 1998). Thus, *kin selection*—helping a relative to survive—may produce genetic benefits for the helper.

There is considerable evidence that kin selection occurs among birds, squirrels, and other animals. The more closely the animals are related, the more likely they are to risk their lives for one another. Studies in a wide variety of cultures show the same pattern of helping among humans (Essock-Vitale & McGuire, 1985). For example, people in the United States are three times as likely to donate a kidney to a relative as to a non-relative (Borgida, Conner, & Monteufel, 1992).

FOCUS ON RESEARCH METHODS

Does Family Matter?

In and of themselves, the data on kidney donations do not confirm evolutionary theories of helping and altruism. The tendency to donate to relatives could also be due to the effects of empathy toward more familiar people, pressure from family members, or other social influence processes. To control for the effects of these confounding variables, some researchers have turned to the laboratory to study the role of evolutionary forces in helping behavior.

■ What was the researchers' question?

Eugene Burnstein, Christian Crandell, and Shinobu Kitayama (1994) wanted to know whether people faced with a choice of whose life they should save will act in a manner consistent with the concept of kin selection. These investigators reasoned that if kin selection does affect helping, the more genetically related two people are—the more genes they share in common—the more inclined they should be to save one another's life. However, if the underlying reason for this kind of helping is actually to preserve one's genes in others, the tendency to save a close relative should be lessened if that relative is unlikely to produce offspring and thereby help preserve the helper's genes.

■ How did the researchers answer this question?

The most direct way to test the accuracy of these predictions would be to put people's lives in danger and then observe which (if any) of their relatives try to save them. But an experiment of this nature would be unthinkable, so instead, Burnstein and his colleagues used a simulation, or *analogue*, methodology. Specifically, they asked people to imagine a series of situations and then to say how they would respond if the situation were real.

The participants in this analogue experiment were 110 men and 48 women enrolled at universities in Japan and the United States. The first independent variable was the kind of help that was needed. On the basis of random assignment, some participants were asked to imagine life-or-death situations in which there was time to save only one of three people who were asleep in separate rooms of a burning house. The remaining participants were asked to imagine everyday situations in which they had time to help only one of three people who each needed a small favor. The other independent variables were the characteristics of the people needing help in each situation—their age, sex, physical health, and genetic relatedness to the potential helper. The dependent variable was the participants' choice of which person they would help first.

■ What did the researchers find?

In line with evolutionary theory, the participants were more than twice as likely to say they would save the life of a close relative than that of an unrelated friend. Also, the more closely related the endangered people were to the potential helpers, the more likely they were to be saved. Did these results occur simply because people tend to help closer relatives in any situation? Probably not; when the participants imagined situations in which only small favors were involved, they were only slightly more likely to help a close relative than a distant one.

The other major prediction of evolutionary theory was supported as well. Several different findings indicated that even close relatives might not be saved if they are unlikely to produce offspring. For example, the participants were more willing to do a small favor for a seventy-five-year-old relative than for a ten- or eighteen-year-old relative, but they were much more likely to save the lives of the younger relatives. Similarly, they were more likely to do the favor for a sick relative than for a healthy one; but in a life-or-death situation, they chose to save the healthy relative more often than the sick one (see Figure 18.9). Finally, the participants were more likely to save the life of a female relative than that of a male relative, unless the female was past childbearing age. There were no substantial differences between the responses of students in the United States and those in Japan.

■ What do the results mean?

The results of this experiment generally support the concept of kin selection, which says that we are inclined to help close relatives because in the long run it helps us. Specifically, if we save the life of a relative and that relative is able to produce offspring, we have really helped ourselves because more of our genes will be represented in the next generation. Evolutionary psychologists see these results as providing confirmation that kin selection affects the decisions people make about saving the life of another person, and thus that there is an evolutionary basis for helping.

■ What do we still need to know?

The findings reported by Burnstein and his colleagues are consistent with the predictions of evolutionary theory, but they must be interpreted with caution and in light of

---

FIGURE 18.9

Kin Selection and Helping

In this analogue experiment, students said they would be more likely to save the life of a healthy relative than that of a sick one, but more likely to do a favor for the sick relative. Results like these have been cited in support of the evolutionary approach to helping behavior (Burnstein, Crandell, & Kitayama, 1994).

Source: Burnstein, Crandell, & Kitayama, 1994.

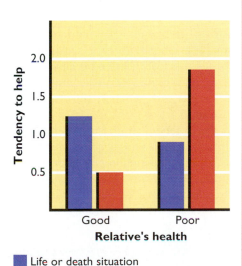

in review

THEORIES OF HELPING BEHAVIORS

Theory	Basic Premise	Important Variables
Arousal: cost-reward	People help in order to reduce the unpleasant arousal caused by another person's distress. They attempt to minimize the costs of doing this.	Factors that affect the costs of helping and of not helping.
Empathy-altruism	People sometimes help for utterly altruistic reasons. They are motivated by a desire to increase another person's well-being.	The amount of empathy that one person feels for another.
Evolutionary	People help relatives because it increases the chances that the helper's genes will survive in future generations.	The biological relationship between the helper and the recipient of help.

the methods that were used to obtain them. Analogue studies give clues to behavior—and allow experimental control—in situations that approximate, but may not precisely duplicate, those outside the laboratory. They tend to be used when it would be unethical or impractical to expose people to "the real thing." The more closely the analogue approximates the natural situation, the more confident we can be that conclusions drawn about behavior observed in the laboratory will apply, or generalize, to the world beyond the laboratory.

In an analogue experiment such as this, we might question how closely the natural situation was approximated. For one thing, the participants predicted what their responses would be in hypothetical situations. Those responses might be different if the students were actually in the situations described. Thus, the analogue methodology in this study allowed the researchers to show that kin selection *could* play a role in human helping behavior; they did not demonstrate that it *did*.

The study also failed to identify the mechanisms whereby biological tendencies are translated into thoughts that lead to helpful actions (Batson, 1998). That is, it is highly unlikely that the participants were thinking, "I'll help a close relative because it will preserve my genes." What *were* they thinking? We do not yet know. More generally, psychologists have been unable to pin down the specific processes whereby the social tendencies we inherit from our ancestors might cause us to act or think in a certain way.

Finally, even if evolutionary theory explains some general human tendencies to help, it cannot predict the behavior of specific individuals in specific situations (Batson, 1998). Like all behavior, helping and altruism depend on the interplay of many genetic and environmental factors—including interactions between particular people and particular situations. (See "In Review: Theories of Helping Behaviors" for a summary of the major reasons why people help and the conditions under which they are most likely to do so.)

COOPERATION, COMPETITION, AND CONFLICT

When people interact with one another while attempting to reach some goal, three kinds of behavior can result: cooperation, competition, or conflict. **Cooperation** is any type of behavior in which people work together to attain a goal. For example, several law students might form a study group to help one another pass a difficult exam. People can also engage in **competition,** trying to attain a goal for themselves while denying that goal to others. The same students might later compete with one another for a single job opening at a prestigious law firm. Finally, **conflict** results when one person or group believes that another stands in the way of achieving the goal. When the students become attorneys and represent opposing parties in a legal dispute, they will be in conflict. One way in which psychologists have learned about all three of these behaviors is by studying social dilemmas (Gifford & Hine, 1997b).

Social Dilemmas

Social dilemmas are situations in which an action that produces rewards for one individual will, if adopted by all others, produce negative consequences for everyone. For instance, it might be in a factory owner's self-interest to save the costs of pollution-control; but if all factories do the same, the air and water will eventually become poisonous for everyone. One particular kind of social dilemma that psychologists have studied extensively is called the two-person "prisoner's dilemma" (Pruitt, 1998).

The Prisoner's Dilemma   The **prisoner's dilemma** is based on a scenario in which two people are separated immediately after being arrested for a serious crime (Lord, 1997). The district attorney believes they are guilty but does not have the evidence to convict them. Each prisoner can either confess or not. If they both refuse to confess, each will be convicted of a minor offense and will be jailed for one year. If they both confess, the district attorney will recommend a five-year sentence. However, if one prisoner remains silent and one confesses, the district attorney will allow the confessing prisoner to go free, whereas the other will serve the maximum ten-year sentence.

Each prisoner faces a dilemma. Figure 18.10(A) outlines the possible outcomes. Obviously, the strategy that will guarantee the best *mutual* outcome—short sentences for both prisoners—is cooperation: Both should remain silent. But the prisoner who remains silent runs the risk of receiving a long sentence if the other prisoner confesses, and the prisoner who confesses has the chance of gaining individually if the other prisoner does not talk. Thus, each prisoner has an incentive to compete for freedom by confessing. But if they *both* compete and confess, each will end up going to jail for longer than if nothing was said.

In the typical prisoner's dilemma experiment, two people sit at separate control panels. Each of them has a red button and a black button, one of which is to be pushed on each of many trials. Pressing the black button is a cooperative response; pressing the red button is a competitive response. For example, if, on a given trial, both participants press their black buttons, each wins five dollars. If both press the red button, they only earn one dollar. However, if one player presses the red button and the other presses the black button, the one who pressed the red button will win ten dollars and the other will win nothing.

Figure 18.10(B) shows the possible outcomes for each trial. Over the course of the experiment, the combined winnings of the players are greatest if each presses the black button—that is, if they cooperate. By pressing the black button, however, a player becomes open to exploitation, because on any trial the other might press the red button and take all the winnings. Indeed, each player stands to benefit the most individually by pressing the red button occasionally. Thus, the prisoner's dilemma is what psychologists call a *mixed-motive conflict*—there are good reasons to cooperate and also good reasons to compete.

What happens when people play this game? Overall, there is a strong tendency to respond competitively; people find it difficult to resist the competitive choice on any

FIGURE 18.10

The Prisoner's Dilemma

In the prisoner's dilemma, mutual cooperation benefits each person and mutual competition is harmful to both, but one party can exploit the cooperativeness of the other. These diagrams show the potential payoffs for prisoners—and research participants.

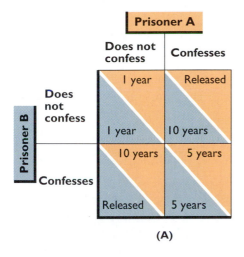

(A)

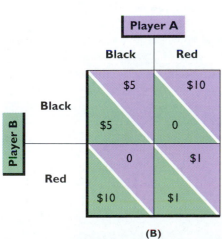

(B)

given trial (Komorita & Parks, 1995). This choice wins them more money on that trial, but in the long run they gain less than they would have gained through cooperation.

If acting competitively leads to smaller rewards in the long run, why do people persist in competing? There seem to be two reasons (Komorita, 1984). First, winning more than an opponent seems to be rewarding in itself. In the prisoner's dilemma game, many people want to outscore an opponent even if the result is that they win less money overall. Second, and more important, once several competitive responses are made, the competition seems to feed on itself (Insko et al., 1990). Each person becomes distrustful of the other, and cooperation becomes increasingly difficult. The more competitive one person acts, the more competitive the other becomes (McClintock & Liebrand, 1988).

Resource Dilemmas   In recent years, psychologists interested in cooperation, competition, and conflict have concentrated on another kind of social dilemma, called a resource dilemma (Pruitt, 1998). In a **resource dilemma,** people share some common resource, thus creating inherent conflicts between the interests of the individual and those of the group and also between people's short-term and long-term interests (Schroeder, 1995). There are two kinds of resource dilemmas. In the *commons dilemma,* people have to decide how much to take from a common resource; in the *public goods dilemma,* people must decide how much to contribute to a common resource. As an example of the commons dilemma, consider a situation in which farmers all draw water for their crops from the same lake. Each individual farmer would benefit greatly from unrestricted use of the water, but if all the farmers do the same, the water will soon be gone. Tax laws provide an example of the public goods dilemma. In the short run, you would benefit greatly if you did not pay taxes, but if everyone failed to pay, no one would have police and fire protection, highway repairs, or other necessary government services. How can people facing such dilemmas be prompted to cooperate?

Fostering Cooperation

Communication can reduce people's tendency to act competitively (Pruitt, 1998). Unfortunately, however, not all communication increases cooperation, just as not all contact between ethnic groups reduces prejudice. If the communication takes the form of a threat, people apparently interpret the threat itself as a competitive response and are likely to respond competitively (Gifford & Hine, 1997b). Furthermore, the com-

A Social Dilemma

If everyone in North America used public transportation or commuted in car pools, and if they drove small cars with fuel-efficient engines that minimize exhaust emissions, the problems of air pollution, traffic and parking, and highway construction and maintenance would be greatly reduced. However, most people like to drive to work alone, at the wheel of a car that is fun to drive and be seen in, but that may guzzle gas and take up a lot of space. In short, the choice of daily transportation reflects a social dilemma; what is good for the individual in the short run is bad for society in the long run.

"There's quite a power struggle going on."

munication must be relevant. In one social dilemma study, cooperation increased only when people spoke openly about the dilemma and how they would be rewarded for various responses. Praising each other for past cooperation was most beneficial (Orbell, van de Kragt, & Dawes, 1988).

People can also communicate implicitly through the strategy they use. In the prisoner's dilemma, the most effective strategy for producing long-term cooperation is to use basic learning principles and play *tit-for-tat*, rewarding cooperative responses with cooperation and punishing exploitation by generating exploitative strategies of one's own. Cooperating after a cooperative response and competing after a competitive response produces a high degree of cooperation over time (Nowak, May, & Sigmund, 1995). Apparently, the players learn that the only way to come out ahead is to cooperate. There is even evidence from computer simulation studies that societies whose members use cooperative strategies with each other are more likely to survive and prosper than are those whose members act competitively (Nowak, May, & Sigmund, 1995).

Interpersonal Conflict

In social dilemmas and other situations in which people are *interdependent*—that is, when what one person does always affects the other—cooperation usually leads to the best outcomes for everyone. This doesn't mean, however, that cooperation always occurs. One might think that people from collectivist cultures, in which cooperation is emphasized, would be less likely to act selfishly in a social dilemma. This may be true in general, but conflict in such situations does appear in all cultures (Smith & Bond, 1999). Conflict is especially likely when people are involved in a **zero-sum game.** These are situations in which what one person gains is subtracted from the other person's resources; the sum of the gains and losses is zero. Election campaigns, lawsuits over a deceased relative's estate, and competition between children for a coveted toy are all examples of zero-sum games.

There are four major causes of interpersonal conflict (Baron & Byrne, 1994). One is competition for scarce resources. If a business has only five offices with windows, for example, employees will compete for them. Some managers report spending as much as 20 percent of their time dealing with interpersonal conflicts based on such competition (Thomas & Schmidt, 1976).

A second major cause of interpersonal conflict is revenge. People reciprocate not only positive actions but also negative ones. Some people who feel exploited or deprived or otherwise aggrieved spend months, even years, plotting ways of getting back at those they hold responsible (Baron & Richardson, 1994).

Interpersonal conflict may also arise because people attribute unfriendly or selfish motives to others (Gifford & Hine, 1997a). For example, if people who must share some resource, such as copy paper, attribute a shortage of that resource to each other's selfishness rather than to factors over which they have no control, such as an inadequate supply, conflict is likely to emerge (Samuelson & Messick, 1995). Sometimes these attributions are accurate, but often conflict results from the kinds of attributional errors discussed in Chapter 17.

Attributional errors are related to a final source of interpersonal conflict: faulty communication. A comment intended as a compliment is sometimes interpreted as a snide remark; constructive criticism is sometimes perceived as a personal attack. Such miscommunication may start a cycle of increasingly provocative actions, in which each person believes the other is being aggressive and unfair (Pruitt & Carnevale, 1993).

Managing Conflict Interpersonal conflict can damage relationships between people and impair the effectiveness of organizations, but it can also lead to beneficial changes. Industrial-organizational psychologists have found that often it is much better to manage conflict effectively than to try to eliminate it. The most common way of managing organizational conflict is through *bargaining.* Each side—labor and management, for example—produces a series of offers and counteroffers until a solution that is acceptable to both emerges. At its best, bargaining can produce a win-win situation in which each side receives what is most important and gives up what is less important (Carnevale & Pruitt, 1992).

If bargaining fails, *third-party interventions* may be useful. Like a therapist working with a couple, an outside mediator can often help the two sides focus on important issues, defuse emotions, clarify positions and proposals, and make suggestions that allow each side to compromise without losing face (Pruitt, 1998).

Other techniques for managing conflict, especially conflict over resources, involve the introduction of *superordinate goals* or a *superordinate identity* (Williams, Jackson, & Karau, 1995). For example, if people who are competing for scarce resources can be made to feel that they are all part of the same group and share the same goals, they will act less selfishly and manage the limited resources more efficiently.

In short, although interpersonal conflict can be harmful if left unchecked, it can also be managed in a way that benefits the group. Much as psychotherapy can help people resolve personal conflict in a way that leads to growth, interpersonal conflict within an organization can be handled in a way that leads to innovations, increased loyalty and motivation, and other valuable changes.

GROUP PROCESSES

Although Western industrialized cultures tend to emphasize individuals over groups, the fact remains that most important governmental and business decisions in those cultures and elsewhere are made by groups, not individuals (Cannon-Bowers & Salas, 1998). Sometimes group decisions are effective; at other times they are disastrous. When Scott O'Grady, a U.S. fighter pilot, was shot down over Bosnia in 1995, a daring and successful rescue was organized by a group of senior military personnel. But a few years earlier, in Somalia, other senior officers made decisions that turned the attempted rescue of trapped U.S. soldiers into a military debacle in which several rescuers lost their lives. In Chapter 8, on cognition and language, we describe some of the factors that influence the nature and quality of group decisions. Here, we consider some of the social psychological processes that often occur in groups to alter the behavior of their members and the quality of their collective efforts.

Group Leadership

A good leader can help a group pursue its goals; a poor one can impede a group's functioning. What makes a good leader? Early research suggested that the personalities of good and bad leaders were about the same, but we now know that certain personality traits often distinguish effective from ineffective leaders. For example, using tests similar to those that measure the big-five traits described in Chapter 14, Robert Hogan and his colleagues (1994) found that effective leaders tend to score high on dominance, emotional stability, agreeableness, and conscientiousness. Other researchers have found that, in general, effective leaders are intelligent, success-oriented, and flexible (Levine & Moreland, 1998).

Having particular personality traits does not guarantee good leadership ability, however. People who are effective leaders in one situation may be ineffective in another (Yukl & Van Fleet, 1992). The reason is that effective leadership also depends on the characteristics of the group members, the task at hand, and, most important, the interaction between these factors and the leader's style.

Two main styles of leadership have been identified. **Task-oriented leaders** provide close supervision, lead by giving directives, and generally discourage group discussion (Yukl & Van Fleet, 1992). Their style may not endear them to group members. In contrast, **person-oriented leaders** provide loose supervision, ask for group members' ideas, and are generally concerned with subordinates' feelings. They are usually well liked by the group, even when they must reprimand someone (Boyatzis, 1982).

Research on leadership effectiveness and gender provides one explanation as to why one leadership style is not invariably better than another. According to Alice Eagly and her associates, men and women in Western cultures tend to have different leadership

A Seasoned Leader

Corporate executives such as Katherine Graham, publisher of the *Washington Post,* bring impressive leadership skills to the running of their complex organizations. To help future leaders hone their skills, management training programs focus on the importance of leader-situation interactions; they also alert women and members of ethnic minorities to the unique pressures they are likely to face on the job (Morrison & Von Glinow, 1990).

styles (Eagly & Johnson, 1990; Eagly, Karau, & Makhijani, 1995). Men tend to be more task-oriented; women, more person-oriented. One interpretation of these differences is that the gender-role learning processes described in Chapter 12 lead men and women to "specialize" in different leadership behaviors.

Overall, men and women are equally capable leaders, but men tend to be more effective when success requires a more task-oriented leader, and women tend to be more effective when success requires a more person-oriented leader. In other words, people of each gender tend to be most effective when they are acting in a manner consistent with gender-role traditions (Eagly & Karau, 1991; Eagly, Karau, & Makhijani, 1995). This may be one reason some people do not like female leaders who act in a "masculine" manner or occupy leadership positions traditionally held by men (Eagly, Makhijani, & Klonsky, 1992). In certain circumstances, such responses create bias against women leaders, particularly among male members of the groups they lead (Eagly, Makhijani, & Klonsky, 1992).

Most contemporary theories of leadership are known as *contingency* theories (Levine & Moreland, 1998) because they suggest that leadership effectiveness is contingent, or depends, on factors such as the leader's relations with group members and the nature of the group's task. They note, for example, that task-oriented leaders tend to be most effective when the group is working under time pressure, when the task is unstructured, and when circumstances make it unclear as to what needs to be done first and how the duties should be divided. People stranded in an elevator in a burning building, for example, need a task-oriented leader. Conversely, person-oriented leaders tend to be most effective when the task is structured and there are no severe time limitations (Chemers, 1987). These people would be particularly successful, for example, in managing an office in which the workers know their jobs well.

Groupthink

The emphasis on group decisions in most large organizations is based on the belief that a group of people working together will make better decisions than will individuals working alone. As noted in Chapter 8, this belief is generally correct; yet, under certain circumstances, groups have been known to make amazingly bad decisions (Levine & Moreland, 1995). Consider two examples. First, in the late 1930s, U.S. government leaders decided not to take special precautions to defend Pearl Harbor. The Japanese

The Dangers of Groupthink

Groupthink appeared to influence decisions by both sides during the 1993 standoff between federal agents and members of David Koresh's Branch Davidians near Waco, Texas. After fifty-one days, the agents saw no alternative but to batter holes in the compound and pump in tear gas; Koresh and his followers decided to set their compound afire. All but nine of nearly one hundred cult members died in the inferno, including twenty-five children.

LINKAGES

How does stress affect group decision making? (a link to Health, Stress, and Coping)

attack there on December 7, 1941, killed 2,500 people. Second, in 1986, National Aeronautics and Space Administration (NASA) officials ignored engineers' warnings about the effects of cold weather and decided to launch the space shuttle *Challenger*. The spacecraft exploded seventy-three seconds after liftoff, killing all aboard. After analyzing these and other disastrous governmental decisions, Irving Janis (1989) proposed that they can be attributed to a phenomenon called **groupthink.** Groupthink occurs, he said, when group members are unable to realistically evaluate the options available to them or to fully consider the potential negative consequences of a contemplated decision.

Groupthink is particularly likely when three conditions exist: (1) The group is isolated from outside influences (Turner et al., 1992); (2) the group is working under time pressure or other intense stressors (Worchel & Shackelford, 1991); and (3) the leader is not impartial. This last condition appeared to play a crucial role in President Kennedy's decision to support a disastrously unsuccessful invasion of Cuba by anti-Castro Cubans in 1961. Before the final decision was made, several advisers were told that Kennedy had made up his mind and that it was time to "close ranks with the president." This situation created enormous pressure for conformity (McCauley, 1989).

When these three conditions exist, groups tend to become very close-minded and to rationalize their decision as the only reasonable one. They dismiss other options and quickly suppress any dissenting voices. As a result, the group becomes more and more certain that its decision cannot possibly be wrong. Although some researchers have questioned the prevalence and dangers of groupthink (Aldag & Fuller, 1993), most researchers agree that it does occur, at least under conditions similar to those originally identified by Janis (Baron, Kerr, & Miller, 1992).

Some psychologists have worked on developing techniques to help groups avoid groupthink. One is to designate someone to play "devil's advocate," constantly challenging the group's emerging consensus and offering alternatives (Janis, 1985; Risen, 1998). Another is to encourage the expression of diverse opinions by making them anonymous. The group members might sit at separate computers and type out all the options that occur to them. Each option is displayed for all to see on an electronic mail system that protects the sender's identity; the group then discusses the options through e-mail without knowing who is saying what. Research on this procedure suggests that it is effective in stimulating logical debate and making people less inhibited about disagreeing with the group (O'Brien, 1991).

LINKAGES

As noted in Chapter 1, all of psychology's many subfields are related to one another. Our discussion of how the presence of other people affects a person's motivation to perform illustrates just one way in which the topic of this chapter, social influence, is linked to the subfield of motivation and emotion (Chapter 11). The linkage diagram shows ties to other subfields as well, and there are many more ties throughout the book. Looking for linkages among subfields will help you see how they fit together and better appreciate the big picture that is psychology.

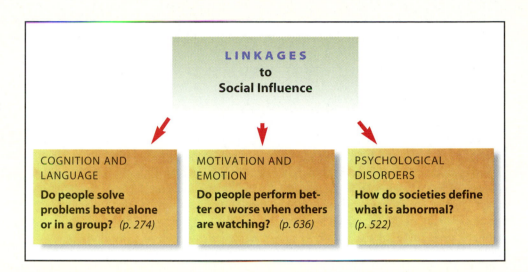

LINKAGES to Social Influence

COGNITION AND LANGUAGE	MOTIVATION AND EMOTION	PSYCHOLOGICAL DISORDERS
Do people solve problems better alone or in a group? *(p. 274)*	**Do people perform better or worse when others are watching?** *(p. 636)*	**How do societies define what is abnormal?** *(p. 522)*

SUMMARY

SOCIAL INFLUENCE

Norms establish the rules for what should and should not be done in a particular situation. Descriptive norms indicate what most other people do and create pressure to do the same. Injunctive norms provide specific information about what others approve or disapprove. *Deindividuation* is a psychological state in which people temporarily lose their individuality, their normal inhibitions are relaxed, and they may perform aggressive or illegal acts that they would not do otherwise.

CONFORMITY AND COMPLIANCE

When behavior or beliefs change as the result of unspoken or implicit group pressure, *conformity* has occurred; when the change is the result of a request, *compliance* has occurred.

The Role of Norms

People tend to follow the normative responses of others, and groups create norms when none already exist.

Why Do People Conform?

People sometimes exhibit public conformity without private acceptance; at other times, the responses of others have a genuine impact on private beliefs. People conform because they want to be right, because they want to be liked, and because they tend to be rewarded for doing so.

When Do People Conform?

People are most likely to conform when the situation is ambiguous, as well as when others in the group are in unanimous agree-ment. Up to a point, conformity usually increases as the number of people holding the majority view grows larger. Persistent and unanimous *minority influence* can also produce some conformity.

Inducing Compliance

Effective strategies for inducing compliance include the foot-in-the-door technique, the door-in-the-face procedure, and the low-ball approach.

OBEDIENCE

Obedience involves complying with an explicit demand, typically from an authority figure. Research by Stanley Milgram indicates that levels of obedience are high even when obeying an authority appears to result in pain and suffering for another person.

Factors Affecting Obedience

Obedience declines when the status of the authority figure declines, as well as when others are observed to disobey. Some people may be more likely to obey orders than others.

Evaluating Milgram's Studies

Because participants in these studies experienced considerable stress, the experiments have been questioned on ethical grounds. Nevertheless, Milgram's research showed that people do not have to be disordered to inflict pain on others.

AGGRESSION

Aggression is an act intended to harm another person.

Why Are People Aggressive?

Freud saw aggression as due partly to self-destructive instincts. More recent theories attribute aggressive tendencies to genetic factors, brain dysfunctions, and hormonal influences. Learning is also important; people learn to display aggression by watching others and by being rewarded for aggressive behavior. There are wide cultural differences in the incidence of aggression.

When Are People Aggressive?

A variety of emotional factors plays a role in aggression. The *frustration-aggression hypothesis* suggests that frustration can lead to aggression, particularly if cues that invite or promote aggression are present. Recent research indicates that stress and negative feelings play a major role in aggression. Arousal from sources unrelated to aggression, such as exercise, can also make aggressive responses more likely, especially if aggression is already a dominant response in that situation. Research in *environmental psychology* suggests that factors such as high temperature, air pollution, noise, and crowding increase the likelihood of aggressive behavior, particularly among people who are already angry.

ALTRUISM AND HELPING BEHAVIOR

Human behavior is also characterized by *helping behavior and altruism.*

Why Do People Help?

There are three major theories of why people help others. According to the *arousal: cost-reward theory,* people help in order to reduce the unpleasant arousal they experience when others are in distress. Their specific reaction to a suffering person depends on the costs associated with helping or not helping. Helping behavior is most likely when the costs of helping are low and the costs of not helping are high. Perceptions of cost are affected by the clarity of the need for help, diffusion of responsibility, and personality traits. Environmental factors also affect willingness to help. *Empathy-altruism theory* suggests that helping can be truly unselfish if the helper feels empathy for the person in need. Evolutionary theory suggests that humans have an innate tendency to help others, especially relatives, because doing so increases the likelihood that family genes will survive.

COOPERATION, COMPETITION, AND CONFLICT

Cooperation is behavior in which people work together to attain a goal; *competition* exists when individuals try to attain a goal while denying that goal to others; *conflict* occurs when a person or group believes that someone stands in the way of something of value.

Social Dilemmas

In *social dilemmas,* selfish behavior that benefits individuals in the short run may spell disaster for an entire group in the long run. Two kinds of social dilemmas are the *prisoner's dilemma* and *resource dilemmas.* When given a choice between cooperation and competition in a social dilemma, people often compete with one another. This is true even though they may receive fewer rewards for competing than for cooperating.

Fostering Cooperation

Communication between competing parties can increase cooperation, especially if the communication is nonthreatening and relevant to the situation. One of the most effective strategies for producing long-term cooperation in a prisoner's dilemma is playing tit-for-tat—that is, rewarding cooperative responses with cooperation and punishing exploitation by generating exploitative strategies of one's own.

Interpersonal Conflict

In *zero-sum games,* competition is almost inevitable because there can be only one winner. Competition for scarce resources, revenge, attribution of another's behavior to unfriendly motives, and faulty communication are frequent sources of interpersonal conflict. Bargaining, third-party interventions, and reminders about broader goals and shared identity are helpful procedures for managing conflict.

GROUP PROCESSES

Many of the world's most important decisions are made by groups.

Group Leadership

No single personality type or behavioral style always results in good leadership. *Task-oriented leaders* are most effective when the task is unstructured and the group is working under time pressure. *Person-oriented leaders* are most effective when the task is structured and there are no severe time limitations. Contingency theories of leadership effectiveness propose that success depends on the extent to which a leader's style fits the characteristics of the group and its tasks.

Groupthink

The pattern of thinking called *groupthink* is most likely to occur when a group is isolated from outside forces, when it lacks a truly impartial leader, and when its decisions are made under stress.

KEY TERMS

aggression (647)

altruism (654)

arousal: cost-reward theory (655)

competition (661)

compliance (637)

conflict (661)

conformity (637)

cooperation (661)

deindividuation (635)

empathy-altruism theory (657)

environmental psychology (652)

frustration-aggression hypothesis (649)

groupthink (666)

helping behavior (654)

minority influence (640)

norms (634)

obedience (642)

person-oriented leaders (664)

prisoner's dilemma (661)

resource dilemma (662)

social dilemmas (661)

social facilitation (636)

social impairment (636)

social loafing (636)

task-oriented leaders (664)

zero-sum game (663)

Behavioral Genetics

Think about some trait on which you are well above or well below average. Perhaps it relates to your skill at sports, languages, or music, or even to some aspect of your personality. Have you ever wondered what made you the way you are? If you are shy, for example, it is easy to think of possible environmental explanations. Perhaps you are shy because, as a child, you had few opportunities to meet new children or because you had embarrassing or unpleasant experiences when you did meet them. Maybe your parents are shy and thus served as the role models you imitated. Such environmental explanations are certainly reasonable, but it is also possible that you *inherited* a tendency toward shyness from your parents.

Issues such as this are addressed by researchers in the field of *behavioral genetics,* the study of how genes affect behavior (see Chapter 2). These researchers have developed methods to explore the genetic as well as the environmental origins of behavioral differences among people. The results of behavioral genetics research make it clear that heredity has a surprisingly strong influence, not just on shyness but on personality more generally (Chapter 14), on mental abilities (Chapter 10), on psychological disorders (Chapter 15), and on many other aspects of human behavior and mental processes. However, behavioral genetics is just as much the study of environment as of genetics. In the process of trying to separate genetic from environmental factors, researchers have made several important discoveries about the impact of the environment.

In this appendix, we discuss behavioral genetics in more detail than in Chapter 2. We begin with a review of the biochemical mechanisms underlying genetics and heredity. We then offer a brief history of genetic research in psychology, followed by a discussion of what research on genetic influences can, and cannot, tell us about the origins of human differences. Finally, we describe some findings from behavioral genetics research that illuminate several important aspects of human behavior and mental processes.

THE BIOLOGY OF GENETICS AND HEREDITY

What does it mean to say that someone has genetically inherited some physical feature or behavioral trait? The answer lies in **genetics,** the biology of inheritance. The story begins with the chemistry of the human body and with the chromosomes contained within each of its cells. Most human cells contain forty-six chromosomes, arranged in twenty-three matching pairs. These **chromosomes** are long, thin structures that are made up of thousands of genes. **Genes** are the biochemical units of heredity that govern the development of an individual by controlling the synthesis of protein. They are composed of **deoxyribonucleic acid (DNA)**—strands of sugar, phosphate, and nitrogen-containing molecules twisted around each other in a double spiral (see Figure 1). It is the particular order in which the nitrogen-containing molecules are arranged in the DNA that determines, through the production of *ribonucleic acid (RNA),* which protein each gene will produce. Protein molecules, in turn, form the physical structure of each cell and also direct the activity of the cell. Thus, as a function of DNA, the genes

| The human body contains 100 trillion *cells*. | There is a *nucleus* inside each human cell (except red blood cells). | Each nucleus contains 46 *chromosomes*, arranged in 23 pairs. | One *chromosome* of every pair is from each parent. | The chromosomes are filled with tightly coiled strands of *DNA*. | *Genes* are segments of DNA that contain instructions to make proteins — the building blocks of life. |

FIGURE 1

Genetic Building Blocks

Genetic Diversity

Diversity in genetic makeup gives rise to the infinite variability that serves as the basis for evolution through natural selection (see Chapter 1). Abnormalities in genetic makeup can lead to a wide range of problems, however. For example, children born with a trio instead of a pair of chromosome 21 develop the distinctive physical appearance and slowed intellectual growth known as Down syndrome (see Chapter 10).

contain a coded message that provides a blueprint for constructing every aspect of a physical human being, including eye color, height, blood type, inherited disorders, and the like—and all in less space than the period that ends this sentence.

New cells are constantly being produced by the division of existing cells. Most of the body's cells divide through a process called *mitosis,* in which the cell's chromosomes duplicate themselves, so that each new cell contains copies of the twenty-three pairs of chromosomes in the original.

A different kind of cell division occurs when a male's sperm cells and a female's egg cells (called *ova*) are formed. This process is called *meiosis.* In meiosis, the chromosome pairs are not copied. Instead, they are randomly split and rearranged, leaving each new sperm and egg cell with just one member of each chromosome pair, or twenty-three single chromosomes. No two of these special new cells are quite the same, and none contains an exact copy of the person who produced it. So, at conception, when a male's sperm cell *fertilizes* the female's ovum, a truly new cell is formed. This fertilized cell, called a *zygote,* carries twenty-three pairs of chromosomes—half of each pair from the mother and half from the father. Thus, the zygote represents a unique heritage, a complete genetic code for a new person that combines randomly selected aspects from both parents. As described in the chapter on human development, the zygote divides first into copies of itself and then into the billions of specialized cells that form a new human being.

Whether or not genes express themselves in the individual who carries them depends on whether they are dominant or recessive. *Dominant* genes are outwardly expressed whenever they are present; *recessive* genes are expressed only when they are paired with a similar gene from the other parent. For example, phenylketonuria (PKU)—a disorder seen in about 1 in 10,000 newborns—is caused by a recessive gene. When inherited from both parents, this gene disrupts the body's ability to control phenylalanine, an amino acid found in milk and other foods. As a result, this acid is converted into a toxic substance that can cause severe mental retardation. (Discovery of this genetic defect made it possible to prevent retardation in PKU children simply by ensuring that they did not consume foods high in phenylalanine.) PKU is an example of a single-gene disorder, but relatively few human characteristics are controlled by just one gene or even just one pair of genes. Most characteristics are **polygenic,** meaning that they are controlled by many genes. Even a person's eye color and height are affected by more than one pair of genes.

The genes contained in the forty-six chromosomes inherited from parents make up an individual's **genotype.** Because identical twins develop from one fertilized egg cell, they are described as *monozygotic;* they have exactly the same genotype. So, why don't all identical twins look exactly alike? Because they do not have the same **phenotype.** An individual's phenotype is the set of observable characteristics that result from the interaction of heredity and environment. Thus, in twins and nontwins alike, the way people actually look and act is influenced by the combination of genes they carry as well as by environmental factors—in other words, by both nature and nurture.

A BRIEF HISTORY OF GENETIC RESEARCH IN PSYCHOLOGY

The field now known as behavioral genetics began in the late 1800s with the work of Sir Francis Galton. A cousin of Charles Darwin, Galton was so impressed with Darwin's book on evolution that he decided to study heredity in the human species, especially as it related to human behavior. Toward this end, Galton suggested the family, twin, and adoption study designs that are the mainstays of human behavioral genetics research today (see Chapter 2). He even coined the phrase *nature-nurture* to refer to genetic and environmental influences. Galton's most famous behavioral genetics study was one in which he showed that genius runs in families. Unfortunately, Galton went too far in interpreting the evidence from this family study when he concluded that "nature prevails enormously over nurture" (Galton, 1883, p. 241). As noted in Chapter 2, family similarity can be due to environmental as well as hereditary factors. Still, Galton's work helped to stimulate psychologists' interest in the influence of genetics. The first twin and adoption studies were conducted in 1924. Both focused on IQ, and both suggested the existence of an important genetic contribution to intelligence.

However, research on the influence of genetics on behavior and mental processes was inhibited for a while because of two factors. The first was the impact of John B. Watson's behaviorism, which, as mentioned in Chapter 1, suggested that we are what we learn. In 1925, Watson insisted "that there is no such thing as an inheritance of capacity, talent, temperament, mental constitution and characteristics. These things again depend on training that goes on mainly in the cradle" (Watson, 1925, pp. 74–75). The second factor discouraging attention to human genetics was its association with the view proclaimed by Adolph Hitler and his Nazis that certain groups of people were "genetically inferior." This view led to the Holocaust during World War II, a campaign of genocide during which millions of Jews and other allegedly "inferior" people were killed, some of them in horrifyingly ill-conceived genetic "experiments."

Genetic research on human behavior all but stopped during the 1930s and 1940s, but research on animals continued, leading not only to the first textbook on behavioral genetics in 1960 (Fuller & Thompson, 1960) but also to increased interest in human genetics. In 1963 an influential article reviewed family, twin, and adoption findings and concluded that genetic influences are important in determining IQ (Erlenmeyer-Kimling & Jarvik, 1963). Around the same time, another study revealed that the children of schizophrenic parents, even those adopted by nonschizophrenic families, are significantly more likely to develop schizophrenia than adopted children whose biological parents are not schizophrenic, thus suggesting a strong genetic contribution to this psychological disorder (Heston, 1966).

In the early 1970s, however, interest in human behavioral genetics faded again, this time because of reactions to two publications. The first was a paper by Arthur Jensen suggesting that differences in average IQ between Blacks and Whites might be partly due to genetic factors (Jensen, 1969). The second was a book by Richard Herrnstein in which he argued that genetics might contribute to social class differences (Herrnstein, 1973). The furious public and scientific response to these publications—which included branding the authors as racists—inhibited genetic research in psychology, even though very few behavioral geneticists were, in fact, studying ethnic or class differences. It was not until later in the 1970s, and into the 1980s, that major genetic studies were again conducted in psychology and psychiatry.

Today most psychologists recognize the role of both genetics and environment in behavior and mental processes, including the controversial area of mental abilities (Snyderman & Rothman, 1987). Indeed, in 1992 the American Psychological Association selected behavioral genetics as one of two themes best representing the past, present, and, especially, the future of psychological research (Plomin & McClearn, 1993). To some, though, the study of human behavioral genetics still carries a hint of racism and class elitism. Such concerns were resurrected a few years ago by a controversial book entitled *The Bell Curve,* which considers the role of genetics in ethnic differences in intelligence and the implications of intelligence for social class structure (Herrnstein & Murray, 1994; see also Chapter 10).

THE FOCUS OF RESEARCH IN BEHAVIORAL GENETICS

Much of the controversy about behavioral genetics, and about nature and nurture in general, comes from misunderstandings about what behavioral genetics researchers study and, more specifically, what it means to say that genes influence behavior.

For one thing, behavioral genetics is the study of genetic and environmental factors responsible for the *differences* between individuals or groups of individuals, not for the characteristics of a single individual. Consider height, for example. Much of the *variability* (i.e., differences) in height that we see among people—actually about 80 percent of it—can be explained by genetic differences among them rather than by environmental differences. But how do psychologists come up with such an estimate for height, or any other trait? One way is to compare the correlations found among identical twins (who are genetically identical) to those found among fraternal twins (who share no more genes than other siblings). With regard to height, these correlations work out to be around .85 for identical twins and around .45 for fraternal twins (Plomin, 1994b). *Heritability*—a measure of the extent to which differences among people on some attribute is due to genetic factors—is estimated by subtracting the correlation for fraternal twins from the correlation for identical twins and multiplying the difference by two (Rowe, 1997). Applying this formula here, we would get $.85 - .45 \times 2 = .80$—an estimate suggesting that 80 percent of the differences among people in height is due to heredity. Results from *adoption studies*—studies of related individuals raised by different families—corroborate this estimate (e.g., Grilo & Pogue-Geile, 1991). By extension, we can conclude that individuals who are genetically related but raised separately are just as similar in height as relatives reared together and, further, that genetically unrelated individuals reared together are no more similar in height than random pairs of individuals. In short, height is highly *heritable.*

However, these findings do *not* mean that a person who is six feet tall grew five of those feet because of genes and the other foot because of environment! Nor do they imply that height is entirely determined by genetics. Remember that identical twins do not correlate perfectly for height. Indeed, the correlation of .85 mentioned earlier indicates that some genetically identical twins differ in height, suggesting that nongenetic factors play a role in height differences among people in general. Nevertheless, if a person is, say, shorter than average, genetic factors are *probably* the primary cause. We say "probably" because finding a genetic influence on height involves referring only to the origins of *average* individual differences in the population. A *particular* person's height could be due solely to an early illness or other growth-stunting *environmental* factors.

To see how this logic applies to conclusions about psychological characteristics, suppose a researcher found that the heritability of a personality trait is 50 percent. This result would mean that approximately half of the *differences between people* on that trait is attributable to genetic factors. It would not mean that each person inherits half of the trait and gets the other half from environmental influences. As in our height example, behavioral geneticists want to know how much variability among people can be accounted for by genetic and environmental factors. The results of their research allow generalizations about the influence of nature and nurture on certain characteristics, but those generalizations do not necessarily apply to the origin of a particular person's characteristics.

Another misconception about genetic influences is that they are "hard-wired" and thus have inevitable effects. This is true in the case of single-gene disorders such as PKU, but more complex traits—intelligence, for example—are influenced by many genes as well as by many environmental factors. So genetic influence means just that—*influence* (Plomin, Owen & McGuffin, 1994). Genes can affect a trait without completely determining whether or not it will appear.

THE ROLE OF GENETIC FACTORS IN PSYCHOLOGY

It is no coincidence that the areas of psychology in which genes have been found to play an important role are areas that focus on individual differences—mental abilities, personality, and psychological disorders. Much less is known about individual differences in areas such as sensation, perception, consciousness, learning, memory, and motivation and emotion. Consequently, much less behavioral genetics research has been conducted on these variables. Nonetheless, enough is known about genetic factors to suggest that they probably influence every area of psychology to some extent. In the following sections, we consider behavioral genetics research results that tell a little more of the story about how genes can have an impact on behavior and mental processes.

Genetic Influences Over the Life Span

One particularly interesting finding about genetic influences on general mental ability is that they continue to increase throughout the life span (McGue et al., 1993; Plomin, 1986). That is, the proportion of individual differences (variance) in IQ scores that can be explained by genetic factors increases from 40 percent in childhood to 60 percent in adolescence and young adulthood and then to 80 percent later in life. This increase in the magnitude of genetic influence can be seen, for example, in the expanding difference between IQ correlations for identical twins and those for fraternal twins as they grow older: Identical twins become more similar in IQ over the life span, whereas fraternal twins become less similar as the years go by. This finding refutes the common assumption that environmental influences become increasingly important as accidents, illnesses, and other experiences accumulate throughout life. We still do not have enough data available to permit firm conclusions about whether the magnitude of genetic influences on other traits also changes as people grow up.

How can it be that genetic influences become more important over time? One possible explanation is that genetic predispositions lead people to select and even create environments that foster the continued development of their abilities.

Genes Affecting Multiple Characteristics

Behavioral genetics research has also revealed that genes affecting one characteristic can sometimes affect others as well. For example, it appears that the same genetic factors affecting anxiety also affect depression (Kendler et al., 1992). Thus, if we could identify specific genes responsible for genetic influences on anxiety, we would expect to find that the same genes were associated with the appearance of depression.

A similar finding has emerged for mental ability and scholastic achievement. Tests of scholastic achievement show almost as much genetic influence as do tests of mental ability. Moreover, tests of scholastic achievement correlate substantially with tests of mental ability. To what extent is a common set of genes responsible for this overlap? Research suggests that the answer is "almost entirely." It appears that the genes influencing performance on mental ability tests are the same ones that influence students' performance at school (Wadsworth, 1994).

Identifying Genes Related to Behavior

One of the most exciting new developments in behavioral genetics involves identifying the specific genes responsible for genetic influences in psychology (Plomin, 1995). For example, there are hundreds of rare, single-gene disorders that affect behavior. One of these is Huntington's disease, an ultimately fatal disorder that involves loss of motor control and progressive deterioration of the central nervous system. Huntington's disease emerges only in adulthood, beginning with personality changes, forgetfulness, and other behavioral problems. It is caused by a single dominant gene whose identification in 1983 made it possible to determine who will get this disease—even though the mechanism for the disorder is still not understood and prevention is not yet possible.

Researchers are also tracking down the numerous genes involved in the appearance of Alzheimer's disease. (As described in Chapter 3, Alzheimer's causes memory loss and increasing confusion in many older people.) One of these, a gene that contributes to the risk for late-onset Alzheimer's disease, was identified in 1993. This gene increases the risk for Alzheimer's disease about fivefold. However, it is not the sole or inevitable cause of this disease—many people with Alzheimer's disease do not have the gene, and many people with the gene do not have the disease. But this gene is by far the strongest risk factor known for Alzheimer's disease, and its discovery may mark the beginning of a new era in which specific genes—or regions of DNA near specific genes—will be identified as influencing disorders and psychological traits. Recent additional examples include reports of linkages between DNA and reading disability (Cardon et al., 1994), homosexuality (Hamer et al., 1993; Hu et al., 1995), intelligence (Chorney et al., 1998), the personality traits of novelty-seeking (Benjamin et al., 1996; Ebstein et al., 1997) and emotional stability (Lesch et al., 1996), attention deficit disorder (LaHoste et al., 1996), heroin use (Ebstein & Belmaker, 1997), alcoholism (Noble, 1996), and smoking (Lerman et al., 1998). Studies of animals suggest that genes may even be associated with fearfulness (Flint et al., 1995). These continuing discoveries will help fill in the details about a variety of characteristics and disorders that are influenced by many genes and many environmental factors.

BEHAVIORAL GENETICS AND ENVIRONMENTAL INFLUENCES

As suggested earlier, research on genetic influences in psychology has also provided some of the best evidence for the importance of environmental influences, because it has shown that genetics cannot explain everything about human behavior. Indeed, we must remember the crucial role of environmental influences—particularly at this point in history, when explanations for human behavior seem to increasingly favor nature over nurture.

For example, as already noted, twin and adoption studies have provided evidence of the importance of genetic factors in schizophrenia and, as a result, many researchers are now trying to identify the specific genes involved. Enthusiasm for genetic explanations of schizophrenia makes it easy to forget, however, that environmental factors can be at least as important as genes. As described in Chapter 15, for example, when one member of an identical-twin pair is schizophrenic, the chances are about 40 percent that the other member of the pair is also schizophrenic. This result surely provides evidence of a strong genetic contribution to schizophrenia, but it also suggests that schizophrenia appears in both identical twins *only* 40 percent of the time. Most of the time, the identical twin of a person with schizophrenia will not display the disorder. Such differences within pairs of identical twins can be due only to the operation of environmental factors.

Indeed, research generally suggests that genetic factors account for less than half of the variance among individuals for many psychological characteristics. This means that at least half of the variance among individuals on these characteristics is due to environmental factors. These environmental—or, more properly, *nongenetic*—factors encompass everything other than genetic inheritance. They include such biological factors as prenatal conditions and events, nutrition, and illnesses, as well as more traditional environmental factors such as parenting, schooling, and peer influences.

Thus, one of the most important findings to emerge from behavioral genetics research has concerned not genetics but the environment. Such research also suggests that, for psychologists, the most important environmental influences are likely to be those that different family members do *not* share. Psychologists need to find out more about these *nonshared factors* and how they act to create differences in children—twins or not—who grow up in the same family.

So far, research on this topic has shown that children growing up in the same family actually experience quite different environments, especially in relation to their parents. Siblings perceive that their parents treat them very differently—and, indeed, observational studies back up such perceptions of differential treatment (Plomin, 1994a). Even events such as parental divorce, which would seem to be shared by all children in the family, appear to be experienced quite differently by each child, depending especially upon age, personality, and the nature of the relationship with each parent (Plomin, 1994a).

Research is also beginning to focus on environmental influences beyond the family—such as relationships with teachers or friends—that are even more likely than home-related factors to be different for different children. If you have a brother or sister, think about a psychological trait on which you and your sibling differ—confidence, for example. Why do you think you two are different on that trait? Perhaps one of you experienced a loss of self-confidence when faced by the demands of an impatient grade-school teacher or after being betrayed by a childhood friend.

Such events sometimes occur randomly, but it is also possible that differences in your genetic makeup were in some way responsible for these different experiences. Unless you and your sibling are identical twins, you share only about 50 percent of your genes. Perhaps genetically influenced differences between the two of you—in emotionality or other aspects of temperament, for example—caused parents, peers, and others to respond to each of you differently.

This brings us to the second major discovery about the environment to emerge from research on behavioral genetics: Environmental influences that appear to cause differences between siblings might themselves be caused by genetic differences between the siblings. Indeed, in the past decade, most of the measures used by psychologists to assess environmental factors have been shown to be influenced by genetic factors (Plomin & Bergeman, 1991). These measures include, for example, adolescents' ratings of how their parents treated them, observations of parent-child interactions, and questionnaires about life events and social support. If scores on measures such as these reflected only environmental factors, then the scores of identical twins should be no more similar than those of fraternal twins. By the same token, there should be little similarity in the environmental-experience scores of genetically related individuals who grew up in different families.

The results reported by behavioral geneticists do not fit these expectations (Braungart, Plomin & Fulker, 1992; Plomin, 1994b). For example, parents differ in terms of how responsive they are to their children, but these differences in responsiveness correlate with the children's mental ability—a trait that has a clear genetic component. Thus, as described in Chapters 10 and 12, parental responsiveness can influence cognitive development, and—as behavioral genetics research suggests—children's inherited mental abilities can alter the responsiveness of their parents. That is, parents tend to be more responsive to bright children who ask lots of questions and are interested in the answers.

Outside the family, too, genetic factors appear to play a role in generating environmental experiences. For example, research on the characteristics of children's peer groups shows that children tend to choose their friends—and to be chosen as friends—partly on the basis of genetically influenced traits, such as mental ability and temperament (Manke et al., 1995). Several studies also suggest that genetic factors can increase or decrease the likelihood of family conflicts and other social stressors that threaten one's physical and psychological well-being (Pike et al., in press).

An important implication of genetic influences on environmental events is that measuring the impact of family relationships, peer influences, and other environmental factors on behavior and mental processes may be more difficult than psychologists thought. A measure that is aimed at assessing an environmental factor may in fact be affected by the genetic characteristics of the people being studied.

In human development, nature and nurture work together, as described in Chapter 12. Children select, modify, and create environments that are correlated with their genetic inclinations. As developmental psychologists have long argued, children are not formless blobs of clay passively molded by the environment. Rather, they are active participants in their experiences. The findings we have described here suggest that genetics plays an important role in those experiences (Plomin, 1994b).

SUMMARY

Behavioral genetics is the study of how genes affect behavior.

THE BIOLOGY OF GENETICS AND HEREDITY

Research on the ways in which nature and nurture interact to shape behavior and mental processes requires a knowledge of *genetics,* the biology of inheritance. The genetic code that transmits characteristics from one generation to the next is contained in the *DNA* that comprises the *genes* that make up *chromosomes.* Dominant genes are expressed whenever they are present; recessive genes are expressed only when inherited from both parents. Most human characteristics are controlled by more than one gene or gene pair; they are *polygenic.* The genes in a person's forty-six chromosomes make up the *genotype;* the *phenotype*—how people actually look and act—is influenced by genes and the environment.

A BRIEF HISTORY OF GENETIC RESEARCH IN PSYCHOLOGY

Galton's work in the nineteenth century helped to stimulate psychologists' interest in the influence of genetics on behavior. The popularity of research in this area has waxed and waned over the years, but today most psychologists recognize the role of genetic as well as environmental influences on many aspects of behavior and mental processes.

THE FOCUS OF RESEARCH IN BEHAVIORAL GENETICS

Behavioral genetics research identifies the genetic and environmental factors responsible for differences between individuals, not for the characteristics of a particular person. Though genes can influence a trait, they may not completely determine whether that trait appears.

THE ROLE OF GENETIC FACTORS IN PSYCHOLOGY

Genetic factors probably influence to some extent every aspect of behavior and mental processes.

Genetic Influences Over the Life Span

Genetic influences on general mental ability appear to increase over time, possibly because genetic predispositions lead people to select and even create environments that foster the continued development of abilities that are in line with those predispositions.

Genes Affecting Multiple Traits

Genes that affect one trait, such as anxiety, can sometimes also affect others, such as depression.

Identifying Genes Related to Behavior

Current research in behavioral genetics is identifying specific genes responsible for specific characteristics—especially rare, single-gene disorders such as Huntington's disease.

BEHAVIORAL GENETICS AND ENVIRONMENTAL INFLUENCES

Research in behavioral genetics has actually provided evidence for the importance of environmental influences, too, because it shows that genetics alone cannot account for such characteristics as intelligence, personality, and mental disorders. Some of the most important environmental influences are likely to be those which members of the same family do not share. In short, neither nature nor nurture is conducting the performance of the other: They are playing a duet.

KEY TERMS

chromosomes A-1
deoxyribonucleic acid
 (DNA) A-1

genes A-1
genetics A-1

genotype A-2
phenotype A-2

polygenic A-2

Statistics in Psychological Research

Understanding and interpreting the results of psychological research depends on *statistical analyses,* which are methods for describing and drawing conclusions from data. Chapter 2 introduced some terms and concepts associated with *descriptive statistics*—the numbers that psychologists use to describe and present their data—and with *inferential statistics*—the mathematical procedures used to draw conclusions from data and to make inferences about what they mean. Here, we present more details about these statistical analyses that will help you to evaluate research results.

DESCRIBING DATA

To illustrate our discussion, consider a hypothetical experiment on the effects of incentives on performance. The experimenter presents a list of mathematics problems to two groups of participants. Each group must solve the problems within a fixed time, but for each correct answer, the low-incentive group is paid ten cents whereas the high-incentive group gets one dollar. The hypothesis to be tested is the **null hypothesis,** the assertion that the independent variable manipulated by the experimenter will have no effect on the dependent variable measured by the experimenter. In this case, the null hypothesis holds that the size of the incentive (the independent variable) will not affect performance on the mathematics task (the dependent variable).

Assume that the experimenter has obtained a random sample of participants, assigned them randomly to the two groups, and done everything possible to avoid the confounds and other research problems discussed in Chapter 2. The experiment has been run, and the psychologist now has the data: a list of the number of correct answers given by each participant in each group. Now comes the first task of statistical analysis: describing the data in a way that makes them easy to understand.

The Frequency Histogram

The simplest way to describe the data is to draw up something like Table 1, in which all the numbers are simply listed. After examining the table, you might discern that the high-incentive group seems to have done better than the low-incentive group, but the difference is not immediately obvious. It might be even harder to see if more participants had been involved and if the scores included three-digit numbers. A picture is worth a thousand words, so a more satisfactory way of presenting the same data is in a picture-like graphic known as a **frequency histogram** (see Figure 1).

Construction of a histogram is simple. First, divide the scale for measuring the dependent variable (in this case, the number of correct solutions) into a number of categories, or "bins." The bins in our example are 1–2, 3–4, 5–6, 7–8, and 9–10. Next, sort the raw data into the appropriate bin. (For example, the score of a participant who had 5 correct answers would go into the 5–6 bin, a score of 8 would go into the 7–8 bin, and so on.) Finally, for each bin, count the number of scores in that bin and draw a bar up to the height of that number on the vertical axis of a graph. The set of bars makes up the frequency histogram.

TABLE 1

A Simple Data Set

Here are the test scores obtained by thirteen participants performing under low-incentive conditions and thirteen participants performing under high-incentive conditions.

Low Incentive	High Incentive
4	6
6	4
2	10
7	10
6	7
8	10
3	6
5	7
2	5
3	9
5	9
9	3
5	8

FIGURE 1

Frequency Histograms

The height of each bar of a histogram represents the number of scores falling within each range of score values. The pattern formed by these bars gives a visual image of how research results are distributed.

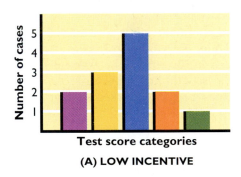

(A) LOW INCENTIVE

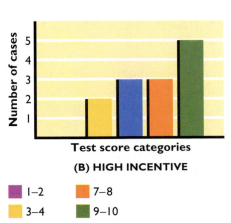

(B) HIGH INCENTIVE

- ■ 1–2
- ■ 3–4
- ■ 5–6
- ■ 7–8
- ■ 9–10

Because we are interested in comparing the scores of two groups, there are separate histograms in Figure 1: one for the high-incentive group and one for the low-incentive group. Now the difference between groups that was difficult to see in Table 1 becomes clearly visible: More people in the high-incentive group obtained high scores than in the low-incentive group.

Histograms and other pictures of data are useful for visualizing and better understanding the "shape" of research data, but in order to analyze data statistically, we need to use other ways of handling the data that make up these graphic presentations. For example, before we can tell whether two histograms are different statistically or just visually, the data they represent must be summarized using **descriptive statistics.**

Descriptive Statistics

The four basic categories of descriptive statistics (1) measure the number of observations made; (2) summarize the typical value of a set of data; (3) summarize the spread, or variability, in a set of data; and (4) express the correlation between two sets of data.

N   The easiest statistic to compute, abbreviated as N, simply describes the number of observations that make up the data set. In Table 1, for example, $N = 13$ for each group, or 26 for the entire data set. Simple as it is, N plays a very important role in more sophisticated statistical analyses.

Measures of Central Tendency   It is apparent in the histograms in Figure 1 that there is a difference in the pattern of scores between the two groups. But how much of a difference? What is the typical value, the *central tendency,* that represents each group's performance? As described in Chapter 2, there are three measures that capture this typical value: the mode, the median, and the mean. Recall that the *mode* is the value or score that occurs most frequently in the data set. The *median* is the halfway point in a set of data: Half the scores fall above the median, half fall below it. The *mean* is the arithmetic average. To find the mean, add the values of all the scores and divide by the number of scores.

Measures of Variability   The variability, or spread, or dispersion of a set of data is often just as important as its central tendency. This variability can be quantified by measures known as the *range* and the *standard deviation.*

As described in Chapter 2, the **range** is simply the difference between the highest and the lowest value in a data set. For the data in Table 1, the range for the low-incentive group is $9 - 2 = 7$; for the high-incentive group, the range is $10 - 3 = 7$.

The **standard deviation,** or **SD,** measures the average difference between each score and the mean of the data set. To see how the standard deviation is calculated, consider the data in Table 2. The first step is to compute the mean of the set—in this case, $20/5 = 4$. Second, calculate the difference, or *deviation* (D), of each score from the mean by subtracting the mean from each score, as in column 2 of Table 2. Third, find the average of these deviations. However, if you calculated the average by finding the arithmetic mean, you would sum the deviations and find that the negative deviations exactly balance the positive ones, resulting in a mean difference of 0. Obviously there is more than zero variation around the mean in the data set. So, instead of employing the arithmetic mean, we compute the standard deviation by first squaring the deviations (which removes any negative values), summing these squared deviations, dividing by N, and then taking the square root of the result. These simple steps are outlined in more detail in Table 2.

The Normal Distribution   Now that we have described histograms and reviewed some descriptive statistics, we will re-examine how these methods of representing research data relate to some of the concepts discussed elsewhere in the book.

In most subareas in psychology, when researchers collect many measurements and plot their data in histograms, the pattern that results often resembles that shown for the low-incentive group in Figure 1. That is, the majority of scores tend to fall in the middle of the distribution, with fewer and fewer occurring as one moves toward the extremes. As more and more data are collected, and as smaller and smaller bins are used (perhaps containing only one value each), the histograms tend to smooth out until they resemble the bell-shaped curve known as the **normal distribution,** or *normal curve,* which is shown in Figure 2(A). When a distribution of scores follows a truly normal curve, its mean, median, and mode all have the same value. Furthermore, if the curve is normal, we can use its standard deviation to describe how any particular score stands in relation to the rest of the distribution.

IQ scores provide an example. They are distributed in a normal curve, with a mean, median, and mode of 100 and an SD of 16—as shown in Figure 2(B). In such a distribution, half of the population will have an IQ above 100, and half will be below 100. The shape of the true normal curve is such that 68 percent of the area under it lies within one standard deviation above and below the mean. In terms of IQ, this means that 68 percent of the population has an IQ somewhere between 84 (100 minus 16) and 116 (100 plus 16). Of the remaining 32 percent of the population, half falls more than 1 SD above the mean, and half falls more than 1 SD below the mean. Thus, 16 percent of the population has an IQ above 116, and 16 percent scores below 84.

The normal curve is also the basis for percentiles. A **percentile score** indicates the percentage of people or observations that fall below a given score in a normal

TABLE 2

Calculating the Standard Deviation

The standard deviation of a set of scores reflects the average degree to which those scores differ from the mean of the set.

Raw Data	Difference from Mean = D	D²
2	$2 - 4 = -2$	4
2	$2 - 4 = -2$	4
3	$3 - 4 = -1$	1
4	$4 - 4 = 0$	0
9	$9 - 4 = 5$	25
Mean = 20/5 = 4		$\Sigma D^2 = 34$

$$\text{Standard deviation} = \sqrt{\frac{\Sigma D^2}{N}} = \sqrt{\frac{34}{5}} = \sqrt{6.8} = 2.6$$

Note: Σ means "the sum of."

FIGURE 2

The Normal Distribution

Many kinds of research data approximate the symmetrical shape of the normal curve, in which most scores fall toward the center of the range.

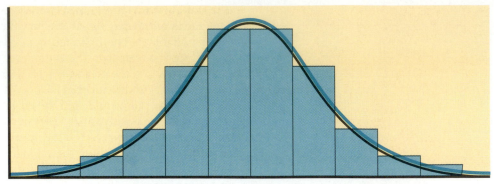

(A) NORMAL DISTRIBUTION, SHOWING THE SMOOTHED APPROXIMATION TO THE FREQUENCY HISTOGRAM

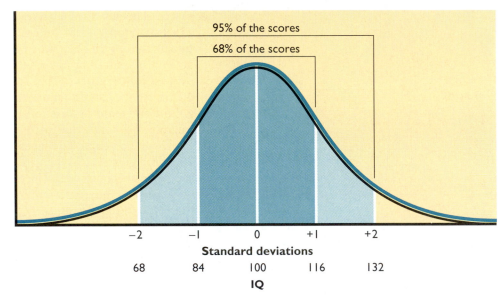

(B) THE NORMAL DISTRIBUTION OF IQ

distribution. In Figure 2(B), for example, the mean score (which is also the median) lies at a point below which 50 percent of the scores fall. Thus, the mean of a normal distribution is at the 50th percentile. What does this say about IQ? If you score 1 SD above the mean, your score is at a point above which only 16 percent of the population falls. This means that 84 percent of the population (100 percent minus 16 percent) must be below that score; so this IQ score is at the 84th percentile. A score at 2 SDs above the mean is at the 97.5 percentile, because only 2.5 percent of the scores are above it in a normal distribution.

Scores may also be expressed in terms of their distance in standard deviations from the mean, producing what are called **standard scores.** A standard score of 1.5, for example, is 1.5 standard deviations from the mean.

Correlation   Histograms and measures of central tendency and variability describe certain characteristics of one dependent variable at a time. However, psychologists are often concerned with describing the *relationship* between two variables. Measures of correlation are frequently used for this purpose. We discussed the interpretation of the *correlation coefficient* in Chapter 2; here we describe how to calculate it.

Recall that correlations are based on the relationship between two numbers associated with each participant or observation. The numbers may represent, say, a person's height and weight or the IQs of a parent and child. Table 3 contains this kind of data for four participants from our incentives study who took the test twice. (As you may recall from Chapter 10, the correlation between their scores would be a measure of *test-retest reliability.*) The formula for computing the Pearson product-moment correlation, or *r*, is as follows:

$$r = \frac{\Sigma(x - M_x)(y - M_y)}{\sqrt{\Sigma(x - M_x)^2 \, \Sigma(y - M_y)^2}}$$

where:

x = each score on variable 1 (in this case, test 1)

y = each score on variable 2 (in this case, test 2)

M_x = the mean of the scores on variable 1

M_y = the mean of the scores on variable 2

The main function of the denominator in this formula is to ensure that the coefficient ranges from +1.00 to −1.00, no matter how large or small the values of the variables being correlated. The "action element" of this formula is the numerator. It is the result of multiplying the amounts by which each of two observations (*x* and *y*) differ from the means of their respective distributions (M_x and M_y). Notice that, if the two variables "go together" (so that, if one is large, the other is also large, and if one is small, the other is also small), then either both will tend to be above the mean of their distribution or both will tend to be below the mean of their distribution. When this is the case, $x - M_x$ and $y - M_y$ will both be positive, or they will both be negative. In either case, their product will always be positive, and the correlation coefficient will also be positive. If, on the other hand, the two variables go opposite to one another, such that, when one is large, the other is small, one of them is likely to be smaller than the mean of its distribution, so that either $x - M_x$ or $y - M_y$ will have a negative sign, and the other will have a positive sign. Multiplying these differences together will always result in a product with a negative sign, and *r* will be negative as well.

Now compute the correlation coefficient for the data presented in Table 3. The first step (step a in the table) is to compute the mean (*M*) for each variable. M_x turns out to be 3 and M_y is 4. Next, calculate the numerator by finding the differences between each *x* and *y* value and its respective mean and by multiplying them (as in step b of Table 3). Notice that, in this example, the differences in each pair have like signs, so the correlation coefficient will be positive. The next step is to calculate the terms in the denominator; in this case, as shown in steps c and d in Table 3, they have values of 18 and 4. Finally, place all the terms in the formula and carry out the arithmetic (step e). The result in this case is an *r* of +.94, a high and positive correlation suggesting that performances on repeated tests are very closely related. A participant doing well the first time

TABLE 3

Calculating the Correlation Coefficient

Though it appears complex, calculation of the correlation coefficient is quite simple. The resulting *r* reflects the degree to which two sets of scores tend to be related, or to co-vary.

Participant	Test 1	Test 2	$(x - M_x)(y - M_y)$ [b]
A	1	3	$(1 - 3)(3 - 4) = (-2)(-1) = +2$
B	1	3	$(1 - 3)(3 - 4) = (-2)(-1) = +2$
C	4	5	$(4 - 3)(5 - 4) = (1)(1) = +1$
D	6	5	$(6 - 3)(5 - 4) = (3)(1) = +3$
	[a]$M_x = 3$	$M_y = 4$	$\Sigma(x - M_x)(y - M_y) = +8$

[c]$\Sigma(x - M_x)^2 = 4 + 4 + 1 + 9 = 18$

[d]$\Sigma(y - M_y)^2 = 1 + 1 + 1 + 1 = 4$

[e]$r = \dfrac{\Sigma(x - M_x)(y - M_y)}{\sqrt{\Sigma(x - M_x)^2 \Sigma(y - M_y)^2}} = \dfrac{8}{\sqrt{18 \times 4}} = \dfrac{8}{\sqrt{72}} = \dfrac{8}{8.48} = +.94$

is very likely to do well again; a person doing poorly at first will probably do no better the second time.

INFERENTIAL STATISTICS

The descriptive statistics from the incentives experiment tell the experimenter that the performances of the high- and low-incentive groups differ. But there is some uncertainty. Is the difference large enough to be important? Does it represent a stable effect or a fluke? The researcher would like to have some *measure of confidence* that the difference between groups is genuine and reflects the effect of incentive on mental tasks in the real world, rather than the effect of random or uncontrolled factors. One way of determining confidence would be to run the experiment again with a new group of participants. Confidence that incentives produced differences in performance would grow stronger if the same or a larger between-group difference occurs again. In reality, psychologists rarely have the opportunity to repeat, or *replicate,* their experiments in exactly the same way three or four times. But **inferential statistics** provide a measure of how likely it was that results came about by chance. They put a precise mathematical value on the confidence or probability that rerunning the same experiment would yield similar (or even stronger) results.

Differences Between Means: The *t* Test

One of the most important tools of inferential statistics is the ***t* test.** It allows the researcher to ask how likely it is that the difference between two means occurred by chance rather than as a function of the effect of the independent variable. When the *t* test or other inferential statistic says that the probability of chance effects is small enough (usually less than 5 percent), the results are said to be *statistically significant.* Conducting a *t* test of statistical significance requires the use of three descriptive statistics.

The first component of the *t* test is the size of the observed effect, the difference between the means. Recall that the mean is calculated by summing a group's scores and dividing by the number of scores. In the example shown in Table 1, the mean of the high-incentive group is 94/13, or 7.23, and the mean of the low-incentive group is 65/13, or 5. Thus, the difference between the means for the high- and low-incentive groups is $7.23 - 5 = 2.23$.

Second, the standard deviation of scores in each group must be known. If the scores in a group are quite variable, the standard deviation will be large, indicating that chance may have played a large role in producing the results. The next replication of the study might generate a very different set of group scores. If the scores in a group are all very similar, however, the standard deviation will be small, which suggests that the same result would probably occur for that group if the study were repeated. Thus, the *difference* between groups is more likely to be significant when each group's standard deviation is small. If variability is high enough that the scores of two groups overlap (in Table 1, for example, some people in the low-incentive group actually did better on the math test than some in the high-incentive group), the mean difference, though large, may not be statistically significant.

Third, we need to take the sample size, *N*, into account. The larger the number of participants or observations, the more likely it is that a given difference between means is significant. This is so because, with larger samples, random factors within a group—the unusual performance of a few people who were sleepy or anxious or hostile, for example—are more likely to be canceled out by the majority, who better represent people in general. The same effect of sample size can be seen in coin tossing. If you toss a quarter five times, you might not be too surprised if heads comes up 80 percent of the time. If you get 80 percent heads after one hundred tosses, however, you might begin to suspect that this is probably not due to chance alone and that some other effect, perhaps some bias in the coin, is significant in producing the results. (For the same reason, a relatively small correlation coefficient—between diet and grades, say—might be statistically significant if it was based on 50,000 students. As the number of participants increases, it becomes less likely that the correlation reflects the influence of a few oddball cases.)

To summarize, as the differences between the means get larger, as N increases, and as standard deviations get smaller, t increases. This increase in t raises the researcher's confidence in the significance of the difference between means.

Now we will calculate the t statistic and show how it is interpreted. The formula for t is:

$$t = \frac{(M_1 - M_2)}{\sqrt{\frac{(N_1 - 1)S_1^2 + (N_2 - 1)S_2^2}{N_1 + N_2 - 2}\left(\frac{N_1 + N_2}{N_1 N_2}\right)}}$$

where:

M_1 = mean of group 1

M_2 = mean of group 2

N_1 = number of scores or observations for group 1

N_2 = number of scores or observations for group 2

S_1 = standard deviation of group 1 scores

S_2 = standard deviation of group 2 scores

Despite appearances, this formula is quite simple. In the numerator is the difference between the two group means; t will get larger as this difference gets larger. The denominator contains an estimate of the standard deviation of the *differences* between group means; in other words, it suggests how much the difference between group means would vary if the experiment were repeated many times. Since this estimate is in the denominator, the value of t will get smaller as the standard deviation of group differences gets larger. For the data in Table 1,

$$t = \frac{(M_1 - M_2)}{\sqrt{\frac{(N_1 - 1)S_1^2 + (N_2 - 1)S_2^2}{N_1 + N_2 - 2}\left(\frac{N_1 + N_2}{N_1 N_2}\right)}}$$

$$= \frac{7.23 - 5}{\sqrt{\frac{(12)(5.09) + (12)(4.46)}{24}\left(\frac{26}{169}\right)}}$$

$$= \frac{2.23}{\sqrt{.735}} = 2.60 \text{ with 24 df}$$

To determine what a particular t means, we must use the value of N and a special statistical table called, appropriately enough, the *t table*. We have reproduced part of the t table in Table 4.

First, find the computed values of t in the row corresponding to the **degrees of freedom,** or **df,** associated with the experiment. In this case, degrees of freedom are simply $N_1 + N_2 - 2$ (or two less than the total sample size or number of scores). Since our experiment had 13 participants per group, df = 13 + 13 − 2 = 24. In the row for 24 df in Table 4, you will find increasing values of t in each column. These columns correspond to decreasing p values, the probabilities that the difference between means occurred by chance. If an obtained t value is equal to or larger than one of the values in the t table (on the correct df line), then the difference between means that generated that t is said to be significant at the .10, .05, or .01 level of probability. Suppose, for example, that an obtained t (with 19 df) was 2.00. Looking along the 19 df row, you find that 2.00 is larger than the value in the .05 column. This allows you to say that the

TABLE 4

The *t* Table

This table allows the researcher to determine whether an obtained *t* value is statistically significant. If the *t* value is larger than the one in the appropriate row in the .05 column, the difference between means that generated that *t* score is usually considered statistically significant.

df	*p* Value .10 (10%)	*p* Value .05 (5%)	*p* Value .01 (1%)
4	1.53	2.13	3.75
9	1.38	1.83	2.82
14	1.34	1.76	2.62
19	1.33	1.73	2.54
22	1.32	1.71	2.50
24	1.32	1.71	2.49

probability that the difference between means occurred by chance was no greater than .05, or 5 in 100. If the *t* had been less than the value in the .05 column, the probability of a chance result would have been greater than .05. As noted earlier, when an obtained *t* is not large enough to exceed *t* table values at the .05 level, at least, it is not usually considered statistically significant.

The *t* value from our experiment was 2.60, with 24 df. Because 2.60 is greater than all the values in the 24 df row, the difference between the high- and low-incentive groups would have occurred by chance less than 1 time in 100. In other words, the difference is statistically significant.

Beyond the *t* Test

Many experiments in psychology are considerably more complex than simple comparisons between two groups. They often involve three or more experimental and control groups. Some experiments also include more than one independent variable. For example, suppose we had been interested not only in the effect of incentive size on performance but also in the effect of problem difficulty. We might then create six groups whose members would perform easy, moderate, or difficult problems with low or high incentives.

In an experiment like this, the results might be due to the incentive, the problem difficulty, or the combined effects (known as the *interaction*) of the two. Analyzing the size and source of these effects is typically accomplished through procedures known as *analysis of variance*. The details of analysis of variance are beyond the scope of this book; for now, note that the statistical significance of each effect is influenced by differences between means, standard deviation, and sample size in much the same way as described for the *t* test.

For more detailed information about how analysis of variance and other inferential statistics are used to understand and interpret the results of psychological research, consider taking courses in research methods and statistical or quantitative methods.

SUMMARY

Psychological research generates large quantities of data. Statistics are methods for describing and drawing conclusions from data.

DESCRIBING DATA

Researchers often test the *null hypothesis,* which is the assertion that the independent variable will have no effect on the dependent variable.

The Frequency Histogram

Graphic representations such as *frequency histograms* provide visual descriptions of data, making the data easier to understand.

Descriptive Statistics

Numbers that summarize a set of data are called *descriptive statistics.* The easiest statistic to compute is *N*, which gives the number of observations made. A set of scores can be described by two other types of descriptive statistics: a measure of central tendency, which describes the typical value of a set of data, and a measure of variability. Measures of central tendency include the mean, median, and mode; variability is typically measured by the *range* and by the standard deviation. Sets of data often follow a *normal distribution,* which means that most scores fall in the middle of the range, with fewer and fewer scores occurring as one moves toward the extremes. In a truly normal distribution the mean, median, and mode are identical. When a set of data shows a normal distribution, a data point can be cited in terms of a *percentile score,* which indicates the percentage of people or observations falling below a certain score, and in terms of *standard scores,* which indicate the distance, in standard deviations, that a score is located from the mean. Another type of descriptive statistic, a correlation coefficient, is used to measure the correlation between sets of scores.

INFERENTIAL STATISTICS

Researchers use *inferential statistics* to quantify the probability that conducting the same experiment again would yield similar results.

Differences Between Means: The *t* Test

One inferential statistic, the *t test,* assesses the likelihood that differences between two means occurred by chance or reflect the effect of an independent variable. Performing a *t* test requires using the difference between the means of two sets of data, the *standard deviation* of scores in each set, and the number of observations or participants. Interpreting a *t* test requires that *degrees of freedom* also be taken into account. When the *t* test indicates that the experimental results had a low probability of occurring by chance, the results are said to be statistically significant.

Beyond the *t* Test

When more than two groups must be compared, researchers typically rely on analysis of variance in order to interpret the results of an experiment.

KEY TERMS

GLOSSARY

Absolute threshold   The minimum amount of stimulus energy that can be detected 50 percent of the time. (See also *internal noise*.) *(p. 141)*

Acetylcholine   A neurotransmitter used by neurons in the peripheral and central nervous systems in the control of functions ranging from muscle contraction and heart rate to digestion and memory. Alzheimer's disease is associated with the neurons that use acetylcholine. *(p. 82)*

Accessory structure   A structure, such as the lens of the eye, that modifies a stimulus. In some sensory systems, this modification is the first step in sensation. *(p. 97)*

Accommodation   (1) The ability of the lens to change its shape and bend light rays so that objects are in focus. (p. 138) (2) The process of modifying schemas as an infant tries out familiar schemas on objects that do not fit them. *(pp. 108, 153)*

Achievement tests   Measures of what a person has accomplished or learned in a particular area. *(p. 327)*

Acoustic encoding   The mental representation of information as a sequence of sounds. *(p. 214)*

Action potential   An impulse that travels down an axon when the neuron becomes depolarized and sodium rushes into the cell. This kind of nerve communication is all or none: The cell either fires at full strength or does not fire at all. *(p. 55)*

Active sleep   See *rapid eye movement (REM) sleep*.

Actor-observer bias   The tendency to attribute other people's behavior to internal causes while attributing one's own behavior (especially errors and failures) to external causes. *(p. 614)*

Actualizing tendency   According to Rogers, an innate inclination toward growth that motivates all people to seek the full realization of their highest potential. *(p. 502)*

Acuity   Visual resolution or clarity, which is greatest in the fovea because of its large concentration of cones. *(p. 110)*

Adaptation   The process through which responsiveness to an unchanging stimulus decreases over time. *(p. 97)*

Addiction   Development of a physical need for a psychoactive drug. *(pp. 310, 523)*

Affective disorder   See *mood disorder*.

Age regression   A phenomenon displayed by some hypnotized people that involves recalling and re-enacting behaviors from childhood. *(p. 177)*

Aggression   An act that is intended to cause harm or damage to another person. *(p. 647)*

Agonists   Drugs that bind to a receptor and mimic the effects of the neurotransmitter that normally fits that receptor. *(p. 309)*

Agoraphobia   A strong fear of being alone or away from the security of home. *(p. 529)*

AI   See *artificial intelligence*.

Alcoholism   A pattern of continuous or intermittent drinking that may lead to addiction and almost always causes severe social, physical, and other problems. *(p. 553)*

Algorithms   Systematic procedures that cannot fail to produce a solution to a problem—but often not the most efficient way to produce a solution. (See also *heuristics*.) *(p. 258)*

Altered state of consciousness   (also called *alternate state of consciousness*)   A condition that exists when quantitative and qualitative changes in mental processes are extensive enough that the person or objective observers notice significant differences in psychological and behavioral functioning. *(p. 297)*

Altruism   An unselfish concern with another's welfare. *(p. 654)*

Amplitude   The difference between the peak and the baseline of a waveform. *(p. 100)*

Amygdala   A structure in the forebrain that, among other things, associates features of stimuli from two sensory modalities, such as linking the shape and feel of objects in memory. *(p. 68)*

Analgesia   The absence of the sensation of pain in the presence of a normally painful stimulus. The brain appears to use serotonin and endorphins to block painful stimuli. *(p. 129)*

Anal stage   The second of Freud's psychosexual stages, usually occurring during the second year of life, in which the focus of pleasure and conflict shifts from the mouth to the anus. The demand for toilet training conflicts with the child's instinctual pleasure in having bowel movements at will. *(p. 486)*

Anchoring heuristic   A shortcut in the thought process that involves adding new information to existing information to reach a judgment. *(p. 260)*

Androgens   Masculine hormones that circulate in the bloodstream and regulate sexual motivation in both sexes. The principal androgen is testosterone, and relatively more androgens circulate in men than in women. *(p. 372)*

Anorexia nervosa   An eating disorder characterized by self-starvation and dramatic weight loss. *(p. 369)*

ANS   See *autonomic nervous system*.

Antagonists   Drugs that bind to a receptor and prevent the normal neurotransmitter from binding. *(p. 309)*

Anterograde amnesia   A loss of memory for any event that occurs after a brain injury. (See also *retrograde amnesia*.) *(p. 241)*

Antidepressant   A drug that relieves depression. *(p. 594)*

Antipsychotic   A drug that alleviates the symptoms of schizophrenia or other severe forms of psychological disorder. *(p. 558)*

Antisocial personality disorder   A personality disorder involving a long-term, persistent pattern of impulsive, selfish, unscrupulous, even criminal behavior. *(p. 551)*

Anxiety disorder   A condition in which intense feelings of apprehension are long-standing or disruptive. (See also *generalized anxiety disorder, panic disorder, phobia,* and *obsessive-compulsive disorder*.) *(p. 528)*

Anxiolytic   A drug that reduces feelings of tension and anxiety. (See also *tranquilizer*.) *(p. 595)*

Aptitude tests   Tests designed to measure a person's capacity to learn certain things or perform certain tasks. *(p. 327)*

Arousal   A general level of activation that is reflected in several physiological systems and can be measured by electrical activity in the brain, heart action, muscle tension, and the state of many other organ systems. *(p. 362)*

Arousal: cost-reward theory   A theory that attributes helping behavior to people's efforts to reduce the unpleasant arousal they feel when confronted with a suffering victim. *(p. 655)*

Arousal theories   A theory of motivation stating that people are motivated to behave in ways that maintain what is, for them, an optimal level of arousal. *(p. 362)*

Artificial concepts   A concept that can be clearly defined by a set of rules or properties, so that each member of the concept has all of the defining properties and no nonmember does. (See also *natural concepts*.) *(p. 255)*

Artificial intelligence (AI)   The field that studies how to program computers to imitate the products of human perception, understanding, and thought. *(p. 268)*

Assertiveness and social skills training   A set of methods for teaching clients who are anxious or unproductive in social situations how to interact with others more comfortably and effectively. (p. 573)

Assimilation   The process of taking in new information about objects by trying out existing schemas on objects that fit those schemas. (p. 411)

Association cortex   Those parts of the cerebral cortex that receive information from more than one sense or combine sensory and motor information to perform such complex cognitive tasks as abstract thought or associating words with images. (p. 74)

Attachment   A deep, affectionate, close, and enduring relationship with the single person with whom a baby has shared many experiences. (p. 425)

Attention   The process of directing and focusing certain psychological resources, usually by voluntary control, to enhance information processing, performance, and mental experience. (p. 164)

Attitude   A predisposition toward a particular cognitive, emotional, or behavioral reaction to an object, individual, group, situation, or action. (p. 616)

Attribution   The process of explaining the causes of people's behavior, including one's own. (See also *attributional bias*.) (pp. 394, 609)

Auditory nerve   The bundle of axons that carries stimuli from the hair cells of the cochlea to the brain to facilitate hearing. (p. 102)

Auditory scene analysis   The perceptual process through which sounds are mentally represented and interpreted. (p. 149)

Authoritarian parents   Firm, punitive, and unsympathetic parents who value obedience from the child and authority for themselves, do not encourage independence, are detached, and seldom praise the child. The result of this parenting style is often an unfriendly, distrustful, and withdrawn child. (p. 431)

Authoritative parents   Parents who reason with the child, encourage give and take, are firm but understanding, and give the child more responsibility as he or she gets older. Children of this type of parents are usually friendly, cooperative, self-reliant, and socially responsible. (p. 431)

Autoimmune disorders   Physical problems caused when cells of the body's immune system attack normal body cells as if they were foreign invaders. (p. 91)

Autonomic nervous system (ANS)   A subsystem of the peripheral nervous system that carries messages between the central nervous system and the heart, lungs, and other organs and glands in the body. The ANS regulates the activity of these organs and glands to meet varying demands placed upon the body and also provides information to the brain about that activity. (p. 61)

Availability heuristic   A shortcut in the thought process that involves judging the frequency or probability of an event or hypothesis by how easily the hypothesis or examples of the event can be brought to mind. Thus, people tend to choose the hypothesis or alternative that is most mentally available. (p. 261)

Aversive conditioning   A method for reducing unwanted behaviors by using classical conditioning principles to create a negative response to some stimulus. (p. 574)

Avoidance conditioning   A type of learning in which an organism responds to a signal in a way that avoids exposure to an aversive stimulus. (p. 187)

Avoidant personality disorder   A personality disorder characterized by avoidance of social situations and extreme sensitivity to criticism or rejection by others. (p. 521)

Axons   The fibers that carry signals from the body of a neuron out to where communication occurs with other neurons. Each neuron generally has only one axon leaving the cell body, but that one axon may have many branches. (p. 54)

Babblings   Repetitions of syllables; the first sounds infants make that resemble speech. (p. 279)

Basilar membrane   The floor of the fluid-filled duct that runs through the cochlea. Waves passing through the fluid in the duct move the basilar membrane, and this movement deforms hair cells that touch the membrane. (See also *cochlea*.) (p. 102)

Behavioral approach (also called *behavioral model*)   Personality theories based on the assumption that human behavior is determined mainly by what a person has learned in life, especially by the rewards and punishments the person has experienced in interacting with other people. According to this approach, the consistency of people's learning histories, not an inner personality structure, produces characteristic behavior patterns. (p. 14)

Behavioral genetics   The study of the effect of genes on behavior. (p. 46)

Behavior modification   Treatments that use operant conditioning methods to change behavior by helping, often literally teaching, clients to act differently. (p. 571)

Behavior therapy   Treatments that use classical conditioning principles to change behavior by helping, often literally teaching, clients to act differently. (p. 571)

Biased sample   A group of research participants selected from a population each of whose members did not have an equal chance of being chosen for study. (p. 38)

Big-Five model   A model based on the five traits found in many factor-analytic studies of personality that have been proposed as the basic components of human personality: neuroticism, extraversion, openness to experience, agreeableness, and conscientiousness. (p. 493)

Binocular disparity   A depth cue based on the difference between the two retinal images. It exists because each eye receives a slightly different view of the world. This difference, which decreases with distance, is measured by the brain, which combines the two images to create the perception of a single image located at a particular distance. (p. 153)

Biofeedback training   Training methods whereby people can monitor and attempt to control normally unconscious physiological processes such as blood pressure, skin conductance, and muscle tension. (p. 453)

Biological approach (also called *biological model*)   A view in which behavior and behavior disorders are seen as the result of physical processes, especially those relating to the brain and to hormones and other chemicals. (p. 13)

Biological psychologists (also called *physiological psychologists*)   Psychologists who analyze the biological factors influencing behavior and mental processes. (p. 17)

Biological psychology (also called *physiological psychology*)   The psychological specialty that researches the physical and chemical changes that cause and occur in response to behavior and mental processes. (p. 52)

Bipolar cells   Cells through which a visual stimulus passes after going to the photoreceptor cells and before going to the ganglion cells. (p. 111)

Bipolar I disorder   A condition in which a person alternates between the two emotional extremes of depression and mania. (p. 541)

Bisexual   People who engage in sexual activities with partners of both sexes. (p. 374)

Blind spot   The point at which the axons from all of the ganglion cells converge and exit the eyeball. This exit point has no photoreceptors and is therefore insensitive to light. (p. 117)

Blood-brain barrier   The aspect of the structure of blood vessels supplying the brain that allows only certain substances to leave the blood and interact with brain tissue. (p. 309)

Bottom-up processing   Aspects of recognition that depend first on the information about the stimulus that comes up to the brain from the sensory receptors. (See also *top-down processing*.) (p. 158)

Brightness   The overall intensity of all of the wavelengths that make up light. (p. 113)

Brown-Peterson procedure   A method for determining how long unrehearsed information remains in short-term memory. It involves presenting a stimulus to individuals, preventing them from rehearsing it by having them perform a counting task, and then testing recall of the stimulus. (p. 224)

Bulimia nervosa   An eating disorder that involves eating massive quantities of food and then eliminating the food by self-induced vomiting or the use of strong laxatives. (p. 370)

Burnout   A gradually intensifying pattern of physical, psychological, and behavioral dysfunctions in response to a continuous flow of stressors. (p. 460)

Case study   A research method involving the intensive examination of some phenomenon in a particular individual, group, or situation. It is especially useful for studying complex or relatively rare phenomena. (p. 33)

Catatonic schizophrenia A type of schizophrenia characterized by a movement disorder in which the individual may alternate between total immobility or stupor (sometimes holding bizarre, uncomfortable poses for long periods) and wild excitement. *(p. 517)*

Central nervous system (CNS) The part of the nervous system encased in bone, including the brain and the spinal cord, whose primary function is to process information provided by the sensory systems and decide on an appropriate course of action for the motor system. *(p. 61)*

Cerebellum The part of the hindbrain whose function is to control finely coordinated movements and to store learned associations that involve movement, such as those movements required in dancing or athletics. *(p. 66)*

Cerebral cortex The outer surface of the cerebrum, consisting of two cerebral hemispheres. It is physically divided into four areas, called the frontal, parietal, occipital, and temporal lobes. It is divided functionally into the sensory cortex, the motor cortex, and the association cortex. *(p. 71)*

Cerebral hemisphere One-half, either right or left, of the round, almost spherical, outermost part of the cerebrum. *(p. 71)*

Cerebrum (also called *telencephalon*) The largest part of the forebrain; it is divided into the right and left cerebral hemispheres and contains the striatum and the limbic system. *(p. 68)*

Chromosomes Long, thin structures in every biological cell that contain genetic information in the form of more than a thousand genes strung out like a chain. *(p. A-1)*

Chunks Stimuli that are perceived as one unit or a meaningful grouping of information. Most people can hold five to nine (seven plus or minus two) chunks of information in short-term memory. (p. 223)

Circadian rhythm A cycle, such as waking and sleeping, that repeats about once a day. *(p. 302)*

Classical conditioning A procedure in which a neutral stimulus is paired with a stimulus that elicits a reflex or other response until the neutral stimulus alone comes to elicit a similar response. *(p. 178)*

Client-centered therapy (also called *person-centered therapy*) A type of therapy in which the client decides what to talk about and when, without direction, judgment, or interpretation from the therapist. This type of treatment is characterized by three important and interrelated therapist attitudes: unconditional positive regard, empathy, and congruence. (See also *congruence, empathy,* and *unconditional positive regard.*) *(p. 568)*

Clinical psychologists Psychologists who seek to assess, understand, and correct abnormal behavior. *(p. 19)*

Closure A Gestalt grouping principle stating that people tend to fill in missing contours to form a complete object. *(p. 148)*

CNS See *central nervous system.*

Cochlea A fluid-filled spiral structure in the ear in which auditory transduction occurs. *(p. 102)*

Coding Translation of the physical properties of a stimulus into a pattern of neural activity that specifically identifies those physical properties. *(p. 98)*

Cognitive approach A way of looking at human behavior that emphasizes research on how the brain takes in information, creates perceptions, forms and retrieves memories, processes information, and generates integrated patterns of action. *(p. 15)*

Cognitive-behavioral approach An approach to personality that views personality as a label summarizing the unique patterns of thinking and behavior that a person learns. *(p. 471)*

Cognitive-behavior therapy Treatment methods that help clients change the way they think as well as the way they behave. Cognitive obstacles are brought to light, and the therapist encourages the client to try new ways of thinking. *(p. 571)*

Cognitive dissonance theory A theory that proposes that uneasiness results when people's cognitions about themselves or the world are inconsistent with one another. Dissonance motivates people to take some action to make the cognitions consistent. *(p. 618)*

Cognitive map A mental representation, or picture, of the environment. *(pp. 200, 254)*

Cognitive psychologists Psychologists whose research focus is on analysis of the mental processes underlying judgment, decision making,

problem solving, imagining, and other aspects of human thought or cognition. *(p. 17)*

Cognitive psychology The study of the mental processes by which information from the environment is modified, made meaningful, stored, retrieved, used, and communicated to others. *(p. 250)*

Cognitive restructuring A therapy technique or process for coping with stress that involves replacing stress-provoking thoughts with more constructive thoughts in order to make stressors less threatening and disruptive. *(p. 478)*

Cognitive therapy An organized problem-solving approach in which the therapist actively collaborates with clients to help them notice how certain negative thoughts precede anxiety and depression. *(p. 576)*

Common fate A Gestalt grouping principle stating that objects moving in the same direction and at the same speed are perceived as belonging together. *(p. 149)*

Community psychologists Psychologists who work to obtain psychological services for people in need of help and to prevent psychological disorders by working for changes in social systems. *(p. 19)*

Community psychology A movement whose goal is to minimize or prevent psychological disorders through promoting changes in social systems and through community mental health programs designed to make treatment methods more accessible to the poor and others who are unserved or underserved by mental health professionals. *(p. 598)*

Common region A principle of perceptual organization in which elements located within some perimeter or other boundary tend to be grouped together. *(p. 149)*

Competition Any type of behavior in which individuals try to attain a goal for themselves while denying that goal to others. *(p. 661)*

Complementary colors Colors that result in gray when lights of those two colors are mixed. Complementary colors are roughly opposite each other on the color circle. *(p. 115)*

Compliance Adjusting one's behavior because of an explicit or implicit request. *(p. 637)*

Computational approach An approach to perception that focuses on how perception occurs; it tries to explain how computations by the nervous system translate raw sensory stimulation into an experience of reality. *(p. 139)*

Concepts Classes or categories of objects, events, or ideas that have common properties. (See also *artificial concepts* and *natural concepts.*) *(p. 254)*

Concrete operations According to Piaget, the third stage of cognitive development, during which children can learn to count, measure, add, and subtract; their thinking is no longer dominated by visual appearances. *(p. 417)*

Conditioned response (CR) In classical conditioning, the response that the conditioned stimulus elicits. *(p. 178)*

Conditioned stimulus (CS) In classical conditioning, the originally neutral stimulus that, through pairing with the unconditioned stimulus, comes to elicit a conditioned response. *(p. 178)*

Conditions of worth According to Rogers, the feelings an individual experiences when the entire person, instead of a specific behavior, is evaluated. The person may feel that his or her worth as a person depends on displaying the right attitudes, behaviors, and values. *(p. 503)*

Cones Photoreceptors in the retina that use one of three varieties of iodopsin, a color-sensitive photopigment, to distinguish colors. (See also *rods.*) *(p. 110)*

Confirmation bias The tendency to pay more attention to evidence in support of one's hypothesis about a problem than to evidence that refutes that hypothesis. *(p. 266)*

Conflict The result of a person or group believing that another person or group stands in the way of achieving a valued goal. *(p. 661)*

Conformity Changing one's behavior or beliefs to match those of other group members, generally as a result of real or imagined, though unspoken, group pressure. *(p. 637)*

Confounding variable In an experiment, any factor that affects the dependent variable along with or instead of the independent variable. Confounding variables include random variables, the placebo effect, and experimenter bias. *(p. 35)*

Congruence In client-centered therapy, a consistency between the way therapists feel and the way they act toward the client; therapists' unconditional positive regard and empathy must be real, not manufactured. *(p. 569)*

Conscious level The level at which mental activities that people are aware of from moment to moment occur. (See also *preconscious level.*) *(p. 292)*

Consciousness The awareness of external stimuli and our own mental activity. *(p. 290)*

Conservation The ability to recognize that the important properties of a substance, such as number, volume, or weight, remain constant despite changes in shape, length, or position. *(p. 417)*

Constructivist approach A view of perception taken by those who argue that the perceptual system uses fragments of sensory information to construct an image of reality. (See also *ecological approach.*) *(p. 139)*

Contact hypothesis The idea that stereotypes and prejudice toward a group will diminish as contact with the group increases. *(p. 622)*

Context-dependent Referring to memories that can be helped or hindered by similarities or differences between the context in which they are learned and that in which they are recalled. *(p. 228)*

Continuity A Gestalt grouping principle stating that sensations that appear to create a continuous form are perceived as belonging together. *(p. 148)*

Continuous reinforcement schedule In operant conditioning, a pattern in which a reinforcer is delivered every time a particular response occurs. *(p. 192)*

Control group In an experiment, the group that receives no treatment or provides some other base line against which to compare the performance or response of the experimental group. *(p. 35)*

Conventional moral reasoning Reasoning that reflects a concern about other people as well as the belief that morality consists of following rules and conventions. *(p. 439)*

Convergence (1) The receiving of information by one bipolar cell from many photoreceptors. Convergence allows bipolar cells to compare the amount of light on larger regions of the retina and increases the sensation of contrast. *(p. 111)* (2) A depth cue involving the rotation of the eyes to project the image of an object on each retina. The closer an object is, the more cross-eyed the viewer must become to achieve a focused image of it. *(p. 153)*

Convergent thinking The ability to apply the rules of logic and what one knows about the world in order to narrow down the number of possible solutions to a problem or perform some other complex cognitive task. *(p. 350)*

Conversion disorder A somatoform disorder in which a person appears to be, but actually is not, blind, deaf, paralyzed, insensitive to pain in various parts of the body, or even pregnant. (See also *somatoform disorder.*) *(p. 533)*

Cooperation Any type of behavior in which several people work together to attain a goal. *(p. 661)*

Cornea The curved, transparent, protective layer through which light rays enter the eye. *(p. 108)*

Corpus callosum A massive bundle of fibers that connects the right and left cerebral hemispheres and allows them to communicate with each other. Severing the corpus callosum causes difficulty in performing tasks that require information from both hemispheres, such as recognizing and naming objects. *(p. 75)*

Correlation In research, the degree to which one variable is related to another; the strength and direction of the relationship is measured by a correlation coefficient. Correlation does not guarantee causation. *(p. 41)*

Correlation coefficient A statistic, r, that summarizes the strength and direction of a relationship between two variables. Correlation coefficients vary from 0.00 to 1.00. The plus or minus sign indicates the direction, positive or negative, of a relationship. An r of 1.00 or −1.00 indicates a perfect correlation, which means that if you know the value of one variable, you can predict with certainty the value of the other variable. *(p. 42)*

Counseling psychologists See *clinical psychologists.*

Couples therapy A form of therapy that focuses on improving communication between partners. *(p. 579)*

Creativity The capacity to produce original solutions or novel compositions. *(p. 349)*

Critical period An interval during which certain kinds of growth must occur if development is to proceed normally. *(p. 407)*

Critical thinking The process of assessing claims and making judgments on the basis of well-supported evidence. *(p. 28)*

Crystallized intelligence The specific knowledge gained as a result of applying fluid intelligence. It produces verbal comprehension and skill at manipulating numbers. (See also *fluid intelligence.*) *(p. 342)*

Culture The accumulation of values, rules of behavior, forms of expression, religious beliefs, occupational choices, and the like, for a group of people who share a common language and environment. *(p. 23)*

Cyclothymic disorder A more common bipolar disorder characterized by an alternating pattern of less extreme mood swings. *(p. 541)*

Dark adaptation The increasing ability to see in the dark as time passes, due to the synthesis of more photopigments by the photoreceptors. *(p. 109)*

Data Numbers that represent research findings and provide the basis for research conclusions. *(p. 30)*

Decay The gradual disappearance of the mental representation of a stimulus. *(p. 236)*

Deep structure An abstract representation of the relationships expressed in a sentence; the various underlying meanings of a given sentence. *(p. 275)*

Defense mechanisms Psychological responses that help protect a person from anxiety and the other negative emotions accompanying stress; they do little or nothing to eliminate the source of stress. *(p. 485)*

Deficiency orientation According to Maslow, a preoccupation with meeting perceived needs for material things a person does not have that can lead to perceiving life as a meaningless exercise in disappointment and boredom. *(p. 503)*

Degrees of freedom The total sample size or number of scores in a data set, less the number of experimental groups. *(p. A-15)*

Deindividuation A hypothesized psychological state occurring in group members that results in loss of individuality and a tendency to do things not normally done when alone. *(p. 635)*

Delusions False beliefs, such as those experienced by people suffering from schizophrenia or extreme depression. *(p. 539)*

Dendrites In a neuron, the fibers that receive signals from the axons of other neurons and carry that signal to the cell body. A neuron can have up to several hundred dendrites. *(p. 54)*

Deoxyribonucleic acid (DNA) The molecular structure of a gene that provides the genetic code. Each DNA molecule consists of two strands of sugar, phosphate, and nitrogen-containing molecules twisted around each other in a double spiral. *(p. A-1)*

Dependent variable In an experiment, the factor affected by the independent variable. *(p. 34)*

Depressants Psychoactive drugs that inhibit the functioning of the central nervous system. *(p. 311)*

Depth perception Perception of distance, one of the most important factors underlying size and shape constancy. Depth perception allows us to experience the world in three-dimensional depth, not as a two-dimensional movie. *(p. 135)*

Descriptive statistics Numbers that summarize a set of research data. *(p. 40)*

Developmental psychologists Psychologists who seek to understand, describe, and explore how behavior and mental processes change over the course of a lifetime. *(p. 18)*

Developmental psychology The psychological specialty that documents the course of people's social, emotional, moral, and intellectual development over the life span and explores how development in different domains fits together, is affected by experience, and relates to other areas of psychology. *(p. 404)*

Diathesis-stress model An integrative approach to psychological disorders that recognizes that each person inherits certain physical predispositions that leave him or her vulnerable to problems that may or may not appear, depending on what kinds of situations that person confronts. People who must deal with particular stressors may or may not develop psychopathology, depending on their predisposition and ability to cope with those stressors. *(p. 522)*

Difference threshold   See *just-noticeable difference.*

Discrimination   Differential treatment of various groups; the behavioral component of prejudice. (See also *prejudice.*) *(p. 621)*

Discriminative stimuli   Stimuli that signal whether reinforcement is available if a certain response is made. *(p. 190)*

Diseases of adaptation   Illnesses that are caused or promoted by stressors. *(p. 458)*

Disorganized schizophrenia   A rare type of schizophrenia characterized by a variety of jumbled and unrelated delusions and hallucinations. The person may display incoherent speech, strange facial grimaces, and meaningless ritual movements and may neglect personal hygiene and lose bowel and bladder control. *(p. 517)*

Dissociation theory   A theory that defines hypnosis as a condition in which people relax central control of mental processes and share some of that control with the hypnotist, who is allowed to determine what the person will experience and do. According to this theory, hypnosis is a socially agreed-upon opportunity to display one's ability to let mental functions become dissociated. (See also *role theory* and *state theory.*) *(p. 307)*

Dissociative amnesia   A psychological disorder marked by a sudden loss of memory, which results in the inability to recall one's own name, occupation, or other identifying information. *(p. 535)*

Dissociative disorders   Rare conditions that involve sudden and usually temporary disruptions in a person's memory, consciousness, or identity. *(p. 535)*

Dissociative fugue   A sudden loss of memory and the assumption of a new identity in a new locale. *(p. 535)*

Dissociative identity disorder   (previously known as *multiple personality disorder*)   The most famous and least commonly seen dissociative disorder, in which a person reports having more than one identity, and sometimes several, each of which speaks, acts, and writes in a very different way. *(p. 535)*

Divergent thinking   The ability to think along many alternative paths to generate many different solutions to a problem. *(p. 350)*

DNA   See *deoxyribonucleic acid.*

Dopamine   A neurotransmitter used in the parts of the brain—such as the substantia nigra and the striatum—that regulate movement. Dopamine is also involved in the the experience of pleasure. Malfunctioning dopamine systems are related to the appearance of movement disorders such as Parkinson's disease, as well as to schizophrenia. *(p. 84)*

Double-blind design   A research design in which neither the experimenter nor the participants know who is in the experimental group and who is in the control group. This design helps prevent experimenter bias (a confounding variable). *(p. 36)*

Dreams   Story-like sequences of images, sensations, and perception that last anywhere from several seconds to many minutes and occur mainly during REM sleep (though they may take place at other times). *(p. 305)*

Drive   In drive reduction theory, a psychological state of arousal, created by an imbalance in homeostasis that prompts an organism to take action to restore the balance and, in the process, reduce the drive. (See also *need, primary drives,* and *secondary drives.*) *(p. 361)*

Drive reduction theory   A theory of motivation stating that much motivation arises from constant imbalances in homeostasis. (See also *drive* and *homeostasis.*) *(p. 361)*

Dysthymic disorder   A pattern of depression in which the person shows the sad mood, lack of interest, and loss of pleasure associated with major depressive disorder, but to a lesser degree. (See also *major depressive disorder.*) *(p. 539)*

Ecological approach   An approach to perception maintaining that humans and other species are so well adapted to their natural environment that many aspects of the world are perceived automatically and at the sensory level, without requiring higher-level analysis and inferences. (See also *constructionist approach.*) *(p. 140)*

ECT   See electroconvulsive therapy.

Educational psychologists   Psychologists who study methods by which instructors teach and students learn, and who apply their results to improving such methods. *(p. 19)*

Ego   In psychodynamic theory, that part of the personality that makes compromises and mediates conflicts between and among the demands of the id, the superego, and the real world; the ego operates according to the reality principle. (See also *id* and *reality principle.*) *(p. 484)*

Elaboration likelihood model   A model of attitude change suggesting that people who have the motivation and ability to carefully evaluate an argument change their attitudes by considering the argument's content (the central route), while those with less motivation or ability tend to take a peripheral route and overrely on various (often irrelevant) persuasion cues. *(p. 617)*

Elaborative rehearsal   A memorization method that involves thinking about how new information relates to information already stored in long-term memory. *(p. 218)*

Electra complex   A pattern proposed by Freud in which young girls develop an attachment to their fathers and compete with their mothers for their father's attention. *(p. 486)*

Electroconvulsive therapy (ECT)   A brief electric shock administered to the brain, usually to reduce profound depression that does not respond to drug treatments. *(p. 590)*

Embryo   The developing individual from the fourteenth day after fertilization until the third month after fertilization. *(p. 407)*

Emotion   A transitory, valenced experience that is felt as happening to the self, is generated, in part, by the cognitive appraisal of a situation, and is accompanied by both learned and reflexive physical responses. *(p. 387)*

Empathy   In client-centered therapy, the therapist's attempt to appreciate how the world looks from the client's point of view. Empathy requires an internal perspective, a focus on what the client might be thinking and feeling. *(p. 569)*

Empathy-altruism theory   A theory that suggests that people help others because of empathy with their needs. *(p. 657)*

Empirically supported therapies   Treatments for psychological disorders whose effectiveness has been validated by controlled experimental research. *(p. 583)*

Encoding   The process of putting information into a form that the memory system can accept and use; the process of constructing mental representations of physical stimuli. *(p. 214)*

Encoding specificity principle   A retrieval principle stating that the ability of a cue to aid retrieval effectively depends on the degree to which it taps into information that was encoded at the time of the original learning. *(p. 227)*

Endocrine system   Cells that form organs called glands and communicate with one another by secreting chemicals called hormones. *(p. 87)*

Endorphin   One of a class of neurotransmitters that can bind to the same receptors that opiates, such as morphine and heroin, bind to and that produces the same behavioral effects of pain relief, euphoria, and, in high doses, sleep. *(p. 85)*

Environmental psychologists   Psychologists who study the effects of the physical environment on behavior and mental processes. *(p. 20)*

Environmental psychology   The study of the relationship between people's physical environment and their behavior. *(p. 652)*

Episodic memory   A person's recall of a specific event that happened while he or she was present. *(p. 215)*

Escape conditioning   A type of learning in which an organism learns to make a particular response in order to terminate an aversive stimulus. *(p. 187)*

Estrogens   Feminine hormones that circulate in the bloodstream of both men and women; relatively more estrogens circulate in women. One of the main estrogens is estradiol. (See also *progestins.*) *(p. 372)*

Ethnic identity   The part of a person's identity associated with the racial, religious, or cultural group to which the person belongs. *(p. 437)*

Ethologists　Scientists who study animals in their natural environment to observe how environmental cues affect behavior. *(p. 14)*

Evoked brain potential　A small, temporary change in EEG voltage that is evoked by some stimulus. One such change is the P300, a positive swing in electrical voltage that occurs about 300 milliseconds after a stimulus. It can be used to determine if a stimulus distracts a person's attention from a given task. *(p. 253)*

Evolutionary approach　An approach to psychology that emphasizes the inherited, adaptive aspects of behavior and mental processes. *(p. 13)*

Excitatory postsynaptic potential (EPSP)　A postsynaptic potential that depolarizes the neuronal membrane, bringing the cell closer to threshold for firing an action potential. *(p. 58)*

Expected value　The total benefit to be expected if a decision, though not always correct, were repeated several times. *(p. 271)*

Experiments　Situations in which the researcher manipulates one variable and then observes the effect of that manipulation on another variable, while holding all other variables constant. *(p. 34)*

Experimental group　In an experiment, the group that receives the experimental treatment; its performance or response is compared with that of one or more control groups. *(p. 35)*

Experimental psychologists　Psychologists who conduct experiments aimed at understanding learning, memory, perception, and other basic behavioral and mental processes. *(p. 17)*

Experimenter bias　A confounding variable that occurs when an experimenter unintentionally encourages participants to respond in a way that supports the hypothesis. *(p. 36)*

Expert systems　Computer programs that help people solve problems in a fairly restricted, specific area, such as the diagnosis of diseases. *(p. 269)*

Explicit memory　The process through which people deliberately try to remember something. *(p. 216)*

Extinction　The gradual disappearance of a conditioned response or operant behavior due to elimination either of the association between conditioned and unconditioned stimuli or of rewards for certain behaviors. *(pp. 179, 574)*

Factor analysis　A statistical technique that involves computing correlations between large numbers of variables. Factor analysis is commonly used in the study of intelligence and intelligence tests. *(p. 342)*

Familial retardation　Cases of mild retardation for which no environmental or genetic cause can be found. Most of the people in this group come from families in the lower socioeconomic classes and are more likely than those suffering from a genetic defect to have a relative who is also retarded. *(p. 352)*

Family therapy　A type of treatment inspired by the psychodynamic theory that many psychological disorders are rooted in family conflicts. It involves two or more individuals from the same family, one of whose problems make him or her the initially identified client, although the family itself ultimately becomes the client. *(p. 578)*

Feature detectors　Cells in the cortex that respond to a specific feature of an object. *(p. 120)*

Fetal alcohol syndrome　A pattern of defects found in babies born to alcoholic women that includes physical malformations of the face and mental retardation. *(p. 408)*

Fetus　The developing individual from the third month after conception until birth. *(p. 407)*

FI　See *fixed-interval schedule.*

Fiber tracts　Axons that travel together in bundles. They are also known as *pathways. (p. 63)*

Fight-or-flight syndrome　The physical reactions initiated by the sympathetic nervous system that prepare the body to fight or to run from a threatening situation. These reactions include increased heart rate and blood pressure, rapid or irregular breathing, dilated pupils, perspiration, dry mouth, increased blood sugar, decreased gastrointestinal motility, and other changes. (See also *sympathetic nervous system.*) *(pp. 89, 390)*

Figure　That part of the visual field that has meaning, stands in front of the rest, and always seems to include the contours or borders that separate it from the relatively meaningless background. (See also *ground.*) *(p. 133)*

Five-factor model　See *Big-Five model.*

Fixed-interval (FI) schedule　In operant conditioning, a type of partial reinforcement schedule that provides reinforcement for the first response that occurs after some fixed time has passed since the last reward. *(p. 193)*

Fixed-ratio (FR) schedule　In operant conditioning, a type of partial reinforcement schedule that provides reinforcement following a fixed number of responses. *(p. 192)*

Flooding　A procedure for reducing anxiety that involves keeping a person in a feared, but harmless, situation. Once deprived of his or her normally rewarding escape pattern, the client has no reason for continued anxiety. *(p. 574)*

Fluid intelligence　The basic power of reasoning and problem solving. Fluid intelligence produces induction, deduction, reasoning, and understanding of relationships between different ideas. (See also *crystallized intelligence.*) *(p. 342)*

Forebrain　The most highly developed part of the brain; it is responsible for the most complex aspects of behavior and mental life. *(p. 68)*

Formal operational period　According to Piaget, the fourth stage in cognitive development, usually beginning around age eleven. It is characterized by the ability to engage in hypothetical thinking, including the imagining of logical consequences and the ability to think and reason about abstract concepts. *(p. 438)*

Formal reasoning　The process of following a set of rigorous procedures for reaching valid conclusions. *(p. 258)*

Fovea　A region in the center of the retina where cones are highly concentrated. *(p. 110)*

FR　See *fixed-ratio schedule.*

Free-floating anxiety　See *generalized anxiety disorder.*

Frequency　The number of complete waveforms, or cycles, that pass by a given point in space every second. For sound waves, the unit of measure is called a hertz (Hz); one hertz is one cycle per second. *(p. 100)*

Frequency histogram　A graphic presentation of data that consists of a set of bars, each of which represents how frequently different values of variables occur in a data set. *(p. A-9)*

Frequency matching (also called *volley theory*)　A theory of hearing that explains how frequency is coded: The firing rate of a neuron matches the frequency of a sound wave. For example, one neuron might fire at every peak of a wave; so a 20-hertz sound could be coded by a neuron that fires twenty times per second. *(p. 104)*

Frustration-aggression hypothesis　A proposition that the existence of frustration always leads to some form of aggressive behavior. *(p. 649)*

Functional analysis　A method of understanding behavior (and thus the person) that involves analyzing exactly what responses occur under what conditions. This approach emphasizes the role of operant conditioning. (See also *operant conditioning.*) *(p. 497)*

Functional fixedness　A tendency to think about familiar objects in familiar ways that may prevent using them in other, more creative ways. *(p. 266)*

Fundamental attribution error　A bias toward overattributing the behavior of others to internal factors. *(p. 613)*

g　A general intelligence factor that Charles Spearman postulated as accounting for positive correlations between people's scores on all sorts of mental ability tests. *(p. 342)*

GABA　A neurotransmitter that inhibits the firing of neurons. Disruptions in GABA systems are related to the appearance of anxiety, epilepsy, and Huntington's disease, a disorder characterized by uncontrollable movements and loss of cognitive ability. *(p. 84)*

Ganglion cells　The cells in the retina that generate action potentials. They are stimulated by bipolar cells; their axons extend out of the retina and travel to the brain. *(p. 112)*

GAS　See *general adaptation syndrome.*

Gate control theory　A theory of pain suggesting a functional gate in the spinal cord that either lets pain impulses travel upward to the brain or blocks their progress. *(p. 129)*

Gender roles　General patterns of work, appearance, and behavior that a society associates with being male or female. *(p. 433)*

Gender schemas　The generalizations children develop about what toys, activities, and occupations are "appropriate" for males versus females. *(p. 434)*

Genes The biological instructions inherited from both parents and located on the chromosomes that provide the blueprint for physical development throughout the life span. (See also *deoxyribonucleic acid, genotype,* and *phenotype.*) (p. A-1)

General adaptation syndrome (GAS) A consistent and very general pattern of responses triggered by the effort to adapt to any stressor. The syndrome consists of three stages: alarm reaction, resistance, and exhaustion. (p. 456)

Generalized anxiety disorder A condition that involves relatively mild but long-lasting anxiety that is not focused on any particular object or situation. (p. 530)

Generativity The concern of adults in their thirties with producing or generating something. (p. 444)

Genetics The biology of inheritance. (p. A-1)

Genital stage The fifth and last of Freud's psychosexual stages, which begins during adolescence when the person begins to mature physically and sexual impulses begin to appear at the conscious level. The young person begins to seek out relationships through which sexual impulses can be gratified. This stage spans the rest of life. (p. 486)

Genotype The full set of genes, inherited from both parents, contained in twenty-three pairs of chromosomes. (p. A-2)

Gestalt psychologists A group of psychologists who suggested, among other things, that there are six principles or properties behind the grouping of stimuli that lead the human perceptual system to glue raw sensations together in particular ways, organizing stimuli into a world of shapes and patterns. (See also *closure, continuity, proximity, similarity,* and *simplicity.*) (p. 148)

Gestalt therapy A form of treatment based on the assumption that clients' problems arise when people behave in accordance with other people's expectations rather than on the basis of their own true feelings. Gestalt therapy seeks to create conditions in which clients can become more unified, more self-aware, and more self-accepting. (p. 570)

Glands Organs that secrete hormones into the bloodstream. (p. 88)

Glial cells Cells in the nervous system that hold neurons together and help them communicate with one another. (p. 54)

Glutamate A neurotransmitter that helps strengthen synaptic connections between neurons, thereby facilitating learning and memory. (p. 84)

Gradient A continuous change across the visual field. (See also *movement gradient* and *texture gradient.*) (p. 136)

Grammar A set of rules for combining the symbols, such as words, used in a given language. (See also *language.*) (p. 274)

Ground The meaningless, contourless part of the visual field; the background. (See also *figure.*) (p. 133)

Group polarization The tendency for groups to make decisions that are more extreme than the decision an individual group member would make. (p. 273)

Group therapy Psychotherapy involving five to ten individuals. Clients can be observed interacting with one another; they can feel relieved and less alone as they listen to others who have similar difficulties, which tends to raise each client's hope and expectations for improvement; and they can learn from one another. (p. 576)

Groupthink A pattern of thinking that, over time, renders group members unable to evaluate realistically the wisdom of various options and decisions. (p. 666)

Growth orientation According to Maslow, drawing satisfaction from what is available in life, rather than focusing on what is missing. (p. 503)

Gustation The sense that detects chemicals in solutions that come into contact with receptors inside the mouth; the sense of taste. (p. 121)

Habituation The process of adapting to stimuli that do not change. (p.176)

Hallucinations False perceptions, such as hearing voices or, less commonly, perceiving nonexistent sights, smells, tastes, and touches. (See also *positive symptoms.*) (p. 545)

Health promotion The process of altering or eliminating behaviors that pose risks to health and at the same time fostering healthy behavior patterns. (p. 474)

Health psychologists Psychologists who study the effects of behavior and mental processes on health and illness, and vice versa. (p. 19)

Health psychology A field in which psychologists conduct and apply research aimed at promoting human health and preventing illness. (p. 452)

Height in the visual field A depth cue whereby more distant objects are higher in the visual field than those nearby. (p. 135)

Helping behavior Any act that is intended to benefit another person. (p. 654)

Heterosexual Sexual motivation that is focused on members of the opposite sex. (p. 374)

Heuristics Mental shortcuts or rules of thumb. (See also *anchoring heuristic, availability heuristic,* and *representativeness heuristic.*) (p. 260)

Hindbrain An extension of the spinal cord contained inside the skull. Nuclei in the hindbrain, especially in the medulla, control blood pressure, heart rate, breathing, and other vital functions. (p. 64)

Hippocampus A structure in the forebrain associated with the formation of new memories. (p. 68)

Homeostasis The tendency for organisms to keep their physiological systems at a stable, steady level by constantly adjusting themselves in response to change. (p. 361)

Homosexual Sexual motivation that is focused on members of a person's own sex. (p. 374)

Hormones Chemicals that are secreted by a gland into the bloodstream, which carries them throughout the body, enabling the gland to stimulate remote cells with which it has no direct connection. (p. 88)

Hue The essential color determined by the dominant wavelength of a light. Black, white, and gray are not considered hues because they have no predominant wavelength. (p. 113)

Humanistic approach An approach to psychology that views behavior as controlled by the decisions that people make about their lives based on their perceptions of the world. (See also *phenomenological approach.*) (p. 15)

Hunger The general state of wanting to eat. (p. 364)

Hypnosis An altered state of consciousness brought on by special induction techniques and characterized by varying degrees of responsiveness to suggestions for changes in experience and behavior. (pp. 28, 306)

Hypnotic susceptibility The degree to which people respond to hypnotic suggestions. (p. 177)

Hypochondriasis A strong, unjustified fear of physical illness. (p. 534)

Hypothalamus A structure in the forebrain that regulates hunger, thirst, and sex drives; it has many connections to and from the autonomic nervous system and to other parts of the brain. (p. 68)

Hypothesis In scientific research, a prediction stated as a specific, testable proposition about a phenomenon. (p. 29)

Id In psychodynamic theory, a personality component containing a reservoir of unconscious psychic energy (sometimes called libido) that includes the basic instincts, desires, and impulses with which all people are born. The id operates according to the pleasure principle, seeking immediate satisfaction, regardless of society's rules or the rights or feelings of others. (See also *pleasure principle.*) (p. 484)

Identity crisis A phase during which an adolescent attempts to develop an integrated image of himself or herself as a unique person by pulling together self-knowledge acquired during childhood. (p. 438)

Immediate memory span The maximum number of items a person can recall perfectly after one presentation of the items, usually six or seven items. (See also *chunks.*) (p. 223)

Immune system The body's first line of defense against invading substances and microorganisms. The immune system includes T-cells, which attack virally infected cells; B-cells, which form antibodies against foreign substances; and natural killer cells, which kill invaders like tumor cells and virally infected cells. (pp. 90, 445)

Implicit memory The unintentional recollection and influence of prior experiences. (p. 216)

Incentive theory A theory of motivation stating that behavior is goal directed; actions are directed toward attaining desirable stimuli, called positive incentives, and toward avoiding unwanted stimuli, called negative incentives. (p. 363)

Independent variable   The variable manipulated by the researcher in an experiment. *(p. 34)*

Industrial-organizational psychologists   Psychologists who study ways to improve efficiency, productivity, and satisfaction among workers and the organizations that employ them. *(p. 19)*

Inferential statistics   A set of procedures that provides a measure of how likely it is that research results came about by chance. These procedures put a precise mathematical value on the confidence or probability that rerunning the same experiment would yield similar (or even stronger) results. *(pp. 40, A-14)*

Informal reasoning   The process of evaluating a conclusion, a theory, or a course of action on the basis of the credibility of evidence. *(p. 260)*

Information processing   The process of taking in, remembering or forgetting, and using information. It is one model for understanding people's cognitive abilities. *(p. 397)*

Information-processing approach   An approach to the study of intelligence that focuses on mental operations, such as attention and memory, that underlie intelligent behavior. *(pp. 342, 397)*

Information-processing model   A model of memory in which information must pass through sensory memory, short-term memory, and long-term memory in order to become firmly embedded in memory. *(p. 220)*

Information-processing system   The procedures for receiving information, representing information with symbols, and manipulating those representations so that the brain can interpret and respond to the information. *(pp. 251, 265)*

Inhibitory postsynaptic potential (IPSP)   A postsynaptic potential that hyperpolarizes the neuronal membrane, taking the cell farther from the threshold for firing an action potential. *(p. 58)*

Insight   In problem solving, a sudden understanding about what is required to produce a desired effect. *(p. 201)*

Insomnia   The most common sleeping problem, in which a person feels tired during the day because of trouble falling asleep or staying asleep at night. *(p. 300)*

Instincts   Innate, automatic dispositions toward responding in a particular way when confronted with a specific stimulus; instincts produce behavior over which an animal has no control. *(p. 359)*

Instinct theory   A view that explains human behavior as motivated by automatic, involuntary, and unlearned responses. *(p. 359)*

Instrumental conditioning   A process through which responses are learned that help produce some rewarding or desired effect. *(p. 185)*

Intelligence   Those attributes that center around reasoning skills, knowledge of one's culture, and the ability to arrive at innovative solutions to problems. *(p. 323)*

Intelligence quotient   An index of intelligence once calculated by dividing one's tested mental age by one's chronological age and multiplying by 100. Today, IQ is a number that reflects the degree to which a person's score on an intelligence test deviates from the average score of others in his or her age group. *(p. 326)*

Interference   The process through which either the storage or the retrieval of information is impaired by the presence of other information. (See also *proactive interference* and *retroactive interference*.) *(p. 236)*

Intermittent reinforcement schedule   See *partial reinforcement schedule*.

Internal noise   The spontaneous, random firing of nerve cells that occurs because the nervous system is always active. Variations in internal noise can cause absolute thresholds to vary. *(p. 129)*

Interneurons   Cells in the retina through which photoreceptor cells make connections to other types of cells in the retina. *(p. 111)*

Interpersonal conflict   A process of social dispute in which one person believes that another stands in the way of something of value. *(p. 621)*

Interposition   A depth cue whereby closer objects block one's view of things farther away. *(p. 151)*

Ions   Molecules that carry a positive or negative electrical charge. *(p. 55)*

IQ score   See *intelligence quotient*.

IQ test   A test designed to measure intelligence on an objective, standardized scale. *(p. 325)*

Iris   The part of the eye that gives it its color and adjusts the amount of light entering it by constricting to reduce the size of the pupil or relaxing to enlarge it. *(p.108)*

Jet lag   A syndrome of fatigue, irritability, inattention, and sleeping problems caused by air travel across several time zones. *(p. 302)*

JND   See *just-noticeable difference*.

Just-noticeable difference (JND)   (also called *difference threshold*)   The smallest detectable difference in stimulus energy. (See also *Weber's law*.) *(p. 145)*

Kinesthesia   The sense that tells you where the parts of your body are with respect to one another. *(p. 132)*

Language   Symbols and a set of rules for combining them that provides a vehicle for the mind's communication with itself and the most important means of communicating with others. *(p. 274)*

Latency period   The fourth of Freud's psychosexual stages, usually beginning during the fifth year of life, in which sexual impulses lie dormant and the child focuses attention on education and other matters. *(p. 486)*

Latent learning   Learning that is not demonstrated at the time it occurs. *(p. 200)*

Lateral geniculate nucleus (LGN)   A region of the thalamus in which the axons from most of the ganglion cells in the retina finally end and form synapses. *(p. 117)*

Lateral inhibition   The enhancement of the sensation of contrast that occurs when greater response to light in one photoreceptor cell suppresses the response of a neighboring cell. *(p. 111)*

Lateralized   Referring to the tendency for one cerebral hemisphere to excel at a particular function or skill compared to the other hemisphere. *(p. 76)*

Law of effect   A law stating that if a response made in the presence of a particular stimulus is followed by a reward, that same response is more likely to be made the next time the stimulus is encountered. Responses that are not rewarded are less likely to be performed again. *(p. 185)*

Learned helplessness   A phenomenon that occurs when an organism has or believes that it has no control over its environment. The typical result of this situation or belief is to stop trying to exert control. *(p. 198)*

Learning   The modification through experience of pre-existing behavior and understanding. *(p. 175)*

Lens   The part of the eye directly behind the pupil. Like the lens in a camera, the lens of the eye is curved so that it bends light rays, focusing them on the retina, at the back of the eye. *(p. 108)*

Levels-of-processing model   A view stating that differences in how well something is remembered reflect the degree or depth to which incoming information is mentally processed. How long the information stays in memory depends on how elaborate the mental processing and encoding becomes. *(p. 218)*

LGN   See *lateral geniculate nucleus*.

Libido   See *id*.

Light and shadow   A feature of visual stimuli that contributes to depth perception. *(p. 136)*

Light intensity   A physical dimension of light waves that refers to how much energy the light contains; it determines the brightness of light. (See also *light wavelength*.) *(p. 107)*

Light wavelength   A physical dimension of light waves that refers to their length. At a given intensity, different light wavelengths produce sensations of different colors. (See also *light intensity*.) *(p. 108)*

Likelihood principle   The notion that people perceive objects in the way that experience tells them is the most likely physical arrangement. *(p.149)*

Limbic system   A set of brain structures that play important roles in regulating emotion and memory. The limbic system is a system because its components have major interconnections and influence related functions. *(p. 69)*

Linear perspective   A depth cue whereby the closer together two converging lines are, the greater the perceived distance. *(p. 152)*

Locus coeruleus   A small nucleus in the brainstem that contains most of the cell bodies of neurons that use norepinephrine in the brain. *(p. 66)*

Long-term memory (LTM)   The stage of memory in which semantic encoding dominates, and for which the capacity to store new information is believed to be unlimited. *(p. 224)*

Looming   A motion cue involving a rapid expansion in the size of an image so that it fills the available space on the retina. People tend to perceive a looming object as an approaching stimulus, not as an expanding object viewed at a constant distance. *(p. 153)*

Loudness   A psychological dimension of sound determined by the amplitude of a sound wave; waves with greater amplitude produce sensations of louder sounds. Loudness is described in units called decibels. *(p. 100)*

Lucid dreaming   The awareness that a dream is a dream while it is happening. This phenomenon is evidence that sleep does not involve a total loss of consciousness or mental functioning. *(p. 305)*

Magnetic resonance imaging (MRI)   A highly advanced technique that detects naturally occurring magnetic fields surrounding atoms in brain tissue to create exceptionally clear pictures of the structures of the brain. *(p. 61)*

Magnitude estimation   The process of judging the size of the difference between two stimuli. *(p. 146)*

Maintenance rehearsal   Repeating information over and over to keep it active in short-term memory. This method is ineffective for encoding information into long-term memory. (See also *elaborative rehearsal*.) *(p. 218)*

Major depressive disorder   A condition in which a person feels sad and hopeless for weeks or months, often losing interest in all activities and taking pleasure in nothing. Weight loss and lack of sleep or, in some cases, overeating and excessive sleeping are frequent accompaniments, as are problems in concentrating, making decisions, and thinking clearly. *(p. 539)*

Mania   An elated, very active emotional state. *(p. 541)*

Matching hypothesis   A hypothesis that people are most likely to be attracted to others who are similar to themselves in physical attractiveness. *(p. 627)*

Maturation   Natural growth or change, triggered by biological factors, that unfolds in a fixed sequence relatively independent of the environment. *(p. 405)*

Mean   A measure of central tendency that is the arithmetic average of the scores in a set of data; the sum of the values of all the scores divided by the total number of scores. *(p.41)*

Median   A measure of central tendency that is the halfway point in a set of data: Half the scores fall above the median, half fall below it. *(p. 41)*

Medical model   An approach that views mental disorder as caused by physical illness or an imbalance in bodily processes. (See also *neurobiological model*.) *(p. 493)*

Meditation   A set of techniques designed to create an altered state of consciousness characterized by inner peace, calmness, and tranquillity. *(p. 179)*

Medulla   An area in the hindbrain that controls blood pressure, heart rate, breathing, and other vital functions through the use of reflexes and feedback systems. *(p. 64)*

Menopause   The process whereby a woman's reproductive capacity ceases. *(p. 441)*

Mental ability   A capacity to perform the higher mental processes of reasoning, remembering, understanding, problem solving, and decision making. *(p. 322)*

Mental chronometry   The timing of mental events that allows researchers to infer what stages exist during cognition. (See also *evoked potential* and *information-processing system*.) *(p. 266)*

Mental model   A cluster of propositions that represents people's understanding of how things work and guides their interaction with those things. *(p. 256)*

Mental set   The tendency for old patterns of problem solving to persist, even when they might not be the most efficient method for solving a given problem. *(p. 266)*

Metacognition   The knowledge of what strategies to apply, when to apply them, and how to deploy them in new situations so that new specific knowledge can be gained and different problems mastered. *(p. 353)*

Method of savings   A method for measuring forgetting by computing the difference between the number of repetitions needed to learn, say, a list of words and the number of repetitions needed to relearn it after some time has elapsed. *(p. 235)*

Midbrain   A small structure that lies between the hindbrain and the forebrain. The midbrain relays information from the eyes, ears, and skin, and controls certain types of automatic behaviors in response to information received through those structures. *(p. 67)*

Midlife transition   A point at around age forty when adults take stock of their lives, reappraise their priorities, and, sometimes, modify their lives and relationships. *(p. 423)*

Minority influence   A phenomenon whereby members of a numerical minority in a group alters the view of the majority. *(p. 640)*

Mnemonics   Strategies for placing information in an organized context in order to remember it. Two powerful methods are the peg-word system and the method of loci. *(p. 243)*

Mode   A measure of central tendency that is the value or score that occurs most frequently in a data set. *(p. 41)*

Modeling   A method of therapy in which desirable behaviors are demonstrated as a way of teaching them to clients. *(p. 572)*

Mood disorder (also called *affective disorder*)   A condition in which a person experiences extremes of mood for long periods, shifts from one mood extreme to another, and experiences moods that are inconsistent with the happy or sad events around them. *(p. 539)*

Morpheme   The smallest unit of language that has meaning. (See also *phoneme*.) *(p. 275)*

Motion parallax   A depth cue whereby a difference in the apparent rate of movement of different objects provides information on the relative distance of those objects. *(p. 153)*

Motivation   The influences that account for the initiation, direction, intensity, and persistence of behavior. *(p. 358)*

Motive   A reason or purpose for behavior. *(p. 358)*

Motor cortex   The part of the cerebral cortex whose neurons control voluntary movements in specific parts of the body. Some neurons control movement of the hand; others stimulate movement of the foot, the knee, the head, and so on. *(p. 73)*

Motor systems   The parts of the nervous system that influence muscles and other organs to respond to the environment in some way. *(p. 61)*

Movement gradient   The graduated difference in the apparent movement of objects across the visual field. Faster relative movement across the visual field indicates closer distance. *(p. 136)*

Multiple intelligences   Howard Gardner's theory that people are possessed of eight semi-independent kinds of intelligence, only three of which are measured by standard IQ tests. *(p. 345)*

Multiple personality disorder   See *dissociative identity disorder*.

Myelin   A fatty substance that wraps around some axons and increases the speed of action potentials. *(p. 56)*

Narcissistic personality disorder   A personality disorder characterized by an exaggerated sense of self-importance combined with self-doubt. *(p. 521)*

Narcolepsy   A daytime sleep disorder in which a person switches abruptly and without warning from an active, often emotional waking state into several minutes of REM sleep. In most cases the muscle paralysis associated with REM causes the person to collapse on the spot and to remain briefly immobilized even after awakening. *(p. 300)*

Narrative   A mental representation of information in the form of a story. *(p. 256)*

Natural concepts   Concepts that have no fixed set of defining features but instead share a set of characteristic features. Members of a natural concept need not possess all of the characteristic features. *(p. 255)*

Naturalistic observation   The process of watching without interfering as a phenomenon occurs in the natural environment. *(p. 32)*

Need   In drive reduction theory, a biological requirement for well-being that is created by an imbalance in homeostasis. (See also *drive, primary drives,* and *secondary drives*.) *(p. 361)*

Need achievement   A motive influenced by the degree to which a person establishes specific goals, cares about meeting those goals, and experiences feelings of satisfaction by doing so; it is often measured by the Thematic Apperception Test. *(p. 378)*

Negative feedback system An arrangement in which the output of a system is monitored, such that output above a certain level will terminate further output until activity returns to an acceptable level. (*p. 89*)

Negative reinforcers Unpleasant stimuli, such as pain. The removal of a negative reinforcer following some response is likely to strengthen the probability of that response recurring. The process of strengthening behavior by following it with the removal of a negative reinforcer is called negative reinforcement. (See also *positive reinforcers*.) (*p. 186*)

Negative symptoms A category of schizophrenic symptoms. They include the absence of feelings of pleasure, lack of speech, and flat affect. (See also *positive symptoms*.) (*p. 547*)

Nervous system A complex combination of cells whose primary function is to allow an organism to gain information about what is going on inside and outside the body and to respond appropriately. (*p. 52*)

Neural networks Neurons that operate together to perform complex functions. Neuroscientists involved in artificial intelligence research are seeking to duplicate these networks on high-speed computers. (*p. 59*)

Neurobiological model A more contemporary name for the medical model of psychological disorder, which reflects a focus on disturbances in the anatomy and chemistry of the brain and other biological processes. (*p. 520*)

Neuroleptic See *antipsychotic*.

Neuromodulators Neurotransmitters that in some circumstances modify the response to other neurotransmitters at a synapse. (*p. 77*)

Neurons The fundamental units of the nervous system; nerve cells. Neurons have the ability to communicate with one another. (*p. 54*)

Neurotransmitters Chemicals that assist in the transfer of signals from the axon of one neuron (presynaptic cell) across the synapse to the receptors on the dendrite of another neuron (postsynaptic cell). (*p. 57*)

Neurotransmitter system A group of neurons that communicates by using the same neurotransmitter, such as acetylcholine or dopamine. (*p. 82*)

Nightmares Frightening, sometimes recurring dreams that take place during REM sleep. (*p. 302*)

Night terrors A rapid awakening from stage 4 sleep, often accompanied by a horrific dream that causes the dreamer to sit up staring, let out a bloodcurdling scream, and experience a state of intense fear that may last up to thirty minutes. This phenomenon is especially common in children, but milder versions occur among adults. (*p. 302*)

Noise Stimulation caused by a source other than the main stimulus, or signal. (*p.144*)

Nonconscious level A segment of mental activity devoted to those processes that are totally inaccessible to conscious awareness, such as blood flowing through veins and arteries, the removal of impurities from the blood, and the measuring of blood sugar by the hypothalamus. (*p. 292*)

Noradrenaline See *norepinephrine*.

Norepinephrine (also called *noradrenaline*) A neurotransmitter involved in arousal, as well as in learning and mood regulation. (*p. 83*)

Norm (1) A description of the frequency at which a particular score occurs, which allows scores to be compared statistically. (*p. 308*) (2) A learned, socially based rule that prescribes what people should or should not do in various situations. (*p. 328*)

Normal distribution A dispersion of scores such that the mean, median, and mode all have the same value. When a distribution has this property, the standard deviation can be used to describe how any particular score stands in relation to the rest of the distribution. (*p. A-11*)

Nuclei Collections of nerve cell bodies in the central nervous system. (*p. 63*)

Null hypothesis The assertion that the independent variable manipulated by the experimenter will have no effect on the dependent variable measured by the experimenter. (*p. A-9*)

Obedience A form of compliance in which people comply with a demand, rather than with a request, because they think they must or should do so; obedience can be thought of as submissive compliance. (See also *compliance*.) (*p. 642*)

Obesity A condition in which a person is severely overweight, often by as much as one hundred pounds. (*p. 368*)

Objective tests Personality tests that ask direct, unambiguous questions about the individual being assessed. (*p. 508*)

Object permanence The knowledge, resulting from an ability to form mental representations of objects, that objects exist even when they are not in view. (*p. 413*)

Observational learning Learning how to perform new behaviors by watching the behavior of others. (*p. 202*)

Obsessive-compulsive disorder An anxiety disorder in which a person becomes obsessed with certain thoughts or images or feels a compulsion to do certain things. If the person tries to interrupt obsessive thinking or compulsions, severe agitation and anxiety usually result. (*p. 530*)

Oedipus complex According to psychodynamic theory, during the phallic stage a boy's id impulses involve sexual desire for the mother and the desire to eliminate, even kill, the father, who is competition for the mother's affection. The hostile impulses create a fear of retaliation so strong that the ego represses the incestuous desires. Then the boy identifies with the father and begins to learn male sex-role behaviors. (See also *phallic stage*.) (*p. 486*)

Olfaction The sense that detects chemicals that are airborne, or volatile; the sense of smell. (*p. 121*)

Olfactory bulb The brain structure that receives messages regarding olfaction, or the sense of smell. (*p. 122*)

One-word stage A stage of language development during which children build their vocabularies one word at a time, tend to use one word at a time, and tend to overextend the use of a single word. (*p. 279*)

Operant A response that has some effect on the world; it is a response that operates on the environment in some way. (See also *operant conditioning*.) (*p. 186*)

Operant conditioning A virtual synonym for instrumental conditioning; a process studied by B. F. Skinner in which an organism learns to respond to the environment in a way that helps produce some desired effect. Skinner's primary aim was to analyze how behavior is changed by its consequences. (*p. 186*)

Operational definitions Statements that define variables describing the exact operations or methods used in research. (*p. 30*)

Opiates Psychoactive drugs, such as opium, morphine, or heroin, that have the ability to produce both sleep-inducing and pain-relieving effects. (*p. 315*)

Opponent-process theory A theory of color vision stating that the visual elements sensitive to color are grouped into three pairs: a red-green element, a blue-yellow element, and a black-white element. Each element signals one color or the other—red or green, for example—but never both. (*p. 115*)

Optic chiasm Part of the bottom surface of the brain where half of the optic nerve fibers cross over to the opposite side of the brain; beyond the chiasm the fibers ascend into the brain itself. (*p. 117*)

Optic nerve A bundle of fibers composed of axons from ganglion cells that carries visual information to the brain. (*p. 117*)

Oral stage The first of Freud's psychosexual stages, occurring during the first year of life, in which the mouth is the center of pleasure. (*p. 485*)

Otoliths Small crystals in the fluid-filled vestibular sacs of the inner ear that, when shifted by gravity, stimulate nerve cells that inform the brain of the position of the head relative to the earth. (*p. 131*)

Pain disorder A somatoform disorder marked by complaints of severe, often constant, pain with no physical cause. (*p. 534*)

Panic disorder Anxiety in the form of terrifying panic attacks that come without warning or obvious cause. These attacks last for a few minutes and are marked by heart palpitations, pressure or pain in the chest, dizziness or unsteadiness, sweating, and faintness. They may be accompanied by feeling detached from one's body or feeling that people and events are not real. The person may think he or she is about to die or go crazy. (*p. 530*)

Papillae Structures that contain groups of taste receptors; the taste buds. (*p. 123*)

Parallel distributed processing (PDP) models An approach to understanding object recognition in which various elements of the object are thought to be simultaneously analyzed by a number of widely distributed but connected neural units in the brain. When applied to memory, these models suggest that new experiences don't just provide new facts that are later retrieved individually; they also change people's overall knowledge base, altering in a more general way their understanding of the world and how it operates. *(pp. 161, 219)*

Paranoid schizophrenia A type of schizophrenia characterized by delusions of persecution or grandeur accompanied by anxiety, anger, superiority, argumentativeness, or jealousy; these feelings sometimes lead to violence. *(p. 517)*

Parasympathetic system The subsystem of the autonomic nervous system that typically influences activity related to the protection, nourishment, and growth of the body. (See also *autonomic nervous system.*) *(p. 390)*

Partial reinforcement extinction effect A phenomenon in which behaviors learned under a partial reinforcement schedule are far more difficult to extinguish than those learned on a continuous reinforcement schedule. Individuals on a partial reinforcement schedule usually are not immediately aware that their behavior is no longer being reinforced; they are used to not being rewarded for every response. However, individuals on a continuous reinforcement schedule are accustomed to being reinforced for each response and are more sensitive to the lack of reward. *(p. 194)*

Partial reinforcement schedule (also called *intermittent reinforcement schedule*) In operant conditioning, a pattern of reinforcement in which a reinforcer is administered only some of the time after a particular response occurs. (See also *fixed interval schedule, fixed ratio schedule, variable interval schedule,* and *variable ratio schedule.*) *(p. 192)*

Pathways See *fiber tracts.*

Percentile score The percentage of people or observations that fall below a given score in a normal distribution. *(p. A-11)*

Perception The process through which people take raw sensations from the environment and interpret them, using knowledge, experience, and understanding of the world, so that the sensations become meaningful experiences. *(p. 138)*

Perceptual constancy The perception of objects as constant in size, shape, color, and other properties despite changes in their retinal image. *(p. 155)*

Perceptual organization The task of determining what edges and other stimuli go together to form an object. *(p. 147)*

Performance scale Five subtests in the Wechsler scales that include tasks that require spatial ability and the ability to manipulate materials; these subtests provide a performance IQ. (See also *verbal scale.*) *(p. 326)*

Peripheral nervous system (PNS) All of the nervous system that is not housed in bone. It has two main subsystems: the somatic nervous system and the autonomic nervous system. *(p. 61)*

Permissive parents Parents who give their child complete freedom and whose discipline is lax. Children of this type of parents are often immature, dependent, and unhappy, lack self-reliance and self-control, and seek parental help for even the slightest problems. *(p. 431)*

Personality The pattern of psychological and behavioral characteristics by which each person can be compared and contrasted with other people; the unique pattern of characteristics that emerges from the blending of inherited and acquired tendencies to make each person an identifiable individual. *(p. 483)*

Personality disorders Long-standing, inflexible ways of behaving that are not so much severe mental disorders as styles of life, which, from childhood or adolescence, create problems, usually for others. (p. 550)

Personality psychologists Psychologists who focus on the unique characteristics that determine individuals' behavior. *(p. 18)*

Person-centered therapy See *client-centered therapy.*

Person-oriented Referring to leaders who provide loose supervision, ask for group members' ideas, and are generally concerned with subordinates' feelings; they are usually well liked by those they lead. *(p. 664)*

Phallic stage The third of Freud's psychosexual stages, lasting from approximately ages three to five, in which the focus of pleasure shifts to the genital area; the Oedipus complex occurs during this stage. (See also *Oedipus complex.*) *(p. 486)*

Phenomenological approach (also called *phenomenological model*) A view of personality based on the assumption that each personality is created out of each person's unique way of perceiving and interpreting the world. Proponents of this view believe that one's personal perception of reality shapes and controls behavior from moment to moment. *(p. 501)*

Phenotype How an individual looks and acts, which depends on how a person's inherited characteristics interact with the environment. *(p. A-2)*

Pheromones Chemicals that are released by one animal and detected by another, and then shape that second animal's behavior or physiology. Often, though not always, the pheromone is detected by the olfactory system. *(p. 123)*

Phobia An anxiety disorder that involves a strong, irrational fear of an object or situation that does not objectively justify such a reaction. The phobic individual usually realizes that the fear makes no sense but cannot keep it from interfering with daily life. *(p. 528)*

Phoneme The smallest unit of sound that affects the meaning of speech. (See also *morpheme.*) *(p. 274)*

Photopigments Chemicals contained in photoreceptors that respond to light and assist in changing light into neural activity. *(p. 109)*

Photoreceptors Nerve cells in the retina that code light energy into neural activity. (See also *rods* and *cones.*) *(p. 109)*

Physical dependence See *addiction.*

Physiological psychologists See *biological psychologists.*

Physiological psychology See *biological psychology.*

Pinna The crumpled, oddly shaped part of the outer ear that collects sound waves. *(p. 92)*

Pitch How high or low a tone sounds; the psychological dimension determined by the frequency of sound waves. High-frequency waves are sensed as sounds of high pitch. *(p. 101)*

Placebo A physical or psychological treatment that contains no active ingredient but produces an effect because the person receiving it believes it will. In an experiment, the placebo effect (a confounding variable) occurs when the participant responds to the belief that the independent variable will have an effect, rather than to the actual effect of the independent variable. *(p. 36)*

Place theory (also called *traveling wave theory*) A theory of hearing stating that hair cells at a particular place on the basilar membrane respond most to a particular frequency of sound. High-frequency sounds produce a wave that peaks soon after it starts down the basilar membrane. Lower-frequency sounds produce a wave that peaks farther along the basilar membrane. *(p. 104)*

Pleasure principle In psychodynamic theory, the operating principle of the id, which guides people toward whatever feels good. (See also *id.*) *(p. 484)*

Polygenic Describing characteristics that are determined by more than one gene or pair of genes. *(p. A-2)*

Positive reinforcement See *positive reinforcers.*

Positive reinforcers Stimuli that strengthen a response if they follow that response. They are roughly equivalent to rewards. Presenting a positive reinforcer after a response is called positive reinforcement. (See also *negative reinforcers.*) *(pp. 186, 542)*

Positive symptoms A category of schizophrenic symptoms. They include disorganized thoughts, hallucinations, and delusions. (See also *negative symptoms.*) *(p. 546)*

Positron emission tomography (PET scanning) A technique that detects and creates a visual image of activity in various parts of the brain. *(p. 61)*

Postconventional moral reasoning Reasoning that reflects moral judgments based on personal standards or universal principles of justice, equality, and respect for human life. *(p. 439)*

Postsynaptic potential The change in the membrane potential of a neuron that has received stimulation from another neuron. *(p. 58)*

Posttraumatic stress disorder (PTSD) A pattern of adverse and disruptive reactions following a traumatic event. One of its most common features is re-experiencing the original trauma through nightmares or vivid memories. *(p. 461)*

Preconscious level   A segment of mental activity devoted to sensations and everything else that is not currently conscious, but of which people can easily become conscious at will. The amount of material at this level far surpasses what is present at the conscious level at any given moment. (See also *conscious level*, *nonconscious level*, *subconscious level*, and *unconscious level*.) *(p. 292)*

Preconventional moral reasoning   Reasoning that is not based on the conventions or rules that guide social interactions in society. *(p. 439)*

Prefrontal lobotomy   A form of psychosurgery in which a sharp instrument is inserted into the brain and used to destroy brain tissue. *(p. 558)*

Prejudice   A positive or negative attitude toward an entire group of people. (See also *discrimination*.) *(p. 620)*

Preoperational period   According to Piaget, the second stage of cognitive development, during which children begin to understand, create, and use symbols to represent things that are not present. *(p. 416)*

Primacy effect   A characteristic of recall in which recall for the first two or three items in a list is particularly good. (See also *recency effect*.) *(p. 227)*

Primary auditory cortex   The area in the temporal lobe of the cerebral cortex that is first to receive information about sounds. It is connected to areas of the brain involved in language perception and production. *(p. 106)*

Primary cortex   The area of cerebral cortex that is first to receive information about a particular sense, such as vision or hearing. See also *primary auditory cortex* and *primary visual cortex*.) *(p. 99)*

Primary drives   Drives that arise from basic biological needs. (See also *drive*, *need*, and *secondary drives*.) *(p. 361)*

Primary reinforcers   Reinforcers that meet an organism's most basic needs, such as food, water, air, and moderate temperatures. A primary reinforcer does not depend on learning to exert its influence. (See also *secondary reinforcer*.) *(p. 191)*

Primary visual cortex   An area in the occipital lobe, at the back of the brain, to which neurons in the lateral geniculate nucleus relay visual input. *(p. 117)*

Prisoner's dilemma   A social dilemma in which mutual cooperation guarantees the best mutual outcome; mixed cooperative and competitive responses by each person guarantee a favorable outcome for one person and an unfavorable outcome for the other; and mutual competition guarantees the worst mutual outcome. (See also *social dilemma*.)*(p. 661)*

Proactive interference   A cause of forgetting in which previously learned information, now residing in long-term memory, interferes with the ability to remember new information. (See also *retroactive interference*.) *(p. 237)*

Procedural memory   A type of memory that contains information about how to do things. *(p. 215)*

Progestins   Feminine hormones that circulate in the bloodstream of both men and women; relatively more progestins circulate in women. One of the main progestins is progesterone. (See also *estrogens*.) *(p. 372)*

Progressive relaxation training   A procedure for learning to relax that involves tensing a group of muscles for a few seconds, then releasing that tension and focusing attention on the resulting feelings of relaxation; the procedure is repeated at least once for each of sixteen muscle groups throughout the body. Progressive relaxation training is a popular physiological method for coping with stress and an important part of systematic desensitization, a method for treating phobias. *(p. 478)*

Projective tests   Personality tests made up of relatively unstructured stimuli, such as inkblots, which can be perceived and responded to in many ways; particular responses are seen as reflecting the individual's needs, fantasies, conflicts, thought patterns, and other aspects of personality. *(p. 510)*

Propositions   The smallest units of knowledge that can stand as separate assertions, may be true or false, and may represent a relationship between a concept and a property of that concept or between two or more concepts. *(p. 256)*

Proprioceptive   The sensory systems that allow us to know about where we are and what each part of our body is doing. (See also *kinesthesia* and *vestibular sense*.) *(p. 131)*

Prototype   A member of a natural concept that possesses all or most of its characteristic features. *(p. 255)*

Proximity   A Gestalt grouping principle stating that the closer objects are to one another, the more likely they are to be perceived as belonging together. *(p. 148)*

Psychedelics   Psychoactive drugs, such as LSD, PCP, and marijuana, that alter consciousness by producing a temporary loss of contact with reality and changes in emotion, perception, and thought. *(p. 315)*

Psychiatrists   Medical doctors who have completed special training in the treatment of mental disorders. Psychiatrists can prescribe drugs. *(p. 563)*

Psychoactive drugs   Chemical substances that act on the brain to create some psychological effect. *(p. 309)*

Psychoanalysis   A method of psychotherapy that seeks to help clients gain insight by recognizing, understanding, and dealing with unconscious thoughts and emotions presumed to cause their problems and work through the many ways in which those unconscious causes appear in everyday behavior and social relationships. *(p. 564)*

Psychodynamic approach (also called *psychodynamic model*)   A view developed by Freud that emphasizes the interplay of unconscious mental processes in determining human thought, feelings, and behavior. *(p. 14)*

Psychological dependence   A condition in which a person continues drug use despite adverse effects, needs the drug for a sense of well-being, and becomes preoccupied with obtaining the drug if it becomes unavailable. *(p. 310)*

Psychological model   An approach that views mental disorder as arising from inner turmoil or other psychological processes. *(p. 521)*

Psychologists   In the realm of treatment, therapists whose education includes completion of a master's or doctoral degree in clinical or counseling psychology, often followed by additional specialized training. Unlike psychiatrists, psychologists are not authorized to prescribe drugs. *(p. 563)*

Psychology   The science of behavior and mental processes. *(p. 3)*

Psychometric approach   A way of studying intelligence that emphasizes the analysis of the products of intelligence, especially scores on intelligence tests. *(p. 341)*

Psychoneuroimmunology   The field that examines the interaction of psychological and physiological processes that affect the ability of the body to defend itself against disease. *(p. 470)*

Psychopathology   Patterns of thinking and behaving that are maladaptive, disruptive, or uncomfortable for the person affected or for those with whom he or she comes in contact. *(p. 517)*

Psychopharmacology   The study of psychoactive drugs and their effects. *(p. 309)*

Psychophysics   An area of research that focuses on the relationship between the physical characteristics of environmental stimuli and the conscious psychological experience those stimuli produce. Psychophysical researchers seek to understand how people make contact with and become conscious of the world. *(p. 140)*

Psychosexual stages   In psychodynamic theory, periods of personality development in which internal and external conflicts focus on particular issues. There are five stages during which pleasure is derived from different areas of the body. (See also *anal stage*, *genital stage*, *latency period*, *oral stage*, and *phallic stage*.) *(p. 485)*

Psychosurgery   Procedures that destroy various regions of the brain in an effort to alleviate psychological disorders; this surgery is done infrequently and only as a last resort. *(p. 591)*

Psychotherapy   The treatment of psychological disorders through psychological methods, such as analyzing problems, talking about possible solutions, and encouraging more adaptive ways of thinking and acting. *(p. 562)*

PTSD   See *posttraumatic stress disorder*.

Puberty   The condition of being able for the first time to reproduce; it occurs during adolescence and is characterized by fuller breasts and rounder curves in females and by broad shoulders and narrow hips in males. Facial, underarm, and pubic hair grows. Voices deepen, and acne may appear. *(p. 436)*

Punishment   The presentation of an aversive stimulus or the removal of a pleasant stimulus; punishment decreases the frequency of the immediately preceding response. *(pp. 188, 575)*

Pupil   An opening in the eye, just behind the cornea, through which light passes. (The pupil appears black because there is no light source inside the eyeball and very little light is reflected out of the eye.) *(p. 108)*

Quantitative psychologists   Psychologists who develop statistical methods for evaluating and analyzing data from psychological research. *(p. 19)*

Quasi-experiments   Research studies whose designs approximate the control of a true experiment (*quasi-* means resembling) but may not include manipulation of the independent variable, random assignment of participants to groups, or other elements of experimental control. *(p. 37)*

Quiet sleep (also called *slow-wave sleep*)   Sleep stages 1 through 4, which are accompanied by slow, deep breathing; a calm, regular heartbeat; and reduced blood pressure. *(p. 298)*

Random assignment   The procedure by which random variables are evenly distributed in an experiment—specifically, through placement of participants in experimental and control groups by means of a coin flip or some other random process. *(p. 35)*

Random sample   A group of research participants selected from a population each of whose members had an equal chance of being chosen for study. *(p. 38)*

Random variables   In an experiment, confounding variables in which uncontrolled or uncontrollable factors affect the dependent variable along with or instead of the independent variable. Random variables can include factors such as differences in the participants' backgrounds, personalities, and physical health, as well as differences in experimental conditions. *(p. 35)*

Range   A measure of variability that is the difference between the highest and the lowest value in a data set. *(p. 41)*

Rapid eye movement (REM) sleep   A stage of sleep during which the EEG resembles that of someone who is active and awake; the heart rate, respiration, blood pressure, and other physiological patterns are also very much like those occurring during the day. At the same time, the sleeper begins rapid eye movements beneath closed lids, and muscle tone decreases to the point of paralysis. *(p. 299)*

Rational-emotive therapy (RET)   A treatment that involves identifying self-defeating, problem-causing thoughts that clients have learned and using modeling, encouragement, and logic to help the client replace these maladaptive thought patterns with more realistic and beneficial ones. *(p. 575)*

Reaction time   The elapsed time between the presentation of a stimulus and an overt response to it. *(p. 252)*

Reality principle   According to psychodynamic theory, the operating principle of the ego that involves, for example, compromises between the unreasoning demands of the id to do whatever feels good and the demands of the real world to do what is acceptable. (See also *ego*.) *(p. 484)*

Reasoning   The process by which people evaluate and generate arguments and reach conclusions. *(p. 257)*

Recency effect   A characteristic of recall in which recall is particularly good for the last few items on a list. (See also *primacy effect*.) *(p. 227)*

Receptive field   The portion of the world that affects a given neuron. For example, in the auditory system, one neuron might respond only to sounds of a particular pitch; that pitch is its receptive field. *(p. 112)*

Receptors   (1) Sites on the surface of the postsynaptic cell that allow only one type of neurotransmitter to fit into them and thus trigger the chemical response that may lead to an action potential. *(p. 57)* (2) Cells that are specialized to detect a certain type of energy and convert it into neural activity. This conversion process is called transduction. *(p. 57)*

Reconditioning   The relearning of a conditioned response following extinction. Because reconditioning takes much less time than the original conditioning, some change in the organism must persist even after extinction. *(p. 179)*

Reduced clarity   A depth cue whereby an object whose retinal image is unclear is perceived as being farther away. *(p. 136)*

Reference group   A category of people to which people compare themselves. *(p. 605)*

Reflection   Restating or paraphrasing what the client has said, which shows that the therapist is actively listening and helps make the client aware of the thoughts and feelings he or she is experiencing. *(p. 569)*

Reflexes   Involuntary, unlearned reactions in the form of swift, automatic, and finely coordinated movements in response to external stimuli. Reflexes are organized completely within the spinal cord. *(pp. 64, 410)*

Refractory period   A short rest period between action potentials; it is so short that a neuron can send action potentials down its axon at rates of up to one thousand per second. *(p. 56)*

Reinforcer   A stimulus event that increases the probability that the response that immediately preceded it will occur again. (See also *positive reinforcers* and *negative reinforcers*.) *(p. 186)*

Relative deprivation   The sense that a person is not doing as well as others in the same reference group. *(p. 605)*

Relative size   A depth cue whereby larger objects are perceived as closer than smaller ones. *(p. 151)*

Reliability   The degree to which a test can be repeated with the same results. Tests with high reliability yield scores that are less susceptible to insignificant or random changes in the test taker or the testing environment. *(p. 328)*

REM behavior disorder   A sleep disorder in which a person fails to show the decreased muscle tone normally seen in REM sleep, thus allowing the sleeper to act out dreams, sometimes with dangerous results. *(p. 302)*

REM sleep   See *rapid eye movement (REM) sleep*.

Representativeness heuristic   A shortcut in the thought process that involves judging the probability that a hypothesis is true or that an example belongs to a certain class of items by first focusing on the similarities between the example and a larger class of events or items and then determining whether the particular example represents essential features of the larger class. *(p. 261)*

Residual schizophrenia   The designation for persons who have displayed symptoms of schizophrenia in the past, but not in the present. *(p. 517)*

Resilience   A quality through which children develop normally in spite of family instability, abuse, and other severe environmental risk factors. *(p. 435)*

Resource dilemma   A situation in which people share some common resource, thus creating conflicts between the short-term interests of individuals and the long-term interests of the group. (See also *resource dilemma*.) *(p. 662)*

Response criterion   The internal rule a person uses to decide whether or not to report a stimulus; it reflects the person's motivation and expectations. *(p. 144)*

RET   See *rational-emotive therapy*.

Reticular formation   A network of nuclei and fibers threaded throughout the hindbrain and midbrain. This network alters the activity of the rest of the brain. *(p. 66)*

Retina   The surface at the back of the eye onto which the lens focuses light rays. *(p. 108)*

Retrieval   The process of recalling information stored in memory and bringing it into consciousness. *(p. 215)*

Retrieval cues   Stimuli that allow people to recall things that were once forgotten and help them to recognize information stored in memory. *(p. 227)*

Retroactive interference   A cause of forgetting in which new information placed in memory interferes with the ability to recall information already in memory. *(p. 237)*

Retrograde amnesia   A loss of memory for events prior to some critical brain injury. Often, a person will be unable to remember anything that occurred in the months, or even years, before the injury. In most cases, the memories return gradually, but recovery is seldom complete. (See also *anterograde amnesia*.) *(p. 241)*

Rods   Photoreceptors in the retina that allow sight even in dim light because their photopigment contains rhodopsin, a light-sensitive chemical. Rods cannot discriminate colors. (See also *cones*.) (p. 110)

Role theory   A theory that states that hypnotized participants act in accordance with a special social role, which demands compliance. According to this theory, the procedures for inducing hypnosis provide a socially acceptable reason to follow the hypnotist's suggestions. (See also *dissociation theory* and *state theory*.) (p. 307)

Rules of logic   Sets of statements that provide a formula for drawing valid conclusions. (p. 258)

s   A group of special abilities, or intelligences, that Charles Spearman saw as accompanying general intelligence (g). (p. 342)

Sampling   The process of selecting participants who are members of the population that the researcher wishes to study. (p. 38)

Satiety   The condition of no longer wanting to eat. (p. 364)

Saturation   The purity of a color. A color is more pure, more saturated, if a single wavelength is relatively more intense—contains more energy—than other wavelengths. (p. 113)

Schemas   Basic units of knowledge; generalizations based on experience of the world. Schemas organize past experience and provide a framework for understanding future experience; a coherent, organized set of beliefs and expectations that can influence the perception of others and objects. (pp. 160, 231, 256, 411)

Schizophrenia   A pattern of severely disturbed thinking, emotion, perception, and behavior that constitutes one of the most serious and disabling of all mental disorders. (p. 544)

Schizotypal personality disorder   A pattern of emotional and behavior disorder that is similar to, but significantly less intense than, schizophrenia. (p. 521)

School psychologists   Psychologists who test IQs, diagnose students' academic problems, and set up programs to improve students' achievement. (p. 19)

Scripts   Mental representations of familiar sequences of activity, usually involving people's behavior. (p. 256)

SD   See *standard deviation*.

Secondary drives   Stimuli that acquire the motivational properties of primary drives through classical conditioning or other learning mechanisms. (See also *drive, need,* and *primary drives*.) (p. 362)

Secondary reinforcer   A reward that people or animals learn to like. Secondary reinforcers gain their reinforcing properties through association with primary reinforcers. (p. 191)

Second-order conditioning   A phenomenon in learning when a conditioned stimulus acts like a UCS, creating conditioned stimuli out of events associated with it. (p. 181)

Selective attention   The focusing of mental resources on only part of the stimulus field. (p. 222)

Self-concept   The way one thinks of oneself. (p. 503)

Self-efficacy   According to Bandura, learned expectations about the probability of success in given situations; a person's expectation of success in a given situation may be enough to create that success and even to blunt the impact of minor failures. (p. 499)

Self-esteem   The evaluations people make about how worthy they themselves are as human beings. (p. 605)

Self-fulfilling prophecy   An impression-formation process in which an initial impression elicits behavior in another that confirms the impression. (p. 609)

Self-perception theory   A theory that holds that when people are unsure of their attitude in a situation, they consider their behavior in light of the circumstances and then infer what their attitude must have been. (p. 620)

Self-regulation   The ability to control one's emotions and behavior. (p. 433)

Self-schemas   Mental representations that people form of themselves. (p. 606)

Self-serving bias   The cognitive tendency to attribute one's successes to internal characteristics while blaming one's failures on external causes. (p. 614)

Semantic encoding   The mental representation of an experience by its general meaning. (p. 215)

Semantic memory   A type of memory containing generalized knowledge of the world that does not involve memory of specific events. (p. 215)

Semantics   In language, the rules that govern the meaning of words and sentences. (See also *syntax*.) (p. 275)

Semicircular canals   Arc-shaped tubes in the inner ear containing fluid that, when shifted by head movements, stimulate nerve cells that provide information to the brain about the rate and direction of those movements. (p. 131)

Sensations   Messages from a sense, which comprise the raw information that affects many kinds of behavior and mental processes. (p. 96)

Sense   A system that translates data from outside the nervous system into neural activity, giving the nervous system, especially the brain, information about the world. (p. 96)

Sensitivity   The ability to detect a stimulus; sensitivity is influenced by neural noise, the intensity of the stimulus, and the capacity of the sensory system. (p. 144)

Sensorimotor period   The first in Piaget's stages of cognitive development, when the infant's mental activity is confined to sensory perception and motor skills. (p. 413)

Sensory cortex   The part of the cerebral cortex located in the parietal, occipital, and temporal lobes that receives stimulus information from the skin, eyes, and ears, respectively. (p. 72)

Sensory memory   A type of memory that is very primitive and very brief, but lasts long enough to connect one impression to the next, so that people experience a smooth flow of information. (See also *sensory registers*.) (p. 221)

Sensory receptors   Specialized cells that detect certain forms of energy. (p. 97)

Sensory registers   Memory systems that hold incoming information long enough for it to be processed further. (See also *sensory memory*.) (p. 221)

Sensory systems   The parts of the nervous system that provide information about the environment; the senses. (p. 60)

Serotonin   A neurotransmitter used by cells in those parts of the brain involved in the regulation of sleep, mood, and eating. (p. 83)

Sex hormones   Chemicals in the blood of males and females that have both organizational and motivational effects on sexual behavior. (p. 372)

Sexual dysfunctions   Problems with sex that involve sexual motivation, arousal, or orgasmic response. (p. 377)

Sexual response cycle   The pattern of arousal during and after sexual activity. (p. 370)

Shaping   In operant conditioning, a procedure that involves reinforcing responses that come successively closer to the desired response. (p. 191)

Short-term memory (STM) (also called *working memory*)   A stage of memory in which information can last less than half a minute unless rehearsed. (p. 222)

Signal-detection theory   A formal mathematical model of what determines a person's report that a near-threshold stimulus has or has not occurred. (p. 143)

Similarity   A Gestalt grouping principle stating that similar elements are perceived to be part of a group. (p. 148)

Simplicity   A Gestalt grouping principle stating that people tend to group stimulus features in a way that provides the simplest interpretation of the world. (p. 148)

Sleep apnea   A sleep disorder in which people briefly but repeatedly stop breathing during the night. (p. 301)

Sleepwalking   A phenomenon that starts primarily in non-REM sleep, especially in stage 4, and involves walking while one is asleep. It is most common during childhood. In the morning sleepwalkers usually have no memory of their travels. (p. 302)

Slow-wave sleep   See *quiet sleep*.

Social cognition   Mental processes associated with people's perceptions of and reactions to other people. (p. 604)

Social-cognitive approach   An approach to personality that views personality as a label summarizing the unique patterns of thinking and behavior that a person learns. (p. 497)

Social comparison   Using other people as a basis of comparison for evaluating oneself. (p. 605)

Social dilemmas Situations in which actions that produce rewards for one individual will produce negative consequences if they are adopted by everyone. *(p. 661)*

Social facilitation A phenomenon in which the mere presence of other people improves a person's performance on a given task. *(p. 636)*

Social identity The beliefs we hold about the groups to which we belong. Social identity is part of the self-concept. *(p. 606)*

Social impairment A reduction in human performance due to the presence of other people. *(p. 636)*

Socialization The process by which parents, teachers, and others teach children the skills and social norms necessary to be well-functioning members of society. *(p. 409)*

Social loafing Exerting less effort when performing a group task (in which one's contribution cannot be identified) than when performing the same task alone. *(p. 636)*

Social perception The processes through which people interpret information about others, draw inferences about them, and develop mental representations of them. *(p. 607)*

Social phobias Strong, irrational fears relating to social situations. Common examples include fear of being negatively evaluated by others or publicly embarrassed by doing something impulsive, outrageous, or humiliating. *(p. 529)*

Social psychologists Psychologists who study how people influence one another's behavior and attitudes, especially in groups. *(p. 17)*

Social psychology The psychological subfield that explores the effects of the social world on the behavior and mental processes of individuals, pairs, and groups. *(p. 604)*

Social referencing A phenomenon in which other people's facial expressions, tone of voice, and bodily gestures serve as guidelines for how to proceed in uncertain situations. *(p. 399)*

Social support network The friends and social contacts on whom one can depend for help and support. *(p. 464)*

Sociocultural explanations Explanations of mental disorder that emphasize the role of such social and cultural factors as gender and age, physical situation, cultural values and expectations, and historical era. *(p. 522)*

Somatic nervous system The subsystem of the peripheral nervous system that transmits information from the senses to the central nervous system and carries signals from the CNS to the muscles that move the skeleton. *(p. 61)*

Somatic senses (also called *somatosensory systems*) A sense that is spread throughout the body, not located in a specific organ. Somatic senses include touch, temperature, pain (the skin senses), and kinesthesia. *(p. 125)*

Somatization disorders Somatoform disorders whereby individuals have numerous physical complaints without verifiable physical illness. *(p. 534)*

Somatoform disorders Psychological problems whereby individuals show the symptoms of some physical (somatic) disorder, even though there is no physical cause. (See also *conversion disorder.*) *(p. 533)*

Somatosensory systems See *somatic senses.*

Sound A repetitive fluctuation in the pressure of a medium like air. *(p. 99)*

Spatial codes In the sensory systems, coding attributes of a stimulus in terms of the location of firing neurons relative to their neighbors. *(p. 98)*

Specific nerve energies A doctrine that states that stimulation of a particular sensory nerve provides codes for that one sense, no matter how the stimulation takes place. *(p. 98)*

Specific phobias Phobias that involve fear and avoidance of heights, blood, animals, and other specific stimuli and situations. *(p. 528)*

Spinal cord The part of the central nervous system contained within the spinal column that receives signals from peripheral senses (such as touch and pain) and relays them to the brain. It also conveys messages from the brain to the rest of the body. *(p. 63)*

Spontaneous recovery The reappearance of the conditioned response after extinction and without further pairings of the conditioned and unconditioned stimuli. *(p. 179)*

Sport psychologists Psychologists who explore the relationships between athletic performance and such psychological variables as motivation and emotion. *(p. 19)*

Spreading activation A principle that, in semantic network theories of memory, explains how information is retrieved. *(p. 229)*

Standard deviation (SD) A measure of variability that is the average difference between each score and the mean of the data set. *(p. 41)*

Standard score A value that indicates the distance, in standard deviations, between a given score and the mean of all the scores in a data set. *(p. A-12)*

Stanford-Binet A test for determining a person's intelligence quotient, or IQ. *(p. 324)*

State-dependent Referring to memories that are aided or impeded by a person's internal state. *(p. 228)*

State of consciousness The characteristics of consciousness at any particular moment—for example, what reaches awareness, what levels of mental activity are most prominent, and how efficiently a person is functioning. *(p. 297)*

State theory A theory that proposes that hypnosis does indeed create an altered state of consciousness. (See also *dissociation theory* and *role theory.*) *(p. 307)*

Statistically significant In statistical analysis, a term used to describe the results of an experiment when the outcome of a statistical test indicates that the probability of those results occurring by chance is small (usually less than 5 percent). *(p. 43)*

Stereotypes Impressions or schemas of an entire group of people that involve the false assumption that all members of the group share the same characteristics. *(p. 620)*

Stimulants Psychoactive drugs that have the ability to increase behavioral and mental activity. Amphetamines and cocaine do so primarily by augmenting the action of the neurotransmitters dopamine and norepinephrine. *(p. 313)*

Stimulus discrimination A process through which individuals learn to differentiate among similar stimuli and respond appropriately to each one. (See also *stimulus generalization.*) *(p. 180)*

Stimulus generalization A phenomenon in which a conditioned response is elicited by stimuli that are similar but not identical to the conditioned stimulus. The greater the similarity between a stimulus and the conditioned stimulus, the stronger the conditioned response will be. *(p. 179)*

Storage The process of maintaining information in the memory system over time. *(p. 215)*

Stress The process of adjusting to circumstances that disrupt, or threaten to disrupt, a person's equilibrium. *(p. 453)*

Stressors Events or situations to which people must adjust. *(p. 453)*

Stress reaction The physical, psychological, and behavioral responses people display in the face of stressors. *(p. 431)*

Striatum A structure within the forebrain that is involved in the smooth initiation of movement. *(p. 68)*

Stroboscopic motion An illusion in which lights or images flashed in rapid succession are perceived as moving. *(p. 154)*

Subliminal stimuli Stimuli that are too weak or brief to be perceived. *(p. 140)*

Substance abuse The self-administration of psychoactive drugs in ways that deviate from a culture's social norms. *(p. 310)*

Substance-related disorders Problems that involve use of psychoactive drugs for months or years in ways that harm the user or others. *(p. 552)*

Substantia nigra An area of the midbrain involved in the smooth initiation of movement. *(p. 68)*

Sudden infant death syndrome (SIDS) A disorder in which a sleeping baby stops breathing but does not awaken and suffocates. *(p. 301)*

Superego According to psychodynamic theory, the component of personality that tells people what they should and should not do. Its two subdivisions are the conscience, which dictates what behaviors are wrong, and the ego ideal, which sets perfectionistic standards for desirable behaviors. *(p. 484)*

Suprachiasmatic nuclei   Nuclei in the hypothalamus that generate biological rhythms. (*p. 68*)

Supraliminal stimuli   Stimuli that fall above the absolute threshold and thus are consistently perceived. (*p. 140*)

Surface structures   The strings of words that people produce; the order in which words are arranged. (*p. 275*)

Survey   A research method that involves giving people questionnaires or special interviews designed to obtain descriptions of their attitudes, beliefs, opinions, and intentions. (*p. 33*)

Syllogisms   In the reasoning process, arguments made up of two propositions, called premises, and a conclusion based on those premises. (See also *propositions*.) (*p. 259*)

Sympathetic system   The subsystem of the autonomic nervous system that usually prepares the organism for vigorous activity, including the fight-or-flight syndrome. (See also *autonomic nervous system* and *fight-or-flight syndrome*.) (*p. 390*)

Synapse   The tiny gap between neurons across which the neurons communicate. (*p. 55*)

Synaptic plasticity   The ability to create synapses and to change the strength of synapses. (*p. 78*)

Syntax   In language, the set of rules that govern the formation of phrases and sentences. (See also *semantics*.) (*p. 275*)

Systematic desensitization   A behavioral method for treating anxiety in which clients visualize a graduated series of anxiety-provoking stimuli while maintaining a state of relaxation. (*p. 571*)

Task-oriented   Referring to leaders who provide close supervision, lead by giving directives, and generally discourage group discussion. (*p. 664*)

Telegraphic   Pertaining to utterances that are brief and to the point and that leave out any word not absolutely essential to the meaning the speaker wishes to convey; children's first sentences, consisting of two-word utterances. (*p. 280*)

Temperament   An individual's basic, natural disposition; the beginning of an individual's identity or personality, which is evident from infancy. (*p. 424*)

Temporal codes   In the sensory systems, coding attributes of a stimulus in terms of changes in the timing of neural firing. (*p. 98*)

Teratogens   Harmful substances, such as alcohol and other drugs, that can cause birth defects. (*p. 407*)

Terminal drop   A sharp decline in mental functioning that tends to occur in late adulthood, a few years or months before death. (*p. 446*)

Test   A systematic procedure for observing behavior in a standard situation and describing it with the help of a numerical scale or a category system. (*p. 328*)

Texture   A Gestalt grouping principle stating that when features of stimuli have the same texture (such as the orientation of certain elements) they tend to be grouped together. (*p. 148*)

Texture gradient   A graduated change in the texture, or grain, of the visual field, whereby changes in texture across the retinal image are perceived as changes in distance; objects with finer, less detailed textures are perceived as more distant. (*p. 151*)

Thalamus   A structure in the forebrain that relays signals from the eyes and other sense organs to higher levels in the brain and plays an important role in processing and making sense out of this information. (*p. 68*)

Theory   An integrated set of propositions that can be used to account for, predict, and even control certain phenomena. (*p. 30*)

Thinking   The manipulation of mental representations, performed in order to form new representations. (*p. 251*)

Timbre   The quality of sound that identifies it, so that, for example, a middle C played on the piano is clearly distinguishable from a middle C played on a trumpet. The timbre depends on the mixture of frequencies and amplitudes that make up the sound. (*p. 101*)

Token economy   A system for improving the behavior of severely disturbed or mentally retarded clients in institutions that involves rewarding desirable behaviors with tokens that can be exchanged for snacks, field trips, access to television, or other privileges. (*p. 574*)

Tolerance   A condition in which increasingly larger drug doses are needed to produce a given effect. (*p. 310*)

Top-down processing   Those aspects of recognition that are guided by higher-level cognitive processes and psychological factors like expectations. (See also *bottom-up processing*.) (*p. 157*)

Topographical representation   A map of each sense, contained in the primary cortex. Any two points that are next to each other in the stimulus will be represented next to each other in the brain. (*p. 99*)

Trait approach   A perspective on personality that views it as the combination of stable characteristics that people display over time and across situations. (*p. 489*)

Tranquilizer   A class of drugs used to reduce mental and physical tension and symptoms of anxiety. (See also *anxiolytic*.) (*p. 560*)

Transduction   The second step in sensation, which is the process of converting incoming energy into neural activity through receptors. (*p. 97*)

Transfer-appropriate processing model   A model of memory that suggests that a critical determinant of memory is how the encoding process matches up with what is ultimately retrieved. (*p. 218*)

Transferred excitation   The process of carrying over arousal from one experience to an independent situation, which is especially likely to occur when the arousal pattern from the nonemotional source is similar to the pattern associated with a particular emotion. (*p. 394*)

Triarchical theory of intelligence   A theory proposed by Robert Sternberg that sees intelligence as involving analytical, creative, and practical dimensions. (*p. 343*)

Trichromatic theory   The theory postulated by Young and Helmholtz that there are three types of visual elements, each of which is most sensitive to different wavelengths, and that information from these three elements combines to produce the sensation of color. (*p. 114*)

Tympanic membrane   A tightly stretched membrane (also known as the eardrum) in the middle ear that generates vibrations that match the sound waves striking it. (*p. 102*)

Unconditional positive regard   In client-centered therapy, the therapist's attitude that expresses caring for and acceptance of the client as a valued person. (*p. 568*)

Unconditioned response (UCR)   In classical conditioning, the automatic or unlearned reaction to a stimulus. (See also *conditioned response*.) (*p. 178*)

Unconditioned stimulus (UCS)   In classical conditioning, the stimulus that elicits a response without conditioning. (See also *conditioned stimulus*.) (*p. 178*)

Unconscious level   A segment of mental activity proposed by Freud that contains sexual, aggressive, and other impulses, as well as once-conscious but unacceptable thoughts and feelings of which an individual is completely unaware. (See also *conscious level, nonconscious level, preconscious level,* and *subconscious level*.) (*p. 292*)

Undifferentiated schizophrenia   Patterns of disordered thought, behavior, and emotions that are characteristic of schizophrenia but that cannot easily be placed in any specific schizophrenic subtype. (*p. 517*)

Utility   In rational decision making, any subjective measure of value. (*p. 271*)

Validity   The degree to which a test measures what it is supposed to measure. (*p. 329*)

Variable-interval (VI) schedule   In operant conditioning, a type of partial reinforcement schedule that provides reinforcement for the first response after some varying period of time. For example, in a VI 60 schedule the first response to occur after an average of one minute would be reinforced, but the actual time between reinforcements could vary from, say, 1 second to 120 seconds. (*p. 193*)

Variable-ratio (VR) schedule   A type of partial reinforcement schedule that provides reinforcement after a varying number of responses. For example, on a VR 30 schedule, a rat might sometimes be reinforced after ten bar presses, sometimes after fifty bar presses, but an average of thirty responses would occur before reinforcement is given. (*p. 192*)

Variables   Specific factors or characteristics that can take on different values in research. (*p. 30*)

Verbal scale   Six subtests in the Wechsler scales that measure verbal skills as part of a measure of overall intelligence. (See also *performance scale*.) (*p. 326*)

Vestibular sacs Organs in the inner ear that connect the semicircular canals and the cochlea, and contribute to the body's sense of balance. *(p. 131)*

Vestibular sense The proprioceptive sense that provides information about the position of the body in space and about its general movements. It is often thought of as the sense of balance. *(p. 131)*

VI See *variable-interval schedule.*

Vicarious conditioning Learning the relationship between a response and its consequences (either reinforcement or punishment) or the association between a conditioned stimulus and a conditioned response by watching others. *(p. 202)*

Visible light Electromagnetic radiation that has a wavelength from about 400 nanometers to about 750 nanometers. (A nanometer is one-billionth of a meter.) *(p. 107)*

Visual encoding The mental representation of stimuli as pictures. *(p. 214)*

Volley theory See *frequency matching.*

Vomeronasal organ A portion of the mammalian olfactory system that is sensitive to nonvolatile pheromones. *(p. 123)*

VR See *variable-ratio schedule.*

Wavelength The distance from one peak to the next in a waveform. *(p. 100)*

Weber's law A law stating that the smallest detectable difference in stimulus energy, the just-noticeable difference *(JND)*, is a constant fraction, *K*, of the intensity of the stimulus, *I*. The constant varies for each sensory system and for different aspects of sensation within those systems. In algebraic terms, Weber's law is *JND = KI*. (See also *just-noticeable difference.*) *(p. 145)*

Withdrawal syndrome A complex of symptoms associated with the termination of administration of a habit-forming substance. *(p. 310)*

Words Units of language composed of one or more morphemes. (See also *morpheme.*) *(p. 275)*

Working memory See *short-term memory.*

Zero-sum game A social situation in which one person's gains are subtracted from another person's resources, such that the sum of the gains and losses is zero. *(p. 663)*

Zygote A new cell, formed from the union of a father's sperm and a mother's ovum, that carries the genetic heritage of each. *(p. 407)*

Abbott, B. B., Schoen, L. S., & Badia, P. (1984). Predictable and unpredictable shock: Behavioral measures of aversion and physiological measures of stress. *Psychological Bulletin, 96,* 45–71.

Abeles, N. (1985). Proceedings of the American Psychological Association, 1985. *American Psychologist, 41,* 633–663.

Abraham, H. D., & Wolf, E. (1988). Visual function in past users of LSD: Psychophysical findings. *Journal of Abnormal Psychology, 97,* 443–447.

Abramis, D. J. (1994). Work role ambiguity, job satisfaction, and job performance: Meta-analyses and review. *Psychological Reports, 75,* 1411–1433.

Abramowitz, J. S. (1996). Variants of exposure and response prevention in the treatment of obsessive-compulsive disorder: A meta-analysis. *Behavior Therapy, 27,* 583–600.

Abramowitz, J. S. (1997). Effectiveness of psychological and pharmacological treatments for obsessive-compulsive disorder: A quantitative review. *Journal of Consulting and Clinical Psychology, 65,* 44–52.

Abrams, R. (1992). *Electroconvulsive therapy.* New York: Oxford University Press.

Abrams, R. (1993). ECT technique: Electrode placement, stimulus type, and treatment frequency. In C. E. Coffey (Ed.), *The clinical science of electroconvulsive therapy.* Washington, DC: American Psychiatric Press.

Abramson, L. Y., Metalsky, G. I., & Alloy, L. B. (1989). Hopelessness depression: A theory-based subtype. *Psychological Review, 96,* 358–372.

Abramson, L. Y., Seligman, M. E. P., & Teasdale, J. D. (1978). Learned helplessness in humans: Critique and reformulation. *Journal of Abnormal Psychology, 87,* 49–74.

Achenbach, T. M. (1997). *Empirically based assessment of child and adolescent psychopathology.* Thousand Oaks, CA: Sage.

Acitelli, L. K. (1992). Gender differences in relationship awareness and marital satisfaction among young married couples. *Personality and Social Psychology Bulletin, 18,* 102–110.

Ackerman, D. (1995). *Mystery of the senses.* Boston: WGBH-TV/Washington, DC: WETA-TV.

Ackerman, P. L. (1994). Intelligence, attention, and learning: Maximal and typical performance. In D. K. Detterman (Ed.), *Current topics in human intelligence* (Vol. 4). Norwood, NJ: Ablex.

Acocella, J. (1998, April 6). The politics of hysteria. *New Yorker,* pp. 64–79.

Adam, K., & Oswald, I. (1977). Sleep is for tissue restoration. *Journal of the Royal College of Physicians London, 11,* 376–388.

Ader, D. N., & Johnson, S. B. (1994). Sample description, reporting, and analysis of sex in psychological research: A look at APA and APA division journals in 1990. *American Psychologist, 49,* 216–218.

Ader, R., & Cohen, N. (1993). Psychoneuroimmunology: Conditioning and stress. *Annual Review of Psychology, 44,* 53–85.

Ader, R., Felten, D., & Cohen, N. (1990). Interactions between the brain and the immune system. *Annual Review of Pharmacology and Toxicology, 30,* 561–602.

Adler, A. (1927). *The practice and theory of individual psychology.* Paterson, NJ: Littlefield Adams. (Reprinted in 1963)

Adler, A. (1963). *The practice and theory of individual psychology.* Paterson, NJ: Littlefield Adams. (Original work published in 1927)

Adler, T. (1993, March). Bad mix: Combat stress, decisions. *APA Monitor,* p. 1.

Adolphs, R., Tranel, D., & Damasio, A. R. (1998). The human amygdala in social judgment. *Nature, 393*(6684), 470–474.

Adolphs, R., Tranel, D., Damasio, H., & Damasio, A. (1994). Impaired recognition of emotion in facial expressions following bilateral damage to the human amygdala. *Nature, 372*(6507), 669–672.

Adorno, T. W., Frenkel-Brunswik, E., Levinson, D. J., & Sanford, R. N. (1950). *The authoritarian personality.* New York: Harper & Row.

Agarwal, D. P. (1997). Molecular genetic aspects of alcohol metabolism and alcoholism. *Pharmacopsychiatry, 30*(3), 79–84.

Agnew, C. R., Van Lange, P. A. M., Rusbult, C. E., & Langston, C. A. (1998). Cognitive interdependence: Commitment and the mental representation of close relationships. *Journal of Personality and Social Psychology, 74,* 939–954.

Ahmed, A., & Ruffman, T. (1998). Why do infants make A not B errors in a search task, yet show memory for the location of hidden objects in a nonsearch task? *Developmental Psychology, 34,* 441–453.

Aiello, J. R., & Kolb, K. J. (1995). Electronic performance monitoring and social context: Impact on productivity and stress. *Journal of Applied Psychology, 80,* 339–353.

Aiken, L. R. (1994). *Psychological testing and assessment* (8th ed.). Boston: Allyn & Bacon.

Aiken, L. R. (1996). *Personality assessment methods and practices* (2nd ed.). Seattle: Hogrefe & Huber Publishers.

Ainsworth, M. D. S. (1973). The development of infant-mother attachment. In B. M. Caldwell & H. N. Ricciuti (Eds.), *Review of child development research: Vol. 3.* Chicago: University of Chicago Press.

Ainsworth, M. D. S. (1989). Attachments beyond infancy. *American Psychologist, 44,* 709–716.

Ainsworth, M. D. S., Blehar, M. D., Waters, E., & Wall, S. (1978). *Patterns of attachment: A psychological study of the Strange Situation.* Hillsdale, NJ: Lawrence Erlbaum Associates.

Aitchison, J. (1983). *The articulate mammal: An introduction to psycholinguistics* (2nd ed.). New York: Universe.

Al-Kubaisy, T., Marks, I. M., Logsdail, S., Marks, M. P., Lovell, K., Sungur, M., & Araya, R. (1992). Role of exposure homework in phobia reduction: A controlled study. *Behavior Therapy, 23,* 599–621.

Alaoui-Ismaili, O., Vernet-Maury, E., Dittmar, A., Delhomme, G., & Chanel, J. (1997). Odor hedonics: Connection with emotional response estimated by autonomic parameters. *Chemical Senses, 22,* 237–248.

Albee, G. (1968). Conceptual models and manpower requirements in psychology. *American Psychologist, 23,* 317–320.

Albee, G. (1985, February). The answer is prevention. *Psychology Today.*

Alberti, R. E., & Emmons, M. L. (1986). *Your perfect right: A guide to assertive living* (5th ed.). San Luis Obispo, CA: Impact Publishers.

Aldag, R. J., & Fuller, S. R. (1993). Beyond fiasco: A reappraisal of the groupthink phenomenon and a new model of group decision processes. *Psychological Bulletin, 113,* 533–552.

Alderete, E., Eskenazi, B., & Sholtz, R. (1995). Effect of cigarette smoking and coffee drinking on time to conception. *Epidemiology, 6*(4), 403–408.

Alexander, C. N., Langer, E. J., Newman, R. I., & Chandler, H. M. (1989). Transcendental meditation, mindfulness, and longevity: An experimental study with the elderly. *Journal of Personality and Social Psychology, 57,* 950–964.

ALI (American Law Institute). (1962). *Model penal code: Proposed offical draft.* Philadelphia: ALI.

Alicke, M., LoSchiavo, F. M., Zerbst, J., & Zhang, S. (1997). The person who outperforms me is a genius: Maintaining perceived competence in upward social comparisons. *Journal of Personality and Social Psychology, 73,* 781–789.

Allen, B. L. (1991). Cognitive research in information science: Implications for design. In M. Williams (Ed.), *Annual Review of Information Science and Technology, 26,* 3–37.

Allen, J. B., Kenrick, D. T., Linder, D. E., & McCall, M. A. (1989). Arousal and attraction: A response-facilitation alternative to misattribution and negative-reinforcement models. *Journal of Personality and Social Psychology, 57,* 261–270.

Allen, L. S., & Gorski, R. A. (1992). Sexual orientation and the size of the anterior commissure in the human brain. *Proceedings of the National Academy of Sciences of the United States of America, 89,* 7199–7202.

Allen, L. S., Hines, M., Shryne, J. E., & Gorski, R. A. (1989). Two sexually dimorphic cell groups in the human brain. *Journal of Neuroscience, 9,* 497–506.

Allison, S. T., Messick, D. M., & Goethals, G. R. (1989). On being better but not smarter than others: The Muhammad Ali effect. *Social Cognition, 7,* 275–296.

Allport, G. W. (1961). *Pattern and growth in personality.* New York: Holt, Rinehart & Winston.

Allport, G. W., & Odbert, H. S. (1936). Trait names: A psycholexical study. *Psychological Monographs, 47*(1, Whole No. 211).

Alston, J. H. (1920). Spatial condition of the fusion of warmth and cold in heat. *American Journal of Psychology, 31,* 303–312.

Altemeyer, B. (1988). *Right-wing authoritarianism.* Winnipeg: University of Manitoba Press.

Altemeyer, B. (1994). Reducing prejudice in right-wing authoritarians. In M. Zanna & J. Olson (Eds.), *The psychology of prejudice: The Ontario Symposium* (Vol. 7, pp. 131–148). Hillsdale, NJ: Lawrence Erlbaum Associates.

Altmann, G. T. M. (1997). *The ascent of Babel: An exploration of language, mind, and understanding.* New York: Oxford University Press.

Aluja-Fabregat, A., & Torrubia-Beltri, R. (1998). Viewing of mass media violence, perception of violence, personality and academic achievement. *Personality and Individual Differences, 25,* 973–989.

Alvarez, F. J., Delrio, M. C., & Prada, R. (1995). Drinking and driving in Spain. *Journal of Studies on Alcohol, 56*(4), 403–407.

Alvaro, E. M., & Crano, W. D. (1997). Indirect minority influence: Evidence for leniency in source evaluation and counterargumentation. *Journal of Personality and Social Psychology, 72,* 949–964.

Amabile, T. M. (1989). *Growing up creative.* New York: Random House.

Amabile, T. M., Goldfarb, P., & Brackfield, S. C. (1990). Social influences on creativity: Evaluation, coaction, and surveillance. *Creativity Research Journal, 3,* 6–21.

Amabile, T. M., Hennessey, B. A., & Grossman, B. S. (1986). Social influences on creativity: The effects of contracted-for reward. *Journal of Personality & Social Psychology, 50,* 14–23.

Amabile, T. M., Hill, K. G., Hennessey, B. A., & Tighe, E. M. (1994). The Work Preference Inventory: Assessing intrinsic and extrinsic motivational orientations. *Journal of Personality and Social Psychology, 66*(5), 950–967.

Amaro, H. (1995). Love, sex, and power: Considering women's realities in HIV prevention. *American Psychologist, 50,* 437–447.

Ambrosini, M. V., Langella, M., Gironi-Carnivale, U. A., & Giuditta, A. (1992). The sequential hypothesis of sleep function: III. The structure of postacquisition sleep in learning and nonlearning rats. *Physiology and Behavior, 51,* 217–226.

American Psychiatric Association (1993, April). Practice guide for major depressive disorder in adults. *American Journal of Psychiatry, 150* (Suppl.), 1–26.

American Psychiatric Association (1994). *Diagnostic and statistical manual of mental disorders* (4th ed.). Washington, DC: American Psychiatric Association.

American Psychological Association. (1974). *Standards for educational and psychological test and manuals.* Washington, DC: APA.

American Psychological Association. (1981). Ethical principles of psychologists. *American Psychologist, 36,* 633–638.

American Psychological Association. (1985). *Standards for Educational and Psychological Testing.* Washington, DC: APA.

American Psychological Association. (1992a, May). APA continues to refine its ethics code. *APA Monitor.*

American Psychological Association. (1992b). Ethical principles of psychologists and code of conduct. *American Psychologist, 47,* 1597–1611.

American Psychological Association (1993). *Violence and youth: Psychology's response.* Washington: DC: APA.

American Psychological Association. (1995a). Directory Survey. Washington, DC: APA.

American Psychological Association (1995b). *Intelligence: Knowns and unknowns: Report.* Washington, D.C.: APA.

American Psychological Association (1995c). *Report of the task force on the changing gender composition of psychology.* Washington, DC: APA.

American Psychological Association (1995d). Sex, race/ethnicity data available. *Trends in Education, 2,* 2–3.

American Psychological Association. (1996, December). *Task Force Report: On-line psychotherapy and counseling.* Washington, DC: APA.

Anastasi, A. (1997). *Psychological testing* (7th ed.). Upper Saddle River, NJ: Prentice-Hall.

Andersen, S. M., Reznik, I., & Manzella, L. M. (1996). Eliciting facial affect, motivation, and expectancies in transference: Significant-other representations in social relations. *Journal of Personality and Social Psychology, 71,* 1108–1129.

Anderson, C. A. (1997). Effects of violent movies and trait hostility on hostile feelings and aggressive thoughts. *Aggressive Behavior, 23,* 161–178.

Anderson, C. A. (in press). Aggression and violence. In A. E. Kazdin (Ed.), *The encyclopedia of psychology.* Washington, DC: American Psychological Association.

Anderson, C. A., & Anderson, K. P. (1998). Temperature and aggression: Paradox, controversy, and a (fairly) clear picture. In R. G. Geen & E. Donnerstein (Eds.), *Human aggression* (pp. 248–298). San Diego: Academic Press.

Anderson, C. A., & Bushman, B. J. (1997). External validity of "trivial" experiments: The case of laboratory aggression. *Review of General Psychology, 1,* 19–41.

Anderson, E. M., & Lambert, M. J. (1995). Short-term dynamically oriented psychotherapy: A review and meta-analysis. *Clinical Psychology Review, 9*(6), 503–514.

Anderson, J. (1996, April 29 and May 6). Black and blue. *New Yorker.*

Anderson, J. A. (1995). *An introduction to neural networks.* Cambridge, MA: MIT Press.

Anderson, J. R. (1990a). *The adaptive character of thought.* Hillsdale, NJ: Lawrence Erlbaum Associates.

Anderson, J. R. (1990b). *Cognitive psychology and its implications* (3rd ed.). New York: W. H. Freeman.

Anderson, J. R. (1992). Problem solving and learning. *American Psychologist, 48,* 35–44.

Anderson, J. R. (1995a). *Cognitive psychology and its implications* (4th ed.). New York: W. H. Freeman.

Anderson, J. R. (1995b). *Learning and memory: An integrated approach.* New York: John Wiley & Sons.

Anderson, R. C., Reynolds, R. E., Schallert, D. L., & Goetz, E. T. (1977). Frameworks for comprehending discourse. *American Educational Research Journal, 14,* 367–382.

Andreasen, N. C. (1997). Linking mind and brain in the study of mental illnesses: A project for a scientific psychopathology. *Science, 275,* 1586–1593.

Andreasen, N. C., Arndt, S., Alliger, R., Miller, D., & Flaum, M. (1995). Symptoms of schizophrenia. *Archives of General Psychiatry, 52,* 341–351.

Andreasen, N. C., Arndt, S., Swayze, V., II, Cizadlo, T., Flaum, M., O'Leary, D., Ehrhandt, J. C., & Yuh, W. T. C. (1994). Thalamic abnormalities in schizophrenia visualized through magnetic resonance image averaging. *Science, 266,* 294–298.

Anrep, G. V. (1920). Pitch discrimination in the dog. *Journal of Physiology, 53,* 367–385.

Anthony, T., Cooper, C., & Mullen, B. (1992). Cross-racial facial identification: Five studies of sex differences in facial prominence. *Personality and Social Psychology Bulletin, 18,* 296–301.

Antonuccio, D. O., Danton, W. G., & DeNelsky, G. Y. (1995). Psychotherapy versus medication for depression: Challenging the conventional wisdom with data. *Professional Psychology: Research and Practice, 26,* 574–585.

Aponte, J. F., Rivers, R. Y., & Wohl, J. (1995). *Psychological interventions and cultural diversity.* Boston: Allyn & Bacon.

Applebaum, P. (1994). *Almost a revolution: Mental health law and the limits of change.* New York: Oxford University Press.

Archambault, C. M., Czyzewski, D., Cordua y Cruz, G. D., Foreyt, F. P., & Mariotto, M. J. (1989). Effects of weight cycling in female rats. *Physiology and Behavior, 46,* 417–421.

Arenberg, D. (1982). Changes with age in problem solving. In F. I. M. Craik & S. Trehub (Eds.), *Aging and cognitive processes* (pp. 221–236). New York: Plenum.

Arlow, J. (1995). Psychoanalysis. In R. J. Corsini & D. Wedding (Eds.), *Current psychotherapies* (5th ed., pp. 15–50). Itasca, IL: Peacock.

Armstrong, M. S., & Vaughan, K. (1996). An orienting response model of eye movement desensitization. *Journal of Behavior Therapy and Experimental Psychiatry, 27,* 21–32.

Arndt, J., Greenberg, J., Pyszczynski, T., & Solomon, S. (1997). Subliminal exposure to death-related stimuli increases defense of the cultural worldview. *Psycological Science, 8,* 379–385.

Aronoff, J., Barclay, A. M., & Stevenson, L. A. (1988). The recognition of threatening stimuli. *Journal of Personality and Social Psychology, 54,* 647–655.

Aronson, E. (1990). Applying social psychology to desegregation and energy conservation. *Personality and Social Psychology Bulletin, 16,* 118–132.

Aronson, E. (1995). *The social animal* (7th ed.). New York: W. H. Freeman.

Aronson, E., Wilson, T. D., & Akert, R. M. (1999). *Social psychology* (3rd ed.). New York: Longman.

Arterberry, M., Yonas, A., & Bensen, A. S. (1989). Self-produced locomotion and development of responsiveness to textural gradients. *Developmental Psychology, 25,* 976–982.

Arvey, R. D. (1986). General ability in employment. *Journal of Vocational Behavior, 29,* 415–420.

Asch, S. E. (1951). Effects of group pressure upon the modification and distortion of judgments. In H. Guetzkow (Ed.), *Groups, leadership, and men.* Pittsburgh: Carnegie Press.

Asch, S. E. (1955). Opinions and social pressure. *Scientific American, 193,* 31–35.

Asch, S. E. (1956). Studies of independence and conformity: A minority of one against a unanimous majority. *Psychological Monographs, 70,* 1–70.

Ashcraft, M. H. (1989). *Human memory and cognition.* Glenview, IL: Scott, Foresman.

Ashton, H. (1995). Protracted withdrawal from benzodiazepines: The post-withdrawal syndrome. *Psychiatric Annals, 25(3),* 174–179.

Aslin, R. N., Jusczyk, P. W., & Pisoni, D. B. (1998). Speech and auditory processing during infancy: Constraints on and precursors to language. In W. Damon (Ed.), *Handbook of child psychology* (5th ed., pp. 147–198). New York: Wiley.

Aspinwall, L. G., & Taylor, S. E. (1992). Modeling cognition adaptation: A longitudinal investigation of the impact of individual differences and coping on college adjustment and performance. *Journal of Personality and Social Psychology, 63,* 989–1003.

Aspinwall, L. G., & Taylor, S. E. (1997). A stitch in time: Self-regulation and proactive coping. *Psychological Bulletin, 121,* 417–436.

Associated Press. (1992, April 23). *Rape survey raises count.*

Associated Press. (1997, October 22). Forty percent in senior classes fail at science. *Chicago Tribune.*

Aston-Jones, G., Chiang, C., & Alexinsky, T. (1991). Discharge of noradrenergic locus coeruleus neurons in behaving rats and monkeys suggests a role in vigilance. *Progress in Brain Research, 88,* 501–520.

Atkinson, G., & Reilly, T. (1996). Circadian variation in sports performance. *Sports Medicine, 21*(4), 292–312.

Atkinson, J. W., & Raynor, J. O. (1974). *Personality, motivation, and achievement.* Washington, DC: Hemisphere.

Atkinson, R. C., & Shiffrin, R. M. (1968). Human memory: A proposed system and its control processes. In K. Spence (Ed.), *The psychology of learning and motivation:* Vol. 2. New York: Academic Press.

Attneave, F. (1971). *Image, object, and illusion.* San Francisco: Freeman.

Au, T. K. (1992). Counterfactual reasoning. In G. R. Semin & K. Fiedler (Eds.), *Language, interaction and social cognition.* London: Sage.

Auld, F., & Hyman, M. (1991). *Resolution of inner conflict: An introduction to psychoanalytic therapy.* Washington, DC: American Psychological Association.

Averill, J. S. (1980). On the paucity of positive emotions. In K. R. Blankstein, P. Pliner, & J. Polivy (Eds.), *Advances in the study of communication and affect: Vol. 6. Assessment and modification of emotional behavior.* New York: Plenum.

Aviezer, O., Van IJzendoorn, M. H., Sagi, A., & Schuengel, C. (1994). Children of the dream revisited: 70 years of collective early child care in Israeli kibbutzim. *Psychological Bulletin, 116,* 99–117.

Ax, R. K., Forbes, M. R., & Thompson, D. D. (1997). Prescription privileges for psychologists: A survey of predoctoral interns and directors of training. *Professional Psychology: Research and Practice, 28,* 509–514.

Ayanian, J., & Cleary, P. (1999). Perceived risks of heart disease and cancer among cigarette smokers. *Journal of the American Medical Association, 281,* 1019–1021.

Ayllon, T., & Azrin, N. H. (1968). The token economy: *A motivational system for therapy and rehabilitation.* New York: Appleton-Century-Crofts.

Azar, B. (1995a, January). DNA-environment mix forms intellectual fate. *American Psychological Association Monitor,* p. 24.

Azar, B. (1995b, May). Several genetic traits linked to alcoholism. *APA Monitor.*

Azar, B. (1996a, November). Project explores landscape of midlife. *APA Monitor,* p. 26.

Azar, B. (1996b, June). Schools the source of rough transitions. *APA Monitor,* p. 14.

Azar, B. (1996c, November). Some forms of memory improve as people age. *APA Monitor,* p. 27.

Azar, B. (1997a, March). Computers learn to mimic human traits. *APA Monitor,* p. 1.

Azar, B. (1997b, September). Economists collaborate with psychologists. *APA Monitor,* p. 19.

Azar, B. (1997c, December). Maternal emotions may influence fetal behaviors. *APA Monitor,* p. 17.

Baars, B. J. (1998). Metaphors of consciousness and attention in the brain. *Trends in Neuroscience, 21*(2), 58–62.

Babcock, R., & Salthouse, T. (1990). Effects of increased processing demands on age differences in working memory. *Psychology and Aging, 5,* 421–428.

Backman, L., & Nilsson, L. (1991). Effects of divided attention on free and cued recall of verbal events and action events. *Bulletin of the Psychonomic Society, 29,* 51–54.

Baddeley, A. (1982). *Your memory: A user's guide.* New York: Macmillan.

Baddeley, A. (1992). Working memory. *Science, 255,* 556–559.

Baddeley, A., & Hitch, G. (1974). Working memory. In G. H. Bower (Ed.), *The psychology of learning and motivation* (Vol. 8, pp. 47–89). New York: Academic Press.

Bagwell, C. L., Newcomb, A. F., & Bukowski, W. M. (1998). Preadolescent friendship and peer rejection as predictors of adult adjustment. *Child Development, 69,* 140–153.

Bahrick, H. P., Bahrick, P. O., & Wittlinger, R. P. (1975). Fifty years of memory for names and faces: A cross-cultural approach. *Journal of Experimental Psychology: General,* 104, 54–75.

Bahrick, H. P., & Hall, L. K. (1991). Lifetime maintenance of high school mathematics content. *Journal of Experimental Psychology: General, 120,* 20–33.

Bahrick, H. P., Hall, L. K., & Berger, S. A. (1996). Accuracy and distortion in memory for high school grades. *Psychological Science, 7*(5), 265–271.

Bahrick, H. P., Hall, L. K., Noggin, J. P., & Bahrick, L. E. (1994). Fifty years of language maintenance and language dominance in bilingual Hispanic immigrants. *Journal of Experimental Psychology: General, 123,* 264–283.

Bailey, A. J. (1993). The biology of autism. *Psychological Medicine, 23,* 7–11.

Bailey, J. M., & Benishay, D. S. (1993). Familial aggregation of female sexual orientation. *American Journal of Psychiatry, 150,* 272–277.

Bailey, J. M., Bobrow, D., Wolfe, M., & Mikach, S. (1995). Sexual orientation of adult sons of gay fathers. *Developmental Psychology, 31*(1), 124–129.

Bailey, J. M., & Pillard, R. C. (1991). A genetic study of male sexual orientation. *Archives of General Psychiatry, 48,* 1089–1096.

Bailey, J. M., & Zucker, K. J. (1995). Childhood sex-typed behavior and sexual orientation: A conceptual analysis and quantitative review. Special Issue: Sexual orientation and human development. *Developmental Psychology, 31,* 43–55.

Baillargeon, R. (1992). A model of physical reasoning in infancy. In C. Rovee-Collier & L. P. Lipsett (Eds.), *Advances in infancy research.* Norwood, NJ: Ablex.

Baillargeon, R. (1994a). How do infants learn about the physical world? *Current Directions in Psychological Science, 3,* 133–139.

Baillargeon, R. (1994b). Physical reasoning in young infants: Seeking explanations for impossible events. *British Journal of Development Psychology, 12,* 9–33.

Baillargeon, R. (1995). Physical reasoning in infancy. In M. S. Gazzaniga (Ed.), *The cognitive neurosciences* (pp. 181–204). Cambridge, MA: MIT Press.

Baillargeon, R. (1998). Infants' understanding of the physical world. In M. Sabourin et al. (Eds.), *Advances in psychological science: Vol. 2. Biological and cognitive aspects* (pp. 503–529). Hove, UK: Taylor & Francis.

Baker, L. T., Vernon, P. A., & Ho, H. (1991). The genetic correlation between intelligence and speed of information processing. *Behavior Genetics, 21,* 351–367.

Balaban, M. T. (1995). Affective influences on startle in five-month-old infants: Reactions to facial expressions of emotion. *Child Development, 66*(1), 28–36.

Balakireva, M., Stocker, R. F., Gendre, N., & Ferveur, J. F. (1998). Voila, a new Drosophila courtship variant that affects the nervous system: Behavioral, neural, and genetic characterization. *Journal of Neuroscience, 18*(11), 4335–4343.

Baldwin, M. W. (1992). Relational schemas and the processing of social information. *Psychological Bulletin, 112,* 461–484.

Ball, K., & Sekuler, R. (1992). Cues reduce direction uncertainty and enhance motion detection. *Perception and Psychophysics, 30,* 119–128.

Ball, S. G., Buchwald, A. M., & Waddell, M. T. (1995). Depression and generalized anxiety symptoms in panic disorder: Implications for comorbidity. *Journal of Nervous and Mental Disorders, 183*(5), 304–308.

Balleine, B., & Dickinson, A. (1994). Role of cholecystokinin in the motivational control of instrumental action in rats. *Behavioral Neuroscience, 108*(3), 590–605.

Baltes, P. B. (1993). The aging mind: Potential and limits. *The Gerontologist, 33,* 580–594.

Baltes, P. B. (1994, August). *Life-span developmental psychology: On the overall landscape of human development.* Invited address presented at the annual meeting of the American Psychological Association, Los Angeles.

Baltes, P. B., & Baltes, M. M. (1990). *Successful aging.* New York: Cambridge University Press.

Baltes, P. B., Staudinger, U. M., Maercker, A., & Smith, J. (1995). People nominated as wise: A comparative study of wisdom-related knowledge. *Psychology and Aging, 10,* 155–166.

Bancroft, J. (1994). Homosexual orientation: The search for a biological basis. *British Journal of Psychiatry, 164,* 437–440.

Bandura, A. (1965). Influence of a model's reinforcement contingencies on the acquisition of imitative responses. *Journal of Personality and Social Psychology, 1,* 589–595.

Bandura, A. (1983). Psychological measurement of aggression. In R. G. Green and C. I. Donnerstein (Eds.), *Aggression: Theoretical and empirical reviews* (Vol. 1). New York: Academic Press.

Bandura, A. (1986). *Social foundations of thought and action: A social cognitive theory.* Englewood Cliffs, NJ: Prentice-Hall.

Bandura, A. (1997). *Self-efficacy: The exercise of control.* New York: Freeman.

Bandura, A., Blanchard, E. B., & Ritter, B. (1969). The relative efficacy of desensitization and modeling approaches for inducing behavioral, affective, and attitudinal changes. *Journal of Personality and Social Psychology, 13,* 173–199.

Bandura, A., Ross, D., & Ross, S. A. (1963). Imitation of film-mediated aggressive models. *Journal of Abnormal and Social Psychology, 66,* 3–11.

Banich, M. (1997). *Neuropsychology: The neural bases of mental function.* Boston: Houghton Mifflin.

Banich, M. T., & Heller, W. (1998). Evolving perspectives on lateralization of function. *Current Directions in Psychological Science, 7,* 1–2.

Banich, M. T., Stolar, N., Heller, W., & Goldman, R. B. (1992). A deficit in right-hemisphere performance after induction of a depressed mood. *Neuropsychiatry, Neuropsychology, and Behavioral Neurology, 5*(1), 20–27.

Banks, W. P., & Krajicek, D. (1991). Perception. *Annual Review of Psychology, 42,* 305–332.

Bar, M., & Biederman, I. (1998). Subliminal visual priming. *Psychological Science, 9,* 464–469.

Barber, J. P., Crits-Christoph, P., & Paul, C. C. (1993). Advances in measures of psychodynamic formulations. *Journal of Consulting and Clinical Psychology, 61,* 574–585.

Barclay, J. R., Bransford, J. D., Franks, J. J., McCarrell, N. S., & Nitsch, K. (1974). Comprehension and semantic flexibility. *Journal of Verbal Learning and Verbal Behavior, 13,* 471–481.

Bardo, M. T. (1998). Neuropharmacological mechanisms of drug reward: Beyond dopamine in the nucleus accumbens. *Critical Reviews of Neurobiology, 12*(1–2), 37–67.

Bardo, M. T., Donohew, R. L., & Harrington, N. G. (1996). Psychobiology of novelty-seeking and drug-seeking behavior. *Behavioral Brain Research, 77*(1–2), 23–43.

Bargh, J. A., Chen, M., & Burrows, L. (1996). Automaticity of social behavior: Direct effects of trait construct and stereotype activation on action. *Journal of Personality and Social Psychology, 71,* 245–262.

Barker, L. M. (1997). *Learning and behavior: Biological, psychological, and sociocultural perspectives* (2nd ed.). Upper Saddle River, NJ: Prentice-Hall.

Barlow, D. H. (1988). *Anxiety and its disorders: The nature and treatment of panic and anxiety.* New York: Guilford.

Barner, E. L., & Gray, S. L. (1998). Donepezil use in Alzheimer disease. *Annals of Pharmacotherapy, 32,* 70–77.

Baron, R. A., & Byrne, D. (1994). *Social psychology: Understanding human interaction* (7th ed.). Boston: Allyn & Bacon.

Baron, R. A. , & Richardson, D. C. (1994). *Human aggression* (2nd ed.) New York: Plenum.

Baron, R. S., Kerr, N. L., & Miller, N. (1992). *Group process, group decision, group action.* Pacific Grove, CA: Brooks/Cole.

Barondes, S. H. (1994). Thinking about Prozac. *Science, 263,* 1102–1103.

Barrett, G. V., & Depinet, R. L. (1991). A reconsideration of testing for competence rather than for intelligence. *American Psychologist, 46,* 1012–1024.

Barrick, M. R., & Mount, M. K. (1991). The Big Five personality dimensions and job performance: A meta-analysis. *Personnel Psychology, 44,* 1–26.

Barron, F., & Harrington, D. M. (1981). Creativity, intelligence, and personality. *Annual Review of Psychology, 52,* 439–476.

Barsalou, L. W. (1991). Deriving categories to achieve goals. In G. H. Bower (Ed.), *The psychology of learning and motivation.* New York: Academic Press.

Barsalou, L. W. (1993). Flexibility, structure, and linguistic vagary in concepts: Manifestations of a compositional system of perceptual symbols. In A. F. Collins, S. E. Gathercole, M. A. Conway, & P. E. Morris (Eds.), *Theories of memory.* Hove, Eng.: Erlbaum.

Barsky, A. J., Wool, C., Barnett, M. C., & Cleary, P. D. (1994). Histories of childhood trauma in adult hypochondriacal patients. *American Journal of Psychiatry, 151,* 397–401.

Bartlett, J. C. (1993). Tonal structure of melodies. In T. J. Tighe & W. J. Dowling (Eds.), *Psychology and music: The understanding of melody and rhythm* (pp. 39–61). Hillsdale, NJ: Lawrence Erlbaum Associates.

Bartol, C. (1991). Predictive validation of the MMPI for small-town police officers who fail. *Professional Psychology: Research and Practice, 22,* 127–132.

Bartone, P., Gifford, R., Wright, K., Marlowe, D., & Martin, J. (1992). *U.S. soldiers remain healthy under Gulf War stress.* Paper presented at the 4th annual convention of the American Psychological Society, San Diego.

Bartoshuk, L. M. (1991). Taste, smell, and pleasure. In R. C. Bollef (Ed.), *The hedonics of taste.* Hillsdale, NJ: Lawrence Erlbaum Associates.

Bartoshuk, L. M., Duffy, V. B., Reed, D., & Williams, A. (1996). Supertasting, earaches and head injury: Genetics and pathology alter our taste worlds.

Neuroscience Biobehavior Review, 20, 79–87.

Bartoshuk, L. M., & Wolfe, J. M. (1990). Conditioned taste aversion in humans: Are there olfactory versions? *Chemical Senses, 15,* 551.

Bartus, R. T., Dean, R. L., III, Beer, B., and Lippa, A. S. (1982). The cholinergic hypothesis of geriatric memory dysfunction. *Science, 217,* 408–417.

Bashore, T. R., & Rapp, P. E. (1992). Are there alternatives to traditional polygraph procedures? *Psychological Bulletin, 113*(1), 3–22.

Bass, E., & Davis, L. (1988). *The courage to heal: A guide for women survivors of child sexual abuse.* New York: Harper & Row.

Bates, E. (1993, March). *Nature, nurture, and language development.* Paper presented at the biennial meeting of the Society for Research in Child Development, New Orleans.

Bateson, G., Jackson, D. D., Haley, J., & Weakland, J. (1956). Toward a history of schizophrenia. *Behavioral Science, 1,* 251–264.

Batson, C. D. (1998). Altruism and prosocial behavior. In D. Gilbert, S. T. Fiske, and G. Lindzey (Eds.), *Handbook of social psychology,* Vol. 2 (4th ed., pp. 282–316). Boston: McGraw-Hill.

Batson, C. D., Sager, K., Garst, E., & Kang, M. (1997). Is empathy-induced helping due to self-other merging? *Journal of Personality and Social Psychology, 73,* 495–509.

Battaglia, G., Yeh, S. Y., & De Souza, E. B. (1988). MDMA-induced neurotoxicity: Parameters of degeneration and recovery of brain serotonin neurons. *Pharmacology, Biochemistry and Behavior, 29,* 269–274.

Baucom, D. H., Shoham, V., Mueser, K. T., Daiuto, A. D., & Stickle, T. R. (1998). Empirically supported couple and family interventions for marital distress and adult mental health problems. *Journal of Consulting and Clinical Psychology, 66,* 53–88.

Bauer, P. J. (1996). What do infants recall of their lives?: Memory for specific events by one- to two-year-olds. *American Psychologist, 51,* 29–41.

Baumeister, R. (1998). The self. In D. Gilbert, S. T. Fiske, and G. Lindzey (Eds.), *Handbook of social psychology,* Vol. 1 (4th ed., pp. 680–740). Boston: McGraw-Hill.

Baumeister, R. F., & Leary, M. R. (1995). The need to belong: Desire for interpersonal attachments as a fundamental human motivation. *Psychological Bulletin, 117*(3), 497–529.

Baumrind, D. (1971). Current patterns of parental authority. *Developmental Psychology Monographs, 4*(1, part 2).

Baumrind, D. (1986). *Familial antecedents of social competence in middle childhood.* Unpublished monograph, Institute of Human Development, University of California, Berkeley.

Bayer, R. (1981). *Homosexuality and American psychiatry.* New York: Basic Books.

Beardsley, R. S., Gardocki, G. J., Larson, D. B., & Hidalgo, J. (1988). Prescribing of psychotropic medication by primary-care physicians and psychiatrists. *Archives of General Psychiatry, 45,* 1117–1119.

Beatty, J. (1995). *Principles of behavioral neuroscience.* Dubuque: Brown and Benchmark.

Beauchamp, G. K., Katahira, K., Yamazaki, K., Mennella, J. A., Bard, J., & Boyse, E. A. (1995). Evidence suggesting that the odortypes of pregnant women are a compound of maternal and fetal odortypes. *Proceedings of the National Academy of Sciences of the United States of America, 92,* 2617–2621.

Beauchamp-Turner, D. L., & Levinson, D. M. (1992). Effects of meditation on stress, health, and affect. *Medical Psychotherapy: An International Journal, 5,* 123–131.

Beck, A. T. (1967). *Depression: Clinical, experimental and theoretical aspects.* New York: Harper & Row.

Beck, A. T. (1976). *Cognitive therapy and the emotional disorders.* New York: International Universities Press.

Beck, A. T. (1995). Cognitive therapy: A 30-year retrospective. In S. O. Lilienfeld (Ed.), *Seeing both sides: Classic controversies in abnormal psychology* (pp. 303–311). Pacific Grove, CA: Brooks/Cole. (Original work published in 1991)

Beck, A. T., Brown, G., Berchick, R. J., Stewart, B. L., & Steer, R. A. (1990). Relationship between hopelessness and ultimate suicide: A replication with psychiatric outpatients. *American Journal of Psychiatry, 147,* 190–195.

Beck, A. T., & Emery, G. (1985). *Anxiety disorders and phobias: A cognitive perspective.* New York: Basic Books.

Beck, A. T., Rush, A. J., Shaw, B. F., & Emery, G. (1979). *Cognitive therapy of depression.* New York: Guilford.

Beck, A. T., Sokol, L., Clark, D., Berchick, R., & Wright, F. (1992). A crossover study of focused cognitive therapy for panic disorder. *American Journal of Psychiatry, 149,* 778–783.

Beck, A. T., & Weishaar, M. E. (1995). Cognitive therapy. In R. J. Corsini & D. Wedding (Eds.), *Current psychotherapies* (5th ed., pp. 229–261). Itasca, IL: Peacock.

Beck, M. (1992, December 7). The new middle age. *Newsweek*, pp. 50–56.

Becker, J. A. (1994). "Sneak-shoes," "sworders" and "nose-beards": A case study of lexical innovation. *First Language, 14,* 195–211.

Bedard, J. (1989). Expertise in auditing: Myth or reality? *Accounting, Organizations and Society, 14,* 113–131.

Bedard, J., & Chi, M. T. H. (1992). Expertise. *Current Directions in Psychological Science, 1,* 135–139.

Begley, S. (1997, September 29). Hope for "snow babies." *Newsweek*, pp. 62–63.

Bell, B. E., & Loftus, E. F. (1989). Trivial persuasion in the courtroom: The power of (a few) minor details. *Journal of Personality and Social Psychology, 56,* 669–679.

Bell, P. A., Fisher, J. D., Baum, A., & Greene, T. (1990). *Environmental psychology* (3rd ed.). Forth Worth, TX: Holt, Rinehart & Winston.

Bell, P. F., Digman, R. H., Jr., & McKenna, J. P. (1995). Should psychologists obtain prescription privileges? A survey of family physicians. *Professional Psychology: Research and Practice, 26,* 371–376.

Bell-Dolan, D., & Anderson, C. A. (in press). Attributional process: An integration of social and clinical psychology. In R. M. Kowalski & M. R. Leary (Eds.), *The social psychology of emotional and behavioral problems: Interfaces of social clinical psychology.*

Bellezza, F. S. (1981). Mnemonic devices: Classification, characteristics, and criteria. *Review of Educational Research, 51,* 247–275.

Bellezza, F. S. (1993). Does "perplexing" describe the self-reference effect? Yes! In T. K. Srull & R. S. Wyer (Eds.), *The mental representation of trait and autobiographical knowledge about the self: Advances in social cognition: Vol. V.* Hillsdale, NJ: Lawrence Erlbaum Associates.

Belmont, J. M., & Butterfield, E. C. (1971). Learning strategies as determinants of memory deficiencies. *Cognitive Psychology, 2,* 411–420.

Belsky, J., & Kelly, J. (1994). *The transition to parenthood.* New York: Dell.

Belsky, J., Spritz, B., & Crnic, K. (1996). Infant attachment security and affective-cognitive information processing at age 3. *Psychological Science, 7,* 111–114.

Bem, D. J. (1967). Self-perception: An alternative interpretation of cognitive dissonance phenomena. *Psychological Review, 74,* 183–200.

Ben-Shakhar, G. & Furedy, J. J. (1990). *Theories and applications in the detection of deception: A psychophysiological and international perspective.* New York: Springer-Verlag.

Ben-Shlomo, Y. (1997). The epidemiology of Parkinson's disease. *Baillieres Clinical Neurology, 6,* 55–68.

Benca, R. M., Obermeyer, W. H., Thisted, R. A., & Gillin, J. C. (1992). Sleep and psychiatric disorders. A meta-analysis. *Archives of General Psychiatry, 49,* 651–658.

Benecke, M. (1999). Spontaneous human combustion: Thoughts of a forensic biologist. *Skeptical Inquirer, 22,* 47–51.

Benedetti, F., & Amanzio, M. (1997). The neurobiology of placebo analgesia: From endogenous opioids to cholecystokinin. *Progress in Neurobiology, 52,* 109–125.

Benet-Martinez, V., & John, O. P. (in press). *Los cinco grandes* across five cultures and ethnic groups: Multi-trait, multi-method analyses of the Big Five in Spanish and English. *Journal of Personality and Social Psychology.*

Benjamin, J., Li, L., Patterson, C., Greenberg, B. D., Murphy, D. L., & Hamer, D. H. (1996). Population and familial association between the D_4 dopamine receptor gene and measures of novelty seeking. *Nature Genetics, 12,* 81–84.

Bennet, W. M. (1994). Marijuana has no medicinal value. *Hospital Practice, 29*(4), 26–27.

Bennett, H. L., Giannini, J. A., & Davis, H. S. (1985). Nonverbal response to intra-operational conversation. *British Journal of Anaesthesia, 57,* 174–179.

Benson, H. (1975). *The relaxation response.* New York: Morrow.

Berenbaum, S. A., & Resnick, S. M. (1997). Early androgen effects on aggression in children and adults with congenital adrenal hyperplasia. *Psychoneuroendocrinology, 22,* 505–515.

Berg, E. P., Engel, B. A., & Forrest, J. C. (1998). Pork carcass composition derived from a neural network model of electromagnetic scans. *Journal of Animal Science, 76,* 18–22.

Bergin, A. E. (1971). The evaluation of therapeutic outcomes. In A. E. Bergin & S. L. Garfield (Eds.), *Handbook of psychotherapy and behavior change: An empirical analysis* (pp. 217–270). New York: Wiley.

Berkowitz, B. (1965). Changes in intellect with age: IV. Changes in achievement and survival in older people. *Journal of Genetic Psychology, 107,* 3–14.

Berkowitz, L. (1994). Is something missing? Some observations prompted by the Cognitive-neoassociationist view of anger and emotional aggression. In L. R. Huesmann (Ed.), *Human aggression: Current perspectives* (pp. 35–60). New York: Plenum.

Berkowitz, L. (1998). Affective aggression: The role of stress, pain, and negative affect. In R. G. Geen & E. Donnerstein (Eds.), *Human aggression* (pp. 49–72). San Diego: Academic Press.

Berlin, L. J., Cassidy, J., & Belsky, J. (1995). Loneliness in young children and infant-mother attachment: A longitudinal study. *Merrill-Palmer Quarterly, 41,* 91–103.

Berliner, D. C. (1993). The 100-year journey of educational psychology: From interest, to disdain, to respect for practice. In T. Fagan & G. VandenBos (Eds.), *Exploring applied psychology: Origins and critical analyses.* Washington, DC: American Psychological Association.

Berliner, D. L., Monti-Bloch, L., Jennings-White, C., & Diaz-Sanchez, V. (1996). The functionality of the human vomeronasal organ (VNO): Evidence for steroid receptors. *Journal of Steroid Biochemical Molecular Biology, 58,* 259–265.

Berman, A. L., & Jobes, D. A. (1991). *Adolescent suicide: Assessment and intervention.* Washington, DC: American Psychological Association.

Berman, R. F. (1991). Electrical brain stimulation used to study mechanisms and models of memory. In J. L. Martinez & R. P. Kesner (Eds.), *Learning and memory: A biological view* (2nd ed.). San Diego, CA: Academic Press.

Bermond, B., Fasotti, L., Nieuwenhuyse, B., & Schuerman, J. (1991). Spinal cord lesions, peripheral feedback and intensities of emotional feelings. *Cognition and Emotion, 5,* 201–220.

Bernard, L. L. (1924). *Instinct.* New York: Holt, Rinehart & Winston.

Bernstein, D. A. (1970). The modification of smoking behavior: A search for effective variables. *Behaviour Research and Therapy, 8,* 133–146.

Bernstein, D. A., & Borkovec, T. D. (1973). *Progressive relaxation training: A manual for the helping professions.* Champaign, IL: Research Press.

Bernstein, D. A., Borkovec, T. D., & Hazlette-Stevens, H. (in press). *Progressive relaxation training: A manual for the helping professions* (rev. ed.). Westport, CT: Greenwood.

Bernstein, D. A., & Stec, A. M. (Eds.). (1999). *The psychology of everyday life.* Boston: Houghton Mifflin.

Bernstein, I. L. (1978). Learned taste aversions in children receiving chemotherapy. *Science, 200,* 1302–1303.

Berridge, K. C. (1999). Pleasure, pain, desire and dread: Biopsychological components and relations. In D. Kahneman, E. Diener, & N. Schwarz (Eds.), *Understanding the quality of life: Scientific perspectives on enjoyment and suffering.* New York: Russell Sage Foundation.

Berry, J. W., & Bennett, J. A. (1992). Cree conceptions of cognitive competence. *International Journal of Psychology, 27,* 73–88.

Berry, J. W., Poortinga, Y. A., Segall, M. H., & Dasen, P. R. (1992). *Cross-cultural psychology: Research and applications.* New York: Cambridge University Press.

Berscheid, E., & Reis, H. T. (1998). Attraction and close relationships. In D. Gilbert, S. T. Fiske, and G. Lindzey (Eds.), *Handbook of social psychology,* Vol. 2 (4th ed., pp. 193–281). Boston: McGraw-Hill.

Bersoff, D. N. (1995). *Ethical conflicts in psychology.* Washington, DC: American Psychological Association.

Besson, M., Faita, F., Peretz, I., Bonnel, A.-M., & Requin, J. (1998). Singing in the brain: Independence of lyrics and tunes. *Psychological Science, 9,* 494–498.

Best, D. (1992, June). *Cross-cultural themes in developmental psychology.* Paper presented at workshop on cross-cultural aspects of psychology. Western Washington University, Bellingham.

Best, J. B. (1995). *Cognitive Psychology* (4th ed.). Minneapolis, MN: West Publishing Company.

Bettman, J. R., Johnson, E. J., & Payne, J. W. (1990). A componential analysis of cognitive effort in choice. *Organizational Behavior and Human Decision Processes, 45,* 111–139.

Beyerstein, B. L. (1997, September/October). Why bogus therapies seem to work. *Skeptical Inquirer, 21,* 29–34.

Biaggio, M., Paget, T. L., & Chenoweth, M. S. (1997). A model for ethical management of faculty-student dual relationships. *Professional Psychology: Research and Practice, 28,* 184–189.

Biederman, I. (1987a). Matching image edges to object memory. *Proceedings of the IEEE First International Conference on Computer Vision,* pp. 364–392.

Biederman, I. (1987b). Recognition by components. *Psychological Review, 94,* 115–147.

Biederman, I., Cooper, E. E., Fox, P. W., & Mahadevan, R. S. (1992). Unexceptional spatial memory in an exceptional memorist. *Journal of Experimental Psychology: Learning, Memory, and Cognition, 18,* 654–657.

Bigelow, A., MacLean, J., Wood, C., & Smith, J. (1990). Infants' responses to child and adult strangers: An investigation of height and facial configuration variables. *Infant Behavior and Development, 13,* 21–32.

Biklen, D. (1990). Communication unbound: Autism and praxis. *Harvard Educational Review, 60,* 290–314.

Billig, M., & Tajfel, H. (1973). Social categorization and similarity in intergroup behavior. *European Journal of Social Psychology, 3,* 27–52.

Billing, J., & Sherman, P. W. (1998). Antimicrobial functions of spices: Why some like it hot. *Quarterly Review of Biology, 73,* 3–49.

Binet, A., & Simon, T. (1905). Methodes nouvelles pour le diagnostic du niveau intellectuel des anormaux. *L'Annee Psychologique, 11,* 191–244.

Bishop, K. M., & Wahlsten, D. (1997). Sex differences in the human corpus callosum: Myth or reality? *Neuroscience Biobehavioral Reviews, 21,* 581–601.

Bittigau, P., & Ikonomidou, C. (1997). Glutamate in neurologic diseases. *Journal of Child Neurology, 12,* 471–485.

Bjork, R. A., & Vanhuele, M. (1992). Retrieval inhibition and related adaptive peculiarities of human memory. *Advances in Consumer Research, 19,* 155–160.

Bjorklund, D. F., & Green, B. L. (1992). The adaptive nature of cognitive immaturity. *American Psychologist, 47,* 46–54.

Black, J. E., & Greenough, W. T. (1991). Developmental approaches to the memory process. In J. L. Martinez & R. P. Kesner (Eds.), *Learning and memory: A biological view* (2nd ed.). San Diego: Academic Press.

Blackwell, B. (1973). Psychotropic drugs in use today. *Journal of the American Medical Association, 225,* 1637–1641.

Blagrove, M. (1996). Problems with the cognitive psychological modeling of dreaming. *Journal of Mind and Behavior, 17,* 99–134.

Blair, I. V., & Banaji, M. (1996). Automatic and controlled processes in stereotype priming. *Journal of Personality and Social Psychology, 70,* 1142–1163.

Blake, J., & de Boysson-Bardies, B. (1992). Patterns in babbling: A cross-linguistic study. *Journal of Child Language, 19,* 51–74.

Blake, R. (1998). What can be "perceived" in the absence of visual awareness? *Current Directions in Psychological Science, 6,* 157–162.

Blanchard, E. B., & Andrasik, F. (1985). Management of chronic headaches: A psychological approach. New York: Pergamon Press.

Blass, T. (1991). Understanding behavior in the Milgram obedience experiment: The role of personality, situations, and their interactions. *Journal of Personality and Social Psychology, 60,* 398–413.

Blatchford, P., Burke, J., Farquhar, C., & Plewis, I. (1989). Teacher expectations in infant school: Associations with attainment and progress, curriculum coverage and classroom interaction. *British Journal of Educational Psychology, 59,* 19–30.

Blatt, S. J., & Ford, R. (1994). *Therapeutic change: An object relations perspective.* New York: Plenum.

Blatt, S. J., & Maroudas, C. (1992). Convergence of psychoanalytic and cognitive behavioral theories of depression. *Psychoanalytic Psychology, 9,* 157–190.

Blazer, D. G., Kessler, R. C., McGonagle, K. A., & Swartz, M. S. (1994). The prevalence and distribution of major depression in a national community sample: The national comorbidity survey. *American Journal of Psychiatry, 151,* 979–986.

Blehar, M., & Rosenthal, N. (1989). Seasonal affective disorders and phototherapy. *Archives of General Psychiatry, 46,* 469–474.

Block, J. A. (1971). *Lives through time.* Berkeley: Bancroft Books.

Block, J. A. (1995). A contrarian view of the five-factor approach. *Psychological Bulletin, 117,* 187–215.

Block, R. I., & Ghoneim, M. M. (1993). Effects of chronic marijuana use on human cognition. *Psychopharmacology, 110*(1–2), 219–228.

Bloom, A. H. (1981). *The linguistic shaping of thought: A study of the impact of language on thinking in China and the West.* Hillsdale, NJ: Lawrence Erlbaum Associates.

Bloom, L. (1995). *The transition from infancy to language: Acquiring the power of expression.* New York: Cambridge University Press.

Blum, L. N., Nielsen, N. H., & Riggs, J. A. (1998). Alcoholism and alcohol abuse among women. *Journal of Women's Health, 7,* 861–871.

Blumberg, M. S., & Lucas, D. E. (1994). Dual mechanisms of twitching during sleep in neonatal rats. *Behavioral Neuroscience, 108*(6), 1196–1202.

Blume, E. S. (1990). *Secret survivors: Uncovering incest and its aftereffects in women.* New York: Ballantine.

Blundell, J. E., & Halford, J. C. G. (1998). Serotonin and appetite regulation: Implications for the pharmacological treatment of obesity. *CNS Drugs, 9,* 473–495.

Bogartz, R. S., Shinskey, J. L., & Speaker, C. J. (1997). Interpreting infant looking: The event set x event set design. *Developmental Psychology, 33,* 408–422.

Bogen, J. E. (1995). On the neurophysiology of consciousness: I. An overview. *Consciousness and Cognition, 4,* 52–62.

Bolles, R. C. (1975). *Theory of motivation* (2nd ed.). New York: Harper & Row.

Bond, G., Aiken, L., & Somerville, S. (1992). The Health Beliefs Model and adolescents with insulin-dependent diabetes mellitus. *Health Psychology, 11,* 190–198.

Bond, R., & Smith, P. B. (1996). Culture and conformity: A meta-analysis of studies using Asch's (1952b, 1956) line judgment task. *Psychological Bulletin, 119,* 111–137.

Bongar, B., & Beutler, L. E. (Eds.). (1995). *Comprehensive textbook of psychotherapy: Theory and practice.* New York: Oxford University Press.

Bonica, J. J. (1992). Importance of the problem. In G. M. Aronoff (Ed.), *Evaluation and treatment of chronic pain.* Baltimore: Williams & Wilkins.

Bonwell, C. C., & Eison, J. A. (1991). *Active learning: Creating excitement in the classroom.* Washington, DC: George Washington University.

Borgida, E., Conner, C., & Monteufel, L. (1992). Understanding living kidney donors: A behavioral decision-making perspective. In S. Spacapan & S. Oskamp (Eds.), *Helping and being helped* (pp. 183–212). Newbury Park, CA: Sage.

Borkowski, J. G., Weyhing, R. S., & Turner, L. A. (1986). Attributional retraining and the teaching of strategies. *Exceptional Children, 53,* 130–137.

Borman, W. C., Hanson, M. A., & Wedge, J. W. (1997). Personnel selection. *Annual Review of Psychology, 48,* 299–337.

Bornstein, R. F. (1992). Subliminal mere exposure effects. In R. F. Bornstein & T. S. Pittman (Eds.), *Perception without awareness: Cognitive, clinical, and social perspectives* (pp. 191–210). New York: Guilford.

Borum, R. & Grisso, T. (1995). Psychological test use in criminal forensic evaluations. *Professional Psychology: Research and Practice. 26,* 465–473.

Boss, P. (1999). *Ambiguous loss: Learning to live with unresolved grief.* Cambridge, MA: Harvard University Press.

Botwinick, J. (1961). Husband and father-in-law: A reversible figure. *American Journal of Psychology, 74,* 312–313.

Botwinick, J. (1966). Cautiousness in advanced age. *Journal of Gerontology, 21,* 347–353.

Botwinick, J. (1977). Intellectual abilities. In J. E. Birren & K. W. Schaie (Eds.), *Handbook of the psychology of aging.* New York: Van Nostrand Reinhold.

Bouchard, T. J., Jr., Lykken, D. T., McGue, M., Segal, N. L., & Tellegen, A. (1990). Sources of human psychological differences: The Minnesota study of twins reared apart. *Science, 250,* 223–228.

Bouchard, T., et al. (1981). Familial studies of intelligence: A review. *Science, 212*(4498), 1055–1059.

Bower, G. H. (1975). Cognitive psychology: An introduction. In W. K. Estes (Ed.), *Handbook of learning and cognitive processes: Vol. 1.* Hillsdale, NJ: Lawrence Erlbaum Associates.

Bower, J. E., Kemeny, M. E., Taylor, S. E., & Fahey, J. L. (1999). Cognitive processing, discovery of meaning, CD4 decline, and AIDS-related mortality among bereaved HIV-seropositive men. *Journal of Consulting and Clinical Psychology, 66,* 979–986.

Bowerman, M. (1996). The origins of children's spatial semantic categories: Cognitive versus linguistic determinants. In J. J. Gumperz & S. C. Levinson (Eds.), *Rethinking linguistic relativity: Studies in the social and cultural foundations of language, No. 17* (pp. 145–176). Cambridge, UK: Cambridge University Press.

Bowlby, J. (1973). *Attachment and loss: Vol. 2. Separation.* New York: Basic Books.

Bowlby, J. (1980). *Loss: Sadness and depression.* New York: Basic Books.

Boyatzis, R. E. (1982). *The competent manager.* New York: Wiley.

Bozarth, M. A., & Wise, R. A. (1984). Anatomically distinct opiate receptor fields mediate reward and physical dependence. *Science, 224,* 516–518.

Bradbury, T. N., Campbell, S. M., & Fincham, F. D. (1995). Longitudinal and behavioral analysis of masculinity and femininity in marriage. *Journal of Personality and Social Psychology, 68,* 328–341.

Bradley-Johnson, S., Graham, D. P., & Johnson, C. M. (1986). Token reinforcement on WISC-R performance for white, low-socioeconomic, upper and lower elementary-school-age students. *Journal of School Psychology, 24,* 73–79.

Bradshaw, G. L. (1993a). Why did the Wright brothers get there first? Part 1. *Chemtech, 23*(6), 8–13.

Bradshaw, G. L. (1993b). Why did the Wright brothers get there first? Part 2. *Chemtech, 23*(7), 16–22.

Bradshaw, G. L., & Shaw, D. (1992). Forecasting solar flares: Experts and artificial systems. *Organizational Behavior and Human Decision Performance, 53*, 135–157.

Brainerd, C. J., & Reyna, V. F. (1998). When things that were never experienced are easier to "remember" than things that were. *Psychological Science, 9*, 484–489.

Brainerd, C. J., Reyna, V. F., & Brandse, E. (1995). Are children's false memories more persistent than their true memories? *Psychological Science, 6*, 359–364.

Brakke, K. E., & Savage-Rumbaugh, E. S. (1996). The development of language skills in pan II: Production. *Language and Communication, 16*, 361–380.

Brandimonte, M. A., Hitch, G. J., & Bishop, D. V. M. (1992). Influence of short-term memory codes on visual image processing: Evidence from image transformation tasks. *Journal of Experimental Psychology: Learning, Memory, and Cognition, 18*, 157–165.

Brandtstadter, J., & Renner, G. (1990). Tenacious goal pursuit and flexible goal adjustment: Explication and age-related analysis of assimilative and accommodative strategies of coping. *Psychology and Aging, 5*, 58–67.

Bransford, J. D., & Johnson, M. K. (1972). Contextual prerequisites for understanding: Some investigations of comprehension and recall. *Journal of Verbal Learning and Verbal Behavior, 11*, 717–726.

Bransford, J. D., & Stein, B. S. (1993). *The ideal problem solver* (2nd ed.). New York: W. H. Freeman.

Braungart, J. M., Plomin, R., & Fulker, D. W. (1992). Genetic mediation of the home environment during infancy: A sibling adoption study of the HOME. *Developmental Psychology, 28*, 1048–1055.

Breakey, W. R., & Thompson, J. W. (Eds.). (1997). *Mentally ill and homeless: Special programs for special needs*. Langhorne, PA: Harwood.

Breedlove, S. M. (1994). Sexual differentiation of the human nervous system. *Annual Review of Psychology, 45*, 389–418.

Breggin, P. (1991). *Toxic psychiatry*. New York: St. Martin's Press.

Bregman, A. S. (1990). *Auditory scene analysis*. Cambridge, MA: Bradford/MIT Press.

Brehm, J. W., & Self, E. A. (1989). The intensity of motivation. *Annual Review of Psychology, 40*, 109–131.

Brehm, S. (1992). *Intimate relationships*. New York: McGraw-Hill.

Breier, A., Buchanan, R. W., Elkashef, A., Munson, R. C., Kirkpatrick, B., & Gellad, F. (1992). Brain morphology and schizophrenia: A magnetic resonance imaging study of limbic, prefrontal cortex, and caudate structures. *Archives of General Psychiatry, 49*, 921–926.

Breland, K., & Breland, M. (1966). *Animal behavior*. New York: Macmillan.

Brelsford, J. W. (1993). Physics education in a virtual environment. In *Proceedings of the 37th Annual Meeting of the Human Factors and Ergonomics Society*. Santa Monica, CA: Human Factors.

Brennan, P. A., & Mednick, S. A. (1994). Learning theory approach to the deterrence of criminal recidivism. *Journal of Abnormal Psychology, 103*, 430–440.

Brennen, T., Baguley, T., Bright, J., & Bruce, V. (1990). Resolving semantically induced tip-of-the-tongue states for proper nouns. *Memory & Cognition, 18*, 339–347.

Brenner, L., & Ritter, R. C. (1995). Peptide cholecystokinin receptor antagonist increases food intake in rats. *Appetite, 24*, 1–9.

Breslin, P. A., & Beauchamp, G. K. (1997). Salt enhances flavour by suppressing bitterness. *Nature, 387*, 563.

Breuer, J., & Freud, S. (1895/1974). Studies on hysteria. In J. A. Strachey (Ed. & Trans.), *The Pelican Freud library* (Vol 3.*)*. Harmondsworth, UK: Penguin.

Breuer, J., & Freud, S. (1896). *Studies on hysteria*. New York: Avon. (Reprinted in 1966)

Brewer, J. B., Zhao, Z., Desmond, J. E., Glover, G. H., & Gabriel, J. D. E. (1998). Making memories: Brain activity that predicts how well visual experience will be remembered. *Science, 281*, 1185–1187.

Brewer, M. B., & Brown, R. J. (1998). Intergroup relations. In D. Gilbert, S. T. Fiske, and G. Lindzey (Eds.), *Handbook of social psychology*, Vol. 2 (4th ed., pp. 554–594). Boston: McGraw-Hill.

Brewer, W. F., & Pani, J. R. (1984). The structure of human memory. In G. H. Bower (Ed.), *The psychology of learning and motivation: Vol. 17*. New York: Academic Press.

Brewer, W. F., & Treyens, J. C. (1981). Role of schemata in memory for places. *Cognitive Psychology, 13*, 207–230.

Brewerton, T. D., Lydiard, R. B., Herzog, D. B., & Brotman, A. W. (1995). Comorbidity of Axis I psychiatric disorders in bulimia nervosa. *Journal of Clinical Psychiatry, 56*(2), 77–80.

Brigham, C. C. (1923). *A study of American intelligence*. Princeton, NJ: Princeton University Press.

Brigham, C. C. (1930). Intelligence tests of immigrant groups. *Psychological Review, 37*, 158–165.

Brinckerhoff, L. C., Shaw, S. F., & McGuire, J. M. (1993). *Promoting postsecondary education for students with learning disabilities*. Austin, TX: Pro-ed.

Brislin, R., (1993). *Understanding culture's influence on behavior*. Fort Worth: Harcourt, Brace, Jovanovich.

Brock, J. W., Farooqui, S. M., Ross, K. D., & Payne, S. (1994). Stress-related behavior and central norepinephrine concentrations in the REM sleep-deprived rat. *Physiology and Behavior, 55*(6), 997–1003.

Brock, T. C., Green, M. C., & Reich, D. A. (1998). New evidence of flaws in the *Consumer Reports* study of psychotherapy. *American Psychologist, 53*, 62–72.

Brody, J. E. (1998, September 15). Personal health: Teenagers and sex—Younger and more at risk. *New York Times* (Web Archive).

Brody, N. (1992). *Intelligence*. San Diego: Academic Press.

Brody, N., & Ehrlichman, H. (1998). *Personality psychology: The science of individuality*. Upper Saddle River, NJ: Prentice-Hall.

Broman, C. L. (1993). Social relationships and health-related behavior. *Journal of Behavioral Medicine, 16*, 335–350.

Bronstein, P., Duncan, P., Clauson, J., Abrams, C. L., Yannett, N., Ginsburg, G., & Milne, M. (1998). Preventing middle school adjustment problems for children from lower-income families: A program for aware parenting. *Journal of Applied Developmental Psychology, 19*, 129–152.

Brooks-Gunn, J., Gross, R. T., Kraemer, H. C., Spiker, D., & Shapiro, S. (1992). Enhancing the cognitive outcomes of low birth weight, premature infants: For whom is the intervention most effective? *Pediatrics, 89*, 1209–1215.

Brown, A. L., Campione, J. C., Webber, L. S., & McGilly, K. (1992). Interactive learning environments: A new look at assessment and instruction. In B. Gifford & M. C. O'Connor (Eds.), *Changing assessments: Alternative views of aptitude, achievement, and instruction*. Boston; Kluever.

Brown, J. (1958). Some tests of the decay theory of immediate memory. *Quarterly Journal of Experimental Psychology, 10*, 12–21.

Brown, J. D., & McGill, K. L. (1989). The cost of good fortune: When positive life events produce negative health consequences. *Journal of Personality and Social Psychology, 57*, 1103–1110.

Brown, R., & Kulik, J. (1977). Flashbulb memories. *Cognition, 5*, 73–99.

Brown, R., & McNeill, D. (1966). The "tip-of-the-tongue" phenomenon. *Journal of Verbal Learning and Verbal Behavior, 5*, 325–337.

Brown, R. A. (1973). *First language*. Cambridge, MA: Harvard University Press.

Brownell, K. D., & Rodin, J. (1994). The dieting maelstrom: Is it possible and advisable to lose weight? *American Psychologist, 49*(9), 781–791.

Bruce, H. M. (1969). Pheromones and behavior in mice. *Acta Neurologica Belgica, 69*, 529–538.

Bruck, M., Cavanagh, P., & Ceci, S. J. (1991). Fortysomething: Recognizing faces at one's 25th reunion. *Memory & Cognition, 19*, 221–228.

Brunvald, J. H. (1989). *Curses! Broiled again! The hottest urban legends going*. New York: Norton.

Brunvald, J. H. (1995). Lights out! A faxlore phenomenon. *Skeptical Inquirer, 19*, 32–37.

Bruyer, R. (1991). Covert face recognition in prosopagnosia. *Brain and Cognition, 15*, 223–235.

Bryant, R. A., & McConkey, K. M. (1989). Hypnotic blindness: A behavioral and experiential analysis. *Journal of Abnormal Psychology, 98*, 71–77.

Bryant, W. R., & Lask, B. (1995). Eating disorders: An overview. *Journal of Family Therapy, 17*(1), 13–30.

Buchanan, R. W., & Carpenter, W. T. (1994). Domains of psychopathology: An approach to the reduction of the heterogeneity in schizophrenia. *Journal of Nervous and Mental Disease, 182*, 193–204.

Buchanan, R. W., Strauss, M., Kirkpatrick, B., Holstein, C., Breier, A., & Carpenter, W. T., Jr., (1994). Neuropsychological impairments in deficit vs. nondeficit forms of schizophrenia. *Archives of General Psychiatry, 51*, 804–811.

Buchsbaum, M. S., Haier, R. J., Potkin, S. G., Nuehterlein, K., Bracha, H. S., Katz, M., Lohr, J., Wu, J., Lottenberg, S., Jerabek, P. A., Trenary, M., Tafalla, R., Reynolds, C., & Bunney, W. E. (1992). Frontostriatal disorder of cerebral metabolism in never-medicated schizophrenics. *Archives of General Psychiatry, 49*, 935–942.

Buck, L. B. (1996). Information coding in the vertebrate olfactory system. *Annual Review of Neuroscience, 19*, 517–544.

Bugental, D. B., & Goodnow, J. J. (1998). Socialization processes. In W. Damon & N. Eisenberg (Eds.), *Handbook of child psychology: Vol. 3. Social, emotional, and personality development* (5th ed., pp. 389–462). New York: Wiley.

Bui, K.-V. T, Peplau, L. A., & Hill, C. T. (1996). Testing the Rusbult model of relationship commitment and stability in a 15-year study of heterosexual couples. *Personality and Social Psychology Bulletin, 22,* 1244–1257.

Bullough, V. L. (1995, August). Sex matters. *Scientific American,* pp. 105–106.

Burchard, R. E. (1992). Coca chewing and diet. *Current Anthropology, 33*(1), 1–24.

Burger, J. M., & Petty, R. E. (1981). The low-ball compliance technique: Task or person commitment? *Journal of Personality and Social Psychology, 40,* 492–500.

Burish, T., & Jenkins, R. (1992). Effectiveness of biofeedback and relaxation training in reducing the side effects of cancer chemotherapy. *Health Psychology, 11,* 17–23.

Burke, H. B., Hoang, A., Iglehart, J. D., & Marks, J. R. (1998). Predicting response to adjuvant and radiation therapy in patients with early-stage breast carcinoma. *Cancer, 82,* 874–877.

Burke, K. C., Burke, J. K., Jr., Regier, D. A., & Rae, D. S. (1990). Age at onset of selected mental disorders in five community populations. *Archives of General Psychiatry, 47,* 511–518.

Burleson, M. H., Gregory, W. L., & Trevarthen, W. R. (1995). Heterosexual activity: Relationship with ovarian function. *Psychoneuroendocrinology, 20*(4), 405–421.

Burman, B., & Margolin, G. (1992). Analysis of the association between marital relationships and health problems: An interactional perspective. *Psychological Bulletin, 112,* 39–63.

Burns, M. O., & Seligman, M. E. P. (1989). Explanatory style across the life span: Evidence for stability over 52 years. *Journal of Personality and Social Psychology, 56,* 471–477.

Burnstein, E., Crandell, C., & Kitayama, S. (1994). Some Neo-Darwinian decision rules for altruism: Weighing cues for inclusive fitness as a function of the biological importance of the decision. *Journal of Personality and Social Psychology, 67,* 773–789.

Burr, C. (1993). Homosexuality and biology. *Atlantic Monthly, 271,* 47–65.

Burr, D. C., Morrone, C., & Fiorentini, A. (1996). Spatial and temporal properties of infant colour vision. In F. Vital-Durand, J. Atkinson, J., & O. J. Braddick (Eds.), *Infant vision* (pp. 63–77). Oxford: Oxford University Press.

Burris, C. T., Branscombe, N. R., & Klar, Y. (1997). Maladjustment implications of group gender-role discrepancies: An ordered distinction model. *European Journal of Social Psychology, 27,* 675–685.

Bushman, B. J. (1993). Human aggression while under the influence of alcohol and other drugs: An integrative research review. *Current Directions in Psychological Science, 2,* 148–152.

Bushman, B. J. (1998). Priming effects of media violence on the accessibility of aggressive constructs in memory. *Personality and Social Psychology Bulletin, 24,* 537–545.

Buske-Kirschbaum, A., Kirschbaum, C., Stierle, H., Jabaij, L., & Hellhammer, D. (1994). Conditioned manipulation of natural killer (NK) cells in humans using a discriminative learning protocol. *Biological Psychology, 38,* 143–155.

Buss, A. (1995). *Personality: Temperament, social behavior, and the self.* Boston: Allyn & Bacon.

Buss, A. H. (1989). Personality as traits. *American Psychologist, 44,* 1378–1388.

Buss, A. H. (1997). Evolutionary perspectives on personality traits. In R. Hogan, J. Johnson, & S. Briggs (Eds.), *Handbook of personality psychology* (pp. 345–366). San Diego: Academic Press.

Buss, D. M. (1995a). Evolutionary psychology: A new paradigm for psychological science. *Psychological Inquiry, 6,* 1–30.

Buss, D. M. (1995b). The future of evolutionary psychology. *Psychological Inquiry, 6,* 81–87.

Buss, D. M. (1995c). Psychological sex differences: Origins through sexual selection. *American Psychologist, 50,* 164–168.

Buss, D. M., & Kenrick, D. T. (1998). Evolutionary social psychology: Intergroup relations. In D. Gilbert, S. T. Fiske, and G. Lindzey (Eds.), *Handbook of social psychology,* Vol. 2 (4th ed., pp. 982–1026). Boston: McGraw-Hill.

Buss, D. M., & Shackelford, T. K. (1997). Human aggression in evolutionary perspective. *Clinical Psychology Review, 17,* 605–619.

Byrne, D., & Nelson, D. (1965). Attraction as a linear function of proportion of positive reinforcements. *Journal of Personality and Social Psychology, 1,* 659–663.

Cabral, G. A., & Dove Pettit, D. A. (1998). Drugs and immunity: Cannabinoids and their role in decreased resistance to infectious disease. *Journal of Neuroimmunology, 83,* 116–123.

Cacioppo, J. T., Berntson, G. G., Malarkey, W. B., Kiecolt-Glaser, J. K., Sheridan, J. F., Poehlmann, K. M., Burleson, M. H., Ernst, J. M., Hawkley, L. C., & Glaser, R. (in press). Autonomic, neuroendocrine, and immune responses to psychological stress: The reactivity hypothesis. *Annals of the New York Academy of Sciences.*

Cacioppo, J. T., Bernston, G. G., & Petty, R. E. (1997). Persuasion. *Encyclopedia of human biology* (Vol. 6, pp. 679–690). San Diego: Academic Press.

Cacioppo, J. T., Malarkey, W. B., Kiecolt-Glaser, J. K., Uchino, B. N., Sgoutas-Emch, S. A., Sheridan, J. F., Berntson, G. G., & Glaser, R. (1995). Heterogeneity in neuroendocrine and immune responses to brief psychological stressors as a function of autonomic cardiac activation. *Psychosomatic Medicine, 57,* 154–164.

Cacioppo, J. T., Petty, R. E., & Crites, S. L. (1993). Attitude change. In V. S. Ramachandran (Ed.), *Encyclopedia of human behavior.* San Diego, CA: Academic Press.

Cacioppo, J. T., Petty, R. E., Feinstein, J. A., & Jarvis, W. B. G. (1996). Dispositional differences in cognitive motivation: The life and times of individuals varying in the need for cognition. *Psychological Bulletin, 119,* 197–253.

Cacioppo, J. T., Poehlmann, K. M., Kiecolt-Glaser, J. K., Malarkey, W. B., Burleson, M. H., Berntson, G. G., & Glaser, R. (1998). Cellular immune responses to acute stress in female caregivers of dementia patients and matched controls. *Health Psychology, 17,* 182–189.

Cadoret, R. J., Yates, W. R., Troughton, E., Woodworth, G., & Stewart, M. A. (1995). Adoption study demonstrating two genetic pathways to drug abuse. *Archives of General Psychiatry, 52,* 42–52.

Cahill, S. P., Carrigan, M. H., & Evans, I. M. (1998). The relationship between behavior theory and behavior therapy: Challenges and promises. In J. J. Plaud & G. H. Eifert (Eds.), *From behavior theory to behavior therapy* (pp. 294–319). Boston: Allyn & Bacon.

Cai, Z., & Kimelberg, H. K. (1997). Glutamate receptor–mediated calcium responses in acutely isolated hippocampal astrocytes. *Glia, 21,* 380–389.

Cairns, R. B., Gariepy, J., & Hood, K. E. (1990). Development, microevolution, and social behavior. *Psychological Review, 97,* 49–65.

Campbell, D. T., & Stanley, J. C. (1966). *Experimental and quasi-experimental designs for research.* Chicago: Rand McNally.

Campbell, S. B. (1986). Developmental issues. In R. Gittelman (Ed.), *Anxiety disorders of childhood* (pp. 24–57). New York: Guilford.

Campbell, S. S., & Murphy, P. J. (1998). Extraocular circadian phototransduction in humans. *Science, 279,* 396–399.

Campfield, L. A., Smith, F. J., & Burn, P. (1998). Strategies and potential molecular targets for obesity treatment. *Science, 280*(5368), 1383–1387.

Campion, M. A., Palmer, D. K., & Campion, J. E. (1998). Structuring employment interviews to improve reliability, validity, and users' reactions. *Current Directions in Psychological Science, 7,* 77–82.

Campione, J. C., Brown, A. L., & Ferrara, R. A. (1982). Mental retardation and intelligence. In R. J. Sternberg (Ed.), *Handbook of human intelligence.* Cambridge: Cambridge University Press.

Campos, J., Langer, A., & Krowitz, A. (1970). Cardiac responses on the visual cliff in prelocomotor human infants. *Science, 170,* 196–197.

Campos, J. J. (1980). Human emotions: Their new importance and their role in social referencing. *Research and Clinical Center for Child Development, 1980–81 Annual Report,* 1–7.

Canavero, S. Bonicalzi, V. De Lucchi, R., Davini, O., Podio, V., & Bisi, G (1998). *Clinical Journal of Pain, 14,* 268–269.

Canino, I. A., & Spurlock, J. (1994). *Culturally diverse children and adolescents: Assessment, diagnosis, and treatment.* New York: Guilford.

Cann, A., & Ross, D. A. (1989). Olfactory stimuli as context cues in human memory. *American Journal of Psychology, 102,* 91–102.

Cannon, T. D. (1998). Neurodevelopmental influences in the genesis and epigenesis of schizophrenia: An overview. *Applied and Preventive Psychology, 7,* 47–62.

Cannon, T. D., Mednick, S. A., Parnas, J., Schulsinger, F., Praestholm, J., & Vestergaard, A. (1993). Developmental brain abnormalities in the offspring of schizophrenic mothers. *Archives of General Psychiatry, 50,* 551–564.

Cannon, T. D., Zorrilla, L. E., Shtasel, D., Gur, R. E., Gur, R. C., Marco, E. J., Moberg, P., & Price, A. (1994). Neuropsychological functioning in siblings discordant for schizophrenia and healthy volunteers. *Archives of General Psychiatry, 51,* 651–661.

Cannon, W. B. (1927/1987). The James-Lange theory of emotions: A critical examination and an alternative theory. Special issue: 100 years of the American Journal of Psychology. *American Journal of Psychology, 100*(3–4), 567–586.

Cannon, W. B., & Washburn, A. L. (1912). An explanation of hunger. *American Journal of Physiology, 29,* 444–454.

Cannon-Bowers, J. A., & Salas, E. (1998). Team performance and training in complex environments: Recent findings from applied research. *Current Directions in Psychological Science, 7,* 83–87.

Cao, Y., Vikingstad, E. M., Huttenlocher, P. R., Towle, V. L., & Levin, D. N. (1994). Functional magnetic resonance studies of the reorganization of the human head sensorimotor area after unilateral brain injury in the perinatal period. *Proceedings of the National Academy of Sciences of the United States of America, 91,* 9612–9616.

Caplan, P. J. (1995). *They say you're crazy. How the world's most powerful psychiatrists decide who's normal.* Reading, MA: Addison-Wesley.

Capron, C., & Duyme, M. (1989). Assessment of effects of socio-economic status on IQ in a full cross-fostering study. *Nature, 340,* 552–553.

Caramazza, A., & Hillis, A. E. (1991). Lexical organization of nouns and verbs in the brain. *Nature, 349,* 788–790.

Cardon, L. R., Smith, S. D., Fulker, D. W., Kimberling, W. J., Pennington, B. F., & DeFries, J. C. (1994). Quantitative trait locus for reading disability on chromosome 6. *Science, 266,* 276–279.

Carli, L. L., Ganley, R., & Pierce-Otay, A. (1991). Similarity and satisfaction in romantic relationships. *Personality and Social Psychology Bulletin, 17,* 419–426.

Carlin, A. S., Hoffman, H. G., & Weghorst, S. (1997). Virtual reality and tactile augmentation in the treatment of spider phobia: A case report. *Behaviour Research and Therapy, 35,* 153–158.

Carlson, M., Marcus-Newhall, A., & Miller, N. (1990). Effects of situational aggression cues: A quantitative review. *Journal of Personality and Social Psychology, 58,* 622–633.

Carlson, N. R. (1998). *Physiology of behavior.* Boston: Allyn & Bacon.

Carmichael, L. L., Hogan, H. P., & Walter, A. A. (1932). An experimental study of the effect of language on the reproduction of visually perceived form. *Journal of Experimental Psychology, 15,* 73–86.

Carnegie Task Force on Learning in the Primary Grades. (1996). *Years of promise: A comprehensive learning strategy for America's children.* New York: Carnegie Corporation.

Carnevale, P. J., & Pruitt, D. G. (1992). Negotiation and mediation. *Annual Review of Psychology, 43,* 531–582.

Carraher, T., Schliemann, A. D., & Carraher, D. W. (1988). Mathematical concepts in everyday life. In C. G. Saxe & M. Gearhart (Eds.), *Children's mathematics: Vol. 41. New directions for child development* (pp. 71–87). San Francisco: Jossey-Bass.

Carraher, T. N., Carraher, D., & Schliemann, A. D. (1985). Mathematics in the streets and in the schools. *British Journal of Developmental Psychology, 3,* 21–29.

Carrey, G., & DiLalla, D. L. (1994). Personality and psychopathology: Genetic perspectives. *Journal of Abnormal Psychology, 103,* 32–43.

Carroll, J. B. (1991). No demonstration that g is not unitary. *Intelligence, 15,* 423–436.

Carroll, K. M., Rounsaville, B. J., & Nich, C. (1994). One-year follow-up of psychotherapy and pharmacotherapy for cocaine dependence: Delayed emergence of psychotherapy effects. *Archives of General Psychiatry, 51*(12), 989–997.

Carstensen, L. (1997, August). *Psychology and the aging revolution: Changes in social needs and social goals across the lifespan.* Paper presented at the annual convention of the American Psychological Association.

Carter, M. M., Hollon, S. D., Carson, R., & Shelton, R. C. (1995). Effects of a safe person on induced distress following a biological challenge in panic disorder with agoraphobia. *Journal of Abnormal Psychology, 104,* 156–163.

Cartwright, R. D. (1978). *A primer on sleep and dreaming.* Reading, MA: Addison-Wesley.

Cartwright, R. D. (1993). Who needs their dreams? The usefulness of dreams in psychotherapy. *Journal of the American Academy of Psychoanalysis, 21*(4), 539–547.

Carver, C. S., & Scheier, M. F. (1995). *Perspectives on personality.* (3rd ed.) Boston, MA: Allyn & Bacon.

Carver, C. S., Scheier, M. F., & Weintraub, J. K. (1989). Assessing coping strategies: A theoretically based approach. *Journal of Personality and Social Psychology, 56,* 267–283.

Casas, J. M. (1995). Counseling and psychotherapy with racial/ethnic minority groups in theory and practice. In B. Bongar & L. E. Beutler (Eds.), *Comprehensive textbook of psychotherapy: Theory and practice* (pp. 311–335). New York: Oxford University Press.

Caspi, A. (1998). Personality development across the life course. In W. Damon & N. Eisenberg (Eds.), *Handbook of child psychology: Vol. 3. Social, emotional, and personality development* (5th ed., pp. 311–388). New York: Wiley.

Caspi, A., Begg, D., & Dickson, N., Harrington, H., Langley, J., Moffitt, T. E., & Silva, P. A. (1997). Personality differences predict health-risk behaviors in young adulthood: Evidence from a longitudinal study. *Journal of Personality and Social Psychology, 73,* 1052–1063.

Caspi, A., Bem, D. J., & Elder, G. H., Jr. (1989). Continuities and consequences of interactional styles across the life course. *Journal of Personality, 57,* 375–406.

Caspi, A., Henry, B., McGee, R. O., Moffitt, T. E., & Silva, P. A. (1995). Temperamental origins of child and adolescent behavior problems: From age 3 to Age 15. *Child Development, 66,* 55–68.

Caspi, A., & Silva, P. A. (1995). Temperamental qualities at age 3 predict personality traits in young adulthood: Longitudinal evidence from a birth cohort. *Child Development, 66,* 468–498.

Caterina, M. J., Schumacher, M. A., Tominaga, M., Rosen, T. A., Levine, J. D., & Julius, D. (1997). The capsaicin receptor: A heat-activated ion channel in the pain pathway. *Nature, 389,* 816–824.

Cattell, R. B. (1963). Theory of fluid and crystallized intelligence: A critical experiment. *Journal of Educational Psychology, 54,* 1–22.

Cattell, R. B., Eber, H. W., & Tatsuoka, M. (1970). *Handbook for the sixteen personality factor questionnaire (16PF).* Champaign, IL: Institute for Personality Testing.

Cavaliere, F. (1996, February). Bilingual schools face big political challenges. *APA Monitor,* p. 36.

Ceci, S. J., & Liker, J. K. (1986). A day at the races: A study of IQ, expertise and cognitive complexity. *Journal of Experimental Psychology: General, 115,* 255–266.

Centers for Disease Control (1998). *Violence: Suicide in the United States.* Atlanta: Centers for Disease Control.

Centers for Disease Control and Prevention (1996). Update: Mortality attributable to HIV infection among persons aged 25–44 years. *United States Morbidity and Mortality Weekly Report, 45,* 121–125.

Cerf, C., & Navasky, V. (1998). *The experts speak: The definitive compendium of authoritative misinformation.* New York: Villard.

Cernoch, J. M., & Porter, R. H. (1985). Recognition of maternal axillary odors by infants. *Child Development, 56,* 1593–1598.

Chaiken, A. L., Sigler, E., & Derlega, V. J. (1974). Nonverbal mediators of teacher expectancy effects. *Journal of Personality and Social Psychology, 30,* 144–149.

Chambless, D. L. (1990). Spacing of exposure sessions in the treatment of agoraphobia and simple phobia. *Behavior Therapy, 21,* 217–229.

Chambless, D. L., & Hollon, S. D. (1998). Defining empirically supported therapies. *Journal of Consulting and Clinical Psychology, 66,* 7–18.

Champion, V., & Huster, G. (1995). Effect of interventions on stage of mammography adoption. *Journal of Behavioral Medicine, 18,* 159–188.

Chan, D. W., & Lee, H. B. (1995). Patterns of psychological test use in Hong Kong in 1993. *Professional Psychology: Research and Practice, 26,* 292–297.

Chance, P. (1988, April). Knock wood. *Psychology Today.*

Chao, R. K. (1994). Beyond parental control and authoritarian parenting style: Understanding Chinese parenting through the cultural notion of training. *Child Development, 65,* 1111–1119.

Chapdelaine, A., Levesque, M. J., & Cuardo, R. M. (in press). Playing the dating game: Do we know who others would like to date? *Journal of Basic and Applied Social Psychology.*

Charlton, T., Gunter, B., & Coles, D. (1998). Broadcast television as a cause of aggression? Recent findings from a naturalistic study. *Emotional and Behavioural Difficulties, 3,* 5–13.

Charness, N. (1987). Component processes in bridge bidding and novel problem-solving tasks. *Canadian Journal of Psychology, 41,* 223–243.

Chartrand, T., Pinckert, S., & Burger, J. M. (in press). Time delay requestor and the foot-in-the-door. *Journal of Applied Social Psychology.*

Chase, T. N. (1998). The significance of continuous dopaminergic stimulation in the treatment of Parkinson's disease. *Drugs, 55* (Suppl. 1), 1–9.

Chase, W. G., & Ericsson, K. A. (1981). Skilled memory. In J. R. Anderson (Ed.), *Cognitive skills and their acquisition.* Hillsdale, NJ: Lawrence Erlbaum Associates.

Chemers, M. M. (1987). Leadership processes: Intrapersonal, interpersonal, and societal influences. In C. Hendrick (Ed.), *Group processes.* Newbury Park, CA: Sage.

Chen, M., & Bargh, J. A. (1997). Nonconscious behavioral confirmation processes: The self-fulfilling consequences of automatic stereotype activation. *Journal of Experimental Social Psychology, 33,* 541–560.

Chi, M. T., Feltovitch, P. J., & Glaser, R. (1981). Representation of physics knowledge by novices and experts. *Cognitive Science, 5,* 121–152.

Chisholm, K. (1997, June). Trauma at an early age inhibits ability to bond. *APA Monitor*, p. 11.

Cho, Z. H., Chung, S. C., Jones, J. P., Park, J. B., Park, H. J., Lee, H. J., Wong, E. K., & Min, B. I. (1998). New findings of the correlation between acupoints and corresponding brain cortices using functional MRI. *Proceedings of the National Academy of Science USA, 95*, 2670–2673.

Chomsky, N. (1965). *Aspects of the theory of syntax.* Cambridge, MA: MIT Press.

Choo, K. L., & Guilleminault, C. (1998). Narcolepsy and idiopathic hypersomnolence. *Clinical Chest Medicine, 19*(1), 169–181.

Chorney, M. L., Chorney, K., Sense, N., Owen, M. J., Daniels, J., McGuffin, P., Thompson, L. A., Detterman, D. K., Benbow, C. P., Lubinski, D., Eley, T. C., & Plomin, R. (1998). A quantitative trait locus (QTL) associated with cognitive ability in children. *Psychological Science, 9*, 159–166.

Christensen, K. A., Stephens, M. A. P., & Townsend, A. L. (1998). Mastery in women's multiple roles and well-being: Adult daughters providing care to impaired parents. *Health Psychology, 17*, 163–171.

Chu, J. (1994). Active learning in epidemiology and biostatistics. *Teaching and Learning in Medicine, 6*, 191–193.

Chuansheng, C., Shin-Ying, L., & Stevenson, H. W. (1995). Response style and cross-cultural comparisons of rating scales among East Asian and North American students. *Psychological Science, 6*, 170–175.

Chugani, H. T., & Phelps, M. E. (1986). Maturational changes in cerebral function in infants determined by 18FDG positron emission tomography. *Science, 231*, 840–843.

Churchland, P. S., & Sejnowski, T. J. (1992). *The computational brain.* Cambridge, MA: MIT Press/Bradford Books.

Chwalisz, K., Diener, E., & Gallagher, D. (1988). Autonomic arousal feedback and emotional experience: Evidence from the spinal cord injured. *Journal of Personality and Social Psychology, 54*, 820–828.

Cialdini, R. B. (1993). *Influence: Science and practice* (3rd ed.). New York: HarperCollins.

Cialdini, R. B. (1995). Principles and techniques of social influence. In A. Tesser (Ed.), *Advanced social psychology* (pp. 257–282). New York: McGraw-Hill.

Cialdini, R. B., Baumann, D. J., & Kenrick, D. T. (1981). Insights from sadness: A three-step model of the development of altruism as hedonism. *Developmental Review, 1*, 207–223.

Cialdini, R. B., Brown, S. L., Lewis, C., & Neuberg, S. (1997). Reinterpreting the empathy-altruism hypothesis: When one into one equals oneness. *Journal of Personality and Social Psychology, 73*, 481–494.

Cialdini, R. B., Reno, R. R., & Kallgren, C. A. (1990). A focus theory of normative conduct: Recycling the concept of norms to reduce littering in public places. *Journal of Personality and Social Psychology, 58*, 1015–1026.

Cialdini, R. B., & Trost, M. (1998). Social influence: Social norms, conformity, and compliance. In D. Gilbert, S. T. Fiske, and G. Lindzey (Eds.), *Handbook of social psychology*, Vol. 2 (4th ed., pp. 151–192). Boston: McGraw-Hill.

Clark, D. C., & Fawcett, J. (1992). Review of empirical risk factors for evaluation of the suicidal patient. In B. Bongar (Ed.), *Suicide: Guidelines for assessment, management, and treatment* (pp. 16–48). New York: Oxford University Press.

Clark, D. C., Gibbons, R. D., Fawcett, J., & Scheftner, W. A. (1989). What is the mechanism by which suicide attempts predispose to later suicide attempts? A mathematical model. *Journal of Abnormal Psychology, 98*, 42–49.

Clark, D. M., Salkovskis, P. M., Ost, L.-G., Breitholtz, E., Koehler, K. A., Westling, B. E., Jeavons, A., & Gelder, M. (1997). Misinterpretation of body sensations in panic disorder. *Journal of Consulting and Clinical Psychology, 65*, 203–213.

Clark, E. V. (1983). Meanings and concepts. In P. H. Mussen, J. H. Flavell, & E. M. Markman (Eds.), *Handbook of child psychology: Vol. 3. Cognitive development* (4th ed., pp. 787–840). New York: Wiley.

Clark, G. M. (1998). Research advances for cochlear implants. *Auris Nasus Larynx, 25*, 73–87.

Clark, L. A., Watson, D., & Reynolds, S. (1995). Diagnosis and classification of psychopathology: Challenges to the current system and future directions. *Annual Review of Psychology, 46*, 121–153.

Clark, L. F. (1994). Social cognition and health psychology. In R. S. Wyer & T. K. Srull (Eds.), *Handbook of social cognition* (2nd ed.). Hillsdale, NJ: Lawrence Erlbaum Associates.

Clark, M. (1994). Close relationships. In R. S. Wyer & T. K. Srull (Eds.), *Handbook of social cognition* (2nd ed.). Hillsdale, NJ: Lawrence Erlbaum Associates.

Clark, M. S., & Pataki, S. P. (1995). Interpersonal processes influencing attraction and relationships. In A. Tesser (Ed.), *Advanced social psychology* (pp. 283–332). New York: McGraw-Hill.

Clarke-Stewart, K. A. (1989). Infant day care: Maligned or malignant? *American Psychologist, 44*, 266–273.

Clarke-Stewart, K. A., & Fein, G. G. (1983). Early childhood programs. In P. H. Mussen (Ed.), *Handbook of child psychology: Vol. 2. Infancy and developmental psychobiology.* New York: Wiley.

Clarkin, J. F., & Carpenter, D. (1995). Family therapy in historical perspective. In B. Bongar & L. E. Beutler (Eds.), *Comprehensive textbook of psychotherapy: Theory and practice* (pp. 205–227). New York: Oxford University Press.

Clary, E. G., & Orenstein, L. (1991). The amount and effectiveness of help: The relationship of motives and abilities to helping behavior. *Personality and Social Psychology Bulletin, 17*, 58–64.

Clary, E. G., Snyder, M., Ridge, R. D., Copeland, J., Stukas, A. A., Haugen, J., & Meine, P. (1998). Understanding and assessing the motivations of volunteers: A functional approach. *Journal of Personality and Social Psychology, 74*, 1516–1530.

Clausen, J., Sersen, E., & Lidsky, A. (1974). Variability of sleep measures in normal subjects. *Psychophysiology, 11*, 509–516.

Clay, R. (1996a, September). Is a psychology diploma worth the price of tuition? *APA Monitor*, p. 54.

Clay, R. (1996b, December). Some elders thrive on working into late life. *APA Monitor*, p. 35.

Clay, R. (1997, July). Do hearing devices impair deaf children? *APA Monitor*, pp. 1, 29.

Clements, L. B., York, R. O., & Rohrer, G. E. (1995). The interaction of parental alcoholism and alcoholism as a predictor of drinking-related locus of control. *Alcoholism Treatment Quarterly, 12*, 97–110.

Clementz, B. A., McDowell, J. E., & Zisook, S. (1994). Saccadic system functioning among schizophrenia patients and their first-degree biological relatives. *Journal of Abnormal Psychology, 103*, 277–287.

Clendenen, V. I., Herman, C. P., & Polivy, J. (1995). Social facilitation of eating among friends and strangers. *Appetite, 23*, 1–13.

Clifton, R. K. (1992). The development of spatial hearing in human infants. In L. A. Werner & E. W. Rubel (Eds.), *Developmental psychoacoustics* (pp. 135–157). Washington, DC: American Psychological Association.

Clifton, R. K., Rochat, P., Litovsky, R., & Perris, E. (1991). Object representation guides infants' reaching in the dark. *Journal of Experimental Psychology: Human Perception and Performance, 17*, 323–329.

Cloninger, C. (1987). Neurogenic adaptive mechanisms in alcoholism. *Science, 236*, 410–416.

Coccaro, E. F. (1989). Central serotonin and impulsive aggression. *British Journal of Psychiatry, 155*, 52–62.

Cohen, C. E. (1981). Person categories and social perception: Testing some boundaries of the processing effects of prior knowledge. *Journal of Personality and Social Psychology, 40*, 441–452.

Cohen, J. (1994). The earth is round (p<.05). *American Psychologist, 49*, 997–1003.

Cohen, J., & Servan-Schreiber, D. (1992). Context, cortex, and dopamine: A connectionist approach to behavior and biology in schizophrenia. *Psychological Review, 99*, 45–77.

Cohen, M. S. (1993). Three paradigms for viewing decision biases. In G. A. Klein, J. Orasanu, R. Calderwood, & C. E. Zasmbok (Eds.), *Decision making in action: Models and methods.* Norwood, NJ: Ablex.

Cohen, N. J., & Corkin, S. (1981). The amnesic patient H.M.: Learning and retention of a cognitive skill. *Neuroscience Abstracts, 7*, 235.

Cohen, S., Doyle, W. J., Skoner, D. P., Gwaltney, J. M., Jr., & Newsom, J. T. (1995). State and trait negative affect as predictors of objective and subjective symptoms of respiratory viral infections. *Journal of Personality and Social Psychology, 68*, 159–169.

Cohen, S., & Herbert, T. B. (1996). Health psychology: Psychological factors and physical disease from the perspective of human psychoneuroimmunology. In J. Spence, D. Foss, & J. Darley (Eds.), *Annual review of psychology* (Vol. 42). El Camino, CA: Annual Review, Inc.

Cohen, S., & Syme, S. L. (1985). Issues in the study and application of social support. In S. Cohen & S. L. Syme (Eds.), *Social support and health.* New York: Academic Press.

Cohen, S., & Williamson, G. (1991). Stress and infectious disease. *Psychological Bulletin, 109*, 5–24.

Colby, A., Kohlberg, L., Gibbs, J., & Lieberman, M. (1983). A longitudinal study of moral judgment. *Monographs of the Society for Research in Child Development, 48*(1, Serial No. 200).

Cole, K. N., Mills, P. E., Dale, P. S., & Jenkins, J. R. (1991). Effects of preschool integration for children with disabilities. *Exceptional Children, 58,* 36–45.

Coleman, D. (1992). Why do I feel so tired? Too little, too late. *American Health, 11*(4), 43–46.

Coles, M. (1989). Modern mind-brain reading: Psychophysiology, physiology & cognition. *Psychophysiology, 26,* 251–269.

Coley, R. L., & Chase-Lansdale, P. L. (1998). Adolescent pregnancy and parenthood: Recent evidence and future directions. *American Psychologist, 53,* 152–166.

College Board (1994, August 25). *News from the college board.* Media release. New York: College Board Publications.

Collins, A. M., & Loftus, E. F. (1975). A spreading activation theory of semantic processing. *Psychological Review, 82,* 407–428.

Collins, G. (1997, May 30). Trial near in new legal tack in tobacco war. *New York Times,* p. A10.

Colombo, M., D'Amato, M. R., Rodman, H. R., & Gross, C. G. (1990). Auditory association cortex lesions impair auditory short-term memory in monkeys. *Science, 247,* 336–338.

Colwill, R. M. (1994). Associative representations of instrumental contingencies. *Psychology of Learning and Motivation, 31,* 1–72.

Compas, B. E., Haaga, D. A. F., Keefe, F. J., Leitenberg, H., & Williams, D. A. (1998). Sampling of empirically supported psychological treatments from health psychology: Smoking, chronic pain, cancer, and bulimia nervosa. *Journal of Consulting and Clinical Psychology, 66,* 89–112.

Condon, J. W., & Crano, W. D. (1988). Inferred evaluation and the relationship between attitude similarity and interpersonal attraction. *Journal of Personality and Social Psychology, 54,* 789–797.

Conel, J. L. (1939/1967). *The postnatal development of the human cerebral cortex* (Vols. 1, 8). Cambridge, MA: Harvard University Press.

Connor, L. T., Balota, D. A., & Neely, J. H. (1992). On the relation between feeling of knowing and lexical decision: Persistent subthreshold activation of topic familiarity? *Journal of Experimental Psychology: Learning, Memory, and Cognition, 18,* 544–554.

Conrad, R. (1964). Acoustic confusions in immediate memory. *British Journal of Psychology, 55,* 75–84.

Consumer Reports (1995, November). Mental health: Does therapy help? pp. 734–739.

Cook, S. W. (1985). Experimenting on social issues: The case of school desegregation. *American Psychologist, 40,* 452–460.

Cook, T., & Mineka, S. (1987). Second-order conditioning and overshadowing in the observational conditioning of fear in monkeys. *Behaviour Research and Therapy, 25,* 349–364.

Cook, T., & Mineka, S. (1990). Selective association in the observational conditioning of fear in rhesus monkeys. *Journal of Experimental Psychology: Animal Behavior Processes, 16,* 372–389.

Cooper, H. (1979). Pygmalion grows up: A model for teacher expectation communication and performance influence. *Review of Educational Research, 49,* 389–410.

Cooper, L. A., Schacter, D. L., Ballesteros, S., & Moore, C. (1992). Priming and recognition of transformed three-dimensional objects: Effects of size and reflection. *Journal of Experimental Psychology: Learning, Memory, and Cognition, 18,* 43–57.

Cooper, M. L., Russell, M., Skinner, J. B., Frone, M. R., & Mudar, P. (1992). Stress and alcohol use: The moderating effects of gender, coping, and alcohol expectancies. *Journal of Abnormal Psychology, 101,* 139–152.

Cooper, R. M., & Zubek, J. P. (1958). Effects of enriched and restricted early environments on the learning ability of bright and dull rats. *Canadian Journal of Psychology, 12,* 159–164.

Coovert, M. D., & Reeder, G. D. (1990). Negativity effects in impression formation: The role of unit formation and schematic expectations. *Journal of Experimental Social Psychology, 26,* 49–62.

Copeland, J., & Snyder, M. (1995). When counselors confirm: A functional analysis. *Personality and Social Psychology Bulletin, 21,* 1210–1220.

Coppen, A., Metcalf, M., & Wood, K. (1982). Lithium. In E. S. Paykel (Ed.), *Handbook of affective disorders.* New York: Guilford.

Corbetta, M., Miezin, F. M., Dobmeyer, S., Shulman, G. L., & Petersen, S. E. (1991). Selective and divided attention during visual discriminations of shape, color, and speed: Functional anatomy by positron emission tomography. *Journal of Neuroscience, 11,* 2383–2402.

Cordova, J. V., & Jacobson, N. S. (1993). Couple distress. In D. H. Barlow (ed.), *Clinical handbook of psychological disorders: A step-by-step treatment manual* (2nd ed.). New York: Guilford.

Coren, S. (1999). Psychology applied to animal training. In A. Stec & D. Bernstein (Eds.), *Psychology: Fields of application.* Boston: Houghton Mifflin.

Coren, S., Ward, L., & Enns, J. (1994). *Sensation and perception.* Fort Worth: Harcourt Brace.

Cork, R. C., Kihlstrom, J. F., & Hameroff, S. R. (1992). Explicit and implicit memory dissociated by anesthetic technique. *Society for Neuroscience Abstracts, 22,* 523.

Cornblatt, B., & Erlenmeyer-Kimling, L. E. (1985). Global attentional deviance in children at risk for schizophrenia: Specificity and predictive validity. *Journal of Abnormal Psychology, 94,* 470–486.

Cornelius, R. R. (1996). *The science of emotion.* Upper Saddle River, NJ: Prentice-Hall.

Cornoldi, C., DeBeni, R., & Baldi, A. P. (1989). Generation and retrieval of general, specific, and autobiographic images representing concrete nouns. Acta *Psychologica, 72,* 25–39

Coryell, W., Scheftner, W., Keller, M., Endicott, J., Maser, J., & Klerman, G. (1993). The enduring consequences of mania and depression. *American Journal of Psychiatry, 150,* 720–727.

Costa, P. T., Jr., & McCrae, R. (1992). *Revised NEO Personality Inventory: NEO PI and NEO Five-Factor Inventory (NEO FFI: Professional Manual).* Odessa, FL: Psychological Assessment Resources, Inc.

Costa, P. T., Jr., & McCrae, R. R. (1995). Primary traits of Eysenck's P-E-N system: Three- and five-factor solutions. *Journal of Personality and Social Psychology, 69,* 308–317.

Costa, P. T., Jr., & McCrae, R. R. (1997). In R. Hogan, J. A. Johnson, & S. R. Briggs (Eds.), Longitudinal stability of adult personality. *Handbook of personality psychology* (pp. 269–290). San Diego: Academic Press.

Costello, E., Costello, A., Edelbrock, C., Burns, B., Dulcan, M., Brent, D., & Janiszewski, S. (1988). Psychiatric disorders in pediatric primary care. *Archives of General Psychiatry, 45,* 1107–1116.

Costermans, J., Lories, G., & Ansay, C. (1992). Confidence level and feeling of knowing in question answering: The weight of inferential processes. *Journal of Experimental Psychology: Learning, Memory, and Cognition, 18,* 142–150.

Cotman, C. W., Monaghan, D. T., & Ganong, A. H. (1988). Excitatory amino acid neurotransmission: NMDA receptors and Hebb-type synaptic plasticity. *Annual Review of Neuroscience 11,* 61–80.

Courneya, K. S. (1995). Understanding readiness for regular physical activity in older individuals: An application of the theory of planned behavior. *Health Psychology, 14,* 80–87.

Cowan, N. (1988). Evolving concepts of memory storage, selective attention, and their mutual constraints within the human information-processing system. *Psychological Bulletin, 104,* 163–191.

Cowan, W. M. (1979). The development of the brain. *Scientific American, 241,* 112–133.

Cowey, A. (1994). Cortical visual areas and the neurobiology of higher visual processes. In M. J. Farah & G. Ratcliff (Eds.), *The neurophysiology of high-level vision: Collected tutorial essays* (pp. 3–31). Hillsdale, NJ: Lawrence Erlbaum Associates.

Coyne, J. C, & Whiffen, V. E. (1995). Issues in personality as diathesis for depression: The case of sociotropy-dependency and autonomy-self-criticism. *Psychological Bulletin, 4,* 278–287.

Cozzarelli, C. (1993). Personality and self-efficacy as predictors of coping with an abortion. *Journal of Personality and Social Psychology, 65,* 1224–1236.

Craig, A. D., & Bushnell, M. C. (1994). The thermal grill illusion: Unmasking the burn of cold pain. *Science, 265,* 252–254.

Craig, A. D., Bushnell, M. C., Zhang, E. B. T., and Blomqvist, A. (1994). A thalamic nucleus specific for pain and temperature sensation. *Nature, 372,* 770–773.

Craik, F. I. M., & Rabinowitz, J. C. (1984). Age differences in the acquisition and use of verbal information. In H. Bouma & D. G. Bouwhuis (Eds.), *Attention and performance: Vol. 10.* Hillsdale, NJ: Lawrence Erlbaum Associates.

Craik, K. H. (1996). Environmental psychology: A core field within psychological science. *American Psychologist, 51,* 1186–1187.

Crandall, C. S., Preisler, J. J., & Aussprung, J. (1992). Measuring life event stress in the lives of college students: The Undergraduate Stress Questionnaire (USQ). *Journal of Behavioral Medicine, 15,* 627–662.

Crano, W. D., & Chen., X. (1998). The leniency contract and persistence of majority and minority influence. *Journal of Personality and Social Psychology, 74,* 1437–1450.

Crawford, H. J., Brown, A. M., & Moon, C. E. (1993). Sustained attentional and dis-attentional abilities: Differences between low and highly hypnotizable persons. *Journal of Abnormal Psychology, 102*(4), 534–543.

Crawford, J. (1989). *Bilingual education: History, politics, theory, and practice.* New York: Crane.

Crawford, J. G. (1998). Alzheimer's disease risk factors as related to cerebral blood flow: Additional evidence. *Medical Hypotheses, 50,* 25–36.

Crawley, J. N., & Corwin, R. L. (1994). Biological actions of cholecystokinin. *Peptides, 15*(4), 731–755.

Crick, F., & Koch, C. (1998). Consciousness and neuroscience. *Cerebral Cortex, 8,* 97–107.

Crick, N. (1997, June). Abused children have more conflicts with friends. *APA Monitor,* p. 32.

Crick, N. R., Casas, J. F., & Mosher, M. (1997). Relational and overt aggression in preschool. *Developmental Psychology, 33,* 579–588.

Critchley, E. M. (1991). Speech and the right hemisphere. *Behavioural Neurology, 4*(3), 143–151.

Cronbach, L. J. (1975). Five decades of public controversy over mental testing. *American Psychologist, 30,* 1–14.

Cronbach, L. J. (1990). *Essentials of psychological testing* (5th ed.). New York: Harper & Row.

Cross-National Collaborative Group. (1992). The changing rate of major depression: Cross-national comparisons. *Journal of the American Medical Association, 268,* 3098–3105.

Cross, S. E., & Madson, L. (1997). Models of the self: Self-construals and gender. *Psychological Bulletin, 122,* 5–37.

Crouchman, M. (1985). What mothers know about their newborns' visual skills. *Developmental Medicine and Child Neurology, 27,* 455–460.

Crow, S. J., & Mitchell, J. E. (1996). Pharmocologic treatments for eating disorders. In J. K. Thompson (Ed.), *Body image, eating disorders, and obesity* (pp. 345–362). Washington, DC: American Psychological Association.

Crystal, D. S., Chen, C., Fuligni, A. J., Stevenson, H. W., Hsu, C.-C., Ko, H.-J., Kitamura, S., & Kimura, S. (1994). Psychological maladjustment and academic achievement: A cross-cultural study of Japanese, Chinese, and American high school students. *Child Development, 65,* 738–153.

Culbertson, F. M. (1997). Depression and gender. An international review. *American Psychologist, 52,* 25–31.

Curcio, C. A., Sloan, D. R., Jr., Packer, O., Hendrickson, A. E., & Kalina, R. E. (1987). Distribution of cones in human and monkey retina: Individual variability and radial asymmetry. *Science, 236,* 579–582.

Curim, I. S., & Sarin, R. K. (1992). Robustness of expected utility model in predicting individual choices. *Organizational Behavior and Human Decision Processes, 52,* 544–568.

Curtis, J. E., Grabb, E., & Baer, D. (1992). Voluntary association membership in 15 countries: A comparative analysis. *American Sociological Review, 57,* 139–152.

Cutler, W. B., Friedmann, E., & McCoy, N. L. (1998). Pheromonal influences on sociosexual behavior in men. *Archives of Sexual Behavior, 27,* 1–13.

Cutting, J. E., & Kozlowski, L. T. (1977). Recognizing friends by their walk: Gait perception without familiarity cues. *Bulletin of the Psychonomic Society, 9,* 353–356.

D'Esposito, M., Detre, J. A., Alsop, D. C., & Shin, R. K. (1995). The neural basis of the central executive system of working memory. *Nature, 378,* 279–281.

Dabbs, J., & Morris, R. (1990). Testosterone, social class, and antisocial behavior in a sample of 4462 men. *Psychological Science, 1,* 209–211.

Dabbs, J. M., Carr, T. S., Frady, R. L., & Riad, J. K. (1995). Testosterone, crime, and misbehavior among 692 male prison inmates. *Personality and Individual Differences, 18,* 627–633.

Dadds, M. R., Spence, S. H., Holland, D. E., Barrett, P. M., & Laurens, K. R. (1997). Prevention and early intervention for anxiety disorders: A controlled trial. *Journal of Consulting and Clinical Psychology, 65,* 627–635.

Dahlstrom, W. G. (1992). The growth in acceptance of the MMPI. *Professional Psychology: Research and Practice, 23,* 345–348.

Dale, P. S. (1976). *Language and the development of structure and function.* New York: Holt, Rinehart & Winston.

Daly, G., Hawi, Z., Fitzgerald, M., & Gill, M. (1999). Mapping susceptibility loci in attention deficit hyperactivity disorder: Preferential transmission of parental alleles at DAT1, DBH and DRD5 to affected children. *Molecular Biology, 4,* 192–196.

Daly, M., & Wilson, M. (1988). *Homicide.* New York: Aldine de Gruyter.

Damon, W., & Hart, D. (1982). The development of self-understanding from infancy through adolescence. *Child Development, 53,* 841–864.

Damos, D. (1992). *Multiple task performance.* London: Taylor & Francis.

Dana, R. H. (1988). Culturally diverse groups and MMPI interpretation. *Professional Psychology: Research and Practice, 19,* 490–495.

Dark, V. J., & Benbow, C. P. (1993). Cognitive differences among the gifted: A review and new data. In D. K. Detterman (Ed.), *Current topics in human intelligence* (Vol. 3). Norwood, NJ: Ablex.

Darkes, J., & Goldman, M. S. (1993). Expectancy challenge and drinking reduction. *Journal of Clinical and Consulting Psychology, 61,* 344–353.

Darwin, C. E. (1872/1965). *The expression of emotions in man and animals.* Chicago: University of Chicago Press.

Dasgupta, A. M., Juza, D. M., White, G. M., & Maloney, J. F. (1995). Memory and hypnosis: A comparative analysis of guided memory, cognitive interviews, and hypnotic hypermnesia. *Imagination, Cognition, and Personality, 14,*(2), 117–130.

Davidson, J. M., Camargo, C. A., & Smith, E. R. (1979). Effects of androgen on sexual behavior in hypogonadal men. *Journal of Clinical Endocrinological Metabolism, 48,* 955–958.

Davidson, K., Hall, P., & MacGregor, M. (1996). Gender differences in the relation between interview-derived hostility scores and resting blood pressure. *Journal of Behavioral Medicine, 19,* 185–201.

Davidson, K., & Prkachin, K. (1997). Optimism and unrealistic optimism have an interacting impact on health-promoting behavior and knowledge changes. *Personality and Social Psychology Bulletin, 23,* 617–625.

Davidson, R. J., Ekman, P., Saron, C., Senulis, J., & Friesen, W. V. (1990). Approach-withdrawal and cerebral asymmetry: Emotional expression and brain physiology: I. *Journal of Personality and Social Psychology, 58,* 330–341.

Davis, J. D., Gallagher, R. J., Ladove, R. F., & Turansky, A. J. (1969). Inhibition of food intake by a humoral factor. *Journal of Comparative and Physiological Psychology, 67,* 407–414.

Davis, K. D., Taylor, S. J., Crawley, A. P., Wood, M. L., & Mikulis, D. J. (1997). Functional MRI of pain- and attention-related activations in the human cingulate cortex. *Journal of Neurophysiology, 77,* 3370–3380.

Davis, K. L., Kahn, R. S., Ko, G., & Davidson, M. (1991). Dopamine in schizophrenia: A review and reconceptualization. *American Journal of Psychiatry, 148,* 1474–1486.

Davis, M., Falls, W. A., Campeau, S., & Kim, M. (1993). Fear-potentiated startle: A neural and pharmacological analysis. *Behavioural Brain Research, 58*(1–2), 175–198.

Davis, M., Rainnie, D., & Cassell, M. (1994). Neurotransmission in the rat amygdala related to fear and anxiety. *Trends in Neuroscience, 17,* 208–214.

Davis, M. H. (1994). *Empathy: A social psychological approach.* Madison, WI: Brown & Benchmark.

Davis, M. H., Luce, C., & Kraus, S. J. (1994). The heritability of characteristics associated with dispositional empathy. *Journal of Personality, 60,* 369–391.

Davis, R. A., & Moore, C. C. (1935). Methods of measuring retention. *Journal of General Psychology, 12,* 144–155.

Davison, G. C. (1998). Being bolder with the Boulder Model: The challenge of education and training in empirically supported treatments. *Journal of Consulting and Clinical Psychology, 66,* 163–167.

Davison, G. C., & Neale, J. M. (1990). *Abnormal psychology* (5th ed.). New York: Wiley.

Dawe, L. A., Platt, J. R., & Welsh, E. (1998). Spectral-motion aftereffects and the tritone paradox among Canadian subjects. *Perception and Psychophysics, 60,* 209–220.

Dawes, R. (1998). Behavioral judgment and decision making. In D. Gilbert, S. T. Fiske, and G. Lindzey (Eds.), *Handbook of social psychology,* Vol. 1 (4th ed., pp. 497–549). Boston: McGraw-Hill.

Dawes, R. M., (1994). *House of cards: Psychology and psychotherapy built on myth.* New York: Free Press.

Dawkins, K., & Potter, W. (1991). Gender differences in pharmacokinetics and pharmacodynamics of psychotropics: Focus on women. *Psychopharmacology Bulletin, 27,* 417–426.

Dawson, T. M., & Dawson, V. L. (1995). Nitric oxide: Actions and pathological roles. *The Neuroscientist, 1,* 7–18.

DeAngelis, T. (1995a, February). Firefighters' PTSD at dangerous levels. *APA Monitor,* pp. 36–37.

DeAngelis, T. (1995b, February). APA group tries to boost diversity of the profession. *APA Monitor,* p. 40.

DeAngelis, T. (1996, March). Women's contributions large: recognition isn't. *APA Monitor,* pp. 12–13.

De Benedittis, G., Lornenzetti, A., & Pieri, A. (1990). The role of stressful life events in the onset of chronic primary headache. *Pain, 40,* 65–75.

DeBeurs, E., van Balkom, A. J. L. M., Lange, A., Koele, P., & van Dyck, R. (1995). Treatment of panic disorder with agoraphobia: Comparison of fluvoxamine, placebo, and psychological panic management combined with exposure and of exposure in vivo alone, *American Journal of Psychiatry, 152*(5), 683–691.

de Castro, J. M., & Goldstein, S. J. (1995). Eating attitudes and behaviors pre- and postpubertal females: Clues to the etiology of eating disorders. *Physiology and Behavior, 58*(1), 15–23.

de Charms, R., Levy, J., & Wertheimer, M. (1954). A note on attempted evaluations of psychotherapy. *Journal of Clinical Psychology, 10,* 233–235.

De Houwer, A. (1995). Bilingual language acquisition. In P. Fletcher & B. MacWhinney (Eds.), *The handbook of child language* (pp. 219–250). Cambridge, MA: Blackwell Publishers.

de Lacoste-Utamsing, C., & Holloway, R. L. (1982). Sexual dimorphism in the human corpus callosum. *Science, 216,* 1431–1432.

de Rios, M. D. (1992). Power and hallucinogenic states of consciousness among the Moche: An ancient Peruvian society. In C. A. Ward (Ed.) *Altered states of consciousness and mental health: A cross-cultural perspective.* Newberry Park, CA: Sage.

de Silva, P. (1994). Psychological treatment of sexual problems. *International Review of Psychiatry, 6*(2–3), 163–173.

Deacon, T., Schumacher, J., Dinsmore, J., Thomas, C., Palmer, P., Kott, S., Edge, A., Penney, D., Kassissieh, S., Dempsey, P., & Isaacson, O. (1997). Histological evidence of fetal pig neural cell survival after transplantation into a patient with Parkinson's disease. *Nature Medicine, 3,* 350–353.

Deary, I. J., & Caryl, P. G. (1993). Intelligence, EEG and evoked potentials. In P. A. Vernon (Ed.), *Biological approaches to the study of human intelligence.* Norwood, NJ: Ablex.

Deaux, K. (1996). Social identification. In E. T. Higgins & A Kruglanski (Eds.), *Social psychology: Handbook of basic principles* (pp. 777–798). New York: Guilford.

Deaux, K., & LaFrance, M. (1998), Gender. In D. Gilbert, S. T. Fiske, and G. Lindzey (Eds.), *Handbook of social psychology,* Vol. 1 (4th ed., pp. 778–828). Boston: McGraw-Hill.

Deaux, K., & Stark, B. E. (1996, May). *Identity and motive: An integrated theory of volunteerism.* Paper presented at the annual meeting of the Society for the Psychological Study of Social Issues, Ann Arbor, MI.

DeBell, C., & Jones, R. D. (1997). As good as it seems? A review of EMDR experimental research. *Professional Psychology: Research and Practice, 28,* 153–163.

Delehanty, S. G., Dimsdale, J. E., & Mills, P. (1991). Psychosocial correlates of reactivity in Black and White men. *Journal of Psychosomatic Research, 35,* 451–460.

Delgado, P. L., Price, L. H., Miller, H. L., Salomon, R. M., Aghajanian, G. K., Heniger, G. R., & Charney, D. S. (1994). Serotonin and the neurobiology of depression. *Archives of General Psychiatry, 51,* 865–874.

Delmolino, L. M., & Romanczyk, R. G. (1995). Facilitated communication: A critical review. *The Behavior Therapist, 18,* 27–30.

DeLoache, J. S. (1987). Rapid change in the symbolic functioning of very young children. *Science, 238,* 1556–1557.

Demare, D., Briere, J., & Lips, H. M. (1988). Violent pornography and self-reported likelihood of sexual aggression. *Journal of Research in Personality, 22,* 140–153.

Dement, W. (1960). The effect of dream deprivation. *Science, 131,* 1705–1707.

Dement, W., & Kleitman, N. (1957). Cyclic variations in EEG during sleep and their relation to eye movements, body motility and dreaming. *Electroencephalography and Clinical Neurophysiology, 9,* 673–690.

Denmark, F., Russo, N. F., Frieze, I. H, & Sechzer, J. A. (1988). Guidelines for avoiding sexism in psychological research. *American Psychologist, 43,* 582–585.

Dennett, D. C. (1991). *Consciousness explained.* Boston: Little, Brown.

Denton, G. (1980). The influence of visual pattern on perceived speed. *Perception, 9,* 393–402.

Denton, K., & Krebs, D. (1990). From the scene to the crime: The effect of alcohol and social context on moral judgment. *Journal of Personality and Social Psychology, 59,* 242–248.

Derogowski, J. B. (1989). Real space and represented space: Cross-cultural perspectives. *Behavior and Brain Sciences, 12,* 51–73.

Derryberry, D., & Tucker, D. M. (1992). Neural mechanisms of emotion. *Journal of Consulting and Clinical Psychology, 60,* 329–338.

DeRubeis, R. J., & Crits-Christoph, P. (1998). Empirically supported individual and group psychological treatments for adult mental disorders. *Journal of Consulting and Clinical Psychology, 66,* 37–52.

Deschaumes, M. C., Dittmar, A., Sicard, G., & Vernet, M. E. (1991). Results from six autonomic nervous system responses confirm "autonomic response specificity" hypothesis. *Homeostasis in Health and Disease, 33*(5–6), 225–234.

Desmarais, S., & Curtis, J. (1997). Gender and perceived pay entitlement: Testing for effects of experience with income. *Journal of Personality and Social Psychology, 72,* 141–150.

Deutsch, M., & Gerard, H. B. (1955). A study of normative and informative social influences on individual judgments. *Journal of Abnormal and Social Psychology, 51,* 629–636.

Devilly, G. J., Spruce, S. H., & Rapee, R. M. (1998). Statistical and reliable change with eye movement desensitization and reprocessing: Treating trauma with a veteran population. *Behavior Therapy, 29,* 435–455.

Devine, P. G. (1989). Stereotypes and prejudice: Their automatic and controlled components. *Journal of Personality and Social Psychology, 56,* 5–18.

Devine, P. G. (1995). Prejudice and out-group perception. In A. Tesser (Ed.), *Advanced social psychology* (pp. 467–524). New York: McGraw-Hill.

Devinsky, O. (1997). Neurological aspects of the conscious and unconscious mind. *Annals of the New York Academy of Science, 835,* 321–329.

Devor, E. J. (1994). A developmental–genetic model of alcoholism: Implications for genetic research. *Journal of Consulting and Clinical Psychology, 62,* 1108–1115.

DeVries, R. (1969). Constancy of generic identity in the years three to six. *Monographs of the Society for Research in Child Development, 34*(3, Serial No. 127).

DeWitt, L. A., & Samuel, A. G. (1990). The role of knowledge-based function in music perception. *Journal of Experimental Psychology: General, 119,* 123–144.

DeWolff, M. S., & van IJzendoorn, M. H. (1997). Sensitivity and attachment: A meta-analysis on parental antecedents of infant attachment. *Child Development, 68,* 571–591.

DiClemente, R. J., & Wingood, G. M. (1995). A randomized controlled trial of an HIV sexual risk-reduction intervention for young African-American women. *Journal of the American Medical Association, 274,* 1271–1276.

Dietz, W. (1991). Physical activity and childhood obesity. *Nutrition, 7,* 295-296.

Dion, K. K. (1992). Stereotyping based on physical attractiveness. Issues and conceptual perspectives. In C. P. Herman, M. P. Zanna, & E. T. Higgins (Eds.), *The Ontario Symposium: Vol 3. Physical appearance, stigma, and social behavior* (pp. 209–239). Beverly Hills, CA: Sage.

Ditto, P. H., & Lopez, D. F. (1992). Motivated skepticism: Use of differential decision criteria for preferred and nonpreferred conclusions. *Journal of Personality and Social Psychology, 63,* 568–584.

Dixon, M., Brunet, A., &Lawrence, J.-R. (1990). Hynotizability and automaticity: Toward a parallel distributed processing model of hynotic responding. *Journal of Abnormal Psychology, 99,* 336–343.

Dodson, C., & Reisberg, D. (1991). Indirect testing of eyewitness memory: The (non)effect of misinformation. *Bulletin of the Psychonomic Society, 29,* 333–336.

Doll, R., Peto, R., Wheatley, K., Gray, R., & Sutherland, I. (1994). Mortality in relation to smoking: 40 years of observations on male British doctors. *British Medical Journal, 309*(6959), 901–911.

Dollard, J., Doob, L., Miller, N., Mowrer, O. H., & Sears, R. R. (1939). *Frustration and aggression.* New Haven, CT: Yale University Press.

Donegan, N. H., & Thompson, R. F. (1991). The search for the engram. In J. L. Martinez & R. P. Kesner (Eds.), *Learning and memory: A biological view* (2nd ed.). San Diego, CA: Academic Press.

Donlon, T. F. (Ed.). (1984). *College board technical handbook for the SAT.* New York: College Entrance Examination Board.

Donnerstein, E. (1984a). Aggression. In A. S. Kahn (Ed.), *Social psychology.* Dubuque, IA: William C. Brown.

Donnerstein, E. (1984b). Pornography: Its effects on violence against women. In N. M. Malamuth & E. Donnerstein (Eds.), *Pornography and sexual aggression.* New York: Academic Press.

Donnerstein, E., & Linz, D. (1995). The mass media: A role in injury causation and prevention. *Adolescent Medicine: State of the Art Reviews, 6,* 271–284.

Donnerstein, E., Slaby, R. G., & Eron, L .D. (1995). The mass media and youth aggression. In L. Eron, J. Gentry, & P. Schlegel (Eds.), *Reason to hope: A psychosocial perspective on violence and youth* (pp. 219–250). Washington, DC: American Psychological Association.

Dordain, G., & Deffond, D. (1994). Pyridoxine neuropathies: Review of the literature. *Therapie, 49*(4), 333–337.

Dovidio, J. F., Allen, J., & Schroeder, D. A. (1990). The specificity of empathy-induced helping: Evidence for altruism. *Journal of Personality and Social Psychology, 59,* 249–260.

Dovidio, J. F., & Gaertner, S. L. (1998). On the nature of contemporary prejudice: The causes, consequences, and challenges of aversive racism. In J. L. Eberhardt & S. T. Fiske (Eds.), *Confronting racism: The problem and the response* (pp. 3–32). Thousand Oaks, CA: Sage Publications.

Dovidio, J. F., Gaertner, S. L., & Validzic, A. (1998). Intergroup bias: Status, differentiation, and a common in-group identity. *Journal of Personality and Social Psychology, 75,* 109–120.

Dovidio, J. F., & Penner, L. A. (in press). Helping and altruism. In M. Clark & M. Hewstone (Eds.), *Handbook of social psychology: Interpersonal processes*. Boston: Blackwell.

Dovidio, J. F., Piliavin, J. A., Gaertner, S. L., Schroeder, D. A., & Clark, R. D., III (1991). The arousal: cost-reward model and the process of intervention: A review of the evidence. In M. Clark (Ed.), *Review of personality and social psychology: Vol. 12. Prosocial behavior* (pp. 86–118). Newbury Park, CA: Sage.

Dovidio, J. F., Smith, J. K., Donnella, A. G., & Gaertner, S. L. (1997). Racial attitudes and the death penalty. *Journal of Applied Social Psychology, 27,* 1468–1487.

Dowson, D. I., Lewith, G. T., & Machin, D. (1985). The effects of acupuncture versus placebo in the treatment of headache. *Pain, 21,* 35–42.

Dresner, R., & Grolnick, W. S. (1996). Constructions of early parenting, intimacy and autonomy in young women. *Journal of Social and Personal Relationships, 13,* 25–40.

Drewnowski, A., Henderson, S. A., & Shore, A. B. (1997). Taste responses to naringin, a flavonoid, and the acceptance of grapefruit juice are related to genetic sensitivity to 6-n-propylthiouracil. *American Journal of Clinical Nutrition, 66,* 391–397.

Dreyfus, H. L., & Dreyfus, S. E. (1988). Making a mind versus modeling the brain: Intelligence back at a branchpoint. In S. R. Graubard (Ed.), *The artificial intelligence debate.* Cambridge, MA: MIT Press.

Drucker, D. B., Ackroff, K., Sclafani, A. (1994). Nutrient-conditioned flavor preference and acceptance in rats: Effects of deprivation state and nonreinforcement. *Physiology and Behavior, 56*(4), 701–707.

Drucker-Colin, R. R., & McGaugh, J. L. (Eds.). (1977). *Neurobiology of sleep and memory.* San Diego, CA: Academic Press.

Druckman, D., & Bjork, R. A. (1994). *Learning, remembering, believing: Enhancing human performance.* Washington, DC: National Academy Press.

Druckman, D., Singer, J. E., & VanCott, H. (Eds.). (1998). *Enhancing organizational performance.* Washington, DC: National Academy Press.

DuBois, D. L., Felner, R. D., Brand, S., Adan, A. M., & Evans, E. G. (1992). A prospective study of life stress, social support, and adaptation in early adolescence. *Child Development, 63,* 542–557.

DuBreuil, S. C., Garry, M., & Loftus, E. F. (in press). Tales from the crib. In S. J. Lynn & K. M. McConkey (Eds.), *Truth in memory.* New York: Guilford.

Duck, S., & Barnes, M. H. (1992). Disagreeing about agreement: Reconciling differences about similarity. *Communication Monographs, 59,* 199–208.

Duckitt, J. H. (1994). *The social psychology of prejudice.* Westport, CT: Praeger.

Duffy, V. B., Fast, K., Cohen Z., Chodos, E., and Bartoshuk, L. M. Genetic taste status associates with fat food acceptance and body mass index in adults. *Chemical Senses,* in press, 1999.

Dujovne, V., & Houston, B. (1991). Hostility-related variables and plasma lipid levels. *Journal of Behavioral Medicine, 14,* 555–564.

Duke, C. R., & Carlson, L. (1993). Applying implicit memory measures: Word fragment completion in advertising tests. *Journal of Consumer Psychology.*

Duncan, G. J., Brooks-Gunn, J., & Klebanov, P. K. (1994). Economic deprivation and early childhood development. *Child Development, 65,* 296–318.

Dunn, J., Brown, H., Slomkowski, C., Tesla, C., & Youngblade, L. (1991). Young children's understanding of other people's feelings and beliefs: Individual differences and their antecedents. *Child Development, 62,* 1352–1366.

Dunn, J. F., & Plomin, R. (1990). *Separate lives: Why siblings are so different.* New York: Basic Books.

Dunn, T. M., Schwartz, M., Hatfield, R. W., & Wiegele, M. (1996). Measuring effectiveness of eye movement desensitization and reprocessing (EMDR) in non-clinical anxiety: A multi-subject, yoked control design. *Journal of Behavior Therapy and Experimental Psychiatry, 27,* 231–239.

Durand, V. M., & Barlow, D. H. (1997). *Abnormal psychology.* Pacific Grove, CA.

Dustman, R., Emmerson, R., Ruhling, R., Shearer, D., Seinhaus, L., Johnson, S., Bonekat, H., & Shigeoka, J. (1990). Age and fitness effects on EEG, ERPs, visual sensitivity, and cognition. *Neurobiology of aging, 11,* 193–200.

Dutton, D. G., & Aron, A. P. (1974). Some evidence for heightened sexual attraction under conditions of high anxiety. *Journal of Personality and Social Psychology, 30,* 510–517.

Dweck, C. S. (1986). Motivational processes affecting learning. Special Issue: Psychological science and education. *American Psychologist, 1*(10), 1040–1048.

Dweck, C. S., Davidson, W., Nelson, S., & Enna, B. (1978). Sex differences in learned helplessness: II. The contingencies of evaluative feedback in the classroom, and III. An experimental analysis. *Developmental Psychology, 14,* 268–276.

Dweck, C. S., & Gilliard, D. (1975). Expectancy statements as determinants of reactions to failure: Sex differences in persistence and expectancy change. *Journal of Personality and Social Psychology, 32,* 1077–1084.

Eagly, A. H. (1987). *Sex differences in social behavior: A social-role interpretation.* Hillsdale, NJ: Lawrence Erlbaum Associates.

Eagly, A. H. (1996). Differences between women and men: Their magnitude, practical importance, and political meaning. *American Psychologist, 51,* 158–159.

Eagly, A. H., & Chaiken, S. (1998). In D. Gilbert, S. T. Fiske, and G. Lindzey (Eds.), *Handbook of social psychology,* Vol. 1 (4th ed., pp. 269–322). Boston: McGraw-Hill.

Eagly, A. H., & Johnson, B. T. (1990). Gender and leadership style: A meta-analysis. *Psychological Bulletin, 108,* 233–256.

Eagly, A. H., & Karau, S. J. (1991). Gender and the emergence of leaders: A meta-analysis. *Journal of Personality and Social Psychology, 60,* 685–710.

Eagly, A. H., Karau, S. J., & Makhijani, M. G. (1995). Gender and the effectiveness of leaders: A meta-analysis. *Psychological Bulletin, 117,* 125–145.

Eagly, A. H., Makhijani, M. G., & Klonsky, B. G. (1992). Gender and evaluation of leaders: A meta-analysis. *Psychological Bulletin, 111,* 3–22.

Eberhardt, J. L., & Fiske, S. T. (1998). Confronting racism: The problem and the response. In J. L. Eberhardt & S. T. Fiske (Eds.), *Confronting racism: The problem and the response* (pp. 1–2). Thousand Oaks, CA: Sage Publications.

Eberts, R., & MacMillan, A. C. (1985). Misperception of small cars. In R. Eberts & C. Eberts (Eds.), *Trends in ergonomics/human factors III.* Amsterdam: Elsevier.

Ebstein, R. P., & Belmaker, R. H. (1997). Saga of an adventure gene: Novelty seeking, substance abuse and the dopamine D4 receptor (D4DR) exon 111 repeat polymorphism. *Molecular Psychiatry, 2,* 381–384.

Ebstein, R. P., Nemanov, L., Klotz, I., Gritsenko, I., & Belmaker, R. H. (1997). Additional evidence for an association between the dopamine D4 receptor (D4DR) exon III repeat polymorphism and the human personality trait of novelty seeking. *Molecular Psychiatry, 2,* 472–477.

Eccles, J., Lord, S., & Buchanan, C. M. (1996). School transitions in early adolescence: What are we doing to our young people? In J. A. Graber, J. Brooks-Gunn, A. C. Peterson (Eds.), *Transitions through adolescence: Interpersonal domains and context* (pp. 251–284). Mahwah, NJ: Lawrence Erlbaum Associates.

Eccles, J. S., Lord, S. E., & Roeser, R. W. (1996). Round holes, square pegs, rocky roads, and sore feet: The impact of stage-environment fit on young adolescents' experiences in schools and families. In D. Cicchetti & S. L. Toth (Eds.), *Adolescence: Opportunities and challenges* (pp. 47–91). Rochester: University of Rochester Press.

Echeburua, E., de Corral, P., Garcia Bajos, E., & Borda, M. (1993). Interactions between self-exposure and alprazolam in the treatment of agoraphobia without current panic: An exploratory study. *Behavioural and Cognitive Psychotherapy, 21,* 219–238.

Educational Testing Service (1987). *ETS sensitivity review process.* Princeton, NJ: ETS.

Educational Testing Service (1995). *Performance assessment.* Princeton, NJ: College Board.

Edwards, A. E., & Acker, L. E. (1972). A demonstration of the long-term retention of a conditioned GSR. *Psychosomatic Science, 26,* 27–28.

Edwards, G. (1987). The alcohol dependence syndrome: A concept as stimulus to enquiry. *British Journal of Addiction, 81,* 171–183.

Eells, T. D. (Ed.). (1997). *Handbook of psychotherapy case formulation.* New York: Guilford.

Egan, M. F., & Weinberger, D. R. (1997). Neurobiology of schizophrenia. *Current Opinion in Neurobiology, 7,* 701–707.

Egas Moñiz, A. (1948). How I came to perform prefrontal leucotomy. *Proceedings of the First International Congress of Psychosurgery* (pp. 7–18). Lisbon: Edicos Atica.

Egbert, L. D., Battit, G. E., Welch, C. E., & Bartlett, M. K. (1964). Reduction of post-operative pain by encouragement and instruction of patients: A study of doctor-patient rapport. *New England Journal of Medicine, 270,* 825–827.

Egeland, J. A., Gerhard, D. S., Pauls, D. L., Sussex, J. N., Kidd, K. K., Allen, C. R., Hostetter, A. M., & Housman, D. E. (1987). Bipolar affective disorders linked to DNA markers on chromosome 11. *Nature, 325,* 783–787.

Ehlers, A. (1995). A 1-year prospective study of panic attacks: Clinical course and factors associated with maintenance. *Journal of Abnormal Psychology, 104,* 164–172.

Ehrlichman, H., & Halpern, J. N. (1988). Affect and memory: Effects of pleasant and unpleasant odors on retrieval of happy and unhappy memories. *Journal of Personality and Social Psychology, 55,* 769–779.

Eich, E. (1989). Theoretical issues in state dependent memory. In H. L. Roediger & F. I. M. Craik (Eds.), *Varieties of memory and consciousness.* Hillsdale, NJ: Lawrence Erlbaum Associates.

Eich, E., & Metcalfe, J. (1989). Mood dependent memory for internal versus external events. *Journal of Experimental Psychology: Learning, Memory, and Cognition, 15,* 443–455.

Eich, J. E., Weingartner, H., Stillman, R. C., & Gillin, J. C. (1975). State dependent accessibility of retrieval cues in the retention of a categorized list. *Journal of Verbal Learning and Verbal Behavior, 14,* 408–417.

Eichelman, B. (1983). The limbic system and aggression in humans. *Neuroscience and Bio-behavioral Reviews, 7,* 391–394.

Eichenbaum, H., Otto, T., & Cohen, N. J. (1994). Two functional components of the hippocampal memory system. *Behavior and Brain Sciences, 17*(3), 449–517.

Eichorn, D. H., Clausen, J. A., Haan, N., Honzik, M. P., & Mussen, P. H. (1981). *Present and past in middle life.* New York: Academic Press.

Einhorn, H., & Hogarth, R. (1982). Prediction, diagnosis and causal thinking in forecasting. *Journal of Forecasting, 1,* 23–36.

Eisenberg, N. (1997, June). Consistent parenting helps children regulate emotions. *APA Monitor,* p. 17.

Eisenberg, N. (1998). Introduction. In W. Damon & N. Eisenberg (Eds.), *Handbook of child psychology: Vol. 3. Social, emotional, and personality development* (5th ed., pp. 1–24). New York: Wiley.

Eisenberg, N., Carol, G., Murphy, B., & van Court, P. (1995). Prosocial development in late adolescence: A longitudinal study. *Child Development, 66,* 1179–1197.

Eisenberg, N., Cialdini, R. B., McCreath, H., & Shell, R. (1987). Consistency-based compliance: When and why do children become vulnerable? *Journal of Personality and Social Psychology, 52,* 1174–1181.

Eisenberg, N., & Fabes, R. A. (1998). Prosocial development. In W. Damon & N. Eisenberg (Eds.), *Handbook of child psychology: Vol. 3. Social, emotional, and personality development* (5th ed., pp. 701–778). New York: Wiley.

Eisenberg, N., Fabes, R. A., & Murphy, B. C. (1995). Relations of shyness and low sociability to regulation and emotionality. *Journal of Personality and Social Psychology, 68,* 505–518.

Eisenman, R. (1993). Belief that drug usage in the United States is increasing when it is really decreasing: An example of the availability heuristic. *Bulletin of the Psychonomic Society, 31,* 249–252.

Eisenman, R. (1994). Conservative sexual values: Effects of an abstinence program on student attitudes. *Journal of Sex Education and Therapy, 20*(2), 75–78.

Ekman, P. (1993). Facial expression and emotion. *American Psychologist, 48,* 384–392.

Ekman, P. (1994). Strong evidence for universals in facial expressions: A reply to Russell's mistaken critique. *Psychological Bulletin, 115*(2), 268–287.

Ekman, P., & Davidson, R. J. (1993). Voluntary smiling changes regional brain activity. *Psychological Science, 4*(5), 342–345.

Ekman, P., Davidson, R. J., & Friesen, W. V. (1990). The Duchenne smile: Emotional expression and brain physiology II. *Journal of Personality and Social Psychology, 58,* 342–353.

Ekman, P., Friesen, W. V., & Ellsworth, P. (1972). *Emotion in the human face: Guidelines for research and a review of findings.* New York: Pergamon Press.

Ekman, P., Friesen, W. V., & O'Sullivan, M. (1988). Smiles when lying. *Journal of Personality and Social Psychology, 54,* 414–420.

Ekman, P., Levenson, R. W., & Friesen, W. V. (1983). Autonomic nervous system activity distinguishes among emotions. *Science, 221,* 1208–1210.

Elashoff, J. D. (1979). Box scores are for baseball. *Brain and Behavioral Sciences, 3,* 392.

Eliot, A. J., & Devine, P. G. (1994). On the motivational nature of dissonance: Dissonance as psychological discomfort. *Journal of Personality and Social Psychology, 67,* 382–394.

Elkins, I. (1994). The NIMH treatment of depression collaborative research program: Where we began and where we are. In A. E. Bergin & S. L. Garfield (Eds.), *Handbook of psychotherapy and behavior change.* New York: Wiley.

Elkins, I., Shea, T., Watkins, J., Imber, S., Sotsky, S., Collins, J., Glass, D., Pilkonis, P., Leber, W., Docherty, J., Fiester, S., & Perloff, M. (1989). National Institute of Mental Health treatment of depression collaborative research program. *Archives of General Psychiatry, 46,* 971–982.

Elliott, C. L., & Greene, R. L. (1992). Clinical depression and implicit memory. *Journal of Abnormal Psychology, 101,* 572–574.

Ellis, A. (1962). *Reason and emotion in psychotherapy.* New York: Lyle Stuart.

Ellis, A. (1993). Reflections on rational-emotive therapy. *Journal of Consulting and Clinical Psychology, 61,* 199–201.

Ellis, A. (1995). Rational emotive behavior therapy. In R. J. Corsini & D. Wedding (Eds.), *Current psychotherapies* (5th ed., pp. 162–196). Itasca, IL: Peacock.

Ellis, A. (1997). Using rational emotive behavior therapy techniques to cope with disability. *Professional Psychology: Research and Practice, 28,* 17–22.

Ellis, A., & Bernard, M. E. (1985). *Clinical applications of rational-emotive therapy.* New York: Plenum.

Ellis, N. R. (1991). Automatic and effortful processes in memory for spatial location. *Bulletin of the Psychonomic Society, 29,* 28–30.

Elmquist, J. K., Scammell, T. E., & Saper, C. B. (1997). Mechanisms of CNS response to systemic immune challenge: The febrile response. *Trends in Neuroscience, 20,* 565–570.

Endsley, M. R. (1988). Design and evaluation for situation awareness enhancement. *Proceedings of the Human Factors and Ergonomics Society 32nd Annual Meeting* (pp. 97–101). Santa Monica, CA: Human Factors Society.

Engel, A. K., Konig, P., Kreiter, A. K., Schillen, T. B., & Singer, W. (1992). Temporal coding in the visual cortex: New vistas on integration in the nervous system. *Trends in Neuroscience, 15,* 218–226.

Engel, S., Zhang, X., & Wandell, B. (1997). Colour tuning in human visual cortex measured with functional magnetic resonance imaging. *Nature, 388,* 68–71.

Engeland, H. V. (1993). Pharmacotherapy and behaviour therapy: Competition or cooperation? *Acta Paedopsychiatrica International Journal of Child and Adolescent Psychiatry, 56*(2), 123–127.

Engen, T., Gilmore, M. M., & Mair, R. G. (1991). Odor memory. In T. V. Getchell et al. (Eds.), *Taste and smell in health and disease.* New York: Raven Press.

Enns, C. Z. (1994). On teaching about the cultural relativism of psychological constructs. *Teaching of Psychology, 21,* 205–211.

Enright, R. D., Lapsley, D. K., & Levy, V. M., Jr. (1983). Moral education strategies. In M. Pressley & J. R. Levin (Eds.), *Cognitive strategy research: Educational application.* New York: Springer-Verlag.

Epping-Jordan, M. P., Watkins, S. S., Koob, G. F., & Markou, A. (1998). Dramatic decreases in brain reward function during nicotine withdrawal. *Nature, 393,* 76–79.

Epstein, L. H., Valoski, A., Wing., R. R., & McCurley, J. (1994). Ten-year outcomes of behavioral family-based treatment for childhood obesity. *Health Psychology, 13,* 373–383.

Epstein, Y. M., Woolfolk, R. L., & Lehrer, P. M. (1981). Physiological, cognitive, and nonverbal responses to repeated experiences of crowding. *Journal of Applied Social Psychology, 11,* 1–13.

Erdberg, P. (1990). Rorschach assessment. In G. Goldstein & M. Hersen (Eds.), *Psychological Assessment* (2nd ed.). New York: Pergamon Press.

Erdelyi, M. H. (1985). *Psychoanalysis: Freud's cognitive psychology.* San Francisco: W. H. Freeman.

Ericsson, K. A., & Charness, N. (1994). Expert performance: Its structure and acquisition. *American Psychologist, 49,* 725–747.

Ericsson, K. A., & Kintsch, W. (1995). Long-term working memory. *Psychological Review, 102*(2), 211–245.

Ericsson, K. A., Krampe, R. T., & Tesch-Römer, C. (1993). The role of deliberate practice in the acquisition of expert performance. *Psychological Review, 100,* 363–406

Ericsson, K. A., & Simon, H. A. (1994). *Protocol analysis: Verbal reports as data* (rev. ed.). Cambridge, MA: MIT Press.

Ericsson, K. A., & Staszewski, J. (1989). Skilled memory and expertise: Mechanisms of exceptional performance. In D. Klahr & K. Kotovsky (Eds.), *Complex information processing: The impact of Herbert A. Simon.* Hillsdale, NJ: Lawrence Erlbaum Associates.

Erikson, E. H. (1968). *Identity: Youth and crisis.* New York: W. W. Norton.

Eriksson, P. S., Perfilieva, E., Bjrk-Eriksson, T., Alborn, A. Nordborg, C., Peterson, D.A. & Gage, F. H. (1998) Neurogenesis in the adult human hippocampus. *Nature Medicine, 4*, 1313–1317.

Erlenmeyer-Kimling, L., & Jarvik, L. F. (1963). Genetics and intelligence: A review. *Science, 142,* 1477–1479.

Eron, L. D., Huesmann, L. R., Lefkowitz, M. M., & Walder, L. O. (1996). Does television violence cause aggression? In D. F. Greenberg (Ed.), *Criminal careers: Vol. 2. The international library of criminology, criminal justice and penology* (pp. 311–321). Aldershot, Eng.: Dartmouth Publishing Company.

Essock-Vitale, S. M., & McGuire, M. T. (1985). Women's lives viewed from an evolutionary perspective: II. Patterns of helping. *Ethology and Sociobiology, 6,* 155–173.

Esterson, A. (1993). *Seductive mirage: An exploration of the work of Sigmund Freud.* Chicago: Open Court.

Esterson, A. (1998). Jeffrey Masson and Freud's seduction theory: A new fable based on old myths. *History of the Human Sciences, 11,* 1–21.

Evans, D. A., Hebert, L. E., Beckett, L. A., Scherr, P. A., Albert, M. S., Chown, M. J., Pilgrim, D. M., & Taylor, J. O. (1997). Education and other measures of socioeconomic status and risk of incident Alzheimer's disease in a defined population of older persons. *Archives of Neurology, 54,* 1399–1405.

Evans, G. W., Hygge, S., & Bullinger, M. (1995). Chronic noise and psychological stress. *Psychological Science, 6,* 333–338.

Evans, J., Barsten, J., & Pollard, P. (1983). On the conflict between logic and belief in syllogistic reasoning. *Memory & Cognition, 11,* 295–306.

Evans, P. (1989). *Motivation and emotion.* New York: Routledge.

Evans, R. I. (in press). Social influences in etiology and prevention of smoking in children and adolescents. In A. Baum, T. Revenson, & J. Singer (Eds.), *Handbook of health psychology.* Hillsdale, NJ: Lawrence Erlbaum Associates.

Everaerd, W., & Laan, E. (1994). Cognitive aspects of sexual functioning and dysfunctioning. *Sexual and Marital Therapy, 9,* 225–230.

Exner, J. E., Jr., & Ona, N. (1995). *RIAP-3: Rorschach Interpretation Assistance Program—version 3.* Odessa, FL: Psychological Assessment Resources.

Eysenck, H. J. (1952). The effects of psychotherapy: An evaluation. *Journal of Consulting Psychology, 16,* 319–324.

Eysenck, H. J. (1961). The effects of psychotherapy. In H. J. Eysenck (Ed.), *Handbook of abnormal psychology.* New York: Basic Books.

Eysenck, H. J. (1966). *The effects of psychotherapy.* New York: International Science Press.

Eysenck, H. J. (1978). An exercise in mega-silliness. *American Psychologist, 33,* 517.

Eysenck, H. J. (1987). Speed of information processing, reaction time, and the theory of intelligence. In P. A. Vernon (Ed.), *Speed of information-processing and intelligence* (pp. 21–67). Norwood, NJ: Ablex.

Eysenck, H. J. (1990a). Genetic and environmental contributions to individual differences: The three major dimensions of personality. *Journal of Personality, 58,* 245–261.

Eysenck, H. J. (1990b). Biological dimensions of personality. In L. A. Pervin (Ed.), *Handbook of personality: Theory and research.* (pp. 244–276). New York: Guilford.

Eysenck, H. J. (1994). A biological theory of intelligence. In D. K. Detterman (Ed.), *Current topics in human intelligence* (Vol. 4). Norwood, NJ: Ablex.

Eysenck, H. J., & Rachman, S. (1965). *The causes and cures of neurosis: An introduction to modern behavior therapy based on learning theory and the principle of conditioning.* San Diego: Knapp.

Eysenck, M. W., & Keane, M. T. (1995). *Cognitive psychology: A student's handbook* (3rd ed.). Hillsdale, NJ: Lawrence Erlbaum Associates.

Fabes, R. A., Shepard, S. A., Guthrie, I. K., & Martin, C. L. (1997). Roles of temperamental arousal and gender-segregated play in young children's social adjustment. *Developmental Psychology, 33,* 693–702.

Facchinetti, F., Centini, G., Parrini, D., Petroglia, F., D'Antona, N., Cosmi, E. V., & Genazzani, A. R. (1982). Opioid plasma levels during labor. *Gynecology & Obstetrics Investigations, 13,* 155–163.

Faedda, G., Tondo, L., Teicher, M., Baldessarini, R., Gelbard, H., & Floris, G. (1993). Seasonal mood disorders: Patterns of seasonal recurrence in mania and depression. *Archives of General Psychiatry, 50,* 17–23.

Fagot, B. I. (1995). Psychosocial and cognitive determinants of early gender-role development. *Annual Review of Sex Research, 6,* 1–31.

Fagot, B. I. (1997). Attachment, parenting, and peer interactions of toddler children. *Developmental Psychology, 33,* 489–499.

Fagot, B. I., & Gauvain, M. (1997). Mother-child problem solving: Continuity through the early childhood years. *Developmental Psychology, 33,* 480–488.

Fairweather, G. W., & Fergus, E. O. (1993). *Empowering the mentally ill.* Austin: Fairweather.

False Memory Syndrome Foundation. (1997). Outcome of recent malpractice suits against therapists brought by former patients claiming negligent encouragement or implantation of false memories. *FMSF Newsletter, 6,* 7–9.

Farberman, R. (1999, February). As managed care grows, public unhappiness rises. *APA Monitor,* p. 14.

FBI (Federal Bureau of Investigation). (1997). *Crime in the United States, 1996.* Washington, DC: U.S. Government Printing Office.

Feather, N. T., Volkmer, R. E., & McKee, I. R. (1992). A comparative study of the value priorities of Australians, Australian Baha'is, and expatriate Iranian Baha'is. *Journal of Cross-Cultural Psychology, 23,* 95–106.

Feighner, J., Merideth, C., & Hendrickson, G. (1982). A double blind comparison of buspirone and diazepam in outpatients with generalized anxiety disorder. *Journal of Clinical Psychiatry, 43,* 103–107.

Feighner, J. P. (1997). Are the new antidepressants Venlafaxine and Nefazodone really different? *Harvard Mental Health Letter, 13*(8), 8.

Feinberg, L., & Campbell, I. G. (1993). Total sleep deprivation in the rat transiently abolishes the delta amplitude response to darkness: Implications for the mechanism of the "negative delta rebound." *Journal of Neurophysiology, 70*(6), 2695–2699.

Feingold, A., & Mazzella, R. (1998). Gender differences in body image are increasing. *Psychological Science, 9,* 190–195.

Feist, J., & Feist, G. J. (1998). *Theories of personality* (4th ed.). Boston: McGraw-Hill.

Felten, D. L., Cohen, N., Ader, R., Felten, S. Y., Carlson, S. L., & Roszman, T. L. (1991). Central neural circuits involved in neural-immune interactions. In R. Ader (Ed.), *Psychoneuroimmunology* (2nd ed.). New York: Academic Press.

Felten, S. Y., Madden, K. S., Bellinger, D. L., Kruszewska, B., Moynihan, J. A., & Felten, D. L. (1998). The role of the sympathetic nervous system in the modulation of immune responses. *Advances in Pharmacology, 42,* 583–587.

Feng-Chen, K. C., & Wolpaw, J. R. (1996). Operant conditioning of H-reflex changes synaptic terminals on primate motoneurons. *Proceedings of the National Academy of Science USA, 93,* 9206–9211.

Fenson, L., Dale, P. S., Reznick, J. S., & Bates, E. (1994). Variability in early communicative development. *Monographs of the Society for Research in Child Development, 59,* 173.

Fenton, W. S., & McGlashan, T. H. (1991). Natural history of schizophrenia subtypes: 1. Longitudinal study of paranoid, hebephrenic, and undifferentiated schizophrenia. *Archives of General Psychiatry, 48,* 969–977.

Fenton, W. S., & McGlashan, T. H. (1994). Antecedent, symptoms progression, and long-term outcome of the deficit syndrome in schizophrenia. *American Journal of Psychiatry, 151,* 351–356.

Fergusson, D. M., & Horwood, L. J. (1997). Early onset cannabis use and psychosocial adjustment in young adults. *Addiction, 92,* 279–296.

Fergusson, D. M., Lloyd, M., & Horwood, L. J. (1991). Family ethnicity, social background and scholastic achievement: An eleven-year longitudinal study. *New Zealand Journal of Educational Studies, 26,* 49–63.

Fernández-Dols, J.-M. & Ruiz-Belda, M.-A. (1995). Are smiles a sign of happiness?: Gold medal winners at the Olympic Games. *Journal of Personality and Social Psychology, 69,* 1113–1119.

Ferraro, R., Lillioja, S., Fontvieille, A. M., Rising, R., Bogardus, C., & Ravussin, E. (1992). Lower sedentary metabolic rate in women compared with men. *Journal of Clinical Investigation, 90,* 780–784.

Ferretti, R. P., & Butterfield, E. C. (1989). Intelligence as a correlate of children's problem solving. *American Journal of Mental Retardation, 93,* 424–433.

Feske, U., & Goldstein, A. J. (1997). Eye movement desensitization and reprocessing treatment for panic disorder: A controlled outcome and partial dismantling study. *Journal of Consulting and Clinical Psychology, 65,* 1026–1035.

Festinger, L. (1954). A theory of social comparison processes. *Human Relations, 7,* 117–140.

Festinger, L. (1957). *A theory of cognitive dissonance.* Evanston, IL: Row, Petersen.

Festinger, L., & Carlsmith, J. M. (1959). Cognitive consequences of forced compliance. *Journal of Abnormal and Social Psychology, 58,* 203–210.

Field, T., Henteleff, T., Hernandez-Reif, M., Martinez, E., Mavunda, K., Kuhn, C., & Schanberg, S. (1998). Children with asthma have improved pulmonary functions after massage therapy. *Journal of Pediatrics, 132,* 854–858.

Field, T., Hernandez-Reif, M., Seligman, S., Krasnegor, J., Sunshine, W., Rivas-Chacon, R., Schanberg, S., & Kuhn, C. (1997). Juvenile rheumatoid arthritis: Benefits from massage therapy. *Journal of Pediatric Psychology, 22,* 607–617.

Field, T., Ironson, G., Scafidi, F., Nawrocki, T., Goncalves, A., Burman, I., Pickens, J., Fox, N., Schanberg, S., & Kuhn, C. (1996). Massage therapy reduces anxiety and enhances EEG pattern of alertness and math computations. *International Journal of Neuroscience, 86,* 197–205.

Fielding, J. E. (1991). The challenge of workplace health promotion. In S. M. Weiss, J. E. Fielding, & A. Baum (Eds.), *Perspectives in behavioral medicine* (pp. 13–28). Hillsdale, NJ: Lawrence Erlbaum Associates.

Fillmore, K. M., & Caetano, R. (1980, May 22). *Epidemiology of occupational alcoholism.* Paper presented at the National Institute on Alcohol Abuse and Alcoholism's Workshop on Alcoholism in the Workplace, Reston, VA.

Fink, M. (1993). Who should get ECT? In C. E. Coffey (Ed.), *The clinical science of electroconvulsive therapy.* Washington, DC: American Psychiatric Press.

Fink, M. (1997). What is the role of ECT in the treatment of mania? *Harvard Mental Health Letter, 13*(12), 8.

Fischer, K. W., & Bidell, T. (1991). Constraining nativist inferences about cognitive capacities. In S. Carey & R. Gelman (Eds.), *The epigenesis of mind: Essays on biology and cognition* (pp. 199–235). Hillsdale, NJ: Lawrence Erlbaum Associates.

Fischer, K. W., & Bidell, T. R. (1993, Fall). Beyond the stage debate: Keeping the constructor in constructivism. *Society for Research in Child Development Newsletter,* pp. 5ff.

Fischer, K. W., & Hencke, R. W. (1996). Infants' construction of actions in context: Piaget's contribution to research on early development. *Psychological Science, 7,* 204–209.

Fischer, P. J., & Breakey, W. R. (1991). The epidemiology of alcohol, drug, and mental disorders among homeless persons. *American Psychologist, 46,* 1115–1128.

Fischoff, B., & MacGregor, D. (1982). Subjective confidence in forecasts. *Journal of Forecasting, 1,* 155–172.

Fischoff, B., & Slovic, P. (1980). A little learning. . . . Confidence in multicue judgment tasks. In R. Nickerson (Ed.), *Attention and performance: VIII.* Hillsdale, NJ: Lawrence Erlbaum Associates.

Fisher, C. B., & Fyrberg, D. (1994). Participant partners: College students weigh the costs and benefits of deceptive research. *American Psychologist, 49,* 417–427.

Fisher, C. B., & Younggren, J. N. (1997). The value and utility of the 1992 ethics code. *Professional Psychology: Research and Practice, 28,* 582–592.

Fisher, S., & Greenberg, R. (1996). *Freud scientifically appraised.* New York: John Wiley.

Fisher, W. A., Fisher, J. D., & Rye, B. J. (1995). Understanding and promoting AIDS-preventive behavior: Insights from the theory of reasoned action. *Health Psychology, 14,* 255–264.

Fiske, A. P., Kitayama, S., Markus, H. R., & Nisbett, R. E. (1998). The cultural matrix of social psychology. In D. T. Gilbert, S. T. Fiske, & G. Lindzey (Eds.), *Handbook of social psychology,* Vol. 2 (4th ed., pp. 915–981). Boston: McGraw-Hill.

Fiske, S. (1995). Social cognition. In A. Tesser (Ed.), *Advanced social psychology* (pp. 149–194). New York: McGraw-Hill.

Fiske, S. T. (1998). Stereotyping, prejudice, and discrimination. In D. Gilbert, S. T. Fiske, and G. Lindzey (Eds.), *Handbook of social psychology,* Vol. 2 (4th ed., pp. 357–414). Boston: McGraw-Hill.

Fitzgerald, T. E., Tennen, H., Affect, G. S., & Pransky, G. (1993). The relative importance of dispositional optimism and control appraisals in quality of life after coronary artery bypass surgery. *Journal of Behavioral Medicine. 16,* 25–43.

Fitzpatrick, D. C., Olsen, J. F., & Suga, N. (1998). Connections among functional areas in the mustached bat auditory cortex. *Journal of Comparative Neurology, 391,* 366–396.

Fivush, R., Gray, J. T., & Fromhoff, F. A. (1987). Two-year-olds talk about the past. *Cognitive Development, 2,* 393–409.

Fivush, R., Haden, C., & Adam, S. (1995). Structure and coherence of preschoolers' personal narratives over time: Implications for childhood amnesia. *Journal of Experimental Child Psychology, 60,* 32–56.

Flavell, J. H. (1996). Piaget's legacy. *Psychological Science, 7,* 200–203.

Flier, J. S., & Maratos-Flier, E. (1998). Obesity and the hypothalamus: Novel peptides for new pathways. *Cell, 92,* 437–440.

Flint, J., Corley, R., DeFries, J. C., Fulker, D. W., Gray, J. A., Miller, S., & Collins, A. C. (1995). A simple genetic basis for a complex psychological trait in laboratory mice. *Science, 269,* 321–327.

Flynn, J. R. (1994). IQ gains over time. In R. Sternberg (Ed.), *Encyclopedia of human intelligence* (pp. 617–623). New York: MacMillan.

Flynn, J. T. (1999). Searching for justice: The discovery of IQ gains over time. *American Psychologist, 54,* 5–20.

Foa, E. B., Franklin, M. E., Perry, K. J., & Herbert, J. D. (1996). Cognitive biases in generalized social phobia. *Journal of Abnormal Psychology, 105,* 433–439.

Foa, E. B., & Kozak, M. J. (1995). DSM-IV field trial: Obsessive-compulsive disorder. *American Journal of Psychiatry, 152,* 90–96.

Foley, T., & Spates, C. R. (1995). Eye movement desensitization of public-speaking anxiety: A partial dismantling. *Journal of Behavior Therapy and Experimental Psychiatry, 26,* 321–329.

Folk, C. L., Remington, R. W., & Wright, J. H. (1994). The structure of attentional control: Contingent attentional capture by apparent motion, abrupt onset, and color. *Journal of Experimental Psychology: Human Perception and Performance, 20,* 317–329.

Folkman, S. (1984). Personal control and stress and coping processes: A theoretical analysis. *Journal of Personality and Social Psychology, 46,* 839–852.

Folkman, S., & Lazarus, R. (1988). *Manual for the ways of coping questionnaire.* Palo Alto, CA: Consulting Psychologists Press.

Folkman, S., Lazarus, R., Dunkel-Shetteer, DeLongis, A., & Gruen, R. (1986b). Dynamics of a stressful encounter: Cognitive appraisal, coping, and encounter outcomes. *Journal of Personality and Social Psychology, 50,* 992–1003.

Folkman, S., Lazarus, R. S., Gruen, R. J., & DeLongis, A. (1986a). Appraisal, coping, health status, and psychological symptoms. *Journal of Personality and Social Psychology, 50,* 571–579.

Foote, S. L., Bloom, F. E., & Aston-Jones, G. (1983). Nucleus locus coeruleus: New evidence of anatomical and physiological specificity. *Physiology Review, 63,* 844–914.

Ford, D. E., & Kamerow, D. B. (1989). Epidemiological study of sleep disturbances and psychiatric disorders: An opportunity for prevention? *Journal of the American Medical Association, 262,* 1479–1484.

Foreyt, J. P., Brunner, R. L., Goodrick, G. K., & Cutter, G. (1995). *International Journal of Eating Disorders, 17*(3), 263–275.

Forgas, J. P., & Fiedler, K. (1996). Us and them: Mood effects on intergroup discrimination. *Journal of Personality and Social Psychology, 70,* 28–40.

Forsyth, D. R. (1992). An introduction to group dynamics. Monterey, CA: Brooks/Cole.

Foulke, E. (1991). Braille. In M. A. Heller & W. Shiff (Eds.), *The psychology of touch.* Hillsdale, NJ: Lawrence Erlbaum Associates.

Foulkes, D. (1985). *Dreaming: A cognitive-psychological analysis.* Hillsdale, NJ: Lawrence Erlbaum Associates.

Fowles, D. (1992). Schizophrenia: Diathesis-stress revisited. *Annual Review of Psychology, 43,* 303–336.

Fox, M. L., Dwyer, D. J., & Ganster, D. C. (1993). Effects of stressful job demands and control on physiological and attitudinal outcomes in a hospital setting. *Academy of Management Journal, 36,* 289–318.

Fox, N. (1997, June). Consistent parenting helps children regulate emotions. *APA Monitor,* p. 17.

Fox, P. T., Ingham, R. J., Ingham, J. C., Hirsch, T. B., Downs, J. H., Martin, C., Jerabek, P., Glass, T., & Lancaster, J. L. (1996). A PET study of the neural systems of stuttering. *Nature, 382,* 158–161.

Fozard, J., Wolf, E., Bell, B., Farland, R., & Podolsky, S. (1977). Visual perception and communication. In J. Birren & K. Schaie (Eds.), *Handbook of the psychology of aging.* New York: Van Nostrand Reinhold.

Frances, A. J., Pincus, H. A., & Widiger, T. A. (1996). DSM-IV and international communication in psychiatric diagnosis. In Y. Honda, M. Kastrup, & J. E. Mezzich (eds.) *Psychiatric diagnosis: A world perspective.* New York: Springer.

Frank, G. (1976). Measures of intelligence and critical thinking. In I. B. Weiner (Ed.), *Clinical methods in psychology.* New York: Wiley.

Frank, J. S. (1973). *Persuasion and healing* (rev. ed.). Baltimore: Johns Hopkins University Press.

Frank, L. G., Glickman, S. E., & Licht, P. (1991). Fatal sibling aggression, precocial development, and androgens in neonatal spotted hyenas. *Science, 252,* 702–704.

Frank, M. G., Ekman, P., & Friesen, W. V. (1993). Behavioral markers and recognizability of the smile of enjoyment. *Journal of Personality and Social Psychology, 64*(1), 83–93.

Frankenberg, W. K., & Dodds, J. B. (1967). The Denver developmental screening test. *Journal of Pediatrics, 71,* 181–191.

Frankmann, S. P., & Green, B. G. (1987). Differential effects of cooling on the intensity of taste. *Annals of the New York Academy of Science, 510,* 300–303.

Frasure-Smith, N., Lesperance, F., & Talajic, M. (1995). The impact of negative emotions on prognosis following myocardial infarction: Is it more than depression? *Health Psychology, 14,* 388–398.

Freed, E. X. (1971). Anxiety and conflict: Role of drug-dependent learning in the rat. *Quarterly Journal of Studies on Alcohol, 32,* 13–29.

Freedland, R. L., & Bertenthal, B. I. (1994). Developmental changes in interlimb coordination: Transition to hands-and-knees crawling. *Psychological Science, 5,* 26–32.

Freedman, J. L. (1992). Television violence and aggression: What psychologists should tell the public. In P. Suedfeld & P. E. Tetlock (Eds.), *Psychology and social policy.* New York: Hemisphere.

Freedman, J. L., & Fraser, S. C. (1966). Compliance without pressure: The foot-in-the-door technique. *Journal of Personality and Social Psychology, 4,* 195–202.

Freeman, W., & Watts, J. W. (1942). *Psychosurgery.* Springfield, IL: Charles C. Thomas.

Fremgen, A., & Fay, D. (1980). Overextensions in production and comprehension: A methodological clarification. *Journal of Child Language, 7,* 205–211.

Freud, A. (1946). *The ego and the mechanisms of defense.* New York: International Universities Press.

Freud, S. (1900). The interpretation of dreams. In J. Strachey (Ed.), *The standard edition of the complete psychological works of Sigmund Freud: Vol. 8.* London: Hogarth Press.

Freud, S. (1924). The loss of reality in neurosis and psychosis. *Collected papers, 2,* 277–282.

Frey, P. L., & Gaertner, S. L. (1986). Helping and the avoidance of inappropriate interracial behavior: A strategy that perpetuates a nonprejudiced self-image. *Journal of Personality and Social Psychology, 50,* 1083–1090.

Fride, E., & Mechoulam, R. (1993). Pharmacological activity of the cannabinoid receptor agonist, anandamide, a brain constituent. *European Journal of Pharmacology, 231,* 313–314.

Fridlund, A. (1994). *Human facial expression: an evolutionary view.* New York: Academic Press.

Fridlund, A., Sabini, J. P., Hedlund, L. E., Schaut, J. A., Shenker, J. I., & Knauer, M. J. (1990). Audience effects on solitary faces during imagery: Displaying to the people in your head. *Journal of Nonverbal Behavior, 14*(2), 113–137.

Fried, I., Wilson, C. L., MacDonald, K. A., & Behnke, E. J. (1998). Electric current stimulates laughter. *Nature, 391,* 650.

Fried, P. A., Watkinson, B., & Gray, R. (1992). A follow-up study of attentional behavior in 6-year-old children exposed prenatally to marijuana, cigarettes, and alcohol. *Neurotoxicity and Teratology, 14*(5), 299–311.

Friedman, E., Clark, D., & Gershon, S. (1992). Stress, anxiety, and depression: Review of biological, diagnostic, and nosologic issues. *Journal of Anxiety Disorders, 6,* 337–363.

Friedman, H. S., Tucker, J. S., Schwartz, J. E., Martin, L. R., Tomlinson-Keasey, C., Wingard, D. L., & Criqui, M. H. (1995a). Childhood conscientiousness and longevity: Health behaviors and cause of death. *Journal of Personality and Social Psychology, 68,* 696–703.

Friedman, H. S., Tucker, J. S., Schwartz, J. E., Tomlinson-Keasey, C., Martin, L. R., Wingard, D. L., & Criqui, M. H. (1995b). Psychosocial and behavioral predictors of longevity: The aging and death of the "Termites." *American Psychologist, 50,* 69–78.

Friedman, H. S., Tucker, J. S., Tomlinson-Keasey, C., Schwartz, J. E., Wingard, D. L., & Criqui, M. H. (1993). Does childhood personality predict longevity? *Journal of Personality and Social Psychology, 65,* 176–185.

Friedman, J. M., & Polifka, J. E. (1996). *The effects of drugs on the fetus and nursing infant.* Baltimore: Johns Hopkins University Press.

Friedman, M., & Rosenman, R. H. (1959). Association of specific overt behavior patterns with blood and cardiovascular findings: Blood cholesterol level, blood clotting time, incidence of arcus senilis, and clinical coronary artery disease. *Journal of the American Medical Association, 169,* 1286–1296.

Friedman, M., & Rosenman, R. H. (1974). *Type A behavior and your heart.* New York: Knopf.

Friedman, M. A., & Brownell, K. D. (1995). Psychological correlates of obesity: Moving to the next research generation. *Psychological Bulletin, 117*(1), 3–20.

Frisby, J. P. (1980). *Seeing: Illusion, brain, and mind.* Oxford: Oxford University Press.

Fritzler, B. K., Hecker, J. E., & Losee, M. C. (1997). Self-directed treatment with minimal therapist contact: Preliminary findings for obsessive-compulsive disorder. *Behaviour Research and Therapy, 35,* 627–631.

Fromkin, V., Krashen, S., Curtiss, S., Rigler, D., & Rigler, M. (1974). The development of language in Genie: A case of language acquisition beyond the critical period. *Brain and Language, 1,* 81–107.

Fromkin, V., & Rodman, R. (1992). *An introduction to language* (5th ed.). New York: Holt, Rinehart & Winston.

Fuhriman, A. J., & Burlingame, G. M. (1995). *The handbook of group psychotherapy: An empirical and clinical synthesis.* New York: Wiley-Interscience.

Fuller, J. L., & Thompson, W. R. (1960). *Behavior genetics.* New York: Wiley.

Funder, D. C. (1993). Explaining traits. *Psychological Inquiry, 5,* 125–127.

Funder, D. C., & Colvin, C. R. (1997). Congruence of others' and self-judgments of personality. In R. Hogan, J. Johnson, & S. Briggs (Eds.), *Handbook of personality psychology* (pp. 617–648). San Diego: Academic Press.

Furstenberg, F. F., Jr., and Cherlin, A. J. (1991). *Divided families: What happens to children when parents part.* Cambridge, MA: Harvard University Press.

Fuson, K. C., & Kwon, Y. (1992). Effects on children's addition and subtraction of the system of number words and other cultural tools. In J. Bideaud & C. Meljac (Eds.), *Pathways to number.* Villeneueve d'asq, France: University de Lille.

Gabrieli, J. D. E., Fleischman, D. A., Keane, M. M., Reminger, S. L., & Morrell, F. (1995). Double dissociation between memory systems underlying explicit and implicit memory in the human brain. *Psychological Science, 6,* 76–82.

Gaertner, S. L., & Dovidio, J. F. (1986). The aversive form of racism. In J. F. Dovidio & S. L. Gaertner (Eds.), *Prejudice, discrimination, and racism* (pp. 61–89). Orlando, FL: Academic Press.

Gaertner, S. L., Dovidio, J. F., & Bachman, B. A. (1997). Revisiting the contact hypothesis: The induction of a common group identity. *International Journal of Intercultural Relations, 20,* 271–290.

Galanter, E. (1962). Contemporary psychophysics. In R. Brown (ed.), *New directions in psychology* (Vol. 1). New York: Holt, Rinehart, Winston.

Galef, B. G., & Wright, T. J. (1995). Groups of naive rats learn to select nutritionally adequate foods faster than do isolated rats. *Animal Behaviour, 49*(2), 403–409.

Gallagher, M. (1998, January 26). Day careless. *National Review,* pp. 37–41.

Gallagher, M., & Chiba, A. A. (1996). The amygdala and emotion. *Current Opinions in Neurobiology, 6*(2), 221–227.

Galton, F. (1883). *Inquiries into human faculty and its development.* London: Macmillan.

Games, D., Adams, D., Alessandrini, R., Barbour, R., Berthelette, P., Blackwell, C., Carr, T., Clemens, J., Donaldson, T., Gillespie, F., Guido, T., Hagopian, S., Johnsonwood, K., Khan, K., Lee, M., Leibowitz, P., Lieberburg, I., Little, S., Masliah, E., McConlogue, L., Montoyazavala, M., Mucke, L., Paganini, L., Penniman, E., Power, M., Schenk, D., Seubert, P., Snyder, B., Soriano, F., Tan, H., Vitale, J., Wadsworth, S., Wolozin, B., & Zhao, J. (1995). Alzheimer-type neuropathology in transgenic mice overexpressing V717F beta-amylois precursor protein. *Nature, 73,* 523–527.

Ganchrow, J. R., Steiner, J. E., & Daher, M. (1983). Neonatal facial expressions in response to different qualities and intensities of gustatory stimuli. *Infant Behavior and Development, 6,* 189–200.

Gara, M. A., Woolfolk, R. L., Cohen, B. D., Goldston, R. B., Allen, L. A., & Novalany, J. (1993). Perception of self and other in major depression. *Journal of Abnormal Psychology, 102,* 93–100.

Garb, H. N. (1997). Race bias, social class bias, and gender bias in clinical judgment. *Clinical Psychology: Science and Practice, 4,* 99–120.

Garb, H. N., Florio, C. M., & Grove, W. M. (1998). The validity of the Rorschach and the Minnesota Multiphasic Personality Inventory: Results from meta-analyses. *Psychological Science, 9,* 402–404.

Garber, R. J. (1992). Long-term effects of divorce on the self-esteem of young adults. *Journal of Divorce and Remarriage, 17,* 131–138.

Garcia, J., & Koelling, R. A. (1966). Relation of cue to consequences in avoidance learning. *Psychonomic Science, 4,* 123–124.

Garcia, J., Rusiniak, K. W., & Brett, L. P. (1977). Conditioning food-illness aversions in wild animals: Caveat Canonici. In H. Davis & H. M. B. Hurwitz (Eds.), *Operant-Pavlovian interactions.* Hillsdale, NJ: Lawrence Erlbaum Associates.

Gardner, H. (1993). *Multiple intelligences: The theory in practice.* New York: Basic Books.

Gardner, H. (1998). Are there additional intelligences? The case for naturalistic, spiritual, and existential intelligence. In J. Kane (Ed.), *Education, information, and transformation.* Englewood Cliffs, NJ: Prentice-Hall.

Gardner, M. (1988). *Perplexing puzzles and tantalizing teasers.* New York: Dover.

Gardner, R., Heward, W. L., & Grossi, T. A. (1994). Effects of response cards on student participation and academic achievement: A systematic replication with inner-city students during whole-class science instruction. *Journal of Applied Behavior Analysis, 27,* 63–71.

Gardner, R. A., & Gardner, B. T. (1978). Comparative psychology and language acquisition. *Annals of the New York Academy of Science, 309,* 37–76.

Garfield, S. L. (1998). Some comments on empirically supported treatments. *Journal of Consulting and Clinical Psychology, 66,* 121–125.

Garland, A. F., & Zigler, E. (1993a). Adolescent suicide prevention: Current research and social policy implications. *American Psychologist, 48,* 169–182.

Garris, Paul A., Kilpatrick, M., Bunin, M. A., Michael, D., Walker, Q. D., & Wightman, R. M. (1999). Dissociation of dopamine release in the nucleus accumbens from intracranial self-stimulation. *Nature, 398,* 67–69.

Garry, M., & Loftus, E. (1994). Pseudomemories without hypnosis. *International Journal of Clinical and Experimental Hypnosis, 42*(4), 363-373.

Gatewood, R. D., & Field, H. S. (1994). *Human resource selection* (3rd ed.). Ft. Worth, TX: Dryden Press.

Gawande, A. (1998a, March 30). No mistake. *New Yorker.*

Gawande, A. (1998b, September 21). The pain perplex. *New Yorker.*

Gazzaniga, M. S., & LeDoux, J. E. (1978). *The integrated mind.* New York: Plenum.

Geary, D. C., Fan, L., & Bow-Thomas, C. C. (1992). Numerical cognition: Loci of ability differences comparing children from China and the United States. *Psychological Sciences, 3,* 180–185.

Geary, J. (1997, May 5). Should we just say no to smart drugs? *Time,* p. 149.

Geen, R. G. (1991). Social motivation. *Annual Review of Psychology, 42,* 377–399.

Geen, R. G. (1998a). Process and personal variables in affective aggression. In R. G. Geen & E. Donnerstein (Eds.), *Human aggression* (pp. 2–24). San Diego: Academic Press.

Geen, R. G. (1998b). Aggression and antisocial behavior. In D. Gilbert, S. T. Fiske, and G. Lindzey (Eds.), *Handbook of social psychology,* Vol. 2 (4th ed., pp. 317–356). Boston: McGraw-Hill.

Geen, R. G., & McCown, E. J. (1984). Effects of noise and attack on aggression and physiological arousal. *Motivation and Emotion, 8,* 231–241.

Gelernter, J., Goldman, D., & Risch, N. (1993). The A1 allele at the D_2 dopamine receptor gene and alcoholism: A reappraisal. *Journal of the American Medical Association, 269,* 1673–1677.

Gellhorn, E., & Loofbourrow, G. N. (1963). *Emotions and emotional disorders.* New York: Harper & Row.

Gelman, R., & Baillargeon, R. (1983). A review of some Piagetian concepts. In P. H. Mussen (Ed.), *Handbook of child psychology* (Vol. 3). New York: Wiley.

Gerbner, G., Gross, L., Morgan, M., & Signorielli, N. (1986). Living with television: The dynamics of the cultivation process. In J. Bryant & D. Zillmann (Eds.), *Perspectives on media effects.* Hillsdale, NJ: Lawrence Erlbaum Associates.

Gerschman, J. A., Reade, P. C., & Burrows, G. D. (1980). Hypnosis and dentistry. In G. D. Burrows & L. Dennerstein (Eds.), *Handbook of hypnosis and psychosomatic medicine.* Amsterdam: Elsevier.

Geschwind, N. (1979). Specializations of the human brain. *Scientific American, 241,* 180–199.

Gfeller, J. D. (1994). Hypnotizability enhancement: Clinical implications of empirical findings. *American Journal of Clinical Hypnosis, 37*(2), 107-116.

Gibbon, J., Malapani, C., Dale, C. L., & Gallistel, C. (1997). Toward a neurobiology of temporal cognition: Advances and challenges. *Current Opinion in Neurobiology, 7,* 170–184.

Gibson, E. J., & Walk, R. D. (1960). The visual cliff. Scientific American, *202,* 64–71.

Gibson, J. J. (1979). *The ecological approach to visual perception.* Boston: Houghton Mifflin.

Gidron, B., Chesler, M. A., & Chesney, B. K. (1991). Cross-cultural perspectives on self-help groups: Comparisons between participants and nonparticipants in Israel and the United States. *American Journal of Community Psychology, 19,* 667–681.

Gidron, Y., & Davidson, K. (1996). Development and preliminary testing of a brief intervention for modifying CHD-predictive hostility components. *Journal of Behavioral Medicine, 19,* 203–220.

Gifford, R., & Hine, D. (1997a). "I'm cooperative, but you are greedy": Some cognitive tendencies in a common dilemma. *Canadian Journal of Behavioural Science, 29,* 257–265.

Gifford, R., & Hine, D. (1997b). Toward cooperation in the commons dilemma. *Canadian Journal of Behavioural Science, 29,* 167–178.

Gilbert, C. D. (1992). Horizontal integration and cortical dynamics. *Neuron, 9,* 1–13.

Gilbert, D. (1998). Ordinary personology. In D. Gilbert, S. T. Fiske, and G. Lindzey (Eds.), *Handbook of social psychology,* Vol. 2 (4th ed., pp. 89–150). Boston: McGraw-Hill.

Gilbert, D. T., & Malone, P. S. (1995). The correspondence bias. *Psychological Bulletin,* 117, 21–38.

Gilbert, R. M. (1984). Caffeine consumption. In G. A. Spiller (Ed.), *The methylxanthine beverages and foods: Chemistry, consumption, and health effects.* New York: Liss.

Giles, T. R. (1990). Bias against behavior therapy in outcome reviews: Who speaks for the patient? *The Behavior Therapist, 13,* 86–90.

Gillette, M. U. (1986). The suprachiasmatic nuclei: Circadian phase-shifts induced at the time of hypothalamic slice preparation are preserved in vitro. *Brain Research, 379,* 176–181.

Gilliard, D. K., & Beck, A. J. (1998). *Prison and jail inmates at midyear 1997.* Washington, DC: Bureau of Justice Statistics.

Gilligan, C. (1982). *In a different voice: Psychological theory and women's development.* Cambridge, MA: Harvard University Press.

Gilligan, C. (1993). Adolescent development reconsidered. In A. Garrod (Ed.), *Approaches to moral development: New research and emerging themes.* New York: Teachers College Press.

Gilligan, C., & Wiggins, G. (1987). The origins of morality in early childhood relationships. In J. Kagan & S. Lamb (Eds.), *The emergence of morality.* Chicago: University of Chicago Press.

Gilman, A. G., Goodman, L. S., Rall, T. W., & Murad, F. (1985). *Goodman and Gilman's the pharmacological basis of therapeutics* (7th ed.). New York: Macmillan.

Gilmore, M. M., & Murphy, C. (1989). Aging is associated with increased Weber ratios for caffeine, but not for sucrose. *Perception and Psychophysics, 46,* 555–559.

Gilovich, T. (1997). Some systematic biases of everyday judgment. *Skeptical Inquirer, 21,* 31–35.

Givens, B. (1995). Low doses of ethanol impair spatial working memory and reduce hippocampal theta activity. *Alcoholism Clinical and Experimental Research, 19*(3), 763–767.

Gladwell, M. (1996, September 30). The new age of man. *New Yorker,* pp. 56–67.

Glanz, J. (1997). Sharpening the senses with neural "noise." *Science, 277,* 1759.

Glanzer, M., & Cunitz, A. (1966). Two storage mechanisms in free recall. *Journal of Verbal Learning and Verbal Behavior, 5,* 351–360.

Glaser, R., & Bassok, M. (1989). Learning theory and the study of instruction. *Annual Review of Psychology, 40,* 631–666.

Gleitman, L., & Landau, B. (1994). *The acquisition of the lexicon.* Cambridge, MA: MIT Press.

Gleuckauf, R., & Quittner, A. (1992). Assertiveness training for disabled adults in wheelchairs: Self-report, role-play, and activity pattern outcomes. *Journal of Consulting and Clinical Psychology, 60,* 419–425.

Glicksohn, J. (1991). Altered sensory environments, altered states of consciousness, and altered-state cognition. *Journal of Mind and Behavior, 14*(1), 1–11.

Glover, J. A., Krug, D., Dietzer, M., George, B. W., & Hannon, M. (1990). "Advance" advance organizers. *Bulletin of the Psychonomic Society, 28,* 4–6.

Goddard, H. H. (1917). Mental tests and the immigrant. *Journal of Delinquency, 2,* 243–277.

Gold, M. S. (1994). The epidemiology, attitudes, and pharmacology of LSD use in the 1990s. *Psychiatric Annals, 24*(3), 124–126.

Goldberg, J. F., Harrow, M., & Grossman, L. S. (1995). Course and outcome in bipolar affective disorder: A longitudinal follow-up study. *American Journal of Psychiatry, 152,* 379–384.

Goldberg, L. R. (1993). The structure of phenotypic personality traits. *American Psychologist, 48,* 26–34.

Goldberg, L. R. (1995). What the hell took so long? Donald W. Fiske and the Big-Five factor structure. In P. E. Shrout & S. T. Fiske (Eds.), *Personality research, methods, and theory: A festschrift honoring Donald W. Fiske* (pp. 29–43). Hillsdale, NJ: Lawrence Erlbaum Associates.

Goldberg, L. R., & Saucier, G. (1995). So what do you propose we use instead? A reply to Block. *Psychological Bulletin, 11,* 221–225.

Goldenberg, I., & Goldenberg, H. (1995). Family therapy. In R. J. Corsini & D. Wedding (Eds.), *Current psychotherapies* (5th ed.). Itasca, IL: Peacock.

Goldfried, M. R., & Davison, G. C. (1994). *Clinical behavior therapy.* New York: Wiley Interscience.

Goldman, M. S., Darkes, J., & Del Boca, F. K. (in press). Expectancy mediation of biopsychosocial risk for alcohol use and alcoholism. In I. Kirsch (Ed.), *Expectancy, experience, and behavior.* Washington, DC: APA Books.

Goldman, M. S., Del Boca, F. K., & Darkes, J. (in press). Alcohol expectancy theory: The application of cognitive neuroscience. In H. Blane & K. Leonard (Eds.), *Psychological theories of drinking and alcoholism*. New York: Guilford.

Goldman-Rakic, P. S. (1987). Development of cortical circuitry and cognitive function. *Child Development, 58*, 601–622.

Goldman-Rakic, P. S. (1994). Specification of higher cortical functions. In S. H. Bromay & J. Grafman (Eds.), *Atypical cognitive deficits in developmental disorders*. Hillsdale, NJ: Lawrence Erlbaum Associates.

Goldman-Rakic, P. S. (1995). Cellular basis of working memory. *Neuron, 14*, 477–485.

Goldstein, E. B. (1999). *Sensation and perception* (5th ed.). Pacific Grove, CA: Brooks-Cole.

Goldstein, I., Lue, T. F., Padma-Nathan, H., Rosen, R. C., Steers, W. D., & Wicker, P. A. (1998). Oral sildenafil in the treatment of erectile dysfunction: Sildenafil Study Group. *New England Journal of Medicine, 338*, 1397–1404.

Goleman, D. (1995). *Emotional intelligence*. New York: Bantam Books.

Golomb, J., Kluger, A., De Leon, M. J., Ferris, S. H., Convit, A., Mittelman, M. S., Cohen, J., Rusinek, H., De Santi, S., & George, A. E. (1994). Hippocampal formation size in normal human aging: A correlate of delayed secondary memory performance. *Learning and Memory, 1*, 45–54.

Goode, K. T., Haley, W. E., Roth, D. L., & Ford, G. L. (1998). Predicting longitudinal changes in caregiver physical and mental health: A stress process model. *Health Psychology, 17*, 190–198.

Goodenough, F. L. (1932). Expression of the emotions in a blind-deaf child. *Journal of Abnormal and Social Psychology, 27*, 328–333.

Goodkin, K., Blaney, N., Feaster, D., Fletcher, M. A., Baum, M., Mantero-Atienza, E., Klimas, N., Millon, C., Szapocznik, J., & Eisdorfer, C. (1992). Active coping style is associated with natural killer cell cytotoxity in asymptomatic HIV-1 seropositive homosexual men. *Journal of Psychosomatic Research, 36*, 635–650.

Goodwin, C. (1992). A conceptualization of motives to seek privacy for nondeviant consumption. *Journal of Consumer Psychology, 1*, 261–284.

Goodwin, F. K., & Jamison, K. R. (Eds.). (1990). *Manic-depressive illness*. New York: Oxford University Press.

Gordon, T. (1970). *Parent effectiveness training: The no-lose program for raising responsible children*. New York: Wyden.

Gorman, J. M., Liebowitz, M. R., Fyer, A. J., & Stein, J. (1989). A neuroanatomical hypothesis for panic disorder. *American Journal of Psychiatry, 146*, 148–161.

Gosling, S. D. (1998). Personality dimensions in spotted hyenas (Crocuta crocuta). *Journal of Comparative Psychology, 112*, 107–118.

Gosselin, P., & Matthews, W. J. (1995). Eye movement desensitization and preprocessing in the treatment of test anxiety: A study of the effects of expectancy and eye movement. *Journal of Behavior Therapy and Experimental Psychiatry, 26*, 331–337.

Gossop, M., Griffiths, P., Powis, B., & Strang, J. (1994). Cocaine; Patterns of use, route of administration, and severity of dependence. *British Journal of Psychiatry, 164*(5), 660–664.

Gotlib, I. H., & Hammen, C. L. (1992). *Psychological aspects of depression: Toward cognitive interpersonal integration*. Chichester, Eng: John Wiley & Sons.

Gottesman, A. (1992, July 19). Asking witness to point out suspect can court embarrassment. *Chicago Tribune,*.

Gottesman, I. I. (1991). *Schizophrenia genesis*. New York: W. H. Freeman.

Gottfredson, L. S. (1997). Why *g* matters: The complexity of everyday life. *Intelligence, 24*, 79–132.

Gottfried, A. (1997, June). Parents' role is critical to children's learning. *APA Monitor*, p. 24.

Gottfried, A. W. (1984). *Home environment and early cognitive development*. Orlando, FL: Academic Press.

Gottlieb, B. H., & Peters, L. (1991). A national demographic portrait of mutual aid group participants in Canada. *American Journal of Community Psychology, 19*, 651–666.

Gottman, J. M., Coan, J., Carrere, S., & Swanson, C. (1998). Predicting marital happiness and stability from newlywed interactions. *Journal of Marriage and the Family, 60*, 5–22.

Gould, E., Tanapat, P., McEwen, B. S., Flugge, G., & Fuchs, E. (1998). Proliferation of granule cell precursors in the dentate gyrus of adult monkeys is diminished by stress. *Proceedings of the National Academy of Science USA, 95*, 3168–3171.

Gould, R. A., Otto, M. W., Pollack, M. H., & Yap, L. (1997). Cognitive behavioral and pharmacological treatment of generalized anxiety disorder: A preliminary meta-analysis. *Behavior Therapy, 28*, 285–305.

Gould, S. J. (1983). *The mismeasure of man*. New York: W. W. Norton.

Grady, D. (1998, October 13). High chlamydia rates found in teenagers. *New York Times* (Web Archive).

Graham, S. (1992). "Most of the subjects were white and middle class." *American Psychologist, 47*, 629–639.

Gray, A., Jackson, D. N., & McKinley, J. B. (1991). The relation between dominance, anger, and hormones in normally aging men: Results from the Massachusetts male aging study. *Psychosomatic Medicine, 53*, 375–385.

Green, A. I., & Patel, J. K. (1996). The new pharmacology of schizophrenia. *Harvard Mental Health Letter, 13*(6), 5–7.

Green, D. M., & Swets, J. A. (1966). *Signal detection theory and psychophysics*. New York: Wiley.

Green, E. J., Greenough, W. T., & Schlumpf, B. E. (1983). Effects of complex or isolated environments on cortical dendrites of middle-aged rats. *Brain Research, 264*(2), 233–240.

Green, J. P., & Lynn, S. J. (1995). Hypnosis, dissociation, and simultaneous task performance. *Journal of Personality and Social Psychology, 69*, 728–735.

Green, M. (1991). Visual search, visual strains, and visual architecture. *Perception and Psychophysics, 50*, 388–404.

Green, R. A., Cross, A. J., & Goodwin, G. M. (1995). Review of the pharmacology and clinical pharmacology of 3,4-methylenedioxymethamphetamine (MDMA or "ecstacy"). *Psychopharmacology, 119*, 247 260.

Greenberg, L. S., Rice, L. N., Elliot, R. (1993). *Process-experiential therapy: Facilitating emotional change*. New York: Guilford.

Greenblatt, D., Harmatz, J., & Shader, R. I. (1993). Plasma alprazolam concentrations: Relation to efficacy and side effects in the treatment of panic disorder. *Archives of General Psychiatry, 50*, 715–732.

Greene, E., & Loftus, E. F. (1998). Psycholegal research on jury damage awards. *Current Directions in Psychological Science, 7*, 50–54.

Greenfield, P. M. (1994). Video games as cultural artifacts. *Journal of Applied Developmental Psychology, 15*, 3–12.

Greenfield, P. M. (1995, Winter). Culture, ethnicity, race, and development: Implications for teaching theory and research. *Society for Research in Child Development Newsletter*, pp. 3ff.

Greenfield, P. M., & Childs, C. P. (1991). Developmental continuity in biocultural context. In R. Cohen & A. W. Siegel (Eds.), *Context and development* (pp. 135–159). Hillsdale, NJ: Lawrence Erlbaum Associates.

Greenfield, P. M., & Suzuki, L. K. (1998). Culture and human development: Implications for parenting, education, pediatrics, and mental health. In W. Damon, I. E. Sigel, & K. A. Renninger (Eds.), *Handbook of child psychology: Vol. 4. Child psychology in practice* (5th ed., pp. 1059–1112). New York: Wiley.

Greenough, W. T. (1997, November). We can't focus just on ages 0 to 3. *APA Monitor*, p. 3.

Greenough, W. T., Black, J. E., & Wallace, C. S. (1987). Experience and brain development. *Child Development, 58*, 539–559.

Greenwald, A. G. (1992). New look 3: Unconscious cognition reclaimed. *American Psychologist, 47*, 766–779.

Greenwald, A. G., & Banaji, M. R. (1995). Implicit social cognition: Attitudes, self-esteem, and stereotypes. *Psychological Review, 102*, 4–27.

Greenwald, A. G., & Draine, S. C. (1997). Do subliminal stimuli enter the mind unnoticed? Tests with a new method. In J. D. Cohen & J. W. Schooler (Eds.), *Scientific approaches to consciousness: Carnegie Mellon Symposia on cognition* (pp. 83–108). Mahwah, NJ: Lawrence Erlbaum Associates.

Greenwald, A. G., Draine, S. C., & Abrams, R. L. (1996). Three cognitive markers of unconscious semantic activation. *Science, 273*, 1699–1702.

Greenwald, A. G., Klinger, M. R., & Schuh, E. S. (1995). Activation by marginally perceptible ("subliminal") stimuli: Dissociation of unconscious from conscious cognition. *Journal of Experimental Psychology: General, 124*(1), 22–42.

Greenwald, A. G., McGhee, D. E., & Schwartz, J. L. K. (1998). Measuring individual differences in implicit cognition: The implicit association test. *Journal of Personality and Social Psychology, 74*, 1464–1480.

Greenwald, A. G., & Spangenberg, E. R. (1991). Double-blind tests of subliminal self-help audiotapes. *Psychological Science, 2*, 119–122.

Greenwald, J. (1991, December 22). Smart as you wanna be. *Los Angeles Times Magazine*.

Greenwald, R. (1996). The information gap in the EMDR controversy. *Professional Psychology: Research and Practice, 27*, 67–72.

Greer, A. E., & Buss, D. M. (1994). Tactics for promoting sexual encounters. *Journal of Sex Research, 31*(3), 185–201.

Gregg, V., Gibbs, J. C., & Basinger, K. S. (1994). Patterns of developmental delay in moral judgment by male and female delinquents. *Merrill-Palmer Quarterly, 40,* 538–553.

Griffitt, W. B., & Guay, P. (1969). "Object" evaluation and conditioned affect. *Journal of Experimental Research in Personality, 4,* 1–8.

Grilo, C. M., Pogue-Geile, M. F. (1991). The nature of environmental influences on weight and obesity: A behavior genetic analysis. *Psychological Bulletin, 110,* 520–537.

Grinspoon, L., Bakalar, J. B., Zimmer, L., & Morgan, J. P. (1997). Marijuana addiction. *Science, 277,* 749, 750–752.

Grisso, T., & Appelbaum, P. S. (1995). The MacArthur Treatment Competence Study: Vol. 3. Abilities of patients to consent to psychiatric and medical treatments. *Law and Human Behavior, 19,* 149–174.

Gritz, E., & St. Jeor, S. (1992). Task Force 3: Implications with respect to intervention and prevention. *Health Psychology, 11*(suppl.), 17–25.

Grob, C., & Dobkin-de-Rios, M. (1992). Adolescent drug use in cross-cultural perspective. *Journal of Drug Issues, 22*(1) 121–138.

Grochowicz, P. M., Schedlowski, M., Husband, A. J., King, M. G., Hibberd, A. D., & Bowen, K. M. (1991). Behavioral conditioning prolongs heart allograft survival in rats. *Brain Behavior and Immunity, 5,* 349–356.

Gross, J. (1998, March 15). Sergeant Major's accusers fault excess army loyalty. *New York Times,* pp. A1, A12.

Grossberg, S. (1988). *Neural networks and natural intelligence.* Cambridge, MA: MIT Press.

Grosz, H. I., & Zimmerman, J. (1970). A second detailed case study of functional blindness: Further demonstration of the contribution of objective psychological data. *Behavior Therapy, 1,* 115–123.

Grotevant, H. D. (1998). Adolescent development in family contexts. In W. Damon & N. Eisenberg (Eds.), *Handbook of child psychology: Vol. 3. Social, emotional, and personality development* (5th ed., pp. 1097–1150). New York: Wiley.

Groth-Marnat, G. (1997). *Handbook of psychological assessment* (3rd ed.). New York: Wiley.

Grunberg, N. E. (1994). Overview: Biological processes relevant to drugs of dependence, *Addiction, 89*(11), 1443–1446.

Grusec, J. E. (1991). Socialization of concern for others in the home. *Developmental Psychology, 27,* 338–342.

Grusec, J. E., & Goodnow, J. J. (1994). Impact of parental discipline methods on the child's internalization of values. *Developmental Psychology, 30,* 4–19.

Guerin, D. W., Gottfried, A. W., & Thomas, C. W. (1997). Difficult temperament and behaviour problems: A longitudinal study from 1.5 to 12 years. *International Journal of Behavioral Development, 21,* 71–90.

Guerlain, S. (1993). Factors influencing the cooperative problem-solving of people and computers. *Proceedings of the Human Factors and Ergonomics Society 37th Annual Meeting* (pp. 387–391). Santa Monica, CA: Human Factors Society.

Guerlain, S. (1995). Using the critiquing approach to cope with brittle expert systems. *Proceedings of the Human Factors and Ergonomics Society 39th Annual Meeting, I* (pp. 233–237). Santa Monica, CA: Human Factors Society.

Guilford, J. P. (1959). Traits of creativity. In H. H. Anderson (Ed.), *Creativity and its cultivation.* New York: Harper & Row.

Guilford, J. P., & Hoepfner, R. (1971). *The analysis of intelligence.* New York: McGraw-Hill.

Gunnoe, M. L., & Mariner, C. L. (1997). Toward a developmental-contextual model of the effects of parental spanking on children's aggression. *Archives of Pediatrics and Adolescent Medicine, 151,* 768–775.

Guntheroth, W. G., & Spiers, P. S. (1992). Sleeping prone and the risk of sudden infant death syndrome. *Journal of the American Medical Association, 267,* 2359–2362.

Gur, R. C., Mozley, L. H., Mozley, P. D., Resnick, S. M., Karp, J. S., Alavi, A., Arnold, S. E., & Gur, R. E. (1995). Sex differences in regional cerebral glucose metabolism during a resting state. *Science, 267,* 528–531.

Gur, R. C., Skolnic, B. E., & Gur, R. E. (1994). Effects of emotional discrimination tasks on cerebral blood flow: Regional activation and its relation to performance. *Brain and Cognition, 25*(2), 271–286.

Gustavson, C. R., Garcia, J., Hawkins, W. G., & Rusiniak, K. W. (1974). Coyote predation control by aversive conditioning. *Science, 184,* 581–583.

Ha, H., Tan, E. C., Fukunaga, H., & Aochi, O. (1981). Naloxone reversal of acupuncture analgesia in the monkey. *Experimental Neurology, 73,* 298–303.

Haber, R. N. (1979). Twenty years of haunting eidetic imagery: Where's the ghost? *The Behavioral and Brain Sciences, 2,* 583–629.

Hackel, L. S., & Ruble, D. N. (1992). Changes in the marital relationship after the first baby is born: Predicting the impact of expectancy disconfirmation. *Journal of Personality and Social Psychology, 62,* 944–957.

Hacking, I. (1995). *Rewriting the soul: Multiple personality and the sciences of memory.* Princeton, NJ: Princeton University Press.

Hackman, J. R. (1998). Why don't teams work? In R. S. Tindale, J. Edwards, & E. J. Posavac (Eds.), *Applications of theory and research on groups to social issues.* New York: Plenum.

Haddock, G., & Zanna, M. P. (1998a). Affect, cognition, and the prediction of social attitudes. In W. Stroebe & M. Hewstone (Eds.), *European Review of Social Psychology,* Vol. 10. New York: John Wiley.

Haddock, G., & Zanna, M. P. (1998b). Authoritarianism, values, and the favorability of anti-gay attitudes. In G. M. Herek (Ed.), *Stigma and sexual orientation: Understanding prejudice against lesbians, gay men, and bisexuals. Psychological perspectives on lesbian and gay issues, Vol. 4* (pp. 82–107). Newbury Park, CA: Sage Publications.

Hahdahl, K., Iversen, P. M., & Jonsen, B. H. (1993). Laterality for facial expressions: Does the sex of the subject interact with the sex of the stimulus face? *Cortex, 29*(2), 325–331.

Hahlweg, K., & Markman, H. J. (1988). Effectiveness of behavioral marital therapy: Empirical status of behavioral techniques in preventing and alleviating marital distress. *Journal of Consulting and Clinical Psychology, 56,* 440–447.

Haines, V. A., Hurlbert, J. S., & Beggs, J. J. (1996). Exploring the determinants of support provision: Provider characteristics, personal networks, community contexts, and support following life events. *Journal of Health and Social Behavior, 37,* 252–264.

Haldeman, D. C. (1994). The practice and ethics of sexual orientation conversion therapy. *Journal of Consulting and Clinical Psychology, 62*(2), 221–227.

Halford, G. S., Maybery, M. R., O'Hare, A. W., & Grant, P. (1994). The development of memory and processing capacity. *Child Development, 65,* 1338–1356.

Hall, C. C. I. (1997). Cultural malpractice: The growing obsolescence of psychology with the changing U.S. population. *American Psychologist, 52,* 642–651.

Hall, C. S., Lindzey, G., & Campbell, J. P. (1998). *Theories of personality* (4th ed.). New York: Wiley.

Hall, G. (1991). *Perceptual and associative learning.* Oxford: Clarendon Press.

Hall, G. C. N. (1995). The preliminary development of theory-based community treatment of sexual offenders. *Professional Psychology: Research and Practice, 26,* 478–483.

Hall, G. C. N., & Hirschman, R. (1991). Toward a theory of sexual aggression: A quadriparite model, *Journal of Consulting and Clinical Psychology, 59,* 662–669.

Hall, P., & Davidson, K. (1996). The misperception of aggression in behaviorally hostile men. *Cognitive Therapy and Research, 20,* 377–389.

Hall, W. (1997). The recent Australian debate about the prohibition on cannabis use. *Addiction, 92,* 1109–1115.

Halpern, D. F. (1997). Sex differences in intelligence. *American Psychologist, 52,* 1091–1102.

Halverson, C. F., Jr., & Wampler, K. S. (1997). Family influences on personality development. In R. Hogan, J. Johnson, & S. Briggs (Eds.), *Handbook of personality psychology* (pp. 241–267). San Diego: Academic Press.

Hamer, D. H., Hu, S., Magnuson, V. L., Hu, N., & Pattatucci, A. M. L. (1993). A linkage between DNA markers on the X chromosome and male sexual orientation. *Science, 261,* 321–327.

Hamilton, D. L., & Sherman, J. (1994). Social stereotypes. In R. S. Wyer & T. K. Srull (Eds.), *Handbook of social cognition* (2nd ed.). Hillsdale, NJ: Lawrence Erlbaum Associates.

Hamilton, N. G. (1994). Object relations theory. In V. S. Ramachandran (Ed.), *Encyclopedia of human behavior* (Vol. 3, pp. 321–332). San Diego: Academic Press.

Hamilton, W. D. (1964). The evolution of social behavior: Parts I and II. *Journal of Theoretical Biology, 7,* 1–52.

Hamm, A. O., Vaitl, D., & Lang, P. J. (1989). Fear conditioning, meaning, and belongingness: A selective association analysis. *Journal of Abnormal Psychology, 98,* 395–406.

Hammen, C. (1991). *Depression runs in families: The social context of risk and resilience in children of depressed mothers.* New York: Springer-Verlag.

Hammer, E. (1968). Projective drawings. In A. I. Rabin (Ed.), *Projective techniques in personality assessment.* New York: Springer.

Hammond, W. R., & Yung, B. (1993). Minority student recruitment and retention practices among schools of professional psychology: A national survey and analysis. *Professional Psychology: Research and Practice, 24*, 3–12.

Hancock, E. (1996, February). High control at work makes for a healthy heart. *Johns Hopkins Magazine*, p. 31.

Hanges, P. (1997, August). Stereotypes still stymie female managers. *APA Monitor*, p. 41.

Hanson, G., & Venturelli, P. J. (1995). *Drugs and society* (4th ed.). Boston: Jones & Bartlett.

Hanson, S. J., & Burr, D. J. (1990). What connectionist models learn: Learning and representations in connectionist networks. *Behavioral and Brain Sciences, 13*, 471–518.

Happe, F. G. E., Winner, E., & Brownell, H. (1998). The getting of wisdom: Theory of mind in old age. *Developmental Psychology, 34*, 358–362.

Harackiewicz, J. M. &Elliot, A. J. (1993). Achievement goals and intrinsic motivation. *Journal of Personality and Social Psychology, 65*(5), 904–915.

Harasty, J., Double, K. L., Halliday, G. M., Kril, J. J., & McRitchie, D. A. (1997). Language-associated cortical regions are proportionally larger in the female brain. *Archives of Neurology, 54*, 171–176.

Hardaway, R. (1990). Subliminally activated symbiotic fantasies: Facts or artifacts. *Psychological Bulletin, 107*, 177–195.

Hardimann, P. T., Dufresne, R., & Mestre, J. (1989). The relation between problem categorization and problem solving among experts and novices. *Memory & Cognition, 17*, 627–638.

Hare, R. D. (1993). *Without conscience: The disturbing world of the psychopaths among us*. New York: Pocket Books.

Harlow, H. F. (1949). The formation of learning sets. *Psychological Review, 56*, 51–65.

Harlow, H. F. (1959, June). Love in infant monkeys. *Scientific American*, 68–74.

Harmon-Jones, E., Brehm, J. W., Greenberg, J., Simon, L., & Nelson, D. E. (1996). Evidence that the production of negative consequences is not necessary to produce cognitive dissonance. *Journal of Personality and Social Psychology, 72*, 515–525.

Harris, G. C., & Aston-Jones, G. (1995). Involvement of D2 dopamine receptors in the nucleus acumbens in opiate withdrawal syndrome. *Nature, 371*, 155–157.

Harris, J. E., & Morris, P. E. (Eds.) (1984). *Everyday memories, actions, and absent-mindedness*. New York: Academic Press.

Harris, J. R. (1995). Where is the child's environment? A group socialization theory of development. *Psychological Review, 102*, 458–489.

Harris, J. R. (1998). *The nurture assumption*. New York: Free Press.

Harris, R. J., Sardarpoor-Bascom, F., & Meyer, T. (1989). The role of cultural knowledge in distorting recall for stories. *Bulletin of the Psychonomic Society, 27*, 9–10.

Hart, A. J. (1995). Naturally occurring expectation effects. *Journal of Personality and Social Psychology, 68*, 109–115.

Hart, D., & Yates, M. (1997). The interrelation of self and identity in adolescence: A developmental account. In R. Vasta (Ed.), *Annals of child development: Vol. 12. A research annual* (pp. 207–243), London: Jessica Kingsley Publishers.

Harter, S. (1998). The development of self representations. In W. Damon & N. Eisenberg (Eds.), *Handbook of child psychology: Vol. 3. Social, emotional, and personality development* (5th ed., pp. 553–618). New York: Wiley.

Hartman, B. K., Cozzari, C., Berod, A., Kalmbach, S. J., & Faris, P. L. (1986). Central cholinergic innervation of the locus coeruleus. *Society for Neuroscience Abstracts, 12*, 770.

Hartmann, H. (1958). *Ego psychology and the problem of adaptation*. New York: International Universities Press.

Hartung, C. M., & Widiger, T. A. (1998). Gender differences in the diagnosis of mental disorders: Conclusions and controversies of DSM-IV. *Psychological Bulletin, 123*, 260–278.

Hartup, W. W., & Stevens, N. (1997). Friendships and adaptation in the life course. *Psychological Bulletin, 121*, 355–370.

Harvard Mental Health Letter. (1994). Brief psychodynamic therapy—Part I, Vol. 10, pp. 1–3.

Harvard Mental Health Letter. (1995a). Update on mood disorders—Part II, Vol. 11(7), pp. 1–4.

Harvard Mental Health Letter. (1995b). Schizophrenia update—Part II, Vol. 11(12), pp. 1–5.

Harvard Mental Health Letter. (1998a). Mood disorders: An overview—Part II, Vol. 14(7), pp. 1–5.

Harvard Mental Health Letter. (1998b). Mood disorders: An overview—Part III, Vol. 14(8), pp. 1–5.

Harwood, R. L., Schulze, P. A., & Wilson, S. P. (1995, March). *Cultural values and acculturation among lower-class Puerto Rican mothers living in the United States*. Poster presented at the biennial meeting of the Society for Research in Child Development, Indianapolis.

Haskell, I., & Wickens, C. D. (1993). Two- and three-dimensional displays for aviation. *International Journal of Aviation Psychology, 4*.

Hassmen, P. & Koivula, N. (1997) Mood, physical working capacity, and cognitive performance in the elderly as related to physical activity. *Aging, 9*, 136–42.

Hastie, R. (1986). Review essay: Experimental evidence on group accuracy. In B. Grofman & G. Owen (Eds.), *Information pooling and group decision making* (pp. 129–264). Greenwich, CT: JAI Press.

Hastie, R., Penrod, S. D., & Pennington, N. (1984). *Inside the jury*. Cambridge, MA: Harvard University Press.

Hatfield, E. (1988). Passionate and companionate love. In R. J. Sternberg & M. L. Barnes (Eds.), *The psychology of love*. New Haven: Yale University Press.

Hatfield, E., & Rapson, R. L. (1995). *Love and sex: Cross-cultural perspectives*. Boston: Allyn & Bacon.

Hauser, P., Zametkin, A. J., Martinez, P., Vitiello, B., Matochik, J. A., Mixson, J., & Weinstraub, B. D. (1993). Attention deficit hyperactivity disorder in people with generalized resistance to thyroid hormone. *New England Journal of Medicine, 328*, 997–1001.

Hausmann, S., & Wucherpfennig, K. W. (1997). Activation of autoreactive T cells by peptides from human pathogens. *Current Opinion in Immunology, 9*, 831–838.

Hawkins, H. L., Kramer, A. R., & Capaldi, D. (1993). Aging, exercise, and attention. *Psychology and Aging, 7*, 643–653.

Hawkins, J. D., Catalano, R. F., Kosterman, R., Abbott, R., & Hill, K. G. (1999). Preventing adolescent health-risk behaviors by strengthening protection during childhood. *Archives of Pediatrics and Adolescent Medicine, 153*, 226–234.

Hayes, N. (1997, July). The distinctive skills of a psychology graduate. *APA Monitor*, p. 33.

Hayflick, L. (1994). *How and why we age*. New York: Ballantine Books.

Hays, P. A. (1995). Multicultural applications of cognitive-behavior therapy. *Professional Psychology: Research and Practice, 26*, 309–315.

Hays, R., Turner, H., & Coates, T. (1992). Social support, AIDS-related symptoms, and depression among gay men. *Journal of Consulting and Clinical Psychology, 60*, 463–469.

He, L. F. (1987). Involvement of endogenous opioid peptides in acupuncture analgesia. *Pain, 31*, 99–121.

Healy, D. J., Haroutunian, V., Powchik, P., Davidson, M., Davis, K. L., Watson, S. J., & Meador-Woodruff, J. H. (1998). AMPA receptor binding and subunit mRNA expression in prefrontal cortex and striatum of elderly schizophrenics. *Neuropsychopharmacology, 19*, 278–286.

Hebb, D. O. (1949). *The organization of behavior*. New York: Wiley.

Hebb, D. O. (1955). Drives and the C.N.S. (conceptual nervous system). *Psychological Review, 62*, 243–254.

Hecker, J. E., Losee, M. C., Fritzler, B. K., & Fink, C. M. (1996). Self-directed versus therapist-directed cognitive behavioral treatment for panic disorder. *Journal of Anxiety Disorders, 10*, 253–265.

Hecker, J. E., & Thorpe, G. L. (1992). *Agoraphobia and panic: A guide to psychological treatment*. Boston: Allyn & Bacon.

Hedge, A., & Yousif, Y. H. (1992). Effects of urban size, urgency, and cost of helpfulness: A cross-cultural comparison between the United Kingdom and the Sudan. *Journal of Cross-Cultural Psychology, 23*, 107–115.

Hegarty, J. D., Baldessarini, R. J., Tohen, M., Waternaux, C., & Oepen, G. (1994). One hundred years of schizophrenia: A meta-analysis of the outcome literature. *American Journal of Psychiatry, 151*, 1409–1416.

Heider, E. (1972). Universals of color naming and memory. *Journal of Experimental Psychology, 93*, 10–20.

Heilbrun, A. B., & Witt, N. (1990). Distorted body image as a risk factor in anorexia nervosa: Replication and clarification. *Psychological Reports, 66*, 407–416.

Heine, S. J., & Lehman, D. R. (1995). Culture, dissonance, and self-affirmation. Unpublished manuscript. University of British Columbia, Vancouver.

Heine, S. J., & Lehman, D. R. (1997). Culture, dissonance, and self-affirmation. *Personality and Social Psychology Bulletin, 23*, 389–400.

Helgesen, S. (1998). *Everyday revolutionaries: Working women and the transformation of American life*. New York: Doubleday.

Heller, W. (1993). Neuropsychological mechanisms of individual differences in emotion, personality, and arousal. *Neuropsychology, 7*(4), 486–489.

Heller, W., Etienne, M. A., & Miller, G. A. (1995). Patterns of perceptual asymmetry in depression and anxiety: Implications for neuropsychological models of emotion and psychopathology. *Journal of Abnormal Psychology, 104*(2), 327–333.

Heller, W., Nitschke, J. B., & Miller, G. A. (1998). Lateralization in emotion and emotional disorders. *Current Directions in Psychological Science, 7,* 26–32.

Helmers, K. F., & Krantz, D. S. (1996). Defensive hostility, gender and cardiovascular levels and responses to stress. *Annals of Behavioral Medicine, 18,* 246–254.

Helmers, K. F., Krantz, D. S., Merz, C. N. B., Klein, J., Kop, W. J., Gottdiener, J. S., & Rozanski, A. (1995). Defensive hostility: Relationship to multiple markers of cardiac ischemia in patients with coronary disease. *Health Psychology, 14,* 202–209.

Helms, J. E. (1992). Why is there no study of cultural equivalence in standardized cognitive ability testing? *American Psychologist, 47,* 1083–1101.

Helson, R., & Moane, G. (1987). Personality change in women from college to midlife. *Journal of Personality and Social Psychology, 53,* 176–186.

Helzer, J. E., Canino, G. J., Yeh, E., Bland, R. C., Lee, C. K., Hwu, H., & Newman, S. (1990). Alcoholism—North America and Asia: A comparison of population surveys with the diagnostic interview schedule. *Archives of General Psychiatry, 47,* 313–319.

Henderson, C. E., Phillips, H. S., Pollock, R. A., Davies, A. M., Lemeulle, C., Armanini, M., Simpson, L. C., Moffet, B., Vandlen, R. A., Koliatsos, V. E., & Rosenthal, A. (1994). GDNF—A potent survival factor for motorneurons present in peripheral nerve and muscle. *Science, 266,* 1062–1064.

Henderson-Smart, D. J., Ponsonby, A. L., & Murphy, E. (1998). Reducing the risk of sudden infant death syndrome: A review of the scientific literature. *Journal of Paediatric Child Health, 34,* 213–219.

Hendrick, C., & Hendrick, S. (1986). A theory and method of love. *Journal of Personality and Social Psychology, 50,* 392–402.

Henker, B., & Whalen, C. K. (1989). Hyperactivity and attention deficits. *American Psychologist, 44,* 216–223.

Hense, R. L., Penner, L. A., & Nelson, D. L. (1995). Implicit memory for age stereotypes. *Social Cognition, 13,* 399–416.

Herbert, J. D., Lilienfeld, S. O., Lohr, J. M., Montgomery, R. W., O'Donohue, W. T., Rosen, G. M., & Tolin, D. F. (in press). Science and pseudoscience in the development of eye movement desensitization and reprocessing: Implications for clinical psychology. *Clinical Psychology Review.*

Hergenhahn, B. R., & Olson, M. (1997). *An introduction to theories of learning* (5th ed.). Upper Saddle River, NJ: Prentice-Hall.

Herman, L. M., Richards, D. G., & Wolz, J. P. (1984). Comprehension of sentences by bottlenosed dolphins. *Cognition, 16,* 129–219.

Herrmann, D. J., & Searleman, A. (1992). Memory improvement and memory theory in historical perspective. In D. Herrmann, H. Weingartner, A. Searlman, & C. McEvoy (Eds.), *Memory improvement: Implications for memory theory.* New York: Springer-Verlag.

Herrnstein, R. (1973). *I.Q. in the meritocracy.* Boston: Little, Brown.

Herrnstein, R. J., & Murray, C. (1994). *The bell curve: Intelligence and class structure in American Life.* New York: Free Press.

Herzog, D. B. (1982). Bulimia: The secretive syndrome. *Psychosomatics, 22,* 481–487.

Hesse, J., Mogelvang, B., & Simonsen, H. (1994). Acupuncture versus metropolol in migraine prophylaxis: A randomized trial of trigger point inactivation. *Journal of Internal Medicine, 235,* 451–456.

Heston, L. L. (1966). Psychiatric disorders in foster home–reared children of schizophrenic mothers. *British Journal of Psychiatry, 112,* 819–825.

Hetherington, E. M., Bridges, M., & Insabella, G. M. (1998). What matters? What does not? Five perspectives on the association between marital transitions and children's adjustment. *American Psychologist, 53,* 167–184.

Hetherington, E. M., & Clingempeel, W. G. (1992). Coping with marital transitions. *Monographs of the Society for Research in Child Development, 57*(2–3, Serial No. 227).

Hickok, G., Bellugi, U., & Klima, E. S. (1996). The neurobiology of sign language and its implications for the neural basis of language. *Nature, 381,* 699–702.

Higgins, E. T. (1989). Knowledge accessibility and activation: Subjectivity and suffering from unconscious sources. In J. S. Uleman & J. A. Bargh (Eds.), *Unintended thought.* New York: Guilford.

Higgins, E. T., Vookles, J., & Tykocinski, O. (1992). Self and health: How patterns of self-beliefs predict emotional and physical problems. *Social Cognition, 10,* 125–150.

Hildreth, E. C., & Ullman, S. (1989). The computational study of vision. In M. I. Posner (ed.), *Fundamentals of cognitive science* (pp. 581–630). Cambridge, MA: MIT Press.

Hilgard, E. R. (1965). *Hypnotic susceptibility.* New York: Harcourt, Brace & World.

Hilgard, E. R. (1977). *Divided consciousness: Multiple controls in human thought and action.* New York: Wiley.

Hilgard, E. R. (1979). *Personality and hypnosis: A study of imaginative involvement.* Chicago: University of Chicago Press.

Hilgard, E. R. (1980). Consciousness in contemporary psychology. *Annual Review of Psychology, 31,* 1–26.

Hilgard, E. R. (1992). Divided consciousness and dissociation. *Consciousness and Cognition, 1,* 16–31.

Hilgard, E. R., Morgan, A. H., & MacDonald, H. (1975). Pain and dissociation in the cold pressor test: A study of "hidden reports" through automatic key-pressing and automatic talking. *Journal of Abnormal Psychology, 84,* 280–289.

Hill, B. (1968). *Gates of horn and ivory.* New York: Taplinger.

Hill, C. T., & Peplau, L. A. (1998). Premarital predictors of relationship outcomes: A 15-year follow-up of the Boston Couples Study. In T. N. Bradbury (Ed.), *The developmental course of marital dysfunction* (pp. 237–278). New York: Cambridge University Press.

Hill, D. L., & Mistretta, C. M. (1990). Developmental neurobiology of salt taste sensation. *Trends in Neuroscience, 13,* 188–195.

Hill, D. L., & Przekop, P. R., Jr. (1988). Influences of dietary sodium on functional taste receptor development: A sensitive period. *Science, 241,* 1826–1828.

Hill, J. O., & Peters, J. C. (1998). Environmental contributions to the obesity epidemic. *Science, 280,* 1371–1374.

Hill, T., Lewicki, P., Czyzewska, M., & Boss, A. (1989). Self-perpetuating biases in person perception. *Journal of Personality and Social Psychology, 57,* 373–386.

Hillman, D. C., Siffre, M., Milano, G., & Halberg, F. (1994). Free-running psychophysiologic circadians and three-month pattern in a woman isolated in a cave. *New Trends in Experimental and Clinical Psychiatry, 10*(3), 127–133.

Hilton, H. (1986). *The executive memory guide.* New York: Simon & Schuster.

Hines, M., & Green, R. (1991). Human hormonal and neural correlates of sex-typed behavior. *Review of Psychiatry, 10,* 536–555.

Hinshaw, S. P., Zupan, B. A., Simmel, C., Nigg, J. T., & Melnick, S. (1997). Peer status in boys with and without attention-deficit hyperactivity disorder: Predictions from overt and covert antisocial behavior, social isolation, and authoritative parenting beliefs. *Child Development, 68,* 880–896.

Hinsz, V. B. (1990). Cognitive and consensus processes in group recognition memory performance. *Journal of Personality and Social Psychology, 59,* 705–718.

Hinton, G. E. (1992, September). How neural networks learn for expense. *Scientific American, 267,* 145–151.

Hinton, J. (1967). *Dying.* Harmondsworth, UK: Penguin.

Hintzman, D. (1991). Human learning and memory. *Annual Review of Psychology,* 110–130.

Hiroto, D. S. (1974). Locus of control and learned helplessness. *Journal of Experimental Psychology, 102,* 187–193.

Hirsch-Pasek, K., Treiman, R., & Schneiderman, M. (1984). Brown and Hanlon revisited: Mothers' sensitivity to ungrammatical forms. *Journal of Child Language, 11,* 81–88.

Hirschfeld, J. A. (1995). The "Back-to-Sleep" campaign against SIDS. *American Family Physician, 51,*(3), 611–612.

Ho, D. Y., & Chiu, C. (1998). Component ideas of individual, collectivism, and social organization. In U. Kim, C. Kagitcibasi, & H. C. Triandis (Eds.), *Individualism and collectivism: Theory, method, and applications.* Thousand Oaks, CA: Sage.

Hobson, J. A. (1988). *The dreaming brain.* New York: Basic Books.

Hobson, J. (1997). Dreaming as delirium: A mental status analysis of our nightly madness. *Seminar in Neurology, 17,* 121–128.

Hobson, J. A., & Stickgold, R. (1994). Dreaming: A neurocognitive approach. *Consciousness and Cognition, 3,* 1–15.

Hoffert, M. J. (1992). The neurophysiology of pain. In G. M. Aronoff (Ed.), *Evaluation and treatment of chronic pain.* Baltimore: Williams & Wilkins.

Hofstadter, D. (1995). *Fluid concepts and creative analogies.* New York: Basic Books.

Hogan, R., Curphy, G. J., & Hogan, J. (1994). What we know about leadership: Effectiveness and personality. *American Psychologist, 49,* 493–504.

Hogan, R. J., & Ones, D. (1997). Conscientiousness and integrity at work. In R. Hogan, J. Johnson, & S. Briggs (Eds.), *Handbook of personality psychology* (pp. 849–873). San Diego: Academic Press.

Hogarth, R. M., & Einhorn, H. J. (1992). Order effects in belief updating: The belief adjustment model. *Cognitive Psychology, 24,* 1–55.

Hohmann, G. W. (1966). Some effects of spinal cord lesions on experienced emotional feelings. *Psychophysiology, 3,* 143–156.

Holahan, C. J. (1986). Environmental psychology. *Annual Review of Psychology, 37,* 381–407.

Holahan, C. J., & Moos, R. H. (1986). Personality, coping, and family resources in stress resistance: A longitudinal analysis. *Journal of Personality and Social Psychology, 51,* 389–395.

Holahan, C. J., Moos, R. H., Holahan, C. K., & Brennan, P. L. (1997). Social context, coping strategies, and depressive symptoms: An expanded model with cardiac patients. *Journal of Personality and Social Psychology, 72,* 918–928.

Holahan, C. K. (1994). Women's goal orientations across the life cycle: Findings from the Terman Study of the Gifted. In B. F. Turner & L. E. Troll (Eds.), *Women growing older* (pp. 35–67). Thousand Oaks, CA: Sage.

Holcomb, L., Gordon, M. N., McGowan, E., Yu, X., Benkovic, S., Jantzen, P., Wright, K., Saad, I., Mueller, R., Morgan, D., Sanders, S., Zehr, C., O'Campo, K., Hardy, J., Prada, C. M., Eckman, C., Younkin, S., Hsiao, K., & Duff, K. (1998). Accelerated Alzheimer-type phenotype in transgenic mice carrying both mutant amyloid precursor protein and presenilin 1 transgenes. *Nature Medicine, 4,* 97–100.

Holden, C. (1991). Probing the complex genetics of alcoholism. *Science, 251,* 163–164.

Holden, C. (1996). Small refugees suffer the effects of early neglect. *Science, 274,* 1076–1077.

Holden, C. (1998). New clues to alcoholism risk. *Science, 280,* 1348–1349.

Holland, J. G. (1960). Teaching machines: An application of principles from the laboratory. *Journal of the Experimental Analysis of Behavior, 3,* 275–287.

Hollis, K. A. (1997). Contemporary research on Pavlovian conditioning: A "new" functional analysis. *American Psychologist, 52,* 956–964.

Hollon, S., Shelton, R., & Loosen, P. (1991). Cognitive therapy and pharmacotherapy for depression. *Journal of Consulting and Clinical Psychology, 59,* 88–99.

Hollopeter, G., Erickson, J. C., & Palmiter, R. D. (1998). Role of neuropeptide Y in diet-, chemical- and genetic-induced obesity of mice. *International Journal of Obesity and Related Metabolic Disorders, 22,* 506–512.

Holman, B. R. (1994). Biological effects of central nervous system stimulants. *Addiction, 89*(11), 1435–1441.

Holmberg, S. D. (1996). The estimated prevalence and incidence of HIV in 96 large U.S. metropolitan areas. *American Journal of Public Health, 86,* 642–654.

Holmes, D. S. (1984). Meditation and somatic arousal reduction: A review of the experimental evidence. *American Psychologist, 39,* 1–10.

Holmes, D. S. (1991). *Abnormal psychology.* New York: HarperCollins.

Holmes, T. H., & Rahe, R. H. (1967). The social readjustment rating scale. *Journal of Psychosomatic Research,* 11, 213–218.

Holway, A. H., & Boring, E. G. (1941). Determinants of apparent visual size with distance variant. *American Journal of Psychology, 54,* 21–37.

Hooker, E. (1993). Reflections of a 40-year exploration: A scientific view on homosexuality. *American Psychologist, 48,* 450–453.

Hopf, H. C., Muller, F. W., & Hopf, N. J. (1992). Localization of emotional and volitional facial paresis. *Neurology, 42*(10), 1918–1923.

Hoptman, M. J., & Davidson, R. J. (1994). How and why do the two cerebral hemispheres interact? *Psychological Bulletin, 116,* 195–219.

Horgan, J. (1996, December). Why Freud isn't dead. *Scientific American,* pp. 106–111.

Horn, J. L. (1982). The theory of fluid and crystallized intelligence in relation to concepts of cognitive psychology and aging in adulthood. In F. I. M. Craik and S. Trehub (Eds.), *Aging and cognitive processes.* New York: Plenum.

Horne, J. A. (1988). *Why we sleep: The functions of sleep in humans.* Oxford: Oxford University Press.

Horney, K. (1937). *Neurotic personality of our times.* New York: W. W. Norton.

Horowitz, L. M., Rosenberg, S. E., & Bartholomew, K. (1993). Interpersonal problems, attachment styles, and outcome in brief dynamic psychotherapy. *Journal of Consulting and Clinical Psychology, 61,* 549–560.

Houpt, T. R. (1994). Gastric pressure in pigs during eating and drinking. *Physiology and Behavior, 56*(2), 311–317.

House, J. S., Landis, K. R. & Umberson, D., (1988). Structures and processes of social support. *Annual Review of Sociology, 14,* 293–318.

Houston, B., & Vavac, C. (1991). Cynical hostility: Developmental factors, psychosocial correlates and health behaviors. *Health Psychology, 10,* 9–17.

Howard-Pitney, B., LaFramboise, T., Basil, M., September, B., & Johnson, M. (1992). Psychological and social indicators of suicide ideation and suicide attempts in Zuni adolescents. *Journal of Consulting and Clinical Psychology, 60,* 473–476.

Howard, D. V. (1983). *Cognitive psychology.* New York: Macmillan.

Howard, K. E., Kopta, S. M., Krause, M. S., & Orlinsky, D. E. (1986). The dose-effect relationship in psychotherapy. *American Psychologist, 41,* 159–164.

Howe, M. J. A. (1970). Using students' notes to examine the role of the individual learner in acquiring meaningful subject matter. *Journal of Educational Research, 64,* 61–63.

Howe, M. J. A., Davidson, J. W., & Sloboda, J. A. (1998). Innate talent: Reality or myth? *Behavioral and Brain Sciences, 21,* 399–442.

Howe, M. L. (1995, March). *Differentiating cognitive and sociolinguistic factors in the decline of infantile amnesia.* Paper presented at the biennial meeting of the Society for Research in Child Development, Indianapolis.

Hoy, A. W. (1999). Psychology applied to education. In A. M. Stec & D. A. Bernstein (Eds.), *Psychology: The fields of application.* Boston: Houghton Mifflin.

Hoyle, R. H. (1993). Interpersonal attraction in the absence of explicit attitudinal information. *Social Cognition, 11,* 309–320.

Hoyt, M. F. (1995). Brief psychotherapies. In A. S. Gurman & S. B. Messer (Eds.), *Essential psychotherapies: Theory and practice* (pp. 441–487). New York: Guilford.

Hsiao, K., Chapman, P., Nilsen, S., Eckman, C., Harigaya, Y., Younkin, S., Yang, F., & Cole, G. (1996). Correlative memory deficits, Abeta elevation, and amyloid plaques in transgenic mice. *Science, 274,* 99–102.

Hu, S., Patatucci, A. M. L., Patterson, C., Li, L., Fulker, D. W., Cherny, S. S., Kruglyak, L., & Hamer, D. H. (1995). Linkage between sexual orientation and chromosome Xq28 in males but not females. *Nature Genetics, 11,* 248–256.

Hubble, M. A., Duncan, B. L., & Miller, S. D. (Eds.). (1999). *The heart and soul of change: What works in psychotherapy.* Washington, DC: American Psychological Assocation.

Hubel, D. H., & Wiesel, T. N. (1979). Brain mechanisms of vision. *Scientific American, 241,* 150–162.

Hudson, J. A., & Sheffield, E. G. (1998). Deja vu all over again: Effects of reenactment on toddlers' event memory. *Child Development, 69,* 51–67.

Hudspeth, A. J. (1997). How hearing happens. *Neuron, 19,* 947–950.

Huesmann, L. R. (1995). *Screen violence and real violence: Understanding the link.* Auckland, NZ: Media Aware.

Huesmann, L. R. (1998). The role of social information processing and cognitive schema in the acquisition and maintenance of habitual aggressive behavior. In R. G. Geen & E. Donnerstein (Eds.), *Human aggression.* San Diego: Academic Press.

Huesmann, L. R., & Eron, L. D. (1986). *Television and the aggressive child: A cross-national comparison.* Hillsdale, NJ: Lawrence Erlbaum Associates.

Huesmann, L. R., Laperspetz, K., & Eron, L. D. (1984). Intervening variables in the TV violence-aggression relation: Evidence from two countries. *Developmental Psychology, 20,* 746–775.

Huesmann, L. R., & Miller, L. S. (1994). Long-term effects of repeated exposure to media violence in childhood. In L. R. Huesmann (Ed.), *Human aggression: Current perspectives* (pp. 153–186). New York: Plenum.

Huesmann, L. R., Moise, J., Podolski, C., & Eron, L. (1997, April). Longitudinal relations between early exposure to television violence and young adult aggression: 1977–1992. Paper presented at the annual meeting of the Society for Research in Child Development. Washington, DC.

Hughes, J. R., Higgins, S. T., & Bickel, W. K. (1994). Nicotine withdrawal versus other drug withdrawal syndromes: Similarities and dissimilarities. *Addiction, 89*(11), 1461–1470.

Hull, C. L. (1943). *Principles of behavior.* New York: Appleton-Century-Crofts.

Hull, C. L. (1951). *Essentials of behavior.* New Haven, CT: Yale University Press.

Humphrey, D. H., & Dahlstrom, W. G. (1995). The impact of changing from the MMPI to the MMPI-2 on profile configurations. *Journal of Personality Assessment, 64,* 428–439.

Humphreys, L. G. (1984). General intelligence. In C. R. Reynolds & R. T. Brown (Eds.), *Perspectives on bias in mental testing.* New York: Plenum.

Humphreys, L. G. (1988). Trends in levels of academic achievement of blacks and other minorities. *Intelligence, 12,* 231–260.

Humphreys, L. G., & Davey, T. C. (1988). Continuity in intellectual growth from 12 months to 9 years. *Intelligence, 12,* 183–197.

Hunt, C. B. (1980). Intelligence as an information processing concept. *British Journal of Psychology, 71*, 449–474.

Hunt, D. M., Dulai, K. S., Bowmaker, J. K., & Mollon, J. D. (1995). The chemistry of John Dalton's color blindness. *Science, 267*, 984–988.

Hunt, E. (1983). On the nature of intelligence. *Science, 219*, 141–146.

Hunt, M. (1982). *The universe within.* New York: Simon & Schuster.

Hunt, R., & Rouse, W. B. (1981). Problem solving skills of maintenance trainees in diagnosing faults in simulated power plants. *Human Factors, 23*, 317–328.

Hunter, J. E. (1986). Cognitive ability, cognitive aptitudes, job knowledge, and job performance, *Journal of Vocational Behavior, 29*, 340–362.

Hunter, J. N. (1997). Needed: A ban on the significance test. *Psychological Science, 8*, 3–7.

Hurt, H., Brodsky, N. L., Betancourt, L., & Braitman, L. E. (1995). Cocaine-exposed children: Follow-up through 30 months. *Journal of Developmental and Behavioral Pediatrics, 16*(1), 29–35.

Huston, A. C., & Wright, J. C. (1989). The forms of television and the child viewer. In G. Comstock (Ed.), *Public communication and behavior* (Vol. 2). San Diego, CA: Academic Press.

Huttenlocher, P. R. (1990). Morphometric study of human cerebral cortex development. *Neuropsychologia, 28*, 517–527.

Huttenlocher, P. R. (1994). Synaptogenesis in human cerebral cortex. In G. Dawson & K. W. Fischer (Eds.), *Human behavior and the developing brain* (pp. 137–152). New York: Guilford.

Huttenlocher, P. R., & Dabholkar, A. S. (1997). Regional differences in synaptogenesis in human cerebral cortex. *Journal of Comparative Neurology, 387*, 167–178.

Hyde, J. S. (1986). Gender differences in aggression. In J. S. Hyde & M. C. Linn (Eds.), *The psychology of gender: Advances through meta-analysis.* Baltimore: Johns Hopkins University Press.

Hyde, J. S. (1994). Can meta-analysis make feminist transformations in psychology? *Psychology of Women Quarterly, 18*, 451–462.

Hyde, J. S., Fennema, E., & Lamon, S. J. (1990). Gender differences in mathematics performance: A meta-analysis. *Psychological Bulletin, 107*, 139–155.

Hyman, I. A. (1995). Corporal punishment, psychological maltreatment, violence, and punitiveness in America: Research, advocacy, and public policy. *Applied and Preventive Psychology, 4*, 113–130.

Hyman, I. E., & Pentland, J. (1996). The role of mental imagery in the creation of false childhood memories. *Journal of Memory and Language, 35*, 101–117.

Ibrahim, F. (1991). Contributions of cultural worldview to generic counseling and development. *Journal of Counseling and Development, 70*, 13–19.

Ickovics, J., & Rodin, J. (1992). Women and AIDS in the United States: Epidemiology, natural history, and mediating mechanisms. *Health Psychology, 11*, 1–16.

Ilgen, D. R., & Klein, H. J. (1989). Organizational behavior. *Annual Review of Psychology, 40*, 327–351.

Illinois Department of Corrections (1993). *Statistical presentation.* Springfield, IL.

Inciardi, J. A., Surratt, H. L., & Saum, C. A. (1997). *Cocaine-exposed infants: Social, legal, and public health issues.* Thousand Oaks, CA: Sage.

Infant Health and Development Program. (1990). Enhancing the outcomes of low-birth-weight, premature infants. *Journal of the American Medical Association, 263*, 3035–3042.

Inoue-Nakamura, N., & Matsuzawa, T. (1997). Development of stone tool use by wild chimpanzees (Pan troglodytes). *Journal of Comparative Psychology, 111*, 159–173.

Insko, C. A., Schopler, J., Hoyle, R. H., Dardis, G. J., & Graetz, K. A. (1990). Individual-group discontinuity as a function of fear and greed. *Journal of Personality and Social Psychology, 58*, 68–79.

Ironson, G., Wynings, C., Schneiderman, N., Baum, A., Rodriguez, M., Greenwood, D., Benight, C., Antoni, M., LaPerriere, A., Huang, H. B .S., Klimas, N., & Fletcher, M. A. (1997). Posttraumatic stress symptoms, intrusive thoughts, loss, and immune function after Hurricane Andrew. *Psychosomatic Medicine, 59*, 128–141.

Iwahashi, K., Matsuo, Y., Suwaki, H., Nakamura, K., & Ichikawa, Y. (1995). CYP2E1 and ALDH2 genotypes and alcohol dependence in Japanese. *Alcoholism Clinical and Experimental Research, 19*(3), 564–566.

Iwamura, Y., Iriki, A., & Tanaka, M. (1994). Bilateral hand representation in the postcentral somatosensory cortex. *Nature, 369*, 554–556.

Izard, C. (1993). Organizational and motivational functions of discrete emotions. In M. Lewis and J. M. Haviland (Eds.), *Handbook of emotions.* New York: Guilford.

Izard, C. E. (1977). *Human emotions.* New York: Plenum.

Jacobs, M. K., & Goodman, G. (1989). Psychology and self-help groups: Predictions on a partnership. *American Psychologist, 44*, 536–545.

Jacobson, E. (1938). *Progressive relaxation.* Chicago: University of Chicago Press.

Jacobson, J. W., Mulick, J. A., & Schwartz, A. A. (1995). A history of facilitated communication. *American Psychologist, 50*, 750–765.

Jacobson, N. S., & Hollon, S. D. (1996). Cognitive-behavior therapy versus pharmacotherapy: Now that the jury's returned its verdict, it's time to present the rest of the evidence. *Journal of Consulting and Clinical Psychology, 64*, 74–80.

Jacoby, L. L., Marriott, M. J., & Collins, J. G. (1990). The specifics of memory and cognition. In T. K. Srull & R. S. Wyer (Eds.), *Advances in social cognition: Vol. III. Content and process specificity in the effects of prior experiences.* Hillsdale, NJ: Lawrence Erlbaum Associates.

Jagger, C., Clarke, M., & Stone, A. (1995). Predictors of survival with Alzheimer's disease: A community-based study. *Psychological Medicine, 25*, 171–177.

Jahnke, J. C., & Nowaczyk, R. H. (1998). *Cognition.* Upper Saddle River, NJ: Prentice-Hall.

James, W. (1884). Some omissions of introspective psychology. *Mind, 9*, 1–26.

James, W. (1890). *Principles of psychology.* New York: Holt.

James, W. (1892). *Psychology: briefer course.* New York: Holt.

Jancke, L., & Kaufmann, N. (1994). Facial EMG responses to odors in solitude and with an audience. *Chemical Senses, 19*(2), 99–111.

Janicak, P., Sharma, R., Israni, T., Dowd, S., Altman, E., & Davis, J. (1991). Effects of unilateral-nondominant vs. bilateral ECT on memory and depression: A preliminary report. *Psychopharmacology Bulletin, 27*, 353–357.

Janig, W. (1996). Neurobiology of visceral afferent neurons: Neuroanatomy, functions, organ regulations and sensations. *Biological Psychology, 5*, 29–51.

Janis, I. L. (1985). International crisis management in the nuclear age. *Applied Social Psychology Annual, 6*, 63–86.

Janis, I. L. (1989). *Crucial decisions: Leadership in policy making and crisis management.* New York: Free Press.

Janowiak, J. J., & Hackman, R. (1994). Meditation and college students' self-actualization and rated stress. *Psychological Reports, 75*(2), 1007-1010.

Janowitz, H. D. (1967). Role of gastrointestinal tract in the regulation of food intake. In C. F. Code (Ed.), *Handbook of physiology: Alimentary canal 1.* Washington, DC: American Physiological Society.

Jason, L. A., McMahon, S. D., Salina, D., Hedeker, D, Stockton, M., Dunson, K., & Kimball, P. (1995). Assessing a smoking cessation intervention involving groups, incentives, and self-help manuals. *Behavior Therapy, 26*, 393–408.

Jenike, M., Baer, L., Ballantine, T., Martuza, R., Tynes, S., Giriunas, I., Buttolph, L., & Cassem, N. (1991). Cingulotomy for refractory obsessive-compulsive disorder: A long-term follow-up of 33 patients. *Archives of General Psychiatry, 48*, 548–555.

Jenkins, J. G., & Dallenbach, K. M. (1924). Obliviscence during sleep and waking. *American Journal of Psychology, 35*, 605–612.

Jenkins, M. R., & Culbertson, J. L. (1996). Prenatal exposure to alcohol. In R. L. Adams, O. A. Parsons, J. L. Culbertson, & S. J. Nixon (Eds.), *Neuropsychology for clinical practice: Etiology, assessment, and treatment of common neurological disorders* (pp. 409–452). Washington, DC: American Psychological Association.

Jensen, A. R. (1969). How much can we boost IQ and scholastic achievement? *Harvard Educational Review, 39*, 1–123.

Jensen, A. R. (1993). Why is reaction time correlated with psychometric g? *Current Directions in Psychological Science, 2*, 53–55.

Jensen, J. P., Bergin, A. E., & Greaves, D. W. (1990). The meaning of eclecticism: New survey and analysis of components. *Professional Psychology: Research and Practice, 21*, 124–130.

Jensen, M., & Karoly, P. (1991). Control beliefs, coping efforts, and adjustment to chronic pain. *Journal of Consulting and Clinical Psychology, 59*, 431–438.

Jernigan, T. L., Trauner, D. A., Hesselink, J. R., & Tallal, P. A. (1991). Maturation of human cerebrum observed in vivo during adolescence. *Brain, 114*, 2037–2049.

Jerusalinsky, D., Kornisiuk, E., & Izquierdo, I. (1997). Cholinergic neurotransmission and synaptic plasticity concerning memory processing. *Neurochemical Research, 22*, 507–515.

Jhanwar, U. M., Beck, B., Jhanwar, Y. S., & Burlet, C. (1993). Neuropeptide Y projection from the arcuate nucleus to the parvocellular division of the paraventricular nucleus: Specific relation to the ingestion of carbohydrate. *Brain Research, 631*(1), 97–106.

Johansson, C. B., Momma, S., Clarke, D. L., Risling, M., Lendsahl, U., & Frisen, J. (1999). Identification of a neural stem cell in the adult mammalian central nervous system. *Cell, 96*, 25–34.

Johansson, G. (1975). Visual motion perception. *Scientific American, 232,* 76–88.

Johnson, J. (1997). Units of analysis for the description and analysis of behavior. In R. Hogan, J. Johnson, & S. Briggs (Eds.), *Handbook of personality psychology* (pp. 73–96). San Diego: Academic Press.

Johnson, J. M., Seikel, J. A., Madison, C. L., & Foose, S. M. (1997). Standardized test performance of children with a history of prenatal exposure to multiple drugs/cocaine. *Journal of Communication Disorders, 30,* 45–73.

Johnson, J. S., & Newport, E. L. (1989). Critical period effects in second language learning. *Cognitive Psychology, 21,* 60–99.

Johnson, J., & Vickers, Z. (1993). Effects of flavor and macronutrient composition of food servings on liking, hunger and subsequent intake. *Appetite, 21*(1), 25–39.

Johnson, L. E., & Thorpe, G. L. (1994). Review of psychotherapy and counseling with minorities: A cognitive approach to individual differences, by Manuel Ramirez. *Behavioural and Cognitive Psychotherapy, 22,* 185–187.

Johnson, M. A., Dziurawiec, S., Ellis, H., & Morton, J. (1991). Newborns' preferential tracking of face-like stimuli and its subsequent decline. *Cognition, 4,* 1–19.

Johnson, S. L., McPhee, L., & Birch, L. L. (1991). Conditioned preferences: Young children prefer flavors associated with high dietary fat. *Physiology and Behavior, 50,* 1245–1251.

Johnson, W. G., & Torgrud, L. J. (1996). Assessment and treatment of binge eating disorder. In J. K. Thompson (Ed.), *Body image, eating disorders, and obesity* (pp. 321–344). Washington, DC: American Psychological Association.

Johnson, W. R., & Neal, D. (1998). In C. Jencks & M. Phillips (Eds.), *The black-white test score gap.* Washington, DC: Brookings Institute Press.

Johnstone, E. C., & Frith, C. D. (1996). Validation of three dimensions of schizophrenic symptoms in a large unselected sample of patients. *Psychological Medicine, 26,* 669–679.

Jones, B. E. (1991). Paradoxical sleep and its chemical/structural substrates in the brain. *Neuroscience, 40,* 637–656.

Jones, G. V. (1989). Back to Woodworth: Role of interlopers in the tip-of-the-tongue phenomenon. *Memory & Cognition, 17,* 69–76.

Jones, G. V. (1990). Misremembering a common object: When left is not right. *Memory & Cognition, 18,* 174–182.

Jones, L. V., & Appelbaum, M. I. (1989). Psychometric methods. *Annual Review of Psychology, 40,* 23–44.

Jones, W. H. S. (1923). (Ed. and Trans.). *Hippocrates,* Vol. 1. London: William Heinemann.

Jordan, N. C., Huttenlocher, J., & Levine, S. C. (1992). Differential calculation abilities in young children from middle- and low-income families. *Developmental Psychology, 28,* 644–653.

Jorgensen, R. S., Johnson, B. T., Kolodziej, M. E., & Schreer, G. E. (1996). Elevated blood pressure and personality: A meta-analytic review. *Psychological Bulletin, 120,* 293–320.

Joseph, B., Overmier, J. B., & Thompson, T. (1997). Food- and nonfood-related differential outcomes in equivalence learning by adults with Prader-Willi syndrome. *American Journal of Mental Retardation, 101,* 374–386.

Josephson, W. L. (1987). Television violence and children's aggression: Testing the priming, social script, and disinhibition predictions. *Journal of Personality and Social Psychology, 53,* 882–890.

Jouriles, E. N., Mehta, P., McDonald, R., & Francis, D. J. (1997). Psychometric properties of family members' reports of parental physical aggression toward clinic-referred children. *Journal of Consulting and Clinical Psychology, 65,* 309–318.

Joy, J. E., Watson, S. J., Jr., & Benson, J. A., Jr. (1999). *Marijuana and medicine: Assessing the science base.* Washington, DC: National Academy Press.

Julien, R. M. (1995). *A primer of drug action* (7th ed.). New York: W. H. Freeman.

Jung, C. G. (1916). *Analytical psychology.* New York: Moffat.

Jung, C. G. (1933). *Psychological types.* New York: Harcourt, Brace and World.

Jussim, L. (1989). Teacher expectations: Self-fulfilling prophecies, perceptual biases, and accuracy. *Journal of Personality and Social Psychology, 57,* 469–480.

Just, N., & Alloy, L. B. (1997). The response styles theory of depression: Tests and an extension of the theory. *Journal of Abnormal Psychology, 106,* 221–229.

Kaczmarek, L., Kossut, M., & Skangiel-Kramska, J. (1997). Glutamate receptors in cortical plasticity: Molecular and cellular biology. *Physiological Review, 77,* 217–255.

Kagan, J., & Snidman, N. (1991). Temperamental factors in human development. *American Psychologist, 46,* 856–862.

Kagan, J. R., Snidman, N., Arcus, D., & Resnick, J. S. (1994). *Galen's prophecy: Temperament in human nature.* New York: Basic Books.

Kahen, V., Katz, L. F., & Gottman, J. M. (1994). Linkages between parent-child interaction and conversations of friends. *Social Development, 3,* 238–254.

Kahn, D. A. (1995). New strategies in bipolar disorder: Part II. Treatment. *Journal of Practical Psychiatry and Behavioral Health, 3,* 148–157.

Kahneman, D., & Tversky, A. (1984). Choices, values, and frames. *American Psychologist, 29,* 341–356.

Kales, A., & Kales, J. (1973). Recent advances in the diagnosis and treatment of sleep disorders. In G. Usdin (Ed.), *Sleep research and clinical practice.* New York: Brunner/Mazel.

Kalish, H. I. (1981). *From behavioral science to behavior modification.* New York: McGraw-Hill.

Kaniasty, K., & Norris, F. H. (1993). A test of the social support deterioration model in the context of natural disaster. *Journal of Personality and Social Psychology, 64,* 395–408.

Kanki, B. J., & Foushee, H. C. (1990). Crew factors in the aerospace workplace. In S. Oskamp & S. Spacepan (Eds.), *People's reactions to technology* (pp. 18–31). Newbury Park, CA: Sage.

Kanner, A. D., Coyne, J. C., Schaefer, C., & Lazarus, R. S. (1981). Comparison of two modes of stress measurement: Daily hassles and uplifts versus major life events. *Journal of Behavioral Medicine, 4,* 1–39.

Kanner, B. (1995). *Are you normal?* New York: St. Martin's Press.

Kaplan, M. F. (1987). The influencing process in group decision making. In C. Hendrick (Ed.), *Group processes.* Newbury Park, CA: Sage.

Kaplan, M. F., & Miller, C. E. (1987). Group decision making and normative vs. informational influence: Effects of type of issue and assigned decision rule. *Journal of Personality and Social Psychology, 53,* 306–313.

Kaplan, R. M. (1991). Health-related quality of life in patient decision-making. *Journal of Social Issues, 47,* 69–90.

Kaplan, R. M., Orleans, C. T., Perkins, K. A., & Pierce, J. P. (1995). Marshaling the evidence for greater regulation and control of tobacco products: A call for action. *Annals of Behavioral Medicine, 17,* 3–14.

Kapur, S., & Mann, J. J. (1993). Antidepressant action and the neurobiologic effects of ECT: Human studies. In C. E. Coffey (Ed.), *The clinical science of electroconvulsive therapy.* Washington, DC: American Psychiatric Press.

Karau, S. J., & Williams, K. D. (1997). The effects of group cohesiveness on social loafing and social compensation. *Group Dynamics, 1,* 156–168.

Kardes, F. (1999). Psychology applied to consumer behavior. In A. M. Stec & D. A. Bernstein (Eds.), *Psychology: Fields of application.* Boston: Houghton Mifflin.

Karni, A., Meyer, G., Adams, M., Turner, R., & Ungerleider, L. G. (1994). The acquisition and retention of a motor skill: A functional MRI study of long-term motor cortex plasticity. *Abstracts of the Society for Neuroscience, 20,* 1291.

Karni, A., Meyer, G., Rey-Hipolito, C., Jezzard, P., Adams, M. M., Turner, R., & Ungerleider, L. G. (1998). The acquisition of skilled motor performance: Fast and slow experience-driven changes in primary motor cortex. *Proceedings of the National Academy of Science USA, 95,* 861–868.

Karni, A., Tanne, D., Rubenstein, B. S., Askenasy, J. J. M., & Sagi, D. (1994). Dependence on REM sleep of overnight improvement of a perceptual skill. *Science, 265,* 679–682.

Karon, B. P., & Widener, A. J. (1997). Repressed memories and World War II: Lest we forget. *Professional Psychology: Research and Practice, 28*(4), 338–340.

Karp, D. A. (1991). A decade of reminders: Changing age consciousness between fifty and sixty years old. In B. B. Hess & E. W. Markson (Eds.), *Growing old in America* (pp. 67–92). New Brunswick, NJ: Transaction.

Kassin, S. M. (1997). The psychology of confession evidence. *American Psychologist, 52,* 221–233.

Kassin, S. M., Rigby, S., & Castillo, S. R. (1991). The accuracy-confidence correlation in eyewitness testimony: Limits and extensions of the retrospective self-awareness effect. *Journal of Personality and Social Psychology, 61,* 698–707.

Kastenbaum, R., Kastenbaum, B. K., & Morris, J. (1989). *Strengths and preferences of the terminally ill: Data from the National Hospice Demonstration Study.*

Kato, S., Wakasa, Y., & Yamagita, T. (1987). Relationship between minimum reinforcing doses and injection speed in cocaine and pentobarbital self-administration in crab-eating monkeys. *Pharmacology, Biochemistry, and Behavior, 28,* 407–410.

Katz, S. E., & Landis, C. (1935). Psychologic and physiologic phenomena during a prolonged vigil. *Archives of Neurology and Psyciatry, 34,* 307–317.

Katzell, R. A., & Thompson, D. E. (1990). Work motivation: Theory and practice. *American Psychologist, 45,* 144–153.

Kauffman, N. A., Herman, C. P., & Polivy, J. (1995). Hunger–induced finickiness in humans. *Appetite, 24,* 203–218.

Kaufman, M. H. (1997). The teratogenic effects of alcohol following exposure during pregnancy, and its influence on the chromosome constitution of the pre-ovulatory egg. *Alcohol and Alcoholism, 32,* 113–128.

Kavanagh, D. J. (1992). Recent developments in expressed emotion in schizophrenia. *British Journal of Psychiatry, 160,* 601–620.

Kawachi, I., Colditz, G. A., & Stone, C. B. (1994). Does drinking coffee increase the risk of coronary heart disease? Results from a meta-analysis. *British Heart Journal, 72(3),* 269–275.

Kawakami, K., Dion, K. L., & Dovidio, J. F. (1998). Racial prejudice and stereotype activation. *Personality and Social Psychology Bulletin, 24,* 407–416.

Kaye, J. A., Swihart, T., Howieson, D., Dame, A., Moore, M. M., Karnos, T., Camicioli, R., Ball, M., Oken, B., & Sexton, G. (1997). Volume loss of the hippocampus and temporal lobe in healthy elderly persons destined to develop dementia. *Neurology, 48,* 1297–1304.

Kaye, W. H., Gwirtsman, H. E., George, D. T., & Jimerson, D. C. (1988). CSF 5-HIAA concentrations in anorexia nervosa: Reduced values in underweight subjects normalize after weight gain. *Biological Psychiatry, 23(1),* 102–105.

Kazdin, A. E. (1994a). *Behavior modification in applied settings* (5th ed.). Pacific Grove, CA: Brooks/Cole.

Kazdin, A. E. (1994b). Methodology, design, and evaluation in psychotherapy research. In A. E. Bergin & S. L. Garfield (Eds.), *Handbook of psychotherapy and behavior change.* New York: Wiley.

Kazdin, A. E., & Weisz, J. R. (1998). Identifying and developing empirically supported child and adolescent treatments. *Journal of Consulting and Clinical Psychology, 66,* 19–36.

Keating, D. P. (1990). Adolescent thinking. In S. S. Feldman & G. R. Elliott (Eds.), *At the threshold: The developing adolescent* (pp. 4–89). Cambridge, MA: Harvard University Press.

Keeling, P. J., & Roger, A. J. (1995). The selfish pursuit of sex. *Nature, 375,* 283.

Keesey, R. E., & Powley, T. L. (1975). Hypothalamic regulation of body weight. *American Scientist, 63,* 558–565.

Keesey, R. E., & Powley, T. L. (1986). The regulation of body weight. *Annual Review of Psychology, 37,* 109–133.

Kehoe, E. J., & Macrae, M. (1998). Classical conditioning. In W. O'Donohue (Ed.), *Learning and behavior therapy* (pp. 36–58). Boston: Allyn & Bacon.

Keinan, G., Friedland, N., & Ben-Porath, Y. (1987). Decision making under stress: Scanning of alternatives under physical threat. *Acta Psychologica, 64,* 219–228.

Keller, A., Ford, L. H., & Meacham, J. A. (1978). Dimensions of self-concept in preschool children. *Developmental Psychology, 14,* 483–489.

Kelley, K. W. (1985). Immunological consequences of changing environmental stimuli. In G. P. Moberg (Ed.), *Animal stress.* Bethesda, MD: American Physiological Society.

Kellman, P. J., & Banks, M. S. (1998). Infant visual perception. In W. Damon, D. Kuhn, & R. Siegler (Eds.), *Handbook of child psychology: Vol. 2. Cognition, language and perception* (5th ed., pp. 103–146). New York: Wiley.

Kelly, G. A. (1980). A psychology of the optimal man. In A. W. Landfield & L. M. Leitner (Eds.), *Personal construct psychology: Psychotherapy and personality.* New York: Wiley.

Kelly, H. H. (1973). The processes of causal attribution. *American Psychologist, 28,* 107–128.

Kelly, J. A., Sikkema, K. J., Winett, R. A., Solomon, L. J., Roffman, R. A., Heckman, T. G., Stevenson, L. Y., Perry, M. J., Norman, A. D., & Desiderato, L. J. (1995). Factors predicting continued high-risk behavior among gay men in small cities: Psychological, behavioral, and demographic characteristics related to unsafe sex. *Journal of Consulting and Clinical Psychology, 63,* 101–107.

Kelly, T. H., Foltin, R. W., Emurian, C. S., & Fischman, M. W. (1990). Multidimensional behavioral effects of marijuana. *Progress in Neuro-Psychopharmacology and Biological Psychiatry, 14,* 885–902.

Kemeny, M. E., & Dean, L. (1995). Effects of AIDS-related bereavement on HIV progression among New York City gay men. *AIDS Education and Prevention, 7,* 36–47.

Kempermann, G., Kuhn, H. G., & Gage, F. H. (1997). More hippocampal neurons in adult mice living in an enriched environment. *Nature, 386,* 493–495.

Kendall-Tackett, K. A., Williams, L. M., & Finkelhor, D. (1993). Impact of sexual abuse on children: A review and synthesis of recent empirical studies. *Psychological Bulletin, 113,* 164–180.

Kendler, K., & Diehl, N. S. (1993). The genetics of schizophrenia: A current genetic-epidemiologic perspective. *Schizophrenia Bulletin, 19,* 87–112.

Kendler, K. S., Kessler, R. C., Walters, E. E., MacLean, C., Neale, M. C., Heath, A. C., & Eaves, L. J. (1995). Stressful life events, genetic liability, and onset of an episode of major depression in women. *American Journal of Psychiatry, 152,* 833–842.

Kendler, K. S., Neale, M. C., Kessler, R. C., Heath, A. C., & Eaves, L. J. (1992). Major depression and generalized anxiety disorder: Same genes, (partly) different environments? *Archives of General Psychiatry, 49,* 716–722.

Kenrick, D. T. (1994). Evolutionary social psychology: From sexual selection to social cognition. In M. Zanna (Ed.), *Advances in experimental social psychology* (Vol. 26, pp. 75–122). San Diego, CA: Academic Press.

Kenrick, D. T., Groth, G., Trost, M., & Sadalla, E. K. (1993). Integrating evolutionary and social exchange perspectives on relationships: Effects of gender, self-appraisal, and involvement level on mate selection. *Journal of Personality and Social Psychology, 64,* 951–969.

Kenrick, D. T., Keefe, R. C., Bryan, A. Barr, A., & Brown, S. (1995). Age preferences and mate choice among homosexuals and heterosexuals: A case for modular psychological mechanisms. *Journal of Personality and Social Psychology, 69,* 1166–1172.

Kenrick, D. T., & Trost, M. R. (1997). Evolutionary approaches to relationships. In S. Duck (Ed.), *Handbook of personal relationships: Theory, research and interventions* (2nd ed., pp. 151–177). Chichester, Eng.: John Wiley & Sons.

Kent, S., Rodriguez, F., Kelley, K. W., & Dantzer, R. (1994). Reduction in food and water intake induced by microinjection of interleukin-1b in the ventromedial hypothalamus of the rat. *Physiology and Behavior, 56(5),* 1031–1036.

Kernberg, O. (1976). *Object relations theory and clinical psychoanalysis.* New York: Jason Aronsen.

Kerns, K. (1991). Data-link communication between controllers and pilots: A review and synthesis of the simulation literature. *International Journal of Aviation Psychology, 1,* 181–204.

Kessel, R. C., & Kardon, R. H. (1979). *Tissues and organs: A text atlas of scanning electron microscopy.* San Francisco: Freeman.

Kessler, R. (1997). The effects of stressful life events on depression. In J. T. Spence, J. M. Darley, & D. J. Foss (Eds.), *Annual Review of Psychology, 48,* 191–214.

Kessler, R. C., McGonagle, K. A., Zhao, S., Nelson, C. B., Hughes, M., Eshleman, S., Wittchen, H. U., & Kendler, K. S. (1994). Lifetime and 12-month prevalence of DSM-III-R psychiatric disorders in the United States. *Archives of General Psychiatry, 51,* 8–19.

Kety, S. S., Wender, P. H., Jacobsen, B., Ingraham, L. J., Jansson, L., Faber, B., & Kinney, D. K. (1994). Mental illness in the biological and adoptive relatives of schizophrenic adoptees. *Archives of General Psychiatry, 51,* 442–455.

Kiecolt-Glaser, J. K., & Glaser, R., (1992). Psychoneuroimmunology: Can psychological interventions modulate immunity? *Journal of Consulting and Clinical Psychology, 60,* 569–575.

Kiecolt-Glaser, J. K., Page, G. G., Marucha, P. T., MacCallum, R. C., & Glaser, R. (1998). Psychological influences on surgical recovery: Perspectives from psychoneuroimmunology. *American Psychologist, 53,* 1290–1218.

Kiesler, D. J. (1996). *Contemporary interpersonal theory and research.* New York: John Wiley & Sons.

Kiesler, S., & Sproull, L. (1992). Group decision making and communications technology. *Organizational Behavior and Human Decision Processes, 52,* 96–123.

Kiewra, K. A. (1989). A review of note-taking: The encoding storage paradigm and beyond. *Educational Psychology Review, 1,* 147–172.

Kihlstrom, J. F. (1993). What does the self look like? In T. K. Srull & R. S. Wyer (Eds.), *The mental representation of trait and autobiographical knowledge about the self: Advances in social cognition: Vol. V.* Hillsdale, NJ: Lawrence Erlbaum Associates.

Kihlstrom, J. F. (1995). The trauma-memory argument. *Consciousness and Cognition, 4,* 63–67.

Kihlstrom, J. F. (1996). Unconscious processes in social interaction. In S. R. Hameroff, A. W. Kaszniak, A. C. Scott. (Eds.), *Toward a science of consciousness: The first Tucson discussions and debates. Complex adaptive systems* (pp. 93–104). Cambridge, MA: MIT Press.

Kihlstrom, J. F., & Klein, S. B. (1994). The self as a knowledge structure. In R. S. Wyer & T. K. Srull (Eds.), *Handbook of social cognition* (2nd ed.). Hillsdale, NJ: Lawrence Erlbaum Associates.

Kilgard, M. P., & Merzenich, M. M. (1998). Cortical map reorganization enabled by nucleus basalis activity. *Science, 279,* 1714–1718.

Kinney, H. C., Korein, J., Panigrahy, A., Dikkes, P., & Goode, R. (1994). Neuropathological findings in the brain of Karen Ann Quinlan: The role of the thalamus in the persistent vegetative state. *New England Journal of Medicine, 330*(21), 1469–1475.

Kinnunen, T., Zamansky, H. S., & Block, M. L. (1994). Is the hypnotized subject lying? *Journal of Abnormal Psychology, 103*(2), 184–191.

Kinsey, A. C., Pomeroy, W. B., & Martin, C. E. (1948). *Sexual behavior in the human male.* Philadelphia: Saunders.

Kinsey, A. C., Pomeroy, W. B., Martin, C. E., & Gebhard, P. H. (1953). *Sexual behavior in the human female.* Philadelphia: Saunders.

Kirchler, E., & Zani, B. (1995). Why don't they stay home? Prejudice against ethnic minorities in Italy. *Journal of Community and Applied Social Psychology, 5,* 59–65.

Kirk, S. A., & Kutchins, H. (1992). *The selling of DSM. The rhetoric of science in psychiatry.* New York: Aldine de Gruyter.

Kirn, J. R., & Schwabl, H. (1997). Photoperiod regulation of neuron death in the adult canary. *Journal of Neurobiology, 33,* 223–231.

Kirsch, I. (1994a). Defining hypnosis for the public. *Contemporary Hypnosis, 11*(3), 142–143.

Kirsch, I. (1994b). Clinical hypnosis as a nondeceptive placebo: Empirically derived techniques. *American Journal of Clinical Hypnosis, 37*(2), 95–106.

Kirsch, I., & Lynn, S. J. (1995). The altered state of hypnosis: Changes in theoretical landscape. *The American Psychologist, 50,* 846–858.

Kirschenbaum, D. S., & Fitzgibbons, M. L. (1995). *Behavior Therapy, 26*(1), 43–68.

Kishioka, S., Miyamoto, Y., Fukunaga, Y., Nishida, S., & Yamamoto, H. (1994). Effects of a mixture of peptidase inhibitors (Amastatin, Captopril and Phosphoramidon) on met enkephalin, beta-endorphin, dynorphin (1–13) and electroacupuncture-induced antinociception in rats. *Japanese Journal of Pharmacology, 1994, 66,* 337–345.

Kitano, H., Chi, I., Rhee, S., Law, C., & Lubben, J. (1992). Norms and alcohol consumption: Japanese in Japan, Hawaii, and California. *Journal of Studies on Alcohol, 53,* 33–39.

Kitayama, S., Markus, H. R., Matsumoto, H., & Norasakkunkit, V. (1997). Individual and collective processes in the construction of the self: Self-enhancement in the United States and self-criticism in Japan. *Journal of Personality and Social Psychology, 72,* 1245–1267.

Klatzky, R. L. (1980). *Human memory: Structures and processes* (2nd ed.). San Francisco: W. H. Freeman.

Klaus, M. H., & Kennell, J. H. (1976). *Maternal infant bonding: The impact of early separation or loss on family development.* St. Louis: Mosby.

Klein, D. C., & Seligman, M. E. P. (1976). Reversal of performance deficits and perceptual deficits in learned helplessness and depression. *Journal of Abnormal Psychology, 85,* 11–26.

Klein, D. N. (1993). False suffocation alarms, spontaneous panics, and related conditions: An integrative hypothesis. *Archives of General Psychiatry, 50,* 306–316.

Klein, G. (1997). The recognition-primed decision (RPD) model: Looking back, looking forward. In C. E. Zsambok & G. Klein (Eds.), *Naturalistic decision making* (pp. 285–292). Mahwah, NJ: Lawrence Erlbaum Associates.

Klein, J. G. (1991). Negativity effects in impression formation: A test in the political arena. *Personality and Social Psychology Bulletin, 17,* 412–418.

Klein, M. (1960). *The psychoanalysis of children.* New York: Grove Press.

Klein, M. (1991). The emotional life and ego-development of the infant with special reference to the depressive position. In P. King & R. Steiner (Eds.), *The Klein-Freud controversies: 1941–1945* (pp. 752–777). London: Tavistock/Routledge.

Kleinknecht, R. A. (1991). *Mastering anxiety: The nature and treatment of anxious conditions.* New York: Plenum.

Kleinman, A. (1991, April). *Culture and DSM-IV: Recommendations for the introduction and for the overall structure.* Paper presented at the National Institute of Mental Health–sponsored Conference on Culture and Diagnosis, Pittsburgh, PA.

Klepp, K.-I., Kelder, S. H., & Perry, C. L. (1995). Alcohol and marijuana use among adolescents: Long-term outcomes of the class of 1989 study. *Annals of Behavioral Medicine, 17,* 19–24.

Klerman, G. L., & Weissman, M. M. (Eds.). (1993). *New applications of interpersonal therapy.* Washington, DC: American Psychiatric Press.

Klesges, R. C., Shelton, M. L., & Klesges, L. M. (1993). Effects of television on metabolic rate: Potential implications for childhood obesity. *Pediatrics, 91,* 281–286.

Klich, N. R., & Feldman, D. C. (1992). The role of approcal and achievement needs in feedback-seeking behavior. *Journal of Managerial Issues, 4*(4), 554–570.

Kline, S., & Groninger, L. D. (1991). The imagery bizarreness effect as a function of sentence complexity and presentation time. *Bulletin of the Psychonomic Society, 29,* 25–27.

Klinger, M. R., & Greenwald, A. G. (1995). Unconscious priming of association judgements. *Journal of Experimental Psychology: Learning, Memory, and Cognition, 21*(3), 569–581.

Klosko, J. S., Barlow, D. H., Tassinari, R., & Cerny, J. A. (1990). A comparison of alprazolam and behavior therapy in treatment of panic disorder. *Journal of Consulting and Clinical Psychology, 58,* 77–84.

Kluger, A. N., & DeNisi, A. (1998). Feedback interventions: Toward the understanding of a double-edged sword. *Current Directions in Psychological Science, 7,* 67–72.

Knapp, S., & VandeCreek, L. (1997). Jaffee v. Redmond: The Supreme Court recognizes a psychotherapist-patient privilege in federal courts. *Professional Psychology: Research and Practice, 28,* 567–572.

Koch, C., & Davis, J. L. (Eds.). (1994). *Large-scale neuronal theories of the brain.* Cambridge, MA: MIT Press.

Koelega, H. S. (1993). Stimulant drugs and vigilance performance: A review. *Psychopharmacology, 111*(1), 1–16.

Koenigsberg, H. W. (1994). The combination of psychotherapy and pharmacotherapy in the treatment of borderline patients. *Journal of Psychotherapy Practice and Research, 3*(2), 93–107.

Koepp, M. J., Gunn, R. N., Lawrence, A. D., Cunningham, V. J., Dagher, A., Jones, T., Brooks, D. J., Bench, C. J., & Grasby, P. M. (1998). Evidence for striatal dopamine release during a video game. *Nature, 393,* 266–268.

Kohlberg, L., & Gilligan, C. (1971). The adolescent as a philosopher: The discovery of the self in a postconventional world. *Daedalus, 100,* 1051–1086.

Köhler, W. (1924). *The mentality of apes.* New York: Harcourt Brace.

Kohut, H. (1971). *Analysis of the self.* New York: International Universities Press.

Kohut, H. (1984). Selected problems of self-psychological theory. In J. D. Lichtenberg & S. Kaplan (Eds.), *Reflections on self psychology* (pp. 387–416). Hillsdale, NJ: Lawrence Erlbaum Associates.

Komatsu, S.-I., & Naito, M. (1992). Repetition priming with Japanese Kana scripts in word-fragment completion. *Memory & Cognition, 20,* 160–170.

Komorita, S. S. (1984). Coalition bargaining. In L. Berkowitz (Ed.), *Advances in experimental social psychology: Vol. 18.* New York: Academic Press.

Komorita, S. S., & Parks, C. D. (1995). Interpersonal relations: Mixed-motive interaction. *Annual Review of Psychology, 46,* 183–207.

Konkol, R. J., Murphey, L. J., Ferriero, D. M., Dempsey, D. A., & Olsen, G. D. (1994). Cocaine metabolites in the neonate: Potential for toxicity. *Journal of Child Neurology, 9*(3), 242–248.

Koob, G. F., & Bloom, F. E. (1988). Cellular and molecular mechanisms of drug dependence. *Science, 242,* 715–723.

Koob, G. F., Roberts, A. J., Schulteis, G., Parsons, L. H., Heyser, C. J., Hyytia, P., Merlo-Pich, E., & Weiss, F. (1998). Neurocircuitry targets in ethanol reward and dependence. *Alcohol: Clinical and Experimental Research, 22*(1), 3–9.

Koocher, G. P. (1995). Ethics in psychotherapy. In B. Bongar & L. E. Beutler (Eds.), *Comprehensive textbook of psychotherapy: Theory and practice* (pp. 456–473). New York: Oxford University Press.

Koppenaal, L., & Glanzer, M. (1990). An examination of the continuous distractor task and the "long-term recency effect." *Memory & Cognition, 18,* 183–195.

Kordower, J. H., Freeman, T. B., Snow, B. J., Vingerhoets, F. J. G., Mufson, E. J., Sanberg, P. R., Hauser, R. A., Smith, D. A., Nauert, G. M., Perl, D. P., & Olanow, C. W. (1995). Neuropathological evidence of graft survival and striatal reinnervation after the transplantation of fetal mesencephalic tissue in a patient with Parkinson's disease. *The New England Journal of Medicine, 332,* 1118–1124.

Korteling, J. (1991). Effects of skill integration and perceptual competition on age-related differences in dual-task performance. *Human Factors, 33,* 35–44.

Kosslyn, S. M. (1976). Can imagery be distinguished from other forms of internal representation? Evidence from studies of information retrieval times. *Memory & Cognition, 4,* 291–297.

Kosslyn, S. M. (1988). Aspects of a cognitive neuroscience of mental imagery. *Science, 240,* 1621–1626.

Kosslyn, S. M. (1994a). *Image and brain: The resolution of the imagery debate.* Cambridge, MA: MIT Press.

Kosslyn, S. M. (1994b). *Image and mind.* Cambridge, MA: Harvard University Press.

Kraft, C. (1978). A psychophysical approach to air safety: Simulator studies of visual illusions in night approaches. In H. L. Pick, H. W. Leibowitz, J. E. Singer, A. Steinschneider, & H. W. Stevenson (Eds.), *Psychology: From research to practice.* New York: Plenum.

Kraft, J. M. (1996). Prenatal alcohol consumption and outcomes for children: A review of the literature. In R. L. Parrott & C. M. Condit (Eds.), *Evaluating women's health messages: A resource book* (pp. 175–189). Thousand Oaks, CA: Sage.

Krakauer, J. (1997). *Into thin air.* New York: Villard.

Kramer, A., Larish, J., & Strayer, D. (1995). Training for attentional control in dual task settings: A comparison of young and old adults. *Journal of Experimental Psychology: Applied, 2,* 50–76.

Krantz, D., Contrada, R., Hill, D., & Friedler, E. (1988). Environmental stress and biobehavioral antecedents of coronary heart disease. *Journal of Consulting and Clinical Psychology, 56,* 333–341.

Krantz, D., & Durel, L. (1983). Psychobiological substrates of the Type A behavior pattern. *Health Psychology, 2,* 393–411.

Kranzler, H. R., & Anton, R. F. (1994). Implications of recent neuropsychopharmacologic research for understanding the etiology and development of alcoholism. *Journal of Consulting and Clinical Psychology, 62,* 1116–1126.

Kraus, S. J. (1995). Attitudes and the prediction of behavior: A meta-analysis of the empirical literature. *Personality and Social Psychology Bulletin, 21,* 58–75.

Krauzlis, R. J., & Lisberger, S. G. (1991). Visual motion commands for pursuit eye movements in the cerebellum. *Science, 253,* 568–571.

Krebs, R. L. (1967). *Some relations between moral judgment, attention, and resistance to temptation.* Unpublished doctoral dissertation, University of Chicago, Chicago, IL.

Krechevsky, M., & Gardner, H. (1994). Multiple intelligences in multiple contexts. In D. K. Detterman (Ed.), *Current topics in human intelligence* (Vol. 4). Norwood, NJ: Ablex.

Kristof, N. D. (1997, August 17). Where children rule. *New York Times Magazine.*

Krosnick, J. A., Betz, A. L., Jussim, L. J., & Lynn, A. R. (1992). Subliminal conditioning of attitudes. *Personality and Social Psychology Bulletin, 18,* 152–162.

Krueger, J. (1998). Enhancement bias in descriptions of self and others. *Personality and Social Psychology Bulletin, 24,* 505–516.

Krykouli, S. E., Stanley, B. G., Seirafi, R. D., & Leibowitz, S. F (1990). Stimulation of feeding by galanin: Anatomical localization and behavioral specificity of this peptide's effects in the brain. *Peptides, 11*(5), 995–1001.

Kubler-Ross, E. (1975). *Death: The final stage of growth.* Englewood Cliffs, NJ: Prentice-Hall.

Kuhs, H., & Tolle, R. (1991). Sleep deprivation therapy. *Biological Psychiatry, 29,* 1129–1148.

Kulynych, J. J., & Stromberg, C. (1998). Legal Update #11: Telecommunication in psychological practice. *Register Report, 24*(1/2), 9–18.

Kunkel, D., Wilson, B. J., Linz, D., Potter, J., Donnerstein, E., Smith, S. L., Blumenthal, E., & Gray, T. (1996). *The national television violence study.* Studio City, CA: Mediascope.

Kunz, P. R., & Woolcott, M. (1976). Season's greetings: From my status to yours. *Social Science Research, 5,* 269–278.

Kurtz, L. F. (1997). *Self-help and support groups: A handbook for practitioners.* Thousand Oaks, CA: Sage.

Kutchins, H., & Kirk, S. A. (1997). *Making us crazy: The psychiatric bible and the creation of mental disorders.* New York: Free Press.

Kwan, M., Greenleaf, W. J., Mann, J., Crapo, L., & Davidson, J. M. (1983). The nature of androgen action on male sexuality: A combined laboratory-self-report study on hypogonadal men. *Journal of Clinical Endocrinology and Metabolism, 57,* 557–562.

Kwan, V. S. Y., Bond, M. H., & Singelis, T. M. (1997). Pancultural explanations for life satisfaction: Adding relationship harmony to self-esteem. *Journal of Personality and Social Psychology, 73,* 1038–1051.

Kyriacou, C. P. (1994). Working round the clock with mouse 25. *Trends in Neuroscience, 17*(8), 313–314.

Laan, E., Everaerd, W., Van Aanhold, M. T., & Rebel, M. (1993). Performance demand and sexual arousal in woman. *Behavior Research and Therapy, 31,* 25–36.

LaBar, K. S., Gatenby, J. C., Gore, J. C., LeDoux, J. E., & Phelps, E. A. (1998). Human amygdala activation during conditioned fear acquisition and extinction: A mixed-trial fMRI study. *Neuron, 20,* 937–945.

LaBerge, S. (1993). Lucid dreaming. In M. Carskadon (Ed.), *Encyclopedia of sleep and dreaming* (pp. 338–341). New York: Macmillan.

Labouvie-Vief, G. (1992). A new-Piagetian perspective on adult cognitive development. In R. J. Sternberg & C. A. Berg (Eds.), *Intellectual development.* New York: Cambridge University Press.

Labouvie-Vief, G. (1982). Discontinuities in development from childhood. In T. M. Field, A. Huston, H. C. Quay, L. Troll, & G. E. Finley (Eds.), *Review of human development.* New York: Wiley.

Lacayo, A. (1995). Neurologic and psychiatric complications of cocaine abuse. *Neuropsychiatry, Neuropsychology, and Behavioral Neurology, 8*(1), 53–60.

Lacayo, R. (1995, June 12). Violent reaction. *Time, 145*(24), 38–44.

Lachman, R., Lachman, J. L., & Butterfield, E. C. (1979). *Cognitive psychology and information processing.* Hillsdale, NJ: Lawrence Erlbaum Associates.

Ladd, G. W., & LeSieur, K. D. (1995). Parents and children's peer relationships. In M. H. Bornstein (Ed.), *Handbook of parenting: Vol. 4. Applied and practical parenting* (pp. 377–409). Mahwah, NJ: Lawrence Erlbaum Associates.

Laforge, R. G., Greene, G. W., & Prochaska, J. O. (1994). Psychosocial factors influencing low fruit and vegetable consumption. *Journal of Behavioral Medicine, 17,* 361–388.

LaFromboise, T. D., Foster, S., & James, A. (1996). *Ethics in multicultural counseling.* Thousand Oaks, CA: Sage.

Lagerspetz, K. M. J., & Lagerspetz, K. Y. H. (1983). Genes and aggression. In E. C. Simmel, M. E. Hahn, & J. K. Walters (Eds.), *Aggressive behavior: Genetic and neural approaches.* Hillsdale, NJ: Lawrence Erlbaum Associates.

Lahey, B. B., Loeber, R., Hart, E. L., Frick, P. J., & Applegate, B. (1995). Four-year longitudinal study of conduct disorder in boys: Patterns and predictors of persistence. *Journal of Abnormal Psychology, 104,* 83–93.

LaHoste, G. J., Swanson, J. M., Wigal, S. S., Glabe, C., Wigal, T., King, N., & Kennedy, J. L. (1996). Dopamine D4 receptor gene polymorphism is associated with attention deficit hyperactivity disorder. *Molecular Psychiatry, 1,* 128–131.

Lamb, M., & Sternberg, K. M. (1990). Do we really know how day care affects children? *Journal of Applied and Developmental Psychology, 11,* 351–379.

Lamb, M. E. (1976). Parent-infant interaction in 8-month-olds. *Child Psychiatry and Human Development, 7,* 56–63.

Lamb, M. E. (1998). Assessments of children's credibility in forensic contexts. *Current Directions in Psychological Science, 7,* 43–46.

Lambert, M. J. (1989). The individual therapist's contribution to psychotherapy process and outcome. *Clinical Psychology Review, 9,* 469–486.

Lambert, M. J., & Bergin, A. E. (1994). The effectiveness of psychotherapy. In A. E. Bergin & S. L. Garfield (Eds.), *Handbook of psychotherapy and behavior change* (4th ed.). New York: Wiley.

Lambert, M. J., & Hill, C. E. (1994). Assessing psychotherapy outcomes and processes. In A. E. Bergin & S. L. Garfield (Eds.), *Handbook of psychotherapy and behavior change* (4th ed.). New York: Wiley.

Land, M. F., & Fernald, R. D. (1992). The volution of eyes. Annual *Review of Neuroscience, 15,* 1–29.

Landau, B. (1986). Early map use as an unlearned ability. *Cognition, 22,* 201–223.

Landrine, H. (1991). Revising the framework of abnormal psychology. In P. Bronstein & K. Quina (Eds.), *Teaching a psychology of people.* Washington, DC: American Psychological Association.

Landsdale, M., & Laming, D. (1995). Evaluating the fragmentation hypothesis: The analysis of errors in cued recall. *Acta Psychologica, 88,* 33–77.

Lang, A. R., Goeckner, D. J., Adesso, V. J., & Marlatt, G. A. (1975). Effects of alcohol on aggression in male social drinkers. *Journal of Abnormal Psychology, 84,* 508–518.

Lang, P. J. (1995). The emotion probe: Studies of motivation and attention. *American Psychologist, 50*(5), 372–385.

Lang, P. J., & Melamed, B. G. (1969). Avoidance conditioning therapy of an infant with chronic ruminative vomiting. *Journal of Abnormal Psychology, 74,* 1–8.

Langer, E. J., Beck, P., Janoff-Bulman, R., & Timko, C. (1984). An exploration of relationships among mindfulness, longevity, and senility. *Academic Psychology Bulletin, 6,* 211–226.

Lanyon, R. I., & Goodstein, L. D. (1997). *Personality assessment* (3rd ed.). New York: Wiley.

Lapointe, L. (1990). *Aphasia and related neurogenic language disorders.* New York: Thieme Medical Publishers.

Larson, G. E., & Saccuzzo, D. P. (1989). Cognitive correlates of general intelligence: Toward a process theory of g. *Intelligence, 13,* 5–32.

Larson, J. R., Jr., Christensen, C., Franz, T. M., & Abbott, A. S. (in press). Diagnosing: The pooling, management, and impact of shared and unshared case information in team-based medical decision making. *Journal of Personality and Social Psychology.*

Larson, M. C., Gunnar, M. R., & Hertsgaard, L. (1991). The effects of morning naps, car trips, and maternal separation on adrenocortical activity in human infants. *Child Development, 62,* 362–372.

Larzelere, R. E. (1996). A review of the outcomes of parental use of nonabusive or customary physical punishment. *Pediatrics, 98,* 824–828.

Lashley, K. S. (1950). In search of the engram. *Symposium of the Society of Experimental Biology, 4,* 454–482.

Latané, B. (1981). The psychology of social impact. *American Psychologist, 36,* 343–356.

Latané, B., & Rodin, J. (1969). A lady in distress: Inhibiting effects of friends and strangers on bystander intervention. *Journal of Experimental Social Psychology, 5,* 189–202.

Lau, M. A., Pihl, R. O., & Peterson, J. B. (1995). Provocation, acute alcohol intoxication, cognitive performance, and aggression. *Journal of Abnormal Psychology, 104,* 150–155.

Laumann, E. O., Gagnon, J. H., Michael, R. T., & Michaels, S. (1994). *The social organization of sexuality: Sexual practices in the United States.* Chicago: University of Chicago Press.

Law, D. J., Pellegrino, J. W., & Hunt, E. B. (1993). Comparing the tortoise and the hare: Gender differences and experience in dynamic spatial reasoning tasks. *Psychological Science, 4,* 35–40.

Lawford, B. R., Young, R. M., Rowell, J. A., Qualichefski, J., Fletcher, B. H., Syndulko, K., Ritchie, T., & Noble, E. P. (1995). Bromocriptine in the treatment of alcoholics with the D_2 dopamine receptor A_1 allele. *Nature Medicine, 1*(4), 337–341.

Lawless, H. T., & Engen, T. (1977). Associations to odors: Interference, memories and verbal learning. *Journal of Experimental Psychology, 3,* 52–59.

Lazarus, A. A. (1971). *Behavior therapy and beyond.* New York: McGraw-Hill.

Lazarus, R. S., & Folkman, S. (1984). *Stress, appraisal, and coping.* New York: Springer-Verlag.

Lazarus, R. S., Opton, E. M., Nomikos, M. S., & Rankin, M. O. (1965). The principle of short-circuiting of threat: Further evidence. *Journal of Personality, 33,* 622–635.

Leaper, C., Anderson, K. J., & Sanders, P. (1998). Moderators of gender effects on parents' talk to their children: A meta-analysis. *Developmental Psychology, 34,* 3–27.

LeDoux, J. E. (1995). Emotion: Clues from the brain. *Annual Review of Psychology, 46,* 209–235.

Lee, V. E., Brooks-Gunn, J., & Schnur, E. (1988). Does Head Start work? A 1-year follow-up comparison of disadvantaged children attending Head Start, no preschool, and other preschool programs. *Developmental Psychology, 24,* 210–222.

Lefcourt, H. M., Davidson, K., Prkachin, K. M., & Mills, D. E. (1997). Humor as a stress moderator in the prediction of blood pressure obtained during five stressful tasks. *Journal of Research in Personality, 31,* 523–542.

Legerstee, M., Anderson, D., & Schaffer, A. (1998). Five- and eight-month-old infants recognize their faces and voices as familiar and social stimuli. *Child Development, 69,* 37–50.

Lehman, H. E. (1967). Schizophrenia: IV. Clinical features. In A. M. Freedman, H. I. Kaplan, & H. S. Kaplan (Eds.), *Comprehensive textbook of psychiatry.* Baltimore: Williams & Wilkins.

Leibel, R. L., Rosenbaum, M., & Hirsch, J. (1995). Changes in energy expenditure resulting from altered body weight. *New England Journal of Medicine, 332*(10), 621–628.

Leibowitz, H. W., Brislin, R., Perlmutter, L., & Hennessy, R. (1969). Ponzo perspective illusion as a manifestation of space perception. *Science, 166,* 1174–1176.

Leibowitz, S. F., Xuereb, M., & Kim, T. (1992). Blockade of natural and neuropeptide Y-induced carbohydrate feeding by a receptor antagonist PYX-2. *Neuroreport: An international journal for the rapid communication of research in neuroscience, 3*(11), 1023–1026.

Leigh, B. C., Schafer, J., & Temple, M. T. (1995). Alcohol use and contraception in first sexual experiences. *Journal of Behavorial Medicine. 18*(1), 81–95.

Leiner, H. C., Leiner, A. L., & Dow, R. S. (1993). Cognitive and language functions of the human cerebellum. *Trends in Neuroscience, 16,* 444–447.

Leinhardt, G., Seewald, A., & Engel, M. (1979). Learning what's taught: Sex differences in instruction. *Journal of Educational Psychology, 71,* 432–439.

Leippe, M. R., Manion, A. P., & Romanczyk, A. (1992). Eyewitness persuasion: How and how well do fact finders judge the accuracy of adults' and children's memory reports? *Journal of Personality and Social Psychology, 63,* 181–197.

Lenneberg, E. H. (1967). *Biological foundations of language.* New York: Wiley.

Leonard, B. E. (1992). *Fundamentals of psychopharmacology.* New York: John Wiley & Sons.

Leonard, B. E. (1997). The role of noradrenaline in depression: A review. *Journal of Psychopharmacology (Oxford), 11,* S39–S47.

Lepore, L., & Brown, R. (1997). Category and stereotype activation: Is prejudice inevitable? *Journal of Personality and Social Psychology, 72,* 275–287.

Lepore, S. J., Evans, G., & Schneider, M. (1991). Dynamic role of social support in the link between chronic stress and psychological distress. *Journal of Personality and Social Psychology, 61,* 899–909.

Lepore, S. J. (1995a). Measurement of chronic stressors. In S. Cohen, R. C. Kessler, & L. U. Gordon (Eds.), *Measuring stress: A guide for health and social scientists.* New York: Oxford University Press.

Lepore, S. J. (1995b). Cynicism, social support, and cardiovascular reactivity. *Health Psychology, 14,* 210–216.

Lerman, C., Caporaso, N., Main, D., Audrain, J., Boyd, N. R., Bowman, E. D., & Shields, P. G. (1998). Depression and self-medication with nicotine: The modifying influence of the dopamine D4 receptor gene. *Health Psychology, 17,* 56–62.

Lesch, K. P., Bengel, D., Heils, A., Sabol, S., Z. Greenburg, B. D., Petri, S., Benjamin, J., Muller, C. R., Hamer, D. H., & Murphy, D. L. (1996). Association of anxiety-related traits with a polymorphism in the serotonin transporter gene regulatory region. *Science, 274,* 1527–1530.

Lettvin, J. Y., Maturana, H. R., McCulloch, W. S., & Pitts, W. H. (1959). What the frog's eye tells the frog's brain. *Proceedings of the Institute of Radio Engineers 47,* 1940–1951.

LeVay, S. (1991). A difference in hypothalamic structure between heterosexual and homosexual men. *Science, 253,* 1034–1037.

Levenson, H., & Strupp, H. H. (1997). Cyclical maladaptive patterns: Case formulation in time-limited dynamic psychotherapy. In T. D. Eells (Ed.), *Handbook of psychotherapy case formulation* (pp. 84–115). New York: Guilford.

Levenson, R. W., Ekman, P., & Friesen, W. V. (1990). Voluntary facial action generates emotion-specific autonomic nervous system activity. *Psychophysiology, 27*(4), 363–384.

Levenson, R. W., Ekman, P., Heider, K., & Friesen, W. V. (1992). Emotion and autonomic nervous system activity in the Minangkabau of West Sumatra. *Journal of Personality and Social Psychology, 62*(6), 972–988.

Levenson, R. W., & Ruef, A. M. (1992). Empathy: A physiological substrate. *Journal of Personality and Social Psychology, 63,* 234–246.

Leventhal, H., & Tomarken, A. J. (1986). Emotion: Today's problems. *Annual Review of Psychology, 37,* 565–610.

Levine, J. M. & Moreland, R. (1990). Progress in small group research. *Annual Review of Psychology, 41,* 55–63.

Levine, J. M., & Moreland, R. L. (1998). Small groups. In D. Gilbert, S. T. Fiske, and G. Lindzey (Eds.), *Handbook of social psychology,* Vol. 2 (4th ed., pp. 415–469). Boston: McGraw-Hill.

Levine, M. W., & Schefner, J. M. (1981). *Fundamentals of sensation and perception. Reading,* MA: Addison-Wesley.

Levine, R., Sato, S., Hashimoto, T., & Verna, J. (1995). Love and marriage in eleven cultures. *Journal of Cross-Cultural Psychology, 26,* 554–571.

Levine, R. V., Martinez, T. M., Brase, G., & Sorenson, K. (1994). Helping in 36 U.S. cities. *Journal of Personality and Social Psychology, 67,* 69–82.

Levinson, D. J., Darrow, C. N., Klein, E. B., Levinson, M. H., & McKee, B. (1978). *The seasons of a man's life.* New York: Knopf.

Levinson, S. C. (1996). Language and space. *Annual Review of Anthropology, 25,* 353–382.

Levinthal, C. F. (1996). *Drugs, behavior, and modern society.* Boston: Allyn & Bacon.

Levy, R. L., Cain, K. C., Jarrett, M., & Heitkemper, M. M. (1997). The relationship between daily life stress and gastrointestinal symptoms in women with irritable bowel syndrome. *Journal of Behavioral Medicine, 20,* 177–194.

Levy-Shiff, R. (1994). Individual and contextual correlates of marital change across the transition to parenthood. *Developmental Psychology, 30,* 591–601.

Lewicki, P. (1985). Nonconscious biasing of single instances of subsequent judgments. *Journal of Personality and Social Psychology, 48,* 563–574.

Lewicki, P. (1992). Nonconscious acquisition of information. *American Psychologist, 47,* 796–801

Lewinsohn, P. M., & Rosenbaum, M. (1987). Recall of parental behavior by acute depressives, remitted depressives, and nondepressives. *Journal of Personality and Social Psychology, 52,* 611–619.

Lewontin, R. (1976). Race and intelligence. In N. J. Block & G. Dworkin (Eds.), *The IQ controversy: Critical readings.* New York: Pantheon.

Ley, R. (1994). The "suffocation alarm" theory of panic attacks: A critical commentary. *Journal of Behavior Therapy and Experimental Psychiatry, 25,* 269–273.

Li, Y. J., & Low, W. C. (1997). Intraretrosplenial cortical grafts of fetal cholinergic neurons and the restoration of spatial memory function. *Cell Transplant, 6*(1), 85–93.

Liben, L. (1978). Perspective-taking skills in young children: Seeing the world through rose-colored glasses. *Developmental Psychology, 14,* 87–92.

Lichstein, K. L., & Riedel, B. W. (1994). Behavioral assessment and treatment of insomnia: A review with an emphasis on clinical application. *Behavior Therapy, 25,* 659–688.

Licht, B. G., & Dweck, C. S. (1984). Determinants of academic achievement: The interaction of children's achievement orientations with skill area. *Developmental Psychology, 20,* 628–636.

Lichtman, A. H., Dimen, K. R., & Martin, B. R. (1995). Systemic or intrahippocampal cannabinoid administration impairs spatial memory in rats. *Psychopharmacology, 119,* 282–290

Lichtman, S. W., Pisarska, K., Berman, E. R., Pestone, M., Dowling, H., Offenbacher, E., Weisel, H., Heshka, S., Matthews, D. E., & Heymsfield, S. B. (1992). Discrepancy between self-reported and actual caloric intake and exercise in obese subjects. *New England Journal of Medicine, 327,* 1893–1898.

Lickey, M., & Gordon, B. (1991). *Medicine and mental illness: The use of drugs in psychiatry.* San Francisco: W. H. Freeman.

Lieberman, A., & Pawl, J. (1988). Clinical applications of attachment theory. In J. Bellsky & T. Nezworski (Eds.), *Clinical applications of attachment.* Hillsdale, NJ: Lawrence Erlbaum Associates.

Lieberman, M. A. (1996). Perspective on adult life crises. In V. L. Bengtson (Ed.), *Adulthood and aging: Research on continuities and discontinuities* (pp. 146–168). New York: Springer Publishing.

Lieberman, M. A., & Tobin, S. (1983). *The experience of old age.* New York: Basic Books.

Lieberman, P. (1991). *Uniquely human.* Cambridge, MA: Harvard University Press.

Liebert, R., & Sprafkin, J. (1988). *The early window: Effects of television on children and youth* (3rd ed.). New york: Pergamon press.

Liebert, R. M., & Spiegler, M. D. (1994). *Personality: Strategies and issues.* Pacific Grow, CA: Brooks/Cole.

Lieppe, M. R., & Eisenstadt, D. (1994). Generalization of dissonance reduction: Decreasing prejudice throuh induced compliance. *Journal of Personality and Social Psychology, 67,* 395–413.

Light, L. L. (1991). Memory and aging: Four hypotheses in search of data. *Annual Review of Psychology, 42,* 333–376.

Lillywhite, A. R., Wilson, S. J., & Nutt, D. J. (1994). Successful treatment of night terrors and somnambulism with paroxetine. *British Journal of Psychiatry, 16,* 551–554.

Lima, S. D., Hale, S., & Myerson, J. (1991). How general is general slowing? Evidence from the lexical domain. *Psychology and Aging, 6,* 416–425.

Lin, K.-M., Poland, R., & Nakasaki, G. (1993). (Eds.). *Psychopharmacology and psychobiology of ethnicity.* Washington, DC: American Psychiatric Association Press.

Lin, L., Umahara, M., York, D. A., & Bray, G. A. (1998). Beta-casomorphins stimulate and enterostatin inhibits the intake of dietary fat in rats. *Peptides, 19,* 325–331.

Lindsey, K. P., & Paul, G. L. (1989). Involuntary commitments to public mental institutions: Issues involving the overrepresentation of blacks and assessment of relevant functioning. *Psychological Bulletin, 106,* 171–183.

Lintern, G. (1991). An informational perspective on skill transfer in human-machine systems. *Human Factors, 33,* 251–266.

Linville, P. W., & Carlston, D. E. (1994). Social cognition of the self. In P. G. Devine, D. L. Hamilton, & T. M. Ostrom (Eds.), *Social cognition: Impact on social psychology* (pp. 144–195). San Diego, CA: Academic Press.

Linz, D., Donnerstein, E., & Penrod, S. (1987). The findings and recommendations of the Attorney General's Commission on Pornography: Do the psychological facts fit the political fury? *American Psychologist, 42,* 946–953.

Linz, D., Wilson, B. J., & Donnerstein, E. (1992). Sexual violence in the mass media: Legal solutions, warnings, and mitigation through education. *Journal of Social Issues, 48,* 145–172.

Liu, C., Weaver, D. R., Jin, X., Shearman, L. P., Pieschl, R. L., Gribkoff, V. K., & Reppert, S. M. (1997). Molecular dissection of two distinct actions of melatonin on the suprachiasmatic circadian clock. *Neuron, 19,* 91–102.

Liu, L. G. (1985). Reasoning counterfactually in Chinese: Are there any obstacles? *Cognition, 21,* 239–270.

Livingstone, M. S., & Hubel, D. H. (1987). Psychological evidence for separate channels for the perception of form, color, movement and depth. *Journal of Neuroscience, 7,* 3416–3468.

Locurto, C. (1991a). Beyond IQ in preschool programs? *Intelligence, 15,* 295–312.

Locurto, C. (1991b). Hands on the elephant: IQ, preschool programs, and the rhetoric of inoculation—a reply to commentaries. *Intelligence, 15,* 335–349.

Loehlin, J. C. (1989). Partitioning environmental and genetic contributions to behavioral development. *American Psychologist, 44,* 1285–1292.

Loehlin, J. C. (1992). *Genes and environment in personality development.* Newbury Park, CA: Sage.

Loesh, K. P., Bongel, D., Heils, A., Zhang Sabol, S., Greenburg, B. D., Petri, S., Benjamin, J., Muller, C. R., Hamer, D. H., & Murphy, D. L. (1996). Association of anxiety-related traits with a polymorphism in the serotonin transporter gene regulatory region. *Science, 274,* 1527–1530.

Loevinger, J. (1997). Stages of personality development. In R. Hogan, J. Johnson, & S. Briggs (Eds.), *Handbook of personality psychology* (pp. 199–208). San Diego: Academic Press.

Loewenstein, G. (1994). The psychology of curiosity: A review and reinterpretation. *Psychological Bulletin, 116*(1), 75–98.

Loewi, O. (1921). Uber umorle Ubertragbarkeit der Herznervenwirkung I. Mitteilung. *Pflugers Archive, 189,* 239–242.

Loftus, E. F. (1979). *Eyewitness testimony.* Cambridge, MA: Harvard University Press.

Loftus, E. F. (1992). When a lie becomes memory's truth: Memory distortion after exposure to misinformation. *Psychological Science, 3,* 121–123.

Loftus, E. F. (1993). The reality of repressed memories. *American Psychologist, 48,* 518–537.

Loftus, E. F. (1997a). Memory for a past that never was. *Current Directions in Psychological Science, 6,* 60–65.

Loftus, E. F. (1997b). Repressed memory accusations: Devastated families and devastated patients. *Applied Cognitive Psychology, 11,* 25–30.

Loftus, E. F. (1998). The price of bad memories. *Skeptical Inquirer, 22,* 23–24.

Loftus, E. F., Garry, M., & Feldman, J. (1994). Forgetting sexual trauma: What does it mean when 38% forget? *Journal of Consulting and Clinical Psychology, 62,* 1177–1191.

Loftus, E. F., & Ketcham, K. (1991). *Witness for the defense.* New York: St. Martin's Press.

Loftus, E. F., & Ketcham, K. (1994). *The myth of repressed memory: False memories and allegations of sexual abuse.* New York: St. Martin's Press.

Loftus, E. F., & Palmer, J. C. (1974). Reconstruction of automobile destruction: An example of the interaction between language and memory. *Journal of Verbal Learning and Verbal Behavior, 13,* 585–589.

Loftus, E. F., & Pickrell, J. E. (1995). The formation of false memories. *Psychiatric Annals, 25*(12), 720–725.

Loftus, G. R. (1996). Psychology will be a much better science when we change the way we analyze data. *Current Directions in Psychological Science, 5,* 161–171.

Logue, A. W. (1985). Conditioned food aversion in humans. *Annals of the New York Academy of Sciences, 104,* 331–340.

Lohr, J. M., Lilienfeld, S. O., Tolin, D. F., & Herbert, J. D. (in press). Eye movement desensitization and reprocessing: An analysis of specific versus nonspecific factors. *Journal of Anxiety Disorders.*

LoLordo, V. M. (1979). Selective associations. In A. Dickinsen & R. A. Boakes (Eds.), *Mechanisms of learning and motivation* (pp. 367–398). Hillsdale, NJ: Lawrence Erlbaum Associates.

London Daily Telegraph. (1998, September 19). "'Cat' that turned out to be a clock."

Loomis, J. M., Da Silva, J. A., Philbeck, J. W., & Fukusima, S. S. (1996). Visual perception of location and distance. *Current Directions in Psychological Science, 5,* 72–77.

Lopes, L. L. (1982). *Procedural debiasing* (Tech. Rep. WHIPP 15). Madison: University of Wisconsin, Human Information Processing Program.

Lopez, M., & Takemoto-Chock, N. (1992, April). Assessment of adolescent stressors: *The adolescent Life Events Scale.* Paper presented at the meetings of the Western Psychological Association, Portland, OR.

Lopez, S. R. (1989). Patient variable biases in clinical judgment: Conceptual overview and methodological considerations. *Psychological Bulletin, 106,* 184–203.

Lord, C. G. (1997). *Social psychology.* Fort Worth: Harcourt, Brace.

Lowe, M. R., Kopyt, D., & Buchwald, J. (1996). Food intake underestimation: Its nature and potential impact on obesity treatment. *The Behavior Therapist, 19,* 17–20.

Luborsky, L. (1972). Another reply to Eysenck. *Psychological Bulletin, 78,* 406–408.

Luborsky, L. (1984). *Principles of psychoanalytic psychotherapy: A manual for supportive expressive treatment.* New York: Basic Books.

Luborsky, L. (1997). The core conflictual relationship theme: A basic case formulation method. In T. D. Eells (Ed.), *Handbook of psychotherapy case formulation* (pp. 58–83). New York: Guilford.

Luborsky, L., Singer, B., & Luborsky, L. (1975). Comparative studies of psychotherapies: Is it true that everyone has won and all must have prizes? *Archives of General Psychiatry, 32,* 995–1008.

Luchins, A. S. (1942). Mechanization in problem solving: The effect of Einstellung. *Psychological Monographs, 54*(6, Whole No. 248).

Luria, Z. (1992, February). *Gender differences in children's play patterns.* Paper presented at University of Southern California, Los Angeles.

Lutsky, N. (1995). When is "obedience" obedience? Conceptual and historical commentary. *Journal of Social Issues, 51,* 55–65.

Lutz, C. (1987). Goals, events and understanding in Ifaluk emotion theory. In N. Quinn & D. Holland (Eds.), *Cultural models in language and thought.* Cambridge, Eng.: Cambridge University Press.

Lynam, D. R. (1996). The early identification of chronic offenders: Who is the fledgling psychopath? *Psychological Bulletin, 120,* 209–234.

Lyness, K. S., & Thompson, D. E. (1997). Above the glass ceiling? A comparison of matched samples of female and male executives. *Journal of Applied Psychology, 82,* 359–375.

Lynn, S. J., Lock, T. G., Myers, B., & Payne, D. G. (1997). Recalling the unrecallable: Should hypnosis be used to recover memories in psychotherapy? *Current Directions in Psychological Science, 6,* 79–83.

Lynn, S. J., Myers, B., & Malinoski, P. (in press). Hypnosis, pseudomemories, and clinical guidelines: A sociocognitive perspective. In J. D. Read & D. S. Lindsay (Eds.), *Recollections of trauma: Scientific studies and clinical practice.* New York: Plenum.

Lynn, S. J., & Rhue, J. W. (1986). The fantasy-prone person: Hypnosis, imagination, and creativity. *Journal of Personality and Social Psychology, 51,* 404–408.

Lyubomirsky, S., & Nolen-Hoeksema, S. (1995). Effects of self-focused rumination on negative thinking and interpersonal problem solving. *Journal of Personality and Social Psychology, 69,* 176–190.

Lyubomirsky, S., & Ross, L. (1997). Hedonic consequences of social comparison: A contrast of happy and unhappy people. *Journal of Personality and Social Psychology, 73,* 1141–1157.

MacAndrew, C., & Edgerton, R. B. (1969). *Drunken comportment.* Chicago: Aldine.

MacArthur Foundation. (1999). *Research network on successful midlife development.* The John D. and Catherine T. MacArthur Foundation, Vero Beach, FL.

MacDonald, M., & Bernstein, D. A. (1974). Treatment of a spider phobia with in vivo and imaginal desensitization. *Journal of Behavior Therapy and Experimental Psychiatry, 5,* 47–52.

Mack, J. (1994). *Abduction: Human encounters with aliens.* New York: Scribners.

MacKenzie, B. (1984). Explaining race differences in IQ: The logic, the methodology, and the evidence. *American Psychologist, 39,* 1214–1233.

Mackie, D. M., Hamilton, D. L., Susskind, S. J., & Rosselli, F. (1996). Social psychological foundations of prejudice. In C. N. Macrae, C. Stangor, & M. Hewstone (Eds.), *Stereotypes and stereotyping* (pp. 41–78). New York: Guilford.

MacLeod, C. M. (1988). Forgotten but not gone: Savings for pictures and words in long-term memory. *Journal of Experimental Psychology: Learning, Memory, and Cognition,* 14, 195–212.

Madden, T. J., Ellen, P. S., & Ajzen, I. (1992). A comparison of the theory of planned behavior and the theory of reasoned action. *Personality and Social Psychology Bulletin, 18,* 3–9.

Maddux, J. (1993). Social cognitive models of health and exercise behavior: An introduction and review of conceptual issues. *Journal of Applied Sport Psychology, 5,* 116–140.

Maddux, J. (in press). Expectancies and the social cognitive perspective: Basic principles, processes and variables. In I. Kirsch (Ed.), *Expectancy, experience, and behavior.* Washington, DC: American Psychological Association.

Maddux, J. E., & DuCharme, K. A. (1997). Behavioral intentions in theories of health behavior. In D. S. Gochman (Ed.), *Handbook of health behavior research: Vol. 1: Personal and social determinants* (pp. 133–151). New York: Plenum.

Magee, J. C., & Johnston, D. (1997). A synaptically controlled, associative signal for Hebbian plasticity in hippocampal neurons. *Science, 275,* 209–213.

Maguire, T., Hattie, J., & Haig, B. (1994). Construct validity and achievement assessment. *Alberta Journal of Educational Research, 40*(2), 109–126.

Mahler, M. S. (1968). *On human symbiosis and the vicissitudes of individuation: Infantile psychosis.* New York: Basic Books.

Mahrer, A. R., & Nadler, W. P. (1986). Good moments in psychotherapy: A preliminary review, a list, and some promising research avenues. *Journal of Consulting and Clinical Psychology, 54,* 10–15.

Main, M. (1996). Introduction to the special section on attachment and psychopathology: *Vol. 2.* Overview of the field of attachment. *Journal of Consulting and Clinical Psychology, 64,* 237–243.

Major, B., Sciacchitano, A. M., & Crocker, J. (1993). In-group versus out-group comparisons and self-esteem. *Personality and Social Psychology Bulletin, 19,* 711–721.

Malamuth, N. M. (1998). The confluence model as an organizing framework for research on sexually aggressive men: Risk moderators, imagined aggression, and pornography consumption. In R. G. Geen & E. Donnerstein (Eds.), *Human aggression* (pp. 230–247). San Diego: Academic Press.

Malamuth, N. M., & Check, J. V. P. (1983). Sexual arousal to rape depictions: Individual differences. *Journal of Abnormal Psychology, 92,* 55–67.

Malamuth, N. M., Heavy, C., & Linz, D. (1993). Predicting men's antisocial behavior against women: The interaction model of sexual aggression. In N. G. Hall & R. Hirschman (Eds.), *Sexual aggression: Issues in etiology and assessment, treatment and policy* (pp. 63–97). New York: Hemisphere.

Malamuth, N. M., Sockloskie, R. J., Koss, M. P., & Tanaka, J. S. (1991). Characteristics of aggressors against women: Testing a model using a national sample of college students. *Journal of Consulting and Clinical Psychology, 59,* 670–681.

Malarkey, W. B., Kiecolt-Glaser, J. K., Pearl, D., & Glaser, R. (1994). Hostile behavior during marital conflict alters pituitary and adrenal hormones. *Psychosomatic Medicine, 56,* 41–51.

Malenka, R. C. (1995). LTP and LTD: Dynamic and interactive processes of synaptic plasticity. *The Neuroscientist, 1,* 35–42.

Manderscheid, R., & Barrett, S. (Eds.) (1987). *Mental health, United States, 1987* (National Institute of Mental Health, DHHS Pub. No. ADM 87–1518). Washington, DC: U.S. Government Printing Office.

Manfield, P. (Ed.). (1998). *Extending EMDR: A casebook of innovative applications.* New York: W. W. Norton.

Manke, B., McGuire, S., Reiss, D., Hetherington, E. M., & Plomin, R. (1995). Genetic contributions to children's extrafamilial social interactions: Teachers, best friends, and peers. *Social Development, 4,* 238–256.

Mann, J. J. (1998). The neurobiology of suicide. *Nature Medicine, 4,* 25–30.

Mann, K., Roschke, J., Nink, M., Aldenhoff, J., Beyer, J., Benkert, O., & Lehnert, H. (1992). Effects of corticotropin-releasing hormone administration in patients suffering from sleep apnea syndrome. *Society for Neuroscience Abstracts, 22,* 196.

Mannuzza, M., Schneider, F. R., Chapman, T. F., Liebowitz, M. R., Klein, D. F., & Fyer, A. J. (1995). Generalized social phobia. *Archives of General Psychiatry, 52,* 230–237.

Marcus, G. F. (1996). Why do children say "breaked"? *Current Directions in Psychological Science, 5,* 81–85.

Marcus, G. F., Pinker, S., Ullman, M., Hollander, M., Rosen, T. J., & Xu, F. (1992). Overregularization in language acquisition. *Monographs of the Society for Research in Child Development, 57*(4, Serial No. 228).

Markovif, B. M., Dimitrijevif, M., Jankovif, B. D. (1993). Immunomodulation by conditioning: Recent developments. *International Journal of Neuroscience, 71,* 231–249.

Markowitz, J. C., & Swartz, H. A. (1997). Case formulation in interpersonal psychotherapy of depression. In T. D. Eells (Ed.), *Handbook of psychotherapy case formulation* (pp. 192–222). New York: Guilford.

Markus, H. R., & Kitayama, S. (1991). Culture and the self: Implications for cognition, emotion, and motivation. *Psychological Review, 98,* 224–253.

Markus, H. R., & Kitayama, S. (1997). Culture and the self: Implications for cognition, emotion, and motivation. In L. A. Peplau & S. Taylor (Eds.), *Sociocultural perspectives in social psychology* (pp. 157–216). Upper Saddle River, NJ: Prentice-Hall.

Markus, H. R., Kitayama, S., & Heiman, R. J. (1996). Culture and "basic" psychological principles. In E. T. Higgins & A. W. Kruglanski (Eds.), *Social psychology: Handbook of basic principles* (pp. 857–913). New York: Guilford.

Marmar, C. R. (1990). Psychotherapy process research: Progress, dilemmas, and future directions. *Journal of Consulting and Clinical Psychology, 58,* 265–272.

Marshall, W. L. (1989). Pornography and sex offenders. In D. Zillmann & J. Bryant (Eds.), *Pornography: Research advances and policy considerations.* Hillsdale, NJ: Lawrence Erlbaum Associates.

Martin, B., & Hoffman, J. (1990). Conduct disorders. In M. Lewis & S. M. Miller (Eds.), *Handbook of developmental psychopathology.* New York: Plenum.

Martindale, C. (1981). *Cognition and consciousness.* Homewood, IL: Dorsey Press.

Martindale, C. (1991). *Cognitive psychology: A neural-network approach.* Pacific Grove, CA: Brooks/Cole.

Martinez, J. L., Schulteis, G., & Weinberger, S. B. (1991). How to increase and decrease the strength of memory traces: The effects of drugs and hormones. In J. L. Martinez & R. P. Kesner (Eds.), *Learning and memory: A biological view* (2nd ed.). San Diego: Academic Press.

Marzuk, P. M., Tardiff, K., Leon, A. C., Hirsch, C. S., Stajic, M., Portera, L., Hartwell, N., & Iqbal, I. (1995). Fatal injuries after cocaine use as a leading cause of death among young adults in New York City. *New England Journal of Medicine, 332*(26), 1753–1757.

Masand, P., Popli, A. P., & Welburg, J. B. (1995). Sleepwalking. *American Family Physician, 51*(3), 649–653.

Maslach, C. (1979). Negative emotional biasing of unexplained arousal. *Journal of Personality and Social Psychology, 37,* 953–969.

Maslach, C , & Goldberg, J. (1998). Prevention of burnout: New perspectives. *Applied and Preventive Psychology, 7,* 63–74.

Masling, J., & Bornstein, R. F. (1991). Perception without awareness and electrodermal responding: A strong test of subliminal psychodynamic activation effects. *Journal of Mind and Behavior, 12,* 33–47.

Masling, J. (1992). In R. F. Bornstein & T. Pittman (Eds.), *Perception without awareness* (pp. 259–276). New York: Guilford.

Maslow, A. H. (1943). A theory of human motivation. *Psychological Review, 50,* 370–396.

Maslow, A. H. (1970). *Motivation and personality* (2nd ed.). New York: Harper & Row.

Maslow, A. H. (1971). *The farther reaches of human nature.* New York: McGraw-Hill.

Mason, W. A. (1997). Discovering behavior. *American Psychologist, 52,* 713–720.

Massaro, D. W., & Cowan, N. (1993). Information processing models: Microscopes of the mind. *Annual Review of Psychology, 44,* 383–425.

Massaro, D. W., & Stork, D. G. (1998). Speech recognition and sensory integration. *American Scientist, 86,* 236–244.

Masson, J. M. (1983). *Assault on the truth: Freud's suppression of the seduction theory.* New York: Farrar, Straus, & Giroux.

Masson, M. E. J., & MacLeod, C. M. (1992). Reenacting the route to interpretation: Enhanced perceptual identification without prior perception. *Journal of Experimental Psychology: General, 121,* 145–176.

Masten, A. S., & Coatsworth, J. D. (1998). The development of competence in favorable and unfavorable environments: Lessons from research on successful children. *American Psychologist, 53,* 205–220.

Masters, J. C., Burish, T. G., Hollon, S. D., & Rimm, D. C. (1987). *Behavior therapy: Techniques and empirical findings* (3rd ed.). San Diego: Harcourt Brace Jovanovich.

Masters, W. H., & Johnson, V. E. (1966). *Human sexual response.* Boston: Little, Brown.

Matlin, M. W. (1998). *Cognition* (4th ed.). Ft. Worth: Harcourt Brace College Publishers.

Matson, J., Sevin, J., Fridley, D., & Love, S. (1990). Increasing spontaneous language in autistic children. *Journal of Applied Behavior Analysis, 23,* 227–223.

Matsumoto, D., and Ekman, P. (1989). American-Japanese cultural differences in intensity ratings of facial expressions of emotion. *Motivation and Emotion, 13,* 143–157.

Mattson, M. P., Guo, Q., Furukawa, K., & Pedersen, W. A. (1998). Presenilins, the endoplasmic reticulum, and neuronal apoptosis in Alzheimer's disease. *Journal of Neurochemistry, 70,* 1–14.

Maupin, H. E., & Fisher, J. R. (1989). The effects of superior female performance and sex-role orientation in gender conformity. *Canadian Journal of Behavioral Science, 21,* 55–69.

Mayer, D. J., & Price, D. D. (1982). A physiological and psychological analysis of pain: A potential model of motivation. In D. W. Pfaff (Ed.), *The physiological mechanisms of motivation.* New York: Springer-Verlag.

Mayer, F. S., & Sutton, K. (1996). *Personality: An integrative approach.* Upper Saddle River, NJ: Prentice-Hall.

Mayer, R. E. (1992). *Thinking, problem solving, and cognition* (2nd ed.). New York: W. H. Freeman.

Mays, D. T., & Franks, C. M. (1985). *Negative outcome in psychotherapy and what to do about it.* New York: Springer-Verlag.

McAdams, D. P. (1996). Alternative futures for the study of human individuality. *Journal of Personality, 30,* 374–388.

McAdams, D. P. (1997). A conceptual history of personality psychology. In R. Hogan, J. Johnson, & S. Briggs (Eds.), *Handbook of personality psychology* (pp. 4–40). San Diego: Academic Press.

McAuley, E. (1992). The role of efficacy cognitions in the prediction of exercise behavior in middle-aged adults. *Journal of Behavioral Medicine, 15,* 65–88.

McBride, T. D., Calsyn, R. J., Morse, G. A., Klinkenberg, W. D., & Allen, G. A. (1998). Duration of homeless spells among severely mentally ill individuals—A survival analysis. *Journal of Community Psychology, 26,* 473–490.

McCahill, T. A., Meyer, L. C., & Fischman, A. (1979). *The aftermath of rape.* Lexington, MA: Lexington Books.

McCarthy, G. (1995). Functional neuroimaging of memory. *The Neuroscientist, 1,* 155–163.

McCartney, K., Harris, M., & Bernieri, F. (1990). Growing up and growing apart: A developmental meta-analysis of twin studies. *Psychological Bulletin, 107,* 226–237.

McCarty, M. F. (1995). Optimizing exercise for fat loss. *Medical Hypotheses, 44*(5), 325–330.

McCauley, C. (1989). The nature of social influence in groupthink: Compliance and internalization. *Journal of Personality and Social Psychology, 57,* 250–260.

McClelland, D. C. (1958). Risk-taking in children with high and low need for achievement. In J. W. Atkinson (Ed.), *Motives in fantasy, action, and society.* Princeton, NJ: Van Nostrand.

McClelland, D. C. (1985). *Human motivation.* Glenview, IL: Scott, Foresman.

McClintock, C. G., & Liebrand, W. B. G. (1988). Role of interdependence structure, individual value orientation, and another's strategy in social decision making: A transformational analysis. *Journal of Personality and Social Psychology, 55,* 396–409.

McCloskey, D. I. (1978). Kinesthetic sensibility. *Physiological Reviews, 58,* 763.

McCloskey, M. (1983). Naive theories of motion. In D. Gentner & K. Stevens (Eds.), *Mental models.* Hillsdale, NJ: Lawrence Erlbaum Associates.

McCormick, D. A., & Thompson, R. F. (1984). Cerebellum essential involvement in the classically conditioned eyelid response. *Science, 223,* 296–299.

McCrae, R. R., & Costa, P. T. (1994). The stability of personality: Observations and evaluations. *Current Directions in Psychological Science, 3,* 173–175

McCrae, R. R., & Costa, P. T. Jr. (1996) Toward a new generation of personality theories. Theoretical contexts for the five-factor model. In J. S. Wiggins (Ed.) *The five-factor model of personality: Theoretical perspectives* (pp. 51–87). New York: Guilford.

McCrae, R. R., & Costa, P. T., Jr. (1997). Personality trait structure as a human universal. *American Psychologist, 52,* 509–516.

McCrae, R., & John, O. (1992). An introduction to the five-factor model and its applications. *Journal of Personality, 60,* 175–215.

McDougall, W. (1904). The sensations excited by a single momentary stimulation of the eye. *British Journal of Psychology, 1,* 78–113.

McDougall, W. (1908). *An introduction to social psychology.* London: Methuen.

McDowd, J., Vercruyssen, M., & Birren, J. (1991). Aging, divided attention, and dual-task performance. In D. Damos (Ed.), *Multiple Task Performance.* Bristol, PA: Taylor & Francis.

McEwen, B. S. (1994). How do sex and stress hormones affect nerve cells? *Annals of the New York Academy of Science, 743,* 1–18.

McEwen, B. S. (1998). Protective and damaging effects of stress mediators. *New England Journal of Medicine, 338,* 171–179.

McFadden, D., & Pasanen, E. G. (1998). Comparison of the auditory systems of heterosexuals and homosexuals: Click-evoked otoacoustic emissions. *Proceedings of the National Academy of Science USA, 95,* 2709–2713.

McGarvey, R. (1989, February). Recording success. *USAIR Magazine,* pp. 94–102.

McGehee, D. S., Heath, M. J. S., Gelber, S., Devay, P., &Role, L. W. (1995). Nicotine enhancement of fast excitation synaptic transmissions in CNS by presynaptic receptors. *Science, 269,* 5231, 1692–1696.

McGlone, J. (1980). Sex differences in human brain asymmetry: A critical survey. *The Behavioral and Brain Sciences, 3,* 215–263.

McGregor, I., Newby-Clark, I. R., & Zanna, M. P. (in press). Epistemic discomfort is moderated by simultaneous accessibility on inconsistent elements. In E. Harmon-Jones & J. Mills (Eds.), *Cognitive dissonance theory 40 years later: A revival with revisions and controversies.*

McGue, M. (1992). When assessing twin concordance, use the probandwise not the pairwise rate. *Schizophrenia Bulletin, 18,* 171–176.

McGue, M., Bouchard, Jr., T. J., Iacono, W. G., & Lykken, D. T. (1993). Behavioral genetics of cognitive ability: A life-span perspective. In R. Plomin & G. E. McClearn (Eds.), *Nature, nurture and psychology* (pp. 59–76). Washington, DC: American Psychological Association.

McGue, M., Pickens, R., & Svikis, D. (1992). Sex and age effects on the inheritance of alcohol problems: A twin study. *Journal of Abnormal Psychology, 101,* 3–17.

McGuire, P. A. (1998, November). California enacts drug-training law for psychologists. *APA Monitor,* p. 24.

McGuire, W. J. (1968). Personality and susceptibility to social influence. In E. F. Borgatta & W. W. Lambert (Eds.), *Handbook of personality theory and research.* Chicago: Rand McNally.

McIntosh, D. N., Silver, R. C., & Wortman, C. B. (1993). Religion's role in adjustment to a negative life event: Coping with the loss of a child. *Journal of Personality and Social Psychology, 65,* 812–821.

McIntosh, J. L. (1992). Suicide of the elderly. In B. Bonger (Ed.), *Suicide: Guidelines for assessment, management, and treatment.* New York: Oxford University Press.

McKenna, J. J., Thoman, E. B., Anders, T. F., Sadeh, A., Schechtman, V. L., & Glotzbach, S. F. (1993). Infant-parent co-sleeping in an evolutionary perspective: Implications for understanding infant sleep development and the sudden infant death syndrome. *Sleep, 16*(3), 263–282.

McKinney, W. T. (1988). *Models of mental disorders: A new comparative psychiatry.* New York: Plenum.

McKnight, J. D., & Glass, D. C. (1995). Perceptions of control, burnout, and depressive symptomatology: A replication and extension. *Journal of Consulting and Clinical Psychology, 63,* 490–494.

McLaughlin, C. S., Chen, C., Greenberger, E., & Biermeier, C. (1997). Family, peer, and individual correlates of sexual experience among Caucasian and Asian-American late adolescents. *Journal of Research on Adolescence, 7,* 33–53.

McLeod, J. D., Kessler, R. C., & Landis, K. R. (1992). Speed of recovery from major depressive episodes in a community sample of married men and women. *Journal of Abnormal Psychology, 101,* 277–286.

McLeod, P., & Dienes, Z. (1996). Do fielders know where to go to catch the ball or only how to get there? *Journal of Experimental Psychology: Human Perception and Performance, 22,* 531–543.

McLoyd, V. C. (1998). Socioeconomic disadvantage and child development. *American Psychologist, 53,* 185–204.

McNeil, J. E., & Warrington, E. K. (1993). Prosopagnosia: A face-specific disorder. *Quarterly Journal of Experimental Psychology: Human Experimental Psychology, 46A*(1), 1–10.

McPhail, T. L., & Penner, L. A. (1995, August). *Can similarity moderate the effects of aversive racism?* Paper presented at the 103rd annual meeting of the American Psychological Association, New York.

Medin, D. L., & Ross, B. H. (1997). *Cognitive psychology* (2nd ed.). Fort Worth, TX: Harcourt Brace Jovanovich.

Mednick, S. A. (1958). A learning theory approach to research in schizophrenia. *Psychological Bulletin, 55,* 316–327.

Meehan, P., Lamb, J., Saltzman, L., & O'Carroll, P. (1992). Attempted suicide among young adults: Progress toward a meaningful estimate of prevalence. *American Journal of Psychiatry, 149,* 41–44.

Mehle, T. (1982). Hypothesis generation in an automobile malfunction inference task. *Acta Psychologica, 52,* 87–116.

Mehta, S. I. (1995). A method for instant assessment and active learning. *Journal of Engineering Education, 84,* 295–298.

Meichenbaum, D. (1977). *Cognitive behavior modification: An integrative approach.* New York: Plenum.

Meichenbaum, D. H. (1995). Cognitive-behavioral therapy in historical perspective. In B. Bongar & L. E. Beutler (Eds.), *Comprehensive textbook of psychotherapy: Theory and practice* (pp. 140–158). New York: Oxford University Press.

Meijer, G. A., Westerterp, K. R., van Hulsel, A. M., & ten Hoor, F. (1992). Physical activity and energy expenditure in lean and obese adult human subjects. *European Journal of Applied Physiology and Occupational Physiology, 65,* 525–528.

Meins, E., Fernyhough, C., Russell, J., & Clark-Carter, D. (1998). Security of attachment as a predictor of symbolic and mentalising abilities: A longitudinal study. *Social Development, 7,* 1–24.

Mellers, R. A., Schwartz, A., & Cooke, D. J. (1998). Judgments and decision making. In J. T. Spence, J. M. Darley, & D. J. Foss (Eds.), *Annual Review of Psychology, 49,* 447–477.

Mello, N. K., Mendelson, J. H., Bree, M. P., & Lukas, S. E. (1989). Buprenorphine suppresses cocaine self-administration by rhesus monkeys. *Science, 245,* 859–862.

Meltzoff, J. (1997). *Critical thinking about research.* Washington, DC: American Psychological Association.

Melzack, R., & Wall, P. D. (1965). Pain mechanisms: A new theory. *Science, 150,* 971–979.

Menaker, M., & Vogelbaum, M. A. (1993). Mutant circadian period as a marker of suprachiasmatic nucleus function. *Journal of Biological Rhythms, 8,* 93–98.

Mendoza, R., Smith, M., Poland, R., Lin, K-M., & Strickland, T. (1991). Ethnic psychopharmacology: The Hispanic and Native American perspective. *Psychopharmacology Bulletin, 27,* 449–461.

Menini, A., Picco, C., & Firestein, S. (1995, February 2). Quantal-like current fluctuations induced by odorants in olfactory receptor cell. *Nature, 373,* 435–437.

Merritt, J. O. (1979). None in a million: Results of mass screening for eidetic ability using objective tests published in newspapers and magazines. *The Behavioral and Brain Sciences, 2,* 612.

Merzenich, M. M., Jenkins, W. M., Johnston, P., Schreiner, C., Miller, S. L., & Tallal, P. (1996). Temporal processing deficits of language-learning impaired children ameliorated by training. *Science, 271,* 77–81.

Mesquita, B., &Frijda, N. H. (1992). Cultural variations in emotions: A review. *Psychological Bulletin, 112,* 179–204.

Messer, S. B., & Wolitzky, D. L. (1997). The traditional psychoanalytic approach to case formulation. In T. D. Eells (Ed.), *Handbook of psychotherapy case formulation* (pp. 26–57). New York: Guilford.

Messick, S. (1982). Test validity and the ethics of assessment. *Diagnostica, 28*(1), 1–25.

Messick, S. (1989). Validity. In R. L. Linn (Ed.), *Educational measurement* (3rd ed., pp. 13–103). New York: Macmillan.

Metalsky, G. I., Joiner, T. E., Jr., Hardin, T. S., & Abramson, L. Y. (1993). Depressive reactions to failure in a naturalistic setting: A test of the hopelessness and self-esteem theories of depression. *Journal of Abnormal Psychology, 102,* 101–109.

Meyer, B. H. F. L., Ehrhardt, A. A., Rosen, L. R., & Gruen, R. S. (1995). Prenatal estrogens and the development of homosexual orientation. *Developmental Psychology, 31*(1), 12–21.

Meyer, R. G. (1975). A behavioral treatment of sleepwalking associated with test anxiety. *Journal of Behavior Therapy and Experimental Psychiatry, 6,* 167–168.

Meyers, C., & Jones, T. B. (1993). *Promoting active learning: Strategies for the college classroom.* San Francisco: Jossey-Bass.

Mezzich, J. E., Kleinman, A., Fabrega, H., & Parron, D. L. (Eds.). (1996). *Culture and psychiatric diagnosis.* Washington, DC: American Psychiatric Press.

Middlebrooks, J. C., Clock, A. E., Xu, L., & Green, D. M. (1994, May 6). A panoramic code for sound location by cortical neurons. *Science, 264,* 842–844.

Mignot, E. (1998). Genetic and familial aspects of narcolepsy. *Neurology, 50,* 16–22.

Mikelson, K. D., Kessler, R. C., & Shaver, P. R. (1997). Adult attachment in a nationally representative sample. *Journal of Personality and Social Psychology, 72,* 1092–1106.

Milberger, S., Biederman, J., Faraone, S. V., & Chen, L. (1997). Further evidence of an association between attention-deficit/hyperactivity disorder and cigarette smoking: Findings from a high-risk sample of siblings. *American Journal on Addictions, 6,* 205–217.

Milgram, S. (1963). Behavioral study of obedience. *Journal of Abnormal and Social Psychology, 67,* 371–378.

Milgram, S. (1965). Some conditions of obedience and disobedience to authority. *Human Relations, 18,* 57–76.

Milgram, S. (1970). The experience of living in cities. *Science, 167,* 1461–1468.

Milgram, S. (1974). *Obedience to authority.* New York: Harper & Row.

Milgram, S. (1977, October). Subject reaction: The neglected factor in the ethics of experimentation. *Hastings Center Report,* pp. 19–23.

Milgram, S., & Jodelet, D. (1976). Psychological maps of Paris. In H. M. Proshansky, W. H. Itelson, & L. G. Revlin (Eds.), *Environmental psychology.* New York: Holt, Rinehart & Winston.

Millar, S. (1994). *Understanding and representing space theory and evidence from studies with blind and sighted children.* New York: Oxford University Press.

Miller, C. L., Miceli, P. J., Whitman, T. L., & Borkowski, J. G. (1996). Cognitive readiness to parent and intellectual-emotional development in children of adolescent mothers. *Developmental Psychology, 32,* 533–541.

Miller, G. A. (1956). The magical number seven, plus or minus two: Some limits on our capacity to process information. *Psychological Review, 63,* 81–97.

Miller, G. A. (1991). *The science of words.* New York: Scientific American Library.

Miller, J. G. (1999). Cultural psychology: Implications for basic psychological theory. *Psychological Science, 10,* 85–91.

Miller, J. G. (1994). Cultural diversity in the morality of caring: Individually oriented versus duty-based interpersonal moral codes. *Cross-cultural Research, 28,* 3–39.

Miller, J. G., & Bersoff, D. M. (1994). Cultural influences on the moral status of reciprocity and the discounting of endogenous motivation. *Personality and Social Psychology Bulletin, 20,* 592–607.

Miller, J. G., & Bersoff, D. M. (1995). Development in the context of everyday family relationships: Culture, interpersonal morality, and adaptation. In M. Killen & D. Hart (Eds.), *Morality in everyday life: A developmental perspective* (pp. 259–282). Cambridge, Eng.: Cambridge University Press.

Miller, J. G., & Bersoff, D. M. (1998). The cultural matrix of social psychology. In D. Gilbert, S. T. Fiske, and G. Lindzey (Eds.), *Handbook of social psychology,* Vol. 2 (4th ed., pp. 915–981). Boston: McGraw-Hill.

Miller, J. L., & Eimas, P. D. (1995). Speech perception: From signal to word. *Annual Review of Psychology, 46,* 467–492.

Miller, K. F., Smith, C. M., Zhu, J., & Zhang, H. (1995). Preschool origins of cross-national differences in mathematical competence: The role of number-naming systems. *Psychological Science, 6,* 56–60.

Miller, L. K. (1999). The savant syndrome: Intellectual impairment and exceptional skill. *Psychological Bulletin, 125,* 31–46.

Miller, L. T., & Vernon, P. A. (1992). The general factor in short-term memory, intelligence, and reaction time. *Intelligence, 16,* 5–29.

Miller, L. T., & Vernon, P. A. (1997). Developmental changes in speed of information processing in young children. *Developmental Psychology, 33,* 549–554.

Miller, M. G., & Teates, J. F. (1985). Acquisition of dietary self-selection in rats with normal and impaired oral sensation. *Physiology and Behavior, 34*(3), 401–408.

Miller, N., & Davidson-Podgorny, G. (1987). Theoretical models of intergroup relations and the use of cooperative teams as an intervention for desegregated settings. In C. Hendrick (Ed.), *Group processes and intergroup relations.* Newberry Park, CA: Sage.

Miller, N. E. (1959). Liberalization of basic S-R concepts: Extensions to conflict behavior, motivation, and social learning. In S. Koch (Ed.), *Psychology: A study of science: Vol. 2.* New York: McGraw-Hill.

Miller, N. E., Bailey, C. U., & Stevenson, J. A. F. (1930). Decreased hunger but increased food intake resulting from hypothalmic lesions. *Science 112,* 256–259.

Miller, T. Q., Heath, L., Molcan, J. R., & Dugoni, B. L. (1991). Imitative violence in the real world: A reanalysis of homicide rates following championship prize fights. *Aggressive Behavior, 17,* 121–134.

Millon, T., & Davis, R. D. (1996). *Disorders of personality. DSM-IV and beyond* (2nd ed.). New York: Wiley.

Milner, B. (1965). Visually-guided maze learning in man: Effects of bilateral hippocampal, bilateral frontal, and unilateral cerebral lesions. *Neuropsychologia, 3,* 317–338.

Milner, B. (1966). Amnesia following operation on temporal lobes. In C. W. M. Whitty & O. L. Zangwill (Eds.), *Amnesia.* London: Butterworth.

Milner, D. (1983). *Children and race.* Beverly Hills, CA: Sage.

Minimi, H., & Dallenbach, K. M. (1946). The effect of activity upon learning and retention in the cockroach. *American Journal of Psychology, 59,* 1–58.

Minshew, N. J., Payton, J. B., & Sclabassi, R. J. (1986). Cortical neurophysiologic abnormalities in autism. *Neurology, 36*(Suppl. 1), 194.

Minuchin, S., & Fishman, H. (1981). *Family therapy techniques.* Cambridge, MA: Harvard University Press.

Mischel, W., & Shoda, Y. (1995). A cognitive-affective system of personality: Reconceptualizing situations, dispositions, dynamics, and influences. *Psychological Review, 90,* 394–402.

Mischel, W., & Shoda, Y. (1998). Reconciling dynamics and dispositions. *Annual Review of Psychology, 49,* 229–258.

Mitchell, D. B. (1991). Implicit memory, explicit theories. *Contemporary Psychology, 36,* 1060–1061.

Mitchell, K. J., & Zaragoza, M. S. (1996). Repeated exposure to suggestion and false memory: The role of contextual variability. *Journal of Memory and Learning, 35,* 246–260.

Miyake, K., Chen, S., & Campos, J. J. (1985). Infant temperament, mother's mode of interaction, and attachment in Japan: An interim report. In I. Bretherton & E. Waters (Eds.), Growing points of attachment theory and research. *Monographs of the Society for Research in Child Development, 50*(1–2, Serial No. 209).

Moergen, S., Merkel, W., and Brown, S. (1990). The use of covert sensitization and social skills training in the treatment of an obscene telephone caller. *Journal of Behavior Therapy and Experimental Psychiatry, 21,* 269–275.

Mogenson, G. J. (1976). Neural mechanisms of hunger: Current status and future prospects. In D. Novin, W. Wyrwicka, & G. Bray (Eds.), *Hunger: Basic mechanisms and clinical applications.* New York: Raven.

Moghaddam, F. M. (1998). *Social psychology: Exploring universals across cultures.* New York: Freeman.

Mohr, D. C. (1995). Negative outcome in psychotherapy: A critical review. *Clinical Psychology: Science and Practice, 2,* 1–27.

Moldin, S. O., & Gottesman, I. I. (1997). At issue: Genes, experience, and chance in schizophrenia—positioning for the 21st century. *Schizophrenia Bulletin, 23,* 547–561.

Molsa, P. K., Marttila, R. J., & Rinne, U. K. (1995). Long-term survival and predictors of mortality in Alzheimer's disease and multi-infarct dementia. *Acta Neurologica Scandinavica, 91,* 159–164.

Monroe, S., Thase, M., & Simons, A. (1992). Social factors and psychobiology of depression: Relations between life stress and rapid eye movement sleep latency. *Journal of Abnormal Psychology, 101,* 528–537.

Montague, C. T., Farooqi, I. S., Whitehead, J. P., Soos, M. A., Rau, H., Wareham, N. J., Sewter, C. P., Digby, J. E., Mohammed, S. N., Hurst, J. A., Cheetham, C. H., Earley, A. R., Barnett, A. H., Prins, J. B., & O'Rahilly, S. (1997). Congenital leptin deficiency is associated with severe early-onset obesity in humans. *Nature, 387,* 903–908.

Monteith, M. J., Zuwerink, J. R., & Devine, P. G. (1994). Prejudice and prejudice reduction: Classic challenges and contemporary approaches. In P. G. Devine, D. L. Hamilton, & T. M. Ostrom (Eds.), *Social cognition: Impact on social psychology* (pp. 324–346). San Diego, CA: Academic Press.

Moore, R. Y. (1997). Circadian rhythms: Basic neurobiology and clinical applications. *Annual Review of Medicine, 48,* 253–266.

Moran, A. (1996). *The psychology of concentration in sports performance: A cognitive analysis.* Hove East Essex, UK: Psychology Press.

Moreland, R. L., & Beach, S. R. (1992). Exposure effects in the classroom: The development of affinity among students. *Journal of Experimental Social Psychology, 28,* 255–276.

Morgan, C. D., & Murray, H. A. (1935). A method for investigating fantasy: The thematic apperception test. *Archives of Neurology and Psychiatry, 34,* 289–306.

Morganstern, J., Labouvie, E., McCrady, B. S., Kahler, C. W., & Frey, R. M. (1997). Affiliation with Alcoholics Anonymous after treatment: A study of its therapeutic effects and mechanism of action. *Journal of Consulting and Clinical Psychology, 65,* 768–777.

Morgenthaler, J., & Dean, W. (1990). *Smart drugs and nutrients.* Santa Cruz, CA: B & J Publications.

Morin, C. M., Kowatch, R. A., Barry, T., & Walton, E. (1993). Cognitive-behavior therapy for late-life insomnia. *Journal of Consulting and Clinical Psychology, 61,* 137–146.

Morisse, D., Batra, L., Hess, L., Silverman, R., & Corrigan, P. (1996). A demonstration of a token economy for the real world. *Applied and Preventative Psychology, 5,* 41–46.

Morris, C. D., Bransford, J. D., & Franks, J. J. (1977). Levels of processing versus transfer appropriate processing. *Journal of Verbal Learning and Verbal Behavior, 16,* 519–533.

Morris, J. S., Ohman, A., & Dolan, R. J. (1998). Conscious and unconscious emotional learning in the human amygdala. *Nature, 393,* 467–470.

Morris, M. W., & Peng, K. (1994). Culture and cause: American and Chinese attributions for social and physical events. *Journal of Personality and Social Psychology, 67,* 949–971.

Morrison, A. M., & Von Glinow, M. A. (1990). Women and minorities in management. *American Psychologist, 45,* 200–208.

Mortimer, R. G., Goldsteen, K., Armstrong, R. W., & Macrina, D. (1988). *Effects of enforcement, incentives, and publicity on seat belt use in Illinois.* University of Illinois, Dept. of Health & Safety Studies, Final Report to Illinois Dept. of Transportation (Safety Research Report 88–11).

Moscovici, S. (1985). Social influence and conformity. In G. Lindzey & E. Aronson (Eds.), *The handbook of social psychology: Vol. 2* (3rd ed.). New York: Random House.

Moscovici, S. (1994). Three concepts: Minority, conflict, and behavioral style. In S. Moscovici, A. Mucchi-Faina, & A. Maass. *Minority influence* (pp. 233–251). Chicago: Nelson-Hall.

Mosier, K. L. (1997). Myths of expert decision making and automated decision aids. In C. E. Zsambok & G. Klein (Eds.), *Naturalistic decision making* (pp. 319–330). Mahwah, NJ: Lawrence Erlbaum Associates.

Motowidlo, S. J., Borman, W. C., & Schmit, M. J. (1997). A theory of individual differences in task and contextual performance. *Human Performance, 10,* 71–83.

Muchinsky, P. (1993). *Psychology applied to work* (4th ed.). Pacific Grove, CA: Brooks/Cole.

Muir, J. L. (1997). Acetylcholine, aging, and Alzheimer's disease. *Pharmacological and Biochemical Behavior, 56*(4), 687–696.

Mukherjee, S., Sackheim, H. A., & Schnur, D. B. (1994). Electroconvulsive therapy of acute manic episodes: A review of 50 years' experience. *American Journal of Psychiatry, 151,* 169–176.

Mullen, B. (1986). Atrocity as a function of lynch mob composition: A self-attention perspective. *Personality and Social Psychology Bulletin, 12,* 187–197.

Murphy, K. R. (1993). *Honesty in the workplace.* Pacific Grove, CA: Brooks/Cole.

Murr, A., & Rogers, A. (1995, March 27). Gray matters. *Newsweek,* pp. 48–54.

Murray, B. (1995, June). Head Start sharpens focus on mental health. *APA Monitor* (p. 39).

Murray, B. (1996, February). Psychology remains top college major. *APA Monitor,* (pp. 1, 42).

Murray, E. A., & Mishkin, M. (1985). Amygdalectomy impairs crossmodal association in monkeys. *Science, 228,* 604–606.

Murray, H. A. (1938). *Explorations in personality.* New York: Oxford University Press.

Murray, H. A. (1971). *Thematic Apperception Test.* Cambridge: Harvard University Press.

Murthy, C. V., & Panda, S. C. (1987). A study of intelligence, socio-economic status and birth order among children belonging to SC-ST and non-SC-ST groups. *Indian Journal of Behaviour, 11,* 25–30.

Myers, B. J. (1987). Mother-infant bonding as a critical period. In M. H. Bornstein (Ed.), *Sensitive periods in development: Interdisciplinary perspectives.* Hillsdale, NJ: Lawrence Erlbaum Associates.

Myers, D. G., & Diener, E. (1995). Who is happy? *Psychological Science, 6,* 10–19.

Myers, P. I., & Hammill, D. D. (1990). *Learning disabilities: Basic concepts, assessment practices, and instructional strategies.* Austin, TX: Pro-ed.

Myerson, J., Rank, M. R., Raines, F. Q., & Schnitzler, M. A. (1998). Race and general cognitive ability. *Psychological Science, 9,* 139–142.

Nader, K., Bechara, A., & Van der Kooy, D. (1997). Neurobiological constraints on behavioral models of motivation. *Annual Review of Psychology, 48,* 85–114.

Naëgelé, B., Thouvard, V., Pépin, J.-L., Lévy, P., Bonnet, C., Perret, J. E., Pellat, P., & Feuerstein, C. (1995). Deficits of cognitive functions in patients with sleep apnea syndrome. *Sleep, 18*(1), 43–52.

Naglieri, J. A., Das, J. P., Stevens, J. J., & Ledbetter, M. F. (1991). Confirmatory factor analysis of planning, attention, simultaneous, and successive cognitive processing tasks. *Journal of School Psychology, 29,* 1–17.

Nalbantoglu, J., Tirado-Santiago, G., Lahsaini, A., Poirier, J., Goncalves, O., Verge, G., Momoli, F., Welner, S. A., Massicotte, G., Julien, J. P., & Shapiro, M. L. (1997). Impaired learning and LTP in mice expressing the carboxy terminus of the Alzheimer amyloid precursor protein. *Nature, 387,* 500–505.

Narayanan, L., Menon, S., & Levine, E. L. (1995). Personality structure: A culture-specific examination of the five-factor model. *Journal of Personality Assessment, 64,* 51–62.

National Advisory Mental Health Council. (1996). Basic behavioral science research for mental health: Vulnerability and resilience. *American Psychologist, 51,* 22–28.

National Cancer Institute. (1994). *National Cancer Institute fact book, 1994.* Washington, DC: U.S. Department of Health and Human Services.

National Center for Health Statistics. (1996). *Health, United States 1995.* Hyattsville, MD: U.S. Public Health Service.

National Computer Systems. (1992). *Catalog of assessment instruments, reports, and services.* Minneapolis: NCS.

National Institute of Mental Health. (1998). *Mental illness in America: The National Institute of Mental Health agenda.* Washington, DC: NIMH.

National Institute on Drug Abuse Research Report Series. (1997). *Heroin abuse and addiction.* Washington, DC: National Institute of Drug Abuse.

National Institute on Drug Abuse. (1996). *National household survey on drug abuse.* Washington, DC: National Clearinghouse for Alcohol and Drug Information.

National Institute on Drug Abuse. (1997). *Research report: Heroin addiction and abuse.* Washington, DC: National Institute on Drug Abuse.

National Joint Committee on Learning Disabilities (1994). *Collective perspective on issues affecting learning disabilities.* Austin, TX: Pro-ed.

National Science Foundation (1994). Characteristics of doctoral scientists and engineers in the United States: 1991. NSF Publication #94-307, Arlington, VA.

Navon, D., & Gopher, D. (1979). On the economy of the human-processing system. *Psychological Review, 86,* 214–255.

Needleman, H. (1996). Bone lead levels and delinquent behavior. *Journal of the American Medical Association, 275,* 363–369.

Neeper, S. A., Gomez-Pinilla, F., Choi, J., & Cotman, C. (1995). Exercise and brain neurotrophins. *Nature, 373,* 109.

Nehlig, A., Daval, J. L., & Debry, G. (1992). Caffeine and the central nervous system: Mechanisms of action, biochemical, metabolic and psychostimulant effects. *Brain Research Review, 17,* 139–170.

Neisser, U. (1967). *Cognitive psychology.* New York: Appelton-Century-Crofts.

Neisser, U. (1998). *The rising curve: Long-term gains in I.Q. and related measures.* Washington, DC: American Psychological Association.

Neisser, U., Boodoo, G., Bouchard, T. J., Boykin, A. W., Brody, N., Ceci, S. J., Halpern, D. F., Loehlin, J. C., Perloff, R., Sternberg, R. J., & Urbina, S. (1996). Intelligence: Knowns and unknowns. *American Psychologist, 51,* 77–101.

Neitz, M., & Neitz, J. (1995, February 17). Numbers and ratios of visual pigment genes for normal red-green color vision. *Science, 267,* 1013–1016.

Nelson, C. A. (1997). The neurobiological basis of early memory development. In N. Cowan (Ed.), *The development of memory in childhood: Studies in developmental psychology* (pp. 41–82). Hove, Eng.: Psychology Press/Erlbaum/Taylor & Francis.

Nelson, C. A., & Bloom F. E. (1997). Child development and neuroscience. *Child Development, 68,* 970–987.

Nelson, D. L. (1999). Implicit memory. In D. E. Morris & M. Gruneberg (Eds.), *Theoretical aspects of memory.* London: Routledge.

Nelson, D. L., McKinney, V. M., & Bennett, D. (in press). Conscious and automatic uses of memory in cued recall and recognition. In B. H. Challis & B. M. Velichkovsky (Eds.), *Stratification of consciousness and cognition.* Amsterdam: John Benjamins Press.

Nelson, D. L., McKinney, V. M., Gee, N., & Janczura, G. A. (in press). Interpreting the influence of implicitly activated memories on recall and recognition. *Psychological Review.*

Nelson, K. (1986). Event knowledge and cognitive development. In K. Nelson (Ed.), Event knowledge: *Structure and function in development.* Hillsdale, NJ: Lawrence Erlbaum Associates.

Nelson, K. (1993). The psychological and social origins of autobiographical memory. *Psychological Science, 4,* 7–14.

Nelson, R. J., Demas, G. E., Huang, P. L., Fishman, M. C., Dawson, V. L., Dawson, T. M., & Snyder, S. H. (1995). Behavioral abnormalities in male mice lacking neuronal nitric oxide synthase. *Nature, 378,* 383–386.

Neugarten, B. L. (1977). Personality and aging. In J. E. Birren & K. W. Schaie (Eds.), *Handbook of the psychology of aging.* New York: Van Nostrand Reinhold.

Neumann, C. S., Grimes, K., Walker, E. F., & Baum, K. (1995). Developmental pathways to schizophrenia: Behavioral subtypes. *Journal of Abnormal Psychology, 104,* 558–566.

Neville, H. A., Heppner, M. J., Louie, C. E., Thompson, C. E., Brooks, L., & Baker, C. E. (1996). The impact of multicultural training on white racial identity attitudes and therapy competencies. *Professional Psychology: Research and Practice, 27,* 83–89.

Neville, H. J., Bavelier, D., Corina, D., Rauschecker, J., Karni, A., Lalwani, A., Braun, A., Clark, V., Jezzard, P., & Turner, R. (1998). Cerebral organization for language in deaf and hearing subjects: Biological constraints and effects of experience. *Proceedings of the National Academy of Science USA,* 95, 922–929.

Newcomb, A. F., & Bagwell, C. L. (1995). Children's friendship relations: A meta-analytic review. *Psychological Bulletin, 117,* 306–347.

Newcombe, N., & Fox, N. A. (1994). Infantile amnesia: Through a glass darkly. *Child Development, 65,* 31–40.

Newell, A., & Simon, H. A. (1972). *Human problem solving.* Englewood Cliffs, NJ: Prentice-Hall.

Newman, J. P., Wolff, W. T., & Hearst, E. (1980). The feature positive effect in adult human subjects. *Journal of Experimental Psychology: Human Learning and Memory, 6,* 630–650.

Newport, E. L., and Meier, R. (1985). The acquisition of American Sign Language. In D. I. Slobin (Ed.), *The cross-linguistic study of language acquisition.* Hillsdale, NJ: Lawrence Erlbaum Associates.

Newsom, J. T., & Schulz, R. (1998). Caregiving from the recipient's perspective: Negative reactions to being helped. *Health Psychology, 17,* 172–181.

NIAA (National Institute on Alcohol and Alcoholism). (1994). *Alcohol Health and Research World, 18,* 243, 245.

NIAAA (National Institute on Alcohol and Alcoholism). (1998, May 13). News release.

NICHD Early Child Care Research Network (1997). The effects of infant child care on infant-mother attachment security: Results of the NICHD Study of Early Child Care. *Child Development, 68,* 860–879.

Nichols, M. P., & Schwartz, R. C. (1991). *Family therapy: Concepts and methods* (2nd ed.). Boston: Allyn & Bacon.

Nichols, R. (1978). Twin studies of ability, personality, and interests. *Homo, 29,* 158–173.

Nicholson, A. N., Pascoe, P. A., Spencer, M. B., Stone, B. M., Roehis, T., & Roth, T. (1986). Sleep after transmeridian flights. *Lancet, 2,* 1205–1208.

Nicholson, I. R., & Neufeld, R. W. J. (1993). Classification of the schizophrenias according to symptomatology: A two factor model. *Journal of Abnormal Psychology, 102,* 259–270.

Nicholson, R. A., & Berman, J. S. (1983). Is follow-up necessary in evaluating psychotherapy? *Psychological Bulletin, 93*(2), 261–278.

Nickell, J. (1994). *Psychic sleuths: ESP and sensational cases.* Amherst, NY: Prometheus Books.

Nickell, J. (1996, November/December). Not-so-spontaneous human combustion. *Skeptical Inquirer, 20,* 17–20.

Nickell, J. (1997, January/February). Sleuthing a psychic sleuth. *Skeptical Inquirer, 21,* 18–19.

Nickerson, R. A., & Adams, M. J. (1979). Long-term memory for a common object. *Cognitive Psychology, 11,* 287–307.

Niedenthal, P. M., Setterlund, M. B., & Wherry, M. B. (1992). Possible self-complexity and affective reactions to goal-relevant evaluation. *Journal of Personality and Social Psychology, 63,* 5–16.

Nielsen Media. (1990). *1990 report on television.* New York: Nielsen Media, Inc.

Nietzel, M. T. (1999). Psychology applied to the legal system. In A. M. Stec & D. A. Bernstein (Eds.), *Psychology: Fields of application.* Boston: Houghton Mifflin.

Nietzel, M. T., & Bernstein, D. A. (1987). *Introduction to clinical psychology* (2nd ed.). New York: Prentice-Hall.

Nietzel, M. T., Bernstein, D. A., & Milich, R. (1998). *Introduction to clinical psychology* (5th ed.). Englewood Cliffs, NJ: Prentice-Hall.

Nietzel, M. T., Speltz, M. L., McCauley, E. A., & Bernstein, D. A. (1998). *Abnormal psychology.* Boston: Allyn & Bacon.

NIH (Technology Assessment Conference Panel) (1992). Methods for voluntary weight loss and control. *Annals of Internal Medicine, 116,* 942–949.

Nijhawan, R. (1997). Visual decomposition of colour through motion extrapolation. *Nature, 386,* 66–69.

Nilsson, G. (1996, November). Some forms of memory improve as people age. *APA Monitor,* p. 27.

NIMH (National Institute of Mental Health). (1985). *Electroconvulsive therapy: Consensus development conference statement.* Bethesda, MD: U.S. Department of Health and Human Services.

Niznikiewicz, M. A., O'Donnell, B. F., Nestor, P. G., Smith, L., Law, S., Karapelou, M., Shenton, M. E., & McCarley, R. W. (1997). ERP assessment of visual and auditory language processing in schizophrenia. *Journal of Abnormal Psychology, 106,* 85–94.

Noble, F. P. (1996, March/April). The gene that rewards alcoholism. *Scientific American,* pp. 52–61.

Nolan, R. P., Spanos, N. P., Hayward, A. A., & Scott, H. A. (1995). The efficacy of hypnotic and nonhypnotic response-based imagery for self-managing recurrent headache. *Imagination, Cognition, and Personality, 14*(3), 183–201.

Nolen-Hoeksema, S. (1990). *Sex differences in depression.* Stanford, CA: Stanford University Press.

Nolen-Hoeksma, S., Morrow, J., & Fredrickson, N. (1993). Response styles and the duration of episodes of depressed mood. *Journal of Abnormal Psychology, 102,* 20–28.

Noll, R. B. (1994). Hypnotherapy for warts in children and adolescents. *Journal of Developmental and Behavioral Pediatrics, 15*(3), 170–173.

Noordsy, D. L., Schwab, B., Fox, L., & Drake, R. E. (1996). The role of self-help programs in the rehabilitation of persons with severe mental illness and substance abuse disorders. *Community Mental Health Journal, 32,* 71–81.

Norman, D. A. (1988). *The psychology of everyday things.* New York: Basic Books.

Nottebohm, F. (1985). Neuronal replacement in adulthood. *Annals of the New York Academy of Science, 457,* 143–161.

Novak, M. A. (1991, July). Psychologists care deeply about animals. *APA Monitor,* p. 4.

Nowak, M. A., May, R. M., & Sigmund, K. (1995). The arithmetics of mutual help. *Scientific American, 272,* 76–81.

Nowak, M. A., & Sigmund, K. (1998). Evolution of indirect reciprocity by image scoring. *Nature, 393,* 573–577.

Nugent, F. (1994). *An introduction to the profession of counseling.* Columbus, OH: Merrill.

Nurnberger, J. (1993). Genotyping status report for affective disorder. *Psychiatric Genetics, 3,* 207–214.

O'Brien, T. L. (1991, September 2). Computers help thwart "groupthink" that plagues meetings. *Chicago Sun Times.*

O'Farrell, T. J. (1995). Marital and family therapy. In R. K. Hester & W. R. Miller (Eds.), *Handbook of alcoholism treatment approaches* (2nd ed., pp. 195–220). Boston: Allyn & Bacon.

O'Farrell, T. J., & Murphy, C. M. (1995). Marital violence before and after alcoholism treatment. *Journal of Consulting and Clinical Psychology, 63,* 256–262.

O'Hare, D., & Roscoe, S. (1991). *Flight deck performance: The human factor.* Ames: Iowa University Press.

O'Leary, K. D., Malone, J., & Tyree, A. (1994). Physical aggression in early marriage: Prerelationship and relationship effects. *Journal of Consulting and Clinical Psychology, 62,* 594–602.

Oakland, T., & Glutting, J. J. (1990). Examiner observations of children's WISC-R test-related behaviors: Possible socioeconomic status, race, and gender effects. *Psychological Assessment, 2,* 86–90.

Oatley, K. (1993). Those to whom evil is done. In R. S. Wyer & T. K. Srull (Eds.), *Toward a general theory of anger and emotional aggression: Advances in social cognition, Vol. VI.* Hillsdale, NJ: Lawrence Erlbaum Associates.

Oden, M. H. (1968). The fulfillment of promise: 40-year follow-up of the Terman gifted group. *Genetic Psychology Monographs, 17,* 3–93.

Offenbach, S., Chodzko-Zajko, W., & Ringel, R. (1990). Relationship between physiological status, cognition, and age in adulot men. *Bulletin of the Psychonomics Society, 28,* 112–114.

Ofshe, R., & Watters, E. (1994). *Making monsters: False memories, psychotherapy, sexual hysteria.* New York: Scribners.

Ogles, B. M., Lambert, M. J., & Sawyer, J. D. (1995). Clinical significance of the National Institute of Mental Health treatment of depression collaborative research program data. *Journal of Consulting and Clinical Psychology, 63,* 321–326.

Ohira, H., & Kurono, K. (1993). Facial feedback effects on impression formation. *Perceptual and Motor Skills, 77*(3, Pt. 2), 1251–1258.

Öhman, A., Dimberg, U., & Ost, L. G. (1985). Animal and social phobias: A laboratory model. In S. Reiss & R. R. Bootzin (Eds.), *Theoretical issues in behavior therapy.* Orlando, FL: Academic Press.

Öhman, A., & Soares, J. F. (1994). "Unconscious anxiety": Phobic responses to masked stimuli. *Journal of Abnormal Psychology, 103*(2), 231–240.

Olds, J. (1973). Commentary on positive reinforcement produced by electrical stimulation of septal areas and other regions of rat brain. In E. S. Valenstein (Ed.), *Brain stimulation and motivation: Research and commentary.* Glenview, IL: Scott, Foresman.

Olds, J., & Milner, P. (1954). Positive reinforcement produced by electrical stimulation of septal areas and other regions of the rat brain. *Journal of Comparative and Physiological Psychology, 47,* 419–427.

Oliner, S. P., & Oliner, P. M. (1988). *The altruistic personality: Rescuers of Jews in Nazi Europe.* New York: Free Press.

Olio, K. A. (1994). Truth in memory. *American Psychologist, 49,* 442–443.

Olness, K., & Ader, R. (1992). Conditioning as an adjunct in the pharmacotherapy of lupus erythmatosus. *Developmental and Behavioral Pediatrics, 13,* 124–125.

Olney, J. W., Wozniak, D. F., & Farber, N. B. (1997). Excitotoxic neurodegeneration in Alzheimer's disease: New hypothesis and new therapeutic strategies. *Archives of Neurology, 54,* 1234–1240.

Olpe, H. R., Steinmann, M. W., & Jones, R. S. G. (1985). Electrophysiological perspectives on locus coeruleus: Its role in cognitive versus vegetative functions. *Physiological Psychology, 13,* 179–187.

Olson, G. M., & Sherman, T. (1983). Attention, learning, and memory in infants. In P. H. Mussen (Ed.), *Handbook of child psychology: Vol. 2. Infancy and developmental psychobiology.* New york: Wiley.

Olson, J. M. (1992). Self-perception of humor: Evidence for discounting and augmentation effects. *Journal of Personality and Social Psychology, 62,* 369–377.

Olson, J. M., & Zanna, M. P. (1993). Attitudes and attitude change. In L. W. Porter & M. R. Rosenzweig (Eds.), *Annual review of psychology* (Vol. 44, pp. 117–154). Palo Alto, CA: Annual Reviews Inc.

Olson, L. (1997). Regeneration in the adult central nervous system. *Nature Medicine, 3,* 1329–1335.

Omoto, A. M., & Snyder, M. (1995). Sustained helping without obligation: Motivation, longevity of service, and perceived attitude change among AIDS volunteers. *Journal of Personality and Social Psychology, 68,* 671–686.

Ones, D., & Viswesvaran, C. (1996). Bandwidth-fidelity dilemma in personality measurement for personnel selection. *Journal of Organizational Behavior, 17,* 609–626.

Ones, D. S., Viswesvaran, C., & Schmidt, F. L. (1993). Comprehensive meta-analysis of integrity test validities: Findings and implications for personnel selection and theories of job performance. *Journal of Applied Psychology, 78,* 679–703.

Orbell, J. M., van de Kragt, A. J. C., & Dawes, R. M. (1988). Explaining discussion-induced cooperation. *Journal of Personality and Social Psychology, 54,* 811–819.

Oren, D. A., & Terman, M. (1998). Tweaking the human circadian clock with light. *Science, 279,* 333–345.

Orme-Johnson, D. (1992). Personal communication, April 20.

Orne, M. T., & Evans, F. J. (1965). Social control in the psychological experiment: Antisocial behavior and hypnosis. *Journal of Personality and Social Psychology, 1,* 189–200.

Orne, M. T., Sheehan, P. W., & Evans, F. J. (1968). Occurrence of posthypnotic behavior outside the experimental setting. *Journal of Personality and Social Psychology, 9,* 189–196.

Ornitz, E. M. (1989). Autism: At the interface of sensory and information processing. In G. Dawson (Ed.), *Autism: Nature, diagnosis, and treatment.* New York: Guilford.

Osborne, J. (1997). Race and academic disidentification. *Journal of Educational Psychology, 89,* 728–735.

Oskamp, S. (1991). *Attitudes and opinions.* Englewood Cliffs, NJ: Prentice-Hall.

Oskamp, S., & Schultz, P. W. (1998). *Applied social psychology* (2nd ed.). Upper Saddle River, NJ: Prentice-Hall.

Öst, L.-G. (1992). Blood and injection phobia: Background and cognitive, physiological and behavioral variables. *Journal of Abnormal Psychology, 101,* 68–74.

Öst, L.-G., Hellström, K., & Kåver, A. (1992). One- versus five-session exposure in the treatment of needle phobia. *Behavior Therapy, 23,* 263–282.

Öst, L.-G., Salkovskis, P. M., & Hellström, K. (1991). One-session therapist-directed exposure vs. self-exposure in the treatment of spider phobia. *Behavior Theapy, 22,* 407–422.

Ostrom, T. M., Skowronski, J. J., & Nowack, A. (1994). The cognitive foundations of attitudes: It's a wonderful construct. In P. G. Devine, D. L. Hamilton, & T. M. Ostrom (Eds.), *Social cognition: Impact on social psychology* (pp. 196–258). San Diego, CA: Academic Press.

Ouimette, P. C., Finney, J. W., & Moos, R. H. (1997). Twelve-step and cognitive-behavioral treatment for substance abuse: A comparison of treatment effectiveness. *Journal of Consulting and Clinical Psychology, 65,* 230–240.

Overmier, J. B., & Seligman, M. E. P. (1967). Effects of inescapable shock upon subsequent escape and avoidance learning. *Journal of Comparative and Physiological Psychology, 63,* 23–33.

Overton, D. A. (1984). State dependent learning and drug discriminations. In L. L. Iverson, S. D. Iverson, & S. H. Snyder (Eds.), *Handbook of psychopharmacology* (Vol. 18). New York: Plenum.

Oyserman, D. (1993). The lens of personhood: Viewing the self and others in a multicultural society. *Journal of Personality and Social Psychology, 65,* 993–1009.

Paik, H., & Comstock, G. (1994). The effects of television violence on antisocial behavior: A meta-analysis. *Communication Research, 21,* 516–546.

Paivio, A. (1986). *Mental representations: A dual coding approach.* New York: Oxford University Press.

Paivio, S. C., & Greenberg, L. S. (1995). Resolving "unfinished business": Efficacy of experiential therapy using empty-chair dialogue. *Journal of Consulting and Clinical Psychology, 63,* 419–425.

Palace, E. M., & Gorzalka, B. B. (1990). The enhancing effects of anxiety on arousal in sexually dysfunctional and functional woman. *Journal of Abnormal Psychology, 99,* 403–411.

Palmer, F. H., & Anderson, L. W. (1979). Long-term gains from early intervention: Findings from longitudinal studies. In E. Zigler & J. Valentine (Eds.), *Project Head Start: A legacy of the war on poverty.* New York: Free Press.

Palmer, S. E. (1992). Common region: A new principle of perceptual grouping. *Cognitive Psychology, 24,* 436–447.

Palmisano, M., & Herrmann, D. (1991). The facilitation of memory performance. *Bulletin of the Psychonomic Society, 29,* 557–559.

Paloski, W. H. (1998). Vestibulospinal adaptation to microgravity. *Otolaryngol Head and Neck Surgery, 118,* S39–S44.

Paloutzian, R. F., & Kirkpatrick, L. A. (1995). Introduction: The scope of religious influences on personal and societal well-being. *Journal of Social Issues, 51,* 1–11.

Pan, H. S., Neidig, P. H., & O'Leary, K. D. (1994). Predicting mild to severe husband-to-wife physical aggression. *Journal of Consulting and Clinical Psychology, 62,* 975–981.

Panksepp, J. (1998). Attention deficit hyperactivity disorders, psychostimulants, and intolerance of childhood playfulness: A tragedy in the making? *Current Directions in Psychological Science, 7,* 91–98.

Paoletti, M. G. (1995). Biodiversity, traditional landscapes and agroecosystem management. *Landscape and Urban Planning, 31*(1–3), 117–128.

Papp, L., Klein, D., Martinez, J., Schneier, F., Cole, R., Liebowitz, M., Hollander, E., Fryer, A., Jordan, F., & Gorman, J. (1993). Diagnostic and substance specificity of carbon monoxide–induced panic. *American Journal of Psychiatry, 150,* 250–257.

Parke, R. D. (1996). *Fatherhood.* Cambridge, MA: Harvard University Press.

Parke, R. D., & Buriel, R. (1998). Socialization in the family: Ethnic and ecological perspectives. In W. Damon & N. Eisenberg (Eds.), *Handbook of child psychology: Vol. 3. Social, emotional, and personality development* (5th ed., pp. 463–552). New York: Wiley.

Parke, R. D., & O'Neil, R. (1997). The influence of significant others on learning about relationships. In S. Duck (Ed.), *Handbook of personal relationships: Theory, research and interventions* (2nd ed., pp. 29–59). Chichester, Eng.: John Wiley & Sons.

Parkes, C. M. P., & Weiss, R. S. (1983). *Recovery from bereavement.* New York: Basic Books.

Parkin, A. J., & Walter, B. M. (1991). Aging, short-term memory, and frontal dysfunction. *Psychobiology, 19,* 175–179.

Parnas, J., Cannon, T., Jacobsen, B., Schulsinger, H., Schulsinger, F., & Mednick, S. (1993). Lifetime DSM-III-R diagnostic outcomes in the offspring of schizophrenic mothers. *Archives of General Psychiatry, 50,* 707–714.

Parnell, L. (1997). *EMDR: The revolutionary new therapy for freeing the mind, clearing the body, and opening the heart.* New York: Norton.

Parnetti, L., Senin, U., & Mecocci, P. (1997). Cognitive enhancement therapy for Alzheimer's disease: The way forward. *Drugs, 53*(5), 752–768.

Parrott, R. F. (1994). Central effects of CCK ligands in pigs making operant responses for food. Pharmacology, *Biochemistry, and Behavior, 49*(3), 463–469.

Pascarella, E. T. & Terenzini, P. T. (1991). *How college affects students: Findings and insights from twenty years of research.* San Francisco, CA: Jossey-Bass.

Patrick, C. J., Craig, K. D., & Prkachin, K. M. (1986). Observer judgments of pain: Facial action determinants. *Journal of Personality and Social Psychology, 50,* 1291–1298.

Patrick, C. J., Cuthbert, B. N., & Lang, P. J. (1994). Emotion in the criminal psychopath: Fear imaging processing. *Journal of Abnormal Psychology, 103,* 523–534.

Patterson, F. G. (1978). The gestures of a gorilla: Language acquisition in another pongid. *Brain and Language, 5,* 72–97.

Patterson, G. R. (1974). Intervention for boys with conduct problems: Multiple settings, treatments, and criteria. *Journal of Consulting and Clinical Psychology, 42,* 471–481.

Patterson, G. R., DeBaryshe, B. D., & Ramsey, E. (1989). A developmental perspective on antisocial behavior. *American Psychologist, 44,* 329–335.

Pattie, F. A. (1935). A report of attempts to produce uniocular blindness by hypnotic suggestion. *British Journal of Medical Psychiatry, 15,* 230–241.

Pauk, W., & Fiore, J. P. (1989). *Succeed in college!* Boston: Houghton Mifflin.

Paul, G. L. (1969). Behavior modification research: Design and tactics. In C. M. Franks (Ed.), *Behavior therapy: Appraisal and status* (pp. 29–62). New York: McGraw-Hill.

Paul, G. L. (2000). Milieu therapy. In A. E. Kazdin (ed), *The encyclopedia of psychology.* Washington, D.C.: American Psychological Association.

Paul, G. L., & Lentz, R. J. (1977). *Psychosocial treatment of chronic mental patients: Milieu versus social learning programs.* Cambridge, MA: Harvard University Press.

Paul, G. L., Stuve, P., & Cross, J. V. (1997). Real-world inpatient programs: Shedding some light—A critique. *Applied and Preventive Psychology, 6,* 193–204.

Paulhus, D. L., Fridhandler, B., & Hayes, S. (1997). Psychological defense: Contemporary theory and research. In R. Hogan, J. Johnson, & S. Briggs (Eds.), *Handbook of personality psychology* (pp. 544–588). San Diego: Academic Press.

Pauls, D. L., Alsobrook, J. P., II, Goodman, W., Rasmussen, S., & Leckman, J. F. (1995). A family study of obsessive-compulsive disorder. *American Journal of Psychiatry, 152,* 76–84.

Paulus, P. B. (1988). *Prison crowding: A psychological perspective.* New York: Springer-Verlag.

Paunonen, S., Jackson, D., Trzebinski, J., & Forsterling, F. (1992). Personality structure across cultures: A multi-method evaluation. *Journal of Personality and Social Psychology, 62,* 447–456.

Pavkov, T., Lewis, D., & Lyons, J. (1989). Psychiatric diagnosis and racial bias: An empirical investigation. *Professional Psychology: Research and Practice, 20,* 364–368.

Payne, J. W., Bettman, J. R., & Johnson, E. J. (1992). Behavioral decision research: A constructive processing perspective. *Annual Review of Psychology, 43,* 87–131.

Peck, J. W. (1978). Rats defend different body weights depending on palatability and accessibility of their food. *Journal of Comparative and Physiological Psychology, 92,* 555–570.

Pederson, P. (1994). A culture-centered approach to counseling. In W. J. Lonner & R. S. Malpass (Eds.), *Psychology and culture.* Boston: Allyn & Bacon.

Penfield, W., & Rasmussen, T. (1968). *The cerebral cortex of man: A clinical study of localization of function.* New York: Hafner.

Pennebaker, J. W. (1993). Putting stress into words: Health, linguistic, and therapeutic implications. *Behaviour Research and Therapy, 31,* 539–548.

Pennebaker, J. W., Colder, M., & Sharp, L. K. (1990). Accelerating the coping process. *Journal of Personality and Social Psychology, 58,* 528–537.

Pennebaker, J. W., Kiecolt-Glaser, J. K., & Glaser, R. (1988). Disclosure of traumas and immune function: Health implications for psychotherapy. *Journal of Consulting and Clinical Psychology, 56,* 239–245.

Pennebaker, J. W., & O'Heeron, R. C. (1984). Confiding in others and illness rate among spouses of suicide and accidental death victims. *Journal of Abnormal Psychology, 93,* 473–476.

Penner, L. A., & Craiger, J. P. (1992b). The weakest link: The performance of individual group members. In R. W. Swezey & E. Salas (Eds.), *Teams: Their training and performance* (pp. 57–74). Norwood, NJ: Ablex.

Penner, L. A., & Finkelstein, M. A. (1998). Dispositional and structural determinants of volunteerism. *Journal of Personality and Social Psychology, 74,* 525–537.

Penner, L. A., Fritzsche, B. A., Craiger, J. P., & Friefeld, T. R. (1995). Measuring the prosocial personality. In J. Butcher & C. D. Spielberger (Eds.), *Advances in personality assessment* (Vol. 10, pp. 147–163). Hillsdale, NJ: Lawrence Erlbaum Associates.

Penner, L. A., Knoff, H., Batchshe, G., Nelson, D. L., & Spielberger, C. D. (Eds.). (1994). *Contributions of psychology to science and math education.* Washington, DC: American Psychological Association.

Penrose, L., & Penrose, R. (1958). Impossible objects: A special type of visual illusion. *British Journal of Psychology, 49,* 31–33.

Pepeu, G. (1994). Memory disorders: Novel treatments, clinical perspective. *Life Sciences, 55,* 2189–2194.

Perls, F. S., Hefferline, R. F., & Goodman, P. (1951). *Gestalt therapy.* New York: Julian Press.

Peroutka, S. J. (1989). "Ecstacy": A human neurotoxin? *Archives of General Psychiatry, 46,* 191.

Peroutka, S. J., Newman, H., & Harris, H. (1988). The subjective effects of 3, 4-methylenedioxymethamphetamine in recreational users. *Neuropharmacology, 1*(4), 273–277.

Perris, E. E., Myers, N. A., & Clifton, R. K. (1990). Long-term memory for a single infancy experience. *Child Development, 61,* 1796–1807.

Persons, J. B., & Silberschatz, G. (1998). Are results of randomized controlled trials useful to psychotherapists? *Journal of Consulting and Clinical Psychology, 66,* 126–135.

Pervin, L. A. (1993). *Personality: Theory and research* (6th ed.). New York: Wiley.

Pervin, L. A. (1994). A critical analysis of current trait theory. *Psychological Inquiry, 5,* 103–113.

Pervin, L. A. (1996). *The science of personality.* New York: John Wiley and Sons.

Pervin, L. A., & John, O. P. (1997). *Personality: Theory and research* (7th ed.). New York: John Wiley & Sons.

Petersen, S. E., van Mier, H., Fiez, J. A., & Raichle, M. E. (1998). The effects of practice on the functional anatomy of task performance. *Proceedings of the National Academy of Science USA, 95,* 853–860.

Peterson, A. C. (1987, September). Those gangly years. *Psychology Today,* pp. 28–34.

Peterson, C. (1995, April). *The preschool child witness: Errors in accounts of traumatic injury.* Paper presented at the biennial meeting of the Society for Research in Child Development, Indianapolis.

Peterson, C. C. (1996). The ticking of the social clock: Adults' beliefs about the timing of transition events. *International Journal of Aging and Human Development, 42,* 189–203.

Peterson, C., & Barrett, L. C. (1987). Explanatory style and academic performance among university freshmen. *Journal of Personality and Social Psychology, 53,* 603–607.

Peterson, C., Maier, S. F., & Seligman, M. E. (1993). *Learned helplessness: A theory for the age of personal control.* New York: Oxford University Press.

Peterson, C., & Seligman, M. E. P. (1984). Causal explanations as a risk factor for depression: Theory and evidence. *Psychological Review, 91,* 347–374.

Peterson, C., Seligman, M. E. P., Yurko, K. H., Martin, L. R., & Friedman, H. S. (1998). Catastrophizing and untimely death. *Psychological Science, 9,* 127–130.

Peterson, G. B., Linwick, D., & Overmier, J. B. (1987). On the comparative efficacy of memories and expectancies as cues for choice behavior in pigeons. *Learning and Motivation, 18,* 1–20.

Peterson, L. R., & Peterson, M. J. (1959). Short-term retention of individual verbal items. *Journal of Experimental Psychology, 58,* 193–198.

Peterson, S. E., Snyder, A., Fox, P. T., & Raichle, M. E. (1990). Activation of extrastriate and frontal cortical areas by visual words and and word-like stimuli. *Science, 249,* 1041–1044.

Petitto, J., Folds, J., Ozer, H., Quade, D., & Evans, D. (1992). Abnormal diurnal variation in circulating natural killer cell phenotypes and cytotoxic activity in major depression. *American Journal of Psychiatry, 149,* 694–696.

Petrie, K. J., Booth, R. J., Pennebaker, J. W., & Davison, K. P. (1995). Disclosure of trauma and immune response to a Hepatitis B vaccination program. *Journal of Consulting and Clinical Psychology, 63,* 787–792.

Petrill, S. A., Plomin, R., Berg, S., Johansson, B., Pederson, N. L., Ahern, F., & McClearn, G. E. (1998). The genetic and environmental relationship between general and specific cognitive abilities in twins age 80 and older. *Psychological Science, 9,* 183–189.

Pettigrew, T. F. (1979). The ultimate attribution error: Extending Allport's cognitive analysis of prejudice. *Personality and Social Psychology Bulletin, 5,* 461–476.

Pettigrew, T. F. (1997). Generalized intergroup contact effects on prejudice. *Personality and Social Psychology Bulletin, 23,* 173–185.

Petty, R. (1995). Attitude change. In A. Tesser (Ed.), *Advanced social psychology* (pp. 195–257). New York: McGraw-Hill.

Petty, R., Cacioppo, J. T., & Schumann, D. (1983). Central and peripheral routes to advertising effectiveness: The moderating role of involvement. *Journal of Consumer Research, 10,* 134–148.

Petty, R. E., & Wegener, D. T. (1998). Attitude change: Multiple roles for persuasion variables. In D. Gilbert, S. T. Fiske, and G. Lindzey (Eds.), *Handbook of social psychology: Vol. 1* (4th ed., pp. 323–390). Boston: McGraw-Hill.

Peuskens, J. (1995). Risperidone in the treatment of patients with chronic schizophrenia: A multi-national, multi-centre, double-blind, parallel-group study versus haloperidol. *British Jorunal of psychiatry, 1966,* 712–726.

Phares, E. J. (1991). *Introduction to personality* (3rd ed.). New York: Harper-Collins.

Phelps, B. J., & Exum, M. E. (1992, Spring). Subliminal tapes: How to get the message across. *Skeptical Inquirer, 16,* 282–286.

Phelps, M. E., & Mazziotta, J. C. (1985). Positron emission tomography: Human brain function and biochemistry. *Science, 228,* 799–809.

Phillips, D. P. (1983). The impact of media violence on U.S. homicides. *American Sociological Review, 48,* 560–568.

Phillips, D. P., & Cartensen, L. L. (1986). Clustering of teenage suicides after television news stories about suicide. *New England Journal of Medicine, 315,* 685–689.

Phinney, J. S. (1996). When we talk about American ethnic groups, what do we mean? *American Psychologist, 51,* 918–927.

Piaget, J. (1952). *The origins of intelligence in children.* New York: International Universities Press.

Pierce, G., Sarason, I., & Sarason, B. (1991). General and specific support expectations and stress as predictors of perceived supportivness: An experimental study. *Journal of Personality and Social Psychology, 63,* 297–307.

Pike, A., McGuire, S., Hetherington, E. M., Reiss, D., & Plomin, R. (in press). Family environment, adolescent depressive symptoms, and antisocial behavior: A multivariate genetic analysis. *Developmental Psychology.*

Pike, K. M., Loeb, K., & Vitousek, K. (1996). Cognitive-behavioral therapy for anorexia nervosa and bulimia nervosa: Assessment and treatment of binge eating disorder. In J. K. Thompson (Ed.), *Body image, eating disorders, and obesity* (pp. 253–302). Washington, DC: American Psychological Association.

Piliavin, J. A., Dovidio, J. F., Gaertner, S. L., & Clark, R. D., III (1981). *Emergency intervention.* New York: Academic Press.

Pillard, R. C., & Bailey, J. M. (1998). Human sexual orientation has a heritable component. *Human Biology, 70,* 347–365.

Pillow, D. R., Zautra, A. J., & Sandler, I. (1996). Major life events and minor stressors: Identifying mediational links in the stress process. *Journal of Personality and Social Psychology, 70,* 381–394.

Pinault, D., Smith, Y., & Deschenes, M. (1997). Dendrodendritic and axoaxonic synapses in the thalamic reticular nucleus of the adult rat. *Journal of Neuroscience, 17,* 3215–3233.

Pinel, J. P. J. (1993). *Biopsychology.* Boston: Allyn & Bacon.

Pi-Sunyer, F. X. (1994). The fattening of America. *Journal of the American Medical Association, 272*(3), 238–239.

Pittman, T. (1998). Motivation. In D. Gilbert, S. T. Fiske, and G. Lindzey (Eds.), *Handbook of social psychology, Vol.: 1* (4th ed., pp. 549–583). Boston: McGraw-Hill.

Plomin, R. (1986). *Development, genetics, and psychology.* Hillsdale, NJ: Lawrence Erlbaum Associates.

Plomin, R. (1989). Environment and genes: Determinants of behavior. *American Psychologist, 44,* 105–111.

Plomin, R. (1994a). The Emanuel Miller memorial lecture 1993: Genetic research and the identification of environmental influences. *Journal of Child Psychology and Psychiatry, 35,* 817–834.

Plomin, R. (1994b). *Genetics and experience: The developmental interplay between nature and nurture.* Newbury Park, CA: Sage.

Plomin, R. (1995). Molecular genetics and psychology. *Current Directions in Psychological Science, 4,* 1–4.

Plomin, R., & Bergeman, C. S. (1991). The nature of nurture: Genetic influence on "environmental" measures. *Behavioral and Brain Sciences, 14,* 373–427. (With Open Peer Commentary)

Plomin, R., Chipuer, H. M., & Loehlin, J. C. (1990). Behavioral genetics and personality. In L. A. Pervin (Ed.), *Handbook of personality: Theory and research* (pp. 225–243). New York: Guilford Press.

Plomin, R., DeFries, J. C., & McClearn, G. E. (1990). *Behavior genetics: A primer.* New York: W. H. Freeman.

Plomin, R., Fulker, D. W., Corley, R., & DeFries, J. C. (1997). Nature, nurture, and cognitive development from 1 to 16 years: A parent-offspring adoption study. *Psychological Science, 8,* 442–447.

Plomin, R., & McClearn, G. E. (Eds.). (1993). *Nature, nurture and psychology.* Washington, DC: American Psychological Association.

Plomin, R., Owen, M. J., & McGuffin, P. (1994). The genetic basis of complex human behaviors. *Science, 264,* 1733–1739.

Plous, S. (1993). *The psychology of judgment and decision making.* New York: McGraw-Hill.

Plous, S. (1996). Attitudes toward the use of animals in psychological research and education: Results from a national survey of psychologists. *American Psychologist, 51,* 1167–1180.

Pollack, I. (1953). The assimilation of sequentially coded information. *American Journal of Psychology, 66,* 421–435.

Pollack, V. (1992). Meta-analysis of subjective sensitivity to alcohol in sons of alcoholics. *American Journal of Psychiatry, 149,* 1534–1538.

Polusny, M. A., & Follette, V. M. (1995). Long-term correlates of child sexual abuse: Theory and review of the empirical literature. *Applied and Preventive Psychology, 4,* 143–166.

Polusny, M. A., & Follette, V. M. (1996). Remembering childhood abuse: A national survey of psychologists' clinical practices, beliefs, and personal experiences. *Professional Psychology: Research and Practice, 27,* 41–52.

Pomerantz, J. R., & Kubovy, M. (1986). Theoretical approaches to perceptual organization. In K. R. Boff, L. Kaufman, and J. P. Thomas (Eds.), *Handbook of perception and human performance* (pp. 36.1–36.46). New York: Wiley.

Pomerleau, C. S., & Pomerleau, O. F. (1992). Euphoriant effects of nicotine in smokers. *Psychopharmacology, 108,* 460–465.

Poole, D. A., Lindsay, D. S., Memon, A., & Bull, R. (1995). Psychotherapy and the recovery of memories of childhood sexual abuse: U.S. and British practitioners' opinions, practices, and experiences. *Journal of Consulting and Clinical Psychology, 63,* 426–437.

Pope, H. G., Jr., Gruber, A. J., & Yurgelun-Todd, D. (1995). The residual neuropsychological effects of cannabis: The current status of research. *Drug and Alcohol Dependence, 38,* 25–34.

Pope, H. G., & Yurgelun-Todd, D. (1996). The residual cognitive effects of heavy marijuana use in college students. *Journal of the American Medical Association, 275,* 521–527.

Pope-Davis, D. B., Reynolds, A. L., Dings, J. G., & Nielson, D. (1995). Examining multicultural counseling competencies of graduate students in psychology. *Professional Psychology: Research and Practice, 26,* 322–329.

Popp, C. A., Diguer, L., Luborsky, L., Faude, J., Johnson, S., Morris, M., Schaffer, N., Schaffler, P., & Schmidt, K. (1996). Repetitive relationship themes in waking narratives and dreams. *Journal of Consulting and Clinical Psychology, 64,* 1073–1078.

Porges, S. W., Doussard, R. J. A., & Maita, A. K. (1995). Vagal tone and the physiological regulation of emotion. *Monographs of the Society for Research on Child Development, 59*(2–3), 167–186, 250–283.

Porkka-Heiskanen, T., Strecker, R. E., Thakkar, M., Bjorkum, A. A., Greene, R. W., & McCarley, R. W. (1997). Adenosine: A mediator of the sleep-inducing effects of prolonged wakefulness. *Science, 276,* 1265–1268.

Porter, R. H. (1991). Human reproduction and the mother-infant relationship. In T. V. Getchell et al. (Eds.), *Taste and smell in health and disease.* New York: Raven Press.

Porter, R. H., Cernich, J. M., & McLaughlin, F. J. (1983). Maternal recognition of neonates through olfactory cues. *Physiology and Behavior, 30,* 151–154.

Posner, M. I. (1978). *Chronometric explorations of the mind.* Hillsdale, NJ: Lawrence Erlbaum Associates.

Posner, M. I., Nissen, M. J., & Ogden, W. C. (1978). Attended and unattended processing modes: The role of set for spatial location. In H. L. Pick & I. J. Saltzman (Eds.), *Modes of perceiving and processing information.* Hillsdale, NJ: Lawrence Erlbaum Associates.

Posner, M. I., & Peterson, S. E. (1990). The attention system of the human brain. *Annual Review of Neurosciences, 13,* 24–42.

Post, R. M. (1992). Transduction of psychosocial stress into the neurobiology of recurrent affective disorder. *American Journal of Psychiatry, 149,* 999–1010.

Powch, I. G., & Houston, B. K. (1996). Hostility, anger-in, and cardiovascular activity in White women. *Health Psychology, 15,* 200–208.

Powley, T. L., & Keesey, R. E. (1970). Relationship of body weight to the lateral hypothalamicsyndrome. *Journal of Comparative and Physiological Psychology, 70,* 25–36.

Pratkanis, A. R. (1992). The cargo-cult science of subliminal persuasion. *Skeptical Inquirer, 16,* 260–273.

Pratkanis, A. R., & Aronson, E. (1991). *Age of propaganda: The everyday use and abuse of persuasion.* New York: W. H. Freeman.

Pratkanis, A. R., Eskenazi, J., & Greenwald, A. G. (1994). What you expect is what you believe (but not necessarily what you get): A test of the effectiveness of self-help audiotapes. *Basic and applied social psychology, 15,* 251–276.

Preciado, J. (1994). The empirical basis of behavior therapy applications with Hispanics. *The Behavior Therapist, 17,* 63–65.

Preece, J., Sharp, H., Benyon, D., Holland, S., & Carey, T. (1994). *Human-computer interaction.* Reading, MA: Addison-Wesley.

Premack, D. (1965). Reinforcement theory. In D. Levine (Ed.), *Nebraska symposium on motivation.* Lincoln: University of Nebraska Press.

Premack, D. (1971). Language in chimpanzees? *Science, 172,* 808–822.

Prentice-Dunn, S., & Rogers, R. W. (1989). Deindividuation and the self-regulation of behavior. In P. B. Paulus (Ed.), *Psychology of group influence* (2nd ed.). Hillsdale, NJ: Lawrence Erlbaum Associates.

Prescott, J. W. (1996). The origins of human love and violence. *Pre- and Peri-Natal Psychology Journal, 10,* 143–188.

Prilleltensky, I. (1997). Values, assumptions, and practices: Assessing the moral implications of psychological discourse and practice. *American Psychologist, 52,* 517–535.

Prinzmetal, W. (1992). The word superiority effect does not require a T-scope. *Perception and Psychophysics, 51,* 473–484.

Prochaska, J. O. (1994). Strong and weak principles for progressing from precontemplation to action on the basis of twelve problem behaviors. *Health Psychology, 13,* 47–51.

Prochaska, J. O., & DiClemente, C. C. (1992). Stages of change in the modification of problem behaviors. In M. Hersen, R. M. Eisler, & P. M. Miller (Eds.), *Progress in behavior modification.* Sycamore, IL: Sycamore Press.

Prochaska, J. O., DiClemente, C., & Norcross, J. (1992). In search of how people change: Application to addictive behaviors. *American Psychologist, 47,* 1102–1114.

Prochaska, J. O., & Norcross, J. C. (1994). *Systems of psychotherapy: A transtheoretical analysis* (3rd ed.). Pacific Grove, CA: Brooks/Cole.

Prochaska, J. O., Velicer, W. F., Rossi, J. S., Goldstein, M. G., Marcus, B. H., Rakowski, W., Fiore, C., Harlow, L. L., Redding, C. A., Rosenbloom, D., & Rossi, S. R. (1994). Stages of change and decisional balance for 12 problem behaviors. *Health Psychology, 13,* 39–46.

Proctor, R. & Van Zandt, T. (1994). *Human factors in simple and complex systems.* Boston: Allyn & Bacon.

Pruitt, D. G. (1998). Social conflict. In D. Gilbert, S. T. Fiske, and G. Lindzey (Eds.), *Handbook of social psychology,* Vol. 2 (4th ed., pp. 470–503). Boston: McGraw-Hill.

Pruitt, D. G., & Carnevale, P. J. (1993). *Negotiation in social conflict.* Pacific Grove, CA: Brooks/Cole.

Pryor, T. (1995). Diagnostic criteria for eating disorders: DSM–IV revisions. *Psychiatric Annals, 25*(1), 40–45.

Purcell, D. G., & Stewart, A. L. (1991). The object-detection effect: Configuration enhances perception. *Perception and Psychophysics, 50,* 215–224.

Quintana, S. M. (1998). Children's developmental understanding of ethnicity and race. *Applied and Preventive Psychology, 7,* 27–45.

Rabbitt, P. (1977). Changes in problem solving ability in old age. In J. E. Birren & K. W. Schaie (Eds.), *Handbook of the psychology of aging.* New York: Van Nostrand Reinhold.

Rachman, S. J. (1990). *Fear and courage* (2nd ed.). San Francisco: W. H. Freeman.

Rada, J. B., & Rogers, R. W. (1973). *Obedience to authority: Presence of authority and command strength.* Paper presented at the annual convention of the Southeastern Psychological Association.

Radecki, T. E. (1990, April–June). Cartoon monitoring. *National Coalition on Television Violence News,* p. 9.

Raeff, C., Greenfield, P. M., & Quiroz, B. (1995, March). *Developing interpersonal relationships in the cultural contexts of individualism and collectivism.* Paper presented at the biennial meeting of the Society for Research in Child Development, Indianapolis.

Raguram, R., & Bhide, A. (1985). Patterns of phobic neurosis: A retrospective study. *British Journal of Psychiatry, 147,* 557–560.

Raine, A., Brennan, P., & Mednick, S. (1994). Birth complications combined with early maternal rejection at age 1 year predispose to violent crime at age 18 years. *Archives of General Psychiatry, 51,* 984–988.

Raine, A., Buschbaum, M. S., Stanley, J., Lottenberg, S., Abel, L., & Stoddard, J. (1994). Selective reductions in prefrontal glucose metabolism in murderers. *Biological Psychiatry, 36,* 365–373.

Raine, A., Venables, P., & Williams, M. (1990). Relationships between central and autonomic measures of arousal at age 15 years and criminality at age 24 years. *Archives of General Psychiatry, 47,* 1003–1007.

Rainville, P., Duncan, G. H., Price, D. D., Carrier, B., & Bushnell, M. C. (1997). Pain affect encoded in human anterior cingulate but not somatosensory cortex. *Science, 277,* 968–971.

Rakowski, W., Ehrich, B., Dube, C., Pearlman, D. N., Goldstein, M. G., Peterson, K. K., Rimer, B. K., & Woolverton, H., III (1996). Screening mammography and constructs from the transtheoretical model: Associations using two definitions of the stages-of-adoption. *Annals of Behavioral Medicine, 18,* 91–100.

Ramachandran, V. S. (1988, August). Perceiving shape from shading. *Scientific American,* pp. 76–83.

Ramey, C. T. (1992). High-risk children and IQ: Altering intergenerational patterns. *Intelligence, 16,* 239–256.

Ramey, C. T. (1995, June). *Biology and experience codetermine intellectual development: Beyond additive models.* Paper presented at the convention of the American Psychological Society, New York.

Ramey, C. T., Bryant, D. M., Wasik, B. H., Sparling, J. J., Fendt, K. H., & LaVange, L. M. (1992). Infant health and development program for low birth weight, premature infants: Program elements, family participation, and child intelligence. *Pediatrics, 89,* 454–465.

Ramey, C. T., & Ramey, S. L. (1998). Early intervention and early experience. *American Psychologist, 53,* 109–121.

Ramirez, S. Z., Wassef, A., Paniagua, F. A., & Linskey, A. O. (1996). Mental health providers' perceptions of cultural variables in evaluating ethnically diverse clients. *Professional Psychology: Research and Practice, 27,* 284–288.

Ranta, S., Jussila, J., & Hynynen, M. (1990). Recall of awareness during cardiac anaesthesia: Influence of feedback information to the anaesthesiologists. *Acta Aneasthesiolgia Scandinavica, 40,* 554–560.

Rapee, R., Brown, T., Antony, M., & Barlow, D. (1992). Response to hyperventilation and inhalation of 5.5% carbon dioxide-enriched air across DSM-III anxiety disorders. *Journal of Abnormal Psychology, 101,* 538–552.

Raskin, D. C. (1986). The polygraph in 1986: Scientific, professional and legal issues surrounding applications and acceptance of polygraph evidence. *Utah Law Review* 1986, 29–74.

Raskin, N. J., & Rogers, C. R. (1995). Person-centered therapy. In J. J. Corsini & D. Wedding (Eds.), *Current psychotherapies* (5th ed., pp. 128–161). Itasca, IL: Peacock.

Ratner, C. (1994). The unconscious: A perspective from sociohistorical psychology. *Journal of Mind and Behavior, 15*(4), 323–342.

Rauschecker, J. P. (1997). Processing of complex sounds in the auditory cortex of cat, monkey, and man. *Acta Otolaryngol Supplement (Stockh), 532,* 34–38.

Rauscher, F. H., Shaw, G. L., Levine, L. J., Wright, E. L., Dennis, W. R., & Newcomb, R. L. (1997). Music training causes long-term enhancement of preschool children's spatial-temporal reasoning. *Neurological Research, 19,* 2–8.

Ray, D. W., Wandersman, A., Ellisor, J., & Huntington, D. E. (1982). The effects of high density in a juvenile correctional institution. *Basic and Applied Social Psychology, 3,* 95–108.

Reber, A. S. (1992). The cognitive unconscious: An evolutionary perspective. *Consciousness and Cognition: An International Journal, 1*(2), 93–133.

Recanzone, G. H. (1998). Rapidly induced auditory plasticity: The ventriloquism aftereffect. *Proceedings of the National Academy of Science USA, 95,* 869–875.

Redd, M., & de Castro, J. M. (1992). Social facilitation of eating: Effects of social instruction on food intake. *Physiology and Behavior, 52,* 749–754.

Redd, W. H. (1984). Psychological intervention to control cancer chemotherapy side effects. *Postgraduate Medicine, 75,* 105–113.

Reder, L. M., & Ritter, F. E. (1992). What determines initial feeling of knowing? Familiarity with question terms, not the answer. *Journal of Experimental Psychology: Learning, Memory, and Cognition, 18,* 435–451.

Reed, G. M., Kemeny, M. E., Taylor, S. E., Wang, H.-Y. J., & Visscher, B. R. (1994). "Realistic acceptance" as a predictor of decreased survival time in gay men with AIDS. *Health Psychology, 13,* 299–307.

Reed, S. K. (1992). *Cognition: Theory and applications* (3rd ed.). Pacific Grove, CA: Brooks/Cole.

Reedy, M. N. (1983). Personality and aging. In D. S. Woodruff & J. E. Birren (Eds.), *Aging: Scientific perspectives and social issues* (2nd ed.). Monterey, CA: Brooks/Cole.

Reeves, R. A., Baker, G. A., Boyd, J. G., & Cialdini, R. B. (1991). The door-in-the-face technique: Reciprocal concessions vs. self-presentational explanations. *Journal of Social Behavior and Personality, 6,* 545–558.

Regier, D. A., Narrow, W., Rae, D., Manderschied, R., Locke, B., & Goodwin, F. (1993). The de facto U.S. mental and addictive disorders service system: Epidemiologic catchment area prospective 1-year prevalence rates of disorders and services. *Archives of General Psychiatry, 50,* 85–94.

Reinisch, J. M., Ziemba-Davis, M., & Sanders, S. A. (1991). Hormonal contributions to sexually dimorphic behavioral development in humans. *Psychoneuroendocrinology, 16,* 213–278.

Reisenzein, R. (1983). The Schachter theory of emotion: Two decades later. *Psychological Bulletin, 94,* 239–264.

Reisman, J. M. (1976). *A history of clinical psychology.* New York: Irvington.

Reiss, A. J., & Roth, J. A. (1993). *Understanding and preventing violence.* Washington, DC: National Academy Press.

Reno, R. R., Cialdini, R. B., & Kallgren, C. A. (1993). The transsituational influence of social norms. *Journal of Personality and Social Psychology, 64,* 104–112.

Rescorla, L. A. (1981). Category development in early language. *Journal of Child Language, 8,* 225–238.

Rescorla, R. A. (1968). Probability of shock in the presence and absence of CS in fear conditioning. *Journal of Comparative and Physiological Psychology, 66,* 1–5.

Rescorla, R. A. (1988). Pavlovian conditioning: It's not what you think it is. *American Psychologist, 43,* 151–159.

Rescorla, R. A., & Wagner, A. R. (1972). A theory of Pavlovian conditioning: Variations in the effectiveness of reinforcement and nonreinforcement. In A. H. Black & W. F. Prokasy (Eds.), *Classical conditioning II.* New York: Appleton Century Crofts.

Resnick, M. (1997). Protecting adolescents from harm: Findings from the National Longitudinal Study of Adolescent Health. *Journal of the American Medical Association, 278,* 823–832.

Reynolds, B. A., & Weiss, S. (1992). Generation of neurons and astrocytes from isolated cells of the adult mammalian central nervous system. *Science, 255,* 1707–1710.

Reynolds, D. V. (1969). Surgery in the rat during electrical analgesia induced by focal brain stimulation. *Science, 164,* 444–445.

Rholes, W. S., Simpson, J. A., Blakely, B. S., Lanigan, L., & Allen, E. A. (1997). Adult attachment styles, the desire to have children, and working models of parenthood. *Journal of Personality, 65,* 357–385.

Rice, M. E. (1997). Violent offender research and implications for the criminal justice system. *American Psychologist, 52,* 414–423.

Richardson, P. H., & Vincent, C. A. (1986). Acupuncture for the treatment of pain: A review of evaluative research. *Pain, 24,* 15–40.

Richardson-Klavehn, A., & Bjork, R. A. (1988). Measures of memory. *Annual Review of Psychology, 39,* 475–543.

Rickels, K., Schweizer, E., Weiss, S., & Zavodnick, S. (1993). Maintenance drug treatment of panic disorder. II: Short- and long-term outcome after drug taper. *Archives of General Psychiatry, 50,* 61–68.

Riedel, W. J., & Jolles, J. (1996). Cognition enhancers in age-related cognitive decline. *Drugs and Aging, 8,* 245–274.

Riedy, C. A., Chavez, M., Figlewicz, D. P., & Woods, S. C. (1995). Central insulin enhances sensitivity to cholecystokinin. *Physiology and Behavior, 58*(4), 755–760.

Riegel, K. F. (1975). Toward a dialectical theory of development. *Human Development, 18,* 50–64.

Riger, S. (1992). Epistemological debates, feminist voices: Science, social values, and the study of women. *American Psychologist, 47,* 730–740.

Riggio, R. E. (1989). *Introduction to industrial/organizational psychology.* Glenview, IL: Scott, Foresman.

Rinn, W. E. (1984). The neuropsychology of facial expressions: A review of the neurological and psychological mechanisms for producing facial expressions. *Psychological Bulletin, 95,* 52–77.

Rioux, S. (1998). *The motivational basis of organizational citizenship behavior.* Unpublished doctoral dissertation, University of South Florida.

Rips, L. J. (1994). *The psychology of proof: Deductive reasoning in human thinking.* Cambridge, MA: MIT Press.

Risen, J. (1998). CIA seeks "curmudgeon" to signal its mistakes. *New York Times,* July 7.

Roberts, G. C., & Treasure, D. C. (1999). Sport psychology. In D. A. Bernstein & A. M. Stec (Eds.), *The psychology of everyday life.* Boston: Houghton Mifflin.

Robertson, J., & Robertson, J. (1971). Young children in brief separation: A fresh look. *Psychoanalytic Study of the Child, 26,* 264–315.

Robins, L. N., & Regier, D. A. (Eds.). (1991). *Psychiatric disorders in America: The Epidemiologic Catchment Area study.* New York: Free Press.

Robins, R., & John, O. (1997). The quest for self-insight: Theory and research on accuracy and bias. In R. Hogan, J. Johnson, & S. Briggs (Eds.), *Handbook of personality psychology* (pp. 649–679). San Diego: Academic Press.

Robins, R. W., Gosling, S. D., & Craik, K. H. (1999). An empirical analysis of trends in psychology. *American Psychologist, 54,* 117–128.

Robinson, J. H., & Pritchard, W. S. (1995). "The scientific case that nicotine is addictive": Reply. *Psychopharmacology, 117*(1), 16–17.

Robinson, J. L., Zahn-Waxler, C., & Emde, R. N. (1994). Patterns of development in early empathic behavior: Environmental and child constitutional influences. *Social Development, 3,* 125–145.

Rock, I. (1983). *The logic of perception.* Cambridge, MA: MIT Press.

Rodin, J., & Langer, E. J. (1977). Long-term effects of a control-relevant intervention with the institutionalized aged. *Journal of Personality and Social Psychology, 35,* 879–902.

Rodin, J., & Salovey, P. (1989). Health psychology. *Annual Review of Psychology, 40,* 533–580.

Rodriguez de Fonseca, F., Carrera, M. R. A., Navarro, M., Koob, G. F., & Weiss, F. (1997). Activation of corticotropin-releasing factor in the limbic system during cannabinoid withdrawal. *Science, 276,* 2050–2054.

Roediger, H. L., III. (1990). Implicit memory: Retention without remembering. *American Psychologist, 45,* 1043–1056.

Roediger, H. L., III, Guynn, M. J., & Jones, T. C. (1995). Implicit memory: A tutorial review. In G. d'Ydewalle, P. Eelen, & P. Bertelson (Eds.), *International perspectives on psychological science: Vol. 2. The state of the art* (pp. 67–94). Hove, Eng.: Lawrence Erlbaum Associates.

Roediger, H. L., III, Jacoby, D., & McDermott, K. B. (1996). Misinformation effects in recall: Creating false memories through repeated retrieval. *Journal of Memory and Learning, 35,* 300–318.

Roediger, H. L., III, & McDermott, K. B. (1995). Creating false memories: Remembering words not presented in lists. *Journal of Experimental Psychology: Learning, Memory, and Cognition, 21,* 803–814.

Roehrich, L., & Goldman, M. S. (1995). Implicit priming of alcohol expectancy memory processes and subsequent drinking behavior. *Experimental and Clinical Psychopharmocology, 3,* 402–410.

Roffwarg, H. P., Hermann, J. H., & Bowe-Anders, C. (1978). The effects of sustained alterations of waking visual input on dream content. In A. M. Arkin, J. S. Antrobus, & S. J. Ellman (Eds.), *The mind in sleep.* Hillsdale, NJ: Lawrence Erlbaum Associates.

Roffwarg, H. P., Muzio, J. N., & Dement, W. C. (1966). Ontogenetic development of the human sleep-dream cycle. *Science, 152,* 604–619. (Revised 1969.)

Rogers, C. R. (1951). *Client-centered therapy.* Boston: Houghton Mifflin.

Rogers, C. R. (1961). *On becoming a person.* Boston: Houghton Mifflin.

Rogers, C. R. (1970). *Carl Rogers on encounter groups.* New York: Harper & Row.

Rogers, C. R. (1980). *A way of being.* Boston: Houghton Mifflin.

Rogers, J., Madamba, S. G., Staunton, D. A., & Siggins, G. R. (1986). Ethanol increases single unit activity in the inferior olivary nucleus. *Brain Research, 385,* 253–262.

Rogers, R. (1995). *Diagnostic and structured interviewing: A handbook for psychologists.* Odessa, FL: Psychological Assessment Resources.

Rogers, T. B. (1995). *The psychological testing enterprise: An introduction.* Belmont, CA: Wadsworth.

Rogers, Y. (1989). Icon design for the user interface. *International Review of Ergonomics, 2,* 129–154.

Rogoff, B., & Waddell, K. J. (1982). Memory for information organized in a scene by children from two cultures. *Child Development, 53,* 1224–1228.

Rohan, M. J., & Zanna, M. P. (1996). Value transmission in families. In C. Seligman, J. M. Olson, & M. P. Zanna (Eds.), *The psychology of values: The Ontario symposium* (Vol. 8, pp. 253–276). Mahwah, NJ: Lawrence Erlbaum Associates.

Rolls, E. T. (1997). Taste and olfactory processing in the brain and its relation to the control of eating. *Critical Review of Neurobiology, 11,* 263–287.

Roper Organization (1992). *Unusual personal experiences: An analysis of data from three national surveys.* Las Vegas, NE: Bigelow Holding Co.

Rosch, E. (1975). Cognitive representations of semantic categories. *Journal of Experimental Psychology: General, 104,* 192–223.

Rosch, E., Mervis, C. B., Gray, W. D., Johnson, D. M., & Boyes-Braem, P. (1976). Basic objects in natural categories. *Cognitive Psychology, 8,* 382–439.

Rose, D. T., Abramson, L. Y., Hodulik, C. J., Halberstadt, L., & Leff, G. (1994). Heterogeneity of cognitive style among depressed inpatients. *Journal of Abnormal Psychology, 103,* 419–429.

Rose, S. P. R. (1993, April 17). No way to treat a mind. *New Scientist,* pp. 23–26.

Rosellini, L. (1998, April 13). When to spank. *U.S. News & World Report,* pp. 52–58.

Rosen, B. C., & D'Andrade, R. (1959). The psychosocial origins of achievement motivation. *Sociometry, 22,* 188–218.

Rosen, R. (1991). *The healthy company.* Los Angeles: J. P. Tarcher.

Rosenbaum, R. (1995, January 15). The great Ivy League nude posture photo scandal. *New York Times Magazine,* pp. 26–31, 40, 46, 55, 56.

Rosenberg, M. B., Friedmann, T., Roberston, R. C., Tuszynski, M., Wolff, J. A., Breakefield, X. O., & Gage, F. H. (1988). Grafting genetically modifed cells to the damaged brain: Restorative effect of NGF expression. *Science, 242,* 1575–1578.

Rosenfarb, I. S., Goldstein, M. J., Mintz, J., & Nuechterlein, K. H. (1995). Expressed emotion and subclinical psychopathology observable within the transactions between schizophrenic patients and their family members. *Journal of Abnormal Psychology, 104,* 259–267.

Rosenfeld, J. P. (1995). Alternative views of Bashore and Rapp's (1993) alternatives to traditional polygraphy: A critique. *Psychological Bulletin, 117*(1), 159–166.

Rosenstock, I. M. (1974). Historical origins of the health belief model. *Health Education Monographs, 2,* 328–335.

Rosenthal, R. (1994a). Science and ethics in conducting, analyzing, and reporting psychological research. *Psychological Science, 5,* 127–134.

Rosenthal, R. (1994b). Interpersonal expectancy effects: A 30-year perspective. *Current Directions in Psychological Science, 3,* 176–179.

Rosenthal, R. R. (1966). *Experimenter effects in behavioral research.* New York: Appleton-Century-Crofts.

Rosenthal, R. R., & Jacobson, L. (1968). *Pygmalion in the classroom.* New York: Holt, Rinehart & Winston.

Rosenzweig, M. R., & Bennett, E. L. (1996). Psychobiology of plasticity: Effects of training and experience on brain and behavior. *Behavioural Brain Research, 78,* 57–65.

Ross, C. A., Anderson, G., Fleisher, W. P., & Norton, G. R. (1991). The frequency of multiple personality disorder among psychiatric inpatients. *American Journal of Psychiatry, 148,* 1717–1720.

Ross, C. A., Joshi, S., & Currie, R. (1990). Dissociative experiences in the general population. *American Journal of Psychiatry, 147,* 1547–1552.

Ross, S. I., & Jackson, J. M. (1991). Teachers' expectations for Black males' and Black females' academic achievement. *Personality and Social Psychology Bulletin, 17,* 78–82.

Ross, S. M., & Ross, L. E. (1971). Comparison of trace and delay classical eyelid conditioning as a function of interstimulus interval. *Journal of Experimental Psychology, 91,* 165–167.

Roth, M. D., Arora, A., Barsky, S. H., Kleerup, E. C., Simmons, M., & Tashkin, D. P. (1998). Airway inflammation in young marijuana and tobacco smokers. *American Journal of Respiratory Critical Care Medicine, 157,* 928–937.

Rothbart, M., & Lewis, S. (1994). Cognitive processes and intergroup relations: A historical perspective: In P. G. Devine, D. L. Hamilton, & T. M. Ostrom (Eds.), *Social cognition: Impact on social psychology* (pp. 347–382). San Diego, CA: Academic Press.

Rothbart, M. K., & Bates, J. E. (1998). Temperament. In W. Damon & N. Eisenberg (Eds.), *Handbook of child psychology: Vol. 3. Social, emotional, and personality development* (5th ed., pp. 105–176). New York: Wiley.

Rothbaum, B. O., Hodges, L. F., Kooper, R., & Opdyke, D. (1995). Effectiveness of computer-generated virtual reality graded exposure in the treatment of acrophobia. *American Journal of Psychiatry, 152,* 626–628.

Rothblum, E. D. (1994). "I only read about myself on bathroom walls": The need for research on the mental health of lesbians and gay men. *Journal of Clinical and Consulting Psychology, 62*(2), 213–280.

Rottenstreich, Y., & Tversky, A. (1997). Unpacking, repacking, and anchoring: Advances in support theory. *Psychological Review, 104,* 406–415.

Rotter, J. (1982). *The development and application of social learning theory.* New York: Praeger.

Rotter, J. B. (1990). Internal versus external control of reinforcement: A case history of a variable. *American Psychologist, 45,* 489–493.

Rotton, J., & Frey, J. (1985). Air pollution, weather, and violent crimes: Concomitant time-series analysis of archival data. *Journal of Personality and Social Psychology, 49,* 1207–1220.

Rotton, J., Frey, J., Barry, T., Mulligan, M., & Fitzpatrick, M. (1979). The air pollution experience and physical aggression. *Journal of Applied Social Psychology, 9,* 397–412.

Rotton, J., & Kelly, I. W. (1985). Much ado about the full moon: A meta-analysis of lunar-lunacy research. *Psychological Bulletin, 97,* 286–306.

Rouéché, B. (1986, December 8). Cinnabar. *The New Yorker.*

Rovee-Collier, C. (1993). The capacity for long-term memory in infancy. *Current Directions in Psychological Science, 2,* 130–135.

Rowe, D. C. (1997). Genetics, temperament, and personality. In R. Hogan, J. Johnson, & S. Briggs (Eds.), *Handbook of personality psychology* (pp. 367–386). San Diego: Academic Press.

Rowe, W. F. (1993). Psychic detectives: A critical examination. *Skeptical Inquirer, 17,* 159–165.

Rozin, E. (1983). *Ethnic cuisine: The flavor principle cookbook.* Brattleboro, VT: Stephen Greene Press.

Rozin, P. (1982). "Taste-smell confusions" and the duality of the olfactory sense. *Perception and Psychophysics, 31,* 397–401.

Rozin, P., & Shenker, J. (1989). Liking oral cold and hot irritant sensations: Specificity to type of irritant and locus of stimulation. *Chemical Senses, 14*(6), 771–779.

Rubin, B. M. (1998, February 8). When he's retiring and she isn't. *Chicago Tribune,* Sect. 1, pp. 1ff.

Rubin, E. (1915). *Synsoplevede figure.* Copenhagen; Gyldendalske.

Rubin, K. H., Bukowski, W., & Parker, J. G. (1998). Peer interactions, relationships, and groups. In W. Damon & N. Eisenberg (Eds.), *Handbook of child psychology: Vol. 3. Social, emotional, and personality development* (5th ed., pp. 619–700). New York: Wiley.

Rubinow, D. R., & Schmidt, P. J. (1996). Androgens, brain, and behavior. *American Journal of Psychiatry, 153,* 974–984.

Ruble, D. N., & Martin, C. L. (1998). Gender development. In W. Damon & N. Eisenberg (Eds.), *Handbook of child psychology: Vol. 3. Social, emotional, and personality development* (5th ed., pp. 933–1016). New York: Wiley.

Ruffman, T., Perner, J., Naito, M., Parkin, L., & Clements, W. A. (1998). Older (but not younger) siblings facilitate false belief understanding. *Developmental Psychology, 34,* 161–174.

Rugg, M. D., & Coles, M. G. H. (Eds.). (1995). *Electrophysiology of mind.* New York: Oxford University Press.

Rumbaugh, D. M. (Ed.). (1977). *Language learning by a chimpanzee: The Lana project.* New York: Academic Press.

Rumelhart, D. E., & McClelland, J. L. (1986). *Parallel distributed processing: Explorations in the microstructure of cognition: Vol. 1. Foundations.* Cambridge, MA: Bradford.

Rumelhart, D. E., & McClelland, J. L., with the PDP Research Group. (1986). *Parallel distributed processing: Vol. 1. Foundations.* Cambridge, MA: MIT Press.

Rumelhart, D. E., & Todd, P. M. (1992). Learning and connectionist representations. In D. E. Meyer & S. Kornblum (Eds.), *Attention and performance XIV: Synergies in experimental psychology, artificial intelligence, and cognitive neuroscience* (pp. 3–30). Cambridge, MA: MIT Press.

Rusbult, C. E., & Van Lange, P. A. M. (1996). Interdependence processes. In E. T Higgins & A. W. Kruglanski (Eds.), *Social psychology: Handbook of basic principles* (pp. 564–596). New York: Guilford.

Rusbult, C. E., Verette, J., Whitney, G. A., Slovik, L. F., & Lipkus, I. (1991). Accommodation processes in close relationships: Theory and preliminary empirical evidence. *Journal of Personality and Social Psychology, 60,* 53–78.

Rush, A. J. (1993). Mood disorders in DSM-IV. In D. L. Dunner (Ed.), *Current psychiatric therapy* (pp. 189–195). Philadelphia: W. B. Saunders.

Rushton, J. P. (1990). Creativity, intelligence, and psychoticism. *Personality and Individual Differences, 11,* 1291–1298.

Rushton, J. P., Fulker, D. W., Neale, M. C., Nias, D. K. B., & Eysenck, H. J. (1986). Altruism and aggression: The heritability of individual differences. *Journal of Personality and Social Psychology, 50,* 1192–1198.

Russell, J. A. (1991). Culture and the categorization of emotions. *Psychological Bulletin, 110,* 426–450.

Russell, J. A. (1994). Is there universal recognition of emotion from facial expression? A review of the cross-cultural studies. *Psychological Bulletin, 155*(2), 102–141.

Russell, J. A. (1995). Facial expressions of emotion: What lies beyond minimal universality? *Psychological Bulletin, 118,* 379–391.

Rutkowski, G. K., Gruder, C. L., & Romer, D. (1983). Group cohesiveness, social norms, and bystander intervention. *Journal of Personality and Social Psychology, 44,* 545–552.

Rutter, M. L. (1997). Nature-nurture integration. The example of antisocial behavior. *American Psychologist, 52,* 390–398.

Ryan, R. H., & Geiselman, R. E. (1991). Effects of biased information on the relationship between eyewitness confidence and accuracy. *Bulletin of the Psychonomic Society, 29,* 7–9.

Rymer, R. (1992, April 23). A silent childhood. *The New Yorker,* pp. 41–81.

Rymer, R. (1993a). *Genie: A scientific tragedy.* New York: HarperCollins.

Rymer, R. (1993b). *Genie: An abused child's flight from silence.* New York: Harper Collins.

Rynders, J., & Horrobin, J. (1980). Educational provisions for young children with Down's syndrome. In J. Gottlieb (Ed.), *Educating mentally retarded persons in the mainstream* (pp. 109–147). Baltimore: University Park Press.

Saarni, C., Mummer, D. L., & Campos, J. J. (1998). Emotional development: Action, communication, and understanding. In W. Damon & N. Eisenberg (Eds.), *Handbook of child psychology: Vol. 3. Social, emotional, and personality development* (5th ed., pp. 237–310). New York: Wiley.

Sachdev, P., Hay, P., & Cumming, S. (1992). Surgical treatment of obsessive-compulsive disorder. *Archives of General Psychiatry, 49,* 582–583.

Sachs, J. (1967). Recognition memory for syntactic and semantic aspects of connected discourse. *Perception and Psychophysics, 2,* 437–442.

Sack, R. L., Hughes, R. J., Edgar, D. M., & Lewy, A. J. (1997). Sleep-promoting effects of melatonin: At what dose, in whom, under what conditions, and by what mechanisms? *Sleep, 20,* 908–915.

Sackeim, H. A. (1985, June). The case for ECT. *Psychology Today,* pp. 36–40.

Sackeim, H. A., Gur, R. C. J., & Saucy, M. C. (1978). Emotions are expressed more intensely on the left side of the face. *Science, 202,* 434–436.

Sackoff, J., & Weinstein, L. (1988). The effects of potential self-inflicted harm on obedience to an authority figure. *Bulletin of the Psychonomic Society, 26,* 347–348.

Sacks, O. (1985). *The man who mistook his wife for a hat.* New York: Summit Books.

Sacks, O. (1992, July 27). The landscape of his dreams. *The New Yorker.*

Sacks, O. (1996). *An anthropologist on Mars: Seven paradoxical tales.* New York: Vintage Books.

Sage, M. R., & Wilson, A. J. (1994). The blood-brain barrier: An important concept in neuroimaging. *American Journal of Neuroradiology, 15*(4), 601–622.

Sagi, A., van IJzendoorn, M. H., Aviezer, O., Donnell, F., & Mayseless, O. (1994). Sleeping out of home in a kibbutz communal arrangement: It makes a difference for infant-mother attachment. *Child Development, 65,* 992–1004.

Sakmann, B. (1992). Elementary steps in synaptic transmission revealed by currents through single ion channels. *Science, 256,* 503–512.

Saks, M. J. (1992). Obedience versus disobedience to legitimate versus illegitimate authorities issuing good versus evil directives. *Psychological Science, 3,* 221–223.

Sakurai, T., Amemiya, A., Ishii, M., Matsuzaki, I., Chemelli, R. M., Tanaka, H., Williams, S. C., Richardson, J. A., Kozlowski, G. P., Wilson, S., Arch, J. R., Buckingham, R. E., Haynes, A. C., Carr, S. A., Annan, R. S., McNulty, D. E., Liu, W. S., Terrett, J. A., Elshourbagy, N. A., Bergsma, D. J., & Yanagisawa, M. (1998). Orexins and orexin receptors: A family of hypothalamic neuropeptides and G protein-coupled receptors that regulate feeding behavior. *Cell, 92,* 573–585.

Salloum, I. M., Cornelius, J. R., Thase, M. E., Daley, D. C., Kirisci, L., & Spotts, C. (1998). Naltrexone utility in depressed alcoholics. *Psychopharmacological Bulletin, 34,* 111–115.

Salovey, P., Mayer, J. D., & Rosenhan, D. L. (1991). Mood and helping: Mood as a motivator of helping and helping as a regulator of mood. In M. S. Clark (Ed.), *Review of personality and social psychology: Vol. 12. Prosocial behavior* (pp. 215–237). Newbury Park, CA: Sage.

Salovey, P., Rothman, A. J., & Rodin, J. (1998). Health behavior. In D. Gilbert, S. T. Fiske, and G. Lindzey (Eds.), *Handbook of social psychology,* Vol. 2 (4th ed., pp. 684–732). Boston: McGraw-Hill.

Salovey, P., & Sluyter, D. J. (Eds.). (1997). *Emotional development and emotional intelligence: Educational implications.* New York: Basic Books.

Salthouse, T. A. (1990). Working memory as a processing resource in cognitive aging. *Developmental Review, 10,* 101–124.

Salthouse, T. A. (1993). Speed and knowledge as determinants of adult age differences in verbal tasks. *Journal of Gerontology, 48,* 29–36.

Salthouse, T. A., Babcock, R. L., & Shaw, R. J. (1991). Effects of adult age on structural and operational capacities in working memory. *Psychology and Aging, 6,* 118–127.

Salthouse, T. A., & Prill, K. A. (1987). Inferences about age impairments in inferential reasoning. *Psychology and Aging, 2,* 43–51.

Salvi, R. J., Chen, L., Trautwein, P., Powers, N., & Shero, M. (1998). Hair cell regeneration and recovery of function in the avian auditory system. *Scandinavian Audiology Supplement, 48,* 7–14.

Samuel, S. E., & Gorton, G. E. (1998). National survey of psychology internship directors regarding education for prevention of psychologist-patient sexual exploitation. *Professional Psychology: Research and Practice, 29,* 86–90.

Samuelson, C. D., & Messick, D. M. (1995). When do people want to change the rules for allocating shared resources? In D. Schroeder (Ed.), *Social dilemmas: Perspectives on individuals and groups* (pp. 143–162). Westport, CT: Praeger.

Sanberg, P. R., Borlongan, C. V., Othberg, A. I., Saporta, S., Freeman, T. B., & Cameron, D. F. (1997). Testis-derived Sertoli cells have a trophic effect on dopamine neurons and alleviate hemiparkinsonism in rats. *Nature Medicine, 3,* 1129–1132.

Sanders, M. R., & Dadds, M. R. (1993). *Behavioral family intervention.* Boston: Allyn & Bacon.

Sanderson, W. C., Rapee, R. M., & Barlow, D. H. (1989). The influence of an illusion of control on panic attacks induced via inhalation of 5.5 carbon dioxide-enriched air. *Archives of General Psychiatry, 46,* 157–162.

Sandler, N. D. (1993). Panic gluttons: The cellular telephone scare shows what can happen when purveyors of junk science feed public fear. *Technology Review, 96,* 72–73.

Sanes, J. N., Donoghue, J. P., Thangaraj, V., Edelman, R. R., & Warach, S. (1995). Shared neural substrates controlling hand movements in human motor cortex. *Science, 268,* 1775–1777.

Sanna, L. J. (1992). Self-efficacy theory: Implications for social facilitation and social loafing. *Journal of Personality and Social Psychology, 62,* 774–786.

Sarason, B. R., Sarason, I. G., & Gurung, R. A. R. (1997). Close personal relationships and health outcomes: A key to the role of social support. In S. Duck (Ed.), *Handbook of personal relationships* (pp. 547–573). New York: Wiley.

Sarason, I., Johnson, J., & Siegel, J. (1978). Assessing impact of life changes: Development of the life experiences survey. *Journal of Clinical and Consulting Psychology, 46,* 932–946.

Sarason, I. G. (1984). Stress, anxiety, and cognitive interference: Reactions to tests. *Journal of Personality and Social Psychology, 46*(4), 929–938.

Sarason, I. G., Sarason, B. R., Keefe, D. E., Hayes, B. E., & Shearin, E. N. (1986). Cognitive interference: Situational determinants and traitlike characteristics. *Journal of Personality and Social Psychology, 51,* 215–226.

Sato, T. (1997). Seasonal affective disorder and phototherapy: A critical review. *Professional Psychology: Research and Practice, 28,* 164–169.

Saudino, K. J. (1998). Moving beyond the heritability question: New directions in behavioral genetic studies of personality. *Current Directions in Psychological Science, 6,* 86–89.

Saudino, K. J., & Plomin, R. (1997). Cognitive and temperamental mediators of genetic contributions to the home environment during infancy. *Merrill-Palmer Quarterly, 43,* 1–23.

Saufley, W. H., Otaka, S. R., & Bavaresco, J. L. (1985). Context effects: Classroom tests and context independence. *Memory & Cognition, 13,* 522–528.

Sauter, S., Murphy, L., & Hurrell, J. (1990). Prevention of work-related psychological disorders: A national strategy proposed by the National Institute for Occupational Safety and Health (NIOSH). *American Psychologist, 45,* 1146–1158.

Savage-Rumbaugh, E. S. (1990). Language acquisition in a non-human species: Implications for the innateness debate. *Developmental Psychobiology, 23,* 599–620.

Savage-Rumbaugh, E. S., Murphy, J., Sevcik, R. A., Brakke, K. E., Williams, S. L., & Rumbaugh, D. M. (1993). Language comprehension in ape and child. *Monographs of the Society for Research in Child Development, 58*(3–4).

Savage-Rumbaugh, S., & Brakke, K. E. (1996). Animal language: Methodological and interpretive issues. In M. Bekoff & D. Jamieson (Eds.), *Readings in animal cognition* (pp. 269–288). Cambridge, MA: MIT Press.

Savage-Rumbaugh, E. S., Pate, J. L., Lawson, J., Smith, S. T., & Rosenbaum, S. (1983). Can a chimpanzee make a statement? *Journal of Experimental Psychology: General, 112,* 469–487.

Saveliev, S. V., Lebedev, V. V., Evgeniev, M. B., & Korochkin, L. I. (1997). Chimeric brain: theoretical and clinical aspects. *International Journal of Developmental Biology, 41,* 801–808.

Savin-Williams, R. C., & Demo, D. H. (1984). Developmental change and stability in adolescent self-concept. *Developmental Psychology, 20,* 1100–1110.

Sayers, J. (1991). *Mother of psychoanalysis.* New York: Norton.

Scarr, S., & Carter-Saltzman, L. (1982). Genetics and intelligence. In R. Sternberg (Ed.), *Handbook of human intelligence.* Cambridge, Eng.: Cambridge University Press.

Scarr, S., & Weinberg, R. A. (1976). IQ test performance of black children adopted by white families. *American Psychologist, 31,* 726–739.

Schachar, R., & Logan, G. (1990). Impulsivity and inhibitory control in normal development and childhood psychopathology. *Developmental Psychology, 26,* 710–720.

Schachter, S., & Singer, J. (1962). Cognitive, social and physiological determinants of emotional state. *Psychological Review, 69,* 379–399.

Schacter, D. L. (1992). Understanding implicit memory: A cognitive neuroscience approach. *American Psychologist, 47,* 559–569.

Schacter, D. L. (1999). The seven sins of memory: Insights from psychology and cognitive neuroscience. *American Psychologist, 54,* 182–203.

Schacter, D. L., Chiu, C.-Y. P., & Ochsner, K. N. (1993). Implicit memory: A selective review. *Annual Review of Neuroscience, 16,* 159–182.

Schacter, D. L., Church, B., & Treadwell, J. (1994). Implicit memory in amnesic patients: Evidence for spared auditory priming. *Psychological Science, 5,* 20–25.

Schacter, D. L., & Cooper, L. A. (1993). Implicit and explicit memory for novel visual objects: Structure and function. *Journal of Experimental Psychology: Learning, Memory, and Cognition, 19*(5), 995–1009.

Schacter, D. L., Cooper, L. A., Delaney, S. M., Peterson, M. A., & Tharan, M. (1991). Implicit memory for possible and impossible objects: Constraints on the construction of structural descriptions. *Journal of Experimental Psychology: Learning, Memory, and Cognition, 17,* 3–19.

Schacter, D. L., & Tulving, E. (1982). Amnesia and memory research. In L. S. Cermak (Ed.), *Human memory and amnesia.* Hillsdale, NJ: Lawrence Erlbaum Associates.

Schaefer, J., Sykes, R., Rowley, R., & Baek, S. (1988, November). *Slow country music and drinking.* Paper presented at the 87th annual meetings of the American Anthropological Association, Phoenix, AZ.

Schaffer, C. E., Davidson, R. J., & Saron, C. (1983). Frontal and parietal EEG asymmetry in depressed and non-depressed subjects. *Biological Psychiatry, 18,* 753–762.

Schaffer, H. R. (1996). *Social development.* Oxford: Blackwell.

Schaie, K. W. (1993). The Seattle logitudinal study of adult intelligence. *Current Directions in Psychological Science, 2*(6), 171–175.

Schaie, K. W. (1996). Intellectual development in adulthood. In J. E. Birren, K. Schaie, R. P. Abeles, M. Gatz, & T. A. Salthouse (Eds.), *Handbook of the psychology of aging* (4th ed., pp. 266–286). San Diego: Academic Press.

Schaie, K. W., & Hertzog, C. (1983). Fourteen year cohort-sequential analysis of adult intellectual development. *Developmental Psychology, 19,* 531–543.

Schanberg, S. M., & Field, T. M. (1987). Sensory deprivation stress and supplemental stimulation in the rat pup and preterm human neonate. *Child Development, 58,* 1431–1447.

Schank, R. C., & Abelson, R. (1977). *Scripts, plans, goals, and understanding.* Hillsdale, NJ: Lawrence Erlbaum Associates.

Scheerer, M., Rothmann, R., & Goldstein, K. (1945). A case of "idiot savant": An experimental study of personality organization. *Psychol. Monognomics, 58*(4).

Scheier, M. F., & Carver, C. S. (1987). Dispositional optimism and physical well-being: The influence of generalized outcome expectancies on health. *Journal of Personality, 55,* 169–210.

Scheier, M. F., Carver, C. S. & Bridges, M. W. (1994). Distinguishing optimism from neuroticism (and trait anxiety, self-mastery, and self-esteem): A reevaluation of the Life Orientation Test. *Journal of Personality and Social Psychology, 67,* 1063–1078.

Scheier, M. F., Matthews, K. A., Owens, J. F., Magovern, G. J., Lefebvre, R. C., Abbott, R. A., & Carver, C. S. (1989). Dispositional optimism and recovery from coronary artery bypass surgery: The beneficial effects on physical and psychological well-being. *Journal of Personality and Social Psychology, 57,* 1024–1040.

Schenck, C. H., & Mahowald, M. W. (1992). Motor dyscontrol in narcolepsy: Rapid eye movement (REM) sleep without atonia and REM sleep behavior disorder. *Annals of Neurology, 32*(1), 3–10.

Schieber, M. H., & Hibbard, L. S. (1993, July 23). How somatotopic is the motor cortex hand area? *Science, 261,* 489–492.

Schiff, M., Duyme, M., Dumaret, A., Stewart, J., Tomkiewicz, S., & Feingold, J. (1978). Intellectual status of working class children adopted early into upper-middle class families. *Science, 200,* 1503–1504.

Schiller, P. H. (1996). On the specificity of neurons and visual areas. *Behavior and Brain Research, 76,* 21–35.

Schloss, P., & Williams, D. C. (1998). The serotonin transporter: A primary target for antidepressant drugs. *Journal of Psychopharmacology, 12,* 115–121.

Schmidt, F. L. (1994). The future of personnel selection in the U.S. Army. In M. Rumsey, C. Walker, & J. Harris (Eds.), *Personnel, selection, and classification* (pp. 333–350). Hillsdale, NJ: Lawrence Erlbaum Associates.

Schmidt, N. B., Lerew, D. R., & Jackson, R. J. (1997). The role of anxiety sensitivity in the pathogenesis of panic: Prospective evaluation of spontaneous panic attacks druing acute stress. *Journal of Abnormal Psychology, 106,* 355–364.

Schmidt, R. A., & Bjork, R. A. (1992, July). New conceptualizations of practice: Common principles in three paradigms suggest new concepts for training. *Psychological Science, 3*(4), 207–217.

Schnabel, T. (1987). Evaluation of the safety and side effects of antianxiety agents. *American Journal of Medicine, 82* (Suppl. 5A), 7–13.

Schnapf, J. L., Kraft, T. W., & Baylor, D. A. (1987). Spectral sensitivity of human cone photoreceptors. *Nature, 325,* 439–441.

Schneider, B. (1985). Organizational behavior. *Annual Review of Psychology, 36,* 573–611.

Schneider, R. J., Hough, L. M., & Dunnette, M. (1996). Broadsided by broad traits, or how to sink science in five dimensions or less. *Journal of Organizational Behavior, 17,* 639–655.

Schneider, W., & Bjorklund, D. F. (1998). Memory. In In W. Damon, D. Kuhn, & R. Siegler (Eds.), *Handbook of child psychology: Vol. 2. Cognition, language and perception* (5th ed., pp. 467–521). New York: Wiley.

Schneiderman, B. (1992). *Designing the user interface* (2nd ed.). Reading, MA: Addison-Wesley.

Schneidman, E. S. (1987). A psychological approach to suicide. In G. VandenBos & B. K. Bryant (Eds.), *Cataclysms, crises, and catastrophes: Psychology in action. The master lectures, Vol. 6* (pp. 147–183). Washington, DC: American Psychological Association.

Schreiber, G. B., Robins, M., Striegel-Moore, R., Obarzanek, E., Morrison, J. A., & Wright, D. J. (1996). Weight modification efforts reported by black and white preadolescent girls: National Heart, Lung, and Blood Institute Growth and Health Study. *Pediatrics, 98,* 63–70.

Schroeder, D. A. (1995). An introduction to social dilemmas. In D. Schroeder (Ed.), *Social dilemmas: Perspectives on individuals and groups* (pp. 1–13). Westport, CT: Praeger.

Schroeder, D. A., Penner, L. A., Dovidio, J. F., & Piliavin, J. A. (1995). *The psychology of helping and altruism: Problems and puzzles.* New York: McGraw-Hill.

Schultz, D., & Schultz, S. E. (1998). *Psychology and work today* (7th ed.). Upper Saddle River, NJ: Prentice-Hall.

Schultz, D. P., & Schultz, S. E. (2000). *A history of modern psychology.* (7th ed.). Fort Worth, TX: Harcourt Brace.

Schulz, R. (1978). *The psychology of death, dying, and bereavement.* Reading, MA: Addison-Wesley.

Schulz, R., Bookwala, J., Knapp, J. E., Scheier, M., & Williamson, G. (1996). Pessimism, age, and cancer mortality. *Psychology and Aging, 11,* 304–309.

Schuster, D. H. (1964). A new ambiguous figure: A three stick clevis. *American Journal of Psychology, 77,* 673.

Schwartz, B., & Reisberg, D. (1991). *Learning and memory.* New York: W. W. Norton.

Schwartz, B., & Robbins, S. J. (1995). *Psychology of learning and behavior* (4th ed.). New York: W. W. Norton.

Schwartz, C., Kagan, J., & Snidman, N. (1995, May). Inhibition from toddlerhood to adolescence. Paper presented at the annual meeting of the American Psychiatric Association, Miami.

Schwartz, R. H., Voth, E. A., & Sheridan, M. J. (1997). Marijuana to prevent nausea and vomiting in cancer patients: A survey of clinical oncologists. *South Medical Journal, 90,* 167–172.

Schwarz, N. (1999). Self-reports: How the questions shape the answers. *American Psychologist, 54,* 93–105.

Schwarz, N., Groves, R. M., & Schuman, H. (1998). Survey methods. In D. T. Gilbert, S. T. Fiske, & G. Lindzey (Eds.), *Handbook of social psychology*, Vol. 1 (4th ed., pp. 143–179). Boston: McGraw-Hill.

Schweinhart, L. J., & Weikart, D. P. (1991). Response to "Beyond IQ in preschool programs?" *Intelligence, 15,* 313–315.

Schwender, D., Klasing, D., Daunderer, M., Maddler, C., Poppel, E., & Peter, K. (1995). Awareness during general anesthetic: Definition, incidence, clinical relevance, causes, avoidance, and medicolegal aspects. *Anaesthetist, 44,* 743–754.

Schwenk, K. (1994, March 18). Why snakes have forked tongues. *Science, 263,* 1573–1577.

Scribner, S. (1977). Modes of thinking and ways of speaking: Culture and logic reconsidered. In P. N. Johnson-Laird & P. C. Watson (Eds.), *Thinking: Readings in cognitive science.* New York: Cambridge University Press.

Seab, J. P., Jagust, W. J., Wong, S. T. S., Roos, M. S., Reed, B. R., & Budinger, T. F. (1988). Quantitative NMR measurements of hippocampal atrophy in Alzheimer's disease. *Magnetic Reasonance in Medicine, 8,* 200–208.

Seamon, J. G., Ganor-Stern, D., Crowley, M. J., & Wilson, S. M. (1997). A mere exposure effect for transformed three-dimensional objects: Effects of reflection, size, or color changes on affect and recognition. *Memory and Cognition, 25,* 367–374.

Searle, L. V. (1949). The organization of hereditary maze-brightness and maze-dullness. *Genetic Psychology Monographs, 39,* 279–325.

Sears, R. (1977). Sources of satisfaction of the Terman gifted men. *American Psychologist, 32,* 119–128.

Secord, D., & Peevers, B. (1974). The development and attribution of person concepts. In T. Mischel (Ed.), *Understanding other persons.* Oxford: Blackwell.

Sedikides, C., Campbell, W. K., Reeder, G., & Elliot, A. J. (1998). The self-serving bias in relational context. *Journal of Personality and Social Psychology, 74,* 378–386.

Seeman, M. V. (Ed.). (1995). *Gender and psychopathology.* Washington, DC: American Psychiatric Press.

Segal, L., & Suri, J. F. (1999). Psychology applied to product design. In A. M. Stec & D. A. Bernstein (Eds.), *Psychology: Fields of application.* Boston: Houghton Mifflin.

Segal, N. L. (1993). Twin, sibling, and adoption methods: Tests of evolutionary hypotheses. *American Psychologist, 48,* 943–956.

Segall, M. H., Dasen, P. R., Berry, J. W., & Poortinga, Y. H. (1990). *Human behavior in global perspective: An introduction to cross-cultural psychology.* Elmwood, NY: Pergamon Press.

Segerstrom, S. C., Taylor, S. E., Kemeny, M. E., & Fahey, J. L. (in press). Optimism is associated with mood, coping, and immune changes in response to stress. *Journal of Personality and Social Psychology.*

Seiger, A., Nordberg, A., Vonholst, H., Backman, L., Ebendal, T., Alafuzoff, I., Amberla, K., Hartvig, P., Herlitz, A., Lilja, A., Lundquist, H., Langstrom, B., Meyerson, B., Persson, A., Viitanen, M., Winblad, B., & Olson, L. (1993). Intracranial infusion of purified nerve growth factor to an Alzheimer patient: the 1st attempt of a possible future treatment strategy. *Behavioral Brain Research, 57,* 255–261.

Sejnowski, T. J., Chattarji, S., & Stanton, P. K. (1990). Homosynaptic long-term depression in hippocampus and neocortex. *Seminars in the Neurosciences, 2,* 355–363.

Sekuler, R., & Blake, R. (1994). *Perception* (3rd ed.). New York: Mc Graw-Hill.

Selco, S. L., & Cohen, N. J. C. (1996). *Processing operation–dependent priming in a symmetry detection task.* Unpublished manuscript, University of Illinois.

Seligman, M. E. P. (1975). *Helplessness: On depression, development, and death.* San Francisco: W. H. Freeman.

Seligman, M. E. P. (1991). *Learned optimism.* New York: Knopf.

Seligman, M. E. P. (1995). The effectiveness of psychotherapy: The *Consumer Reports* study. *American Psychologist, 50,* 965–974.

Seligman, M. E. P. (1996). Good news for psychotherapy: The *Consumer Reports* study. *Independent Practitioner, 16,* 17–20.

Seligman, M. E. P., Castellon, C., Cacciola, J., Shulman, P., Luborsky, L., Ollove, M., & Downing, R. (1988). Explanatory style change during cognitive therapy for unipolar depression. *Journal of Abnormal Psychology, 97,* 13–18.

Seligman, M. E. P., Klein, D. C., & Miller, W. R. (1976). Depression. In H. Leitenberg (Ed.), *Handbook of behavior modification and behavior therapy.* Englewood Cliffs, NJ: Prentice-Hall.

Seligman, M. E. P., & Schulman, P. (1986). Explanatory style as a predictor of productivity and quitting among life insurance agents. *Journal of Personality and Social Psychology, 50,* 832–838.

Sell, R. L., Wells, J. A., & Wypij, D. (1995). The prevalence of homosexual behavior and attraction in the United States, the United Kingdom, and France: Results of national population-based samples. *Archives of Sexual Behavior, 24*(3), 235–248.

Selman, R. L. (1981). The child as a friendship philosopher. In S. R. Asher & J. M. Gottman (Eds.), *The development of children's friendships.* New York: Cambridge University Press.

Selye, H. (1956). *The stress of life.* New York: McGraw-Hill.

Selye, H. (1976). *The stress of life* (2nd ed.). New York: McGraw-Hill.

Seppa, N. (1997, June). Children's TV remains steeped in violence. *APA Monitor,* p. 36.

Serpell, R. (1994). The cultural construction of intelligence. In W. J. Lonner & R. S. Malpass (Eds.), *Psychology and culture.* Boston: Allyn & Bacon.

Servan-Schreiber, E., & Anderson, J. R. (1990). Learning artificial grammars with competitive chunking. *Journal of Experimental Psychology: Learning, Memory, and Cognition, 16,* 592–608.

Service, R. F. (1994, October 14). Neuroscience: Will a new type of drug make memory-making easier? *Science, 266,* 218–219.

Sevcik, R. A., & Savage-Rumbaugh, E. S. (1994). Language comprehension and use by great apes. *Language and Communication, 14,* 37–58.

Shadish, W. R., Cook, T. D., & Campbell, D. T. (in press). *Experimental and quasi-experimental designs for generalized causal inference.* Boston: Houghton Mifflin.

Shaffer, D. R. (1973). *Children's responses to a hypothetical proposition.* Unpublished manuscript, Kent State University.

Shaffer, D. R. (1999). *Developmental psychology: Childhood and adolescence.* Pacific Grove, CA: Brooks/Cole.

Shalev, A. Y., Bonne, M., & Eth, S. (1996). Treatment of posttraumatic stress disorder: A review. *Psychosomatic Medicine, 58,* 165–182.

Shapiro, D. E., & Schulman, C. E. (1996). Ethical and legal issues in e-mail therapy. *Ethics and Behavior, 6,* 107–124.

Shapiro, D. H., & Walsh, R. N. (Eds.) (1984). *Meditation: Classical and contemporary perspectives.* New York: Aldine.

Shapiro, F. (1989a). Eye movement desensitization: A new treatment for post-traumatic stress disorder. *Journal of Behavior Therapy and Experimental Psychiatry, 20,* 211–217.

Shapiro, F. (1989b). Efficacy of the eye movement desensitization procedure in the treatment of traumatic memories. *Journal of Traumatic Stress, 2,* 199–223.

Shapiro, F. (1991). Eye movement desensitization and reprocessing procedure: From EMD to EMD/R—A new treatment model for anxiety and related traumata. *The Behavior Therapist, 15,* 133–135.

Shapiro, F. (1995). *Eye movement desensitization and reprocessing: Basic principles, protocols, and procedures.* New York: Guilford.

Shapiro, F. (1996). Eye movement desensitization and reprocessing (EMDR): Evaluation of controlled PTSD research. *Journal of Behavior Therapy and Experimental Psychiatry, 27,* 209–218.

Shaver, P. R., & Clark, C. L. (1996). Forms of adult romantic attachment and their cognitive and emotional underpinnings. In G. G. Noam & K. W. Fischer (Eds.), *Development and vulnerability in close relationships: The Jean Piaget symposium series* (pp. 29–58). Mahwah, NJ: Lawrence Erlbaum Associates.

Shaw, J. S., III. (1996). Increases in eyewitness confidence resulting from persistent questioning. *Journal of Experimental Psychology: Applied, 2,* 126–146.

Shaw, S. F., Cullen, J. P., McGuire, J. M., & Brinckerhoff, L. C. (1995). Operationalizing a definition of learning disabilities. *Journal of Learning Disabilities.*

Shaywitz, B. A., Shaywitz, S. E., Pugh, K. R., Constable, R. T., Skudlarski, P., Fulbright, R. K., Bronen, R. A., Fletcher, J. M., Shankweller, D. P., Katz, L., & Gore, J. C. (1995). Sex differences in the functional organization of the brain for language. *Nature, 373,* 607–609.

Shepherd, C. (1994, March 31). News of the weird. *Daily Illini.*

Shepperd, J. A. (1993). Productivity loss in performance groups: A motivation analysis. *Psychological Bulletin, 113,* 67–81.

Sher, K., Walitzer, K., Wood, P., & Brent, E. (1991). Characteristics of children of alcoholics: Putative risk factors, substance use and abuse, and psychopathology. *Journal of Abnormal Psychology, 100,* 427–448.

Sherif, M. (1937). An experimental approach to the study of attitudes. *Sociometry, 1,* 90–98.

Sherman, J. W., & Klein, S. B. (1994). Development and representation of personality impressions. *Journal of Personality and Social Psychology, 67,* 972–983.

Sherman, S. J. (1980). On the self-erasing nature of errors of prediction. *Journal of Personality and Social Psychology, 39,* 211–221.

Sherwin, B. B., & Gelfand, M. M. (1987). The role of androgen in the maintenance of sexual functioning in oophorectomized women. *Psychosomatic Medicine, 49,* 397–409.

Sherwin, B. B., Gelfand, M. M., & Brender, W. (1985). Androgen enhances sexual motivation in females: A prospective crossover study of sex steroid administration in the surgical menopause. *Psychosomatic Medicine, 47,* 339–351.

Shewchuk, R. M., Richards, J. S., & Elliott, T. R. (1998). Dynamic processes in health outcomes among caregivers of patients with spinal cord injuries. *Health Psychology, 17,* 125–129.

Shiffman, S. (1993). Smoking cessation treatment: Any progress? *Journal of Consulting and Clinical Psychology, 61,* 718–722.

Shiffman, S., Engberg, J. B., Paty, J. A., & Perz, W. G. (1997). A day at a time: Predicting smoking lapse from daily urge. *Journal of Abnormal Psychology, 106,* 104–116.

Shiloh, S. (1996). Genetic counseling: A developing area of interest for psychologists. *Professional Psychology: Research and Practice, 27,* 475–486.

Shobe, K. K., & Kihlstrom, J. F. (1997). Is traumatic memory special? *Current Directions in Psychological Science, 6,* 70–74.

Shrout, P. E. (1997). Should significance tests be banned? Introduction to a special section exploring the pros and cons. *Psychological Science, 8,* 1–2.

Shweder, R. A., Much, N. C., Mahapatra, M., & Park, L. (1994). The "big three" of morality (autonomy, community, and divinity), and the "big three" explanations of suffering, as well. In A. Brandt & P. Rozin (Eds.), *Morality and health.* Stanford, CA: Stanford University Press.

Siddle, D. A. T., Packer, J. S., Donchin, E., & Fabiani, M. (1991). Mnemonic information processing. In J. R. Jennings & M. G. H. Coles (Eds.), *Handbook of cognitive psychophysiology: Central and autonomic nervous system approaches* (pp. 449–510). Chichester, Eng.: John Wiley & Sons.

Siegal, M. (1997). *Knowing children: Experiments in conversation and cognition* (2nd ed.). Hove, Eng.: Psychology Press/Erlbaum/Taylor & Francis.

Siegel, J. M., & Rogawski, M. A. (1988). A function for REM sleep: Regulation of noradrenergic receptor sensitivity. *Brain Research Review, 13,* 213–233.

Siegel, S., Hirson, R. E., Krank, M. D., & McCully, J. (1982). Heroin "overdose" death: The contribution of drug associated environmental cues. *Science, 216,* 430–437.

Siegler, R. S. (1994). Cognitive variability: A key to understanding cognitive development. *Current Directions in Psychological Science, 3,* 1–4.

Siegler, R. S. (1995). Children's thinking: How does change occur? In W. Schneider & F. Weinert (Eds.), *Memory performance and competencies: Issues in growth and development.* Hillsdale, NJ: Lawrence Erlbaum Associates.

Silbersweig, D. A., Stern, E., Frith, C., Cahill, C., Holmes, A., Grootoonk, S., Seaward, J., McKenna, P., Chua, S. E., Schnorr, L., Jones, T., & Frackowiak, R. S. J. (1995, November). A functional neuroanatomy of hallucinations in schizophrenia. *Nature, 378,* 176–179.

Silbert, M. H., & Pines, A. M. (1984). Pornography and sexual abuse of women. *Sex Roles, 10,* 857–868.

Silver, B., Poland, R., & Lin, K.-M. (1993). Ethnicity and pharmacology of tricyclic antidepressants. In K.-M. Lin, R. Poland, & G. Nakasaki (Eds.), *Psychopharmacology and psychobiology of ethnicity.* Washington, DC: American Psychiatric Association Press.

Silver, E. (1995). Punishment or treatment? Comparing the lengths of confinement of successful and unsuccessful insanity defendants. *Law and Human Behavior, 19,* 375–388.

Silver, R. L., & Wortman, C. B. (1980). Coping with undesirable life events. In J. Garber & M. E. P. Seligman (Eds.), *Human helplessness: Theory and applications* (pp. 279–340). New York: Academic Press.

Silverman, K., Evans, A. M., Strain, E. C., & Griffiths, R. R. (1992). Withdrawal syndrome after the double-blind cessation of caffeine consumption. *New England Journal of Medicine, 327,* 1109–1114.

Silverstein, L. B. (1996). Evolutionary psychology and the search for sex differences. *American Psychologist, 51,* 160–161.

Silviera, J. M. (1971). *Incubation: The effect of interruption timing and length on problem solution and quality of problem processing.* Unpublished doctoral dissertation, University of Oregon, Eugene.

Sims, J. H., & Baumann, D. D. (1972). The tornado threat: Coping styles of the north and south. *Science, 17,* 1386–1392.

Sinclair, R. C., Hoffman, C., Mark, M. M., Martin, L. L., & Pickering, T. L. (1994). Construct accessibility and the misattribution of arousal. *Psychological Science, 5*(1), 15–19.

Sinha, M. K., & Caro, J. F. (1998). Clinical aspects of leptin. *Vitamins and Hormones, 54,* 1–30.

Sinha, P., & Poggio, T. (1996). I think I know that face. *Nature, 384,* 404.

Skinner, B. F. (1938). *The behavior of organisms.* New York: Appleton.

Skinner, B. F. (1958). Teaching machines. *Science, 128,* 969–977.

Skinner, B. F. (1961a). *Cumulative record* (3rd ed.). Englewood Cliffs, NJ: Prentice-Hall.

Skinner, B. F. (1961b). Teaching machines. *Scientific American* (November), pp. 91–102.

Slamecka, N. J., & McElree, B. (1983). Normal forgetting of verbal lists as a function of their degree of learning. *Journal of Experimental Psychology: Learning, Memory, and Cognition, 9,* 384–397.

Slater, A., Mattock, A., Brown, E., & Bremner, J. G. (1991). Form perception at birth. *Journal of Experimental Child Psychology, 51,* 395–406.

Sleek, S. (1998, May). Diet, nutrition and sex: New teen data have it all. *APA Monitor,* p. 27.

Sleek, S. (1999, February). Programs aim to attract minorities to psychology. *APA Monitor,* p. 47.

Slomkowski, C., & Dunn, J. (1996). Young children's understanding of other people's beliefs and feelings and their connected communication with friends. *Developmental Psychology, 32,* 442–447.

Slovic, P. (1984). *Facts versus fears: Understanding perceived risk.* Paper presented at science and public policy seminar sponsored by the Federation of Behavioral and Psychological and Cognitive Sciences, Washington, DC.

Small, G. W., Rabins, P. V., Barry, P. P., Buckholtz, N. S., DeKosky, S. T., Ferris, S. H., Finkel, S. I., Gwyther, L. P., Khachaturian, Z. S., Lebowitz, B. D., McRae, T. D., Morris, J. C., Oakley, F., Schneider, L. S., Streim, J. E., Sunderland, T., Teri, L. A., & Tune, L. E. (1997). Diagnosis and treatment of Alzheimer's disease and related disorders: Consensus statement of the American Association for Geriatric Psychiatry, the Alzheimer's Association, and the American Geriatrics Society. *Journal of American Medical Association, 278,* 1363–1371.

Small, I. F., Small, J. G., & Milstein, V. (1986). Electroconvulsive therapy. In P. A. Berger & H. K. H. Brodie (Eds.), *American handbook of psychiatry: Biological psychiatry* (2nd ed., Vol. 8). New York: Basic Books.

Smith, A., & Weissman, M. (1992). Epidemiology. In E. S. Paykel (Ed.), *Handbook of affective disorders* (2nd ed.). New York: Guilford.

Smith, A. C., III, & Kleinman, S. (1989). Managing emotions in medical school: Students' contacts with the living and the dead. *Social Psychology Quarterly, 52,* 56–69.

Smith, A. P., & Maben, A. (1993). Effects of sleep deprivation, lunch, and personality on performance, mood, and cardiovascular function. *Physiology and Behavior, 54*(5), 967–972.

Smith, D., & Dumont, F. (1995). A cautionary study: Unwarranted interpretations of the Draw-a-Person test, *Professional Psychology: Research and Practice, 26,* 298–303.

Smith, E. (1998). Mental representation and memory. In D. Gilbert, S. T. Fiske, and G. Lindzey (Eds.), *Handbook of social psychology,* Vol. 1 (4th ed., pp. 391–445). Boston: McGraw-Hill.

Smith, E. R. (1993). Social identity and social emotions: Toward new conceptualizations of prejudice. In D. M. Mackie & D. L. Hamilton (Eds.), *Affect, cognition, and stereotyping* (pp. 297–315). San Diego, CA: Academic Press.

Smith, H. S., & Cohen, L. H. (1993). Self-complexity and reactions to a relationship breakup. *Journal of Clinical and Social Psychology, 12,* 367–384.

Smith, J., & Baltes, P. B. (1990). A study of wisdom-related knowledge: Age/cohort differences in responses to life-planning problems. *Developmental Psychology, 26,* 494–505.

Smith, L. B., & Sera, M. D. (1992). A developmental analysis of the polar structure of dimensions. *Cognitive Psychology, 24,* 99–142.

Smith, M. (1988). Recall of spatial location by the amnesic patient HM. Special issue: Single case-studies in amnesia—Theoretical Advances. *Brain and Cognition, 7,* 178–183.

Smith, M. L., Glass, G. V., & Miller, T. I. (1980). *The benefits of psychotherapy.* Baltimore: Johns Hopkins University Press.

Smith, P. B., & Bond, M. H. (1999). *Social psychology across cultures: Analysis and perspectives* (2nd ed.). Boston: Allyn & Bacon.

Smith, R. S., Guilleminault, C., & Efron, B. (1997). Circadian rhythms and enhanced athletic performance in the National Football League. *Sleep, 20,* 362–365.

Smith, S., & Freedman, D. G. (1983, April). *Mother-toddler interaction and maternal perception of child temperament in two ethnic groups: Chinese-American and European-American.* Paper presented at the meeting of the Society for Research in Child Development, Detroit, MI.

Smith, S. L., & Donnerstein, E. (1998). Harmful effects of exposure to media violence: Learning of aggression, emotional desensitization, and fear. In R. G. Geen & E. Donnerstein (Eds.), *Human aggression* (pp. 230–247). San Diego: Academic Press.

Smith, S. M., Glenberg, A. M., & Bjork, R. A. (1978). Environmental context and human memory. *Memory & Cognition, 6,* 342–355.

Smith, S. M., Vela, E., & Williamson, J. E. (1988). Shallow input processing does not induce environmental context-dependent recognition. *Bulletin of the Psychonomic Society, 26,* 537–540.

Smith, S. S., O'Hara, B. F., Persico, A. M., Gorelick, D. A., Newlin, D. B., Vlahov, D., Solomon, L., Pickens, R., & Uhl, G. R. (1992). Genetic vulnerability to drug abuse. The D_2 dopamine receptor Taq i B1 restriction fragment length polymorphism appears more frequently in polysubstance abusers. *Archives of General Psychiatry, 49,* 723–727.

Smith, V. L. (1991). Prototypes in the courtroom: Lay representations of legal concepts. *Journal of Personality and Social Psychology, 44,* 787–797.

Smythe, M. M., Collins, A. F., Morris, P. E., & Levy, P. (1995). *Cognition in action* (2nd ed.). Hillsdale, NJ: Lawrence Erlbaum Associates.

Smythies, J. (1997). The functional neuroanatomy of awareness: With a focus on the role of various anatomical systems in the control of intermodal attention *Consciousness and Cognition, 6,* 455–481.

Snarey, J. (1987). A question of morality. *Psychological Bulletin, 97,* 202–232.

Snodgrass, S. R. (1994). Cocaine babies: A result of multiple teratogenic influences. *Journal of Child Neurology, 9*(3), 227–233.

Snow, R. E. (1995). Pygmalion and intelligence? *Current Directions in Psychological Science, 4,* 169–171.

Snowden, L. R., & Cheung, F. (1990). Use of inpatient mental health services by members of ethnic minority groups. *American Psychologist, 45,* 347–355.

Snyder, C. R. (1997). Unique invulnerability: A classroom demonstration in estimating personal mortality. *Teaching of Psychology, 24,* 197–199.

Snyder, M., & Cantor, N. (1998). Understanding personality and social behavior: A functionalist strategy. In D. Gilbert, S. T. Fiske, and G. Lindzey (Eds.), *Handbook of social psychology,* Vol. 1 (4th ed., pp. 635–679). Boston: McGraw-Hill.

Snyder, M., & Haugen, J. A. (1995). Why does behavioral confirmation occur? A functional perspective on the role of the target. *Personality and Social Psychology Bulletin, 21,* 963–974.

Snyderman, M., & Rothman, S. (1987). Survey of expert opinion on intelligence and aptitude testing. *American Psychologist, 42,* 137–144.

Soetens, E., Casaer, S., D'Hooge, R., & Hueting, J. E. (1995). Effect of amphetamine on long-term retention of verbal material. *Psychopharmacology, 119,* 155–162.

Sokoloff, L. (1981). Localization of functional activity in the central nervous system by measurement of glucose utilization with radioactive deoxyglucose. *Journal of Cerebral Blood Flow and Metabolism, 1,* 7–36.

Solomon, A. (1998, January 12). Anatomy of melancholy. *New Yorker,* pp. 46–61.

Solomon, R. L. (1980). The opponent-process theory of acquired motivation: The costs of pleasure and the benefits of pain. *American Psychologist, 35,* 691–712.

Solomon, R. L., & Corbit, J. D. (1974). An opponent-process theory of motivation: I. Temporal dynamics of affect. *Psychological Review, 81,* 119–145.

Solomon, R. L., Kamin, L. J., & Wynne, L. C. (1953). Traumatic avoidance learning: The outcomes of several extinction procedures with dogs. *Journal of Abnormal and Social Psychology, 48,* 291–302.

Solso, R. L. (1998). *Cognitive psychology* (5th ed.). Boston: Allyn & Bacon.

Sommer, R. (1999). Applying environmental psychology. In D. A. Bernstein & A. M. Stec (Eds.), *The psychology of everyday life.* Boston: Houghton Mifflin.

Sorce, J., Emde, R., Campos, J., & Klinnert, M. (1981, April). *Maternal emotional signaling: Its effect on the visual cliff behavior of one-year-olds.* Paper presented at the meetings of the Society for Research in Child Development, Boston, MA.

Spaeth, A. (1997, May 19). The golden shaft. *Time,* pp. 54–58.

Spangler, G., Fremmer-Bombik, E., & Grossman, K. (1996). Social and individual determinants of infant attachment security and disorganization. *Infant Mental Health Journal, 17,* 127–139.

Spangler, W. (1992). Validity of questionnaire and TAT measures of need for achievement: Two meta-analyses. Psychological *Bulletin, 112,* 140–154.

Spanos, N. P. (1994). Multiple identity enactments and multiple personality disorder: A sociocognitive perspective. *Psychological Bulletin, 116,* 143–165.

Spanos, N. P. (1996). *Multiple identities and false memories: A sociocognitive perspective.* Washington, DC: American Psychological Association.

Spanos, N. P., Burnley, M. C. E., & Cross, P. A. (1993). Response expectancies and interpretations as determinants of hypnotic responding. *Journal of Personality and Social Psychology, 65*(6), 1237–1242.

Spanos, N. P., Cross, P. A., Dickson, K., & DuBreuil, S. C. (1993). Close encounters: An examination of UFO experiences. *Journal of Abnormal Psychology, 102,* 624–632.

Spearman, C. E. (1904). General intelligence objectively determined and measured. *American Journal of Psychology, 15,* 201–293.

Spearman, C. E. (1927). *The abilities of man.* New York: Macmillan.

Spelke, E. S., Breinlinger, K., Macomber, J., & Jacobson, K. (1992). Origins of knowledge. *Psychological Review, 99,* 605–632.

Spencer, S., Steele, C. M., & Quinn, D. (1997). *Under suspicion on inability: Stereotype threats and women's math performance.* Unpublished manuscript.

Sperry, R. W. (1968). Hemisphere deconnection and unity in conscious awareness. *American Psychologist, 23,* 723–733.

Sperry, R. W. (1974). Lateral specialization in the surgically separated hemispheres. In F. O. Schmitt & F. G. Wordon (Eds.), *The neurosciences third study program.* Cambridge, MA: MIT Press.

Spiegel, D. (Ed.) (1994). *Dissociation: Culture, mind, and body.* Washington, DC: American Psychiatric Press.

Spielman, A. J., Saskin, P., & Thorpy, M. J. (1987). Treatment of chronic insomnia through restriction of time in bed. *Sleep, 10,* 45–56.

Spitz, H. H. (1991). Commentary on Locurto's "Beyond IQ in preschool programs?" *Intelligence, 15,* 327–333.

Spitz, H. H. (1997). *Nonconscious movements: From mystical messages to facilitated communication.* Hillsdale, NJ: Lawrence Erlbaum Associates.

Spitzer, R., First, M., Williams, J., Kendler, K., Pincus, A., & Tucker, G. (1992). Now is the time to retire the term "Organic Mental Disorders." *American Journal of Psychiatry, 149,* 240–244.

Spitzer, R. L., Severino, S. K., Williams, J. B., & Parry, B. L. (1989). Late luteal phase dysphoric disorder and DSM-III-R. *American Journal of Psychiatry, 146,* 892–897.

Spitzer, R. L., Skodol, A. E., Gibbon, M., & Williams, J. B. W. (1983). *Psychopathology: A casebook,* New Yokr: McGraw-Hill.

Sprecher, S., Hatfield, E., Anthony, C., & Potapova, E. (1994). Token resistance to sexual intercourse and consent to unwanted sexual intercourse: College students' dating experiences in three countries. *Journal of Sex Research, 31*(2), 125–132.

Sprecher, S., Sullivan, Q., & Hatfield, E. (1994). Mate selection preferences: Gender differences examined in a national sample. *Journal of Personality and Social Psychology, 66,* 1074–1080.

Springer, K., & Belk, A. (1994). The role of physical contact and association in early contamination sensitivity. *Developmental Psychology, 30*(6), 864–868.

Springer, S. P., & Deutsch, G. (1989). *Left brain, right brain.* San Francisco: W. H. Freeman.

Squire, L. (1987). *Memory and brain.* New York: Oxford University Press.

Squire, L. R. (1986). Mechanisms of memory. *Science, 232,* 1612–1619.

Squire, L. R. (1992). Memory and the hippocampus: A synthesis from findings with rats, monkeys, and humans. *Psychological Review, 99,* 195–231.

Squire, L. R., Amara, D. G., & Press, G. A. (1992). Magnetic resonance imaging of the hippocampal formation and mamillary nuclei distinguish medial temporal lobe and diencephalic amnesia. *Journal of Neuroscience, 10,* 3106–3117.

Squire, L. R., & McKee, R. (1992). The influence of prior events on cognitive judgments in amnesia. *Journal of Experimental Psychology: Learning, Memory, and Cognition, 18,* 106–115.

Squire, L. R., & Zola, S. M. (1996). Structure and function of declarative and non-declarative memory systems. *Proceedings of the National Academy of Sciences, USA, 93*(24), 13515–13522.

Squire, L. R., & Zola-Morgan, S. (1991). The medial temporal lobe memory system. *Science, 253,* 1380–1386.

St. Lawrence, J. S. (1993). African-American adolescents' knowledge, health-related attitudes, sexual behavior, and contraceptive decisions: Implications for the prevention of adolescent HIV infection. *Journal of Counsuling Clinical Psychology, 61,* 104–112.

Staddon, J. E. R., & Ettinger, R. H. (1989). *Learning: An introduction to the principles of adaptive behavior.* San Diego: Harcourt Brace Jovanovich.

Standing, L., Conezio, J., & Haber, R. N. (1970). Perception and memory for pictures: Single-trial learning of 2500 visual stimuli. *Psychonomic Science, 19,* 73–74.

Stankov, L. (1989). Attentional resources and intelligence: A disappearing link. *Personality and Individual Differences, 10,* 957–968.

Stanley, B. G., Willett, V. L., Donias, H. W., & Ha-Lyen, H. (1993). The lateral hypothalamus: A primary site mediating excitatory aminoacid-elicited eating. *Brain Research, 630*(1–2), 41–49.

Stanton-Hicks, M., & Salamon, J. (1997). Stimulation of the central and peripheral nervous system for the control of pain. *Journal of Clinical Neurophysiology, 14,* 46–62.

Stasser, G., Stewart, D., & Wittenbaum (1995). Expert roles and information exchange during discussion: The importance of knowing who knows what. *Journal of Experimental Social Psychology, 31,* 244–265.

Statistical Abstracts of the United States (1997). Washington, DC: National Data Book.

Statistics Canada (1998). *Causes of Death, 1995.* Ottawa: Ministry of Industry, Science, and Technology, Health Statistics Division.

Staubli, U., Izrael, Z., & Xu, F. (1996). Remembrance of odors past: Enhancement by central facilitation of AMPA receptors. *Behavioral Neuroscience, 110,* 1067–1073.

Stearns, C. Z., & Stearns, P. N. (1986). *Anger: The struggle for emotional control in America's history.* Chicago: University of Chicago Press.

Steele, C. M. (1986, January). What happens when you drink too much? *Psychology Today.*

Steele, C. M. (1988). The psychology of self-affirmation: Sustaining the integrity of the self. In L. Berkowitz (Ed.), *Advances in experimental social psychology* (Vol. 21, pp. 261–302). New York: Academic Press.

Steele, C. M. (1997). A threat in the air: How stereotypes shape intellectual identity and performance. *American Psychologist, 52,* 613–629.

Steele, C. M., & Aronson, J. (1995). Stereotype threat and the intellectual performance of African-Americans. *Journal of Personality and Social Psychology, 69,* 797–811.

Steele, T. D., McCann, U. D., & Ricaurte, G. A. (1994). 3,4-methylenedioxymethamphetamine (MDMA, ecstacy): Pharmacology and toxicology in animals and humans. *Addiction, 89*(5), 539–51.

Stein, D. M., & Lambert, M. J. (1995). Graduate training in psychotherapy: Are therapy outcomes enhanced? *Journal of Consulting and Clinical Psychology, 63,* 182–196.

Steinberg, L. (1990). Autonomy, conflict, and harmony in the family relationship. In S. S. Feldman & G. R. Elliott (Eds.), *At the threshold: The developing adolescent* (pp. 255–276). Cambridge, MA: Harvard University Press.

Steinberg, L., Dornbusch, S. M., & Brown, B. B. (1992). Ethnic differences in adolescent achievement: An ecological perspective. *American Psychologist, 47,* 723–729.

Steinberg, L., Lamborn, S. D., Darling, N., Mounts, N. S., & Dornbusch, S. M. (1994). Over-time changes in adjustment and competence among adolescents from authoritative, authoritarian, indulgent, and neglectful families. *Child Development, 65,* 754–770.

Steketee, G., & Goldstein, A. J. (1994). Reflections on Shapiro's reflections: Testing EMDR within a theoretical context. *The Behavior Therapist, 17,* 156–157.

Stella, N., Schweitzer, P., & Piomelli, D. (1997). A second endogenous cannabinoid that modulates long-term potentiation. *Nature, 388,* 773–778.

Stepanski, E., Glinn, M., Zorick, F., & Roehrs, T. (1994). Heart rate changes in chronic insomnia. *Stress Medicine, 10*(4), 261–266.

Stephens, R. S., Roffman, R. A., & Simpson, E. E. (1994). Treating adult marijuana dependence: A test of the relapse prevention model. *Journal of Consulting and Clinical Psychology. 62*(1), 92–99.

Steriade, M., & McCarley, R. W. (1990). *Brainstem control of wakefulness and sleep.* New York: Plenum.

Stern, K., & McClintock, M. K. (1998). Regulation of ovulation by human pheromones. *Nature, 392*(6672), 177–179.

Stern, Y., Tang, M. X, Denaro, J., & Mayeux, R. (1995). Increased risk of mortality in Alzheimer's disease patients with more advanced educational and occupational attainment. *Annals of Neurology, 37,* 590–595.

Sternberg, R. J. (1985). *Beyond IQ: A triarchic theory of human intelligence.* Cambridge, Eng.: Cambridge University Press.

Sternberg, R. J. (1988a). *The triarchic mind.* New York: Cambridge Press.

Sternberg, R. J. (1988b). Triangulating love. In R. J. Sternberg & M. L. Barnes (Eds.), *The psychology of love.* New Haven: Yale University Press.

Sternberg, R. J. (1989). Domain generality versus domain specificity: The life and impending death of a false dichotomy. *Merrill-Palmer Quarterly, 35,* 115–130.

Sternberg, R. J. (1996). *Successful intelligence.* New York: Simon & Schuster.

Sternberg, R. J., & Kaufman, J. C. (1998). Human abilities. *Annual Review of Psychology, 49,* 479–502.

Sternberg, R. J., & Lubert, T. I. (1992). Buy low and sell high: An investment approach to creativity. *Current Directions in Psychological Science, 1*(1), 1–5.

Sternberg, R. J., Wagner, R. K., Williams, W. M., & Horvath, J. A. (1995). Testing common sense. *American Psychologist, 50,* 912–927.

Sternberg, R. J., & Williams, W. M. (1997). Does the graduate record examination predict meaningful success of graduate training of psychologists? A Case Study. *American Psychologist, 52,* 630–641.

Stevens, A. (1996). *Private myths: Dreams and dreaming.* Cambridge, MA: Harvard University Press.

Stevens, A., & Coupe, P. (1978). Distortions in judged spatial relations. *Cognitive Psychology, 10,* 422–437.

Stevens, D. G. (1995, July 29). New Doppler radar off to stormy start. *Chicago Tribune.*

Stevens, J. C., & Hooper, J. E. (1982). How skin and object temperature influence touch sensation. *Perception and Psychophysics, 32,* 282–285.

Stevenson, H. W., Azuma, H., & Hakuta, K. (1986). *Child development and education in Japan.* New York: W. H. Freeman.

Stewart, R. E., DeSimone, J. A., & Hill, D. L. (1997). New perspectives in a gustatory physiology: Transduction, development, and plasticity. *American Journal of Physiology, 272,* C1–C26.

Stickgold, R., Pace-Schott, E., & Hobson, J. A. (1994). A new paradigm for dream research: Mentation reports following spontaneous arousal from REM and NREM sleep recorded in a home setting. *Consciousness and Cognition, 3,* 16–29.

Stickgold, R., Rittenhouse, C. D., & Hobson, J. A. (1994). Dream splicing: A new technique for assessing thematic coherence in subjective reports of mental activity. *Consciousness and Cognition, 3*(1), 114–128.

Stigler, J. (1992, March). *Cultural differences in cognitive development and education.* Paper presented at the Claremont Conference on Cognitive Development, Claremont CA.

Stipek, D. J., & Ryan, R. H. (1997). Economically disadvantaged preschoolers: Ready to learn but further to go. *Developmental Psychology, 33,* 711–723.

Stoff, D. M., Breiling, J., & Maser, J. D. (Eds.). (1997). *Handbook of antisocial behavior.* New York: John Wiley & Sons.

Stone, J. S., Oesterle, E. C., & Rubel, E. W. (1998). Recent insights into regeneration of auditory and vestibular hair cells. *Current Opinion in Neurology, 11,* 17–24.

Stone, J., Wiegand, A. W., Cooper, J., & Aronson, E. (1997). When exemplification fails: Hypocrisy and the motive for self-integrity. *Journal of Personality and Social Psychology, 72,* 54–65.

Storms, M. D., & Nisbett, R. E. (1970). Insomnia and the attribution process. *Journal of Personality and Social Psychology, 16,* 319–328.

Strain, E. C., Mumford, G. K., Silverman, K., & Griffiths, R. R. (1994). Caffeine dependence syndrome: Evidence from case histories and experimental evaluations. *Journal of the American Medical Association, 272*(13), 1043–1048.

Street, W. R. (1994). *A chronology of noteworthy events in American psychology.* Washington, DC: American Psychological Association.

Strickland, T., Ranganath, V., Lin, K-M., Poland, R., Mendoza, R., & Smith, M. (1991). Psychopharmacologic considerations in the treatment of Black American populations. *Psychopharmacology Bulletin, 27,* 441–448.

Stromberg, C., Schneider, J., & Joondeph, B. (1993, August). Dealing with potentially dangerous patients. *The Psychologist's Legal Update,* No. 2, pp. 3–12.

Stromberg, C. D., Haggarty, D. J., Leibenluft, R. F., McMillian, M. H., Mishkin, B., Rubin, B. L., & Trilling, H. R. (1988). *The psychologist's legal handbook.* Washington, DC: Council for the National Register of Health Service Providers in Psychology.

Stroop, J. R. (1935). Studies of interference in serial verbal reactions. *Journal of Experimental Psychology, 18,* 643–662.

Strupp, H. H., & Hadley, S. W. (1979). Specific versus non-specific factors in psychotherapy. *Archives of General Psychiatry, 36,* 1125–1136.

Stuart, G., Spruston, N., Sakmann, B., & Hausser, M. (1997). Action potential initiation and backpropagation in neurons of the mammalian CNS. *Trends in Neuroscience, 20,* 125–131.

Stunkard, A. J., & Wadden, T. A. (1992). Psychological aspects of severe obesity. *American Journal of Clinical Nutrition, 55,* 524S–532S.

Sturchler-Pierrat, C., Abramowski, D., Duke, M., Wiederhold, K. H., Mistl, C., Rothacher, S., Ledermann, B., Burki, K., Frey, P., Paganetti, P. A., Waridel, C., Calhoun, M. E., Jucker, M., Probst, A., Staufenbiel, M., & Sommer, B. (1997). Two amyloid precursor protein transgenic mouse models with Alzheimer's disease-like pathology. *Proceedings of the National Academy of Science USA, 94,* 13287–13292.

Subrahmanyam, K., & Greenfield, P. M. (1994). Effect of video game practice on spatial skills in girls and boys. *Journal of Applied Developmental Psychology, 15,* 13–32.

Suddath, R. L., Christison, G. W., Torrey, E. F., Casanova, M. F., & Weinberger, D. R. (1990). Anatomical abnormalities in the brains of monopsychotic twins discordant for schizophrenia. *New England Journal of Medicine, 322,* 789–794.

Sudhalter, V., & Braine, M. D. S. (1985). How does comprehension of passives develop? A comparison of actional and experiential verbs. *Journal of Child Language, 12,* 455–470.

Sue, D. (1992). *Asian and Caucasian subjects' preference for different counseling styles.* Unpublished manuscript, Western Washington University.

Sue, S. (1998). In search of cultural competence in psychotherapy and counseling. *American Psychologist, 53,* 440–448.

Sue, S., & Okazaki, S. (1990). Asian-American educational achievements: A phenomenon in search of an explanation. *American Psychologist, 45,* 913–920.

Sue, S., Zane, N., & Young, K. (1994). Research on psychotherapy with culturally diverse populations. In A. E. Bergin & S. L. Garfield (Eds.), *Handbook of psychotherapy and behavior change.* New York: Wiley.

Suh, E., Diener, E., Oishi, S., & Triandis, H. C. (1998). The shifting basis of life satisfaction judgments across cultures: Emotions versus norms. *Journal of Personality and Social Psychology, 74,* 482–493.

Suinn, R. M. (1995). Schizophrenia and bipolar disorder: Origins and influences. *Behavior Therapy, 26,* 557–571.

Sullivan, H. S. (1954). *The psychiatric interview.* New York: W. W. Norton.

Sullivan, K. T., & Bradbury, T. N. (1996). Preventing marital dysfunction: The primacy of secondary strategies. *The Behavior Therapist, 19,* 33–36.

Sullivan, L., & Stankov, L. (1990). Shadowing and target detection as a function of age: Implications for the role of processing resources in competing tasks and in general intelligence. *Australian Journal of Psychology, 42,* 173–185.

Suls, J., & Fletcher, B. (1985). The relative efficacy of avoidant and nonavoidant coping strategies: A meta-analysis. *Health Psychology, 4,* 249–288.

Suls, J., & Wan, C. K. (1993). The relationship between trait hostility and cardiovascular reactivity: A quantitative review and analysis. *Psychophysiology, 30,* 1–12.

Summala, H., & Mikkola, T. (1994). Fatal accidents among car and truck drivers: Effects of fatigue, age, and alcohol consumption. *Human Factors, 36*(2), 315–326.

Sundberg, N., & Sue, D. (1989). Research and research hypotheses about effectiveness in intercultural counseling. In P. Pederson, J. Draguns, W. Lonner, & J. Trimble (Eds.), *Counseling across cultures* (3rd ed.). Honolulu: University of Hawaii Press.

Susser, E., & Lin, S. (1992). Schizophrenia after prenatal exposure to the Dutch hunger winter of 1944–1945. *Archives of General Psychiatry, 49,* 983–988.

Sutker, P. B., Davis, M. J., Uddo, M., & Ditta, S. R. (1995). War zone stress, personal resources, and PTSD in Persian Gulf War returnees. *Journal of Abnormal Psychology, 104,* 444–452.

Suzdak, P. D., Glowa, J. R., Crawley, J. N., Schwartz, R. D., Skolnick, P., & Paul, S. M. (1986). A selective imidazobenzodiazepine antagonist of ethanol in the rat. *Science, 234,* 1243–1247.

Svendsen, C. N., Caldwell, M. A., Shen, J., ter Borg, M. G., Rosser, A. E., Tyers, P., Karmiol, S., & Dunnett, S. B. (1997). Long-term survival of human central nervous system progenitor cells transplanted into a rat model of Parkinson's disease. *Experimental Neurology, 148,* 135–146.

Swaab, D. E., & Hofman, M. A. (1990). An enlarged suprachiasmatic nucleus in homosexual men. *Brain Research, 537,* 141–148.

Swan, G. E. (1996, December). Some elders thrive on working into late life. *APA Monitor,* p. 35.

Swan, G. E., & Carmelli, D. (1996). Curiosity and mortality in aging adults: A 5-year follow-up of the Western Collaborative Group Study. *Psychology and Aging, 11,* 449–453.

Swann, W. B., Jr., De La Ronde, C., & Hixon, J. G. (1994). Authenticity and positivity strivings in marriage and courtship. *Journal of Personality and Social Psychology, 66,* 857–869.

Sweller, J., & Gee, W. (1978). Einstellung: The sequence effect and hypothesis theory. *Journal of Experimental Psychology: Human Learning and Memory, 4,* 513–526.

Swets, J. A. (1992). The science of choosing the right decision threshold in high-stakes diagnostics. *American Psychologist, 47,* 522–532.

Swithers, S. E., & Hall, W. G. (1994). Does oral experience terminate ingestion? *Appetite, 23*(2), 113–138.

Syzmanski, S., Lieberman, J. A., Alvir, J. M., Mayerhoff, D., Loebel, A., Geisler, S., Chakos, M., Koreen, A., Jody, D., Kane, J., Woerner, M., & Cooper, T. (1995). Gender differences in onset of illness, treatment response, course, and biologic indexes in first-episode schizophrenia patients. *American Journal of Psychiatry, 152,* 698–703.

Szasz, T. S. (1987). *Insanity: The idea and its consequences.* New York: Wiley.

Tagliabue, J. (1999, January 28). Devil gets his due, but Catholic church updates exorcism rites. *International Herald Tribune,* p. 6.

Takayama, H., Ray, J., Raymon, H. K., Baird, A., Hogg, J., Fisher, L. J., & Gage, F. H. (1995). Basic fibroblast growth factor increases dopaminergic graft survival and function in a rat model of Parkinson's disease. *Nature Medicine, 1,* 54–64.

Takayama, Y., Sugishita, M., Kido, T., Ogawa, M., & Akiguchi, I. (1993). A case of foreign accent syndrome without aphasia caused by a lesion of the left precentral gyrus. *Neurology, 43,* 1361–1363.

Takei, N., Sham, P., O'Callaghan, E., Murray, G. K., Glover, G., & Murray, R. M. (1994). Prenatal exposure to influenza and the development of schizophrenia: Is the effect confined to females? *American Journal of Psychiatry, 151,* 117–119.

Takeuchi, A. H., & Hulse, S. H. (1993). Absolute pitch. *Psychological Bulletin, 113,* 345–361.

Tallal, P., Miller, S. L., Bedi, G., Byma, G., Wang, X., Nagarajan, S. S., Schreiner, C., Jenkins, W. M., & Merzenich, M. M. (1996). Language comprehension in language-learning impaired children improved with acoustically modified speech. *Science, 271,* 81–84.

Tamis-LeMonda, C. S., Bornstein, M. H., Cyphers, L., Toda, S., & Ogino, M. (1992). Language and play at one year: A comparison of toddlers and mothers in the United States and Japan. *International Journal of Behavioral Development,* 19–42.

Tanaka-Matsumi, J., & Higginbotham, H. N. (1994). Clinical application of behavior therapy across ethnic and cultural boundaries. *The Behavior Therapist, 17,* 123–126.

Tanda, G., Pontieri, F. E., & Di Chiara, G. (1997). Cannabinoid and heroin activation of mesolimbic dopamine transmission by a common mu1 opioid receptor mechanism. *Science, 276,* 2048–2050.

Tannen, D. (1994). *Gender and discourse.* New York: Oxford University Press.

Tanner, J. M. (1978). *Foetus into man: Physical growth from conception to maturity.* London: Open Books, 1978.

Tanner, J. M. (1992). Growth as a measure of nutritional and hygienic status of a population. *Hormone Research, 38,* 106–115.

Tarr, S. J., & Pyfer, J. L. (1996). Physical and motor development of neonates/infants prenatally exposed to drugs in utero: A meta-analysis. *Adapted Physical Activity Quarterly, 13,* 269–287.

Tartaglia, L. A., Dembski, M., Weng, X., Deng, N., Culpepper, J., Devos, R., Richards, G., Campfield, L. A., Clark, F. T., Deeds, J., Muir, C., Sanker, S., Moriarty, A., Moore, K. J., Smutko, J. S., Mays, G. G., Woolf, E. A., Monroe, C. A., & Tepper, R. I. (1996). Identification and expression cloning of a leptin receptor, OB-R. *Cell, 83,* 1263–1271.

Task Force on Promotion and Dissemination of Psychological Procedures (1995). Training in and dissemination of empirically validated psychological treatments: Report and recommendations. *Clinical Psychologist, 48,* 3–23.

Tasker, F., & Golombok, S. (1995). Adults raised as children in lesbian families. *American Journal of Orthopsychiatry, 65*(2), 203–215.

Tatman, S. M., Peters, D. B., Greene, A. L., & Bongar, B. (1997). Graduate students' attitudes toward prescription privileges training. *Professional Psychology: Research and Practice, 28,* 515–517.

Taub, A. (1998). Thumbs down on acupuncture. *Science, 279,* 159.

Taubes, G. (1998). Weight increases worldwide? *Science, 280,* 1368.

Tavris, C. (1992). *The mismeasure of woman.* New York: Simon & Schuster.

Taylor, R. L., & Richards, S. B. (1991). Patterns of intellectual differences of Black, hispanic, and White children. *Psychology in the Schools, 28,* 5–8.

Taylor, S. (1996). Meta-analysis of cognitive-behavioral treatments for social phobia. Journal of *Behavior Therapy and Experimental Psychiatry, 27,* 1–9.

Taylor, S. E. (1998a). *Health psychology* (4th ed.). New York: McGraw-Hill.

Taylor, S. E. (1998b). The social being in social psychology. In D. Gilbert, S. T. Fiske, & G. Lindzey (Eds.), *Handbook of social psychology,* Vol. 1 (4th ed., pp. 58–95). Boston: McGraw-Hill.

Taylor, S. E., & Aspinwall, L. G. (1996). Mediating processes in psychosocial stress: Appraisal, coping, resistance, and vulnerability. In H. B. Kaplan (Ed.), *Perspectives on psychosocial stress.* New York: Academic Press.

Taylor, S. E., Kemeny, M. E., Aspinwall, L. G., Schneider, S. G., Rodriguez, R., & Herbert, M. (1992). Optimism, coping, psychological distress, and high-risk sexual behavior among men at risk for acquired immunodeficiency syndrome (AIDS). *Journal of Personality and Social Psychology, 63,* 460–473.

Taylor, S. E., & Lobel, M. (1989). Social comparison activity under threat: Downward evaluation and upward contacts. *Psychological Review, 96.*

Taylor, S. P., & Hulsizer, M. R. (1998). Psychoactive drugs and human aggression. In R. G. Geen & E. Donnerstein (Eds.), *Human aggression* (pp. 139–167). San Diego: Academic Press.

Tecott, L. H., Sun, L. M., Akana, S. F., Strack, A. M., Lowenstein, D. H., Dallman, M. F., & Julius, D. (1995). Eating disorder and epilepsy in mice lacking 5-HT$_{2C}$ serotonin receptors. *Nature, 374,* 542–546.

Teghtsoonian, R. (1992). In defense of the pineal gland. *Behavioral and Brain Sciences, 15,* 224–225.

Teigen, K. H. (1994). Yerkes-Dodson: A law for all seasons. *Theory and Psychology, 4*(4), 525–547.

Teitelbaum, P. (1961). Disturbances in feeding and drinking behavior after hypothalamic lesions. In M. R. Jones (Ed.), *Nebraska symposium on motivation.* Lincoln: University of Nebraska Press.

Teitelbaum, P. (1957). Random and food-directed activity in hyperphagic and normal rats. *Journal of Comparative and Physiological Psychology, 50,* 386–490.

Tellegen, A., Lykken, D. T., Bouchard, T. J., Wilcox, K. J., Segal, N. L., & Rich, S. (1988). Personality similarity in twins reared apart and together. *Journal of Personality and Social Psychology, 54,* 1031–1039.

Ter Riet, G., Kleijnen, J., & Knipschild, P. (1990). Acupuncture and chronic pain: A criteria-based meta-analysis. *Journal of Clinical Epidemiology, 43,* 1191–1199.

Terman, L. M. (1916). *The measurement of intelligence.* Boston: Houghton Mifflin.

Terman, L. M., & Oden, M. H. (1947). *The gifted child grows up: Vol. 4. Genetic studies of genius.* Stanford, CA: Stanford University Press.

Terman, L. M., & Oden, M. H. (1959). *The gifted group at midlife.* Stanford, CA: Stanford University Press.

Terrace, H. S., Petitto, L. A., Sanders, D. L., & Bever, J. G. (1979). Can an ape create a sentence? *Science, 206,* 891–902.

Tesser, A. (1988). Toward a self-evaluation maintenance model of social behavior. In L. Berkowitz (Ed.), *Advances in experimental social psychology* (Vol. 21, pp. 181–227). San Diego, CA: Academic Press.

Tesser, A. (1993). The importance of heritability in psychological research: The case of attitudes. *Psychological Review, 100,* 129–142.

Tharinger, D. J., Lambert, N. M., Bricklin, P. M., Feshbach, N., Johnson, N. F., Oakland, T. D., Paster, V. S., & Sanchez, W. (1996). Education reform: Challenges for psychology and psychologists. *Professional Psychology: Research and Practice, 27,* 24–33.

Thelen, E. (1992). Development as a dynamic system. *Current Directions in Psychological Science, 1,* 189–193.

Thelen, E. (1995). Motor development: A new synthesis. *American Psychologist, 50,* 79–95.

Theunisson, E. (1994). Factors influencing the design of perspective flight path displays for guidance and navigation. *Displays, 15,* 241–254.

Thibodeau, R., & Aronson, E. (1992). Taking a closer look: Reasserting the role of the self-concept in dissonance theory. *Personality and Social Psychology Bulletin, 18,* 591–602.

Thomas, A., & Chess, S. (1977). *Temperament and development.* New York: Brunner/Mazel.

Thomas, E. L., & Robinson, H. A. (1972). *Improving reading in every class: A sourcebook for teachers.* Boston: Allyn & Bacon.

Thomas, K. W., & Schmidt, W. H. (1976). A survey of managerial interests with respect to conflict. *Academy of Management Journal, 19,* 315–318.

Thompson, D. B., Ravussin, E., Bennett, P. H., & Bogardus, C. (1997). Structure and sequence variation at the human leptin receptor gene in lean and obese Pima Indians. *Human Molecular Genetics, 6,* 675–679.

Thompson, J. K. (1996). Introduction: Assessment and treatment of binge eating disorder. In J. K. Thompson (Ed.), *Body image, eating disorders, and obesity* (pp. 1–22). Washington, DC: American Psychological Association.

Thompson, R. A. (1998). Early sociopersonality development. In W. Damon & N. Eisenberg (Eds.), *Handbook of child psychology: Vol. 3. Social, emotional, and personality development* (5th ed., pp. 25–104). New York: Wiley.

Thompson, S. C., Sobolow-Shubin, A., Galbraith, M. E., Schwankovksy, L., & Cruzen, D. (1993). Maintaining perceptions of control: Finding perceived control in low control circumstances. *Journal of Personality and Social Psychology, 64,* 293–304.

Thompson, W. G. (1995). Coffee: Brew or bane. *American Journal of the Medical Sciences, 308*(1), 49–57.

Thomson, C. P. (1982). Memory for unique personal events: The roommate study. *Memory & Cognition, 10,* 324–332.

Thorndike, E. L. (1898). Animal intelligence: An experimental study of the associative processes in animals. *Psychological Monographs, 2*(Whole No. 8).

Thorndike, E. L. (1905). *The elements of psychology.* New York: Seiler.

Thorndike, R. L., Hagan, E., & Sattler, J. (1986). *Stanford-Binet* (4th ed.). Chicago: Riverside.

Thorpe, G. L., & Olson, S. L. (1997). *Behavior therapy: Concepts, procedures, and applications* (2nd ed.). Boston: Allyn & Bacon.

Thurstone, L. (1938). *Primary Mental Abilities.* Psychometric Monographs, Whole No. 1.

Tian, H.-G., Nan, Y., Hu, G., Dong, Q.-N., Yang, X.-L., Pietinen, P., & Nissinen, A. (1995). Dietary survey in a Chinese population. *European Journal of Clinical Nutrition, 49,* 27–32.

Tidwell, M. C. O., Reis, H. T., & Shaver, P. R. (1996). Attachment, attractiveness, and social interaction: A diary study. *Journal of Personality and Social Psychology, 71,* 729–745.

Tiihonen, J., Kuikka, J., Bergstrom, K., Hakola, P., Karhu, J., Ryynänen, O.-P., & Föhr, J. (1995). Altered striatal dopamine re-uptake site densities in habitually violent and non-violent alcoholics. *Nature Medicine, 1*(7), 654-657.

Tiller, J., Schmidt, U., Ali, S., & Treasure, J. (1995). Patterns of punitiveness in women with eating disorders. *International Journal of Eating Disorders, 17*(4), 365–371.

Timberlake, W. (1980). A molar equilibrium theory of learned performance. In G. H. Bower (Ed.), *The psychology of learning and motivation,* Vol. 14 (pp. 1–58). San Diego: Academic Press.

Timberlake, W., & Farmer-Dougan, V. A. (1991). Reinforcement in applied settings: Figuring out ahead of time what will work. *Psychological Bulletin, 110*(3), 379–391.

Tinbergen, N. (1989). *The study of instinct.* Oxford: Clarendon.

Tolin, D. F., Montgomery, R. W., Kleinknecht, R. A., & Lohr, J. M. (1996). An evaluation of eye movement desensitization and reprocessing (EMDR). In S. Knapp, L. VandeCreek, & T. L. Jackson (Eds.), *Innovations in clinical practice: A source book.* Sarasota, FL: Professional Resource Press.

Tolman, E. C., & Honzik, C. H. (1930). Introduction and removal of reward and maze performance in rats. *University of California Publication in Psychology, 4,* 257–275.

Tomes, H. (1999). The need for cultural competence. *APA Monitor,* April, p.31.

Townsend, J. M., Kline, J., & Wasserman, T. H. (1995). Low-investment copulation: Sex differences in motivational and emotional reactions. *Ethology and Sociobiology, 16*(1), 25–51.

Trabasso, T. R., & Bower, G. H. (1968). *Attention in learning.* New York: Wiley.

Tracor, Inc. (1971). *Community reaction to aircraft noise: Vol. 1* (NASA Report CR–1761). Washington, DC: National Aeronautics and Space Administration.

Treffert, D. A. (1988). The idiot savant: A review of the syndrome. *American Journal of Psychiatry, 145,* 563–572.

Treisman, A. (1988). Features and objects: The 14th Bartlett memorial lecture. *Quarterly Journal of Experimental Psychology, 40,* 201–237.

Tremblay, A., & Bueman, B. (1995). Exercise-training, macronutrient balance and body weight control. *International Journal of Obesity, 19*(2), 79–86.

Tremblay, R. E., Pagani-Kurtz, L., Mâsse, L., Vitaro, F., & Pihl, R. O. (1995). A bimodal preventive intervention for disruptive kindergarten boys: Its impact through mid-adolescence. *Journal of Consulting and Clinical Psychology, 63,* 560–568.

Tremblay, R. E., Pihl, R. O., Vitaro, F., & Dobkin, P. (1994). Predicting early onset of male antisocial behavior from preschool behavior. *Archives of General Psychiatry, 51,* 732–739.

Triandis, H. C. (1964). Cultural influences upon cognitive processes. In L. Berkowitz (Ed.), *Advances in experimental social psychology.* New York: Academic Press.

Triandis, H. C. (1994). *Culture and social behavior.* New York: McGraw-Hill.

Triandis, H. C. (1996). The psychological measurement of cultural syndromes. *American Psychologist, 51,* 407–415.

Triandis, H. C. (1997). Cross-cultural perspectives on personality. In R. Hogan, J. Johnson, & S. Briggs (Eds.), *Handbook of personality psychology* (pp. 439–464). San Diego: Academic Press.

Troll, L. E. (1982). *Continuations: Adult development and aging.* Monterey, CA: Brooks/Cole.

Tronick, E. Z. (1989). Emotions and emotional communication in infants. *American Psychologist, 44,* 112–119.

Trope, Y., Cohen, O., & Alfieri, T. (1991). Behavior identification as a mediator of dispositional inference. *Journal of Personality and Social Psychology, 61,* 873–883.

Trower, P. (1995). Adult social skills: State of the art and future directions. In W. O'Donohue & L. Krasner (Eds.), *Handbook of psychological skills training: Clinical techniques and applications* (pp. 54–80). Boston: Allyn & Bacon.

Trujillo, C. M. (1986). A comparative evaluation of classroom interactions between professors and minority and non-minority college students. *American Educational Research Journal, 23,* 629–642.

Trujillo, K. A., & Akil, H. (1991). Inhibition of morphine tolerance and dependence by the NMDA receptor antagonist MK–801. *Science, 251,* 85–87.

Trull, T. J., & Sher, K. J. (1994). Relationship between the five-factor model of personality and Axis I disorders in a nonclinical sample. *Journal of Personality and Social Psychology, 103,* 350–360.

Tryon, R. C. (1940). Genetic differences in maze-learning ability in rats. *Yearbook of the National Society for the Study of Education, 39,* 111–119.

Tryon, W. W. (1995). Resolving the cognitive behavioral controversy. *The Behavior Therapist, 18,* 83–86.

Tseng, W., Kan-Ming, M., Li-Shuen, L., Guo-Qian, C., Li-Wah, O., & Hong-Bo, Z. (1992). Koro epidemics in Guangdong China. *Journal of Nervous and Mental Disease, 180,* 117–123.

Tuerkheimer, A. M., & Vyse, S. A. (1997, March/April). The book of predictions: Fifteen years later. *Skeptical Inquirer, 21,* 40–42.

Tulving, E. (1979). Relation between encoding specificity and levels of processing. In L. S. Cermak & F. I. M. Craik (Eds.), *Levels of processing in human memory.* Hillsdale, NJ: Lawrence Erlbaum Associates.

Tulving, E. (1982). *Elements of episodic memory.* New York: Oxford University Press.

Tulving, E. (1993). Self-knowledge of an amnesic individual is represented abstractly. In T. K. Srull & R. S. Wyer (Eds.), *The mental representation of trait and autobiographical knowledge about the self: Advances in social cognition: Vol. V.* Hillsdale, NJ: Lawrence Erlbaum Associates.

Tulving, E., Hayman, C. A. G., & Macdonald, C. A. (1991). Long-lasting perceptual priming and semantic learning in amnesia: A case experiment. *Journal of Experimental Psychology: Learning, Memory, and Cognition, 17,* 595–617.

Tulving, E., & Psotka, J. (1971). Retroactive inhibition in free recall: Inaccessibility of information available in the memory store. *Journal of Experimental Psychology, 87,* 1–8.

Tulving, E., & Schacter, D. L. (1990). Priming and human memory systems. *Science, 247,* 301–306.

Tulving, E., Schacter, D. L., & Stark, H. (1982). Priming effects in word-fragment completion are independent of recognition memory. *Journal of Experimental Psychology: Learning, Memory, and Cognition, 8,* 336–342.

Tulving, E., & Thomson, D. M. (1973). Encoding specificity and retrieval processes in episodic memory. *Psychological Review, 80,* 352–373.

Turiel, E. (1998). The development of morality. In W. Damon & N. Eisenberg (Eds.), *Handbook of child psychology: Vol. 3. Social, emotional, and personality development* (5th ed., pp. 863–932). New York: Wiley.

Turkington, C. (1987). Special talents. *Psychology Today,* pp. 42–46.

Turkkan, J. S. (1989). Classical conditioning: The new hegemony. *Behavioral & Brain Sciences, 12,* 121–179.

Turner, A. M., & Greenough, W. T. (1985). Differential rearing effects on rat visual cortex synapses: I. Synaptic and neuronal density and synapses per neuron. *Brain Research, 329,* 195–203.

Turner, B. G., Beidel, D. C., Hughes, S., & Turner, M. W. (1993). Test anxiety in African-American school children. *School Psychology Quarterly, 8,* 140–152.

Turner, C. F., Miller, H. G., & Rogers, S. M. (1998). Survey measurement of sexual behaviors: Problems and progress. In J. Bancroft (Ed.), *Researching Sexual Behavior.* Bloomington: Indiana University Press.

Turner, C. F., Miller, H. G., Smith, T. K., Cooley, P. C., & Rogers, S. M. (1996). Telephone and audio computer-assisted self-interviewing (T-ACASI) and survey measurements of sensitive behaviors: Preliminary results. In R. Banks, J. Fairgrieve, & L. Gerrard (Eds.), *Survey and statistical computing 1996.* Chesham, Bucks, UK: Association for Survey Computing.

Turner, J. C. (1991). *Social influence.* Pacific Grove, CA: Brooks/Cole.

Turner, M. E., Pratkanis, A. R., Probasco, P., & Leve, C. (1992). Threat, cohesion, and group effectiveness: Testing a social identity maintenance prospective on group-think. *Journal of Personality and Social Psychology, 63,* 781–796.

Tversky, A. (1972). Elimination by aspects: A theory of choice. *Psychological Review, 79,* 281–299.

Tversky, A., & Kahneman, D. (1974). Judgment under uncertainty: Heuristics and biases. *Science, 185,* 1124–1131.

Tversky, A., & Kahneman, D. (1981). The framing of decisions and the psychology of choice. *Science, 211,* 453–458.

Tversky, A., & Kahneman, D. (1991). Loss aversion in riskless choice: A reference dependent model. *Quarterly Journal of Economics, 106,* 1039–1061.

Tversky, A., & Kahneman, D. (1993). Probabilistic reasoning. In A. Goldman (Ed.), *Readings in philosophy and cognitive science* (pp. 43–68). Cambridge, MA: MIT Press.

Tversky, B. (1991). Spatial mental models. In G. Bower (Ed.), *The psychology of learning and motivation: Advances in research and theory* (Vol. 27, pp. 109–145). San Diego: Academic Press.

Tversky, B., & Tuchin, M. (1989). A reconciliation of the evidence on eyewitness testimony: Comments on McCloskey and Zaragoza. *Journal of Experimental Psychology: General, 118,* 86–91.

U.S. Bureau of the Census (1996). *Statistical abstract of the United States* (117th ed.). Washington, DC: U.S. Government Printing Office.

U.S. Bureau of the Census (1997). *Statistical abstract of the U.S.: 1997.* Washington, DC.

U.S. Department of Commerce, Bureau of the Census. (1992). *Statistical Abstract of the United States* (112th ed.). Washington, DC: U.S. Government Printing Office.

U.S. Department of Justice. (1997). *Lifetime likelihood of going to state or federal prison.* Washington, DC: Bureau of Justice Statistics.

U.S. Department of Justice (1998). *Alcohol and crime: An analysis of national data on the prevalence of alcohol involved in crime.* Washington, DC: USDJ.

USDHHS (U.S. Department of Health and Human Services). (1990). *Seventh annual report to the U.S. Congress on alcohol and health.* Rockville, MD: National Institute on Alcohol Abuse and Alcoholism.

USDHHS (U.S. Department of Health and Human Services). (1992). *NCPS AIDS community demonstration projects: What we have learned, 1985–1990.* Washington, DC: USDHHS.

USDHHS (U.S. Department of Health and Human Services). (1997, September 9). Substance Abuse and Mental Health Services Administration news release.

Ullmann, L., & Krasner, L. (1975). *A psychological approach to abnormal behavior* (2nd ed.). Englewood Cliffs, NJ: Prentice-Hall.

Ungerleider, L. G., Courtney, S. M., & Haxby, J. V. (1998). A neural system for human visual working memory. *Proceedings of the National Academy of Science USA, 95,* 883–890.

Valencia-Flores, M., Castano, V. A., Campos, R. M., Rosenthal, L., Resendiz, M., Vergara, P., Aguilar-Roblero, R., Garcia Ramos, G., & Bliwise, D. L. (1998). The siesta culture concept is not supported by the sleep habits of urban Mexican students. *Journal of Sleep Research, 7,* 21–29.

Valenstein, E. S. (Ed.) (1980). *The psychosurgery debate.* San Francisco: W. H. Freeman.

Valenza, E., Simion, F., Assia, V. M., & Umilta, C. (1996). Face preference at birth. *Journal of Experimental Psychology: Human Perception and Performance, 22,* 892–903.

Vallacher, R. R., & Nowak, A. (1997). The emergence of dynamical social psychology. *Psychological Inquiry, 8,* 73–99.

Van Bezooijen, R., Otto, S. A., & Heenan, T. A. (1983). Recognition of vocal expression of emotion: A three-nation study to identify universal characteristics. *Journal of Cross-Cultural Psychology, 14,* 387–406.

Van de Ven, P. (1994). Comparisons among homophobic reactions of undergraduates, high school students, and young offenders. *Journal of Sex Research, 31*(2), 117–124.

Van Essen, D. C., Anderson, C. H., & Felleman, D. J. (1992). Information processing in the primate visual system: An integrated systems perspective. *Science, 255,* 419–423.

van IJzendoorn, M. H. (1995). Adult attachment representations, parental responsiveness, and infant attachment: A meta-analysis on the predictive validity of the Adult Attachment Interview. *Psychological Bulletin, 117,* 387–403.

Van Lange, P. A. M., & Sedikides, C. (1998). Being more honest but not necessarily more intelligent than others: Generality and explanations for the Muhammad Ali effect. *European Journal of Social Psychology, 28,* 675–680.

van Reekum, R., Black, S. E., Conn, D., & Clarke, D. (1997). Cognition-enhancing drugs in dementia: A guide to the near future. *Canadian Journal of Psychiatry, 42* (Suppl. 1), 35S–50S.

Van Sickel, A. D. (1992). Clinical hypnosis in the practice of anesthesia. *Nurse Anesthesiologist, 3,* 67–74.

Van Tol, H., Caren, M., Guan, H-C., Ohara, K., Bunzow, J., Civelli, O., Kennedy, J., Seeman, P., Niznik, H., & Jovanovic, V. (1992). Multiple dopamine D_4 receptor variants in the human population. *Nature, 358,* 149–152.

Vanderweele, D. A. (1994). Insulin is a prandial satiety hormone. *Physiology and Behavior, 56*(3), 619–622.

Vargha-Khadem, F., Isaacs, E., & Mishkin, M. (1994). Agnosia, alexia and a remarkable form of amnesia in an adolescent boy. *Brain, 117,* 683–703.

Verfaellis, M., & Cermak, L. S. (1991). Neuropsychological issues in amnesia. In J. L. Martinez & R. P. Kesner (Eds.), *Learning and memory: A biological view* (2nd ed.). San Diego, CA: Academic Press.

Vernet, M. E., Robin, O., & Dittmar, A. (1995). The ohmic perturbation duration, an original temporal index to quantify electrodermal responses. *Behavioural Brain Research, 67*(1), 103–107.

Vernon, P. A. (Ed.) (1987). *Speed of information-processing and intelligence.* Norwood, NJ: Ablex.

Victor, M., Adams, R. D., & Collins, G. H. (1971). *The Wernicke-Korsakoff Syndrome.* Philadelphia: F. A. Davis.

Vincent, C. A., & Richardson, P. H. (1986). The evaluation of therapeutic acupuncture: Concepts and methods. *Pain, 24,* 1–13.

Vincent, K. R. (1991). Black/White IQ differences: Does age make a difference? *Journal of Clinical Psychology, 47,* 266–270.

Voelker, R. (1997). "Decent research and closure" needed on medical marijuana, says head of NIH panel. *Journal of the American Medical Association, 278,* 802.

Vogeltanz, N. D., Sigmon, S. T., & Vickers, K. S. (1998). Feminism and behavior analysis: A framework for women's health research and practice. In J. J. Plaud & G. H. Eifert (Eds.), *From behavior theory to behavior therapy* (pp. 269–293). Boston: Allyn & Bacon.

von Bekesy, G. (1960). *Experiments in hearing.* New York: McGraw-Hill.

Vuchinich, R. E., & Sobell, M. B. (1978). Empirical separation of physiological and expected effects of alcohol on complex perceptual motor performance. *Psychopharmacology, 60,* 81–85.

Vyse, S. A. (1997). *Believing in magic: The psychology of superstition.* New York: Oxford University Press.

Waagenaar, W. A. (1989). *Paradoxes of gambling behavior.* Hillsdale, NJ: Lawrence Erlbaum Associates.

Wade, C. (1988, April). *Thinking critically about critical thinking in psychology.* Paper presented at the annual meeting of the Western Psychological Association, San Francisco, CA.

Wadsworth, S. (1994). School achievement. In J. C. DeFries, R. Pomin,, & D. W. Fulker (Eds.), *Nature and nurture during middle childhood* (pp. 86–101). Cambridge, MA: Blackwell.

Wakefield, J. C. (1992). The concept of mental disorder: On the boundary between biological facts and social values. *American Psychologist, 47,* 373–388.

Walberg, H. J. (1987). Studies show curricula efficiency can be attained. *NASSP Bulletin, 71,* 15–21.

Waldrop, M. M. (1987). The working of working memory. *Science, 237,* 1564–1567.

Wali, S. O., & Kryger, M. H. (1995). Medical treatment of sleep apnea. *Current Opinions in Pulmonary Medicine, 1,* 498–503.

Walker, E. F., & Diforio, D. (1998). Schizophrenia: A neural diathesis-stress model. *Psychological Review, 104,* 667–685.

Walker, L. (1991). The feminization of psychology. *Psychology of Women Newsletter of Division, 35,* 1, 4.

Walker, L. J. (1989). A longitudinal study of moral reasoning. *Child Development, 60,* 157–166.

Walker-Andrews, A. S., Bahrick, L. E., Raglioni, S. S., & Dias, I. (1991). Infants' bimodal perception of gender. *Ecological Psychology, 3,* 55–75.

Wallace, C., Liberman, R., MacKain, S., Blackwell, G., & Eckman, T. (1992). Effectiveness and replicability of modules for teaching social and instrumental skills to the severely mentally ill. *American Journal of Psychiatry, 149,* 654–685.

Wallace, R. K., & Benson, H. (1972). The physiology of meditation. *Scientific American, 226,* 84–90.

Wallen, K., & Lovejoy, J. (1993). Sexual behavior: Endocrine function and therapy. In J. Schulkin (Ed.), *Hormonal pathways to mind and brain.* New York: Academic Press.

Waller, N. G., & Shaver, P. R. (1994). The importance of nongenetic influences on romantic love styles: A twin-family study: *Psychological Science, 3,* 268–274.

Wallerstein, J. S., & Blakeslee, S. (1989). *Second chances: Men, women and children a decade after divorce.* New York: Ticknor and Fields.

Wallman, J., Gottlieb, M. D., Rajaram, V., & Fugate-Wentzek, L. A. (1987). Local retinal regions control local eye growth and myopia. *Science, 237,* 73–76.

Walsh, W., & Banaji M. (1997). The collective self. In J. Snodgrass & R. Thompson (Eds.), *The self across psychology: Self-recognition, self-awareness, and the self* (pp. 193–214). New York: New York Academy of Sciences.

Walters, G. (1992). Drug-seeking behavior: Disease or lifestyle? *Professional Psychology, 23,* 139–145.

Walton, G. E., Bower, N. J. A., & Bower, T. G. R. (1992). Recognition of familiar faces by newborns. *Infant Behavior and Development, 15,* 265–269.

Wang, X., Merzenich, M. M., Sameshima, K., & Jenkins, W. M., (1995). Remodelling of hand representation in adult cortex determined by timing of tactile stimulation, *Nature, 378,* 71–75.

Warburton, D. M. (1995). Effects of caffeine on cognition and mood without caffeine abstinence. *Psychopharmacology, 119,* 66–70.

Ward, C. (1994). Culture and altered states of consciousness. In W. J. Lonner & R. S. Malpass (Eds.), *Psychology and culture.* Boston: Allyn & Bacon.

Ward, L. M. (1997). Involuntary listening aids hearing. *Psychological Science, 8,* 112–118.

Warner, L., Kessler, R., Hughes, M., Anthony, J., & Nelson, C. (1995). Prevalence and correlates of drug use and dependence in the United States. *Archives of General Psychiatry, 52,* 219–229.

Warot, D., et al. (1991). Comparative effects of ginkgo biloba extracts on psychomotor performances and memory in healthy subjects. *Therapies, 46,* 33–36.

Warrington, E., K., & Weiskrantz, L. (1970). The amnesic syndrome: Consolidation of retrieval? *Nature, 228,* 626–630.

Wasik, B. H., Ramey, C. T., Bryant, D. M., & Sparling, J. J. (1990). A longitudinal study of two early intervention strategies: Project CARE. *Child Development, 61,* 1682–1696.

Watanabe, S., Sakamoto, J., & Wakita, M. (1995). Pigeons' discrimination of paintings by Monet and Picasso. *Journal of Experimental Analysis of Behavior, 63,* 165–174.

Watanabe, T., & Sugita, Y. (1998). REM sleep behavior disorder (RBD) and dissociated REM sleep. *Nippon Rinsho, 56*(2), 433–438.

Waterman, A. S. (1982). Identity development from adolescence to adulthood: An extension of theory and a review of research. *Developmental Psychology, 18,* 341–358.

Watkins, C. E., Campbell, V. L., Nieberding, R., & Hallmark, R. (1995). Contemporary practice of psychological assessment by clinical psychologists. *Professional psychology: Research and Practice, 26,* 54–60.

Watson, J. B. (1913). Psychology as the behaviorist views it. *Psychological Review, 20,* 158–177.

Watson, J. B. (1919). *Psychology from the standpoint of a behaviorist.* Philadelphia: Lippincott.

Watson, J. B. (1925). *Behaviorism.* London: Kegan Paul, Trench, Trubner.

Watson, M. W. (1981). The development of social roles: A sequence of social-cognitive development. *New Directions for Child Development, 12,* 33–41.

Watson, R. I. (1963). *The great psychologists: From Aristotle to Freud.* Philadelphia: Lippincott.

Watt, N. F., & Saiz, C. (1991). Longitudinal studies of premorbid development of adult schizophrenics,. In E. F. Walker (Ed.), *Schizophrenia: A life-course in developmental perspective.* San Diego, CA: Academic Press.

Watts, R. L., Subramanian, T., Freeman, A., Goetz, C. G., Penn, R. D., Stebbins, G. T., Kordower, J. H., & Bakay, R. A. (1997). Effect of stereotaxic intrastriatal cografts of autologous adrenal medulla and peripheral nerve in Parkinson's disease: Two-year follow-up study. *Experimental Neurology, 147,* 510–517.

Weary, G., & Edwards, J. A. (1994). Social cognition and clinical psychology: Anxiety and the processing of social information. In R. S. Wyer & T. S. Srull (Eds.), *Handbook of social cognition* (2nd ed.). Hillsdale, NJ: Lawrence Erlaum Associates.

Weber, R. J. (1992). *Forks, phonographs, and hot air balloons: A field guide to inventive thinking.* New York: Oxford University Press.

Wechsler, D. (1939). *The measurement of adult intelligence.* Baltimore: Williams & Wilkins.

Wechsler, D. (1949). *The Wechsler Intelligence Scale for Children.* New York: Psychological Corporation.

Weekes, J. R., Lynn, S. J., Green, J. P., & Brentar, J. T. (1992). Pseudomemory in hypnotized and task-motivated subjects. *Journal of Abnormal Psychology, 101,* 356–360.

Weeks, D., & Weeks, J. (1995). *Eccentrics: A study of sanity and strangeness.* New York: Villard.

Wegner, D. M., & Bargh, J. A. (1998). Control and automaticity in social life. In D. Gilbert, S. T. Fiske, and G. Lindzey (Eds.), *Handbook of social psychology, Vol. 1* (4th ed. pp. 446–498). Boston: McGraw-Hill.

Weigent, D. A., & Blalock, J. E. (1997). Production of peptide hormones and neurotransmitters by the immune system. *Chemical Immunology, 69,* 1–30.

Weinberg, R. A. (1989). Intelligence and IQ: Landmark issues and great debates. *American Psychologist, 44,* 98–104.

Weinberg, R. A., Scarr, S., & Waldman, I. D. (1992). The Minnesota transracial adoption study: A follow-up of IQ test performance at adolescence. *Intelligence, 16,* 117–135.

Weiner, B. (1980). *Human motivation.* New York: Holt, Rinehart & Winston.

Weiner, B. (1993). On sin versus sickness: A theory of perceived responsibility and social motivation. *American Psychologist, 48*(9), 957–965.

Weisman, A., Lopez, S. R., Karno, M., & Jenkins, J. (1993). An attributional analysis of expressed emotion in Mexican-American families with schizophrenia. *Journal of Abnormal Psychology, 102,* 601–606.

Weiss, B., & Weisz, J. R. (1995). Relative effectiveness of behavioral versus nonbehavioral child psychotherapy. *Journal of Consulting and Clinical Psychology, 63,* 317–320.

Weiss, D. S., Marmar, C. R., Metzler, T. J., & Ronfeldt, H. M. (1995). Predicting symptomatic distress in emergency services personnel. *Journal of Consulting and Clincal Psychology, 63,* 361–368.

Weiss, S., & Moore, M. (1990). Cultural differences in the perception of magazine alcohol advertisements by Israeli Jewish, Moslem, Druze, and Christian high school students. *Drug and Alcohol Dependence 26,* 209-215.

Weisstein, N., & Harris, C. S. (1974). Visual detection of line segments: An object superiority effect. *Science, 186,* 752–755.

Weisz, J. R., Weiss, B., Han, S. S., Granger, D. A., & Morton, T. (1995). Effects of psychotherapy with children and adolescents revisited: A meta-analysis of treatment outcome studies. *Psychological Bulletin, 117,* 450–468.

Weltzin, T. E., Bulik, C. M., McConaha, C. W., & Kaye, W. H. (1995). Laxative withdrawal and anxiety in bulimia nervosa. *International Journal of Eating Disorders, 17*(2), 141–146.

Werner, E. E. (1995). Resilience in development. *Current Directions in Psychological Science, 4,* 81–85.

Wertheimer, M. (1987). *A brief history of psychology* (3rd ed.). New York: Holt, Rinehart & Winston.

Westen, D. (1998). The scientific legacy of Sigmund Freud: Toward a psychodynamically informed psychological science. *Psychological Bulletin, 124,* 333–371.

Whimbey, A. (1976). *Intelligence can be taught.* New York: Bantam.

Whitaker, L. (1998, April 30). Personal communication.

Whitam, F. L., Diamond, M., &Martin, J. (1993). Homosexual orientation in twins: A report on 61 pairs and three triplet sets. *Archives of Sexual Behavior, 22*(3), 187–206.

Whitbourne, S. K., Zuschlag, M. K., Elliot, L. B., & Waterman, A. D. (1992). Psychosocial development in adulthood: A 22-year sequential study. *Journal of Personality and Social Psychology, 63,* 260–271.

White, D. E., & Glick, J. (1978). *Competence and the context of performance.* Paper presented at the meeting of the Jean Piaget Society, Philadelphia.

White, F. J. (1998). Nicotine addiction and the lure of reward. *Nature Medicine, 4,* 659–660.

White, M. (1987). *The Japanese educational challenge: A commitment to children.* New York: Free Press.

Whorf, B. L. (1956). *Language, thought and reality.* Cambridge and New York: MIT Press and Wiley.

Wickelgren, W. (1977). Speed-accuracy tradeoff and information processing dynamics. *Acta Psychologica, 41,* 67–85.

Wickens, C. D. (1989). Attention. In D. Holding (Ed.), *Human skills.* New York: Wiley.

Wickens, C. D. (1992a). *Engineering psychology and human performance* (2nd ed.). New York: HarperCollins.

Wickens, C. D. (1992b). Virtual reality and education. *In Proceedings of the IEEE International Conference on Systems, Man and Cybernetics.* New York: IEEE.

Wickens, C. D., & Carswell, C. M. (1997). Information processing. In G. Salvendy (Ed.), *Handbook of human factors and ergonomics* (2nd ed., pp. 89–122). New York: Wiley Interscience.

Wickens, C. D., Gordon, S. E., & Liu, Y. (1998). *An introduction to human factors engineering.* New York: Longman.

Wickens, C. D., Stokes, A., Barnett, B., & Hyman, F. (1992). The effects of stress on pilot judgment in a MIDIS simulator. In O. Svenson & J. Maule (Eds.), *Time pressure and stress in human judgment and decision making.* New York: Plenum.

Wickrama, K., Conger, R. D., & Lorenz, F. O. (1995). Work, marriage, lifestyle, and changes in men's physical health. *Journal of Behavioral Medicine, 18,* 97–112.

Widiger, T. A., & Costa, P. T. (1994). Personality and personality disorders. *Journal of Abnormal Psychology, 103,* 78–91.

Widiger, T. A., & Kelso, K. (1983). Psychodiagnosis of Axis II. *Clinical Psychology Review, 3,* 491–510.

Widiger, T. A., & Sanderson, C. J. (1995). Assessing personality disorders. In J. N. Butcher (Ed.), *Clinical personality assessment. Practical approaches* (pp. 380–394). New York: Oxford University Press.

Widiger, T. A., & Smith, G. T. (1994). Substance use disorder: Abuse, dependence, and dyscontrol. *Addiction, 89,* 267–282.

Widom, C. S. (1989a). The cycle of violence. *Science, 244,* 160–166.

Widom, C. S. (1989b). Does violence beget violence? A critical examination of the literature. *Psychological Bulletin, 106,* 3–28.

Wiebe, D. J., & Smith, T. W. (1997). Personality and health: Progress and problems in psychomatics. In R. Hogan, J. Johnson, & S. Briggs (Eds.), *Handbook of personality psychology* (pp. 891–918). San Diego: Academic Press.

Wiedenfeld, S., O'Leary, A., Bandura, A., Brown, S., Levine, S., & Raska, K. (1990). Inpact of perceived self-efficacy in coping with stressors on components of the immune system. *Journal of Personality and Social Psychology, 59,* 1082–1094.

Wiegersma, S., & Meertse, K. (1990). Subjective ordering, working memory, and aging. *Experimental Aging Research, 16,* 73–77.

Wiener, E., & Nagel, D. (1988). *Human factors in aviation.* Orlando, FL: Academic Press.

Wiertelak, E. P., Maier, S. F., & Watkins, L. R. (1992). Cholecystokinin antialgesia: Safety cues abolish morphine analgesia. *Science, 256,* 830–833.

Wiggins, J. S. (1997). In defense of traits. In R. Hogan, J. Johnson, & S. Briggs (Eds.), *Handbook of personality psychology* (pp. 97–118). San Diego: Academic Press.

Wiggins, J. S., & Trapnell, P. D. (1997). Personality structure: The return of the Big Five. In R. Hogan, J. Johnson, & S. Briggs (Eds.), *Handbook of personality psychology* (pp. 737–766). San Diego: Academic Press.

Wiley, M. G., & Crittenden, K. S. (1992). By your attributions you shall be known: Consequences of attributional accounts for professional and gender identities. *Sex Roles, 27*(5–6), 259–276.

Williams, D. A., Butler, M. M., & Overmier, J. B. (1990). Expectancies of reinforcer location and quality as cues for a conditional discrimination in pigeons. *Journal of Experimental Psychology: Animal Behavior Processes, 16,* 3–13.

Williams, G. V., & Goldman-Rakic, P. S. (1995). Modulation of memory fields by dopamine D1 receptors in prefrontal cortex. *Nature, 376,* 572–575.

Williams, J. E., & Best, D. L. (1990). *Measuring stereotypes: A multination study* (Rev. ed.). Newbury Park, CA: Sage.

Williams, K. D., Jackson, J. M., & Karau, S. J. (1995). In D. Schroeder (Ed.), *Social dilemmas: Perspectives on individuals and groups* (pp. 117–142). Westport, CT: Praeger.

Williams, K. D., & Sommer, K. L. (1997). Social ostracism by coworkers: Does rejection lead to loafing or compensation? *Personality and Social Psychology Bulletin, 23,* 693–706.

Williams, L. M. (1993). Recall of childhood trauma: A prospective study of women's memories of child sexual abuse. *Journal of Consulting and Clinical Psychology, 62,* 1167–1176.

Williams, L. M. (1994b). What does it mean to forget child sexual abuse? A reply to Loftus, Garry, and Feldman (1994). *Journal of Consulting and Clinical Psychology, 62,* 1182–1186.

Williams, M. H. (1992). Exploitation and inference: Mapping the damage from therapist-patient sexual involvement. *American Psychologist, 47,* 412–421.

Williams, R. B., Jr., & Barefoot, J. C. (1988). Coronary-prone behavior: The emerging role of the hostility complex. In B. K. Houston & C. R. Snyder (Eds.), *Type A behavior pattern: Current trends and future directions* (pp. 189–221). New York: Wiley.

Willis, W. D., Jr. (1988). Dorsal horn neurophysiology of pain. *Annals of the New York Academy of Science, 531,* 76–89.

Wills, T. A. (1991). Similarity and self-esteem in downward comparison. In J. M. Suls & T. A. Wills (Eds.), *Social comparison: Contemporary theory and research* (pp. 23–50). Hillsdale, NJ: Lawrence Erlbaum Association.

Wilson, B. A. (1987). *Rehabilitation of memory.* New York: Guilford.

Wilson, D. L., Silver, S. M., Covi, W. G., & Foster, S. (1996). Eye movement desensitization and reprocessing: Effectiveness and autonomic correlates. *Journal of Behaviour Therapy and Experimental Psychiatry, 27,* 219-229.

Wilson, G. T. (1985). Limitations of meta-analysis in the evaluation of the effects of psychological therapy. *Clinical Psychology Review, 5,* 35–47.

Wilson, G. T. (1995). Behavior therapy. In R. J. Corsini & D. Wedding (Eds.), *Current psychotherapies* (5th ed., pp. 197–228). Itasca, IL: Peacock.

Wilson, G. T. (1997). Dissemination of cognitive behavioral treatments: Commentary. *Behavior Therapy, 28,* 473–475.

Wilson, G. T., Nathan, P. E., O'Leary, K. D., & Clark, L. A. (1996). *Abnormal psychology.* Boston: Allyn & Bacon.

Wilson, S. A., Becker, L. A., & Tinker, R. H. (1997). Fifteen-month follow-up of eye movement desensitization and reprocessing (EMDR) treatment for posttraumatic stress disorder and psychological trauma. *Journal of Consulting and Clinical Psychology, 65,* 1047–1056.

Wilson, W. J. (1997). *When work disappears: The world of the new urban poor.* New York: Vintage Books.

Wimmer, H., & Perner, J. (1983). Beliefs about beliefs: Representation and constraining function of wrong beliefs in young children's understanding of deception. *Cognition, 13,* 103–128.

Wincze, J. P., Richards, J., Parsons, J., & Bailey, S. (1996). A comparative survey of therapist sexual misconduct between an American state and an Australian state. *Professional Psychology: Research and Practice, 27,* 289–294.

Winkler, J., Suhr, S. T., Gage, F. H., Thal, L. J., & Fisher, L. J. (1995). Essential role of neocortical acetylcholine in spatial memory. *Nature, 375,* 484–487.

Winn, P. (1995). The lateral hypothalamus and motivated behavior: An old syndrome reassessed and a new perspective gained. *Current Directions in Psychological Science, 4,* 182–187.

Winokur, G., Coryell, W., Keller, M., Endicott, J., & Leon, A. (1995). A family study of manic-depressive (Bipolar I) disease. *Archives of General Psychiatry, 52,* 367–373.

Winter, D. G. (1996). *Personality: Analysis and interpretation of lives.* New York: McGraw-Hill.

Wise, R. A. (1996). Neurobiology of addiction. *Current Opinions in Neurobiology, 6*(2), 243–251.

Wise, R. A., & Rompre, P. P. (1989). Brain dopamine and reward. *Annual Review of Psychology, 40,* 191–225.

Wiseman, R., West, D., & Stemman, R. (1996, January/February). Psychic crime detectives: A new test for measuring their successes and failures. *Skeptical Inquirer, 21,* 38–58.

Witelson, S. F. (1992). Cognitive neuroanatomy: A new era. *Neurology, 42,* 709–713.

Witt, S. D. (1997). Parental influence on children's socialization to gender roles. *Adolescence, 32,* 253–259.

Wittchen, H. U., Zhao, S., Kessler, R. C., & Eaton, W. W. (1994). DSM-III-R: Generalized anxiety disorder in the national comorbidity survey. *Archives of General Psychiatry, 51,* 355–364.

Wittenbaum, G. M., & Stasser, G. (1996). Management of information in small groups. In J. L. Nye & A. M. Brower (Eds.), *What's social about cognition? Social cognition in small groups* (pp. 3–28). Newbury Park, CA: Sage.

Wohl, J. (1995). Traditional individual psychotherapy and ethnic minorities. In J. F. Aponte, R. Y. Rivers, & J. Wohl (Eds.), *Psychological interventions and cultural diversity* (pp. 74–91). Boston: Allyn & Bacon.

Wolke, R. L. (1997, March/April). A real cool con. *Skeptical Inquirer, 21,* 43–44.

Wolman, C., van den Broek, P., & Lorch, R. F. (1997). Effects of causal structure and delayed story recall by children with mild mental retardation, children with learning disabilities, and children without disabilities. *Journal of Special Education, 30,* 439–455.

Wolpe, J. (1958). *Psychotherapy by reciprocal inhibition.* Stanford, CA: Stanford University Press.

Wolpe, J. (1982). *The practice of behavior therapy* (3rd ed.). New York: Pergamon Press.

Wolpe, J., & Plaud, J. J. (1997). Pavlov's contributions to behavior therapy: The obvious and the not so obvious. *American Psychologist, 52,* 966–972.

Wong, B. Y. L. (1986). Metacognition and special education: A review of a view. *Journal of Special Education, 20,* 9–29.

Wong, S. E., Martinez-Diaz, J. A., Massel, H. K., Edelstein, B. A., Wiegand, W., Bowen, L., & Liberman, R. P. (1993). Conversational skills training with schizophrenic inpatients: A study of generalization across settings and conversants. *Behavior Therapy, 24,* 285–304.

Woodall, K. L., & Matthews, K. A. (1993). Changes in and stability of hostile characteristics: Results from a 4-year longitudinal study of children. *Journal of Personality and Social Psychology, 64,* 491–499.

Woodhead, M. (1988). When psychology informs public policy: The case of early childhood intervention. *American Psychologist, 43,* 443–454.

Woods, S. C., Seeley, R. J., Porte, D., Jr., & Schwartz, M. W. (1998). Signals that regulate food intake and energy homeostasis. *Science, 280,* 1378–1383.

Woodworth, R. S., & Schlosberg, H. (1954). *Experimental psychology.* New York: Holt.

Woolfolk-Hoy, A. (1999). Psychology applied to education. In A. Stec & D. Bernstein (Eds.), *Psychology: Fields of application.* Boston: Houghton Mifflin.

Woolley, J. D. (1997). Thinking about fantasy: Are children fundamentally different thinkers and believers from adults? *Child Development, 68,* 991–1011.

Worchel, S., & Shackelford, S. L. (1991). Groups under stress: The influence of group structure and environment on process and performance. *Personality and Social Psychology Bulletin, 17,* 640–647.

Wren, C. (1998, September 22). For crack babies, a future less bleak. *New York Times* (Web Archive).

Wright, E. F., Voyer, D., Wright, R. D., & Roney, C. (1995). Supporting audiences and performance under pressure: The home-ice disadvantage in hockey championships. *Journal of Sport Behavior, 18*(1), 21–28.

Wurtman, R. J., & Wurtman, J. J. (1995). Brain serotonin, carbohydrate-craving, obesity and depression. *Obesity Research, 3* (Suppl. 4), 477S–480S.

Wynn, K. (1992). Addition and subtraction by human infants. *Nature, 358,* 749–750.

Wynn, K. (1995). Infants possess a system of numerical knowledge. *Current Directions in Psychological Science, 4,* 172–177.

Wynn, K. (1996). Infants' individuation and enumeration of actions. *Psychological Science, 7,* 164–169.

Wynn, K., & Chiang, W.-C. (1998). Limits to infants' knowledge of objects: The case of magical appearance. *Psychological Science, 9,* 448–455.

Xin, Y., Weiss, K. R., & Kupfermann, I. (1996). An identified interneuron contributes to aspects of six different behaviors in Aplysia. *Journal of Neuroscience, 16,* 5266–5279.

Xu, M., Hu, X. T., Cooper, D. C., Moratalla, R., Graybiel, A. M., White, F. J., & Tonegawa, S. (1994). Elimination of cocaine-induced hyperactivity and dopamine-mediated neurophysiological effects in dopamine D_1 receptor mutant mice. *Cell, 79,* 945-955.

Yahr, P., & Jacobsen, C. H. (1994). Hypothalamic knife cuts that disrupt mating in male gerbils sever efferents and forebrain afferents of the sexually dimorphic area. *Behavioral Neuroscience, 108*(4), 735–742.

Yakimovich, D., & Saltz, E. (1971). Helping behavior: The cry for help. *Psychonomic Science, 23,* 427–428.

Yalom, I. D. (1995). *The theory and practice of group therapy* (4th ed.). New York: Basic Books.

Yang, K., & Bond, M. (1990). Exploring implicit personality theories with indigenous or imported constructs: The Chinese case. *Journal of Personality and Social Psychology, 58,* 1087–1095.

Yantis, S. (1993). Stimulus-driven attentional capture. *Current Directions in Psychological Science, 2,* 156–161.

Yates, J. F., Lee, J. W., & Shinotsuka, H. (1992). *Cross-national variation in probability judgment.* Paper presented at the 33rd annual meeting of the Psychonomic Society, St. Louis.

Yerkes, R. M. (Ed.) (1921). Psychological examining in the U.S. Army. *Memoirs of the National Academy of Sciences,* No. 15.

Yesavage, J. A., Leirer, V. O., Denari, M., & Hollister, L. E. (1985). Carry-over effects of marijuana intoxication on aircraft pilot performance: A preliminary report. *American Journal of Psychiatry, 142,* 1325–1329.

Yonas, A., Artiberry, M. E., & Granrud, C. D. (1987). Space perception in infancy. In R. Vasta (Ed.), *Annals of child development* (Vol. 4). Greenwich, CT: JAI Press.

Yonkers, K., Kando, J., Cole, J., & Blumenthal, S. (1992). Gender differences in pharmacokinetics and pharmacodynamics of psychotropic medication. *American Journal of Psychiatry, 149,* 587–595.

York, J. L., & Welte, J. W. (1994). Gender comparisons of alcohol consumption in alcoholic and nonalcoholic populations. *Journal of Studies on Alcohol, 55*(6), 743–750.

Young, A. W., Aggleton, J. P., Hellawell, D. J., &Johnson, M. (1995). Face processing impairments after amygdalotomy. *Brain, 118*(1), 15–24.

Young, A. W., & De Haan, E. H. F. (1992). Face recognition and awareness after brain injury. In A. D. Milner & M. D. Rugg (Eds.), *The neuropsychology of consciousness.* San Diego, CA: Academic Press.

Young, F. A., Leary, G. A., Baldwin, W. R., West, D. C., Box, R. A., Harris, E., & Johnson, C. (1969). The transmission of refractive errors within Eskimo families. *American Journal of Opometry, 46,* 676–685.

Young, M. (1971). Age and sex differences in problem solving. *Journal of Gerontology, 26,* 331–336.

Youniss, J., & Yates, M. (1997). *Community service and social responsibility in youth.* Chicago: University of Chicago Press.

Yousif, Y., & Korte, C. (1995). Urbanization, culture, and helpfulness: Cross-cultural studies in England and the Sudan. *Journal of Cross-Cultural Psychology, 26,* 474–489.

Yukl, G., & Van Fleet, D. D. (1992). Theory and research on leadership in organizations. In M. D. Dunnette & L. M. Hough (Eds.), *Handbook of industrial and organizational psychology* (2nd ed., Vol. 3, pp. 147–198). Palo Alto, CA: Consulting Psychologists Press.

Yukl, G. A., Latham, G. P., & Pursell, E. D. (1976). The effectiveness of performance incentives under continuous and variable ratio schedules of reinforcement. *Personnel Psychology, 29,* 221–232.

Yule, G. (1996). *The study of language* (2nd ed.). New York: Cambridge University Press.

Yutrzenka, B. A. (1995). Making a case for training in ethnic and cultural diversity in increasing treatment efficacy. *Journal of Consulting and Clinical Psychology, 63,* 197–206.

Zahn-Waxler, C., Friedman, R. J., Cole, P. M., Mizuta, I., & Hiruma, N. (1996). Japanese and United States preschool children's responses to conflict and distress. *Child Development, 67,* 2462–2477.

Zahn-Waxler, C., Radke-Yarrow, M., Wagner, E., & Chapman, M. (1992). Development of concern for others. *Developmental Psychology, 28,* 1038–1047.

Zahrani, S. S., & Kaplowitz, S. A. (1993). Attributional biases in individualistic and collectivist cultures: A comparison of Americans with Saudis. *Social Psychology Quarterly, 56*(3), 223–233.

Zajonc, R. B. (1965). Social facilitation. *Science, 149,* 269–274.

Zajonc, R. B. (1998). Emotions. In D. Gilbert, S. T. Fiske, and G. Lindzey (Eds.), *Handbook of social psychology,* Vol. 1 (4th ed., pp. 591–634). Boston: McGraw-Hill.

Zeki, S. (1992). The visual image in mind and brain. *Scientific American, 267,* 68–76.

Zelinski, E., Schaie, K. W., & Gribben, K. (1977, August). *Omission and commission errors: Task-specific adult lifespan differences.* Paper presented at the convention of the American Psychological Association, San Francisco.

Zhang, G., & Simon, H. A. (1985). STM capacity for Chinese words and idioms: Chunking and acoustical loop hypothesis. *Memory & Cognition, 13,* 193–201.

Zhang, Y., Proenca, R., Maffei, M., Barone, M., Leopold, L., & Friedman, J. M. (1994). Positional cloning of the mouse obese gene and its human homologue. *Nature, 372,* 425–432.

Zhou, J.-N., Hofman, M. A., Gooren, L. J. G., & Swaab, D. F. (1995). A sex difference in the human brain and its relation to transsexuality. *Nature, 378,* 68–70.

Zigler, E., & Seitz, V. (1982). Social policy and intelligence. In R. J. Sternberg (Ed.), *Handbook of human intelligence.* Cambridge, Eng.: Cambridge University Press.

Zigler, E., & Styfco, S. J. (1994). Head Start: Criticisms in a constructive context. *American Psychologist, 49*(2), 127–132.

Zigler, E., Taussig, C., & Black, K. (1992). Early childhood intervention: A promising preventive for juvenile delinquency. *American Psychologist, 47,* 997–1006.

Zigler, E. F., & Stevenson, M. F. (1993). *Children in a changing world* (2nd ed.). Pacific Grove, CA: Brooks/Cole.

Zillmann, D. (1984). *Connections between sex and aggression.* Hillsdale, NJ: Lawrence Erlbaum Associates.

Zillmann, D. (1988). Cognition-excitation interdependencies in aggressive behavior. *Aggressive Behavior, 14,* 51–64.

Zillmann, D., Baron, R. A., & Tamborini, R. (1981). Social costs of smoking: Effects of tobacco smoke on hostile behavior. *Journal of Applied Social Psychology, 11,* 548–561.

Zillmann, D., Katcher, A. H., & Milavsky, B. (1972). Excitation transfer from physical exercise to subsequent aggressive behavior. *Journal of Experimental Social Psychology, 8,* 247–259.

Zimbardo, P. G. (1973). The psychological power and pathology of imprisonment. In E. Aronson & R. Helmreich (Eds.), *Social psychology,* New York: Van Nostrand.

Zimmerman, M., Reischl, T., Seidman, E., Rappaport, J., Toro, P., & Salem, D. (1991). Expansion strategies of a mutual help organization. *American Journal of Community Psychology, 19,* 251–279.

Zinbarg, R. E., & Barlow, D. H. (1996). Structure of anxiety and the anxiety disorders: A hierarchical model. *Journal of Abnormal Psychology, 105,* 181–193.

Zinbarg, R. E., & Mineka, S. (1991). Animal models of psychopathology: II. Simple phobia. *The Behavior Therapist, 14,* 61–65.

Zola-Morgan, S., & Squire, L. R. (1990). The neuropsychology of memory: Parallel findings in humans and nonhuman primates. *Annals of the New York Academy of Sciences, 608,* 434–456.

Zorumski, C., & Isenberg, K. (1991). Insights into the structure and function of GABA-benzodiazepine receptors: Ion channels and psychiatry. *American Journal of Psychiatry, 148,* 162–173.

Zsambok, C. E., & Klein, G. (1997). *Naturalistic decision making.* Hillsdale, NJ: Lawrence Erlbaum Associates.

Zubin, J., & Spring, B. (1977). Vulnerability—A new view of schizophrenia. *Journal of Abnormal Psychology, 86,* 103–126.

Zuckerman, M. (1984). Sensation seeking: A comparative approach to a human approach. *The Behavioral and Brain Sciences, 7,* 413–471.

Zuckerman, M. (1990). Some dubious premises in research and theory on racial differences. *American Psychologist, 45,* 1297–1303.

Zuckerman, M. (1999). *Vulnerability to psychopathology: A biosocial model.* Washington, DC: American Psychological Association.

Zuercher-White, E. (1997). *Treating panic disorder and agoraphobia: A step-by-step clinical guide.* Oakland, CA: New Harbinger.

Zuger, A. (1998, July 28). A fistful of aggression is found among women. *New York Times,* pp. B8, B12.

Zweben, J. E. (1996). Integrating psychotherapy and 12-step approaches. In A. M. Washton (Ed.), *Psychotherapy and substance abuse: A practitioner's handbook.* New York: Guilford.

NAME INDEX

Abbott, A. S., 274
Abbott, B. B., 462
Abbott, R., 599
Abbott, R. A., 466, 509
Abel, L., 648
Abeles, N., 394
Abelson, R., 256, 278
Abraham, H. D., 315
Abramis, D. J., 381
Abramowitz, J. S., 581, 597
Abramowski, D., 71
Abrams, C. L., 437
Abrams, R., 590, 591
Abramson, L. Y., 199, 543
Achenbach, T. M., 555
Acitelli, L. K., 629
Acker, L. E., 183
Ackerman, D., 103
Ackerman, P. L., 343
Ackroff, K., 367
Acocella, J., 536, 537
Adam, K., 304
Adam, S., 420
Adams, D., 70
Adams, M. J., 225
Adams, M. M., 90
Adan, A. M., 436
Ader, D. N., 39
Ader, R., 91, 183, 470
Adesso, V. J., 311
Adler, A., 487, 502, 565
Adler, T., 462
Adolphs, R., 387
Adorno, T. W., 621
Afflect, G. S., 467
Agarwal, D. P., 313
Aggleton, J. P., 129
Aghajanian, G. K., 541
Agnew, C. R., 627
Aguilar-Roblero, R., 300
Ahern, F., 335
Ahmed, A., 414
Aiello, J. R., 636
Aiken, L., 476
Aiken, L. R., 327, 333, 490
Ainsworth, M. D. S., 426, 427, 487
Aitchison, J., 281
Ajzen, I., 616
Akana, S. F., 71
Akert, R. M., 266, 617, 623, 627, 635, 639, 640, 651, 652, 657
Akiguchi, I., 75
Akil, H., 315
Al-Kubaisy, T., 574
Alafuzoff, I., 79
Alavi, A., 77
Albee, G., 598, 599
Albert, M. S., 87
Alberti, R. E., 573
Alborn, A., 78, 79
Albright, M., 380
Alcoholics Anonymous, 577
Aldag, R. J., 666
Aldenhoff, J., 556

Alderete, E., 314
Alessandrini, R., 70
Alexander, C. N., 447
Alexinsky, T., 66
Alfieri, T., 613
Ali, M., 605
Ali, S., 370
Alicke, M., 605
Allen, C. R., 541
Allen, E. A., 487
Allen, G. A., 599
Allen, J., 657
Allen, J. B., 77, 394
Allen, L. A., 543
Allen, L. S., 376
Alliger, R., 546, 547
Alloy, L. B., 199, 543
Allport, G. W., 490–491, 492, 497
Alsobrook, J. P., 531
Alsop, D. C., 242
Alston, J. H., 12
Altemeyer, B., 621
Altman, E., 590
Altmann, G. T. M., 276
Aluja-Fabregat, A., 205
Alvarez, F. J., 311
Alvaro, E. M., 640
Alvir, J. M., 544
Alzheimer, A., 69, 70
Amabile, T., 350, 381
Amanzio, M., 130
Amara, D. G., 242
Amaro, H., 474
Amberla, K., 79
Ambrosini, M. V., 305
Amemiya, A., 365
American College Testing Assessment, 327
American Law Institute, 557
American Psychiatric Association, 310, 378, 524, 544, 590
American Psychological Association, 12, 20, 45, 204, 328, 329, 331, 512, 583, 588
Anastasi, A., 329
Anders, T. F., 301
Anderson, C. A., 204, 205, 610, 647, 648, 649, 652, 653
Anderson, C. H., 118
Anderson, D., 419
Anderson, E. M., 581
Anderson, G., 536
Anderson, J., 624
Anderson, J. A., 269
Anderson, J. R., 208, 218, 220, 224, 244, 267, 269, 478
Anderson, K., 293
Anderson, K. J., 434
Anderson, K. P., 648, 652, 653
Anderson, L. W., 339
Anderson, R. C., 278
Andrasik, F., 478
Andreasen, N. C., 546, 547
Annan, R. S., 365

Ansay, C., 230
Anthony, C., 373
Anthony, J., 555
Anthony, T., 622
Anton, R. F., 555
Antoni, M., 461
Antonuccio, D. O., 597
Antony, M., 531
Aochi, O., 131
Aponte, J. F., 587
Appelbaum, M. I., 331, 332
Applebaum, P., 558
Applegate, B., 552, 555, 556
Arafat, Y., 641
Araya, R., 574
Arch, J. R., 365
Archambault, C. M., 369
Arcus, D., 424
Arenberg, D., 442
Aristotle, 258
Arlow, J., 565
Armanini, M., 79
Armstrong, N., 99
Armstrong, R. W., 193
Arndt, J., 293
Arndt, S., 546, 547
Arnold, S. E., 77
Aron, A. P., 395
Aronoff, J., 398
Aronson, E., 266, 617, 619, 621, 623, 627, 635, 639, 640, 651, 652, 657
Aronson, J., 341
Arora, A., 318
Arterberry, M., 163
Arvey, R. D., 331
Asch, S. E., 638, 639
Ashcraft, M. H., 267
Ashton, H., 300
Askenasy, J. J. M., 305
Aslin, R. N., 409
Aspinwall, L. G., 463, 466, 467, 476, 615
Assia, V. M., 409
Associated Press, 204
Aston-Jones, G., 66, 310
Atkinson, J. W., 336
Atkinson, R. C., 220
Au, T. K., 260
Audrain, J., A6
Auld, F., 565
Aussprung, J., 455
Averill, J. S., 391
Aviezer, O., 428
Ax, R. K., 563
Ayanian, J., 615
Ayllon, T., 574
Azar, B., 15, 21, 407, 424, 436, 443, 445, 554
Azrin, N. H., 574
Azuma, H., 422

Baars, B. J., 292, 295
Babcock, R. L., 348
Bachman, B. A., 623
Backman, L., 79, 238, 239

Baddeley, A., 218, 222, 242
Badia, P., 462
Baek, S., 41
Baer, D., 382
Baer, L., 591
Baguley, T., 230
Bagwell, C. L., 32, 432
Bahrick, H. P., 226, 420
Bahrick, L. E., 226, 414
Bahrick, P. O., 420
Bailey, A. J., 556
Bailey, C. U., 365
Bailey, J. M., 375, 376
Bailey, S., 588
Baillargeon, R., 414–416, 418
Baird, A., 79
Bakalar, J. B., 317
Bakay, R. A., 78
Baker, C. E., 588
Baker, G. A., 641
Baker, L. T., 343
Balaban, M. T., 398
Balakireva, M., 375
Baldessarini, R., 542, 544
Baldi, A. P., 223
Baldwin, J. M., 9
Baldwin, M. W., 14
Baldwin, W. R., 109
Ball, K., 166
Ball, M., 69
Ball, S. G., 300
Ballantine, T., 591
Balleine, B., 363
Balota, D. A., 229
Baltes, P. B., 442
Banaji, M., 606, 625
Banaji, M. R., 218
Bancroft, J., 377
Bandura, A., 202, 204, 462, 475, 498–499, 500, 507, 573, 649
Banich, M., 16
Banich, M. T., 77, 388
Banks, M. S., 409
Banks, W. P., 159
Bar, M., 293
Barber, J. P., 489
Barbour, R., 70
Barclay, A. M., 398
Barclay, J. R., 227
Bard, J., 123
Bard, P., 395
Bardo, M. T., 84, 362, 396
Barefoot, J. C., 471
Bargh, J. A., 293, 621, 624
Barker, L. M., 176, 186
Barlow, D. H., 463, 530, 531, 532, 550, 574, 597
Barner, E. L., 87
Barnes, M. H., 626, 629
Barnett, A. H., 369
Barnett, B., 268
Barnett, M. C., 534
Baron, R. A., 629, 648, 649, 653, 663
Baron, R. S., 636, 666

CREDITS

Chapter 11: **p. 360:** Frans Lanting/Minden Pictures. **p. 361:** Warner Bros./Courtesy Kobal.) **p. 362:** Okoniewski/The Image Works. **p. 365:** Richard Howard. **p. 367:** Peter Menzel/Stock Boston. **p. 368:** Kopstein/Monkmeyer. **p. 369:** Reuters/Kansas City Star/Archive Photos. **p. 374:** Bill Aron/PhotoEdit. **p. 375:** James Wilson/Woodfin Camp. **p. 378,** *Figure 11.8:* Reprinted by permission of the publisher from Henry A. Murray, THEMATIC APPERCEPTION TEST, Cambridge, Mass.: Harvard University Press, Copyright © 1943 by the President and Fellows of Harvard College © 1971 by Henry A. Murray. **p. 380:** AP/Wide World Photos. **p. 381:** David Joel/Tony Stone Images. **p. 383:** Bob Daemmrich/The Image Works. **p. 386:** Joe Hoyle/The Daily Illini. **p. 388:** From *The Neurological Examination,* 4th ed., by R. N. DeJong, New York: Lipincott/Harper & Row, 1979. **p. 393:** Courtesy of Paul Ekman. Appeared in "Autonomic nervous system distinguishes among emotions," by Ekman, P., Levenson, R. W. & Fresen, W. V., *Science* 221, 1983. **p. 394:** Robert E. Daemmrich/ Tony Stone Images. **p. 397:** *(bottom left)* Eastcott/Momatiuk/Woodfin Camp. **p. 397:** *(bottom center)* Rick Smolan/Stock Boston. **p. 397:** *(bottom right)* Jonathan Blair/Woodfin Camp.

Chapter 12: **p. 404:** Les Stone/Sygma. **p. 406:** *(top)* B. Anderson/Monkmeyer. **p. 406:** *(bottom)* C. Salvador/Sygma. **p. 407:** Photo Lennart Nilsson/Albert Bonniers Forlag AB, *Behold Man,* Little, Brown and Company. **p. 408:** John Chiasson/Gamma-Liaison. **p. 409:** Reproduced, with permission, from Nelson, C.A. (1987). The recognition of facial expressions in the first two years of life: Mechanisms of development. *Child Development,* 58, 889–909. **p. 410:** Petit Format/J. Da Cunha/Photo Researchers. **p. 413:** George Zimbel/Monkmeyer. **p. 414:** Joe McNally/Sygma. **p. 415:** Courtesy of Carolyn Rovee-Collier. **p. 421:** Laima Druskis/Stock Boston. **p. 424:** David Young-Wolff/PhotoEdit. **p. 425:** Harlow Primate Laboratory, University of Wisconsin. **p. 426:** AP/Wide World Photos. **p. 427:** Laurence Monneret/Tony Stone Images. **p. 432:** Nathan Nourok/PhotoEdit. **p. 433:** Bill Aron/PhotoEdit. **p. 434:** Wanstall/The Image Works. **p. 443:** Wojnarowicz/The Image Works. **p. 444:** Bob Daemmrich/Stock Boston. **p. 445:** *(top)* Penny Tweedie/Tony Stone Images. **p. 445:** *(bottom)* M. Greenlar/The Image Works.

Chapter 13: **p. 452:** Lori Adamski Peek/Tony Stone Images. **p. 453:** Piet van Lier/Impact Visuals. **p. 454:** Liz Gilbert/Sygma. **p. 459:** *(top)* Kelvin Boyes/FSP/Liaison Agency. **p. 460:** Photofest. **p. 461:** David Alan Harvey/Woodfin Camp. **p. 465:** *(top)* Lauren Greenfeld/Sygma. **p. 465:** *(bottom)* P. Durand/Sygma. **p. 466:** Steve Liss/Sygma. **p. 470:** Boehringer Ingelheim, International GmbH/photo Lennart Nilsson, *The Incredible Machine,* National Geographic Society. **p. 472:** Esbin-Anderson/The Image Works. **p. 473:** Huntly Hersch/Index Stock Imagery. **p. 474:** Farley/Monkmeyer. **p. 475:** Leslie O'Shaughnessy/Medical Images.

Chapter 14: **p. 484:** Mary Evans Picture Library. **p. 487:** Corbis-Bettmann. **p. 488:** Harriet Russell Stanley Fund, New Britain Museum of American Art. **p. 491:** Michael Powers/Stock Boston. **p. 493:** Robert Caputo/AURORA. **p. 494:** Bruce Plotkin/Tony Stone Images. **p. 496:** AP/Wide World Photos. **p. 498:** Mark Richards/PhotoEdit. **p. 500:** *(left)* Andy King/Sygma. **p. 500:** *(right)* Titan Sports/ Sygma. **p. 501:** AP/Wide World Photos. **p. 502:** Ilene Perlman/Stock Boston. **p. 503:** Richard Pasley/Stock Boston. **p. 505:** Tom Wagner/Odyssey/Chicago. **p. 512:** Charlotte Miller.

Chapter 15: **p. 519:** *(top)* Dunn/Monkmeyer. **p. 519:** *(bottom)* Grox-J. M. News/Sipa Press. **p. 520:** J.L. Dugast/Sygma. **p. 521:** Culver Pictures. **p. 529:** David Woo/Stock Boston. **p. 530:** Abe Rezny/The Image Works. **p. 532:** Copyright ©99 PhotoDisc, Inc. **p. 533:** Dr. Susan Mineka. **p. 535:** Photofest. **p. 540:** P. Chauvel/Sygma. **p. 542:** Dan McCoy/Rainbow. **p. 545:** D. Silbersweig M.D./E. Stern M.D. **p. 547:** Grunnitus/Monkmeyer. **p. 548:** Office of Scientific Information, National Institute of Mental Health. **p. 550:** Reuters/HO/Archive Photos. **p. 553:** Michael Weisbrot/Stock Boston. **p. ???** Bob Daemmrich/The Image Works. **p. 557:** Independent Record/Sygma.

Chapter 16: **p. 563:** *(top)* Stock Montage. **p. 563:** *(bottom)* Hank Morgan/Rainbow. **p. 565:** Photograph ©Edmund Engleman. **p. 566:** M. Grecco/Stock Boston. **p. 569:** Michael Rougier, Life Magazine ©Time Inc. **p. 570:** Zigy Kaluzny/Tony Stone Images. **p. 572:** Georgia Tech photo by Gary Meek. **p. 574:** *(top)* Renate Hiller/Monkmeyer. **p. 574:** *(bottom)* Rich Friedman/Black Star. **p. 575:** Courtesy Albert Ellis, Institute for Rational-Emotive Therapy. **p. 576:** Courtesy Aaron T. Beck, M.D. **p. 577:** James Wilson/Woodfin Camp. **p. 578:** Will Hart/PhotoEdit. **p. 587:** Spencer Grant/PhotoEdit. **p. 588:** Michael Newman/ PhotoEdit. **p. 589:** AP/Wide World Photos. **p. 589:** *(bottom)* Stock Montage.

p. 590: Will & Deni McIntyre/Photo Researchers. **p. 599:** Dith Pran/New York Times Co./Archive Photos.

Chapter 17: **p. 605:** George L. Walker III/Liaison Agency. **p. 606:** Bob Daaemmrich/The Image Works. **p. 608:** Jerry Wachter/Photo Researchers. **p. 609:** Tom McCarthy/Rainbow. **p. 612:** Peter Ginter/Material World. **p. 613:** Bob Daemmrich/The Image Works. **p. 617:** David Woo/Stock Boston. **p. 619:** Evan Agostini/Liaison Agency. **p. 623:** Robert Brenner/PhotoEdit. **p. 626:** David Joel/Tony Stone Images. **p. 628:** D.P.A./The Image Works. **p. 630:** Myrleen Ferguson/PhotoEdit.

Chapter 18: **p. 634:** AP/Wide World Photos. **p. 635:** David Leeson/The Image Works. **p. 637:** AP/Wide World Photos. **p. 638:** *(left)* Nabeel Turner/Tony Stone Images. **p. 638:** *(right)* Corbis-Bettmann. **p. 641:** AP/Wide World Photos. **p. 642:** John Chiasson/Liaison Agency. **p. 643:** Stanley Milgram, 1972; by permission of Alexandra Milgram. **p. 644:** AP/Wide World Photos. **p. 645:** Reka Hazir/Sygma. **p. 649:** Reuters/Lorda Shreif/Archive Photos. **p. 653:** Eduardo Citrinblum/Outline. **p. 654:** *(top)* John Barr/Liaison Agency. **p. 654:** *(bottom)* Elizabeth Crews/Stock Boston. **p. 655:** Robert Brenner/PhotoEdit. **p. 658:** Mark C. Burnett/Photo Researchers. **p. 662:** Michael Newman/PhotoEdit. **p. 665:** Catherine Karnow/ Woodfin Camp. **p. 666:** AP/Wide World Photos.

Tables and Illustrations

Figure 1.1, p. 5: Husband and father-in law: Reversible Figure" by J. Botwinick in *American Journal of Psychology,* 1961, 74: 312–313. Copyright 1961 by the Board of Trustees of the University of Illinois. Used with the permission of the University of Illinois Press. **Figure 1.2, p. 6:** Morris, Michael W. and Kaiping Peng (1994). Culture and Cause: American and Chinese Attributions for Social and Physical Events. *Journal of Personality and Social Psychology,* Vol. 67, No. 6, 949–97. Adapted from Figure 8. Copyright © 1994 by the American Psychological Association. Adapted with permission.

Figure 3.12, p. 65: Peterson, S.E., van Mier, H., Fiez, J. A., & Raichle, M. E. (1998). The Effects of practice on the functional anatomy of task performance. *Proceedings of the National Academy of Science USA, 95,* 853–860. Copyright 1998 National Academy of Sciences, U.S.A. **Figure 3.13, p. 65:** Cho, Z. H., Chung, S. C., Jones, J.P., Park, J.B., Park, H. J., Lee, H. J., Wong, E. K., & Min, B. I. (1988). New findings of the correlation between acupoints and corresponding brain cortices using functional MRI. *Proceedings of the National Academy of Science USA, 95,* 5, pp. 2670–2673. Copyright 1998 National Academy of Sciences, U.S.A. **Figure 3.18, p. 73:** Reprinted with the permission of Simon & Schuster from *The Cerebral Cortex of Man* by Wilder Penfield and Theodore Rasmussen. Copyright 1950 Macmillan Publishing Company; copyright renewed © 1978 Theodore Rasmussen.

Table 4.1, p. 101: *Fundamentals of Sensation and Perception* by M. W. Levine and J. M. Shefner, Addison Wesley, 1981. Reprinted by permission of the author. **Figure 4.6, p. 104:** G.L. Rasmussen and W.F. Windle, *Neural Mechanisms of the Auditory and Vestibular Systems,* 1960. Courtesy of Charles C. Thomas, Publisher, Springfield, Illinois. **Figure 4.21, p. 118:** Jared Schneidman Design. **Figure 4.13, p. 131:** From Sensation and Perception by H. R. Schiffman, 1990, Wiley, p. 275, Figure 14.6. Reprinted by permission of John Wiley & Sons, Inc.

Figure 5.3, p. 139: From Solso, Robert L., *Cognitive Psychology,* 5/e. Copyright © 1998 by Allyn & Bacon. Reprinted by permission. **Table 5.1, p. 140:** Galanter, E. (1962), "Contemporary Psychophysics," in R. Brown (Ed.) *New Directions in Psychology.* New York: Holt, Rinehart & Winston. Reprinted by permission of the author. **Figure 5.6, p. 146:** Parts B and D from *Seeing: Illusion, Brain and Mind,* pp. 14 and 105, by Frisby, J. P., 1980, Oxford: Oxford University Press. By permission of Oxford University Press. **Figure 5.7, p. 147:** From: *Image, Object, and Illusion* by Held © 1971 by W. H. Freeman and Company. Used with permission. **Figure 5.16, p. 158:** Illustration from *Sensation and Perception,* Fourth Edition by Stanley Coren, Lawrence M. Ward, and James T. Enns, copyright © 1994 by Harcourt, Brace & Company, reprinted by permission of the publisher. **Figure 5.21, p. 161:** Reprinted with permission from figures by Weisstein & Harris, *Science,* 1974, 186, 752–755. Copyright © 1974 by American Association of the Advancement of Science. **Figure 5.22, p. 161:** Taken from Beiderman, I., *Matching Image Edges to Object Memory,* from the Proceedings of the IEEE First International Conference on Computer Vision, pp. 364–392, 1987, IEEE. © 1997 IEEE. **Figure 5.23, p. 162:** Romelhart, D.E., and McClelland, J.L. (1986) *Parallel Distributing*